CASES AND STATUTES ON EVIDENCE

AUSTRALIA AND NEW ZEALAND
The Law Book Company Ltd.
Sydney : Melbourne : Perth

CANADA AND U.S.A.
The Carswell Company Ltd.
Agincourt, Ontario

INDIA
N.M. Tripathi Private Ltd.
Bombay
and
Eastern Law House Private Ltd.
Calcutta
M.P.P. House
Bangalore

ISRAEL
Steimatzky's Agency Ltd.
Jerusalem : Tel Aviv : Haifa

PAKISTAN
Pakistan Law House
Karachi

CASES AND STATUTES

ON

EVIDENCE

Second Edition

by

P. B. CARTER

of the Middle Temple, Barrister and Honorary Bencher;
Emeritus Fellow of Wadham College, Oxford;
Honorary Reader, Inns of Court School of Law

LONDON
SWEET & MAXWELL
1990

First Edition 1981
Reprinted 1982
Second Edition 1990

Published in 1990 by
Sweet & Maxwell Limited of
South Quay Plaza, 183 Marsh Wall, London E14 9FT
Laserset by P.B. Computer Typesetting,
Pickering, N. Yorks.
Reproduced, printed and bound in Great Britain by
BPCC Hazell Books
Aylesbury, Bucks, England
Member of BPCC Ltd

British Library Cataloguing in Publication Data

Carter, P. B. (Peter Basil)
Cases and statutes on evidence. — 2nd ed
1. England. Criminal courts. Evidence.
Law
I. Title   II. Cockle, Ernest
344.205′6

ISBN 0–421–32990–4

PREFACE

During the eight years that have elapsed since the publication of the last edition of this book, not only have there been major statutory changes in the law of evidence, but there has also been (on a seemingly unprecedented scale) a flood of reported cases directly dealing with, or bearing upon, this branch of the law. An easy way of accommodating these developments in this new edition would have involved a substantial increase in its size. In fact a reduction (as compared with the last edition) of some 150 pages has been achieved. Financial considerations dictated this, — increased production costs inevitably being reflected in the selling price. I hope that law teachers and other users of the book will excuse the exclusion or truncation of any of their favourite materials.

In spite of the contraction in overall size, I have been able to effect some increase in the introductory text in each Chapter in Part One, and in the annotation of the materials more generally.

I am particularly indebted to Dr Rosemary Pattenden, of the University of East Anglia Law School, for her skilful assistance in the preparation of much of the material on Statutes and Rules set in Part Two and Part Three respectively.

I would like to thank, too, Mrs Maureen Clarke for once again deciphering and reducing to immaculate typescript much of my illegible manuscript.

Finally I wish to express my appreciation to Messrs. Sweet and Maxwell for all their help in the production of this book.

August 1, 1989

P. B. Carter

CONTENTS

Part Two: Statutes on Evidence

Part Three: Rules on Evidence

ACKNOWLEDGMENTS

The author and publishers wish to thank the following for permission to reprint extracts from the sources indicated:

Australian Law Reports

Butterworth & Co. (Publishers) Ltd.
The All England Law Reports

Canada Law Book Ltd.
Dominion Law Reports

Carswell Company Ltd.
Supreme Court Reports

Incorporated Council of Law Reporting for England and Wales
Law Reports

Law Book Co. Ltd.
Commonwealth Law Reports

TABLE OF CASES

[References to pages where extracts from judgments are set out are printed in **bold** type. Reference to summaries are printed in *italics* and all other references in roman type.]

TABLE OF STATUTES

[References to pages where legislation is set out in full are printed in **bold** type.]

Part One

CASES ON EVIDENCE

Chapter 1

SOME GENERAL CONSIDERATIONS

I

EVIDENCE has been said to denote "the *means* by which any alleged matter of fact, the truth of which is submitted to investigation, is established or disproved."[1] The law of evidence comprises the legal rules regulating those means. It is a part of adjectival as distinct from substantive law—but it is nonetheless law. Rules of substantive law are characteristically couched in terms of given fact situations. They indicate the legal significance of a set of facts which are either admitted or have been established. A party to a dispute may admit facts and adduce arguments as to the substantive law: alternatively or additionally he may dispute some or all of the facts. Such disputed facts may be said to be in issue and thus open to proof or disproof. Adjectival law is largely concerned with the regulation of this process: it embraces not only the law of evidence but also the law of procedure more generally, including pre-trial and post-trial procedure. Perhaps no clearly cut distinction can be drawn between evidence and other adjectival matters. To some extent this sub-classification depends upon historical and pedagogical considerations, but the focus of the law of evidence is upon the trial process itself and more particularly upon the fact-finding element in that process. It is concerned, within this general context, with such matters as the relative roles of judge and jury, the rights and duties of the parties, the nature of proof, the availability of witnesses, documents and other media of proof, the admissibility of evidence, and similar matters. Although the distinction between adjectival law (of which the law of evidence forms a part) and substantive can be seen as a distinction between rules governing the establishment of facts and rules determining the effect of admitted or established facts, there are grey borderline areas, such as, for example, the law relating to the incidence of the burden of proof, to irrebuttable presumptions or to estoppels. Indeed the law of evidence cannot be studied in isolation from substantive law—especially the criminal law.

Essentially the law of evidence is concerned with the regulation of an investigation—that of fact-finding. This investigation is historical rather than scientific. The experimental methods of the natural sciences are not normally apt. When occasional resort is had to them, for example by the use of blood-tests or even of psychiatric evidence, this is strictly incidental to an enquiry as to past events. But to describe the fact-finding process simply as an historical investigation could be misleading: indeed, it has several characteristics which would be anathema to historians. These characteristics reflect, or should reflect, the context

---

[1] Wills, *Circumstantial Evidence* (7th ed., 1937), p. 2.

3

and purpose of the investigation. That purpose is not the mere acquisition of knowledge: it is the just settlement of a dispute. The results of the investigation have practical and often immediate consequences: they are likely to affect specifically the position of identifiable human beings. The context of the investigation is a trial, and, more particularly in common law jurisdictions, a trial conducted by adversary rather than inquisitorial methods. There are thus inherent constraints which the professional historian would find intolerable. These include the following: (1) Evidence is marshalled and presented very largely by interested persons. A party in civil proceedings and the accused in criminal proceedings is not impartial: he is concerned not so much with establishing the whole truth as with winning his case. He can within fairly broad limits decide which evidence to offer and which to withhold. (2) A conclusion has to be reached one way or another even though the evidence may be inadequate. (3) It has to be reached quickly, and in a court of last resort it is final. (4) The tradition of trial by peers requires that the investigators be untrained. (5) The dogma that the trier of fact must judge according to the evidence seriously restricts the liberty of the investigators to inform themselves. (6) The evidence according to which they must judge is usually itself that of a non-expert and presented in the unfamiliar and somewhat forbidding atmosphere of a courtroom.

Adjudicative fact-finding smacks then of being an historical investigation carried out by untrained investigators required to act upon non-expert sources of information presented by biased protagonists, these untrained investigators being required to reach a decision which will be final and binding, to do so regardless of the adequacy of the evidence and to do so quickly. The constraints which foster such a situation may be largely unavoidable, stemming as they do from important social policies, such as the fairness of trial by peers, considerations of natural justice and the need for speed and finality. But, given that the adversary trial system, as we know it, is by and large the most acceptable, it is of paramount importance that rules be evolved in an attempt to mitigate the disadvantages which the inherent constraints impose. This is a major concern of the law of evidence.[2]

Another, but much less central, concern of the law of evidence is to accommodate certain policies extrinsic to the efficiency of the trial process. Sometimes even highly relevant evidence is excluded on the grounds of public policy. Again a witness by claiming testimonial privilege is sometimes allowed to decline to answer a question, although by doing so he is reducing the likelihood of the trial leading to a just result. Here the problem is not the amelioration of disadvantages inherent in the trial technique, but rather the reconciliation of the requirements of an efficient trial with countervailing external policies requiring, for example, that evidence be withheld on the ground that its production would be liable to jeopardise national security or that the privacy of certain communications should be protected.

II

The English law of evidence is still basically a case-law subject. Not only is there no code, but the interventions of the legislature in this branch of

---

[2] See Hart and McNaughton, *Evidence and Inference in the Law* (1958), pp. 48 *et seq.*

the law have been piecemeal. There are on the statute book some Acts of Parliament, such as the Criminal Evidence Act 1898 and the Civil Evidence Act 1968, which deal exclusively with evidentiary questions. Moreover, in very recent years there have been significant statutory changes in the law of criminal evidence.[3] Also there has been a tendency, very marked in recent decades, to include individual sections dealing with particular evidentiary aspects in statutes primarily concerned with matters of substantive law. Excerpts from no less than 79 statutes have been included in Part Two of this book, and it would have been easy to increase this number. But, despite this proliferation, the common law has proved remarkably (and in some respects depressingly) hardy: there remain many extensive areas of the subject in which there has been no statutory intervention, and, moreover, much of the statutory change that has been effected has been within a common law framework and is permeated by common law doctrine.

III

There follows a catalogue of some basic terminology of the law of evidence. The definitions are brief and almost inevitably incomplete and imprecise. What is presented here purports to be no more than an introductory guide.

Fact in issue. A fact in issue is a fact, which as a matter of substantive law must be established if a particular party to legal proceedings is to succeed, and the existence of which is denied by the opposing party. (Sometimes the substantive law prescribes alternatives, for example for the formation of a contract the use of the seal or consideration.) Whether a fact is in issue depends upon the substantive law and the parties' allegations and denials. In civil cases these latter are largely contained in the pleadings.

Occasionally the term "fact in issue" is used more loosely so as to cover any relevant fact the existence of which is the subject of dispute between the parties.

Judicial evidence. Proof or disproof of a fact in issue is normally achieved by adducing judicial evidence. This usually takes the form of testimony, documentary evidence or real evidence. Sometimes the adduction of evidence is dispensed with if, for example, judicial notice is taken of a fact, or reliance is placed upon a presumption, or an estoppel is successfully pleaded.

Testimony. The assertion of a witness in court offered as evidence of the truth of that which is asserted.

Documentary evidence. A document produced for inspection by the court for the purpose of showing the fact, and/or the truth, of its *contents*. If production is simply to show its physical existence or a physical characteristic (*e.g.* that it is torn), it is most usefully classified as real evidence.

---

[3] See Pts. VII and VIII of the Police and Criminal Evidence Act 1984, and Pts. II and III of the Criminal Justice Act 1988 (both Part Two, *infra*).

Real evidence. A material object (other than a document tendered to show its contents) produced for inspection by the court.

Relevant or evidentiary fact. A fact the existence of which would directly or indirectly tend to suggest, either by itself or in conjunction with other facts, the existence or non-existence of a fact in issue.

Material fact. This term is used in several different senses. Most often it is used synonymously with the term relevant fact, but sometimes it connotes a fact in issue. Again, it has been used simply to emphasise the weight or importance of a piece of evidence. Occasionally materiality is contrasted with relevance: this is when the latter term is used loosely so as to include a tendency to show the existence or non-existence of a fact even though that fact may itself neither be in issue nor bear upon a fact in issue.

Relevant evidence. Evidence which either by itself or in conjunction with other evidence tends to show the existence or non-existence of a relevant fact or a fact in issue. Relevant evidence is succinctly defined in Rule 401 of the United States Federal Rules of Evidence as "evidence having any tendency to make the existence of any fact that is of consequence to the determination of the action more probable or less probable than it would be without the evidence." Relevance depends upon rational inference in the light of human experience. Relevance is a matter of degree: the concept covers the whole scale of probative worth. Moreover, it contains a subjective element in so far as different judges of fact have had differing experiences and may have differing inclinations regarding the drawing of inferences. Although relevance is essentially not a matter of law, the law may tacitly prescribe a minimum standard where probative worth is slight, tenuous or controversial. Conversely, as a distinguished American commentator put it, "... considerable leeway is allowed ... for proof of facts that do not bear directly on the purely legal issues, but merely fill in the background of the narrative and give it interest, colour and lifelikeness."[4] Any doubt as to the relevance of a piece of evidence will be resolved by the judge as a threshold element in the determination of its admissibility.

Admissible evidence. Evidence which is relevant and which is not excluded by any rule of the law of evidence. Admissibility is a matter of law and is determined by the judge.

Weight or cogency of evidence. The probative worth, weight or cogency of admissible evidence is normally assessed by the jury or trier of fact.

Sufficient evidence. The notion of sufficiency is a manifestation of judicial control over the trier of fact's assessment of evidence. A judge must direct, acquittal in a criminal case, or a finding for a particular party in a civil case, if the evidence could not justify a contrary finding. Again he must withdraw an issue from the jury if in the light of all the evidence adduced on that issue an affirmative finding would be unreasonable. It is to be observed that, whereas relevance and

---

[4] *McCormick on Evidence* (3rd. ed., 1984), p. 541.

admissibility relate to a particular piece of evidence, sufficiency relates to all the evidence adduced in a case on a particular issue.

Prima facie evidence. This term is commonly used in two distinct senses. It may connote evidence which is adequate to warrant, but not to require, a finding of fact; or it may connote evidence of a fact which *must* be accepted as persuasive in the absence of adequate evidence to the contrary. The former of these two primary usages is probably the more valuable. Also, the qualifying words prima facie are occasionally inserted gratuitously, the term simply connoting *some* evidence; at other times the words may serve to emphasise the inconclusive nature of that evidence.

Preliminary fact. A fact the existence of which controls or conditions the applicability of a rule of evidence. Such facts are determined by the judge, who probably for this purpose may sometimes rely upon evidence which would not be admissible at the trial of the merits. The judge's investigation of such a preliminary issue is sometimes referred to as the *voir dire* or as a trial within a trial.

The hearsay rule. Assertions which are not made at the trial by the witness who is testifying are inadmissible as evidence of the truth of that which is asserted. The rule applies to testimony, to documentary evidence and to certain non-verbal conduct.

Original evidence. Evidence of the fact that a statement was made tendered without reference to the truth of that statement. Sometimes such evidence is said (somewhat confusingly) to be circumstantially relevant.

Circumstantial evidence. Facts of which proof is tendered, which are not themselves in issue, but from which the existence or non-existence of a fact in issue might reasonably be directly or indirectly inferred. Occasionally the term is used more broadly so as to cover facts the existence of which is merely consistent with the existence or non-existence of a fact in issue.

Direct evidence. This term is commonly used in two distinct senses. In one, it contrasts with hearsay; in the other it contrasts with circumstantial evidence.

IV

Clearly a student of the law of evidence must at the outset attune himself or herself to the distinction between questions of law and questions of fact and to the respective roles of judge and jury in jury trials. The judge, who has general charge of the proceedings, decides questions of law and practice, including questions relating to the admissibility of evidence. The latter may involve an investigation of a preliminary fact, and sometimes this will be carried out in the absence of the jury. The jury decides questions of fact and so assesses the weight to be attached to evidence found to be admissible. Similarly, whereas the testimonial competence of a witness, being a matter of law, is determined by the judge, evaluation of a competent witness's testimony is a matter for the jury. If the competence of the witness itself depends upon the determination of a preliminary fact (*e.g.* whether a child understands the nature of the oath), that preliminary fact will be found by the judge. So, too, if the credibility of a witness might be affected by the existence of some fact (*e.g.* that he has been convicted of perjury on previous occasions), the determination of that fact will be for the judge, whereas the significance to be attached to it, if found, will be for the jury.

Although questions of fact are generally decided by the jury, the judge may withdraw an issue from the jury on the ground of insufficiency. Moreover, in his summing-up when going through the evidence he may within limits comment upon its worth.

It is now generally accepted that in criminal cases a judge has an overriding discretion to exclude a piece of otherwise admissible evidence, if in his opinion its reception might seriously prejudice the fairness of the accused's trial.[5] There is, however, seemingly strong authority[6] for the view that a judge has no corresponding inclusionary discretion. In civil cases nothing approaching a clearly articulated discretion, even to exclude, was developed at common law; but some statutory enactments have assumed the existence of unspecified discretions[7] to exclude evidence, and others have expressly introduced specific and very limited inclusionary discretions.[8] It is to be noted that the question of the existence or non-existence of a true discretion has often been blurred by two different tendencies. First, an intrinsically flexible rule of law involving the balancing of countervailing factors has sometimes been dubbed "discretionary."[9] Secondly, the undoubted *de facto* power of a judge to encourage (often effectively) counsel not to press for the admission of a particular piece of evidence has been seen as involving an element of what is then loosely termed "discretion."[10]

In criminal matters trial by jury is confined to offences tried upon indictment. When a trial is before lay justices of the peace, it is the duty of the Clerk to the Justices to advise on matters of law, including the law of evidence; and lay magistrates should accept this advice. The position of a stipendiary magistrate is theoretically the same, but in practice he tends to be in a real, as well as a formal, sense judge of law as well as of fact. The great majority of civil actions are heard by a judge sitting alone, who is judge of both law and fact. But in all cases the maintenance of the distinction between the determination of a point

---

[5] The Police and Criminal Evidence Act, s.72(2) and s.82(3), 1984 expressly preserve this discretion in relation to evidence admissible under respectively Pt. VII and Pt. VIII of that Act. See, too, the curiously worded and perhaps superfluous s.78 considered in the *Note* on *R.* v. *List* [1966] 1 W.L.R. 9 (Assizes) (pp. 14–15, *infra*). The Criminal Justice Act 1988, s.28(1)(*b*) makes provision in relation to evidence admissible under Pt. II of that Act generally similar to s.72(2) and s.82(3) of the 1984 Act. For these enactments see Part Two, *infra*.

[6] See, *e.g. Sparks* v. *R.* [1964] A.C. 964 (P.C.), *infra*.

[7] See, *e.g.* Civil Evidence Act 1968, s.18(5) and Civil Evidence Act 1972, s.5(3) (both Part Two, *infra*).

[8] See, *e.g.* Civil Evidence Act 1968, s.8(3)(*a*) (Part Two, *infra*) effected by R.S.C., Ord. 38, r. 29 (Part Three, *infra*).

[9] See, *e.g.* the position relating to the exclusion of illegally obtained evidence (Chap. 17, *infra*).

[10] For instance, a judge might in any circumstances discourage counsel from pressing a priest to reveal the secrets of the confessional, although as a matter of law no privilege attaches to the priest-penitent relationship.

of law and a finding of a fact is important: for example, a judge sitting without a jury must himself disregard evidence which he has found to be legally inadmissible; also the rules relating to appeals differ.

At the same time it must be recognised that in modern times the primary role of the law of evidence is in criminal proceedings, whether jury trials or trials before (mostly lay) magistrates. It is to be observed, too, that many of the rules that go to make up the law of evidence have as their focus the safeguarding of the position of the accused in this context.

The cases in this Chapter are concerned with some aspects of the interaction of the roles of judge and jury.

A. JUDGE AND JURY: ADMISSIBILITY AND PRELIMINARY QUESTIONS OF FACT

BARTLETT v. SMITH

12 L.J.Ex. 287; 7 Jur. 448; 11 M. & W. 483; 152 E.R. 895 (Exchequer: 1842)

The admissibility of evidence, documentary or otherwise, is a question of law for the judge; and, if admissibility depends on certain facts, the judge should himself adjudicate upon such facts without submitting them to the jury, if any.

It was objected by the defendant at the trial that a bill of exchange with a foreign stamp could not be read, on the ground that it was drawn in this country. Evidence of that fact was tendered and refused at that stage, but was afterwards received as part of the defendant's case and submitted to the jury. It was held that the judge ought to have received evidence of the place of drawing, in the first instance, to enable him to decide upon the admissibility of the bill, and that he ought not to have submitted the evidence to the jury.

LORD ABINGER C.B.: . . . All facts which are necessary to be proved with a view to the reception of evidence, are for the consideration of the judge, and he is to receive evidence respecting them for his own satisfaction. He might indeed, if he pleased, ask the opinion of the jury, but still the decision ought to be his own. A judge should receive evidence as to the competency of a witness, or the sufficiency of a stamp, which is good upon the face of it, and ought to determine those questions for himself, instead of submitting them to the jury. . . .

PARKE AND ALDERSON BB. delivered the judgment to the same effect, and ROLFE B. concurred.

Note.—Where the admissibility of a piece of evidence depends upon the existence of a particular fact or facts (preliminary facts) the burden of proving such fact or facts rests upon the party alleging their existence. It is, for example, for the prosecution to prove that a confession was not obtained by oppression (Police and Criminal Evidence Act 1984, s.76(2), Part Two, *infra.*), or that a declarant was dying so as to render his declaration admissible (*R.* v. *Jenkins* (1869) L.R. 1 C.C.R. 187 and see Chap. 14, Section A, *infra.*). There is, however, remarkably little explicit general authority as to the *degree* of proof required. As a matter of common sense proof on balance of probabilities should suffice, except that in a criminal case, when evidence is tendered by the prosecution, proof beyond reasonable doubt ought to be necessary. See *R. v. Minors* [1989] 1 W.L.R. 441, 448 (C.A.).

For the position in relation to matters of testimonial competence or compellability, see *R. v. Yacoob* (1981) 72 Cr.App.R. 313 (C.A.), Chap. 8, *infra*. For the position in a particular statutory context, see *R. v. Ewing* [1983] Q.B. 1039 (C.A.), Chap. 3, *infra*.

The judge retains throughout the trial the power to reconsider the admissibility of evidence upon which he has already ruled; but the occasions on which he should allow counsel to invite him to exercise this power are extremely rare. Moreover, in some statutory contexts, exercise of this power may be subject to specific control: see *R. v. Sat Bhambra* (1988) 88 Cr.App.R. 55 (C.A.).

Doe d. Jenkins v. **Davies** (1847) 10 Q.B. 314. The issue in an action of ejectment was to whether a person was legitimate. She was dead. The disputed evidence was a declaration made by her to a solicitor when she had handed him a document concerning her parents' marriage. Its admissibility as an exception to the hearsay rule depended upon whether it was made by a legitimate member of the family. It was argued that the judge ought not to have heard evidence tending to show that the declarant was legitimate when considering the admissibility of the declaration, because legitimacy was itself the substantive issue in the case. Lord Denman C.J., rejecting this argument, said (at p. 324): "...neither the admissibility nor the effect of the evidence is altered by the accident that the fact which is for the Judge as a condition precedent is the same fact which is for the jury in the issue."

Ajodha v. **The State** [1982] A.C. 204 (P.C.) The context of this appeal was the application of what was then prevailing common law doctrine, namely that the admissibility of evidence of a confession by an accused when tendered by the prosecution depended upon whether it had been made voluntarily. Lord Bridge of Harwich, delivering the opinion of the Privy Council, said (p. 214): "The primary question for their Lordships' decision in these appeals can be stated in its simplest form as follows: when the prosecution proposes to tender in evidence a written statement of confession signed by the accused and the accused denies that he is the author of the statement but admits that the signature or signatures on the document are his and claims that they were obtained from him by threat or inducement, does this raise a question of law for decision by the judge as to the admissibility of the statement?" His Lordship noted (p. 221) that "A purist might say that in considering the issue of authorship, the judge was usurping the function of the jury; but, if it is necessary to consider the issue of authorship before the judge can be satisfied that the statement was signed voluntarily, there is in truth no usurpation but only a discharge by the judge of his necessary function in deciding the question of admissibility." Lord Bridge distinguished (p. 222) between (1) cases in which an issue of fact (such as that of authorship in the instant case) bears upon voluntariness and thus upon admissibility, and has, therefore, to be determined by the judge as part of the process of ruling on admissibility; and (2) cases in which an issue of fact has no bearing on admissibility and is therefore simply a matter for the jury. At the same time in the former type of case the issue may have to be reconsidered by the jury when assessing weight. Lord Bridge said (p. 221): "If the judge rules the statement to have been voluntarily signed and therefore admissible...the issues both as to authorship and as to the manner in which the signature was obtained will again have to be canvassed before and left for consideration by the jury."

R. v. **Murray** [1951] 1 K.B. 391 (C.C.A.). The accused was indicted for housebreaking and theft, and the only evidence against him was his signed confession. He denied that it had been made voluntarily, but the Recorder ruled that it was admissible. After the return of the jury, he refused to allow the accused's counsel to cross-examine the police officers, or to examine the accused, as to whether the confession was voluntary. The accused's conviction was quashed. Lord Goddard C.J. said (pp. 392–393): "The Recorder was wrong in the course which he took. It was quite right for him to hear evidence in the absence of the jury and to decide on the admissibility of the confession; and, since he could find nothing in the evidence to cause him to think that the confession had been improperly obtained, to admit it. But its weight and value were matters for the jury, and in considering such matters they were entitled to take into account the opinion which they had formed, on the way in which it had been obtained. (Counsel) was perfectly entitled to cross-examine the police again in the presence of the jury as to the circumstances in which the confession was obtained, and to try again to show that it had been obtained by means of a promise or favour. If he could have persuaded the jury of that, he was entitled to say to them: 'You ought to disregard the confession because its weight is a matter for you.'... The weight and value of the evidence are always matters for the jury. Here the jury were told that they were not to consider that matter at all. That is a complete misdirection on a point of law."

Note.—As to the modern law relating to the admissibility of confessions, see Chap. 17, *infra.*

R. v. REYNOLDS

[1950] K.B. 606; 66 T.L.R. (Pt. I) 333; [1950] 1 All E.R. 335; 34 Cr.App.R. 60
(Court of Criminal Appeal: 1950)

The examination of a child-witness by the judge must be conducted in the presence of the jury.

LORD GODDARD C.J. (delivering the judgment of the court which included BYRNE and MORRIS JJ.): The appellant was convicted at Hertfordshire Quarter Sessions of indecent assault on a child... Another point occurred to the court in this case which is of the greatest importance.... The chairman then said: "The question whether the child is capable of taking the oath or not is entirely a question for me.... The only question at the moment is whether... submissions should be made in the absence of the jury. I think perhaps that would be the better course. Members of the jury, I do not know what is coming; it may be that it is something you should not hear until after the case. Therefore I must ask you to retire."

Evidently the clerk of the peace, in putting the question "Do you wish the jury to be here?", was thinking of the practice which obtains in the courts that if there is a discussion on the question whether a confession is admissible or not, or has been obtained by methods which would render it inadmissible the jury are always told to retire. Obviously the reason for this is that it is almost impossible, while evidence is being taken as to the circumstances in which the confession has been obtained, to prevent the terms of the confession from coming out. The whole question at that stage is whether or not the confession can go before the jury. Therefore, the jury are outside the court while that question is argued, so that they cannot hear the terms of a confession which, it may be held afterwards, is not admissible.

The state of affairs in the present case is entirely different. After the jury had retired, the school-attendance officer was called who had had a good deal to do with this child and knew the school to which she had been sent. It was a school, not for mentally deficient children, but for those who are mentally retarded. This child evidently came from a somewhat squalid home, and her degree of education was very slight, that is, presumably, less than ordinary for a child of her age which was then 12 years—she was 11 years old at the time of the assault. The officer was called, gave evidence, and was cross-examined. His evidence occupied some three or four pages of the shorthand note. All that was done in the absence of the jury, and the question is whether that was such an irregularity that this conviction cannot be allowed to stand. In the opinion of the court it was.

In such a case as the present, what is the first thing which the chairman has to decide? Section 38 of the Children and Young Persons Act 1933, provides: "Where, in any proceeding against any person for any offence any child of tender years called as a witness does not in the opinion of the court understand the nature of the oath, his evidence may be received, though not given upon oath, if, in the opinion of the court, he is possessed of sufficient intelligence to justify the reception of the evidence, and understands the duty of speaking the truth." So, when a child is put into the witness-box, the chairman or presiding judge must first decide whether the child in his opinion understands the nature of the oath. Then he may have to go on and consider whether, if the child does not possess sufficient intelligence to understand the nature of the oath, he is possessed of sufficient intelligence to justify the reception of his unsworn evidence on the ground that he understands the duty of speaking the truth. . . .

Certainly no member of the present court has ever known of a case in which a witness has been called to inform the court whether a child is capable or not of giving evidence. I am not saying that there may not be cases—perhaps this is one—in which the chairman may not want some assistance, especially if he hears that the child is at a particular sort of school. It is not on that ground that the court thinks that there has been a fatal mistake here. It is for this reason: obviously, why the court decided in *Rex* v. *Dunne* ((1928) 21 Cr.App.R. 176) that the evidence of the child must be given in the presence of the jury was that, although the duty of deciding whether the child may be sworn or not lies on the judge and is not a matter for the jury, it is most important that the jury should hear the answers which the child gives and see the demeanour of the child when she is questioned, because it will enable the jury to come to a conclusion as to the weight which they should attach to her evidence. If that was the reason why the court in *Rex* v. *Dunne* held that it was essential that the evidence should be given in the presence of the jury, in this case that is so a fortiori it seems to me, when a witness is called to assist the court by telling it what his experience may be of the child and of the character or impression that he may have formed of the child. The jury would then have all the facts before them with regard to the child's truthfulness, or reputation for truthfulness, and all the information which could be given on the question whether the child was one who would be likely to tell the truth and on whose evidence they could rely.

I may say—and I am sure that I do so with the concurrence of my brethren—that it should be regarded as most exceptional that any evidence should be given in a criminal trial otherwise than in the presence of the jury. As I have said, there is one well known exception to this rule which has been laid down in mercy and fairness to prisoners, namely, that any evidence with regard to whether a confession was properly made ought to be given in the absence of the jury; but the class of evidence given in the present case ought to be given in the face of the jury and in open court. On these grounds we have come to the conclusion—it may be unfortunate for many reasons—that this conviction cannot stand and must be quashed.

Note.—The actual decision in R. v. Dunne could have been seen as resting on the fact that the questioning of the child took place in the absence of the accused. R. v. Reynolds, however, seems to lay down a broad principle to the effect that investigation of the voluntariness of a confession and "most exceptional" cases apart, the determination of a preliminary fact must be in the presence of the jury. See too, R. v. Lal Khan (1981) 73 Cr.App.R. 190 (C.A.). However the rule has been criticised and is only defensible if the "evidence" tendered on the preliminary issue would be admissible if tendered in the course of the trial of the general issues. Probably the judge should have some discretion as provided for, e.g. in the United States Federal Rules (see supra), in The People (Attorney-General) v. Keating [1953] I.R. 200, the Irish Court of Criminal Appeal set aside a conviction on the ground that the investigation of a child's competence had not taken place in the presence of the jury and of the accused. The judge had questioned the child in another trial two days previously and had then formed the impression that she was fit to give evidence, and he had simply relied on this in the instant case.

R. v. LIST

[1966] 1 W.L.R. 9; [965] 3 All E.R. 710; 50 Cr.App.R. 81 (Assizes 1965)

In a criminal case a judge may in his discretion exclude otherwise admissible evidence if its likely prejudicial effect so outweighs its probative value that its reception might result in an unjust conviction.

On a charge of receiving stolen goods knowing them to have been stolen, contrary to the Larceny Act 1916, s.33(1), the prosecution (in order to prove guilty knowledge) sought to adduce evidence under section 43(1)(b) of that Act showing that the defendant had within five years preceding the date of the offence been convicted of offences involving fraud or dishonesty. The defence objected to the admission of this evidence.

ROSKILL J. (having referred to the facts and read section 43(1) of the Larceny Act 1916): . . .
. . . [Defence counsel's] second proposition was that in every case where it is sought to adduce evidence by virtue of section 43, the trial judge has a discretion to disallow the admission of such evidence (even though it be admissible in law) if, on the facts of a particular case, there is a risk of injustice being done by reason of such evidence being admitted. He says here, and says with force, that the real issue being the issue of possession, it will be difficult for the jury to appreciate that this evidence, if admitted, is not relevant to that issue but is only relevant to the issue of guilty knowledge at the time of receipt if there ever was such receipt. I think there is force in this . . . and unless,

therefore, I am compelled as a matter of law to admit this evidence, I would not, if it is a matter for my discretion, admit it.

Am I then compelled, as a matter of law to allow this evidence to be given? . . .

. . . A trial judge always has an overriding duty in every case to secure a fair trial, and if in any particular case he comes to the conclusion that, even though certain evidence is strictly admissible, yet its prejudicial effect once admitted is such as to make it virtually impossible for a dispassionate view of the crucial facts of the case to be thereafter taken by the jury, then the trial judge, in my judgment, should exclude that evidence.

. . . I have reached my decision, first as a matter of the construction of the statute and, second, as a matter of principle, the principle being that a trial judge, as has been repeatedly said, has an overriding discretion to exclude any evidence the prejudicial effect of which hopelessly outweighs its probative value. In my judgment that is the position here, and I therefore do not propose to allow this evidence to be adduced.

Note.—The Larceny Act 1916, s.43(1), was repealed by the Theft Act 1968 and re-enacted with modification in section 27(3) (Part Two, *infra*).

In a very similar case, *R.* v. *Herron* [1967] 1 Q.B. 107 (C.C.A.), Roskill J.'s ruling on the discretion point was expressly approved by the Court of Criminal Appeal. That the judge has an exclusionary discretion has been established in other categories of case, particularly in connection with the similar fact rule (see, *e.g. Noor Mohamed* v. *R.* [1949] A.C. 182 (P.C.), and Chapter 20, *infra*) and with the Criminal Evidence Act 1898, s.1, proviso *(f)* (ii) (Part Two, *infra*; and see *Selvey* v. *D.P.P.* [1970] A.C. 304 (H.L.) and Chapter 23, *infra*). It is, however, now generally accepted that these cases are but illustrations of a more general rule, as Lord Salmon said in *R.* v. *Sang* [1980] A.C. 402 (H.L.): "I cannot, however, accept that a judge's undoubted duty to ensure that the accused has a fair trial is confined to such cases. In my opinion the category of such cases is not and never can be closed except by statute." For recent consideration of some of the factors relevant to the exercise of this discretion, and for emphasis upon caution in resorting to it, see *Scott* v. *The Queen* [1989] 2 W.L.R. 924 (P.C.).

The importance of this common law discretion to exclude in the interests of the fairness of the trial must now be reconsidered in the light of particularly section 78 of the Police and Criminal Evidence Act 1984 (Part Two, *infra*). Whether section 78 is regarded as rendering the common law discretion largely otiose, or the section is seen as itself being superfluous, is perhaps not simply a matter of words. There is certainly room for the view that in the exercise of any discretion, the avowed purpose of which is promotion of the fairness of the trial, a judge will be better served by the pragmatic and flexible techniques of the common law than by rules of statutory interpretation. Moreover, it is to be noted that the 1984 Act expressly provides that nothing in Parts VII or VIII (which deal with evidence) shall prejudice any existing discretion to exclude (sections 72(2) and 82(3)). See, too, the Criminal Justice Act 1988, s.28(1)(*b*).

Section 78 was in fact introduced at a late stage of the passage of the legislation through Parliament. It represented an inadequate response to an amendment tabled in the House of Lords by Lord Scarman which had a very different purpose—namely to render inadmissible evidence on the ground that it had been obtained by illegal, improper or deceptive conduct on the part of law enforcement officers. (See Chapter 17, *infra*). The reference in section 78 to "the circumstances in which the evidence was obtained" no doubt derives from these antecedents; but the reference is incongruous in the context of the purpose of the section as enacted. As was pointed out by the Supreme Court of Canada in *R.* v. *Wray* [1971] S.C.R. 272, it will be only in a very rare case that the way in which evidence was obtained will affect the fairness of the proceedings in which is it used. Without prejudice to the merits of Lord Scarman's original amendment, the position now would certainly be clearer if section 78 in its present form had never been enacted.

At the same time it is to be noted that at common law there is also a separate, if severely limited, discretion to exclude certain real evidence (see especially *R.* v. *Sang* [1980] A.C. 402 (H.L.), Chapter 17, *infra*) on the explicit ground of the unacceptability of the way in which it was obtained. This discretion is seemingly unaffected by section 78: see section 82(3).

Sparks v. **R.** [1964] A.C. 964 (P.C.). At the trial of the appellant for indecently assaulting a girl under four years of age, the judge had held to be inadmissible evidence by the child's mother a statement made to her by the child shortly after the assault to the effect that "it was a coloured boy." The defendant was a 27-year-old white man. The child did not testify at the trial. The appellant was found guilty, and one of the grounds of his appeal was that this evidence had been wrongly excluded. However, the Privy Council held that the evidence was inadmissible, it being hearsay and not falling within any recognised exception to the rule that excludes hearsay in criminal cases. The matter was regarded as being one simply of legal admissibility. Lord Morris of Borth-y-Gest, in the course of delivering the opinion of the Privy Council, said (p. 978): "It was said that it was manifestly unjust for the jury to be left throughout the whole trial with the impression that the child could not give any clue to the identity of her assailant. The cause of justice is, however, best served by adherence to rules which have long been recognised and settled." (The appeal was in the event allowed, but on quite different grounds.)

Note.—The assumption of the Privy Council that no inclusionary discretion exists is seemingly unqualified. That this is the position was re-affirmed by Lord Reid in *Myers* v. *D.P.P.* [1965] A.C. 1001 (H.L.) at p. 1024, and there is indeed virtually no authority to the contrary. At the same time it is perhaps a matter for conjecture as to what the position would have been had, for example, the declarant been an adult of unquestioned reliability who had died before the trial.

B. JUDGE AND JURY: SUFFICIENCY OF EVIDENCE

METROPOLITAN RY. v. JACKSON

(1877) 3 App.Cas. 193; 47 L.J.C.P. 303; 37 L.T. 679; *sub nom. Jackson* v. *Metropolitan Ry.*, 26 W.R. 175 (H.L.: 1877)

Whether the party starting has made out a prima facie case, that is, whether there is sufficient evidence to be left to the jury from which they may legally and properly infer the matter in issue, is a question of law for the judge; whether such evidence establishes the matter in issue is a question of fact for the jury, if any.

This was an action for damages for personal injury, caused by the alleged negligence of a servant of the defendant company in shutting a railway-carriage door on the plaintiff's thumb.

LORD CAIRNS L.C.: . . .
The question is, was there at the trial any evidence of this negligence which ought to have been left to the jury? . . . The judge has a certain duty to discharge and the jurors have another and a different duty. The judge has to say whether any facts have been established by evidence from which negligence *may be* reasonably inferred; the jurors have to

say whether, from those facts, when submitted to them, negligence *ought to be* inferred. It is, in my opinion, of the greatest importance in the administration of justice that these separate functions should be maintained, and should be maintained distinct. It would be a serious inroad on the province of the jury, if, in a case where there are facts from which negligence may reasonably be inferred, the judge were to withdraw the case from the jury upon the ground that, in his opinion, negligence ought not to be inferred; and it would, on the other hand place in the hands of the jurors a power which might be exercised in the most arbitrary manner, if they were at liberty to hold that negligence might be inferred from any state of facts whatever. . . .

LORD O'HAGAN: . . . Your Lordships have never held that, when negligence is alleged, any state of facts assumed to bear upon the issue can be made the subject of inference by jurors, although not really connected with the issue before them. The consequences of such a doctrine would be disastrous, and it is of high importance that the authority of the judge should restrain a latitude of decision which might often in the result be very inconsistent with reason and justice. . . .

LORD BLACKBURN: . . . I think it has always been considered a question of law to be determined by the judge, subject, of course, to review, whether there is evidence which, if it is believed, and the counter-evidence, if any, not believed, would establish the facts in controversy. It is for the jury to say whether and how far the evidence is to be believed. And if the facts, as to which evidence is given, are such that from them a farther inference of fact may legitimately be drawn, it is for the jury to say whether that inference is to be drawn or not. But it is for the judge to determine, subject to review, as a matter of law whether from those facts that farther inference may legitimately be drawn. . . .

LORD GORDON: . . . The duty of a judge in such a case is an exceedingly delicate one, as the line of division between what is proper to be submitted to the jury, as necessary to support a charge of negligence in point of law, and what may be submitted to the jury as sufficient to support a charge of negligence in point of fact, is often a very narrow one. But I agree . . . that there is in every case a preliminary question, which is one of law, namely, whether there is any evidence on which the jury could properly find the question for the party on whom the onus of proof lies. If there is not, the judge ought to withdraw the question from the jury, and direct a nonsuit if the onus is on the plaintiff, or direct a verdict for the plaintiff if the onus is on the defendant. . . .

Note.—The judge may first have to rule upon sufficiency of evidence in response to a submission, made in criminal proceedings by the defence at the end of the presentation of the prosecution case, or made in civil proceedings by the opponent (generally the defendant) at the end of the presentation of the case of the party first introducing evidence (generally the plaintiff). At this stage the judge has to consider whether the evidence so far adduced could (even without further contradiction) warrant a conviction or affirmative finding by any reasonable jury.

Furthermore, even if such a submission is not made, or if made is rejected, the judge must ultimately direct acquittal in a criminal case, or a finding for a particular party in a civil case, if he considers the totality of evidence adduced by both parties insufficient to warrant a conviction or contrary finding by any reasonable jury.

Also the judge must sometimes withdraw a particular issue from the jury for lack of sufficiency if, having regard to all the evidence adduced relevant to that issue, he considers that no reasonable jury could find for its proponent.

The general doctrine relative to the roles of judge and jury as propounded in the *Metropolitan Railway* v. *Jackson* is classic and has been re-stated many times. However, two comments on the actual formulation of that doctrine, in respectively the speeches of Lord Cairns and Lord Blackburn, may be made in the interests of completeness.

In the passage from the Lord Chancellor's speech set out above two judicial duties could be seen as having been telescoped. The judge is under a duty to explain to the jury the nature of the applicable legal rule—in the instant case this would involve propounding the legal standard of negligence. He is under a *separate* duty to decide whether the evidence adduced is as a matter of law sufficient to warrant a finding by any reasonable jury that there has been compliance with that rule. If he determines that there has been no such compliance the need to discharge the former duty is obviated.

As Lord Blackburn pointed out, it is for the jury to decide whether evidence is to be believed and, if it is believed, what inferences are to be drawn from it. The judge may find evidence insufficient to be put to the jury, but only on the ground that, on the assumption that the proponent's evidence is believed, the required inference could not be "legitimately" drawn. That a judge cannot withdraw an issue from the jury simply because the evidence tendered by its proponent is palpably not to be believed seemingly represents orthodox doctrine. This limitation upon judicial control may be difficult to defend. Moreover, it may not always be strictly adhered to in practice; and in *R*. v. *Galbraith* [1981] 1 W.L.R. 1039 (C.A.) Lord Lane C.J., reading the judgment of the court, although restating orthodoxy, did add (p. 1042): "There will, of course, as always in this branch of the law, be borderline cases. They can safely be left to the discretion of the judge."

R. v. **Smith and Doe** (1987) 85 Cr.App.R. 197 (C.A.). The two accused were charged with burglary. At the close of the prosecution case the trial judge rejected a submission that there was no case to answer. The judge then informed the jury that he would have stopped the case if he had thought that there was no case to answer. The trial then proceeded, and the accused, who did not give evidence, were convicted. Their appeal against conviction was allowed by the Court of Appeal. Watkins L.J. said (p. 200): "The question as to whether or not there is a sufficiency of evidence is one which is exclusively for the judge following submissions made to him in the absence of the jury. His decision should not be revealed to the jury lest it wrongly influences them. There is a risk that they might convict because they think the judge's view is a sufficient indication that the evidence is strong enough for that purpose."

R. v. **Abbott** [1955] 2 Q.B. 497 (C.C.A.). A man and a woman were jointly charged. A submission for the man, made after the evidence for the prosecution had been called, that there was no case to answer against him, was rejected. The man's conviction was quashed on appeal. The trial judge, although taking the view (shared by the Court of Criminal Appeal) that there was really no evidence against him, had thought that to withdraw the case against the man from the jury would be unfair to the woman co-accused. Lord Goddard C.J. said (p. 504): "That was not the line to take. If there was no evidence against the appellant he was entitled to be acquitted and to leave the dock." The judge is under a duty, not only to put an issue to the jury if there is sufficient evidence to warrant a reasonable affirmative finding, but also to withdraw an issue from the jury if there is insufficient evidence to warrant such a finding.

R. v. COCKLEY

79 Cr.App.R. 181 (C.A.: 1984)

In a criminal case, where a trial judge is held to have rightly rejected a submission of no case to answer, an appeal court will not quash a conviction on the ground of insufficiency except on the basis of a review of the whole of the evidence. However, if a trial judge has erred in law in rejecting such a submission, an appeal court cannot review the whole of the defence evidence; nor can it uphold a conviction by way of resort to the proviso to section 2(1) of the Criminal Appeal Act 1968 on the ground that no miscarriage of justice had occurred.

The accused was convicted of having in his possession an offensive weapon, a knife, in a public place without lawful authority. The trial judge had admitted prosecution evidence that the appellant had earlier in the day been involved in another incident in an alley way in which knives were used. The accused appealed on the grounds *inter alia* that this evidence had been wrongly admitted; that, even if rightly admitted, its prejudicial effect was totally disproportionate to its probative value and the trial judge ought to have excluded it in his discretion; and that the case should have been withdrawn from the jury.

BRISTOW J. (delivering the judgment of the court which included MAY L.J. and MACPHERSON J.):
. . .
The trial judge has of course a discretion to exclude admissible evidence if in his judgment its prejudicial effect would be disproportionate to its probative value. But such a discretion is to be exercised to promote, not to defeat, the course of justice. All evidence against an accused person is necessarily prejudicial to him. It is a matter of striking a proper balance between proof and prejudice, and this Court will be slow to interfere with the exercise of the discretion by the trial judge, who must have a far better sense of the immediate trial priorities than we can have on appeal. That said, we add that we think that the admission of the police evidence of what Cockley said about the alleway confrontation was in this case absolutely proper.
The importance of the matter was this. At the close of the prosecution case counsel submitted on Cockley's behalf that there was no case against him to answer.... Counsel submitted to this Court that had the police evidence relating to the alleyway incident not been admitted, the trial judge should have withdrawn the case against Cockley from the jury, following guidance given by this Court in *Galbraith* (1981) 73 Cr.App.R. 124. Since in the judgment of this Court the police evidence was rightly admitted, it is not necessary for us to come to a decision upon that submission.
Once the defence evidence was called, counsel accepts that there was evidence before the jury which, if they accepted it, must have led to Cockley's conviction.
. . .
Counsel canvassed before us what the situation might be if we came to the conclusion that the trial judge had been wrong in law not to withdraw the case against Cockley from the jury....
In our judgment it is not the law that if, on appeal to this Court, it is established that a trial judge has erred in law by not upholding a

submission of no case to go to the jury, it is open to this Court nevertheless to look at the whole of the evidence given below in deciding whether or not to quash the conviction which followed the judge's error of law. Had he not gone wrong in law the judge would have been bound to tell the jury there and then, whether or not he immediately directed them to acquit, that they were no longer concerned with the case against defendant X, and that they were from then on only concerned with his co-accused, Y and Z. It is clear that the proviso could not be invoked on appeal in that situation, because if the judge had not erred in law the case against X would have finished there and then and become *res judicata*. No evidence given by witnesses called in the defence of Y and Z, however much they implicated X, could thereafter affect X's situation. . . .

Having regard however to our decision that the trial judge was right not to withdraw Cockley's case from the jury these questions do not arise. The appeal is dismissed.

PAYNE v. HARRISON

[1961] 2 Q.B. 403; [1961] 2 All E.R. 873 (C.A.: 1961)

In civil cases, with or without a jury, when a defendant submits that there is no case to answer but subsequently gives evidence, an appellate court is entitled to consider the whole of the evidence.

The plaintiff was the widow of a man killed while driving a vehicle on the highway, and sued the owner and driver of the other colliding vehicle for negligence. At the conclusion of the plaintiff's case, counsel for the defendants submitted that there was no case to go to the jury. The judge rejected this submission, the defendant driver gave evidence, and the jury returned a verdict of £2,500 damages for the plaintiff, who obtained judgment accordingly. On appeal, it was argued for the defendants that the rejection on the submission of no case was erroneous. However, it was held that there was sufficient evidence to go to the jury, and that the appellate court should consider the whole of the evidence relating to negligence, including that of the defendant.

HOLROYD PEARCE L.J.: . . . There is no authority which directly covers this case. In *Great Western Ry.* v. *Rimell* (1856) 18 C.B. 575 the defendant at the end of the plaintiff's case submitted that there was no evidence to go to the jury. The judge held that there was, and the defendant then called evidence. It was held that the defendant did not, by calling witnesses preclude himself from appealing on the ground that the judge had ruled erroneously. . . . But that case was different from the present in that at the end of all the evidence on both sides there was not a scintilla of evidence to go the jury (*per* Crosswell J.). The defendant's evidence left the situation unaltered and the judge was wrong when in his summing-up he told the jury that they could find in the plaintiffs' favour. The defendant's submission that there was no evidence to go to the jury was well founded not only when it was made but also when all the evidence had been called on both sides.

In *Groves* v. *Cheltenham and East Gloucestershire Building Society*

[1913] 2 K.B. 100 (D.C.), the defendants in a county court before a judge alone at the close of the plaintiff's case submitted that there was no case to answer. That submission was rejected and the defendants called evidence. The court said clearly that if on the whole of the evidence called the judge was entitled to find for the plaintiff, even if he was wrong in not nonsuiting at the conclusion of the plaintiff's case, the court ought not to overrule his decision. It did, however, come to the conclusion that on the whole of the evidence the plaintiff could not succeed. . . .

(Counsel) submits that that case can be distinguished on the ground that it was an appeal from a judge alone. In my judgment, however, the principle which underlies the decision is equally applicable to a jury case and it is founded on justice and common sense. Certainly the judges in that case said nothing to suggest that there was any difference in principle between considerations in a jury case and those in a non-jury case.

. . . . [His Lordship referred to certain criminal cases including *R.* v. *Abbott, supra*]. . . . in certain respects the criminal courts may be prepared to extend to a defendant a latitude at the expense of the prosecution which the civil courts should not extend to a defendant at the expense of the plaintiff.

As to the exact rights of a defendant in a jury case in respect of submissions, there is some divergence of view which is irrelevant for the purposes of this case. . . .

Thus there is authority for the view that the defendant has no right until all the evidence is concluded to have a ruling on a submission that there is no case to answer. Assuming, without deciding, that a judge in a jury case has a discretion to rule without putting the defendant to his election whether he will call evidence, the judge is certainly not bound to give a ruling until the evidence is concluded. When the evidence is concluded the defendant, of course, has a right to a ruling whether there is any evidence to go to the jury, and if there is no such evidence he has a right to judgment.

In this case, therefore, the judge certainly need not have ruled on the defendant's submission at that stage. He could have deferred his ruling and thereby made the defendant elect. Even assuming that the judge did rule incorrectly, the defendant was thereby left in the position in which at the least the judge had every right to place him, namely, he was compelled to elect. Either he could call no evidence and stand on his submission before the judge, and if necessary before this court, or he could call evidence. He took the latter course. He cannot now, when it has proved disadvantageous, revert to the former course. Events have moved on since he made his choice. Truth has superseded hypothesis. It has been shown by evidence that the defendant was negligent, and the process of the law has given the plaintiff a judgment to which she thus became entitled. There is nothing here which suffices to "lure it back to cancel half a line." It would be a denial of justice now to deprive the plaintiff of that judgment by assessing the case artificially on a fragment of evidence when the whole has, by the defendant's choice, become available.

The question whether the judge was right in his ruling does not, therefore, arise. Now that the defendant has himself provided evidence of his own negligence, an interlocutory assessment of the evidence as it stood at the time when the plaintiff closed her case has become academic and irrelevant. If it were relevant I would hold on the facts (which it is unnecessary to recapitulate) that there was just sufficient evidence on the plaintiff's case to justify the judge in leaving it to the jury. I would therefore dismiss the appeal.

WILLMER and PEARSON L.JJ. delivered concurring judgments.

D.P.P. v. **Stonehouse** [1978] A.C. 55 (H.L.). The defendant was charged with attempting to obtain property by deception. At his trial the judge directed the jury, not that the conduct of the defendant could constitute an attempt, but that it did. The jury convicted the defendant, and the Court of Appeal upheld the conviction. The House of Lords affirmed this decision but only by virtue of resort to the proviso to section 2(1) of the Criminal Appeal Act 1968 on the ground that no miscarriage of justice resulted from the misdirection. Lord Salmon said (pp. 79–80): "Whilst there is no doubt that if a judge is satisfied that there is no evidence before the jury which could justify them in convicting the accused and that it would be perverse for them to do so, it is the judge's duty to direct them to acquit. This rule, which has long been established, is to protect the accused against being wrongly convicted. But there is no converse rule—although there may be some who think that there should be. If the judge is satisfied that, on the evidence, the jury would not be justified in acquitting the accused and indeed that it would be perverse of them to do so, he has no power to pre-empt the jury's verdict by directing them to convict. The jury alone have the right to decide that the accused is guilty. In an appropriate case (and this was certainly such a case) the judge may sum up in such a way as to make it plain that he considers that the accused is guilty and should be convicted. I doubt however whether the most effective way of doing so would be for the judge to tell the jury that it would be perverse for them to acquit. Such a course might well be counter-productive." Lord Edmund-Davies said (p. 88): "My Lords, the erroneous direction in the instant case is but one example of a prevalent (though fortunately not universal) tendency in our courts in these days to withdraw from the jury issues which are solely theirs to determine.... Whether this tendency springs from distrust of the jury's capacity or from excessive zeal in seeking to simplify their task, it needs careful watching, and there are welcome signs that judges are awakening to that fact: see for example, *R.* v. *Guttridge* [1973] R.T.R. 135, *R.* v. *Clemo (Note)* [1973] R.T.R. 176 and *R.* v. *Martin* (1972) 57 Cr.App.R. 279. And it has to be said that, while the possibility of a perverse verdict cannot be wholly eliminated, the risk that directions to convict may lead to quashings can be obviated by clarity in identifying the contested issue, by commenting on the evidence (maybe even in strong terms, provided that they fall short of a direction, as Lord Devlin stressed in *Chandler* v. *Director of Public Prosecutions* [1964] A.C. 763, 806), and by then trusting the jury to play their constitutional part in the criminal process." Lord Keith of Kinkel said (p. 94): "It is the function of the presiding judge at a trial to direct the jury upon the relevant rules of law. This includes the duty, if the judge takes the view that the evidence led, if accepted, cannot in law amount to proof of the crime charged, of directing the jury that they must acquit. It is the function of the jury, on the other hand, no only to find the facts and to draw inferences from the facts, but in modern practice also to apply the law, as they are directed upon it, to the facts as they find them to be. I regard this division of function as being of fundamental importance, and I should regret very much any tendency on the part of presiding judges to direct juries that, if they find certain facts to have been established, they must necessarily convict. A lawyer may think that the result of applying the law correctly to a certain factual situation is perfectly clear, but nevertheless the evidence may give rise to nuances which he has not observed, but which are apparent to the collective mind of a lay jury. It may be suggested that a direction to convict would only be given in exceptional circumstances, but that involves the existence of a discretion to decide whether such circumstances exist, and with it the possibility that the discretion may be wrongly exercised. Thus the field for appeals against conviction would be widened. The wiser and sounder course, in my opinion, is to adhere to the principle that, in every case where a jury may be entitled to convict, the application of the law to the facts is a matter for the jury and not for the judge. I see no reason to doubt that the good sense and responsible outlook of juries will enable them to perform this task successfully."

Lord Diplock (p. 70) and Lord Dilhorne (p. 74) expressed the view that a judge is not forbidden to tell the jury that particular acts of a defendant, if established, are so closely connected with the offence that they amount in law to an attempt to commit, if a verdict to the contrary would be perverse. This minority view does not represent the law. See *R.* v. *Challinor* (1985) 80 Cr.App.R. 253 (C.A.).

Note. See the subsequently enacted Criminal Attempts Act 1981, s.4(3) (Part Two, *infra*).

C. JUDGE AND JURY:
MATTERS OF CONSTRUCTION

MORRELL v. FRITH

3 M. & W. 402; 150 E.R. 1201; 7 L.J.Ex. 172; 1 H. & H. 100; 2 Jur. 619; 8 C. & P. 246 (Exchequer: 1838)

The construction of a document is generally a question of law for the judge; but where extrinsic evidence is required and allowed to explain it, as where peculiar terms or expressions are used, such evidence is for the jury, if any.

The question was whether a letter was a sufficient acknowledgment in writing to take the case out of the statute of limitation. The judge was of opinion that it was not sufficient; and, although requested by the plaintiff's counsel to leave the question to the jury, he declined to do so, and directed a nonsuit. On an application for a new trial, it was held that he was right.

LORD ABINGER C.B.: . . . One case in which the effect of a written document must be left to a jury, is, where it requires parol evidence to explain it, as in the ordinary case of mercantile contracts in which peculiar terms and abbreviations are employed. So also, where a series of letters form part of the evidence in the cause, they must be left, with the rest of it, to the jury. But where the question arises on the construction of one document only, without reference to any extrinsic evidence to explain it, it is the safest course to adhere to the rule, that the construction of written documents is a question of law for the court.

The intention of the parties is a question for the jury, and, in some cases, in cases of libel for instance, the meaning of the document is part of that intention, and therefore must be submitted to the jury. But where a legal right is to be determined from the construction of a written document which either is unambiguous or of which the ambiguity arises only from the words themselves, that is a question to be decided by the judge. . . .

PARKE B.: . . . The construction of a doubtful instrument itself is not for the jury, although the facts by which it may be explained are. . . .

ALDERSON B.: . . . Where it is a letter only, and there is no evidence beyond the written instrument itself, the construction of it is for the court only, and not for the jury. The case of mercantile documents is altogether different. There the meaning of the words themselves is in question, being words that are used in a particular and technical sense; it is as if the document were in a foreign language, and the truth or propriety of the translation were in question.

BOLLAND B. concurred.

Note.—The case of libel deserves special note. Prior to 1792 in prosecutions for libel the general practice was for the jury to decide merely questions of publication and of truth of the innuendoes (if any), these clearly being questions of fact. The judge decided whether the writing was defamatory or not, this being a question of law. However, in order to curb this power of the judge Fox's Libel Act 1792 provided that in criminal prosecutions for libel the jury shall, after direction by the judge on the law, give a general verdict upon the whole matter; thus in effect construing the writing provided the judge holds it to be capable of a defamatory meaning. This rule has now been applied to civil proceedings for libel (*Nevill* v. *Fine Arts and General Insurance Co. Ltd.* [1897] A.C. 68 (H.L.).)

As to parol or extrinsic evidence of documents, see Chapter 24, *infra*.

COZENS v. BRUTUS

[1973] A.C. 854; [1972] 2 All E.R. 1297; 56 Cr.App.R. 799 (H.L.: 1972)

The proper construction of a statute is a question of law. However, the ordinary meaning of an English word is a question of fact unless the court determines that the word has been used in an unusual sense. Normally, therefore, if it is alleged that the wrong meaning has been ascribed to a word, the only question of law that is normally raised is as to whether the finding was unreasonable in the sense that no reasonable tribunal acquainted with the ordinary use of language could have so found.

LORD REID. My Lords, the charge against the appellant is that on June 28, 1971, during the annual tournament at the All England Lawn Tennis Club, Wimbledon, he used insulting behaviour whereby a breach of the peace was likely to be occasioned, contrary to section 5 of the Public Order Act 1936, as amended.

. . . .

The magistrates came to the conclusion that the appellant's behaviour was not insulting within the terms of the offence alleged. They did not consider the other points raised in argument but dismissed the information without calling upon the appellant.

On a case stated a Divisional Court set aside the judgment of the magistrates and remitted the case to them to continue the hearing of the case. They certified as a point of law of general public importance [1972] 1 W.L.R. 484, 488:

"whether conduct which evidences a disrespect for the rights of others so that it is likely to cause their resentment or give rise to protests from them is insulting behaviour within the meaning of section 5 of the Public Order Act 1936."

Section 5 is in these terms:

"Any person who in any public place or at any public meeting uses threatening, abusive or insulting words or behaviour with intent to provoke a breach of the peace or whereby a breach of the peace is likely to be occasioned, shall be guilty of an offence."

Subsequent amendments do not affect the question which we have to consider.

It is not clear to me what precisely is the point of law which we have to decide. The question in the case stated for the opinion of the court is "Whether, on the above statement of facts, we came to a correct determination and decision in point of law." This seems to assume that the meaning of the word "insulting" in section 5 is a matter of law. And the Divisional Court appear to have proceeded on that footing.

In my judgment that is not right. The meaning of an ordinary word of the English language is not a question of law. The proper construction of a statute is a question of law. If the context shows that a word is used in an unusual sense the court will determine in other words what that unusual sense is. But here there is in my opinion no question of the word "insulting" being used in any unusual sense. It appears to me, for reasons which I shall give later, to be intended to have its ordinary meaning. It is for the tribunal which decides the case to consider, not as law but as fact, whether in the whole circumstances the words of the statute do or do not as a matter of ordinary usage of the English language cover or apply to the facts which have been proved. If it is alleged that the tribunal has reached a wrong decision there can be a question of law but only of a limited character. The question would normally be whether their decision was unreasonable in the sense that no tribunal acquainted with the ordinary use of language could reasonably reach that decision.

. . . .

So the question of law in this case must be whether it was unreasonable to hold that the appellant's behaviour was not insulting. To that question there could in my view be only one answer—No. . . .

. . . I do not agree that there can be conduct which is not insulting in the ordinary sense of the word but which is "insulting for the purpose of this section." If the view of the Divisional Court was that in this section the word "insulting" has some special or unusually wide meaning, then I do not agree. Parliament has given no indicat that the word is to be given any unusual meaning. Insulting means insulting and nothing else.

. . . .
I would allow the appeal with costs.

LORD MORRIS OF BORTH-Y-GEST, VISCOUNT DILHORNE AND LORD KILBRANDON delivered judgments to the same effect. LORD DIPLOCK agreed.

R. v. Feely [1973] 1 Q.B. 530 (C.A.). The word "dishonestly" in the Theft Act 1968, s.1(1), relates only to the state of mind of the person who did the act amounting to appropriation. That is a question of fact and should have been left to the jury. As it was not, the conviction should be quashed. "We do not agree that judges should define what 'dishonestly' means. This word is in common use whereas the word 'fraudulently' which was used in section 1(1) of the Larceny Act 1916 had acquired, as a result of case law, a special meaning. Jurors, when deciding whether an appropriation was dishonest can be reasonably expected to, and should, apply the current standards of ordinary decent people" (*per* Lawton L.J., delivering the judgment of the court at pp. 537–538).

Note.—Although basically benign in its implied emphasis upon the role of the common-sense of the jury and of the magistracy, this aspect of the doctrine laid down in *Cozens* v. *Brutus* has rightly not been applied with undue rigidity. Words, even if in general use, must sometimes be given a legal meaning (or at least legal limits must be placed upon their meaning) in particular contexts. For example, in *R.* v, *Magginis* [1987] A.C. 303 the House of Lords appears to have regarded the word "supply" in the Misuse of Drugs Act 1971 section 5(3) in this way. So, too, in *R.* v. *Caldwell* [1982] A.C. 341 the House of Lords considered the legal limits upon the meaning of the term "recklessly." In such cases a word, although in general use, is in effect being specifically used in what Lord Reid in *Cozens* v. *Brutus* referred to as an "unusual sense."

Cozens v. *Brutus* and *R.* v. *Feely* were respectively non-jury and jury criminal cases. There is some early authority (*e.g. Neilson* v. *Harford* (1841) 8 M. & W. 806, 823) for the view that, in a civil case tried with a jury, the ordinary meaning of words is a matter of construction for the judge. Given the contemporary paucity of such cases the matter is no longer important.

Sometimes a statute may prescribe that the meaning of a word shall be treated as a question of law: see, *e.g.* the Perjury Act 1911, s.1(6).

D. JUDGE AND JURY:
ISSUES OF REASONABLENESS

HERNIMAN v. SMITH

[1928] A.C. 305; 107 L.J.K.B. 225; [1938] 1 All E.R. 1 (H.L.: 1937)

In an action for malicious prosecution, it is the function of the jury (if any) to decide the facts operating on the mind of the prosecutor, if these are disputed, and of the judge to decide whether those facts constitute reasonable cause for the prosecution.

The accused had been convicted of conspiracy to defraud and false pretences but his conviction was quashed on appeal. He subsequently brought this action for damages for malicious prosecution and obtained judgment for £5,000; but it was held by the Court of Appeal that there was no case to go to the jury and the judgment was set aside. The plaintiff appealed to the House of Lords.

LORD ATKIN:.... The judge had left to the jury the following questions: (1) Has it been proved that the defendant commenced and proceeded with the prosecution without any honest belief that the plaintiff was guilty of fraud? (2) Has it been proved that the defendant failed or neglected to take reasonable care to inform himself of the true facts before commencing or proceeding with the prosecution? (3) Has it been proved that the defendant, in commencing or proceeding with the prosecution, was actuated by other motives than a desire to bring to justice one whom he honestly believed to be guilty?

The jury answered all three questions in the affirmative. The judge thereupon held that there was an absence of reasonable and probable cause,... and entered judgment for the plaintiff....

It is well settled that the question of the absence of reasonable and probable cause is for the judge. At the same time it is, I think, clear that the question is one of fact and not law: see *Lister* v. *Perryman* (1870) L.R. 4 H.L. 521, *per* Lord Chelmsford and Lord Westbury (at 535, 538). It is this circumstance of the decision of a material question of fact being confided to the judge that has given rise to disputes in a trial by jury as to what is the function of the jury. There is a danger lest the questions asked in this case, which are taken from the questions formulated by Cave J. in 1882 in the well-known case of *Abrath* v. *North Eastern Ry.* (1883) 11 Q.B.D. 440 should be asked in every case. This, it seems to me, would be to take the decision of the issue out of the hands of the judge to whom in the interests of prosecutor and accused alike it has been confided. The jury no doubt have important functions to perform. They are to find for the judge what the relevant facts are, when they are disputed. If there is any evidence of a lack of honest belief in the guilt of the accused on the part of the prosecutor, the fact whether he honestly believed or not is a disputed but essential fact on which the judge is to draw his conclusion and is a question for the jury. Questions may arise as to what the true facts are upon which the prosecutor acted. Were the statements, which he says were made to him, in fact made? Were the documents, which he says he saw, in fact seen by him and in the form in which he says he saw them? If the evidence on which he acted for any cause reasonably apparent to him might be unreliable or incomplete, was he aware or should he in the circumstances of the particular case have been aware that there was other reliable evidence available? If there are specific points of genuine dispute between the parties in regard to such circumstances, the facts should be ascertained by the jury. But to ask the general question whether the defendant took reasonable care to inform himself of the true state of the facts appears to me in many cases merely to ask the jury what the judge has to decide for himself. The facts upon which the prosecutor acted should be ascertained; in principle, other facts upon which he did not act appear to be irrelevant. When the judge knows the facts operating on the prosecutor's mind, he must then decide whether they afford reasonable or probable cause for prosecuting the accused....

On the whole of the facts, therefore . . . I come to the same conclusion as the Court of Appeal, that there was no evidence on which the judge could leave any question to the jury, and that he should have decided that there was no want of reasonable and probable cause. Neither of the first two questions should have been left to the jury. There was no evidence to go to the jury in support of the affirmative of either of them. Whether independently of the want of reasonable and probable cause there was any evidence of malice is a question which in the circumstances becomes irrelevant. I think that this appeal should be dismissed.

LORDS RUSSELL OF KILLOWEN, MACMILLAN, MAUGHAM and ROCHE agreed.

Note.—Herniman v. *Smith* was followed in *Tempest* v. *Snowden* [1952] 1 K.B. 130 (C.A.); *Glinski* v. *McIver* [1962] A.C. 726 (H.L.). The same rule seems to apply to actions for false imprisonment, when the defence is that the defendant had a reasonable and honest belief that the arrest of the plaintiff was justified. So, too, it is for the judge to determine whether the terms of a covenant in restraint of trade are reasonably necessary for the protection of the covenantee: *Dowden and Pook Ltd.* v. *Pook* [1904] 1 K.B. 45. But it is to be emphasised that these are exceptional cases for normally (and in a criminal case almost always) what is reasonable is a matter for the jury. The following matters, amongst others, have been held to be generally questions of fact for the jury—actual knowledge, real intention, express malice, good faith, due diligence and negligence.

BURDEN OF PROOF

THE term burden (or onus) of proof has been used in several differing senses, but most authorities agree that it has two primary meanings. These are usually respectively designated the legal burden of proof and the evidential burden of proof.[1]

The legal burden denotes an obligation to persuade. It was referred to by Wigmore as the "risk of non-persuasion," and in a recent House of Lords case[2] it has been dubbed the "probative burden." To be precisely meaningful the term must be related to a particular fact in issue rather than to a whole case. To speak, therefore, of the legal burden in criminal cases being upon the prosecution is only to make a generalisation, albeit a useful one; *viz.* that in respect of the great majority of issues liable to arise in criminal cases the legal burden of proof will rest upon the prosecution. Again, to speak of the legal burden in civil cases being upon the plaintiff is to make a similar, although here less accurate and therefore less useful, generalisation. What is to be remembered is that the legal burden may be differently placed in respect of different issues arising in the same case. The position can somewhat cumbrously be put thus: that the legal burden of proof in respect of a particular issue or disputed question of fact (fact in issue) is upon a party means that, if, after all the evidence has been adduced, there is then not what the law deems to be an adequate balance of evidence in favour of that issue being decided for that party, that issue must as a matter of law be decided against that party. Rules relating to the quantum of proof (Chapter 3, *infra*) prescribe what the law does regard as an adequate balance in this context: these rules indicate the degree of persuasion required in order to discharge a legal burden. In a civil action proof on balance of probabilities suffices, whereas what is required of the prosecution in criminal cases is proof beyond reasonable doubt.

The evidential burden of proof denotes an obligation to raise an issue and to adduce sufficient evidence, sometimes referred to as a prima facie case, to warrant putting that issue before the trier of fact. To describe the evidential burden as a burden of *proof* is therefore something of a misnomer. The evidential burden, like the legal burden, relates to a particular issue and may be differently placed in respect of the different issues which may arise in a case. The evidential burden is

---

[1] For an analysis of the relationship between these two concepts which is both thought-provoking and misconceived, see McNaughten (1955) 68 Harvard Law Review 1382.
[2] *D.P.P.* v. *Morgan* [1976] A.C. 182.

discharged by evidence sufficient to warrant, but not necessarily to require, an affirmative finding by a reasonable jury. Although it is for the judge to decide whether there is such a sufficiency, he is bound, if the evidence is sufficient, to put the issue to the jury, and, if it is insufficient, to withhold it from the jury. Whereas it is for the jury or trier of fact to determine whether a legal burden has been satisfied, discharge of an evidential burden is the exclusive concern of the judge.

The legal and evidential burdens in respect of one and the same issue will often rest on the same party, but they may be on opposing parties. For example, if an accused in a criminal case wishes to rely upon the defence of provocation, he must raise that issue and must adduce sufficient evidence to warrant it being put to the jury; but, if he does this, the prosecution is then under an obligation to prove beyond reasonable doubt that he was not in fact provoked. The evidential burden or the obligation to "pass the judge" rests upon the accused, but the "risk of non-persuasion" will fall upon the prosecution.

The placing or incidence of either burden, legal or evidential, on any given issue, being a matter of law, will depend upon case law precedent or the construction of a statute. It is sometimes said that the legal burden rests upon him who affirms rather than him who denies; but this by itself is an uncertain guide. The placing of legal and evidential burdens often reflects the way in which a relevant rule of substantive law is formulated, for example, proof of what is described as a defence will often rest upon the defendant; and, especially in civil cases, it may project the policies underlying that particular rule.[3] In criminal cases, however, more general considerations apply. Thus at common law, although the evidential burden in respect of a defence may be upon the accused, the legal burden in respect of all issues except insanity is upon the prosecution. A statute may, however, by means of a "reverse onus clause" expressly place the legal burden in respect of a designated issue upon the accused. When this is done the issue normally relates to an exemption, qualification or other defence: see, for example, the Merchant Shipping Act 1894, s.697; Sexual Offences Act 1956, s.47 (Part Two, *infra*); the Magistrates' Courts Act 1980, s.101 (Part Two, *infra*). In the absence of an express "reverse onus clause" the matter remains one of statutory interpretation, but a bias in favour of the accused does, and should, permeate. The subject has recently been reviewed by the House of Lords in R. v. *Hunt*.[4]

A legal burden, once placed, cannot usefully be seen as being shifted (except in a purely tactical sense) by the mere adduction of evidence. On the other hand, as its initial placing is determined by a rule of law, so it may be seen to shift as a result of the coming into operation of some other legal rule such as a compelling, although rebuttable, presumption of law. This process is sometimes couched in terms of the legal shifting of a burden of proof, but at other times in terms of the operation of a legal presumption. The use of the latter terminology is probably the most felicitous, and the matter is dealt with in Chapter 4 (*infra*) on presumptions. Quite apart from this, there may, of course, come a point in the course of a trial at which the legal burden

---

[3] See Stone (1944) 60 L.Q.R. 262 (especially pp. 270–284) in which *Joseph Constantine Steamship Line Ltd.* v. *Imperial Smelting Corporation Ltd.* [1942] A.C. 154 (H.L.) (*infra*) is discussed.
[4] [1987] A.C. 352 (H.L.) (*infra*).

upon an issue seems, in the light of the evidence so far adduced, to have
been. satisfied. In such circumstances there is a real sense in which
considerations of prudence (but not of law) impose an obligation upon
the opponent. He is then sometimes said to bear a tactical burden of
proof; or again sometimes it is said that the legal burden of proof has
tactically shifted to him.

The rules governing the right to begin relate to the incidence of the
evidential burden of proof. See *Mercer* v. *Whall* (1845) 14 L.J.Q.B. 267
(Q.B.) and *Note* thereto *infra.*

The evidential burden too may shift in a purely tactical sense; that is
to say it may appear at a given moment in the trial to have been
satisfied. A rule of law, such as a presumption, may cause the burden to
be shifted legally; this too, is considered in Chapter 4 (*infra.*). However,
for the evidential burden to be shifted as a matter of law simply by the
adduction of evidence, that evidence would have to be so convincing as
to require a directed finding. In such circumstances a contrary finding
could be set aside as unreasonable by an appellate court. It is to be
noted, however, that in criminal proceedings when (as is mostly the
case) the legal burden is upon the prosecution there can be no directed
finding against the accused and an acquittal cannot be set aside as
unreasonable.[5]

The doctrine of *res ipsa loquitur* in some of its various manifestations
bears upon the incidence of the legal and evidential burdens of proof in
civil cases. Mostly, however, the doctrine reflects the operation of a
presumption and it is treated under that heading (Chapter 4, *infra*).

The importance accorded to problems of burden of proof derives in
large measure from the nature of the adversary process.

A. INCIDENCE AND DISTRIBUTION OF BURDENS: CIVIL LITIGATION

AMOS v. HUGHES

1 Mood. & R. 464; 174 E.R. 160 (Nisi Prius: 1835)

*The burden of proof of the issues is upon the party who would be
unsuccessful in the case if no evidence at all were given; and such party
has the right to begin.*

In an action for a breach of contract to emboss calico in a
workmanlike manner, the defendant pleaded that he had done the work
properly, and the question arose as to which party was entitled to begin.

ALDERSON B. ruled that the plaintiff was entitled. He said questions
of this kind were not to be decided by simply ascertaining on which side
the affirmative, in point of form, lay: the proper test is, which party
would be successful if no evidence at all were given? Now here,

---

[5] A Divisional Court may, however, on an appeal by the prosecution remit a case to
magistrates who have wrongly found that there was no case to answer.

supposing no evidence to be given on either side, the defendant would be entitled to the verdict for it is not to be assumed that the work was badly executed; therefore the onus lies on the plaintiff.

Note.—The incidence of the legal burden of proof, therefore, reflects the substantive law.

In practice problems as to its incidence usually arise in one of two contexts: (a) either at the court of trial or on appeal in cases where there is not enough evidence to lead to any definite conclusion, the question arises which side must suffer for the inability to each to carry the matter to a definite result; (b) on appeal, in criminal cases particularly, objection may be taken that the appropriate direction to the jury was not given.

The subject of the evidential burden usually arises in two other contexts; (a) to determine which party has the right to begin in a civil trial; (b) at the court of trial or in an appellate court when considering whether the evidence constitutes a prima facie case.

Soward v. **Leggatt** (1836) 7 C. & P. 613 (Nisi Prius). The plaintiff, being the landlord of the defendant, alleged that the latter "did not repair" the premises in question. The defendant pleaded that he "did well and sufficiently repair" the same. It was held that, notwithstanding that the defendant's pleading was the grammatical affirmative, the burden of proof was upon the plaintiff.

Lord Abinger C.B. said (p. 615): "Looking at these things according to common sense, we should consider what is the substantive fact to be made out, and on whom it lies to make it out. It is not so much the form of the issue which ought to be considered, as the substance and effect of it. In many cases, a party, by a little difference in the drawing of his pleadings might make it either affirmative or negative, as he pleased. The plaintiff here says, 'You did not repair'; he might have said, 'You let the house become dilapidated.' I shall endeavour by my own view to arrive at the substance of the issue, and I think in the present case that the plaintiff's counsel should begin."

Mercer v. **Whall** (1845) 14 L.J.Q.B. 267 (Q.B.). An attorney's clerk brought an action for unliquidated damages for wrongful dismissal. The defendant pleaded that the dismissal had been for misconduct. It was held that the plaintiff had the right to begin because he bore the evidential burden of proof with regard to the amount of damages. Otherwise, the defendant would have been entitled to begin because there would then have been no issue upon which the plaintiff bore the evidential burden (that burden in respect of the issue of misconduct being on the defendant).

Note.—The position is now embodied in R.S.C. Order 35, r. 7(6), but subject to the judge's discretion to direct otherwise (r. 7(1)) (Part Three, *infra*).

In criminal cases on a plea of not guilty the prosecution will normally have the right to begin. If, however, there is an agreed statement of fact under section 9, or a formal admission under section 10 of the Criminal Justice Act 1967, the accused may have the right to begin. He may also have the right to begin if there is a dispute of fact arising out of a special plea such as *autrefois convict*.

Williams v. **East India Co.** (1802) 3 East 192 (K.B.). The plaintiff alleged that the defendants, who had chartered his ship, had put on board dangerous substances without due notice to the captain or to any other person concerned in the navigation. It was held that the burden lay on the plaintiff to prove even such a negative averment because the law presumed innocence of such a criminal neglect of duty.

Note.—The so-called presumption of innocence in criminal cases casts the burden of proof of guilt upon the prosecution (see *Woolmington* v. *D.P.P.* [1935] A.C. 462 (H.L.),

Chapter 2, *supra*). As the judgment above indicates, the presumption of innocence may also be applicable to civil cases. As to the standard of proof of criminality in civil cases, see *Hornal* v. *Neuberger Products Ltd.* [1957] 1 Q.B. 247 (C.A.), Chapter 3, *supra*.

Wakelin v. **London and South Western Ry.** (1886) 12 App.Cas. 41 (H.L.). This was an action brought by the widow of the deceased under the Fatal Accidents Act 1846 alleging that her husband had met his death owing to the negligence of the defendants. The only evidence was that the deceased's dead body was found lying at the side of the railway line near a level crossing. Lord Halsbury L.C. said (p. 445): "My Lords it is incumbent upon the plaintiff in this case to establish by proof that the husband's death had been caused by some negligence of the defendants.... That is the fact to be proved. If that fact is not proved the plaintiff fails, and if in the absence of direct proof the circumstances which are established are equally consistent with the allegation of the plaintiff as with the denial of the defendants, the plaintiff fails for the very simple reason that the plaintiff is bound to establish the affirmative of the proposition: "*Ei qui affirmat non ei qui negat incumbit probatio.*" ...

In this case I am unable to see any evidence of how this unfortunate calamity occurred. One may surmise, and it is but surmise and not evidence, that the unfortunate man was knocked down by a passing train while on the level crossing; but assuming in the plaintiff's favour that fact to be established, is there anything to show that the train ran over the man rather than the man ran against the train? ...

Note.—Compare *Jones* v. *G.W. Ry.* (1930) 144 L.T. 194, where the House of Lords distinguished *Wakelin's* case without "whittling down" the principles laid down there (Lord Hailsham L.C. at p. 197). The evidence in the *Jones* case was such that the inference could reasonably be drawn that as a matter of fact, the accident was occasioned by the negligence of the respondents. The matter was therefore properly left to the jury, whose finding that it had been so occasioned stood.

Wilsher v. **Essex Area Health Authority** [1988] A.C. 1074 (H.L.). See Chapter 4, Section B, *infra*.

JOSEPH CONSTANTINE STEAMSHIP LINE LTD. v. IMPERIAL SMELTING CORPORATION LTD.

[1942] A.C. 154; 110 L.J.K.B. 433; 165 L.T. 27; 57 T.L.R. 485; [1941] 2 All E.R. 165; 46 Com.Cas. 258; 70 Ll.L.R. 1; [1941] W.N. 112 (H.L.: 1941)

The burden of proof lies normally upon the party who affirms and not upon the party who denies. This rule applies to a plaintiff who asserts an exception to the defence pleaded.

A ship on charter was damaged by the explosion of her boiler while in harbour and before she sailed, with the result that she was unable to commence her voyage. The charterers claimed damages from the owners of the ship, whose defence was that the impossibility of performance resulting from the explosion amounted to frustration and they were not liable. The charterers contended that frustration did not arise unless the shipowners proved affirmatively that the explosion was not attributable to any default or negligence of theirs. In reply, the shipowners said that, having proved that the explosion disabled the vessel, the defence of frustration protected them unless the charterers showed affirmatively some default which would deprive the shipowners of the benefit of this defence. There were at least three possible hypotheses which would account for the disaster, and the arbitrator came to the conclusion that the evidence did not warrant his finding which of these actually did cause it, nor was he able to find affirmatively that the shipowners' negligence or that of their servants did not cause the accident. In the circumstances, therefore, the decision turned on which side carried the burden of proof. The House of Lords held that it lay upon the charterers to establish affirmatively that there had been such negligence or default as would vitiate the defence of frustration, and that they had failed to discharge this burden.

VISCOUNT SIMON L.C.: ... I reach the conclusion ... that the Court of Appeal was mistaken in holding that once the frustration in fact was established and any inference of default alleged to arise from the fact that the ship was under the control of the appellants' servants was negatived, it lay on the appellants to go further and satisfy the arbitrator positively that the frustration occurred without their default. ...

VISCOUNT MAUGHAM: ... I think the burden of proof in any particular case depends on the circumstances under which the claim arises. In general, the rule which applies is *"Ei qui affirmat non ei qui negat incumbit probatio."* It is an ancient rule founded on considerations of good sense and it should not be departed from without strong reasons. The position as to proof of non-responsibility for the event in such a case as the present is not very different from the position of a plaintiff in an action for negligence where contributory negligence on his part is alleged. In such a case the plaintiff must prove that there was some negligent act or omission on the part of the defendant which caused or materially contributed to the injury, but it is for the defendant to prove affirmatively, if he so contends, that there was contributory negligence on the part of the person injured, though here again the onus may easily be shifted. ...

If, however, I am right in the opinion above expressed that the onus of establishing absence of default did not rest on the appellants, the mere possibility of default on their part is not sufficient to disentitle them to rely on the principle of frustration. ...

LORDS RUSSELL OF KILLOWEN, WRIGHT and PORTER agreed with the motion that the appeal be allowed.

Sutton v. **Sadler** (1857) 3 C.B.(N.S.) 87 (C.P.). The heir-at-law of a testator brought an action against the devisee alleging the insanity of the testator. The devisee produced the will, proved its execution and called evidence of the testator's competency. The plaintiff heir-at-law gave some evidence of his insanity. The trial judge directed the jury that unless the heir proved insanity the devisee was entitled to succeed. The Court of Common Pleas held this to be a misdirection. Although proof of the execution of a rational will placed an evidential burden upon the heir-at-law to adduce sufficient evidence of insanity for the issue to be put to the jury, the legal burden of proof on that issue was then upon the defendant devisee. A new trial was accordingly ordered.

Note.—This case illustrates the general proposition that the evidential and legal burdens in respect of one and the same issue may be placed upon opposing parties.

B. INCIDENCE AND DISTRIBUTION OF BURDENS: CRIMINAL TRIALS

WOOLMINGTON v. DIRECTOR OF PUBLIC PROSECUTIONS

[1935] A.C. 462; 104 L.J.K.B. 433; 153 L.T. 232; 51 T.L.R. 446; 25 Cr.App.R. 72; 30 Cox C.C. 234 (H.L.: 1935)

In a criminal case it is always the duty of the prosecution to prove the guilt of the accused beyond reasonable doubt. Subject to statutory exceptions and the defence of insanity, the Crown must prove every ingredient in the crime.

On a charge of murder the judge directed the jury that once the Crown had proved the killing by the prisoner, it must be presumed to be murder and that it was for the prisoner to prove circumstances which would reduce the crime to manslaughter, or which would excuse the homicide as an accident. It was held that this was a misdirection and the conviction was quashed.

LORD SANKEY L.C.: . . . If it is proved that the conscious act of the prisoner killed a man and nothing else appears in the case, there is evidence upon which the jury may, not must, find him guilty of murder. It is difficult to conceive so bare and meagre a case, but that does not mean that the onus is not still on the prosecution.

If at any period of trial it was permissible for the judge to rule that the prosecution had established its case, and that the onus was shifted on the prisoner to prove that he was not guilty and that unless he discharged that onus the prosecution was entitled to succeed, it would be enabling the judge in such a case to say that the jury must in law find the prisoner guilty and so make the judge decide the case and not the jury, which is not the common law. It would be an entirely different case from those exceptional instances of special verdicts where a judge asks the jury to find certain facts and directs them that on such facts the prosecution is entitled to succeed. Indeed, a consideration of such special verdicts shows that it is not till the end of the evidence that a verdict can properly be found and that at the end of the evidence it is not for the prisoner to establish his innocence but for the prosecution to establish his guilt. Just as there is evidence on behalf of the prosecution so there may be evidence on behalf of the prisoner which may cause a doubt as to his guilt. In either case, he is entitled to the benefit of the doubt. But while the prosecution must prove the guilt of the prisoner, there is no such burden laid on the prisoner to prove his innocence and it is sufficient for him to raise a doubt as to his guilt; he is not bound to satisfy the jury of his innocence.

This is the real result of the perplexing case of *R.* v. *Schama* (1914) 84 L.J.K.B. 396 (C.C.A.), which lays down the same proposition, although perhaps in somewhat involved language. Juries are always told that if conviction there is to be the prosecution must prove the case beyond reasonable doubt. This statement cannot mean that in order to be acquitted the prisoner must "satisfy" the jury. This is the law as laid down in the Court of Criminal Appeal in *R.* v. *Davies* (1913) 29 T.L.R. 350, the headnote of which correctly states that where intent is an ingredient of a crime there is no onus on the defendant to prove that the act alleged was accidental. Throughout the web of the English criminal law one golden thread is always to be seen that it is the duty of the prosecution to prove the prisoner's guilt subject to what I have already said as to the defence of insanity and subject also to any reasonable exception. If, at the end of and on the whole of the case, there is a reasonable doubt, created by the evidence given by either the prosecution or the prisoner, as to whether the prisoner killed the deceased with a malicious intention, the prosecution has not made out the case and the prisoner is entitled to an acquittal. No matter what the charge or where the trial, the principle that the prosecution must prove the guilt of the prisoner is part of the common law of England and no attempt to whittle it down can be entertained. When dealing with a murder case the Crown must prove (a) death as the result of a voluntary act of the accused; and (b) malice of the accused. It may prove malice either expressly or by implication. For malice may be implied where death occurs as the result of a voluntary act of the accused which is (i) intentional; and (ii) unprovoked. When evidence of death and malice has been given (this is a question for the jury) the accused is entitled to show, by evidence or by examination of the circumstances adduced by the Crown, that the act on his part which caused death was either unintentional or provoked. If the jury are either satisfied with this explanation or, upon a review of all the evidence, are left in reasonable doubt whether, even if his explanation be not accepted, the act was unintentional or provoked, the prisoner is entitled to [the benefit of the doubt]. It is not the law of England to say, as was said in the summing-up in the present case: "if the Crown satisfy you that this woman died at the prisoner's hands then he has to show that there are circumstances to be found in the evidence which has been given from the witness-box in this case which alleviate the crime so that it is only manslaughter or which excuse the homicide altogether by showing it was a pure accident...."

LORDS HEWART, ATKIN, TOMLIN and WRIGHT concurred.

Note.—The words in square brackets were substituted in *Mancini* v. *D.P.P.* (immediately *infra*). For *obiter* consideration of the significance of the *Woolmington* case see *Jayasena* v. *R.* [1970] A.C. 618 (P.C.). As to the standard of proof see Chapter 3, *infra.*

MANCINI v. DIRECTOR OF PUBLIC PROSECUTIONS

[1942] A.C. 1; 111 L.J.K.B. 84; 165 T.L.R. 353; [1941] 3 All E.R. 272; 28 Cr.App.R. 65 (H.L.: 1941)

The prosecution bears the legal burden of negativing provocation, but the issue will not be put to the jury unless the accused discharges the evidential burden relating to it.

The appellant had been convicted of murder.

VISCOUNT SIMON L.C.: ... In the present case, the appellant's counsel contended that the learned judge should have directed the jury as to what would amount to provocation sufficient to reduce the felonious act to manslaughter, and should have told them that, if they took the view that the appellant's act was provoked in this sense, they should acquit him of murder, and moreover that if, without being satisfied on the point, they felt a reasonable doubt whether the act was or was not so provoked, the appellant was still entitled to be acquitted of murder and should be found guilty only of manslaughter. All this, however, depends on the view that there was evidence before the jury which might, if believed, be regarded as amounting to sufficient provocation. It is here, I think, that the contention for the appellant breaks down....

... Before, therefore, Macnaghten J.'s summing-up can be criticised on the ground that it did not deal adequately with the topic of provocation, we have to see what was the extent of the provocation as disclosed by the evidence which the jury had to consider, ...

... In my opinion, moreover, there was not sufficient evidence (once the story of being attacked with the pen-knife was discarded) to justify a verdict of manslaughter arising from the use of the dagger.

As regards the more general question with which the Attorney-General asks the House to deal, I would formulate the following proposition:—

(1) *Woolmington's* case [1942] A.C. 1 is concerned with explaining and reinforcing the rule that the prosecution must prove the charge it makes beyond reasonable doubt, and, consequently, that if, on the material before the jury, there is a reasonable doubt, the prisoner should have the benefit of it. The rule is of general application in all charges under the criminal law. The only eceptions arise, as explained in *Woolmington's* case, in the defence of insanity and in offences where onus of proof is specially dealt with by statute. Thus, when a prisoner is charged with murder and felonious homicide is proved against him, if the jury, when considering the evidence as a whole at the conclusion of the case, are left in reasonable doubt whether the homicide proved is not manslaughter, the jury should return a verdict of manslaughter. *Woolmington's* case was one in which the defence to the charge of murder was that of pure accident in circumstances not alleged to amount to criminal negligence. The prisoner gave evidence to that effect and my noble and learned friend, Lord Sankey, lays it down that "if the jury are either satisfied with his explanation or, upon a review of all the evidence, are left in reasonable doubt whether, even if his explanation be not accepted, the act was unintentional ..., the prisoner is entitled to be acquitted." A proposition to the same effect, but in different language, had been laid down by Lord Reading C.J., in connection with a charge of receiving recently stolen goods, in *Rex* v. *Abramovitch* (1914) 11 Cr.App.R. 45, 49 and was approved in the *Woolmington* decision. The law on this subject is thus finally established and is, I think, perfectly clear.

(2) The language employed by Lord Sankey does not assert and does not imply that in every charge of murder, whatever the circumstances, the judge ought to devote part of his summing-up to directing the jury on the question of manslaughter or the jury ought to consider it. If the evidence before the jury at the end of the case does not contain material on which a reasonable man could find a verdict of manslaughter instead of murder, it is no defect in the summing-up that manslaughter is not dealt with. Taking, for example, a case in which no evidence has been

given which would raise the issue of provocation, it is not the duty of the judge to invite the jury to speculate as to provocative incidents, of which there is no evidence and which cannot be reasonably inferred from the evidence. The duty of the jury to give the accused the benefit of the doubt is a duty which they should discharge having regard to the material before them, for it is on the evidence, and the evidence alone, that the prisoner is being tried, and it would only lead to confusion and possible injustice if either judge or jury went outside it.

(3) There is no prescribed formula for summing-up in a trial for murder, but the essential rules on this particular matter are as above stated. A good example of the proper direction is, as this House in *Woolmington's* case pointed out, that of Finlay J. (as he then was) at the abortive trial.

(4) Our attention was called to the recent decision of the Court of Criminal Appeal in *Rex* v. *Prince* [1941] 3 All E.R. 37, where the court reduced the jury's verdict of murder to manslaughter on the ground that the trial judge did not give a direction to the jury in accordance with the decision in *Woolmington's* case. *Prince's* case was one in which the defence pleaded that there was provocation sufficient to reduce the charge to manslaughter. The Court of Criminal Appeal must have proceeded on the view that the jury were not adequately directed that reasonable doubt whether such provocation existed, as opposed to confident assurance that it did, was sufficient to require the milder view to be taken. There is no reason to repeat to the jury the warning as to reasonable doubt again and again, provided that the direction is plainly given.

(5) In *Woolmington's* case, the sentence already quoted, which ends "the prisoner is entitled to be acquitted," should, of course, be understood as meaning "the prisoner is entitled to the benefit of the doubt." If the jury are left in reasonable doubt whether the act was "unintentional," *i.e.* a pure accident without criminal negligence, the verdict should be not guilty. If they are left in reasonable doubt whether the act was "provoked," *i.e.* perpetrated under the impulse of provocation as above defined, the prisoner should be found guilty of manslaughter.

... There is no error of law in Macnaghten J.'s summing-up and I, therefore, move that the appeal be dismissed.

VISCOUNT SANKEY and LORDS RUSSELL OF KILLOWEN, WRIGHT and PORTER concurred.

Chan Kau v. **The Queen** [1955] A.C. 207 (P.C.). The accused had been convicted of murder. A verdict of manslaughter was substituted on the ground that the issue of provocation had been wrongly withdrawn from the jury. The Privy Council also indicated that on the issue of self-defence, although the evidential burden was on the accused, if this had been satisfied, the legal burden would have been on the prosecution.

R. v. **Lobell** [1957] 1 Q.B. 547 (C.C.A.) the appellant had been convicted of wounding with intent to cause grievous bodily harm. He had set up the defence of self-defence which there was some evidence to support. The trial judge had directed the jury that it was for the defence to establish that plea to their satisfaction. The conviction was quashed. Lord Goddard C.J., reading the judgment of the court, said (pp. 551–552): "It must, however, be understood that maintaining the rule that the onus always remains on the prosecution does not mean that the Crown must give evidence-in-chief to rebut a suggestion of self-defence before that issue is raised, or indeed need give any evidence on the subject at all. If an issue relating to self-defence is to be left to the jury there must be some evidence from which a jury would be entitled to find that issue in favour of the accused, and ordinarily no doubt such evidence would be given by the defence. But there is a difference between leading evidence which would enable a jury to find an issue in favour of a defendant and in putting the onus upon him. The truth is that the jury must come to a verdict on the whole of the evidence that has been laid before them. If on a consideration of all the evidence the jury are left in doubt whether the killing or wounding may not have been in self-defence the proper verdict would be not guilty. A convenient way of directing the jury is to tell them that the burden of establishing guilt is on the prosecution, but that they must also consider the evidence for the defence which may have one of three results: it may convince them of the innocence of the accused, or it may cause them to doubt, in which case the defendant is entitled to an acquittal, or it may and sometimes does strengthen the case for the prosecution. It is perhaps a fine distinction to say that before a jury can find a particular issue in favour of an accused person he must give some evidence on which it can be found but none the less the onus remains on the prosecution; what it really amounts to is that if in the result the jury are left in doubt where the truth lies the verdict should be not guilty, and this is as true of an issue as to self-defence as it is to one of provocation, though of course the latter plea goes only to a mitigation of the offence. Had the judge in the present case gone on to say that it was not for the accused to establish his plea with the same degree of certainty as is necessary to establish a case for the prosecution it might have been that we should have had to consider whether this was a case for the application of the proviso. There was certainly here material on which a jury might have found self-defence. But that it was the duty of the accused to satisfy them on this point was on several occasions stressed in the summing-up and we do not feel by any means satisfied that if what we now hold was the correct direction that had been given the jury would be sure to have convicted. For these reasons we quashed the conviction at the close of the argument."

R. v. **Gill** [1963] 1 W.L.R. 841 (C.C.A.). In a criminal case it is for the accused to raise a defence of duress. "The Crown are not called upon to anticipate such a defence and destroy it in advance. The defendant, either by the cross-examination of the prosecution witness or by evidence called on his behalf, or by a combination of the two, must place before the court such material as makes duress a live issue fit and proper to be left to the jury. But, once he has succeeded in doing this, it is then for the Crown to destroy that defence in such a manner as to leave in the jury's minds no reasonable doubt that the accused cannot be absolved on the grounds of the alleged compulsion" (*per* Edmund Davies J. at p. 846, giving the judgment of the court). As, when viewed as a whole, the summing-up has made it clear that the legal burden on the issue of duress remained on the prosecution, the appeal was dismissed.

R. v. **Bone** [1968] 1 W.L.R. 983 (C.A.). The appellant's conviction for housebreaking and larceny was quashed because the trial judge had failed to direct the jury that it was for the prosecution to negative his defence of duress. "Duress, like self-defence and like drunkenness, is something which must in the first instance be raised by the defence: but at the end of the day it is always for the prosecution to prove their case, which involves negativing the defence which has been set up. It has been said in many cases, particularly self-defence cases, that to ensure that the jury are not confused it is not in general sufficient to give the general direction at the beginning in regard to the burden and standard of proof, but the jury should be told specifically that it is for the prosecution to negative, in that case, the self-defence" (*per* Lord Parker C.J. at p. 985, delivering the judgment of the court).

R. v. Gannon (1988) 87 Cr.App.R. 254 (C.A.). The appellant had been convicted of taking a vehicle without the consent of the owner contrary to the Theft Act 1968, s.12. Section 2(6) provides that: "A person does not commit an offence under this section by anything done in the belief that he has lawful authority to do it. . . . " The Court of Appeal held that although the onus of proving absence of belief of lawful authority lay on the prosecution, the issue of belief in lawful authority had first to be raised by the appellant who had to adduce sufficient evidence for the issue to be put to the jury. Kenneth Jones J. said (p. 256): "The onus was of course on the prosecution to prove the absence of the belief—*MacPherson* [1973] R.T.R. 157. But before that stage was reached, it was of course for the appellant to raise the issue. That means that he was required to call evidence or at least be able to point to some evidence which tended to show that he did hold the belief referred to in section 12(6). This he did not do." The appeal was dismissed.

The People (Attorney-General) v. Quinn [1965] I.R. 366 (S.C. Eire). The appellant had been convicted of manslaughter. At his trial he had pleaded self-defence. The Irish Supreme Court, allowing his appeal, quashed the conviction and ordered a new trial. One of the reasons for this was that the trial judge's direction as to the onus of proof on the issue of self-defence had been inadequate. Walsh J., in the course of his judgment (with which the other members of the Supreme Court agreed) said (pp. 382–383): "When the evidence in a case, whether it be the evidence offered by the prosecution or by the defence, discloses a possible defence of self-defence the onus remains throughout upon the prosecution to establish that the accused is guilty of the offence charged. The onus is never upon the accused to raise a doubt in the minds of the jury. In such case the burden rests on the prosecution to negative the possible defence of self-defence which has arisen and if, having considered the whole of the evidence, the jury is either convinced of the innocence of the prisoner or left in doubt whether or not he was acting in necessary self-defence they must acquit. Before the possible defence can be left to the jury as an issue there must be some evidence from which the jury would be entitled to find that issue in favour of the appellant. If the evidence for the prosecution does not disclose this possible defence then the necessary evidence will fall to be given by the defence. In such a case, however, where it falls to the defence to give the necessary evidence it must be made clear to the jury that there is a distinction, fine though it may appear, between adducing the evidence and the burden of proof and that there is no onus whatever upon the accused to establish any degree of doubt in their minds. In directing the jury on the question of the onus of proof it can only be misleading to a jury to refer to "establishing" the defence "in such a way as to raise a doubt." No defence has to be "established" in any case apart from insanity. In a case where there is evidence, whether it be disclosed in the prosecution case or in the defence case, which is sufficient to leave the issue of self-defence to the jury the only question the jury has to consider is whether they are satisfied beyond reasonable doubt that the accused killed the deceased (if it be a case of homicide) and whether the jury is satisfied beyond reasonable doubt that the prosecution has negatived the issue of self-defence. If the jury is not satisfied beyond reasonable doubt on both of these matters the accused must be acquitted."

M'Naughten's Case (1843) 10 Cl. & F. 200 (H.L.). It was held that the legal burden of establishing the common law defence of insanity does rest upon the accused.

Note.—This position was re-affirmed in *Woolmington* v. *D.P.P.* (*supra*). In *R.* v. *Windle* [1952] 2 Q.B. 826 Lord Goddard C.J., delivering the judgment of the Court of Criminal Appeal said (at p. 831): "It is common knowledge that it is for the defence to prove insanity, and if no evidence is given of insanity as understood by the law, there is no issue on the question to be left to the jury any more than in the case of any other issue which may be raised in a case and which is unsupported by evidence. Of course, it generally happens that if in a criminal proceeding the case is withdrawn from the jury, it is because the prosecution have failed to prove the case. If that is the opinion of the judge, it is his duty to withdraw it. So too, where the law puts on the defendant the burden of proving an issue—and there are a number of cases besides the issue of insanity in which a statute puts the proof of certain facts on the defence—and the defence fails to give any evidence of those facts, it is right for the judge to tell the jury that the defence raised is not going to be left to them because there is no evidence to support it." The Homicide Act 1957, s.2 (Part Two, *infra*) similarly places upon the accused the legal burden of establishing the statutory defence of diminished responsibility. (The burden is discharge by proof in the same way as this type of burden is discharged in civil cases: for the defence of insanity see *Sodeman* v. *R.* [1936] 2 All E.R. 1138, 1140 (P.C.); and for the defence of diminished responsibility see *R.* v. *Dunbar* [1958] 1 Q.B. 1 (C.C.A.); and on the standard of proof generally see Chapter 3, *infra*.)

R. v. **Podola** [1960] 1 Q.B. 325 (C.C.A.). The accused, indicted for capital murder, raised as a preliminary issue his fitness to plead, and this was contested by the prosecution. It was laid down that in such circumstances there is a burden upon the defence to satisfy the jury on balance of probabilities of the accused's insanity; but that, conversely, if the prosecution alleges, and the defence disputes, unfitness to plead, there is a burden upon the prosecution to establish unfitness.

BRATTY v. ATTORNEY-GENERAL FOR NORTHERN IRELAND

[1963] A.C. 386; [1961] 3 All E.R. 523; 46 Cr.App.R. 1 (H.L.: 1961)

There is a burden on the accused to adduce positive evidence in respect of some defences, including that of sane automatism.

The accused was charged with the murder of a girl by strangling her. His defences were automatism, or incapacity to form a murderous intention, or insanity. The judge left the defence of insanity only to the jury, who rejected it and convicted the accused. The Court of Criminal Appeal in Northern Ireland and the House of Lords upheld the conviction.

Viscount Kilmuir L.C.: . . . Automatism was defined by the Court of Criminal Appeal in this case "as connoting the state of a person who, though capable of action, is not conscious of what he is doing. . . . It means unconscious involuntary action, and it is a defence because the mind does not go with what is being done." . . .

The first portion of the argument before them that "automatism" should have been left to the jury was summarised by the Court of Criminal Appeal as being that the whole of the evidence on the issue of insanity was relevant on the issue whether automatism itself existed, however it was caused; in view of the onus being on the defence to show on a preponderance of probability that the necessary constituents of the M'Naughten formula were present, it was therefore submitted that, although the evidence might have failed to prove some constituent of insanity, the lack of consciousness itself might have seemed a genuine possibility to the jury, and the jury might at least have had a reasonable doubt as to whether the appellant was conscious of his acts so as to be guilty of murder. . . .

The Court of Criminal Appeal rejected that "first portion of the argument" on the ground that the learned judge was right in not leaving to the jury the defence of automatism, in so far as it purported to be founded on a defect of reason from disease of the mind within the M'Naughten Rules. In this I think that they were right. To establish the defence of insanity within the M'Naughten Rules the accused must prove on the preonderance of probabilities first a defect of reason from a disease of the mind, and, secondly, as a consequence of such a defect, ignorance of the nature and quality (or the wrongfulness) of the acts. We have to consider a case in which it is sought to do so by medical evidence to the effect that the conduct of the accused might be compatible with psychomotor epilepsy, which is a disease of the mind affecting the reason, and that psychomotor epilepsy could cause ignorance of the nature and quality of the acts done, but in which the medical witness can assign no other cause for that ignorance. Where the possibility of an unconscious act depends on, and only on, the existence of a defect of reason from disease of the mind within the M'Naughten Rules, a rejection by the jury of this defence of insanity necessarily implies that they reject the possibility.

. . . .

What I have said does not mean that, if a defence of insanity is raised unsuccessfully, there can never, in any conceivable circumstances, be room for an alternative defence based on automatism. For example, it may be alleged that the accused had a blow on the head, after which he acted without being conscious of what he was doing or was a sleepwalker. There might be a divergence of view as to whether there was a defect of reason from disease of the mind. . . . The jury might not accept the evidence of a defect of reason from disease of the mind, but at the same time accept the evidence that the prisoner did not know what he was doing. If the jury should take that view of the facts they would find him not guilty. But it should be noted that the defence would only have succeeded because the necessary foundation had been laid by positive evidence which, properly considered, was evidence of something other than a defect of reason from disease of the mind. In my opinion, this analysis of the two defences (insanity and automatism) shows that where the only cause alleged for the unconsciousness is a defect of reason from disease of the mind, and that cause is rejected by the jury, there can be no room for the alternative defence of automatism. Like the Court of Criminal Appeal, I cannot therefore accept the submission that the whole of the evidence directed to the issue of insanity should have been left to the jury to consider whether there was automatism due to another cause. It was conceded before this House and this is stated in the judgment of the Court of Criminal Appeal, that there was nothing to show or suggest that there was any other pathological cause for automatism.

I next consider the submission that even so the question of automatism ought to have been left to the jury. . . .

. . . It is necessary that a proper foundation be laid before a judge can leave "automatism" to the jury. That foundation, in my view, is not forthcoming merely from unaccepted evidence of a defect of reason from disease of the mind. There would need to be other evidence on which a jury could find non-insane automatism. What the Court of Criminal Appeal say about the onus of proof must be read in the context of evidence directed simultaneously to defences of insanity and automatism.

Certain very relevant problems were discussed in *Hill* v. *Baxter* [1958] 1 Q.B. 277 (D.C.), where the court (Lord Goddard C.J., Devlin and Pearson JJ.) held that, in spite of the justices accepting the defendant's evidence that he became unconscious while driving, there was no evidence which justified the justices in finding that the defendant was not fully responsible in law for his actions.... Devlin J. (at 284, 285) used these words, with which I respectfully agree and which are relevant to the present case: "It would be quite unreasonable to allow the defence to submit at the end of the prosecution's case that the Crown had not proved affirmatively and beyond a reasonable doubt that the accused was at the time of the crime sober, or not sleep-walking or not in a trance or blackout." Later he continued: "In my judgment there is not to be found in the case stated evidence of automatism of a character which would be fit to leave to a jury... he was not saying that he was a victim of disease of the mind. Unless there was evidence that this irrationality was due to some cause other than disease of the mind, the justices were not entitled simply to acquit.... "

I have already dealt with the unsuccessful attempt to prove psychomotor epilepsy and the concession before us that there was nothing in the evidence to show or suggest that there was any other pathological cause. If one subtracts the medical evidence directed to the establishment of psychomotor epilepsy, I am of opinion that there was not any evidence on which a jury could properly have considered the existence of automatism. Counsel for the petitioner directed our attention to the petitioner's statement, to his evidence and to his previous conduct. In my view they do not provide evidence fit to be left to a jury on this question. They could not form the basis of reasonable doubt....

LORDS TUCKER and HODSON agreed with the speeches of the Lord Chancellor and Lord Morris. LORD DENNING reached the same conclusion.

LORD MORRIS OF BORTH-Y-GEST:...In the conceivably possible case that I have postulated (of a violent act committed by a sleep-walker) it would not necessarily be the duty of the prosecution in leading their evidence as to the commission of the act specifically to direct such evidence to negativing the possibility of the act having been committed while sleep-walking. If, however, during the trial the suggested explanation of the act was advanced and if such explanation was so supported that it had sufficient substance to merit consideration by the jury, then the onus which is upon the prosecution would not be discharged unless the jury, having considered the explanation, were sure that guilt in regard to the particular crime charged was established so that they were left in no reasonable doubt. The position would be analogous to that which arises where a defence of self-defence is raised. Though the onus is upon the prosecution to negative that defence, the obligation to do so only arises effectively when there is a suggestion of such defence (see *R.* v. *Lobell* [1957] 1 Q.B. 547 (C.C.A.)).

Before an explanation of any conduct is worthy of consideration such explanation must be warranted by the established facts or be supported by some evidence that has been given by some witness. Though questions as to whether evidence should or should not be accepted or as to the weight to be attached to it are for the determination of the jury, it is a province of the judge to rule whether a theory or a submission has the support of evidence so that it can properly be passed to the jury for their consideration. As human behaviour may manifest itself in infinite varieties of circumstances it is perilous to generalise but it is not every facile mouthing of some easy phrase of excuse that can amount to an explanation. It is for the judge to decide whether there is evidence fit to be left to a jury which could be the basis for some suggested verdict. . . .

There were three medical witnesses called (either by the prosecution or by the defence) during the trial. In questions that were put to them and in the course of their evidence the only pathological explanation of what the appellant might have been suffering from what was suggested or in any way canvassed was the possibility that he might have been suffering from psychomotor epilepsy. Psychomotor epilepsy was said to be a functional disorder amounting to defect of reason due to disease of the mind. There was some evidence that during an attack of psychomotor epilepsy a person might commit a violent act unconsciously. There was no medical evidence which was directed to the suggestion of "automatism" other than automatism of an epileptic character. . . .

The non-medical evidence which was relied upon as supporting the suggestion that the appellant had acted in a state of automatism was the evidence of the appellant himself and all the evidence as to his general behaviour and backwardness and his characteristics and all the evidence relating to the circumstances attending the death of the deceased. . . . The appellant said in the witness box that he did not at the time know what he was doing or "did not realise exactly" what he was doing or realise at the time what he had done or did not remember what he had done. He also said that he had not "meant to do any harm." A consideration of his evidence and of the other evidence in the case leads me to the view that it did not provide a proper foundation for a submission that (apart from any question of insanity) the actions of the appellant had been unconscious and involuntary. There was no sufficient evidence, fit to be left to a jury, on which a jury might conclude that the appellant had acted unconsciously and involuntarily or which might leave a jury in reasonable doubt whether this might be so. . . .

R. v. **Burns** (1973) 58 Cr.App.R. 364 (C.A.). Where issues of both insanity and automatism arise, it is important that the summing-up should distinguish between them with regard to burden of proof. Whereas the burden of proving insanity is upon the accused, Stephenson L.J., delivering the judgment of the court, said (pp. 374–375): "It is not for the defence to prove automatism, it is for the prosecution to negative it once the defence lays a foundation for it. Nowhere does the judge draw that distinction between the two 'defences,'. . . Nowhere does the judge tell the jury that, if they thought other factors than disease of the mind might be a cause of his unawareness, they should consider automatism even if they rejected insanity, or that, if they thought one or more of those factors might not be known to the appellant to be likely to produce unawareness, they should acquit him altogether. We . . . have come to the conclusion that there was some evidence of other factors operating upon a disease of the appellant's mind, and of the possibility that he did not appreciate the effect which they might have. There was therefore misdirection or non-direction on the issue of automatism.... We have then to consider whether this verdict is in consequence unsatisfactory or unsafe or whether we can apply the proviso confident that no miscarriage of justice has occurred. In our judgment this is a clear case for the application of the proviso and the jury's verdict can safely stand."

R. v. Turner (1816) 5 M. & S. 206. This was a prosecution against a carrier for having pheasants and hares in his possession without being qualified by law to do so. There were numerous different qualifications recognised by the game laws. As the accused knew which qualification, if any, applied to him, the Court of King's Bench held that the burden of proof was upon him to show that qualification, notwithstanding that the absence of qualification was affirmatively alleged by the prosecution. Otherwise the prosecution would have been obliged to negative expressly the whole truth of every possible qualification. Bayley J. said (p. 211): "I have always understood it to be a general rule, that if a negative averment be made by one party, which is peculiarly within the knowledge of the other, the party within whose knowledge it lies, and who asserts the affirmative, is to prove it, and not he who avers the negative. And if we consider the reason of the thing in this particular case, we cannot but see that it is next to impossible that the witness for the prosecution should be prepared to give any evidence of the defendant's want of qualification ... there is no hardship in casting the burden of the affirmative proof on the defendant, because he must be presumed to know his own qualification, and to be able to prove it ... But if the onus of proving the negative is to lie on the other party, it seems to me that it will be the cause of many offenders escaping conviction. I cannot help thinking, therefore, that the onus must lie on the defendant, and that when the prosecutor has proved everything which, but for the defendant's being qualified, would subject the defendant to the penalty, he has done enough; and the proof of qualification is to come in as matter of defence...."

Note.—This doctrine suggesting, as it does, a rule of statutory interpretation has been invoked many times. However, more recently it has usually been confined to cases in which the factual basis of a negative averment was peculiarly within the knowledge of the accused. It posits no general rule that, whenever facts are peculiarly within the knowledge of an accused, he will bear the burden of proving a defence based on such facts: see, *e.g.* *R. v. Spurge* [1961] 2 Q.B. 205 (C.C.A.). Moreover, the doctrine and some of its implications must now be reviewed in the light of the decision of the House of Lords in *R. v. Hunt* [1987] A.C. 352 (*infra*).

R. v. HUNT

[1987] A.C. 352; [1987] 1 All E.R. 1; 84 Cr.App.R. 163 (H.L.: 1986)

A statutory exception to the rule that the legal burden of proof in a criminal case is upon the prosecution may be express or implied. This is so whether the offence is triable summarily or upon indictment. Where a linguistic construction does not clearly indicate where the burden of proof lies, the court may look to other factors in order to discover the intention of Parliament. These considerations include the mischief at which the provision is directed, and also practical considerations such as, in particular, the relative degrees of likely difficulty for the respective parties in discharging the burden.

The appellant had been convicted, under section 5(2) of the Misuse of Drugs Act 1971, of unlawful possession of a controlled drug, morphine. Section 5 of that Act provides: "(1) Subject to any regulations under section 7 of this Act for the time being in force, it shall not be lawful for a person to have a controlled drug in his possession. (2) Subject to section 28 of this Act and subsection (4) below, it is an offence for a person to have a controlled drug in his possession in contravention of subsection (1) above." Section 28 and section 5(4) set out certain defences. Section 7(1) empowers the Secretary of State by regulation to: "(a) except from section ... 5(1) of this Act such controlled drugs as may be specified in the regulations; and (b) make such other provision as he thinks fit for the purpose of making it unlawful for persons to do things which ... it would otherwise be unlawful for them to do." By regulation 4 of, and Schedule 1 to, the Misuse of Drugs Regulations 1973 (S.I. 1973 No. 797), made pursuant to section 7 of the Act, the Secretary of State directed that section 5(1) "shall not have effect in relation to" any preparation of morphine containing "not more than 0.2 per cent. of morphine calculated as anhydrous morphine base" and compounded in such a way that the morphine cannot readily be recovered and does not constitute a risk to health.

Police officers had found at the appellant's home a paper fold containing 154 milligrams of a white powder which, when analysed, was found to be morphine mixed with caffeine and antropine. The prosecution called no evidence at the trial as to the proportion of morphine in the powder, and, at the end of the prosecution's case, the defence submitted that there was no case to answer. The judge rejected this submission. The appellant then changed his plea to guilty, and a conviction was recorded. The Court of Appeal (Criminal Division) dismissed the appellant's appeal against conviction, but gave leave to appeal to the House of Lords and certified the following point of law of general public importance: "Whether, in a prosecution for possession of a preparation or product containing morphine under section 5 of the Misuse of Drugs Act 1971, where the morphine is of an unspecified amount and compounded with other ingredients, and where the defence seeks to rely upon the exception to the said section 5 set out in regulation 4(1) of and paragraph 3 of Schedule 1 to the Misuse of Drugs Regulations 1973 (as amended), the burden falls upon the defence to show that the said preparation or product comes within the said exception." The House of Lords allowed the appeal and quashed the appellant's conviction.

LORD TEMPLEMAN: ...

The appellant was accused of "possessing a controlled drug, contrary to section 5(2) of the Misuse of Drugs Act 1971." The evidence established possession of a powder containing "morphine mixed with caffeine and atropine." If the powder contained not more than 0.2 per cent. of morphine, calculated and compounded in the manner specified in the regulations, then the accused did not possess a controlled drug "contrary to section 5(2)." The prosecution only tendered facts which might or might not amount to an offence.

. . . .

The present appeal is not concerned with defences. By section 5(2) it is an offence to be in possession of a controlled drug in contravention of section 5(1). Possession of a powder containing not more than 0.2 per cent. of morphine based and compounded in the manner specified in regulation 4 does not contravene section 5(1) and therefore does not contravene section 5(2). Possession of a powder which contains morphine and does not comply with the conditions specified by regulation 4 contravenes section 5(1) and section 5(2). The prosecution only proved possession of a powder containing morphine. The appellant was therefore entitled to be acquitted.

LORD GRIFFITHS: . . .

The appellant challenges the decision of the Court of Appeal by two entirely distinct arguments. It is submitted that on the true construction of the Act and the Regulations the Court of Appeal were wrong to hold that the burden was upon the defendant to prove that the powder fell within Schedule 1 to the Regulations—an argument depending upon a close consideration of this particular legislation. But the appellant also raises an argument of far wider ranging significance based upon the decision of this House in *Woolmington* v. *Director of Public Prosecutions* [1935] A.C. 462 and involving the submission that the leading case of *Reg.* v. *Edwards* [1975] Q.B. 27 was wrongly decided by the Court of Appeal.

I propose first to consider the argument based upon *Woolmington* v. *Director of Public Prosecutions*. The starting point is the celebrated passage in the speech of Viscount Sankey L.C., at pp. 481–482:

"Throughout the web of the English criminal law one golden thread is always to be seen, that it is the duty of the prosecution to prove the prisoner's guilt subject to what I have already said as to the defence of insanity and subject also to any statutory exception. . . ."

The appellant submits that in using the phrase "any statutory exception" Lord Sankey L.C. was referring to statutory exceptions in which Parliament had by the use of express words placed the burden of proof on the accused, in the same way as the judges in *M'Naghten's Case* (1843) 10 Cl. & Fin. 200 had expressly placed the burden of proving insanity upon the accused. There are, of course, many examples of such statutory drafting of which a number are to be found in this Act—see section 5(4): "In any proceedings for an offence under subsection (2) above in which it is proved that the accused had a controlled drug in his possession, it shall be a defence for him to prove— . . ."—see also section 28(2)(3). . . .

The appellant also relies upon a passage in the speech of Viscount Simon L.C. in *Mancini* v. *Director of Public Prosecutions* [1942] A.C. 1 in which he said, at p. 11:

"*Woolmington's* case is concerned with explaining and reinforcing the rule that the prosecution must prove the charge it makes beyond reasonable doubt, and, consequently, that if, on the material before the jury, there is a reasonable doubt, the prisoner should have the benefit of it. The rule is of general application in all charges under the criminal law. The only exceptions arise, as explained in *Woolmington's* case, in the defence of insanity and in offences where onus of proof is specially dealt with by statute."

It is submitted that the use of the word "specially" indicates that Lord Simon L.C. considered that the reference in *Woolmington* [1935] A.C. 462 was limited to express statutory burdens of proof.

From this premise, it is argued that as it is well settled that if a defendant raises any of the common law defences such as accident, self-defence, provocation or duress and there is evidence to support such a defence the judge must leave it to the jury with a direction that the burden is on the prosecution to negative that defence, so it must follow that if a defendant raises any statutory defence the same rule must apply, and provided there is evidence to support such a defence the burden lies on the prosecution to negative it, the only exceptions to this rule being those cases in which the statute has by express words placed the burden of proving the defence upon the defendant.

However, in *Woolmington* the House was not concerned to consider the nature of a statutory defence or upon the burden of proving it might lie. The House was considering a defence of accident to a charge of murder and were concerned to correct a special rule which appeared to have emerged in charges of murder whereby once it was proved that the defendant had killed the deceased a burden was held to lie upon the defendant to excuse himself by proving that it was the result of an accident or that he had been provoked to do so or had acted in self-defence. This in effect relieved the prosecution of the burden of proving an essential element in the crime of murder, namely the malicious intent and placed the burden upon the accused to disprove it. It was this aberration that was so trenchantly corrected by Lord Sankey L.C. in the passage already cited [1935] A.C. 462, 481–482. In *Mancini* the House dealt with the duty of the judge to lay before the jury any line of defence which the facts might reasonably support and they also dealt with the particular nature of the defence of provocation. In neither appeal was the House concerned with a statutory defence and no argument was addressed on the nature or scope of statutory exceptions.

Before the decision in *Woolmington* [1935] A.C. 462 there had been a number of cases in which in trials on indictment the courts had held that the burden of establishing a statutory defence fell upon the defendant although the statute did not expressly so provide: see for example *Rex v. Turner* (1816) 5 M. & S. 206, a decision under the Gaming Acts, and *Apothecaries' Co. v. Bentley* (1824) 1 C. & P. 538 and *Rex v. Scott* (1921) 86 J.P. 69, decisions in which it was held that the defendant had the burden of proving that he was licensed to perform an otherwise prohibited act.

I cannot accept that either Viscount Sankey L.C. or Lord Simon L.C. intended to cast doubt on these long-standing decisions without having had the benefit of any argument addressed to the House on the question of statutory exceptions. I am, therefore, unwilling to read the reference to "any statutory exception" in *Woolmington*, at p. 481, in the restricted sense in which the appellant invites us to read it. It is also to be observed that Lord Devlin in *Jayesena* v. *The Queen* [1970] A.C. 618, a decision of the Privy Council, commenting upon *Woolmington* said, at p. 623:

> "The House laid it down that, save in the case of insanity or of a statutory defence, there was no burden laid on the prisoner to prove his innocence and that it was sufficient for him to raise a doubt as to his guilt."

Lord Devlin does not appear to restrict a statutory defence to one in which the burden of proof is expressly placed upon the defendant.

In *Reg.* v. *Edwards* [1975] Q.B. 27, the defendant had been convicted in the Crown Court of selling intoxicating liquor without a justices' licence contrary to section 160(1)(*a*) of the Licensing Act 1964. Section 160(1)(*a*) provides:

"Subject to the provisions of this Act, if any person—(a) sells or exposes for sale by retail any intoxicating liquor without holding a justices' licence or canteen licence authorising him to hold an excise licence for the sale of that liquor . . . he shall be guilty of an offence under this section."

The prosecution had called no evidence that the defendant did not have a licence and he appealed on the ground that the burden was on the prosecution to establish the lack of a licence. The Court of Appeal held that the burden was on the defendant to prove that he held a licence and that as he had not done so he was rightly convicted.

After an extensive review of the authorities the Court of Appeal held that the same rule applied to trials on indictment as was applied to summary trial by section 81 of the Magistrates' Courts Act 1952 which provided: . . . .

[Section 80 of that Act has, as Lord Griffiths pointed out, now been repealed and re-enacted in identical language in section 101 of the Magistrates' Courts Act 1980. This is set out in Part Two, *infra*.]

. . . .

There have been a number of cases considered by the Court of Appeal since *Woolmington* v. *Director of Public Prosecutions* [1935] A.C. 462 concerning the burden of proof in licensing cases both on indictment and on summary trial. There is no indication in any of these cases that the court considered that there should be any difference of approach to the burden of proof according to whether the case was tried summarily or on indictment: see *Rex* v. *Oliver* [1944] K.B. 68, *Rex* v. *Putland and Sorrell* [1946] 1 All E.R. 85, *John* v. *Humphreys* [1955] 1 W.L.R. 325, *Robertson* v. *Bannister* [1973] R.T.R. 109; see also *Reg.* v. *Ewens* [1967] 1 Q.B. 322 in which it was held that the Drugs (Prevention of Misuse) Act 1964 on its true construction placed an onus on the defendant to show that he was in possession of a prohibited drug by virtue of the issue of a prescription by a duly qualified medical practitioner.

Mr. Zucker relied upon three recent decisions of the Court of appeal which he submitted support his submission that a statutory defence only places an evidentiary burden on the defendant to raise the defence and that if this is done the burden remains on the prosecution to negative the defence. They are *Reg.* v. *Burke* (1978) 57 Cr.App.R. 220, *Reg.* v. *MacPherson* [1973] R.T.R. 157, *Reg.* v. *Cousins* [1982] Q.B. 526. In none of these cases was *Reg.* v. *Edwards* [1975] Q.B. 27 either cited in argument or referred to in the judgment. In each case the Court of Appeal construed the relevant statutory provision as requiring the burden of proof to be discharged by the prosecution. I do not regard these cases as intending to cast any doubt upon the correctness of the decision in *Reg.* v. *Edwards*, or as support for the proposition for which they were cited.

Whatever may have been its genesis I am satisfied that the modern rule was encapsulated by Lord Wilberforce in *Nimmo* v. *Alexander Cowan & Sons Ltd.* [1968] A.C. 107, 130, when speaking of the Scottish section which was then the equivalent of the present section 101 of the Magistrates' Courts Act 1980:

"I would think, then, that the section merely states the orthodox principle (common to both the criminal and the civil law) that exceptions, etc., are to be set up by those who rely on them."

I would summarise the position thus far by saying that *Woolmington* [1935] A.C. 462 did not lay down a rule that the burden of proving a statutory defence only lay upon the defendant if the statute specifically so provided: that a statute can, on its true construction, place a burden of proof on the defendant although it does not do so expressly: that if a burden of proof is placed on the defendant it is the same burden whether the case be tried summarily or on indictment, namely, a burden that has to be discharged on the balance of probabilities.

The real difficulty in these cases lies in determining upon whom Parliament intended to place the burden of proof when the statute has not expressly so provided. It presents particularly difficult problems of construction when what might be regarded as a matter of defence appears in a clause creating the offence rather than in some subsequent proviso from which it may more readily be inferred that it was intended to provide for a separate defence which a defendant must set up and prove if he wishes to avail himself of it. This difficulty was acutely demonstrated in *Nimmo* v. *Alexander Cowan & Sons Ltd.* [1968] A.C. 107. Section 29(1) of the Factories Act 1961 provides:

> "There shall, so far as is reasonably practicable, be provided and maintained safe means of access to every place at which any person has at any time to work, and every such place shall, so far as is reasonably practicable, be made and kept safe for any person working there."

The question before the House was whether the burden of proving that it was not reasonably practicable to make the working place safe lay upon the defendant or the plaintiff in a civil action. However, as the section also created a summary offence the same question would have arisen in a prosecution. In the event, the House divided three to two on the construction of the section, Lord Reid and Lord Wilberforce holding that the section required the plaintiff or prosecution to prove that it was reasonably practicable to make the working place safe, the majority, Lord Guest, Lord Upjohn and Lord Pearson, holding that if the plaintiff or prosecution proved that the working place was not safe it was for the defendant to excuse himself by proving that it was not reasonably practicable to make it safe. However, their Lordships were in agreement that if the linguistic construction of the statute did not clearly indicate upon whom the burden should lie the court should look to other considerations to determine the intention of Parliament such as the mischief at which the Act was aimed and practical considerations affecting the burden of proof and, in particular, the ease or difficulty that the respective parties would encounter in discharging the burden. I regard this last consideration as one of great importance for surely Parliament can never lightly be taken to have intended to impose an onerous duty on a defendant to prove his innocence in a criminal case, and a court should be very slow to draw any such inference from the language of a statute.

When all the cases are analysed, those in which the courts have held that the burden lies on the defendant are cases in which the burden can be easily discharged. This point can be demonstrated by what, at first blush, appear to be two almost indistinguishable cases that arose under wartime regulations. In *Rex* v. *Oliver* [1944] K.B. 68 the defendant was prosecuted for selling sugar without a licence. The material part of the Sugar (Control) Order 1940 (S.R. & O. 1940 No. 1068) by article 2 provided:

"Subject to any directions given or except under and in accordance with the terms of a licence permit or other authority granted by or on behalf of the Minister no...wholesaler shall by way of trade...supply...any sugar."

The Court of Criminal Appeal held that this placed the burden upon the defendant to prove that he had the necessary licence to sell sugar. In *Rex* v. *Putland and Sorrell* [1946] 1 All E.R. 85, the defendant was charged with acquiring silk stockings without surrendering clothing coupons. The material part of the Consumer Rationing (Consolidation) Order 1944 (S.R. & O. 1944 No. 800), article 4 provided: "A person shall not acquire rationed goods...without surrendering...coupons." The Court of Criminal Appeal there held that the burden was upon the prosecution to prove that the clothing had been bought without the surrender of coupons. The real distinction between these two cases lies in the comparative difficulty which would face a defendant in discharging the burden of proof.

In *Oliver's* case [1944] K.B. 68 it would have been a simple matter for the defendant to prove that he had a licence if such was the case but in the case of purchase of casual articles of clothing it might, as the court pointed out in *Putland's* case, be a matter of the utmost difficult for a defendant to establish that he had given the appropriate number of coupons for them. It appears to me that it was this consideration that led the court to construe that particular regulation as imposing the burden of proving that coupons had not been surrendered upon the prosecution.

In *Reg.* v. *Edwards* [1975] Q.B. 27, 39–40 the Court of Appeal expressed their conclusion in the form of an exception to what they said was the fundamental rule of our criminal law that the prosecution must prove every element of the offence charged. They said that the exception

"is limited to offences arising under enactments which prohibit the doing of an act save in specified circumstances or by persons of specified classes or with specified qualifications or with the licence or permission of specified authorities."

I have little doubt that the occasions upon which a statute will be construed as imposing a burden of proof upon a defendant which do not fall within this formulation are likely to be exceedingly rare. But I find it difficult to fit *Nimmo* v. *Alexander Cowan & Sons Ltd.* [1968] A.C. 107 into this formula, and I would prefer to adopt the formula as an excellent guide to construction rather than as an exception to a rule. In the final analysis each case must turn upon the construction of the particular legislation to determine whether the defence is an exception within the meaning of section 101 of the Act of 1980 which the Court of Appeal rightly decided reflects the rule for trials on indictment. With this one qualification I regard *Reg.* v. *Edwards* as rightly decided.

. . . .

With these considerations in mind I turn now to the question of construction. The essence of the offence is having in one's possession a prohibited substance. In order to establish guilt the prosecution must therefore prove that the prohibited substance is in the possession of the defendant. As it is an offence to have morphine in one form but not an offence to have morphine in another form the prosecuting must prove that the morphine is in the prohibited form for otherwise no offence is established. . . .

The Court of Appeal rejected this construction primarily because they considered that all the regulations made pursuant to section 7 of the Act should be similarly construed as placing a burden on the defendant. But this approach does not, in my view, give sufficient weight to the difference between the two regulatory powers given to the Secretary of State by section 7(1). Under section 7(1)(a), a power is given to provide that it shall not be an offence to possess certain drugs—this is achieved by exempting them in regulation 4. Under section 7(1)(b), a power is given to clothe certain persons with immunity for what would otherwise be unlawful acts and this is achieved by the remainder of the regulations in Part II of the Regulations of 1973. These latter regulations provide special defences to what would otherwise be unlawful acts and would, I accept, place a burden upon defendants to bring themselves within the exceptions if it were necessary to do so. I say "if it were necessary to do so" because of the extreme improbability that an exempted person would be charged with an offence.

However, I regard regulation 4 as in a quite different category from the other regulations in Part II. It deals not with exceptions to what would otherwise be unlawful but with the definition of the essential ingredients of an offence. This can be strikingly demonstrated by reference to regulation 4(2) which provides:

> "Sections 4(1) (which prohibits the production and supply of controlled drugs) and 5(1) of the Act shall not have effect in relation to poppy-straw."

Poppy-straw is shown in Part I of Schedule 2 to the Act as a Class A drug. But Parliament having removed poppy-straw from the Schedule by the regulation where is there room for any burden to lie on a defendant if he is charged with possessing poppy-straw? The defendant's answer is simply that it s not an offence to possess poppy-straw? Clearly, one cannot approach the problem of poppy-straw by saying that the prosecution establishes a prima facie case by proving the possession of poppy-straw because it is a controlled drug within Part I of Schedule 2 to the Act when poppy-straw has been withdrawn from the Schedule for the purposes of an offence under section 5(1). Both parts of regulation 4 must be similarly construed and by a parity of reasoning the prosecution cannot establish a prima facie case of possessing morphine by pointing to morphine in the Schedule when the regulation has provided that it is not an offence to possess morphine in a particular form. The prosecution must prove as an essential element in the offence the possession of a prohibited substance and the burden therefore lies upon the prosecution to prove not only that the powder contained morphine but also that it was not morphine in the form permitted by regulation 4(1) and Schedule 1 thereunder.

I do not share the anxieties of the Court of Appeal that this may place an undue burden on the prosecution. It must be extremely rare for a prosecution to be brought under the Act of 1971 without the substance in question having been analysed. If it has been analysed there will be no difficulty in producing evidence to show that it does not fall within Schedule 1 to the Regulations. I pause here to observe that the analyst was in court during this trial and could, no doubt, have given this evidence if called upon to do so. In future the evidence can, of course, be included in the analyst's report. On the other hand if the burden of proof is placed upon the defendant he may be faced with very real practical difficulties in discharging it. The suspected substance is usually seized by the police for the purposes of analysis and there is no statutory provision entitling the defendant to a proportion of it. Often there is very little of the substance and if it has already been analysed by the prosecution it may have been destroyed in the process. In those cases, which I would surmise are very rare, in which it is intended to prosecute without an analyst's report there will have to be evidence from which the inference can be drawn that the substance was a prohibited drug and such evidence may well permit of the inference that it was not one of the relatively harmless types of compounds containing little more than traces of the drugs which are contained in Schedule 1 to the Regulations.

Finally, my Lords, as this question of construction is obviously one of real difficulty I have regard to the fact that offences involving the misuse of hard drugs are among the most serious in the criminal calendar and, subject to certain special defences the burden whereof is specifically placed upon the defendant, they are absolute. In these circumstances, it seems to me right to resolve any ambiguity in favour of the defendant and to place the burden of proving the nature of the substance involved in so serious an offence upon the prosecution.

For these reasons, my Lords, I would answer the certified question in the negative. I would allow this appeal and quash the conviction.

LORD ACKNER: . . . This appeal raises in essence three relatively short points, with which I will seek to deal seriatim.

1. *In order to place a burden of proof upon the defendant, does Parliament have expressly so to provide or can it do so by necessary implication?*

. . . .

It is, of course, axiomatic that a statute may impose upon the accused the burden of proof of a particular defence to a statutory offence and may do so either expressly or by necessary implication. Whichever method Parliament uses it has created a "statutory exception" and there is no difference in the quality or status of such an exception. As at the date of the decision in *Woolmington's* case, there were numerous examples of statutes in which the onus of proof of a particular defence had been placed upon the accused, either expressly or, on a proper construction of the Act, by necessary implication. There is no warrant to be found either in the words used by the Lord Chancellor [in *Woolmington's* case] or in their context for suggesting that "statutory exception" is limited to *express* statutory exception. In *Mancini* v. *Director of Public Prosecutions* [1942] A.C. 1, 11 Viscount Simon L.C. referred to Lord Sankey's second exception as covering no more than "offences where onus of proof is specially dealt with by statute." I take the word "specially" to mean no more than that the onus of proof is made the subject of a statutory provision, be this express or implied. Lord Simon was not purporting to narrow the exception identified by Lord Sankey, but merely to repeat it. If he had intended to narrow it to *express* statutory exceptions, this would have been so stated, but the resultant anomaly would then have required justification. Since, *ex hypothesi*, Parliament had by necessary implication from the words used in the statute made known its intention, by what authority could that intention be ignored? It is a constitutional platitude to state that where Parliament makes its intention known, either expressly or by necessary implication, the courts must give effect to what Parliament has provided. While the very nature of this appeal demonstrates the desirability of Parliamentary draftsmen, whenever it is the intention of Parliament to place a burden of proof upon the accused, so to provide in express terms, the proposition advanced by the appellant cannot be sustained.

2. *Where does the incidence of the burden of proof lie in the offence charged?*

Where Parliament has made no express provision as to the burden of proof, the court must construe the enactment under which the charge is laid. But the court is not confined to the language of the statute. It must look at the substance and the effect of the enactment. . . .

While I accept that the Court of Appeal were entitled to have regard to the practical consequences of holding that the burden of proof rested on one party or the other and were not restricted to the formal wording of the relevant statutory provisions, those practical considerations pointed in my judgment to the burden of negativing the possibility of the drug being within one of the exceptions in Schedule 1 to the Regulations of 1973 resting on the prosecution.

3. *What is the weight of the burden of proof when it rests upon an accused?*

Where the burden of proof rests on the prosecution to negative the possibility of the drug falling within one of the exceptions, it is, of course, common ground that the prosecution must prove its case beyond reasonable doubt. It was, however, strongly urged upon your Lordships that if the burden had been upon the defence, as indeed it is conceded to be if reliance is being placed upon regulation 6, that burden is only an evidential one, that is to say an obligation to establish through evidence from the prosecution and/or evidence from the defence that there is material which raises such a defence, so that it becomes a live issue in the case.

Although, in the light of my decision on the first two points, this question does not arise, I have no hesitation in rejecting Mr. Zucker's submission for the following reasons. (i) It is accepted that when Parliament by express words provides that the proof of the excuse shall lie upon the accused, the legal burden of proof, that is to say the ultimate burden of proof, is placed upon the defendant, and that is discharged "on the balance of probabilities." It cannot logically follow that if, *ex hypothesi*, Parliament has by necessary implication placed the burden upon the accused, the weight of that burden should be quite different. (ii) The hypothesis is that by necessary implication Parliament has provided in a statute that *proof* of a particular exculpatory matter shall lie on the accused. However, the discharge of an evidential burden *proves* nothing—it merely raises an issue. Accordingly, the mere raising of an issue by the defence would not satisfy the obligation which Parliament has imposed. . . .

LORDS KEITH OF KINKEL and MACKAY OF CLASHFERN concurred.

Gatland v. Metropolitan Police Commissioner [1968] 2 Q.B. 279 (D.C.). The accused had been charged that without lawful authority or excuse he had deposited a thing, namely a metal hopper, on a highway in consequence whereof a user of the highway had been endangered, contrary to section 140 of the Highways Act, 1959 and the company had been charged with aiding and abetting Gatland. It was held that, although it was for the accused to establish any lawful authority or excuse, and although he had failed to do so, it was for the prosecution to prove, not only that the article in question has been deposited upon a highway, but also that in consequence thereof a user of the highway is injured or endangered. As there had been no evidence that any user of the highway had been injured or endangered in consequence of the deposit, the conviction had been rightly quashed.

R. v. Cousins [1982] 1 Q.B. 526 (C.A.). The appellant was convicted of making a threat to kill in contravention of section 16 (as substituted by the Criminal Law Act 1977, s.65(4) and Sched. 12) of the Offences against the Person Act 1861. The section runs: "A person who without lawful excuse makes to another a threat, intending that the other would fear it would be carried out, to kill that other or a third person shall be guilty of an offence...." The defence was that the accused had lawful excuse within section 16 in that *inter alia* he was acting in self-defence. The Court of Appeal quashed his conviction on the ground that on the facts a lawful excuse could exist within section 16 and that the trial judge had been wrong in withdrawing from the jury the issue as to whether the appellant had a lawful excuse. Milmo J., delivering the judgment of the court, said (p. 530): "In order to obtain the conviction of the appellant...the onus lay on the prosecution to establish.... (c) that there was no lawful excuse for making the threat.... As to (c), if there was evidence of facts which could give rise to lawful excuse, it was the duty of the judge to direct the jury to these facts and having reminded them that the onus lay with the prosecution to prove the absence of lawful excuse, to have left it to the jury to decide whether the existence of lawful excuse had been disposed of. On the other hand if there was no evidence of any facts which would give rise to a lawful excuse, it was the duty of the judge to direct the jury accordingly."

R. v. BENNETT AND OTHERS

(1979) 68 Cr.App.R. 168 (C.A.: 1978)

Sometimes, although the evidential burden rests upon the accused, the prosecution may be under an obligation either to call evidence or make it available to the defence.

The appellants had been convicted of *inter alia* conspiring to contravene the provisions of the Misuse of Drugs Act 1971. Their appeal (which was dismissed) was largely concerned with points of substantive law, but the Court of Appeal laid down certain guidelines as to the evidentiary obligations of the parties in cases of common law conspiracies.

BROWNE L.J. reading the following judgment of the Court (which included ORR L.J. and MAIS J.): In our judgment, the position of the Court, at any rate in cases of common law conspiracy, is as follows: (a) The burden of proof of course rests on the Crown; (b) If the Crown has in its possession evidence which might show that at the time when the agreement was made the carrying out of the agreement would have been impossible (as in *D.P.P.* v. *Nock* [1978] A.C. 979; 67 Cr.App. 116, where the evidence came from the Police Forensic Laboratory—see p. 981 and p. 118 of the respective reports) it is the duty of the Crown either to call the evidence or to make it available to the defence; (c) If the Crown has no such evidence, it is not their duty in the first instance to call evidence that the carrying out of the agreement would have been possible; the evidential burden of proving impossibility then shifts to the defence; (d) The probative burden remains on the Crown, and if there is some evidence of impossibility the question must be left to the jury with appropriate directions; (e) If there is no evidence of impossibility, the judge need not direct the jury about it. . . .

Note.—In *R.* v. *Dickie* [1984] 1 W.L.R. 1031 (C.A.) it was said (p. 1037) that the prosecution "has the obligation, if it has evidence in its possession of insanity which would assist the defence to establish that the defendant was in that condition when the crime was committed, to make that evidence available to the defence in good time, so that in its discretion it may make proper use of it."

C. BURDENS AND EVIDENCE

Abrath v. **North Eastern Ry.** (1883) 11 Q.B.D. 440 (C.A.). In an action for malicious prosecution the plaintiff alleged that the plaintiff had instituted proceedings against him without reasonable and probable cause. It was held that the burden was on the plaintiff to prove, not only the prosecution, but also the want of reasonable and probable cause. Bowen L.J. said (pp. 457–458, 462): "Now in an action for malicious prosecution the plaintiff has the burden throughout of establishing that the circumstances of the prosecution were such that a judge can see no reasonable or probable cause for instituting it. In one sense this is the assertion of a negative, and we have been pressed with the proposition that when a negative is to be made out the onus of proof shifts. That is not so. If the assertion of a negative is an essential part of the plaintiff's case, the proof of the assertion still rests upon the plaintiff. The terms "negative" and "affirmative" are after all relative and not absolute. In dealing with a question of negligence that term may be considered either as negative or affirmative according to the definition adopted in measuring the duty which is neglected. Wherever a person asserts affirmatively as part of his case that a certain state of facts is present or is absent, or that a particular thing is insufficient for a particular purpose, that is an averment which he is bound to prove positively. It has been said that an exception exists in those cases where the facts lie peculiarly within the knowledge of the opposite party. The counsel for the plaintiff have not gone the length of contending that in all those cases the onus shifts, and that the person within whose knowledge the truth peculiarly lies is bound to prove or disprove the matter in dispute. I think a proposition of that kind cannot be maintained, and that the exceptions supposed to be found amongst cases relating to the game laws may be explained on special grounds. . . .

The ground of our decision comes back to what was suggested. Who had to make good their point as to the proposition whether the defendants had taken reasonable and proper care to inform themselves of the true state of the case? The defendants were not bound to make good anything. It was the plaintiff's duty to show the absence of reasonable care. . . . "

Note.—The decision was affirmed on appeal: (1886) 11 App.Cas. 247 (H.L.).

PICKUP v. THAMES INSURANCE CO.

(1878) 3 Q.B.D. 594; 47 L.J.Q.B. 749; 39 L.T. 341 (C.A.: 1878)

The legal burden of proof is not shifted as a matter of law by the mere adduction of evidence.

In an action on a policy of marine insurance it was proved at the trial that the vessel put back from inability to proceed 11 days after she started on her voyage: the judge directed the jury that the time which elapsed between setting sail and putting back was sufficiently short to shift the onus of proof from the underwriters, and make it incumbent on the assured to prove that the unseaworthiness arose from causes occurring subsequently to setting sail. The Court of Appeal held, affirming the judgment of the Queen's Bench Division, that this was a misdirection. In the Queen's Bench Division Cockburn C.J. said "If a vessel very shortly after leaving port founders, or becomes unable to prosecute her voyage, in the absence of any external circumstances to account for such disaster or inability the irresistible inference arises, that her misfortune has been due to inherent defects existing at the time at which the risk attached. But this is not by reason of any legal presumption or shifting of the burden of proof, but simply as matter of reason and common sense brought to bear upon the question as one of fact, inasmuch as in the absence of every other possible cause the only conclusion, which can be arrived at, is that inherent unseaworthiness must have occasioned the result."

BRETT L.J.: I agree with the judgment of the Queen's Bench Division.

A good deal has been said on the argument about "the burden of proof" and "presumption." The burden of proof upon a plea of unseaworthiness to an action on a policy of marine insurance lies upon the defendant, and so far as the pleadings go it never shifts, it always remains upon him. But when facts are given in evidence, it is often said certain presumptions which are really inferences of fact, arise, and cause the burden of proof to shift; and so they do as a matter of reasoning, and, as a matter of fact, for instance, where a ship sails from a port, and soon after she has sailed sinks to the bottom of the sea, and there is nothing in the weather to account for such a disaster, it is a reasonable presumption to be made that she was unseaworthy when she started; and a jury may be properly told that, upon such uncontradicted evidence, they may presume as a matter of reasoning and inference from the facts, the vessel must have been in an unseaworthy condition when she started; that is, when she started she was not in a fit state to encounter the ordinary perils of the voyage, and if a jury, with no other evidence than that I have stated, were to find the contrary, it would not be a finding against any principle of law, but it would be such a finding against the reasonable inference from the facts that it would amount to a verdict against evidence. And as a guide on the question of fact, and the mode in which the jury are to draw inferences, I think the jury might be told what is laid down in 2 Arnould on Marine Insurance (5th ed.), p. 666, namely, that where a ship becomes so leaky or disabled as to be unable to proceed on her voyage soon after sailing on it, and this cannot be ascribed to any violent storm or extraordinary peril of the sea, the fair and natural presumption is that it arose from causes existing

before her setting out on her voyage, and, consequently, that she was
not seaworthy when she sailed. That is only telling them, if no other
facts are shown, "I should advise you, as reasonable men, to find that
the ship was unseaworthy when she started." . . .

THEISIGER L.J.: I agree that this case must go back for a new
trial. . . .
What was the position of the facts in the case at the time when the
learned judge gave his direction? On the one hand there had been
evidence—I do not give any opinion as to the strength or weakness of
that evidence—but there had been evidence that the ship had met with
some severe weather during the course of the 11 days which elapsed
between her leaving Rangoon and the time when she set sail to return
to Rangoon. On the other hand there was evidence that, upon her
return to Rangoon, upon the first survey some traces of worming were
discovered, and upon later surveys taking place, at a considerable period
after her return to Rangoon, her bottom was found to be very seriously
worm-eaten, so much so as to be quite sufficient to account for the
return to Rangoon.
Under those circumstances, what direction, either in fact or in law,
could the learned judge give to the jury? It seems to me that he could
not direct the jury that the burden of proof was shifted either in fact or
in law. All that he could say was this: "The burden of proof remains as
it originally remained, namely, that if there had been no evidence on
the one side, or on the other, the plaintiff would have been entitled to a
verdict on the question as to whether the ship was or was not seaworthy
at the commencement of the voyage. There being evidence on both
sides, it is for you, the jury to consider whether the evidence as to the
weather was such as to induce you to think that the loss was due to the
weather, and therefore to a peril insured against; or whether the
evidence which has been given as to the worming, coupled with the
evidence as to the weather, satisfies you that the weather was
insufficient to account for the loss, while the worming was amply
sufficient." That seems to me to be the whole extent to which, under
the circumstances of the case, the learned judge could fairly direct the
jury. . . .

COTTON L.J. agreed that there had to be a new trial.

Note.—Although the legal burden may not be shifted by the mere adduction of
evidence, it may be shifted as a result of the coming into operation of a compelling
presumption of law (see Chapter 4, *infra*). In *Abrath* v. *North Eastern Ry.* (see *supra*)
Bowen L.J. said (at p. 456): ". . . it is to be observed that very often the burden of proof
will be shifted within the scope of a particular issue by presumptions of law which have to
be explained to the jury."

Ajum Goolam Hossen & Co. v. Union Marine Insurance Co. [1901] A.C. 362
(P.C.). The facts were generally similar to those in *Pickup* v. *Thames Insurance
Co.* (*supra*). Lord Lindley, giving the opinion of the Privy Council, said (at
p. 366): "The underwriters have the great advantage of the undoubted fact that
the vessel capsized and sank in less than 24 hours after leaving port without
having encountered any storm or other known cause sufficient to account for the
catastrophe; and there is no doubt that if nothing more were known, they would

be entitled to succeed in the action. If nothing more were known, unseaworthiness at the time of sailing would be the natural inference to draw; there would be a presumption of unseaworthiness which a jury ought to be directed to act upon, and which a Court ought to act upon if unassisted by a jury. But if, as in this case, other facts material to the inquiry as to the unseaworthiness of the ship are proved, those facts must also be considered; and they must be weighed against the unaccountable loss of the ship so soon after sailing, and unless the balance of evidence warrants the conclusion that the ship was unseaworthy when she sailed, such unseaworthiness cannot be properly treated as established, and the defence founded upon it must fail. The law on this point was finally settled in *Pickup* v. *Thames and Mersey Marine Insurance Co.* ((1878) 3 Q.B.D. 594) which followed *Anderson* v. *Morice* ((1874) L.R. 10 C.P. 58)."

Note.—Although the reference to it is technically *obiter*, the position is that in civil proceedings the balance of evidence in favour of the party bearing the legal burden on a particular issue may be so overwhelming that, not only will a finding in his favour be demanded by common sense, but a judge would then be justified in directing such a finding. In this extreme case the equivalent of an evidential burden may perhaps usefully be said to have resulted from the mere adduction of evidence. But where in a criminal case a legal burden is on the prosecution there cannot be a direction that the weight of evidence is such as to discharge that burden or to place the equivalent of an evidential burden upon the accused. On the other hand, the Queen's Bench Divisional Court, on an appeal by the prosecutor against a finding of no case to answer, may remit a case to magistrates on the ground that the weight of evidence was such that there was a case to answer.

Chapter 3

DEGREES OF PERSUASION

THE terms "standard of proof" and "*quantum* of proof" are often used interchangeably and they refer to the size of the legal burden of proof. The rules relating to standard or *quantum* of proof indicate the degree of persuasion necessary for the discharge of that burden. It is the duty of the trier of fact to determine whether the probative force of the evidence that has been adduced tending to show discharge of the legal burden on a particular issue adequately exceeds the probative force of the evidence tending to show the contrary. Essentially, the rules relating to standard or *quantum* of proof prescribe what constitutes an adequate excess in this context. This is a matter of law. On the other hand it is a function of the trier of fact to weigh and to assess the evidence. It is accordingly, for the trier of fact to decide whether there is such an excess and, if so, whether it measures up to the required *quantum*; but in a jury trial the judge must, of course, direct the jury as to the nature of that *quantum* or standard.[1]

The common law knows two distinct standards of proof. In a civil case, all that is usually required is persuasion on balance of probabilities. The standard of proof in criminal cases has traditionally been defined as proof beyond reasonable doubt. The imposition of this heavy burden upon the prosecution, leading as it may to acquittal even though the trier of fact feels it more probable than not that the accused is guilty, reflects a compromise between a strong aversion to the possibility of an innocent man being convicted and a less strong reaction to the prospect of a guilty man being acquitted. This fundamental policy has no applicability even in a criminal case when the legal burden of proof on a particular issue is exceptionally placed upon the accused. Nor does it reach to civil litigation in which the existence of all or some of the ingredients of a crime is in issue. In each of these situations proof on balance of probabilities suffices.

The doctrine that the obligation placed upon the prosecution in a criminal case is an obligation to persuade beyond reasonable doubt received the *imprimatur* of the House of Lords in *Woolmington* v. *D.P.P.*,[2] but in recent decades there has been a considerable amount of

---

[1] Usually it is unnecessary for a trial judge to direct the jury more than once in a summing-up on the burden and standard of proof. However, there are circumstances in which a repetition of that direction to the jury is necessary: see *R.* v. *Gibson* [1983] 1 W.L.R. 1038 (C.A.).

[2] [1935] A.C. 462 (H.L.). Chap. 2, *supra*; see, too, *Mancini* v. *D.P.P.* [1942] A.C. 1, 11 (H.L.).

59

case law concerned with the proper instruction to be given to a jury on this subject. Much of this stems from two Court of Criminal Appeal cases, *R.* v. *Kritz*[3] and *R.* v. *Summers*,[4] in which reservations were expressed as to the wisdom of using the phrase "beyond reasonable doubt." It has been emphasised that there is no duty upon the judge to use this, or any other, particular phrase: it is the effect of the summing-up as a whole, seen in the context of the actual trial, that is important. On the other hand, words and phrases acquire meaning by usage, and for this reason it is submitted that very often use of the phrase "proof beyond reasonable doubt" will be positively helpful simply because it is the time-honoured phrase. Elaborate attempts to explain to the jury what is meant by reasonable are, however, generally to be avoided.

Matrimonial causes are civil proceedings, but the common law civil standard—proof on mere balance of probabilities—emerged in the context of litigation largely concerned with the apportionment of loss, and it is not necessarily apt in, for example, a petition for divorce. Moreover, the degree of persuasion required on the various issues which may arise in divorce proceedings can be seen as a matter of statutory construction. The Matrimonial Causes Act 1973, s.1 provides that the court shall not grant a divorce on the ground that the marriage has broken down irretrievably unless the petitioner "satisfies the court" of one or more specified facts, and that, if the court is so "satisfied on the evidence," it shall generally grant a divorce unless it is 'satisfied on all the evidence" that the marriage has not broken down irretrievably. Most of the authorities concerned with *quantum* of proof in matrimonial causes predate the Divorce Reform Act 1969 (now replaced by the Matrimonial Causes Act 1973) which eliminated the concept of the matrimonial offence (*e.g.* adultery) as such and introduced the pattern of the current law. For this reason evaluation of the somewhat confused case-law may be more tentative, but it is to be noted that the key word "satisfied" has been consistently used by the legislature. It was held that a judge could be satisfied of the non-existence of condonation (a bar to divorce under the old legislation) by proof on balance of probabilities. At the same time there is strong but not uncontradicted authority for the view that for the court to be satisfied of the existence of grounds for divorce proof beyond reasonable doubt is required.

That the legislature has never in this connection made use of the familiar formulation of either of the established common law standards is perhaps some indication of an intention to set up a standard *sui generis*, namely a standard rather higher than the normal civil standard but less exacting than proof beyond reasonable doubt. Divorce involves an alteration of the status of the parties. The alteration is of a type which can have consequences for them and for strangers which are serious and far-reaching. It is improbable that it was the intention of the legislature that the burden upon a party seeking to prove facts, which in law will bring about such changes, should be the lightest possible—no more than an obligation to prove them on the merest balance of probabilities. As has been pointed out this traditional civil standard of proof was itself developed in a very different context—that of litigation mostly concerned with the allocation of responsibility for irreversible damage that has already occurred.

---

[3] [1950] 1 K.B. 82, *infra*.
[4] (1952) 36 Cr.App.R. 14, *infra*.

At all events, although there have been dicta to the contrary, the fact that a finding of adultery might cast serious doubt upon the legitimacy of a child is not necessarily a crucial consideration. A finding of adultery does not itself render a child illegitimate. If an issue of legitimacy does arise a child conceived or born in lawful wedlock must be presumed to be legitimate, although this presumption can since 1969[5] be rebutted by evidence that it is more likely than not that he or she is illegitimate. At the same time on an issue of the paternity the standard of proof has been held still to be higher than the normal civil standard although not as high as proof beyond reasonable doubt.[6]

The notion has been canvassed that each of the two traditional common law standards of proof are themselves capable of infinite variation according to the seriousness of the issue and/or the gravity of the consequences of a finding.[7] This it is submitted, the eminence of its judicial proponents notwithstanding, can constitute a starting point for two fallacious lines of reasoning, which could give rise to considerable confusion. Of course, it may well be that, for example, the commission of a serious crime is often intrinsically less likely than is the commission of a petty crime, and this is then one factor to be taken into account when assessing probabilities: " . . . the very elements of gravity become a part of the whole range of circumstances which have to be weighed in the scale when deciding as to the balance of probabilities."[8] But to go further and to require a higher degree of persuasion simply because the issue is felt to be a serious one (or a correspondingly lower degree because it is felt to be non-serious) is unwarranted. The policy of the law is that a man ought not to be convicted of even a minor crime except on proof beyond reasonable doubt, but that a plaintiff in a civil action ought not be required to prove the wrong of which he complains more convincingly simply because it is a grievous wrong. So, too, conjecture as to the gravity or otherwise of the consequences of a finding of fact has no rational bearing upon the fact-finding process, which is concerned only with probabilities. A court must not be deterred from reaching a conclusion by regret or alarm at the possible gravity of its consequences, any more than it should jump or move easily to a conclusion because its consequences appear trivial. To allow juries and magistrates to be influenced when weighing evidence by their subjective assessment of the gravity of the issue and/or their estimate of the likely consequences of a finding is not only contrary to principle but in jury cases it could give rise to serious practical difficulty. As Edmund Davies L.J. said in *Bastable* v. *Bastable*[9]: " 'In proportion as the offence is grave, so ought the proof to be clear,' observed Lord Denning in *Blyth* v. *Blyth*,[10] but with the utmost deference I take leave to doubt that such a distinction could effectively be made by a jury, or indeed by many judges and lawyers. I should have thought, with respect, that an offence

---

[5] Family Law Reform Act 1969, s.26 (Part Two, *infra*).
[6] See *Serio* v. *Serio* (1983) 13 Fam. Law 255 (C.A.) (*infra*); *Avon C.C.* v. *G.* (1988) 152 J.P.N. 78; *W.* v. *K.* (Proof of Paternity) (1988) 18 Fam. Law 64.
[7] Denning L.J. in *Bater* v. *Bater* [1951] P.35 (C.A.) (*infra*); Lord Denning in *Blyth* v. *Blyth* [1966] A.C. 643, 669 (H.L.) (*infra*); Dixon J. (as he then was) in *Briginshaw* v. *Briginshaw* (1938) 60 C.L.R. 336 in the High Court of Australia.
[8] See Morris L.J. in *Hornal* v. *Neuberger Products Ltd.* [1957] 1 Q.B. 247, 266 (C.A.) (*infra*).
[9] [1968] 1 W.L.R. 1685 (C.A.) (*infra*).
[10] [1966] A.C. 643, 669 (H.L.) *infra*.

is either proved or it is not proved, in accordance with the standard (civil or criminal) appropriate to the case under consideration."[11] The true position has been lucidly stated by the High Court of Australia in *Rejfek* v. *McElroy*[12]: "The standard of proof to be applied in a case and the relationship between the degree of persuasion of the mind according to the balance of probabilities and gravity or otherwise of the fact of whose existence the mind is to be persuaded are not to be confused. The difference between the criminal standard of proof and the civil standard of proof is no mere matter of words: it is a matter of critical substance. No matter how grave the fact which is to be found in a civil case, the mind has only to be reasonably satisfied and has not with respect to any matter in issue in such a proceeding to attain that degree of certainty which is indispensable to the support of a conviction upon a criminal charge."[13]

Discharge of the evidential, as distinct from the legal, burden calls for "such evidence as, if believed and if left uncontradicted and unexplained, could be accepted by the jury as proof" (*per* Lord Devlin in *Yayasena* v. *The Queen* [1970] A.C. 618, 624 (P.C.)). In other words the evidence must be sufficient to justify (but not necessarily require) a finding that the legal burden on the issue is discharged. The meaning of "as proof" in this context will obviously depend upon the *quantum* of the particular legal burden. If a fact has to be proved beyond reasonable doubt, the evidence necessary to warrant such a finding will be greater than the evidence which would warrant a finding on balance of probabilities. So too where in a criminal case the evidential burden is upon the accused but the legal burden on the same issue is upon the prosecution, all that is required of the accused is to adduce evidence which "might leave a jury in reasonable doubt" (*per* Lord Morris of Borth-y-Gest in *Bratty* v. *Att.-Gen. for Northern Ireland* [1963] A.C. 386, 419 (H.L. (*infra*).

MILLER v. MINISTER OF PENSIONS

[1948] L.J.R. 203; 177 L.T. 536; **[1947] 2 All E.R. 372;** (1947) 63 T.L.R. 474 (K.B.: 1947)

Two standards of proof distinguished.

---

[11] At pp. 1691–1692.
[12] (1965) 112 C.L.R. 517.
[13] At pp. 521–522; cited with approval by Edmund Davies L.J. in *Bastable* v. *Bastable* [1968] 1 W.L.R. 1685 (C.A.) at p. 1691. In *Lawrence* v. *Chester Chronicle* [1986] C.L.Y. 1986 (C.A.), a defamation case, the Court of Appeal has confirmed that it is not generally necessary to direct the jury that the more serious the allegation made, the higher the standard of proof required, save in unusual cases. *R.* v. *Hants C.C., Ex p. Ellerton* [1985] 1 W.L.R. 749 (C.A.), concerned with disciplinary proceedings in the fire services, is perhaps such a case. There it was held that, such proceedings being domestic and not criminal, the appropriate standard is the civil standard, but the standard is higher or lower according to the nature and gravity of a particular contravention of the Fire Services (Discipline) Regulations 1948. See, too, *In re G. (a minor)* [1987] 1 W.L.R. 1461 (Fam.Div.), where it was said that in care and wardship proceedings the normally applicable civil standard on the issue of sexual abuse might in certain circumstances be increased.

This was an appeal by the appellant, the widow of an army officer, from a decision of a pensions appeal tribunal. She was entitled to a pension on account of her husband's long service, but she claimed the higher pension granted to widows of soldiers whose death was due to war service. The tribunal rejected this claim.

DENNING J.... The first point of law in the present appeal is whether the tribunal properly directed itself as to the burden of proof. The proper direction is covered by decisions of this court. It is as follows.
   1. In cases falling under art. 4(2) and art. 4(3) of the Royal Warrant Concerning Retired Pay, Pensions, etc., 1943 (which are generally cases where the man was passed fit at the commencement of his service, but is later afflicted by a disease which leads to his death or discharge) there is a compelling presumption in the man's favour which must prevail unless the evidence proves beyond reasonable doubt that the disease was not attributable to or aggravated by war service, and for that purpose the evidence must reach the same degree of cogency as is required in a criminal case before an accused person is found guilty. That degree is well settled. It need not reach certainty, but it must carry a high degree of probability. Proof beyond reasonable doubt does not mean proof beyond the shadow of a doubt. The law would fail to protect the community if it admitted fanciful possibilities to deflect the course of justice. If the evidence is so strong against a man as to leave only a remote possibility in his favour which can be dismissed with the sentence "of course it is possible, but not in the least probable," the case is proved beyond reasonable doubt, but nothing short of that will suffice.
   2. In cases falling under art. 4(2) and art. 4(4) (which are generally cases where the man was fit on his discharge, but incapacitated later by a disease) there is no compelling presumption in his favour, and the case must be decided according to the preponderance of probability. If at the end of the case the evidence turns the scale definitely one way or the other, the tribunal must decide accordingly, but if the evidence is so evenly balanced that the tribunal is unable to come to a determinate conclusion one way or the other, then the man must be given the benefit of the doubt. This means that the case must be decided in favour of the man unless the evidence against him reaches the same degree of cogency as is required to discharge a burden in a criminal case. That degree is well settled. It must carry a reasonable degree of probability, but not so high as is required in a criminal case. If the evidence is such that the tribunal can say: "We think it more probable than not," the burden is discharged, but, if the probabilities are equal, it is not.
   The present case falls under the first category. [His Lordship then referred to expert evidence which had been given.] ....
   The question is: What degree of doubt do those opinions impart? Do they give rise to a reasonable doubt or not? That was essentially a matter for the tribunal.
   The weight to be attached to the various opinions and the assessment of the degree of probability were essentially matters for the tribunal. They came to the conclusion that the whole of the probabilities were that war service played no part. They recognised the existence of a possibility the other way, but dismissed it as too remote saying, in effect: "Of course, it is possible, but not in the least probable." I cannot say they could not reasonably come to that conclusion. The appeal, is, therefore, dismissed.

Newis et Ux. v. Lark and Hunt (1571 2 Plow. 403, 412; 75 E.R. 609, 621) contains an early indication of the civil standard applicable at common law: "But where the matter is so far gone that the parties are at issue, . . . so that the jury is to give a verdict one way or the other, there, if the matter is doubtful, they may found their verdict upon that which appears the most probable. . . . "

Bonnington Castings Ltd. v. Wardlaw [1956] A.C. 613 (H.L.), confirms the applicability of this civil standard in a statutory context: "In my judgment, the employee must in all cases prove his case by the ordinary standard of proof in civil actions: he must make it appear at least that on a balance of probabilities the breach of duty caused or materially contributed to his injury" (*per* Lord Reid at p. 620).

Re Bramblevale Ltd. [1970] Ch. 128 (C.A.). Proof of contempt of court even in civil proceedings must be beyond reasonable doubt.

Note.—See, too, *Rooney* v. *Snaresbrook Crown Court* (1979) 68 Cr.App.R. 78 (C.A.); *Dean* v. *Dean* [1987] 1 F.L.R. 517 (C.A.).

R. v. Marlow Justices, Ex parte O'Sullivan [1984] Q.B. 381 (D.C.). The prosecutor laid information against the defendant, who entered into a recognisance before Justices in the sum of £1,000 to be of good behaviour for a period of 12 months, and the information was not heard. Later the prosecutor made a complaint that the defendant was in breach of the recognisance. The Divisional Court held that the Justices had acted properly in finding the allegations in the complaint proved on balance of probabilities and ordering the recognisance to be forfeited. Webster J., giving the judgment of the court, distinguished earlier decisions which he accepted (p. 385) as "clear authority for the proposition that the criminal standard of proof must be applied in determining whether a person is liable to be sentenced for an offence, upon conviction of which he entered into a recognisance to be of good behaviour, on the ground that he has breached that recognisance." In the instant case the only liability of the defendant, if the breach of recognisance was proved, was forfeiture of his recognisance. His Lordship concluded (p. 387): "that an application to forfeit or estreat a recognisance constitutes, both substantively and procedurally, a civil proceeding in which the appropriate standard of proof is the civil, not the criminal, standard."

R. v. Ewing [1983] Q.B. 1039 (C.A.). At the trial of the appellant on 24 counts charging theft, forgery of valuable securities and uttering forged documents, it was disputed that documents bore his handwriting. The trial judge stated that he was satisfied on the balance of probabilities that other documents used by handwriting experts for comparison purposes were written by the appellant and ruled that they were admissible under section 8 of the Criminal Procedure Act 1865 (see Part Two *infra*). The Court of Appeal held that the judge ought to have satisfied himself beyond reasonable doubt that those other documents were in the handwriting of the accused. O'Connor L.J., reading the judgment of the Court, said (pp. 1046–1047): "In our judgment, the words in section 8, 'any writing proved to the satisfaction of the judge to be genuine,' do not say anything about the standard of proof to be used, but direct that it is the judge, and not the jury, who is to decide, and the standard of proof is governed by common law: see the passage from Lord Pearce's speech in *Blyth* v. *Blyth* [1966] A.C. 643, 672. It follows that when the section is applied in civil cases, the civil standard of proof is used, and when it is applied in criminal cases, the criminal standard should be used. Were it otherwise, the situation created would be unacceptable, where conviction depends on proof that disputed handwriting is that of the accused person and where that proof depends upon comparison of the disputed writing with samples alleged to be genuine writings of the accused; we cannot see how his case can be said to be proved beyond reasonable doubt, if the prosecution only satisfy the judge, on a balance of probabilities, that the allegedly genuine samples were in fact genuine. The jury may be satisfied beyond a reasonable doubt that the crucial handwriting is by the same hand as the allegedly genuine writings, but if there is a reasonable doubt about the genuineness of such writing, then that must remain a reasonable doubt about the fact that the disputed writing was that of the accused and the case is not proved." His Lordship however concluded (p. 1048): "If the judge had directed himself that he should apply the criminal standard of proof, ... he must have said that he was satisfied that these documents were in the genuine writing of the appellant, and this ground of appeal must fail." (See, too, *R.* v. *Minors* [1989] 1 W.L.R. 441, 448 (C.A.).)

   R. v. **Kritz** [1950] 1 K.B. 82 (C.C.A.). This is the first of a series of cases in which the proper jury direction on the criminal standard was reconsidered. Lord Goddard C.J. said (pp. 89–90): "The only other point which has been seriously argued is that because the Common Serjeant told the jury that they must be reasonably satisfied, and did not use the words 'satisfied beyond reasonable doubt,' he was not sufficiently stating the onus of proof. It would be a great misfortune, in criminal cases especially, if the accuracy of a summing-up were made to depend upon whether or not the judge or the chairman had used a particular formula of words. It is not the particular formula that matters: it is the effect of the summing-up. If the jury are made to understand that they have to be satisfied and must not return a verdict against a defendant unless they feel sure, and that the onus is all the time on the prosecution and not on the defence, then whether the judge uses one form of language or another is neither here nor there.... It is right that they should be reminded in a criminal case that they must be fully satisfied of the guilt of the accused person and should not find a verdict against him unless they feel sure. That is the direction which I myself constantly give to juries. When once a judge begins to use the words 'reasonable doubt' and to try to explain what is a reasonable doubt and what is not, he is much more likely to confuse the jury than if he tells them in plain language: 'It is the duty of the prosecution to satisfy you of the prisoner's guilt' " (*per* Lord Goddard C.J. at pp. 89–90 in the *Law Reports*).

   R. v. **Summers** (1952) 36 Cr.App.R. 14 (C.C.A.). "If a jury is told that it is their duty to regard the evidence and see that it satisfies them so that they can feel sure when they return a verdict of Guilty, that is much better than using the expression 'reasonable doubt' and I hope in future that that will be done. I never use the expression when summing up. I always tell a jury that, before they convict they must feel sure and must be satisfied that the prosecution have established the guilt of the prisoner" (*per* Lord Goddard C.J. at p. 15).

   R. v. **Hepworth and Fearnley** [1955] 2 Q.B. 600 (C.C.A.). "It may be ... that I misled courts because I said in *R.* v. *Summers*—and I still adhere to it—that I thought that it was very unfortunate to talk to juries about 'reasonable doubt' because ... it is very difficult to tell a jury what is a reasonable doubt.... It may be that in some cases the word 'satisfied' is enough. Then, it is said that the jury in a civil case has to be satisfied and, therefore, one is only laying down the same standard of proof as in a civil case ... one would be on safe ground if one said in a criminal case to a jury: 'You must be satisfied beyond reasonable doubt' and one could also say: 'You, the jury, must be completely satisfied,' or better still: 'You must feel sure of the prisoner's guilt.' But I desire to repeat what I said in *R.* v. *Kritz*: 'It is not the formula that matters: it is the effect of the summing-up' " (*per* Lord Goddard C.J. at p. 603).

Dawson v. **The Queen** (1961) 106 C.L.R. 1 (H.C.Aust.). Dixon C.J., speaking of the phrase "satisfied beyond reasonable doubt," said: '. . . it is a mistake to depart from the time-honoured formula. It is, I think, used by ordinary people and understood well enough by the average man in the community. The attempts to substitute other expressions, of which there have been many examples not only here but in England, have never prospered. It is wise as well as proper to avoid such expressions" (at p. 18).

R. v. **Allan** [1969] 1 All E.R. 91 (C.C.A.). "It has been said in cases a good many times—and it is not necessary to cite them—that merely to say that the jury must be 'satisfied' without any clear indication of the degree of satisfaction required is an inadequate direction. But equally it has been said a good many times that it is not a matter of some precise formula or particular form of words being used" (*per* Fenton Atkinson L.J. at p. 92).

The People (Attorney-General) v. **Byrne** [1974] I.R. 1 (C.C.A., Eire): "The correct charge to a jury is that they must be satisfied beyond reasonable doubt of the guilt of the accused, and it is helpful if that degree of proof is contrasted with that in a civil case. It is also essential, however, that the jury should be told that the accused is entitled to the benefit of the doubt and that, when two views on any point of the case are possible on the evidence, they should adopt that which is favourable to the accused unless the state has established the other beyond reasonable doubt" (*per* Kenny J. at p. 9).

Green v. **The Queen** (1971) 126 C.L.R. 28 (H.C.Aust.). "A reasonable doubt is a doubt which the particular jury entertain in the circumstances. Jurymen themselves set the standard of what is reasonable in the circumstances. It is that ability which is attributed to them which is one of the virtues of our mode of trial: to their task of deciding facts they bring to bear their experience and judgment. . . . A reasonable doubt which a jury may entertain is not to be confined to a 'rational doubt,' or a 'doubt founded on reason' " (*per* Barwick C.J. at pp. 32–33).

Note.—For the distinction between scientific and legal proof see *R.* v. *Bracewell* (1979) 68 Cr.App.R. 44 (C.A.) at p. 49.

Walters v. **R.** [1969] 2 A.C. 26 (P.C.). A petition for special leave to appeal from an order of the Court of Appeal of Jamaica dismissing the petitioner's application for leave to appeal against his conviction was dismissed. Lord Diplock (delivering the opinion of the Board) said (pp. 29–31): "At the trial of the petitioner the judge thought it desirable to explain to the jury what was meant by the time-honoured phrase 'a reasonable doubt.' In the course of doing so he said: 'a reasonable doubt is that quality and kind of doubt which, when you are dealing with matters of importance in your own affairs, you allow to influence you one way or the other. . . . ' It is the duty of each individual juror to make up his own mind as to whether the evidence that the defendant committed the offence with which he is charged is so strong as to convince him personally of the defendant's guilt. Inevitably, because of differences of temperament or experience some jurors will take more convincing than others. That is why there is safety in numbers. And shared responsibility and the opportunity for discussion after retiring serves to counteract individual idiosyncrasies. By the time he sums up the judge at the trial has had an opportunity of observing the jurors. In their Lordships' view it is best left to his discretion to choose the most appropriate set of words in which to make *that* jury understand that they must not return a verdict against a defendant unless they are sure of his guilt; and if the judge feels that any of them, through unfamiliarity with court procedure, are in danger of thinking that they are engaged in some task more esoteric than applying to the evidence adduced at the trial the common sense with which they approach matters of importance to them in their ordinary lives, then the use of such analogies as that used by Small J. in the present case, whether in the words in which he expressed it or in those used in any of the other cases to which reference has been made, may be helpful and is in their Lordships' view unexceptionable. Their Lordships would deprecate any attempt to lay down some precise formula or to draw fine distinctions between one set of words and another. It is the effect of the summing-up as a whole that matters."

Note.—In *R.* v. *Gray* (1974) 58 Cr.App.R. 177 (C.A.) the only direction regarding the standard of proof had been in the following terms: "The burden of proof here, of course, lies upon the prosecution and it remains upon the prosecution from the very start to the very end of the case. It is never any part of the accused's duty to prove his innocence and the standard of proof is a high one. It must be proved, it is sometimes said, beyond reasonable doubt, and that means simply a doubt based upon good reason and not a fanciful doubt. It is the sort of doubt which might affect you in the conduct of your everyday affairs. That is the standard of proof which is required." Of this Megaw L.J. (delivering the judgment of the Court of Appeal) said (at p. 183): "If the learned judge had referred, for example, to the sort of doubt which may affect the mind of a person in the conduct of important affairs, there could be, in the view of the Court, no proper criticism. Indeed that was the very sort of direction which was approved by the Judicial Committee of the Privy Council in *Walters* v. *R.* [1969] 2 A.C. 26. But in this case the direction is open to legitimate criticism. The reference to 'the conduct of your everyday affairs' might in this context suggest to the jury too low a standard of proof; because a doubt which would influence a decision on an important matter might sensibly be disregarded in a decision on some 'everyday affair.' "

R. v. **Yap Chuan Ching** (1976) 63 Cr.App.R. 7 (C.A.). The appellant had been convicted of theft. Despite the apparent clarity of the issue and "a clear and impeccable summing up" the jury had appeared to have difficulty in reaching a verdict. After almost three hours the judge had summoned them back and made enquiries as to the prospects of their doing so. In the course of discussion with the foreman, the latter appeared to seek further instructions. The judge gave the jury a further direction in these terms: "It is the duty of the prosecution to prove the charge on the whole of the evidence beyond a reasonable doubt. A reasonable doubt, it has been said, is a doubt to which you can give a reason as opposed to a mere fanciful sort of speculation such as 'Well, nothing in this world is certain, nothing in this world can be proved.' As I say, that is the definition of a reasonable doubt—something to which you can assign a reason. It is sometimes said the sort of matter which might influence you if you were to consider some business matter. A matter, for example, of a mortgage concerning your house, or something of that nature. Does that assist?" The foreman said, "Yes, it does." Then, following a further retirement of four minutes, the jury returned a verdict convicting the appellant by a majority of 11 to 1 of theft on one count and acquitting him of the charge of theft on the second count. The appellant's appeal, which was dismissed, centred on this final direction. In the course of delivering the judgment of the Court of Appeal Lawton L.J. said (pp. 9–11): "Perhaps it is not irrelevant in the year 1976 for the Court to take judicial notice of the fact that one of the popular forms of entertainment nowadays on television is a series of reconstructed trials which have a striking degree of realism. Most jurors nowadays know something about the burden and standard of proof before they ever get into the jury box. It is against that background that we turn now to the judge's summing-up. He dealt with the burden of proof at the beginning of the summing-up. In the judgment of this Court, that is the best place in a summing-up to deal with it. He did so in these terms: 'So far as the law is concerned, the first matter is one which, quite rightly, has already been referred to, namely, that in this, as in every criminal case, it is for the prosecution to prove the charge, or charges, and to prove them so that you are sure that they have been made out—to prove them beyond a reasonable doubt—those being two different ways of saying what is really the same thing. If you are not satisfied to that degree, then your verdict, or verdicts, must necessarily be ones of not guilty.' Nothing could have been clearer, nothing could have been more accurate.... The task therefore for us has been to consider what was the effect of the summing-up as a whole, including the final direction. Mr. Latham attacked that final direction on three grounds. He said that it was unsatisfactory for a judge to define a 'reasonable doubt' as one for which a reason could be given; he pointed to a criticism of that phrase which was made by Lord Justice Edmund Davies (as he then was) in *Stafford and Luvaglio* (1968) 53 Cr.App.R. 1. Edmund Davies L.J., sitting with Fenton Atkinson L.J. and Waller J. said at p. 2: 'We do not, however, ourselves agree with the trial judge when, directing the jury upon the standard of proof, he told them to "Remember that a reasonable doubt is one for which you could give reasons if you were asked," and we dislike such a description or definition.' So do we. It does not help juries. But that is not the problem in this case. The problem is whether its use made this conviction unsafe. The next ground of complaint was that by using the mortgage of a house analogy, the learned judge was doing something which had been condemned a number of times in this Court. Counsel called our attention to two recent decisions. One was *Gray* (1973) 58 Cr.App.R. 177. In that case the phrase which was disapproved of was 'doubt which might affect you in the conduct of your everyday affairs.' The other, even more recently, is the decision of this Court, on January 13, 1976, in *Knott.* In that case the phrase 'the sort of doubt that can influence you as prudent men and women in the conduct of your everyday affairs.' In the past this Court has criticised trial judges for using that kind of analogy. The use of any analogy is to be avoided whenever possible. The final criticism was that when giving the direction of which complaint is made, the judge did not emphasise once again that the jury had to be sure. But we have no doubt that by the time the jury retired for the last time, they must have appreciated that they had to be sure before they could return a verdict of guilty. Nevertheless, in most cases—but not in this one—judges would be well advised not to attempt any gloss upon what is meant by 'sure' or what is meant by 'reasonable doubt.' In the last two decades there have been numerous cases before this Court, some of which have been successful, some of which have not, which have come here because judges have thought it helpful to a jury to comment of what the standard of proof is. Experience in this Court has shown that such comments usually create difficulties. They are more likely to confuse than help. But the exceptional case does sometimes arise. This is the sort of case in which, as I have already pointed out, the jury possibly wanted help as to what was meant by 'doubt.' The judge thought they wanted help and he tried to give them some. He was right to try and that is all he was doing. He seems to have steered clear of the formulas which have been condemned in this Court such as 'such doubt as arises in your everyday affairs or your everyday life'; or using another example which has been before the Court, 'the kind of doubts which you may have when trying to make up your minds what kind of motor car to buy. [Defence counsel] said that the judge did not stress that the relevant doubts were those which have to be overcome in *important* business affairs. What he did was to pick an example, which for sensible people would be an important matter. We can see nothing wrong in his so doing.... We point out and emphasise that if judges stopped trying to define that which is almost impossible to define there would be fewer appeals. We hope there will not be any more for some considerable time."

Ferguson v. **The Queen** [1979] 1 W.L.R. 94 (P.C.). Lord Scarman, giving the opinion of the Board, said (pp. 98–99) "In *Walters* v. *The Queen* [1969] 2 A.C. 26

their Lordships had to consider a direction almost identical in part with that in this case.... The Board expressed the view in that case that the formula used in summing up does not matter so long as it is made clear to the jury, whatever words are used, that they must not return a verdict against a defendant unless they are sure of his guilt. Their Lordships' Board agree with these comments, with one reservation. Though the law requires no particular formula, judges are wise, as a general rule, to adopt one. The time-honoured formula is that the jury must be satisfied beyond reasonable doubt. As Dixon C.J. said in *Dawson* v. *The Queen* (1961) 106 C.L.R. 1, 18, attempts to substitute other expressions have never prospered. It is generally sufficient and safe to direct a jury that they must be satisfied beyond reasonable doubt so that they feel sure of the defendant's guilt. Nevertheless, other words will suffice, so long as the message is clear."

McGreevy v. **D.P.P.** [1973] 1 W.L.R. 276 (H.L.). The House of Lords considered the "rule" in *Hodge's Case*. In *R.* v. *Hodge* (1838) 2 Lewin 227, Alderson B., summing up in a murder trial at which the Crown evidence against the accused was entirely circumstantial, directed the jury that before they found him guilty they must be satisfied "not only that those circumstances were consistent with his having committed the act, but they must also be satisfied that the facts were such as to be inconsistent with any other rational conclusion than that the prisoner was the guilty person." Their Lordships held that there is no rule of law requiring such a direction. The fact that the case against the accused depends wholly or substantially on circumstantial evidence does not impose upon the judge a duty to give the jury any additional or special direction: it is enough to direct them that they must be satisfied of the guilt of the accused beyond reasonable doubt.

Note.—McGreevy v. *D.P.P.* has been in effect followed by the High Court of Australia in *Barca* v. *R.* (1975) 133 C.L.R. 82; but in a later High Court case, *Grant* v. *R.* (1976) 11 A.L.R. 503, Barwick C.J. did say (p. 504): "The trial judge,... in the case where circumstantial evidence is relied on by the prosecution, must consider whether or not the case calls for the assistance of the jury by giving a direction specifically directed to the application of the onus of proof to circumstantial evidence." *McGreevy* v. *D.P.P.* was not followed in New Zealand in *Police* v. *Pereira* [1977] 1 N.Z.L.R. 547. There is a large body of Canadian case law in which the *Hodge* direction has been held to be mandatory, but the Supreme Court has recently restricted its scope: see especially *R.* v. *Mitchell* [1964] S.C.R. 471; 46 D.L.R. (2d) 384, *John* v. *R.* [1971] S.C.R. 781; 15 D.L.R. (3d) 692 and *R.* v. *Cooper* (1977) 74 D.L.R. (3d) 731. In *Holland* v. *U.S.* (1954) 348 U.S. 121; 75 S.Ct. 127, the Supreme Court of the United States actually prohibited the use by federal trial judges of an additional instruction along the lines of the *Hodge* formulation.

R. v. **Carr-Briant** [1943] K.B. 607 (C.C.A.) The accused was a director of a firm which contracted to do work for a government department, payments for work done being made on the certificate of an engineer employed by the department. The accused gave or lent the engineer £60; and he was charged with an offence under the Prevention of Corruption Acts, 1906 and 1916, which provide that in such circumstances the money shall be deemed to have been paid or given corruptly, unless the contrary is proved. The trial judge directed that the burden of proof resting on the appellant to negative corruption was as heavy as that resting in a normal case on the prosecution. The accused's conviction was quashed. Humphreys J. said (pp. 610 and 612): "We see no reason why the rebuttable presumption created by the section should not be construed in the same manner as similar words in other statutes or similar presumptions at common law, for instance, the presumption of sanity in the case of an accused person who is setting up the defence of insanity.... In our judgment, in any case where, either by statute or at common law, some matter is presumed against an accused person "unless the contrary is proved," the jury should be directed that it is for them to decide whether the contrary is proved, that the burden of proof required is less than that required at the hands of the prosecution in proving the case beyond a reasonable doubt, and that the burden may be discharged by evidence satisfying the jury of the probability of that which the accused is called upon to establish."

Hurst v. **Evans** [1917] 1 K.B. 352 (K.B.D.). An insurance policy excluded liability for loss by theft or dishonesty of any servant in the exclusive employment of the assured. In an action by the assured against one of the underwriters the evidence established a loss by theft and tended to implicate in the theft a servant in the exclusive employment of the plaintiff. Lush J. held that, assuming the burden of proving theft by the plaintiff's servant lay on the defendant, such theft might be established by evidence which would be insufficient to secure a conviction: "I do not think that the evidence in a civil case must necessarily be the same as in a criminal case arising out of the same matter . . ." (at p. 357).

Hornal v. **Neuberger Products Ltd.** [1957] 1 Q.B. 247 (C.A.). On the sale of a lathe to the plaintiff, a director of the defendant company was alleged to have falsely stated that the machine had been reconditioned by a named firm. If it could be proved beyond reasonable doubt that he did in fact make the representation knowing that it was untrue, he would be guilty of fraudulent misrepresentation. In a civil action for damages for breach of warranty, or in the alternative for fraud, with respect to the latter claim the county court judge was satisfied on balance of probabilities that the false statement had been made as alleged, and he applied that standard of proof. But he also stated that he would not have been satisfied if the criminal standard or proof had been applicable. On appeal it was held that the judge had applied the correct standard.

Post Office v. **Estuary Radio Ltd.** [1967] 1 W.L.R. 1396 (C.A.). The defendant operated a wireless transmitting station at a tower in the Thames estuary. The Post Office sought an injunction under section 14(7) of the Wireless Telegraphy Act 1949, to restrain him from using apparatus for wireless telegraphy at the tower contrary to section 1(1) of the Act, as applied by section 6(1). It was necessary for the Post Office to show that the tower was within United Kingdom internal waters. The Court of Appeal rejected the defendants' contention that, since the facts alleged would, if proved, constitute a criminal offence under section 14 of the Wireless Telegraphy Act 1949, an onus lay on the plaintiffs to prove them beyond reasonable doubt. The Court followed *Hornal* v. *Newberger Products Ltd.*

The Michael [1979] Ll.L.R. 55 (Q.B.Comm.Ct.). A question arose in civil proceedings as to whether barratry, in the shape of the deliberate scuttling of a ship, had been perpetrated. Kerr J. found this to be the case on a "clear balance of possibility." His approach seems to have been similar to that sometimes taken to the proof of fraud: a slightly loaded civil standard is applied.

Bater v. **Bater** [1951] P. 35. (C.A.). The Court held that on a petition for divorce on the ground of cruelty it was no misdirection for the trial judge to state that the petitioner must prove her case beyond reasonable doubt. Bucknill L.J., with whom Somervell L.J. agreed, said (at p. 36): "I regard proceedings for divorce as proceedings of very great importance, not only to the parties, but to the State. . . . I think that, if a high standard of proof is required because of the importance of a case to the parties and also the community, divorce proceedings are the kind of case which requires that high standard." Denning L.J. said (at pp. 36–38): "The difference of opinion which has been evoked about the standard of proof in recent cases may well turn out to be more a matter of words than anything else. It is of course true that by our law a higher standard of proof is required in criminal cases than in civil cases. But this is subject to the qualification that there is no absolute standard in either case. In criminal cases the charge must be proved beyond reasonable doubt, but there may be degrees of proof within that standard. As Best C.J., and many other great judges have said, "in proportion as the crime is enormous, so ought the proof to be clear." So also in civil cases, the case may be proved by a preponderance of probability, but there may be degrees of probability within that standard. The degree depends on the subject-matter. A civil court, when considering a charge of fraud, will naturally require for itself a higher degree of probability than that which it would require when asking if negligence is established. It does not adopt so high a degree as a criminal court, even when it is considering a charge of a criminal nature; but still it does require a degree of probability which is commensurate with the occasion. Likewise, a divorce court should require a degree of probability which is proportionate to the subject-matter. I do not think that the matter can be better put than it was by Lord Stowell in *Loveden* v. *Loveden* (1810) 2 Hagg.Con. 1, 3. "The only general rule that can be laid down upon the subject is, that the circumstances must be such as would lead the guarded discretion of a reasonable and just man to the conclusion." The degree of probability which a reasonable and just man would require to come to a conclusion—and likewise the degree of doubt which would prevent him coming to it—depends on the conclusion to which he is required to come. It would depend on whether it was a criminal case or a civil case, what the charge was, and what the consequences might be; and if he were left in real and substantial doubt on the particular matter, he would hold the charge not to be established: he would not be satisfied about it. But what is a real and substantial doubt? It is only another way of saying a reasonable doubt; and a reasonable doubt is simply that degree of doubt which would prevent a reasonable and just man from coming to the conclusion. So the phrase "reasonable doubt" takes the matter no further. It does not say that the degree of probability must be as high as 99 per cent. or as low as 51 per cent. The degree required must depend on the mind of the reasonable and just man who is considering the particular subject-matter. In some cases 51 per cent. would be enough, but not in others. When this is realised, the phrase "reasonable doubt" can be used just as aptly in a civil case or a divorce case as in a criminal case; and indeed it was so used by my Lord in *Davis* v. *Davis* [1950] P. 125 and *Gower* v. *Gower* 66 T.L.R. (Pt. I) 717 to which we have been referred. The only difference is that, because of our high regard for the liberty of the individual, a doubt may be regarded as reasonable in the criminal courts, which would not be so in the civil courts. I agree therefore with my brothers that the use of the phrase "reasonable doubt" by the commissioner in this case was not a misdirection any more than it was in *Briginshaw* v. *Briginshaw* (1938) 60 C.L.R. 336.

If, however, the commissioner had put the case higher and said that the case had to be proved with the same strictness as a crime is proved in a criminal court, then he would, I think, have misdirected himself, because that would be the very error which this court corrected in *Davis* v. *Davis* [1950] P. 125. It would be adopting too high a standard. The divorce court is a civil court, not a criminal court, and it should not adopt the rules and standards of the criminal court. I agree that the appeal should be dismissed."

Note.—For a criticism of the views of Denning L.J. see pp. 61–62, *supra*. The Court of Appeal hearing was some months prior to the House of Lords' hearing of *Preston-Jones* v. *Preston-Jones* (*infra*).

PRESTON-JONES v. PRESTON JONES

[1951] A.C. 391; [1951] W.N. 16; [1951] 1 T.L.R. 8; [1951] 1 All E.R. 124; 49
L.G.R. 417 (H.L.: 1950)

*In proceedings for divorce the standard of proof of adultery is proof
beyond reasonable doubt.*

A husband's petition for divorce alleged adultery by the wife based on
the fact that the husband was not in England during the period when
her child was conceived. The child, which was normal, was born on
August 13, 1946. The husband was absent between August 18, 1945,
and February 6, 1946. It was held that the alleged adultery had been
proved beyond reasonable doubt.

LORD SIMONDS:... It is plain, my Lords, that these appeals raise a
question of peculiar difficulty, which I may state in this way: "If a
husband proves that his wife has given birth to a normal child 360 days
after he could have had intercourse with her, and no proof of any
adulterous intercourse by her is given, what, if any, further evidence is
required that the child is not his child?"
Let me first get one difficulty out of the way. A question was raised as
to the standard of proof. The result of a finding of adultery in such a
case as this is in effect to bastardise the child. That is a matter in which
from time out of mind strict proof has been required. But that does not
mean that a degree of proof is demanded such as in a scientific inquiry
would justify the conclusion that such and such an event is impossible.
In this context at least no higher proof of a fact is demanded than that it
is established beyond all reasonable doubt: see *Head* v. *Head* 1 Sim &
S. 150. To prove that a period of so many days between fruitful coition
and the time of conception is in a scientific sense impossible is itself, I
suppose, a scientific impossibility. The utmost that a court of law can
demand is that it should be established beyond all reasonable doubt that
a child conceived so many days after a particular coitus cannot be the
result of that coitus. I would add that since writing this opinion I have
had the advantage of reading that of my noble and learned friend Lord
MacDermott and concur in what he says upon this matter....
The question, as I see it, is whether the court ought to accept this
evidence as adequate to justify a finding that beyond all reasonable
doubt the child was not the child of the husband. I have no hesitation in
answering this question in the affirmative....

[LORD NORMAND did not deal with the point. LORD OAKSEY
dissented on the need for further medical evidence.]

LORD MORTON OF HENRYTON:... In *Ginesi* v. *Ginesi* [1948] P. 179,
the Court of Appeal, after a survey of the authorities, held that a
petitioner must prove adultery "beyond reasonable doubt." In my view
the burden of proof is certainly no heavier than this, and counsel for the
appellant did not intend that it was any lighter....

LORD MACDERMOTT:... The duty of the court, on hearing a petition
for divorce is, in so far as material, to pronounce a decree if "satisfied
on the evidence" that the case for the petition has been proved, and to
dismiss the petition if not so satisfied: see s.178, subs. 2, of the Supreme

Court of Judicature (Consolidation) Act, 1937. The standard of proof to be observed by the court in exercising this jurisdiction was the subject of controversy in the present case. For the husband it was argued that the adultery alleged had to be proved beyond reasonable doubt. For the wife, on the other hand, it was submitted that, as the result of a finding of adultery would, in effect, be to bastardise the child, the petitioner, in order to succeed, would have to go further and show that it was impossible for him to be the father. This, in my opinion, is putting the onus too high. . . .

The evidence must, no doubt, be clear and satisfactory, beyond a mere balance of probabilities, and conclusive in the sense that it will satisfy what Lord Stowell, when Sir William Scott, described in *Loveden* v. *Loveden* (1810) 2 Hag.Con. 1, 3 as "the guarded discretion of a reasonable and just man"; but these desiderata appear to me entirely consistent with the acceptance of proof beyond reasonable doubt as the standard required. Such, in my opinion, is the standard required by the statute. If a judge is satisfied beyond reasonable doubt as to the commission of the matrimonial offence relied upon by a petitioner as ground for divorce, he must surely be "satisfied" within the meaning of the enactment, and no less so in cases of adultery where the circumstances are such as to involve the paternity of a child. On the other hand, I am unable to subscribe to the view which, though not propounded here, has had its adherents, namely, that on its true construction the word "satisfied" is capable of connoting something less than proof beyond reasonable doubt. The jurisdiction in divorce involves the status of the parties and the public interest requires that the marriage bond shall not be set aside lightly or without strict inquiry. The terms of the statute recognise this plainly, and I think it would be quite out of keeping with the anxious nature of its provisions to hold that the court might be "satisfied," in respect of a ground for dissolution, with something less than proof beyond reasonable doubt. I should, perhaps, add that I do not base my conclusions as to the appropriate standard of proof on any analogy drawn from the criminal law. I do not think it is possible to say, at any rate since the decision of this house in *Mordaunt* v. *Moncreiffe* (1874) L.R. 2 Sc. & D. 374, that the two jurisdictions are other than distinct. The true reason, as it seems to me, why both accept the same general standard—proof beyond reasonable doubt—lies not in any analogy, but in the gravity and public importance of the issues with which each is concerned. . . .

Note.—See *Note* on *Bastable* v. *Bastable* (*infra.*).

Blyth v. **Blyth** [1966] A.C. 643 (H.L.). On a husband's petition for divorce on the ground of his wife's adultery the husband sought to rebut the presumption of condonation arising from an act of sexual intercourse between them after the known adultery, which would then have been a bar to divorce. The Commissioner, dismissing the petition on the ground of condonation, held the evidence tendered in rebuttal to be inadmissible, but added that had it been admissible he would have found on a rather slender balance of probabilities that the husband had not intended to condone the adultery. The Court of Appeal, dismissing the husband's appeal, held the evidence admissible, but that the appropriate standard of proof of non-condonation was proof beyond reasonable doubt. By a majority (Lord Denning, Lord Pearce and Lord Pearson) the House of Lords, Lord Morris of Borth-y-Gest and Lord Morton of Henryton dissenting, held that the appropriate standard was that of mere preponderance of probability. Of the majority Lord Pearson and seemingly Lord Pearce would distinguish between proof of grounds for divorce and proof of the non-existence of a bar to divorce. Of Lord MacDermott's holding in *Preston-Jones* v. *Preston-Jones* that adultery is to be proved beyond reasonable doubt Lord Pearce said (at p. 673): "I do not regard his observation as necessarily inconsistent, or intended to be inconsistent, with the view that in other less serious matters to be investigated under the section a court could be satisfied with less cogent evidence. I do not believe that he would have so expressed himself had he anticipated that his words would be used to assert that proof of innocence of connivance, which is a wholly different matter, could not be established on a mere balance of probabilities."

Lord Denning, however, seems to have blurred this distinction. He took the view that even adultery may be proved on balance of probabilities. His Lordship said (at p. 669): "In short it comes to this: so far as the *grounds* for divorce are concerned, the case, like any civil case, may be proved by a preponderance of probability, but the degree of probability depends on the subject-matter. In proportion as the offence is grave, so ought the proof to be clear. So far as the *bars* to divorce are concerned, like connivance or condonation, the petitioner need only show that on balance of probability he did not connive or condone or as the case may be...."

Note.—See *Note* on *Bastable* v. *Bastable* (*infra*).

Bastable v. **Bastable** [1968] 1 W.L.R. 1686 (C.A.). A husband was granted a divorce on the grounds of his wife's desertion and her adultery with the co-respondent. The wife did not dispute the desertion but she and the co-respondent appealed against the finding of adultery. The Court of Appeal, held that adultery had not been proved and dismissed the co-respondent from the suit. Willmer L.J. (with whom Winn L.J. agreed) said: "In the present case, what is charged is 'an offence.' True it is not a criminal offence; it is a matrimonial offence. It is for the husband petitioner to satisfy the court that the offence has been committed. Whatever the popular view may be, it remains true to say that in the eyes of the law the commission of adultery is a serious matrimonial offence. It follows, in my view, that a high standard of proof is required in order to satisfy the court that the offence has been committed.... The case, I think, was very near the borderline. Had it been a matter of merely assessing an ordinary balance of probabilities as between plaintiff and defendant in normal civil litigation, I might have found myself able to agree with the judge. Bearing in mind, however, that the standard of proof to be exacted in a matrimonial cause of this sort is on any view a high one, I find myself unable to agree with the view of the judge" (at pp. 1687 and 1690). Edmund Davis L.J. pointed out that Lord Denning's remarks in *Blyth* v. *Blyth* [1966] A.C. 643 about the standard of proof appropriate to the establishment of a matrimonial offence (as distinct from a bar such as condonation) "must ex necessitatis be regarded as *obiter*" (at p. 1692). Edmund Davies L.J., himself, treated the question as open but was able to agree with the majority because in his view the petitioner had not satisfied even the normal civil standard.

Note.—As has already been indicated (p. 60, *supra*) the Divorce Reform Act 1969 abolished the pre-existing specific grounds for divorce, which were largely based upon the notion of the matrimonial offence, and replaced them with one ground, namely that the marriage has irretrievably broken down. The relevant parts of the 1969 Act are now re-enacted in the Matrimonial Causes Act 1973. Section 1(2) of this Act provides that a marriage shall not be dissolved unless "the petitioner satisfies the court of one or more of the following facts... [adultery; unreasonable behaviour; desertion; two years separation coupled with consent; five years separation]." Section 1(4) provides that "If the court is satisfied on the evidence of any such fact as is mentioned in sub-section (2) of this section, then, unless it is satisfied on all the evidence that the marriage has not broken down irretrievably, it shall... grant a decree of divorce." Most of the cases concerned with the standard of proof in matrimonial causes pre-date the changes in the substantive law wrought by the 1969 Act. The matter is one of statutory construction; but it is to be noted that in the contemporary Act the same word, namely "satisfied," is used as was used in the pre-1969 legislation. In the circumstances it is perhaps not unreasonable to suppose that by way of analogy *Preston-Jones* v. *Preston-Jones* and *Bastable* v. *Bastable* will be seen as relevant to the construction of section 1(2), and *Blyth* v. *Blyth* as relevant to the construction of section 1(4), of the 1973 Act.

Serio v. **Serio** (1983) 13 Fam. Law 255 (C.A.). In divorce proceedings the husband denied that the wife's son was a child of the family. The County Court judge held that on balance of probabilities the husband was not the father. The Court of Appeal allowed the wife's appeal, holding that the standard of proof required on an issue of paternity is somewhat higher. Although the purpose of section 26 of the Family Law Act 1969 had been to do away with the old principle that there had to be proof beyond reasonable doubt to rebut the presumption of legitimacy, it did not provide that the standard of proof should be the same as would apply, say, in a commercial action or an action for negligence.

Note.—Although perhaps justifiable in policy terms, this approach does not lie too easily with the wording of section 26 (Part Two, *infra*). See, too, *Avon C.C.* v. *G.* (1988) 152 J.P.N. 78; *W.* v. *K.* (Proof of Paternity) (1988) 18 Fam. 64. The approach provides a further illustration of the inappropriateness of applying in family law matters the traditional civil standard of proof.

In custody, access and wardship applications the standard of proof is the balance of probabilities. This is so even in access proceedings brought in the County Court under the Matrimonial Proceedings Act 1973, when there is an allegation that a parent has sexually abused the children: *Re H*; *Re K.* (1989) 139 N.L.J. 864 (C.A.)

Chapter 4

PRESUMPTIONS

THE effect of a presumption is to facilitate or dispense with proof, or occasionally to prohibit disproof. This is the loose common theme that runs through the use of the terminology of presumptions. Usage of this terminology has however been somewhat promiscuous.

Sometimes resort is had to it when the terminology of burden of proof would be more apt. To speak, for example, of the presumption of innocence is to indicate that the legal burden of proof of guilt (or the ingredients of guilt) is upon the prosecution or him who asserts it.[1] So, too, to speak of the presumption of sanity in a criminal[2] case is to refer to the common law anomaly that the legal burden of proof of insanity within the *M'Naghten*[3] rules rests upon the accused. Similarly when reference was made in *Bratty* v. *Att.-Gen. for Northern Ireland*[4] to "the presumption of mental capacity" what was being adverted to was the rule that the evidential (although here not the legal) burden of non-insane automatism rests upon the accused.

Again the term presumption when qualified by some such adjective as "conclusive" or "irrebuttable," is sometimes used in the formulation of a rule of substantive law. The Children and Young Persons Act 1933, s.50[5] provides that it "shall be conclusively presumed" that a child under the age of 10 cannot be guilty of any offence. The rule of law set out there does not pertain to proof but rather propounds a substantive defence to a criminal prosecution. It may be noted that at other times, although resort may be had to the use of adjectival terminology in stating a rule of substantive law, the term presumption is itself eschewed. For example, the Civil Evidence Act 1968, s.13[6] provides that in defamation proceedings evidence that a person stands convicted of an offence shall be "conclusive evidence" that he committed it. To express a rule of substantive law in adjectival terms is merely a device of presentation, and whether the word presumption is used in this context is of no particular moment.

Various attempts have been made to classify presumptions for legal purposes. A conventional threefold classification is into presumptions of

---

[1] For the use of the term "presumption of innocence" in civil cases see *Williams* v. *East India Co.* (1802) 3 East 192 (K.B.), Chap. 2, Section A *supra*.
[2] The term "presumption of sanity" is used in civil cases in a different sense (see *infra*).
[3] *M'Naghten's Case* (1843) 10 Cl. and Finn. 200.
[4] [1963] A.C. 386, *per* Lord Kilmuir at p. 407 and *per* Lord Denning at p. 413.
[5] Part Two, *infra*; as amended by the Children and Young Persons Act 1963, s.16(1).
[6] Part Two, *infra*.

fact, rebuttable presumptions of law and irrebuttable presumptions of law. Whereas the last-mentioned category represents an infelicitous use of terminology, when lawyers speak of presumptions they usually mean rebuttable presumptions, and it is with these that this Chapter is concerned. However, the classification of rebuttable presumptions as being simply either of fact or of law is inadequate.

All rebuttable presumptions are couched in terms of basic facts and presumed facts.[7] The basic fact or set of facts of such a presumption must be established for the presumption to be brought into operation. The presumed fact or facts may or must, with varying degrees of permission or compulsion, be deemed to exist once the basic fact or facts have been proved. To be useful a classification of rebuttable presumptions must reflect differences in the legal consequences of proof of the basic fact or facts. They might be classified according to the way in which they can be rebutted. Unfortunately, however, not only do decisions and *dicta* vary in this regard as between presumptions (which is understandable), but they often differ too with respect to the same presumption. Moreover, this inconsistency cannot be explained in terms of chronological development. In these circumstances it would, as a learned author has pointed out, "be unreasonable to expect anything approaching neat precision in this area of the law."[8] Four patterns of rebuttable presumption are perhaps discernible, but it cannot be stated with confidence upon which pattern certain presumptions are based. Those four patterns are as follows.

(1) **Presumptions of fact.** These are no more than rebuttable rational inferences drawn in the light of experience and common sense. The basic fact tends to show the existence of the presumed fact. The law does no more than recognise factual probability. Presumptions of fact tend to be cases of commonplace or stereotyped relevance. On proof of the basic fact the presumed fact may be taken for granted in the absence of adequate evidence to the contrary. The presumption of the continuance of life provides an example: upon proof that a person was alive and well a month ago, it will be assumed in the absence of adequate evidence suggesting the contrary that he is alive today. The presumption of intention (certainly in criminal cases and probably in civil cases) is another example of a presumption of fact: see the Criminal Justice Act 1967, s.8.[9] Of course, even a presumption of fact may be so strong that, if it is not rebutted, a finding of the non-existence of the presumed fact would be set aside as unreasonable.

(2) **Permissive presumptions of law.** Here, as with all presumptions of law, upon proof of the basic fact certain legal consequences follow. These consequences do not necessarily only reflect factual probability. In the case of a permissive presumption the law permits a finding of the presumed fact even though the evidence is not otherwise sufficient to warrant such a finding. In other words the party bearing the evidential burden is relieved of the necessity of satisfying it. Thus in a jury trial, where proof of the basic fact is the only evidence of the existence of the

---

[7] So-called "irrebuttable presumptions" can usually by a slight verbal manipulation be pressed into a similar general mould.
[8] Cross, *Evidence* (6th ed., 1985), p. 132.
[9] Part Two, *infra*.

presumed fact, the issue as to the existence or non-existence of the
latter is to be determined by the jury. The common law presumption
arising from the possession of recently stolen goods seems to fall into
this category: see, *e.g. R. v. Hepworth and Fearnley.*[10] A statutory
illustration is to be found in the Road Traffic Regulation Act 1984,
s.89(4)[11] which provides that the issue of a bus timetable by an
employer "may be produced as prima facie evidence" that the employer
incited an employee to commit a speeding offence. The common law
presumption as to regularity, often expressed in the maxim *omnia
praesumuntur rite esse acta,* has sometimes been regarded in this way;
but at other times it has been treated as an evidential presumption.

(3) **Evidential presumptions of law.** The effect of such a presumption
is to place the equivalent of an evidential burden upon an opponent. It
is compelling but only in a limited sense. Once the opponent has
adduced sufficient evidence for the possibility of the non-existence of the
presumed fact to be put to the jury, the force of the presumption is
spent: the incidence of the legal burden is unaffected. It is in this sense
that, for example, the term presumption is defined in the United States
Federal Rules of Evidence. Rule 301 states "In . . . civil actions . . . a
presumption imposes on the party against whom it is directed the
burden of going forward with evidence to rebut or meet the
presumption, but does not shift to such a party the burden of proof in
the sense of the risk of non-persuasion, which remains throughout the
trial upon the party on whom it was originally cast." Some English
statutes providing that fact A *shall* be prima facie evidence of fact B
have been construed as giving rise to this type of presumption. The
common law presumption of regularity is perhaps an evidential (rather
than a permissive) presumption. On the other hand the common law
presumption of death is perhaps an evidential, rather than a compelling,
presumption.

(4) **Compelling presumptions of law.** The effect of a compelling
presumption is to shift the legal burden of proof. In the Canadian Law
Reform Commission's Evidence Code the term presumption was used in
this sense. Section 14(2) ran "In civil proceedings a presumption
imposes upon the party against whom it operates the obligation of
satisfying the trier of fact that the non-existence of the presumed fact is
more probable than its existence. . . . " Section 14(3) contains a
corresponding provision for criminal cases. The modern presumption of
legitimacy is an example of a compelling presumption. Exceptionally the
effect of a presumption of this type is not only to shift the legal burden
but also to increase its *quantum.* Thus formerly at common law the
presumption of legitimacy, to the effect that a person born or conceived
in lawful wedlock is legitimate, imposed upon the opponent an
obligation to disprove legitimacy beyond reasonable doubt, although the
obligation which, in the absence of the presumption, would have rested
on the proponent would have been to prove legitimacy simply on
balance of probability. However, the Family Law Reform Act 1969,
s.26[12] now provides that in civil cases this presumption places upon the

---

[10] [1955] 2 Q.B. 600 (C.C.A.), *infra.*
[11] See, too, the Road Traffic Offenders Act 1988, s.12 (both Part Two, *infra*).
[12] Part Two, *infra.*

opponent the obligation to show that "it is more probable than not" that the *propositus* is illegitimate: in other words, like most compelling presumptions, it simply shifts, without increasing, the legal burden. Indeed, very often whether the position is formulated in terms of the shifting of or reallocation of the burden of proof, or in the terms of a presumption, is simply a matter of technique of exposition.

Some writers, although seemingly and perhaps significantly few judges,[13] have concerned themselves with the possibility of two presumptions conflicting. If there were to be an interaction between two presumptions of differing categories of cogency, it would seem that the legal effect of that belonging to the category of greater cogency should be cumulative to, or if necessary should prevail over, the legal effect of that belonging to the category of lesser cogency. An apparently more difficult problem could arise in the event of two compelling presumptions coming into conflict. If the presumptions were of equal force (for example, if each did no more than shift the legal burden of proof) they should cancel each other out leaving the issue to be decided on the evidence, the risk of non-persuasion remaining where it would be were no presumption involved. This, indeed, seems to be the gist of such authority as there is. It could, however, be contended that the compelling presumption with a clearly stronger policy underpinning should prevail.

Presumptions are the creatures of common law, equity or statute. It would obviously be impossible to refer to authorities illustrating every rebuttable presumption, and the excerpts from cases set out in this Chapter purport to do no more than exemplify some of the more important common law and equitable presumptions. However, a majority of presumptions are statutory. Differing statutory terms are used, and in each such case the problem is ultimately one of individual interpretation. This further adds to the difficulty of classifying presumptions. Some examples of statutory terminology are set out below:

Evidence. Children and Young Persons Act 1933, s.100; Cheques Act 1957, s.3.

Prima facie evidence. Documentary Evidence Act 1868, s.2; Bankers' Books Evidence Act 1879, s.3; Partnership Act 1890, s.2(3).

Prima facie evidence without further proof. Prosecution of Offences Act 1985, s.26.

Sufficient evidence. Merchant Shipping Act 1894, s.691(3).

Deemed. Bills of Exchange Act 1882, s.27; Official Secrets Act 1911, s.1(2); Children and Young Persons Act 1933, ss.17, 99(1).

Prima facie deemed. Bills of Exchange Act 1882, s.30.

Presumed. Children and Young Persons Act 1933, s.17.

Presumed (or deemed), unless the contrary is proved. Official Secrets Act 1911, s.1(2); Children and Young Persons Act 1933, ss.4(2), 99(2).

Conclusively presumed. Children and Young Persons Act 1933, s.50.

---

[13] But see *Axon* v. *Axon* (1937) 59 C.L.R. 395 (High Court of Australia).

A. SOME TYPICAL PRESUMPTIONS

R. v. Lumley (1869) L.R. I.C.C.R. 196 (C.C.C.R.). On a trial for bigamy, it was proved that the prisoner, a woman, married A in 1836, left him in 1843, and married another man in 1847. Nothing was heard of A after the prisoner left him, nor was any evidence given of his age, but the judge, holding that there was a presumption of law that A was alive at the date of the second marriage, withdrew the case from the jury, in effect directing them to return a verdict of guilty. It was held by the Court for Crown Cases Reserved that there was no presumption of law either in favour of, or against, the continuance of A's life up to 1847; but that it was a question for the jury as a matter of fact whether or not A was alive at the date of the second marriage. The conviction was quashed. Lush J. said (198): "... it is incumbent on the prosecution to prove to the satisfaction of the jury that the husband or wife, as the case may be, was alive at the date of the second marriage. This is purely a question of fact. The existence of the party at an antecedent date may, or may not, afford a reasonable inference that he is living at the subsequent date. If, for example, it was proved that he was in good health on the day preceding the marriage, the inference would be strong, almost irresistible, that he was living on the latter day, and the jury would in all probability find that he was so. If, on the other hand, it were proved that he was then in a dying condition, and nothing further was proved, they would probably decline to draw that inference. Thus, the question is entirely for the jury. The law makes no presumption either way...."

Note.—See also *Chard* v. *Chard* [1956] P. 259 (*infra*).

R. v. STEANE

[1947] K.B. 997; [1947] L.J.R. 969; 63 T.L.R. 403; 177 L.T. 122; [1947] 1 All E.R. 813; 32 Cr.App.R. 61 (C.C.A.: 1947)

There is a presumption of intention; that is, that a person may be presumed to intend the natural consequences of his deliberate actions.

The accused was a British subject who broadcast for Germany during the last Great War, and was indicted for doing acts with intent to assist the enemy, contrary to a statutory regulation. His defence was that he acted under duress. The judge directed the jury that the accused must be presumed to have intended to assist the enemy, and he was convicted. On appeal the conviction was quashed, as another inference was possible.

LORD GODDARD C.J. read the judgment of the court (which included ATKINSON and CASSELLS JJ.): ... In the opinion of the court, there was undoubtedly evidence from which a jury could infer that the acts done by the appellant were acts likely to assist the enemy.

The far more difficult question that arises, however, is in connection with the direction to the jury with regard to whether those acts were done with the intention of assisting the enemy. The case as opened, and indeed as put by the learned judge, appears to this court to be this: A man is taken to intend the natural consequences of his acts: if, therefore, he does an act which is likely to assist the enemy, it must be assumed that he did it with the intention of assisting the enemy.... While no doubt the motive of a man's act and his intention in doing the act are, in law, different things, it is, none the less, true that in many offences a specific intention is a necessary ingredient and the jury have to be satisfied that a particular act was done with that specific intent, although the natural consequences of the act might, if nothing else were proved, be said to show the intent for which it was done.... No doubt, if the prosecution prove an act the natural consequence of which would be a certain result and no evidence or explanation is given, then a jury may, on a proper direction, find that the prisoner is guilty of doing the act with the intent alleged, but if on the totality of the evidence there is room for more than one view as to the intent of the prisoner, the jury should be directed that it is for the prosecution to prove the intent to the jury's satisfaction, and if, on a review of the whole evidence, they either think that the intent did not exist or they are left in doubt as to the intent, the prisoner is entitled to be acquitted....

Note.—This case clearly suggested that the presumption of intention is no more than a presumption of fact. Subsequently, in *D.P.P.* v. *Smith* [1961] A.C. 290 the House of Lords decided that in certain circumstances there is a presumption of law that normal people intend the natural consequences of their acts. However, the Criminal Justice Act 1967, s.8 (Part Two, *infra*), now makes it clear that in criminal proceedings any presumption of intention is not one of law. The Act does not refer expressly to a presumption of intention, or state that it is one of fact; but this appears to be the effect of the relevant section. See *R.* v. *Wallett* [1968] 2 Q.B. 367 (C.A.) and *R.* v. *Moloney* [1985] A.C. 905 (H.L.).

In *R.* v. *Moloney* Lord Bridge of Harwich, having said (p. 929) that "Section 8 of the Criminal Justice Act 1967 leaves us at liberty to go back to decisions before that of this House in *Director of Public Prosecutions* v. *Smith* [1961] A.C. 290," continued "I know of no clearer exposition of the law than that in the judgment...delivered by Lord Goddard C.J. in *R.* v. *Steane*...where he said [Lord Bridge then recited the last nine lines of the passage from Lord Goddard's judgment set out above]." Lord Bridge had previously observed that "we should now no longer speak of presumptions in this area but rather of inferences." The practical scope of this "presumption" is particularly limited in the context of proof of a specific intent. Lord Bridge said (p. 925): "But looking on their facts at the decided cases where a crime of specific intent was under consideration...they suggest to me that the probability of the consequence taken to have been foreseen must be little short of overwhelming before it will suffice to establish the necessary intent."

In civil proceedings the view that the presumption of intention is merely one of fact has been strongly expressed by Denning L.J. (as he then was) in a number of cases (for example, *Kaslefsky* v. *Kaslefsky* [1951] P. 38 at 46 (C.A.)). It has been considered in matrimonial causes, but the highest courts have not yet given a clear pronouncement on the nature of the presumption (see *Jamieson* v. *Jamieson* [1952] A.C. 525 (H.L.); *Lang* v. *Lang* [1955] A.C. 402 (P.C.); but compare *Gollins* v. *Gollins* [1964] A.C. 644 at 644, 692 (H.L.); *Williams* v. *Williams* [1964] A.C. 698 (H.L.)).

R. v. **B.** [1979] 1 W.L.R. 1185 (C.A.). Two appellants were convicted of blackmail whilst aged 13. The judge had ruled that, although the obligation to rebut the presumption of *doli incapax* was upon the prosecution, it was entitled to adduce evidence of the appellants' backgrounds and characters, including evidence of their previous convictions, for this purpose.

Note.—The presumption of *doli incapax* is a presumption of law to the effect that a person under the age of 14 is incapable of forming the necessary intent to commit a crime. The presumption is compelling, but rebuttable. The burden of proving *mens rea* is normally, of course, in any event upon the prosecution, but in the case of an accused of 14 or more the prosecution is assisted in the discharge of this burden by the presumption of fact that a person intends the natural consequences of his acts. However, if the accused is shown to have been under 14 at the time of the crime charged, the prosecution may be faced with the presumption of *doli incapax* which can be rebutted only by the equivalent of proof beyond reasonable doubt. In order to rebut the presumption the prosecution must prove that the child had known that what it was doing was seriously wrong: *J. M. (A Minor)* v. *Runeckles* (1984) 79 Cr.App.R. 225 (D.C.).

If the accused was under 10 he is irrebuttably presumed not to be guilty: Children and Young Persons Act 1933, s.50, as amended by Children and Young Persons Act 1963, s.16(1) (Part Two, *infra*). It is to be noted that the presumed fact here is the absence of guilt, whereas the presumed fact in the common law presumption of *doli incapax* referred to above seemingly relates only to mental state.

In criminal law there is a further irrebuttable presumption that a boy under 14 is not able to have sexual intercourse. This did not apply in affiliation proceedings (*L.* v. *K.* [1985] Fam. 144 (Fam. Div.)) and probably would not apply in many civil law contexts.

Berryman v. **Wise** (1791) 4 T.R. 366; 100 E.R. 1067 (K.B.). In an action by an attorney for words spoken of him in the way of his profession, it was held that he need not prove that he was an attorney by his certificate or by a copy of the roll of attorneys; and proof that he acted as such was held to be sufficient by the court. Buller J. said that in the case of all peace officers, justices of the peace, constables, etc., it was sufficient to prove that they acted in those characters without producing their appointments.

Note.—There is a presumption of law as to regularity; that is, that public and official acts and duties have been regularly and properly performed; and that persons acting as public officers, or in public capacities, have been regularly and properly appointed.

In *R.* v. *Roberts* (1878) 14 Cox C.C. 101 (C.C.R.), the doctrine was applied to a Deputy Judge of County Courts. Amongst other officials to whom it has been applied may be mentioned solicitors, commissioners for oaths, Masters in Chancery, Post Office employees, churchwardens, vestry clerks and Lords of the Treasury.

For a statutory alternative in the case of a solicitor to reliance upon the principle *omnia praesumuntur rite esse acta*, see now the Solicitors Act 1974, s.18 (Part Two, *infra*).

R. v. *Verelst* (1813) 3 Camp. 432 is clear authority for the view that the maxim "*omnia praesumuntur rite ac solemniter esse acta*" represents a rebuttable presumption of law. It must, however, be used with care in criminal cases. The prosecution cannot rely upon the presumption to establish facts central to the offence charged: *Dillon* v. *The Queen* [1982] A.C. 484 (P.C.).

R. v. HEPWORTH AND FEARNLEY

[1955] 2 Q.B. 600; [1955] 3 W.L.R. 331; [1955] 2 All E.R. 918; 39 Cr.App.R. 152; [1955] Crim.L.R. 576 (C.C.A.: 1955)

The possession of goods recently stolen calls for an explanation by the accused, and, if none is given, the jury is entitled to convict.

The accused men were charged with receiving bales of wool, knowing them to have been stolen, and were convicted. On appeal, the summing-up of the Recorder was said to be defective with regard to the burden of proof and the explanation of the accused. The appeal was allowed.

LORD GODDARD C.J. (delivering the judgment of the court, which included FINNEMORE and DEVLIN JJ.): . . . complaint is made in the case... that the Recorder in summing up did not give the jury any direction with regard to the burden of proof, and did not give them a sufficient direction with regard to the duty of a jury and how they were to regard the evidence and the degree of certainty they were to feel.

First, with regard to the burden of proof it is always desirable that a jury should be told that the burden of proof is on the prosecution. I have no doubt that in most cases they know it, but it is desirable that they should be told that it is for the prosecution to prove the case. It is also most desirable that emphasis should be laid upon that in a receiving case. In such a case it is generally desirable, although there may be circumstances in the particular case which would not render it necessary, to remind the jury first, that the burden of proof remains on the prosecution; secondly, to tell them that if an explanation for possession of the goods is given by the accused, although the jury may not be convinced that it is true, if they think that it may be true it would mean that the prosecution have not proved the case because the jury would remain in some degree of doubt. It is not necessary to use on all occasions the formula which was used in *R. v. Schama and Abramovitch* (1914) 11 Cr.App.R. 45, because that case, which is constantly cited in these matters relating to receiving, as I have said more than once in giving judgment in appeals, lays down no more than this: if the explanation given by the accused persons which, when they have given it becomes part of the sum of evidence in the case, leaves the jury in doubt whether the accused honestly or dishonestly received the goods, they are entitled to be acquitted because the case has not been proved. A case is never proved if any jury is left in any degree of doubt....

... The jury should be told that the possession of goods recently stolen calls for an explanation, and if none is given, or one is given which the jury are convinced is untrue, that entitles them to convict. But if the explanation given leaves them in doubt as to whether the accused received the goods honestly or dishonestly, the prosecution have not proved the case and they should acquit....

Note.—The position of persons charged with receiving stolen goods has been the subject of many decisions, a well-known case of the last century being *R. v. Langmead* (1864) 9 Cox C.C. 464 (C.C.A.). Later cases emphasise that, though the jury need not act on the presumption of knowledge that the goods were stolen arising from the fact of possession, they may do so, when the accused gives no credible explanation (see also *R. v. Garth* (1949) 33 Cr.App.R. 100; [1949] 1 All E.R. 773 (C.C.A.); *R. v. Aves* (1950) 34 Cr.App.R. 159; [1950] 2 All E.R. 330, 159 (C.C.A.). In *R. v. Smith* (1984) 148 J.P. 216; [1983] C.L.Y. 646 (C.A.) it was reiterated that the presumption places no burden upon the accused, and moreover that the jury should be directed that the permission embodied in the doctrine is only available if they are satisfied that no convincing explanation has been given. Indeed, the presumption is in effect no more than one of fact. Twenty years ago Kenny J., delivering the judgment of the Irish Court of Criminal Appeal in *The People (Attorney-General) v. Oglesby* [1966] I.R. 162, said (p. 167): "As counsel for the prosecution placed relevance on what he called 'the doctrine of recent possession,' we wish to say that it does not exist. The so-called doctrine is a convenient way of referring to the inferences of fact which, in the absence of any satisfactory explanation by the accused, may be drawn as a matter of common sense from other facts." More recently in *R. v. Ball* [1983] 1 W.L.R. 801 (C.A.), McCullogh J., giving the judgment of the English Court of Appeal, has said (p. 805), of the "so-called doctrine of recent possession," "It is not even a doctrine. It is in fact no more than an inference which a jury may, or may not, think it right to draw about the state of mind [*i.e.* knowledge that the goods were stolen] of the defendant who is dealing in goods stolen not long beforehand. It is based on common sense."

R. v. Cash [1985] Q.B. 801 (C.A.). The appellant was tried on 11 counts charging contravention of the Theft Act 1968, s.22(1) by dishonestly handling goods stolen in five burglaries, of which the most recent had taken place some nine days before the police had found the goods in his possession. There was overwhelming evidence that the goods had been the subject of the burglaries and that they were in the appellant's possession when found by the police. The appellant nevertheless contended that, in view of the requirement of section 22(1) that the handling be "otherwise than in the course of the stealing," a charge of handling was not established unless the Crown proved affirmatively that the accused was not the thief. This contention was rejected by the Court of Appeal. Lord Lane C.J., giving the judgment of the court restated (p. 804) the doctrine of recent possession thus: "If someone is found in possession of stolen goods soon after they have left the possession of their owner, and he is unable to give any or any reasonably credible explanation of how he came by them, it is open to the jury to infer that he is on the one hand guilty of theft (or burglary if they were stolen in the course of burglary) or on the other hand, guilty of dishonestly handling the goods knowing or believing them to have been stolen." His Lordship noted that it was well established that the corresponding offences of larceny and receiving had been mutually exclusive and he concluded (pp. 804–805) that "The inference which the jury are in a proper case entitled to draw, namely, that a defendant was the guilty handler, includes the inference that he was not the actual thief. There is in our judgment, at least so far as 'recent possession' cases are concerned, no further burden on the prosecution to prove that the defendant was not party to the theft or burglary as the case may be."

The court also relied upon a different and more general ground: the accused must be presumed to be innocent of theft or burglary unless the contrary is proved. "It was not suggested to or by any witness that the appellant was the thief or that the property came into his possession in the course of stealing; there was no evidence that the appellant was the burglar" (p. 805). In the context of this defence to a charge of dishonest handling the legal burden of proof of theft or burglary would appear to rest upon the accused.

Piers v. Piers (1848) 2 H.L. Cas: 331 (H.L.). Two persons had evinced an intention to marry, and a marriage ceremony had in fact been performed; but it was in a private house, and there was no evidence that the necessary special licence had been obtained. The House of Lords nevertheless upheld the validity of the marriage, relying on the common law presumption of the formal validity of a ceremony proved to have been celebrated between persons intending it to constitute a valid marriage. It was heavily emphasised that this presumption is strong and compelling. (It can now probably be rebutted only by the equivalent of proof beyond reasonable doubt to the contrary: *Mahadervan* v. *Mahadervan* [1964] P. 233 (P.D.), *per* Sir Jocelyn Simon P. at p. 246).

Re Peete, Peete v. Crompton [1952] 2 All E.R. 599 (Ch.D.). An application for provision under the Inheritance (Family Provision) Act 1938 was made by a woman who had gone through a ceremony of marriage with the testator in 1919. The ceremony was valid in point of form, but there was doubt as to her capacity to marry (*i.e.* as to the "essential," as distinct from formal, validity of the marriage). She gave evidence that she had been told that her first husband had been killed in an accident in 1916, but this was held to be insufficient to satisfy the burden of proof resting upon her to show that she had capacity to marry the testator and was thus his widow. The presumption of the essential validity of this formally valid marriage, although compelling, was held to be more easily rebuttable than the presumption of the formal validity of a ceremony. (Moreover, it is to be noted that, in cases in which the issue is as to a party's incapacity on grounds other than the subsistence of a prior marriage, the presumption in favour of capacity is probably only evidential).

Re Taylor dec'd. [1961] 1 W.L.R. 9 (C.A.). It was held that where a man and woman are proved to have lived together as, and to have been regarded as, man and wife, there is a presumption even in the absence of evidence of a ceremony of marriage that they are validly married. The evidence adduced by the plaintiff sufficed to give rise to this presumption even though the period of reputation by cohabitation was short. The presumption prevailed because the defendant's evidence in rebuttal was not "clear and firm."

Note.—Although the basic facts and the presumed facts of the three presumptions illustrated in the three cases immediately above differ, the distinction between them has not been consistently maintained in the case law. Moreover, there is some doubt as to the effect of the presumptions—especially the presumption of the validity (seemingly both formal and essential) arising from proof of cohabitation and repute. Again, there have been suggestions that *Piers* v. *Piers* is authority for the view that what is to be presumed from the celebration of a marriage is validity not simply of the ceremony but of the marriage generally (see, *e.g. Mulhern* v. *Clery* [1930] I.R. 649, 697 (S.C. Eire). However, although this might appear only to telescope two presumptions, it would have the effect of according greater strength to the presumption of essential validity than is warranted: see *Re Peete, Peete* v. *Crompton, supra.*

In criminal case the force of these presumptions (like that of the presumption of legitimacy) is greatly reduced when they are invoked against the accused.

CHARD v. CHARD

[1956] P. 259; [1955] 3 W.L.R. 954; [1955] 3 All E.R. 721 (Divorce: 1955)

There is a presumption of law as to death, arising (inter alia) *from seven years' unexplained absence. However, whether death is to be presumed when the basic facts of this presumption have not been established is a question of fact.*

On a husband's petition, the ceremony of marriage in 1933 between the petitioner and the respondent was alleged to be a nullity. The petitioner had been married to another woman in 1909, and he had last heard of her in 1917. The question was whether she should be presumed to be dead in 1933. The court inferred that she was alive then, and held the ceremony of 1933 null.

SACHS J.: On the basis, which I have adopted, that any presumption of continuance of life is simply one of fact, the various decisions cited to me and the dicta therein become reconciled. Further, due weight can thus be given in each case to the different circumstances of any given individual, *e.g.* whether a friendless orphan or a gregarious man in public life, whether in good or in bad health, and whether following a quiet or a dangerous occupation.

Turning next to the question as to presumptions of death (whether before or after a lapse of seven years) the same reasoning to my mind generally applies—save in one set of circumstances to which I will refer later. I respectfully agree with Harman J.'s conclusion in *Re Watkins* [1953] 1 Q.L.R. 1323 that, where no statute applies, there is no "magic" in the mere fact of a period of seven years elapsing without there being positive evidence of a person being alive. It is, generally speaking, a matter in each case of taking the facts as a whole and of balancing, as a jury would, the respective probabilities of life continuing and having ceased . . .

My view is thus that in matters where no statute lays down an applicable rule, the issue of whether a person is, or is not to be presumed dead, is generally speaking one of fact and not subject to a presumption of law.

To that there is an exception which can be assumed without affecting the present case. By virtue of a long sequence of judicial statements, which either assert or assume such a rule, it appears accepted that there is a convenient presumption of law applicable to certain cases of seven years' absence where no statute applies. That presumption in its modern shape takes effect (without examining its terms too exactly) substantially as follows. Where as regards "A.B." there is no acceptable affirmative evidence that he was alive at some time during a continuous period of seven years or more, then if it can be proved first, that there are persons who would be likely to have heard of him over that period, secondly that those persons have not heard of him, and thirdly that all due inquiries have been made appropriate to the circumstances, "A.B." will be presumed to have died at some time within that period. (Such a presumption would, of course, be one of law, and could not be one of fact, because there can hardly be a logical inference from any particular set of facts that a man had not died within 2,555 days but had died within 2,560.) . . .

It is, however, not necessary for me to deal further with the questions raised by (counsel) because in the present case there is no one who has been shown to have been likely to have heard from the 1909 wife in the years 1917 to 1933 or, indeed, from 1933 to date and so such a rule could not operate.

The present case is thus one where there is no suggestion that in 1917 the 1909 wife was other than a woman of normal health, nor any evidence of any fact by reason of which her expectation of life could be regarded as greatly sub-normal. There are many factors which, as previously mentioned, might have led her not to wish to be heard of by the (petitioner) or his family, there is no one known who would naturally have heard of her, and there is no registration of a relevant death.

I accordingly approach the matter on the footing (1) that this is a case in which the court is put upon inquiry as to the validity of the 1933 marriage; (2) that once the husband was shown to have contracted the 1909 marriage it is for him (or his present wife) to prove facts from which a cessation before . . . 1933 of the earliest marriage can be inferred before it can be said that the 1933 marriage is valid (see *MacDarmaid's Case* [1950] P. 218 at 220); (3) that there is in the present case no presumption of law either as to the continuance of life or as to death having supervened; (4) that this is thus one of the class of cases which has to be determined on its own facts.

. . . .

The correct inference in the present case from the known facts is that the 1909 wife was living on May 15, 1933, and not that she was by then dead. . . .

Note.—The common law presumption of death is mirrored in various statutes; for example, in the Offences against the Person Act 1861, s.57, as amended, as a defence to a charge of bigamy, and in the Matrimonial Causes Act 1973, s.19 (Part Two, *infra*), in respect of divorce. Leave to swear to the death of a testator or intestate (sometimes referred to as presuming death) after a shorter period than seven years, may be given in probate matters (see *Re Matthews* [1898] P. 17).

PRUDENTIAL ASSURANCE CO. v. EDMONDS

(1877) 2 App.Cas. 487 (H.L.: 1877)

In order to raise the presumption that a person who has not been heard of for seven years is dead, inquiry must be made amongst those who, if he were alive, would be likely to have heard of him. Whether evidence that he has been heard of is to be believed is a matter for the jury.

The presumption, once the basic facts have been established, can (seemingly) be rebutted by evidence which would warrant, but not necessarily require, a finding that the person is alive.

LORD BLACKBURN: ... Looking at the bill of exceptions as it now stands, we find the facts to be these: *Robert Nutt's* life was insured; the question was, was he to be considered as dead or not? The Plaintiff had failed in proving the actual death of *Robert Nutt*, and then he relied upon the rule of law which is generally laid down in something like these terms; if a man has not been heard of for seven years that raises the presumption that he is dead. It is generally so enunciated. I do not say that that is the correct way of enunciating it, but I think it may be fairly enough put in those words for this purpose. I think, having regard both to the reason of the thing and the decisions, we must take "not being heard of" in a certain sense.... My Lords, it appears from the case of *Doe* v. *Andrew* (15 Q.B. 751) that it is necessary, in order to raise the presumption, that there should have been an inquiry and search made for the man amongst those who, if he was alive, would be likely to hear of him.... In order to raise a presumption that a man is dead from his not having been heard of for seven years, you must inquire amongst those who, if he was alive, would be likely to hear of him, and see whether or no there has been such an absence of hearing of him as would raise the presumption that he was dead.

[Witnesses gave evidence that they had not heard of Robert Nutt for more than seven years but that they had heard that his niece believed that she had seen him in Melbourne. The niece gave evidence that when she at age 20] "was standing in a crowded street in *Melbourne*, in *Australia*, a man passed her whom she recognised as her uncle *Robert Nutt*; that he was well dressed, and apparently well-to-do, and resembled her uncle as she remembered him in *Cheltenham*; that she did not speak to the man, because he was lost in the crowd as she turned to do so; and that she had, on returning to *England* in 1873, told all the relations in *Cheltenham* that she had seen her uncle *Robert Nutt*."

. . .

Supposing the jurymen had found as a fact that they thought she was mistaken, would or would not the grounds have existed upon which the presumption from a seven years' absence would arise that the man not heard of was dead? I think certainly they would. It seems to me that when she said, "I have seen the man in the streets of *Melbourne*," it upset the presumption arising from the relatives, including herself, never having seen or heard of him, and it turned the *onus* the other way. It was possible, however, that it might have been proved that the man she saw was not *Robert Nutt*, but somebody else. If that had been proved, it would have left the matter just as if she had never made that statement. When she said she thought she had seen him, and all the others had heard it from her, although that unexplained and uncontradicted statement affected the *onus*, yet, as soon as it was made out by satisfactory evidence that she was mistaken, the hearing from her was gone, and the presumption would remain as it was before.

The House (LORDS HATHERLEY, O'HAGAN, BLACKBURN and GORDON), although equally divided as to whether the jury had been properly directed, did not doubt that the presumption would have been applicable if the jury did not accept the niece's evidence.

Note.—The extent of the inquiries that must be made, and indeed the need to make them at all, must depend upon the circumstances. Failure to make inquiries may accordingly sometimes be justified: see, *e.g. Bullock* v. *Bullock* [1960] 1 W.L.R. 975. See, too, *Chipchase* v. *Chipchase* (*infra*).

CHIPCHASE v. CHIPCHASE

[1939] P. 391; 108 L.J.P. 154; [1939] 3 All E.R. 895; 55 T.L.R. 1067 (Divorce: 1939)

The effect of the presumption of death is that the propositus may be presumed to have been dead at any time after the elapse of seven years since he was last known to be alive.

THE PRESIDENT (SIR BOYD MERRIMAN): This is an appeal from the Hendon magistrates, who dismissed a complaint by a wife against the husband based on several charges of adultery, desertion and failure to maintain respectively, on the ground that the wife had failed to prove that there was an existing marriage. We have come to the conclusion that it is essential that this case should be reheard by the magistrates, for we think that there are matters in connection with the two points on which they gave their decision to which they have not yet given proper or sufficient attention. . . .

I am going to deal with this point first before coming to the second point. On the face of the wife's evidence she had not heard of her husband for seven years and more at the time when she went through the ceremony of marriage with the man whom she is now charging as her husband; in fact, twelve years or thereabouts had elapsed at the time of the second ceremony of marriage. It is quite true that she was asked questions about the nature of the inquiries she had made, opportunities she had of inquiring from his relatives, and so forth, but her evidence was that she had not heard of her husband from the moment to which I have already referred, at the beginning of 1916, and had no idea whether he was dead or alive.

The magistrates have given their decision that they gave expressly on the ground that, there being no evidence that Leetch was dead, they were of opinion for that reason that the first marriage was still subsisting. It seems to me impossible to say that there was no evidence that Leetch was dead having regard to the presumption which arises in circumstances of this kind. That presumption—I am taking the statement of it from the judgment of Giffard L.J. in *Phené's Trusts* (1869) L.R. 5 Ch. 139)—is that the law presumes a person who has not been heard of for over seven years to be dead, but in the absence of special circumstances draws no presumption from that fact as to the particular period at which he died. I need not read for present purposes the rest of the statement of the legal doctrine. Once it is shown that the wife has not heard of her husband for seven years, that presumption arises. Of course, it is not an irrebuttable presumption and it may take very little evidence to rebut it, having regard to the particular circumstances of a particular case, but, if that proposition is established affirmatively to the satisfaction of the magistrates, then it is impossible to say there is no evidence of a husband having been dead.

It is in that connection, in my opinion, that the question of the nature of any such inquiries that the wife has made arises. There is nothing in this statement of the presumption which I have quoted about reasonable belief, or inquiries, or probability of life, or any of those things to which Mr. Horner has referred us. But, of course, if a person was given ground for supposing that the other party to the marriage was alive and deliberately turned a blind eye and refused to make obvious inquiries, it might very well be that the court would not accept as proved that the party had not been heard of for seven years. It seems to me that it is in discussing this question that the reasonableness of inquiries that have been made in regard to the circumstances of the case, whatever they may be, should be ascertained. It is in this connection that that matter is important, but once it has been established to the satisfaction of the tribunal that the party has not been heard of for seven years, then the presumption arises, although, of course, it is a presumption which can be rebutted.

In this particular case the question is whether the wife was entitled to rely on that presumption. At the time when she went through the ceremony of marriage in 1928 not merely seven but twelve years had elapsed, but it goes without saying that the magistrates have got to judge of that question as it appears to them in 1939. The wife, on the one hand, is entitled to pray in aid the lapse of yet another ten years, during which, she says, she has not heard of her husband. The husband, on the other hand, might be shown by some evidence, the nature of which we are unaware, but which it is suggested is in existence, actually to have been alive in 1928. In taking into account the further lapse of ten years since the ceremony of marriage in 1928 it will, no doubt, be open to the magistrates to discount that further lapse of time in connection with the non-appearance of the husband, by reason of the fact that the marriage itself did not take place in the name of Leetch but took place in the wife's maiden name. Putting it another way, there was nothing in the nature of the second marriage itself to attract the attention of the first husband if, in fact, he was alive. Those are all circumstances which the magistrates will be able to take into account.

At the end of it all, the question remains: Is it established that the husband had not been heard of for twelve years or so before the second ceremony of marriage and is there anything in the evidence to rebut the presumption that he was dead? I do not feel that that approach to the matter has been considered by the magistrates at all. . . .

[*Case remitted to magistrates.*]

Note.—On a strict interpretation of the dicta in *Re Phené's Trusts* (1870) L.R. 5 Ch. 139 (Ch.App.) the first husband would not have been presumed dead until 1939, this being the date of the proceedings; but the more generous view of the nature of the presumed fact, implicit in the *Chipchase* decision, has been adopted in several cases. In *Re Westbrook's Trusts* [1873] W.N. 167 the property of an intestate was divided amongst such of his next-of-kin as were living at a date seven years after his disappearance, but those who died before that date were excluded.

JOHNSON v. BARNES

(1873) L.R. 8 C.P. 527; 42 L.J.C.P. 259; 29 L.T. 65 (Exchequer Chamber: 1873)

There is a presumption of law as to lawful origin; that is, that asserted rights, exercised without interruption for such a length of time that they may fairly be taken to have had a lawful origin, had such lawful origin.

Where the corporation of a borough had from time immemorial exercised exclusively a right of pasturage over certain lands, it was presumed that the corporation was legally entitled to an exclusive right of pasturage over such lands, and not a mere right of common which could not, in the circumstances, have been legal; and this notwithstanding that the right had been described as a right of common in a long series of documents.

KELLY C.B.: ... I think, however, we are bound to presume a legal origin, if such be possible, in favour of a right which appears, from the facts stated in the case, to have existed for many hundreds of years, and that the inaccurate description of such a right in a series of conveyances cannot interfere with the presumption which we should otherwise be entitled to make from the facts with relation to the enjoyment of the right. When we look to these facts, we find that the corporation of Colchester has in fact exercised a right of pasturing an unlimited number of cattle or sheep on certain land around the walls of the town during a certain season of the year, except as to any part of the land under cultivation. ... It seems to me manifest that what the corporation have exercised from time immemorial is a right which, though frequently spoken of as a right of common, was, in fact, an exclusive right of pasturage. ...

Then we come to what has been made one of the most important questions in the case, that is to say, supposing that the right actually exercised has always been in fact a right of exclusive pasturage, and has always been treated and dealt with as such, is the presumption which would naturally arise from the facts destroyed by the effect of a long and numerous series of documents in which the right is spoken of in expressions indicating a right in the nature of a right of common? I do not think we should be justified in giving this effect to the documents, if the result would be to set aside a right which has been so long exercised in fact. ... It appears to me, therefore, on consideration of the whole of the facts and documents in this case, that we are bound, in accordance with one of the best established principles of law, to presume a legal origin, if one were possible, in favour of a long and uninterrupted actual enjoyment of a right. . . .

MARTIN B. and BLACKBURN J. delivered judgments to the same effect. CLEASBY B. and QUAIN and ARCHIBALD JJ. concurred.

Note.—The so-called "presumption of lost grant" was an instance of the presumption of lawful origin in cases where such origin would properly be a "grant." Another illustration is afforded by the dedication of a highway: but see now Highways Act 1980 (Part Two, *infra*).

Family Law Reform Act 1969, s.26. "Any presumption of law as to the legitimacy or illegitimacy of any person may in any civil proceedings be rebutted by evidence which shows it is more probable than not that the person is illegitimate or legitimate, as the case may be, and it shall not be necessary to prove that fact beyond reasonable doubt in order to rebut the presumption."

Note.—The common law presumption of legitimacy is to the effect that a child conceived or born during the subsisting marriage of its mother is legitimate. At common law this presumption was rebutted only by the equivalent of proof beyond reasonable doubt. Not only has the *quantum* of evidence required to rebut the presumption been reduced, but the old rule that such evidence must go to show non-access, or at least no intercourse between the spouses, has finally been discarded. Any type of evidence tending to show illegitimacy may now be tendered in rebuttal of the presumption, but of course, it must be sufficient. In *Re Overbury, Decd., Re Sheppard* v. *Matthews* [1955] Ch. 122 (Ch.D), where a widow remarried six months after her first husband's death and gave birth to a child two months later, it was held that the child was the legitimate offspring of the first husband, there being inadequate evidence to rebut the presumption.

The presumption of legitimacy has no application when they are living apart under a decree of judicial separation or an order of a court of summary jurisdiction (*Ettenfield* v. *Ettenfield* [1940] P. 96 (C.A.)). Indeed there is a rebuttable presumption that a child conceived in such circumstances is illegitimate. But if the parties are living apart under a separation agreement, or if there is a maintenance (as opposed to a separation) order in force against the husband, the presumption of legitimacy continues to operate.

There is some authority that the presumption of legitimacy involves, not only a presumption as to paternity, but also a presumption as to the date of conception: *Knowles* v. *Knowles* [1962] P. 161.

For further implications of section 26 for the standard of proof see the Introduction to Chapter 3 (*supra*); also *Serio* v. *Serio* (1983) 13 Fam. Law 255 (C.A.) (p. 75, *supra*.)

T.(H.H.) v. **T.(E.)** [1971] 1 W.L.R. 429 (P.D.A.). From 1963 until an occasion in December 1966 a husband and wife did not meet. In subsequent divorce proceedings an issue arose as to the paternity of a child born to the wife in September 1967. The meeting of the parties in 1966 had been by chance, and the parties were then in each other's company for about three hours. The husband had taken the wife to a club, and they had a good deal to drink. The wife alleged that before they left the club they had intercourse, in effect against her will, as a result of which the child was conceived. The husband denied that this intercourse had taken place. A blood test showed that it was not impossible that the husband was the father. There was medical statistical evidence that approximately 11 per cent. of Western European men had blood groups compatible with the paternity of the child. Rees J. held that, although the onus of proving the child illegitimate was upon the husband, by virtue of s.26 of the Family Law Reform Act 1969 he need only show it was more probable than not that he was not the father. He had, however, failed to discharge this onus. The learned judge expressly approved a dictum of Lord Reid in *S.* v. *McC. (orse. S.) and M.(D.S. intervener); W.* v. *W.*

[1972] A.C. 24, 41, concerning the effect of section 26: "That means that the presumption of legitimacy now merely determines the onus of proof. Once evidence has been led it must be weighed without using the presumption as a make-weight in the scale of legitimacy. So even weak evidence against legitimacy must prevail if there is no other evidence to counterbalance it. The presumption will only come in at that stage in the very rare case of the evidence being so evenly balanced that the court is unable to reach a decision on it."

Shephard v. **Cartwright** [1955] A.C. 431 (H.L.) A father subscribed for shares in companies and had some of the shares allotted to each of his three children. Five years later, at their father's request, the children signed the documents necessary to transfer the shares to their father. He dealt with the shares as though they were his own, the children signing further documents when required to do so. After his death the children claimed the shares, and it was held that they were entitled to them or their value, as the equitable presumption of advancement was not rebutted. Lord Simonds said (pp. 445–446): "... the law is clear that on the one hand where a man purchases shares and they are registered in the name of a stranger there is a resulting trust in favour of the purchaser; on the other hand, if they are registered in the name of a child or one to whom the purchaser then stood in loco parentis, there is no such resulting trust but a presumption of advancement. Equally it is clear that the presumption may be rebutted but should not, as Lord Eldon said, give way to slight circumstances (Finch v. Finch (1808) 15 Ves. 43). It must then be asked by what evidence can the presumption be rebutted, ... [The law is] correctly stated in ... a passage from Snell's Equity, 24th ed., p. 153, which is as follows: 'The acts and declarations of the parties before or at the time of the purchase, or so immediately after it as to constitute a part of the transaction, are admissible in evidence either for or against the party who did the act or made the declaration. ... But subsequent declarations are admissible as evidence only against the party who made them, and not in his favour.' ... But although the applicable law is not in doubt, the application of it is not always easy. There must often be room for argument whether a subsequent act is part of the same transaction as the original purchase or transfer, and equally whether subsequent acts which it is sought to adduce in evidence ought to be regarded as admissions by the party so acting, and whether, if they are so admitted, further facts should be admitted by way of qualification of those admissions."

Note.—As to informal admissions by parties, see Chapters 13 and 15, infra. Such an admission may be made by a predecessor in interest. For declarations against interest by deceased persons, see Chapter 13, infra.

For a new statutory presumption dealing with the effect of testamentary gifts to spouses, see the Administration of Justice Act 1982, s.22.

B. INTERACTION OF PRESUMPTIONS AND BURDENS

R. v. **Wilson** (1984) 78 Cr.App.R. 247 (C.A.). The accused was convicted of contravening section 30 of the Sexual Offences Act 1956. The section provides: "(1) It is an offence for a man knowingly to live wholly or in part on the earnings of prostitution. (2) For the purposes of this section a man who lives with ... a prostitute ... shall be presumed to be living on the earnings of prostitution, unless he proves the contrary." The Court of Appeal referred (p. 249) with approval to the trial judge's summing up in these terms: "If this woman is a prostitute, and if he [the accused] was living with her, then he must be presumed to be living on her earnings unless he proves the contrary. He has to prove something definite to the contrary." The judge had earlier "made it quite plain to the jury that when this presumption arises the burden of proof shifts to the accused, the standard of proof being on a balance of probabilities and not the full burden which applies to the prosecution" (per Kilner Brown J., giving the judgment of the Court of Appeal, at p. 249).

   Note.—See, too, *R.* v. *Braithwaite*; *R.* v. *Girdham* [1983] 1 W.L.R. 385 concerned with a similar "reverse onus clause" in section 2 of the Prevention of Corruption Act 1916 (see Part Two, *infra*). Of the section the Court of Appeal said (p. 389): "The effect of that is that when the matters in that section have been fulfilled, the burden of proof is lifted from the shoulders of the prosecution and descends upon the shoulders of the defence. It then becomes necessary for the defendant to show, on a balance of probabilities, that what was going on was not reception corruptly as inducement or reward. In an appropriate case it is the judge's duty to direct the jury first of all that they must decide whether they are satisfied so as to feel sure that the defendant received money or gift or consideration, and then to go on to direct them that if they are so satisfied, then under section 2 of the Act of 1916 the burden of proof shifts."

   Patterson v. **Charlton** [1986] R.T.R. 18 (D.C.). Allowing a prosecutor's appeal the Divisional Court held that when a defendant had admitted having driven on a particular day and it had been proved that he had then taken a breath test which had proved positive, the legal burden rested upon him to prove that he was not over the alcohol limit when he was driving.

NG CHUN PUI v. LEE CHUEN TAT

[1988] R.T.R. 298 (P.C.: 1988)

It is misleading to speak of the "doctrine" of res ipsa loquitur having the effect of shifting the legal burden of proof.

   LORD GRIFFITHS (delivering the judgment of the Privy Council, which included LORD BRIDGE OF HARWICH, LORD FRASER OF TULLEYBELTON, LORD ACKNER and SIR JOHN STEPHENSON, on appeal from the Court of Appeal of Hong Kong): By a judgment dated May 15, 1987 Nazareth J. decided liability in favour of the plaintiffs in respect of a road accident that occurred on February 28, 1982. The Court of Appeal by their judgment dated September 23, 1987 allowed the defendants' appeal and reversed the finding of the judge. The plaintiffs now appeal to their Lordships.
   On the afternoon of February 28, 1982 a coach owned by the second defendant left the westbound carriageway of Castle Peak Road, crossed the grass central reservation between the carriageways and collided with a public light bus being driven in the opposite direction in the nearside lane of the eastbound carriageway. The first plaintiffs are the personal representatives of a passenger in the public light bus who was killed in the collision. The remaining plaintiffs are other passengers and the driver, who were all injured in the collision.
   At the trial before Nazareth J. the plaintiffs put in evidence without objection a number of documents including a police sketch plan showing

the dimensions of the road and the positions of the vehicles after the
accident, which showed that the accident had occurred on the
defendants' wrong side of the road and after the bus had crossed the
central reservation, and a vehicle report showing that the defendants'
coach had been in good mechanical order immediately before the
accident.

The plaintiffs called no oral evidence and relied upon the fact of the
accident as evidence of negligence or, as the judge put it, the doctrine
of *res ipsa loquitur*. There can be no doubt that the plaintiffs were
justified in taking this course. In ordinary circumstances if a well-
maintained coach is being properly driven it will not cross the central
reservation of a dual carriageway and collide with on-coming traffic in
the other carriageway. In the absence of any explanation of the
behaviour of the coach the proper inference to draw is that it was not
being driven with the standard of care required by the law and that the
driver was therefore negligent. If the defendants had called no evidence
the plaintiffs would undoubtedly have been entitled to judgment.

The defendants however did call evidence and gave an explanation of
the circumstances that caused the first defendant to lose control of the
coach. This evidence was given both by the driver of the coach, *i.e.* the
first defendant, and a passenger sitting in the front of the coach. Their
evidence corresponded closely with the contemporary accounts that both
of them had given to the police. The judge accepted their evidence and
made the following findings of fact:

"The evidence led by the defendants shows clearly that the coach was
proceeding along a straight stretch of the road possibly a little in excess
of the speed limit of 40 miles per hour. But the speed of the coach is
not alleged to be one of the elements of negligence and I am not
particularly concerned with that. The coach was travelling in the fast or
outer lane and in that lane there was other traffic about two coach
lengths ahead of it. In the inner lane there was a vehicle about 10 to 20
feet ahead and between that vehicle and the coach there was a blue car
travelling a little faster than the coach. Suddenly that blue car, which
did not subsequently stop and has not been traced, cut into the fast lane
some six to eight feet ahead of the coach. That was clearly a very
dangerous manoeuvre and the first defendant reacted to it by braking
and swerving a little to his right. The coach then skidded across the
central reservation, as I have said, colliding with the public light bus."

The judge however was of the view that, despite those findings of
fact, because the plaintiffs had originally relied upon the doctrine of *res
ipsa loquitur*, the burden of disproving negligence remained upon the
defendants and they had failed to discharge it. In their Lordships'
opinion this shows a misunderstanding of the so-called doctrine of *res
ipsa loquitur*, which is no more than the use of a Latin maxim to
describe a state of the evidence from which it is proper to draw an
inference of negligence. Although it has been said in a number of cases,
it is misleading to talk of the burden of proof shifting to the defendant
in a *res ipsa loquitur* situation. The burden of proving negligence rests
throughout the case on the plaintiff. Where the plaintiff has suffered
injuries as a result of an accident which ought not to have happened if
the defendant had taken due care, it will often be possible for the
plaintiff to discharge the burden of proof by inviting the court to draw
the inference that on the balance of probabilities the defendant must
have failed to exercise due care, even though the plaintiff does not
know in what particular respects the failure occurred. One of the

earliest examples of the operation of this doctrine is *Scott* v. *London and St. Katharine Docks Co.* (1865) 3 H. & C. 596. Bags of sugar being lowered by a crane from a warehouse by the defendants' servants fell and struck the plaintiff. Erle C.J. said, at p. 601:

"But where the thing is shown to be under the management of the defendant or his servants, and the accident is such as in the ordinary course of things does not happen if those who have the management use proper care, it affords reasonable evidence, in the absence of explanation by the defendants, that the accident arose from want of care."

So in an appropriate case the plaintiff establishes a prima facie case by relying upon the fact of the accident. If the defendant adduces no evidence there is nothing to rebut the inference of negligence and the plaintiff will have proved his case. But if the defendant does adduce evidence that evidence must be evaluated to see if it is still reasonable to draw the inference of negligence from the mere fact of the accident. Loosely speaking this may be referred to as a burden on the defendant to show he was not negligent, but that only means that faced with a prima facie case of negligence the defendant will be found negligent unless he produces evidence that is capable of rebutting the prima facie case. Resort to the burden of proof is a poor way to decide a case; it is the duty of the judge to examine all the evidence at the end of the case and decide whether he on the facts he finds to have been proved and on the inferences he is prepared to draw he is satisfied that negligence has been established. In so far as resort is had to the burden of proof the burden remains at the end of the case as it was at the beginning upon the plaintiff to prove that his injury was caused by the negligence of the defendants. Their Lordships adopt the following two passages from the decided cases as most clearly expressing the true meaning and effect of the so-called doctrine of *res ipsa loquitur*. In *Henderson* v. *Henry E. Jenkins & Sons* [1970] R.T.R. 70 Lord Pearson said, at pp. 811–82A:

"In an action for negligence the plaintiff must allege, and has the burden of proving, that the accident was caused by negligence on the part of the defendants. That is the issue throughout the trial, and in giving judgment at the end of the trial the judge has to decide whether he is satisfied on a balance of probabilities that the accident was caused by negligence on the part of the defendants, and if he is not so satisfied the plaintiff's action fails. The formal burden of proof does not shift. But if in the course of the trial there is proved a set of facts which raises a prima facie inference that the accident was caused by negligence on the part of the defendants, the issue will be decided in the plaintiff's favour unless the defendants by their evidence provide some answer which is adequate to displace the prima facie inference. In this situation there is said to be an evidential burden of proof resting on the defendants. I have some doubts whether it is strictly correct to use the expression 'burden of proof' with this meaning, as there is a risk of it being confused with the formal burden of proof, but it is a familiar and covenient usage."

In *Lloyde* v. *West Midlands Gas Board* [1971] 1 W.L.R. 749, 755 Megaw L.J. said:

"I doubt whether it is right to describe *res ipsa loquitur* as a 'doctrine.' I think that it is no more than an exotic, although convenient, phrase to describe what is in essence no more than a commonsense approach, not limited by technical rules, to the assessment of the effect of evidence in certain circumstances. It means that a plaintiff prima facie establishes negligence where: (i) it is not possible for him to prove precisely what was the relevant act or omission which set in train the events leading to the accident; but (ii) on the evidence as it stands at the relevant time it is more likely than not that the effective cause of the accident was some act or omission of the defendant or of someone for whom the defendant is responsible, which act or omission constitutes a failure to take proper care for the plaintiff's safety. I have used the words 'evidence as it stands at the relevant time.' I think that this can most conveniently be taken as being at the close of the plaintiff's case. On the assumption that a submission of no case is then made, would the evidence, as it then stands, enable the plaintiff to succeed because, although the precise cause of the accident cannot be established, the proper inference on balance of probability is that that cause, whatever it may have been, involved a failure by the defendant to take due care for the plaintiff's safety? If so, *res ipsa loquitur*. If not, the plaintiff fails. Of course, if the defendant does not make a submission of no case, the question still falls to be tested by the same criterion, but evidence for the defendant, given thereafter, may rebut the inference. The res, which previously spoke for itself, may be silenced, or its voice may, on the whole of the evidence, become too weak or muted."

...Their Lordships will humbly advise Her Majesty that this appeal ought to be dismissed.

Note.—The maxim *res ipsa loquitur* (the thing speaks for itself) has often been treated as equivalent to a rebuttable presumption of law. It has been frequently invoked and it is much discussed in the literature on negligence. But there has been a wide diversity of judicial and other opinion as to the effect of the presumption. On one view the presumption is no more than permissive—its effect is to warrant, but not to require, a finding of negligence. On another view it shifts the legal burden of proof (*Woods* v. *Duncan* [1946] A.C. 401 (H.L.).

In *Ng Chun Pui* v. *Lee Chuan Tat* it has now been confirmed that its effect is to place the equivalent of an evidential burden upon the opponent. An earlier case in which this approach was taken was *The Kite* [1933] P. 154 (P.D.).

Wilsher v. **Essex Area Health Authority** [1988] A.C. 1074 (H.L.). The plaintiff had developed a condition of the eyes which resulted in blindness. A likely cause of the condition, but not a definite or the only possible cause, was that too much oxygen had been administered to him in hospital shortly after his birth. He claimed damages from the defendant Health Authority for negligent medical treatment. Pain J., the trial judge, held the defendants liable since they had failed to prove that the plaintiff's condition had not been caused by the negligence of their employees. The Court of Appeal by a majority dismissed the defendant's appeal, but its further appeal was allowed by a unanimous House of Lords. The House distinguished its earlier decision in *McGhee* v. *National Coal Board* [1973] 1 W.L.R. 1. Of that decision Lord Bridge of Harwich said (p. 1090): "[it] laid down no new principle of law whatever. On the contrary, it affirmed the principle that the onus of proving causation lies on the pursuer or plaintiff. Adopting a robust and pragmatic approach to the undisputed primary facts of the case, the majority concluded that it was a legitimate inference of fact that the defender's negligence had materially contributed to the pursuer's injury. The decision, in my opinion, is of no greater significance than that, and to attempt to extract from it some esoteric principle which in some way modifies, as a matter of law, the nature of the burden of proof of causation which a plaintiff or pursuer must discharge once he has established a relevant breach of duty is a fruitless one." The House held that the issue of causation in the instant case should be retried on this basis before a different judge.

> *Note.*—In the light of this case an earlier decision, also of Pain J., in *Clark* v. *MacLennan* [1983] 1 All E.R. 416, if it is still good law, must (perhaps unfortunately) be regarded as being of limited scope. There Pain J. had held in a medical negligence action that, although the legal burden of proof is upon the plaintiff, in a case where there is a general duty of care and the plaintiff has established (1) a failure by the defendant to take a recognised preventative precaution and (2) that this has been followed by (although not necessarily caused by) the very damage which the precaution was designed to prevent, a burden then rests on the defendant to prove either (1) that he was nevertheless not in breach of the general duty, or (2) that the damage was in fact not caused by that breach. In effect, therefore, when a doctor (as in that case) departs from usual approved medical practice, and injury which that practice was designed to prevent occurs, the doctor will have the burden of proving that he was not negligent. The defendant had failed to discharge that burden.

C. CONFLICTING PRESUMPTIONS

R. v. **Willshire** (1881) 6 Q.B.D. 366 (C.C.R.). In a prosecution for bigamy, it appeared that the prisoner had gone through four marriage ceremonies with A, B, C and D, in 1864, 1868, 1879 and 1880 respectively. Having been convicted in 1868 of marrying B in the lifetime of A, he was now prosecuted for marrying D in the lifetime of C. In defence the prisoner gave evidence of the previous conviction, thus proving that A, his real or first wife, was alive in 1868. The presumption then arose that her life continued to 1879, when the prisoner married C, and that therefore the marriage with C was void, and he had not committed bigamy by marrying D in the lifetime of C. It was held to be a question of fact for the jury whether A was alive or not at the relevant time, the burden of proof being, of course, on the prosecution.

> *Note.*—This case is traditionally cited as a leading authority on conflicting presumptions, *i.e.* on cases in which there is an inconsistency between two presumed facts, but it would appear to be of limited value, as the presumption of continuance of life is only one of fact, whereas that of the validity of the 1879 marriage was an evidential presumption of law. A theoretically difficult case would be one in which two compelling presumptions conflict. See Introduction to this Chapter, p. 79, *supra.*

Chapter 5

FORMAL ADMISSIONS

ANY fact which is formally admitted for the purposes of a civil trial need not be proved. Such a fact ceases to be in issue, and no evidence in proof or disproof of it is admissible.[1] Formal admissions, which are generally conclusive but only for the purposes of the case in which they are made, are to be distinguished from informal admissions. These latter are mere items of evidence admitted by way of exception to the hearsay rule[2] and are, of course, not conclusive. When a party formally admits a fact, he and his adversary are usually saved some time, trouble and expense.

In civil cases formal admissions may be made in various ways. They may be made expressly in the pleadings, or may result from a default in pleading or from a failure to traverse the fact in a pleading. They may result from interlocutory proceedings. These various matters are dealt with by Rules of Court. They include: (1) Admissions made in answer to a notice to admit facts or documents served under R.S.C. Ord. 27.[3] Such a notice calls for the admission of specified facts or documents, and unreasonable failure to admit facts in response to it may make the defaulting party liable to pay the costs involved in proving them. The court has power to allow a party to amend or withdraw an admission so made "on such terms as may be just." (2) Admissions made in answer to interrogatories. By virtue of R.S.C., Ord. 26,[4] a party may with leave of the court address written interrogatories to the other party before the trial. These must be answered by affidavit, and the answers will be admissible at the trial against the party making them. But they are not necessarily conclusive and they may not be used otherwise than in the action in respect of which they are made.[5] Formal admission may also be made prior to the trial either by a party or by letter written with his authority by his solicitor or barrister; but such an admission may be subsequently withdrawn on terms, provided the opponent has not acted upon it so as to give rise to an estoppel. At the trial itself the party or his advocate may admit facts thus rendering inadmissible evidence in proof or disproof of them.

---

[1] See, e.g. Urquhart v. Butterfield (1887) 37 Ch.D. 357, 374 (C.A.) and Pioneer Plastic Containers Ltd. v. Commissioners of Customs and Excise [1967] Ch. 597 (Ch.D.).
[2] Chapter 14, Section D. infra.
[3] Part Three, infra; and see, too, C.C.R., Ords. 14 and 20, Part Three, infra.
[4] Part Three, infra; and see too, C.C.R., Ords. 14 and 20, Part Three, infra.
[5] Riddick v. Thames Board Mills [1977] Q.B. 881 (C.A.); but see, too, Sony Corporation v. Times Electronics [1981] 1 W.L.R. 1293 (Ch.D.).

At common law formal admissions were not allowed in criminal cases.[6] However, an important change was effected by section 10 of the Criminal Justice Act 1967. By virtue of this section a formal admission may now, subject to certain restrictions, be made in any criminal proceedings by, or on behalf of, the prosecution or the defendant before or at the trial, but it may later be withdrawn with leave of the court. For the important safeguards built into this innovation see the text of the section.[7]

SWINFEN v. CHELMSFORD (LORD)

29 L.J. Ex. **383;** 2 L.T. 406; 8 W.R. 545; 6 Jur.(N.S.) 1035; 5 H. & N. 890; 157
E.R. 1436 (Exchequer: 1860)

A barrister (or other advocate) may make any admission on behalf of his client which, in the honest exercise of his judgment, he thinks proper; but he has no authority on matters collateral to the suit.

Lord Chelmsford, the defendant, when Sir Frederick Thesiger, appeared for the plaintiff in a certain case, which he compromised. It was held that he was authorised to do so by virtue of his engagement.

POLLOCK C.B. (delivering the judgment of the court, which included BRAMWELL, CHANNELL and WATSON BB.): . . . The conduct and control of the cause are left necessarily to counsel. If a party desires to retain the power of directing counsel how the suit shall be conducted, he must agree with some counsel willing to bind himself. . . . Although counsel has complete authority over the suit, the mode of conducting it, and all that is incident to it, such as withdrawing the record, withdrawing a juror, or calling a witness, or selecting such as in his discretion he thinks ought to be called, and other matters which properly belong to the suit, and the management and conduct of the trial, he has not, by virtue of his retainer in the suit, any power over matters that are collateral to it. . . .

Note.—*Swinfen* v. *Chelmsford (Lord)* has been followed in *Waugh* v. *H.B. Clifford and Sons* [1982] Ch. 374 (C.A.) where Brightman L.J. (with whose reasoning Cumming-Bruce and Ackner L.JJ. agreed) said (pp. 387–388): " . . . a solicitor (or counsel) may in a particular case have ostensible authority *vis-à-vis* the opposing litigant where he has no implied authority *vis-à-vis* his client. I see no objection to that. All that the opposing litigant need ask himself when testing the ostensible authority of the solicitor or counsel, is the question, whether the compromise contains matter 'collateral to the suit.' The magnitude of the compromise, or the burden which it imposes on the other party, is irrelevant. But much more than that question may need to be asked by a solicitor when deciding whether he can safely compromise without reference to this client."

---

[6] A plea of guilty constitutes an admission of guilt but, as Hawkins J. said in *R.* v. *Riley* (1896) 18 Cox C.C. 285, 295 (C.C.C.R.), it does not constitute an admission of the facts stated in the depositions. Nor, presumably, should it be treated as an admission of the truth of any particular fact which would have been alleged by the prosecution.
    After conviction an accused may make admissions of fact affecting sentence.
[7] Part Two, *infra.*

An admission may be made by a party's solicitor before an action in correspondence or otherwise (*Ellis* v. *Allen* [1914] 1 Ch. 904), or by counsel in the pleadings (see *Warner* v. *Sampson* [1958] 1 Q.B. 404; reversed on another point [1959] 1 Q.B. 297 (C.A.)), or at the trial.

A probation officer has no implied authority to make admissions on behalf of a party to domestic proceedings in a magistrates' court (*Smith* v. *Smith* [1957] 1 W.L.R. 802 (D.C.)).

H. Clark (Doncaster) Ltd. v. **Wilkinson** [1965] 1 Ch. 694 (C.A.). An admission made by counsel in the course of proceedings can be withdrawn unless the circumstances are such as to give rise to an estoppel. Salmon L.J. said (p. 704): "No doubt a statement made by counsel, just like a statement made by the client, if acted upon by the other side to its prejudice, cannot be withdrawn. This is because an estoppel would then arise. Similarly, counsel is the ostensible agent of his client to make an agreement during the course of a trial settling the case. If he does so, his client is bound by the agreement, just as anyone is bound by an agreement made on his behalf by another who is ostensibly his agent to make the agreement. To my mind the circumstances here are quite different. It is not even suggested that the statement made by counsel before the registrar ... was acted on by the respondents. Clearly, if a man were appearing in person and made an admission during the course of any interlocutory proceedings or during the course of the trial and that statement was not acted upon by the other side to its detriment there is no rule of law that prevents him from withdrawing it. I do not see how a man can be any worse off in this respect because, instead of making the admission himself, the admission is made on his behalf by counsel."

Chapter 6

ESTOPPELS

AN estoppel prevents a party to litigation from alleging or disputing the existence of a fact. It prohibits disproof by the party against whom it is raised (the estoppel-denier) and thus dispenses with proof by the party relying upon it (the estoppel-asserter). Historically estoppels have been said to be of three kinds—by record, by deed and by conduct. To be operative an estoppel by record or by deed, and usually an estoppel by conduct, must be pleaded by the estoppel-asserter.

There is some dispute (in part semantic in nature) as to whether estoppels pertain to substantive or adjectival law[1]; but there is a generally accepted principle that resort cannot be had to an estoppel to effect a blatant contravention of substantive law. Thus where a formality is prescribed by statute, an estoppel will not inhibit proof of non-compliance.[2] So, too, a false representation as to age by an infant will not estop him from setting up contractual incapacity[3]; and a corporation is not estopped by acts which are *ultra vires*.[4] On the other hand a defendant might be estopped from pleading that money was paid in respect of a gaming debt, if he had led the plaintiff to believe that it was not so[5]; and an employer has been estopped from pleading that a workman had not instituted proceedings within the statutory period of six months where he had led him to believe his claim was admitted.[6] The apparent inconsistency presented by such cases can perhaps be plausibly, if not convincingly, rationalised by drawing a distinction between contravention of mandatory and facultative rules of law.[7]

Estoppel by record. A judgment is conclusive as against all persons as to the existence of the legal situation that it actually brings about. This is of particular practical importance if the judgment is *in rem*, for example, a decree of divorce is conclusive that the parties are no longer husband and wife.

Quite apart from this, and in addition to it, is the doctrine of estoppel

---

[1] See, *e.g. Amalgamated Property Co.* v. *Texas Bank* [1982] Q.B. 84 (C.A.), *per* Brandon L.J. at pp. 131–132.

[2] *Hunt* v. *Wimbledon Local Board* (1878) 4 C.P.D. 48; but *cf. Western Fish Products Ltd.* v. *Penwith District Council* [1981] 2 All E.R. 204 (C.A.), *per* Megaw L.J. at p. 221.

[3] *R. Leslie Ltd.* v. *Sheill* [1914] 3 K.B. 607, 615 (C.A.).

[4] *British Mutual Banking Co.* v. *Charnwood* (1887) 18 Q.B.D. 714.

[5] *Tatam* v. *Reeve* [1893] 1 Q.B. 44.

[6] *Wright* v. *John Bagnall & Sons Ltd.* [1900] 2 Q.B. 240.

[7] See *Maritime Electric Co.* v. *General Dairies* [1937] A.C. 610 (P.C.), *infra.*

by record *inter partes* or estoppel *per rem judicatam*. By virtue of this doctrine a party to legal proceedings in which judgment has been given, or who claims under a person who was a party thereto, may be estopped from denying the facts upon which such a judgment was based if the judgment is pleaded as an estoppel. It is, however, to be remembered that an application may be made to have an otherwise conclusive judgment set aside if it was obtained by fraud or collusion. Moreover, it is to be emphasised that a judgment does not in this sense estop persons who were neither parties nor privies thereto.

An estoppel by record *inter partes* may operate as a "cause of action" estoppel or as an "issue" estoppel. The former stems from the merger of the cause of action in the judgment: after judgment a party cannot bring another action against the same opposing party for the same cause. The law relating to "issue" estoppel is still at a formative stage. Its nature has been indicated by Lord Denning M.R.: "The rule then is that, once an issue has been raised and distinctly determined between the parties, then, as a general rule, neither party can be allowed to fight that issue all over again."[8] For the doctrine to operate it is essential that there be an identity of parties and of issue.

In matrimonial causes estoppels operate as between the parties but they do not necessarily bind the court.[9]

In a criminal case the analogue of "cause of action" estoppel is a plea of *autrefois acquit* or *autrefois convict*. The doctrine of "issue" estoppel is not generally applicable in criminal cases.

Estoppel by deed. Historically a party to a deed and those claiming through him were estopped from denying the truth of facts stated in the deed including facts stated in recitals. The doctrine is only operative in actions on a deed. Moreover, it does not prevent a party from setting up a plea of fraud, duress or illegality, or from relying on a fact which would entitle him to rescission or rectification. The raising of an estoppel by recitals and probably estoppel by deed generally, is now dependent upon the intention, express or implied, of the parties. If the whole doctrine is based upon intention it could in many respects be subsumed under the category of estoppel by conduct.

Estoppel by conduct. An estoppel by conduct, anciently called an estoppel by matter *in pais*, may arise from a party's conduct, the underlying assertive or representational significance of which it would be unconscionable to permit him to deny. The conduct must be such that a reasonable man would take the representation of fact implicit in it to be true and would believe that it was meant that he should act upon it. As Sir Owen Dixon once said in the High Court of Australia, "The principle upon which estoppel *in pais* is founded is that the law should not permit an unjust departure by a party from an assumption of fact which he has caused another party to adopt or accept for the purpose of their legal relations."[10] An estoppel may arise from agreement, from an express or implied representation (verbal or otherwise) or from negligence—although, at least when the conduct takes the form of

---

[8] *Fidelitas Shipping Co. Ltd.* v. *V./O Exportchleb* [1966] 1 Q.B. 630, 640 (C.A.).
[9] See *Thompson* v. *Thompson* [1957] P. 19 (C.A.), *infra*.
[10] *Grundt* v. *Great Boulder Proprietary Gold Mine Ltd.* (1937) 59 C.L.R. 641, 674 (H.C. of Australia).

negligence the authorities suggest that the estoppel-denier must be shown to have owed an identifiable duty to the estoppel-asserter. A representation, express or implied, upon which it is sought to found an estoppel must be unambiguous and must be of present or past fact[11]: a representation as to intention does not suffice, nor normally does a representation of pure law.

A. ESTOPPEL BY RECORD

The Duchess of Kingston's Case (1776) 20 St. Tr. 355; 1 Leach 146; 1 East P.C. 468; 168 E.R. 175 (H.L.). The Duchess of Kingston was indicted and tried in the House of Lords for bigamy, in marrying the Duke of Kingston in March 1769, during the lifetime of her husband the Earl of Bristol. The Duchess pleaded that, in a suit for jactitation of marriage instituted by her against the Earl of Bristol in the Consistory Court of the Bishop of London, it had been decreed and declared in February 1769 that she was a spinster, and that the Earl of Bristol had wickedly and maliciously boasted and publicly asserted (though falsely) that they were joined and contracted together in matrimony, and he had been admonished to desist from such boasting and asserting of such alleged marriage.

It was ordered by the House that the following questions be put to the Judges: (1) Whether a sentence of the spiritual court against a marriage in a suit for jactitation of marriage is conclusive evidence so as to stop the counsel for the Crown from proving the said marriage in an indictment for polygamy? (2) Whether, admitting such sentence to be conclusive upon such indictment, the counsel for the Crown may be admitted to avoid the effect of such sentence, by proving the same to have been obtained by fraud or collusion?

De Grey C.J. gave the opinion of the Judges, to the following effect: (1) That "a cause of jactitation...ranked as a cause of defamation only.... The sentence has only a negative and qualified effect, *viz.*, 'that the party has failed in his proof, and that the libellant is free from all matrimonial contract, as far as yet appears';...so that, admitting the sentence in its full extent and import, it only proves that it did not yet appear that they were married, and not that they were not married at all...." In this it, unlike, *e.g.* a decree of nullity, was not conclusive as to the legal status of the parties. (2) That, although a person who was a party to legal proceedings in which a judgment as given, or who claims under a person who was a party, may be estopped from denying the facts upon which the judgment was based, as "a general principle, a transaction between two parties, in judicial proceedings, ought not to be binding upon a third." The Crown not being a party to the jactitation proceedings was not, therefore, estopped from denying the facts upon which the judgment in those proceedings had been based. (3) That, even if the judgment were conclusive in the sense that it could "not be impeached from within; yet, like all other acts of the highest judicial authority, it is impeachable from without; although it is not permitted to show that the court was mistaken, it may be shown that they were misled. Fraud is an extrinsic, collateral act; which vitiates the most solemn proceedings of courts of justice. Lord Coke says, it avoids all judicial acts, ecclesiastical or temporal...."

The Chief Justice concluded: "We are therefore unanimously of opinion: First, that a sentence in the spiritual court against a marriage in a suit of jactitation of

---

[11] *Jorden* v. *Money* (1854) 5 H.L.Cas. 185 (H.L.).

marriage is not conclusive evidence so as to stop the counsel for the Crown from proving the marriage in an indictment for polygamy.

Secondly, admitting such sentence to be conclusive upon such indictment, the counsel for the Crown may be admitted to avoid the effect of such sentence by proving the same to have been obtained by fraud or collusion."

Note.—Estoppel by judgment is based on principles expressed in two maxims—*interest rei publicae ut sit finis litium* (the public interest requires finality in lawsuits) and *nemo debet bis vexari pro eadem causa* (no person should be troubled twice with the same cause).

Judgments are of two kinds—*in rem* and *in personam*. The former comprise judgments affecting legal status, *e.g.* a divorce decree or an adjudication in bankruptcy, and are conclusive against all persons, whether parties or strangers. Judgments *in personam* are ordinary judgments between persons not affecting status. They bind parties and privies as to the facts in issue. This limitation has been strictly construed. For example, in *Carl Zeiss Stiftung* v. *Rayner and Keeler Ltd. (No. 2)* [1967] 1 A.C. 853 (H.L.) it was held that a representation by solicitors of a common principle did not give rise to privity in this context. See, too, *Gleeson* v. *Wippell* [1977] 1 W.L.R. 510. It is necessary that a person should have been a party in the same capacity in both proceedings; so a judgment against a man in his personal capacity will not bind him in the capacity of administrator of his wife's estate (see *Marginson* v. *Blackburn Borough Council* [1939] 2 K.B. 426 (C.A.)).

Judgments are conclusive against all persons of their legal effect, as distinguished from the facts upon which they are based. That is to say, a judgment in favour of A against B for damages for negligence is proof against all the world that such judgment has been entered and between those parties, but there is no estoppel in the case of persons not parties to that judgment or their privies from disputing the facts on which it was based (see *Townsend* v. *Bishop* [1939] 1 All E.R. 805).

The estoppel may arise upon a judgment by default (see *New Brunswick Ry.* v. *British and French Trust Corp. Ltd.* [1939] A.C. 1 at 21 (H.L.)), or by consent (see *Kinch* v. *Walcott* [1929] A.C. 482 (P.C.)). In *Khan* v. *Goleccha International* [1980] 1 W.L.R. 1492 the Court of Appeal re-affirmed that an issue is settled so as to ground an estoppel in subsequent proceedings, whether embodied in the court's judgment, or contained in an admission to the court, or implied in a consent order. *cf. Thyssen-Bornemisza* v. *Thyssen-Bornemisza* [1986] Fam. 1 (C.A.).

The judgment is only conclusive of what it actually decides and of matters necessarily implicit in the decision and actually raised before the tribunal by the pleadings (*Hoystead* v. *Commr. of Taxation* [1926] A.C. 155 (P.C.); *New Brunswick Ry.* v. *British and French Trust Corp. Ltd.* (above)).

In *Carl Zeiss Stiftung* v. *Rayner and Keeler Ltd. (No. 2)* [1976] 1 A.C. 853 (H.L.) four Law Lords took the view that issue estoppel can be based on a foreign judgment, although this extension should be applied with caution because of uncertainties arising from differences of procedure in foreign countries. However in *The Sennar (No. 2)* [1985] 1 W.L.R. 490 (H.L.) it was held *per curiam* in the words of Lord Diplock (at p. 493): "It is far too late, at this stage of the development of the doctrine, to question that issue estoppel can be created by the judgment of a foreign court if the court is recognised in English private international law as being a court of competent jurisdiction. Issue estoppel operates regardless of whether or not an English court would regard the reasoning of the foreign judgment as open to criticism."

An estoppel arises only when the same subject-matter is in issue in both actions. As to negligence causing traffic accidents, compare *Marginson* v. *Blackburn Borough Council* [1939] 2 K.B. 426, *Bell* v. *Holmes* [1956] 1 W.L.R. 1359 and *Wood* v. *Luscombe* [1966] 1 Q.B. 169 with *Randolph* v. *Tuck* [1962] 1 Q.B. 175. For the position in matrimonial causes, see *Thompson* v. *Thompson* [1957] P. 19 (C.A.) (*infra*) and *Porter* v. *Porter* [1971] P. 282 (*infra*).

When a decision relates only to a definite period, as in the case of an assessment for rating by a valuation court, it does not operate as an estoppel in respect of a later period (*Society of Medical Officers of Health* v. *Hope* [1960] A.C. 551 (H.L.)).

Vooght v. **Winch** (1819) 2 B. and Ald. 662 (K.B.). In an action for diverting water from a stream, the defendant gave in evidence a judgment in a former action between the same parties for the same cause of action, and insisted that it operated as an estoppel. The judge received it in evidence, but refused to nonsuit the plaintiff, the defendant having pleaded only not guilty, and the plaintiff obtained a verdict. On motion to the court for a nonsuit or new trial, a nonsuit was refused, although a new trial was granted on other grounds. Abbott C.J. said (p. 668): "I am of opinion that the verdict and judgment obtained for the defendant in the former action was not conclusive evidence against the plaintiff upon the plea of not guilty. It would indeed have been conclusive if pleaded in bar to the action by way of estoppel. In that case the plaintiff would not be allowed to discuss the case with the defendant, and for the second time to disturb and vex him by the agitation of the same question. But the defendant has pleaded not guilty, and has thereby elected to submit his case to a jury. Now if the former verdict was proper to be received in evidence by the learned judge, its effect must be left to the jury. If it were conclusive indeed, the learned judge ought immediately to have nonsuited the plaintiff, or to have told the jury that they were bound, in point of law, to find a verdict for the defendant. It appears to me, however, that the party, by not pleading the former judgment in bar, consents that the whole matter shall go to the jury, and leaves it open to them to inquire into the same upon evidence, and they are to give their verdict upon the whole evidence then submitted to them."

Note.—An amendment of a pleading may be allowed in appropriate circumstances, as when the judgment relied on as an estoppel was given after the issue of the writ in subsequent proceedings (see *Morrison Rose & Partners* v. *Hillman* [1961] 2 Q.B. 266 (C.A.)).

The High Court of Australia has held that there are some circumstances in which cause of action estoppel need not always be pleaded: *Laws Holdings Pty. Ltd.* v. *Short and Others* (1972) 46 A.L.J.R. 563.

THOMPSON v. THOMPSON

[1957] P. 19; [1957] 2 W.L.R. 138; [1957] 1 All E.R. 161 (C.A.: 1956)

In matrimonial proceedings estoppels by record do not bind the High Court.

A wife had applied to the High Court for an order for maintenance against her husband, on the ground of his wilful neglect to maintain her, alleging cruelty as a reason for leaving the husband. He had made a similar charge of cruelty by the wife. After a full hearing the application was dismissed. Subsequently the husband petitioned for divorce, alleging cruelty. By her answer the wife denied cruelty, and prayed for a judicial separation on the ground of the husband's cruelty. The husband applied to have this allegation struck out on the ground that her allegations of cruelty had been determined in the maintenance proceedings and he pleaded that she was estopped from raising them again. The Court of Appeal, upholding the registrar and the judge in chambers, held that the wife's allegation of cruelty could be investigated again.

DENNING L.J.: . . . The situation has been neatly summarised by saying that in the divorce court "estoppels bind the parties but do not bind the court": but this is perhaps a little too abbreviated. The full proposition is that, once an issue of a matrimonial offence has been litigated between the parties and decided by a competent court, neither party can claim as of right to reopen the issue and litigate it all over again if the other party objects (that is what is meant by saying that estoppels bind the parties): but the divorce court has the right, and indeed the duty in a proper case, to reopen the issue, or to allow either party to reopen it, despite the objection of the other party (that is what is meant by saying that estoppels do not bind the court). Whether the divorce court should reopen the issue depends on the circumstances. If the court is satisfied that there has already been a full and proper inquiry in the previous litigation, it will often hold that it is not necessary to hold another inquiry all over again: but if the court is not so satisfied it has a right and a duty to inquire into it afresh. If the court does decide to reopen the matter, then there is no longer any estoppel on either party. Each can go into the matter afresh. . . .

To come now to the present case, the question is whether the wife should be allowed to raise again in these proceedings the allegations of cruelty which were all thrashed out at great length in the maintenance proceedings before Mr. Commissioner Grazebrook. At first sight it would seem that she should not be allowed to do it. The court should, it would seem, act on the strict rule of estoppel by *res judicata*. If the wife had herself brought a petition for divorce on the ground of her husband's cruelty, I should have thought it plain that she should not be allowed to harass him again with the self-same charges on which she has already failed. . . . But the trouble in this case is with the husband's own petition. He has in his petition charged his wife with perjury in the prior maintenance proceedings. He has said that she falsely and maliciously swore that he treated her with cruelty and so forth. His charge of perjury is so comprehensive that, in order to investigate it, the court will have to go into her allegations all over again. He has set up this charge of perjury in order to revive any condoned cruelty. If he is bringing up the allegations in this way, I do not see why she should not be allowed to keep them in her answer. The court should allow a departure from a strict estoppel to enable her to do so. It is very unfortunate that all this expense should be had all over again, but he has brought it on his own head by his own pleading. . . .

In the result, I think the appeal should be dismissed; . . .

HODSON and MORRIS L.J. delivered judgments reaching the same conclusion.

Note.—For an earlier manifestation of this approach see *Harriman* v. *Harriman* [1909] P. 123 (C.A.). The same approach is substantially reflected in the Matrimonial Causes Act 1973, s.4. It provides that the jurisdiction of the court in divorce is not precluded by reason only that a party has on the same (or substantially the same) facts as those proved in support of the petition obtained a decree of judicial separation or an order under (or having the same effect as if made under) the Matrimonial Proceedings (Magistrates' Courts) Act 1960 or Part I of the Domestic Proceedings and Magistrates' Courts Act 1978. It provides that the court may treat such decree or order as sufficient proof of the adultery, desertion or other ground on which it was granted, but it shall not grant a divorce without receiving evidence from the petitioner.

In cases *not* coming within the ambit of section 4 it would appear (1) that a court of summary jurisdiction is bound by an earlier finding of the divorce court (*James* v. *James* [1948] 1 All E.R. 214 (D.C.)) or of another court of summary jurisdiction (*Stokes* v. *Stokes* [1911] P. 195); and (2) that the divorce court is bound by its own previous findings (*Finney* v. *Finney* (1868) L.R. 1 P and D 483), but not by findings of courts of summary jurisdiction (*Winnan* v. *Winnan* [1949] P. 174 (C.A.)).

Hayward v. **Hayward** [1961] P. 152 (P.D.). A husband, although he and his wife suspected that their marriage was bigamous and therefore void, had admitted liability in maintenance proceedings in a court of summary jurisdiction. In subsequent nullity proceedings alleging that the marriage was void on the grounds of bigamy it was held that no estoppel precluded the assertion of this invalidity. Status being in issue, policy required that investigation of the truth be permitted. Phillimore J. said (pp. 158–159): "It would surely be remarkable as a proposition of law if this court were to be prevented from declaring the truth, namely, that a marriage is bigamous and so correcting the status of parties to it and of their dependants merely because one or both of them had chosen to assert its validity or because one of them had failed to dispute or had concurred in the assertion of its validity by the other. This court deals not merely with disputes between parties but with status. Marriage is not an ordinary contract—it is an institution which confers status on the parties to it and upon the children that issue from it,.... It is an old maxim that estoppels are odious because they tend to shut out the truth... and it is well settled that they cannot override the law of the land.... If the law declares a bigamous marriage void and criminal, is this court nevertheless to treat it as valid and refuse to declare the truth by reason of the conduct, however unmeritorious, of one or both of the parties to it? The consequences to which this doctrine might lead are surely remarkable."

Porter v. **Porter** [1971] P. 282 (P.D.). A husband had petitioned for divorce alleging desertion. The wife had denied desertion and had alleged cruelty, constructive desertion and adultery. In the event, however, the wife had allowed the petition to proceed undefended and a decree had been pronounced. On a later application for maintenance, the wife sought to argue the husband's cruelty. Ormrod J. held that she was not estopped from doing so. His Lordship said (p. 284): "This then is yet another case on the much argued problem of estoppel in matrimonial causes.... It arises from a conflict between two issues of public policy; on the one hand, the desirability of finality in litigation... and, on the other hand, the importance in the interests of justice to the individuals concerned, that the discretionary powers of the court in ancillary matters should be exercised with a full knowledge of all the relevant facts rather than on a basis, partly of fact, and partly of assumptions, arising from such rules as estoppel. It is particularly difficult to do justice in so personal a field as matrimonial cases if the realities of the situation are allowed to be obscured by the application of rules or principles which in other situations assist the cause of justice." Referring to the judgment of Sachs J. in *Hull* v. *Hull* [1960] P. 118, Ormrod J. continued (p. 285): "Estoppel operates to prevent a party in ancillary proceedings from challenging the ground on which the decree was pronounced in the suit, and from attacking the express findings of fact of the trial judge. Thus a respondent against whom a decree has been pronounced on the ground of adultery cannot be heard in ancillary proceedings to deny such adultery or to set up an absolute bar to a decree on this ground, *e.g.* connivance or condonation.... Similarly, where the trial judge has made specific findings, *e.g.* that the husband did not strike the wife as alleged on a particular paragraph of the pleading that finding is conclusive. Apart from these categories of fact there is no estoppel.... Applying these conclusions to the present appeal, it follows that the wife cannot be heard to deny that she deserted the husband as found by the trial judge.... Accordingly, she cannot set up just cause for leaving the husband, nor can she assert that he has treated her with cruelty within the meaning of the Matrimonial Causes Act 1965 because this would be equivalent to asserting just cause. On the other hand, I see no reason why she should not raise any matters of complaint against the husband by way of mitigation of her desertion. If she is prevented from doing so the court, in the exercise of its discretionary jurisdiction, will be failing to carry out its statutory duty to consider the 'conduct of the parties,' which is not the same thing as asking who obtained the decree and on what ground. ... "

Note.—The role of estoppel in ancillary proceedings is somewhat specialised and in practice limited. See, too, *Porter* v. *Porter* [1969] 1 W.L.R. 1155 (C.A.); *Tumath* v. *Tumath* [1970] P. 78; and *Tebutt* v. *Haynes* [1981] 2 All E.R. 238 (C.A.). Its scope is particularly restricted in custody proceedings: indeed, in *Frost* v. *Frost* [1968] 1 W.L.R. 1221 (C.A.) Salmon L.J. (p. 1228) reserved "the question whether the doctrine of *res judicata* can apply in any circumstances in custody proceedings." See, too, *Rowe* v. *Rowe* [1980] Fam. 47 (C.A.).

Mills v. **Cooper** [1967] 2 Q.B. 459 (D.C.). An accused in a criminal case was not allowed to raise an issue estoppel because the issue in the earlier proceedings (in which he had been acquitted) was not the same as that in the instant case. Lord Parker C.J. doubted (p. 466) whether the doctrine of issue estoppel was ever applicable in criminal cases, but Diplock L.J. said (pp. 468–469): "The doctrine of issue estoppel in civil proceedings is of fairly recent and sporadic development though none the worse for that. Although *Hoystead* v. *Taxation Commissioner* ([1926] A.C. 155) did not purport to break new ground, it can be regarded as the starting point of the modern common law doctrine, the application of which to different kinds of civil actions is currently being worked out in the courts. That doctrine, so far as it affects civil proceedings, may be stated thus: a party to civil proceedings is not entitled to make, as against the other party, an assertion, whether of fact or of the legal consequences of facts, the correctness of which is an essential element in his cause of action or defence, if the same assertion was an essential element in his previous cause of action or defence in previous civil proceedings between the same parties or their predecessors in title and was found by a court of competent jurisdiction in such previous civil proceedings to be incorrect, unless further material which is relevant to the correctness or incorrectness of the assertion and could not by reasonable diligence have been adduced by that party in the previous proceedings has since become available to him."

Note.—Diplock L.J.'s proviso relating to the effects of the availability of new evidence marks a distinction between "cause of action" and "issue" estoppels.

In *Arnold* v. *National Westminster Bank* [1989] Ch. 63 (Ch.D.) Sir Nicholas Browne-Wilkinson V.-C. referred (p. 68) to Diplock L.J.'s formulation as the "classic modern statement of the law." In that case it was held that, where a tenancy agreement provided for regular rent reviews, and where a matter had been litigated as a result of one such review, a party to the agreement was entitled to start fresh proceedings on the same question arising out of a subsequent review if the law had been changed in the interim.

In *R.* v. *Secretary of State for the Environment, ex p. Hackney London Borough Council* [1984] 1 W.L.R. 592 (C.A.) doubts were expressed *per curiam* as to whether the doctrine of issue estoppel is applicable in proceedings, brought under R.S.C., Ord. 53, for judicial review. In *Re Norway's Application (No. 2)* [1988] 3 W.L.R. 603 (C.A.) it was doubted whether a determination as to whether a court has jurisdiction under a statute can be affected by the principle of issue estoppel.

Craddock's Transport Ltd. v. **Stuart** [1970] N.Z.L.R. 499 (New Zealand Court of Appeal). Mrs. S sued C in respect of injuries suffered in a collision between C's truck, which was being driven by K, and a car driven by S in which she was a passenger. C denied that K was negligent and issued a third-party notice to S claiming contribution. The jury found K negligent and acquitted S of any negligence. S then sued C for damages to his car, and sought by reason of the decision in the first trial to estop C from denying that K was negligent or alleging that S was guilty of contributory negligence. C claimed that issue estoppel could not arise because (1) the questions arising in the second proceedings were not necessarily identical with those arising in the first, and (2) the parties were not the same in so far as in the first trial C's defence was undertaken by an insurer, whereas C was not insured in respect of damage to S's car. It was held by a majority that at the first trial the issue was as to whether K or C was in breach of a duty owed to Mrs. S and not as to any duty owed by K to S. Accordingly C was not estopped from denying that K was in breach of any duty to S or alleging that S had not taken proper care for the safety of his own vehicle. For the majority it was thus unnecessary to answer the second question, but the view was expressed that a plea of estoppel, if otherwise well-founded, would be unlikely to fail because the first defence was conducted by an insurer.

R. v. HUMPHRYS

[1977] A.C. 1; [1976] 2 W.L.R. 857; [1976] 2 All E.R. 497; 63 Cr.App.R. 95 (H.L.: 1976)

Issue estoppel cannot be pleaded in criminal proceedings

Humphrys was charged with driving a motor vehicle on July 18, 1972, while disqualified. The only disputed issue was as to whether the police officer was correct in identifying him as the driver whom he had stopped on the day in question. Humphrys gave evidence and denied having driven any vehicle during 1972. He was acquitted. Later he was charged with perjury, the allegation being that at the earlier trial he had given evidence which he knew to be false, *viz.*, that he did not drive a vehicle in 1972. The same police officer was, along with others, a prosecution witness at the perjury trial. The judge rejected a plea of issue estoppel raised by the defence and allowed this police officer to give evidence again identifying Humphrys as the driver whom he had stopped on July 18, 1972. Humphrys was convicted of perjury. The House of Lords, reversing the Court of Appeal, restored this conviction. The House was unanimous in holding that issue estoppel had no applicability in criminal proceedings, but their Lordships expressed varying views as to whether a judge has, in certain circumstances, an inherent jurisdiction to stop proceedings for perjury if they involve essentially a retrial of another offence of which the accused has been acquitted.

LORD DILHORNE: . . . In my opinion issue estoppel has not and never has had a place in English criminal law and it is very undesirable that it should have. . . .

LORD HAILSHAM OF ST. MARYLEBONE: . . . (1) The doctrine of issue estoppel as it has been developed in civil proceedings is not applicable to criminal proceedings. . . . (2) Although the civil doctrine of issue estoppel as it has been developed in civil proceedings is not applicable to criminal proceedings, there is a doctrine applicable to criminal proceedings which is in some ways analogous to issue estoppel, and has sometimes been described by that name. However, (3) the civil doctrine is based on the necessity for finality between private litigants, whereas the doctrine in criminal proceedings is based on the prohibition of double jeopardy, that is, the *maxim nemo debet bis vexari pro una et eadem causa*. It follows (4) that whereas the civil doctrine is equally applicable to either of the two civil parties, the criminal doctrine is available to the accused but not to the Crown. (5) Whereas the civil doctrine applies to all cases where an individual issue can be isolated and identified as determined, the criminal doctrine is not so limited but is primarily concerned with verdicts, and applies to verdicts which are either in form or in substance inconsistent. (6) In general, the doctrine in criminal law precludes the Crown from adducing evidence or making suggestions which are inconsistent with a previous verdict of acquittal when its real effect is determinated. The doctrine is one of substance rather than form. The court will inquire into realities and not mere technicalities. (7) Where a second charge is brought which is different both in substance and in form from an earlier charge, the mere fact that some of the evidence adduced in support of the second charge is inconsistent with innocence on the earlier charge does not preclude the Crown from adducing that evidence in asserting its truth when considering a verdict on the second charge. (8) Where the second charge consists in an allegation that the accused in the first charge has committed perjury in his evidence given on his own behalf in his defence on the former charge, the mere fact that some of the evidence brought in support of the charge of perjury is identical with evidence given in the first charge and inconsistent with innocence on that charge does not preclude the Crown from adducing that evidence or asserting its truth where it is accompanied by other evidence in support of the charge of perjury but (9) where the evidence is substantially identical with the evidence given at the first trial without any addition and the Crown is in substance simply seeking to get behind a verdict of acquittal, the second charge is inadmissible both on the ground that it infringes the rule against double jeopardy and on the ground that it is an abuse of the process of the court whether or not the charge is in form a charge of perjury at the first trial. (10) Except where the formal pleas of *autrefois acquit* or *convict* are admissible, when it is the practice to empanel a jury, it is the duty of the court to examine the facts of the first trial in case of any dispute, and in any case it is the duty of the court to rule as a matter of law on the legal consequences deriving from such facts. In any case it is, therefore, for the court to determine whether on the facts found there is as a matter of law a double jeopardy involved in the later proceedings and to direct a jury accordingly.

LORD SALMON:... The doctrine of issue estoppel is complex and highly technical, even when applied to civil proceedings alone. In this field, however, it is firmly entrenched and performs a useful function. It brings finality to litigation. The whole procedure relating to pleadings in the civil courts is appropriate for defining with precision the issues between the parties. Once these issues have been ascertained and fought out and then finally adjudicated upon in the courts, it would be unjust and absurd if the disappointed party, save in certain exceptional cases which I need not recite, were allowed to reopen the issues and start litigating them all over again. It is in the public interest that litigation should have an end.

In the criminal field, however, besides being complex and technical, the doctrine of issue estoppel would, in my view, also be inappropriate, artificial, unnecessary and unfair. It would be inappropriate because there are no pleadings defining the issues and no judgments explaining how the issues (even if identifiable) were decided. Sometimes, as in the present case, it would be possible to identify the issues. But it would be rarely possible to do so. Since juries give general verdicts "guilty" or "not guilty" it would often be difficult, if not impossible, to do more than guess how they had decided any issue capable of identification.

Even in the rare cases in which the difficulty to which I have alluded could be overcome, issue estoppel would often be artificial and unfair. Take the not infrequent case in which the jury decides an issue in the defendant's favour not because they are satisfied that their solution is correct but because they are left in doubt as to whether the contrary had been proved. In such a case, surely it would be artificial and unjust if the defendant who, quite rightly in my view, enjoys many advantages, should be given the added bonus that the issue should thereafter be presumed for ever to have been irrevocably decided in his favour as between himself and the Crown. This might mean that upon a totally different charge against the same defendant, supported by overwhelming evidence against him, he might quite unjustly escape conviction because of the issue estoppel. Moreover, I think that it is wholly unnecessary to introduce issue estoppel into the criminal field. The doctrine of *autrefois acquit* and *convict* amply protects the accused from being brought into double jeopardy. . . .

It is almost unheard of for those who have been convicted in spite of their lies to be prosecuted for perjury save in the most exceptional circumstances—and rightly so. A charge or perjury after a full trial in respect of another offence, in which the prosecution has failed to persuade a jury that the accused was lying and that he was guilty, could in some circumstances smack of an attempt by a disappointed prosecution to find what it considered to be a more perspicacious jury or tougher judge. This would in reality be putting the accused in double jeopardy. Although the form of charge would be different from that of the charge upon which he had already been tried and acquitted, the true substance of the charge would be the same. It is of great importance that in such a case, if it arose, the courts should not hesitate to exercise their inherent powers in relation to prosecutions which are oppressive and an abuse of the process of the court. There are, however, exceptional cases in which prosecutions for perjury are fully justified after an acquittal, for example, cases in which a man acquitted of a crime subsequently earns substantial sums of money by writing articles for the Press explaining how in fact he committed the crime and deceived the jury by the ingenious lies he had told in the witness box: see *H.M. Advocate* v. *Cairns*, 1967 J.C. 37.

LORD EDMUND-DAVIES: . . . My Lords, I would be for holding that issue estoppel has no place in our criminal law. . . .

. . . I am now satisfied that, in the words of Lord Parker C.J. in *Mills* v. *Cooper* [1967] 2 Q.B. 459, 467: ". . . every court has undoubtedly a right in proceedings its discretion to decline to hear proceedings on the ground that they are oppressive and an abuse of the process of the court." . . .

LORD FRASER OF TULLYBELTON: My Lords, I agree with my noble and learned friends that, for reasons given by them, issue estoppel has no place in the criminal law of England. . . .

The question of whether a court in England can decline to allow a prosecution to proceed, on the ground that it is oppressive, was not argued in this case and I reserve my opinion on it.

Note.—One way in which the flank of the generality of the decision to reject issue estoppel in criminal cases may be partially turned is by an extension of the scope of the plea of *autrefois acquit*. In this connection it is to be noted that the Privy Council case of *Sambasivam* v. *Malaya Federation Public Prosecutor* [1950] A.C. 458, although referred to, was not doubted by their Lordships. See, too, *G. (An infant)* v. *Coltart* [1967] 1 Q.B. 432 (D.C.). The principle embodied in this line of authority is that the prosecution may not in a second trial adduce evidence which is relevant only on the assumption that the accused was guilty of another offence of which he has been acquitted in an earlier trial.

Several of their Lordships referred to decisions of the High Court of Australia, *e.g. R.* v. *Wilkes* (1948) 77 C.L.R. 511, and *Mraz* v. *R.* (1956) 96 C.L.R. 62, indicating the availability of issue estoppel in criminal cases. In the former case Dixon C.J. said *obiter* (p. 518): "Whilst there is not a great deal of authority upon the subject, it appears to me there is nothing wrong in the view that there is an issue estoppel, if it appears by record of itself or as explained by proper evidence, that the same point was determined in favour of a prisoner in a previous criminal trial which is brought in issue on a second criminal trial of the same prisoner.... Such a question must rarely arise because the conditions can seldom be fulfilled which are necessary before an issue estoppel in favour of a prisoner and against the Crown can occur. There must be a prior proceeding determined against the Crown necessarily involving an issue which again arises in a subsequent proceeding by the Crown against the same prisoner. The allegation of the Crown in the subsequent proceeding must itself be inconsistent with the acquittal of the prisoner in the previous proceeding. But if such a condition of affairs arises I see no reason why the ordinary rules of estoppel should not apply. Such rules are not to be confused with those of *res judicata*, which in criminal proceedings are expressed in the pleas of *autrefois acquit* and *autrefois convict*. They are pleas which are concerned with the judicial determination of an alleged criminal liability and in the case of conviction with the substitution of a new liability. Issue estoppel is concerned with the judicial establishment of a proposition of law or fact between parties." However, the position relating to the applicability of the doctrine of issue estoppel in criminal cases in Australia has now been rendered uncertain by the judgments in the more recent High Court case of *R.* v. *Storey* (1978) 140 C.L.R. 364; but it seems clear that the Crown cannot rely on issue estoppel.

Hunter v. **Chief Constable of the West Midlands Police** [1982] A.C. 529 (H.L.). The plaintiffs had been convicted of the murder of 21 people and of injuring 161 others in an I.R.A. bombing incident. At their trial the judge had rejected allegations, made on a *voir dire* (or "trial within a trial") held to determine the voluntariness of their confessions, that these had been induced by violence on the part of the police. When the trial resumed before the jury the plaintiffs had repeated their allegations. The judge in his summing-up had warned the jury that, if the allegations might reasonably be true, their confessions should be regarded as worthless. The jury convicted all six plaintiffs. It was accepted that the plaintiffs had been subjected to considerable physical violence either by the police or by prison officers, but not until after the police had completed their interrogations. Following a subsequent trial of a number of prison officers for assault of which all were acquitted, the plaintiffs instituted civil proceedings against two Chief Constables and also against the Home Office, claiming damages against the police for injuries caused by alleged assaults, which involved the same allegations as had been made on the *voir dire* and at their trial, and also against the Home Office in respect of assaults by prison officers and by other prisoners. The plaintiffs relied on new medico-forensic evidence, which had been given by the defence in the trial of the prison officers, concerning photographs which were said to show that some of the injuries were sustained prior to interrogation, and also on statements from three prison officers to the effect that the plaintiffs were bruised and injured on arrival in prison. The defendant Chief Constables applied for the statements of claim against them to be struck out on the ground *inter alia* that the decision on the *voir dire* gave rise to an issue estoppel. Cantley J. dismissed the application, but the Court of Appeal (Goff L.J. dissenting) allowed the Chief Constables' appeal ([1980] Q.B. 283 *sub nom. McIlkenny* v. *Chief Constable*). A majority (Lord Denning M.R. and Sir George Baker) held that the decision on the *voir dire*, supported as it was by the jury's verdict, did give rise to an issue estoppel, and that the fresh evidence, upon which the plaintiffs relied, could have been available at their trial and that it did not throw any reasonable doubt on the correctness of the *voir dire* holding. Accordingly the claims against the police should be struck out on the basis of issue estoppel. Goff L.J. dissented from this on the ground that, although the *voir dire* and the jury's verdict taken together did constitute a final verdict on the same issues, it was not a finding between the same parties (or their privies), as in the present actions. His Lordship agreed, however, that the statements of claim against the police might in the circumstances be struck out under R.S.C. Ord. 18, r. 19, as an abuse of the process of the court. The plaintiffs' appeal to the House of Lords was dismissed on grounds substantially similar to the approach taken by Goff L.J., Lord Diplock, with whose judgment Lords Russell of Killowen, Keith of Kinkel, Roskill and Brandon of Oakbrook agreed, eschewed reliance upon the doctrine of estoppel but held that where a final decision has been made by a criminal court of competent jurisdiction it is a general rule of public policy that the use of a civil action to initiate a collateral attack on that decision is an abuse of the process of the court. Lord Diplock said (p. 541): "The abuse of process which the instant case exemplifies is the initiation of proceedings in a court of justice for the purpose of mounting a collateral attack upon a final decision against the intending plaintiff which has been made by another court of competent jurisdiction in previous proceedings in which the intending plaintiff had a full opportunity of contesting the decision in the court by which it was made." The House further held that such fresh evidence as the present plaintiffs had sought to adduce fell far short of satisfying the test to be applied in considering whether an exception to this general rule of public policy should be made, which, in the case of a collateral attack in a court of co-ordinate jurisdiction, was whether the fresh evidence entirely changed the aspect of the case.

Note.—The dismissal of the appeal on this general ground rendered consideration of the limits of the doctrine of issue estoppel unnecessary. However, it would seem clear that the loose approach to the requirement of identity of parties accepted by the majority of the Court of Appeal (Lord Denning M.R. and Sir George Baker) is to be rejected. The view of Goff L.J. is preferred: a party to proceedings ought not be estopped from raising an issue by virtue of a decision which was taken in earlier proceedings to which either he or his opponent was not a party. It is to be noted, too, that, whereas in the Court of Appeal Sir George Baker had taken the view ([1980] Q.B. 283, 342) that *R.* v. *Humphrys* (*supra*) was not authority for the proposition that an issue of fact which had been determined in a criminal case cannot give rise to an issue estoppel in later civil proceedings, Lord Diplock, expressing the view of all their Lordships, said (pp. 540–541): "...it would be best, in order to avoid confusion, if the use of the description 'issue estoppel'...were restricted to that species of estoppel *per rem judicatam* which may arise in civil actions between the same parties or their privies, of which the characteristics are stated in a judgment of my own in *Mills* v. *Cooper* [*supra*] and approved by this House in *Reg.* v. *Humphrys* [*supra*], the case in which it was also held that 'issue estoppel' had no place in English criminal law."

Hunter v. *Chief Constable of the West Midlands Police* has been followed in *Somasundaram* v. *M. Julius Melchior and Co. (A Firm)* [1988] 1 W.L.R. 1394 (C.A.).

B. ESTOPPEL BY DEED

Bowman v. **Taylor** (1834) 4 L.J.K.B. 58. A deed, by which the plaintiff granted to the defendant a licence to use looms, recited (*inter alia*) that the plaintiff had invented certain improvements in power looms, and had obtained letters patent and had caused a specification to be enrolled. It was held that the defendant was estopped from pleading that the plaintiff was not the inventor, that it was not a new invention, and that no specification had been enrolled. Lord Denman C.J. said (p. 61): "An estoppel operates because it concludeth a man to allege the truth by reason of the assertion of the party that that fact is true.... If a party has by his deed directly asserted a specific fact, it is impossible to say that he shall not be precluded from disputing that fact, thus solemnly admitted by him on the face of his deed...."

Note.—This states classic common law doctrine. A party to a deed (or instrument under seal) and those in privity with him may be estopped from denying its contents. The estoppel may extend to statements made in the recitals. For the scope of estoppel by deed at the present day see the next case.

GREER v. KETTLE

[1938] A.C. 156; 107 L.J.Ch. 56; 158 L.T. 433; 54 T.L.R. 143; [1937] 4 All E.R. 396 (H.L.: 1937)

A recital in a deed may operate as an estoppel of one party only. The intention of the parties depends on the construction of the document. A recital introduced by mistake does not operate as an estoppel.

The liquidator of the M company claimed the unpaid balance of a loan from the P company, as guarantor of a loan from the M company to the A company. The P company resisted liability on the ground that the guarantee related to a loan secured upon fully paid shares in the I company, whereas the loan was not so secured. The relevant agreement under seal between M and P companies contained a recital that the loan had been advanced on the security of these shares, but in fact the shares had not been validly issued. It was held that the recital was intended as a statement by the M company and not by the P company; that the P company was not estopped by the recital; and that the P company was not liable.

LORD ATKIN agreed with the opinion of LORD RUSSELL OF KILLOWEN and with the following opinion; he stated that LORD MACMILLAN also concurred.

LORD MAUGHAM: ... The case of *Bowman* v. *Taylor* [*supra*] calls for a little examination. The estoppel was founded on a recital in an indenture of May 10, 1824, containing a grant by the plaintiff of a licence to the defendants to use an invention for which the plaintiff had obtained letters patent in the form in use in 1824. The action was for breach of a covenant by the defendant to pay certain royalties. The defendant pleaded (amongst other things) that the plaintiff was not the true and first inventor and that the supposed invention was not a new invention. The deed, however, recited that the plaintiff had invented improvements and obtained letters patent for them, and the defendants were held estopped from denying that the plaintiff was the true and first inventor. There was accordingly judgment for the plaintiff. My Lords, I do not doubt the correctness of the result; but I do doubt whether the recital could properly be taken to be a statement on behalf of the licensee who could have had little knowledge as to possible anticipations of the invention. The decision may be explained on the ground that the deed was entered into on the footing that the recital, whether true or not, must be taken during the continuance of the licence as true. The question of estoppel in relation to licences to use a patent has been the subject since 1834 of nearly a score of decisions in varying circumstances, of which *Clark* v. *Adie* (1877) 2 App.Cas. 423 (H.L.) is perhaps the most authoritative. The decision of the House of Lords in that case was not based on the narrow ground adopted in *Bowman* v. *Taylor*, but on the much wider ground that the licensee of a patent right is bound on the same principle and in the same way as a tenant who has taken a lease of lands from another and who is estopped during the lease from denying his landlord's title. . . .

Patteson J., in his judgment in *Stroughill* v. *Buck* (1850) 14 Q.B. 781 at 787, stated: . . . "When a recital is intended to be a statement which all the parties to the deed have mutually agreed to admit as true, it is an estoppel upon all. But, when it is intended to be the statement of one party only, the estoppel is confined to that party, and the intention is to be gathered from construing the instrument." My Lords, in agreement with the Court of Appeal and with the opinion of my noble and learned friend Lord Russell of Killowen I think that this statement of the law is correct; and I also agree with them in coming to the conclusion that upon the true construction of the recital contained in the guarantee of March 20, 1929, read in conjunction with the charge of even date mentioned in the recital, the fair inference is that the recital is intended to be the statement of the Mercantile Marine and not to be that of the Parent Trust and Finance Co. The latter accordingly are not estopped from relying on the admitted fact that the charge was not secured on the 275,000 fully paid shares of the Iron Industries Ltd., for the simple reason that these shares had never been issued.

My Lords, this conclusion is sufficient for the determination of the present appeal; but it is easy to imagine a deed so framed, perhaps by inadvertence, that such a conclusion, as a mere matter of construction, might be impossible even in a case of a common mistake; and it seems to me to be desirable to point out that there was another road, not depending on a perhaps ill-framed recital, leading more certainly in such a case to the same result.

Estoppel by deed is a rule of evidence founded on the principle that a solemn and unambiguous statement or engagement in a deed must be taken as binding between parties and privies and therefore as not admitting any contradictory proof. It is important to observe that this is a rule of common law, though it may be noted that an exception arises when the deed is fraudulent or illegal. The position in equity is and was always different in this respect, that where there are proper grounds for rectifying a deed, *e.g.* because it is based upon a common mistake of fact, then to the extent of the rectification there can plainly be no estoppel based on the original form of the instrument. It is at least equally clear that in equity a party to a deed could not set up an estoppel in reliance on a deed in relation to which there is an equitable right to rescission or in reliance on an untrue statement or an untrue recital induced by his own representation, whether innocent or otherwise, to the other party. Authority is scarcely needed for so clear a consequence of a rectification order or an admitted or proved right to such an order. The well-known rule of the Chancery courts in regard to a receipt clause in a deed not effecting an estoppel if the money has not in fact been paid is a good illustration of the equity view.... The decision of Lord Romilly in *Brooke* v. *Haymes* (1868) L.R. 6 Eq. 25 is even more closely in point, and it may be added that the statement of the law in that case appears never to have been doubted. The headnote beings as follows: "A party to a deed is not estopped in equity from averring against or offering evidence to controvert a recital therein contrary to the fact, which has been introduced into the deed by mistake of fact, and not through fraud or deception on his part." In a simple case of this kind it would be unnecessary, as that case shows, to counterclaim for rectification, though in a case of any complexity it would certainly be desirable to do so.

Since the Judicature Act 1873, the rule in equity must prevail....

LORD ROCHE concurred.

Note.—A receipt for money or goods does not amount to an estoppel. It is only prima facie evidence and is open to explanation. Even a receipt in a deed appears not to amount to an estoppel generally, either at law or in equity, since the Judicature Act 1873.

For an illustration of the rule that, where a deed is rectifiable, the doctrine of estoppel by deed will not bind the parties to it, see *Wilson* v. *Wilson* [1969] 1 W.L.R. 1470 (Ch.D.).

C. ESTOPPEL BY CONDUCT

Cooke v. **Loxley** (1792) 5 T.R. 4 (K.B.). In an action for use and occupation of land let to the defendant by the predecessor in title of the present plaintiff, to whom the defendant had also paid rent, the defendant offered evidence to the effect that the plaintiff had no title to the land. The evidence was rejected, and on an application for a new trial the judge's decision was upheld. Lord Kenyon C.J. said (p. 5): "... in an action for use and occupation it ought not to be permitted to a tenant, who occupies land by the licence of another, to call upon that other to show the title under which he let the land. This is not a mere technical rule, but is founded in public convenience and policy.... Here the defendant, who occupied the land, did so by the permission of the plaintiff, and then refused to pay his rent under an idea that he might contest the plaintiff's right; but the plaintiff could not be supposed to come to trial prepared to meet such a defence and to make out his title; such an action as the present does not involve the question of title...."

Note.—When the tenancy is created by deed, there may also be an estoppel upon that ground. However, the rule applies equally to tenancies which are not created under seal (see also *Mackley* v. *Nutting* [1949] 2 K.B. 55 (C.A.)). Yet the tenant is not estopped from showing that the title of his landlord has expired since the tenancy commenced, or that the land in question is not comprised in the lease. There is no inconsistency in holding the land and at the same time proving such matters.

Similar cases of estoppel are those bailees, licensees and agents, who cannot deny the title of the bailors, licensors or principals, after having acknowledged them by their dealings.

FREEMAN v. COOKE

18 L.J.Ex. 114; 12 Jur. 777; 2 Exch. 654; 6 D. & L. 187; 154 E.R. 652
(Exchequer: 1848)

*A person who, by his words or conduct, wilfully causes another person to
believe in the existence of a state of things, and induces him to act on
that belief, so as to alter his position for the worse, is estopped from
setting up against the latter person a different state of things as existing
at the time in question.*

*But there is no estoppel unless the words or conduct were intended to
induce the other person so to act, or they were such that a reasonable
man would act upon them, even though he did in fact act upon them
to his prejudice.*

The defendant was sheriff of Yorkshire, and his officer had seized
certain goods under a writ of execution against Joseph and Benjamin
Broadbent. Evidence was given that the goods belonged to William
Broadbent, but that he, expecting an execution against himself, removed
them to the house of his father, Joseph Broadbent; then again,
anticipating a distress for rent on his father (Joseph) he removed them
to the house of his brother, Benjamin Broadbent. When the sheriff's
officer entered the house of Benjamin, William, supposing the writ to be
against himself, gave him notice not to seize the goods as they were the
property of Benjamin. The officer then produced his writ, which was
against Benjamin. Then William said the goods belonged to another
brother, and finally that they belonged to himself. The officer seized and
sold the goods as the goods of Benjamin. William having become
bankrupt, an action was brought by his assignees to recover the goods in
question, and it was contended by the defendant that the statements of
William operated as conclusive evidence, or an estoppel, that the
property was not his. It was held that it was not so.

PARKE B. (delivering the judgment of the court, which included
ALDERSON, ROLFE and PLATT B.B.): ... The only question is whether it
be an estoppel. It is contended that it was, upon the authority of the
rule laid down in *Pickard* v. *Sears* (1837) 6 A. & E. 469. That rule is,
that "where one by his words or conduct *wilfully* causes another to
believe in the existence of a certain state of things, and induces him to
act on that behalf, or to alter his own previous position, the former is
concluded from averring against the latter a different state of things as
existing at the time." ... By the term "wilfully," however, in that rule,
we must understand, if not that the party represents that to be true
which he knows to be untrue, at least that he means his representation
to be acted upon, and that it is acted upon accordingly; and if, whatever
a man's meaning may be, he so conducts himself that a reasonable man
would take the representation to be true, and believe that it was meant
he should act upon it, and did act upon it as true, the party making the
representation would be equally precluded from contesting its truth; and
conduct by negligence or omission, when there is a duty cast upon a
person by usage of trade or otherwise to disclose the truth, may often
have the same effect—as, for instance, a retiring partner omitting to
inform the customers of the firm, in the usual mode, that the continuing
partners were no longer authorised to act as his agents, is bound by all

contracts made by them with third persons on the faith of their being authorised. . . .

It is not found that the bankrupt intended to induce the officers to seize the goods as those of Benjamin, and whatever intention he had on his first statement was done away with by an opposite statement before the seizure took place; nor can it be said that any reasonable man would have seized the goods on the faith of the bankrupt's representations taken all together. In truth, in most cases to which the doctrine in *Pickard* v. *Sears* is to be applied, the representation is such as to amount to the contract or licence of the party making it. Here there is no pretence for saying it amounted to a licence, and a contract is out of the question.

Note.—The representation, either express or by conduct, upon which it is sought to found an estoppel must not relate to intention in the future (*Jorden* v. *Money* (1854) 5 H.L.Cas. 185), and must normally be one of fact not of law (*Territorial and Auxiliary Forces Association of the County of London* v. *Nichols* [1949] 1 K.B. 35 (C.A.); *Kai Nam* v. *Ma Kam Chan* [1956] A.C. 358 (P.C.)). But a statement of the legal effect of a document may found an estoppel (see *Sidney Bolsom Investment Trust Ltd.* v. *E. Karmios & Co. (London) Ltd.* [1956] 1 Q.B. 529 (C.A.)).

An arrangement made without consideration, by which one party promises to forbear from exercising a legal right, and under which the other party acts, may serve as a defence to an action by the promisor, by way of analogy to a legal estoppel (*Central London Property Trusts Ltd.* v. *High Trees House Ltd.* [1947] K.B. 130; compare *Combe* v. *Combe* [1951] 2 K.B. 215 (C.A.)).

Amalgamated Property Co. v. **Texas Bank** [1982] Q.B. 84 (C.A.). The plaintiff company owned a subsidiary company which borrowed money from the defendant bank through a subsidiary owned by the bank. The plaintiff executed a guarantee to secure all money owed by the plaintiff's subsidiary to the defendants. The plaintiff's subsidiary defaulted. The plaintiffs ran into severe financial difficulty and were ordered to be compulsorily wound up. Acting through their liquidator, they claimed a declaration that they were under no liability to the defendant bank in respect of the loan. The trial judge, dismissing this claim, held that, although the bank could not rely directly on the terms of the guarantee, the plaintiffs were estopped from contending that it did not cover the loan. The Court of Appeal dismissed the appeal. Lord Denning M.R. said (p. 122): "When the parties to a transaction proceed on the basis of an underlying assumption—either of fact or of law—whether due to misrepresentation or mistake makes no difference—on which they have conducted the dealings between them—neither of them will be allowed to go back on that assumption when it would be unfair or unjust to allow him to do so." Here the parties had acted upon the agreed assumption that the plaintiffs were liable for the loan. They were, therefore, estopped from denying that they were bound to discharge the debt. It was a case of "estoppel by convention."

Note.—Brandon L.J., dealing with an argument advanced by the plaintiffs that the bank was seeking to use the estoppel "as a sword rather than a shield," considered the position if the bank had brought an action against the plaintiffs before they went into liquidation. The bank could then have pleaded an estoppel precluding the plaintiffs from questioning the interpretation of the guarantee which both parties had assumed (rightly or wrongly) to be correct for the purpose of their transactions. His Lordship said (pp. 131–132): "In this way the bank, while still in form using the estoppel as a shield, would in substance be founding a cause of action on it. This illustrates what I would regard as the true proposition of law, that, while a party cannot in terms found a cause of action on an estoppel, he may, as a result of being able to rely on an estoppel, succeed on a cause of action on which, without being able to rely on that estoppel, he would necessarily have failed."

Greenwood v. **Martins Bank Ltd.** [1933] A.C. 51 (H.L.). The plaintiff's wife had forged her husband's signature to cheques drawn on the defendant bank, and had used the proceeds for her own purposes. The husband discovered the forgeries but did not disclose them to the bank for some months. Eventually he threatened to do so, and the wife committed suicide. In an action by the husband against the bank for the amounts paid out of his account on the forged cheques, it was held by the Court of Appeal and the House of Lords that the husband was estopped from relying on the forgeries. Lord Tomlin said (pp. 57–58): "Mere silence cannot amount to a representation, but, when there is a duty to disclose, deliberate silence may become significant and amount to a representation. The existence of a duty on the part of the customer of a bank to disclose his knowledge of such a forgery as the one in question in this case as rightly admitted.... The appellant's silence, therefore, was deliberate and intended to produce the effect which it in fact produced—namely, the leaving of the respondents in ignorance of the true facts so that no action might be taken by them against the appellant's wife. The deliberate abstention from speaking in those circumstances seems to me to amount to a representation to the respondents that the forged cheques were in fact in order, and assuming that detriment to the respondents followed there were, it seems to me, present all the elements essential to estoppel...."

Note.—A more recent and more rational tendency in cases of estoppel by representation (as distinct from estoppel by negligence) is to focus not so much upon the existence of an identifiable duty as upon general notions of unconscionability. This is reflected in the words of Oliver J. in *Taylors Fashions Ltd.* v. *Liverpool Trustees Co.* [1982] Q.B. 133, 151–152 (Ch.D.): "...principle...requires a very much broader approach which is directed rather at ascertaining whether, in particular individual circumstances, it would be unconscionable for a party to be permitted to deny that which, knowingly, or unknowingly, he has allowed another to encourage or assume to his detriment, than to inquiring whether the circumstances can be fitted within the confines of some preconceived formula serving as a universal yardstick for every form of unconscionable behaviour."

In *Pacol* v. *Trade Lines* [1982] Com.L.R. 92 Webster J. indicated that silence or acquiescence can found an estoppel by agreement or representation where a reasonable man would expect the person against whom the estoppel is raised, acting honestly and reasonably, to bring the true facts to the attention of the other party known by him to be under a mistake as to their respective rights and obligations.

COVENTRY, SHEPPARD & CO. v. GREAT EASTERN RY.

(1883) 11 Q.B.D. 776; 52 L.J.Q.B. 694; 49 L.T. 641 (C.A.: 1883)

When the negligence of the defendant causes a person to believe in the existence of a supposed fact, and that person acts on the belief with resulting damage, the defendant may be estopped from denying the existence of the supposed fact.

A railway company negligently issued two delivery orders, not purporting to be duplicates, in respect of one consignment of wheat, whereby a fraudulent person was enabled to obtain two advances of money as on two separate consignments. The company was held to be estopped by negligence from disputing that there were two consignments.

BRETT M.R.: This judgment must be affirmed. It can be upheld only on the ground of estoppel, that is, that the defendants were prevented by their own conduct from relying upon the facts that there were not two parcels of goods. . . .

The negligence of the defendants was to the prejudice of the plaintiffs and allowed the fraud to be perpetrated upon them. It seems to me, therefore, that the defendants are estopped as against the plaintiffs, their negligence having been the immediate cause of the advance. . . .

LINDLEY and FRY L.JJ. agreed.

Note.—Estoppel by negligence differs from other forms of estoppel by conduct in that it derives from a duty owed generally: the estoppel asserter is thus often a third party. Indeed, this type of estoppel could be more appropriately seen as simply part of the substantive law of negligence. A person who puts certain types of document into circulation owes a duty of care to anyone whom he ought reasonably to foresee may be a victim of their misuse. Doubts exist as to the extent of this duty. Moreover, as in any negligence case, there may also be doubts as to whether there has been an actual breach of the duty in particular circumstances. Contrast the above case with the two cases immediately following.

Mercantile Bank of India Ltd. v. Central Bank of India Ltd. [1938] A.C. 287 (P.C.). A firm of merchants pledged railway receipts entitling them to certain goods with the Central Bank as security for a loan. The Central Bank later returned the receipts to the merchants to enable them to claim possession of the goods. The receipts were then delivered to the Mercantile Bank in order to obtain another loan. It was held that the Central Bank was not estopped from asserting its prior claim to the goods. There was no relationship of contract or agency between the banks, and the Central Bank had no reason to suppose that the receipts would be handed to the Mercantile Bank. The Central Bank had committed no breach of duty owed to the Mercantile Bank or to anyone else. There was a local practice well known to both banks under which receipts were returned by pledgees to their owners to enable them to get possession of goods.

Moorgate Mercantile Co. Ltd. v. Twitchings [1977] A.C. 890 (H.L.). The plaintiffs, a finance company, were members of an organisation (H.P.I.) set up to prevent fraud arising out of hire-purchase agreements. A finance company would inform H.P.I. of any hire-purchase agreement that they had entered into in respect of a motor vehicle, so that, in the event of it being improperly offered for sale, the offeree could by contacting H.P.I. ascertain whether the vehicle was subject to a subsisting hire-purchase agreement. The plaintiffs had let a car on hire-purchase to one McLorg; but, owing to a mistake or oversight on their part, H.P.I. had not been informed. McLorg, falsely asserting that he was the owner of the car, offered it for sale to the defendant, a dealer. The defendant contacted H.P.I. who told him that the car was not registered with their organisation. The defendant thereupon bought the car and later re-sold it. The plaintiffs sued the defendant for its conversion. A bare majority of the House of Lords (reversing a majority judgment of the Court of Appeal, and restoring the trial judge) held that the plaintiffs were under no legal duty to the defendant to register (or to take reasonable care in regard to registering) with H.P.I. the hire-purchase agreement in question, and that therefore an estoppel by negligence could not arise so as to bar their claim against the defendant. Lord Edmund-Davies, a member of the majority, said (p. 919): "It is, of course, *desirable* that finance companies who are members of H.P.I. should promptly and accurately notify H.P.I. of any new agreement entered into, and this both in their own interests and in that of dealer-members of that organisation. But they are, as I think, under no sort of obligation to join it at all.... In most situations it is better to be careful than careless, but it is quite another thing to elevate all carelessness into a tort. Liability has to be based on a legal duty not to be careless, and I can find none in this case." Lord Wilberforce in his dissenting judgment rejected (p. 902) the argument that there was an estoppel by representation: "To constitute an estoppel a representation must be clear and must unequivocally state the fact which, ultimately, the maker is to be prevented from denying. The answer given by H.P.I. to the respondent's inquiry cannot in my opinion bear the meaning for which the respondent must contend.... It is quite clear that the answer given by H.P.I., both intrinsically and as it was understood by this particular motor dealer, conveyed nothing more than information as to the state of the records of H.P.I.; it did not profess to and did not say anything as to the ownership or lack of ownership of any finance house member of H.P.I." His Lordship would, however, hold (p. 906) "that a finance company belonging to the H.P.I. scheme is under a duty towards dealers, members of H.P.I., to take reasonable care to register any hire purchase agreement to which it is a party so that if in reliance on the absence of any such registration a dealer acts to his prejudice the finance company is estopped from asserting his title against that dealer." Lord Salmon, the other dissentient, would have dismissed the appeal, but on the basis of estoppel by representation as well as estoppel by negligence.

MARITIME ELECTRIC CO. v. GENERAL DAIRIES LTD.

[1937] A.C. **610**; 106 L.J.P.C. 81; 156 L.T. 444; 53 T.L.R. 391; [1937] 1 All E.R. 748 (P.C.: 1937)

An estoppel is only a rule of evidence and cannot avail to release a person from an obligation to obey the mandatory terms of a statute.

The appellants, a statutory undertaking, had over a period of time mistakenly charged the respondents less for the supply of electricity than they were statutorily obliged to do. The respondents, believing the accounts rendered by the appellants to be accurate, had acted upon them to their prejudice. The appellants, after discovering their mistake, sought to recover the unpaid balances of the amounts that ought to have been charged. To the respondents plea of estoppel, one objection raised by the appellants was that the statutory obligation imposed upon them to charge, and upon the respondents to pay, the correct amounts precluded estoppel. This objection was rejected by the Supreme Court of Canada (reversing the judgment of the Supreme Court of New Brunswick). The appellants appealed to the Privy Council.

LORD MAUGHAM (delivering the judgment of the Board, which included LORDS ATKIN, THANKERTON, RUSSELL OF KILLOWEN and ALNESS): ... The specific question for determination here is can the duty so cast by statute upon both parties to this action, be defeated or avoided by a mere mistake in the computation of accounts?

In the view of their Lordships the answer to this question in the case of such a statute as is now under consideration must be in the negative. The sections of the Public Utilities Act which are here in question are sections enacted for the benefit of a section of the public, that is, on grounds of public policy in a general sense. In such a case—and their Lordships do not propose to express any opinion as to statutes which are not within this category—where, as here, the statute imposes a duty of a positive kind, not avoidable by the performance of any formality, for the doing of the very act which the plaintiff seeks to do, it is not open to the defendant to set up an estoppel to prevent it. This conclusion must follow from the circumstances that an estoppel is only a rule of evidence which under certain special circumstances can be invoked by a party to an action; it cannot therefore avail in such a case to release the plaintiff from an obligation to obey such a statute, nor can it enable the defendant to escape from a statutory obligation of such a kind on his part. It is immaterial whether the obligation is onerous or otherwise to the party suing. The duty of each party is to obey the law.... the Court should first of all determine the nature of the obligation imposed by the statute, and then consider whether the admission of an estoppel would nullify the statutory provision.... If we now turn to the authorities it must be admitted that reported cases in which the precise point now under consideration has been raised are rare. It is, however, to be observed that there is not a single case in which an estoppel has been allowed in such a case to defeat a statutory obligation of an unconditional character....

....

Their Lordships having thus arrived at the conclusion that estoppel is not open to the respondents....

Chapter 7

JUDICIAL NOTICE

Two fundamental dogmas of the law of evidence are that issues of fact (as distinct from those of law) are to be determined by the jury or "trier of fact," and that they are to be determined according to the evidence, that is to say, on the basis of the evidence presented in court. The doctrine of judicial notice and related doctrines and practices mark, in various ways and in varying degrees, rejection of those dogmas.

There are certain matters of fact which are considered too notorious to require proof or to be susceptible to disproof. Such matters are the subject of judicial notice in its simplest form. The judge will take notice of their existence and of their nature without requiring evidence in proof or allowing it in attempted disproof. Any matter of such common knowledge that it would be an insult to the intelligence to require its demonstration is dealt with in this way: for example, the fact that Christmas Day falls on December 25, that the sun rises in the east, that Peking is in China or that Queen Victoria is dead. Facts which, although notorious, are only locally so are also covered by the doctrine, a typical example of this being a fact of local geography. Moreover, the doctrine of judicial notice has been extended so as to apply to facts which, although not notorious, are capable of demonstration by resort to sources of virtually indisputable accuracy readily accessible to persons in the situation of members of the court. Facts of this latter type include, *e.g.* the fact that November 1, 1944 was a Wednesday, the time of sunset in a particular place on a particular day, the longitude and latitude of Peking and the day and place of Queen Victoria's death. Judicial notice of such facts is sometimes said to be taken only "after enquiry."

When a fact is judicially noticed proof of it is not only unnecessary, it is also excluded. The doctrine is thus not a mode of proof: it narrows the scope of proof. When a judge takes judicial notice of a fact he in effect declares that he will find that fact to exist (or will direct the jury to do so) without it being established by evidence. The taking of judicial notice involves a conclusive determination by the judge of a question of fact, and therefore constitutes *pro tanto* a usurpation of the function of the jury or trier of fact. The judge does not have to make his determination "according to the evidence," but if the fact noticed, although capable of ascertainment, is not notorious, the judge has to acquaint himself with it. He may achieve this in any way he thinks appropriate and he may, if he wishes, inform himself in open court by a procedure which superficially resembles that of proof. For example experts may appear and be questioned by him and by the parties. But the process is essentially different from proof in that resort to it is not necessary, it is not governed by the rules of evidence and there is no right to rebut the "evidence" tendered.

Justification for the practice of taking judicial notice is to be found in several different considerations. Most obviously it leads to the saving of time and expense. Moreover, it reduces the risk of diversion and confusion which would result from disputation concerning what is really indisputable. In addition it can make for consistency between cases. Finally it is a form of judicial control over the jury: resort to it precludes the possibility of a jury finding the non-existence of the obvious.

The use of the terminology of judicial notice is more widespread than has been so far indicated. Certain other propositions which are really distinct are nevertheless commonly couched in terms of the taking of judicial notice. These include the propositions that a judge is irrebuttably presumed to know the law; that the authenticity of certain sources of law cannot be questioned; and that the courts are obliged to accept a ruling of the executive arm of government on certain public, constitutional or international matters affecting the government of the United Kingdom and sometimes its relations with other States. The first of these propositions means that the judge is deemed omniscient regarding the state of the law of the *forum*. It is not susceptible to proof. He is in this regard unrestricted in his investigation and his conclusions. In contrast with this, if a point of foreign law arises, it is treated as one of fact, and, although nonetheless determined by the judge, it must be proved—usually by expert testimony. By virtue of the second above-mentioned proposition it is not necessary to prove that, for example, an authorised copy of a statute before the court actually corresponds with the Act duly passed by Parliament. The third proposition concerns the relative roles, not of judge and jury, but of the Courts and the Executive.

The notion of judicial notice also manifests itself in another context. Facts have often to be determined for the purpose of intelligent judicial law-making. For example, in *McQuaker* v. *Goddard*[1] it was necessary to decide whether a camel fell for the purposes of tort liability into the legal category of an animal *ferae naturae* or that of an animal *mansuetae naturae*. Rational determination of this point of law involved factual investigation of the habits of camels. One member of the Court of Appeal took the view that this involved taking judicial notice of those habits. It must however be remembered that this process of "legislative" fact-finding is essentially different from the process of "adjudicative" fact-finding, the latter, but never the former, being the province of the jury except when judicial notice is taken. One practical consequence of the distinction between taking judicial notice in the normal sense, *i.e.* of an adjudicative fact, and of taking notice of a legislative fact, is that, whereas the former does not create a precedent, the latter leads to a finding of law to which the doctrine of *stare decisis* may be applicable.

Finally, mention may be made of two matters upon which consideration of the doctrine of judicial notice may impinge and with which it may be confused.

First, in assessing any evidence given in court the trier of fact must obviously draw upon a vast mass of previously acquired factual

---

[1] [1940] 1 K.B. 687 (C.A.).

information, knowledge and experience. This forms the yard-stick by reference to which the significance of evidence is consciously or subconsciously measured. The nature of this yardstick will vary from person to person as their experiences, and reactions to their experiences, have differed. Questions may arise as to whether triers of fact may be assumed to have certain background knowledge for this purpose (see, *e.g. R.* v. *Hunt*[2]). It is to be noted, too, that in some cases the knowledge will be in part highly specialised, but this does not constitute an impediment to its use, not of course as a substitute for evidence, but as part of the yardstick for the assessment of evidence. In *Wetherall* v. *Harrison*[3] a medically-qualified magistrate was allowed to use his medical knowledge and experience in this way.

Secondly, there is the problem of what is sometimes referred to as "jury or magistrate notice." Here the question is as to the extent to which a trier of fact may rely upon knowledge, which he has acquired out of court, of a very fact which is either in issue, or directly relevant to a fact in issue, in the case before him. If the fact is notorious, he is usually, by way of analogy with judicial notice properly so-called, entitled to take notice of it (see, *e.g. R.* v. *Jones*[4]). If, however, the fact, although known to him personally, is not notorious, principle requires that he should try to disregard it or, if necessary, be disqualified. Sometimes however, as was the case in *Ingram* v. *Percival*,[5] principle seems to have been stretched, if not contravened.[6]

R. v. **Luffe** (1807) 8 East. 193 (K.B.). The question arising as to the legitimacy of a child, and the fact appearing that the husband did not have access to the wife until a fortnight before the birth, the court took judicial notice of the fact that, according to the course of nature, he could not have been the father. Lord Ellenborough C.J. said (pp. 201–202): "Here . . . in nature the fact may certainly be known that the husband, who had no access until within a fortnight of his wife's delivery, could not be the actual father of the child. Where the thing cannot certainly be known, we must call in aid such probable evidence as can be resorted to, and the intervention of a jury must, in all cases in which it is practicable, be had to decide thereupon; but where the question arises as it does here, and where it may certainly be known from the invariable course of nature, as in this case it may, that no birth could be occasioned and produced within those limits of time, we may venture to lay down the rule plainly and broadly, without any danger arising from the precedent. . . . "

Note.—Where the alleged period of gestation is not so short as to be manifestly impossible the court will hear experts and may refer to medical textbooks. See *Preston-Jones* v. *Preston-Jones* [1951] A.C. 391 (H.L.) (Chapter 3, *supra*).

---

[2] [1980] R.T.R. 29 (C.A.), *infra.*
[3] [1976] Q.B. 773 (D.C.), *infra.*
[4] [1970] 1 W.L.R. 16 (C.A.), *infra.*
[5] [1969] 1 Q.B. 548 (D.C.), *infra.*
[6] Contrast the situation in *R.* v. *Blick* (1966) 50 Cr.App.R. 280 (C.C.A.) in which it was held that a judge had properly received a note from a juror who had special knowledge of a relevant fact which contradicted evidence already given. The judge had then allowed evidence to be called in rebuttal of that earlier evidence.

See, generally, Carter, *Judicial Notice: Related and Unrelated Concepts*, in *Well and Truly Tried* (ed. Campbell and Waller, 1982).

Other matters judicially noticed as matters of common knowledge include the course of time, ordinary public festivals, the order of months, the meaning of ordinary language, weights and measures, currency and coin, notorious historical, geographical, scientific and other facts, general customs, established professional practices, etc. In the *Oxford Poor Rate Case* (1857) 8 E. & B. 184, Coleridge J. said (p. 204): "... the University of Oxford, without attempting an exact or complete definition of it, may at least be said to be a national institution created for a great national purpose, the advancement, namely, of religion and learning through the nation. We are bound judicially so to regard it...."

BRANDAO v. BARNETT

12 Cl. and F. 787; 3 C.B. 519; 8 E.R. 1622 (H.L.: 1846)

The court will judicially notice all general customs, such as the custom of banker's lien, and other customs of the law merchant, when they have been judicially ascertained and established.

In an action against bankers to recover certain exchequer bills, the defendants set up a general banker's lien by virtue of general custom. It was held that such custom should be judicially noticed.

LORD CAMPBELL: The first question that arises upon this record is, whether judicial notice is to be taken of the general lien of bankers on the securities of their customers in their hands? The exchequer bills, for which this action is brought, are found to be the property of the plaintiff....

The usage of trade by which bankers are entitled to a general lien is not found by the special verdict, and unless we are to take judicial notice of it, the plaintiff is at once entitled to judgment. But, my Lords, I am of opinion that the general lien of bankers is part of the law merchant, and is to be judicially noticed—like the negotiability of bills of exchange or the days of grace allowed for their payment. When a general usage has been judicially ascertained and established, it becomes a part of the law merchant which courts of justice are bound to know and recognise. Such has been the invariable understanding and practice in Westminster Hall for a great many years; there is no decision or dictum to the contrary, and justices could not be administered if evidence were required to be given *toties quoties* to support such usages, and issue might be joined upon them in each particular case....

LORD LYNDHURST agreed.

Note.—Care must be taken to distinguish general from particular customs, the latter not being judicially noticed, but requiring proof on each occasion. *Moult* v. *Halliday* [1898] 1 Q.B. 125 (D.C.), and *Edelstein* v. *Schuler* [1902] 2 K.B. 144.

Besides mercantile liens, the following general customs have, among others, been judicially noticed—the negotiability of instruments, the general practice of conveyancers, the custom or law of the road, customs of navigation, and market overt.

It is to be remembered that what is usually judicially noticed in such cases is the existence of a custom or practice, and this does not preclude evidence that there was a departure from the custom or practice on a particular occasion. In *Davey* v. *Harrow Corporation* [1958] 1 Q.B. 60 (C.A.) a question arose as to the significance to be accorded to a particular line on an Ordnance Survey map. An official from the Ordnance Survey Office testified as to a practice of using such a line to indicate the centre of an existing hedge. Lord Goddard C.J., delivering the judgment of the court, said (p. 69) that "courts in future can take notice of this practice of the Ordnance Survey as at least prima facie evidence of what a line on the map indicates." The term prima facie, it is to be observed, does not indicate the possibility of contradiction of the fact to be noticed, namely the existence of the practice, but rather the possibility of contradiction of a fact which could be deduced from this, namely that the practice had actually been followed in the instant case.

Stockdale v. **Hansard** (1839) 9 A. and E. 1 (Q.B.). In an action for libel, the defence was publication by order of the House of Commons. It was held that the court could determine whether the House of Commons had such privilege as would support the plea, and could judicially notice the nature and extent of parliamentary privilege as part of the law of the land. A court will judicially notice the law of England, including the law and custom of Parliament, and the privileges and course of proceedings of each House of Parliament.

Note.—Before 1921 judicial notice was also taken of the common law in Ireland; but the laws in Eire are not now judicially noticed: *Todd* v. *Todd* [1961] 1 W.L.R. 951. Nor is judicial notice taken of the laws of Scotland and Northern Ireland (except in the House of Lords, or by express statutory provision, *e.g.* Maintenance Orders Act 1950, s.22, Part Two, *infra*), the Channel Islands or the Isle of Man. The laws of these jurisdictions, like foreign laws and generally speaking the laws of Commonwealth countries, must be proved by evidence (see *infra*). But as to proof of colonial statutes, see the Evidence (Colonial Statutes) Act 1907. The effect of the evidence is to be determined by the judge (see Administration of Justice Act 1920, s.15; Supreme Court Act 1981, s.69(5); County Courts Act 1984, s.68 (all Part Two, *infra*)). Foreign law may also be ascertained under the British Law Ascertainment Act 1859 (Part Two, *infra*). Judicial notice is taken of EEC law (see European Communities Act 1972, s.3(2), Part Two, *infra*).

Of course, if a point of English law should happen temporarily not to be in the forefront of a judge's mind, he may refer to, or be referred to, authorities in order to focus his attention on the law in question and to refresh his memory; but this is not "proving" the law.

Every statute passed after 1850 is a Public Act and judicially noticed as such in the absence of express provision to the contrary (see Interpretation Act 1978, s.3, Part Two, *infra*, and Note thereto).

Earlier Public Acts are judicially noticed, but earlier Private Acts in the absence of special provision are not.

Judicial notice of certain official acts is expressly required by statute. These include the following: (1) The signatures of the judges of the superior courts appended to any judicial or official document (Evidence Act 1845, s.2, Part Two, *infra*); (2) The Seal of every county court on all summonses and other process of the court (County Courts Act 1984, s.134); (3) Various miscellaneous matters, *e.g.* authentication of certain foreign documents for the purposes of extradition procedures (Criminal Justice Act 1988, s.13(2), Part Two, *infra*).

Mostyn v. **Fabrigas** (1774) 1 Cowp. 161. In an action for assault and false imprisonment alleged to have been committed in Minorca, then a British possession, by the Governor, a question arose as to the law of the island. Lord Mansfield C.J. said:... "The way of knowing foreign laws is by admitting them to be proved as facts, and the court must assist the jury in ascertaining what the law is. For instance, if there is a French settlement, the construction of which depends upon the custom of Paris, witnesses must be received to explain what the custom is;... In the supreme resort to the King in Council, the Privy Council determines all questions that arise in the plantations, in Gibraltar or Minorca, in Jersey or Guernsey; and they inform themselves, by having the law stated to them...."

Note.—The last sentence states what must be regarded as an exception (to the general rule that law other than that of England and Wales must be proved as fact) if the Privy Council is to be characterised as an English court when hearing an appeal from abroad, for in such cases judicial notice is taken of the law of the jurisdiction whence the appeal comes.

DUFF DEVELOPMENT CO., LTD. v. KELANTAN (GOVERNMENT)

[1924] A.C. 797; 93 L.J.Ch. 343; 131 L.T. 676; 40 T.L.R. 566 (H.L.: 1924)

The court will judicially notice public, constitutional or international matters, affecting the Government of the United Kingdom and its relations with other states, in order that the court and the Government may take the same view and act in unison in dealing with such matters. For such purpose the court should inquire of the Government and thereby acquire the information, and the information so received is conclusive.

The Government of Kelantan applied for an order to set aside an order obtained by the appellants to enforce an award, on the ground that Kelantan was a sovereign independent state. The Secretary of State for the Colonies, in reply to an inquiry by the master, wrote that Kelantan was an independent state and the Sultan the sovereign ruler thereof. It was held that his letter was conclusive.

VISCOUNT CAVE: ... First, it was argued that the Government of Kelantan was not an independent sovereign state, so as to be entitled by international law to the immunity against legal process.... It has for some time been the practice of our courts, when such a question is raised, to take judicial notice of the sovereignty of a state, and for that purpose (in any case of uncertainty) to seek information from a Secretary of State; and when information is so obtained the court does not permit it to be questioned by the parties....

In the present case the reply of the Secretary of State shows clearly that notwithstanding the engagements entered into by the Sultan of Kelantan with the British Government that government continues to recognise the Sultan as a sovereign and independent ruler, and that His Majesty does not exercise or claim any rights of sovereignty or jurisdiction over that country. If after this definite statement a different view were taken by a British court, an undesirable conflict might arise; and, in my opinion, it is the duty of the court to accept the statement of the Secretary of State thus clearly and positively made as conclusive upon the point....

VISCOUNT FINLAY: ... It is settled law that it is for the court to take judicial cognisance of the status of any foreign government. If there can be any doubt on the matter the practice is for the court to receive information from the appropriate department of His Majesty's Government, and the information so received is conclusive.... Such information is not in the nature of evidence: it is a statement by the

Sovereign of this country through one of his Ministers upon a matter which is peculiarly within his cognisance. . . .

LORDS DUNEDIN, SUMNER and CARSON delivered speeches to the same effect, except that Lord Sumner referred to the information supplied as the best evidence.

Note.—The statements with reference to evidence in the speeches of Viscount Finlay and Lord Sumner appear to conflict, but Lord Sumner had previously distinguished mere information on which judicial notice is based from evidence in the ordinary sense (see *Commonwealth Shipping Representative* v. *P. & O. Branch Service* [1923] A.C. 191 at 212 (H.L.)). See also *McQuaker* v. *Goddard* [1940] 1 K.B. 687 (C.A.), *infra.*

The Fagernes [1927] P. 311 (C.A.). A question arose as to whether a collision in the Bristol Channel occurred within the jurisdiction of the High Court. At the request of the Court of Appeal the Attorney-General stated that the Home Secretary instructed him to say that the spot where the collision occurred was not within the limits to which the territorial sovereignty of His Majesty extended. The court by a majority held that this statement was conclusive.

Note.—See, too, the Territorial Sea Act 1987, s.1(3).

Engelke v. **Musman** [1928] A.C. 433 (H.L.). This was an action for arrears of rent in which the defendant claimed immunity from the jurisdiction of the English court on the ground that he was a member of the staff of the German ambassador. "The sole point for determination is the method by which the status of any person who claims the benefit of this privilege is to be determined. For the appellants it is contended that the statement of the Attorney-General on the instruction of the Foreign Office is for this purpose conclusive, while the respondent asserts that any such dispute should be ascertained in the ordinary way according to the rules of evidence" (Lord Buckmaster at pp. 440–446). The House of Lords unanimously held that the certificate was conclusive on the issue of the respondent's status.

R. v. **Botrill, ex parte Keuchenmeister** [1947] 1 K.B. 41 (C.A.) The Foreign Secretary certified *inter alia* that "Germany still exists as a State and German nationality as a nationality . . . His Majesty is still in a state of war with Germany. . . . " The court held that therefore the applicant (for a writ of *habeas corpus*) was still an enemy alien. The certificate was conclusive as to the matters stated.

Carl Zeiss Stiftung v. **Rayner and Keeler Ltd. (No. 2)** [1967] 1 A.C. 853 (H.L.) This was an action for an injunction restraining the sale of certain optical goods under a particular label. A question arose as to whether the plaintiff, incorporated under the legislation of an alleged foreign state, was a legal person for the purposes of the litigation. The Foreign Secretary certified that Her Majesty's Government had not granted any recognition *de jure* or *de facto* to the "state" in question or its government. The House of Lords held this to be conclusive.

Note.—See, too, *Mighell* v. *Sultan of Johore* [1894] 1 Q.B. 149 (C.A.). But an issue as to the incorporation of a body under the law of a *recognised* state is a matter for the law of that state: see *Krajina* v. *Tass Agency* [1949] 2 All E.R. 274 (C.A.).

Protection of Trading Interests Act 1980, s.4. " . . . a certificate signed by or on behalf of the Secretary of State to the effect that [an order under the Evidence

(Proceedings in Other Jurisdictions) Act 1975, s.2 (Part Two, *infra*)] infringes the jurisdiction [of the United Kingdom] or is ... prejudicial [to its sovereignty] shall be conclusive evidence of that fact."

WETHERALL v. HARRISON

[1976] Q.B. 773; [1976] 2 W.L.R. 168; [1976] 1 All E.R. 241; [1976] R.T.R. 125; [1976] Crim.L.R. 54 (Q.B.D.: 1975)

A magistrate (or juryman) is entitled to draw upon his specialised knowledge when assessing evidence, but he may not use that knowledge as evidence. He may inform other members of the bench (or jury) of his views, but he must not attempt to persuade them to use his specialised knowledge as evidence.

LORD WIDGERY C.J.: This is an appeal by case stated by Northampton justices in respect of their adjudication as a magistrates' court ... they were dealing with an information preferred by the prosecutor, who is the appellant before us, against the defendant, alleging that the defendant, without reasonable excuse, had failed to provide a specimen for a laboratory test, contrary to section 9(3) of the Road Traffic Act 1972.
... It will be appreciated that the whole issue in this case was whether there was reasonable excuse for the failure to give a blood sample. The stage had been reached when the defendant was bound to give a blood sample, and if he did not give one then either his excuse was a reasonable excuse or not. The defendant was saying "I could not give a blood sample because I was ill. I had a sort of fit," and the prosecutor through the mouth of Dr. Price was saying "Not at all, he was simulating a fit. There was no earthly reason why he should not give a sample of blood." That was the issue.
Here comes the unusual twist, if I may so describe it, in the case. On the bench was a practising registered medical practitioner, Dr. Robertson, and the bench: "had regard to his professional opinion of the [defendant's] reactions and behaviour according to the evidence, and Dr. Robertson's own reasons are separately attached."
Now I take that to mean that in the retiring room Dr. Robertson, possibly at the invitation of the other members of the bench, gave his views on the matters traversed by Dr. Price, in other words, gave his view as to whether it was a simulated fit or a genuine fit. The justices said not only did they listen to Dr. Robertson's reasons but they also had a layman's experience and viewpoint of war-time inoculations and the fear that they could create in certain individuals.
The matter comes before us really in this form, that we are invited to say whether the justices acted with propriety in having regard to information given to them by Dr. Robertson and drawing on their own war-time experiences so far as they did. In the event, they acquitted the defendant, obviously not being satisfied that his fit was simulated and therefore not being satisfied that he acted without reasonable excuse.
Mr. Barker, in putting the matter before us, is really inviting us to say, for the advantage of justices hereafter, what should happen when a

justice has specialised knowledge of this kind; should he use it or should he not.

In argument we were referred to three authorities. The only one I need refer to, and the most recent, is *Reynolds* v. *Llanelly Associated Tinplate Co. Ltd.* [1948] 1 All E.R. 140. That was concerned with arbitrators and judges and the extent to which they could have regard to their own personal knowledge. I do not think that the position of a justice of the peace is the same, in this regard, as the position of a trained judge.... They are much more like jurymen in this respect.... I do not believe that a serious restriction on a justice's use of his own knowledge or the knowledge of his colleagues can really be enforced. Laymen (by which I mean non-lawyers) sitting as justices considering a case which has just been heard before them lack the ability to put out of their minds certain features of the case. In particular, if the justice is a specialist, be he a doctor, or an engineer or an accountant, or what you will, it is not possible for him to approach the decision in the case as though he had not got that training, and indeed I think it would be a very bad thing if he had to. In a sense, the bench of justices are like a jury, they are a cross-section of people, and one of the advantages which they have is that they bring a lot of varied experience into the court room and use it.

So I start with the proposition that it is not improper for a justice who has special knowledge of the circumstances forming the background to a particular case to draw on that special knowledge in interpretation of the evidence which he has heard. I stress that last sentence, because it would be quite wrong if the justice went on, as it were, to give evidence to himself in contradiction of that which has been heard in court. He is not there to give evidence to himself, still more is he not there to give evidence to other justices; but that he can employ his basic knowledge in considering, weighing up and assessing the evidence given before the court is I think beyond doubt.

Furthermore, I do not see why he should not, certainly if requested to by his fellow justices, tell his fellow justices the way in which his specialised knowledge has caused him to look at the evidence. In no bench of justices should there be a leader, so aggressive that he tries to assume responsibility for the decision and excludes the others, whether he is proceeding on the basis of a specialised subject or not, and that certainly goes for justices with a specialised knowledge, because it would be quite wrong for the doctor in the present case to have gone into the justices' retiring room and immediately proceeded to persuade all the justices because of his specialised knowledge. He ought really to have waited until asked to make a contribution on his specialist subject. Whether he is asked or not, he should not press his views unduly on the rest of the bench. He should tell them in a temperate and orderly way what he thinks about the case, if they want to know, and then leave them to form their own conclusion if they wish so to do. Here again it is most important that the justice with specialised knowledge should not proceed to give evidence himself to his fellow justices contradictory to that which they have heard in the court. He can explain the evidence they have heard: he can give his own view as to how the case should go and how it should be decided; but he should not be giving evidence himself behind closed doors which is not available to the parties.

Applying those principles to the instant case, there was certainly no reason why Dr. Robertson should not, when forming his own conclusion about this case, have referred to his own knowledge, and his own knowledge and experience was that this kind of fit was genuine, and knowing that it would be right that in reviewing and considering the evidence in this case he should have that knowledge in the background and use it if he thought fit. Since his fellow justices obviously knew he was a doctor and I think asked him for the benefit of his views, I see no reason at all why he should not tell them what his views were. That does not seem to me to be contrary to any principle to be applied here, and I do not believe in this case either that the doctor went beyond the scope of the authority which I am trying to apply.

. . . .

O'CONNOR and LAWSON JJ. concurred, and the appeal was dismissed.

Note.—The distinction drawn in *Wetherall* v. *Harrison* has been applied in various fields including, *e.g.* that of labour law (see *Heatons Transport (St. Helens) Ltd.* v. *T.G.W.U.* [1972] I.C.R. 308; *Dugdale* v. *Kraft Foods Ltd.* [1977] I.C.R. 48 and *Hammington* v. *Berker Ltd.* [1980] I.C.R. 248). In the last mentioned an industrial tribunal had relied, when reaching its decision about the future employment prospects of a worker, upon information splied by one of its own members, this being based upon his knowledge and experience of the particular industry. The Employment Appeal Tribunal allowed an appeal. Talbot J. said (p. 252): "The essence . . . of the use of such specialised knowledge and information and experience is that it is to be used . . . for the purpose of weighing up and assessing the evidence and if necessary interpreting it. What must not be done is using that knowledge to substitute for the evidence given in court that derived from that knowledge; nor must it be used for producing some factor of evidence which is not evidence before the court with which the parties have not had an opportunity of dealing." For the application of the distinction in arbitrations generally, see *Fox* v. *P.G. Wellfair Ltd.* [1981] Com.L.R. 140 (C.A.).

Kent v. **Stamps** [1982] R.T.R. 273 (D.C.). The accused had been charged with speeding. The prosecution gave evidence that his speed had been measured by an electronic device, a Truvelo meter, which was in good working order. The accused testified that his lorry, which was laden and old, could not reach the speed recorded on the meter as he had just rounded a bend and the road was on a slight upward gradient. Using their local knowledge of the area, the justices accepted the defendant's evidence and dismissed the information. The Divisional Court, dismissing an appeal by the prosecutor, held that the justices were entitled to use their local knowledge to assess the evidence of the meter reading. The court purported to follow *Wetherall* v. *Harrison*. It is to be noted that there was no suggestion that the fact was notorious in the locality. The case is seemingly to be explained on the ground that the justices "were using their knowledge of the locality . . . to assess and weigh up the rival evidence, the rival evidence being the police officer's opinion supported by the Truvelo meter—because of course the evidence in fact is the Truvelo meter reading—as against the defendant's statement that his vehicle in that particular case could not have been doing 40 miles per hour as stated." (Ormrod L.J. at p. 277).

R. v. **Rosser** (1836) 7 Carr. and Payne 648; 173 E.R. 284 (C.C.C.). The accused was indicted for stealing in a dwelling house a watch and seals stated in the indictment to be of the value of £7. A prosecution witness gave evidence that the property was worth this sum. After the summing up the jury enquired whether they were at liberty to put a value on the property themselves. Vaughan J. said:

"If you see any reason to doubt the evidence on the subject, you are at liberty to do so. Any knowledge you may have on the subject you may use. Some of you may perhaps be in the trade." Parke B. said (p. 649): "If a gentleman is in the trade, he must be sworn as a witness. That general knowledge, which any man can bring to the subject may be used without; but if it depends on any knowledge of the trade, the gentleman must be sworn." The verdict was guilty of stealing goods under the value of £5.

Note.—These two statements may at first sight appear to conflict; but perhaps Vaughan J. was countenancing the use of background knowledge (including that of a specialist type) for the purpose of assessing evidence that had been given, whereas Parke B. was concerned to prohibit the use of specialist knowledge as a substitute for that evidence. In practice the distinction may often be blurred.

R. v. Hunt [1980] R.T.R. 29 (C.A.). A question arose as to whether there was evidence from which the jury could conclude that the impairment of an accused's ability to drive properly was attributable to intoxication. Bridge L.J., delivering the judgment of the Court of Appeal, said (pp. 33–34): "...It may at one time have been the case that lay people had no knowledge of the quantity of alcohol in the blood, measured in milligrammes per millilitre, which was likely to affect a person and to cause intoxication. But if that was ever the situation, in our judgment, it is certainly not the situation today. The breathalyser laws have been with us for 12 years. Now, in our judgment, it is a matter of the commonest of common knowledge that if a person has in his blood a concentration of alcohol nearly two-and-a-half times the legal limit under section 6, he is likely to be intoxicated to a substantial degree. It seems to us quite plain that from the mere fact of such a concentration, the jury is entitled, without the assistance of expert evidence, to infer that intoxication, in such a case as the present, was responsible for the impairment of the driver's ability to drive, which resulted in the relevant accident."

R. v. Jones [1970] 1 W.L.R. 16 (C.A.). The defendant had been convicted under section 1 of the Road Safety Act 1967 of attempting to drive a motor vehicle with blood alcohol concentration above the prescribed limit. One of the points taken in his defence was that it had not been proved that he had been "given an opportunity to provide a specimen of breath for a breath test" within section 2(7) of the Act, because it had not been proved that the device used, the Alcotest R80, was "a device of a type approved...by the Secretary of State" so as to be within the definition of "breath test" in section 7. The Court of Appeal rejected this contention. Edmund Davies L.J. said (p. 20): "...the number of cases in which it has been proved that the Alcotest R80 device is of an approved type has by now become so large and so widely reported that, in our judgment, a court (including the jury) is entitled to take judicial notice of that fact, and its formal proof is accordingly no longer necessary."

Note.—*R.* v. *Jones* was followed in *Bentley* v. *Northumbria Police* [1984] R.T.R. 276 (D.C.). It would appear that, whereas in *R.* v. *Hunt* the question was as to whether the jury could be assumed to possess certain background general knowledge for the purpose of assessing the significance of the evidence, in *R.* v. *Jones* the jury was permitted to take notice without proof of a fact in issue because that fact had become notorious. However, in *Ingram* v. *Perceval* (*infra*) the magistrates were seemingly so permitted even though the fact was not shown to be notorious.

INGRAM v. PERCIVAL

[1969] 1 Q.B. 548; 3 W.L.R. 663; [1968] 3 All E.R. 657 (Q.B.D.: 1968)

Justices may and should take into consideration matters of which, of their own knowledge, they are aware, and particularly such matters in regard to the locality.

LORD PARKER C.J.: This is an appeal by way of case stated from a decision of Sunderland justices who convicted the defendant of an offence against section 11 of the Salmon and Freshwater Fisheries Act, 1923. That section makes it an offence to place a fixed engine of any description for taking or facilitating the taking of salmon or migratory trout or for detaining, or obstructing the free passage of, salmon or migratory trout in any inland or tidal waters.

The justices found as a fact that on July 11, 1967, the defendant had used a net for taking salmon and migratory trout in waters near the North Pier at Sunderland, and that that net was a fixed engine in that it was made secure by anchors and left unattended for taking salmon or trout . . . and the sole question here is whether that place where the net was fixed was in tidal waters. The magistrates came to the conclusion that it was and convicted the defendant.

. . . . The question therefore is whether the justices were entitled to find that at this position where the net was found, there was a perceptible, a real, ebb and flow of the tide, notwithstanding that it was fixed, as I understand it, below low water mark. In connection with that, the justices say this:

" . . . We considered that tidal waters consist of waters affected by a lateral or horizontal flow of water as distinct from a vertical rise and fall and it is within our knowledge that such a flow extends beyond low water mark and is experienced at more than 100 yards from the shore. We therefore held that in this case the net was in tidal waters."

Accordingly, on the view I take of this case, the result depends upon whether the justices were entitled to make use of the knowledge which they said that they had. In my judgment they were fully entitled to do so. It has always been recognised that justices may and should—after all, they are local justices—take into consideration matters which they know of their own knowledge, and particularly matters in regard to the locality, whether it be on the land, as it seems to me, or in water. In my judgment they were fully entitled to use that knowledge, and on that ground I would dismiss this appeal. . . .

Finally, I would say that each case must depend upon the evidence as to the ebb and flow, and in cases where justices have not got a local knowledge of the particular place where a net is fixed, there must be evidence as to whether at that place there is in any real sense an ebb or flow, whether a lateral movement or a vertical movement.

WALLER J. . . . I also agree with the observation by my Lord in relation to the justices using their local knowledge as to whether or not this particular water was tidal.

FISHER J. I agree with both the judgments which have been delivered.

[A petition to appeal to the House of Lords was dismissed].

R. v. Field and others (Justices), ex parte White (1895) 64 L.J.M.C. 158 (D.C.).
In order to establish a defence to a prosecution under the Food and Drugs Act

1875, s.6, it had to be shown that cocoa must necessarily contain a quantity of foreign ingredients. No evidence was adduced to show this, but justices, relying on their own knowledge, held for the accused. The Queen's Bench Divisional Court refused to disturb the justices' finding, although Wills J. said (pp. 159–160): "I do not say that the justices pursued an altogether prudent course: and perhaps if the occasion arose again they would be wiser to hear evidence, and keep themselves technically right."

McQUAKER v. GODDARD

[1940] 1 K.B. 687; 109 L.J.K.B. 673; 162 L.T. 232; 56 T.L.R. 409; [1940] 1 All E.R. 471 (C.A.: 1940)

The judge may consult books of reference, as an aid to judicial notice; and may supplement such books by oral statements.

The plaintiff was bitten by a camel while visiting the defendant's zoological gardens. The question was whether the camel was a domestic or a wild animal for purposes of the law relating to liability for animals. Five witnesses gave sworn evidence as to the characteristics of camels.

CLAUSON L.J. (agreeing with SCOTT and MACKINNON L.JJ. in dismissing the appeal): . . . I should like, however, to add a word as to the part taken in the matter by the evidence given as to the facts of nature in regard to camels. That evidence is not, it must be understood, in the ordinary sense evidence bearing upon an issue of fact. In my view the exact position is this. The judge takes judicial notice of the ordinary course of nature, and in this particular case of the ordinary course of nature—in regard to the position of camels among other animals. The reason why the evidence was given was for the assistance of the judge in forming his view as to what the ordinary course of nature in this regard in fact is, a matter of which he is supposed to have complete knowledge. The point is best explained by reading a few lines from that great work, the late Mr. Justice Stephen's *Digest of the Law of Evidence*. In the 12th edition, Article 62 is as follows: "No evidence of any fact of which the court will take judicial notice need be given by the party alleging its existence; but the judge, upon being called upon to take judicial notice thereof, may, if he is unacquainted with such fact, refer to any person or to any document or book of reference for his satisfaction in relation thereto, or may refuse to take judicial notice thereof unless and until the party calling upon him to take such notice produces any such document or book of reference." From that statement it appears that the document or book of reference only enshrines the knowledge of those who are acquainted with the particular branch of natural phenomena; and in the present case, owing to some extent to the fact that there appears to be a serious flaw in a statement in a well known book of reference on the matter here in question, the learned judge permitted, and properly permitted, oral evidence to be given before him by persons who had, or professed to have, special knowledge with regard to this particular branch of natural history. When that evidence was given and weighed up with the statements in the books of reference which were referred to, the facts became perfectly plain; and the learned judge was able without any difficulty whatever to give a correct statement of the natural phenomena material to the matter in question, of which he was bound to take judicial notice.

Note.—It may perhaps be questioned whether Stephen actually contemplated "evidence" on oath by witnesses as a basis of judicial notice.

No mention was made of judicial notice in the judgment of Branson J. at first instance, or in the judgments of Scott and MacKinnon L.JJ. in the Court of Appeal; nor does the point appear to have been raised by counsel. However Scott L.J., in refusing leave to the House of Lords, did say (p. 701): "On the facts proved, of which the learned judge and this Court are entitled to take judicial notice . . . the law is clear that in England, as elsewhere, the camel is a domestic animal."

Regarded as a case on judicial notice *McQuaker* v. *Goddard* is to be seen as involving the taking of such notice of legislative rather than adjudicative facts (see p. 136, *supra*). The investigation of the nature and habits of camels was undertaken in the context of a piece of judicial law-making—namely the allocation of the camel to one legal category rather than another for the purposes of determining tort liability.

The taking of judicial notice in *R.* v. *Simpson* (1984) 78 Cr.App.R. 115 (C.A.) that a flick knife is an offensive weapon *per se* for the purposes of section 1(1) of the Prevention of Crime Act 1953 would similarly appear to involve taking notice of a legislative fact.

R. v. **Yap Chuan Ching** (1976) 63 Cr.App.R. 7 (C.A.) (Chapter 3, *supra*). Lawton L.J., delivering the judgment of the Court of Appeal when considering the correctness of the trial judge's direction on the quantum of proof in a criminal case, said (p. 9): "Perhaps it is not irrelevant in the year 1976 for the Court to take judicial notice of the fact that one of the popular forms of entertainment nowadays on television is a series of reconstructed trials which have a striking degree of realism. Most jurors nowadays know something about the burden and standard of proof before they ever get into the jury box."

Note.—This would appear to be a reference to judicial notice of a legislative rather than an adjudicative fact. What is being noticed is a fact which bears upon the proper formulation of a rule of law, albeit adjectival law. The fact that most jurors nowadays know something about notions of burden and standard of proof bears upon the rules of the law of evidence which prescribe what shall constitute adequate directions on these matters.

Chapter 8

ORAL EVIDENCE AND TESTIMONIAL COMPETENCE AND COMPELLABILITY

USUALLY, although there are exceptions, the evidence of a witness is given orally. The materials in this Chapter are concerned with the rights of the parties to give oral testimony themselves, their rights and the right of the judge to call competent witnesses to testify, limitations upon testimonial competence, the extent to which a person may be compelled to testify and the right of the judge to comment upon the failure of the accused to testify in a criminal case.

The common law disqualification of parties and their spouses from themselves testifying on the ground of their interest in the outcome of the proceedings has been largely abolished.[1] A non-party witness may be called to give evidence by either party or, in a criminal case in certain circumstances by the judge. In civil cases the judge may call a witness only with the consent of the parties.[2]

Any witness, whether a party or not, must be testimonially competent. The ordinary individual is competent and is presumed to be so. The law of competence is therefore most usefully seen as a law of incompetence in that it is comprised of exceptions to this general rule. The principal grounds of testimonial incompetence in modern times are lack of age and defective intellect. A competent witness is also compellable if he can lawfully be obliged to give evidence; and the basic rule is that all competent witnesses are compellable, but there are some exceptional cases of bare competence. Apart from sovereign and diplomatic immunities, many of which are recognised or created by statute,[3] and a particular immunity enjoyed by bankers and bank officials under the Bankers Books Evidence Act 1879, s.6,[4] the principal cases of bare competence relate to the accused and, to a now limited extent, his or her spouse in criminal proceedings.

---

[1] See the Evidence Acts 1843 and 1851, Evidence Amendment Act 1853, Evidence Further Amendment Act 1869 and Criminal Evidence Act 1898 (Part Two, *infra*).

[2] The High Court of Australia has apparently held that the judge does not have a discretion to call a witness even in a criminal trial unless the parties consent: *Titheradge v. R.* (1917) 24 C.L.R. 107. See, too, *R. v. McDowell* [1984] Crim.L.R. 486; [1984] C.L.Y. 610 (C.A.).

[3] See the Diplomatic Privileges Act 1964, s.2(1), Sched. 1, Arts. 1, 31(2), 37(1), (2); Consular Relations Act 1968, s.1(1), Sched. 1, Arts. 1(1), 44, 58(2); International Organisations Act 1968; Diplomatic and other Privileges Act 1971, s.4; State Immunity Act 1978.

[4] Part Two, *infra*.

The accused is a competent witness in his own defence but he is not compellable.[5] An accused is also a competent, but again not a compellable, witness for anyone tried jointly with him. He will, however, be compellable for the prosecution (or for any accused) if he has pleaded guilty, or if he is tried separately.

The position of the spouse of the accused has been radically altered by the Police and Criminal Evidence Act 1984, s.80.[6] The general rule now is that the accused's spouse is a competent witness for the prosecution.[7] The only exception is where spouses are jointly charged with an offence. Then neither shall be competent for the prosecution unless he or she has pleaded guilty or for some other reason (e.g. that the prosecution has withdrawn the case) is no longer liable to be convicted.[8] In certain cases the spouse of the accused is not only competent but also compellable. These are (a) cases in which the offence charged involves an assault on, or injury or threat of injury to, the spouse or a person under the age of 16 at the material time; (b) cases in which the offence charged is a sexual offence against a person under the age of 16 at the material time; and (c) the offence charged is an inchoate offence in respect of an offence falling into one of these categories.[9] In other cases the spouse, although competent, is not a compellable witness for the prosecution.[10] The spouse is competent, and usually compellable, for the defence.[11] The only case in which he or she is not compellable is that in which he or she is jointly charged with the accused.[12] A spouse is a competent witness for the co-accused,[13] but is only compellable in situations in which he or she would be compellable as a prosecution witness.[14]

A spouse of the accused means a person to whom the accused is validly married at the time of the proceedings. It does not therefore include an ex-spouse, but it does include a husband or wife although judicially separated.

Generally, a party's failure to testify or to call a compellable witness may be the subject of comment by his opponent or by the judge,[15] and rational inferences may be drawn from it. But there are restrictions in the case of the accused and that of his or her spouse in criminal proceedings. In these cases comment by the prosecution is statutorily prohibited,[16] and, although the judge has the right to comment, his discretion in this regard is not unrestricted and has been made the subject of appellate control. Counsel for one accused has, however, a seemingly unrestricted right to make relevant comments upon the failure

---

[5] Criminal Evidence Act 1898, s.1, proviso (a).
[6] See Part Two, infra, and the commentary on s.80 generally.
[7] s.80(1)(a).
[8] s.80(4).
[9] s.80(3).
[10] The spouse is, however, seemingly compellable for the prosecution if the proceedings are brought by him or her: see the Theft Act 1968, s.30(2), (Part Two, infra).
[11] s.80(2).
[12] s.80(4).
[13] s.80(1)(b).
[14] s.80(3).
[15] For exceptional restrictions on the judge's powers in this regard, see R. v. Gallagher [1974] 3 All E.R. 118 (C.A.).
[16] Criminal Evidence Act 1898, s.1, proviso (b), and the Police and Criminal Evidence Act 1984, s.80(8).

of a co-accused to testify and to invite the drawing of inferences from such failure.

A witness, before he or she is permitted to give evidence, must take an oath or make an affirmation to the effect that his or her evidence will be true, the modern law on the subject being embodied in the Oaths Act 1978[17] which consolidates earlier enactments. An important exception to this general rule is contained in section 38 of the Children and Young Persons Act 1933,[18] which allows a child of tender years, although incompetent to give sworn evidence, to give unsworn evidence in criminal cases provided that "in the opinion of the court, he is possessed of sufficient intelligence to justify the reception of the evidence, and understands the duty of speaking the truth."[19] The other cases in which unsworn evidence may be received are miscellaneous and unimportant. The common law right of the accused to make an unsworn statement, although expressly preserved by the Criminal Evidence Act 1898, s.1, proviso (h), was essentially abolished by the Criminal Justice Act 1982, s.72.[20] The right to address the court to the extent that counsel as a solicitor could, and the right to make unsworn statements in mitigation of sentence, are, however, retained. It may be noted that a person called pursuant to a *subpoena duces tecum* for the sole purpose of producing a document need not be sworn if there is another witness who can identify the document. Such a person is, however, *ex hypothesi* not giving oral testimony.

Oral evidence is normally given from the witness box, but in exceptional circumstances and subject to certain safeguards a criminal court may allow a witness who is outside the United Kingdom to give evidence through a closed circuit television link.[21] Similar provision is made for the reception of the evidence of a child under 14 when the accused is charged with certain offences against the person.[22]

R. v. Baines [1909] 1 K.B. 258 (K.B.D.). The defendant caused to be issued and served *subpoenas ad testificandum*, requiring the Prime Minister and the Home Secretary to attend and give evidence at the Leeds Assizes, on the trial of an indictment against him for breach of the peace and unlawful assembly. The Ministers applied to the King's Bench Division for an order that the *subpoenas* served on them should be set aside, on the ground that the issue thereof was an abuse of the process of the court. They supported their application by affidavits. The court set aside the *subpoenas*. Bigham J. said (p. 261): "There can be no doubt as to the jurisdiction of the court to interfere where it is satisfied that its process is being used for indirect or improper objects. It must not be supposed that the position which the applicants occupy affords them any privilege. They stand in the same position as any other of His Majesty's subjects. But the court

---

[17] Part Two, *infra*.

[18] Part Two, *infra*.

[19] See, too, for special provisions relating to children's evidence by deposition or written statements in certain circumstances, the Children and Young Persons Act 1933, ss.42 and 43, and the Magistrates' Courts Act 1980, s.103 (all Part Two, *infra*). See, too, the Criminal Justice Act 1988, s.32 (Part Two, *infra*).

[20] Part Two, *infra*.

[21] Criminal Justice Act 1988, s.32 (Part Two, *infra*).

[22] Criminal Justice Act 1988, s.32(1)(b) and (2) (Part Two, *infra*.).

has to inquire whether its process has been issued against them with the object and expectation on reasonable grounds of obtaining from them evidence which can be relevant.... I do not believe, as a matter of fact, that they saw or could have seen or that they heard or could have heard anything that can be material to the inquiry at Leeds. We have before us the affidavits of the applicants, in which they both swear that they are wholly unable to give any evidence which can possibly be relevant to any issue which may arise. I believe that to be true. Therefore it would be an idle waste of time and money to require them to go down to Leeds to give evidence. The applicants further say that no application has been made to them by the defendants for any proof of the evidence to be given by them. This statement satisfies me that this process has not been issued for the simple and proper purpose of obtaining evidence; but for a different and ulterior purpose, a purpose to which the process of the court ought not to be applied. It is sufficient to say, first, that I am satisfied that neither of the applicants can give relevant evidence, and, secondly, that the process of the court has not been issued for the purpose of obtaining relevant evidence, but for other reasons."

Note.—The case illustrates the exception to the general rule that a party to legal proceedings may *subpoena* any person as a witness without leave of the court. See also *McKinley* v. *McKinley* [1960] 1 W.L.R. 120, where an unnecessary *subpoena* to a magistrates' clerk was set aside. But an application to set aside a *subpoena* may be refused, when the ground for the application is privilege, which the witness can claim after he has attended in pursuance to the *subpoena* (see *Broome* v. *Broome* [1955] P. 190).

If a person who is not *subpoenaed* happens to be present in a civil court, he probably cannot be compelled to give evidence against his will, except in a county court (County Courts Act 1984, s.55). If he voluntarily submits to be sworn, it seems that he is bound to answer all questions put to him on pain of attachment (see *R.* v. *Flavell* (1884) 14 Q.B.D. 364 (D.C.)). In criminal cases, a person present in court, though not served with a *subpoena*, may be obliged to give evidence (*R.* v. *Sadler* (1830) 4 C. & P. 218).

In some courts a summons (or even warrant) takes the place of a *subpoena*; and in criminal cases a witness order or a witness summons is now prescribed by the Criminal Procedure (Attendance of Witnesses) Act 1965 (Part Two, *infra*).

Evidence may be taken before the hearing of proceedings in court. In the High Court evidence may be so taken by the following methods: (1) affidavits (see R.S.C., Ord. 39); (2) commissions; (3) letters of request (*ibid.*); (4) interrogatories (Ord. 26); and (5) perpetuation of testimony (Ord. 39, r. 15). Some rules from these orders are printed in Part Three, *infra*.

In cases of indictable offences depositions are taken by the justices before whom a person is charged (see Magistrates' Courts Rules 1981; Part Three, *infra*). Several other provisions have been made for using depositions in criminal cases, which include the Criminal Law Amendment Act 1867, the Criminal Justice Act 1925, and the Children and Young Persons Act 1933, as amended. Some of the relevant provisions are printed in Part Two, *infra*. There is a judicial discretion to allow depositions taken before a coroner to be read as evidence at a subsequent trial: *R.* v. *Black* (1909) 74 J.P.R. 71.

Re Enoch and Zaretzky, Bock & Co.'s Arbitration [1910] 1 K.B. 327 (C.A.). An arbitrator called a witness without the consent of the parties. It was held that an arbitrator is in the same position as a judge in civil cases, and that neither has any right to call witnesses against the will of the parties. At the same time, as Fletcher Moulton L.J. said (p. 333): "It is well known that if a party calls a witness he may not then attack his general credibility. There may be a person whom it would be desirable to have before the court. Neither party wishes to take the responsibility of first vouching his personal credibility, or that he is a witness fit to be called, and the judge may relieve the parties in this way, by letting him go into the box as a witness of neither party...."

Note.—See also *Coulson* v. *Disborough* [1894] 2 Q.B. 316 (C.A.). When a witness has been called by a party, a judge may recall him; and this rule applies when a case has been transferred from a judge to an official referee (*Fallon* v. *Calvert* [1960] 2 Q.B. 201 (C.A.)).

An exception to the general rule occurs in a case of civil contempt, when the judge may call a witness (*Yianni* v. *Yianni* [1966] 1 W.L.R. 120).

R. v. HARRIS

[1927] 2 K.B. 587; 96 L.J.K.B. 1069; 137 L.T. 535; 43 T.L.R. 774; 20 Cr.App.R. 86; 28 Cox C.C. 432 (C.C.A.: 1927)

At a criminal trial the judge has the right to call a witness not called by either the prosecution or the defence. But after the defence is closed, he should do so only where a matter has been raised ex improviso *on the part of the prisoner.*

The apellant was tried together with four other persons before the Recorder of Liverpool. Two of the prisoners were charged with stealing and pleaded guilty; the appellant and the two other prisoners were charged with receiving and pleaded not guilty. After the appellant had given evidence denying guilty knowledge and had closed her case, the Recorder called one of the prisoners who had pleaded guilty but had not yet been sentenced, who gave evidence against the appellant, and she was convicted. It was held that this procedure was irregular, and the conviction was quashed.

AVORY J. (delivering the judgment of the court, which included LORD HEWART C.J. and SALTER J.): Two questions arise. . . . The first is whether the course taken by the Recorder in calling the prisoner Benton as a witness when the case for the defence had closed was in accordance with the well-recognised rule that governs proceedings at criminal trials. . . .

As to the first point, it has been clearly laid down by the Court of Appeal, in *Re Enoch and Zaretzky, Bock & Co.* (*supra*) that in a civil suit the judge has no right to call a witness not called by either party, unless he does so with the consent of both of the parties. It also appears to be clearly established that the rule does not apply to a criminal trial where the liberty of a subject is at stake and where the sole object of the proceedings is to make certain that justice should be done as between the subject and the state. The cases of *R.* v. *Chapman* (1838) 8 C. & P. 558, and *R.* v. *Holden* (1838) 8 C. & P. 606, establish the proposition that the presiding judge at a criminal trial has the right to call a witness not called by either the prosecution or the defence, and without the consent of either the prosecution or the defence, if in his opinion this course is necessary in the interests of justice. It is true that in none of the cases has any rule been laid down limiting the point in the proceedings at which the judge may exercise that right. But it is obvious that injustice may be done to an accused person unless some limitation is put upon the exercise of that right, and for the purpose of this case we adopt the rule laid down by Tindal C.J. in *R.* v. *Frost* (1839) 4 St.Tr.N.S. 86 at 386, where the Chief Justice said: "There is no doubt that the general rule is that where the Crown begins its case like a plaintiff in a civil suit, they cannot afterwards support their case by calling fresh witnesses, because they are met by certain evidence that contradicts it. They stand or fall by the evidence they have given. They must close their case before the defence begins, but if any matter arises *ex improviso*, which no human ingenuity can foresee, on the part of a defendant in a civil suit, or a prisoner in a criminal case, there seems to me no reason why that matter which so arose *ex improviso* may not be answered by contrary evidence on the part of the Crown." That rule applies only to a witness called by the Crown and on behalf of the Crown, but we think that the rule should also apply to a case where a witness is called in a criminal trial by the judge after the case for the defence is closed, and that the practice should be limited to a case where a matter arises *ex improviso*, which no human ingenuity can foresee, on the part of a prisoner, otherwise injustice would ensue. . . .

In the circumstances, without laying down that in no case can an additional witness be called by the judge after the case for the defence has been closed, we are of opinion that in this particular case the course that was adopted was irregular, and was calculated to do injustice to the appellant Harris.

Note.—*R. v. Harris* was followed in *R. v. Day* (1940) 27 Cr.App.R. 168 (C.C.A.); but compare *R. v. Tregear* [1967] 2 Q.B. 574 (C.A.).

In *R. v. Cleghorn* [1967] 2 Q.B. 584 (C.A.). Lord Parker C.J., giving the judgment of the Court of Appeal, said (pp. 587–588): "It is abundantly clear that a judge in a criminal case, where the liberty of the subject is at stake and where the sole object of the proceedings is to make certain that justice should be done as between the subject and the state, should have a right to call a witness who has not been called by either party. It is clear, of course, that the discretion to call such a witness should be carefully exercised, and indeed, as was said in *R. v. Edwards* by Erle J. ((1848) 3 Cox C.C. 82, 83): 'There are, no doubt, cases in which a judge might think it a matter of justice so to interfere; but generally speaking we ought to be careful not to overrule the discretion of counsel, who are, of course, more fully aware of the facts of the case than we can be.' "

Recently in *R. v. Roberts* (1985) 80 Cr.App.R. 89, the Court of Appeal applied the *dicta* of Avory J. in *R. v. Harris* and of Lord Parker C.J. in *R. v. Cleghorn* and held that the trial judge had rightly exercised his discretion in refusing to call a witness although counsel for one of two accused had requested that he do so.

The judge has a discretion to recall a witness, even after a submission that there is no case to answer (*R. v. McKenna* (1956) 40 Cr.App.R. 65). But new evidence cannot be given even by a previous witness after the summing-up (*R. v. Browne* (1943) 29 Cr.App.R. 106 (C.C.A.); *R. v. Owen* [1952] 2 Q.B. 362 (C.C.A.); *R. v. Corless* (1972) 52 Cr.App.R. 341 (C.A.); *R. v. Davis* (1976) 62 Cr.App.R. 194, 201 (C.A.)); yet a witness for the defence who arrived during the summing-up has been allowed to give evidence (*R. v. Sanderson* (1953) 37 Cr.App.R. 32 (C.C.A.)). A witness for the prosecution should certainly not give evidence after the retirement of the jury or magistrates (*R. v. Gearing* (1965) 50 Cr.App.R. 18; *Webb v. Leadbetter* [1966] 1 W.L.R. 245 (D.C.). As to real evidence see *Lawrence* [1968] 1 W.L.R. 341 (C.A.); but compare *R. v. Martin* (1872) L.R. 1 C.C.R. 378; *R. v. Nixon* [1968] 1 W.L.R. 577 (C.A.).

For the circumstances in which further evidence may be called by a party after the close of his case, see Chapter 9, Section D, *infra*.

R. v. Yacoob (1981) 72 Cr.App.R. 313 (C.A.). The competence and compellability of a prosecution witness depended upon whether she had lawfully married the accused in 1971. A marriage certificate of that fact was produced; but so also was a certificate of her marriage to another man in 1968. The trial judge held that she was competent and compellable as a prosecution witness because the presumption of the validity of the later marriage was rebutted by the production of the certificate of her prior marriage, and that the onus was upon the defence to prove incompetence. On the defendant's appeal against conviction the Court of Appeal held that the trial judge had erred in imposing the burden of proof upon the defence; but that, nevertheless, as the 1968 marriage was subsisting in 1971 (and, indeed, at the date of the trial), the witness was not the wife of the accused. Watkins L.J., giving the judgment of the Court of Appeal, said (pp. 316–317): "The beginning of a trial is obviously the appropriate time for the issue of the competence and compellability of a prosecution witness to be raised and determined. Whether the issue can be properly concluded in the absence of oral evidence from at least the witness whose competence is challenged depends upon the circumstances affecting that person.... As to the burden of proof in this context, it is for the prosecution, once the issue of the competence of one of its witnesses is raised, to prove that that person is competent to testify.... The burden will be discharged if the trial judge is satisfied beyond a reasonable doubt upon admissible and sufficient evidence of competence."

Note.—Preliminary facts controlling the competence or compellability of a witness are, of course, to be determined by the judge. It is for the party rendering the witness to establish such a fact when competence or compellability is challenged on the basis of its alleged non-existence. In the case of a prosecution witness the fact must be established beyond reasonable doubt. All this is in accord with general principle (See *Note* to *Bartlett* v. *Smith* (1842) 12 L.J.Ex. 287, Chapter 1, Section A, *supra*). Watkin L.J.'s use of the phrase "admissible and sufficient evidence" could, however, be misleading. The judge in determining an issue of preliminary fact is not restricted by the rules of evidence—he could for example be persuaded beyond reasonable doubt by strong but technically inadmissible hearsay evidence.

It is not to be supposed that Watkin L.J.'s statement, that the beginning of the trial is the appropriate time for issues of competence or compellability to be raised and determined, is intended to preclude absolutely the propriety of their being raised later in certain circumstances. In *Jacobs* v. *Layboun* (1843) 11 M. & W. 685 (Exch.) it was held that the trial judge had erred in rejecting an objection to a witness's competence on the ground that it had been made too late. Lord Abinger C.B. said (pp. 692–692): "Now a witness may, on his examination on the *voir dire*, appear perfectly competent; and the circumstances showing him not to be so may appear afterwards.... I do not see why counsel should be restrained from enquiring at any moment into a witness's competency...." See, too *Attorney-General* v. *O'Sullivan* [1930] I.R. 552, 556 (C.C.A., Eire).

R. v. **Brasier** (1779) 1 Leach. 199 (C.C.R.). In a prosecution for assault with intent to commit rape the question arose whether the proposed evidence of a child under seven years of age was admissible. The question was submitted to the 12 judges, who held that the evidence was not admissible as the child did not have sufficient understanding of the nature of an oath, without which evidence could not then be given. The assembled 12 judges gave a unanimous opinion (p. 200): "That no testimony whatever can be legally received except upon oath and that an infant, though under the age of seven years, may be sworn in a criminal prosecution, provided such infant appears, on strict examination by the court, to possess a sufficient knowledge of the nature and consequences of an oath, for there is no precise or fixed rule as to the time within which infants are excluded from giving evidence, but the admissibility of their evidence depends upon the sense and reason they entertain of the danger and impiety of falsehood, which is to be collected from their answers to questions propounded to them by the court; but if they are found incompetent to take an oath their evidence cannot be received."

Note.—It is to be observed that the decision in the above case was based on the fact that the child appeared not to possess sufficient understanding of the nature and consequences of an oath. At the time of this decision no evidence could usually be given without an oath. This is not now the case. The Children and Young Persons Act 1933, s.38 (Part Two, *infra*) provides for an exception in *criminal* proceedings (see *R. v. Surgenor* (1940) 27 Cr.App.R. 175 (C.C.A.)). The general rule, however, still applies in civil proceedings; and also in criminal proceedings when the witness is not of tender years. The question of competence, being a preliminary issue, is for the judge to determine (see Chapter 1, *supra*). Where a child of tender years is tendered as a witness there is an obligation upon the judge to investigate whether he or she has sufficient understanding of the solemnity of the occasion and the added responsibility to tell the truth which is involved in taking the oath: *R. v. Lal Khan* (1981) 73 Cr.App.R. 190 (C.A.), where it was held that the trial judge should not have allowed a child aged 12 to give sworn evidence without enquiry. The child's competence should be ascertained in open court (*R. v. Dunne* (1929) 21 Cr.App.R. 176 (C.C.A.); *R. v. Reynolds* [1950] 1 K.B. 606 (C.C.A.), both Chapter 1, Section A, *supra*). But it is undesirable for a child of five years of age to be called as a witness (*R. v. Wallwork* (1958) 42 Cr.App.R. 153 (C.C.A.) at p. 160).

It has been held that it is not necessary to seek the leave of the High Court before calling a ward to give evidence if the child has been interviewed by the police in connection with contemplated criminal proceedings before being made a ward of court: *In re K. (Minors)* [1988] Fam. 1 (Fam. Div.). A Practice Direction (*Wards: Witness at Trial* [1987] 1 W.L.R. 1739) has now laid down that, when the police wish to interview a child who is already a ward of court, application must be made for leave for them to do so. A subsequent Practice Direction (*Ward: Witness at Trial (No. 2)* [1988] 1 W.L.R. 989) has, however, introduced an element of flexibility into the requirement. Also, when such leave is granted it will (presumably) not then be necessary to seek further leave to call the ward to give evidence.

R. v. HAYES

[1977] 1 W.L.R. 234; [1977] 2 All E.R. 288; 64 Cr.App.R. 194 (C.A.: 1977)

The important consideration when a judge has to decide whether a child should be sworn is whether the child has a sufficient appreciation of the solemnity of the occasion and added responsibility to tell the truth which is involved in taking an oath; but the child's acceptance of the divine sanction of the oath is not essential. The determination by the judge of an issue of fact in this context should not lightly be disturbed.

BRIDGE L.J. (giving the judgment of the court which included WIEN and KENNETH JONES JJ.): This is an application for leave to appeal against the defendant's conviction...of four counts of indecency with small boys....

The sole issue in the case was one of identification. Three small boys, Martin, Trevor and George, aged at the time of the alleged offences 11, 10 and 8, but at the time of the trial 12, 11 and 9, respectively, gave evidence that on a day in the Christmas holidays, 1975, either shortly before or shortly after Christmas, they had approached a man at about seven o'clock in the evening, when it was dark but in a street-lighted area, to ask him the time and had been invited by him, in language which I do not need to quote, to engage in acts of gross indecency with him. The boys walked away and the man followed for some distance. They crossed over a road, the man then got over a wall into some playing fields and renewed his invitation. One of the boys, the youngest, George, got over the wall and the act of gross indecency alleged was that the boy had put his hand on the man's erect penis....

...This was a case where unless one at least of the boys who gave evidence was able to give evidence on oath, the case for the Crown would have failed: . . . In fact, two of the boys, Trevor and Martin, were sworn after being examined on the *voir dire* by the judge. The youngest boy, George, was permitted to give unsworn evidence.

The first submission is that the judge wrongly exercised his discretion in the light of the boys' answers to questions in permitting Trevor and Martin to be sworn and that accordingly there was an irregularity in the proceedings.

The stronger of the two cases in support of that submission is furnished by the transcript of the questions and answers in the case of the boy Martin. The transcript does read rather surprisingly considering that this was a boy of 12 at the time he was called to give evidence. It is not necessary to refer to more than a few of the questions and answers. He was asked if he had religious instruction at school, and shook his head. Then the judge said: "You don't? Do they teach you about the Bible? Have they told you about God or Jesus?" and he answered "No." "(Q) Do you know what I mean by God? Have you heard of God? (A) No." Later, there follows this series of questions and answers: "(Q) Do you think there is a God? (A) Yes . . . (Q) You know what it means to tell the truth don't you? (A) Yes. (Q) You know it's important to tell the truth? (A) Yes. (Q) Not to tell lies. You understand that it is important particularly today when you are here? (A) Yes. (Q) Will you promise before God that you will tell the truth? (A) Yes (Q) And you will stick to that? (A) Yes." The boy was then permitted to take the oath.

If the series of questions and answers started with the question "Do you think there is a God" and the answer "Yes" there would really be no substance in Mr. Charlesworth's [defence counsel's] complaints, but the fact that the earlier questions and answers, on their face, reveal the boy declaring that he is wholly ignorant of the existence of God does lend some force to the submission that if the essence of the sanction of the oath is a divine sanction, and if it is an awareness of that divine sanction which the court is looking for in a child of tender years, then here was a case where, on the face of it, that awareness was absent. The court is not convinced that that is really the essence of the court's duty in the difficult situation where the court has to determine whether a young person can or cannot properly be permitted to take an oath before giving evidence. It is unrealistic not to recognise that, in the present state of society, amongst the adult population the divine sanction of an oath is probably not generally recognised. The important consideration, we think, when a judge has to decide whether a child should properly be sworn, is whether the child has a sufficient appreciation of the solemnity of the occasion and the added responsibility to tell the truth, which is involved in taking an oath, over and above the duty to tell the truth which is an ordinary duty of normal social conduct.

Against the background of those general considerations of principle, we think it right also to approach the matter on the footing that this is very much a matter within the discretion of the trial judge and we think that this court, although having jurisdiction to interfere if clearly satisfied that the trial judge's discretion was wrongly exercised, should hesitate long before doing so. The judge sees and hears the boy or girl, which means very much more than the bare written word, and it may easily be that the judge comes to the conclusion that the way in which he has initially been phrasing his questions has been such that the child to whom the questions are directed has not sufficiently understood them, and he may then attempt to phrase his questions in a different way.

Mr. Charlesworth very frankly concedes that the watershed dividing children who are normally considered old enough to take the oath and children normally considered too young to take the oath, probably falls between the ages of 8 and 10. Both boys here were over the age of 10, as already stated. Martin was 12 and Trevor was 11. In all the circumstances we are not satisfied in either case—it is unnecessary to review the detail of the questions and answers in the other case—that there was any failure on the part of the judge to investigate the fitness of these two boys to take the oath, or that in his decision to permit them to do so he erred in any way....

Note.—The necessity for at least one boy to give sworn evidence derived from the proviso in section 38(1) of the Children and Young Persons Act 1933. This proviso was repealed by the Criminal Justice Act 1988, s.34(1).

R. v. **Bellamy** (1986) 82 Cr.App.R. 222 (C.A.). The complainant in a rape case being mentally handicapped, the trial judge investigated her competence as a witness. He questioned her social worker about the complainant's belief in a knowledge of God and about her understanding of the importance of telling the truth. He held her to be a competent witness, but that she lacked a sufficient belief in the existence of God to take the oath. He allowed her to affirm under the Oaths Act 1978, s.5 (Part Two, *infra*). The accused was convicted and appealed on the ground that the complainant should have been required to give sworn evidence. The Court of Appeal held, following *R.* v. *Hayes* (*supra*) and *R.* v. *Campbell* [1983] Crim.L.R. 174 (C.A.), that the trial judge had been wrong to investigate the complainant's theological understanding since an awareness of the divine sanction is no longer necessary. Moreover, having found her competent to be a witness, and given that she did not object to her being sworn, the judge should have allowed her to take the oath. The appeal was, however, dismissed, resort being had to the proviso to section 2(1)(c) of the Criminal Appeal Act 1968 (Part Two, *infra*).

R. v. HILL

20 L.J.M.C. 222; 2 Den. C.C. 254; 15 Jur. 470; 169 E.R. 495; 5 Cox 259 (C.C.R.: 1851)

Persons suffering from mental disabilities are not necessarily incompetent as witnesses. Whether they are competent or not depends on the character and extent of their malady. A person who is insane on one matter, but understands an oath, may be capable of giving evidence on matters unaffected by his derangement.

On a trial for manslaughter, evidence was given by one Donelly, who was a patient in a lunatic asylum. Before he was called as a witness, an attendant at the asylum stated, "Donelly labours under the delusion that he has a number of spirits about him which are continually talking to him; that is his only delusion." The medical superintendent at the asylum stated the same, and added, "I believe him to be quite capable of giving an account of any transaction that happened before his eyes. I have always found him so. It is solely with reference to the delusion about the spirits that I attribute to him being a lunatic." Other medical evidence was given to the effect that a man might have a delusion on one subject without its affecting his mind generally. The witness was held competent to prove the act of killing.

LORD CAMPBELL C.J.: . . . If there be a delusion in the mind of a party tendered as a witness, it is for the judge to see whether the party tendered has a sense of religion and understands the nature and sanction of an oath; and then if the judge admits him as a witness, it is for the jury to say what degree of credit is to be given to his testimony. Various old authorities have been brought forward to show that a person *non compos mentis* is not a competent witness; but the question is in what sense the expression *non compos mentis* is used. If by that term is meant one who does not understand the sanction of an oath, of course he ought not to be admitted as a witness; but he may be *non compos* in another sense, and yet understand the sanction of an oath and be capable of giving material testimony. . . . He had a clear apprehension of the obligation of an oath, and was capable of giving a trustworthy account of any transaction which took place before his eyes, and he was perfectly rational upon all subjects except with respect to his particular delusion. . . .

COLDERIDGE J.: . . . He appeared to be unusually well instructed in the nature and obligation of an oath, and prima facie therefore to be quite competent to give evidence proper for the consideration of the jury. If his evidence had in the course of the trial been so tainted with insanity as to be unworthy of credit, it was the proper function of the jury to disregard it, and not to act upon it.

LORD CAMPBELL C.J.: The rule contended for would have excluded the evidence of Socrates, for he believed that he had a spirit always prompting him.

TALFOURD J. and ALDERSON and PLATT BB. concurred.

Note.—The references to understanding the sanction of the oath might now be modified in the light of the more secular approach to the competency of children taken in *R.* v. *Hayes (supra)*.

R. v. **Pitt** [1983] Q.B. 25 (C.A.). The appellant was charged with two offences of assault causing actual bodily harm to his eight-month-old baby. His wife made a witness statement which was prejudicial to him. She was called as a prosecution witness but during her examination-in-chief she gave answers inconsistent with that statement. The judge allowed a prosecution application to treat her as hostile, and she was cross-examined on her witness statement. The appellant successfully appealed against conviction. The Court of Appeal was not satisfied that the wife fully understood that the wife (as the law then stood) was not obliged to give evidence. Pain J. giving the judgment of the court said (p. 29): "The choice, whether to give evidence or not is hers. She does not lose that choice because she makes a witness statement or gives evidence at the committal proceedings. She retains the right of refusal up to the point when, with full knowledge of that right, she takes the oath in the witness box." His lordship later added (p. 31): "It seems to us to be desirable that where a wife is called as a witness for the prosecution of her husband, the judge should explain to her in the absence of the jury, that before she takes the oath she has the right to refuse to give evidence, but that if she chooses to give evidence she may be treated like any other witness." Pain J. had already made it clear (p. 30) that: "There is, in our view, no objection in law which will preclude a judge from giving leave to treat as hostile a wife who chooses to give evidence for the prosecution of her husband."

Note.—For the position relating to hostile witnesses generally, see Chapter 9, Section A, *infra*, and the Criminal Procedure Act 1865, s.3 (Part Two, *infra*). In the light of the Police and Criminal Evidence Act 1984, s.80(3)(*a*), (Part Two, *infra*), the wife in *R.* v. *Pitt* would now in fact have been compellable; but the decision remains authority in cases coming within the general rule that a spouse of an accused cannot be compelled to give evidence for the prosecution.

Monroe v. **Twistleton** (1802) Peake Add.Cas. 219. A plaintiff *in assumpsit* was not allowed to call the divorced wife of the defendant to prove a contract allegedly concluded during their marriage.

Note.—The combined effect of the Evidence Amendment Act 1853 and the Evidence Further Amendment Act 1869 was to render the spouse of a party in civil proceedings both competent and compellable. It would seem highly incongruous if there are limitations upon the competence or compellability of an ex-spouse. However, unless and until *Monroe* v. *Twistleton* is overruled, or the words "husbands" and "wives" in the 1853 Act are construed so as to include ex-husbands and ex-wives, this would seem, at least theoretically, to be the position. In criminal cases an ex-spouse no longer qualifies as a spouse: Police and Criminal Evidence Act 1984, s.80(5) (Part Two, *infra*).

R. v. BATHURST

[1968] 2 Q.B. 99; [1968] 2 W.L.R. 1092; [1968] 1 All E.R. 1175; 52 Cr.App.R. 251 (C.A.: 1968).

There may be cases in which an accused ought to testify even though the only disputed issue is as to diminished responsibility, but such cases in which the judge can properly comment on his failure to do so must be very rare.

In cases in which a burden rests upon the accused any comment by the judge should take a different form from that which it takes in other cases.

LORD PARKER C.J. (delivering the judgment of the court which included WINN and ASHWORTH JJ.): ... this defendant, Eric Wilfred Bathurst, was convicted of the murder of a young woman.... He now appeals by leave of the full court against his conviction.

.... The killing was admitted; the sole defence was diminished responsibility, and the sole question here is whether the verdict was properly one of murder or should be one of manslaughter....

The defence sought to set up the defence of diminished responsibility. They called two psychiatrists, a Dr. Milne and a Dr. Dransfield, who both gave evidence to the effect that the defendant was suffering at the time from reactive depression, that that was a mental illness, and that his mental responsibility at the time of the killing was substantially diminished.

The defendant himself gave no evidence, and the prosecution in rebuttal called Dr. O'Brien and Dr. Fiddian, who gave evidence that in their view the depression was not of such a degree as to be described as a mental illness, and accordingly that he was not suffering from diminished responsibility within the meaning of section 2 of the Homicide Act 1957. It is to be observed that the jury were out for only 25 minutes and returned a verdict of murder.

The reason why the court gave leave to appeal in this case was having regard to a very strong comment that the trial judge made in relation to the fact that this defendant had chosen to remain silent and not go into the witness box and give evidence. I will read the full passage: "As someone said earlier in this case . . . this is not a question of insanity; this is a question of an intelligent man"—may I interpose there to say that he was a man at the time of the killing of about 40, earning nearly £1,500 a year as an area sales manager of a cash register company. The learned judge went on: "I emphasise that for this reason, namely, the accused person is under no obligation to give evidence; he has a right to do so if he wishes, but he cannot be required to give evidence. That is something that is often referred to in criminal cases as the privilege of silence. He is entitled to take the attitude 'Well, you the prosecution get on with it, and put before the court such facts as you can, and I will say nothing.' That is the right of everyone in a criminal case. This man has chosen to remain silent in this case and remain in the dock, even in relation to a matter where there is a burden of proof upon him. You will, of course, bear in mind that while he is perfectly entitled to remain silent, that is his right, nevertheless the fact that he is entitled to give evidence on his own behalf gives him an opportunity of adding to the material at your disposal on which you could come to a conclusion, and he has not afforded you that opportunity; he has chosen to remain where he is, and the evidence about him, the evidence of the symptoms, or many of them, which the doctors describe depends entirely on what they have said. It may help you to reflect that your task might well have been easier if he had given evidence. He has not. You see, it would be quite wrong, I think, if you said to yourselves 'Oh well, all this must be nonsense, because he has not given evidence.' But common sense compels you to reflect, does it not, that while he might or might not have added a great deal to the case he has abstained from making the contribution that he might have done. You may ask yourselves why. It is entirely a matter for you. Of course, we have the advantage of knowing that he has enjoyed the guidance of experienced counsel." That undoubtedly is a strong comment, and the court in granting leave was concerned to consider the question how far any comment was justified in the case of a man who was pleading diminished responsibility, and if justified in certain circumstances, whether this comment was justified on the facts of this case.

. . . [T]his court feels strongly that while it may be that there are cases in which a defendant ought to go into the witness box, albeit his plea is one of diminished responsibility, yet the cases when comment on his failure to do so can properly be made must be very rare. One has only to go back to one's own experience at the Bar, and I think the experience of all practising barristers today, to realise that in almost every case counsel defending a prisoner raising this defence would prevent him if he could from going into the witness box. He may well be suffering from delusions, he may be on the border of insanity; it would be the last thing that any counsel would do to allow his client to go into the witness box, and in those cases at any rate any comment on his failure to do so would be clearly unfair.

Having said that, the court is prepared to concede that there may be cases where a defendant ought to go into the box, and where his failure to do so may be commented on, albeit the plea is one of diminished responsibility. There might be a case where the prosecution, by cross-examining the psychiatrist called for the defence, indicated that they were challenging some particular point, and a point which could only be spoken to by the defendant as opposed to some relations, friends, or the like, and in such a case, probably a very rare case, some comment might be justified.

But to turn to the present case, the court is quite satisfied that the comment here was unjustified. Mr. Cobb very properly had probed the matter, cross-examining the psychiatrists called for the defence, suggesting to them that what they spoke to was only what the prisoner himself had said, but never from beginning to end suggesting that what the prisoner had said was lies, that he was malingering, that he was deceiving the doctor. Indeed, so far as the facts of this case were concerned, it is to be observed that when psychiatrists were called in rebuttal, one of them said that he had no reason to believe but that what he had been told was the truth. It is perfectly true that what the prisoner had told the medical experts for the defence and what he had told the medical experts for the prosecution, was different. What had happened was that Dr. Milne for the defence had questioned the prisoner, and in answer had obtained a lot of information which was not given to Dr. O'Brien, the prosecution expert, for the very good reason that Dr. O'Brien had not questioned him on those matters. But from beginning to end in this case, in the opinion of the court, there was no real challenge of the truthfulness of this man in answering questions, and giving information to the medical experts.

In those circumstances this court feels it was not right to comment, as the trial judge did, on his failure to give evidence, and in particular in the passage: "But common sense compels you to reflect, does it not, that while he might or might not have added a great deal to the case he has abstained from making the contribution that he might have done. You may ask yourselves why."

It may be a matter of speculation, but it certainly looks as if the trial judge was inviting the answer to that question to be: well, if he did go into the witness box he would have said that what he told the doctors was lies.

That is enough to dispose of this case; but the court would like to point out that the form of the comment, if comment is justified in any particular case on a plea of diminished responsibility, is a comment which is undoubtedly different from the comment which is justified when the burden is on the prosecution. Then, as is well known, the accepted form of comment is to inform the jury that, of course, he is not bound to give evidence, that he can sit back and see if the prosecution have proved their case, and that while the jury have been deprived of the opportunity of hearing his story tested in cross-examination, the one thing they must not do is to assume that he is guilty because he has not gone into the witness box.

When one comes to this sort of case, the case where the burden is on the defence and the defendant does not go into the witness box, the comment is directed to something quite different; it would more likely take this form, that he is not bound to go into the witness box, nobody can force him to go into the witness box, but the burden is upon him, and if he does not, he runs the risk of not being able to prove his case.

.... In all the circumstances this court feels that the only safe course is to set aside that verdict, and substitute one of manslaughter.

Note.—See, too, *R.* v. *Bradshaw* (1986) 82 Cr.App. 79 (C.A.) (Chapter 18, *infra*).

R. v. MUTCH

[1973] 1 All E.R. 178; 57 Cr.App.R. 196; [1973] Crim.L.R. 111 (C.A.: 1972)

The judge, in any comment upon the failure of the accused to testify, must in the normal case warn the jury not to assume from this failure that the accused is guilty. There may be the rare exceptional cases in which admitted or well-established facts so clearly implicate the accused that an innocent explanation is called for.

LAWTON L.J. (with whom CHAPMAN and WIEN JJ. agreed):
This is an appeal by Kenneth Mutch against his conviction for robbery.... The appeal raises the question whether the trial judge was justified in telling the jury that they were entitled to draw inferences unfavourable to the appellant because of his absence from the witness box.

The Crown's case against the appellant was that on May 17, 1971, he had gone with another man to a grocer's shop in Liverpool. This man had put his arm round a young female assistant's throat whilst the appellant had taken £104.81 from the till. Both then ran away. At the trial the assaulted girl and another female assistant had identified the appellant as one of the robbers; but there were features about the former's identification which weakened it somewhat. A young male assistant, who chased the robbers, saw one of them disappear into one of a block of houses where the appellant's father lived.

The appellant was arrested on July 16, 1971, and, when told why, he made comments which amounted to a denial. He was released on bail and it was alleged against him by the Crown that, whilst on bail and for the purpose of confusing any one attending an identification parade of which he was the suspect member, he had tried to alter his appearance by tinting his hair and moustache and by reshaping the latter. As a result of these suspicions on the part of the police, no formal identification parade was held.

As his trial there was clearly a case for him to answer. He elected not to give evidence. He called two witnesses to prove that he had not altered his appearance as alleged. The trial judge, when summing up, commented on the appellant's absence from the witness box in these terms: "In this case there is another matter about which I have to give you a direction and it is this: as you are aware, the [appellant] himself has not given evidence. That is an attitude that he is perfectly entitled to adopt. He has called evidence which, of course, you must consider with the rest of the evidence in the case. He has not gone into the witness box himself and he is perfectly entitled to take up that attitude. He is entitled to sit back in the dock where he is and say to the prosecution, 'Now you prove it,' and that is what he does say apart, of course, from the two witnesses relative to his appearance that he has called. But, at the same time, members of the jury, you must not think that in not giving evidence he is not doing what he is perfectly entitled to do. He is entitled to sit where he is as he has done and please do not think that the onus of proof is in any way shifting, it isn't. It remains fairly and squarely upon the shoulders of the prosecution but, at the same time, I have to tell you this: the jury are entitled to draw inferences unfavourable to the prisoner where he is not called to establish an innocent explanation of facts proved by the prosecution which, without such explanation, tell for his guilt. I will give you that again because it is extremely important: the jury are entitled to draw inferences unfavourable to the prisoner where he is not called to establish an innocent explanation of facts proved by the prosecution which, without such explanation, tell for his guilt. He is entitled not to give evidence and the burden of proof does not shift in the slightest, but you are entitled to have in mind that passage that I have just read to you when you come to make your assessment as to where the proof of this matter lies."

It was submitted that the judge was wrong to tell the jury that they were entitled to draw inferences unfavourable to the appellant because of his absence from the witness box and that he had made his error worse by repeating what he had said. There is nothing in the complaint about repetition. In repeating what he had said the judge was doing nothing more than helping the jury to understand what he thought, and rightly thought, was a somewhat complicated and involved legal formula. The legal concept underlying the formula is one which is founded on authorities over 60 years old. The problem is whether it was applicable in a case such as this where the sole issue was whether an identification was correct. If it was applicable, accused persons faced with evidence of identity, however weak it may be, will be doing themselves no good but positive harm by not giving evidence because the unfavourable inferences to be drawn from their silence may be regarded as strengthening the prosecution's weak evidence to such an extent as to warrant a conviction.

. . . . *R.* v. *Corrie* ((1904) 20 T.L.R. 365) . . . has no doubt been quoted as an authority by the editors of Archbold because of the following passage in the judgment of Lord Alverstone C.J. (p. 365, *cf.* 68 J.P. 296, 297): "No inference should be drawn in support of a weak case from the fact that the defendants were not called; but when transactions were capable of an innocent explanation, then, if the defendants could have given it, it was not improper, once a prima facie case had been established, for the jury to draw a conclusion from their not being called."

In our judgment . . . Lord Alverstone C.J.'s inference to the accused not being called was but one way of stating that an inference can be drawn from uncontested or clearly established facts which point so strongly to guilt as to call for an explanation; if no explanation is given when the circumstances are such that an innocent man would be expected either to give an explanation or deny the basic facts, this is a factor which can be taken into consideration: see *Bessela* v. *Stern* ((1877) 2 C.P.D. 265). . . .

Since the first decade of this century, there have been many cases in which this court and its predecessor have had to rule whether comments about an accused's absence from the witness box or a failure to disclose a defence when questioned by the police were permissible, and as Salmon L.J. pointed out in *R.* v. *Sullivan* ((1966) 51 Cr.App.R. 102, 105): "The line dividing what may be said and what may not be said is a very fine one, and it is perhaps doubtful whether in a case like the present it would be even perceptible to the members of any ordinary jury." Nevertheless, as long as the law recognises the so-called right to silence, judges must keep their comments on the correct side of the line even though the differences between what is permissible and what is not may have little significance for many jurors. In the circumstances of this case there would be no point in reviewing the cases, some of which are not easy to reconcile, as we are firmly of the opinion that the trial judge used a form of words which was inappropriate to the case and the evidence which he was summing up. The words he used might have been permissible if the evidence had established a situation calling for "confession and avoidance"; they were not proper for one of flat denial as this case was. The court is of the opinion that the trial judge was led into error by the passage in Archbold (37th ed., 1969, p. 500, para. 1308) to which we have already referred. The concept there set out has a limited application and it would be helpful to both judges and practitioners if this was made clear.

Judges who are minded to comment on an accused's absence from the witness box should remember, first, Lord Oaksey's comment in *Waugh* v. *R.* ([1950] A.C. 203, 211): "It is true that it is a matter for the judge's discretion whether he shall comment on the fact that a prisoner has not given evidence; but the very fact that the prosecution are not permitted to comment on that fact shows how careful a judge should be in making such comment"; and, secondly, that in nearly all cases in which a comment is thought necessary (the *R.* v. *Corrie* . . . type of cases being rare exceptions) the form of comment should be that which Lord Parker C.J. described in *R.* v. *Bathurst* ([1968] 2 Q.B. 99, 107–108) as the accepted form, namely, that—"the accused is not bound to give evidence, that he can sit back and see if the prosecution have proved their case, and that, while the jury have been deprived of the opportunity of hearing his story tested in cross-examination, the one thing that they must not do is to assume that he is guilty because he has not gone into the witness box." The trial judge in this case went very near to encouraging this assumption.

For these reasons the court allowed the appeal and quashed the conviction because we adjudged that it was unsafe and unsatisfactory to allow it to stand.

Note.—Other cases in which comment may be justified include the case in which defence counsel has put forward a plausible, but dubious, explanation of his client's failure to testify; and, of course, the case in which the comment itself takes the form of a necessary explanation of the accused's failure to give evidence.

R. v. **Sparrow** [1973] 1 W.L.R. 488 (C.A.). Lawton L.J., delivering the judgment of the court, said (pp. 495–496): "In the present case, the charge was murder, and the evidence went to establish that when the police officer was shot by the co-defendant the appellant was standing close by and that after the shooting the pair of them drove off together and that one of them within a short time in the presence of the other reloaded the pistol; there has to be added to that the submission of the appellant's counsel that the prosecution's evidence was consistent with the possibility that the joint enterprise between the co-defendant and the appellant was merely to frighten the police officer with a pistol (which the appellant knew was loaded) and that the co-defendant departed from it by pressing the trigger a number of times. In the judgment of this court, if the trial judge had not commented in strong terms upon the appellant's absence from the witness box he would have been failing in his duty. The object of a summing up is to help the jury and in our experience a jury is not helped by a colourless reading out of the evidence as recorded by the judge in his notebook. The judge is more than a mere referee who takes no part in the trial save to intervene when a rule of procedure or evidence is broken. He and the jury try the case together and it is his duty to give them the benefit of his knowledge of the law and to advise them in the light of his experience as to the significance of the evidence, and when an accused person elects not to give evidence, in most cases but not all the judge should explain to the jury what the consequences of his absence from the witness box are, and if, in his discretion, he thinks that he should do so more than once he may, but he must keep in mind always his duty to be fair.... In *R.* v. *Bathurst* [1968] 2 Q.B. 99 Lord Parker C.J. gave judges some guidance, but what he said was, as he appreciated, *obiter*. It was in these terms, at p. 107: '...as is well known, the accepted form of comment is to inform the jury that, of course, he'— the defendant—'is not bound to give evidence, that he can sit back and see if the prosecution have proved their case, and that while the jury have been deprived of the opportunity of hearing his story tested in cross-examination, the one thing they must not do is to assume that he is guilty because he has not gone into the witness box.' In many cases, a direction in some such terms as these will be all that is required; but we are sure that Lord Parker C.J. never intended his words of guidance to be regarded as a judicial directive to be recited to juries in every case in which a defendant elects not to give evidence. What is said must depend upon the facts of each case and in some cases the interests of justice call for a stronger comment. The trial judge, who has the feel of the case, is the person who must exercise his discretion in this matter to ensure that a trial is fair. A discretion is not to be fettered by laying down rules and regulations for its exercise.... What, however, is of the greatest importance in Lord Parker C.J.'s advice to judges is his reference to the need to avoid telling juries that the absence from the witness box is to be equated with guilt.... How should these principles be applied in this case? In our judgment there is nothing in the complaint about the cumulative effects of the comments, particularly as the trial judge at the beginning of his summing up explained accurately and clearly that the appellant had a right to remain silent and to rest his defence on the presumption that he was innocent until proved guilty.... Our law, however, does not require a defendant to give evidence and a judge must not either by express words or impliedly give jurors to understand that a defence cannot succeed unless the defendant gives evidence. Unfortunately, probably by a slip of the tongue, that is what the trial judge did when he said to the jury: 'Is it not essential that he should go into the witness box and tell you that himself and be subject to cross-examination about it? Well, he did not do so and there it is.' He did overstep the limits of justifiable comment; he should not have said what he did. How far did these few words in a long summing up affect the jury's verdict? This must always be a matter of speculation, but we are confident on the facts of this case that the jury would have come to the same verdict if the trial judge had not said what he did. There has been no miscarriage of justice. The appeal is dismissed." The conviction of murder, rather than manslaughter, therefore stood.

R. v. **Wickham** (1971) 55 Cr.App.R. 199 (C.A.). It was held that, where there is a conflict in the evidence relating to two defendants, counsel for one has the right to comment upon the failure of the other to testify, and the judge has no discretion to prevent such comment. Fenton Atkinson L.J. (delivering the judgment of the Court of Appeal) said (pp. 203–204): "The Criminal Evidence Act 1898 restricts the prosecution from making such comment, but says nothing to restrict counsel for the co-accused, and it is perhaps important to notice that when one looks at section 1(*f*)(iii), when the right is given to the co-accused to cross-examine about character any other person charged [in the same proceedings], in that instance the court has no discretion to prevent such cross-examination when evidence has been given against a co-accused. . . . It seems right to this Court that, whereas there is a fetter on the prosecution, a co-accused ought to be free through his counsel to put his case as he in his discretion thinks fit."

Chapter 9

PRESENTATION AND CREDIBILITY OF ORAL EVIDENCE

AFTER a witness has been sworn or has affirmed[1] he is questioned by the advocate of the party calling him. This questioning is known as examination-in-chief. Although the purpose of examination-in-chief is to elicit testimony in support of the version of the facts which the party calling the witness seeks to establish, generally speaking resort may not be had to the asking of leading questions in order to achieve this. Also, although a witness will often be permitted, subject to certain safeguards, to refresh his memory by referring to a previously prepared document,[2] there are severe restrictions upon the putting of questions about his former statements with a view either to their being treated as evidence of the facts stated therein or to their being used to bolster his credibility by demonstrating consistency. Such statements are often referred to as "self-serving."[3] A party may call another witness to contradict unfavourable evidence given by a witness whom he has called; but he may not attempt to discredit his own witness unless he first obtains the leave of the judge to treat that witness as hostile.

Immediately after his examination-in-chief a witness may be cross-examined by the opponent's advocate, with a view to casting doubt upon the evidence which he has given and to eliciting evidence favourable to the opponent. Leading questions may be put in cross-examination, but the judge has a power to disallow oppressive questioning. All witnesses who have been examined-in-chief may be cross-examined except one who was called for the sole purpose of producing a document. Moreover, a witness is liable to cross-examination not merely by the opponent of the party calling him but also by all other parties. This is the position even though the witness may not have given evidence unfavourable to the other party (*e.g.* a co-accused) who seeks to cross-examine him; but cross-examination is not then permitted if it is directed not to the merits but to discrediting the witness. There are limits upon the reception of evidence of previous

---

[1] For the exceptional cases in which the requirement of an oath or affirmation is dispensed with see Chapter 8, *supra.*

[2] Generally speaking little attempt is made to prevent a witness from refreshing his memory *before* giving evidence.

[3] For the principal cases in which evidence of a witness's prior statement is admissible to confirm his testimony, although not necessarily as evidence of their truth, see the *Note* following *Corke* v. *Corke & Cook* [1958] P. 93 (C.A.), *infra.*

inconsistent statements of a witness under cross-examination.[4] Moreover, answers given by a witness under cross-examination to questions concerning collateral facts must be treated as final in the sense that, although, of course, they may not be accepted by the jury, cross-examining counsel cannot call further evidence in order to contradict them. To this collateral evidence rule there are, however, some exceptions.[5]

It is to be noted that failure to cross-examine on evidence given in examination-in-chief which an opponent wishes to contradict may be held to imply acceptance of that evidence and thus preclude contradiction. But this is a general rather than an absolute rule, and is especially liable to be disregarded in proceedings before lay justices.

If a witness is cross-examined the advocate for the party who called him may then re-examine him, but such re-examination must be confined to matters arising out of cross-examination, and new matter may be introduced only with leave of the judge. At the same time the course of cross-examination may have had the effect of rendering admissible in re-examination evidence which would not have been admissible in examination-in-chief. So too previously inadmissible evidence of prior consistent statements may only be received if rendered admissible by the course of cross-examination.[6] Leading questions may be asked in re-examination only to the extent that they could have been asked in examination-in-chief.

The materials set out in this Chapter illustrate some of the permissible limits of the examination-in-chief, cross-examination and re-examination of witnesses. The final section of this Chapter contains materials concerned with the very limited extent to which a party may be allowed to call further evidence after closing his case. Additional restrictions upon the cross-examination of the accused in a criminal case, imposed by the Criminal Evidence Act 1898, s.1, proviso (f), read in conjunction with proviso (e),[7] are separately illustrated by the materials set out in Chapter 23.

A. EXAMINATION-IN-CHIEF

Stephen: A Digest of the Law of Evidence, Art. 140 (12th ed., rev. 1936).
Leading Questions. "Questions suggesting the answer which the person putting the

---

[4] The admissibility under cross-examination of a witness's previous statements which are inconsistent with his evidence-in-chief is controlled by the Criminal Procedure Act 1865, ss.4 and 5 (Part Two, *infra*). These sections apply in civil as well as criminal proceedings and re-enact the Common Law Procedure Act 1854, ss.23 and 24. But the purposes for which such a statement, when admitted, may be used are limited. At common law it can be used only to impugn the credibility of the witness, and does not itself constitute evidence of the facts stated (unless it falls within an exception to the hearsay rule, see Chapter 14, *infra*). However, by virtue of the Civil Evidence Act 1968, s.3(1)(a) (Part Two, *infra*), the statement is in civil proceedings also admissible as evidence of any fact of which the maker could have given oral evidence.
[5] See the *Note* following *R.* v. *Riley* (1887) 18 Q.B.D. 481 (C.C.R.), *infra*.
[6] But see, too, Civil Evidence Act 1968, s.2 (Part Two, *infra*).
[7] Part Two, *infra*.

question wishes or expects to receive, or suggesting disputed facts as to which the witness is to testify, must not, if objected to by the adverse party, be asked in examination-in-chief, or in re-examination, except with the permission of the Court, but such questions may be asked in cross-examination."

Note.—The term "leading question" is one of those expressions the meaning of which gives rise to relatively little difficulty in practice but is hard to explain in words. The underlying principle is that a party's own witness must not be "prompted." The gist of the matter is that a question must not be so framed that, with regard to the matter in dispute, it suggests the answer which the questioner hopes to receive. Nor must the question be couched in a way which assumes something to have occurred when the dispute is as to whether that thing did occur. Thus on a trial for assault, where it is in dispute whether any assault ever took place, a witness should not generally be asked, "Did you see the prisoner strike A," but preferably, "Were you walking down Green Street?" "Did something attract your attention?" Nor should the witness be asked before he has deposed that he saw the prisoner strike A "What did A do when the prisoner struck him?" The framing of questions so as to be clear to the witness without "leading" him often requires considerable skill.

It may be said shortly that leading questions may only be put in examination-in-chief (a) on merely introductory matters, such as the name or occupation of the witness, (b) on other matters not in dispute, (c) as to the identification of persons or things, (d) to assist the memory of a witness or to lead his mind to the matter referred to, and (e) for miscellaneous other unobjectionable purposes.

Nicholls v. **Dowding and Kemp** (1815) 1 Stark. 81 (Nisi Prius). In order to prove that the defendants were partners, a witness was asked whether one of them had not interfered in the business of the other. The question was objected to as a leading one, but the court allowed it to be put. Lord Ellenborough C.J. said: "I wish that objections to questions as leading might be a little better considered before they are made. It is necessary, to a certain extent, to lead the mind of the witness to the subject of inquiry. If questions are asked to which the answer "Yes" or "No" would be conclusive, they would certainly be objectionable; but in general no objections are more frivolous than those which are made to questions as leading ones."

Note.—This prohibition on questions answerable by "Yes" or "No" is clearly inadequate as a test for determining whether a question is leading. A question may be framed so as to be answered "Yes" or "No" without the implication that "Yes" rather than "No" (or vice versa) is the hoped-for answer, in which case it is usually unobjectionable. Again, it is harmless advocacy to frame a question to an advocate's own witness so as to invite him to answer it in a way which would damage his case. The indignant "No" in answer consequently carries all the more weight. It must be remembered, too, that the inflection of the voice may render a proper question objectionable or vice versa.

R. v. **Richardson** [1971] 2 Q.B. 484 (C.A.). Before the trial of the defendant on charges of burglary and attempted burglary relating to offences which had taken place about 18 months earlier, four prosecution witnesses were on the initiative of prosecuting counsel shown statements which they had made to the police a few weeks after the alleged offences. The defendant was convicted and appealed on the ground *inter alia* that, as these witnesses had been allowed to refresh their memories before entering the witness box, the evidence was inadmissible. The appeal was dismissed. Sachs L.J. in the course of delivering the judgment of the court said (pp. 489–490): "First, it is to be observed that it is the practice of the courts not to allow a witness to refresh his memory in the witness-box by reference to written statements unless made contemporaneously. Secondly, it has been recognised in a circular issued in April 1969 with the approval of the Lord Chief Justice and the judges of the Queen's Bench Division (the repositories of the common law) that witnesses for the prosecution in criminal cases are normally though not in all circumstances) entitled, if they so request, to copies of any statements taken from them by police officers. Thirdly, it is to be noted that witnesses for the defence are normally, as is known to be the practice, allowed to have copies of their statements and to refresh their memories from them at any time up to the moment when they go into the witness-box—indeed, Mr. Sedgemore was careful not to submit that there was anything wrong about that. Fourthly, no one has ever suggested that in civil proceedings witnesses may not see their statements up to the time when they go into the witness-box. One has only to think for a moment of witnesses going into the box to deal with accidents which took place five or six years previously to conclude that it would be highly unreasonable if they were not allowed to see them.

Is there, then, anything wrong in the witnesses in this case having been offered an opportunity to see that which they were entitled to ask for and to be shown on request? In a case such as the present, is justice more likely to be done if a witness may not see a statement made by him at a time very much closer to that of the incident?

Curiously enough, these questions are very bare of authority. Indeed, the only case which has a direct bearing on this issue is one which was decided not in this country but on appeal in the Supreme Court of Hong Kong in 1966: *Lau Pak Ngam* v. *The Queen* [1966] Crim.L.R. 443. In the view of each member of this court this case contains some sage observations, two of which are apt to be quoted. One of them is: 'Testimony in the witness-box becomes more a test of memory than of truthfulness if witnesses are deprived of the opportunity of checking their recollection beforehand by reference to statements or notes made at a time closer to the events in question.' The other is: 'Refusal of access to statements would tend to create difficulties for honest witnesses but be likely to do little to hamper dishonest witnesses.'

With those views this court agrees. It is true that by the practice of the courts of this country a line is drawn at the moment when a witness enters the witness-box; when giving evidence there in chief he cannot refresh his memory except by a document which, to quote the words of *Phipson on Evidence*, 11th ed. (1970), p. 634, para. 1528: 'must have been written either at the time of the transaction or so shortly afterwards that the facts were fresh in his memory.' (Incidentally, this definition does provide a measure of elasticity and should not be taken to confine witnesses to an over-short period.) This is, moreover, a practice which the courts can enforce: when a witness is in the box the court can see that he complies with it.

The courts, however, must take care not to deprive themselves by new, artificial rules of practice of the best chances of learning the truth. The courts are under no compulsion unnecessarily to follow on a matter of practice the lure of the rules of logic in order to produce unreasonable results which would hinder the course of justice. Obviously it would be wrong if several witnesses were handed statements in circumstances which enabled one to compare with another what each had said. But there can be no general rule (which, incidentally, would be unenforceable, unlike the rule as to what can be done in the witness-box) that witnesses may not before trial see the statements which they made at some period reasonably close to the time of the event which is the subject of the trial. Indeed, one can imagine many cases, particularly those of a complex nature, where such a rule would militate very greatly against the interests of justice."

R. v. **Westwell** [1976] 2 All E.R. 812 (C.A.). On similar facts the Court of Appeal approved *R.* v. *Richardson* (*supra*). Delivering the judgment of the court, Bridge L.J. went on to say (p. 815): "Since hearing the argument in this appeal, our attention has been called to the decision of the Divisional Court in *Worley* v. *Bentley* [1976] 2 All E.R. 449 in which the same point arose. The court held that it was desirable but not essential that the defence should be informed that witnesses have seen their statements. We agree. In some cases the fact that a witness has read his statement before going into the witness box may be relevant to the weight which can properly be attached to his evidence and injustice might be caused to the defendant if the jury were left in ignorance of that fact.

Accordingly, if the prosecution is aware that statements have been seen by witnesses it will be appropriate to inform the defence. But if, for any reason, this is not done, the omission cannot of itself be a ground for acquittal. If the prosecution tell the defence that the witness has been allowed to see his statement the defence can make such use of the information as it thinks prudent, but in any event the defence, where such a fact may be material, can ask the witness directly when giving evidence whether the witness has recently seen his statement. Where such information is material it does not ultimately matter whether it is volunteered by the prosecution or elicited by the defence."

Note.—Where a prosecution witness refreshes his memory from a notebook outside court before giving evidence, the accused is entitled to examine the contents of the notebook and cross-examine the witness on the relevant matters contained in it: *Owen* v. *Edwards* (1983) Cr.App.R. 191 (D.C.).

MAUGHAM v. HUBBARD

6 L.J.(o.s.)K.B. 229; **8 B. & C. 14**; 2 Man. & Ry.K.B. 5; 108 E.R. 948 (K.B.: 1828)

A witness may refresh his memory by referring to any writing or document made by himself at or soon after the transaction in question. But it is not necessary that the witness should have any independent recollection of the fact recorded, if he is prepared to swear to it on seeing the writing or document.
Refreshing a witness's memory by inspecting a document does not make the document evidence at common law.

A witness, called to prove the receipt of a sum of money, was shown an acknowledgment of the receipt of the money signed by himself. On seeing it, he said he had no doubt that he had received it, although he had no recollection of the fact. It was held that this was sufficient parol evidence of the payment of the money, and that the written acknowledgment having been used to refresh the memory of the witness, and not as evidence of the payment, did not require any stamp.

LORD TENTERDEN C.J.: In order to make the paper itself evidence of the receipt of the money it ought to have been stamped. The consequence of its not having been stamped might be that the party who paid the money, in the event of the death of the person who received it, would lose his evidence of such payment. Here the witness, on seeing the entry signed by himself, said that he had no doubt that he had received the money. The paper itself was not used as evidence of the receipt of the money, but only to enable the witness to refresh his memory; and when he said that he had no doubt that he had received the money there was sufficient parol evidence to prove the payment.

BAYLEY J.: Where a witness called to prove the execution of a deed sees his signature to the attestation, and says that he is, therefore, sure that he saw the party execute the deed, that is a sufficient proof of the execution of the deed, though the witness add that he has no recollection of the fact of the execution of the deed.

Note.—As to the rule that an unstamped document, which would ordinarily require stamping, may be used merely to refresh memory, see the Stamp Act 1891 (Part Two, *infra*).

In cases in which the witness's memory is refreshed, not in the sense that his present recollection is actually revived, but only in the sense that he accepts that his past recollection must have been as recorded, English law generally requires that the document used by the witness be the original: *Doe d. Church and Phillips* v. *Perkins* (1790) 3 Term Rep. 749; *Howard* v. *Camfield* (1836) 1 Jur. 71; *R.* v. *Harvey* (1869) 11 Cox C.C. 346; but *cf. Topham* v. *McGregor* (1844) 1 Can. & Kin. 320. More generally contrast the decision of the New Zealand Court of Appeal in *R.* v. *Naidanovici* (1962) N.Z.L.R. 334, where, distinguishing *Maugham* v. *Hubbard*, it held that, when a document is used to refresh the memory of a witness, who prepared it but who has no independent recollection of the transaction recorded in it, and the witness relies upon and adopts the record which he made, his evidence being co-extensive with the contents of the document, the document itself becomes admissible in evidence,—although it must not be treated as separate confirmatory evidence of the witness's oral testimony.

At common law the opposite party is entitled to inspect any writing or document used to refresh a witness's memory in order to check it and to cross-examine upon it. Cross-examination does not make it documentary evidence, but it will do so in so far as it refers to parts of the writing or document other than those used by the witness in refreshing his memory (*Gregory* v. *Tavernor* (1833) 6 C. & P. 280; recently approved and applied in *R.* v. *Britton* [1987] 1 W.L.R. 539 (C.A.)). This appears to reflect the rule that a party who calls for and inspects a document held by the other party is bound to put it in evidence if required to do so (*Wharam* v. *Routledge* (1805) 5 Esp. 235). When a document is "made evidence" in this way, it is not automatically rendered admissible as evidence of the truth of statements contained in it. In *R.* v. *Virgo* (1978) 67 Cr.App.R. 323 the Court of Appeal quashed a conviction because the trial judge had not directed the jury on the limited use that could be made of diaries which had been made evidence following wide-ranging cross-examination. They could be used to show the witness's creditworthiness, but not to show the truth of their contents so as to constitute corroboration.

A prosecution witness may refresh his memory from his statement, and the suggestion that he may do so may come from the judge; but it is better that the witness remain in court to refresh his memory: *R.* v. *Tyagi* [1986] C.L.Y. 588 (C.A.). Documents which were used for refreshing the memory of a witness may now be admissible as evidence in civil cases under the Civil Evidence Act 1968, s.3(2) (Chapter 16 and Part Two, *infra*).

Common examples of writings used to refresh memory are entries in notebooks, diaries and account-books.

R. v. **Simmonds** (1967) 51 Cr.App.R. 316 (C.A.). In the course of delivering the judgment of the court Fenton Atkinson L.J. said (pp. 329–330): "Next we deal with two objections taken at length in the course of the evidence of interviews. The Customs officers who conducted the interviews with the accused did not make any note of what was said at the time, but made up their notes from their recollections, assisted in some cases by written questionnaires they had with them, as soon as they returned to their offices. When they gave evidence at the trial, they had their notes in front of them and read out what was so recorded. Two objections were taken: first that a witness can refresh his memory only from a contemporaneous note, that is a note actually written down as the interview proceeded; and, second, that in any event the witness was not entitled to read from his notes. It was contended that such a practice made nonsense of the system of oral evidence and involved a pretence that the witness was refreshing his memory when, in truth, he had no real memory of what was said. The judge followed what has certainly been the established practice of our criminal courts for a very long time. He held that the notes had been written up at the first convenient opportunity as soon as the officers returned to their offices and that they were entitled to read from their notes. On the first objection, the question of whether a note is to be regarded as contemporaneous is a matter of fact and degree, and, in our view, the judge was plainly right in allowing the witnesses to use notes prepared as soon as they got to their offices, which was, in fact, the first available opportunity. On the second objection, assuming that notes of interviews of such length and complexity have to be introduced in evidence-in-chief, no other course was sensible or practicable. It is the course which is constantly adopted by police officers giving evidence of a long interview or series of interviews with suspected persons, and is certainly a better and fairer practice than the witness trying to learn his evidence by heart. It is a practice long established and not open to objection. These points could, of course, be used to attack the accuracy of the records and were so used by [counsel]...again and again, but the legal submissions were without merit."

Attorney General's Reference (No. 3 of 1979) (1979) 68 Cr.App.R. 411 (C.A.). A police officer made brief jottings of an interview with the defendant and later compiled notes of the interview with the aid of these jottings. The Court of Appeal held that the trial judge had wrongly ruled that the officer could only refresh his memory from the original jottings and not from his notebook. It was sufficient that the notes had been written up when the facts were still fresh in the police officer's memory.

R. v. Mills [1962] 1 W.L.R. 1152 (C.C.A.). A police officer was allowed to refresh his memory by referring to a note which he had written from a tape recording. The recording, which was of conversations between the two appellants, had been made by the officer, who had himself overheard these conversations. He had then used the recording (which was not put in evidence) to assist him when writing up the note. At the trial the officer also gave evidence that he remembered what had been said.

R. v. Kelsey (1982) 74 Cr.App.R. 213 (C.A.). The appellant appealed against his conviction of burglary on the ground that a witness called for the prosecution had wrongly been permitted to refresh his memory about a car registration number by reference to a note made at his (the witness's) dictation by a police officer and verified orally, but not visually, as accurate by the witness at the time. The officer had given evidence that the note produced was the note that the witness saw him making and heard him read back. It was held that in these circumstances the trial judge had been right to allow the witness to refresh his memory about the car's registration number. Taylor J., delivering the judgment of the Court of Appeal, disapproved the dictum of Winn J. in *R. v. Mills* (*supra*) to the effect that a witness can only refresh his memory from a note he has made himself or "from a note made by some other person which he has contemporaneously, in the sense of within a short time, himself seen, read and adopted as accurate." Taylor J. said (p. 217) "...there is no magic in verifying by seeing as opposed to verifying by hearing,—what must be shown is that (the) witness...has verified in the sense of satisfying himself whilst the matters are fresh in his mind (1) that a record has been made, and (2) that it is accurate."

Note.—See too: *Burrough* v. *Martin* (1809) 2 Camp. 112 (where a ship's captain who had inspected his ship's log book throughout a voyage and found the entries in it to be accurate was allowed to refresh his memory from it although the entries were made by the mate); *Dyer* v. *Best* (1866) 4 H. & C. 189; and *R.* v. *Langton* (1876) 2 Q.B.D. 296 (C.C.R.).

R. v. **Cheng** (1976) 63 Cr.App.R. 20. Cheng was one of a number of persons whom police officers kept under observation as suspected drug pedlars. He was later charged with unlawfully supplying a dangerous drug. At his trial one of the policemen who had kept watch was called for the prosecution. He no longer had the notebook in which he had recorded his observations and sought to refresh his memory from a statement which he had prepared from that notebook for use at the committal proceedings. The defence objected because the statement was only a partial and not an exact copy of the notebook, but the trial judge allowed him to refer to it. This ruling was upheld by the Court of Appeal. Lawton L.J., delivering the judgment of the court, said (p. 24): "If the statement...is substantially what is in the notes and there is evidence to that effect, then the judge should allow the witness to refresh his memory from the statement...."

R. v. **Sekhon** (1987) 85 Cr.App.R. 19 (C.A.). The appellant appealed against conviction of offering to supply a controlled drug. At the trial police officers had used a log (compiled by one officer, the entries based upon reports of others having been verified by those others) to refresh their memories. The jury asked to see the log and the trial judge had decided in their absence that it should be made an exhibit. The appeal was on the ground that, although the jury might have been allowed to inspect the log, it was wrong to allow them to have it with them whilst they considered their verdict. It was held that, even if the jury had not raised the matter themselves, it would have been open to the prosecution to introduce the log, since otherwise the cross-examination of the police officers could not have been assessed by the jury. However, the jury should have had explained to them the true status of the log. The judge's failure in this regard was an error; but in the circumstances it did not render the conviction unsafe or unsatisfactory. The appeal was, therefore, dismissed. Woolf L.J., reading the judgment of the court, expressly rejected the submission that a distinction is to be drawn between the use for refreshment purposes, of notes made by the witness himself of matters which he had observed, and a record such as the log. His Lordship stated (pp. 22–23) the position regarding both cases as follows:

"(1) That they can both be referred to by witnesses to refresh their memory if the usual basis for permitting this to be done is established without the record being put before the jury.

(2) That the documents used by the witness for the purpose of refreshing his memory must be available for inspection by the other parties who can cross-examine on the basis of that document if it is relevant to do so. In the majority of cases the fact that there is such cross-examination will not make the record evidence in the case, nor will it be necessary for a jury to inspect the document, and it will not be appropriate for the record to become an exhibit.

(3) Where however the nature of the cross-examination involves a suggestion that the witness has subsequently made up his evidence, which will usually involve, if not expressly at least by implication, the allegation that the record is concocted, the record may be admissible to rebut this suggestion and, if the nature of the record assists as to this, to show whether or not it is genuine, that is

to say whether or not it has the appearance of being a contemporaneous record which has not subsequently been altered.

(4) Where the record is inconsistent with the witness's evidence, it can be admitted as evidence of this inconsistency.

(5) It is also appropriate for the record to be put before the jury where it is difficult for the jury to follow the cross-examination of the witness who has refreshed his memory, without having the record or, in practice, copies of the records before them.

(6) However, subject to the exception mentioned below, in the cases referred to where the record is permitted to go before the jury, it will not be placed before them as evidence of the truth of the contents of the record, and it will not amount to corroboration of the evidence given by the witness refreshing his memory from the record. It will on the one hand be before them for the more limited purpose of being a 'tool'... to assist the jury to evaluate the truth of the evidence given in the witness box by the witness. Whether in these circumstances it is appropriate to treat the document as an exhibit is of no practical importance. In a case involving a lot of documents, it may be appropriate to give it an exhibit number just to identify the document.

(7) There may be cases where it is also convenient to use the record as an *aide memoire* as to the witness's evidence where that evidence is long and involved. However care should be exercised in adopting this course in cases where the evidence, and therefore the record, is bitterly contested, because of the danger that the use of the document for this purpose could result in the jury misunderstanding its status and lead to their wrongly regarding the document as being evidence in itself.

(8) Although normally the document when admitted is not evidence of the truth of its contents, in those cases where it provides, because of its nature, material by which its authenticity can be judged, then in respect of that material and only for the purpose of assessing its authenticity it can amount to evidence in the case."

CORKE v. CORKE AND COOK

[1958] P. 93; [1958] 1 All E.R. 224 (C.A.: 1957)

Evidence of a statement made by a witness on an earlier occasion is generally not admissible to confirm his testimony.

A husband, who was living separately from his wife, went to his wife's house. About midnight the husband and an inquiry agent accused the wife and a lodger of having recently committed adultery together, which they denied. Some 10 minutes later the wife telephoned to her doctor, asking him to examine herself and the lodger, to show that there had not been recent sexual intercourse. The doctor refused. On the husband's petition for divorce, the court admitted evidence of the telephone conversation, and dismissed the suit. On appeal it was held by a majority that this evidence was inadmissible, though the appeal was dismissed on the ground of lack of adequate evidence of adultery.

HODSON L.J. held the evidence inadmissible, but MORRIS L.J. dissented on the question of the admissibility of the evidence.

SELLERS L.J.:...In my view, not only is the evidence of what the wife did and said valueless and might indeed be misleading to the court, but it is not admissible. To what issue, it should be asked, does it go? It does nothing to prove the condition of either the female or male organ respectively of the parties alleged to be involved. It does nothing to disprove the intercourse the husband had alleged. The most that could be said is that the wife was showing a belief in her own story and adding some reason why the court should believe her. In this case I do not think the conduct and statement of the wife have that effect, but it is clear that a skilful witness might well embark on circumstantial matters to bolster up his or her story. Neville J.'s statement in *Jones* v. *South Eastern & Chatham Railway Co.* (87 L.J.K.B. 775, 779) cited by my Lord, "that you are not entitled to give evidence of statements on other occasions by the witness in confirmation of her testimony" neatly and accurately, in my opinion, states the law which is applicable to the question raised by the appellant.

Whether this rule is strictly logical or not, it is one which keeps the evidence to the main issues in dispute and tends to avoid deception of the court by a resourceful witness....

...The wife's conduct and statement cannot, in my view, be regarded as revealing consciousness of innocence. They reveal at the most a consciousness that the doctor would not find any physical proof of guilt. I apprehend that the dishonest may be resourceful in giving an air of innocence to their transactions. To say "You can take my finger-prints" would establish nothing unless finger-prints for comparison were available. If the wife's statement in question was not admissible in her favour, the doctor's evidence of what the wife said was even more clearly inadmissible. Were it to be held otherwise, one wonders where ingenuity in bolstering up a witness's evidence would stop.

The idea of telephoning the doctor originated in this case not from the wife but from the lodger, the co-respondent, and after some discussion the parties got dressed and went out to a telephone kiosk. There was abundant time to weigh up the advantages of such a course and to prepare, if necessary, for the requested examination. I would hold that the appellant should succeed on the legal point of the inadmissibility of evidence, which was his sole ground of appeal, and that the commissioner's first view that the evidence was inadmissible was correct.

Nevertheless, the appeal as a whole should be dismissed.

Note.—See, too, *e.g. Fox* v. *General Medical Council* [1960] 1 W.L.R. 1017 (P.C.) *per* Lord Radcliffe at pp. 1024–1025: "The purpose of such evidence of a witness's previous statement is and can only be to support his credit, when his veracity has been impugned, by showing a consistency in his account which adds some probative value to his evidence in the box. Generally speaking, as is well known, such confirmatory evidence is not admissible, the reason presumably being that all trials, civil and criminal, must be conducted with an effort to concentrate evidence upon what is capable of being cogent and, as was remarked by Humphreys J. in *Rex* v. *Roberts* (1942) 1 All E.R. 187 (C.C.A.), it does not help to support the evidence of a witness, who is the accused person, to know that he has frequently told other persons before the trial what his defence was. Evidence to that effect is therefore in a proper sense immaterial."

There are some well-established, but diverse and specific, exceptions to the rule that evidence of a witness's prior statements is inadmissible to confirm his testimony. These include (1) complaints of sexual assaults; (2) statements admitted in re-examination to rebut allegations of recent fabrication; (3) some previous statements said to be admissible as part of the *res gestae* (see too Chapter 15, *infra*); (4) statements made by an accused when confronted with incriminating facts; (5) previous identifications of an accused; (6) statements in writing by a witness adduced in a civil case under the Civil Evidence Act 1968 (Part Two, *infra*). The first five of these categories of exceptional case are illustrated by the immediately following cases.

R. v. LILLYMAN

[1896] 2 Q.B. 167; 65 L.J.M.C. 195; 74 L.T. 730; 12 T.L.R. 473; 18 Cox C.C. 346; 44 W.R. 654 (C.C.R.: 1896)

In cases of rape and some other sexual offences, the fact that a complaint was made by the prosecutrix shortly after the alleged occurrence, and particulars of the complaint, so far as they relate to the charge, may be given in evidence by the prosecution. The complaint is evidence of the consistency of the conduct and assertions of the prosecutrix, and as being inconsistent with her consent.
The judge ought to inform the jury that the statement is not evidence of the facts complained of, and must not be so regarded by them.

On a charge of attempted rape and indecent assault the mistress of the prosecutrix, being a person to whom she would naturally complain, was allowed to state what the prosecutrix told her about the incident, in the absence of the prisoner, very shortly after the commission of the act.

Hawkins J. (delivering the judgment of the court, which included Lord Russell C.J., Pollock B., Cave and Wills JJ.): ... It is necessary in the first place to have a clear understanding as to the principles upon which evidence of such a complaint, not on oath, nor made in the presence of the prisoner, nor forming part of the *res gestae*, can be admitted. It clearly is not admissible as evidence of the facts complained of; those facts must therefore be established, if at all, upon oath by the prosecutrix or other credible witness, and, strictly speaking, evidence of them ought to be given before evidence of the complaint is admitted. The complaint can only be used as evidence of the consistency of the conduct of the prosecutrix with the story told by her in the witness-box, and as being inconsistent with her consent to that of which she complains.

In every one of the old textbooks, proof of complaint is treated as a most material element in the establishment of a charge of rape or other kindred charge.... It is too late, therefore, now to make serious objection to the admissibility of evidence of the fact that a complaint was made, provided it was made as speedily after the acts complained of as could reasonably be expected....

After very careful consideration we have arrived at the conclusion that we are bound by no authority to support the existing usage of limiting evidence of the complaint to the bare fact that a complaint was made, and reason and good sense are against our doing so. The evidence is admissible only upon the ground that it was a complaint of that which is charged against the prisoner; it can be legitimately used only for the purpose of enabling the jury to judge for themselves whether the conduct of the woman was consistent with her testimony on oath given in the witness-box.... In reality, affirmative answers to such stereotyped questions as these, "Did the prosecutrix make a complaint" (a very leading question, by the way) "of something done to herself?" "Did she mention a name?" amount to nothing to which any weight ought to be attached; they tend rather to embarrass than to assist a thoughtful jury, for they are consistent either with there having been a complaint or no complaint of the prisoner's conduct. To limit the evidence of the complaint to such questions and answers is to ask the jury to draw important inferences from imperfect materials, perfect materials being at hand, and in the cognisance of the witness in the box. In our opinion, nothing ought unnecessarily to be left to speculation or surmise.

It has been sometimes urged that to allow the particulars of the complaint would be calculated to prejudice the interests of the accused and that the jury would be apt to treat the complaint as evidence of the facts complained of. Of course, if it were so left to the jury, they would naturally so treat it. But it never could be legally so left, and we think it is the duty of the judge to impress upon the jury in every case that they are not entitled to make use of the complaint as any evidence whatever of those facts, or for any other purpose than that we have stated. With such direction we think the interests of an innocent accused would be more protected than they are under the present usage. For when the whole statement is laid before the jury they are less likely to draw wrong and adverse inferences, and may sometimes come to the conclusion that what the woman said amounted to no real complaint of any offence committed by the accused. . . .

Note.—The complaint should be made as soon as reasonably practicable after the offence occurred (see *R.* v. *Osborne* [1905] 1 K.B. 551 (C.C.R.) (*infra*); *R.* v. *Cummings* [1948] 1 All E.R. 551 (C.C.A.)).

R. v. OSBORNE

[1905]1 K.B. 551; 74 L.J.K.B. 311; 92 L.T. 393; 21 T.L.R. 288; 53 W.R. 494
(C.C.R.: 1906)

Evidence of a complaint made in the absence of the accused is admissible only in cases of rape and other sexual offences. The fact that the complaint has been made in answer to a question does not of itself render it inadmissible; but it must not have been elicited by questions of a leading and inducing or intimidating character.

Such evidence is admissible, whether consent is or is not a material element in the charge, in order to show the consistency of the conduct of the prosecutrix with her evidence.

On a charge of indecent assault on a girl aged 12, Keziah Parkes, evidence was given by another girl, aged 11, to the effect that she had left the prosecutrix with the prisoner shortly before the alleged offence, arranging to return soon. On her way back she met the prosecutrix running home, and said to her, "Why are you going home? Why did you not wait until we came back?" The answer, incriminating the prisoner, was admitted in evidence.

RIDLEY J. (delivering the judgment of the court, which included LORD ALVERSTONE C.J., KENNEDY, CHANNELL and PHILLIMORE JJ.):...It was contended for the prisoner that the evidence was inadmissible—first, because the answer made by the girl was not a complaint, but a statement of conversation, having been made in answer to a question; and secondly, because, as Keziah Parkes was under the age of thirteen, her consent was not material to the charge.

As to the first point.... It appears to us that the mere fact that the statement is made in answer to a question in such cases is not of itself sufficient to make it inadmissible as a complaint. Questions of a suggestive or leading character will, indeed, have that effect, and will render it inadmissible; but a question such as this, put by the mother or other person, "What is the matter?" or "Why are you crying?" will not do so. These are natural questions which a person in charge will be likely to put. On the other hand, if she were asked "Did So-and-so (naming the prisoner) assault you?" "Did he do this and that to you?" then the result would be different, and the statement ought to be rejected. In each case the decision on the character of the question put, as well as other circumstances, such as the relationship of the questioner to the complainant, must be left to the discretion of the presiding judge. If the circumstances indicate that but for the questioning there probably would have been no voluntary complaint, the answer is inadmissible. If the question merely anticipates a statement which the complainant was about to make, it is not rendered inadmissible by the fact that the questioner happens to speak first....

Upon the second point it was contended that, although under the decision of *R. v. Lillyman* [1896] 2 Q.B. 167 (C.C.R.) the particulars of a complaint made may in some circumstances be given in evidence on a charge of rape, that ruling does not extend to a charge of criminal knowledge or indecent assault where, as in the present case, consent is not legally material....

But...it appears to us that, in accordance with principle, such complaints are admissible, not merely as negativing consent, but because they are consistent with the story of the prosecutrix. In all ordinary cases, indeed, the principle must be observed which rejects statements made by anyone in the prisoner's absence. Charges of this kind form an exceptional class, and in them such statements ought, under the proper safeguards, to be admitted. Their consistency with the story told is, from the very nature of such cases, of special importance. Did the woman make a complaint at once? If so, that is consistent with her story. Did she not do so? That is inconsistent. And in either case the matter is important for the jury....

We are, at the same time, not insensible of the great importance of carefully observing the proper limits within which such evidence should be given. It is only to cases of this kind that the authorities on which our judgment rests apply; and our judgment also is to them restricted. It applies only where there is a complaint not elicited by questions of a leading and inducing or intimidating character, and only when it is made at the first opportunity after the offence which reasonably offers itself. Within such bounds we think the evidence should be put before the jury; the judge being careful to inform the jury that the statement is not evidence of the facts complained of, and must not be regarded by them, if believed, as other than corroborative of the complainant's credibility, and, where consent is in issue, of the absence of consent.

Note.—Evidence of a complaint may be received even though the prosecutrix does not testify as to the complaint: *Breen* v. *R.* (1976) 50 A.L.J.R. 534 (H.C. of Australia). Evidence of a complaint of a sexual offence against a young male person is admissible (*R.* v. *Camelleri* [1922] 2 K.B. 122 (C.C.A.)). See also *R.* v. *Wannell* (1922) 17 Cr.App.R. 53, where a complaint by a youth of 19 was admitted. However, in *R.* v. *Christie* [1914] A.C. 545 (H.L.) (Chapter 14, *infra*), the House of Lords declined to consider the application of the rule to a young boy. There is some conflict of rather meagre authority as to whether evidence of a complaint of non-sexual violence is admissible in any proceedings (see *R.* v. *Folley* (1896) 60 J.P. 569 and *R.* v. *Wink* (1834) 6 C. & P. 397, but contrast *Beatty* v. *Cullingworth* (1896) 60 J.P. 740; affirmed on appeal, *The Times*, January 14, 1897; see, too, dicta in *R.* v. *Osborne* [1905] 1 K.B. 551, 561 (C.C.R.); *Jones* v. *South Eastern and Chatham Ry.* (1917) 87 L.J.K.B. 775, 778 (C.A.) and *Gillie* v. *Posho Ltd.* [1939] 2 All E.R. 196, 200–201 (P.C.)). But such evidence does seem to be admissible in matrimonial causes (see *Berry* v. *Berry* (1898) 78 L.T. 688; *Fromhold* v. *Fromhold* [1952] 1 T.L.R. 1526, 1528 (C.A.)).

R. v. **Wallwork** (1958) 42 Cr.App.R. 153 (C.C.A.). The accused was charged with incest with his five-year-old daughter. The child was placed in the witness box but was unable to give evidence. Her grandmother was permitted to give details of a complaint made by the child to her. The Court of Criminal Appeal, although dismissing the appeal on the ground that no substantial miscarriage of justice had been caused, held the evidence to have been wrongly admitted. Lord Goddard C.J., delivering the judgment of the court, said (pp. 161–162): "In cases of rape or indecent assault it has always been held that evidence of a complaint and the terms of the complaint may be given, but they may be given only for a particular purpose, not as evidence of the fact complained of,... The evidence may be and is tendered for the purpose of showing consistency in her conduct and consistency with the evidence she has given in the box.... The child had given no evidence because when the poor little thing was put into the witness-box, she said nothing and could not remember anything. The learned judge had expressly told the jury to disregard her evidence altogether. Therefore, there was no evidence given by her with regard to which it was necessary to say what she had said to her grandmother was consistent;... the evidence [of the grandmother] ought not to have been given and the learned judge ought to have told the jury to disregard it. It was not evidence against the appellant of the facts on which the complaint was founded, and therefore we are bound to say that there was a wrongful admission of evidence in this case."

Note.—See, too, *Sparks* v. *R.* [1964] A.C. 964 (P.C.), Chapters 13 and 15 (*infra*).

Kilby v. **R.** (1973) 129 C.L.R. 460 (H.C.Aust.). The appellant had been convicted of rape. He sought special leave to appeal to the High Court of Australia on the ground *inter alia* that the judge was in error in not instructing the jury that the absence of a complaint by the prosecutrix at the earliest reasonable opportunity was evidence of her consent to intercourse. The High Court refused leave. Barwick C.J. said (pp. 466–472): "The submission is founded on the proposition that because evidence of proximate complaint is evidence, as it was said, that the woman had not consented, the lack of complaint must be evidence of consent. But, in my opinion, even granting the premises, the conclusion does not follow. Further, evidence of a complaint at the earliest reasonable opportunity is exceptionally admitted only as evidence of consistency in the account given by the woman claiming to have been raped: that is to say, it is admitted as matter going to her credit (see *R.* v. *Lillyman* [1896] 2 Q.B. 167, 170 *per* Hawkins J.; *Sparks* v. *R.* [1964] A.C. 964, 979). Because the account with which the complaint is said to show consistency is an account of intercourse without consent, it has often been said that the evidence of the complaint is evidence negating consent. In my opinion, this manner of expressing the function of the evidence of proximate complaint is not correct: though, as it shows consistency in her account of rape, the fact of the complaint buttresses her evidence of no consent or, as it was said in *R. v. Lillyman*, is inconsistent with consent. At times also it is said with technical inaccuracy that the evidence of such a complaint is corroborative of the woman's evidence of the rape. It is quite clearly not so corroborative.... [T]he admissibility of that evidence in modern times can only be placed, in my opinion, upon the consistency of statement or conduct which it tends to show, the evidence having itself no probative value as to any fact in contest but, merely and exceptionally constituting a buttress to the credit of the woman who has given evidence of having been subjected to the sexual offence. To understand the reasons for the admissibility and the use which can properly be made of the evidence of recent complaint is to deny the validity of the applicant's proposition that lack of complaint is probative of consent. I can see no ground in logic for saying that because evidence of complaint is admitted to show consistency in the story told by the woman, evidence of non-complaint is evidence of her consent to intercourse. In my opinion, quite apart from the fact that there may be many reasons why a complaint is not made, the want of a complaint does not found on inference of consent. It does tell against the consistency of the woman's account and accordingly is clearly relevant to her credibility in that respect...."

Nominal Defendant v. **Clements** (1961) 104 C.L.R. 476 (High Court of Australia). Dixon C.J. said (at p. 479): "If the credit of a witness is impugned as to some material fact to which he deposes upon the ground that his account is a late invention or has been lately devised or reconstructed, even though not with conscious dishonesty, that makes admissible a statement to the same effect as the account he gave as a witness, if it was made by the witness contemporaneously with the event or at a time sufficiently early to be inconsistent with the suggestion that his account is a late invention or reconstruction. But, inasmuch as the rule forms a definite exception to the general principle excluding statements made out of court and admits a possibly self-serving statement made by the witness, great care is called for in applying it. The judge at the trial must determine for himself upon the conduct of the trial before him whether a case for applying the rule of evidence has arisen and, from the nature of the matter, if there be an appeal, great weight should be given to his opinion by the appellate court. It is evident however that the judge at the trial must exercise care in assuring himself not only that the account given by the witness in his testimony is attacked on the ground of recent invention or reconstruction or that a foundation for such an attack has been laid by the party, but also that the contents of the statement are in fact to the like effect as his account given in his evidence and that having regard to the time and circumstances in which it was made it rationally tends to answer the attack. It is obvious that it may not be easy sometimes to be sure that counsel is laying a foundation for impugning the witness's account of a material incident or fact as a recently invented, devised or reconstructed story. Counsel himself may proceed with a subtlety which is the outcome of caution in pursuing what may prove a dangerous course. That is one reason why the trial judge's opinion has a peculiar importance."

Note.—This statement received the express approval of the Court of Appeal in *R. v. Oyesiku* (1972) 56 Cr.App.R. 240, 246–247. For earlier English authority see *R. v. Benjamin* (1913) 8 Cr.App.R. (C.C.A.); see, too, *R. v. Coll* (1889) 25 L.R.Ir. 522.

See, too, the Civil Evidence Act 1968, s.3(1)(*b*) (Part Two, *infra*) which provides that in civil proceedings a witness's prior statement proved for the purpose of rebutting an allegation of recent fabrication shall also be available as "evidence of any fact stated therein of which direct oral evidence would be admissible." But in criminal cases such evidence, formally at least, is only circumstantial evidence negativing fabrication.

R. v. Fowkes, *The Times*, March 8, 1856 (Assizes); and see Stephen, *A Digest of the Law of Evidence* (12th rev. ed., 1948), p. 8. The accused, who was commonly known as "the butcher," was charged with murder. The son of the dead man testified that he and a police officer were sitting in a room with his father when a face appeared at the window through which the fatal shot was fired. The witness stated that he thought that the face was that of the accused, and he was allowed to add that on seeing the face he had shouted "There's Butcher." The police officer, who had not seen the face, was also allowed to testify that he had heard the son shout this.

Note.—Evidence of a witness's previous consistent statement which forms part of the *res gestae* may in criminal cases be admissible, under the exception to the hearsay rule associated with that term (see Chapter 15, *infra*), to show its truth as well as consistency. In civil cases, however, compliance with the provisions of Civil Evidence Act 1968 (Part Two, *infra*) would be necessary in order for it to be received to show its truth.

R. v. Storey (1968) 52 Cr.App.R. 334 (C.A.). The police found a large quantity of cannabis in the accused's flat. She told them that it belonged to a man who had brought it there against her will. If this were true it would afford a complete answer to the crime with which she was charged. At the close of the prosecution case a submission by the defence that there was no case to answer was rejected by the judge. The Court of Appeal upheld this ruling on the ground that the defendant's statement to the police was not evidence of the facts stated therein, but only of her reaction to police inquiries. This evidence of the accused's reaction was not sufficient to negative the evidence of possession suggested by the presence of cannabis in her flat so as to justify a finding of no case to answer. Widgery L.J., delivering the judgment of the court on this aspect of the case, said (pp. 337–338): "The question which arises in this case is whether the fact that she gave shortly afterwards an explanation which, if true, would provide a completely innocent explanation is enough to produce a situation in which the learned judge's duty was to say that there was no case to answer.... We think it right to recognise that a statement made by the accused to the police, although it always forms evidence in the case against him, is not in itself evidence of the truth of the facts stated. A statement made voluntarily by an accused person to the police is evidence in the trial because of its vital relevance as showing the reaction of the accused when first taxed with the incriminating facts. If, of course, the accused admits the offence, then as a matter of shorthand one says that the admission is proof of guilt, and, indeed, in the end it is. But if the accused makes a statement which does not amount to an admission, the statement is not strictly evidence of the truth of what was said, but is evidence of the reaction of the accused which forms part of the general picture to be considered by the jury at the trial."

Note.—See, too, *R. v. Barbery* (1975) 62 Cr.App.R. 248 (C.A.); *R. v. Donaldson* (1976) 64 Cr.App.R. 59 (C.A.); *R. v. McCarthy (G.J.)* (1980) 71 Cr.App.R. 142 (C.A.) and *R. v. Pearce* (1979) 69 Cr.App.R. 365, 369–370 (C.A.).

R. v. Fannon (1922) 22 S.R.(N.S.W.) 427. Ferguson J. (delivering the judgment of the Supreme Court of New South Wales) said (at p. 430): "The most trustworthy evidence of identification, that by which the jury must always be chiefly guided is that given in the witness box by witnesses who can say on oath 'That is the man,' and whose evidence can be tested by cross-examination. In cases where there has been a considerable lapse of time between the offence and the trial, and where there might be a danger of the witness's recollection of the prisoner's features having become dimmed, no doubt it strengthens the value of the evidence if it can be shown that in the meantime, soon after the commission of the offence, the witness saw and recognised the prisoner. And even where there has been no delay of the sort, in any case where a witness of the offence has not yet seen a person whom the police have afterwards arrested on the charge of having committed it, the question whether or not such a witness recognises the person arrested as the offender may be of the greatest importance either in detecting the guilty or in clearing the innocent. Upon these grounds evidence has been admitted in criminal trials from time immemorial of the identification of the accused witnesses out of Court. The practice has been for the witnesses to be asked to pick the person they recognise from a number of other persons so chosen as to remove as far as possible any suspicion of outside suggestion."

Note.—See too *R.* v. *Christie* [1914] A.C. 545 (H.L.); *R.* v. *Osbourne and Virtue* [1973] Q.B. 678 (C.A.).

EWER v. AMBROSE

3 B. & C. 746; 3 L.J.(o.s.)K.B. 128; 5 Dow. & Ry.K.B. 629; 107 E.R. 910
(K.B.: 1825)

If a witness gives evidence which is unfavourable to the party calling him, the party may contradict him by other witnesses; but he may not call general evidence to show that his own witness is not to be believed.

In an action for money had and received, the defence being that the defendant was jointly liable with a partner against whom judgment had been recovered, a witness was called by the defendant to prove the partnership, but he proved the contrary. It was held that the defendant could not discredit his own witness, but he could contradict him by other witnesses.

HOLROYD J.: I take the rule of law to be that, if a witness proves a case against the party calling him, the latter may show the truth by other witnesses. But it is undoubtedly true that, if a party calls a witness to prove a fact, he cannot, when he finds the witness proves the contrary, give general evidence to show that that witness is not to be believed on his oath, but he may show by other evidence that he is mistaken as to the fact which he is called to prove....

LITTLEDALE J.: Where a witness is called by a party to prove his case, and he disproves that case, I think the party is still at liberty to prove his case by other witnesses. It would be a great hardship if the rule were otherwise, for if a party had four witnesses upon whom he relied to prove his case, it would be very hard that, by calling first the one who happened to disprove it, he should be deprived of the testimony of the other three.... The order in which the witnesses happen to be called ought not, therefore, to make any difference....

Stephen, Digest of the Law of Evidence (12th ed.) art. 147. "If a witness appears to the judge to be hostile to the party calling him, that is to say, not desirous of telling the truth to the court at the instance of the party calling him, the judge may in his discretion permit his examination by such party to be conducted in the manner of a cross-examination to the extent to which the judge considers necessary for the purpose of doing justice."

GREENOUGH v. ECCLES

28 L.J.C.P. 160; 7 W.R. 341; 5 Jur.(N.S.) 766; 5 C.B.(N.S.) 786; 141 E.R. 315
(Common Pleas: 1859)

Although a party calling a witness may not discredit him generally if he proves unfavourable, yet if he proves actually hostile, the party may, by leave of the judge, show that the witness has made a previous inconsistent statement.

A witness called by the defendants supported the plaintiff's case.

WILLIAMS J.: The question in this case is whether, in construing the terms of the 22nd section of the Common Law Procedure Act, 1854 "in case the witness shall prove adverse," the word "adverse" ought to be understood as meaning merely "unfavourable," or as meaning "hostile."
... The section lays down three rules as to the power of a party to discredit his own witness: first, he shall not be allowed to impeach his credit by general evidence of his bad character. Secondly, he may contradict him by other evidence. Thirdly, he may prove that he has made at other times a statement inconsistent with his present testimony.
These three rules appear to include the principal questions that have ever arisen on the subject.... The law relating to the first two of these rules was settled before the passing of the Act, while, as to the third, the authorities were conflicting....
The section requires the judge to form an opinion that the witness is adverse, before the right to contradict or prove that he has made inconsistent statements is to be allowed to operate. This is reasonable and indeed necessary, if the word "adverse" means "hostile," but wholly unreasonable and unnecessary if it means "unfavourable." On these grounds we think the preferable construction is that, in case the witness shall, in the opinion of the judge, prove "hostile," the party producing him may not only contradict him by other witnesses, as he might heretofore have done, and may still do, if the witness is unfavourable, but may also, by leave of the judge, prove that he has made inconsistent statements....

WILLES J. agreed.

COCKBURN C.J.: ... The solution by my learned brothers is a solution of a difficulty, otherwise incapable of any solution, but I am not satisfied therewith, and without actually dissenting from their judgment, I do not altogether assent to it.

Note.—Section 22 of the Common Law Procedure Act 1854, which in the above case came before the court for construction, provided that "A party producing a witness shall not be allowed to impeach his credit by general evidence of bad character, but he may, in case the witness shall, in the opinion of the judge, prove adverse, contradict him by other evidence, or, by leave of the judge, prove that he has made at other times a statement inconsistent with his present testimony." The section was repealed, but it is re-enacted by the Criminal Procedure Act 1865, which applies to both civil and criminal cases (Part Two, *infra*).

Section 3 of this Act permits the "adverse" witness to be questioned, by the counsel who called him, as to a previous inconsistent statement; and, if necessary, it permits proof that the witness made such a statement. In *R. v. Booth* (1982) 74 Cr.App.R. 123 (C.A.) it was reaffirmed that leave of the judge is required before a party can put inconsistent statements to his own hostile witness. The effect of the procedure in criminal cases is merely to cancel the hostile testimony; it does not result in substituting for that testimony the previous statement (see *R. v. Harris* (1927) 20 Cr.App.R. 144 (C.C.A.) and *R. v. Golder* [1960] 1 W.L.R. 1169 (C.C.A.), *infra*). But in civil cases the position is otherwise: see the Civil Evidence Act 1968, s.3(1) (Part Two, *infra*).

Section 4 of the 1865 Act (Part Two, *infra*) does not apply to cross-examination of a party's own hostile witness: *R. v. Booth, supra*.

Witnesses who must be called to prove attestation are regarded as the court's witnesses, and evidence of previous inconsistent statements by them is admissible, even though they are not hostile (see *Oakes v. Uzzell* [1932] P. 19).

Price v. **Manning** (1889) 42 Ch.D. 372 (C.A.). The plaintiff called the defendant as a witness to prove a point in his case. The defendant was cross-examined. On his re-examination the plaintiff's counsel put questions to him in the nature of cross-examination, treating him as a hostile witness. The trial judge refused to allow this to be done. The Court of Appeal upholding the trial judge's exercise of his discretion emphasised that the discretion is operative even if a party's witness is the opposing party. Lopes L.J. said (p. 374): "Whether the witness called by one party is a litigant or non-litigant, it is a matter of discretion in the presiding judge whether the witness has shown himself so hostile as to justify his cross-examination by the party calling him. This rule applies in a case when an opponent is called as a witness."

Note.—It must be observed that the judge can only allow a party to "cross-examine" his own witness within the limited provisions of the Criminal Procedure Act 1865, at least in that he cannot allow him to discredit generally a witness whom he has produced as a reliable person. For a curious situation where the plaintiff called one of two co-defendants as his witness, see *Tedeschi v. Singh* [1948] Ch. 319.

As to treating one's own witness as hostile in re-examination compare *Cartwright v. W. Richardson & Co. Ltd.* [1955] 1 W.L.R. 340; *Hilton v. Lancashire Dynamo Nevelin Ltd.* [1964] 1 W.L.R. 952; *Harvey v. Smith-Wood* [1964] 2 Q.B. 171; Civil Evidence Act 1968, s.3(1) (Part Two, *infra*).

R. v. THOMPSON

64 Cr.App.R. 96 (C.A.: 1976)

The common law right of the judge in his discretion to allow cross-examination by a party when his witness proves to be hostile is not destroyed by section 3 of the Criminal Procedure Act 1965.

LORD PARKER C.J. (delivering the judgment of the court which included CANTLEY and JUPP JJ.): ... [T]he appellant was convicted of two counts of incest with his daughter Anne, one of indecent assault on the same girl, one of attempted incest with his daughter Sylvia, and one of indecent assault on Sylvia. . . .

The daughter Anne, who was 16 at the time of the trial, was called as a witness. She had given a statement to the police earlier implicating her father in these offences, and at the trial she was called into the witness box to be sworn, and was sworn, but then refused to give evidence.

. . . the learned judge gave counsel permission to treat the witness as hostile. She was asked leading questions accordingly, her statement was put to her, and in the end she agreed that her statement was true and that was of course the basis of the case against the appellant in respect of the daughter Anne. . . .

Section 3 [of the Criminal Procedure Act 1865] provides. . . [the L.C.J. proceeded to read out the first part of the section].

It is to be observed in the text of that section that the party producing a witness is permitted in certain circumstances to contradict, and that he may produce a statement inconsistent with present testimony. The argument of [counsel for the appellant] is that in order to get the benefit of section 3 it is not enough to show, as in this case, that the girl was hostile and stood mute of malice. It is essential, so the argument goes, that there should be a contradiction of a previous statement and an inconsistent current statement, and since in this case there was no such contradiction, the previous statement standing alone and the girl refusing to produce a second statement either consistent or otherwise, it is contended that the section has no application.

We do not find it necessary to express any view upon the section as applied to cases where there is an inconsistent statement. We think this matter must be dealt with by the provisions of the common law in regard to recalcitrant witnesses. Quite apart from what is said in section 3, the common law did recognise that pressure could be brought to bear upon witnesses who refused to co-operate and perform their duties. We have had the advantage of looking at one or two of the earlier cases prior to the Act to which I have already referred and their treatment of this matter.

The first is *Clarke* v. *Saffery* (1824) Ry. & M. 126 . . . [where] in the course of the trial the plaintiff's counsel called the defendant, who was also one of the assignees, as a witness, and objection was taken by the defendant's counsel to the mode of examining the defendant. There does not seem to be a second statement contradicting the earlier one there, yet Best C.J. said, at p. 126: "there is no fixed rule which binds the counsel calling a witness to a particular mode of examining him. If a witness, by his conduct in the box, shows himself decidedly adverse, it is always in the discretion of the judge to allow a cross-examination. . . . "

. . . We are dealing here with a witness who shows himself decidedly adverse, and whereupon, as Best C.J. says, it is always in the discretion of the judge to allow cross-examination. After all, we are only talking about the asking of leading questions. . . .

Then in the case of *Bastin* v. *Carew* (1824) Ry. & M. 127 Lord Abbott C.J. said, at p. 127: "I mean to decide this, and no further. But in each particular case there must be some discretion in the presiding judge as to the mode in which the examination should be conducted, in order best to answer the purposes of justice." That statement, which is consistently supported in later authorities, again seems to us to cover this case admirably. The short question after all is: was the judge right in allowing counsel to cross-examine in the sense of asking leading questions? On the authority of *Clarke* v. *Saffrey* and *Bastin* v. *Carew* it seems to us that he was right and there is no reason to suppose that the subsequent statutory intervention into this subject has in any way destroyed or removed the basic common law right of the judge in his discretion to allow cross-examination when a witness proves to be hostile.

Accordingly . . . this appeal must be dismissed.

R. v. **Prefas and Pryce** (1988) 86 Cr.App.R. 111 (C.A.). The appellant and one, Pryce, were charged with arson. At the scene of the fire three petrol containers were found. A witness had made a statement to the police that they were his containers and that he had given them to a man named Chris—the name by which the appellant was known. The witness had failed to identify the appellant at an identity parade, but had later told a police officer that he had deliberately done so out of fear for the safety of his family. At the end of the witness's evidence-in-chief at the trial the prosecution obtained permission to treat him as hostile on the basis that he was deliberately refraining from telling the truth by not identifying the appellant. The prosecution also obtained leave to call the police officer to prove his previous inconsistent statement. The appellant's appeal against conviction was dismissed: the trial judge had been correct. The Lord Chief Justice said (p. 114) that all the ingredients of the common law requirements for treating the witness as hostile were present.

R. v. **Golder** [1960] 1 W.L.R. 1169 (C.C.A.). The accused was charged with the theft of a gold watch. Lord Parker C.J. (delivering the judgment of the Court of Appeal) said (pp. 1171–1173): "As counsel for the prosecution frankly admitted, the [rest of the prosecution] evidence was not enough to do more than create a case of grave suspicion, and accordingly he sought to rely on a witness, Taylor. Before the committing magistrates she swore that on April 20 the appellant Golder, whom she knew as Chuck, had brought her a gold watch which was, in fact, part of the property stolen in Newmarket early in April. At the trial she went back on her story and counsel for the prosecution obtained leave to treat her as adverse and cross-examined her. He did not, however, succeed in extracting from her an admission that her deposition was true, still less that it was the appellant Golder who handed her the gold watch. In the course of his summing-up the deputy chairman dealt with the question of the watch and the conflicting testimony of Taylor in a way which plainly indicated to the jury that it was open to them to act upon the evidence contained in her deposition notwithstanding her repudiation of it.... In the judgment of this court the direction to the jury in regard to Mrs. Taylor's deposition was wrong in law and, as was intimated at the end of the hearing of the appeals, all three convictions must be quashed. A long line of authority has laid down the principle that while previous statements may be put to an adverse witness to destroy his credit and thus to render his evidence given at the trial negligible, they are not admissible evidence of the truth of the facts stated therein.... In the judgment of this court, when a witness is shown to have made previous statements inconsistent with the evidence given by that witness at the trial, the jury should not merely be directed that the evidence given at the trial should be regarded as unreliable; they should also be directed that the previous statements, whether sworn or unsworn, do not constitute evidence upon which they can act."

Note.—The position could be different if the witness had accepted or adopted his earlier statement. For the position in civil cases see the Civil Evidence Act 1968, s.3(1)(*a*), Part Two, *infra*.

In *Driscoll* v. *R.* (1977) 137 C.L.R. 517 (H.C.Aust.) Gibbs J., after quoting the last sentence (starting "In the judgment . . .") set out above, said (p. 536): "In that passage the Court of Criminal Appeal was dealing succinctly with the proper direction to be given in relation to the two different questions that arise when a witness is shown to have made a previous statement inconsistent with the evidence given by that witness at the trial. The first is as to the use to which the statement previously made out of court may be put, and the second is as to the effect of the previous statement on the value of the testimony given by the witness in court. As to the first of these questions it is clearly settled that the previous statement is admitted merely on the issue of credibility, and is not evidence of the truth of the matters stated in it: *Taylor* v. *R.* (1918) 25 C.L.R. 573; *Deacon* v. *R.* [1947] 3 D.L.R. 772, and *R.* v. *Pearson* [1964] Qd.R. 471. Since the jury, if uninstructed, are not likely to be aware of the limited use to which the previous statement may be put, it is essential that this should be made clear to them by the trial judge. As to the second question, the whole purpose of contradicting the witness by proof of the inconsistent statement is to show that the witness is unreliable. In some cases the circumstances might be such that it would be highly desirable, if not necessary, for the judge to warn the jury against accepting the evidence of the witness. From the point of view of the accused this warning would be particularly necessary when the testimony of the witness was more damaging to the accused than the previous statement. In some cases the unreliability of the witness might be so obvious as to make a warning on the subject almost superfluous. It is possible to conceive other cases in which the evidence given by a witness might be regarded as reliable notwithstanding that he had made an earlier statement inconsistent with his testimony. For these reasons I cannot accept that it is always necessary or even appropriate to direct a jury that the evidence of a witness who has made a previous inconsistent statement should be treated as unreliable. The statement to that effect in *R.* v. *Golder, Jones and Porritt* was obiter, because in that case the trial judge had in fact warned the jury that the evidence was unreliable and the Court of Criminal Appeal was concerned only with the judge's failure to direct the jury that they could not act on the unsworn statement. Although what was said in *R.* v. *Golder, Jones and Porritt* has been cited with approval (see *R.* v. *Oliva* [1965] 3 All E.R. 116 at 123; [1965] 1 W.L.R. 1028 at 1936–7), it cannot be accepted that in cases where a witness has made a previous inconsistent statement there is an inflexible rule of law or practice that the jury should be directed that the evidence should be regarded as unreliable."

B. CROSS-EXAMINATION

Parkin v. **Moon** (1836) 7 C. and P. 408 (Nisi Prius). The plaintiff's counsel was cross-examining one of the defendant's witnesses (who, it seemed, was an unwilling witness for the defendant, but a willing one on the part of the plaintiff), by putting leading questions in the usual way. The defendant's counsel submitted that, in the circumstances, leading questions ought not to be allowed even on cross-examination. It was held that they were admissible. Alderson B. said (p. 409): "I apprehend you may put a leading question to an unwilling witness on the examination-in-chief at the discretion of the judge; but you may always put a leading question in cross-examination whether a witness be unwilling or not."

Wood v. **Mackinson** (1840) 2 Mood. and Rob. 273 (Nisi Prius). The plaintiff's counsel called a witness, who was sworn in the usual way; but, before he had put any question to him, he said he had been misinstructed as to what the witness was able to prove, and he should not examine him at all. The defendant's counsel then claimed the right to cross-examine the witness. It was held that he had no right to do so. Coleridge J. said (pp. 275–6): "[U]pon the whole, it appears to me that the more satisfactory principle to lay down is this, that if there really be a mistake, whether on the part of counsel or officer, and that mistake be discovered before the examination-in-chief has begun, the adverse party ought not to have the right to take advantage of this mistake by cross-examining the witness. Here the learned counsel explains that there has been a mistake, which consists in this, that the witness is found not to be able to speak at all as to the transaction which was supposed to be within his knowledge. This is, I think, such a mistake as entitles the party calling the witness to withdraw him without his being subject to cross-examination. If, indeed, the witness had been able to give evidence of the transaction which he was called to prove, but the counsel had discovered that the witness, besides that transaction, knew other matters inconvenient to be disclosed, and therefore attempted to withdraw him, that would be a different case. I think the defendants have here no right to cross-examine the witness."

Note.—A witness who is called to produce a document and is not sworn cannot be cross-examined (*Summers* v. *Moseley* (1834) 2 Cr. & M. 477), nor can such a witness be cross-examined if he has been sworn unnecessarily (*Rush* v. *Smith* (1834) 1 Cr.M. & R. 94). A witness called by the judge himself cannot be cross-examined without the leave of the judge (see *Coulson* v. *Disborough* [1894] 2 Q.B. 316 (C.A.), as explained in *Re Enoch and Zaretzky, Bock & Co.'s Arbitration* [1910] 1 K.B. 327 (Chapter 8, *supra*).

R. v. **Hilton** [1972] 2 Q.B. 421 (C.A.). Hilton and nine others were tried for aiding and abetting an affray. The first accused gave evidence-in-chief in his own defence. His evidence did not adversely reflect on any of the other nine. Counsel for a number of the accused desired to cross-examine him, but the trial judge refused to allow this on the ground that that accused's evidence had not been in any way adverse to any of the other accused. On appeal Fenton Atkinson L.J. said (pp. 423–424): "In our view the ruling of the learned judge was wrong.... counsel for one of two or more co-accused has for many years past invariably been allowed to cross-examine a co-accused who has given evidence whether or not such evidence was in any way adverse to his client.... [W]e are all quite satisfied that the practice to allow such cross-examination is well established in our courts and that it is necessary for justice to be done. This can be illustrated as follows. A and B are charged with an offence and are separately represented. A gives evidence in his own defence, making no mention of B. B's counsel knows that there is in fact important evidence that A can give in B's favour. If he cannot elicit the matter in cross-examination, he has no right to call A to give evidence a second time as A is not a compellable witness and may be unwilling for a number of reasons to give evidence for a second time.... We agree entirely with the statement of the South African judge, Harcourt J., in the case of *The State* v. *Langa* (1963 (4) S.A. 941, 945)... when he said: 'An accused ought, if a fair trial is what is aimed at, to be at liberty to cross-examine a co-accused or any witness (not called by him) who may not have inculpated him in any way in order to establish facts which may tend to support the alibi.' "

Note.—An accused may not examine a co-accused as to credit (as distinct from the merits of the issue) if he has not given evidence against him. See, too, the Criminal Evidence Act 1898, s.1, proviso (*f*)(iii), Part Two, *infra* and Chapter 23, *infra*.

BROWNE v. DUNN

6 R. 67 (H.L.: 1894)

A witness may be cross-examined as to his credibility, but he should have his attention drawn to any facts with respect to which it is intended to impeach his credit by other witnesses, so as to give him an opportunity of explanation, unless the evidence he gives is so incredible that it is reasonable to let him leave the box without such questions being put.

In an action for libel witnesses were not cross-examined on a material matter. It was held that the jury could not be asked afterwards to disbelieve them.

LORD HERSCHELL L.C.: ... It seems to me to be absolutely essential to the proper conduct of a cause, where it is intended to suggest that a witness is not speaking the truth on a particular point, to direct his attention to the fact by some questions put in cross-examination showing that that imputation is intended to be made, and not to take his evidence and pass it by as a matter altogether unchallenged, and then, when it is impossible for him to explain, as perhaps he might have been able to do if such questions had been put to him, the circumstances which it is suggested indicate that the story he tells ought not to be believed, to argue that he is a witness unworthy of credit. My Lords, I have always understood that if you intend to impeach a witness you are bound, whilst he is in the box, to give him an opportunity of making any explanation which is open to him; and, as it seems to me, that is not only a rule of professional practice in the conduct of a case, but is essential to fair play and fair dealing with witnesses. Sometimes reflections have been made upon excessive cross-examination of witnesses, and it has been complained of as undue; but it seems to me that a cross-examination of a witness which errs in the direction of excess may be far more fair to him than to leave him without cross-examination, and afterwards to suggest that he is not a witness of truth, I mean upon a point on which it is not otherwise perfectly clear that he has had full notice beforehand that there is an intention to impeach the credibility of the story which he is telling. Of course I do not deny for a moment that there are cases in which that notice has been so distinctly and unmistakably given, and the point upon which he is impeached, and is to be impeached, is so manifest, that it is not necessary to waste time in putting questions to him upon it. All I am saying is that it will not do to impeach the credibility of a witness upon a matter on which he has not had any opportunity of giving an explanation by reason of there having been no suggestion whatever in the course of the case that his story is not accepted. ...

LORD HALSBURY: ... To my mind nothing would be more absolutely unjust than not to cross-examine witnesses upon evidence which they have given, so as to give them notice, and to give them an opportunity of explanation, and an opportunity very often to defend their own character, and, not having given them such an opportunity, to ask the jury afterwards to disbelieve what they have said, although not one question has been directed either to their credit or to the accuracy of the facts they have deposed to. ...

LORD MORRIS: ... There is another point upon which I would wish to guard myself, namely, with respect to laying down any hard-and-fast rule as regards cross-examining a witness as a necessary preliminary to impeaching his credit. In this case, I am clearly of opinion that the witnesses, having given their testimony, and not having been cross-examined, having deposed to a state of facts which is quite reconcilable with the rest of the case, it was impossible for the plaintiff to ask the jury at the trial, and it is impossible for him to ask any legal tribunal, to say that those witnesses are not to be credited. But I can quite understand a case in which a story told by a witness may have been of so incredible and romancing a character that the most effective cross-examination would be to ask him to leave the box. I therefore wish it to be understood that I would not concur in ruling that it was necessary, in order to impeach a witness's credit, that you should take him through the story which he had told, giving him notice by the questions that you impeached his credit.

LORD BOWEN concurred.

Note.—See, too, *R.* v. *Fenlon and others* (1980) 71 Cr.App.R. 307 (C.A.).
The rule applies not only to credibility or credit, but also to statements of fact by a witness. Failure to cross-examine implies acceptance of the truth of the evidence given by the witness (*R.* v. *Hart* (1932) 23 Cr.App.R. 202 (C.C.A.)).

ATTORNEY-GENERAL v. HITCHCOCK

16 L.J.Ex. 259; 11 Jur. 478; 1 Exch. 91; 154 E.R. 38 (Exchequer: 1847)

A witness's answer to a question concerning collateral facts or matters is final and cannot be contradicted by other evidence.

The defendant, a maltster, was charged on information with having used a cistern for the making of malt, without making an entry thereof, as required by Act of Parliament. A witness, having sworn that the cistern had been used, was asked if he had not said to one Cook that the Excise officers had offered him £20 to say the cistern had been used; and he denied that he had made such statement. The defendant's counsel thereupon called Cook, and proposed to ask him whether the witness had told him so. The evidence was disallowed.

POLLOCK C.B.: . . . The test of whether an inquiry is collateral or not is, whether the fact to be elicited is material to the issue. If it be, then the witness may be contradicted, or, as is better put by my Brother Alderson, thus: If you ask a witness whether he has not made a certain statement which would be material, and opposed to part of his testimony, you may then call witnesses to prove that he has made the statement, and the jury are at liberty to believe either the one account or the other. . . . The statement which may be contradicted must be one which refers to matter that may be given in evidence, and if answered in one way would contradict part of the witness's testimony, and be material.

There is, however, a distinction between contradicting a witness in particulars stated by him, and those which have reference to his motives, temper, character, and feelings. . . . A witness may be asked how he stands affected towards one of the parties; and if his relation towards them is such as to prejudice his mind, and fill him with sentiments of revenge or other feelings of a similar kind, and if he denies the fact, evidence may be given to show the state of his mind and feelings. But these cases of the witness's connection with the parties in feeling and sentiments are not to be confounded with those other cases where the matter to be admissible in evidence must be connected with the question. . . .

In the present case it could not be proved that a bribe was offered to the witness and not accepted, for such a fact is clearly irrelevant to the matter in issue. The offer of a bribe is a matter of no importance, if it be not accepted, for it does not disparage the party to whom it is offered. . . .

ALDERSON B.: . . . . A witness, however, is not to be examined as to collateral facts. In many cases his doing a particular act is collateral. In such cases his evidence as to the fact is to be received as final; but no witness ought to be called on to prove his whole life; and if contradiction of his testimony were permitted, he ought to be allowed to support it by other evidence, and to prove his innocence; the result of which would be, that an endless amount of collateral issues would have to be tried. The convenient administration of justice, therefore, requires that this course should not be adopted. If the witness has spoken falsely he may be indicted for perjury. When the answer given is not material to the issue, public convenience requires that it be taken as decisive, and that no contradiction be allowed. In the present case, the witness was asked whether he had been offered a bribe to say the cistern had been used. This was not material, nor did it qualify what had gone before, for his being offered a bribe did not show that he was not a fair and credible witness.

ROLFE B. delivered a judgment to the same effect.

Note.—The same rule had previously been expressed by Lawrence J. in these words—"I will permit questions to be put to a witness as to any improper conduct of which he may have been guilty, for the purpose of trying his credit; but when those questions are irrelevant to the issue on the record, you cannot call other witnesses to contradict the answer he gives" (*Harris* v. *Tippett* (1811) 2 Camp. 637).

R. v. **Holmes** (1871) 41 L.J.M.C. 12 (C.C.R.). The accused was charged with indecent assault, which, from the evidence, appeared to amount to an attempt at rape. The defence was consent. The prosecutrix, in her cross-examination, was asked if she had had connection with another man, and she denied it. The man in question was then called to contradict her, but the judge disallowed the evidence. The Court for Crown Cases Reserved affirmed the conviction. Kelly C.B. said (pp. 13–14): "On an indictment for rape, or for attempt to commit a rape, or for an indecent assault, which, upon the circumstances of the case, amounts to an attempt to commit a rape, a question put to the prosecutrix as to an act of connection with a particular person, and denied by her, cannot be contradicted. If a witness is cross-examined as to a collateral fact, the answer must be taken for better or worse, and the witness cannot be contradicted. If the question were admissible it might involve an inquiry into her whole life. . . . There is no doubt the prosecutrix may be asked as to connection with the prisoner on a prosecution for rape. There the fact has a direct bearing on the question before the court, which involves the fact of consent or non-consent on the part of the prosecutrix. . . . "

Note.—The extent to which evidence of the complainant's sexual experience with others is admissible at all is now limited by the Sexual Offences (Amendment) Act 1976, s.2 (Part Two, *infra*), which provides that at a trial for a "rape offence" the complainant may not be cross-examined about her sexual experience with anyone other than the defendant except by leave of the judge.

R. v. RILEY

18 Q.B.D. 481; **56 L.J.M.C. 52;** 56 L.T. 371; 35 W.R. 382; 16 Cox C.C. 191
(C.C.R.: 1887)

In prosecutions for rape, assault with intent to commit rape or indecent assault, evidence of similar conduct on other occasions between the prosecutrix and the accused is admissible, as being relevant to the issue of consent.

LORD COLERIDGE C.J.: ... The indictment charged the prisoner with an assault with intent to commit a rape upon a woman, and the woman having denied previous voluntary connection with the accused, the prisoner proposed to show that she had had such connection with him. That evidence was rejected. It is clear that it was receivable. It has been held again and again that if in such a case evidence as to connection with persons other than the accused is denied by the prosecutrix, evidence offered in contradiction must be rejected. There are good reasons, other than those suggested in argument, for rejecting such evidence. It would be very unfair and sometimes cruel to the prosecutrix to admit such evidence; but, in addition, it does not go to the point in issue. . . .

But rejection of evidence of previous voluntary connection with the prisoner is another matter, because not only does such evidence render it more likely that the woman has consented, but it is a line of examination going to the very point in issue.

Upon principle and authority, I think that the evidence in question was receivable.

POLLOCK B.: I agree. The only question is whether the evidence tendered was relevant to the issue. If it was irrelevant as merely going to the woman's character, as in the case of evidence as to connection by the woman with other men, then it was properly rejected. In my opinion, evidence as to her connection with the prisoner, whether of recent date or not, is clearly relevant to that issue.

STEPHEN, MATHEW and WILLS JJ. concurred. The conviction was quashed.

Note.—This decision is not affected by the Sexual Offences (Amendment) Act 1976 (Part Two, *infra*). But compare *R.* v. *Holmes* (*supra*). See, too, *Thomas* v. *David* (*infra*); also *R.* v. *Clarke* (1817) 2 Stark. 241 (Nisi Prius) and *R.* v. *Cox* (1987) 84 Cr.App. 132 (C.A.). (Chapter 22, *infra*).

Although a witness cannot usually be contradicted when he denies an imputation upon his credit, there are several well-established types of case in which this is permissible. These include (1) cases of denial by him of a previous conviction (see the Criminal Procedure Act 1865, s.6, Part Two, *infra*); (2) cases in which he has made a previous inconsistent statement (see the Criminal Procedure Act 1865, s.4, Part Two, *infra*); (3) to show prejudice or bias; (4) to show a general reputation for untruthfulness and (5) to show mental instability. The following cases illustrate the three latter situations.

For cases in which the witness's previous statement is in writing see the Criminal Procedure Act 1865, s.5 (Part Two, *infra*).

Thomas v. **David** (1836) 7 C. & P. 350 (Nisi Prius). In an action on a promissory note one of the plaintiff's witnesses, who was his female servant, and who was one of the attesting witnesses to the defendant's signature of the promissory note, was asked in cross-examination whether she did not constantly sleep in the same bed with her master. She said that she did not. The defendant was allowed to call a witness to prove that she did. Coleridge J. said (p. 351): "Is it not material to the issue, whether the principal witness who comes to support the plaintiff's case is his kept mistress? If the question had been, whether the witness had walked the streets as a common prostitute, I think that that would have been collateral to the issue, and that, had the witness denied such a charge, she could not have been contradicted; but here, the question is, whether the witness had contracted such a relation with the plaintiff as might induce her the more readily to conspire with him to support a forgery, just in the same way as if she had been asked if she was the sister or daughter of the plaintiff, and had denied that. I think that the contradiction is admissible."

Note.—Similarly, the denial of a witness who is prejudiced against a party may be contradicted by evidence. See, *e.g. R.* v. *Phillips* (1936) 26 Cr.App.R. 17 (C.C.A.), where it was held that the accused should have been allowed to call evidence to rebut his daughter's denial that they had been schooled by their mother to give evidence against him.

R. v. **Mendy** (1976) 64 Cr.App.R. 4 (C.A.). The appellant was charged with assault. At the trial, witnesses were kept out of court before giving evidence in accordance with normal practice. While a detective was giving evidence, a man in the public gallery was seen to be taking notes. He was then seen to leave the court and soon afterwards seen to be talking to the appellant's husband apparently describing the detective's evidence to him. The husband later gave evidence and under cross-examination denied that the incident with the man had occurred. The prosecution was given leave to call witnesses in rebuttal. The Court of Appeal held that this was proper. Geoffrey Lane L.J., delivering the judgment of the court, said (pp. 5–6): "A party may not, in general, impeach the credit of his opponent's witnesses by calling witnesses to contradict him on collateral matters, and his answers thereon will be conclusive.... [N]o one seriously suggests that the issue in the present case was other than collateral. On the other hand, it seems strange, if it be the case, that the court and the jury have to be kept in ignorance of behaviour by a witness such as that in the present case.... The truth of the matter is, as one would expect, that the rule is not all-embracing. It has always been permissible to call evidence to contradict a witness's denial of bias or partiality towards one of the parties and to show that he is prejudicial so far as the case being tried is concerned."

R. v. **Busby** (1982) 75 Cr.App.R. 79 (C.A.). This was an appeal against conviction of offences of burglary and of handling stolen goods. The appellant was alleged to have made certain remarks to the police when interviewed about these offences, which, although not clearly admissible, were very damaging. He did not give evidence at the trial, but his counsel cross-examined two police officers with a view to showing *inter alia* that the appellant had not made the remarks attributed to him, and also that one officer had (in the presence of another) threatened a potential defence witness to stop him giving evidence. Both officers denied that they had threatened this witness. The prosecution objected to this witness then being called to give evidence about the officer's visit to him. The trial judge upheld this objection, but the Court of Appeal held that he had been wrong to do so and quashed the conviction. Eveleigh L.J. (giving the judgment of the court) said (p. 82). "It is not always easy to determine when a question relates to facts which are collateral only, and therefore to be treated as final, and when it is relevant to the issue which has to be tried. . . . In the present case, the evidence if true, would have indicated that the officers were prepared to cheat in furtherance of the prosecution."

Note.—It is to be observed that the distinction, between cases falling outside the collateral facts inhibition, and those which are within it but saved by an exception to it, has not always been clearly drawn.

R. v. Brown and Hedley (1867) 36 L.J.M.C. 59 (C.C.R.). At the close of the case for the prosecution the counsel for the defendant, after having called several witnesses to character, proposed to call witnesses to prove that they would not believe the witnesses for the prosecution on their oaths. The court refused to receive such evidence, but stated a case for the Court for Crown Cases Reserved. The evidence was held admissible. Kelly C.B. said (p. 60): "It has been the practice to admit the evidence rejected in this case for centuries without dispute, . . . So long a practice cannot be altered but by the legislature."

Note.—See, too, *R. v. Richardson* [1969] 1 Q.B. 209 (C.A.), where it was emphasised that, when a witness has given evidence which is challenged as untruthful, it is open to the opponent to call another witness to give evidence, not only that the impugned witness's general reputation as to veracity, but also that his own opinion based on personal knowledge, is such that the impugned witness is not to be believed upon oath.

TOOHEY v. METROPOLITAN POLICE COMMISSIONER

[1965] A.C. 595; [1965] 1 All E.R. 506; 49 Cr.App.R. 148 (H.L.: 1965)

A witness may be discredited by medical evidence to the effect that he is suffering from some disease, defect or abnormality of mind. Such evidence is not confined to general opinion of the witness's unreliability, but may show the reasons for the diagnosis and also the extent to which the witness's credibility is affected.

The appellant was charged with two others with assaulting a youth, Madden, with intent to rob. The defence was that they were trying to help him, but that he became hysterical and accused them of hitting him and of being after his money. A doctor gave evidence for the defence that when Madden was examined at the police station he was in a hysterical state. At the first (abortive) trial the doctor was allowed to state his opinion that Madden was more prone to hysteria than a normal person. At the new trial the doctor's evidence of opinion was held inadmissible, and the appellant was convicted. The Court of Criminal Appeal dismissed his appeal, but the House of Lords quashed the conviction on the ground that the doctor's evidence had been wrongly excluded.

LORD PEARCE: ... My Lords, there are two separate and distinct aspects of this appeal, the first whether the medical evidence was admissible as relevant to the facts in issue at the trial, regardless of whether or not it affected the credibility of Madden as a witness, the second whether it was admissible as showing that Madden's evidence was unreliable....

The second question, whether it was permissible to impeach the credibility of Madden, qua witness, by medical evidence of his hysterical and unstable nature, raises a wider and more important problem which applies to evidence in criminal and civil cases alike.

The Court of Criminal Appeal held that such evidence was not admissible since they were bound by the case of *Gunewardene* [1951] 2 K.B. 600....

Throughout *Gunewardene's* case the court dealt with the problem created by the mental disease and mental abnormality of the witness as if it were identical with the problem of moral discredit and unveracity. The referred to many cases dealing with bad character and reputation, but to none which dealt with mental disturbance....

Human evidence shares the frailties of those who give it. It is subject to many cross-currents such as partiality, prejudice, self-interest and, above all, imagination and inaccuracy. Those are matters with which the jury, helped by cross-examination and common sense, must do their best. But when a witness through physical (in which I include mental) disease or abnormality is not capable of giving a true or reliable account to the jury, it must surely be allowable for medical science to reveal this vital hidden fact to them. If a witness purported to give evidence of something which he believed that he had seen at a distance of 50 yards, it must surely be possible to call the evidence of an oculist to the effect that the witness could not possibly see anything at a greater distance than 20 yards, or the evidence of a surgeon who had removed a cataract from which the witness was suffering at the material time and which would have prevented him from seeing what he thought he saw. So, too, must it be allowable to call medical evidence of mental illness which makes a witness incapable of giving reliable evidence, whether through the existence of delusions or otherwise.

It is obviously in the interest of justice that such evidence should be available. The only argument that I can see against its admission is that there might be a conflict between the doctors and that there would then be a trial within a trial. But such cases would be rare and, if they arose, they would not create any insuperable difficulty, since there are many cases in practice where a trial within a trial is achieved without difficulty. And in such a case (unlike the issues relating to confessions) there would not be the inconvenience of having to exclude the jury since the dispute would be for their use and their instruction....

Gunewardene's case was, in my opinion, wrongly decided. Medical evidence is admissible to show that a witness suffers from some disease or defect or abnormality of mind that affects the reliability of his evidence. Such evidence is not confined to a general opinion of the unreliability of the witness but may give all the matters necessary to show, not only the foundation of and reasons for the diagnosis, but also the extent to which the credibility of the witness is affected.

I would therefore allow the appeal.

LORDS REID, MORRIS OF BORTHY-Y-GEST, HODSON, and DONOVAN concurred.

R. v. Mackenney; R. v. Pinfold (1983) 76 Cr.App.R. 271 (C.A.). The appellants had been convicted of murder. One ground of appeal was that the trial judge had refused to allow the defence to have access to medical reports on the principal prosecution witness which, it was contended, might have shown him to be suffering from some disease or defect or abnormality of mind such as to affect the reliability of his evidence. The Court of Appeal upheld the judge's exercise of his discretion in refusing disclosure of these reports on the ground "that they in no way disclosed (on the contrary in fact) that Childs [the witness] was suffering from any mental disorder, defect or abnormality of mind" (*per* Ackner L.J. at p. 273). The defence had also sought to call evidence of their own, including that of an expert psychologist who had watched Childs giving evidence and had read the trial papers. The Court of Appeal upheld the trial judge's refusal to allow this. The court seems to have indicated that a psychologist with no medical qualifications can never be called to give expert evidence as to whether a witness is suffering from any specific disease or defect or abnormality of mind. Ackner L.J. said (p. 275): "No doubt his training as a psychologist gave him some insight into the medical science of psychiatry. However, not being a medical man, he had of course no experience of direct personal diagnosis. He was thus not qualified to act as a psychiatrist. [His] evidence was not medical evidence, and was not admissible. In fact, his evidence was based essentially on 'an extensive examination of the literature of psychopathy' which he related to Childs' behaviour as observed by him when giving evidence." Moreover, the court emphasised that, although in a proper case medical evidence may be admitted to show that a witness is incapable of giving reliable evidence (or even that his capability is substantially impaired) it is, of course, for the jury alone to consider whether or not the capable witness had in fact given reliable evidence.

C. RE-EXAMINATION

Prince v. Samo (1838) 7 L.J.Q.B. 123 (Q.B.). It was held that proof by a witness, during cross-examination, of part of a conversation with him at a former time (if admissible) did not authorise proof, on re-examination, of all that was said at the same time, but only of so much of the former conversation as was connected with that proved in cross-examination.

Lord Denman C.J. (at pp. 124–125) cited the words of Lord Tenterden in *The Queen's Case* (1820) 2 Brod. Bing. 284, 297: "I think counsel has a right, on re-examination, to ask all questions which may be proper to draw forth an explanation of the sense and meaning of the expressions used by the witness on cross-examination, if they be in themselves doubtful and also of the motive by which the witness was induced to use those expressions; but I think he has no right to go further, and to introduce new matters not suited to the purpose of explaining either the expressions or the motives of the witness."

Note.—The general rule is that re-examination must be confined to matters arising out of cross-examination. No new matter may be introduced without leave of the judge. Such leave may be granted, for instance, on important matters which have been overlooked. But in such a case he will of course allow further cross-examination on such questions. As to allowing witnesses to be recalled, or even to be called after the close of the party's case, in criminal matters, see the note to *R. v. Harris* [1927] 2 K.B. 587 (C.C.A.) (Chapter 8, *supra*).

D. FURTHER RECEPTION OF EVIDENCE

SHAW v. R.

85 C.L.R. 365; 26 A.L.J. 40 (H.C. of Australia: 1952)

A rule of practice and procedure requires that the prosecution put its case completely and finally before the accused responds. Only in very special or exceptional circumstances may there be departure from this rule.

The accused was charged with the murder of a prostitute named Sylvia. He admitted in evidence that he had said to the police (as deposed in evidence by one police officer but contradicted by another) "Go and find the bastard that throttled Sylvia." When asked how he knew that she had been throttled, he replied that he had overheard police talking. After the close of the defence the judge permitted the prosecution to recall police witnesses to establish that at the relevant time nothing had been said from which the accused could have deduced that Sylvia had been throttled. The accused appealed against the judge's ruling that the prosecution be allowed to reopen its case after the accused had unexpectedly confirmed the version of the conversation which was unfavourable to the defence. The High Court of Australia held that, as the prosecution could have called the evidence in question as part of its case, the judge had wrongly exercised his discretion in allowing the prosecution to reopen its case.

DIXON C.J., McTIERNAN, WEBB and KITTO JJ.: ... The rule is adopted from the language attributed to Tindal C.J. in the report of *R. v. Frost* in (1839) 4 State Trials (N.S.) 86, at p. 386. His Lordship is reported to have said: "There is no doubt that the general rule is that where the Crown begins its case like a plaintiff in a civil suit, they cannot afterwards support their case by calling fresh witnesses, because they are met by certain evidence that contradicts it. They stand or fall by the evidence they have given. They must close their case before the defence begins; but if any matter arises, *ex improviso*, which no human ingenuity can foresee, on the part of a defendant in a civil suit, or a prisoner in a criminal case, there seems to me no reason why that matter which so arose *ex improviso* may not be answered by contrary evidence on the part of the Crown." The great limitation contained in this language lies, not in the expression "*ex improviso*," which means no more than "unexpectedly" or "suddenly" but in the words "which no human ingenuity can foresee." In the report in *Carrington & Payne* (1839) 9 C. & P. at p. 159 (173 E.R. 789) the words ascribed to Tindal C.J. are: "But if any matter arises *ex improviso* which the Crown could not foresee, supposing it to be entirely new matter which they may be able to answer by contradictory evidence, they may give evidence in reply." ... In *R. v. Frost* it was probably not intended to state an exhaustive rule. ... The formula adopted from Tindal C.J. has little to commend it. The words "which no human ingenuity can foresee" hardly express a legal principle. They are rhetorical but if literally understood they lay down a test which could almost never be satisfied. Clearly the principle is that the prosecution must present its case completely before the prisoner's answer is made. There are issues the proof of which does not lie upon the prosecution and in such cases it may have a rebutting case, as when the defence is insanity. When the prisoner seeks to prove good character, evidence may be allowed in reply. But the prosecution may not split its case on any issue. The Court possesses a power to allow further evidence to be called but it must be exercised according to rule and the rule is against reopening the Crown case unless the circumstances are most exceptional. We are not disposed to lay down the rule in the terms adopted from Tindal C.J., in *R.* v. *Frost.* It is a matter of practice and procedure and in such matters, even where the procedure is criminal and directed to safeguarding the position of the accused.... It seems to us unsafe to adopt a rigid formula in view of the almost infinite variety of difficulties that may arise at a criminal trial. It is probably enough to say that the occasion must be very special or exceptional to warrant a departure from the principle that the prosecution must offer all its proofs during the progress of the Crown case and before the prisoner is called upon for his defence.

FULLAGAR J. delivered a concurring judgment.

Note.—The rule that parties must call all their evidence before the close of their cases is of general applicability in criminal and civil proceedings; but most of the authorities are concerned with the extent to which the prosecution may adduce evidence in rebuttal in criminal cases. Departure from the general rule is a matter for the discretion of the judge. He is apparently allowed considerable latitude in its exercise in civil cases: see, *e.g. Wright* v. *Willcox* (1850) 9 C.B. 650. In criminal cases, however, the discretion is more limited.

When the prosecution is allowed to adduce further evidence after closing its case, and this is not in rebuttal, or because a new point has arisen, the proper course is to serve a notice of additional evidence, but failure to do so will not be a material irregularity unless some serious prejudice results: *R.* v. *Dartey* (1987) 84 Cr.App.R. 352 (C.A.).

The prosecution can never adduce further evidence, either by calling or recalling a witness, after the completion of the summing-up by the judge: *R.* v. *Owen* [1952] 2 Q.B. 362 (C.C.A.).

R. v. **Day** [1940] 1 All E.R. 402 (C.C.A.). The accused was charged with forgery and obtaining money by a forged instrument. After the defence had been closed the judge allowed the prosecution to call a handwriting expert. Specimens of the accused's admitted handwriting had been in the possession of the prosecution from the beginning of the proceedings. The Court of Criminal Appeal held that the additional evidence did not relate to anything that had arisen *ex improviso* in the course of the trial, but was evidence the possible need for which ought to have been foreseen. The judge had wrongly exercised his discretion, and the accused's conviction was quashed.

R. v. **Milliken** (1969) 53 Cr.App.R. 330 (C.A.). The appellant was convicted of being in possession of housebreaking implements by night. His defence was that the incident in question had never taken place, and at the trial he alleged for the first time that he was the victim of a police "frame-up." The Court of Appeal held that the trial judge had not erred in the exercise of his discretion in allowing the prosecution to adduce evidence in rebuttal of this allegation.

Note.—The court will usually allow evidence in rebuttal to be called in order to make good a purely formal omission, *e.g.* a failure to prove that leave of the Director of Public Prosecutions to bring proceedings had been obtained (*Price* v. *Humphries* [1958] 2 Q.B.D. 353 (D.C.)).

For the position when the defence of an alibi is raised, see the Criminal Justice Act 1967, s.11(4). Part Two, *infra.*

R. v. Milliken was referred to in *R. v. Scott* (1984) 79 Cr.App.R. 49 (C.A.) where Lawton L.J. said (p. 51): "In our judgment the principle is as follows. If the prosecution could reasonably have foreseen that a particular piece of evidence was necessary to prove their case they should have put it before the court as part of their case. They should not wait until the defendant has given evidence to produce that evidence. Much, however, will turn on what is reasonable."

Chapter 10

CORROBORATION

ONE of the most marked features of the law of evidence in common law systems still is the stern and exacting nature of its qualitative requirements for the reception of evidence: much relevant material is excluded because it falls within a suspect category, such as hearsay, opinion or evidence of disposition. There is a complementary laxity in the quantitative standards that are imposed: the general rule, which contrasts with that obtaining in most civil law systems, is that corroboration (or confirmatory or supporting probative material) of otherwise admissible evidence is unnecessary. Indeed, the contradicted, but believed, testimony of one witness can constitute proof beyond reasonable doubt. The explanation of this at first sight rather striking approach of the common law is in part historical and relates to a time when jurors were themselves witnesses; but its survival to modern times reflects the need for there to be a proper relationship between qualitative and quantitative tests for the admissibility of evidence. The more exacting the former are, so the more reasonable it is to allow the latter to be generous.

It is, of course, to be remembered that the common law doctrine is merely permissive: a finding on the basis of the testimony of one witness, although generally allowed, is not required. It is to be noted, too, that courts possess an inherent power to control an unnecessary multiplicity of witnesses in the interests of saving time and expense and of avoidance of confusion.

To the general rule that corroboration is not required there are four categories of qualification. They are:

(1) Cases in which corroboration is required as a matter of law, and in which it must take the form of the testimony of a second witness. These cases are now all statutory; they are few in number and mostly unimportant. Mention may, however, be made of the Treason Act 1795, s.1, which provides that a person shall not be convicted of compassing the death or restraint of the Queen or her heirs except on "the oaths of two lawful and credible witnesses."

(2) Cases in which corroboration is required as a matter of law and may, but need not, take the form of the testimony of a second witness. Here adequate corroboration may be provided by, for example, an informal admission, or documentary, real or circumstantial evidence. Cases falling into this category are also all

statutory. They include the opinion evidence of a Crown witness as to the speed of a motor-vehicle in a prosecution for speeding,[2] the evidence of a prosecution witness as to the falsity of the statement alleged to be false in a prosecution for perjury or a related offence,[3] and the evidence of a Crown witness in a prosecution for procuring a girl for prostitution or a kindred offence.[4] The requirement that the unsworn evidence of a child tendered on behalf of the prosecution be corroborated has been abolished.[5]

(3) Cases in which the law does not require corroboration but in which it does require that the trier of fact be warned of the risks involved in making a finding on uncorroborated evidence. Although some of these cases have evolved historically from rules of practice (*e.g.* that of the evidence of an accomplice in a criminal trial), they now represent rules of law, and so a failure to give the required warning may constitute reversible error. Other cases dealt with under this heading are many of those concerned with the evidence of the complainant in prosecutions for sexual offences, seemingly in proceedings other than trials on indictment[6] the sworn evidence of children, and by way of partial analogy the evidence of certain other suspect witnesses.

(4) Cases in which there are no legal requirements, but in which as a matter of practice corroboration is usually sought before a particular finding is made. An uncorroborated claim against the estate of a deceased person is usually treated with caution. So, too, a court will often look for corroboration of an allegation of facts constituting grounds for matrimonial relief; and there is some authority for the view that a warning to this effect ought to be given whenever adultery is alleged by a party to it.

The materials in this Chapter are concerned with cases falling into the last three of the above-mentioned categories. Their importance should be seen in perspective: even cumulatively they constitute but a small inroad into basic common law doctrine. The delineation of these three categories is not completely exact. This is due in part to continuing historical evolution, especially the gradual hardening of rules of practice into rules of law, but also in part to contemporary doubts and inconsistencies.

The Chapter also contains some materials on the nature of corroboration. For several reasons it is difficult to generalise about this. First, many of the rules requiring corroboration are statutory, and the meaning to be ascribed to these rules will largely depend upon the interpretation of the particular statute, although it is true that many statutes (*e.g.* the Sexual Offences Act 1956)[7] adopt a common form stipulating corroborative evidence which itself implicates the accused in a material particular. Secondly, the policies underlying different corroboration requirements differ and suggest differing interpretations. For example, the evidence of an accomplice is suspect partly because he is liable to be under the specific temptation to shift suspicion from

---

[2] Road Traffic Regulation Act 1984, s.89(2) (Part Two, *infra*).
[3] Perjury Act 1911, s.13 (Part Two, *infra*).
[4] Sexual Offences Act 1956, ss.2 (Part Two, *infra*), 3, 4, 22 and 23.
[5] Criminal Justice Act 1988, s.34(1) amending the Children and Young Persons Act 1933, s.38 (both Part Two, *infra*).
[6] See the Criminal Justice Act 1988, s.34(2) (Part Two, *infra*).
[7] *Ibid.*

himself to the accused. It is therefore not unreasonable to regard as corroborative only evidence which itself actually implicates the accused.[8] By way of contrast in some other cases evidence may be suspect because of doubts as to its general reliability. Any evidence which significantly bolsters that reliability ought therefore to be seen as adequate corroboration. Thirdly, the range of possibly available corroborative evidence is so wide and varying that the formulation of specific requirements is rendered difficult and, indeed, undesirable.

In dealing with problems of corroboration, especially in cases in which a mandatory warning must be given, it is often important to differentiate between the respective roles of the judge and of the jury or trier of fact. This differentiation marks the distinction between the question as to whether a particular item of evidence is capable in law of constituting corroboration, which is a matter for the judge, and the issue as to whether an item, that is so capable, does in fact constitute adequate corroboration, which, being a matter of cogency or weight, is for the jury to determine.

Two elementary, but until recently curiously under-emphasised, points must also be remembered. First, no evidence can constitute corroboration unless it is otherwise relevant and admissible. As Scarman L.J. explained in *R. v. Scarrott*,[9] the corroborative capability of evidence is a consequence of its admissibility and not *vice versa*. Secondly, as Lord Hailsham of St. Marylebone said in *D.P.P. v. Kilbourne*,[10] "Corroboration can only be afforded to or by a witness who is otherwise to be believed. If a witness's testimony falls of its own inanition, the question of his needing, or being capable of giving, corroboration does not arise." The role of corroboration is not, of course, to transform an incredible witness into a credible one. It is to make it more likely that a credible witness will be in fact believed. Lord Hailsham's words that the witness "is otherwise to be believed" are not felicitous.[11] They must be taken to mean that the witness could reasonably be believed, because to take them to mean that he must actually be believed would *ex hypothesi* render corroboration superfluous.

Evidence of identification does not in itself have to be corroborated, nor is the judge under any obligation to warn the jury of the dangers of convicting on such evidence on the ground *simpliciter* that it is uncorroborated.[12] Evidence of identification, particularly evidence of visual identification, is however notoriously prone to unreliability. The Criminal Law Revision Committee[13] saw "mistaken identification as by far the greatest cause of actual or possible wrong convictions"; and, whereas in civil cases the problem is generally treated as one of weight, the Court of Appeal has now laid down[14] guidelines for the protection of the accused in criminal cases. Failure by a judge to follow these

---

[8] See *R. v. Baskerville* [1916] 2 K.B. 658 (C.C.A.) and *Note* thereon, *infra*.
[9] [1978] Q.B. 1016, 1021 (C.A.) (Chap. 20, *infra*).
[10] [1973] A.C. 729, 746 (*infra*). See, too, *R. v. Hester* [1973] A.C. 296, *per* Lord Morris of Borth-y-Gest, at p. 315.
[11] See later comment of Lord Hailsham in *R. v. Spencer* [1987] A.C. 128 at pp. 133–134.
[12] See *Arthurs v. Att.-Gen. for Northern Ireland* (1971) 55 Cr.App.R. 161 (H.L.) and *R. v. Long* (1973) 57 Cr.App.R. 871 (C.A.).
[13] 11th Report, para. 196. See, too, the Report of the Committee on Evidence of Identification in Criminal Cases under the chairmanship of Lord Devlin, Cmnd. 338 (1976).
[14] *R. v. Turnbull* [1977] Q.B. 224 (C.A.), *infra*.

guidelines would appear to constitute reversible error. Although there is obviously some affinity between the policy underlying these guidelines and that underlying the law of corroboration, they are distinct from that law. The guidelines sometimes require "supporting" evidence which may not constitute corroboration in a traditional sense. Conversely, the guidelines may be applicable even though the evidence of identification could be seen as having been corroborated. Nevertheless it is convenient for the guidelines to be considered along with the law of corroboration, and the materials set out in the last section of this Chapter relate to them.

A. CASES IN WHICH CORROBORATION IS REQUIRED

Nicholas v. **Penny** [1950] 2 K.B. 466 (D.C.). The accused was charged with speeding. Lord Goddard C.J. said (pp. 471–472): "*Russell* v. *Beesley* (53 T.L.R. 298) is authority for the proposition that one need not have the evidence of more than one police officer in such a case if it is supported by a speedometer reading, or by some other means by which the evidence given by the officer becomes evidence of fact and not of mere opinion. Section 2, subs. 2(3) of the Road Traffic Act, 1934, provides: 'A person prosecuted for driving a motor-vehicle on a road at a speed exceeding a speed-limit imposed by or under any enactment shall not be liable to be convicted solely on the evidence of one witness to the effect that in the opinion of the witness the person prosecuted was driving the vehicle at a speed exceeding that limit.' [The substance of this provision is now in the Road Traffic Regulation Act 1984, s.89(2) (Part Two, *infra*).] Therefore, if there is only the evidence of a police officer, or any other person, who says, 'I saw the vehicle in question go by and in my opinion it was exceeding' the speed-limit, that is not enough, although if two people say that, it is in law sufficient to justify a conviction. *Russell* v. *Beesley* and other cases show that, if the question depends on the reading of a speedometer, a mechanical device for recording speed, the justices can act upon that and need not have the evidence of two people. The justices in *Russell* v. *Beesley*, being of opinion that in cases of this kind it was not desirable that the evidence of a police officer checking a person's speed from the speedometer of his own car should be accepted unless corroborated by another witness present at the time, dismissed the information without giving any opinion on the legal point raised, and the court (of which I was a member) said that the justices were wrong in that case, and that it was not necessary to call two witnesses provided the evidence given by the one witness who was called was not evidence of mere opinion. In that case the opinion of the witness was supported by his evidence that his speedometer showed a certain speed; but it is only fair to say, in view of the argument of counsel for the defendant in the present case, that there was evidence in that case that the speedometer had been tested." The court went on to hold that justices could convict on the evidence of one police officer as to the speedometer reading of a police car driven at an even distance behind the defendant's car, notwithstanding that no admissible evidence had been adduced as to the accuracy of the speedometer.

Note.—See, too, *Crosland* v. *D.P.P.* [1988] 3 All E.R. 712 (D.C.) where it was held that when a police officer estimates a vehicle's speed on the basis of a calculation from physical and material data, such as skid marks, burn marks, damage to the vehicle, etc., this does not constitute "opinion" within the meaning of the section.

In *Burton* v. *Gilbert* [1984] R.T.R. 162 (D.C.) it was held that a reading on a Muniquip radar speed meter could, in the absence of evidence suggesting that it was not working properly, constitute corroboration of a police officer's opinion as to speed. It is to be noted, too, that evidence of the opinion of a second witness may corroborate the opinion of the first witness: *Brighty* v. *Pearson* [1938] 4 All E.R. 127 (D.C.).

Perjury Act 1911, s.13 (Part Two, *infra*) provides that a person shall not be convicted of an offence under the Act (or of any offence declared by any other Act to be perjury or subornation of perjury or to be punishable as such) "solely upon the evidence of one witness as to the falsity of any statement alleged to be false." It is to be noted that it is only on the issue of falsity that corroboration is required. Although corroboration need not take the form of the testimony of a second witness, in practice this is often in effect required: see the Eleventh Report of the Criminal Law Revision Committee (1972, Cmnd. 4991), para. 191.

R. v. **Goldstein** (1914) 11 Cr.App.R. 27 (C.C.A.). The appellant was convicted of attempting to procure a girl to become a prostitute contrary to the Criminal Law Amendment Act 1885, s.2(1), to which section there was a proviso "that no person shall be convicted of any offence under this section upon the evidence of one witness, unless such witness be corroborated in some material particular by evidence implicating the accused." (Procuration and similar offences are now dealt with in the Sexual Offences Act 1956, ss.2 (Part Two, *infra*), 3, 4, 22 and 23, each of which sections contains a similar proviso). Lord Reading C.J. said (pp. 28–29): "In order that men may be protected from a charge of this character being made against them without corroboration, the law provides that there must be corroboration of some material particular implicating the accused. Now here it is said that the charge of attempted procuration rested on the evidence of the girl alone. It is admitted that there was no corroboration of any material particular implicating the accused, but there were other matters on which the girl gave evidence on which there was corroboration. One of these matters amounted to the commission of a crime by the appellant if the jury accepted her evidence, but not of the crime with which he was charged; it is suggested that that was sufficient corroboration to satisfy the statute. The proposition has only to be stated to be refuted. It is clear that it is intended that the corroborative evidence should implicate the accused in respect of the offence charged; when that fails it is wholly immaterial that there is corroboration of other portions of the evidence. It follows that this conviction must be quashed. . . .

Director of Public Prosecutions v. **Hester** [1973] A.C. 296 (H.L.). The accused was charged with indecent assault on a girl aged 12, contrary to the Sexual Offences Act 1956, s.14(1). The complainant gave evidence on oath. Her sister aged 9 also gave unsworn evidence for the prosecution under the Children and Young Persons Act 1933, s.38(1) (Part Two, *infra*). That subsection at that time provided that "where evidence admitted by virtue of this section is given on behalf of the prosecution the accused shall not be liable to be convicted of the offence unless that evidence is corroborated by some other material evidence in support thereof implicating him." The trial judge directed the jury that the evidence of the unsworn child could amount to corroboration of the evidence of the sworn complainant. The accused was convicted, but his conviction was quashed by the Court of Appeal. The House of Lords held that the evidence of a sworn child can in law be corroborated by the evidence of an unsworn child provided that the latter is itself corroborated; and that in the present case each child's evidence could corroborate that of the other, provided that after proper guidance and warning the jury was satisfied that each was a truthful witness. The prosecution's appeal was, however, dismissed on the more general ground that the conviction was unsafe and unsatisfactory.

Note.—As a result of the enactment of section 34 of the Criminal Justice Act 1988 (Part Two, *infra*) the significance of this case has been greatly reduced for two reasons. First, corroboration is no longer required of the evidence of an unsworn child simply because he or she is unsworn. Secondly, a warning of the dangers of convicting on the sworn evidence of a child, simply because he or she is a child, is no longer necessary. On the other hand in circumstances such as those in *Hester's* case a warning would probably still be required with regard to the evidence of the complainant, not on the ground of her being a child, but on the ground of her being the complainant in a prosecution for a sexual offence (see this Chapter, section B, *infra*). Section 34(3) makes it clear that the unsworn evidence of a child could constitute such corroboration, and could do so even if the complainant's evidence were also unsworn.

B. CASES IN WHICH A WARNING IS MANDATORY

R. v. BASKERVILLE

[1916] 2 K.B. 658; 86 L.J.K.B. 28; 115 L.T. 453 (C.C.A.: 1916)

The judge must warn the jury of the danger of convicting the accused on the uncorroborated testimony of an accomplice.

Evidence corroborating that of an accomplice must be confirmation of a material circumstance and of the identity of the accused person. Such evidence may be circumstantial.

On a charge of indecency the evidence of accomplices was corroborated by the statements of the accused.

LORD READING C.J. (delivering the judgment of the court, which included SCRUTTON, AVORY, ROWLATT and ATKIN JJ.):...There is no doubt that the uncorroborated evidence of an accomplice is admissible in law.... But it has long been a rule of practice at common law for the judge to warn the jury of the danger of convicting a prisoner on the uncorroborated testimony of an accomplice, and, in the discretion of the judge, to advise them not to convict upon such evidence; but the judge should point out to the jury that it is within their legal province to convict upon such unconfirmed evidence.... This rule of practice has become virtually equivalent to a rule of law....

In addition to the rule of practice above mentioned, there are, with regard to certain offences, statutory provisions that no person shall be convicted upon the evidence of one witness, unless such witness be corroborated in some material particular implicating the accused.... In these cases, the law is that the judge, in the absence of such corroborative evidence, must stop the case at the close of the prosecution and direct the jury to acquit the accused. Where no such statutory provision is applicable to the offence charged, and the evidence for the prosecution consists of the uncorroborated testimony of an accomplice, the law is that the judge should leave the case to the jury after giving them the caution already mentioned....

As to the nature and extent of the corroboration required...we have come to the conclusion that the better opinion of the law upon this point is that stated in *R. v. Stubbs* (1855) Dears, C.C. 555, by Parke B., namely, that the evidence of an accomplice must be confirmed not only as to the circumstances of the crime, but also as to the identity of the prisoner. The learned Baron does not mean that there must be confirmation of all the circumstances of the crime, that is unnecessary. It is sufficient if there is confirmation as to the material circumstance of the crime and of the identity of the prisoner. . . .

We hold that evidence in corroboration must be independent testimony which affects the accused by connecting or tending to connect him with the crime. In other words, it must be evidence which implicates him, that is, which confirms in some material particular not only the evidence that the crime has been committed, but also that the prisoner committed it. The test applicable to determine the nature and extent of the corroboration is thus the same whether the case falls within the rule of practice at common law or within that class of offences for which corroboration is required by statute. . . .

The corroboration need not be direct evidence that the accused committed the crime; it is sufficient if it is merely circumstantial evidence of his connection with the crime. . . .

The question was discussed on the hearing of this appeal whether the evidence of an accomplice against two prisoners, corroborated as to one prisoner's participation in the crime, but not as to the other, can be regarded as corroboration with regard to both prisoners. We think the law is correctly stated by Alderson B. in *R.* v. *Jenkins* (1845) 1 Cox C.C. 177. The learned Baron said: "Where there is one witness of bad character giving evidence against both prisoners, a confirmation of his testimony with regard to one, is no confirmation of his testimony as to the other. . . ." . . .

Note.—Whether the rule that in order to qualify as corroboration evidence must itself implicate the accused (as distinct from merely indicate the credibility of the witness) ought to apply in all common law contexts is perhaps questionable (see pp. 191–192, *supra*). In *R.* v. *Olaleye* (1986) 82 Cr.App.R. 337 (C.A.) no reference seems to have been made to the requirement when it was held that, as a principal had been convicted of attempted rape after an impeccable summing-up regarding corroboration, it was unnecessary to apply the corroboration rule to the complainant's evidence affecting the appellant who had been convicted of aiding and abetting the principal—for this would involve what had already been proved namely that the complainant was a reliable witness.

There is no requirement that corroborative evidence must relate to the particular matters spoken to by the accomplice: *R.* v. *Beck* [1982] 1 W.L.R. 461, 470–471 (C.A.).

Corroboration by another accomplice, or even by several accomplices, usually does not suffice (*R.* v. *Noakes* (1832) 5 C. & P. 326). Testimony by the wife of an accomplice may sometimes amount to corroboration (*R.* v. *Allen* [1965] 2 Q.B. 295 (C.C.A.), considering *R.* v. *Payne* (1913) 8 Cr.App.R. 171 (C.C.A.); *R.* v. *Willis* [1916] 1 K.B. 933 (C.C.A.); see, too, *Tropodi* v. *R.* (1961) 104 C.L.R. 1; [1961] A.L.R. 780 (High Court of Australia)).

A statement before trial by an accomplice implicating the accused is not generally admissible against the latter (*R.* v. *Smith* (1966) 51 Cr.App.R. 22 (C.A.)).

DAVIES v. DIRECTOR OF PUBLIC PROSECUTIONS

[1954] A.C. 378; [1954] 1 All E.R. 507; 38 Cr.App.R. 11; [1954] Crim.L.R. 305
(H.L.: 1954)

In a criminal trial it is the duty of the judge to warn the jury that it is dangerous to convict upon the uncorroborated evidence of an accomplice. This practice has the force of a rule of law.

Accomplices include participants in the crime charged, receivers in respect of thieves from whom they receive goods, and parties to crimes which constitute similar facts. Who is an accomplice is a question of fact.

A witness for the prosecution (one Lawson) and the accused were members of a gang of youths who attacked another gang, and one youth was stabbed to death. The witness had been previously convicted of common assault but had been acquitted of the murder of the stabbed youth, for which murder the accused was on trial. It was not proved that the witness knew before the stabbing that the accused had a knife, and the trial judge did not treat the witness as an accomplice to the murder. The Court of Criminal Appeal and the House of Lords held that the witness was not an accomplice, and dismissed the accused's appeal against conviction.

LORD SIMONDS L.C.: ... My Lords, [I] will proceed to deal with three problems raised by the main ground of appeal, namely—(a) What is the scope and effect of the rule that a judge ought to warn juries in connection with the evidence of an "accomplice"? (b) What is an "accomplice" within the rule? (c) Whatever be the true answers to these questions, what (if any) is their application to the evidence of Lawson?

(a)— ... It is clear that an accomplice is and was at all material times a competent witness, and that a conviction based on his evidence, though uncorroborated, could, and can today be supported: and a judge may properly direct a jury that they are entitled if they choose to act on such uncorroborated evidence. But for over a century and a half it has been customary for judges to warn juries that it is dangerous to convict on such evidence, free though they are, if they find it wholly convincing, to do so....

... The true rule has been, in my view, accurately formulated by the appellant's counsel in his first three propositions, more particularly in the third. These propositions as amended read as follows:

"*First proposition*:
In a criminal trial where a person who is an accomplice gives evidence on behalf of the prosecution, it is the duty of the judge to warn the jury that, although they may convict upon his evidence, it is dangerous to do so unless it is corroborated.

Second proposition:
This rule, although a rule of practice, now has the force of a rule of law.

Third proposition:
Where the judge fails to warn the jury in accordance with this rule, the conviction will be quashed, even if in fact there be ample corroboration of the evidence of the accomplice, unless the appellate court can apply the proviso to section 4(1) of the Criminal Appeal Act 1907."

The rule it will be observed applies only to witnesses for the prosecution.

The remaining questions, therefore, on the main issue—(b) and (c)—
What is an "accomplice" within the rule? And has the rule, on the
proper construction of the word "accomplice" contained in it, any
application to Lawson in the present case?

There is in the authorities no formal definition of the term
"accomplice": and your Lordships are forced to deduce a meaning for
the word from the cases in which X, Y and Z have been held to be, or
held liable to be treated as, accomplices. On the cases it would appear
that the following persons, if called as witnesses for the prosecution,
have been treated as falling within the category:

(1) On any view, persons who are *participes criminis* in respect of the
actual crime charged, whether as principals or accessories before or after
the fact (in felonies) or persons committing, procuring or aiding and
abetting (in the case of misdemeanours). This is surely the natural and
primary meaning of the term "accomplice." But in two cases, persons
falling strictly outside the ambit of this category have, in particular
decisions, been held to be accomplices for the purpose of the rule: *viz.*:

(2) Receivers have been held to be accomplices of the thieves from
whom they receive goods on a trial of the latter for larceny (*R.* v.
Jennings (1912) 7 Cr.App.R. 242: *R.* v. *Dixon* (1925) 19 Cr.App.R. 36).

(3) When X has been charged with a specific offence on a particular
occasion, and evidence is admissible, and has been admitted, of his
having committed crimes of this identical type on other occasions, as
proving system and intent and negativing accident; in such cases the
court has held that in relation to such other similar offences, if evidence
of them were given by parties to them, the evidence of such other
parties should not be left to the jury without a warning that it is
dangerous to accept it without corroboration (*R.* v. *Farid* (1945) 30
Cr.App.R. 168). . . .

My Lords, these extensions of the term are imbedded in our case law
and it would be inconvenient for any authority other than the legislature
to disturb them. Neither of them affects this case. Lawson was not a
receiver, nor was there any question of "system"; Lawson, if he was to
be an accomplice at all had to be an accomplice to the crime of murder.
I can see no reason for any further extension of the term "accomplice."
In particular, I can see no reason why, if half a dozen boys fight another
crowd, and one of them produces a knife and stabs one of the
opponents to death, all the rest of his group should be treated as
accomplices in the use of a knife and the infliction of mortal injury by
that means, unless there is evidence that the rest intended or concerted
or at least contemplated an attack with a knife by one of their number,
as opposed to a common assault. If all that was designed or envisaged
was in fact a common assault, and there was no evidence that Lawson, a
party to that common assault, knew that any of his companions had a
knife, then Lawson was not an accomplice in the crime consisting in its
felonious use. . . .

My Lords, I have tried to define the term "accomplice." The branch
of the definition relevant to this case is that which covers "participes
criminis" in respect of the actual crime charged, "whether as principals
or accessories before or after the fact." But, it may reasonably be
asked, who is to decide, or how is it to be decided, whether a particular
witness was a "particeps criminis" in the case in hand? In many or most
cases this question answers itself, or, to be more exact, is answered by
the witness in question himself, by confessing to participation, by
pleading guilty to it, or being convicted of it. But it is indisputable that

there are witnesses outside these straightforward categories, in respect of whom the answer has to be sought elsewhere. The witnesses concerned may never have confessed, or may never have been arraigned or put on trial, in respect of the crime involved. Such cases fall into two classes. In the first, the judge can properly rule that there is no evidence that the witness was, what I will, for short, call a participant. The present case, in my view, happens to fall within this class, and can be decided on that narrow ground. But there are other cases within this field in which there is evidence on which a reasonable jury could find that a witness was a "participant." In such a case the issue of "accomplice vel non" is for the jury's decision: and a judge should direct them that if they consider on the evidence that the witness was an accomplice, it is dangerous for them to act on his evidence unless corroborated: though it is competent for them to do so if, after that warning, they still think fit to do so. . . .

LORDS PORTER, OAKSEY, TUCKER and ASQUITH OF BISHOPSTONE concurred.

Note.—For the proviso to the Criminal Appeal Act 1907, s.4(1) see now the Criminal Appeal Act 1968, s.2(1) (Part Two, *infra*).

It is not essential to use the word "corroboration" in the summing-up: *R.* v. *O'Reilly* [1967] 2 Q.B. 722 (C.C.A.); *R.* v. *Russell* (1968) 52 Cr.App.R. 147 (C.A.).

Once a judge has decided that there is a possibility that a prosecution witness may be an accomplice, he is under a duty to give a clear warning to the jury as to the dangers of acting on his uncorroborated evidence if they find him to be an accomplice; if he thinks that the risk is in fact not very great, he can then say so: *R.* v. *Riley* (1979) 70 Cr.App.1 (C.A.).

In Canada the mandatory warning requirement in relation to the evidence of an accomplice has been discarded. In *Vetrovec* v. *R.* (1982) 136 D.L.R. (3d) 89 Dickson J., delivering the judgment of the Supreme Court of Canada, said (p. 105): "I would hold that there is no special category for 'accomplices.' An accomplice is to be treated like any other witness testifying at a criminal trial and the judge's conduct, if he chooses to give his opinion, is governed by the general rules."

McNee v. **Kay** [1953] V.L.R. 520 (S.C.Vict., Australia). Sholl J. offered a more generous definition of accomplice than that propounded in the *Davies* case, and one which would probably have covered the witness, Lawson, in that case. Sholl J. said (p. 530): " . . . if I were free so to hold, I should consider the true principle to be that that person is an accomplice within the common law rule who is chargeable, in relation to the same events as those found in the charge against the accused, with an offence (whether the same offence or not) of such a character, and who would be if convicted thereof liable to such punishment as might possibly tempt that person to exaggerate or fabricate evidence as to the guilt of the accused."

Note.—See, too, *Horsburgh* v. *R.* [1967] S.C.R. 746; 63 D.L.R. (2d.) 699, where Martland J., speaking for the majority of the Supreme Court of Canada, said (p. 708): "What is necessary to become an accomplice is a participation in the crime involved, and not necessarily the actual commission of it."

R. v. **Loveridge** (1983) 76 Cr.App.R. 125 (C.A.). Two brothers were found guilty of conspiring to steal from various premises. At the trial they had set up inconsistent defences. Both appealed, one of them (Frederick) on the ground that the judge had failed to direct the jury adequately as to what evidence could corroborate his brother's (Christopher's) evidence against him. The appeal was dismissed, the court holding that when a defendant called in his own defence gives evidence against a co-defendant the full warning against uncorroborated evidence, which is appropriate in respect of a witness for the prosecution who may be an accomplice, is not necessary. Ackner L.J., giving the judgment of the court, adverted (pp. 126–127) to the fact that at the trial the judge had at an earlier stage actually given "the time-honoured direction which courts are obliged to give when evidence is given by prosecution witnesses who are accomplices or potential accomplices." His Lordship continued (p. 127): "Until fairly recently, by reason of what is known as the *Prater* decision (1960) 44 Cr.App.R. 83; 1960 2 Q.B. 464, it has been the practice of the courts to give such a direction when there are witnesses of whom it may be said that they might have reasons of their own to advance in giving certain evidence, or where co-defendants implicate, or may be taken to implicate, each other." Ackner L.J. later concluded (p. 128): " ... the learned judge's caution in regard to a co-defendant's evidence being based on the decision in *Prater* ... was more favourable than was necessary, and his omission to complete the *Prater* direction does not, in our judgment, render the verdict of the jury unsafe or unsatisfactory."

Note.—The decision makes it clear that when a defendant gives evidence against a co-defendant the full warning against uncorroborated evidence, appropriate in the case of the prosecution witness who may be an accomplice, is not required. What is less clear is the effect upon the *Prater* case. In that case Edmund Davies L.J., giving the judgment of the Court of Criminal Appeal, had said ([1960] 2 Q.B. 464, 465–466): "For the purposes of this present appeal, this court is content to accept that ... in practice it is desirable that a warning should be given that the witness, whether he comes from the dock, as in this case, or whether he be a Crown witness, may be a witness with some purpose of his own to serve." But later in his judgment he did say: "But every case must be looked at in the light of its own facts. ... " Perhaps since *R.* v. *Loveridge* the decision in *Prater* is to be seen as no longer authority for the view that special treatment is automatically to be accorded to the evidence from a witness who "comes from the dock," but as still supporting the general proposition that as a matter of practice the giving of a warning may well be desirable "in cases where a person may be regarded as having some purpose of his own to serve" (*per* Edmund Davies L.J. at p. 466). This would seem to be consistent with the decision in *R.* v. *Beck* [1982] 1 W.L.R. 461 (C.A.), where it was held that, although a judge should advise a jury to proceed cautiously when there is material suggesting that evidence of a witness might be tainted by an improper motive (the tenor of such advice varying according to the circumstances), the judge is not obliged to give an accomplice warning if the witness is not a prosecution witness who could be an accomplice. In *R.* v. *Spencer*; *R.* v. *Smails* [1987] A.C. 128 (*infra*) the House of Lords expressly stated that *R.* v. *Beck* was rightly decided. See, too, *R.* v. *Knowlden* (1983) 77 Cr.App.R. 94 (C.A.).

R. v. **Royce-Bentley** [1974] 1 W.L.R. 535 (C.A.). The accused was charged with theft. A Crown witness, who could have been an accomplice, gave evidence which was mainly, although not entirely, favourable to the accused. Before summing up the judge consulted both counsel, and counsel for the defence indicated that he would prefer that no direction be given about corroboration. The judge gave no warning. The accused was convicted. The Court of Appeal held that there had been no irregularity. Lord Widgery C.J., delivering the judgment of the court, said: " ... where a trial judge is faced with the situation which arises here, he should of course consult counsel in the absence of the jury before taking any final decision, but having done that, he ought to consider whether on the whole, more harm to the defence would be done by giving the accomplice direction than by not giving it, and if he comes to the conclusion that on the whole more harm would be done in that way, then it is no irregularity on his part in the conduct of the trial if he decides not to give the accomplice direction."

D.P.P. v. **Kilbourne** [1973] A.C. 729 (H.L.). The respondent had been convicted of the offences of buggery and indecent assault on one group of boys in 1970 and of similar offences on another group of boys in 1971. His defence had been one of innocent association. The judge had directed the jury that they were entitled to treat the uncorroborated evidence of the group of boys involved in the 1971 offences, provided they were satisfied that they were speaking the truth, as corroboration of evidence given by the boys involved in the 1970 offences. The House of Lords held that this direction was proper and that the respondent had been rightly convicted. A warning of the dangers of convicting on the uncorroborated evidence of the complainant must be given in prosecutions for sexual offences. Moreover, a warning is in any event necessary in respect of the uncorroborated evidence of any child witness for the prosecution. Lord Hailsham of St. Marylebone L.C. in the course of his judgment said (pp. 746–747): "Corroboration is only required or afforded if the witness requiring corroboration or giving it is otherwise credible. If this evidence is not credible, a witness's testimony should be rejected and the accused acquitted, even if there could be found evidence capable of being corroboration in other testimony. Corroboration can only be afforded to or by a witness who is otherwise to be believed. If a witness's testimony falls of its own inanition the question of his needing, or being capable of giving, corroboration does not arise.... Of course, the moment at which the jury must make up its mind is at the end of the case. They must look at the evidence as a whole before asking themselves whether the evidence of a given witness is credible in itself and whether, if otherwise credible, it is corroborated. Nevertheless, corroboration is a doctrine applying to otherwise credible testimony and not to testimony incredible in itself."

Note.—To the extent that the decision relates to the fact that the witnesses were children it is now to be reviewed in the light of the Criminal Justice Act 1988, s.34 (Part Two, *infra*): see *Note* to *D.P.P.* v. *Hester* [1973] A.C. 296 (H.L.) *supra*. The boys may have been accomplices. If they were, then the decision is also authority for the proposition, as explicitly stated by Lord Hailsham (p. 748), that an accomplice who falls into the third category enumerated by Lord Simonds in *Davies* v. *D.P.P.* (*supra*) can corroborate the evidence of an accomplice to the other crime. Although the general rule is that one accomplice cannot corroborate another accomplice, the danger of collusion is obviously greatly reduced when they are parties to different crimes.

For commentary on Lord Hailsham's reference to the relationship between credibility and corroboration, see p. 192, *supra*: see, too, *Att.-Gen. of Hong Kong* v. *Wong Muk Ping* [1987] A.C. 501 (P.C.).

R. v. **Chance** [1988] Q.B. 932 (C.A.). The appellant had been tried on *inter alia* a count of rape. He did not contest that the complainant had been raped. The judge had indicated to the jury that the sole issue was as to the identity of the perpetrator. They were directed in accordance with *R.* v. *Turnbull* (p. 209, *infra*) about the special need for caution (and the reason for it) before convicting on evidence of identification. They were further directed that independent identification evidence supporting the correctness of the complainant's identification as needed, and potentially corroborative evidence was pointed out to them. The appellant appealed against conviction on the ground that, since a sexual offence was charged, a *Turnbull* direction on the issue of identity was not sufficient and that a full mandatory warning that it would be dangerous to convict on the uncorroborated evidence of the complainant ought to have been given. The Court of Appeal dismissed the appeal. In the course of reading the judgment of the court Roch J. said (pp. 942–943): "The general rule from *Rex* v. *Baskerville* [1916] 2 K.B. 658, which was of course an accomplice case, onwards until at any rate *Reg.* v. *Turnbull* [1977] Q.B. 224 has been, broadly speaking, that in all sexual cases juries should be given the usual warning, namely, that it is dangerous to convict on the uncorroborated evidence of the complainant. That corroboration, it has been said, should be of the fact that the offence was committed and that the defendant committed it. In other words that there must be corroboration both of identification and of the offence: see *James* v. *The Queen* (1970) 55 Cr.App.R. 299, 302. That rule is subject to certain tacit exceptions. We examine it under four heads.

(1) *Where identification is not in issue*

Where for example the defendant gives evidence that it was he who was at the material time with the complainant or had admittedly said as much to the police or does not dispute that he was the man involved but denies the offence, it is not necessary for the judge to go through the charade of giving the usual warning to the jury about the complainant's evidence on identification and then explaining that the defendant's own evidence is potential corroboration. Under those circumstances any warning as to the identification evidence would be otiose and need not be given.

(2) *Where the offence (or more correctly the fact that someone committed the offence) is not in issue*

Here the situation is more complicated. In the unlikely event that there has been a formal admission by the defence there is no difficulty. That part of the case is proved and there is no danger against which the jury needs to be warned: see section 10 of the Criminal Justice Act 1967. What is the judge to do in the much more usual case where there has been no formal admission but equally there has been no suggestion by the defence that there is any doubt as to the commission of the offence and no cross-examination of the complainant to that effect? If, as in the instant case for example, it could not sensibly be suggested that no rape had occurred, it is absurd and gratuitously offensive to the complainant to insist that the usual warning should nevertheless be given. It is a fine distinction between 'I admit' and 'I do not dispute.' On the other hand, where it is suggested by the defendant that the complainant's evidence as to the offence may be unreliable, or, despite the lack of any such suggestion, the judge in his discretion perhaps decides in the interests of justice that it is advisable to do so, the usual warning about the complainant's evidence as to the offence should be given. . . .

(3) *Where the identity of the offender is in issue*

The situation here seems to us to have been altered by the decision in *Reg.* v. *Turnbull* [1977] Q.B. 24. As already pointed out, that decision, albeit not involving a sexual offence, deliberately avoided introducing the concept of corroboration in the strict sense into the problems of identification. Does the fact that the charge is of a sexual nature make any difference to that approach? There may no doubt be occasions when the sexual nature of the offence casts some doubt upon the complainant's identification evidence or adds to it a further peril, but in our judgment that possibility does not require judges on every occasion to give the usual warning. In the ordinary way a full *Turnbull* direction is sufficient, despite the sexual nature of the case. In the rare case where the sexual nature of the case may have affected the complainant's identification evidence or where the judge in his discretion considers it advisable, the *Turnbull* direction should be amplified to include a formal direction as to corroboration, tailored to the particular circumstances of the case.

(4) *Where the offence itself is in issue*

Here the usual warning must always be given.

. . .

Two incidental benefits will accrue from the approach which we have ventured to adopt. First, it will no longer be evidentially advantageous to the burglar to rape the woman householder. Secondly, the judge will not, in cases of this sort, be given the unenviable task of making the suggestion, not advanced by the defence and patently absurd, that the woman householder may have been giving her evidence out of fantasy, spite or neurosis."

Note.—The general position is seemingly the same in cases of sexual offences against males: *R.* v. *Burgess* (1956) 40 Cr.App.R. 144 (C.C.A.).

In *Mattouk* v. *Hassad* [1943] A.C. 588, a civil suit based upon the alleged seduction of the plaintiff's 15-year-old daughter, the Privy Council took the view that there is a rule, at least of practice, that caution be exercised in acting on the victim's uncorroborated evidence in such cases.

For the particular effect of *R.* v. *Chance* on earlier authorities see, *e.g. R.* v. *Trigg* and the *Note* thereon, *infra.*

R. v. **Trigg** [1963] 1 W.L.R. 305 (C.C.A.). At the accused's trial for rape, three girls, including the complainant, gave evidence that a man had approached them in the street and had invited them to go with him for a ride on his motorcycle and that the complainant had accepted the offer. The complainant gave evidence that the man had taken her into the country and raped her. The three girls had identified the defendant at an identification parade as being the man in question. At the trial the fact that the complainant had been raped was not disputed, the only issue being as to the identity of her assailant. The defendant, who was convicted, appealed on the ground *inter alia* that the judge had failed to warn the jury of the danger of convicting on the uncorroborated evidence of the complainant. The appellant's conviction was quashed. In the course of giving the judgment of the Court of Criminal Appeal Ashworth J. said (pp. 308–310): "There was no direction whatever in regard to corroboration... in a sexual case of this sort, the jury must be warned of the danger of acting on the complainant's evidence unless there is corroboration.... In the present case, [counsel for the appellant] conceded, and rightly conceded, that there was material in the evidence which the jury, on proper direction, could accept as corroborative of the complainant's evidence.... So one finds this court in the position that the summing-up contains an omission in regard to corroboration where there was evidence that could have been accepted as such. In these circumstances, the only way in which this conviction can be upheld is by the application of the proviso to section 4(1) of the Criminal Appeal Act, 1907, on the ground that there was no substantial miscarriage of justice.... In principle, this court feels that cases in which no warning as to corroboration is given where such a warning should have been given, should, broadly speaking, not be made the subject of the proviso to section 4(1) of the Criminal Appeal Act 1907. There are cases where the evidence has been such that this court has felt it possible to apply the proviso, but those cases, in the view of this court, must be regarded more as exceptional than as, in any sense, a regular matter."

Note. For the proviso to the Criminal Appeal Act 1907, s.4(1) see now the Criminal Appeal Act 1968, s.2(1) (Part Two, *infra*).

Although, in the light of *R.* v. *Chance*, the need for a full corroboration direction in all cases in which the only issue is identity has been superseded by the adequacy of a *Turnbull*-type direction, it would appear that *R.* v. *Trigg* has survived as a decision because there seemingly had been no direction there which would qualify even as a *Turnbull*-type direction. It would appear, too, that the existence of evidence which, if believed, could constitute corroboration will still not absolve the judge from the need to give a full corroboration warning in cases in which it is otherwise required. However, to be contrasted here is the decision of the High Court of Australia in *R.* v. *Kelleher* (1974) 131 C.L.R. 534; [1974] 4 A.L.R. 450. There in a rape case it was held that the judge's failure to give a warning of the dangers of convicting an accused of a sexual offence on the uncorroborated evidence of the complainant is not automatically an error in law if that evidence is in fact corroborated by substantial evidence. At the same time one of the members of the court, Mason J., did indicate that the judge should often as a matter of practice give such a warning as he "cannot anticipate with certainty that an appellate court will necessarily agree with his evaluation of the corroborating evidence.... " Nor, as the dissenting Gibbs J. pointed out, can he be sure that the jury will believe the evidence which he sees as credible corroboration.

Regarding the reluctance of an appeal court in such cases to resort to the proviso to what is now section 2(1) of the Criminal Appeal Act 1968 (a matter upon which R. v. Trigg has been expressly followed in R. v. Birchall and others (1986) 82 Cr.App.R. 208 (C.A.)), it could be perhaps contended that often that reluctance should be even more marked in cases in which there has been a failure to comply with the generally laxer and more flexible Turnbull guidelines, as distinct from a failure to comply with the sterner and more rigid corroboration warning requirement.

To be contrasted is R. v. Jenkins (1981) 72 Cr.App.R. 354 (C.A.), where the trial judge had failed to warn the jury of the danger of convicting on the uncorroborated evidence of a witness who might be regarded as an accomplice, but resort was had to the proviso on the ground that, there being ample independent evidence implicating the accused, no miscarriage of justice had occurred. Kilner Brown J., giving the judgment of the court, adverted to the fact that R. v. Trigg was a case dealing with a sexual offence.

R. v. Spencer; R. v. Smails [1987] A.C. 128 (H.L.). The appellants, nurses at a secure hospital, were convicted in two separate trials of ill-treating their patients. In both cases the prosecution evidence consisted wholly of that of other inmates, who had serious convictions and/or were mentally ill. In each case the trial judge had directed the jury to approach the evidence with great caution but had given no specific direction as to the danger of convicting without corroboration. The convictions were upheld by the Court of Appeal. The House of Lords (although allowing certain appeals on other grounds) held that the trial judge's direction had in this respect been entirely adequate. Lord Ackner said (p. 141): "Counsel for the appellants has fully accepted... that patients in hospital under the Mental Health Acts are not in a category like accomplices or complainants in sexual cases or young children. To create from them such a new category would clearly involve considerable problems of definition. What sort of patients, and patients with what sort of criminal records are to be included? The submission of the appellants, in essence, is that without use of the word 'danger', in any case analogous to those of the three established categories, and where the evidence of the only or principal witness relied upon by the prosecution is inherently unreliable, such a warning must be inadequate. I cannot agree." The House of Lords, having answered the certified question in the affirmative, declared (p. 146) that: "(1) while it may often be convenient to use the words 'danger' or 'dangerous,' the use of such words is not essential to an adequate warning so long as the jury are made fully aware of the dangers of convicting on such evidence; and (2) Reg. v. Beck [1982] 1 W.L.R. 461, was rightly decided and in a case which does not fall into the three established categories and where there exists potential corroborative material, the extent to which the trial judge should make reference to that material depends on the facts of each case and the overriding rule is that he must put defence fairly and adequately."

Note.—For R. v. Beck see Note on R. v. Loveridge, supra.
The references to the evidence of a child must be reviewed in the light of the Criminal Justice Act 1988, s.34(2) (Part Two, infra).
For confirmation that, even in a case concerned with the evidence of a complainant in a prosecution for a sexual offence, the use of the word "danger" or "dangerous" is not essential, see R. v. Taylor (1985) 80 Cr.App.R. 327 (C.A.). There Lord Lane L.C.J. said (p. 333): "It is true that the learned judge nowhere uses the word 'danger' or 'dangerous.' But it has been said time and time again, and will have to be said again, that there is no magic formula in these cases. It is not necessary for the judge to use the particular form of words which other judges may have used in the past, provided he makes it perfectly plain to the jury that there is a risk, that there is a danger, whatever particular word may be used. Here the learned judge plainly did.... " To be contrasted with this on the facts is R. v. Stewart (1986) 83 Cr.App.R. 327 (C.A.), decided nearly two years later, in which the

court held that the warning given there regarding the evidence of an accomplice and couched in terms of a reminder of the reasons an accomplice might have for giving false evidence, coupled with an injunction to look at her evidence with "considerable care," fell "far short of a decisive warning (however expressed) that if they convicted on the basis of her evidence they were in danger of convicting an innocent man" (*per* Mustill L.J., at p. 335, giving the judgment of the court).

C. CASES IN WHICH CORROBORATION IS OFTEN REQUIRED IN PRACTICE

Re Hodgson, Beckett v. **Ramsdale** (1885) 31 Ch.D. 177 (C.A.). In an administration action the evidence of a member of the claimant firm of bankers was held admissible without corroboration. Hannen P. said (p. 183): "It is said on behalf of the defendants that the evidence is not to be accepted by the court because there is no corroboration of it, and that in the case of a conflict of evidence between living and dead persons there must be corroboration to establish a claim advanced by a living person against the estate of a dead person. We are of opinion that there is no rule of English law laying down such a proposition. The statement of a living man is not to be disbelieved because there is no corroboration, but we must take into account the necessary absence through death of one of the parties to the transaction, and in considering the statement of the survivor it is natural to look for corroboration in support of it; but if the evidence given by the living man does bring conviction to the tribunal which has to try the question, then there is no rule of law which prevents that being acted upon."

Note.—For a more recent decision to the same effect see *Re Cummins, decd.* [1972] Ch. 62 (C.A.).

Alli v. **Alli** [1965] 3 All E.R. 480 (D.C.). A wife brought proceedings before justices against her husband, alleging desertion and wilful neglect to provide reasonable maintenance for her and their child. The wife sought an adjournment of the hearing to enable a *subpoena* to be served on a person who she hoped would give corroborative evidence in support of her case. The justices refused her application, but, after hearing evidence only from the parties, found for her on both allegations. In their reasons they made no reference to the need for, or even the desirability of, corroboration. Counsel for the husband had, however, reminded the justices that the wife's evidence was uncorroborated. The husband's appeal to the Divisional Court was dismissed. Sir Jocelyn Simon P. said (pp. 484–485): "To sum up, then, our view of the authorities so far: (a) where a matrimonial offence is alleged, the court will look for corroboration of the complainant's evidence; (b) the court will normally, before finding a matrimonial offence proved, require such corroboration if, on the face of the complainant's own evidence, it is available; (c) these are not rules of law, but of practice only. They spring from the gravity of the consequences of proof of a matrimonial offence; and because, we would add, experience has shown the risk of a miscarriage of justice in acting on the uncorroborated testimony of a spouse in this class of case; (d) it is, nevertheless, open to a court to act on the uncorroborated evidence of a spouse if it is in no doubt where the truth lies; (e) these statements are equally applicable to proceedings in courts of summary jurisdiction as to those in the High Court. It follows, we think, that justices should remind themselves, as they proceed to adjudication, of the desirability of corroboration, not least where, on the face of the complainant's evidence, it is available, just as they should remind themselves of the onus and standard of proof; see *Saunders* v. *Saunders* ([1975] 1 All E.R. 838, 843 and 846). The question then arises for decision whether it is incumbent on the justices, in their reasons for their decision prepared for this court, to signify that they have had the question of corroboration in mind; and whether the court will quash the decision if there is no such reference? [His Lordship then referred to some apparently inconsistent authorities.] We think that this discrepancy is significant and due to there being two classes of case. In the first—those alleging sexual misconduct and those where the evidence of adultery is that of a willing participant—experience has shown that there is such an exceptional risk of a miscarriage of justice unless the court has in mind the danger of acting on uncorroborated evidence that an appellate court will intervene unless the trial court has expressly warned itself of that danger. However, in other classes of case, the risk is less acute and the absence of an express indication that the desirability of corroboration was in mind will not of itself call for the intervention of the appellate court; though no doubt such absence may, together with other matters, convince the appellate court that the trial court must have proceeded oblivious of the rules of practice to which we have referred, and that it would not be safe to let the decision stand.... We do not, however, consider that the present is such a case."

D. THE NATURE OF CORROBORATION

R. v. **Reeves** (1979) 68 Cr.App.R. 331 (C.A.). The accused was convicted of handling stolen goods. His co-accused, the thief, pleaded guilty and gave evidence against him. The trial judge warned the jury of the danger of acting on the uncorroborated evidence of an accomplice, but he did not identify those parts of the evidence which were capable of constituting corroboration. The Court of Appeal held that the summing-up was defective. Lord Widgery C.J. said (p. 332): "The criticism of the learned judge's treatment of the whole question of corroboration is that, whereas...the general direction is given certainly in adequate terms, what the judge fails to do is to indicate to the jury whether there was in the evidence in this case any matter which could be regarded as corroborative. It is becoming progressively more clearly recognised that this is a very important feature of the summing-up where the judge has to deal with such questions. The reason for that is that an identification of evidence which is capable of corroboration is not always easy. Even lawyers find it difficult sometimes, and it is, therefore, quite vital that the trial judge should not dispose of the matter as this judge did merely by describing the dangers of acting on uncorroborated evidence unless he produces the back-up direction which tells the jury what evidence can be regarded as corroborative for this purpose."

Note.—To the same effect see *R.* v. *Charles and others* (1976) 68 Cr.App.R. 334(n) (C.A.) and *R.* v. *Cullinane* [1984] C.L.Y. 595; [1984] Crim.L.R. 420 (C.A.).

R. v. **Lucas** [1981] Q.B. 720 (C.A.). The appellant was tried on a count in respect of which evidence was given against her by an accomplice. The appellant gave evidence which was challenged as being partly lies. The trial judge gave the corroboration warning but directed the jury that lies told by the appellant in court could be treated as corroborative of the accomplice's evidence. Allowing her appeal against conviction, the Court of Appeal held that, although lies told in court which fulfilled certain criteria were capable of constituting corroboration, the mere fact that the evidence of the appellant was not believed did not enable the jury to treat this as corroboration. Lord Lane C.J. said (pp. 724–726): "To be capable of amounting to corroboration the lie told out of court must first of all be deliberate. Secondly it must relate to a material issue. Thirdly the motive for the lie must be a realisation of guilt and a fear of the truth. The jury should in appropriate cases be reminded that people sometimes lie, for example, in an attempt to bolster up a just cause, or out of shame or out of a wish to conceal disgraceful behaviour from their family. Fourthly the statement must be clearly shown to be a lie by evidence other than that of the accomplice who is to be corroborated, that is to say by admission or by evidence from an independent witness. As a matter of good sense it is difficult to see why, subject to the same safeguards, lies proved to have been told in court by a defendant should not equally be capable of providing corroboration.... Provided that the lies told in court fulfil the four criteria which we have set out above, we are unable to see why they should not be available for the jury to consider in just the same way as lies told out of court. So far as the instant case is concerned,...[the] lie told by the appellant was clearly not shown to be a lie by evidence other than that of the accomplice who was to be corroborated and consequently the apparent direction that a lie was capable of providing corroboration was erroneous. It is for that reason that we have reached the conclusion that the conviction on the... count-...must be quashed...."

Note.—The criteria laid down in *R.* v. *Lucas* have been applied in at least two subsequent Court of Appeal cases, *R.* v. *West* (1984) 79 Cr.App.R. 45 and *R.* v. *Youssef Rahmoun* (1986) 82 Cr.App.R. 217. These were concerned, not with the evidence of an accomplice, but with the evidence of the complainant in rape cases. There would appear to be no reason to suppose that the criteria are not applicable in all corroboration contexts.

Fabrication of a false alibi can constitute corroboration provided the jury is satisfied that the falsity was not due to mistake and that the fabrication was not caused by panic or stupidity: *R.* v. *Thorne* (1977) 66 Cr.App.R. 6 (C.A.).

An accused's failure to give evidence will not of itself constitute corroboration: *R.* v. *Jackson* [1953] 1 W.L.R. 151 (C.C.A.).

R. v. **Redpath** (1962) 46 Cr.App.R. 319 (C.C.A.). The appellant was charged with indecent assault. It was disputed that the complainant, a small girl, had been assaulted at all. The only corroboration of her evidence was her distressed condition immediately afterwards, but the appellant was convicted. The Court of Criminal Appeal held that the complainant's evidence was sufficiently corroborated and that the conviction should stand; but the court struck a cautionary note (p. 321): "Of course, the circumstances will vary enormously, and in some circumstances quite clearly no weight, or little weight, could be attached to such evidence as corroboration. Thus, if a girl goes in a distressed condition to her mother and makes a complaint, while the mother's evidence as to the girl's condition may in law be capable of amounting to corroboration, quite clearly the jury should be told that they should attach little, if any, weight to that evidence, because it is all part and parcel of the complaint. The girl making the complaint might well put on an act and simulate distress."

Note.—In *R.* v. *Wilson* (1973) 58 Cr.App.R. 304 (C.A.) *R.* v. *Redpath* was distinguished on the ground that no specific warning had been given to the jury as to the weight to be given to evidence of distress. Edmund-Davies L.J. said (p. 235): "...while the appearance and emotional state of a complainant may in very special circumstances be regarded as capable of constituting corroboration, it is an approach which has to be very guarded...." Contrast *R.* v. *Chauhan* (1981) 73 Cr.App.R. 232 (C.A.) where *R.* v. *Redpath* was followed, the Court of Appeal holding that the evidence there was of sufficient weight and that the jury had been fully directed in this regard. See, too, the decision of the Irish Court of Criminal Appeal in *The People* (*D.P.P.*) v. *Mulvey* [1987] I.R. 502.

R. v. Cramp (1880) 14 Cox C.C. 390. The defendant was charged with administering "a noxious thing" with intent to cause a miscarriage. There was no other evidence of administration except the woman's to the effect that the accused had given her, and incited her to take excessive quantities of the drug in question, apart from evidence that, when her father had accused him of giving the drug to his daughter "to produce abortion," the defendant had not denied it. Denman J. doubted whether the woman was an accomplice, but held that, even assuming that she was, the defendant's failure to deny the father's accusation constituted adequate corroboration, "especially coupled with the other's evidence, as the evidence of the chemists called to show that he went to one chemist after another and got this [drug] in two bottles about the same time.... "

R. v. Whitehead [1929] 1 K.B. 99 (C.C.A.). The accused was charged with having unlawful carnal knowledge of a girl under 16. Evidence that the accused, when charged by a police officer and cautioned, had made no denial of the charge, could not constitute corroboration. Lord Hewart C.J., delivering the judgment of the court, held that to hold otherwise would be to go far beyond the *dictum* of Lord Alverstone C.J. in *R. v. Tate* [1908] 2 K.B. 680, 683 (C.C.A.), to the effect that: "It may be that in some cases the absence of an indignant refutation of a charge might be some corroboration." It was also held that, evidence that the girl had complained to her mother several months after the offence was committed could not constitute corroboration. *R. v. Lillyman* [1896] 2 Q.B. 167 (C.C.R.) and *R. v. Osborne* [1905] 1 K.B. 551 (C.C.R.) were distinguished as cases in which the complaint was made at the first reasonably available opportunity. (But it is now to be doubted whether evidence of even immediate complaint, although admissible, can constitute corroboration: see *D.P.P. v. Kilbourne* [1973] A.C. 729 (H.L.), *supra, per* Lord Hailsham of St. Marylebone at p. 746).

R. v. Smith (1985) 81 Cr.App.R. 286 (C.A.). The appellant had been convicted of robbery, the prosecution having relied on the evidence of an accomplice. There was also evidence that police officers searching the scene of the crime had found hairs there and the appellant had refused to give hair samples with which they could be compared. It was held that the jury had been properly directed that evidence of this refusal could constitute corroboration. The Court of Appeal held (p. 292) that such evidence was "in a wholly different category from evidence of a failure to answer when a caution has been administered or a failure to answer in sufficient detail," but added that "Each case must be judged on its own particular facts."

Note.—For the corroborative effect of refusal to provide an "intimate sample" (which does not include hair other than pubic hair) see the Police and Criminal Evidence Act 1984, s.62(10) (Part Two, *infra*).

R. v. Hills (1988) 86 Cr.App.R. 26 (C.A.). The appellant was charged with being knowingly concerned with the illegal importation of a controlled drug. He was said to have enlisted as a courier one, Baruch, who, having pleaded guilty, gave evidence for the prosecution against the appellant. The appellant's conviction was quashed. In the course of giving the judgment of the court Lord Lane C.J., having said (pp. 30–31): "Corroboration is not infrequently provided by a combination of pieces of circumstantial evidence, each innocuous on its own, which together tend to show that the defendant committed the crime," continued (p. 31): "The other statements or circumstances are only of value if, having regard to what is in issue, they come from a source or sources independent of the accomplice and go some part of the way towards proving guilt, by tending to show that the offence was committed and that the accused committed it. It is therefore always important to consider: (1) what are the real issues in the case; (2) what the evidence being put forward as corroboration does in fact prove. The proof may of course come from several sources, and in that sense corroboration may be cumulative as already illustrated; (3) whether that evidence: (a) comes from a source or sources independent of the accomplice; (b) goes some significant part of the way towards showing that the offence was committed and that the accused committed it. In the present case the judge purported to identify possible corroboration perhaps without reminding himself sufficiently of the issue in the case (namely, whether the appellant really was involved in Baruch's admitted attempt to import heroin). He then listed the 13 circumstances which in many instances (1) were themselves dependent upon the evidence of the accomplice or (2) did not themselves and without regard to the evidence of the accomplice sufficiently go towards proving guilt. It is moreover impossible to say which of those 13 items the jury may have selected as being potential corroboration. If they selected one or two which were not independent of the evidence of Baruch himself, the result may very well have been that they were using as corroborative evidence something which was not in fact capable of corroboration. For that reason alone we consider there to have been a material misdirection."

R. v. Willoughby (1989) 88 Cr.App.R. 91 (C.A.). The appellant had been convicted of offences against a girl aged 9, who had seen her attacker briefly and had picked him out at an identification parade. In evidence she said that her attacker had spots on his face. At the trial the appellant had a spot on his face; but he said that it had developed while he was waiting for the trial. The Court of Appeal quashed the conviction, holding that the trial judge had wrongly directed the jury that the spot could be corroboration of the girl's evidence. It in no way corroborated her statement that her assailant had spots.

The Court also held that the judge had erred in not directing the jury that it was for it to decide (1) whether any evidence capable of constituting corroboration was true, and (2), if so, whether it did in fact amount to corroboration.

E. EVIDENCE OF IDENTIFICATION IN CRIMINAL CASES

R. v. TURNBULL

[1977] Q.B. 224; [1976] 3 All E.R. 549; 63 Cr.App.R. 132 (C.A.: 1976)

Whenever the case against an accused depends wholly or substantially upon the correctness of one or more identifications of the accused, which the defence alleges to be mistaken, there are special guidelines that must be followed.

Several appellants had variously been convicted of conspiracy to burgle, robbery and unlawful wounding.

LORD WIDGERY C.J. (delivering the judgment of a Court of five judges): . . .
Each of these appeals raises problems relating to evidence of visual identification in criminal cases. Such evidence can bring about miscarriages of justice and has done so in a few cases in recent years. . . .

In our judgment the danger of miscarriages of justice occurring can be much reduced if trial judges sum up to juries in the way indicated in this judgment.

First, whenever the case against an accused depends wholly or substantially on the correctness of one or more identifications of the accused which the defence alleges to be mistaken, the judge should warn the jury of the special need for caution before convicting the accused in reliance on the correctness of the identification or identifications. In addition he should instruct them as to the reason for the need for such a warning and should make some reference to the possibility that a mistaken witness can be a convincing one and that a number of such witnesses can all be mistaken. Provided this is done in clear terms the judge need not use any particular form of words.

Secondly, the judge should direct the jury to examine closely the circumstances in which the identification by each witness came to be made. How long did the witness have the accused under observation? At what distance? In what light? Was the observation impeded in any way, as for example by passing traffic or a press of people? Had the witness ever seen the accused before? How often? If only occasionally, had he any special reason for remembering the accused? How long elapsed between the original observation and the subsequent identification to the police? Was there any material discrepancy between the description of the accused given to the police by the witness when first seen by them and his actual appearance? If in any case, whether it is being dealt with summarily or on indictment, the prosecution have reason to believe that there is such a material discrepancy they should supply the accused or his legal advisers with particulars of the description the police were first given. In all cases if the accused asks to be given particulars of such descriptions, the prosecution should supply them. Finally, he should remind the jury of any specific weaknesses which had appeared in the identification evidence.

Recognition may be more reliable than identification of a stranger; but even when the witness is purporting to recognise someone whom he knows, the jury should be reminded that mistakes in recognition of close relatives and friends are sometimes made.

All these matters go to the quality of the identification evidence. If the quality is good and remains good at the close of the accused's case, the danger of a mistaken identification is lessened; but the poorer the quality, the greater the danger.

In our judgment when the quality is good, as for example when the identification is made after a long period of observation, or in satisfactory conditions by a relative, a neighbour, a close friend, a workmate and the like, the jury can safely be left to assess the value of the identifying evidence even though there is not other evidence to support it: provided always, however, that an adequate warning has been given about the special need for caution. Were the courts to adjudge otherwise, affronts to justice would frequently occur. A few examples, taken over the whole spectrum of criminal activity, will illustrate what the effects upon the maintenance of law and order would be if any law were enacted that no person could be convicted on evidence of visual identification alone.

Here are the examples. A has been kidnapped and held to ransom over many days. His captor stayed with him all the time. At last he was released but he did not know the identity of his kidnapper nor where he had been kept. Months later the police arrested X for robbery and as a result of what they had been told by an informer they suspected him of the kidnapping. They had no other evidence. They arranged for A to attend an identity parade. He picked out X without hesitation. At X's trial, is the trial judge to rule at the end of the prosecution's case that X must be acquitted?

This is another example. Over a period of a week two police officers, B and C, kept observation in turn on a house which was suspected of being a distribution centre for drugs. A suspected supplier, Y, visited it from time to time. On the last day of the observation B saw Y enter the house. He at once signalled to other waiting police officers, who had a search warrant to enter. They did so; but by the time they got in, Y had escaped by a back window. Six months later C saw Y in the street and arrested him. Y at once alleged that C had mistaken him for someone else. At an identity parade he was picked out by B. Would it really be right and in the interests of justice for a judge to direct Y's acquittal at the end of the prosecution's case?

A rule such as the one under consideration would gravely impede the police in their work and would make the conviction of street offenders such as pickpockets, car thieves and the disorderly very difficult. But it would not only be the police who might be aggrieved by such a rule. Take the case of a factory worker, D, who during the course of his work went to the locker room to get something from his jacket which he had forgotten. As he went in he saw a workmate, Z, whom he had known for years and who worked nearby him in the same shop, standing by D's open locker with his hand inside. He hailed the thief by name. Z turned round and faced D; he dropped D's wallet on the floor and ran out of the locker room by another door. D reported what he had seen to his chargehand. When the chargehand went to find Z, he saw him walking towards his machine. Z alleged that D had been mistaken. A direct acquittal might well be greatly resented not only by D but by many others in the same shop.

When, in the judgment of the trial judge, the quality of the identifying evidence is poor, as for example when it depends solely on a fleeting glance or on a longer observation made in difficult conditions, the situation is very different. The judge should then withdraw the case from the jury and direct an acquittal unless there is other evidence which goes to support the correctness of the identification. This may be corroboration in the sense lawyers use that word; but it need not be so if its effect is to make the jury sure that there has been no mistaken identification: for example, X sees the accused snatch a woman's handbag; he gets only a fleeting glance of the thief's face as he runs off but he does see him entering a nearby house. Later he picks out the accused on an identity parade. If there was no more evidence than this, the poor quality of the identification would require the judge to withdraw the case from the jury; but this would not be so if there was evidence that the house into which the accused was alleged by X to have run was his father's. Another example of supporting evidence not amounting to corroboration in a technical sense is to be found in *Reg.* v. *Long* (1973) 57 Cr.App.R. 871. The accused, who was charged with robbery, had been identified by three witnesses in different places on different occasions but each had only a momentary opportunity for observation. Immediately after the robbery the accused had left his home and could not be found by the police. When later he was seen by them he claimed to know who had done the robbery and offered to help to find the robbers. At his trial he put forward an alibi which the jury rejected. It was an odd coincidence that the witnesses should have identified a man who had behaved in this way. In our judgment odd coincidences can, if unexplained, be supporting evidence.

The trial judge should identify to the jury the evidence which he adjudges is capable of supporting the evidence of identification. If there is any evidence or circumstances which the jury might think was supporting when it did not have this quality, the judge should say so. A jury, for example, might think that support for identification evidence could be found in the fact that the accused had not given evidence before them. An accused's absence from the witness box cannot provide evidence of anything and the judge should tell the jury so. But he would be entitled to tell them that when assessing the quality of the identification evidence they could take into consideration the fact that it was uncontradicted by any evidence coming from the accused himself.

Care should be taken by the judge when directing the jury about the support for an identification which may be derived from the fact that they have rejected an alibi. False alibis may be put forward for many reasons: an accused, for example, who has only his own truthful evidence to rely on may stupidly fabricate an alibi and get lying witnesses to support it out of fear that his own evidence will not be enough. Further, alibi witnesses can make genuine mistakes about dates and occasions like any other witnesses can. It is only when the jury is satisfied that the sole reason for the fabrication was to deceive them and there is no other explanation for its being put forward can fabrication provide any support for identification evidence. The jury should be reminded that proving the accused has told lies about where he was at the material time does not by itself prove that he was where the identifying witness says he was.

In setting out these guidelines for trial judges, which involve only changes of practice, not law, we have tried to follow the recommendations set out in the Report which Lord Devlin's Committee made to the Secretary of State for the Home Department in April 1976. We have not followed that report in using the phrase "exceptional circumstances" to describe situations in which the risk of mistaken identification is reduced. . . .

A failure to follow these guidelines is likely to result in a conviction being quashed and will do so if in the judgment of this court on all the evidence the verdict is either unsatisfactory or unsafe.

. . . .

[The court held that, the trial of the first two appellants having correctly followed the practice necessary in cases depending upon identification, their appeals would be dismissed; but that, the practice not having been followed in the trials of the third and fourth appellants, their appeals would be allowed.]

Note.—In *R.* v. *Weeder* (1980) 71 Cr.App.R. 228 the Court of Appeal, again sitting five judges strong, said (p. 231): "When the quality of the identifying evidence is poor the judge should withdraw the case from the jury and direct an acquittal unless there is other evidence which goes to support the correctness of the identification. The identification evidence can be poor, even though it is given by a number of witnesses. They may all have had only the opportunity of a fleeting glance or a longer observation made in difficult conditions, *e.g.* the occupants of a bus who observed the incident at night as they drove past." The court went on to state (p. 231) that: "Where the quality of the identification evidence is such that the jury can be safely left to assess its value, even though there is no other evidence to support it, then the Judge is fully entitled, if so minded, to direct the jury that an identification by one witness can constitute support for the identification by another, *provided* that he warns them in clear terms that even a number of honest witnesses can all be mistaken." Subsequently in *R.* v. *Breslin* (1985) 80 Cr.App.R. 226 the Court of Appeal, having emphasised that it is the quality, rather than the quantity, of identification evidence that matters, held (p. 230) that "the directions and warnings referred to in the passage from *Weeder* [set out above and restated by the court] should be given in all 'identification' cases to which that passage is applicable." The court, noting that *R.* v. *Weeder* had been decided after *R.* v. *Keane* (1977) 65 Cr.App.R. 247 (C.A.), impliedly but clearly rejected the suggestion strongly made in the earlier case that the *Turnbull* guidelines are to be interpreted very flexibly.

In *R.* v. *Keane* it had also been specifically laid down that the falsity of an alibi can be relied upon as supporting an identification only if the jury is satisfied that the sole reason for the fabrication was to deceive them on the issue of identification. This holding is undisturbed.

As the matters dealt with in *R.* v. *Turnbull* are primarily concerned with the assessment of the weight of evidence and only incidentally with admissibility, the holding of a *voir dire* is not appropriate: *R.* v. *Walshe* (1982) 74 Cr.App.R. 85 (C.A.). See, too, *R.* v. *Flemming* (1988) 86 Cr.App.R. 32.

R. v. **Hunjan** (1979) 68 Cr.App.R. 99 (C.A.). The appellant had been convicted of possessing and supplying a controlled drug—morphine—contrary to the Misuse of Drugs Act 1971, s.4. He was granted leave to appeal on the ground that the trial judge had failed to follow the guidelines on identification evidence laid down in *R.* v. *Turnbull, (supra)*. When the appeal was heard the Court of Appeal seems to have treated the guidelines as mandatory subject only to the *proviso* to section 2(1) of the Criminal Appeal Act 1968. Geoffrey Lane L.J., delivering the judgment of the court, said (pp. 103–104): "There is no doubt that there was a misdirection in this case in that the *Turnbull* warnings were not given, or in so far as they were given were not given adequately. The only question which remains then is this: Whether we should apply the *proviso* so as to leave the conviction standing despite the conceded fault in the direction to the jury . . . we have to be convinced that, had the jury been directed correctly, they would nevertheless have come to the same conclusion as that which they, in fact, did. We do not feel confident that they would." The conviction was quashed.

Note.—The Irish Court of Criminal Appeal has also held that failure to comply with guidelines generally similar to those set out in *R.* v. *Turnbull* (see *The People (Attorney-General)* v. *Casey (No. 2)* [1963] I.R. 33) constitutes a misdirection: *The People* v. *Stafford* [1983] I.R. 165.

In *Scott* v. *The Queen* [1989] 2 W.L.R. 924 the Privy Council, allowing an appeal against conviction on account of the trial judge's failure to give an appropriate warning regarding the dangers of identification evidence, said (p. 936) that "it would only be in the most exceptional circumstances that a conviction based on uncorroborated identification evidence should be sustained in the absence of such a warning" and again that failure to give such a warning in these circumstances "is generally to be regarded as a fatal flaw in a summing up . . ."

Chapter 11

PRIVILEGE

THE notion of privilege in the law of evidence denotes a liberty to withhold or prevent the answer to a question or the production of a document or sometimes a physical object. Its operation is not confined to the trial itself: it may be operative in interlocutory proceedings. It manifests itself in two general forms. A witness may, if he so wishes, decline to answer a particular question or to produce a particular piece of documentary or real evidence: this may be usefully described as a case of true testimonial or witness privilege, for the option is exercisable by the witness—in other words it is he who enjoys the right to waive the privilege. The privilege against self-incrimination falls into this category. The second kind of privilege may be referred to as relational, in that it attaches to communications arising out of a particular type of relationship between two or more persons, one of whom, not only may himself decline to give or adduce evidence as to the contents of the communication, but also may prevent other parties to the communication from doing so. Thus the person who has the right to waive this sort of privilege may, or may not, be the witness. The privilege arising from the professional relationship of lawyer and client exemplifies the situation, the privilege being that of the client even when it is the lawyer who is the witness.

Privilege in either of its manifestations must be distinguished on the one hand from bare competence or immunity from compellability, and on the other hand from inadmissibility.

Compellability is concerned with whether a competent witness can be required to give evidence at all, whereas testimonial privilege is concerned with whether a witness, who is already in the witness box, is obliged to answer a particular question or produce a particular document. The protection of a testimonial privilege is equally available, whether the witness claiming it is barely competent and has given evidence of his own free will, or is compellable and has been required to do so.

Privilege differs from inadmissibility in several respects. (1) Matters protected by privilege may be proved by secondary evidence. This is the doctrine of *Calcraft* v. *Guest*[1] (*infra*) and embodies a rule of adjectival law. It is, however, to be borne in mind that as a matter of substantive law a court may in its discretion grant an injunction against the use of material, in which an applicant has a legitimate interest such as the fact

---

[1] [1898] 1 Q.B. 759 (C.A.).

that its utilisation would involve a breach of confidence. Such an injunction was granted in *Ashburton* v. *Pape*[2] (*infra*). Although the apparent conflict between these two doctrines can be formally resolved in terms of the distinction between adjectival and substantive law, the conflict reflects something more fundamental. Whereas the rule in *Calcraft* v. *Guest* emphasises the purely personal nature of a privilege, the doctrine of *Ashburton* v. *Pape* more fully reflects the policy underlying the existence of many privileges. Moreover, in an age of greatly extended means of rapid and accurate reproduction of oral and written statements the distinction between original and secondary evidence in this context is increasingly difficulty to justify. (2) A privilege usually has to be claimed by the person entitled to it. The judge may, and in the case of certain privileges often does, warn the witness that he may be entitled to claim privilege, but there is no rule requiring the judge to do this. Evidence given in ignorance of the availability of even the most palpable privilege is nonetheless admissible.[3] (3) If the person claiming privilege is not a party to the proceedings, there will usually be no appeal against the rejection or upholding of his claim. It may be mentioned, too, that no adverse inference ought to be drawn from the fact that a privilege is claimed.

When the law concedes a privilege justification for it must be found in considerations extrinsic to the efficiency and fairness of the trial process. Whereas the bulk of the exclusionary rules which go to make up the law of evidence are designed (although not always well-designed) to assist that process, to sustain a claim of privilege is cold-bloodedly to permit relevant evidence to be withheld at the risk of causing injustice to a party. Privileges should therefore be narrowly construed and allowed only for overriding reasons of compelling policy. In fact few privileges were known to the Common Law, the most important being those already mentioned—the privilege against self-incrimination and that attaching to the lawyer-client relationship. Several privileges are creatures of statute, many having been enacted in the wake of the abolition in the nineteenth century of the old rules about testimonial disqualification. More recently the pendulum has begun to swing back, in civil cases as a result of the generally limiting provisions of the Civil Evidence Act 1968, ss.14 and 16, and in criminal cases by the Police and Criminal Evidence Act 1984, s.80(9), (both Part Two, *infra*)—although new professional privileges attaching to the relationships of Patent Agent and client, Trade Mark Agent and client and Licensed Conveyancer and client, and a limited privilege relating to disclosure of the identity of an informant, have been created.[4] Finally it may be mentioned that a very recent tendency is discernible, especially in certain Commonwealth jurisdictions, to adopt a more flexible approach to the definition of the traditional categories of privilege. Two illustrations of this are noted at pp. 241–242, *infra*.

The protection accorded to statements made "without prejudice" is often subsumed under the rubric of privilege. Such statements can only be withheld when they are made in the course of, and relate to,

---

[2] [1913] 2 Ch. 469.
[3] *R.* v. *Coote* (1873) 4 L.R.P.C. 599 (P.C.).
[4] Civil Evidence Act 1968, s.15, but now see the Copyright, Designs and Patents Act 1988, s. 280; *ibid.* s. 284; Administration of Justice Act 1985, s.33; Contempt of Court Act 1981, s.10 (all Part Two, *infra*).

negotiations for the settlement of a dispute. It is considered necessary to allow the parties to speak freely when attempting such a settlement and to some extent to disclose their cases to each other in the course of doing so. But the necessary freedom of discussion would not prevail if any admission made could be given in evidence should the negotiation for a settlement break down. Accordingly, communications made "without prejudice" may not, except in special circumstances, be disclosed in court without the consent of both parties. The position has affinities with that of the relational privilege, but the privilege here must be seen as joint. Also, it is doubtful whether secondary evidence of a "without prejudice" communication is admissible. Communications may be expressly stated to be "without prejudice" or this may be implied. It should, of course, be remembered, too, that intrinsic substantive liability cannot be evaded by marking a document "without prejudice": a libel is still a libel although uttered in a document so marked.

A. PRIVILEGE AGAINST SELF-INCRIMINATION

Blunt v. **Park Lane Hotel Ltd.** [1942] 2 K.B. 253. In an action for slander based on the allegation that the plaintiff had been guilty of adultery, the defendants were allowed to administer interrogatories to her in support of their plea of justification. The Court of Appeal held that, formal ecclesiastical censure of laymen for adultery being obsolete, the privilege against self-incrimination did not extend to liability to a finding of adultery. Goddard L.J. propounded (p. 257) a classic formulation of that privilege: "The rule is that no one is bound to answer any question if the answer thereto would, in the opinion of the judge, have a tendency to expose the deponent to any criminal charge, penalty or forfeiture which the judge regards as reasonable likely to be preferred or sued for."

Note.—The privilege is available if the answer to the question would have a tendency to render the bringing of a charge, although not necessarily conviction, likely. As Stephen J. said in *Lamb* v. *Munster* (1882) 10 Q.B.D. 110, 113, "It is not that a man must be guilty of an offence and say substantially, 'I am guilty of the offence, but am not going to furnish evidence of it.' I do not think that the privilege is so narrow as that, for then it would be illusory. . . . it seems to me that a man may say, 'I think the answer would tend to criminate me,' meaning thereby 'would tend to bring a criminal prosecution against me for a crime of which I am in fact innocent, but of which I might on the facts be very probably accused.' "

The privilege in so far as it relates to liability to forfeiture is abrogated in civil cases by the Civil Evidence Act 1968, s.16(1)(*a*) (Part Two, *infra*).

The privilege applies not only to oral testimony but also to the production of documentary (see, *e.g.* *Spokes* v. *Grosvenor Hotel Co.* [1897] 2 Q.B. 124 (C.A.)) and real evidence.

Although the common law privilege against incrimination does not cover liability to a finding of adultery, from 1869 (Evidence Further Amendment Act, s.3) until 1968 (Civil Evidence Act, s.16(5)) there existed in "proceedings instituted in consequence of adultery" a limited statutory privilege relating to admissions of adultery. There is no privilege if the danger apprehended is of liability to proceedings for debt or another civil remedy, not being a penalty or forfeiture, whether in England or abroad (see Witnesses Act 1806 (Part Two, *infra*). The risk of bankruptcy proceedings probably confers no immunity: *Ex parte Haes* [1902] 1 K.B. 98 (C.A.). Privilege is available in respect of evidence the production of which would tend to expose the claimant to fines under Articles 85, 189 and 192 of the European Economic Community Treaty, which cover penalties imposed by administrative action and recoverable under English law: *Re Westinghouse Uranium Contract* [1978] A.C. 547 (H.L.).

It is uncertain whether at common law the privilege extends to answers which would tend to expose to liability under a foreign law, but the Civil Evidence Act 1968, s.14(1)(*a*) (Part Two, *infra*) confines the scope of the privilege in civil cases to incrimination or exposure to proceedings for recovery of a penalty under the law of any part of the United Kingdom. There is no corresponding statute relating to the scope of the privilege in criminal cases. It has been held in Canada (*Spencer v. R.* (1985) 2 S.C.R. 278; 21 D.L.R. (4d) 756); in Australia (*Jackson v. Gamble* [1983] 1 V.R. 552); and in the United States (*Murphy v. Waterfront Commission of New York Harbour* (378 U.S. 52 (1964)) that the privilege does extend generally to cases of incrimination under foreign law.

R. v. Boyes (1861) 30 L.J.Q.B. 301 (Q.B.). A witness declined to answer a question on the ground that the answer would incriminate him in an offence. He was forthwith handed a written pardon, and so could not be prosecuted in the ordinary way. It was no valid objection that he still remained liable to impeachment in Parliament to which a pardon is no bar, by the Act of Settlement, 1700. Cockburn C.J. (delivering the judgment of the Court) said (303–304): "It was contended that a bare possibility of legal peril was sufficient to entitle a witness to protection; nay, further, that the witness was the sole judge as to whether his evidence would bring him into danger of the law, and that the statement of his belief to that effect, if not manifestly made mala fide, should be received as conclusive. With the latter of these propositions we are altogether unable to concur. Upon a review of the authorities, we are clearly of opinion... that, to entitle a party called as a witness to the privilege of silence, the court must see, from the circumstances of the case and the nature of the evidence which the witness is called to give, that there is reasonable ground to apprehend danger to the witness from his being compelled to answer. We, indeed, quite agree that if the fact of the witness being in danger be once made to appear, great latitude should be allowed to him in judging for himself of the effect of any particular question, there being no doubt... that a question, which might appear at first sight a very innocent one might, by affording a link in a chain of evidence, become the means of bringing home an offence to the party answering. Subject to this reservation a judge is, in our opinion, bound to insist on a witness answering, unless he is satisfied that the answer will tend to place the witness in peril. Further than this, we are of opinion that the danger to be apprehended must be real and appreciable with reference to the ordinary operation of law in the ordinary course of things; not a danger of an imaginary and unsubstantial character, having reference to some extraordinary and barely possible contingency, so improbable that no reasonable man would suffer it to influence his conduct. We think that a merely remote and naked possibility, out of the ordinary course of law, and such as no reasonable man would be affected by, should not be suffered to obstruct the administration of justice. The object of the law is to afford to a party, called upon to give evidence in a proceeding *inter alios*, protection against being brought by means of his own evidence within the penalties of the law. But it would be to convert a statutory protection into a means of abuse if it were to be held that a mere imaginary possibility of danger, however remote and improbable, was sufficient to justify the withholding of evidence essential to the ends of justice.

Now, in the present case, no one seriously supposes that the witness runs the slightest risk of an impeachment by the House of Commons.... it was, therefore the duty of the presiding judge to compel him to answer...."

Note.—It may be noted that in the case of the common law privilege of refusing to answer incriminating questions, it is perfectly lawful and proper for the question to be put, and it is for the witness to claim privilege if he thinks fit (*Boyle v. Wiseman* (1855) 10 Exch. 647). (This is to be contrasted with the position of the accused, in those cases in which he may not be cross-examined as to other offences, under the Criminal Evidence

Act, 1898 (Part Two, *infra*)). However, in practice the judge may advise the witness of his
right to plead the privilege against incrimination.

Rank Film Distributors Ltd. v. **Video Information Centre** [1982] A.C. 380
(H.L.). The plaintiffs were owners of the copyright in certain films. On the basis
of evidence that in breach of this copyright the defendants were making and
selling video cassette copies of the films, the plaintiffs on an *ex parte* motion
before the judge obtained orders permitting them to enter the defendants'
premises and seize infringing copies of the films and requiring the defendants to
give discovery of relevant documents and answers to interrogatories relating to the
supply and sale of infringing copies. The House of Lords held that the defendants
were entitled to rely on the privilege against self-incrimination by discovery or
answering interrogatories, since, if they complied with orders of that nature, there
was in the circumstances a real and appreciable risk of criminal proceedings for
conspiracy to defraud being taken against them. The order requiring the
defendants to allow the plaintiffs access to their premises for the purpose of
looking for illicit copy films and to allow their being removed to safe custody was
not seriously contested, and the House confirmed that the privilege against self-
incrimination had no application in that context.

Note.—See now, however, the Supreme Court Act 1981, s.72 (Part Two, *infra*), which
seeks to strike a balance between protection of the holders of certain forms of intellectual
property and of persons against self-incrimination. It seeks to achieve this by statutory
exclusion of the privilege coupled with prohibition upon the use of incriminating answers
in certain subsequent proceedings. See, too, *e.g.* the Theft Act 1968, s.31(1); and the
Criminal Damage Act 1971, s.9 (Part Two, *infra*).

An accused person who elects to give evidence on his own behalf cannot claim privilege
in respect of the offence with which he is charged; Criminal Evidence Act 1898, s.1,
proviso (*e*) (Part Two, *infra*).

Some statutes (consistently with the testimonial nature of the privilege but inconsistently
with its supposed policy basis) provide for compulsory out-of-court answering of
incriminating questions and yet make no provision restricting the admissibility of the
evidence compulsorily given. They relate to the investigation of serious offences like
contravention of the Official Secrets Act 1911, s.1, but also to some road traffic offences.
But contrast legal professional privilege in the Companies Act 1985, s.452(1) and (2), the
Criminal Justice Act 1987, s.2(9) (both Part Two, *infra*) and the Taxes Management Act
1970, ss. 20(3) and 20B(8), as applied in *R.* v. *Inland Revenue, ex p. Goldberg* [1988] 3
W.L.R. 522 (D.C.).

The Civil Evidence Act 1968, s.14(1)(*b*), (Part Two, *infra*) provides that in civil
proceedings the privilege shall extend to answers to questions and the production of
documents or things tending to incriminate (or expose to proceedings for recovery of a
penalty) the spouse of the privileged person. See, too, s.14(3) and (4). There is no
corresponding provision in the Police and Criminal Evidence Act 1984, and it would seem
(as is perhaps implicit in, *e.g. R.* v. *Pitt* [1983] Q.B. 25 (C.A.) (p. 147 *supra*)) that in
criminal cases the privilege does not always protect the spouse of a witness.

B. PRIVILEGE ARISING FROM THE RELATIONSHIP OF LAWYER AND CLIENT

Introductory Note.—"Items subject to legal privilege" are defined, for the purposes of
the Police and Criminal Evidence Act 1984, in section 10 of that Act (Part Two, *infra*).
For the relationship of this with the position at common law, see the judgments of Lord
Griffiths and Lord Goff of Chievely in *R.* v. *Central Criminal Court, ex parte Francis and
Francis* [1989] A.C. 346 (H.L.), *infra*.

WHEELER v. LE MARCHANT

17 Ch.D. 675; **50 L.J. Ch. 793;** 44 L.T. 632; 30 W.R. 235 (C.A.: 1881)

Communications made in professional confidence to counsel, solicitors and their clerks may not be disclosed without the consent of the client. This privilege extends to communications made by other persons on behalf of the client to the legal adviser, if obtained by the latter for the purpose of litigation but not otherwise.

The court ordered production of letters which had passed between the solicitors of the defendants and their surveyor, except such (if any) as the defendants should state by affidavit to have been prepared confidentially after dispute had arisen between the plaintiff and the defendants and for the purpose of obtaining information, evidence or legal advice with reference to litigation existing or contemplated between the parties to the action.

JESSEL M.R.: . . . The principle is of a very limited character. It does not protect all confidential communications which a man must necessarily make in order to obtain advice, even when necessary for the protection of his life or of his honour, to say nothing of his fortune. There are many communications which must be made, because without them the ordinary business of life cannot be carried on, and yet they are not protected. As I have said in the course of the argument, the communication made to a medical man, whose advise is sought by a patient . . . is not protected. Communications made to the priest in the confessional, on matters perhaps considered by the penitent to be more important even than the care of his life or his fortune, are not protected. Communications made to a friend with respect to matters of the most delicate nature, on which advice is sought with respect to a man's honour or reputation, are not protected. Therefore it must not be supposed that there is any principle which says that every confidential communication which, in order to carry on the ordinary business of life, must necessarily be made, is protected. The protection is of a very limited character. It is a protection in this country restricted to the obtaining the assistance of lawyers, as regards the conduct of litigation or the rights of property. It has never gone beyond the obtaining of legal advice and assistance; and all things reasonably necessary in the shape of communication to the legal advisers are protected from production or discovery, in order that that legal advice may be obtained safely and sufficiently. . . .

The actual communication to the solicitor by the client is, of course, protected, and it is equally protected whether that communication is made by the client in person or by an agent on behalf of the client, and whether made to the solicitor in person or to a clerk or subordinate of the solicitor, who acts in his place and under his direction. Again, with the same view, the evidence obtained by the solicitor, or by his direction, or at his instance, even if obtained by the client, is protected if obtained after litigation has been commenced or threatened, or with a view to the defence or prosecution of such litigation. So, again, it does not matter whether the advice is obtained from the solicitor as to a dealing which is not the subject of litigation. What is protected is the communication necessary to obtain legal advice. It must be a communication made to the solicitor in that character and for that purpose.

But what we are asked to protect here is this: The solicitor being consulted in a matter as to which no dispute has arisen, thinks he would like to know some further facts before giving his advice, and applies to a surveyor to tell him what the state of a given property is, or information of that character, and it is said that information given in answer to such application ought to be protected because it is desired or required by the solicitor in order to enable him the better to give legal advice. It appears to me that it is not only extending the rule beyond what has been previously laid down, but beyond what necessity warrants. . . . It is a rule invented and maintained only for the purpose of enabling a man to obtain legal advice with safety. . . .

BRETT L.J.: The proposition laid before us for approval is that where one of the parties to an action has in his possession or control documents which passed between his solicitor and third parties, and which contain either information or advice, those documents are protected in his hands from inspection on the ground that they are documents which passed between the solicitor and the third party for the purpose of enabling the solicitor to give advice to his client, although such information and advice was obtained by the solicitor for that purpose at a time when there was no litigation pending between the parties nor any litigation contemplated. It seems to me that that proposition cannot be acceded to. . . .

COTTON L.J.: . . . It is said communications between a client and his legal advisers, for obtaining legal advice, are privileged, and therefore any communication between the representatives of the client and the solicitor must also be privileged. That is a fallacious use of the word "representatives." If the representative is a person employed as an agent on the part of the client to obtain the legal advice of the solicitor, of course he stands in exactly the same position, as regards protection, as the client, and his communications with the solicitors stand in the same position as the communications of the principal with his solicitor. But these persons were not representatives in that sense. They were representatives in this sense, that they were employed on behalf of the clients, the defendants, to do certain work, but that work was not the communicating with the solicitors to obtain legal advice. So their communications cannot be protected on the ground that they are communications between the client by his representatives and the solicitor.

In fact, the proposition of the defendant comes to this, that all communications between a solicitor and a third person, in the course of his advising his client, are to be protected.

It was conceded that there was no case that went that length . . . to protect such documents. Hitherto such documents have been protected only when they have been made in contemplation of some litigation, or for the purpose of giving advice or obtaining evidence with reference to it. And that is reasonable, because then the solicitor is preparing for the defence, or for bringing the action, and all communications he makes for that purpose, and the communications made to him for the purpose of giving him the information are, in fact, the brief in the action, and ought to be protected. . . .

Note.—The privilege represents simply a rule of evidence and is applied only to prevent disclosure by way of pre-trial discovery, or in the actual course of judicial or quasi-judicial proceedings. It did not, for example, apply in an inquiry or inspection by the Law Society to enforce its Accounts Rules: *Parry Jones* v. *Law Society* [1969] 1 Ch. 1 (C.A.), where Diplock L.J. said (p. 9): "... privilege, of course, is irrelevant when one is not concerned with judicial or quasi-judicial proceedings because, strictly speaking, privilege refers to a right to withhold from a court, or tribunal exercising judicial functions, material which would otherwise be admissible in evidence." There has, however, been some recent statutory projection of the privilege into other contexts: see, *e.g.* the Data Protection Act 1984, s.31(2) (Part Two, *infra*).

The privilege does not attach to documents or to chattels, which were in existence before the relationship of lawyer and client was established, simply because they have been sent to the lawyer for his advice (*R.* v. *Peterborough Justices, ex p. Hicks* [1977] 1 W.L.R. 1371 (D.C.), which concerned a forged power of attorney deposited for legal advice in relation to an impending prosecution); or simply because they have been sent by the lawyer to a third party even if in connection with litigation (*R.* v. *King* [1983] 1 W.L.R. 411 (C.A.), which concerned a document sent by the defence to a handwriting expert for comparison with prosecution documents in connection with an impending prosecution). For a comparison with section 10(1)(*c*) of the Police and Criminal Evidence Act 1984 (Part Two, *infra*), see *R.* v. *Central Criminal Court, ex p. Francis and Francis* [1989] A.C. 346 (H.L.) and *Note* thereto, p. 232, *infra*.

It is the client alone who can waive the privilege: *Wilson* v. *Rastall* (1792) 4 T.R. 753, Waiver may be express or implied. It may result from a failure to claim it, or from the use of a privileged document. So, when counsel cross-examined a witness for the plaintiff as to his previous statement to the defendant (which was privileged as having been prepared in respect of litigation), there was held to be a waiver of the privilege as to the whole statement: *Burnell* v. *British Transport Commission* [1956] 1 Q.B. 187 (C.A.). The question whether the party consented to the waiver was not discussed, but counsel must be regarded as having been acting on his behalf. See, too, *Great Atlantic Insurance* v. *Home Insurance* [1981] 1 W.L.R. 529, where the Court of Appeal held that counsel had without any express authority unintentionally waived the client's privilege in respect of the whole of a memorandum by reading out in court a part of its contents. Neither the client nor his legal advisers claimed any privilege for this part, but the court found that it would have been privileged and that reading it out constituted a waiver not only of this privilege but also of any privilege attaching to the rest of the memorandum which dealt with the same subject-matter. But the mere use of a privileged document in order to facilitate cross-examination (as distinct from in effect using it as evidence) does not constitute waiver: *General Accident Co.* v. *Tanter* [1984] 1 W.L.R. 100 (Q.B.D.). Nor does making a document available to the prosecution in separate criminal proceedings constitute waiver in the civil proceedings to which it relates: *British Coal Corporation* v. *Dennis Rye Ltd.* [1988] 1 W.L.R. 1113 (C.A.).

Although some statutes specifically preserve the privilege in particular contexts (see, *e.g.* the Companies Act 1985, s.732 (Part Two, *infra*)) there has been some limited statutory abrogation of the privilege. See, *e.g.* the Civil Evidence Act 1972, s.2(3) (Part Two, *infra*) which allows for the making of Rules of Court regulating the availability of certain medical and other reports which might otherwise be within the privilege. See, too, *Jones* v. *G.D. Searle & Co. Ltd.* [1979] 1 W.L.R. 101 (C.A.) in which the Limitation Act 1939, s.2D, was construed as creating an exception to the privilege. Eveleigh J. said (p. 106): "I think that the court would be slow to take away a well-established privilege ... and certainly would require some positive indication that the legislation so intended.... However, the wording of section 2D(3)(*f*) refers specifically to the nature of any such advice he may have received. Thus the position is that the court is under a duty to consider the nature of advice received by the plaintiff; and if the court is under a duty to consider the advice ... the court must be in a position to demand evidence as to what the nature of the advice was."

The dictum of Jessel M.R. in *Wheeler* v. *Le Marchant* as to medical men is supported by authority (for example, *Duchess of Kingston's Case* (1776) 20 St.Tr. 355 at 572, 573); but the absence of privilege for confessional communications has not apparently been decided in England, though there are other dicta against its recognition. In practice considerable discretion operates in many of these cases. As Lord Denning M.R. said in *Att.-Gen.* v. *Mulholland* [1963] 2 Q.B. 477, 489: "Take the clergyman the banker or the medical man. None of these is entitled to refuse to answer when directed to by a judge. Let me not be mistaken. The judge will respect the confidences which each member of these honourable professions receives in the course of it, and will not direct him to answer unless not only is it relevant but also it is a proper and, indeed, necessary question in the course of justice to be put and answered." Also, communications to medical men, and to priests or clergymen of any church, may fall within the rule as to statements made without prejudice to a conciliator of a matrimonial dispute. Further, medical reports obtained for the purpose of contemplated litigation may fall within the principle recognised in the judgments above (see *Worrall* v. *Reich* [1955] 1 Q.B. 296 (C.A.)). There is no privilege for communications with accountants (see *Chantrey Martin* v. *Martin* [1953] 2 Q.B. 286 (C.A.)), except upon a similar ground; nor with bankers (see *Tournier* v. *National Provincial and Union Bank of England* [1924] 1 K.B. 461 at 473, 479, 486 (C.A.) and the Bankers' Books Evidence Act 1879 (Part Two, *infra*). But for the position of communications with Patent Agents and with Licensed Conveyancers see respectively the Copyright, Designs and Patents Act 1988, s.280 and the Administration of Justice Act 1985, s.33 (Section C, *infra*).

BALABEL v. AIR INDIA

[1988] Ch. 317; [1988] 2 W.L.R. 1036; [1988] 2 All E.R. 246 (C.A.: 1988)

The purpose of legal professional privilege is to enable legal advice to be sought and given in confidence. This purpose is to be broadly construed; and legal advice is to be taken to include advice as to what should prudently and sensibly be done in the relevant legal context.
In view of the increased range of assistance given by solicitors not all solicitor and client communications are necessarily privileged; but in a conveyancing transaction communications passing in the handling of that transaction are privileged even though they do not incorporate a specific piece of advice, provided that their aim is obtaining appropriate legal advice.

The plaintiffs brought an action against the defendant, an Indian corporation, claiming *inter alia* specific performance of an agreement for an underlease of business premises. In support of the allegation in their statement of claim relating to the negotiations for the underlease the plaintiffs sought discovery of three categories of documents, namely, (1) communications between the defendant and its solicitors other than those seeking or giving legal advice; (2) drafts, working papers, attendance notes and memoranda of the defendant's solicitors relating to the proposed new underlease; and internal communications of the defendant other than those seeking advice from their Indian legal advisers. The defendant's claim of privilege covering these documents was upheld by the Court of Appeal.

TAYLOR L.J.: "This case raises an important point concerning legal professional privilege. Broadly, the issue is whether such privilege extends only to communications seeking or conveying legal advice, or to all that passes between solicitor and client on matters within the ordinary business of a solicitor. . . .
It is common ground that the basic principle justifying legal professional privilege arises from the public interest requiring full and frank exchange of confidence between solicitor and client to enable the latter to receive necessary legal advice. Originally it related only to communications where legal proceedings were in being or in contemplation. This was the rationale which distinguished the solicitor and client

relationship from that between any other professional man and his client. There is no doubt that legal professional privilege now extends beyond legal advice in regard to litigation. But how far?

Mr Lightman, counsel for the defendant, has referred to a long series of decisions from 1833 until today.... [His Lordship referred to several cases including *Minter* v. *Priest* [1929] 1 K.B. 655 (C.A.); [1930] A.C. 558 (H.L.) from which he quoted (p. 1042) from the judgment of Lord Buckmaster]. In the House of Lords [1930] A.C. 558, Lord Buckmaster, with whom Lord Thankerton agreed, said, at p. 568: "The relationship of solicitor and client being once established, it is not a necessary conclusion that whatever conversation ensued was protected from disclosure. The conversation to secure this privilege must be such as, within a very wide and generous ambit of interpretation, must be fairly referable to the relationship, but outside that boundary the mere fact that a person speaking is a solicitor, and the person to whom he speaks is his client affords no protection."...

These cases undoubtedly show a divergence of judicial authority as to the scope of the privilege. It is therefore important to go back to the basic principle justifying such privilege as an exception to the general rule that all relevant evidence is discoverable and admissible. That principle is that a client should be able to get legal advice in confidence....

Although originally confined to advice regarding litigation, the privilege was extended to non-litigious business. Nevertheless, despite that extension, the purpose and scope of the privilege is still to enable legal advice to be sought and given in confidence. In my judgment, therefore, the test is whether the communication or other document was made confidentially for the purposes of legal advice. Those purposes have to be construed broadly. Privilege obviously attaches to a document conveying legal advice from solicitor to client and to a specific request from the client for such advice. But it does not follow that all other communications between them lack privilege. In most solicitor and client relationships, especially where a transaction involves protracted dealings, advice may be required or appropriate on matters great or small at various stages. There will be a continuum of communication and meetings between the solicitor and client. The negotiations for a lease such as occurred in the present case are only one example. Where information is passed by the solicitor or client to the other as part of the continuum aimed at keeping both informed so that advice may be sought and given as required, privilege will attach. A letter from the client containing information may end with such words as "please advise me what I should do." But, even if it does not, there will usually be implied in the relationship an overall expectation that the solicitor will at each stage, whether asked specifically or not, tender appropriate advice. Moreover, legal advice is not confined to telling the client the law; it must include advice as to what should prudently and sensibly be done in the relevant legal context.

It may be that applying this test to any series of communications might isolate occasional letters or notes which could not be said to enjoy privilege. But to be disclosable such documents must be not only privilege-free but also material and relevant. Usually a letter which does no more than acknowledge receipt of a document or suggest a date for a meeting will be irrelevant and so non-disclosable. In effect, therefore, the "purpose of legal advice" test will result in most communications between solicitor and client in, for example, a conveyancing transaction being exempt from disclosure, either because they are privileged or because they are immaterial or irrelevant.

What documents, then, are disclosable on this test? The answer is provided by cases such as *Smith-Bird* v. *Blower* [1939] 2 All E.R. 406 and *Conlon* v. *Conlons Ltd.* [1952] 2 All E.R. 462. In the former case the client's letter to his solicitor informed him of a fait accompli, namely, that he had agreed to sell the property to the plaintiff's agent. . . .

Likewise in *Conlon* v. *Conlons Ltd.* [1952] 2 All E.R. 462, privilege was held not to extend to a communication from a client to his solicitor authorising him to offer terms of settlement. . . .

It follows from this analysis that those dicta in the decided cases which appear to extend privilege without limit to all solicitor and client communication upon matters within the ordinary business of a solicitor and referable to that relationship are too wide. It may be that the broad terms used in the earlier cases reflect the restricted range of solicitors' activities at the time. Their role then would have been confined for the most part to that of lawyer and would not have extended to business adviser or man of affairs. To speak therefore of matters "within the ordinary business of a solicitor" would in practice usually have meant the giving of advice and assistance of a specifically legal nature. But the range of assistance given by solicitors to their clients and of activities carried out on their behalf has greatly broadened in recent times and is still developing. Hence the need to re-examine the scope of legal professional privilege and keep it within justifiable bounds.

By contrast, the formulation adopted by Judge Paul Baker [the trial judge] and quoted earlier in this judgment is in my view too restrictive. It suggests that a communication only enjoys privilege if it specifically seeks or conveys advice. If it does so, it is privileged, notwithstanding it may also contain "narratives of facts or other statements which in themselves would not be protected." However, the second half of the judge's formulation implies that all documents recording information or transactions with or without instructions or recording meetings lack privilege if they do not specifically contain or seek advice. . . . In my judgment that formulation is too narrow. As indicated, whether such documents are privileged or not must depend on whether they are part of that necessary exchange of information of which the object is the giving of legal advice as and when appropriate. Accordingly, I agree with the formulation made by Master Munrow in the present case, subject to the additional words which I have placed in brackets. He said: "Once solicitors are embarked on a conveyancing transaction they are employed to ensure that the client steers clear of legal difficulties, and communications passing in the handling of that transaction are privileged (if their aim is the obtaining of appropriate legal advice) since the whole handling is experience and legal skill in action and a document uttered during the transaction does not have to incorporate a specific piece of legal advice to obtain that privilege."

Judge Paul Baker applied his more restrictive test to the documents in the present case. Those documents have been produced to this court. In the light of the principles stated above, I am of the opinion the defendant's claim that the documents are privileged should have been upheld.

Accordingly I would allow this appeal.

PARKER L.J. and LORD DONALDSON OF LYMINGTON M.R. Agreed.

Brown v. **Foster** (1857) 1 N. and N. 736 (Ex.Ch.) Counsel attended before a magistrate on behalf of a person charged with embezzlement, and a book was produced by the prosecutor in which it was the duty of the accused to have entered a sum of money received by him, and the book then contained no such entry. On a later examination the book was again produced and an entry in the accused's hand was then found. The accused subsequently brought an action for malicious prosecution, and a question arose as to whether the counsel might give evidence, without the plaintiff's consent, as to whether there had been an entry in the book at the time of the first examination. Pollock C.B. said (p. 740): "I entertain no doubt whatever as to the admissibility of the evidence." Martin B. said (p. 740): "I am of the same opinion.... The counsel was called to state, not what he learnt from his client, but whether on a particular occasion he saw a certain book, and whether a certain entry was then in that book. There is no breach of professional confidence in answering those questions. I agree that what passes between counsel and client ought not to be communicated and is not admissible in evidence, but with respect to matters which the counsel sees with his eyes, he cannot refuse to answer."

Note.—A solicitor can be obliged to disclose the identity of his client: *Bursill* v. *Tanner* (1885) 16 Q.B.D. 1. Nor is he prevented from disclosing his residence by the mere circumstance that it became known to him only in his capacity as a solicitor. For the privilege to be applicable it must have been made known to him in confidence for the purpose of obtaining professional advice: *Re Cathcart, ex parte Campbell* (1870) 5 Ch.App. 707 (C.A.).

SCHNEIDER v. LEIGH

[1955] 2 Q.B. 195; [1955] 2 All E.R. 173 (C.A.: 1955)

The privilege accorded to a litigant to protect him in the preparation of his case belongs only to him and his successors in title and does not extend to a proposed witness who becomes a party to a different action.

In other proceedings a plaintiff had claimed damages for personal injuries against a company, whose solicitors had obtained a medical report to which privilege attached. This report had been shown by the plaintiff's solicitors to their client, who regarded it as defamatory. He commenced the present libel proceedings against the doctor who had made the report and sought disclosure of the full report and related correspondence. The defendant doctor claimed the protection of the privilege admitted to be possessed by the defendant company in the other action. The Court of Appeal held that the defendant doctor was not so entitled.

HODSON L.J.... It is conceded by the defendant that the medical reports which form the basis of the libel action were brought into existence in contemplation of the action brought by the plaintiff against the company, and that privilege from production accordingly attaches to the company in the proceedings taken by the plaintiff against it. The question is whether the privilege from production extends beyond the company, so as to protect the defendant in separate proceedings brought against him, although the privilege is not his, but that of the company.

It is essential to bear in mind that the privilege is the privilege of the litigant, accorded to him in order that he may be protected in preparing his case, and not the privilege of his witnesses as such. The litigant can waive the privilege if he chooses, and if he does so the proofs of his witnesses can be shown to the opposing party without the witnesses having any ground for complaint. What is being sought here is, in effect, to extend the umbrella of the protection which the privilege gives the company to the defendant, who is, on the hypothesis that he is the author of the libel, to be looked at for the purpose of this application as a proposed witness on behalf of the company. In this capacity not only has he no privilege of his own, but he is under no duty to assert the right of the company to resist the production of any documents.

I have emphasised that the privilege is the privilege of the company. This statement is subject to the qualification that the privilege ensures for the benefit of successors in title to the party to an action, at any rate, where the relevant interest subsists. (See *Minet* v. *Morgan* (1873) L.R. 8 Ch. 361.) It has been argued for the defendant, however, that the privilege is not limited to the original litigant, that is to say, the company and its successors in title; ... [His Lordship, rejecting this argument, held to the contrary and pointed out that this holding was not] open to the objection that it exposes witnesses in legal proceedings to an undue risk of proceedings for libel. The law already provides the protection necessary to a witness whose proof is taken for the purpose of litigation, since the occasions on which statements are made in such cases are privileged. ...

Mr. Hawser has stated on behalf of his client that if the appeal is allowed he will consent to an order for inspection to take effect only when the action against the company has been disposed of, so that there will be no question of interference with the company's privilege. I would allow the appeal and make an order in terms giving effect to the consent given by counsel for the plaintiff.

ROMER L.J. ... The defendant asks us in the present case to carry the rule which has been evolved for the protection of litigants further than it has ever, so far as I am aware, been carried before, by bringing within its scope not only the litigant himself, but also his prospective witnesses; so that any witness who has been approached by the litigant for a report, and has given it, can claim protection in respect of the contents of the report if he himself becomes a party to subsequent and wholly independent proceedings. For my part I feel quite unable to accept the invitation and (subject to giving effect to the concession which Mr. Hawser offered for the benefit of the Pedigree company, to which Hodson L.J. has referred) I would allow the appeal.

SINGLETON L.J. dissented.

Note.—It would seem that the decision of the majority might have been reached on an alternative ground. The existence of an evidential privilege, a matter of adjectival law, cannot directly alter substantive liability. On this view this privilege would not have been available even if the defendants in the personal injury action had themselves uttered an alleged libel and thus been the defendants in the defamation proceedings. But, of course, the non-availability of the evidential privilege would not preclude the possible availability of the substantive defence of qualified privilege. On the distinction between adjectival and substantive privileges see the judgment of Lord Atkin in *Minter* v. *Priest* [1930] A.C. 558 (H.L.) at pp. 579–580.

Lee v. **South West Thames Regional Health Authority** [1985] 1 W.L.R. 845 (C.A.) The infant plaintiff, having been admitted to hospital, was transferred to a hospital under the Hillingdon Area Health Authority. He was later returned to the first hospital by ambulance provided by the defendant South West Thames Authority. It was subsequently discovered that he had suffered severe brain damage. Notes disclosed by the two hospitals suggested that there had been "a problem in the ambulance transfer." A memorandum prepared by the ambulance crew had been sent to the Hillingdon Authority with a view to it obtaining legal advice as to its possible liability to the plaintiff. The present defendant South West Thames Authority claimed the right to withhold inspection of this memorandum on the ground that it had come into existence after the possibility of litigation had become known to the Hillingdon Authority and had been prepared for the sole purpose of enabling that Authority to obtain legal advice with reference to such litigation. The Court of Appeal upheld the defendant's claim. Sir John Donaldson M.R. distinguished the case from *Schneider* v. *Leigh* "upon the basis that the cause of action being asserted against South West Thames is not a wholly independent cause of action, but arises out of the same incident as that which rendered Hillingdon a likely defendant...." (p. 850).

The Aegis Blaze [1986] 1 Lloyd's Rep. 203 (C.A.). Surveyors, who had been instructed by solicitors in contemplation of litigation, had prepared a survey report on a vessel in 1980. That document was privileged in that litigation. Subsequently the same vessel suffered another casualty and separate litigation followed. The plaintiffs in the later action sought discovery from the defendants of the earlier survey report. The Court of Appeal upheld the defendant's contention that the report was privileged on the ground that the party claiming privilege in this later action was the party entitled to privilege in the earlier action.

R. v. **Craig** [1975] 1 N.Z.L.R. 597 (New Zealand S.C.). Craig was accused of giving perjured evidence on behalf of a plaintiff in earlier civil proceedings. The Crown wished to call the plantiff's solicitor who had briefed Craig's evidence and had taken notes of what he said. However, the plaintiff instructed his solicitor to claim privilege. It was held in the New Zealand Supreme Court that a client's privilege is not only available in the original litigation, although the extent of its availability in other proceedings is not clear. It was further held that, if the communication was originally privileged, the onus was on the Crown to show that there was no ground on which the client could any longer reasonably be regarded as having a recognisable interest in asserting the privilege. Alternatively, the Crown might show that the communication was made in furtherance of crime or fraud (see *R.* v. *Cox and Railton* (*infra*)). The Crown had satisfied neither of these alternatives.

WAUGH v. BRITISH RAILWAYS BOARD

[1980] A.C. 521; [1979] 2 All E.R. 1169 (H.L.: 1979)

A document prepared by a third party will not be protected by professional privilege unless submission to legal advisers in anticipation of litigation was at least the dominant purpose for which it was prepared.

The plaintiff's husband, an employee of the defendants, was killed in a railway accident. In accordance with the defendant Board's usual practice a report was made concerning the circumstances of the accident. This report was made partly for the purpose of discovering whether such accidents could be avoided in the future and partly to inform the Board's solicitor in case of litigation, which at the time was considered probable, or in any event possible. The plaintiff sued the Board alleging that the collision had been caused by its negligence and sought discovery of the report. Discovery was resisted by the Board on the ground of legal professional privilege.

LORD WILBERFORCE: . . . My Lords, before I consider the authorities, I think it desirable to attempt to discern the reason why what is (inaccurately) called legal professional privilege exists. It is sometimes ascribed to the exigencies of the adversary system of litigation under which a litigant is entitled within limits to refuse to disclose the nature of his case until the trial. Thus one side may not ask to see the proofs of the other side's witnesses or the opponent's brief or even know what witnesses will be called: he must wait until the card is played and cannot try to see it in the hand. This argument cannot be denied some validity even where the defendant is a public corporation whose duty it is, so it might be thought, while taking all proper steps to protect its revenues, to place all the facts before the public and to pay proper compensation to those it has injured. A more powerful argument to my mind is that everything should be done in order to encourage anyone who knows the facts to state them fully and candidly—as Sir George Jessel M.R. said, to bare his breast to his lawyer: *Anderson* v. *Bank of British Columbia* (1876) 2 Ch.D. 644, 699. This he may not do unless he knows that his communication is privileged.

But the preparation of a case for litigation is not the only interest which calls for candour. In accident cases " . . . the safety of the public may well depend on the candour and completeness of reports made by subordinates whose duty it is to draw attention to defects": *Conway* v. *Rimmer* [1968] A.C. 910, *per* Lord Reid, at p. 941. This however does not by itself justify a claim to privilege since, as Lord Reid continues: " . . . no one has ever suggested that public safety has been endangered by the candour or completeness of such reports having been inhibited by the fact that they may have to be produced if the interests of the due administration of justice should ever require production at any time."

So one may deduce from this the principle that while privilege may be required in order to induce candour in statements made for the purposes of litigation it is not required in relation to statements whose purpose is different—for example to enable a railway to operate safety.

It is clear that the due administration of justice strongly requires disclosure and production of this report: it was contemporary; it contained statements by witnesses on the spot; it would be not merely relevant evidence, but almost certainly the best evidence as to the cause of the accident. If one accepts that this important public interest can be overridden in order that the defendant may properly prepare his case, how close must the connection be between the preparation of the document and the anticipation of litigation? On principle I would think that the purpose of preparing for litigation ought to be either the sole purpose or at least the dominant purpose of it: to carry the protection further into cases where that purpose was secondary or equal with another purpose would seem to be excessive, and unnecessary in the interest of encouraging truthful revelation. At the lowest such desirability of protection as might exist in such cases is not strong enough to outweigh the need for all relevant documents to be made available.

. . . .

The whole question came to be considered by the High Court of Australia in 1976: *Grant* v. *Downs*, 135 C.L.R. 674. This case involved reports which had "as one of the material purposes for their preparation" submission to legal advisers in the event of litigation. It was held that privilege could not be claimed. In the joint judgment of Stephen, Mason and Murphy JJ. . . . it was held that "legal professional privilege" must be confined to documents brought into existence for the sole purpose of submission to legal advisers for advice or use in legal proceedings. Jacobs J. put the test in the form of a question, at p. 692: " . . . does the purpose [in the sense of intention, the intended use] of supplying the material to the legal adviser account for the existence of the material?"

Barwick C.J. stated it in terms of "dominant" purpose. This is closely in line with the opinion of Lord Denning M.R. in the present case that the privilege extends only to material prepared "wholly or mainly for the purpose of preparing [the defendant's] case." It appears to me that unless the purpose of submission to the legal adviser in view of litigation is at least the dominant purpose for which the relevant document was prepared, the reasons which require privilege to be extended to it cannot apply. On the other hand to hold that the purpose, as above, must be the sole purpose would, apart from difficulties of proof, in my opinion, be too strict a requirement, and would confine the privilege too narrowly: as to this I agree with Barwick C.J. in *Grant* v. *Downs*, 135 C.L.R. 674 and in substance with Lord Denning M.R.

LORD RUSSELL OF KILLOWEN. . . . At the conclusion of the arguments in this appeal I was minded, while agreeing that anything less than the standard of the dominant purpose would not suffice to support a claim for privilege from production, to prefer the higher standard of the sole purpose, in line with as I understand them the judgments of the majority in the High Court of Australia in *Grant* v. *Downs*, 135 C.L.R. 674. It appeared to me that such a standard had the merit of greater simplicity in a decision on a claim for privilege from production, as being a line easier to draw and to apply to the facts of a particular case. However on reflection I am persuaded that the standard of sole purpose would be in most, if not all, cases impossible to attain, and that to impose it would tilt the balance of policy in this field too sharply against the possible defendant. Moreover to select the standard of dominant purpose is not to impose a definition too difficult of measurement. . . . I am in agreement with the speech of my noble and learned friend Lord Wilberforce, and would allow this appeal. . . .

LORDS SIMON OF GLAISDALE, EDMUND-DAVIES and KEITH OF KINKEL delivered concurring speeches.

Note.—The doctrine propounded in *Waugh's* case does not impinge upon the rule that privilege does extend to a situation in which the client is directly seeking legal advice even though litigation is not in contemplation. The Board's report, although prepared internally, seems to have been treated in the same way as would a report prepared by a third party.

In *Buttes Gas and Oil Co.* v. *Hammer (No. 3)* [1981] Q.B. 233 (C.A.) two members of the court (Donaldson and Brightman L.JJ.) held that legal professional privilege is available when two persons having a common interest in anticipated litigation employ a common solicitor and exchange information for the dominant purpose of informing each other of the facts or issues or of advice received in respect of the litigation; and the documents exchanged in such circumstances are privileged in the hands of either such person even though only one of them is a party to the litigation. (Subsequent proceedings in the House of Lords, [1982] A.C. 888, did not affect this point).

In *Neilson* v. *Laugharne* [1981] Q.B. 736 the Court of Appeal, accepting that the test laid down in *Waugh's* case is whether the dominant purpose for which the document in question came into existence was for use in possible litigation, or for obtaining information or advice for general or other purposes, held that statements obtained for the purpose of carrying out the duty to investigate a complaint against the police under section 49 of the Police Act 1964 were not covered by legal professional privilege, although a further purpose in obtaining the statements was to assist in threatened litigation. [The statements were, however, excluded on the ground of public interest. On this point the case was subsequently distinguished in *Peach* v. *Commissioner of Police* [1986] Q.B. 1064 (C.A.). See Chapter 12, *infra*].

In assessing (for the purpose of determining whether a document is privileged) the dominant purpose for which it was prepared, the court must take an objective view of the evidence as a whole: *Guinness Peat Ltd.* v. *Fitzroy Robinson* [1987] 1 W.L.R. 1027 (C.A.).

In re Duncan, decd. [1968] P.306 (P.D.). Ormrod J. held (p. 311): " . . . that all the documents which are communications passing between the plaintiff and his foreign legal advisers are privileged, whether or not proceedings in this or any other court were contemplated when they came into existence"; and (p. 313) that documents (including communications with third parties) "if they were prepared in connection with proposed or actual litigation in a foreign court or courts, . . . are just as entitled to privilege in the present [English] action as if they had been prepared for it."

Note.—The privilege can also extend to proceedings under the rules of the European Economic Community: *A.M. and S. Europe* v. *E.C. Commission* [1983] Q.B. 878 (Eur. Ct.).

R. v. COX AND RAILTON

14 Q.B.D. 153; 54 L.J.M.C. 41; 52 L.T. 25; 33 W.R. 396; 15 Cox C.C. 611
(C.C.R. 1884)

Privilege extends only to those communications between solicitor and client which are made in the legitimate course of professional employment of the solicitor. Communications made in furtherance of any criminal or fraudulent purpose are not privileged.

A solicitor was compelled to disclose what passed between the prisoners and himself, on an occasion when they called to consult him with reference to drawing up a bill of sale which was alleged to be fraudulent.

STEPHEN J. (delivering the judgment of the court, which included LORD COLERIDGE C.J., HAWKINS, WATKIN WILLIAMS, and MATHEW J.J.): ... The conduct of Mr. Goodman, the solicitor, appears to have been unobjectionable. He was consulted in the common course of business, and gave a proper opinion in good faith. The question therefore is, whether, if a client applies to a legal adviser for advice intended to facilitate or to guide the client in the commission of a crime or fraud, the legal adviser being ignorant of the purpose for which his advice is wanted, the communication between the two is privileged. We expressed our opinion at the end of the argument that no such privilege existed. If it did, the result would be that a man intending to commit treason or murder might safely take legal advice for the purpose of enabling himself to do so with impunity, and that the solicitor to whom the application was made would not be at liberty to give information against his client for the purpose of frustrating his criminal purpose. Consequences so monstrous reduce to an absurdity any principle or rule in which they are involved. ...

We are greatly pressed with the argument that, speaking practically, the admission of any such exception to the privilege of legal advisers as that it is not to extend to communications made in furtherance of any criminal or fraudulent purpose would greatly diminish the value of that privilege. The privilege must, it was argued, be violated in order to ascertain whether it exists. The secret must be told in order to see whether it ought to be kept. ...

In each particular case the court must determine upon the facts actually given in evidence, or proposed to be given in evidence, whether it seems probable that the accused person may have consulted his legal adviser, not after the commission of the crime for the legitimate purpose of being defended, but before the commission of the crime, for the purpose of being guided or helped in committing it. We are far from saying that the question whether the advice was taken before or after the offence will always be decisive as to the admissibility of such evidence. Courts must in every instance judge for themselves on the special facts of each particular case, just as they must judge whether a witness deserves to be examined on the supposition that he is hostile or whether a dying declaration was made in the immediate prospect of death. ... Of course, the power in question ought to be used with the greatest care not to hamper prisoners in making their defence, and not to enable unscrupulous persons to acquire knowledge to which they have no right, and every precaution should be taken against compelling unnecessary disclosures.

Note.—For the limited nature of this exception to the privilege see, e.g. Butler v. Board of Trade [1971] Ch. 680 (Ch.D.) infra. See, also, Crescent Farm Sports v. Sterling Offices [1972] Ch. 553 (Ch.D.), per Goff J. at pp. 564–565: "The principle of the exception is that the communication in such circumstances is not in truth within the scope of professional privilege at all, and the plaintiffs submit that it is no part of a solicitor's duty innocently or otherwise to further any breach of duty or wrongful act. In my judgment that is far too wide. ... I do not consider the principle requires any extension. On the contrary I think the wide submission of the plaintiffs would endanger the whole basis of legal professional privilege. It is clear that parties must be at liberty to take advice as to the ambit of their contractual obligations and liabilities in tort and what liability they will incur whether in contract or tort by a proposed course of action without thereby in every case losing professional privilege. I agree that fraud in this connection is not limited to the tort of deceit and includes all forms of fraud and dishonesty such as fraudulent breach of trust, fraudulent conspiracy, trickery and shown contrivances, but I cannot feel that the tort of inducing a breach of contract or the narrow form of conspiracy pleaded in this case come within that ambit." See, too, *Chandler* v. *Church* [1987] C.L.Y. 3059 (Ch.D.), where Hoffman J. held that it did not matter that the fraud alleged was not some past event but was the very conduct of the case itself; however, in such a case the risk of injustice to the party seeking the protection of the privilege was so great, if the allegation were ill-founded, that the case against him had to be very convincing.

R. v. **Central Criminal Court, ex parte Francis and Francis** [1989] A.C. 346 (H.L.). The specific holding by a majority of the House of Lords was that on the true construction of section 10(2) of the Police and Criminal Evidence Act 1984 (Part Two, *infra*) the phrase "items held with the intention of furthering a criminal purpose" covers any document prepared and held with the intention of furthering a criminal purpose, whether the intention be that of the person holding the document or be someone else. Conveyancing documents prepared with the intention of furthering the laundering of proceeds of illegal drug trafficking, although innocently held by a solicitor, fell within the subsection and were not, therefore, protected from disclosure to the police by the lawyer-client privilege.

Note.—The decision also has wider importance. Two members of the majority, Lords Griffiths (pp. 382–385) and Goff of Chieveley (p. 395) expressed the view that section 10 of the 1984 Act was intended to be a statutory enactment of the common law. On this basis henceforth authority on the interpretation of section 10, and corresponding common law authority, can in most respects be treated as interchangeable. Indeed Lord Goff by way of *obiter* postscript intimated that he would "as at present advised . . . be minded, if the matter arose for decision, to interpret section 10(2) . . . in accordance with the common law" rule that legal professional privilege cannot be excluded by the exception established in *R.* v. *Cox and Railton* (*supra*) in cases in which a communication is made by a client to his legal adviser regarding the conduct of his case in criminal or civil proceedings, merely because such communication is untrue and would, if acted upon, lead to the commission of the crime of perjury in such proceedings.

In *R.* v. *Inner London Crown Court, ex p. Baines and Baines* [1988] Q.B. 579 (D.C.) it was held that, whereas advice given by a solicitor to his client during a conveyancing transaction would normally be privileged, a conveyance and a record of the financing of a transaction for the purchase of property could not be subject to legal privilege within the meaning of the section. In *R.* v. *Guildhall Court, ex p. Primlaks* [1989] 2 W.L.R. 841 (D.C.), in which *R.* v. *Central Criminal Court, ex p. Francis and Francis* was applied on the construction of the section, it was stated *per curiam* (at p. 851), of documents sent by a client to his solicitors under cover of correspondence for the purpose of obtaining legal advice, "Such documents would not be within section 10(1)(c) if they were pre-existing documents and were not themselves made in connection with the giving of legal advice or in connection with or in contemplation of legal proceedings". These interpretations would seem, too, to reflect corresponding common law doctrine.

R. v. **Barton** [1973] 1 W.L.R. 115 (Crown Ct.). The accused was charged with fraudulent conversion, theft and falsification of accounts alleged to have been committed in the course of his employment as a legal executive with a firm of solicitors. The defence served on a solicitor, who was a partner in the firm, a subpoena to give evidence at the trial and produce certain documents which had come into existence while the solicitor was acting as the solicitor to the executors or administrators of the estates of deceased persons. The solicitor's claim that the documents were therefore protected by legal professional privilege was rejected. Caulfield J. said (p. 118): "If there are documents in the possession or control of a solicitor which, on production, help to further the defence of an accused man, then in my judgment no privilege attaches. I cannot conceive that our law would permit a solicitor or other person to screen from a jury information which, if disclosed to the jury, would perhaps enable a man either to establish his innocence or to resist an allegation made by the Crown."

Note.—Caulfield J.'s words were cited with approval in *R. v. Ataou* [1988] Q.B. 798 (C.A.), where the Court of Appeal essayed (p. 807) the following principle: "Where a communication was originally privileged and in criminal proceedings privilege is claimed against the defendant by the client concerned or his solicitor, it should be for the defendant to show on the balance of probabilities that the claim cannot be sustained. That might be done by demonstrating that there is no ground on which the client could any longer be reasonably regarded as having a recognisable interest in asserting the privilege. The judge must then balance whether the legitimate interest of the defendant in seeking to breach the privilege outweighs that of the client in seeking to maintain it."

CALCRAFT v. GUEST

[1898] 1 Q.B. 759; 67 L.J.Q.B. 505; 78 L.T. 283; 46 W.R. 420 (C.A.: 1898)

Although privilege is applicable to documents, secondary evidence of them, if available, is admissible.

In an action for trespass to a fishery, after judgment had been given for the plaintiff, the defendant discovered certain documents which had been used in a former action involving the same rights, but defended by a predecessor in title of the present plaintiff. The documents, which had been prepared for the purposes of the old action, included proofs of witnesses and rough notes of evidence used in the defence of the former action. The originals of these documents had been given up to the present plaintiff, after copies had been taken by the solicitors to the defendant, and on appeal in the present action the defendant claimed to use these copies in support of his case. It was contended by him that, as they had not been prepared for the purposes of the present action, they were not privileged; and that, even if the originals were privileged, he was entitled to use the copies as secondary evidence thereof. It was held that, as the originals had been prepared for the purposes of the former action, they retained their privilege in the present proceedings, but the copies were admissible as secondary evidence.

LINDLEY M.R.: I take it that, as a general rule, one may say once privileged always privileged. I do not mean to say that privilege cannot be waived, but that the mere fact that documents used in a previous litigation are held and have not been destroyed, does not amount to a waiver of the privilege. I think that so far as regards professional privilege, *Minet* v. *Morgan* (1873)—Ch. App. 361, covers these documents. Then comes the next question. It appears that the appellant has obtained copies of some of these documents, and is in a position to give secondary evidence of them; and the question is whether he is entitled to do that. That appears to me to be covered by the authority of *Lloyd* v. *Mostyn* (1842) 10 M. & W. 478, (where) Parke B. said, "Where an attorney intrusted confidentially with a document communicates the contents, or suffers another to take a copy, surely the secondary evidence so obtained may be produced. Suppose the instrument were even stolen, and a correct copy taken, would it not be reasonable to admit it?" The matter dropped there; but the other members of the court all concurred in that, which I take to be a distinct authority that secondary evidence in a case of this kind may be received.

RIGBY and VAUGHAN WILLIAMS L.JJ. concurred.

I.T.C. Film Distributors Ltd. v. **Video Exchange Ltd.** [1982] Ch. 431 (Ch.D.). During the course of a copyright action the judge heard certain motions and cross-motions in open court. After the judge had risen in the defendant obtained by a trick some documents which had been brought into court by the plaintiff's solicitors. On the issue as to how far the defendant should be allowed to retain and use these documents, it was held that, although the documents already used could not be excluded, the remainder should be excluded. Warner J. said (p. 440): "I must balance the public interest that the truth should be ascertained, which is the reason for the rule in *Calcraft* v. *Guest* [1898] 1 Q.B. 759, against the public interest that litigants should be able to bring their documents into court without fear that they may be filched by their opponents, whether by stealth or by a trick, and then used by them in evidence." His Lordship added (p. 441): "I do not overlook that for a party to litigation to take possession by stealth or by a trick of documents belonging to the other side within the precincts of the court is probably contempt of court, so that there may be another sanction. But it seems to me, that if it is contempt of court, then the court should not countenance it, by admitting such documents in evidence." Warner J. also mentioned that, had the appropriate writ been issued by the plaintiffs earlier, some relief would very probably have been available along the lines of that granted in *Ashburton* v. *Pape* (see *infra*).

Note.—In *R.* v. *Tompkins* (1977) 67 Cr. App.R. 181 (C.A.) counsel for the prosecution was handed an incriminating note, written by the accused to the defence counsel, which had been found on the floor of the court during an adjournment. The Court of Appeal upheld the propriety of his being allowed to cross-examine the accused on the contents of the note. Distinguishing this case Warner J. said (p. 441) that it "proceeded on the footing that the document in question there had come into the possession of the prosecution fortuitously. The relevance of possible impropriety was not discussed." Seemingly, therefore, the exception to the doctrine of *Calcraft* v. *Guest* formulated in the *I.T.C. Film Distributors* case does not extend to cases in which there has been no impropriety.

Ashburton v. **Pape** [1913] 2 Ch. 469 (C.A.). Pape was a bankrupt, and his discharge was opposed by, amongst others, the plaintiff. Pape obtained by a trick privileged correspondence between the plaintiff and his solicitors and took copies of it before returning it. He proposed to use these copies in pending bankruptcy proceedings. The plaintiff was, however, able to obtain an injunction prohibiting him from doing so. Cozens-Hardy M.R. said (p. 473) of *Calcraft* v. *Guest*: "The court in such an action is not really trying the circumstances under which the document was produced. That is not an issue in [such a] case and the court simply says 'Here is a copy of a document which cannot be produced; it may have been stolen, it may have been picked up in the street, it may have improperly got into the possession of the person who proposes to produce it, but that is not a matter which the court in the trial of the action can go into.' But that does not seem to me to have any bearing upon a case where the whole subject-matter of the action is the right to retain the originals or copies of certain documents which are privileged."

English and American Insurance Co. v. **Herbert Smith** [1988] F.S.R. 232; [1988] C.L.Y. 1596. Papers of counsel for the plaintiff were accidentally sent to the defendant's solicitors, who clients instructed them to read them. The plaintiff obtained an injunction restraining the defendant from making use of any of the information contained in the papers. Browne-Wilkinson V.-C. held that, as the privileged information had not yet been tendered in evidence, the person entitled to legal professional privilege could restrain its use by the other side, including its use in pending proceedings.

Note.—It is to be observed that no impropriety need be involved in the context of the availability of an injunction. Contrast the position under the doctrine of *Calcraft* v. *Guest*, *supra*: see *R.* v. *Tompkins* mentioned in *Note* to *I.T.C. Film Distributors Ltd.* v. *Video Exchange Ltd.*, p. 234, *supra.*

BUTLER v. BOARD OF TRADE

[1971] Ch. 680; [1970] 3 All E.R. 593 (Ch.D.: 1970)

The mere fact that a document is relevant to criminal proceedings is not sufficient to destroy a legal professional privilege. It will only do so if it is shown prima facie that there was a bona fide and reasonably tenable charge of crime or fraud, and that the document was prepared in furtherance of, or as part of, the commission of such crime or fraud.
It would not be a proper exercise of the equitable jurisdiction in confidence to make a declaration, at the suit of an accused in a public prosecution, restraining the Crown from adducing admissible evidence relevant to the crime with which he is charged.

GOFF J.: In this action the plaintiff, who is being prosecuted by the Board of Trade for alleged offences under section 332(3) of the Companies Act, 1948, in connection with two companies now in compulsory liquidation, claims a declaration as follows: "that the defendants," the Board of Trade, "are not entitled by themselves, their servants or agents to publish, disclose, divulge or otherwise make use of the contents of a letter dated July 31, 1964, written to the plaintiff by Phyllis Edith Newman, a solicitor, or any information contained therein."

The object is to prevent the defendants from adducing in evidence against the plaintiff at the criminal trial a copy of a letter written to him by Mrs. Newman, a solicitor then in charge of the practice of another solicitor, one Miss Berman. As the defendants are a department of the Crown it is not possible to obtain interlocutory relief, since an injunction cannot be granted against the Crown, nor will the court make an interlocutory declaration. To overcome that difficulty, if possible, this special case has been presented under R.S.C., Ord. 33, r. 3 pursuant to an order obtained from Master Neave to test whether there is any equity to grant a declaration at the trial.

The facts which have to be assumed are set out in the special case and it is unnecessary to recite them, save paragraphs 7, 8 and 12 which read as follows:

7. "Shortly after the dates of the respective winding up orders a representative of the Official Receiver being the provisional liquidator of Curzon and Capricorn called upon Miss Berman and collected the

papers of the company concerned. A copy of the letter was found amongst these papers.

8. The department of the Official Receiver in Companies Liquidation is a department of the defendants...12. For the purpose of this special case it is to be assumed (i) that the letter was unsolicited by the plaintiff and (ii) that it was written by Mrs. Newman as the plaintiff's own solicitor and not, or not only, as solicitor to Curzon and Capricorn.''

The last-mentioned paragraph postulates alternatives, but I can only deal with the matter on this special case on one footing which must be that most favourable to the plaintiff, that is to say, ignoring the words ''or not only.''

The question for the opinion of the court, set out in paragraph 14, is ''whether there is any equity to prevent the defendants from tendering a copy of the letter in evidence in any of the said criminal proceedings.''

The plaintiff claims that the original of the letter is protected by legal professional privilege, and that therefore the copy is a confidential document, and I agree that if the premise be right the conclusion follows. Further, in my judgment it is right prima facie because, although the special case tells me nothing about the solicitor's instructions, I must, as it seems to me, assume that the advice contained in the letter was given by her as legal adviser and within the ambit of her retainer, and indeed that is really implicit in paragraph 12 of the special case.

It is submitted on behalf of the defendants, however, that as the plaintiff is charged with criminal offences, and the letter is relevant thereto, which it undoubtedly is, the privilege does not apply. Now, it is clear that a sufficient charge of crime or fraud will in certain circumstances destroy the privilege, but there is a dispute between the parties as to what it is necessary to show for that purpose.

The defendants say that relevance is alone sufficient.... The plaintiff submits, however, that it is necessary to go further and to show that the professional advice was in furtherance of the crime or fraud...or in preparation for it...or parts of it....

...the two tests are not the same and in the present case, cannot I think, possibly produce the same result. On the information before me the letter was nothing but a warning volunteered—no doubt wisely, but still volunteered—by the solicitor that if her client did not take care he might incur serious consequences, which she described. I cannot regard that on any showing as being in preparation for or in furtherance or as part of any criminal designs on the part of the plaintiff.

I must, therefore, decide which test is correct, and I prefer the narrower view. First, that appears to me to be the true effect of *Reg.* v. *Cox and Railton* (1884) 14 Q.B.D. 153....

....

Secondly, in my judgment all the members of the House in *O'Rourke* v. *Darbishire* [1920] A.C. 581, with the possible exception of Lord Wrenbury, p. 626, clearly adopted the narrower test and that is binding on me....

In my judgment, therefore, on the limited facts before me the original letter is privileged and the copy confidential.... If one rejects the bare relevance test, as I have done, then what has to be shown prima facie is not merely that there is a bona fide and reasonably tenable charge of crime or fraud but a prima facie case that the communications in question were made in preparation for or in furtherance or as part of it. . . .

There remains, however, the final question whether the law or equity as to breach of confidence operates, in the terms of paragraph 14 of the special case, to give the plaintiff "any equity to prevent the defendants from tendering a copy of the letter in evidence in any of the said criminal proceedings," where if tendered it would, as I see it, clearly be admissible: see *Calcraft* v. *Guest* [1898] 1 Q.E. 759, 764, subject of course to the overriding discretion of the trial court to reject it if it thought its use unfair.

The plaintiff relies on the decision of the Court of Appeal in *Ashburton* v. *Pape* [1913] 2 Ch. 469, where a party to certain bankruptcy proceedings, having by a trick obtained a copy of a privileged letter, Neville J. granted an injunction restraining him and his solicitors from publishing or making use of it, save for the purposes of those proceedings, and the Court of Appeal varied the order by striking out the exception, so that the injunction was unqualified. . . .

I turn back to *Ashburton* v. *Pape*. In the present case there was no impropriety on the part of the defendants in the way in which they received the copy, but that, in my judgment, is irrelevant because an innocent recipient of information conveyed in breach of confidence is liable to be restrained. I wish to make it clear that there is no suggestion of any kind of moral obliquity on the part of the solicitors, but the disclosure was in law a breach of confidence. Nevertheless, *Ashburton* v. *Pape* does differ from the present case in an important particular, namely, that the defendants are a department of the Crown and intend to use the copy letter in a public prosecution brought by them.

. . . .

In my judgment it would not be a right or permissible exercise of the equitable jurisdiction in confidence to make a declaration at the suit of the accused in a public prosecution in effect restraining the Crown from adducing admissible evidence relevant to the crime with which he is charged. It is not necessary for me to decide whether the same result would obtain in the case of a private prosecution, and I expressly leave that point open.

. . . .

For these reasons, in my judgment, the answer to the question propounded in paragraph 14 of the special case is in the negative and action must be dismissed. . . .

Goddard v. **Nationwide Building Society** [1987] Q.B. 670 (C.A.). The two plaintiffs purchased a house with the aid of a mortgage from the defendant. The solicitor acting for the plaintiffs in connection with the purchase also acted for the defendant in connection with the grant of the mortgage. The plaintiffs, claiming that the house was defective to a greater extent than they had been led to believe, brought an action for damages against the defendant for negligence. Having been informed of these proceedings, the solicitor sent the defendant a copy of an attendance note in which were recorded *inter alia* conversations which he had had with the first plaintiff. The defendant pleaded the substance of this note in its defence. The Court of Appeal held that the plaintiffs were entitled to delivery up of the copy of the note to an injunction restraining the defendant from disclosing or making use of any confidential information contained in it. The court had no doubt that the only legal privilege attaching to the original note was, and continued to be, with the plaintiffs. Of the interaction between the doctrines of *Calcraft* v. *Guest* and *Ashburton* v. *Pape* May L.J. said (p. 683): "If a litigant has in his possession copies of documents to which legal privilege attaches he may nevertheless use such copies as secondary evidence in his litigation: however if he has not yet used the document in that way, the mere fact that he intends to do so is no answer to a claim against him by the person in whom the privilege is vested for delivery up of the copies or to restrain him from disclosing or making use of any information contained in them." Nourse L.J. agreed with this formulation. Both of their Lordships regarded the position as being less than satisfactory on account of the importance accorded to timing. As Nourse L.J. said (pp. 684–685): "The crucial point is that the party who deserves protection must seek it before the other party has adduced the confidential communication in evidence or otherwise relied on it at trial."

Nourse L.J. took the opportunity to make some further general observations (pp. 685–686) which included the following: "Second, although the equitable jurisdiction is of much wider application, I have little doubt that it can prevail over the rule of evidence only in cases where privilege can be claimed. The equitable jurisdiction is well able to extend, for example, to the grant of an injunction to restrain an unauthorised disclosure of confidential communications between priest and penitent or doctor and patient. But those communications are not privileged in legal proceedings and I do not believe that equity would restrain a litigant who already had a record of such a communication in his possession from using it for the purposes of his litigation. It cannot be the function of equity to accord a de facto privilege to communications in respect of which no privilege can be claimed. Equity follows the law. Third, the right of the party who desires the protection to invoke the equitable jurisdiction does not in any way depend on the conduct of the third party into whose possession the record of the confidential communication has come.... [This] is directly in point in the present case and our decision necessarily affirms it. Fourth, once it is established that a case is governed by *Lord Ashburton* v. *Pape* [1913] 2 Ch. 469 there is no discretion in the court to refuse to exercise the equitable jurisdiction according to its view of the materiality of the communication, the justice of admitting or excluding it or the like. The injunction is granted in aid of the privilege which, unless and until it is waived, is absolute. In saying this, I do not intend to suggest that there may not be cases where an injunction can properly be refused on general principles affecting the grant of a discretionary remedy, for example on the ground of inordinate delay. Fifth, in a case to which *Lord Ashburton* v. *Pape* can no longer apply, public policy may nevertheless preclude a party who has acted improperly in the proceedings from invoking the rule of evidence: see *I.T.C. Film Distributors Ltd.* v. *Video Exchange Ltd.* [1982] Ch. 431, where the defendant had at an earlier hearing obtained some of the plaintiff's privileged documents by a trick.... I emphasise that that decision proceeded not on an exercise of the court's discretion but on grounds of public policy. Sixth, the distinction between civil proceedings and public prosecutions made in *Butler* v. *Board of Trade* [1971] Ch. 680 was again one which was made on grounds of public policy. The distinction has since been adopted and applied by the Criminal Division of this court in *Reg.* v. *Tompkins*, 67 Cr.App.R. 181. It can now be disregarded only by the House of Lords. Finally, it is to be noted that the Court of Appeal in New Zealand, after an extensive consideration of the authorities, including *Calcraft* v. *Guest*, *Butler* v. *Board of Trade* and *Reg.* v. *Tompkins*, recently declined to apply the rule of evidence in a criminal case and held that the evidence of a police constable who had happened to overhear a privileged conversation between the accused and his solicitor (*i.e.* one which was not itself part of a criminal or unlawful proceeding: see *Reg.* v. *Cox and Railton* (1884) 4 Q.B.D. 153 was not admissible: see *Reg.* v. *Uljee* [1982] 1 N.Z.L.R. 561. The practical result of the decision would seem to be to leave the spirit of *Lord Ashburton* v. *Pape* [1913] 2 Ch. 469 supreme in both civil and criminal proceedings in that jurisdiction, a supremacy for which in my respectful opinion there is much to be said in this."

Note.—It has been held (*Guinness Peat Properties* v. *Fitzroy Robinson Partnership* [1987] 1 W.L.R. 1027 (C.A.)) that exceptionally an injunction may be granted despite the rule that it is too late to claim privilege after inspection. There the plaintiffs' solicitors and their expert would have realised that there had been an obvious error on the part of the defendants' solicitors in permitting them to inspect a letter, and the court had power to intervene in the exercise of its equitable jurisdiction by granting an injunction for the protection of the defendants, who had moved promptly to seek relief as soon as they became aware of their mistake.

C. MISCELLANEOUS PRIVILEGES

Copyright, Designs and Patents Act 1988, s. 280 (Part Two, *infra*). A statutory professional privilege, originally introduced by the Civil Evidence Act 1968, s.15, is now contained in this section. The privilege derives from the relationship of a person and his Patent Agent. A corresponding privilege, deriving from the relationship of a person and his Trade Mark Agent, is created by s. 284 of the Act. Communications within these statutory privileges are likened to communications within the common law privilege deriving from the relationship of a person with his lawyer.

Administration of Justice Act 1985, s.33 (Part Two, *infra*). A new privilege, similar to that attaching to the relationship of lawyer and client (see section B, *supra*), attaching to the relationship of licensed conveyancer (or recognised body) and client is created in respect of communications made to or by the licensed conveyancer (or recognised body) in the course of his (or its) acting as such. The privilege is available in both civil and criminal proceedings.

Contempt of Court Act 1981, s.10 (Part Two, *infra*). A limited statutory privilege is created so as to enable a person to refuse to disclose the source of information contained in a publication for which he is responsible. The privilege is limited in three ways. It relates merely to the source, and not to the content, of the information; it may not be claimed by the supplier, but only by the recipient, of the information; and, most importantly, it is negatived if the court is satisfied "that disclosure is necessary in the interests of justice or national security or for the prevention of disorder or crime."

Note.—At common law the claim of journalists or other media persons to have the sources of their publications protected is not recognised, although the courts perhaps have some discretion in the matter on the basis of public interest: *Att.-Gen.* v. *Clough* [1963] 1 Q.B. 773 (Q.B.D.); *Att.-Gen.* v. *Mulholland* [1963] 2 Q.B. 477 (C.A.); *British Steel Corporation* v. *Granada Television Ltd.* [1982] A.C. 1096 (H.L.), Chapter 12, *infra*. Also, there is a prohibition on interrogatories concerning the source of the defendant's information where qualified privilege or fair comment is pleaded in actions for defamation: R.S.C., Ord. 82, r. 6 (Part Three, *infra*). Moreover, it has been held that a journalist who refused to reveal his source was not in contempt as this information could in the circumstances of the particular case have served no useful purpose; *Att.-Gen.* v. *Lundin* (1982) 75 Cr. App.R. 90 (Div. Ct.).

Secretary of State for Defence v. **Guardian Newspapers Ltd.** [1985] A.C. 339 (H.L.). *The Guardian* newspaper came into possession of a photocopy of a secret document which it published. The Secretary of State for Defence, alleging infringement of the Crown's copyright, sought an order for immediate delivery up of the document, which bore certain marks which, it was believed, could identify the person (*i.e.* the "informant") who had supplied it to the newspaper. The newspaper sought to rely on the Contempt of Court Act 1981, s.10, as enabling it to refuse to disclose the source of its information. The trial judge and the Court of Appeal held that section 10 was not intended to interfere with proprietary rights and that the Crown was entitled to the order sought. The House of Lords unanimously held that section 10 applied in all judicial proceedings irrespective of their nature, or the claim or cause of action in respect of which they had been brought, but nevertheless dismissed the appeal (Lord Fraser of Tulleybelton and Lord Scarman dissenting) on the ground that, although the defendant newspaper had been prima facie entitled to the protection of section 10, that entitlement had been negatived as a result of the Crown adducing evidence sufficient to discharge the burden upon it of showing that immediate delivery up of the document was necessary in the interests of national security. Lord Diplock, who delivered the leading majority judgment said (p. 345): "The section is so drafted as to make it a question of fact not of discretion as to whether in the particular case a requirement for disclosure of sources of information falls within one of the express exceptions introduced by the word 'unless.' If it does not, the statutory right to refuse disclosure of sources of information in the media is absolute." His Lordship went on to intimate that the difference between the majority and the minority of the Lordships was essentially simply on a question of fact, *i.e.* as to whether the evidence did or did not sufficiently establish that the identification of the informant was necessary in the interests of national security. Lord Diplock also uttered a salutary warning (p. 345) that he did "not think that the process of ascertaining the true construction of the section is advanced by dubbing this 'a constitutional right.' " Lord Roskill, another member of the majority, emphasised this when he said (p. 369): " ... the fact that a section affects specific freedoms or confers specific privileges or immunities whether on individuals or on the media does not give it a special constitutional status in our law." Lord Diplock noted, too, that the exceptions listed in the latter part of the section refer to specific interests and that there is no reference to "the public interest" generally.

The four specific interests entitled to protection are (1) justice, (2) national security, (3) the prevention of disorder, and (4) the prevention of crime. Of the first of these Lord Diplock said (p. 350): " ... in my view the expression 'justice,' the interests of which are entitled to protection, is not used in a general sense as the antonym of 'injustice' but in the technical sense of the administration of justice in the course of legal proceedings. ... " In the instant case it was, however, the interests of national security upon which the Crown case relied, and in relation to which the majority were persuaded. They were so persuaded notwithstanding that, as several of their Lordships emphasised, what is required is proof of "necessity." As Lord Diplock said (p. 350): " ... expediency, however great, is not enough; section 10 requires actual necessity to be established; and whether it has or not is a question of fact that the judge has to find in favour of necessity as a condition precedent to his having any jurisdiction to order disclosure of sources of information."

Note.—In the later case of *Maxwell* v. *Pressdram Ltd.* [1987] 1 W.L.R. 298 (C.A.) the issue did turn on the words "interests of justice" in section 10. The trial judge was not satisfied that disclosure was necessary on that ground. The Court of Appeal declined to reverse this finding of fact (inaccurately referred to in the headnote in The Weekly Law Reports as "the judge's exercise of his discretion"). Kerr L.J. said (p. 310): "[The judge] clearly did not regard it as necessary—a word to which he must have attached great importance—to make the order, even in the perhaps somewhat extreme circumstances of this case, but concluded that the matter could be dealt with adequately by a strong direction in his summing up to the jury, as well as by what they had seen and heard by way of cross-examination of all the witnesses." Parker L.J. added (p. 311): "The judge took the view that it had not become necessary in the interests of justice to disclose the sources. It does not follow that that position need necessarily remain so until the end of the case. I do not wish to encourage further applications, but it is abundantly apparent that as a trial proceeds the situation may change from time to time, and the situation might arise, as the result of some evidence being given on behalf of one side or another, that the judge concludes, albeit at a late stage and contrary to what he felt earlier, that the interests of justice did now make it necessary that the source should be disclosed."

In re An Inquiry under the Company Securities (Insider Dealing) Act 1985 [1988] A.C. 660 (H.L.). Section 178 of the Financial Services Act 1986 obliges a journalist to disclose his sources unless he has "reasonable excuse" not to do so. Inspectors, appointed under the Act to investigate whether, in relation to merger situations, there had been contravention of the Company Securities (Insider Dealing) Act 1985, questioned a journalist responsible for two newspaper articles that appeared to have been based on unpublished price-sensitive information. When he refused to answer on the ground that this might in his view lead to the identification of the sources of his information, the inspectors sought the assistance of the court pursuant to section 178. The journalist claimed that he had a "reasonable excuse" within the meaning of section 178(2) and relied upon section 10 of the Contempt of Court Act 1981. The House of Lords held that, although that section did not apply directly to a reference under section 178, it recognised that it is in the public interest that a journalist should be entitled to protect his source of information unless one of the matters of public interest there specified required revelation. The House of Lords followed its earlier decision in *Secretary of State for Defence* v. *Guardian Newspapers Ltd.* (*supra*). It unanimously held that in the instant case the inspectors had produced sufficient evidence that it was "necessary . . . for the prevention of . . . crime" that they should know the journalist's sources, and accordingly that he did not have a "reasonable excuse" within section 178(2). Lord Griffiths, delivering the leading judgment, re-iterated that the burden of proof rests on the party seeking disclosure. In the course of his judgment his Lordship also took the opportunity to consider the meaning of two key words in section 10. He said (p. 704): "I doubt if it is possible to go further than to say that 'necessary' has a meaning that lies somewhere between 'indispensable' on the one hand, and 'useful' or 'expedient' on the other, and to leave it to the judge to decide towards which end of the scale of meaning he will place it on the facts of any particular case. The nearest paraphrase I can suggest is 'really needed.' " The trial judge, adopting a narrow construction of the words "prevention of . . . crime", had held that "it must appear probable that in the absence of disclosure by the journalist further crimes are likely to be committed." The appellant contended that this was correct. However, Lord Griffith said (p. 705): "The phrase 'prevention of crime' carries, to my mind, very different overtones from 'prevention of a crime' or even 'prevention of crimes.' There are frequent articles and programmes in the media on the prevention of crime. . . . The prevention of crime in this broad sense is a matter of public and vital interest in any civilised society. . . . By identifying 'prevention of crime' as one of the four heads of public interest to which the journalist's privilege may occasionally have to yield, I am satisfied that Parliament was using the phrase in its wider and, I think, natural meaning, rather than in the restricted sense for which the appellant contends."

Note.—On the meaning of "prevention of . . . crime" see, too, *X.* v. *Y. and others* [1988] 2 All E.R. 648 (Q.B.D.).

Bell v. **University of Auckland** [1969] N.Z.L.R. 1029 (S.C. New Zealand). The plaintiff, a university lecturer, who had failed to get promotion brought an action against the University alleging breach of contract of employment. An application for the inspection of reports of persons nominated by the plaintiff as referees was rejected *inter alia* because the documents had been obtained under an express pledge of secrecy which had been given on the plaintiff's direct authority. Turner J. said (pp. 1035–1036): "It is of course a commonplace of the law of evidence that a mere pledge of secrecy, however solemnly given, will not hold good when in the course of litigation the transactions which were the subject of that pledge become relevant as part of the case of some person not a party to the pledge of secrecy.... The case before me, however, is a different case. Here the parties to the present action have solemnly agreed before the action that the documents which are now in question should be brought into existence upon the solemn undertaking of both of them that the plaintiff will not be entitled to see the documents. I cannot but think that this situation is one in which, if the existing rules of privilege do not protect the documents from discovery, an addition should be made to the categories of documents regarded as privileged."

Slavutych v. **Baker** (1976) 55 D.L.R. (3d) 224 (S.C. of Canada). A University professor claimed privilege for assertions about a colleague which he had made in a confidential document sent to the Department Chairman as part of the University's procedure for the consideration of tenure. The Supreme Court took the view by way of *obiter dictum* that such a communication should be the subject of privilege.

D. STATEMENTS MADE WITHOUT PREJUDICE

Paddock v. **Forrester** (1842) 3 Scott N.R. 715 (C.P.). A letter was written by one party "without prejudice." The reply thereto was not stated to have been so written. It also was held to be inadmissible. Tindall C.J. said (p. 734): "...it would be hard indeed to hold that a letter which is stated to be written without prejudice is admissible in evidence because the same terms are not adopted in the reply. When used in the letter containing the offer, the words 'without prejudice' must cover the whole correspondence." Coltman J. said (p. 734): "It is of the utmost importance that parties should have the opportunity of free communication without prejudice; and I should be sorry to hold anything that might be in the slightest degree calculated to embarrass or discourage the practice."

Note.—The rule excluding evidence of without prejudice communications does not apply unless at the time the communication was made the dispute had already arisen and negotiation for its settlement, if not in train, was being initiated by the communication: *Re Daintrey, ex parte Holt* [1893] 2 Q.B. 116 (Q.B.D.), followed in *Bucks. C.C.* v. *Moran* [1989] 3 W.L.R. 153 (C.A.), where it was held that the defendant's letter was not within the rule because it was an assertion of his rights and not an offer to negotiate. The words "without prejudice" should be inserted at an early stage of the correspondence by one party or the other, if negotiations are proposed on that footing. But in some circumstances it is not essential that the words "without prejudice" should have been used; as it may be implied that negotiations were conducted on this understanding. So oral communications to a probation officer (see *McTaggart* v. *McTaggart* [1949] P. 94 (C.A.)) or other conciliator by a party to a matrimonial dispute may be treated as having been made without prejudice (*Mole* v. *Mole* [1951] P. 21 (C.A.); *Pool* v. *Pool* [1951] P. 470; *Henley* v. *Henley* [1955] P. 202). See too, the judgment of Lord Griffiths in *Rush and Tompkins Ltd.* v. *Greater London Council* [1988] 3 W.L.R. 939 (H.L.), *infra*.

WALKER v. WILSHER

23 Q.B.D. 335; 58 L.J.Q.B. 501; 5 T.L.R. 649; 37 W.R. 723 (C.A.: 1889)

The terms of negotiations made without prejudice may not be disclosed to the court, except by the consent of both parties.

At the trial of an action, which resulted in a judgment by consent for an agreed sum, application was made to the judge to deprive the plaintiff of his costs on the ground that, at an early stage of the proceedings, as appeared from letters marked "without prejudice" which had passed between the parties, the case could have been settled for the amount finally accepted. The letters, though objected to, were received by the judge as showing "good cause" for depriving the plaintiff of his costs. The plaintiff appealed, and the appeal was allowed.

LORD ESHER M.R.: ... It is, I think, a good rule to say that nothing which is written or said without prejudice should be looked at without the consent of both parties, otherwise the whole object of the limitation would be destroyed. I am therefore of opinion that the learned judge should not have taken these matters into consideration in determining whether there was good cause, and as that was all that was before him on the point, if that is excluded, it follows that there was no good cause, and that the plaintiff should not have been deprived of his costs.

LINDLEY L.J.: ... What is the meaning of the words "without prejudice?" I think they mean without prejudice to the position of the writer of the letter if the terms he proposes are not accepted. If the terms proposed in the letter are accepted, a complete contract is established, and the letter, although written without prejudice, operates to alter the old state of things and to establish a new one. A contract is constituted in respect of which relief by way of damages or specific performance would be given.... No doubt there are cases where such letters may be taken into consideration, as was done the other day in a case in which a question of laches was raised. The fact that such letters have been written and the dates at which they were written may be regarded, and in so doing the rule to which I have adverted would not be infringed. The facts may, I think, be given in evidence, but the offer made and the mode in which that offer was dealt with—the material matters, that is to say, of the letters—must not be looked at without consent. I think, therefore, that there was no good cause for depriving the plaintiff of costs, and that the decision should be reversed.

BOWEN L.J.: ... [I]t would be a bad thing and lead to serious consequences if the courts allowed the action of litigants, on letters written to them without prejudice, to be given in evidence against them or to be used as material for depriving them of costs. It is most important that the door should not be shut against compromises, as would certainly be the case if letters written without prejudice suggesting methods of compromise were liable to be read when a question of costs arose....

Note.—Walker v. *Wilsher* was distinguished in *Cutts* v. *Head* [1984] 1 Ch. 290 (C.A.), where it was held that the heading of a letter "without prejudice" did not preclude its admission on the issue of costs because the letter had contained an express reservation that, should the offer contained in it prove unacceptable, the letter could be brought to the notice of the judge on that issue. See, too, *McDonnell* v. *McDonnell* [1977] 1 W.L.R. 34 (C.A.).

A person cannot protect himself from substantive liability for a communication, by marking it "without prejudice." In *Tomlin* v. *Standard Telephones and Cables Ltd.* [1969] 1 W.L.R. 1378 (C.A.) Lindley L.J.'s formulation in *Walker* v. *Wilsher* (*supra*) of the meaning of the words "without prejudice" was approved and it was held that, if terms offered in a "without prejudice" letter are accepted, a valid contract may be formed. Similarly, a threat made in contravention of patent legislation and contained in a letter marked "without prejudice" has been held nevertheless to constitute an infringement of that legislation (*Kurtz & Co.* v. *Spence & Sons* (1887) 57 L.J.Ch. 238); and a statement in a letter headed "without prejudice" to the effect that the writer is unable to pay his debts has been proved as an act of bankruptcy in bankruptcy proceedings (*Re Daintrey, Ex parte Holt* [1893] 2 Q.B. 116).

RUSH AND TOMKINS LTD. v. GREATER LONDON COUNCIL

[1988] 3 W.L.R. 939; [1988] 3 All E.R. 737 (H.L.: 1988)

The inadmissibility of "without prejudice" correspondence generally extends to subsequent litigation connected with the same subject-matter. The protection accorded to "without prejudice" correspondence also includes protection from discovery to third parties.

The Greater London Council entered into a contract with Rush and Tompkins Ltd. for the construction of a housing development. The latter subsequently engaged a sub-contractor to carry out certain ground works required under the main contract. In 1979 Rush and Tompkins Ltd. started proceedings against the GLC and the sub-contractor, claiming a declaration that the former was liable to reimburse them in respect of any sums for which they might be found liable to pay to the latter under the sub-contract, and an inquiry against both defendants regarding the amount of loss and expense which the latter were entitled to recover from them. Correspondence marked "without prejudice" between the plaintiff Rush and Tompkins Ltd. and the defendant GLC resulted in their reaching a compromise agreement in 1981. As a consequence the plaintiffs discontinued the action against this defendant. The sub-contractor then sought disclosure by the plaintiffs of the "without prejudice" correspondence. The plaintiffs conceded that the correspondence might be relevant to issues between them but refused to disclose. The defendants applied for an order for specific discovery. Discovery was refused by the Official Referee, Judge Esyr Lewis Q.C. The House of Lords, reversing the Court of Appeal, was unanimous in upholding this refusal.

LORD GRIFFITHS: My Lords, this appeal raises a novel point on the right to discovery of documents. . . .

The "without prejudice" rule is a rule governing the admissibility of evidence and is founded upon the public policy of encouraging litigants to settle their differences rather than litigate them to a finish. It is nowhere more clearly expressed than in the judgment of Oliver L.J. in *Cutts* v. *Head* [1984] Ch. 290, 306:

"That the rule rests, at least in part, upon public policy is clear from many authorities, and the convenient starting point of the inquiry is the nature of the underlying policy. It is that parties should be encouraged so far as possible to settle their disputes without resort to litigation and should not be discouraged by the knowledge that anything that is said in the course of such negotiations (and that includes, of course, as much the failure to reply to an offer as an actual reply) may be used to their prejudice in the course of the proceedings.... The public policy justification, in truth, essentially rests on the desirability of preventing statements or offers made in the course of negotiations for settlement being brought before the court of trial as admissions on the question of liability."

The rule applies to exclude all negotiations genuinely aimed at settlement whether oral or in writing from being given in evidence. A competent solicitor will always head any negotiating correspondence "without prejudice" to make clear beyond doubt that in the event of the negotiations being unsuccessful they are not to be referred to at the subsequent trial. However, the application of the rule is not dependent upon the use of the phrase "without prejudice" and if it is clear from the surrounding circumstances that the parties were seeking to compromise the action, evidence of the content of those negotiations will, as a general rule, not be admissible at the trial and cannot be used to establish an admission or partial admission. I cannot therefore agree with the Court of Appeal that the problem in the present case should be resolved by a linguistic approach to the meaning of the phrase "without prejudice." I believe that the question has to be looked at more broadly and resolved by balancing two different public interests namely the public interest in promoting settlements and the public interest in full discovery between parties to litigation.

Nearly all the cases in which the scope of the "without prejudice" rule has been considered, concern the admissibility of evidence at trial after negotiations have failed. In such circumstances no question of discovery arises because the parties are well aware of what passed between them in the negotiations. These cases show that the rule is not absolute and resort may be had to the "without prejudice" material for a variety of reasons when the justice of the case requires it. It is unnecessary to make any deep examination of these authorities to resolve the present appeal but they all illustrate the underlying purpose of the rule which is to protect a litigant from being embarrassed by any admission made purely in an attempt to achieve a settlement. Thus the "without prejudice" material will be admissible if the issue is whether or not the negotiations resulted in an agreed settlement, which is the point that Lindley L.J. was making in *Walker* v. *Wilsher* (1889) 23 Q.B.D. 335 and which was applied in *Tomlin* v. *Standard Telephones & Cables Ltd.* [1969] 1 W.L.R. 1378. The court will not permit the phrase to be used to exclude an act of bankruptcy: see *In re Daintrey, Ex parte Holt* [1893] 2 Q.B. 116 nor to suppress a threat if an offer is not accepted: see *Kitcat* v. *Sharp* (1882) 48 L.T. 64. In certain circumstances the "without prejudice" correspondence may be looked at to determine a question of costs after judgment has been given: see *Cutts* v. *Head* [1984] Ch. 290. There is also authority for the proposition that the admission of an "independent fact" in no way connected with the merits of the cause is admissible even if made in the course of negotiations for a settlement.

Thus an admission that a document was in the handwriting of one of the parties was received in evidence in *Waldridge* v. *Kennison* (1794) 1 Esp. 142. I regard this as an exceptional case and it should not be allowed to whittle down the protection given to the parties to speak freely about all issues in the litigation both factual and legal when seeking compromise and, for the purpose of establishing a basis of compromise, admitting certain facts. If the compromise fails the admission of the facts made for the purpose of the compromise should not be held against the maker of the admission and should therefore not be received in evidence.

I cannot accept the view of the Court of Appeal that *Walker* v. *Wilsher*, 23 Q.B.D. 335 is authority for the proposition that if the negotiations succeed and a settlement is concluded the privilege goes, having served its purpose. In *Walker* v. *Wilsher* the Court of Appeal held that it was not permissible to receive the contents of a "without prejudice" offer on the question of costs and no question arose as to the admissibility of admissions made in the negotiations in any possible subsequent proceedings. There are many situations when parties engaged upon some great enterprise such as a large building construction project must anticipate the risk of being involved in disputes with others engaged on the same project. Suppose the main contractor in an attempt to settle a dispute with one subcontractor made certain admissions it is clear law that those admissions cannot be used against him if there is no settlement. The reason they are not to be used is because it would discourage settlement if he believed that the admissions might be held against him. But it would surely be equally discouraging if the main contractor knew that if he achieved a settlement those admissions could then be used against him by any other subcontractor with whom he might also be in dispute. The main contractor might well be prepared to make certain concessions to settle some modest claim which he would never make in the face of another far larger claim. It seems to me that if those admissions made to achieve settlement of a piece of minor litigation could be held against him in a subsequent major litigation it would actively discourage settlement of the minor litigation and run counter to the whole underlying purpose of the "without prejudice" rule. I would therefore hold that as a general rule the "without prejudice" rule renders inadmissible in any subsequent litigation connected with the same subject-matter proof of any admissions made in a genuine attempt to reach a settlement. It of course goes without saying that admissions made to reach settlement with a different party within the same litigation are also inadmissible whether or not settlement was reached with that party.

. . . .

The only issue that now survives in the present litigation is the subcontractors' counterclaim. For the reasons I have given the contents of the "without prejudice" correspondence between the main contractor and the GLC will not be admissible to establish any admission relating to the subcontractors' claim. Nevertheless, the subcontractors say they should have discovery of that correspondence which one must assume will include admissions even though they cannot make use of them in evidence. . . .

The general rule is that a party is entitled to discovery of all documents that relate to the matters in issue irrespective of admissibility and here we have the admission of the head contractors that the "without prejudice" correspondence would be discoverable unless protected by the "without prejudice" rule. There is little English authority on this question but I think some light upon the problem is to be gained from a consideration of the decision in *Rabin* v. *Mendoza & Co.* [1954] 1 W.L.R. 271....

This authority shows that even as between the parties to "without prejudice" correspondence they are not entitled to discovery against one another....

....

I have come to the conclusion that the wiser course is to protect "without prejudice" communications between parties to litigation from production to other parties in the same litigation. In multi-party litigation it is not an infrequent experience that one party takes up an unreasonably intransigent attitude that makes it extremely difficult to settle with him. In such circumstances it would, I think, place a serious fetter on negotiations between other parties if they knew that everything that passed between them would ultimately have to be revealed to the one obdurate litigant. What would in fact happen would be that nothing would be put on paper but this is in itself a recipe for disaster in difficult negotiations which are far better spelt out with precision in writing.

If the party who obtains discovery of the "without prejudice" correspondence can make no use of it at trial it can be of only very limited value to him. It may give some insight into his opponent's general approach to the issues in the case but in most cases this is likely to be of marginal significance and will probably be revealed to him in direct negotiations in any event. In my view this advantage does not outweigh the damage that would be done to the conduct of settlement negotiations if solicitors thought that what was said and written between them would become common currency available to all other parties to the litigation. In my view the general public policy that applies to protect genuine negotiations from being admissible in evidence should also be extended to protect those negotiations from being discoverable to third parties. Accordingly I would allow this appeal and restore the decision of Judge Esyr Lewis Q.C.

LORDS BRIDGE OF HARWICH, BRANDON OF OAKBROOK, OLIVER OF AYLMERTON and GOFF OF CHIEVELEY concurred.

Theodoropoulas v. **Theodoropoulas** [1964] P. 311 (Winchester Assizes). It was held that, where spouses were endeavouring to effect a reconciliation in the presence of, or through a third person, neither of the parties, nor the third person, could give evidence of the terms of their communications without the assent of both parties. Sir Jocelyn Simon P. said (pp. 313–314): "No doubt when a probation officer or an SSAFA representative or a clergyman is approached, the law will readily infer that the parties have gone to him with a view to reconciliation and on the tacit understanding that nothing said should afterwards be used against them; but, equally, where it is proved that any private individual is enlisted specifically as a conciliator...the law will aid his or her efforts by guaranteeing that any admissions or disclosures by the parties are privileged in subsequent matrimonial litigation.... Moreover, it seems to me the principles ...are just as applicable to communications between the parties themselves with a view to reconciliation as to those conducted through intermediaries.... [The privilege] also extends to excluding the evidence of an independent witness who was fortuitously present when those communications were made and who overheard or read them."

Field v. **Commissioner for Railways for New South Wales** (1957) 99 C.L.R. 285 (H.C. Aust.). The plaintiff was injured when alighting from a train run by the defendant and brought an action for damages for personal injuries. In the course of "without prejudice" negotiations, entered into in the hope of settling the dispute on a compromise basis, the plaintiff was examined by a medical specialist appointed by the defendant. During this examination he gave an account of the accident. At the trial the specialist was called by the defence to repeat what the plaintiff had said to him. The High Court of Australia held by a majority that this had been right. Dixon C.J., Webb, Kitto and Taylor JJ. said (p. 293): "The question really is whether it was fairly incidental to the purposes of the negotiations to which the medical examination was subsidiary or ancillary that the plaintiff should communicate to the surgeon appointed by the Railway Commissioner the manner in which the accident was caused. To answer this question in the affirmative stretches the notion of incidental protection very far. The defendant's contention that it was outside the scope of the purpose of the plaintiff's visit to the doctor to enter upon such a question seems clearly right."

Note.—See, too, the old case of *Waldridge* v. *Kinnison* (1794) 1 Esp. 143 where it was held that the privilege does not extend to statements of fact made in the course of without prejudice negotiations if such statements have no reference to the dispute between the parties, as where one of them casually admits that a document is in his handwriting.

Chapter 12

EVIDENCE EXCLUDED ON GROUNDS OF PUBLIC POLICY

SOMETIMES relevant and otherwise admissible evidence is excluded on grounds of public policy. As in cases of privilege, exclusion is justified in terms of considerations extrinsic to (and often inimical to) the efficiency and fairness of the trial process. However, this branch of the law of evidence is, in several respects, essentially different from the law relating to privilege. What is posited here is a rule of exclusion: thus there is usually no possibility of waiver; resort may not be had to secondary evidence when primary evidence is excluded; and in many cases objection may (or must) be taken by the judge even if not raised by a party or witness. On the other hand historically the terminology of privilege has been used in such phrases as Crown Privilege, State Privilege and public interest privilege—but in recent years this usage has been the object of considerable judicial disapproval.[1] The term currently and more appropriately in vogue is public interest immunity.

Evidence of certain facts connected with previous litigation is excluded on the ground of public policy. For instance, jurors are not permitted to give evidence as to events occurring in the jury room in a case in which they were sitting. But the most important, and by far the most controversial, head of public policy relates to State or "public" interest, and all the materials set out in this chapter are concerned with that subject. The central theme may be propounded with opaque simplicity: evidence must be excluded if its reception would be unduly prejudicial to State or public interests. State or public interest is inevitably, however, a vague and sometimes potentially sinister concept. A related difficulty and danger concerns the way in which the validity of a claim to withhold evidence on this ground is to be determined. Objection that an item of evidence must be excluded because its reception would be unduly prejudicial to State or public interests may be taken by a party or by the court, but (not surprisingly) it is in

---

[1] "Crown Privilege," said Lord Simon of Glaisdale in *R.* v. *Lewes Justices, ex parte Secretary of State for the Home Department* [1973] A.C. 388 (*infra*) at pp. 405–406, "is a misnomer and apt to be misleading." Contrast the reasoned nostalgia expressed by Lord Scarman in *Science Research Council* v. *Nassé* [1980] A.C. 1028 (*infra*) at p. 1087 at the passing of the term "Crown privilege" which "at least emphasised the very restricted area of public interest immunity." In *Air Canada* v. *Secretary of State for Trade* [1983] 2 A.C. 394 (*infra*) Lord Fraser at p. 436 has emphasised: "Public interest immunity is not a privilege which may be waived by the Crown or by any party."

practice often taken by, or on the initiative of, a Cabinet Minister or a senior member of the executive arm of government.

The immediate historical background was provided by the wartime House of Lords decision in *Duncan* v. *Cammell Laird & Co. Ltd.*[2] but the effective starting point for the modern law is to be found in *Conway* v. *Rimmer*.[3] Since the latter case, itself a decision of the House of Lords, the matter has been before their Lordships' House on at least nine further occasions.[4] This is a mark of its difficulty. Considerations of space make it impossible to be other than extremely selective when choosing material, for inclusion in this Chapter, from the more than 40 speeches on the subject which have been delivered in the House of Lords since *Duncan* v. *Cammell Laird & Co. Ltd*. Many important cases have had to be simply summarised or noted.

The general pattern of the emerging law would seem to be along the following lines.

Evidence will only be excluded under this head of public policy if a recognisable public interest in exclusion is demonstrated, and if it is further demonstrated that this public interest clearly outweighs the often conflicting, but ever present, public interest in ensuring that the courts are able to insist upon "parties and witnesses disclosing the truth, the whole truth, and nothing but the truth, when this would assist the decision of matters in dispute." (*Per* Lord Hailsham of Marylebone in *D.* v. *National Society for the Prevention of Cruelty to Children*.[5]) There is still considerable doubt as to what will qualify as a recognisable public interest for this purpose. Usually, but not always, the interest must be of a governmental, quasi-governmental or in a loose sense, "official" nature. The generally accepted (and better) view is that in the event of the two conflicting public interests being adjudged to be in apparent equilibrium, the claim for non-disclosure must be rejected.[6]

It is now clear that in the majority of, but not all, cases it is for the judge to determine whether the existence of a public interest in non-disclosure has been established, and, if it has, whether it sufficiently outweighs the countervailing public interest in the efficacy and fairness of trials. In order that he may perform this task the judge has the right to inspect the disputed evidence. His powers in this regard are, however, subject to a specific right of appeal against inspection and/or disclosure.

It would be impracticable and indeed undesirable to essay a closed catalogue of factors to which a judge may, or should, in appropriate cases have regard when attempting to strike a balance between

---

[2] [1942] A.C. 624 (*infra*).

[3] [1968] A.C. 910 (*infra*).

[4] *R.* v. *Lewes Justices, ex Secretary of State for the Home Department* [1973] A.C. 388; *Norwich Pharmical Co.* v. *Customs and Excise Commissioners* [1974] A.C. 133; *Alfred Crompton Amusement Machines Ltd.* v. *Customs and Excise Commissisoners (No. 2)* [1974] A.C. 405; *D.* v. *National Society for the Prevention of Cruelty to Children* [1978] A.C. 177; *Science Research Council* v. *Nassé, Leyland Cars (B.L. Cars Ltd.)* v. *Nyas* [1980] A.C. 1028; *Burmah Oil Co.* v. *Bank of England* [1980] A.C. 1090; *Lonhro Ltd.* v. *Shell Petroleum Co. Ltd.* [1980] 1 W.L.R. 627; *British Steel Corporation* v. *Granada Televison Ltd.* 1981] A.C. 1096; *Air Canada* v. *Secretary of State for Trade* [1983] 2 A.C. 394.

[5] [1978] A.C. 171, 225 (*infra*).

[6] For the special statuory position for the purposes of an investigation under the Parliamentary Commission [Ombudsman] Act 1967 see ss.8 and 11 of that Act.

conflicting public interests. Moreover, it is obvious that what is called for is usually a quantitative as well as a qualitative assessment. But it may be noted that amongst the factors which have been judicially considered are the following. (1) The basis of the objection to production of a document; was it that revelation of the actual contents would be harmful to the public interest, or, was it rather that the document belonged to a category or class of documents which should as such be kept secret? (2) That publication of the information which it was sought to withhold might endanger national security. (3) That that information related to the formulation and/or execution of high governmental policy. (4) That a responsible Minister of the Crown had in fact personally considered the document and had come to the conclusion that in the public interest its contents should be protected from disclosure. (5) The danger that disclosure would be likely to lead to a "drying up" of sources of important and valuable information. (6) Society's interest in the preservation of the confidentiality of certain relationships. (7) That there might have been available from other sources alternative, equally useful, but less dangerous information. (8) The relevance and cogency of the disputed evidence. (9) Its possible bearing upon the establishment of the innocence of an accused person. (10) The fact that persons whose identity it was sought to withhold were likely to have been wrong-doers. (11) The circumstance that the information which it was sought to withhold had already been made public.

Generally speaking, although some factors will almost always carry very great weight, no single factor is to be treated as automatically conclusive. However, in one situation a specific rule of law is well established. The Director of Public Prosecutions may not, anyhow in civil proceedings, disclose the names of his informants or the information which they gave him and which led to the bringing of a public prosection. This is the doctrine of the old case of *Marks* v. *Beyfus*.[7] It is subject to few limited exceptions, but it has recently been extended by way of analogy in *D.* v. *National Society for the Prevention of Cruelty to Children*.[8]

Most of the leading cases on public policy have in fact been concerned with documentary evidence, but there is no reason to suppose that similar principles do not apply *mutatis mutandis* to oral testimony and to real evidence.[9]

Finally, one source of confusion may be mentioned. Many of the recently decided cases have involved interlocutory matters, in particular the availability of discovery. Although in most civil litigation discovery of documents is in fact almost automatic, this represents no more than a convenient practice, and in the final analysis the availability of discovery is a matter for the discretion of the court: discovery is not to be ordered unless it is necessary for fairly disposing of the case or for saving costs. Some of the factors which may properly bear upon the exercise of this discretion may be virtually indistinguishable from some of the factors which fall to be taken into account by a court when adjudicating upon a claim for non-disclosure on the score of public policy. Despite this

---

[7] (1890) 25 Q.B.D. 492 (*infra*).
[8] [1978] A.C. 171 (*infra*).
[9] See *Marconi's Wireless Telegraph Co. Ltd.* v. *The Commonwealth* (1913) 16 C.L.R. 178 (H.C. of Australia).

similarity the two contexts must, however, be kept separate. The effect of a finding, after weighing conflicting public interests one against the other, that evidence should for reasons of public policy not be given, is that a mandatory rule is activated, and this will override and eliminate the discretion which the court would otherwise exercise in cases in which what is in issue is the availability of discovery.

Duncan v. **Cammell Laird and Co. Ltd.** [1942] A.C. 624 (H.L.). In an action for negligence in relation to the construction of a submarine the defendants were directed by the Board of Admiralty to object to the production of numerous documents in their possession as government contractors. The validity of this direction was upheld by the House of Lords. It was held that the production of a document may be withheld in the public interest either (a) on account of its contents or (b) because it belongs to a class which on the grounds of public policy must as a class be withheld from production. Viscount Simon delivering the unanimous decision of the House further held that a properly taken decision of a responsible Minister that evidence falling into either category should be withheld was binding upon the courts.

CONWAY v. RIMMER AND ANOTHER

[1968] A.C. 910; [1968] 1 All E.R. 874 (H.L.: 1968)

A Minister's affidavit or certificate objecting to the production of a document on the ground of privilege is not conclusive. A judge may inspect the document and order its production, notwithstanding the Minister's objection, though in every case full weight must be given to the Minister's view, which in some cases must prevail. The courts have a duty to balance the public interest in the proper administration of justice against the public interest in withholding any evidence on a Minister's objection to production.

The appellant, a probationer police constable, was charged with stealing a torch from another probationer. At quarter sessions the case was stopped and a verdict of not guilty returned. Shortly thereafter he was dimissed from his post. He now sued the respondent, a superintendent in the same police force, for malicious prosecution, and both parties wished five police probationary and other reports concerning the appellant to be produced. An affidavit by the Home Secretary stated that having personally examined the documents, he objected to production on the grounds that the reports fell within classes of documents comprising confidential police reports to superior officers, or police reports on investigations into crime, and that production of each such class would be injurious to the public interest. The House of Lords allowed the appellant's appeal from the decision of the Court of Appeal which had upheld the objection to production.

LORD REID: . . . I would therefore propose that the House ought now to decide that courts have and are entitled to exercise a power and duty to hold a balance between the public interest, as expressed by a Minister, to withhold certain documents or other evidence, and the public interest in ensuring the proper administration of justice. That does not mean that a court would reject a Minister's view: full weight must be given to it in every case, and if the Minister's reasons are of a character which judicial experience is not competent to weigh, then the Minister's view must prevail. But experience has shown that reasons given for withholding whole classes of documents are often not of that character. . . .

I do not doubt that there are certain classes of documents which ought not to be disclosed whatever their content may be. Virtually everyone agrees that Cabinet minutes and the like ought not to be disclosed until such time as they are only of historical interest. . . .

It appears to me that if the Minister's reasons are such that a judge can properly weigh them, he must, on the other hand, consider what is the probable importance in the case before him of the documents or other evidence sought to be withheld. If he decides that on balance the documents probably ought to be produced, I think that it would generally be best that he should see them before ordering production and if he thinks that the Minister's reasons are not clearly expressed he will have to see the documents before ordering production. I see nothing wrong in the judge seeing documents without their being shown to the parties. . . .

But it is important that the Minister should have a right to appeal before the document is produced. . . .

In my judgment, this appeal should be allowed and these documents ought now to be required to be produced for inspection. If it is then found that disclosure would not in your Lordship's view be prejudicial to the public interest, or that any possibility of such prejudice is, in the case of each of the documents, insufficient to justify its being withheld, then disclosure should be ordered.

LORD MORRIS OF BORTH-Y-GEST: . . . It is, I think, a principle which commands general acceptance that there are circumstances in which the public interest must be dominant over the interests of a private individual. To the safety or the well-being of the community the claims of a private person may have to be subservient. This principle applies in litigation. The public interest may require that relevant documents ought not to be produced. If, for example, national security would be or might be imperiled by the production and consequent disclosure of certain documents, then the interest of litigant must give way. There are some documents which can readily be identified as containing material the secrecy of which it is vital to protect. But where disclosure is desired and is resisted there is something more than a conflict between the public interest and some private interest. There are two aspects of the public interest which pull in contrary directions. It is in the public interest that full effect should be given to the normal rights of a litigant. It is in the public interest that in the determination of disputes the courts should have all relevant material before them. It is, on the other hand, in the public interest that material should be withheld if, by its production and disclosure, the safety or the well-being of the community would be adversely affected. There will be situations in which a decision ought to be made whether the harm that may result from the production of documents will be greater than the harm that may result from their non-production. Who, then, is to hold the scales? Who is to adjudge where the greater weight lies?

We could have a system under which, if a Minister of the Crown gave a certificate that a document should not be produced, the courts would be obliged to give full effect to such certificate and, in every case and without exception, to treat it as binding, final and conclusive. Such a system ... would, in my view, be out of harmony with the spirit which in this country has guided the ordering of our affairs and in particular the administration of justice....

It was the submission of the Attorney-General ... that the primary duty to determine whether the public interest require that a document be withheld rests with the executive government.... He further submitted that the court has in English law no ad hoc discretion to reject a statement of the executive government (if put forward in appropriate form and in good faith and without mistake or misdirection) recording a determination that the public interest requires that a document be withheld. The court, he submitted, must give conclusive effect to such a statement: it must be regarded as a statement upon a matter peculiarly within the knowledge and competence of the executive government: the court cannot reject the statement on the ground that the necessities of justice in the particular case outweigh the public interest averred by the executive.

My Lords, I am unable to regard these submissions as being acceptable. It is one of the main functions of courts to weigh up competing evidence and considerations. I see no peril in leaving such a process to the courts. They are well qualified to perform it. Their day-to-day task is to pay heed to evidence and to argument and then to consider, to weigh and to decide. It is said that a statement by the executive to the effect that the public interest requires that a document should be withheld is a statement upon a matter peculiarly within the knowledge and competence of the executive government and must therefore be accepted by a court. A court would always pay the greatest heed to a statement that production of a document was not in the public interest and in most cases would be likely to give effect to it. There are many matters upon which the executive will be likely to be best qualified to form a view. It will be easy for a court to recognise this and to give full weight to this consideration. The court, however, will be in a position of independence and will as a result often be better placed than a department to assess the weight of competing aspects of the public interest including those with which a particular department is not immediately concerned....

In my view, it should now be made clear that whenever an objection is made to the production of a relevant document it is for the court to decide whether or not to uphold the objection. The inherent power of the court must include a power to ask for a clarification or an amplification of an objection to production though the court will be careful not to impose a requirement which could only be met by divulging the very matters to which the objection related. The power of the court must also include a power to examine the documents privately, a power, I think, which in practice should be sparingly exercised but one which could operate as a safeguard for the executive in cases where a court is inclined to make an order for production, though an objection is being pressed. I see no difference in principle between the consideration of what have been called the contents and the class cases.

....

I have come to the conclusion that the appeal should be allowed and that the best procedure to follow for weighing the public and private interests which are involved in this case will be to have an inspection of the five documents which are in question. It can then be decided whether there should not be an order for the production of some or all of the documents.

LORD UPJOHN: ... My Lords, feeling as I do unfettered by any necessity for a strictly textual adherence to Lord Simon's words [in *Duncan* v. *Cammell Laird and Co. Ltd.*], I think that the principle to be applied can be very shortly stated. On the one side there is the public interest to be protected; on the other side of the scales is the interest of the subject who legitimately wants production of some documents which he believes will support his own or defeat his adversary's case. Both are matters of public interest, for it is also in the public interest that justice should be done between litigating parties by production of all documents which are relevant and for which privilege cannot be claimed under the ordinary rules. They must be weighed in the balance one against the other.

... No doubt there are many cases in which documents by their very nature fall into a class which requires protection such as, only by way of example, Cabinet papers, Foreign Office dispatches, the security of the State, high-level inter-department minutes and correspondence and documents pertaining to the general administration of the naval, military and air force services. Nearly always such documents would be the subject of privilege by reason of their contents but by their "class" in any event they qualify for privilege. So, too, high-level inter-departmental communications, to take, only as an example upon establishment matters, the promotion or transfer of reasonably high level personnel in the service of the Crown. But no catalogue can reasonably be compiled. ...

... It is clear, in my opinion, that the Judiciary must regain its control over the whole of this field of the law. ...

So it seems to me to be quite clear that there is no erosion of our normal ideas of justice *inter partes* if a judge is not satisfied about the Crown's claim to privilege in himself privately inspecting the allegedly privileged documents. But before reaching that stage he may, of course, require further and better affidavits by the Minister and may direct the Minister to attend for cross-examination by any party to the litigation before he inspects the document.

. . . .

My Lords, I would allow this appeal.

LORDS HODSON AND PEARCE delivered judgments to the same effect.

Note.—The House read the documents in question, and, holding that disclosure would not be prejudicial, took the view that they should be made available on the trial of the action.

There is power to prevent the disclosure even of the existence of a document (see Crown Proceedings Act 1947, s.28, Part Two, *infra*; R.S.C., Ord. 77, r. 12(2)).

The rule of exclusion applies to oral communications also (see, for one example, *West* v. *West* (1911) 27 T.L.R. 189, 476 (C.A.)); but the court has refused to act on a certificate by a Minister that it would be contrary to the public interest for a particular witness to give evidence (*Broome* v. *Broome* [1955] P. 190). A witness may not refresh his memory from a privileged document (*Gain* v. *Gain* [1961] 1 W.L.R. 1469).

BURMAH OIL CO. v. BANK OF ENGLAND

[1980] A.C. 1090; [1979] 3 All E.R. 7000 (H.L.: 1979)

Documents, the disclosure of which is opposed, should be produced for inspection where without inspection it would not be possible to decide whether the balance of public interest lay for or against disclosure. No class of documents is absolutely immune from production.

Where a court orders inspection the Crown should have a right to appeal before the document is produced.

An agreement was entered into in 1975 between the Burmah Oil Co. and the Bank of England (acting in close contact with and under the direction of the government) with the object of rescuing the company from financial difficulties arising from the international oil crisis, on terms consistent with the government's national economic policies. A term of this agreement involved the sale and transfer to the Bank of some 78 million ordinary stock units in British Petroleum, held by Burmah Oil, at £2.30 per unit, this being the price required by the government.

The following year Burmah Oil brought an action against the Bank claiming a declaration that the sale was unconscionable and inequitable and an order that the Bank should transfer the stock units back to them at the same price as it had paid. Burmah Oil sought an order for discovery of all documents held by the Bank and relevant to the issues pleaded. The Bank, on government instructions, resisted production of 62 documents in its possession and control. The Crown intervened by the Attorney-General, but the only defendant was the Bank. Objection to production was taken by the Chief Secretary to the Treasury in a certificate stating that he had personally read and considered each of these 62 documents and that he had formed the opinion that their production would be injurious to the public interest. He placed the documents in three categories. Categories A and B consisted of classes of documents relating to the formulation of government policy in the light of the international consequences of the financial collapse of Burmah Oil and its effect on the government's own oil policy, as discussed either at ministerial level or at a lower level with the Bank but related to eventual formulation of ministerial policy. Category C documents concerned commercial or financial information communicated in confidence to the government or the Bank by major business companies and businessmen. With regard to these it was claimed that the preservation of confidence was in the public interest because, if it became known that what was given in confidence might be revealed publicly, such information, necessary for policy decisons, would not be so readily forthcoming.

Before the hearing, as a result of an innocent mistake, Burmah Oil's solicitors and counsel were able to read the 62 documents. The trial judge upheld the claim for non-disclosure without looking at any of the documents. The Court of Appeal, having read the documents at the end of argument, dismissed Burmah Oil's appeal. On Burmah Oil's further appeal to the House of Lords the documents had been reduced from 62 to 10 (2 in category A and 8 in category B). The House (Lord Wilberforce dissenting) held that they should be produced for inspection. Following inspection the House found that none of them contained matter of such evidential value as to make an order for their disclosure necessary for disposing fairly of the case. The appeal was, therefore, dismissed.

LORD WILBERFORCE (dissenting):...My Lords in an interlocutory matter involving a large amount of discretion, which has been concurrently decided by both courts below, I apprehend that your Lordships should be reluctant to intervene and indeed should only do so if of opinion that some different principle of law from that accepted below ought to be applied....

The starting point in the discussion must be the certificate of the Chief Secretary. This is a lengthy and detailed document to which justice cannot be done without setting it out in full. It is perfectly clear that this document represents the result of careful and responsible consideration: that the minister has read and applied his mind to each of the documents: that, to adopt language used by the courts in other cases, the minister has not merely repeated a mechanical formula, that the certificate is not "amorphous" or of a blanket character, but is specific and motivated. Further, the minister has not contented himself with a general assertion that production would be injurious to the public interest, he has stated very fully the reasons why this would in his opinion be so: in summary that they concern discussions at a very high level, as to one category at ministerial level, and as to another the highest official level, as to the formulation of government policy. He has not even contented himself with a general reference to government policy. He has specified this as concerned with (a) the possible effect of a collapse of Burmah upon the £ sterling, upon other British companies with large overseas borrowings, upon the government's North Sea oil policy, and the future production of North Sea oil and correspondingly on the expectation which might be aroused on the part of other private borrowers if Burmah were to receive assistance, (b) the international and other consequences of a sale of the B.P. stock to the bank—which would bring the government shareholding up to 70 per cent.— and (c) as regards possible further financial support to Burmah after January 1975 having regard to the possible consequences of a financial collapse by Burmah.

It is apparent that these identified matters of policy were of the highest national and political importance and that they called for formulation of policy at the highest governmental levels, including the Cabinet, involving directly several ministers in the Treasury, the Department of Energy and the Paymaster General, and, in the first two mentioned departments, handled by the Permanent Under Secretary of State.
. . . .

The claim to "public interest immunity" in respect of these documents is clearly what has come under a rough but accepted categorisation to be known as a "class" claim, not a "contents" claim, the distinction between them being that with a class claim it is immaterial whether the disclosure of the particular contents of particular documents would be injurious to the public interest—the point being that it is the maintenance of the immunity of the class from disclosure in litigation that is important; whereas in a contents claim the protection is claimed for particular contents in a particular document. A claim remains a class even though something may be known about the contents: it remains a class even if parts of documents are revealed and parts disclosed. The appellant did not, I think, dispute this. And, the claim being a class claim, I must state with emphasis that there is not the slightest ground for doubting that the documents in question fall within the class described: indeed the descriptions themselves and references in disclosed documents make it clear that they do. So this is not one of those cases, which anyway are exceptional, where the court feels it necessary to look at the documents in order to verify that fact. We start with a strong and well-fortified basis for an immunity claim.

I now deal with the two main arguments used by the appellants. . . .

The second argument is perhaps more plausible, it is to say that, whatever may have been the need to protect governmental policy from disclosure at the time (1975) all is now past history: the decision has been made; the sale has gone through; Burmah has been saved from collapse. So what is the public interest in keeping up the protective screen?

I think that there are several answers to this. The first (and easiest) is that all is not past history—at least we do not know that it is. Government policy as to supporting private firms in danger of collapse: as to ownership of B.P. stock: as to the development of North Sea oil is ongoing policy; the documents are not yet for the Record Office. They are not, to use a phrase picked out of Lord Reid's speech in *Conway* v. *Rimmer* [1968] A.C. 910, 952, of purely historical interest. Secondly the grounds on which public interest immunity is claimed for this class of document are, no doubt within limits, independent of time. One such ground is the need for candour in communication between those concerned with policy making. It seems now rather fashionable to decry this, but if as a ground it may at one time have been exaggerated, it has now, in my opinion, received an excessive dose of cold water. I am certainly not prepared—against the view of the minister—to discount the need, in the formation of such very controversial policy as that with which we are here involved, for frank and uninhibited advice from the bank to the government, from and between civil servants and between ministers. It does not require much imagination to suppose that some of those concerned took different views as to the right policy and expressed them. The documents indeed show that they did. To remove protection from revelation in court in this case at least could well deter frank and full expression in similar cases in the future.

Another such ground is to protect from inspection by possible critics the inner working of government while forming important governmental policy. I do not believe that scepticism has invaded this, or that it is for the courts to assume the role of advocates for open government. If, as I believe, this is a valid ground for protection, it must continue to operate beyond the time span of a particular episode. Concretely, to reveal what advice was *then* sought and given and the mechanism for seeking and considering such advice, might well make the process of government more difficult *now*. On this point too I am certainly not prepared to be wiser than the minister. So I think that the "time factor" argument must fail.

The basis for an immunity claim, then, having been laid, it is next necessary to consider whether there is any other element of public interest telling in favour of production. The interest of the proper and fair administration of justice falls under this description. It is hardly necessary to state that the mere fact that the documents are or may be "relevant" to the issues, within the extended meaning of relevance in relation to discovery, is not material. The question of privilege or immunity only arises in relation to "relevant" documents and itself depends on other considerations, viz., whether production of these documents (admittedly relevant) is necessary for the due administration of justice. In considering how these two elements are to be weighed one against the other, the proper starting point must be the decision of this House in *Conway* v. *Rimmer* [1968] A.C. 910. . . .

It may well be arguable whether, when one is faced with a claim for immunity from production on "public interest" grounds, and when the relevant public interest is shown to be of a high, or the highest, level of importance, the fact is of itself conclusive, and nothing which relates to the interest in the administration of justice can prevail against it. . . .

. . . I am . . . quite prepared to deal with this case on the basis that the courts may, in a suitable case, decide that a high level governmental public interest must give way to the interests of the administration of justice.

But it must be clear what this involves. A claim for public interest immunity having been made, on manifestly solid grounds, it is necessary for those who seek to overcome it to demonstrate the existence of a counteracting interest calling for disclosure of particular documents. When this is demonstrated, but only then, may the court proceed to a balancing process. In *Conway* v. *Rimmer* [1968] A.C. 910 itself it was known that there were in existence probationary reports on the plaintiff as to which an obviously strong argument could be made that their disclosure was necessary if the plaintiff's claim were to have any hope of succeeding (in the end they turned out to be far from helpful to him): so the court had something very definite to go upon which it could put into the scales against the (minor) public interest of not revealing routine reports. . . . But the present case is quite different. There is not, and I firmly assert this, the slightest ground, apart from pure speculation, for supposing that there is any document in existence, among those which it is sought to withhold, or anything in a document which could outweigh the public interest claim for immunity. I make this assertion good under two heads.

1. A very full and careful disclosure has been made of all documents bearing upon negotiations between Burmah and the bank leading to the sale of the stock. . . .

2. The exact nature of Burmah's claim against the bank is not very clear, but I need not, indeed should not, analyse it for present purposes. . . .

This brings me to the issue of inspection. For now it is said, "Well, let us look at the documents and see—to do so cannot do any harm. If there is nothing there no damage will be done: if there is, we can weigh its importance." As presented (and to be fair to Burmah's very able counsel, such a submission occupied a far from prominent place in their argument) this may appear to have some attraction. But with all respect to those who think otherwise, I am firmly of opinion that we should not yield to this siren song. The existing state of the authorities is against it: and no good case can be made for changing the law. Indeed, to do so would not in my opinion be progress.

As to authority, before *Conway* v. *Rimmer* [1968] A.C. 910, although the court had power to inspect any document, the question whether to exercise it was treated as one for the discretion of the judge, who, it was said, should normally accept the affidavit claiming the immunity: see *Westminister Airways Ltd.* v. *Kuwait Oil Co. Ltd.* [1915] 1 K.B. 134. . . .

In *Conway* v. *Rimmer* [1968] A.C. 910 itself, it was said that the power should be exercised "sparingly" (*per* Lord Morris of Borth-y-Gest,

p. 971), and then only if there are reasons to doubt the accuracy of the certificate or the cogency of the minister's reasons. Inspection should be by way of final check. Or, as Lord Upjohn put it, inspection should be made if the judge "feels any doubt about the reason for [the document's] inclusion as a class document" (p. 995). In *Alfred Crompton Amusement Machines Ltd.* v. *Customs and Excise Commissioners (No. 2)* [1974] A.C. 405 this House upheld the claim to public interest immunity without inspecting the documents, although that course had been taken by the Court of Appeal....

As to principle, I cannot think that it is desirable that the courts should assume the task of inspection except in rare instances where a strong positive case is made out, certainly not upon a bare unsupported assertion by the party seeking production that something to help him may be found, or upon some unsupported—viz., speculative—haunch of its own. In the first place it is necessary to draw a reasonably clear line between the responsibility of ministers on the one hand, and those of the courts on the other. Each has its proper contribution to make towards solution of the problem where the public interest lies—judicial review is not a "bonum in se" it is a part—and a valuable one—of democratic government in which other responsibilities coexist. Existing cases, from *Conway* v. *Rimmer* onwards have drawn this line carefully and suitably. It is for the minister to define the public interest and the grounds on which he considers that production would affect it. Similarly, the court, responsible for the administration of justice, should, before it decides that the minister's view must give way, have something positive or identifiable to put into the scales. To override the minister's opinion by "amorphous" phrases or unsupported contentions, would be to do precisely what the courts will not countenance in the actions of ministers. Secondly, decisions on grounds of public interest privilege fall to be made at first instance, by judges or masters in chambers. They should be able to make these decisions according to simple rules: these are provided by the law as it stands. To invite a general procedure of inspection is to embark the courts on a dangerous course: they have not in general the time nor the experience, to carry out in every case a careful inspection of documents and thereafter a weighing process. The results of such a process may, indeed are likely, to be variable from court to court and from case to case. This case provides an example of opposite conclusions come to upon identical materials: see [1979] 1 W.L.R. 473. This inevitable uncertainty is not likely to do credit to the administration of justice and is bound to encourage appeals.

In the end, I regard this as a plain case: of public interest immunity properly claimed on grounds of high policy on the one hand in terms which cannot be called in question; of nothing of any substance to put in the scale on the other. I return to the point that both courts below have refused to exercise a discretionary power to order production of these documents, or to inspect them. Their decision can only be reserved if they erred in law. To say that they erred in law in not inspecting the documents involves the proposition that there is a duty, either in all cases or at least in such a case as this, to inspect. In my opinion it is not the law, and ought not to be the law, that there is any such duty....

I would dismiss the appeal.

LORD SALMON: ...I have privately inspected the 10 documents, to which I have referred. In my opinion none of them throws much, if any, light on what is necessary for fairly disposing of this case; and I would accordingly dismiss the appeal.

LORD EDMUND-DAVIES: ... Yet, when all is said and done and even accepting that the withheld documents are likely to contain material supportive of the allegation of unconscionability, this House is at present completely in the dark as to the cogency of such material. For example, does it clearly and substantially support the allegation, or only to an insignificant degree? Unless its evidentiary value is clear and cogent, the balancing exercise may well lead to the conclusion that the public interest would best be served by upholding the Chief Secretary's objection to disclosure. On the other hand, if the material provides strong and striking support of the plaintiffs' claim, the court may conclude that, when this is set against such prejudice to the public interest as is likely to arise where any disclosure made in late 1979 regarding even high-policy commercial negotiations conducted in January 1975, the interests of justice demand that disclosure (complete or partial) should be ordered. A judge conducting the balancing exercise needs to know (see *per* Lord Pearce in *Conway* v. *Rimmer* [1968] A.C. 910, 987)

"...whether the documents in question are of much or little weight in the litigation, whether their absence will result in a complete or partial denial of justice to one or other of the parties or perhaps to both, and what is the importance of the particular litigation to the parties and the public. All these are matters which should be considered if the court is to decide where the public interest lies."

A judge may well feel that he cannot profitably embark on such a balancing exercise without himself seeing the disputed documents. ...

LORD KEITH OF KINKEL: ... There are cases where consideration of the terms of the ministerial certificate and of the nature of the issues in the case before it was revealed by the pleadings, taken with the description of the documents sought to be recovered, will make it clear to the court that the balance of public interest lies against disclosure. In other cases the position will be the reverse. But there may be situations where grave doubt arises, and the court feels that it cannot properly decide upon which side the balance falls without privately inspecting the documents. In my opinion the present is such a case. ...

There can be no doubt that the court has power to inspect the documents privately. This was clearly laid down in *Conway* v. *Rimmer* [1968] A.C. 910. I do not consider that exercise of such power, in cases responsibly regarded by the court as doubtful, can be treated as itself detrimental to the public interest. Indeed, I am of opinion that it is calculated to promote the public interest, by adding to public confidence in the administration of justice. ...

Apprehension has on occasion been expressed lest the power of inspection might be irresponsibly exercised, perhaps by one of the lower courts. As a safeguard against this, an appeal should always be available, as indicated in *Conway* v. *Rimmer* [1968] A.C. 910, *per* Lord Reid at p. 953.

. . . .

LORD SCARMAN: ... In his certificate ... the Chief Secretary to the Treasury recognises that the 62 documents, disclosure of which Burmah seeks, relate to the matters in question in this action. He expresses the opinion that their production would be injurious to the public interest. The reason given for his opinion is that it is necessary for the proper functioning of the public service that production of the documents should be withheld. His objection is what has become known as a "class" objection. The Chief Secretary grounds his opinion not upon the contents but upon the class of the documents. . . .

[His Lordship went on to intimate that discovery of documents remains ultimately a matter for discretion,—but a discretion subject to two general rules,—(1) that it is not to be ordered unless necessary for fairly disposing of the case or for saving costs; and (2) that the documents relate to matters in issue, this embracing, not only documents directly relevant, but also documents which may well lead to a relevant train of enquiry: *Compagnie Financière et Commerciale du Pacifique* v. *Peruvian Guano Co.* (1882) 11 Q.B.D. 55. Public interest immunity represents an overriding exception to general law and practice.]

. . . It is said—and this view commended itself to the majority of the Court of Appeal—that the bank has given very full discovery of the documents directly relevant to the critical issue in the action, namely, the conduct by the bank of the negotiations with Burmah: that Burmah knows as much about this issue as does the bank: and that it can be fully investigated and decided upon the documents disclosed and the evidence available to Burmah without recourse to documents noting or recording the private discussions between the bank and the government. Upon this view, Burmah's attempt to see these documents is no more than a fishing expedition.

I totally reject this view of the case. First, as a matter of law, the documents for which immunity is claimed relate to the issues in the action and, according to the *Peruvian Guano* formulation, 11 Q.B.D. 55, may well assist towards a fair disposal of the case. It is unthinkable that in the absence of a public immunity objection and without a judicial inspection of the documents disclosure would have been refused. Secondly, common sense must be allowed to creep into the picture. Burmah's case is not merely that the bank exerted pressure: it is that the bank acted unreasonably, abusing its power and taking an unconscionable advantage of the weakness of Burmah. Upon these questions the withheld documents may be very revealing. This is not "pure speculation." The government was creating the pressure: the bank was exerting it upon the government's instructions. Is a court to assume that such documents will not assist towards an understanding of the nature of the pressure exerted? The assumption seems to me as unreal as the proverbial folly of attempting to understand Hamlet without reference to his position as the Prince of Denmark. I do not understand how a court could properly reach the judge's conclusion without inspecting the documents: and this he refused to do. The judge in my opinion wrongly exercised his discretion when he refused to inspect unless public policy (of which public interest immunity is a manifestation) required him to refuse.

It becomes necessary, therefore, to analyse closely the public interest immunity objection made by the minister and to determine the correct approach of the court to a situation in which there may be a clash of two interests—that of the public service and that of justice.

In *Conway* v. *Rimmer* [1968] A.C. 910 this House had to consider two questions. They were formulated by Lord Reid in these terms, at p. 943:

" ... first, whether the court is to have any right to question the finality of a minister's certificate and, secondly, if it has such a right, how and in what circumstances that right is to be exercised and made effective."

The House answered the first question, but did not, in my judgment, provide, nor was it required to provide, a complete answer to the second.

As I read the speeches in *Conway* v. *Rimmer* the House answered the first question by establishing the principle of judicial review. The minister's certificate is not final. The immunity is a rule of law: its scope is a question of law: and its applicability to the facts of a particular case is for the court, not the minister, to determine. . . .

Having established the principle of judicial review, the House had in *Conway* v. *Rimmer* [1968] A.C. 910 a simple case on the facts to decide. The question was whether routine reports, albeit of a confidential character, upon a former probationary police constable should in the interests of justice be disclosed in an action brought by him against his former superintendent in which he claimed damages for alleged malicious prosecution. There was a public interest in the confidentiality of such reports, but the Home Secretary, in his affidavit objecting to production on the ground of injury to the public interest, did not go so far as to say that it was necessary for the proper functioning of the public service to withhold production. On the other hand, the reports might be of critical importance in the litigation. Granted the existence of judicial review, here was a justiciable issue of no great difficulty. The House decided itself to inspect the documents, and, having done so, ordered production.

In reaching its decision the House did indicate what it considered to be the correct approach to the clash of interests which arises whenever there is a question of public interest immunity. The approach is to be found stated in two passages of Lord Reid's speech: p. 940c–f and p. 952c–g. The essence of the matter is a weighing, on balance, of the two public interests, that of the nation or the public service in non-disclosure and that of justice in the production of the documents. A good working, but not logically perfect, distinction is recognised between the contents and the classes of documents. If a minister of the Crown asserts that to disclose the contents of a document would or might, do the nation or the public service a grave injury, the court will be slow to question his opinion or to allow any interest, even that of justice, to prevail over it. Unless there can be shown to exist some factor suggesting either a lack of good faith (which is not likely) or an error of judgment or an error of law on the minister's part, the court should not (the House held) even go so far as itself to inspect the document. In this sense, the minister's assertion may be said to be conclusive. It is, however, for the judge to determine whether the minister's opinion is to be treated as conclusive. I do not understand the House to have denied that even in "contents" cases the court retains its power to inspect or to balance the injury to the public service against the risk of injustice, before reaching its decision.

In "class" cases the House clearly considered the minister's certificate to be more likely to be open to challenge. Undoubtedly, however, the House thought that there were certain classes of documents, which ought not to be disclosed however harmless the disclosure of their contents might be, and however important their disclosure might be in the interest of justice. Cabinet minutes were cited as an example. But the point did not arise for decision. For the documents in *Conway* v. *Rimmer* [1968] A.C. 910, though confidential, were "routine," in no way concerned with the inner working of the government at a high level; and their production might well be indispensable to the doing of justice in the litigation.

The point does arise in the present case. The documents are "high level." They are concerned with the formulation of policy. They are part of the inner working of the government machine. They contain information which the court knows does relate to matters in issue in the action, and which may, on inspection, prove to be highly material. In such circumstances the minister may well be right in his view that the public service would be injured by disclosure. But is the court bound by his view that it is *necessary* for the proper functioning of the public service that they be withheld from production? And, if non-disclosure is necessary for that purpose, is the court bound to hold that the interest in the proper functioning of the public service is to prevail over the requirements of justice?

If the answer to these two questions is to be in the affirmative . . . [a] properly drawn minister's certificate, which is a bona fide expression of his opinion, becomes final. But the advance made in the law by *Conway* v. *Rimmer* was that the certificate is not final. I think, therefore, that it would now be inconsistent with principle to hold that the court may not—even in a case like the present—review the certificate and balance the public interest of government to which alone it refers, against the public interest of justice, which is the concern of the court.

I do not therefore accept that there are any classes of document which, however harmless their contents and however strong the requirement of justice, may never be disclosed until they are only of historical interest. In this respect I think there may be a difference between a "class" objection and a "contents" objection—though the residual power to inspect and to order disclosure must remain in both instances. A Cabinet minute, it is said, must be withheld from production. Documents relating to the formulation of policy at a high level are also to be withheld. But is the secrecy of the "inner workings of the government machine" so vital a public interest that it must prevail over even the most imperative demands of justice? If the contents of a document concern the national safety, affect diplomatic relations or relate to some state secret of high importance, I can understand an affirmative answer. But if they do not (and it is not claimed in this case that they do), what is so important about secret government that it must be protected even at the price of injustice in our courts?

The reasons given for protecting the secrecy of government at the level of policy-making are two. The first is the need for candour in the advice offered to ministers: the second is that disclosure "would create or fan ill-informed or captious public or political criticism." Lord Reid in *Conway* v. *Rimmer* [1968] A.C. 910, 952, thought the second "the most important reason." Indeed, he was inclined to discount the candour argument.

I think both reasons are factors legitimately to be put into the balance which has to be struck between the public interest in the proper functioning of the public service (*i.e.* the executive arm of government) and the public interest in the administration of justice. Sometimes the public service reasons will be decisive of the issue: but they should never prevent the court from weighing them against the injury which would be suffered in the administration of justice if the document was not to be disclosed. And the likely injury to the cause of justice must also be assessed and weighed. Its weight will vary according to the nature of the proceedings in which disclosure is sought, the relevance of the documents, and the degree of likelihood that the document will be of importance in the litigation. In striking the balance, the court may always, if it thinks it necessary, itself inspect the documents.

Inspection by the court is, I accept, a power to be exercised only if the court is in doubt, after considering the certificate, the issues in the case and the relevance of the documents whose disclosure is sought. Where documents are relevant (as in this case they are), I would think a pure "class" objection would by itself seldom quieten judicial doubts— particularly if, as here, a substantial case can be made out for saying that disclosure is needed in the interest of justice.

I am fortified in the opinion which I have expressed by the trend towards inspection and disclosure to be found both in the United States and in Commonwealth countries. [His Lordship then referred to *Nixon* v. *U.S.* 418 U.S. 683 (S.C., U.S.A.) and *Sankey* v. *Whitlam* (1978) 142 C.L.R. 1 (H.C., Austr.), see *infra*; and later to *Robinson* v. *State of South Australia (No. 2)* [1931] A.C. 704 (P.C.)].

Both *Nixon's* case, 418 U.S. 683 and *Sankey* v. *Whitlam*, 53 A.L.J.R. 11 are far closer to the Scottish and Commonwealth stream of authority than to the English. In the *Glasgow Corporation* case, 1956 S.C. (H.L.) 1, Viscount Simonds said, at p. 11: "that there always has been and is now in the law of Scotland an inherent power of the court to override the Crown's objection to produce documents on the ground that it would injure the public interest to do so."

. . . .

Something was made in argument about the risk to the nation or the public service of an error at first instance. . . . I would respectfully agree with Lord Reid's observations on the point in *Conway* v. *Rimmer* [1968] A.C. 910, 953D: " . . . it is important that the minister should have a right to appeal before the document is produced."

In cases where the Crown is not a party—as in the present case—the court should ensure that the Attorney-General has the opportunity to intervene before disclosure is ordered.

For these reasons I was one of a majority of your Lordships who thought it necessary to inspect the 10 documents. Having done so, I have no doubt that they are relevant and, but for the immunity claim, would have to be disclosed, but their significance is not such as to override the public service objections to their production. Burmah will not suffer injustice by their non-disclosure, while their disclosure would be, in the opinion of the responsible minister, injurious to the public service. I would, therefore, dismiss the appeal.

By way of tail-piece I mention the strange affair of the edited documents. The bank, claiming immunity for part, but not the whole, of certain documents, covered up the parts to the disclosure of which it objected. Burmah's advisers were able to penetrate the cover and read their contents. They did not tell their client what they had seen. Should they now be disclosed, the cover having been blown? The issue evaporated because it became clear in argument that Burmah were ultimately fighting to see only the 10 documents, which a majority of your Lordships has now inspected. But the accident of an insufficient cover cannot weaken the objection of public interest immunity. Even if the parties allow discovery, the court must take the objection of its own motion: and this may have to be done even before the Crown intervenes. There was a difference of opinion as to the importance of the covered up parts. But in view of the course taken by the parties in argument in this House the question does not arise. Burmah's advisers acted with propriety in the handling of the incident.

Note.—In *Sankey* v. *Whitlam*, to which Lord Scarman referred, in the course of the private prosecution by one Sankey of Mr. Gough Whitlam, a former Prime Minister of Australia, and three other former Ministers for offences involving the alleged misuse of loan raising powers whilst in office, a number of *subpoenas duces tecum* were issued on Sankey's behalf to members of the Federal Public Service. The Federal Government objected to the production of some, but not all, of the documents covered by the *subpoenas* on the ground that they belonged to a class of documents which the public interest required should not be disclosed and that disclosure would impede the proper functioning of the Executive Government and the public service. At the committal hearing the Magistrate upheld this claim and refused to order the production of an explanatory memorandum and schedule relating to a meeting of the Executive Council, memoranda and letters passing between ministers and the Departments of the Treasury and Minerals and Energy, a Treasury file note of a meeting with the Prime Minister, a minute from a Treasury official to the Treasurer, and certain Loan Council documents (submissions, loan programmes and minutes). However, Sankey obtained a declaration from the High Court of Australia to the effect that all the claims to immunity from disclosure must fail except those in respect of Loan Council documents, and that these latter should be upheld only subject to limited disclosure necessary to furnish information for the bringing of common law conspiracy charges, such disclosure not being detrimental to the public interest.

It was emphasised that the nature of public interest may vary from case to case. Moreover, the character and purpose of the proceedings in which exclusion is sought may be factors to be considered when balancing conflicting public interests.

R. v. **Lewes Justices, ex parte Secretary of State for the Home Department**; [*Rogers* v. *Secretary of State for the Home Department*] [1973] A.C. 388 (H.L.). Applications to the Gaming Board for certificates of consent in relation to several bingo clubs were refused by the Board. The unsuccessful applicant brought proceedings for criminal libel in respect of a letter written by an assistant Chief Constable to the Board in reply to its request for information about him. The House of Lords held that witness summonses served on the Secretary of the Gaming Board and on the Chief Constable requiring them to give evidence and to produce certain documents, including the assistant Chief Constable's letter and copy, should be set aside. The letter was based on information supplied to the police in confidence and was treated as belonging to a class which in the public interest ought not to be disclosed. If information supplied to the Board were liable to be disclosed, it might be withheld, and the Board would thus be impeded in the performance of its public duty to identify persons of dubious character for the purpose of preventing them from obtaining permission to run gaming establishments.

In the course of his judgment Lord Reid said (pp. 440–401): "The ground put forward has been said to be Crown privilege. I think that that expression is wrong and may be misleading. There is no question of any privilege in the ordinary sense of the word. The real question is whether the public interest requires that the letter shall not be produced and whether that public interest is so strong as to override the ordinary right and interest of a litigant that he shall be able to lay before a court of justice all relevant evidence. A Minister of the Crown is always an appropriate and often the most appropriate person to assert this public interest, and the evidence or advice which he gives to the court is always valuable and may sometimes be indispensable. But in my view it must always be open to any person interested to raise the question and there may be cases where the trial judge should himself raise the question if no one else has done so. In the present case the question of public interest was raised by both the Attorney-General and the Gaming Board. In my judgment both were entitled to raise the matter. Indeed I think that in the circumstances it was the duty of the Board to do as they have done. The claim in the present case is not based on the nature of the contents of this particular letter. It is based on the fact that the Board cannot adequately perform their statutory duty unless they can preserve the confidentiality of all communications to them regarding the character, reputation or antecedents of applicants for their consent.

Claims for "class privilege" were fully considered by this House in *Conway* v. *Rimmer* [1968] A.C. 910. It was made clear that there is a heavy burden of proof on any authority which makes such a claim. But the possibility of establishing such a claim was not ruled out.... There are very unusual features about this case. The Board require the fullest information they can get in order to identify and exclude persons of dubious character and reputation from the privilege of obtaining a licence to conduct a gaming establishment. There is no obligation on anyone to give any information to the Board. No doubt many law abiding citizens would tell what they knew even if there was some risk of their identity becoming known, although many perfectly honourable people do not want to be thought to be mixed up in such affairs. But it is obvious that the best source of information about dubious characters must often be persons of dubious character themselves. It has long been recognised that the identity of police informers must in the public interest be kept secret and the same considerations must apply to those who volunteer information to the Board. Indeed it is in evidence that many refuse to speak unless assured of absolute secrecy.

The letter called for in this case came from the police. I feel sure that they would not be deterred from giving full information by any fear of consequences to themselves if there were any disclosure. But much of the information which they can give must come from sources which must be protected and they would rightly take this into account. Even if the information were given without naming the source, the very nature of the information might, if it were communicated to the person concerned, at least give him a very shrewd idea from whom it had come.

It is possible that some documents coming to the Board could be disclosed without fear of such consequences. But I would think it quite impracticable for the Board or the court to be sure of this. So it appears to me that, if there is not to be very serious danger of the Board being deprived of information essential for the proper performance of their difficult task, there must be a general rule that they are not bound to produce any document which gives information to them about an applicant."

Note.—This case has been expressly followed several times, including in *Hasselblad (G.B.) Ltd.* v. *Orbinson* [1985] Q.B. 475 (C.A.) where, in a libel action based on a letter sent to the European Commission which was investigating a complaint of an alleged breach of Art. 85 of the EEC Treaty, it was held that in the circumstances the public interest in ensuring that the Commission should not be frustrated in attempting to discharge its duty to enforce compliance with the provisions of the Treaty must prevail over the public interest in allowing litigants freedom to have their allegations investigated by the courts.

On the danger that a source of information may dry up see, too, *D.* v. *National Society for the Prevention of Cruelty to Children* [1978] A.C. 171 (H.L.) (*infra*).

AIR CANADA v. SECRETARY OF STATE FOR TRADE

[1983] 2 A.C. 394; [1983] 1 All E.R. 910 (H.L.: 1983)

*When the Crown objects to the production of a class of document on
the basis of public interest immunity, the judge ought not to inspect
the document in question until he is satisfied that it contains material
which, either would give substantial support to a contention of the
party seeking disclosure on an issue arising in the case, or would
assist any of the parties to the proceedings and that disclosure is
necessary for "disposing fairly of the cause or matter" within R.S.C.,
Ord. 24, r. 13(1).*

In 1979 and 1980 the British Airports Authority (BAA), a statutory
body owning and managing several airports, substantially increased
landing charges at Heathrow airport. The plaintiffs, a group of
international airlines, claimed that the increases were excessive and
discriminatory. They brought an action against the Secretary of State
for Trade and BAA alleging that the Secretary's order resulting in the
increases was *ultra vires*. The plaintiffs contended that the Secretary's
power to give financial directions to BAA was limited to the purposes
of the Airports Authority Act 1975 and that, since his dominant
motive in giving instructions to BAA had in fact been to implement
the government policy of reducing the public sector borrowing
requirement, the giving of those instructions had been *ultra vires* and
unlawful. In order to investigate the Secretary's dominant purpose the
plaintiffs sought production of documents for which the Secretary
claimed public interest immunity, and certificates in support of this had
been signed by Permanent Secretaries of the relevant government
departments. The documents in category A consisted of his level
ministerial papers relating to the formulation of government policy,
and those in category B consisted of inter-departmental communications between senior civil servants. Bingham J., the trial judge, was
provisionally inclined to order production of the category A documents
but decided to inspect them first. He made an order for inspection, but
stayed the order pending an appeal. The Court of Appeal allowed an
appeal by the Secretary of State. The plaintiffs appealed to the House
of Lords. That appeal was dismissed.

LORD FRASER OF TULLYBELTON: My Lords this appeal is concerned
with the question of when and in what circumstances the court should
exercise its power to inspect documents which are relevant to an
action, with a view to ordering their production, when their production
has been objected to on behalf of the Crown on the ground that they
fall within a class of documents the production of which would be
injurious to the public interest.

. . . .

The Treasury Solicitor on behalf of the Secretary of State served on
the plaintiffs a list of documents, but he objected to production of
certain of the documents in the list.

... The certificate further provided, *inter alia*: "It is, in my opinion,
necessary for the proper functioning of the public service that the
documents in category A and category B should be withheld from

production. They are all documents falling within the class of documents relating to the formulation of government policy. Such policy was decided at a high level, involving as it did matters of major economic importance to the United Kingdom. The documents in question cannot properly be described as routine documents. . . . " The certificate explains further the reason for objection on lines very similar to the certificate referred to in *Burmah Oil Co. Ltd.* v. *Governor and Company of the Bank of England* [1980] A.C. 1090. . . .

 . . . .

In considering the present law of England on what has come to be called public interest immunity, in relation to the production of documents, it is not necessary to go further back than *Conway* v. *Rimmer* [1968] A.C. 910 where this House decided that a certificate by a minister stating that production of documents of a certain class would be contrary to the public interest, was not conclusive. Lord Reid said, at p. 952: . . . "I do not doubt that there are certain classes of documents which ought not to be disclosed whatever their content may be. Virtually everyone agrees that Cabinet minutes and the like ought not to be disclosed until such time as the are only of historical interest." [This] . . . observation was strictly speaking *obiter* in *Conway* where the documents in question were reports on a probationer police constable by his superiors.

I do not think that even Cabinet minutes are completely immune from disclosure in a case where, for example, the issue in a litigation involves serious misconduct by a Cabinet Minister. Such cases have occurred in Australia (see *Sankey* v. *Whitlam* (1978) 21 A.L.R. 505) and in the United States (see *United States* v. *Nixon* (1974) 418 U.S. 683) but fortunately not in the United Kingdom: see also the New Zealand case of *Environmental Defence Society Inc.* v. *South Pacific Aluminium Ltd. (No. 2)* [1981] 1 N.Z.L.R. 153. But while Cabinet documents do not have complete immunity, they are entitled to a high degree of protection against disclosure. In the present case the documents in category A do not enjoy quite the status of Cabinet minutes, but they approach that level in that they may disclose the reasons for Cabinet decisions and the process by which the decisions were reached. The reasons why such documents should not normally be disclosed until they have become of purely historical interest were considered in *Burmah Oil Co. Ltd.* v. *Governor and Company of the Bank of England* [1980] A.C. 1090, where Lord Wilberforce said this, at p. 1112: [Lord Fraser then quoted from the passage in Lord Wilberforce's judgment commencing: "One such ground is the need for candour . . . " and concluding: " . . . I am certainly not prepared to be wiser than the Minister." set out on p. 258, *supra*.] Although Lord Wilberforce dissented from the majority as to the result in that case, I do not think that his statement of the reasons for supporting public interest immunity were in any way in conflict with the views of the majority.

In the present case, then, we have documents which are admittedly relevant to the matters in issue, in the sense explained in *Compagnie Financière et Commerciale du Pacifique* v. *Peruvian Guano Co.* (1882) 11 Q.B.D. 55, 63, *per* Brett L.J. I am willing to assume that they are, in the words of R.S.C., Ord. 24, r. 13(1), "necessary . . . for disposing fairly of the cause" on the (perhaps not very rigorous) standard which would apply if this were an ordinary case in which public interest immunity had not been claimed. But it has been claimed, and the onus therefore is on the plaintiffs, as the parties seeking disclosure, to show why the documents ought to be produced for inspection by the court privately. The question of whether the court, having inspected them privately, should order them to be produced publicly is a separate question which does not arise at this stage, although as I shall seek to show in a moment it is in my opinion relevant.

. . . .

We were referred to some observations in reported cases to the effect that the court should have all relevant information before it whichever party it might help: see for example *Alfred Crompton Amusement Machines Ltd.* v. *Customs and Excise Commissioners (No. 2)* [1974] A.C. 406, 434D, *per* Lord Cross of Chelsea. As a general rule that is, of course, true, but it is subject to some qualification. The very existence of legal professional privilege and of public interest immunity constitutes qualification. The importance of the general rule was emphasised by all the noble and learned lords who delivered reasoned speeches in *D.* v. *National Society for the Prevention of Cruelty to Children* [1978] A.C. 171 but none of them was considering the present question, or the difference between the inspection stage and the production stage. Nor was any of them contemplating the possibility of a person being compelled to disclose information in his own favour which he preferred to keep private. In an adversarial system such as exists in the United Kingdom, a party is free to withhold information that would help his case if he wishes—perhaps for reasons of delicacy or personal privacy. He cannot be compelled to disclose it against his will. It follows in my opinion that a party who seeks to compel his opponent, or an independent person, to disclose information must show that the information is likely to help his own case. It would be illogical to apply a different rule at the stage of inspection from that which applies at the stage of production. After all, the purpose of inspection by the court in many cases, including the present, would be to let the court see whether there is material in favour of disclosure should be put in the scales to weigh against the material in favour of immunity. Inspection is with a view to the possibility of ordering production, and in my opinion inspection ought not to be ordered unless the court is persuaded that inspection is likely to satisfy it that it ought to take the further step of ordering production.

A great variety of expressions has been used in the reported cases to explain the considerations that ought to influence judges in deciding whether to order inspection. [His Lordship then referred to statements of Lord Reid and Lord Morris in *Conway v. Rimmer* (*supra*) and to statements of Lord Wilberforce, Lord Edmund-Davies and Lord Scarman in the Burmah Oil case (*supra*).]

My Lords, I do not think it would be possible to state a test in a form which could be applied in all cases. Circumstances vary greatly. The weight of the public interest against disclosure will vary according to the nature of the particular documents in question; for example, it will in general be stronger where the documents are Cabinet papers than when they are at a lower level. The weight of the public interest in favour of disclosure will vary even more widely, because it depends upon the probable evidential value to the party seeking disclosure of the particular documents, in almost infinitely variable circumstances of individual cases. The most that can usefully be said is that, in order to persuade the court even to inspect documents for which public interest immunity is claimed, the party seeking disclosure ought at least to satisfy the court that the documents are very likely to contain material which would give substantial support to his contention on an issue which arises in the case, and that without them he might be "deprived of the means of... proper presentation" of his case: see *Glasgow Corporation* v. *Central Land Board,* 1956 S.C.(H.L.) 1, 18, *per* Lord Radcliffe. It will be plain that that formulation has been mainly derived from the speech of my noble and learned friend, Lord Edmund-Davies, in the *Burmah Oil* case [1980] A.C. 1090, 1129, and from the opinion of McNeill J. in *Williams* v. *Home Office* [1981] 1 All E.R. 1151, 1154A. It assumes, of course, that the party seeking disclosure has already shown in his pleadings that he has a cause of action, and that he has some material to support it. Otherwise he would merely be "fishing."

The test is intended to be fairly strict. It ought to be so.... When the claim is a "class" claim judges will often not be well qualified to estimate its strength, because they may not be fully aware of the importance of the class of documents to the public administration as a whole. Moreover, whether the claim is a "class" claim or a "contents" claim, the court will have to make its decision on whether to order production, after having inspected the documents privately, without having the assistance of argument from counsel. It should therefore, in my opinion, not be encouraged to "take a peep" just on the off chance of finding something useful. It should inspect documents only where it has definite grounds for expecting to find material of real importance to the party seeking disclosure.

Applying these considerations to the present appeal, I am of opinion that the case for inspection of the category A documents by the court has not been made out.... The plaintiffs do not make any case that the Secretary of State's true reasons were different from those which he had publicly announced. In these circumstances it seems to me that any information contained in the category A documents would almost certainly tend merely to repeat the information already known to and relied on by the plaintiffs, and published to the world. It is unlikely to add anything material. It is therefore unlikely that access to category A documents would assist the plaintiffs in proving their case....

. . . .

When Bingham J. decided to inspect the documents in category A, he did so on the view that he was not concerned with the question whether they were likely to help the plaintiffs, but that the relevant question for him was whether they were likely to affect the outcome of the case "one way or the other." For the reasons I have endeavoured to explain, I consider that that is an erroneous view, and that his exercise of discretion is accordingly vitiated.

I would dismiss the appeal with costs.

LORD WILBERFORCE:... What then are the criteria upon which a decision should be made to inspect, or not to do so? This matter was discussed at length in the opinions of the House of Lords in the *Burmah Oil* case [1980] A.C. 1090. The main difference of opinion between the majority and the minority opinions related to the likelihood, on the facts of that case, that the documents, inspection of which was claimed, would be supportive of the plaintiffs' case, the minority regarding this likelihood as purely speculative, the majority as amounting to a degree (differently expressed) of probability. Leaving this difference aside as not relevant here, there are three questions which have now to be answered. (1) What is it that the documents must be likely (in whatever degree) to support? (2) What is the degree of likelihood that must be shown? (3) Is that degree of likelihood attained?

(1) On this point there was a difference in opinion between Bingham J. and the Court of Appeal. The learned judge held that documents would be necessary for fairly disposing of a case or (his gloss) for the due administration of justice, if they give substantial assistance to the court in determining the facts upon which the decision in the case would depend. He considered that they were very likely to affect the outcome "one way or the other." The Court of Appeal, on the other hand, held that there must be a likelihood that the documents would support the case of the party seeking discovery.

On this point I agree with the Court of Appeal. In a contest purely between one litigant and another, such as the present, the task of the court is to do, and be seen to be doing, justice between the parties—a duty reflected by the word "fairly" in the rule. There is no higher or additional duty to ascertain some independent truth. . . .

(2) The degree of likelihood (of providing support for the plaintiff's case) may be variously expressed: "likely" was the word used by Lord Edmund-Davies in *Burmah Oil*: a "reasonable probability" by Lord Keith of Kinkel. Both expressions must mean something beyond speculation, some concrete ground for belief which takes the case beyond a mere "fishing" expedition. One cannot attain greater precision in stating what must be a matter of estimation. I would accept either formula.

(3) . . . the judgment of Bingham J. contains this important passage: "If it were necessary for the plaintiffs . . . to show a likelihood that the documents, if produced, would help them I could not on the material put before me conclude that they had done so. There are indications both ways. It would be wrong to guess." I respectfully agree. It was only because the learned judge applied a different test (that they would be "helpful") that he concluded for inspection of category A. On the correct test he would have reached the same conclusion as the Court of Appeal and that which I have been compelled to reach.

I would dismiss the appeal.

LORD EDMUND-DAVIES agreed with the views of LORD FRASER.

LORD SCARMAN: . . .

The issue is specific and within a small compass. The Crown having made its objection to production in proper form, in what circumstances should the court inspect privately the documents before determining whether they, or any of them, should be produced?

The court, of course, has a discretion: but the discretion must be exercised in accordance with principle. . . .

The learned judge, Bingham J., correctly appreciated the principle of the matter. He decided to inspect because he believed that the documents in question were very likely to be "necessary for the just determination of the second and third issues in the plaintiffs' . . . cases." Here I consider he fell into error. For the reasons given in the speech of my noble and learned friend, Lord Templeman, I do not think that the appellants have been able to show that the documents whose production they are seeking are likely to be necessary for fairly disposing of the issues in their "constitutional" case. Indeed, my noble and learned friend has demonstrated that they are unnecessary. Accordingly, for this reason, but for no other, I would hold that the judge was wrong to decide to inspect the documents.

On all other questions I find myself in agreement with the judge. In particular, I am persuaded by his reasoning that the public interest in the administration of justice, which the court has to put into the balance against the public interest immunity, is as he put it: "In my judgment, documents are necessary for fairly disposing of a cause or for the due administration of justice if they give substantial assistance to the court in determining the facts upon which the decision in the cause will depend."

The learned judge rejected, in my view rightly, the view which has commended itself to the Court of Appeal and to some of your Lordships that the criterion for determining whether to inspect or not is whether the party seeking production can establish the likelihood that the documents will assist his case or damage that of his opponent. No doubt that is what he is seeking; no doubt also, it is a very relevant consideration for the court. But it would be dangerous to elevate it into a principle of the law of discovery. Discovery is one of the few exceptions to the adversarial character of our legal process. It assists parties and the court to discover the truth. By so doing, it not only helps towards a just determination: it also saves costs. A party who discovers timeously a document fatal to his case is assisted as effectively, although less to his liking, as one who discovers the winning card; for he can save himself and others the heavy costs of litigation. There is another important aspect of the matter. The Crown, when it puts forward a public interest immunity objection, is not claiming a privilege but discharging a duty. The duty arises whether the document assists or damages the Crown's case or if, as in a case to which the Crown is not a party, it neither helps nor injuries the Crown. It is not for the Crown but for the court to determine whether the document should be produced. Usually, but not always, the critical factor will be whether the party seeking production has shown the document will help him. But it may be necessary for a fair determination or for saving costs, even if it does not. Therefore, although it is likely to make little difference in practice, I would think it better in principle to retain the formulation of the interests to be balanced which Lord Reid gave us in *Conway* v. *Rimmer* [1968] A.C. 910, 940: "It is universally recognised that here there are two kinds of public interest which may clash. There is the public interest that harm shall not be done to the nation or the public service by disclosure of certain documents, and there is the public interest that the administration of justice shall not be frustrated by the withholding of documents which must be produced if justice is to be done." ... Basically, the reason for selecting the criterion of justice, irrespective of whether it assists the party seeking production, is that the Crown may not have regard to party advantage in deciding whether or not to object to production on the ground of public interest immunity. It is its duty to bring the objection, if it believes it to be sound, to the attention of the court. It is for the court, not the Crown, to balance the two public interests, that of the functioning and security of the public service, which is the sphere within which the executive has the duty to make an assessment, and that of justice, upon which the executive is not competent to pass judgment.

For these reasons I would dismiss the appeal.

LORD TEMPLEMAN: . . .

I agree with my noble and learned friend, Lord Scarman, for the reasons he has deployed that the court should inspect the documents if the court considers the disclosure of the documents may materially assist any of the parties to the proceedings. If the plaintiff seeks discovery against the assertion which the defendant feels under a duty to put forward of public interest immunity, the judge may find the documents are wholly or partly favourable to the plaintiff's case or wholly or partly fatal to the plaintiff's case. In either event the judge must decide whether the public interest in maintaining the confidential nature of the document prevails over the public interest in ensuring that justice is achieved. If the public interest in confidentiality prevails the judge will decline to allow the plaintiff to see the documents. If the judge decides in all the circumstances that the claim for public interest immunity is not strong enough to prevail over the public interest in justice, the judge will allow the plaintiff to inspect the documents. In that case either party is free to use the documents for the purposes of the proceedings but is not bound to do so. If both parties in their discretion for the same or different reasons decide not to rely on the documents, the documents will not be revealed to the public. The plaintiff who will only have inspected the documents in order to determine whether or not to make use of them in the proceedings will not be allowed to make use of the documents for any other purpose.

Norwich Pharmacal Co. v. **Customs and Excise Commissioners** [1974] A.C. 133 (H.L.). The appellants were owners and licensees of a patent of a chemical compound which they discovered was being infringed by unknown importers. The Commissioners of Customs and Excise were allowing the importation and charging duty thereon. The appellants sought an order that the Commissioners should disclose the names of the importers. The House of Lords made the order, holding that the public interest in the doing of justice outweighed any public interest in the preservation of the confidentiality of the relationship between the importers and the Commissioners. Amongst the factors to which the Law Lords attached weight in striking the balance between these countervailing public interests were the circumstance that non-disclosure would involve protecting persons who were almost certainly wrongdoers, the fact that it would be difficult to obtain the information from another source, and the unlikelihood that disclosure would involve the Commissioners in any disadvantage which could not be alleviated by an order for costs.

British Steel Corporation v. **Granada Television Ltd.** [1981] A.C. 1096 (H.L.). The appellants broadcast over a television network quotations from a number of secret or confidential documents, which were the property of the respondents and which had been delivered to the appellants by someone whose work with the respondents must have entitled him to have access to highly classified documents. An undertaking to respect his anonymity had been given. The respondents issued a writ and notice of motion claiming *inter alia* an order for delivery up of the documents and copies thereof. The documents were delivered up, but many of them had been mutilated by cutting off anything on them that might have lead to identification of their source. The respondents then amended their notice of motion and their writ so as to claim an order that the appellants should disclose the names of those who supplied the documents to them. The House confirmed that no privilege attaches to the relationship of, on the one hand, the media of information and journalists who write or contribute to them and, on the other hand, the sources and suppliers of their information. However, Lord Wilberforce did say (pp. 1174–1175): "Although, as I have said, the media, and journalists, have no immunity, it remains true that there may be an element of public interest in protecting the relevation of the source.... The court ought not to compel confidence bona fide given to be breached unless necessary in the interests of justice:... There is a public interest in the free flow of information, the strength of which will vary from case to case. In some cases it may be very weak; in others it may be very strong. The court must take this into account. How ought the discretion which the court undoubtedly has to be exercised in this case?... I think that... the balance was strongly in B.S.C.'s favour." Viscount Dilhorne and Lords Fraser of Tullybelton and Russell of Killowen delivered concurring judgments. Lord Salmon's lone dissent was fundamental. He saw the policy issues involved in a different perspective. He concluded his judgment thus (p. 1195): "The immunity of the press to reveal its sources of information save in exceptional circumstances is in the public interest, and has been so accepted by the courts for so long that I consider it is wrong now to sweep this immunity away.... Certainly no such circumstances appear in the present case:... The freedom of the press depends upon this immunity. Were it to disappear so would the sources from which its information is obtained; and the public should be deprived of much of the information to which the public of a free nation is entitled."

Note.—The significance of the decision must now perhaps be seen in the light of the Contempt of Court Act 1981, s.10. (Part Two, *infra*, and see Chapter 11, Section C, *supra*). There must be some overlap between the discretion referred to by Lord Wilberforce and the rather loose formula embodied in the section.

See, too, *X* v. *Y and others* [1988] 2 All E.R. 648 (Q.B.D.) where Rose J. granted a permanent injuction restraining a national newspaper from publishing information obtained from hospital records identifying actual or potential AIDS sufferers. His Lordship held that the public interest in preserving the confidentiality of such records outweighed the public interest in the freedom of the press, because victims of the disease ought not to be deterred by fear of publicity from going to hospital for treatment.

Alfred Crompton Amusement Machines Ltd. v. **Customs and Excise Commissioners (No. 2)** [1974] A.C. 405 (H.L.). A company sought arbitration under section 36 of the Purchase Tax Act 1963 on a purchase tax assessment which had been made on them. The Commissioners claimed to withhold a wide range of internal communications between themselves and their staff and between themselves and third parties. The House of Lords, although re-affirming that the fact that information contained in some of the communications was given by third parties in confidence was not a ground for exclusion, ruled that various memoranda and routine documents should be withheld on the ground that it was in the public interest that they should not be disclosed because knowledge that the Commissioners could not keep such information secret might be harmful to the efficient workings of Purchase Tax legislation. Considerable weight was attached to the importance of preserving the confidentiality of this information. Lord Cross of Chelsea said (pp. 433–434): "Confidentiality is not a separate head of privilege, but it may be a very material consideration to bear in mind when privilege is claimed on the ground of public interest."

Note.—Of this decision the late Sir Rupert Cross wrote, "The case was obviously on the borderline" (*Evidence* (5th ed.), p. 307). It is, however, unfortunately not clear that a majority of their Lordships saw it in this way. Lord Cross of Chelsea, also adverted to what is in effect the incidence of the burden of proof when balancing opposing public interests. He said (p. 434): "In a case where considerations for and against disclosure appear to be fairly evenly balanced the courts should I think uphold a claim to privilege on the ground of public interest and trust to the head of the department concerned to do whatever he can to mitigate the ill-effects of non-disclosure." This view is neither attractive nor generally accepted: see, *e.g. D.* v. *National Society for the Prevention of Cruelty to Children* [1978] A.C. 171 (*infra*), especially *per* Lord Edmund-Davies at p. 246; *London Securities Ltd.* v. *Nicholson* [1980] 1 W.L.R. 948; and *Campbell* v. *Thameside Council* [1982] Q.B. 1065 (C.A.), *per* Ackner L.J. at p. 1075.

Alfred Crompton Machines Ltd. v. *Customs and Excise Commissioners (No. 2)* has, however, been followed by the Court of Appeal in *Neilson* v. *Laugharne* [1981] Q.B. 736 (C.A.), but in this latter case the facts would seem to have been considerably stronger. The documents there contained statements taken in pursuance of an inquiry, instituted under section 49 of the Police Act 1964, for the investigation of a complaint against the police. The Court of Appeal held that it was in the public interest that the whole class of such documents should be withheld from disclosure. The Court saw "a very real danger that the prospect of disclosure on discovery of material gathered in the course of such an inquiry will inhibit the proper conduct of the enquiry and thus frustrate the purpose of the legislature in making the statutory provision for it" (*per* Oliver L.J. at p. 754). *Neilson* v. *Laugharne* has subsequently been distinguished. In *Conerney* v. *Jacklin* [1985] C.L.Y. 1998; [1985] Crim.L.R. 234 (C.A.) it was held that written complaints made to the Police Complaints Board, as distinct from statements made for the purposes of an inquiry under the 1964 Act, were not as a class subject to public interest immunity. Moreover, and more importantly, it was distinguished in *Peach* v. *Commissioner of Police* (*infra*).

Peach v. Commissioner of Police [1986] 1 Q.B. 1064 (C.A.). The Metropolitan Police began an investigation into the death of Blair Peach during a public demonstration. They took various witness statements, which were made available to the coroner at the inquest. The plaintiff, as mother of the deceased and administratrix of his estate, brought an action against the Commissioner of the Metropolis claiming damages under the Law Reform (Miscellaneous Provisions) Act 1934. Amongst the documents for which public interest immunity was claimed by the Commissioner were police reports, statements and correspondence prepared in pursuance of an inquiry under section 49 of the 1964 Police Act. The plaintiff's application for disclosure of certain of these documents was allowed. The Court of Appeal held that, although there had been an inquiry under section 49, the dominant purpose of the inquiry was broader—it was to investigate a violent death that was a matter of public concern and in circumstances in which it was clear from the outset that an inquest would be held and that a prosecution might well follow. Such an inquiry could not be treated simply as a private inquiry into the conduct of the police under section 49. Accordingly, the documents prepared during the investigation were not covered by public interest immunity and they should be disclosed as being relevant to issues in the plaintiff's action. Fox L.J. said (pp. 1078–1079): "In *Neilson* v. *Laugharne* [1981] Q.B. 736 the only investigation was an investigation into the complaints of misconduct by the police. Those complaints were of civil wrongs. Allegations of burglary and of theft had been dropped. The present case is, in my view, essentially different in its nature. Blair Peach had died a violent death. It was a matter of public concern to establish the cause of his death. And that would have been so whether there was a complaint against the police or not.... [The inquiry here] was a major inquiry into a man's death. That was its predominant purpose... its primary purpose was to find out how Blair Peach died and not whether there had been misconduct by a police officer."

MARKS v. BEYFUS

25 Q.B.D. 494; 59 L.J.Q.B. 479; 63 L.T. 733;; 6 T.L.R. 406; 55 J.P. 182; 38 W.R. 705; 17 Cox C.C. 196 (C.A.: 1890)

Prosecutions instituted by the Director of Public Prosecutions are public prosecutions, and the Director should refuse to disclose the names of his informants or the information which they have given him.

In an action against the defendants for maliciously conspiring to prosecute the plaintiff for fraud (upon the trial of which charge he had been acquitted), the plaintiff called the Director of Public Prosecutions as a witness, and asked him to give the names of his informants and to produce the statement on which he had acted in directing the prosecution. The witness declined on grounds of public policy, and his objection was upheld by the judge. The plaintiff unsuccessfully appealed.

LORD ESHER M.R.: ... The ground taken on behalf of the Director of Public Prosecutions is that this was a public prosecution, ordered by the Government (or by an official equivalent to the Government) for what was considered to be a public object, and that therefore the information ought not, on grounds of public policy, to be disclosed. The question whether this was a public prosecution in this sense depends upon the true construction of the statutes by which the office of Director of Public Prosecutions was created. ...

The Director of Public Prosecutions ... is in the position which a person authorised by the Government in former days would have been in—that is to say, a prosecution instituted or conducted by him is a public as distinguished from a private prosecution. ...

In the case of *Att.-Gen.* v. *Briant* (1846) 15 M. & W. 169, Pollock C.B.... says: "... that in a public prosecution a witness cannot be asked such questions as will disclose the informer, if he be a third person ... and we think the principle of the rule applies where a witness is asked if he himself is the informer." Now this rule ... was founded on grounds of public policy, and if this prosecution was a public prosecution the rule attaches; I think it was a public prosecution and that the rule applies. I do not say it is a rule which can never be departed from; if ... the disclosure of the name of the informant is necessary or right in order to show the prisoner's innocence, then one public policy is in conflict with another public policy, and that which says that an innocent man is not to be condemned when his innocence can be proved as the policy that must prevail. But, except in that case, this rule ... is not a matter of discretion; it is a rule of law, and as such should be applied by the judge at the trial. ...

LINDLEY and BOWEN L.JJ. agreed

Note.—In R. v. *Lewes Justices ex parte Secretary of State for the Home Department* [1973] A.C. 388 (*supra*) Lord Simon of Glaisdale said (pp. 407–408) "Sources of police information are a judicially recognised class of evidence excluded on the ground of public policy unless their production is required to establish innocence in a criminal trial." His Lordship elaborated this qualification in *D.* v. *National Society for the Prevention of Cruelty to Children* [1978] A.C. 171 (*infra*) when he said (p. 232): "The public interest that no innocent man should be convicted of crime is so powerful that it outweighs the general public interest that sources of police information should not be divulged, so that exceptionally, such evidence must be forthcoming when required to establish innocence in a criminal trial." But it is for the accused to show such necessity: R. v. *Hennessey and others* (1978), 68 Cr.App.R. 419 (C.A.).

In R. v. *Rankine* [1986]; Q.B. 861 (C.A.) it was held that, as it is in the public interest that assistance should be given by members of the public to the police in the detection of

crime, the rule that a police informant should not be identified (except when the exclusion
of that evidence would be likely to result in a miscarriage of justice) is equally applicable
to the identification of those who have permitted their premises to be used for surveillance
by the police. *R.* v. *Rankine* was followed in *R.* v. *Johnson* [1988] 1 W.L.R. 1377 (C.A.).
But compare *R.* v. *Brown*; *R.* v. *Daley* (1988) 87 Cr.App.R. 52 (C.A.).

   In *Evans* v. *Chief Constable of Surrey* [1988] 1 Q.B. 588 (Q.B.D.) the plaintiff, in civil
proceedings brought against a Chief Constable for wrongful arrest and false imprisonment,
sought discovery of a report which had been sent by the police to the Director of Public
Prosecutions. Wood J. held that the report was not relevant to the plaintiff's case, but
that, even if it were, it was in the public interest that such a document should not be
disclosed.

   D. v. **National Society for the Prevention of Cruelty to Children** [1978] A.C. 171
(H.L.). A plaintiff claimed damages for injuries to her health caused by the
making of false allegations, to the effect that she had maltreated her child, by an
officer of the defendant Society, who was acting on information which had been
supplied to the Society in confidence. The Society sought an order excusing it
from giving discovery of documents disclosing the identity of the informer. His
identity was relevant to the plaintiff's contention that the Society had been
negligent in *inter alia* failing first properly to investigate the complaint. The House
of Lords (reversing the Court of Appeal) held for the defendant Society.

   A majority of their Lordships (Lords Diplock, Hailsham of St. Marylebone,
Simon of Glaisdale and Kilbrandon) invoked the analogy of *Marks* v. *Beyfus*
(*supra*). In this context it was material that the Society was authorised by Act of
Parliament to institute legal proceedings on behalf of children. The actual decision
was on an interlocutory summons regarding discovery but their Lordships held the
doctrine to be equally applicable to disclosure by interrogatories and questions at
trial.

   Lord Edmund-Davies would seem to have based his decision on looser grounds.
His Lordship said (at p. 245): "But where (i) a confidential relationship exists
(other than that of lawyer and client) *and* (ii) disclosure would be in breach of
some ethical or social value involving the public interest, the court has a discretion
to uphold a refusal to disclose relevant evidence provided it considers that, on
balance, the public interest would be better served by excluding such evidence."
The need for the involvement of a public interest is emphasised: confidentiality is
not enough. The reference to a discretion is perhaps unfortunate: once it is clear
that the balance of public interest indicates exclusion, it is generally accepted that
a court must as a matter of law order it. Lord Edmund-Davies went on to
emphasise that the onus of justifying exclusion is upon the party seeking it. He
said (p. 246): "The disclosure of all evidence relevant to the trial of an issue being
at all times a matter of considerable public interest, the question to be determined
is whether it is clearly demonstrated that in the particular case the public interest
would nevertheless be better served by excluding evidence despite its relevance.
If, on balance, the matter is left in doubt, disclosure should be ordered." Lord
Hailsham (with whom Lord Kilbrandon concurred) also emphasised (p. 225) the
prime importance of "the principle that, in all cases before them, the courts
should insist on parties and witnesses disclosing the truth, the whole truth, and
nothing but the truth, when this would assist the decision of the matters in
dispute." Lord Edmund-Davies also said (p. 245): "In conducting the necessary
balancing operation between competing aspects of public interest, the presence (or
absence) of involvement of the central government in the matter of disclosure is
not conclusive either way, though in practice it may affect the cogency of the
argument against disclosure," and his Lordship went on to contemplate the

involvement of local government at least as sufficing. (See, however, his views and those of Lord Scarman in the later case of *Science Research Council* v. *Nassé*; *Leyland Cars (B.L. Cars Ltd.)* v. *Vyas, infra*).

Their Lordships were unanimous in re-affirming that confidentiality is not itself a ground for non-disclosure, nor indeed is it in all cases a necessary component of the basis of exclusion. The public interest to be protected in the instant case was the efficient working of a Society statutorily authorised to bring legal proceedings for the welfare of children. Their Lordships, holding that the categories of public interest are not closed, extended the notion of public interest beyond that of governmental interest.

Note.—See, too, *Gaskin* v. *Liverpool City Council* [1980] 1 W.L.R. 1549 (C.A.) where the general principles propounded by Lord Edmund-Davies were specifically applied in the case of an application for disclosure and production by a local authority of "all case notes and/or records" relating to a child who had been in the care of the authority. This case and the principal case itself were, however, distinguished in *Campbell* v. *Thameside Council* (*infra*).

See, too, *R.* v. *Bournemouth Justices, ex p. Graya* [1987] 1 F.L.R. 36 (Fam.D.), where public interest immunity was held not to extend to confidential information given to a social worker at an adoption agency.

Campbell v. **Tameside Council** [1982] Q.B. 1065 (C.A.). A school teacher employed by the defendant education authority was violently assaulted by an 11 year-old boy in her class room and suffered severe injuries. Before commencing proceedings against the defendants she applied for an order (under the Administration of Justice Act 1970 and R.S.C., Ord. 24, r. 7A) for disclosure of all documents in their possession relating to the boy, including the reports of teachers, psychologists and psychiatrists. The defendants contended that these were confidential documents of a class protected by public interest immunity. Russell J., after he had inspected the documents, ordered the defendants to disclose those in their possession concerning the educational and psychological welfare of the child. The defendants' appeal was dismissed. On examination the documents were clearly of crucial significance on the issue as to whether the defendants knew, or reasonably ought to have known, that the boy was (or was not) of a violent disposition and should (or should not) have been allowed to attend the plaintiff's class. The judge had rightly concluded that there was a real risk of the plaintiff being the victim of a denial of justice if the documents were not disclosed. The balance of public interest was in favour of disclosure. Ackner L.J. said (pp. 1075–1076): "Despite the apparent conflict in the able submissions addressed to us, the basic principles which we must apply in the resolution of this dispute do not seem to me to be much in issue. These are: 1. The exclusion of relevant evidence always calls for clear justification. All relevant documents, whether or not confidential, are subject to disclosure unless upon some recognised ground, including the public interest, their non-disclosure is permissable. 2. Since it has been accepted in this court that the documents for which the respondent seeks discovery are relevant to the contemplated litigation, there is a heavy burden upon the appellants to justify withholding them from disclosure: see in particular *Conway* v. *Rimmer* [1968] A.C. 910 and *Reg.* v. *Lewes Justices, Ex parte Secretary of State for the Home Department* [1973] A.C. 388, 400H, *per* Lord Reid. 3. The fact that information has been communicated by one person to another in confidence is not, of itself, a sufficient ground for protection from disclosure in a court of law, either the nature of the information of the identity of the informant if either of these matters could assist the court to ascertain facts which are relevant to an issue upon which it is adjudicating: *Alfred Crompton Amusement Machines Ltd.* v. *Customs and Excise Commissioners (No. 2)* [1974] A.C. 405, 433–434. The private promise of confidentiality must yield to the general public interest, that in the administration of justice truth will out, unless by reason of the character of the information or the relationship of the recipient of the information to the informant a more important public interest is served by protecting the information or identity of the informant from disclosure in a court of law: *per* Lord Diplock, *D.* v. *National Society for the Prevention of Cruelty to Children* [1978] A.C. 171, 218B. Immunity from disclosure was permitted in that case because the House of Lords recognised the special position of the N.S.P.C.C. in the enforcement process of the provisions of the Children and Young Persons Act 1969, a position which the House saw as comparable with that of a prosecuting authority in criminal proceedings. It applied the rationale of the rule as it applies to police informers, that if their identity was liable to be disclosed in court of law, this source of information would dry up and the police would be hindered in their duty of detecting and preventing crime. 4. Documents in respect of which a claim is made for immunity from disclosure come under a rough but accepted categorisation known as a "class" claim or a "contents" claim. The distinction between them is that with a "class" claim it is immaterial whether the disclosure of the particular contents of particular documents would be injurious to the public interest—the point being that it is the maintenance of the immunity of the "class" from disclosure in litigation that is important. In the "contents" claim, the protection is claimed for particular "contents" in a particular document. A claim remains a "class" even though something may be known about the documents; it remains a "class" even if part of documents are revealed and part disclosed: *per* Lord Wilberforce in *Burmah Oil Co. Ltd.* v. *Governor and Company of the Bank of England* [1980] A.C. 1090, 1111. 5. The proper approach where there is a question of public interest immunity is a weighing, on balance, of the two public interests, that of the nation or the public service in non-disclosure and that of justice in the production of the documents. Both in the "class" objection and the "contents" objection the courts retain the residual power to inspect and to order disclosure: *Burmah Oil* case [1980] A.C. 1090, 1134, *per* Lord Keith of Kinkel; pp. 1143–1144, *per* Lord Scarman. 6. A judge conducting the balancing exercise needs to know whether the documents in question are of much or little weight in the litigation, whether their absence will result in a complete or partial denial of justice to one or other of the parties or perhaps to both, and what is the importance of the particular litigation to the parties and the public. All these are matters which should be considered if the court is to decide where the public interest lies: *per* Lord Pearce in *Conway* v. *Rimmer* [1968] A.C. 910, 987, quoted by Lord Edmund-Davies in the *Burmah Oil* case [1980] A.C. 1090, 1129. Lord Edmund-Davies commented that judge may well feel that he cannot profitably embark on such a balancing exercise without himself seeing the disputed documents and cited in support of that view the observations of Lord Reid and Lord Upjohn in *Conway* v. *Rimmer* [1968] A.C. 910, 953, 995."

Science Research Council v. **Nassé; Leyland Cars (B.L. Cars Ltd.)** v. **Vyas** [1980] A.C. 1028 (H.L.). Two complainants were employed respectively by a research council run on civil service lines and a large industrial concern. They alleged that they were the victims of discrimination by their employers, in that they had been passed over, in the case of one for promotion on the ground of trade union activities and sex, and in the case of the other for transfer on the ground of race. The Industrial Tribunals to which the complaints were made were bound by County Court Rules with regard to discovery, the effect of which was that no order should be made unless in the opinion of the Chairman this was necessary for disposing fairly of the proceedings or saving costs. The defendant employers, although willing to produce confidential reports relating to the complainants, refused to produce such reports relating to other employees who had been applicants for the posts in question. The House of Lords held that no public interest immunity protected such confidential documents. However, the House further held that the Tribunal should, in the free exercise of its discretion, have had regard to their confidentiality as one factor when considering whether discovery was necessary in accordance with the County Court Rules for disposing fairly of the proceedings. As Lord Scarman put it (pp. 1087 and 1088): "The confidential nature of a document does not, by itself, confer 'public interest' immunity from disclosure. The confidential nature of a document or of evidence is no ground for a refusal to disclose the document or give the evidence, if the Court requires it: . . . [but] it does not follow that, because we are outside the field of public interest immunity, the confidential nature of documents is to be disregarded by the court in the exercise of its discretionary power to order discovery of documents." In the instant cases there had been no compliance with appropriate procedures for the exercise of that discretion. The cases were therefore remitted to the Tribunal for the Chairman to examine the documents claimed to be confidential and decide which, if any, of them needed to be disclosed.

HEARSAY: THE RULE OF EXCLUSION

ASSERTIONS which are not made at the trial by the witness who is testifying are inadmissible as evidence of the truth of that which is asserted. Such assertions are hearsay and (except in certain non-adversary proceedings) are generally excluded at common law. The underlying notion is that a witness should speak only of facts which he has personally perceived with one of his five senses. But it is to be emphasised that the hearsay rule is directed against, and only against, evidence of out-of-court assertions which are being tendered as evidence of their truth. Thus, whereas a witness's testimony that X told him that he had seen Y steal would be inadmissible to show that Y had committed theft, the hearsay rule would not preclude its admissibility to show that X had uttered a defamatory statement about Y. In the latter case the statement is said to constitute "original" evidence rather than hearsay: again it is sometimes said to be "circumstantially" relevant.

The position relating to the inadmissibility of hearsay evidence in civil cases was fundamentally changed and put on a statutory basis by Part I[1] of the Civil Evidence Act 1968.[2] As a result there are now in effect two laws of hearsay, one basically common law and the other entirely statutory. The materials in the present Chapter, Chapter 14 and Chapter 15 are concerned with hearsay evidence in criminal cases. Those in the present chapter illustrate the limits of the common law exclusionary rule; those in Chapter 14 the established exceptions (mostly themselves creatures of common law) to that rule[3]; and those in Chapter 15 a cluster of somewhat ill-defined common law exceptions usually associated with the term *res gestae*. Material concerning hearsay in civil cases are set out in Chapter 16. The admissibility of evidence of confessions, which has hearsay, but also other important policy implications, is now based upon the Police and Criminal Evidence Act 1984, sections 76 and 77 (Part Two, *infra*); but some related case-law materials are set out separately in Chapter 17.

The policies underlying the common law rule excluding hearsay evidence are several. The unrestricted reception of hearsay evidence could easily lead to undue protraction of a trial: not only could this be

---

[1] ss.1–10.

[2] Part Two, *infra*. The admissibility of hearsay evidence before magistrates when exercising civil jurisdiction is however at present still governed by the common law and the Evidence Act 1938.

[3] Some of these exceptions are made statutorily applicable in civil cases by their preservation in the Civil Evidence Act 1968, s.9.

time-consuming and expensive, but it could exhaust and confuse the jury. Again, uncontrolled admissibility of hearsay could often enable a party to achieve a tactical advantage of surprise with consequential unfairness to his opponent. But the principal objection to the admission of hearsay evidence is constituted by the possibility of its unreliability coupled with the absence of an opportunity to test that reliability by cross-examination. A hearsay assertion is only most exceptionally made on oath and is usually not made in circumstances of solemnity and seriousness equivalent to those surrounding the giving of evidence in court; the danger of mistake resulting from repetition is almost always present in some measure—particularly in cases of multiple hearsay; there is no opportunity to observe the declarant's demeanour, tone of voice, etc.; and the opponent is unable by cross-examination to probe his powers of perception, his memory, the meaning of language he used or his sincerity.

The common law rule excluding hearsay evidence, as formulated in the opening sentence of this introductory note, affects not only the typical situation in which an assertion is made by a person other than the witness, but also cases of the witness's own earlier out of court assertions. Despite the verbal inelegance introduced in describing this latter type of assertion as hearsay, despite the availability of the declarant for cross-examination and the consequential mitigation of traditional hearsay dangers, and despite the overlap both with the rule against narration (under which evidence of a witness's prior consistent statements is usually excluded) and with the rule limiting the admissibility of evidence of his prior inconsistent statements,[4] this broader formulation of the hearsay rule is probably the most convenient. This is because, when evidence is admitted by way of exception to either of those other rules, it may at common law[5] be used, only to show consistency or inconsistency (and thus the credibility or incredibility of the witness), and not to show the truth of the earlier statement—unless the evidence also falls with an appropriate exception (e.g. as constituting an admission[6] or being part of the res gestae[7]) to the hearsay rule. Moreover, this broader formulation of the common law rule excluding hearsay was used by Stephen[8] and is adopted in the United States Federal Rules of Evidence.[9] Also, it seems to have been assumed by the framers of Part I of the Civil Evidence Act 1968.

At common law no differentiation is made between cases of single hearsay, in which the declarant has communicated as to matters within his personal knowledge directly to the witness, and cases of double or multiple hearsay, in which the communication made to the witness is itself hearsay. This attitude is reflected, not only in the formulation of the exclusionary rule, but also to some extent in the inclusionary exceptions to it. In the Civil Evidence Act 1968, however, a distinction is drawn in respect of oral evidence.

The hearsay rule applies not only to spoken but also to written assertions. It also applies to non-verbal assertions, at least if intended to

---

[4] See Chap. 9, *supra*.
[5] Contrast for civil cases the Civil Evidence Act 1968, s.3(1) (Part Two, *infra*).
[6] See Chap. 14, *infra*.
[7] See Chap. 15, *infra*.
[8] Stephen, *Digest of the Law of Evidence* (12 rev. ed., 1948), Art. 15.
[9] *Federal Rules of Evidence*, Rule 801.

be assertive, such as deliberate gestures. It seems to be accepted that the rule will also render inadmissible oral and written statements which are not assertive in the sense that the maker does not intend to communicate to anyone, for example, the case of a person talking to himself mistakenly thinking that he is not being overheard, or the case of the person who makes an entry in a supposedly private diary. It seems, too, that the rule also renders inadmissible certain (but by no means all) assertions implied from verbal or non-verbal conduct. In these cases a person either has made a statement, or has behaved in a particular way, which was not intended by him to be assertive of the fact that it is being tendered to prove. A well-worn hypothetical example of a non-assertive statement of this type is provided by evidence of the greeting "Hello X" tendered to show the fact of X's presence. The extent to which the rule also applies so as to render inadmissible assertions implied from non-verbal conduct is however far from clear. The late Sir Rupert Cross[10] illustrated the problem (posed by the admissibility of an assertion implied from non-verbal conduct) by a case in which it is sought to show that the victim of an accident was dead at a particular time by calling a witness to testify that at that time he had seen a doctor examine his motionless body and then place it in a mortuary van rather than an ambulance. Had the doctor said that, or otherwise expressly asserted that, the man was dead, evidence of this would have been excluded. As a matter of crude logical analysis a case could obviously be made for, by the same token, excluding the assertion to that effect implied for the doctor's conduct. Baron Parke in an oft-quoted statement in *Wright* v. *Doe* d. *Tatham*[11] seems to have subscribed to this view. In that case an issue was as to a testator's sanity, and letters which had been written to him were tendered as evidence that the writers treated him as being sane. They did not expressly assert his sanity, but it was sought to use the letters as if they had done so. It was as a result of a conflation of the opinion and hearsay rules that the letters were excluded; but Baron Parke, in emphasising the hearsay factor, instanced amongst other similar hypothetical situations that of "the conduct of a deceased captain on a question of seaworthiness, who after examining every part of the vessel embarked in it with his family" and continued "these when deliberately considered, are with reference to the matter in issue in each case, mere instances if hearsay evidence, mere statements, not on oath, but implied in or vouched by the actual conduct of persons by whose acts the litigant parties are not to be bound."[12] But, Baron Parke's words notwithstanding, it is suggested that the adoption of a relentlessly logical application of the hearsay rule to all implied assertions would involve a negation of the rule's ultimate objective, *i.e.* reliability. It would, moreover, in many cases be highly inconvenient.

Assertions which it would be possible to imply from non-verbal conduct not intended to be assertive are very wide-ranging in their nature, and the reliability of such implied assertions can vary a great deal. To appreciate this one only has to contrast, for example, Sir Rupert Cross's hypothetical case mentioned above with the actual facts of *Wright* v. *Doe* d. *Tatham*. The former is the case of a professional

---

[10] See Cross, *Evidence* (5th ed.), at pp. 469–470.
[11] (1837) 7 Ad. & Ell. 313.
[12] *Ibid.* pp. 387–388.

man, whose sincerity there is no reason to doubt, performing his professional duty in public view, making a considered and important decision within his professional expertise and then taking a step the significance of which is unambiguous. Traditional hearsay dangers are thus minimal. The same could not be said of the actual facts of *Wright* v. *Doe* d. *Tatham*; although in some of Parke B's hypothetical cases, such as that of the deceased sea captain mentioned above, the position is perhaps less clear. In these circumstances indiscriminate application of the hearsay rule to assertions implied from non-verbal conduct would not be apt. Nor would its total rejection. In this area of the factual field it would seem to be necessary in each case to look behind the rule and to assess directly the dangers against which the rule is intended to guard. Although seldom articulated by the judges this is probably not far removed from the actual practice of the courts. It is scarcely credible that evidence of the doctor's behaviour would be excluded, and yet the correctness of the actual decision in *Wright* v. *Doe* d. *Tatham* is not doubted. One might perhaps then be tempted to consider whether resort ought not to be had to this kind of flexible approach in relation to the applicability of the hearsay rule more generally. To succumb to this temptation would, however, be to lose sight of the fact that in the law of evidence, dealing as it does with questions that often arise suddenly and unexpectedly in the course of a trial and which have to be resolved quickly, the availability of a clear cut rule is at a distinct premium. But in the area of implied non-verbal assertions that premium is probably too high to pay.

It cannot be over-stressed that the hearsay rule is concerned only with assertions, whether express or implied, which are tendered as evidence of their truth. Cases in which evidence is tendered to show that a statement, true or false, was made, this fact being itself in issue or relevant, are obviously outside the scope of the rule. So, too, words the utterance of which itself has legal effect, sometimes called legally operative words, are not hearsay: words constituting a contractual offer or the acceptance of a contractual offer exemplify this. Again, words, the utterance of which tends to show that a particular state of mind was induced in another, do not present a hearsay problem if what is contended is, not that they were necessarily true, but merely that they were, or might reasonably have been, believed by that other. Also, evidence of a witness's previous statements, when exceptionally admitted in order to bolster or discredit his testimony, do not involve contravention of the hearsay rule. Nor is the rule violated when a witness is allowed to use a previously prepared document for the sole purpose of refreshing his memory.

There are many common law exceptions to the hearsay rule and the list has been added to by statute. The materials selected for inclusion in the present Chapter are intended to illustrate the scope of the rule rather than the exceptions to it. However, it would be unrealistic to suppose that the distinction between evidence received as original evidence and evidence received as admissible hearsay has always been scrupulously observed by the courts. The tendency to blur this distinction is perhaps especially noticeable in cases in which admissibility has been justified by invocation of the doctrine of *res gestae*. Moreover, consequent upon the barren but emphatic holding by a majority of the House of Lords in 1964[13] that hearsay evidence is not to be admitted unless "within some established and existing exception to the

---

[13] *Myers* v. *D.P.P.* [1965] A.C. 1001 (H.L.) (*infra*).

rule,"[14] there have been signs of a judicial tendency to blur the limits of meaning of hearsay itself in order to facilitate the reception of particular items of apparently reliable evidence.[15]

R. v. Eriswell (Inhabitants) 3 T.R. 707; 100 E.R. 815 (K.B.). Two justices of the peace took the evidence of a pauper as to his place of legal settlement. About five years later, other justices made an order for his removal solely upon such evidence. The Court of King's Bench was equally divided as to the propriety of this; so the order stood. Grose J. said: "Now it is a general rule that such evidence is not admissible, except in some few particular cases where the exception (for aught we know) is as ancient as the rule.... No principle was stated to take this out of the general rule, to show why hearsay evidence of the agreement should be permitted in this case any more than any other.... Is the evidence better upon the ground that it was upon oath administered by two justices? Evidence, though upon oath, to affect an absent person, is incompetent, because he cannot cross-examine; as nothing can be more unjust than that a person should be bound by evidence which he is not permitted to hear. But it may be said that it is in this case wise and discreet to depart from the general rule of evidence, and in this instance to admit hearsay evidence of a fact, or evidence on oath administered in the absence of the adverse party. I dread that rules of evidence shall ever depend upon the discretion of judges; I wish to find the rule laid down, and to abide by it. In this case I find the general rule; I find no decided authority that forms an exception to it; and nothing but a clear uncontrovertible decision upon the point; and not the concession of counsel or the obiter dictum of a judge, ought to form an exception to a general rule of law framed in wisdom by our ancestors, and adopted in every case except where the exception is as ancient as the rule...."

Note. In a later case (*R. v. Ferry Frystone (Inhabitants)* (1801) 2 East 54), Lord Kenyon said—"The point upon which the court were divided in opinion, in the case of *The King* v. *Eriswell*, has been since considered to be so clear against the admissibility of the evidence...that it was abandoned by the counsel at the bar in the case of *The King* v. *Nuneham Courtenay* (1801) 1 East 373, without argument." For a limited exception in cases in which the witness in the former proceedings is dead or otherwise unavailable see Chapter 14, *infra*.

STOBART v. DRYDEN

1 M. & W. 615; 5 L.J.Ex. 218; 2 G. 146; 1 Tyr. & Gr. 899; 150 E.R. 581
(Exchequer: 1836)

The statements of a deceased person may not generally be repeated by a witness in criminal proceedings for the purpose of proving the truth of what was stated. The rule applies to both oral and written statements.

The plaintiff sued the defendant on a mortgage deed. The defendant pleaded that the deed had been fraudulently altered by one of the

---

[14] *Ibid. per* Lord Morris at p. 1028.
[15] See, *e.g. R. v. Cook* [1987] Q.B. 417 (C.A.), p. 306, *infra*.

attesting witnesses, who had since died. In support of this plea, the defendant called a witness to prove statements and letters made and written by the deceased attesting witness, tending to show that he had fraudulently altered the deed. It was held that the evidence was inadmissible.

PARKE B. (delivering the judgment of the court, which included LORD ABINGER C.B., BOLLAND and GURNEY BB.):... The general rule is, that hearsay evidence is not admissible as proof of a fact which has been stated by a third person. This rule has been long established as a fundamental principle of the law of evidence; but certain exceptions have also been recognised, some from very early times, upon the ground of necessity or convenience. The simple question for us to decide is, whether such a declaration as this be one of the allowed exceptions to the general rule.... Is evidence of what the subscribing witness has said admissible?

It was contended on the argument that it was, and that it formed an exception to the general rule, and on two grounds; one of them, which I shall mention first, in order to dispose of it, was that, as the plaintiff used the declaration of the subscribing witness, evidenced by his signature, to prove the execution, the defendant might use any declaration of the same witness to disprove it. The answer to this argument is, that evidence of the handwriting in the attestation is not used as a declaration by the witness, but to show the fact that he put his name in that place and manner, in which in the ordinary course of business he would have done, if he had actually seen the deed executed. A statement of the attesting witness by parol, or written on any other document than that offered to be proved, would be inadmissible. The proof of actual attestation of the witness is, therefore, not the proof of a declaration, but of a fact.

The other ground, and the principal one, on which the most reliance was placed, was that it was in the nature of a substitute for the loss of the benefit of the cross-examination of the subscribing witness, if he had been alive and personally examined; by which, either the fact confessed would have been proved; or, if not, the witness would have been liable to be contradicted by proof of his admission; and it was contended that every declaration was admissible which might have been in evidence to impeach the credit of the witness himself on his personal examination.

Let us inquire what the authorities are in support of this exception....

...it is impossible to say that there is any such weight or authority...as to induce us to hold that this case is established and recognised as an exception from the great principle of our law of evidence, that facts, the truth of which depends on parol evidence, are to be proved by testimony on oath.

If we had to determine the question of the propriety of admitting the proposed evidence, on the ground of convenience, apart from the consideration of the expediency of abiding by general rules, we should say that it was at least very doubtful whether, generally speaking, it would not cause greater mischief than advantage in the investigation of truth. An extreme case might occur...where the exclusion of evidence of a death-bed declaration would probably have been the exclusion of one mode of discovering the truth. The same may, perhaps, be said of all solemn assertions *in extremis* by deceased witnesses. But, on the other hand, if any declarations at any time from the mouth of subscribing witnesses who are dead are to be admitted in evidence (and you cannot stop short of that, for no one contends that the exception is to be confined to death-bed declarations, and if so confined, the evidence would be inadmissible in the present case), the result would be that the security of solemn instruments would be much impaired. The rights of parties under wills and deeds would be liable to be affected at remote periods by loose declarations of attesting, witnesses, which those parties would have no opportunity of contradicting, or explaining by the evidence of the witnesses themselves. . . .

Note.—It will be observed that this case illustrates the fact that the rule against hearsay applies not only to oral statements, but also to statements in documents. However, substantial statutory inroads have been made into the latter—see especially the Police and Criminal Evidence Act 1984, Part VII, and the Criminal Justice Act 1988, Part II (both Part Two, *infra*). For common law exceptions to the application of the rule generally see Chapters 14 and 15 (*infra*).

R. v. **Gibson** (1887) 18 Q.B.D. 537 (C.C.R.). The accused was indicted for malicious wounding by throwing a stone at the prosecutor in the street where the accused's house was situated. In evidence the prosecutor stated that, just after he had been hit by the stone, a woman pointed to the door of the accused's house and said, "The person who threw the stone went in there." Shortly afterwards the accused was arrested in this house. He was convicted but the conviction was quashed. Lord Coleridge C.J. said (pp. 540–542): "I am of opinion that this conviction must be quashed. At the trial the statement of a passer-by as to where the prisoner had gone was received in evidence as tending to his identification. . . . I am of the opinion that the true principle which governs the present case is that it is the duty of the judge in criminal trials to take care of the verdict of the just is not founded upon any evidence except that which the law allows. Here evidence which was at law inadmissible was allowed to go to the jury."

Note.—In none of the judgments was the evidence expressly described as hearsay, doubtless because this was well understood by every member of the court. The judgments were mainly directed to the question whether the reception of inadmissible evidence necessitated the quashing of the conviction. A similar point was discussed in *R.* v. *Saunders* [1899] 1 Q.B. 490 (C.C.R.), when the court, citing *R.* v. *Gibson*, quashed convictions because the prosecutor had given evidence of the result of inquiries from third persons. In *R.* v. *Saunders* the evidence was held inadmissible expressly as hearsay. See also *Teper* v. *R.* [1952] A.C. 480 (P.C.), *infra*.

Similarly, on a charge of wounding his wife, an accused was convicted on evidence which included that of a neighbour as to the wife's statement that the accused had shot her. The conviction was quashed on appeal: *R.* v. *Parker* (1960) 45 Cr.App.R. 1 (C.C.A.).

Teper v. **R.** [1952] A.C. 480 (P.C.). See Chapter 15, p. 355, *infra*.

Sparks v. **R.** [1964] A.C. 964 (P.C.). The appellant, a white man, was convicted of indecent assault upon a girl between three and four years old. Shortly after the assault the child, who was not a witness at the trial, had told the mother that "it was a coloured boy." The Privy Council (on appeal from the Supreme Court of Bermuda) held that the trial judge had been right to reject the defence's application to allow the mother to give evidence of this statement. Lord Morris of Borth-y-Gest, delivering the judgment of the Privy Council, said (p. 978): "The mother would clearly be giving hearsay evidence if she were permitted to state what her girl had said to her. It becomes necessary, therefore, to examine the contentions which have been advanced in support of the admissibility of the evidence. It was said that 'it was manifestly unjust for the jury to be left throughout the whole trial with the impression that the child could not give any clue to the identity of her assailant'. The cause of justice is, however, best served by adherence to rules which have long been recognised and settled. If the girl had made a remark to her mother (not in the presence of the appellant) to the effect that it was the appellant who had assaulted her and if the girl was not to be a witness at the trial, evidence as to what she said would be the merest hearsay. In such circumstances it would be the defence who would wish to challenge a contention, if advanced, that it would be 'manifestly unjust' for the jury not to know that the girl had given a clue to the identity of her assailant. If it is said that hearsay evidence should freely be admitted and that there should be concentration in any particular case upon deciding as to its value or weight it is sufficient to say that our law has not been evolved upon such lines but is firmly based upon the view that it is wiser and better that hearsay should be excluded save in certain well defined and rather exceptional circumstances." The Privy Council also rejected the contention that the evidence was admissible as part of the *res gestae* (see Chapter 15, *infra*). The appeal was, however allowed on the ground that evidence of a confession had been wrongly admitted (see Chapter 17, *infra*).

R. v. Attard (1958) 43 Cr.App.R. 90 (C.C.A.). The accused, a Maltese, who neither spoke nor understood English, was charged with murder. The prosecution sought to call evidence by a police officer of an interview which he had had with the accused through an interpreter. This was held to be inadmissible. Gorman J. said (pp. 92–93): "There were present at an interview, at the first stage, the prisoner and the detective-superintendent. At a further stage the detective-superintendent thought it right to get the services of an interpreter in order that there might be no mistake with regard to what was said. Thereafter, the interview went on in this way: a question was put by the superintendent in English, that was then translated into Maltese, and, that having been done, the prisoner answered the question in Maltese. The answer was then translated into English by the interpreter, and then the superintendent, having put the question in English and having got through the interpreter the answer in English, made a note of what was said to him by the interpreter. There may also have been in the course of the interview statements made by the prisoner in Maltese which were not the direct result of questions put to him through the interpreter by the superintendent, and those statements, too, were translated into English by the interpreter, and the superintendent, having heard them, made a note of them. It is sought here by the prosecution to ask the detective-superintendent to tell us that which he in fact wrote down at the time. It is said by Mr. Edward Clarke [defence counsel] that, when there is an interview of that kind, the best person, or the nearest person to the prisoner, is the interpreter, and the interpreter, he does not dispute, can be called to say: "I heard the detective-superintendent put the question. I then translated that question. I said this to the prisoner and the prisoner said this to me"; the interpreter being asked as a sort of intermediary between the non-English speaking prisoner and the English-speaking detective-superintendent.... The interpreter says, Mr. Humphreys [prosecution counsel] is not in the nature of a police officer, but a mere cypher who hears translations and then gives them back in the English language.... In my opinion, in all the circumstances here the submission made by the defence is a correct one and the evidence ought not to be given through the mouth of the detective-superintendent in the witness-box."

Note.—As a result of this decision, the Home Office sent out a circular letter to Chief Officers of Police stating that "it will be necessary in similar cases in the future to ensure that the interpreter is available to give evidence as to oral statements made by the accused, as is already done in the case of written statements. It will be desirable that, whenever practicable, the interpreter should make his own notes of the interview for use in the event of his being called to give evidence. Failing this, the interpreter should be asked to initial the record of the interview made in the notebook of the police officer conducting the interview, so that it can be used by the interpreter to refresh his memory when giving evidence."

To be contrasted with *R.* v. *Attard* is the case of *Gaio* v. *R.* (1961) 104 C.L.R. 419, where the High Court of Australia by a majority adopted a different analysis of the problem. Dixon C.J. said (p. 421): "I think that the translation word by word or sentence by sentence by the interpreter is not an *ex post facto* narrative statement of an event that has passed within the rule against the admissibility of hearsay but is an integral part of one transaction consisting of communication through the interpreter. It is therefore enough if it is proved that what he did was to interpret faithfully. The version as spoken and heard in one language or the other—in the present case English—can then be given in evidence." Fullagar J., with whose judgment Dixon C.J. agreed, said (p. 429) of the interpreter he " . . . is not in any real sense a party to the conversation. He contributes nothing of his own that is material. He is merely the mouthpiece alternately of A and of B. Subject to one condition, therefore, there is no reason why A should not give evidence of the conversation conducted wholly in his own language, or why B should not give evidence of it as a conversation conducted wholly in his own language. The one condition is that the accuracy of the means of communication employed should be verified."

R. v. McLean (1968) 52 Cr.App.R. 80 (C.A.). Gomery, a few minutes after being attacked and robbed, dictated something, which he could not afterwards remember, to Cope. Cope wrote down on a card the registration number of a car, which was alleged to have been involved in the attack and which the appellant was alleged to have hired a few days previously. Gomery did not see what Cope wrote down. At the trial of the appellant for robbery Cope was allowed to produce the card and to give evidence of the number which he had written down. The Court of Appeal held that this evidence was wrongly admitted and quashed the conviction. Edmund Davies L.J., delivering the judgment of the court, said (pp. 83–84): "With the utmost reluctance, which is shared by all three members of this Court, the appeal against conviction is allowed.... The crucial defect in this cases arises in relation to the evidence given by Mr. Cope, Mr. Cope being called to say (in effect): 'I wrote down on a piece of paper—here is the paper—what Mr. Gomery told me was the number of the card. It was HKB 138D.' We confess that we have strained to find some means whereby the testimony of Mr. Cope might be regarded as properly admitted in this case, for it is difficult to see that justice is done by its exclusion. But we are bound to apply the law as we find it, and by reference to such cases as *Jones* v. *Metcalfe* [1967] 3 All E.R. 205. Notwithstanding the submissions of Mr. Briggs, for which we are indebted, it seems to us that for Mr. Cope to be allowed to say that what he was told by Mr. Gomery was that the car involved was HKB 138D is a contravention of the hearsay rule when that remark is adduced as evidence that the car involved in the robbery was in fact HKB 138D, and so we hold.... Mr Cope ought not to have been permitted under our existing rules to give evidence of what Mr. Gomery told him in relation to the number of the car."

Note.—This impeccably, if somewhat relentlessly, logical approach (like that taken by the Northern Ireland Court of Appeal in *R.* v. *Linden* [1984] 12 N.I. 251; [1985] C.L.Y. 2382) may be contrasted with that in effect taken by the British Columbia Court of Appeal in *R.* v. *Penno* (1977) 35 C.C.C. (2d.) 266. There an issue was as to the numbers on tickets attached to two coats hanging in a robbery victim's shop just before the robbery. One witness testified that she had previously helped another witness to take an inventory. She had then looked at the ticket on each coat and had called out the number to the other witness, who had written it on the inventory sheets. The first witness did not check the inventory and at the trial could not remember the numbers which she had called out. The second witness's testimony and the relevant inventory sheet were held to be properly admissible to prove the numbers on the coats. The court took the view that the hearsay rule was not infringed. This is surely wrong, but, as a leading Canadian commentator has pointed out, as the reception of the evidence "did not substantially violate, if it violated at all, any of the interests the hearsay rule functions to protect," that reception was justified (Schiff, "Hearsay and the Hearsay Rule: A Functional View," LVI Canadian Bar Review, 674, 689).

MYERS v. DIRECTOR OF PUBLIC PROSECUTIONS

[1965] A.C. 1001; [1964] 1 All E.R. 877; 48 Cr.App.R. 348 (H.L.: 1964)

As a general rule hearsay evidence is not admissible, and in order to justify its reception authority must be found within some existing established exception to this rule.

LORD REID: My Lords, the appellant was convicted, together with another man, on several counts relating to the theft of motor cars. His scheme was to buy for small sums, but, curiously, not very small sums, wrecked cars together with their log books issued by the local authorities on registration. Having bought a wrecked car he then stole a car as nearly as possible identical with the wrecked car and proceeded to disguise the stolen car so that it corresponded in every respect with the particulars of the wrecked car noted in its log book. He could then, as he thought, safely sell the disguised stolen car together with the genuine log book of the wrecked car.

The log book contains a chassis number and an engine number, and these had therefore to be transferred, together with the wrecked car's number plates, from it to the stolen car. As the chassis number and engine number appear on small plates which can be detached from the chassis or engine it was not difficult to substitute the genuine chassis and number plates taken from the wrecked car for those on the stolen car.

But a great deal of evidence of various kinds was adduced against the appellant....

But there was also very cogent evidence in the case of a few cars derived from records kept by Austins, the manufacturers, at their Longbridge Works, and the question of law in this case is whether that evidence was rightly admitted. It appeared that when each car is being assembled it is accompanied by a card on which it is the duty of the workman concerned to copy particulars of the card. So there is copied on to the card the chassis number and the engine number which the workman sees on the car. But there is also another number, known as the block number, which is indelibly stamped on the engine: and this, too, is entered on the card. These cards were photographed on to microfilms and then destroyed and the microfilms were produced by a witness responsible for these records who also transcribed the particulars from the microfilms. If these records were admissible evidence they proved that when a particular car left the works it bore three particular numbers—the chassis and the engine numbers on detachable plates and the block number. But when the disguised car was examined it bore two numbers which the records showed belonged to the wrecked car and one, the block number, which the records showed belonged to the stolen car. As the latter number was incapable of alteration this evidence proved conclusively that the disguised car was the stolen car and not the wrecked car rebuilt.

The reason why this evidence is maintained to have been inadmissible is that its cogency depends on hearsay. The witness could only say that a record made by someone else showed that, if the record was correctly made, a car had left the works bearing three particular numbers. He could not prove that the record was correct or that the numbers which it contained were in fact the numbers on the car when it was made. This is a highly technical point, but the law regarding hearsay evidence is technical, and I would say absurdly technical. So I must consider whether in the existing state of the law that objection to the admissibility of this evidence must prevail.

It is difficult to make any general statement about the law of hearsay evidence which is entirely accurate, but I think that the books show that in the seventeenth century the law was fluid and uncertain but that early in the eighteenth century it had become the general rule that hearsay evidence was not admissible. Many reasons for the rule have been put forward, but we do not know which of them directly influenced the judges who established the rule. The rule has never been absolute. By the nineteenth century many exceptions had become well established, but again in most cases we do not know how or when the exception came to be recognised. It does seem, however, that in many cases there was no justification either in principle or logic for carrying the exception just so far and no further. One might hazard a surmise that when the rule proved highly inconvenient in a particular kind of case it was relaxed just sufficiently far to meet that case, and without regard to any question of principle. But this kind of judicial legislation became less and less acceptable and well over a century ago the patchwork which then existed seems to have become stereotyped. The natural result has been the growth of more and more fine distinctions. . . .

It was not disputed before your Lordships that to admit these records is to admit hearsay. They only tend to prove that a particular car bore a particular number when it was assembled if the jury were entitled to infer that the entries were accurate, at least in the main; and the entries on the cards were assertions by the unidentifiable men who made them that they had entered numbers which they had seen on the cars. Counsel for the responsible were unable to adduce any reported case or any textbook as direct authority for their admission. Only four reasons for their admission were put forward. It was said that evidence of this kind is in practice admitted at least at the Central Criminal Court. Then it was argued that a judge has a discretion to admit such evidence. Then the reasons given in the Court of Criminal Appeal were relied on. And lastly it was said with truth that common sense rebels against the rejection of this evidence.

At the trial counsel for the prosecution sought to support the existing practice of admitting such records, if produced by the persons in charge of them, by arguing that they were not adduced to prove the truth of the recorded particulars but only to prove that they were records kept in the normal course of business. Counsel for the accused then asked the very pertinent question—if they were not intended to prove the truth of the entries what were they intended to prove? I ask what the jury would infer from them: obviously that they were probably true records. If they were not capable of supporting an inference that they were probably true records, then I do not see what probative value they could have, and their admission was bound to mislead the jury.

The first reason given by the Court of Criminal Appeal for sustaining the admission of the records was that, although the records might not be evidence standing by themselves, they could be used to corroborate the evidence of other witnesses. I regret to say that I have great difficulty in understanding that.... Unless the jury were entitled to regard them as probably true records they afforded no corroboration at all. If the jury were entitled so to regard them, I can see no reason why they should only become admissible evidence after some witnesses have identified the cars for different reasons....

At the end of their judgment the Court of Criminal Appeal gave a different reason. "In our view the admission of such evidence does not infringe the hearsay rule because its probative value does not depend upon the credit of an unidentified person but rather on the circumstances in which the record is maintained and the inherent probability that it will be correct rather than incorrect." That, if I may say so, is undeniable as a matter of common sense. But can it be reconciled with the existing law? I need not discuss the question on general lines because I think that this ground is quite inconsistent with the established rule regarding public records. Public records are prima facie evidence of the fact which they contain but it is quite clear that a record is not a public record within the scope of that rule unless it is open to inspection by at least a section of the public. Unless we are to alter that rule how can be possibly say that a private record not open to public inspection can be prima facie evidence of the truth of its contents? I would agree that it is quite unreasonable to refuse to accept as prima facie evidence a record obviously well kept by public officers and proved never to have been discovered to contain a wrong entry though frequently consulted by officials, merely because it is not open to inspection. But that is settled law. This seems to me to be a good example of the wide repercussions which would follow if we accepted the judgment of the Court of Criminal Appeal. I must therefore regretfully decline to accept this reason as correct in law.

In argument the Solicitor-General maintained that, although the general rule may be against the admission of private records to prove the truth of entries in them, the trial just has a discretion to admit a record in a particular case if satisfied that it is trustworthy and that justice requires its admission. That appears to me to be contrary to the whole framework of the existing law. It is true that a judge has a discretion to exclude legally admissible evidence if justice so requires, but it is a very different thing to say that he has a discretion to admit legally inadmissible evidence. The whole development of the exceptions to the hearsay rule is based on the determination of certain classes of evidence as admissible or inadmissible and not on the apparent credibility of particular evidence tendered. No matter how cogent particular evidence may seem to be, unless it comes within a class which is admissible, it is excluded. Half a dozen witnesses may offer to prove that they heard two men of high character who cannot now be found discuss in detail the fact now in issue and agree on a credible account of it, but that evidence would not be admitted although it might be by far the best evidence available.

It was admitted in argument before your Lordships that not every private record would be admissible. If challenged it would be necessary to prove in some way that it had proved to be reliable, before the judge would allow it to be put before the jury. And I think that some such limitation must be implicit in the last reason given by the Court of Criminal Appeal. I see no objection to a judge having a discretion of this kind though it might be awkward in a civil case. But it appears to me to be an innovation on the existing law which decide inadmissibility by categories and not by apparent trustworthiness. For these reasons I would hold that this evidence ought not to have been admitted at the trial. . . .

LORD MORRIS OF BORTH-Y-GEST and LORD HODSON delivered concurring speeches against the reception of the evidence.

LORD PEARCE (dissenting on the question of admissibility): My Lords, the evidence whose admission is the ground of complaint was fair, clear, reliable and sensible. The question is whether the court was bound by a technical rule to exclude it. No one doubts that the general exclusion of hearsay evidence, subject to exceptions permitted where common sense and the pursuit of truth demand it, is an important and valuable principle. But it is a disservice to that general principle if the courts limit the necessary exceptions so rigidly that the general rule creates a frequent and unnecessary injustice. This case is of importance since a similar situation may arise, not only in the many cases of car-stealing but also in cases of long firm frauds, hire-purchase frauds and the like. . . .

Since the cars are made in large quantities by mass production, many workmen are concerned with the records. Particulars of a car, as it goes along the line, are entered on a card. For ease of storage the cards are photographed on a micro-film and the cards themselves are destroyed. The relevant micro-films in the present case were extracted and the numbers shown on them were scheduled in convenient form. The films and schedules were produced on oath by Legg who was employed in the Technical Investigation Department of the Austin Motor Company Ltd. and was in charge of all their records "for police purposes."

It is not disputed that the log books are admissible as public documents. But they do not contain the cylinder block numbers. It is not disputed that the cards themselves (which contain all the numbers) or a photographic reproduction of them when the originals have been destroyed, either could have been used to "refresh the memory" of the particular workmen who recorded the numbers or, following the more realistic approach developed by *Rex* v. *Bryant and Dickson* (1946) 31 Cr.App.R. 146 (C.C.A.), could have been produced by the particular workmen as records made by them. In that case (*ibid.* 150) Lord Goddard C.J., in the Court of Criminal Appeal, said: "A person who keeps a record as part of his duty is entitled to look at that record and looking at the record give evidence: 'I am satisfied I kept this record, and this, that or the other happened, and it is duly recorded.' " Thus, when the record is proved by the man who made it, it can, though its contents are not remembered, speak for itself. . . .

In the present case, if the anonymous workman who copied down the number could be proved to be dead, the records would be admissible as declarations in the course of duty. Since we do not know whether he is dead or not, the court, it is argued, cannot inform itself from the records. But in this case the fact that he is not on oath and is not subject to cross-examination has no practical importance whatever. It would be no advantage, if he could have been identified, to put him on oath and cross-examine him about one out of many hundreds of repetitious and routine entries made three years before. He could say that to the best of his belief the number was correct; but everybody already knows that. If he pretends to any memory in the matter, he is untruthful; but, even if he is, that in no way reflects on whether he copied down a number correctly in the day's work three years before. Nor is it of any importance how he answers the routine question in cross-examination: "You may have made a mistake?" Everybody knows that he may have made a mistake. The jury knew it without being told, the judge told them so at least once, and both counsel told them so, probably more than once. The only questions that could helpfully be asked on the matter were whether the particular system of recording was good and whether in practice it had been found prone to error. These questions could not be answered by the individual workman but they could be dealt with by Legg if the defence wished to probe into the matter. He and not the workmen would know how efficient the system had been found in practice, and how often, if at all, it has been shown subsequently that mis-recordings must have occurred. The evidence produced is therefore as good as evidence on this point can be; it is the best evidence, though it is, of course, subject, like every other man-made record, to the admitted universal human frailty of occasional clerical error. The fact that the engine and chassis numbers which emanated from precisely the same source are admissible because they have been embodied in a public document, namely, the log-book, show up the absurdity of excluding these records. Has the machinery of justice really got itself into such a position that it must blind its eyes to the truth in such a situation? It is indeed a sad thing if it must condemn an accused by excluding evidence that to eyes of any reasonable man would prove his innocence. For the same situation would rise and the same technicality would be a bar, if the accused could have proved by Austin's records (if they had been admissible) that the car was not stolen, in spite of deceptive human evidence to the contrary. It is no answer to say that in such a case a prosecution would not be brought as things are today. It cannot be right that the prosecution should shoulder a duty not to prosecute in doubtful cases on the ground that it knows that the court will not give the accused a fair trial but will exclude vital evidence in his favour.

I use the words machinery of justice, because the question how far a court will admit evidence and what weight it will give to it is part of the judicial process. It is the method of extracting the truth to which the law is to be applied and it cannot be considered in vacuo without regard to social conditions. The main argument against any change in principles of law is not applicable to the method of ascertaining the truth. When principles of law are disturbed, many persons who have ordered their affairs on the basis of existing legal authority may suffer injustice. There may be unforeseen repercussions in other branches of the law which may lead to confusion and injustices. The admission of records such as those in question can produce no such effect and lead to no injustice.

Either the total admission of hearsay or its total exclusion would lead to injustice and inefficiency in the search for truth. Professor Wigmore, in his book on Evidence (3rd ed., Vol. 5, p. 27, quoted in Cross, 2nd ed., p. 383) was of opinion that the rule has been over-enforced and abused and concluded that "the problem for the coming generation is to preserve the fundamental value of the rule, while allowing the amplest exceptions to it and abstaining from petty meticulous exceptions."

There is not now and never has been a rule for the *total* exclusion of hearsay without exception. Originally hearsay was usual and admissible. Through the sixteenth and the earlier part of the seventeenth centuries there was no objection to it. But in the later seventeenth century objections to it grew and by the early eighteenth century there was a general exclusion of hearsay evidence, with certain exceptions. There was a transitional period when such evidence was accepted as confirmatory though not as sufficient by itself. And during the eighteenth century some hearsay, namely, evidence of prior statements by a witness, might be accepted to confirm the testimony of that witness. The courts were gradually working out their own compromises to obtain satisfactory machinery for handling evidence and ascertaining the truth. They were adopting the hearsay rule in general with such adaptations and exceptions as would make it work and conduce to just decisions.

This process of improvement and evolution was carried out by the inherent power of the courts to conduct its process so as to prevent abuse and secure justice. I see no reason why at some stage the courts should decide that evolution was now complete and that thereafter no further change must occur, however great the absurdity or injustice.

The argument for the appellant is not founded on any decision whose facts approximate to those in the present case. It is based on the negative argument that since hearsay is excluded save for certain excepted classes of case, and since no exception has been introduced which covers this case, the court no longer has a power to introduce such an exception or to adapt any exception to meet this case. Such an argument should be approached with suspicion when applied to the court's power to inform itself of the truth by means which have been gradually evolving over the centuries. Admittedly justice and common sense have in the past demanded various exceptions if the general rule was to be acceptable at all. That the court should be slow to introduce or further adapt exceptions is reasonable. That the court should debar itself forever from introducing further exceptions or adapting them under any circumstances, however unforeseen or unforeseeable, would be unreasonable.
. . . .

In *Woodward* v. *Goulstone* . . . [(1886) 11 App.Cas. 469 Lord Herschell] . . . criticised the broad expression of principle propounded by Jessel M.R. in *Sugden* v. *Lord St. Leonards* (1876) 1 P.D. 154: "It is much broader than would merely support the particular extension of the exceptions which the Master of the Rolls was then upholding; and I cannot help feeling that for the courts to add at will from time to time any new exceptions which appear to be capable of being supported on principles similar to those which have been long established would be introducing a dangerous uncertainty into the law of evidence" (1886) 11 App.Cas. 469, 480.

I find it impossible to accept that there is any "dangerous uncertainty" caused by obvious and sensible improvements in the means by which the court arrives at the truth. One is entitled to choose between the individual conflicting obiter dicta of two great judges and I prefer that of Jessel M.R. His dictum was as follows (1876) 1 P.D. 154, 241: "Now I take it the principle which underlies all these exceptions is the same. In the first place, the case must be one in which it is difficult to obtain other evidence, for no doubt the ground for admitting the exceptions was that very difficulty. In the next place the declarant must be disinterested; that is, disinterested in the sense that the declaration was not made in favour of his interest. And, thirdly, the declaration must be made before dispute or litigation, so that it was made without bias on account of the existence of a dispute or litigation which the declarant might be supposed to favour. Lastly, and this appears to me one of the strongest reasons for admitting it, the declarant must have had peculiar means of knowledge not possessed in ordinary cases." ...

That, I respectfully think, is the correct method of approach, particularly to a problem that deals with the court's method of ascertaining truth. As new situations arise it adapts its practice to deal with the situation in accordance with the basic and established principles which lie beneath the practice. To exalt the practice above the principle would be a surrender to formalism. Since this branch of the law is so untidy, there is but little appeal in "the demon of formalism which tempts the intellect with the lure of scientific order."

While I give weight to the general explicit or implicit disapproval of further extension, expressed obiter in *Woodward* v. *Goulstone*, I cannot accept that from 1886 no further evolution was possible in particular circumstances or sets of circumstances on the general principles expressed by Jessel M.R. Since that date life has greatly changed in various respects. With the necessity created by death the courts were familiar and they had evolved exceptions which dealt reasonably adequately with that phenomenon. With the necessity created by insanity Lord Eldon and Lord Cottenham had dealt and I cannot find that they have been overruled. The necessity created by mass production and modern business they could not then foresee. They did not provide for the anonymity of modern industrial records and the difficulty of tracing those who made them. The individuality of persons in a large factory or business may be difficult or impossible to discover. They do many repetitive and almost automatic tasks concerning which no memory exists. Yet their composite efforts make machines and records whose complexity, efficiency, and accuracy are beyond anything imaginable in 1886. In my view the anonymity of the recorder or the impossibility of tracing him create as valid a necessity as does his death for allowing his business records to be admitted. The principles on which the court sets out to discover the truth about these things remain unchanged, but the way in which those principles are applied must change if the principles are to be honoured and observed.

. . . .

There are on balance strong grounds for admitting the evidence in this case. The evidence is clear and cogent on a vital issue in the case. It is the *best* evidence. There is no authority directed to this point which binds your Lordships to exclude it. The basic principles which have found expression in other sets of circumstances clearly justify it and demand expression in this class of case also. The admission of this evidence is in accordance with a certain degree of practice which is fair and sensible. Its admission cannot disturb or offend any existing legal principles. In so far as the admission throws up by contrast some exclusion in some other class of case as being anomalous, that is no disadvantage. The development of this branch of the law has always been sporadic.

In my opinion, where the person who from his own knowledge made business records cannot be found, and where a business produces by some proper servant, who can speak with knowledge to the method and system of record-keeping, its records reliably kept in the ordinary way of business, they should be admitted as prima facie evidence. I say reliably kept because the judge must clearly have a discretion to exclude from a jury (as he would reject from his own mind in adjudicating) records so ill-kept as not to be worthy of credit. If any question arose about that, he could hear evidence or argument about it in the absence of the jury, as is done, for instance, in the case of confessions.

I would also, if necessary, accept the reasons given by the Court of Criminal Appeal in this case. *Reg.* v. *Rice* [1963] 1 Q.B. 857 was, in my view, correctly decided for the reasons given by Winn J. *ibid.* 871–872. The fact that an air ticket marked with the name of Rice was apparently given up by one of the passengers was somewhat more consistent with Rice having flown on that aeroplane than with his not having flown. It was a piece of confirmatory evidence. It was one of the circumstances which the jury might consider. But it was not evidence (unless the writer of the name Rice on the ticket was called) that someone had given his name as Rice or, *a fortiori*, that it was Rice who had bought the ticket. So, too, if a handkerchief marked with his name had been found. To take another comparable case, suppose that as part of a contractual correspondence a plaintiff or prosecutor produces a telegram officially delivery to him signed with the defendant's name. If it was handed in at a busy telegraph office which has lost all record of it, the telegram could not be strictly proved; but it would not, I think, be ruled out of the case. Since it has not been proved to have been sent by the defendant, it is possible that it was falsely sent by someone else (including the plaintiff himself) or evolved by some mistake of the Post Office. But it is a fact which the jury are entitled to consider in the light of common sense and probability. The same might be said of an invoice from the Austin Motor Co. bearing, *inter alia*, the number of the cylinder block, if it was found in the pocket of the stolen car itself. That would be a circumstance which would fall to be considered on a question of probabilities, but it would not have the weight of a proved record. In all those cases the document is linked up with the witness or the car. Here it may fairly be said that once the car is proved to be an Austin car, it is permissible to prove that the Austin record links up the engine and chassis numbers (which were properly proved by the log-book to be the numbers of this Austin car) with a certain number on the cylinder block. That is a circumstance which can be taken into account. It would not, on its own, carry great weight since the entry has not been strictly proved, but its existence is a fact to be considered.

Let us suppose that in the present case the number attributed to the cylinder block was different, and that the defendant had subpoenaed Legg to produce the records so that he could rely on the disparity as a fact tending to cast doubt on the prosecution's identification. He would not tender the records as strictly proved evidence of the information contained in the records but as "inferential evidence" on the issue of identification. . . . Can it be right to hold that such evidence must be wholly excluded and that the court has no discretion to admit it? In my opinion common sense compels that answer that the existence of the record should be admitted as one of the surrounding circumstances.

For the reasons which I have set out, the evidence in this case was in my opinion properly admitted and I would dismiss the appeal. . . .

LORD DONOVAN agreed with Lord Pearce's dissent on the question of admissibility.

[Although divided as to the admissibility of the evidence, their Lordships were unanimous in holding that the appeal should be dismissed, because even if the evidence were rejected the other evidence of the appellant's guilt was overwhelming.]

Note.—For *R.* v. *Rice* referred to by Lord Pearce see *infra*.

The majority view on admissibility, as applied to the actual facts of *Myers* v. *Director of Public Prosecutions*, was negatived by the Criminal Evidence Act 1965. This was subsequently repealed and its substance re-enacted in the Police and Criminal Evidence Act 1984, ss.68–72. Section 68 has itself now been repealed and replaced in a greatly extended form by Part II of the Criminal Justice Act 1988 (Part Two, *infra*).

In *R.* v. *Shone* (1983) 76 Cr.App.R. 72 (C.A.) it was held that it was open to a witness, whose duty was to keep records, to give evidence of the absence of any entry indicating that articles, which had disappeared, had been sold. The jury was entitled to infer from this that they had not been sold. This would appear to be a case of "negative hearsay," and the decision would seem to imply that the hearsay rule does not necessarily apply to such cases.

R. v. **Rice** [1963] 1 Q.B. 857 (C.A.). Three men were convicted of conspiracy. Objection had been taken at their trial to the admission in evidence of a used airline ticket which bore the names of two of them, Rice and Moore, and which was produced by an airline representative. The judge had overruled this objection, and the ticket was admitted as an exhibit on behalf of the Crown. Rice and Moore appealed on the ground *inter alia* that this piece of evidence had been wrongly admitted. Their appeals were dismissed. Winn J., in the course of delivering the judgment of the Court of Criminal Appeal said (pp. 869 *et seq.*):

"...after objection and discussion, that ticket was produced in evidence by the airline representative whose function it was to deal with flight tickets returned after use. The court has no doubt that the ticket and the fact of the presence of that ticket in the file or other place where tickets used by passengers would in the ordinary course be found, were facts which were in logic relevant to the issue whether or not there flew on those flights two men either of whom was a Mr. Rice or a Mr. Moore. The relevance of that ticket in logic and its legal admissibility as a piece of real evidence both stem from the same root, *viz.*, the balance of probability recognised by common sense and common knowledge that an air ticket which has been used on a flight and which has a name upon it has more likely than not been used by a man of that name or by one of two men whose names are upon it. A comparable document would be a passport, which is more likely on the whole to be in the possession of the person to whom it was issued than that of anyone having no right to it. It is, however, essential, whether for the purposes of logical reasoning or for a consideration of the evidentiary effect in law of any such document, to distinguish clearly between its relevance and its probative significance: the document must not be treated as speaking its contents for what it might say could only be hearsay. Thus a passport cannot say "my bearer is X" nor the air ticket "I was issued to Y."... The court doubts whether the air ticket could constitute admissible evidence that the booking was effected either by Rice or even by any man of that name...."

Note.—Lord Pearce, giving an alternative reason for his dissent in *Myers* v. *D.P.P.* (*supra*), expressed approval of the way in which the airline ticket was treated in *R.* v. *Rice*. However, although the majority judgments in the *Myers* case are primarily concerned with the non-availability of any established exception to the hearsay rule, it is (obviously) implicit in them that the records could not have been treated as original evidence. The authority of *R.* v. *Rice* must therefore be regarded as having been shaken. On the other hand it is to be noted that when Lord Hodson referred to the case in the Privy Council in *Patel* v. *Comptroller of Customs* (*infra*) he did not go so far as to disapprove it. Also, as the late Sir Rupert Cross has pointed out (Cross, *Evidence* (5th ed,, 1979), p. 467), "...if *R.* v. *Rice* was wrongly decided, a court would be driven to such absurd conclusions as that a handkerchief bearing a name, or a passport, are not evidence that a person of the name they bore travelled on the plane on which they were found." See, too, *R.* v. *Lydon, infra.*

Patel v. **Comptroller of Customs** [1965] A.C. 356 (P.C.). The appellant had been convicted of making a false declaration in a customs import entry which he had produced to a customs officer (contrary to the Fiji Customs Ordinance, s.166) in that in respect of five bags of seed instead of declaring the origin of the seed to be Morocco he had declared it to be India. The evidence that the origin of the seed was in fact Morocco consisted in each case of the legend on the inner bag "produce of Morocco." One of the grounds upon which the defendant appealed against conviction was that this evidence had been wrongly admitted. The Privy Council upheld this contention and advised that the conviction be set aside. Lord Hodson said (p. 365): "The only entry as to which the allegation of falsity is made is the word 'India' in the column headed 'country of origin,' which is part of the import entry form signed by the appellant. The only evidence purporting to show that this entry was false is the legend 'produce of Morocco' written upon the bags. Their Lordships are asked by the respondent to say that the inference can be drawn that the goods contained in the bags were produced in Morocco. This they are unable to do. From an evidentiary point of view the words are hearsay and cannot assist the prosecution. This matter need not be elaborated in view of the decision of the House of Lords in *Myers* v. *Director of Public Prosecutions* [1965] A.C. 1001, given after the Fiji courts had considered the case. The decision of the House, however, makes clear beyond doubt that the list of exceptions to the hearsay rule cannot be extended judicially to include such things as label or markings. Nothing is to be gained by comparing the legend in this case with the records considered in *Myers* v. *Director of Public Prosecutions*. Nothing here is known of when and by whom the markings on the bags were affixed and no evidence was called to prove any fact which tended to show that the goods in question in fact came from Morocco. Some reliance was placed by the respondent on *R.* v. *Rice* [1963] 1 Q.B. 857 where a used airline ticket was admitted as an exhibit in a criminal prosecution. It is sufficient to say that the Court of Criminal Appeal in admitting the document said that it must not be treated as speaking its contents, for what it might say could be hearsay."

R. v. **Lydon** (1987) 85 Cr.App.R. 221 (C.A.). The appellant had been convicted of taking a conveyance without authority and robbery of a post office. He had denied involvement. The trial judge had allowed evidence to be given that a gun had been found on a grass verge about a mile from the post office and on the road which would have been used by the getaway car, and that nearby were found two pieces of paper bearing the writing "Sean rules" and "Seanrules 85." The appellant's name was Sean. Ink of similar appearance was found on the gun barrel. The Court of Appeal held that this evidence had been rightly admitted. The reference to Sean involved no assertion. If the jury were satisfied that the gun had been used in the robbery and that the pieces of paper were linked with the gun, the reference to Sean "would fit in" with the appellant having committed the offence. The most important issue for the jury was the accuracy of various items of identification evidence. The probative value of the finding of the pieces of paper was not great, but it was not hearsay. Woolf L.J. said (p. 224) that, "whether or not the case of *Rice* [*supra*] is still good law," the evidence had been rightly admitted in the instant case because the "reference to Sean could be regarded as no more than a statement of fact involving no assertion as to the truth of the contents of the document.... The inference that the jury could draw from the words written on the piece of paper is that the paper had been in the possession of someone who wished to write 'Sean rules' and that person would presumably either be Sean himself or at least be associated with such a person, and thus it creates an inferential link with the appellant.... Similarly, if the gun had been wrapped in a local paper normally only circulating in Neasden, that again, having regard to the fact that the appellant admittedly came from Neasden, would have been relevant circumstantial evidence."

Note.—The justification for the reception of the evidence in *R.* v. *Lydon* (or in *R.* v. *Rice*), as in effect real rather than documentary evidence, must lie in the factual connection between the commission of the offence (or the flight) and the finding of the pieces of paper (or the ticket). Absent that factual connection the pieces of paper (or the ticket) would be being tendered as documentary evidence and would be hearsay.

R. v. **van Vreden** (1973) 57 Cr.App.R. 818 (C.A.). The appellant was convicted on various counts of obtaining pecuniary advantage by deception, obtaining property by deception and attempting to do so. The prosecution case was that he and a co-defendant had used a Barclaycard, issued on South Africa to a Miss Lang, to perpetrate the offences. A document (Exhibit 1), which the prosecution alleged to be the application form which related to the issue of this card, was admitted in evidence. The Court of Appeal, following *Myers* v. *D.P.P.* (*supra*), quashed the appellant's conviction. Lawton L.J., delivering the judgment of the Court, said (pp. 821–822)": There is no reason whatsoever for thinking that Exhibit 1 was not a genuine document. This being so, the inference to be drawn from it is that the card used by the two persons had not been issued to either of them. This the appellant's counsel accepted; but he submitted that the law, because of the hearsay rule, will not allow a jury to infer that which everyone outside a jury box would infer without any hesitation at all. The argument was as follows: someone in South Africa probably approved the application and that person or some other person issued a card to the applicant. Then someone, it may have been he who approved or he who had issued, or even a third person, wrote down on Exhibit 1 a number as the account number. This unknown person was stating on Exhibit 1 what he had done. The production of Exhibit 1 by Mr. Fishwick at the trial effected the same result as if he had produced a statement made by a named clerk in South Africa asserting that he had issued a card to Miss Lang bearing the number which he had entered as the account number. Such a statement would, it was submitted, not be admissible in evidence; the fact that the identity of the clerk is unknown, as are the circumstances in which the entry was made, cannot make admissible that which would be inadmissible if all the relevant facts were known. We have been impelled albeit with reluctance, to accept this argument."

Ares v. **Venner** (1970) 14 D.L.R. (3d.) 4 (S.C. Canada). The plaintiff having been injured in a ski-ing accident, was admitted to the Seton Hospital where he was treated by Doctor Vener. However his condition worsened and as a result his leg was amputated. He sued Dr. Venner, the Seton Hospital and its proprietors alleging negligence. The trial judge, O'Byrne J., found for the plaintiff. This finding was reversed by the Appellate Division of the Alberta Supreme Court. The Supreme Court of Canada allowed the plaintiff's further appeal and restored the finding of the trial judge. Hall J., delivering the judgment of the Supreme Court of Canada, said (p. 9): " ...The main issue in the Appellate Division was as to the admissibility of notes made by the nurses who attended the appellant while he was in Seton Hospital. These notes were tendered in evidence as part of Dr. Venner's discovery evidence which was being read into the record on behalf of the appellant at the trial. Counsel for Dr. Venner objected to the notes being received in evidence, but they were admitted by O'Bryne, J., as being an exception to the hearsay rule.... I think it desirable that the Court should deal with the issue as a matter of law and settle the practice in respect of hospital records and nurses' notes as being either admissible and prima facie evidence of the truth of the statements made therein or not admissible as being excluded by the hearsay rule. The question has not been free from doubt. The need for a restatement of the hearsay rule has long been acknowledged, but differences of opinion exist as to how the change should come about. There are two schools of thought and these are well illustrated in the recent decision in the House of Lords in *Myers* v. *D.P.P.* [1965] A.C. 1001. In the *Myers* case, Lord Reid, with whom Lords Morris and Hodson agreed, presented the case for a legislative solution as follows.... [His Lordship then quoted from the judgment of Lord Reid.]...Lord Donovan presented the case for extension of the rule by judicial decision in these words.... 'The common law is moulded by the judges and it is still their province to adapt it from time to time so as to make it serve the interests of those it binds. Particularly is this so in the field of procedural law. Here the question posed is— "Shall the courts admit as evidence of a particular fact authentic and reliable records by which alone the fact may be satisfactorily proved?" I think the courts themselves are able to give an affirmative answer to that question.' He was supported by Lord Pearce who said...[His Lordship then quoted from the judgment of Lord Pearce.] Although the views of Lords Donovan and Pearce are those of the minority in the *Myers* case, I am of opinion that this Court should adopt and follow the minority view rather than resort to saying in effect: "This judge-made law needs to be restated to meet modern conditions, but we must leave it to [the Federal] Parliament and the 10 [Provincial] legislatures to do the job." Hospital records, including nurses' notes, made contemporaneously by someone having a personal knowledge of the matters then being recorded and under a duty to make the entry or record should be received in evidence as prima facie proof of the facts stated therein. This should, in no way, preclude a party wishing to challenge the accuracy of the records or entries from doing so. Had the respondent here wanted to challenge the accuracy of the nurses' notes, the nurses were present in Court and available to be called as witnesses if the respondent had so wished. I would, accordingly, allow the appeal and restore the judgment of O'Byrne J., with costs here and in the Appellate Division."

Note.—The trial judge had relied on *Wigmore on Evidence*, (3rd ed.), Vol. 6, para. 1707, which advocates the admission of the original or a certified copy of hospital records.

SUBRAMANIAM v. PUBLIC PROSECUTOR

[1956] 1 W.L.R. 965; [1956] Crim.L.R. 621 (P.C.: 1956)

The repetition by a witness of the statement of an absent person is not hearsay, when the evidence is adduced merely to prove that the statement was made, irrespective of its truth.

The accused was charged with being in possession of ammunition, contrary to the emergency regulations of the Federation of Malaya. His defence was that he was acting under duress, and he sought to give evidence of what had been said to him by terrorists. At the trial the judge excluded this evidence as hearsay, and the accused was convicted, but the Privy Council held that the evidence was admissible, and quashed the conviction.

MR. DE SILVA (delivering the opinion of the Board, which included LORDS RADCLIFFE and TUCKER):...In ruling out peremptorily the evidence of conversation between the terrorists and the appellant the trial judge was in error. Evidence of a statement made to a witness by a person who is not himself called as a witness may or may not be hearsay. It is hearsay and inadmissible when the object of the evidence is to establish the truth of what is contained in the statement. It is not hearsay and is admissible when it is proposed to establish by the evidence, not the truth of the statement, but the fact that it was made. The fact that the statement was made, quite apart from its truth, is frequently relevant in considering the mental state and conduct thereafter of the witness or of some other person in whose presence the statement was made. In the case before their Lordships statements could have been made to the appellant by the terrorists, which, whether true or not, if they had been believed by the appellant, might reasonably have induced him in an apprehension of instant death if he failed to conform to their wishes.

In the rest of the evidence given by the appellant statements made to him by the terrorists appear now and again to have been permitted, probably inadvertently, to go in. But, a complete, or substantially complete, version according to the appellant of what was said to him by the terrorists and by him to them has been shut out. This version, if believed, could and might have afforded cogent evidence of duress brought to bear upon the appellant. Its admission would also have meant that the complete story of the appellant would have been before the trial judge and assessors and enabled them more effectively to have come to a correct conclusion as to the truth or otherwise of the appellant's story. . . .

Note.—See, too, *R.* v. *Willis* [1960] 1 W.L.R. 55 (C.C.A.).

MAWAZ KHAN v. R.

[1967] A.C. 454; [1967] 1 All E.R. 80 (P.C.: 1966)

A statement may be received as original evidence for the purpose of asking the trier of fact to find the assertions contained therein to be false and to draw inferences from their falsity.

LORD HODSON (delivering the advice of the Board which included LORDS PEARCE and PEARSON): This is an appeal from a judgment of the Supreme Court of Hong Kong . . . dismissing the appeals of both appellants against their conviction for murder by the Supreme Court sitting in its criminal jurisdiction with a jury. . . . Both were sentenced to death: each made statements, but neither gave evidence in the witness-box.

The main ground of appeal is that the learned trial judge erred in ruling that a statement made by one accused person in the absence of another could be used for any purpose or in any way against the other. To admit such a statement would, it is said, violate the "hearsay" rule.

Before considering the facts of this case it is convenient to state what is meant by the "hearsay" rule, for contravention of the rule makes evidence inadmissible.

The accepted textbooks on the law of evidence are at one in saying that such statements are inadmissible to prove truth of the matters stated. *Wigmore on Evidence* (3rd ed., Vol. 6, page 178) puts the matter clearly in this way:

"The prohibition of the hearsay rule, then, does not apply to all words or utterances merely as such. If this fundamental principle is clearly realised, its application is a comparatively simple matter. The hearsay rule excludes extrajudicial utterances only when offered for a special purpose, namely, as assertions to evidence the truth of the matter asserted."

The rule has been stated to the same effect as their Lordships in *Subramaniam* v. *Public Prosecutor* [1956] 1 W.L.R. 695. . . .

The case for the prosecution rested on circumstantial evidence. . . .

This circumstantial evidence connected both appellants with the scene of the crime, but the Crown relied strongly upon the fact that each of the appellants had in his respective statement sought to set up a joint alibi which was demonstrated to be false.

Each of the appellants separately told the police that they were at a place called the Ocean Club on the night in question and endeavoured to explain their injuries as having been sustained in a fight between them and as having no connection with the killing of the deceased. Many of the details of their statements were contradicted by the evidence of witnesses. The statement of each appellant was used against him, the judge directing the jury:

"A statement which is made by an accused person in the absence of the other is not evidence against the other: it is evidence against the maker of the statement but against him only."

No complaint was made of this direction, but the learned judge went on to say:

"The Crown's case here is not that these statements are true and that what one says ought to be considered as evidence of what actually happened. What the Crown say is that these statements have been shown to be a tissue of lies and that they disclose an attempt to fabricate a joint story. Now, members of the jury, if you come to that conclusion then the fabrication of a joint story would be evidence against both. It would be evidence that they had co-operated after the alleged crime."

It was submitted that the direction of the learned judge that a statement made by one accused person in the absence of the other is not evidence against that other was nullified by the further direction that the jury were entitled to compare the statements and if they came to the conclusion that they were false that would be evidence that they had co-operated after the alleged crime and jointly concocted the story out of a sense of guilt.

Their lordships are of opinion that this submission, which appealed to one member of the Court of Appeal and no doubt impressed the Chief Justice and Rigby A.J., when they made reference to the importance of the question involved, ought not to be sustained.

Their lordships agree with Hogan C.J. and Rigby A.J. in accepting the generality of the proposition maintained by the text writers and to be found in *Subramaniam's* case ([1956] 1 W.L.R. 965) that a statement is not hearsay and is admissible when it is proposed to establish by the evidence, not the truth of the statement, but the fact that it was made.

Not only therefore can the statements of each appellant be used against each appellant individually, as the learned judge directed, but they can without any breach of the hearsay rule be used, not for the purpose of establishing the truth of the assertions contained therein, but for the purpose of asking the jury to hold the assertions false and to draw inferences from their falsity.

The statements were relevant as tending to show that the makers were acting in concert and that such action indicated a common guilt. This is a factor to be taken into account into conjunction with the circumstantial evidence to which reference has been made in determining the guilt or innocence of the accused persons....

Their lordships are of opinion that there was no misdirection of the jury and will accordingly humbly advise Her Majesty that the appeal be dismissed.

R. v. **Chapman** [1969] 2 Q.B. 436 (C.A.). The accused was convicted of having driven a motor vehicle with blood alcohol concentration above the prescribed limit, contrary to the Road Safety Act 1967, s.1(1). Section 2(2)(*b*) of that Act provides that "a person shall not be required to provide such a specimen [of breath for breath test] while at a hospital as a patient if the medical practitioner in immediate charge of his case is not first notified of the proposal to make the requirement or objects to the provision of a specimen on the ground that its provision or the requirement to provide it would be prejudicial to the proper care or treatment of the patient." A breath test had been administered to the accused whilst in hospital. One of the grounds upon which he appealed against conviction was that the evidence of the police officers to the effect that the casualty officer did not object to the provision of specimens of breath and of blood was hearsay and should not have been admitted. It was contended that it would be necessary in such circumstances for the prosecution to call the doctor to prove affirmatively that he did have no objection. The Court of Appeal rejected this contention. Fenton Atkinson L.J. said (p. 440): "What was to be established here was the fact that Dr. Din made no objection, and in our view it was perfectly proper for the police to give that evidence without Dr. Din being called."

Note.—The lack of objection was treated as a legally objective fact. If a doctor states that he has no objection, this could as a matter of substantive law constitute a failure to object even if he is not speaking the truth. His position is not unlike that of a person who makes a contractual offer: he may thereby alter his legal position even if the offer is not in fact genuine.

In *Woodhouse* v. *Hall* (1981) 72 Cr.App.R. 39 (D.C.) offers of immoral services by women in an alleged brothel were seemingly regarded as objective facts. Donaldson L.J. said (p. 42): "I suspect that the justices... thought that this was a hearsay case, because they may have thought that they had to be satisfied as to the truth of what the ladies said or were alleged to have said in the sense that they had to satisfy themselves that the words were not a joke but were meant seriously and something of that sort. But this is not a matter of truth or falsity.... There is no question here of the hearsay rule arising at all. The relevant issue was did these ladies make these offers?" It is submitted that the matter is, however, more complicated than this would suggest. The disputed evidence was being tendered to show the purposes for which premises were being used. If the "offers" were not genuine they would not be relevant. On the other hand what might be contended is that it is unlikely that such "offers" would be made unless they were genuine. But to base admissibility on this latter ground involves accepting (inconsistently with the hearsay rule, but perhaps not unreasonably) that, when the mere fact that a statement was made will in particular circumstances itself strongly suggest that it was true, reception is warranted even though in those circumstances, it is only relevant on the assumption that it was in fact true.

Woodhouse v. *Hall* appears to have been approved by way of *obiter dictum* in *R.* v. *Harry* (1988) 86 Cr.App.R. 105 (C.A.). However, the actual decision in that case was to the effect that evidence of telephone calls made to a flat seeking to obtain drugs from a co-accused was not admissible on behalf of an accused, both having been charged with possessing and supplying a controlled drug. Such evidence would, it was held, offend against the hearsay rule!

See, too, *Police* v. *Machirus* [1977] 1 N.Z.L.R. 288 (Chapter 15, *infra*) where one member (Woodhouse J.) of the New Zealand Court of Appeal seems to have regarded an attempt to make a bet by telephone as an objective fact. The learned judge said (p. 292): "In my opinion, the words said to have been used by the caller in this particular instance were tendered to prove the truth of any assertion but simply to indicate that there had been an apparent attempt to bet. For that reason I do not think the hearsay rule has any application in the case."

Lloyd v. **Powell Duffryn Steam Coal Co. Ltd.** [1914] A.C. 733 (H.L.). See Chapter 15, p. 368, *infra*.

Ratten v. **R.** [1972] A.C. 378 (P.C.). See Chapter 15, p. 357, *infra*.

R. v. **Cook** [1987] Q.B. 417 (C.A.). A victim of robbery and indecent assault described her attacker to a police officer, who pieced together a photofit picture. At the trial of the appellant for robbery and indecent assault he submitted as a preliminary point that the photofit picture was inadmissible in evidence as being hearsay and a previous consistent statement of the victim. The Court of Appeal held that the judge had acted correctly in rejecting this submission. Watkins L.J., giving the judgment of the Court cited the words of Willes J. in *R.* v. *Tolson* (1864) 4 F. & F. 103, 104: "The photograph was admissible because it is only a visible representation of the image or impression made upon the minds of the witnesses by the sight of the person or the object it represents; and, it therefore is, in reality, only another species of the evidence which persons give of identity, when they speak merely from memory." His Lordship then continued (pp. 424–425): "That ruling has never been doubted and is applied with regularity to photographs, including those taken nowadays automatically in banks during a robbery. Such photographs are invaluable aids to identification of criminals. It has never been suggested of them that they are subject to the rule against hearsay. We regard the production of the sketch or photofit by a police officer making a graphic representation of a witness's memory as another form of the camera at work, albeit imperfectly and not produced contemporaneously with the material incident but soon or fairly soon afterwards. As we perceive it the photofit is not a statement in writing made in the absence of a defendant or anything resembling it in the sense that this very old rule against hearsay has ever been expressed to embrace. It is we think sui generis, that is to say, the only one of its kind. It is a thing apart, the admissibility to evidence of which would not be in breach of the hearsay rule. Seeing that we do not regard the photofit as a statement at all it cannot come within the description of an earlier consistent statement which, save in exceptional circumstances, cannot ever be admissible in evidence. The true position is in our view that the photograph, the sketch and the photofit are in a class of evidence of their own to which neither the rule against hearsay nor the rule against the admission of an earlier consistent statement applies."

Note.—It is submitted that the likening of the photofit to a photograph is crucially fallacious. The photofit was based upon the out-of-court assertions of the victim. A photograph is not based upon out-of-court assertions of anyone but is a direct reproduction of events. The production in court of the photofit is in this respect no different from the classic hearsay case in which what is offered in court is oral testimony based on a declarant's out-of-court assertion. Perhaps the Court in *R.* v. *Cook* was indeed conscious of the shortcomings of the likening of a photofit to a photograph when it went on to describe the photofit as *sui generis*. In this event a pertinent question is as to the reason for this unique treatment. The traditional hearsay dangers are liable to be present. Moreover, there is an additional source of possible unreliability,—there are obvious intrinsic limitations upon the accuracy of photofit technique which are operative even when (which may not always be the case) the particular user is highly skilled.

To be contrasted is the clearly correct holding in *Taylor* v. *Chief Constable of Cheshire* [1986] 1 W.L.R. 1479 (D.C.) where it was held that a witness could without infringing the hearsay rule give evidence as to what he had seen on a video recording. The recording was of events in a shop alleged to constitute theft, but the recording had been accidentally destroyed before the trial. Ralph Gibson L.J. (pp. 1486–1487) saw "no effective distinction so far as concerns admissibility between a direct view of the action of an alleged shoplifter by a security officer and a view of those activities by the officer on the video display unit of a camera, or a view of those activities on a recording of what the camera recorded.... Such evidence is not, in my view, inadmissible because of the hearsay principle. It is direct evidence of what was seen to be happening in a particular place at a particular time and, like all direct evidence, may vary greatly in its weight, credibility and reliability."

Chandrasekera v. **R.** [1937] A.C. 220 (P.C.). At a murder trial evidence that the victim, who was unable to speak owing to the nature of her wounds, had made signs indicating that it was the defendant who had cut her throat was admitted. Lord Roche, giving the Opinion of the Privy Council, seems to have regarded this non-verbal, but assertive, conduct as hearsay, but nevertheless admissible by virtue of a statutory exception (contained in the Ceylon Evidence Ordinance 1895, s.32) substantially similar to the common law exception under which dying declarations are sometimes admissible (see Chapter 14, *infra*).

WRIGHT v. Doe d. TATHAM

7 Ad. & Ell. 313; 2 Nev. & P.K.B. 395; 7 L.J.Ex. 340 (Ex. Chamber: 1837)

and

WRIGHT v. TATHAM

4 Bing. N.C. 489; 6 Scott 58; 5 Cl. & Fin. 650; 7 L.J.Ex. 363; 2 Jur. 462 (H.L.: 1838)

The hearsay rule may apply to assertions implied from non-verbal conduct not intended to be assertive.

When a person's mental condition is in issue the contents of letters upon which he has acted may, if relevant, seemingly be admitted as part of the res gestae.

This was an action concerning land owned by John Marsden, deceased. The defendant, Wright, claimed as devisee under Marsden's will. The plaintiff, Tatham, claimed as heir at law, alleging *inter alia* that the will was void on the grounds of the testator's mental incompetence, and he introduced evidence to this effect. Wright sought in rebuttal to produce letters which had been written to Marsden by persons who knew him well to show that they treated him as sane. The trial judge excluded these letters and the jury found for Tatham. Wright filed a bill of exceptions in the Court of Exchequer Chamber.

PARKE B.: It is argued that the letters would be admissible because they are evidence of the *treatment* of the testator as a competent person by individuals acquainted with his habits and personal character, not using the word *treatment* in a sense involving any *conduct* of the testator himself: that they are more than mere statements to a third person indicating an opinion of his competence of those persons; they are acts done *towards* the testator by them, which would not have been done if he had been incompetent, and from which, therefore, a legitimate inference may, it is argued, be derived that he was so. Each of the three letters, no doubt, indicates that in the opinion of the writer the testator was a rational person. He is spoken of in respectful terms in all. Mr. Ellershaw describes him as possessing hospitality and benevolent politeness; and Mr. Marton addresses him as competent to do business to the limited extent to which his letter calls upon him to act; and there is no question but that, if any one of those writers had been living, his evidence, founded on personal observation, that the testator possessed the qualities which justified the opinion expressed or implied in his letters, would be admissible on this issue. But the point to be determined is, whether *these letters* are admissible as proof that *he did possess these qualities*? I am of the opinion that, according to the established principles of the law of evidence, the letters are all inadmissible for such a purpose....

But the question is, whether the contents of these letters are evidence of the *fact to be proved upon this issue*—that is, the actual existence of the qualities which the testator is, in those letters, by implication, stated to possess; and those letters may be considered in this respect to be on the same footing as if they had contained a direct and positive statement that he was competent. *For this purpose* they are mere hearsay evidence, statements of the writers, not on oath, of the truth of the matter in question, with this addition, that they have acted upon the statements on the faith of their being true, by their sending the letters to the testator. That the so acting cannot give a sufficient sanction for the truth of the statement is perfectly plain; for it is clear that, if the same statements had been made by parol or in writing to a third person, ~~that would have been made by parol or in writing to a third person~~, that would have been insufficient; and this is conceded by the learned counsel for the plaintiff in error....

Let us suppose the parties who wrote these letters to have stated the matter therein contained, that is, their knowledge of his personal qualities and capacity for business, on oath before a magistrate, or in some judicial proceeding to which the plaintiff and defendant were not parties. No one could contend that such statement would be admissible on this issue...;

...the supposed conduct of the family or relations of a testator, taking the same precautions in his absence as if he were a lunatic; his election, in his absence, to some high and responsible office; the conduct of a physician who permitted a will to be executed by a sick testator; the conduct of a deceased captain on a question of seaworthiness, who, after examining every part of a vessel, embarked in it with his family; all these, when deliberately considered are, with reference to the matter in issue in each case, mere instances of hearsay evidence, mere statements, not on oath, but implied in or vouched by the actual conduct of persons whose acts the litigant parties are not to be bound. The conclusion at which I have arrived is, that proof of a particular fact, which is not itself a matter in issue, but which is relevant only as implying a statement or opinion of a third person on the matter in issue, is inadmissible in all cases where such a statement or opinion not on oath would be of itself inadmissible; and, therefore, in this case the letters which are offered only to prove the competence of the testator, that is the truth of the implied statements therein contained, were properly rejected, as the mere statements or opinion of the writer would certainly have been inadmissible. . . .

[The Court of Exchequer Chamber (TINDALL C.J., COLTMAN J., GURNEY B., BOSANQUET J., PARKE B. and PARK J.) agreed unanimously that none of the letters was admissible as an implied declaration by its writer. The members of the court were, however, eventually divided on the further question as to whether the deceased had acted on receipt of the letters. Had he been shown to have done so, this would have rendered the content of the letters admissible as part of the *res gestae*. The trial verdict was confirmed. Wright appealed to the House of Lords, where the House put certain questions to Judges. Excerpts from some of the Judges' answers are set out below.]

COLERIDGE J.: The first ground on which the admissibility of the letters is rested, lays all participation, all acts by Mr. Marsden in regard to them, out of the question; it becomes indifferent whether the letters ever reached him or not; the only things material are the writing and sending—the former shows the opinion of the writer, the latter vouches it. . . . I do not, indeed, concede, although it is not perhaps necessary now to decide the point, that the mere opinion of a witness, even on oath, is, as such, admissible evidence upon a question of competency. . . . But if it be, the argument is by no means relieved from another insuperable difficulty: if opinion, merely as such, be evidence, it cannot be proved by hearsay. . . .

Upon principle, then, I think it abundantly clear, that, upon the first ground suggested, these letters are not receivable. . . .

I am now brought to the consideration of the third ground taken by the counsel for the defendant below; that these letters are admissible, because they accompany and explain acts done by Mr. Marsden; in other words, that there is evidence with respect to each of these letters that Mr. Marsden had done some act, which act would in itself be relevant to and admissible upon the point in issue, his competency, and the act itself being admissible, whatever accompanies it and served to explain its character, is relevant and admissible also. The principle here applied is admitted on all hands to be correct. . . . The only question therefore remaining is on of fact, whether there was any evidence of such act by Mr. Marsden in regard to all or any one of these letters. . . . What is the evidence of these facts? none direct; and every circumstance stated is equally consistent with the assumption of competency or incompetency. . . . The facts then being consistent with either view of the case, he must fail whose duty it is to affirmatively to establish either, and who relies on this for proof. . . .

ALDERSON B.: After fully considering the question which your Lordships have put to the judges, I have also arrived at the conclusion that all the three letters ought to be rejected as evidence upon the trial in question.

These letters were addressed to the testator by persons acquainted with him, and whose opinion as to his capacity if properly proved, would be received as evidence in the cause. . . .

If therefore, the letters are to be used as proofs of the opinion of the writers respecting Mr. Marsden's capacity, the objection for their admissibility is, that this opinion is not upon oath, nor is it possible for the opposite party to test by cross-examination the foundation on which it rests. . . .

But then, lastly, it is said that the letters are receivable as having been acted upon by the testator and as explanatory of his acts; and if that were the case, I should agree in the conclusion.

Every act of the testator is evidence, and if these are letters which qualify, or illustrate, or explain any act of his, they are receivable.

But then, the first step to be taken is to show some act of the testator by clear evidence, for that is the foundation of the whole.

Here, that step wholly fails; this is an attempt to raise a superstructure which has nothing to support it.

If the testator had made an indorsement on any one of them, the contents of the letter would have been receivable. But why? Only for the purpose of showing that the indorsement was a rational act, not for the purpose of showing the opinion of the writer. If an answer to the letter had been sent by him, the letter is in like manner receivable to show the rationality of such answer. . . .

PARKE B.: . . . These letters . . . indicate the opinion of the writers that the alleged testator was a rational person and capable of doing acts of ordinary business. But it is perfectly clear that in this case an opinion not given upon oath in a judicial inquiry between the parties is no evidence; for the question is not what the capacity of the testator was reputed to be, but what it really was in point of fact; and though the opinion of a witness upon oath, as to that fact, might be asked, it would only be a compendious mode of ascertaining the result of the actual observation of the witness, from acts done, so to the habits and demeanour of the deceased. Nor is the evidence the more admissible, because the persons writing the letters do not merely express an opinion in writing, but prove their belief of it by acting upon it to the extent of sending the letters and putting them in the course of reaching the person addressed. After all, it is but an expression of an opinion vouched by an act, and by an act not so strong by any means as others done to third persons, which are allowed on all hands to be inadmissible; not even so strong nor so confirmatory of the truth of the communication as a simple letter written to another man. If the opinion of a person be of itself inadmissible, the act which only proves the belief of that person in its truth, and is irrelevant to the issue, except for that purpose, cannot render it admissible.

Besides that, there is another ground, and the only other ground on which these letters are argued to be receivable in evidence, and that is, that there was proof in this case of acts done by the testator or in reference to these letters, or at least one of them, which render the contents admissible by way of explanation of those acts. Those acts are the opening of two of the letters, and placing them in the supposed usual repository of the papers of the deceased, and the opening of the third one, and transmitting it to the attorney. . . .

The answer to this argument is, that there is no direct proof whatever of these acts being done by the testator; and as to indirect proof, to infer that the testator did the acts is to assume the very fact to be proved. . . .

WILLIAMS PATTESON, VAUGHAN and LITTLEDALE JJ., TINDAL C.J., GURNEY B., BOSANQUET J., BOLLAND B. and PARK J. agreed. The House of Lords affirmed the verdict in favour of the plaintiff.

Note.—The state of mind of the testator was primarily relevant at the time when his will was executed, but sanity and other states of mind may be continuing facts.

For the admissibility of declarations as to state of mind as part of the *res gestae*, see Chapter 15, *infra.*

Chapter 14

HEARSAY: EXCEPTIONS TO THE RULE

BASICALLY the materials set out in this Chapter are concerned with the reception of hearsay evidence in criminal[1] cases by way of exception to the common law rule excluding such evidence.[2] Most of the categories of such exceptional admissibility are themselves creatures of the common law, but several statutory provisions, particular the Criminal Justice Act 1988, Part II, make inroads into the exclusionary rule.[3] The applicability in civil cases of some of the exceptions which were established at common law (and which were dealt with in the present Chapter) has been preserved in slightly differing degrees by section 9 of the Civil Evidence Act 1968.[4] Indeed, the practical importance of some of these common law exceptions to the hearsay rule lies, not in their survival as such in criminal cases, but rather in their statutory preservation as in effect independent rules of admissibility in civil cases.

The exceptions to the hearsay rule, with which materials set out, or referred to, in the present Chapter are concerned, have been classified thus: A. Statements by deceased persons; B. Statements in public documents; C. Evidence given in former proceedings; D. Informal admissions; and E. Certain statutory exceptions.

There are six readily identifiable categories of admissible hearsay statements by deceased persons.[5] They are (i) declarations made in the course of duty; (ii) declarations against interest; (iii) declarations as to pedigree; (iv) declarations as to public and general rights; (v) dying declarations; and (vi) declarations by testators as to the contents of their wills. These exceptions are based in part upon the indisputable and permanent non-availability of the declarant as a witness. It is, however, a matter for remark that non-availability for reasons other than death does not suffice: proof, for instance, that the declarant at the time of the

---

[1] Most of these exceptions, like the hearsay rule itself, are also still applicable in civil cases before Magistrates' Courts, because Pt. I of the Civil Evidence Act 1968 is not yet applicable in these courts.

[2] The materials relating to the admissibility of evidence of confessions, which, in addition to constituting an exception to the hearsay rule, has other implications, are set out separately in Chap. 17. Those common law exceptions to the hearsay rule which have been associated with the inclusionary phenomena of *res gestae* have been treated along with consideration of that doctrine in Chap. 15.

[3] Part Two *infra*. See, too, *e.g.* the Criminal Justice Act 1967, s.9, and the Theft Act 1968, s.27(4) (both Part Two, *infra*).

[4] Part Two, *infra*; see, too, Chap. 16, *infra*.

[5] There are in adddition other miscellaneous and less well-defined groups of cases.

trial is incurably insane, or cannot be found or is absent in a remote part of the world is not enough. It is to be noted that the practical importance of the admissibility of statements by deceased persons, as such, is now limited. Dying declarations apart, they are not often material in criminal cases; and of those listed above only declarations as to pedigree and declarations as to public and general rights are included amongst the categories of hearsay evidence the admissibility of which is preserved in civil cases by the Civil Evidence Act 1968, s.9.

The admissibility of statements contained in public documents is now largely covered by a multiplicity of statutes, but the common law exception retains an interstitial role. This is preserved by section 9 of the 1968 Act.

At common law evidence of oral testimony (and sometimes depositions) given by a witness in former proceedings (or an earlier stage of the same proceedings) was, and in criminal cases still is, admissible to prove the facts then stated.[6] Reception of such evidence is subject to following conditions: (1) both proceedings must be between the same parties or persons in privity with them; (2) there must be an identity of issue; (3) the party (or person in privity with him) against whom the evidence is tendered must have had a full opportunity to cross-examine on the former occasion; and (4) the witness must be unavailable as a witness at the later proceedings.

An informal admission by words (or sometimes by silence) and/or non-verbal conduct (including sometimes mere inactivity) by a party, or by a person in privity with him, is admissible against that party as evidence of the fact so admitted.

An informal admission differs fundamentally from a formal admission.[7] The effect of the latter is that the fact admitted ceases to be in issue: in this sense the admission is conclusive. An informal admission is simply a piece of admissible evidence the weight of which is to be assessed by the trier of fact. If the informal admission is made out of court (*i.e.* not by the party, or person in privity with him, whilst testifying in the instant proceedings), a hearsay problem will often be presented because the purpose of tendering evidence of the admission is usually to show its truth. The principal, but not the sole, objective of the law relating to the reception in evidence of informal admissions is the accommodation of this problem.

The reception of an informal admission is also to be kept distinct from the reception, on an issue of credibility, of the previous statement of any witness, whether or not a party. The making of an informal admission may be proved by a witness, or by questioning the party himself if he testifies. In the latter event a double analysis may be involved if the declaration is tendered both as the party's informal admission, and as a prior inconsistent statement with a view to impugning his credibility *qua* witness.

There are several ways in which an informal admission, seen as an exception to the hearsay rule, differs from a declaration against interest. The declarant against interest may be any person provided he is deceased at the time of the proceedings; whereas an admission must

---

[6] This evidence is also still admissible in civil proceedings in Magistrates' Courts: see note (1), *supra*. But admissiblity under this heading in civil cases generally is seemingly eliminated by the Civil Evidence Act 1968. s.1(1) (Part two, *infra*).

[7] See Chap. 6, *supra*..

have been made by a party to the proceedings or by someone in privity with him. A declaration against interest must have been against the pecuniary or proprietary interest of the declarant, who usually had no interest in the outcome of possible proceedings; whereas an admission must be in some way adverse to the party's interest in the outcome of the actual proceedings. The declaration against interest must, at the time it was made, have been known, or thought, by the declarant to be against his interest; whereas an admission must be in fact adverse to the party's interest at the time of proceedings.

As a result of the preservation in the Civil Evidence Act 1968[8] of the common law admissibility of admissions, legal doctrine relating to informal admissions, as such, remains basically the same in both criminal and civil proceedings. There is, however, a long established and important restriction upon the reception of otherwise admissible informal admissions in criminal cases. When such an admission is made by an accused person and concerns a material element of the offence charged it is dubbed a "confession," and to secure its reception in evidence against him there must be compliance with sections 76 and 77 of the Police and Criminal Evidence Act 1984.[9] Materials dealing with the admissibility of confessions and with related matters are set out in Chapter 17.

An admission is admissible evidence against a party only if made by him or by a person in privity with him. The meaning of privity in this context is idiosyncratic. The reception of so-called "vicarious" admissions is based to some extent on actual or implied authorisation and to some extent on identity of interest. There is no privity between joint parties (*e.g.* between co-plaintiffs, co-defendants, co-accuseds or co-respondents) as such. Nor is there automatic privity between spouses. On the other hand an admission by a predecessor in title of a party to the litigation in which it is tendered, is admissible evidence against the party to the extent that it relates to the title and was made at a time when the maker had the interest qualified by the statement. Also, in certain circumstances the statements of a person, to whom a party has referred others for information, may be proved against him as admissions in so far as they relate to the subject-matter of the reference. Again, the admissions of one conspirator will be admitted against his co-conspirators to the extent, but only to the extent, that they relate to acts done in furtherance of the conspiracy. This principle probably extends also the cases other than conspiracy in which the prosecution alleges concerted action by two or more persons in preparation for, or assisting in, the commission of a crime. So far as partners are concerned the Partnership Act 1890, s.15,[10] perpetuating a common law principle, provides that an admission made by a partner concerning partnership affairs and made in the ordinary course of partnership business is evidence against the firm. Similarly there is old authority[11] for the view that an admission made by one of several people, jointly interested in a contract or particular piece of property, is evidence against the others, provided it was made during the subsistence of the interest.

There is, however, considerable uncertainty as to the extent to which

---

[8] s.9(1), (2)(*a*).
[9] Part Two, *infra*.
[10] Part Two, *infra*.
[11] *Jaggers* v. *Binnings* (1815) 1 Stark. 64.

a principal is vicariously bound by the admissions of his agent. A pre-condition of the reception of the admission of an agent is, of course, that a relationship of agency in a broad sense be established.[12] If the making of the admission was authorised by the principal, or if it formed a natural part of an authorised conversation or correspondence, it will be admissible as evidence against him. The agent's authority may be express or implied, it may be imposed by statute, or it may derive from some other rule of substantive law. On the other hand, it is clear that, if the admission was neither authorised nor made in the course of an authorised communication, and, although made during the subsistence of the relationship of principal and agent, was not made in the course of employment, it will not be admissible against the principal.[13] What is uncertain is the position if the admission, although unauthorised and not made in the course of an authorised communication, was made in the course of the agent's employment in the sense in which that phrase is used in the law of torts. Satisfactory resolution of this uncertainty cannot be rationally achieved simply by reference to the purposes of the hearsay rule and factors affecting reliability: consideration of the policies underlying the substantive law of vicarious responsibility must also be involved.

Indeed the general pattern of the law relating to the admissibility of informal admissions can only be fully appreciated if the subject is not seen solely in terms of the hearsay rule and questions of reliability. This segment of the law of evidence relates as well to the nature of the adversary process of trial. There is an underlying notion that a party ought to be "saddled with" responsibility for his admissions, even if in a particular case the admission does not bear any special stamp of reliability. An informal admission has in this respect some affinity with a formal admission, although, unlike the latter, it is in no sense conclusive. This aspect of the matter is reflected in the definition of informal admissions, and also in some of the limitations upon their admissibility; it is to be seen, for example, in the rule that an admission is available only against the party who makes it, and in the width of responsibility for vicarious admissions.

The present Chapter also contains materials relating to a rule of evidence rather different from, but in practice closely associated with, that providing for the reception of informal admissions. This rule is to the effect that statements made in the presence of a party are themselves admissible by way of introduction to evidence of his or her reaction to them, which reaction may prove to constitute an admission or to be otherwise relevant; but, if this latter does in fact not prove to be the case, the evidence of the introductory statement may then have to be disregarded.

There is a considerable number of statutes which provide for the admissibility of hearsay evidence in criminal cases. Most of them are of limited scope in that they are concerned only with proof of specified facts and/or are applicable only in particular proceedings. The Theft Act 1968, s.27(4)[14] is a good (and important) example. It provides that, in proceedings for the theft of goods in transmission or for the handling of goods so stolen, a statutory declaration by the sender (or recipient) that

---

[12] See *R.* v. *Evans* [1981] Crim.L.R. 699 (C.A.) and *Note* thereon, p. 339 *infra*.
[13] *Burr* v. *Ware R.D.C.* [1939] 2 All E.R. 688 (C.A.), *infra*, would seem to support this.
[14] Part Two, *infra*.

the goods were despatched (or received) is admissible as evidence of that fact and of the condition of the goods, provided that due notice has been given to the accused, and that he has not required the maker of the declaration to be called as a witness. There are in addition statutory provisions of more general significance. Two of these are section 9 of the Criminal Justice Act 1967[15] and Part II of the Criminal Justice Act 1988.[16] The former provides for the admission in certain circumstances in criminal cases of agreed statements of facts to the same extent and with the same effect as admissible oral evidence. The main requirements for such admissibility are that the statement should be signed and that it should contain a declaration of the maker's knowledge that it was made subject to penalties in the event of its being used in evidence if the maker knew it to be false or did not care whether it was true; that a copy should have been served on the opposing party; and that no notice of objection should have been received from that party within seven days. However, the parties may agree to waive the requirements relating to notice and non-receipt of objection. The ultimate source of Part II of the Criminal Justice Act 1988 was the Criminal Evidence Act 1965, which was itself enacted in consequence of, and in order to reverse, the majority decision of the House of Lords in *Myers* v. *Director of Public Prosecutions*.[17] More immediately it has replaced and extended the provisions of section 68 of the Police and Criminal Evidence Act 1984. It provides for the reception in criminal proceedings of certain important categories of documentary hearsay. This is without prejudice to any admissibility at common law. Section 69 of the 1984 Act makes provision for the admissibility in criminal proceedings of certain evidence of computer records. Section 29 of the 1988 Act allows for the reception in criminal proceedings of expert reports with leave of the court, the hearsay rule notwithstanding.

A. STATEMENTS BY DECEASED PERSONS

(i) DECLARATIONS MADE IN THE COURSE OF DUTY

PRICE v. TORRINGTON (EARL)

1 Salk. 285; 2 Ld. Raym. 873; Holt, K.B. 300; 90 E.R. 1065; 2 Sm. L.C. (13th ed.) 296 (Nisi Prius: 1703)

Statements made by a person in the regular course of his business or duty are admissible evidence of the facts stated in criminal proceedings after his death. Such statements are known as declarations in the course of a duty.

[This was an action in *indebitatus assumpsit* for beer sold and delivered to the defendant, tried at *nisi prius* before Holt C.J.]

---

[15] Part Two, *infra.*
[16] Part Two, *infra.*
[17] [1965] A.C. 1001. See Chap. 13, *supra.*

The plaintiff being a brewer, brought an action against the Earl of Torrington for beer sold and delivered, and the evidence given to charge the defendant was, that the usual way of the plaintiff's dealing was that the draymen came every night to the clerk of the brewhouse and gave him an account of the beer they had delivered out, which he set down in a book kept for that purpose, to which the draymen set their hands; and that the drayman was dead, but that this was his hand set to the book; and this was held good evidence of a delivery; otherwise of the shop-book itself, without more.

Note.—The last phrase probably refers to a previous decision of Holt C.J. (*Pitman* v. *Maddox* (1699) Holt, K.B. 298) that such statements were inadmissible, unless they fell within the provisions of the Shop-Books Evidence Act 1609, or there was some other ground of admissibility. In the case above the fact that the drayman was dead provided the necessary ground for admitting evidence of his statement. But compare *Brain* v. *Preece* (1843) 11 M. & W. 773, where records of coal sold by a workman were made on behalf of a foreman by a third person; and, after the death of both the workman and the foreman, the records were held inadmissible.

There must be a duty to do the act and also to record it. Moreover, the duty must be owed to another person to do and to record the matter in question (see, for example, *Massey* v. *Allen* (1879) 13 Ch.D. 558; *Mills* v. *Mills* (1920) 36 T.L.R. 772; *Simon* v. *Simon* [1936] P. 17.

A declaration made in the course of duty is evidence only of the precise facts which it was the writer's duty to state or record, and not of other matters which, though contained in the same statement, were collateral to the duty: see *Chambers* v. *Bernasconi (infra)*.

Chambers v. **Bernasconi** (1834) 3 L.J.Ex. 373 (Ex.Ch.). The question being whether A was arrested in a certain parish, a certificate by a deceased officer, stating the fact, time and place of the arrest, was held inadmissible as to the place. Although it was the officer's practice to record the place of arrest, it was his duty merely to record the fact and time, not the place, of the arrest. Lord Denman C.J., delivering the judgment of the court, said (p. 381): "We are all of opinion that, whatever effect may be due to an entry made in the course of any office reporting facts necessary to the performance of a duty, the statement of other circumstances, however naturally they might be thought to find a place in the narrative, is no proof of those circumstances. Admitting, then, for the sake of argument, that the entry tendered was evidence on the fact, and even of the day when the arrest was made (both which facts it might be necessary for the officer to make known to his principal), we are all clearly of opinion that it is not admissible to prove in what particular spot within the bailiwick the caption took place, that circumstance being merely collateral to the duty done."

Note.—In the later case of *Smith* v. *Blakey* (1867) L.R. 2 Q.B. 326, Blackburn J. said— "... [I]t is an essential fact to render such an entry admissible, that not only it should have been made in the due discharge of the business about which the person is employed, but the duty must be to do the very thing to which the entry relates, and then to make a report or record of it." The act must already have been done at the time that the report or record is made. In *Rowlands* v. *De Vecchi* (1882) 1 Cab. & El. 10, an office record of letters to be posted and kept by a clerk who had since died was held inadmissible as evidence that a particular letter entered in the record had in fact been posted. (Contrast the position relating to the admissibility of declarations of intention under the doctrine of *res gestae*, Chapter 15, *infra*).

The Henry Coxon (1878) 47 L.J. Adm. 83 (Admiralty). In an action against the owners of a ship in respect of a collision, entries made in the log book of a ship by the first mate, since deceased, were rejected on three grounds: (1) they were made two days after the occurrence recorded, whereas the duty was to make them immediately; (2) the first mate had an interest to misrepresent, so as to negative any imputation of negligence by himself and the ship's crew; (3) the entries referred not only to his own acts, but those of the crew. Phillmore J. said (p. 83): "Neither do I think that the entry can be considered as contemporaneous; also it was in the interest of the party who made it; and the authorities point to this, that when such evidence is admitted, it must relate to acts done by the person who makes the entry and not by others, but the mate must enter, not only the manoeuvres of his own ship, but also the consequences of the manoeuvres and navigation of the other ship. These different sets of facts are so inextricably mixed up that it is very difficult, if not impossible, to separate them. I therefore, for these reasons, reject this evidence. . . . "

Note.—The case of *Mercer* v. *Denne* [1904] 2 Ch. 534 at 540–542 (on appeal, see p. 325 *infra*), also illustrates the rule that the acts recorded must be those of the declarant and not of other persons. Regarding log-books see the Merchant Shipping Act, 1970, s.68 and s.75.

R. v. **McGuire** (1985) 81 Cr.App.R. 323 (C.A.). The accused was charged with arson of a hotel owned by his wife. The prosecution case was that the fire had been started in or around room 13. A Mr. Draper, a Senior Scientific Officer, had inspected the premises shortly after the fire had been extinguished. He had made working notes as to what he saw and had later appended a report as to his opinion on the seat of the fire. That opinion was that the fire, as likely as not, had started in a different room. This Officer died before the trial. The defence sought to have put in evidence a document containing these working notes and his opinion. The Court of Appeal held that at the trial the judge had rightly admitted the notes but excluded the statement of opinion. The Lord Chief Justice, in the course of reviewing the authorities dating back to *Price* v. *Torrington* (*supra*), observed that, both the exclusion of collateral matters (see, *e.g. Chambers* v. *Bonascioni, supra*), and the contemporaneity or near-contemporaneity, requirement (see, *e.g. The Henry Coxon, supra*), strongly indicated that statements of opinion are not with the exception to the hearsay rule. His Lordship cited *Cross on Evidence* as a statement of the rationale of this exception: "The grounds of the exception appear to be that, in many cases, it would be impossible to obtain other evidence of the servant's acts after his death, and, in most cases, the likelihood of detection if errors were made together with the sanction of dismissal if the duty were unfulfilled afford some guarantee of the trustworthiness of the statement" (now *op. cit.* 6th ed., p. 571). Lord Lane continued (p. 330): "All those considerations applied to the notes made by Mr. Draper of his observations at the scene of the fire: the measurements and so on; and the judge was plainly right to admit those. They do not however, it seems to us, apply in the same way to the opinion of Mr. Draper. First of all, taking the difficulty or impossibility of obtaining other evidence. . . . There is no reason why another expert should not, having apprised himself of the contents of those notes, have come to an opinion as to the seat of the fire. Secondly, it can be noted from a number of the decisions . . . that one of the grounds for admitting the evidence is the mechanical nature of the note-taking, the routing nature, which in itself is some guarantee of the accuracy of the notes. There was nothing mechanical or routine about the opinion. Thirdly, it seems to us, opinions are certainly not subject to the sort of checking by the employer which Professor Cross in this book refers to as a part of the rationale of the exception to the hearsay rule."

(II) DECLARATIONS AGAINST INTEREST

HIGHAM v. RIDGWAY

10 East 109; 103 E.R. 717; 2 Smith L.C. (13th ed.) 284 (K.B.: 1808)

In criminal proceedings, statements made by a person against his pecuniary interest are admissible evidence, after his death, not only of the facts against such interest but also of connected facts in the same statement. Such statements are known as declarations against interest.

Entries in a day-book made by a deceased male midwife, of his having delivered a woman of a child on a certain day, and in his ledger, in which he had made a charge for his attendance marked as "paid," were held evidence of the date of birth of the child. The word "paid" was held to be a statement against the pecuniary interest of the midwife, as affording evidence against him if he had sued for his charges. All the facts stated, including those in the day-book, with which the ledger was connected, were considered part of the same entry, and were held admissible in evidence.

LORD ELLENBOROUGH C.J.: . . . I think the evidence here was properly admitted, upon the broad principle on which receiver's books have been admitted; namely, that the entry made was in prejudice of the party making it. In the case of the receiver, he charges himself to account for so much to his employer. In this case the party repelled by his entry a claim which he would otherwise have had upon the other for work performed, and medicines furnished to the wife; and the period of her delivery is the time for which the former charge is made, the date of which is April 22; when it appears by other evidence that the man-midwife was in fact attending at the house of Wm. Fowden. If this entry had been produced when the party was making a claim for his attendance, it would have been evidence against him that this claim was satisfied. It is idle to say that the word "paid" only shall be admitted in evidence without the context, which explains to what it refers; we must, therefore, look to the rest of he entry, to see what the demand was which he thereby admitted to be discharged. By reference to the ledger, the entry there is virtually incorporated with and made a part of the other entry of which it is explanatory. . . . The discharge in the book in his own handwriting repels the claim which he would otherwise have had against the father from the rest of the evidence as it now appears. Therefore, the entry made by the party was to his own immediate prejudice, when he had not only no interest to make it, if it were not true, but he had an interest the other way, not to discharge a claim, which it appears from the evidence that he had. . . .

LE BLANC, BAYLEY and GROSE JJ. concurred.

Note.—To be admissible as a declaration against interest the declaration must have been against the declarant's interest, and known by him to be so, at the time when it was made. There is, however, a conflict of opinion as to whether it is sufficient to show only prima facie that this was the case or it must be shown that it never could be made available for the declarant. Blackburn J. seems to have subscribed to the latter view in *Smith* v. *Blakey* (1867) L.R. 2 Q.B. 326, 331–332; and there are dicta in later cases to the same effect (*e.g. per* Hamilton L.J. in *Ward* v. *H.S. Pitt & Co.* [1913] 2 K.B. 130, 137 (C.A.); this case is reported together with *Lloyd* v. *Powell Duffryn Steam Coal Co. Ltd.*, which went to the

House of Lords ([1914] A.C. 733) where it was decided on other grounds, see Chapter 15, *infra*). However, in *Re Adams* [1922] P.240 a declaration which was prima facie against interest was admitted, and evidence was rejected that in the circumstances in which it was made it was in fact to the declarant's advantage. See, too, *Coward* v. *Motor Insurance Bureau* [1963] 1 Q.B. 529 (C.A.).

Another condition of admissibility probably is that the declarant must be shown to have had personal knowledge of the facts stated. This was emphasised in the House of Lords in *The Sussex Peerage Case* (1884) 11 Cl. & Finn. 85, 112 (*infra*) and *Sturla* v. *Freccia* (1880) 5 App. Cas. 623, 632–633, and it formed the *ratio* in the Court of Appeal in *Ward* v. *H.S. Pitt & Co.* (*supra*). But contrast, *e.g. Crease* v. *Barrett* (1835) 1 Cr. M. & R. 919.

A record of a future legal liability is not within the rule (*R.* v. *Worth (Inhabitants)* (1843) 4 Q.B. 132; and see *Smith* v. *Blakey* (1867) L.R. 2 Q.B. 326). But a present moral obligation, as under an arrangement to pay money which is not intended to create legal relations, is seemingly within the rule (*Coward* v. *Motor Insurers' Bureau, supra*). The declaration must be unilateral or "bare," so that, if it were made as part of a contractual promise not under seal, it would not qualify as being against interest. So, too, in *Ward* v. *H.S. Pitt & Co.* (*supra*) a declaration by a deceased workman to the effect that he promised to marry the mother of the child upon whose behalf workmen's compensation was being claimed was held by the Court of Appeal to be inadmissible as evidence of that promise, it being given in consideration of her promise to marry him.

PEACEABLE d. UNCLE v. WATSON

4 Taunt. 16; 128 E.R. 232 (Common Pleas: 1811)

Statements made by a person against his proprietary interest are admissible evidence in criminal proceedings after his death.
Statements made by any one in possession of land, tending to limit his interest therein to any less estate than a fee simple, are admissible as declarations against his proprietary interest, possession being evidence of ownership in fee simple, until the contrary appears.

In an action of ejectment, in order to prove the seisin of a person through whom the plaintiff claimed, a witness was asked whether he had ever heard one Clarke (since deceased) say to whom he rented certain houses; but the identity of the houses was not established. Grose J. rejected the evidence and nonsuited the plaintiff. A new trial was granted on the ground appearing below.

SIR J. MANSFIELD C.J.: The opinion of Grose J. is unanswerable. The ground of the rejection is this. Possession is prima facie evidence of seisin in fee simple; the declaration of the possessor that he is tenant to another makes most strongly, therefore, against his own interest, and consequently is admissible, but it must first be shown that he was in possession of the premises for which the ejectment is brought. The learned judge's report, however, seems to go further, and to intimate that he should have rejected the evidence of the declarations whether there had or had not been other evidence to identify the premises which Clarke held, as those that were sued for.

LAWRENCE J. agreed.

Note.—This decision is based on the rule that possession of land is evidence of ownership in fee simple. Otherwise it might be difficult to say that a statement was against the occupier's proprietary interest. The essence of the matter is that the man in possession of land is presumed to be the owner in fee simple till he is shown to have done or said something which rebuts that presumption. So a statement that land is held on a tenancy at an annual rent is against interest (*R.* v. *Overseers . . . of Birmingham* (1861) 1 B. & S. 763). Again, the statement by a deceased occupier of land that it was subject to an equitable charge is admissible (see *Homes* v. *Newman* [1931] 2 Ch. 112).

The operation of the principle is limited by the rule of substantive law that a tenant must not derogate from his landlord's title. In *Papendick* v. *Bridgwater* (1855) 24 L.J.Q.B. 289 (Q.B.) a declaration by a deceased tenant of a farm, to the effect that he was not entitled to common pasture in respect of the farm, was held not to be admissible in evidence against the reversioner, his landlord. There Lord Campbell C.J. said (p. 291): "You cannot receive in evidence a declaration of a tenant which derogates from the title of the landlord. Such evidence, if receivable. would be most mischievous, because a tenant might thus destroy a valuable easement or be enabled to impose a servitude."

Cases as to declarations against proprietary interest may be compared with the case as to admissions by predecessors in title (*Woolway* v. *Rowe* (1834) 1 Ad. & Ell. 114, *infra*).

Sussex Peerage Case (1844) 11 Cl. & Finn. 85 (H.L.). Evidence of a statement made to his son by a deceased clergyman concerning a marriage ceremony at which he had officiated was held to be inadmissible as evidence of the marriage, although it tended to expose the clergyman to criminal liability under the Royal Marriages Act 1772. Lord Brougham said: "The rule as understood now is that the only declarations of deceased persons receivable in evidence are those made against the pecuniary or proprietary interest of the maker."

Note.—It has been pointed out (Baker, *The Hearsay Rule*, p. 70) that, even if declarations exposing the declarant to merely penal (as distinct from pecuniary or proprietary) consequences were admissible, the evidence in this case would seem still to be inadmissible as there was no evidence that the declarant was aware of the dangers to which he was exposing himself, the marriage having been celebrated abroad.

Moreover, in modern times, when most criminal penalties are, and are known to be, pecuniary in nature, the limits of the rule laid down in the *Sussex Peerage Case* become blurred. All that can perhaps be said is that a declaration exposing the declarant to criminal liability (and presumably *a fortiori* to civil liability or mere social stigma) are not *per se*, against interest. In *R.* v. *Turner* (1975) 61 Cr.App.R. 78 (C.A.) it was held *inter alia* that the trial judge had rightly refused to admit evidence that a third party, who was not called as a witness, had confessed to having committed the offence charged. The doctrine of the *Sussex Peerage case* was impliedly accepted by the House of Lords in *R.* v. *Blastland* [1986] A.C. 41 (Chapter 15, *infra*). It may be noted that in *B.* v. *Attorney General* [1965] P.278 Willmer L.J., sitting as a trial judge, considered (at p. 286) it to be arguable that a declaration exposing the declarant "to the risk of being cited as co-respondent in any such divorce proceedings, with all the consequences that might follow from that," would be against interest.

R. v. **O'Brien** [1978] 1 S.C.R. 591; 76 D.L.R. (3d.) 513 (Supreme Court of Canada). O'Brien and Jensen were jointly charged with possession of narcotics for the purpose of trafficking. O'Brien was arrested and convicted; Jensen fled the country. Following O'Brien's conviction, Jensen returned to Canada. He then told O'Brien's counsel that he, Jensen, alone had committed the act. He agreed to testify to that effect, but died before any re-hearing or appeal. The substantial question before the Supreme Court of Canada was to the admissibility of evidence of Jensen's statement to O'Brien's counsel. Dickson J., delivering the unanimous judgment of the Supreme Court, said: "The effect of the rule in the *Sussex Peerage* case, as it has been generally understood, is to render admissible a statement by a deceased that he had received payment of a debt from another or that he held a parcel of land as tenant and not as owner, but to render inadmissible a confession by a deceased that he and not someone else was the real perpetrator of the crime. The distinction is arbitrary and tenuous. There is little or no reason why declarations against penal interest and those against pecuniary or proprietary interest should not stand on the same footing. A person is as likely to speak the truth in a matter affecting his liberty as in a matter affecting his pocketbook. For these reasons and the ever-present possibility that a rule of absolute prohibition could lead to grave injustice I would hold that, in a proper case, a declaration against penal interest is admissible, according to the law of Canada; the rule as to absolute exclusion of declarations against penal interest, established in *The Sussex Peerage* case, should not be followed. There is a further question. Can it be said that Jensen's declarations to Mr. Simons qualifies as a declaration against penal interest? . . . To be admissible there must be a realisation by the declarant that the statement may well be used against him. That is the very thing Jensen wished to avoid. He had no intention of furnishing evidence against himself. His obvious desire was not to create damaging evidence, detrimental to his penal interest. Yet, that is the very basis upon which admissibility of extra judicial declarations of penal interest rests. In my opinion, the statement of Jensen to Mr. Simons failed to meet the requirement for admissibility. Viewed from Jensen's subjectivity, the statements were not against interest." On the facts the evidence was therefore held to have been rightly excluded.

Note.—In the later case of *Demeter* v. *R.* (1977) 75 D.L.R. (3d.) 251 the Supreme Court of Canada again indicated that in many situations declarations of deceased persons against penal interest will be admissible. It is, however, to be noted that in *R.* v. *Pelletier* (1978) 38 C.C.C. (2d.) 515 (Ont. C.A.), one of the few reported cases in which such evidence has been actually held to have been rightly received for the purpose of exculpating an accused, the statement had been made to the police. Moreover, such evidence will never be admitted if it would have an inculpatory effect on an accused: *Lucier* v. *R.* (1982) 132 D.L.R. (3d.) 244 (S.C. Can.). In Australia in a judgment embodying a full review of the authorities and policy considerations, *In re van Beelen* (1974) 9 S.A.S.R. 163 (C.C.A. of South Australia), a declaration against penal interest was held to be inadmissible.

Federal Rules of Evidence (U.S.), Rule 804. " . . . (b) . . . The following are not excluded by the hearsay rule if the declarant is unavailable as a witness . . . :(3) Statement against interest.—A statement which was at the time of its making so far contrary to the declarant's pecuniary or proprietary interest, or so far tended to subject him to civil or criminal liability, or to render invalid a claim by him against another, that a reasonable man in his position would not have made the statement unless he believed it to be true. A statement tending to expose the declarant to criminal liability and offered to exculpate the accused is not admissible unless corroborating circumstances clearly indicate the trustworthiness of the statement."

Note.—Although the qualitative nature of the interest is extended, its quantitative nature is restricted by the use of the words "so far." Notice, too, that under the Federal Rules declarations against interest (like several other declarations admissible at common law only if made by deceased persons) are rendered admissible if the declarant is unavailable (as broadly defined in para. (a) of the Rule 804).

The doctrine of the *Sussex Peerage* case was accepted by the Supreme Court of the United States, only over a powerful dissent by Holmes J. in *Donnelly* v. *United States* (1913) 228 U.S. 243.

Taylor v. **Witham** (1876) 3 Ch.D. 605 (Ch.). The question was whether A (deceased) had lent money to B. An entry by A in his book, "B paid me three months' interest," followed by other entries connected therewith, and pointing to such a loan, was held admissible as evidence of the loan. The entry of such payment, by itself being against interest, was held to render admissible the connected entries, although the latter were actually in the declarant's interest.

Note.—This rule as to the admissibility of the whole declaration should be compared with the rule that, in the case of declarations in course of duty, only so much thereof as it was strictly the declarant's duty to state is legally admissible (see *Chambers* v. *Bernasconi* (1834) 3 L.J. Ex. 373 (Ex.Ch.), *supra*).

In *Taylor* v. *Witham*, Jessell M.R., having stated that for a declaration to have been made against interest it is sufficient if it was "prima facie and in its natural meaning, standing alone" against interest, went on to indicate (p. 607) that any notice to misrepresent goes to the weight rather than to the admissibility of a declaration against interest.

(III) DECLARATIONS AS TO PEDIGREE

Goodright d. Stevens v. **Moss** (1777) 2 Cowp. 591 (K.B.). In an action of ejectment, the question was whether a certain person was the legitimate child of his parents. Declarations by his father and mother, then deceased, that he was born before marriage was held admissible. Lord Mansfield C.J. said (p. 000): "An entry in a father's family Bible, an inscription on a tombstone, a pedigree hung up in the family mansion, are all good evidence. So [too] the declarations of parents in their lifetime...."

Note.—The common law exception to the hearsay rule permitting the reception of declarations as to pedigree is still, as such, available in criminal cases and in civil proceedings before Magistrates Courts: but the practical importance of this is obviously limited. The operation of the rule in other civil litigation is, however, statutorily preserved by section 9 of the Civil Evidence Act 1968, but only to the extent that the evidence would not be admissible under sections 2 or 4 of that Act. If evidence is to be admitted under section 2 or 4, there must have been compliance with the safeguards concerning the serving of notice (although this is obviated if the declarant is dead), and it is to be remembered that admissibility under section 2 is limited to first-hand hearsay; but, if reliance is placed upon section 9, although the notice requirements and other limitations of the Act are not applicable, there must be compliance with the pre-conditions of admissibility at common law. Those preconditions are:

(1) The death of the declarant.

(2) That the declaration relates to an issue of pedigree. An issue as to date of birth is not *per se* an issue as to pedigree (*Haines* v. *Guthrie* (1884) 53 L.J.Q.B. 521 (C.A.)); but it can be when a matter of family relationship is involved; also legitimacy, celibacy, intestacy and failure of issue. The rule applies in an application for a declaration of legitimacy or legitimation under the Family Law Act 1986, s.56, which replaces earlier legislation. In such cases declarations of the deceased father or grandfather, though the father is not legally relation of his illegitimate child, may be received (*Re Davy* [1935] P.1; *Battle* v. *Att.-Gen.* [1949] P.358).

(3) That the declarant is related by blood or marriage (or a combination of both) to the person whose pedigree is in issue. In *Johnson* v. *Lawson* (1824) 2 Bing. 86 (C.P.) a declaration by a deceased person who had been the housekeeper of the *propositus* for 24 years was rejected. Inscriptions on tombstones would naturally be made by strangers, but with family approval, and would amount to declarations by relatives.

(4) That the declaration was made before the dispute in question had arisen (see *Butler* v. *Mountgarret (Viscount)* (1859) 7 H.L.Cas. 633 (H.L.)). However admissibility is not confined to matters within the personal knowledge of the declarant. The matter stated may be mere family tradition or reputation, or hearsay upon hearsay, so long as it is confined to the statements and belief of deceased members of the family. Even a statement to the effect that there was absence of information in a family concerning one of its members would be admissible: *Doe d. Banning* v. *Griffin* (1812) 15 East 293 (K.B.).

(IV) DECLARATIONS AS TO PUBLIC AND GENERAL RIGHTS

Introductory Note.—A developed common law exception to the hearsay rule provides for the reception in evidence of an oral or written declaration made by a deceased person concerning the reputed existence of a public or general right, provided that it was made *ante litem motam*, and provided, in the case of a declaration concerning the reputed existence of a general right, that the declarant had competent knowledge. Public rights are those common to all the community, such as rights to use highways, ferries, and public fisheries. General rights are those common to a considerable class of the community, such as parochial or manorial rights. Declarations may be made in any manner or form, as in oral statements, writings, deeds, depositions, maps, plans, books, presentments of manorial courts, or verdicts, judgments, orders or convictions of competent courts (see *Newcastle (Duke)* v. *Broxtowe (Hundred)* (1832) 4 B. & Ad. 273).

Common law doctrine permitting reception of hearsay statements concerning the reputed existence of public or general rights is still applicable, as such, in all criminal cases and in civil matters arising before magistrates. It is also given statutory force in other civil cases by the Civil Evidence Act 1968, s.9. Additionally, such evidence may be admissible under either section 2 or section 4 of the 1968 Act. It is arguable (see Cross, *Evidence* (6th ed., (1985), p. 505) that even evidence of reputation may be admissible under section 2, notwithstanding the limitation of ₍the scope of that section to first-hand hearsay, because section 9(3)(*b*) provides that evidence of reputation shall be treated as evidence of fact for the purposes of sections 1 to 10 of the Act.

For evidence to be received by virtue of section 9 there must be compliance with the common law pre-conditions of admissibility, but there is obviously no need for this if evidence is admitted under either section 2 or section 4.

R. v. BLISS

7 A. & E. 550; 7 L.J.Q.B. 4; 2 Nev. & P.K.B. 464; Will. Woll. & Dav. 624;
112 E.R. 577 (Q.B.: 1837)

To be admissible declarations as to public or general rights must embody reputation relating directly to the existence of the right itself, and not to particular facts which may support or negative it.
To be admissible as a declaration accompanying a relevant act, the declaration must explain that act.

The question was whether a road was public or private. Evidence of a statement, made by a deceased resident of the locality when he planted a tree to the effect that he was planting it to mark the boundary of the road, was inadmissible.

LORD DENMAN C.J.:...I think the evidence was not admissible. It is not every declaration accompanying an act that is receivable in evidence: if it were so, persons would be able to dispose of the rights of others in the most unjust manner. The facts that Ramplin planted a willow on the spot, and that persons kept within the line pointed out by it, would have been evidence; but a declaration to shew that the party planted it with a particular motive is not so.... Neither was the evidence admissible as shewing reputation. Any statement from a person since deceased is to be received with caution...here the deceased party is reported to have said that the boundary of the road was at a particular spot; that is, that he knew it to be so from what he had himself observed, and not from reputation.

PATTESON J.: In looking at this evidence as proof of reputation, we must consider what is in issue. If the question had been of boundary merely, the statement of the deceased person would have been receivable; but evidence of reputation as to boundary is not let in where the question is whether a road be public or private. If evidence of user had been offered, it would have been very different; and proof of declarations that the line of road in question had always been used as public would have been admissible. It was agreed here that the alleged road was a road of some sort; the evidence was not necessary as to that; and the reputation which it was attempted to introduce was of a particular fact. Then it was said that the declaration might be proved as accompanying an act; but whether it accompanied the act, as explanatory of it, is equivocal; and, at any rate, the declaration signified nothing in this case, the question being not of boundary, but as to the character of the road, whether public or private. The mere fact of the tree being placed there could not, I think, be relevant, unless as introductory to other matters.

COLERIDGE and WILLIAMS JJ. agreed.

Note.—Contrast *Howe* v. *Malkin* (1878) 40 L.T. 196 (C.P.D.) (Chapter 15, *infra*).

Dunraven (Earl) v. **Llewellyn** (1850) 19 L.J.Q.B. 388. The question, between the lord of a manor and the owner of a freehold estate within the manor, was whether a piece of land was part of the lord's waste or part of the defendant's land. After proof had been given that there were many lands held of the manor the tenants of which had always exercised rights of common on the waste of the manor, evidence was offered, on the part of the lord, of declarations of deceased tenants that the land was parcel of the waste. It was held that these declarations were not admissible in evidence; for there is no common law right for all tenants of a manor to have common on the waste of the manor, but each tenant who has the right has it as an incident by law attached to his particular grant; and the numerous private rights of common of the several tenants did not compose one public right, so as to render evidence of reputation admissible. It was also held that evidence of actual enjoyment of a right need not be given in order to render evidence of reputation admissible.

Mercer v. **Denne** [1905] 2 Ch. 538 (C.A.). In an action to establish an immemorial custom for fishermen at Walmer to dry their nets on a plot of land owned by the defendant near the seashore, the defendant tendered the following documents as evidence of reputation (1) A survey made in 1616 of the reparations required to protect Walmer Castle from the sea, and estimates of the cost thereof; (2) Depositions taken in an information brought by the Attorney-General in 1639 against persons who claimed to be entitled to the Manor of Walmer, for destroying a bank between the sea and Walmer and thereby causing expense to the King; (3) Maps and plans of the same locality prepared by the Board of Ordnance between 1641 and 1647. All these documents were produced from the War Office, and were tendered to show that the land in question was, at the various dates above mentioned, below highwater mark, so that the custom claimed could not have been immemorial. The Court of Appeal held that none of these documents was admissible. Stirling L.J. said (p. 564): "The evidence does not in any way relate to the alleged custom, nor even to the plot of land over which the custom is said to be exercisable. It relates to the state of the foreshore adjoining the Castle of Walmer in the early part of the seventeenth century. The object is to establish that at that period the sea flowed twice a day over *locus in quo*, the plot over which the custom is said to be exercisable, and it is said that, by establishing where the sea flowed at that time ... it will be shown that that plot of land was, at that time, subject to the flux and reflux of the sea, and therefore the custom must have arisen at a subsequent date, and consequently does not satisfy the requirements of the law as to period of time at which it began. In my opinion, that is not a matter of reputation. It is laid down in all the cases that, when reputation is admissible, evidence of particular acts ought not to be allowed."

Note.—The surveys, maps and plans were also held not admissible as public documents (see this chapter, Section B, *infra*). The position, so far as rights of way are concerned, is now greatly improved by the Highways Act 1980, s.32 (Part Two, *infra*).

(v) DYING DECLARATIONS

R. v. WOODCOCK

1 Leach 500; 168 E.R. 352; 1 East P.C. 356 (Old Bailey: 1789)

A statement by a deceased person, as to the cause of injuries leading to his death is admissible on a trial for the murder of that person, although the deceased did not expressly refer to his expectation of death. It is sufficient if the circumstances show that he expected death soon, and was without hope.
Such statements are called dying declarations.

The prisoner was charged with the murder of his wife, whose statement was taken on oath by a magistrate. She died about 48 hours afterwards. It was proved to be impossible from the first that she could live long; but although she retained her senses to the last moment, and repeated the circumstances of the ill usage she had received, she never expressed any apprehension or seemed sensible of her approaching dissolution. The statement was held admissible.

EYRE C.B.: ... The general principle on which the species of evidence is admitted is, that they are declarations made in extremity, when the party is at the point of death, and when every hope of this world is gone; when every motive to falsehood is silenced, and the mind is induced by the most powerful considerations to speak the truth; a situation so solemn and so awful is considered by law as creating an obligation equal to that which is imposed by a positive oath administered in a court of justice. But a difficulty also arises with respect to these declarations; for it has not appeared, and it seems impossible to find out, whether the deceased herself apprehended that she was in such a state of mortality as would inevitably oblige her soon to answer before her Maker for the truth or falsehood of her assertions ..., however, my judgment is, that in as much as she was mortally wounded, and was in a condition which rendered almost immediate death inevitable; as she was thought by every person about her to be dying, though it was difficult to get from her particular explanations as to what she thought of herself and her situation; her declarations, made under these circumstances, ought to be considered by a jury as being made under the impression of her approaching dissolution; for, resigned as she appeared to be, she must have felt the hand of death, and must have considered herself as a dying woman.... Declarations so made are certainly entitled to credit; they ought therefore to be received in evidence; but the degree of credit to which they are entitled must always be a matter for the sober consideration of the jury, under all the circumstances of the case....

Note.—A declaration would not now be admitted without evidence of the declarant's appreciation of impending certain death.

Chief Baron Eyre purports to explain the basis of the rule as to dying declarations. The explanation is not wholly convincing. As has been pointed out (Cowen and Carter, *Essays on the Law of Evidence* (1956, reprint 1973) p. 2), "While in many cases the immediate prospect of being confronted by one's Maker is a distinct incentive to speak the truth, in some others, at least, the desire to seize the last opportunity to harm an enemy or the desire to protect a friend may provide an equally impelling incentive to lie. In any case an honest mistake is by no means improbable: a person who has been homicidally attacked and believes himself on the point of death may well be in a distracted, confused, and weakened condition."

R. v. **Mead** (1824) 2 B. and C. 605 (K.B.). The accused had been convicted of perjury. He obtained an order for a new trial, but shot the deceased before it took place. A dying declaration made by the deceased concerning the transaction out of which the prosecution for perjury arose was rejected for two reasons. Abbott C.J. said (p. 608): "...evidence of this description is only admissible where the death of the deceased is the subject of the charge, and the circumstances of the death the subject of the dying declarations."

Note.—From the point of view of reliability it is not clear why the admissibility of dying declarations should be limited to trials for murder or manslaughter. In *R.* v. *Lloyd* (1830) 4 C. & P. 233 (Assizes), a case of robbery, the dying declaration of the person robbed was rejected; so, too, in a case of a rape (*R.* v. *Newton and Carpenter* (1859) 1 F. & F. 641) (Assizes), the declaration of the deceased victim was excluded; also, in *R.* v. *Hutchinson* (Assizes 1822), cited in 2 B. & C. as a note at p. 608, where the accused was charged with using an instrument with intent to procure a miscarriage and the offence had actually resulted in the death of the declarant, evidence was held to be inadmissible as a dying declaration. Although reported English cases in which a dying declaration has been admitted have all been cases of murder or manslaughter, it is to be noted that the limitation propounded in *R.* v. *Mead* is somewhat wider—it is to proceedings where "the death of the deceased is the subject of the charge." There is Canadian authority holding that this covers proceedings for causing death by criminal negligence in the operation of a motor vehicle: *R.* v. *Jurtyn* [1958] O.W.N. 355; 28 C.R. 295 (Court of Appeal for Ontario). There, unlike in a case of, *e.g.* rape, resultant death is an essential ingredient of the offence charged.

The second limitation upon the admissibility of dying declarations which was laid down in *R.* v. *Mead* (*supra*), *i.e.* that such a declaration is only admissible to the extent that it indicates the circumstances of the declarant's own death, is also not easy to defend from the standpoint of reliability.

A dying declaration may be admissible, although it is partly favourable to the accused as showing provocation by the deceased (*R.* v. *Scaife* (1836) 1 Mood. & R. 551).

A dying declaration need not be corroborated (*Nembhard* v. *R.* [1981] 1 W.L.R. 1515 (P.C.)).

R. v. **Pike** (1829) 3 C. and P. 598 (Assizes). The prisoner was indicted for the murder of a child aged four years. It was proposed to put in evidence, as a dying declaration, what the child said shortly before her death. The declaration was held to be inadmissible. Park J. said (p. 598): "We allow the declaration of persons *in articulo mortis* to be given in evidence, if it appear that the person making such declaration was then under the deep impression that he was soon to render an account to his Maker. Now, as this child was but four years old, it is quite impossible that she, however precocious her mind, could have had that idea of a future state which is necessary to make such a declaration admissible. . . . "

Note.—The implicit requirement that the dying declarant would have been a competent witness had he been living would presumably apply equally in the case of a lunatic. However, Park J.'s reasoning notwithstanding, at least this requirement would not now affect the admissibility of the declaration of a known atheist who could have affirmed.

R. v. Jenkins (1869) 38 L.J.M.C. 82 (C.C.R.); L.R. 1 C.C.R. 187. The prisoner was charged with the murder of a woman, who, on her death-bed, accused him of the crime. A magistrate's clerk attended her to take down her statement, writing that it was made "with no hope of my recovery." He then read this statement over to her; but, before she signed it, she desired the addition of the words "at present," so that the words read "with no hope at present of my recovery." It was held that the statement could not be received in evidence, as her objection to sign the statement without the words "at present" suggested some faint hope of recovery. Kelly C.B. said (L.J.M.C., p. 85): "I am of opinion that the result of the cases is, that there must be an unqualified belief, without any hope of recovery, that the declarant is about to die. According to the language of Eyre C.B., every hope of this world must be gone. According to Tindal C.J., any hope of recovery, however slight, must exclude the evidence. Then the burden of proof lies entirely on the prosecution. The judge must be perfectly satisfied beyond a reasonable doubt that the declarant was under the belief that no hope of recovery existed."

Note.—There is some judicial support for the view that the nature of the victim's wound is not a sufficient ground for drawing the inference that he knew that he was dying. In *R. v. Morgan* (1875) 14 Cox C.C. 337 (Kent Assizes), a case in which the victim with his head apparently almost severed and being unable to speak had made a written note about five minutes before he died. Denman J., after consulting his fellow Assize judge, Cockburn C.J., said that neither was prepared to say that the statement "might" not be admissible, but that he could not admit it without reserving a case for the Court for Crown Cases Reserved. Crown counsel then elected not to press for its admission, and the accused was convicted on the rest of the evidence.

R. v. PERRY

[1909] 2 K.B. 697; 78 L.J.M.C. 1034; 101 L.T. 127; 25 T.L.R. 676; 22 Cox C.C. 154 (C.C.A.: 1909)

If proof is given that the declarant realised that death was imminent and that he or she had abandoned all hope of living, it is not necessary to show a belief that death would ensue immediately.

This was an appeal against conviction for murder by means of an illegal operation on April 9. On the morning of the 16th the deceased was asked by her sister, "Maggie, what did you have that woman for?" The deceased replied, "Oh, Gert, I shall go. But keep this a secret. Let the worst come to the worst"; adding a statement of what the prisoner had done to her. The deceased died the same evening. The statement was admitted as a dying declaration, and the appeal was dismissed.

LORD ALVERSTONE C.J. (delivering the judgment of the court, which included DARLING and LAWRENCE JJ.): . . . In *R.* v. *Peel* (1860) 2 F. & F. 21, Willes J. said: "It must be proved that the man was dying and there must be a settled hopeless expectation of death in the declarant." That sentence expresses in very clear and crisp language the rule which I have been trying to explain. In *R.* v. *Gloster* (1888) 16 Cox C.C. 471, Charles J., examining the cases . . . said, "In the latest case of all, *R.* v. *Osman* (1881) 15 Cox C.C. 1, Lush L.J. lays down the principle in these terms: 'A dying declaration is admitted in evidence because it is presumed that no person who is immediately going into the presence of his Maker, will do so with a lie on his lips. But the person making the declaration must entertain a settled hopeless expectation of immediate death. If he thinks he will die tomorrow it will not do.' That is the judgment of Willes J., with this addition, that Lush L.J. inserts the words 'immediate' before 'death.' With the greatest deference I would prefer to adopt the language of Willes J. and say that the declarant must be under a 'settled hopeless expectation of death.' 'Immediate death' must be construed in the sense of death impending, not on the instant, but within a very, very short distance indeed." In other words, the test is whether all hope of life has been abandoned so that the person making the statement thinks that death must follow. I now propose to apply that principle in the present case. . . . If the expression "I shall go" is taken alone, it might mean "I shall die some day"; but, taking into consideration the whole sentence, we concur with Lawrence J. that the statement was made by the deceased with the hopeless expectation of death.

Note.—Provided the declarant's expectation was of "immediate" death in the slightly flexible sense indicated by Lord Alverstone C.J., the declaration will not necessarily be rejected if in fact death did not ensue until a little later. In *R.* v. *Mosely* (1825), 1 Mood. C.C. 97 (Crown Cases Reserved) death did not occur until 11 days after the declaration was made, and in *R.* v. *Bernadotti* (1869) 11 Cox C.C. 316 (Assizes) three weeks elapsed. The fact that the deceased subsequently entertained hope will not exclude the declaration (*R.* v. *Austin* (1912) 8 Cr.App.R. 27 (C.C.A.)). When the deceased fell into a coma, from which he did not recover, before he had completed his statement, the declaration was held to be inadmissible (*Waugh* v. *R.* [1950] A.C. 203 (P.C.)).

When the declaration was oral, it is desirable that the actual words used, and the whole statement, should be proved; but non-compliance with these requirements does not necessarily make the declaration inadmissible (see *R.* v. *Stephenson* [1947] N.I. 110 (C.C.A.)). A dying declaration may apparently be made by signs (*Chandrasekera* v. *R.* [1937] A.C. 220 (P.C.)).

On the whole Willes J.'s oft-quoted words in *R.* v. *Peel* (1860) 2 F. & F. 21 (Assizes) that "there must be a settled hopeless expectation of death in the declarant" have been restrictively applied. Admissibility by virtue of the exception has been accordingly limited. Perhaps this reflects judicial scepticism concerning the adequacy of its rationale.

(VI) POST-TESTAMENTARY DECLARATIONS BY TESTATORS AS TO THE CONTENTS OF THEIR WILLS

Sugden v. **Lord St. Leonards** (1876) 1 P.D. 154 (C.A.). The will of Lord St. Leonards was missing at his death, and was never found. A daughter of the deceased wrote out the contents of the will from memory, there being no draft or copy of it. The daughter had lived with the testator all her life; he had constantly consulted her about the will and explained its provisions to her, and she had from time to time assisted him to alter it. Her statement of the will was in some degree corroborated by other papers of the testator, and also by his verbal statements made after the execution of the will to his friends and relatives. The court held that proof of such statements or declarations made by the testator was admissible as evidence of its contents, and granted probate of the will as written down by the daughter.

Note.—This decision was the subject of much adverse comment, particularly because it allowed secondary evidence of a type not otherwise recognised, namely, the repetition by the witness of what she had heard her father say, and a so-called copy of the will composed from memory. The rule which it embodies has not been preserved for civil cases by the Civil Evidence Act 1968, s.9. Moreover, such a rule will seldom fall to be applied in criminal cases. In retrospect the decision can be seen as a landmark of more general interest. It marks the last occasion on which a new common law exception to the hearsay rule was explicitly created at common law.

See, too, the Inheritance (Provision for Family and Dependants) Act 1975, s.21 (Part Two, *infra*).

B. STATEMENTS IN PUBLIC DOCUMENTS

STURLA v. FRECCIA

5 App. Cas. 623; 50 L.J.Ch. 86; 43 L.T. 209; 29 W.R. 217 (H.L.: 1880)

Entries or statements in public documents, such as official books and registers, whether British or foreign, are evidence against everyone. A public document is one made in pursuance of a legal duty, in relation to a public matter, by a public officer, for public information or reference.

Although foreign public documents are within the rule, yet the report of a committee appointed by a public department in a foreign state, addressed to that department and acted on by the Government, was not admitted in an English court as evidence of the facts stated therein; there being no evidence of any legal duty to make either the entries or any particular inquiries on which they were based, nor any evidence that the report was to be available for public reference.

LORD SELBORNE L.C.: . . . There is abundant proof that the report which contains the passage it is desired to use is an authentic public document of the Genoese Government, to which, so far as the good faith of those who made it is concerned, credit might be justly given on any occasion on which it might properly be used. But . . . it does not appear that any particular rules were prescribed to (the committee) as to the kind of information which they should collect; still less as to the evidence which they were to require to substantiate such information. . . . It appears to me to have been perfectly open to its members to receive any species of information, of hearsay or otherwise, to which they themselves at the moment thought credit could be given; and, therefore I am unable to apply to them any analogy derived from the cases of courts, commissoners, or other persons having a special duty or authority under the English law to make particular kinds of inquiries. . . .

LORD BLACKBURN: ... It is an established rule of law that public documents are admitted for certain purposes. What a public document is, within that sense, is of course the great point which we have now to consider ... the principle, upon which it goes is, that there should be a public inquiry, and a public document, made by a public officer. I do not think that "public" there is to be taken in the sense of meaning the whole world. I think an entry in the books of a manor is public in the sense that it concerns all the people interested in the manor. And an entry probably in a corporation book concerning a corporate matter, or something in which all the corporation is concerned, would be "public" within that sense. But it must be a public document, and it must be made by a public officer. I understand a public document there to mean a document that is made for the purpose of the public making use of it, and being able to refer to it. It is meant to be where there is a judicial, or quasi-judicial, duty to inquire, as might be said to be the case with the bishop acting under the writs issued by the Crown. That may be said to be quasi-judicial. He is acting for the public when that is done; but I think the very object of it must be that it should be made for the purpose of being kept public, so that the persons concerned in it may have access to it afterwards. ... Can the document in this case be said to come within that class of cases? I think it is impossible to look at it in that way. There is not the slightest evidence, or the least circumstance, to lead me to the conclusion that it was ever intended that this private and confidential report should be seen by anyone interested in it. It was meant for private information, to guide the discretion of the Government. It was not, like the bishop's return of the first-fruits, for the public information, to be kept in the office and to be seen by all in the diocese who might be concerned when there came to be any litigation.

LORDS HATHERLEY and WATSON agreed.

R. v. **Halpin** [1975] Q.B. 907 (C.A.). The appellant was convicted of conspiring with others to cheat a local authority by making false claims for work allegedly done by a limited company. The Court of Appeal held that the trial judge had not erred in granting leave to the prosecution to adduce in evidence extracts from the annual returns of the company filed at the Companies Registry in order to show that during the relevant period the appellant and his wife had been the sole shareholders and directors of the company. The Court accepted that it was a condition of admissibility that the official making the record should either have had personal knowledge of the matters which he was recording or should have inquired into the accuracy of the facts. However, on the basis that "the common law should move with the times and should recognise the fact that the official charged with recording matters of public import can no longer in this highly complicated world, as like as not, have personal knowledge of their accuracy," the Court held that the duty could be divided. Geoffrey Lane L.J., giving the judgment of the Court, said (p. 915): "What has happened now is that the function originally performed by one man has had to be shared by two: the first having the knowledge and the statutory duty to record that knowledge and forward it to the Registrar of Companies, the second having the duty to preserve that document and to show it to members of the public under proper conditions as required." The court of Appeal further held that the delay between the events and recording them went to weight rather than to admissibility.

Note.—Statements in public documents are generally admissible evidence of the truth of their contents. In criminal cases this is by virtue of an established common law exception to the hearsay rule or by virtue of some specific statutory enactment. In civil cases they are now admissible by virtue of section 9(1) of the Civil Evidence Act 1968 (Part Two, *infra*) which preserves their common law admissibility: in addition they will in some cases, in which they would not have been admissible at common law, now be statutorily admissible (subject to compliance with the relevant notice procedure) under section 2 or section 4 of that Act.

Public documents include public statutes (see *R.* v. *Sutton* (1816) 3 M. and S. 532 (K.B.)). Recitals of fact in private Acts of Parliament have been regarded as evidence only against the parties to them, even though the Acts may be declared public for the purpose of proof. But recent dicta do not refer to this restriction, in relation to legal rights long beyond the reach of living memory (see *Wyld* v. *Silver* [1963] 1 Q.B. 169 at 187, 194, 196 (C.A.)).

Before the year 1850 it was customary to insert a clause in private Acts of Parliament declaring that they should be deemed public and be judicially noticed. The effect of this clause was to dispense with the necessity, not only of pleading the Act specially, but of producing an examined copy or a copy printed by the printer for the Crown. As to proof of other early private Acts, see Evidence Act 1845, s.3 (Part Two, *infra*). The Interpretation Act 1978 (replacing earlier legislation), lays down that every Act passed after 1850 shall be a public Act and shall be judicially noticed as such, unless the contrary is expressly provided by the Act in question (Part Two, *infra*). As to judicial notice generally, see Chapter 7, *supra*, Other examples of public documents are the *London Gazette*, registers of births, marriages and deaths, surveys of Crown lands, maps, plans and charts attached to enclosure awards and public inquisitions. There is power to declare that foreign registers are public documents, by the Evidence (Foreign, Dominion and Colonial Documents) Act, 1933, as amended (Part Two, *infra*). Ancient documents such as surveys, estimates and petitions for a private character, produced from the Records Office, which do not affect the Queen's property or revenues, are not public documents in the above sense. Nor are confidential plans or reports made to the War Office, not intended as permanent records (*Mercer* v. *Denne* [1905] 2 Ch. 538 (C.A.), *supra*), or other documents not available for public reference (*Ioannou* v. *Demetriou* [1952] A.C. 84 (P.C.)).

A public document must have some relation to members of the public (see *Heyne* v. *Fischel & Co.* (1913) 30 T.L.R. 190). Records prepared by an authority for its own purposes are not public documents, *e.g.* regimental records (*Lilley* v. *Pettit*[1946] K.B. 401 (D.C.)). A draft document is not regarded as public (*White* v. *Taylor* [1969] 1 Ch. 150).

The rules as to public documents have been applied from time to time to a number of analogous documents, which do not necessarily comply with the tests laid down in the speeches extracted above. Court rolls are now specifically treated as public documents by the Law of Property Act 1922, s.144; and many other statutes deal with particular documents.

Books of reference, like dictionaries, may be either admissible as evidence (see now the Civil Evidence Act 1968, s.9(2)(*b*)) or used as an aid to judicial notice, for the purpose of establishing the meaning of words (see *Jarman* v. *Lambert & Cooke Contractors, Ltd.* [1951] 2 K.B. 937; *R.* v. *Agricultural Land Tribunal* [1955] 2 Q.B. 140 at 147, 150, 156 (C.A.)). It appears that maps and plans may be similarly utilised, although they are not necessarily public documents, if they are published and generally offered for sale to the public, as to matters of public notoriety, but not as to matters of private concern.

As to the proof of public documents by secondary evidence, see Chapter 24, *infra*.

C. EVIDENCE IN FORMER PROCEEDINGS

R. v. HALL

[1973] 1 Q.B. 496; [1973] 1 All E.R. 1; 57 Cr.Äp.R. 170; [1973] Crim. L.R. 48
(C.A.: 1972)

Provided the conditions of legal admissibility are fulfilled, the judge in a criminal trial has no discretion to exclude a transcript of evidence given in earlier proceedings unless its reception might be unfairly prejudicial to the accused.

The accused was charged with several forgery offences. At the first trial, at which the jury failed to agree, one, Reeve, gave evidence for the prosecution which was in some respects unsatisfactory. Reeve died before the re-trial. At the re-trial the defence sought to put in evidence his deposition and a transcript of his evidence. The judge admitted the deposition but rejected the transcript. The accused's appeal against conviction was allowed on the ground that the transcript should have been admitted.

FORBES J. (delivering the judgment of the court which included KARMINSKI L.J. and O'CONNOR J.): ... we think it plain that a deposition properly taken before a magistrate on oath in the presence of the accused and where the accused has had the opportunity of cross-examination was at least since 1554 admissible at common law in criminal cases if the original deponent was dead, despite the absence of opportunity to observe the demeanour of the witness. The only difference between such a deposition and the transcript of evidence given at a previous trial is that the transcript is not signed by the witness. Provided it is authenticated in some other appropriate way, as by calling the shorthand writer who took the original note, there seems no reason to think that such a transcript should not be equally receivable in evidence.

This is not to say that transcripts of previous testimony, because of this rule, are always to be received. The judge in a criminal trial still has a discretion to exclude such evidence if he considers it would be unfair to the defendant (though not to the prosecution) to admit it. . . . It may be that the absence of opportunity to observe the demeanour of the witness could be a powerful factor to be taken into account in considering the exercise of such discretion.

The true position, therefore, as we see it is that the transcript of Mr. Reeve's evidence was admissible, but the judge could have refused to receive it in evidence in his discretion if he thought its reception might prejudice the accused. In fact the judge considered that he had no discretion and rules that in law the evidence was not admissible. No question of a wrongful exercise of discretion therefore arises and the ruling was, in our view, wrong. . . .

The conviction will accordingly be quashed.

R. v. **Thompson** [1982] Q.B. 647 (C.A.). The accused was charged with various offences including robbery and blackmail. A witness gave evidence of identification and was cross-examined. The trial was aborted. At the second trial the defence accepted that this witness was unable to travel to court on account of her medical condition, but objected to a transcript of her evidence at the first trial being admitted. The Court of Appeal held that the judge had rightly ruled that the transcript was admissible in law. The conviction was, however, quashed since the overall effect of various matters that had arisen in the course of the trial was to render the verdict unsafe and unsatisfactory. Dunn L.J., delivering the judgment of the Court, reviewed the authorities and concluded (p. 659) that it has been the law for at least the last 150 years that if a former witness's illness is such that he is unlikely to be able to attend court within a reasonable time the transcript will be admissible.

Note.—In addition to death or illness, another ground for reception of a transcript would seem to be that the witness is being kept away by the opponent; but not (it would seem) the mere fact that the witness is out of the jurisdiction: *R.* v. *Scaife* (1851) 17 Q.B.D. 238, 243.

It is clear that in all these cases the evidence given in the earlier proceedings must have been for or against the same accused; it must relate to substantially the same facts; and there must have been an opportunity to examine the witness in the earlier proceedings.

In addition to this common law admissibility the judge has a statutory power to admit the transcript of evidence of a witness given at the first trial when a retrial is ordered by the Court of Appeal: Criminal Appeal Act 1968, s.8(4) and Sched. 2. See, too, for the admissibility of depositions taken before examining magistrates, the Criminal Justice Act 1925, s.13(3) (Part Two, *infra*).

D. INFORMAL ADMISSIONS

SLATTERIE v. POOLEY

6 M. & W. 664; **10 L.J. Ex. 8;** 4 Jur. 1038; 1 H. & W. 18; 151 E.R. 579
(Exchequer: 1840)

Informal admissions are considered primary evidence against a party, and they are admissible to prove even the contents of written documents, without notice to produce, or accounting for the absence of, the originals.

The plaintiff sued upon a deed by which the defendant covenanted to indemnify him against all debts set out in another deed and schedule, which itself was inadmissible as not being duly stamped. An oral admission of the defendant, that a debt in question in the action was the same as one mentioned in such schedule, was admitted.

PARKE B.: . . . The rule as to the production of the best evidence is not at all infringed. It does not apply to the present case. That rule is founded on the supposition that a party is going to offer worse evidence than the nature of the case admits. But what is said by a party to the suit is not open to that objection. . . . We therefore think it is a sound rule that admissions made by a party to a suit may be received against him, although they relate to the contents of a written document.

LORD ABINGER C.B., GURNEY and ROLFE BB. concurred.

Note.—For the admissibility of secondary evidence of documents, see Chapter 24, *infra*. An admission by a person of something, of which he knows nothing, is of no evidential value and is inadmissible: *Comptroller of Customs* v. *Western Electric Co. Ltd.* [1966] A.C. 367 (P.C.). But see, too, *Lustre Hosiery Ltd.* v. *York* (1935) 54 C.L.R. 134 (H.C. of Australia).

R. v. McGregor [1968] 1 Q.B. 371 (C.A.). At the defendant's trial on a charge of receiving he gave evidence in the presence of a police officer. The jury disagreed, and there was a second trial at which the accused did not give evidence. The court admitted evidence from the police officer that at the first trial the defendant had made admissions that he had possession of the handled goods and had given explanations as to how, when they came into his possession, he did not know that they were stolen. The Court of Appeal held that the evidence was rightly admitted.

R. v. Rimmer [1972] 1 W.L.R. 268 (C.A.). The defendant pleaded guilty before a Magistrates' Court to theft. He was remanded until a later date when he asked to change his plea to one of not guilty. He was subsequently allowed to do so, and, having elected for trial, was committed to Quarter Sessions. During his trial evidence was given of the plea of guilty in the Magistrates' Court. On the defendant's appeal against conviction it was contended that this evidence had been improperly admitted. The Court of Appeal held that there is no bar to the reception of an earlier plea of guilty as an informal admission, but that it is an area in which the discretion of the trial judge is especially important. Sachs L.J. (delivering the judgment of the court) said (p. 272): "Whether it [the plea of guilty] has a probative value at all, and whether that probative value exceeds the prejudice which may be thus imported, must depend on the facts of the case. The circumstances in which a withdrawal of a plea is permitted may vary infinitely. One may have a case where a plea, for instance, to a charge of handling is most properly withdrawn because the defendant did not realise that it was necessary for him to have the relevant knowledge that the goods were stolen. On the other hand, the withdrawal of a plea may result from some completely false statement of fact made by the defendant himself as to what has happened between the date of the plea and the date that withdrawal is requested, something which the magistrates cannot and would not check on the spot. Whether in any individual case the evidence as to the previous plea and its withdrawal should be admitted into evidence is plainly a matter for the discretion of the trial judge, who must most carefully examine whether indeed the probative value does exceed the prejudice which would be induced by the admission of such evidence. In the vast majority of cases in practice the result of such an examination would be that the evidence would not be admitted. Indeed, the occasions on which it is likely to be regarded as admissible will, of their nature, be rare. In each case that question must be decided, as it was in the present case, by an examination of the relevant facts upon what is often referred to as a trial within a trial." The court held that in the instant case the evidence had not been properly admitted, but that in the light of the rest of the evidence it would apply the proviso to section 2(1) of the Criminal Appeal Act 1968 and dismiss the appeal.

MORIARTY v. LONDON, CHATHAM & DOVER RY.

L.R. 5 Q.B. 314; 39 L.J.Q.B. 109; 22 L.T. 163; 18 W.R. 625 (Q.B.: 1870)

An admission may be made by conduct only; and it may relate not only to specific facts, but even show that the party's whole case is bad.

The plaintiff sued a railway company for personal injury, and evidence was given that he had gone about suborning false witnesses who had not been present at the accident. It was held that such conduct amounted to an admission that he had no case.

COCKBURN C.J.:... Here, if you can show that a man has been suborning false testimony, and has endeavoured to have recourse to perjury, it is strong to show that he knew perfectly well that his cause of action was an unrighteous one....

BLACKBURN J.:... The jury should be cautioned against giving the evidence too much weight, which they might possibly do, and directed that they were not to punish a man for giving false testimony by taking away his right of action, but only to see whether it shook their belief in his evidence....

LUSH J.:... This species of evidence is receivable as an admission by the party that the case he is putting forward is not the true one. It was an admission by conduct, and receivable on that ground....

Note.—See, too, *Preece* v. *Parry* [1983] Crim.L.R. 170; [1983] C.L.Y. 637 (D.C.), where it was held the evidence of disorderly, violent and abusive conduct towards the police after arrest later the same evening was so inconsistent with the reaction of innocent persons as to be reasonably capable of constituting an admission of an offence under the Public Order Act 1936, s.5, of using threatening words and behaviour at a public house whereby a breach of the peace was likely to be occasioned.

WEIDEMANN v. WALPOLE

[1891] 2 Q.B. 534; **60 L.J.Q.B. 762;** 40 W.R. 114 (C.A.: 1891)

Although silence may amount to an admission when it is natural to expect a reply, when the circumstances are such that a reply cannot reasonably be expected, the party's silence in face of a charge or assertion will not amount to an admission.

In an action for breach of promise of marriage, the fact that the defendant had not answered a letter written to him, calling upon him to perform his promise of marriage, was held not to be an admission by him.

LORD ESHER M.R.:... The letter could only be put in as some evidence of an admission of the truth of the statements contained in it.... There are no doubt mercantile and business cases in which it is the ordinary course of mankind to answer a letter written upon a matter of business, and, if the letter were not answered, the court would take notice of the ordinary course adopted by men of business—namely, to answer a letter where it is not intended to admit the truth of the statements contained in it; and if it were not answered, would take it as some evidence of the truth of the statements in it. But that is not like the case of a letter charging a man with some offence or impropriety. It could not be said that a man must answer such a letter at once, and that if he did not do so it must be taken as an admission that the statements are true. Life would not be bearable if a man had to answer such letters, and if it were to be taken as an admission of guilt if he did not do so. It is the ordinary and wise practice of mankind not to answer such a letter, because, if a man answered it, a correspondence would be entered into, and he would be lost. I have no doubt that the mere fact of not answering a letter containing a statement of a promise to marry is not an admission....

BOWEN L.J.: ...It would be a monstrous thing if it were the law that the mere fact of a man not answering a letter charging him with some offence, or making some claim against him, would necessarily and in all circumstances be evidence of admission of the truth of the charge or statement contained in the letter. There must be some limit placed upon such a proposition to make it consonant with common sense. I think the limit to be placed upon it is, that silence upon the receipt of a letter cannot be taken as evidence of admission of the truth of its contents, unless there are some circumstances in the case which would render it probable that the person receiving the letter, who dissented from the statements, would answer it and deny them....

KAY L.J.: ...I decline to lay down any general rule. There are certain business letters, not the answering of which by the persons who received them has been taken to be an admission by those persons of the truth of the statements contained in them. In other cases, all the circumstances under which the letter was written and received must be looked at in order to determine whether the omission to reply to it does fairly amount to an admission....

Note.—This case may be contrasted with the earlier breach of promise of marriage case of *Bessela* v. *Stern* noted immediately below. Such actions, before they were abolished by the Law Reform (Miscellaneous Provisions) Act 1970, s.1(1), constituted one of the instances in which corroboration was required. The defendant's admission in *Bessela* v. *Stern* was held to be corroboration of the plaintiff's evidence.

Bessela v. **Stern** (1877) 46 L.J.C.P. 467 (C.A.). It was proved that the plaintiff had said to the defendant, "You always promised to marry me, and you don't keep your word." The defendant made no answer to this assertion, but said that he would give the plaintiff money to go away. His silence on the subject of marriage was held to be an admission. Cockburn C.J. said (p. 469): "If the conversation took place, no doubt it is not conclusive; for a man might think it not worthwhile to contradict the assertion of the promise and raise a dispute. On the other hand, it might be said he made no reply to the accusation, because he could not with truth deny it...". Brett L.J. said (p. 470): "The...question is, would it have been natural at the time when the woman made the statement, that the man should have contradicted it? If so, the jury had a right to consider 'his not denying it' as evidence of the truth of what she said...."

PETO v. HAGUE

5 Esp 134; 170 E.R. 763; 1 Smith 417 (Nisi Prius: 1804)

Statements made by an agent in the course of his employment may be admissible against his principal. Those made about other transactions will not bind the principal as admissions. When the agent's authority to act in the particular matter has ceased, the principal cannot be affected by his agent's subsequent statements.

The defendant was a coal-merchant who was sued for a penalty for selling short measure. A witness was proceeding to state what was said to him by one Peely, the defendant's manager, as to a sale about to take place. This was objected to, but was held admissible.

LORD ELLENBOROUGH C.J. said that Peely appeared to be the manager and conductor of the defendant's business; what he might have said respecting a former sale made by the defendant or on another occasion, would not be evidence to affect his master; but what he said respecting a sale of coals, then about to take place, and respecting the disposition of the coals then lying at the wharf, which were the object of sale, was in the course of witness's employment for the defendant, and was evidence to affect his master.

KIRKSTALL BREWERY CO. v. FURNESS RY.

L.R. 9 Q.B. 468: **43 L.J.Q.B. 142;** 30 L.T. 783; 22 W.R. 876 (Q.B.: 1874)

An agent or servant may bind his principal by admissions made within the scope of his authority or duty.

In an action against a railway company for loss of a parcel of money, statements made by the station-master to a police officer, tending to show theft thereof by one of the company's servants, were received as admissions against the company, the station-master being the proper agent to make such statements.

COCKBURN C.J.: . . . I think it impossible to say that a man who has the sole management of a railway station, and had authority to cause a person to be apprehended if he had reasonable and probable cause to suppose that a felony had been committed, could not have authority to give instructions to the police, and could not make such communications as would be admissible in evidence just as if they were made by his principals.

QUAIN J.: . . . In putting the police in motion he was acting within his duty, and within the scope of the authority given to him. . . .

ARCHIBALD J.: . . . Being in charge of the station at the time a felony was committed, it was his duty to put the police in motion. That being so, I think that he was acting within the scope of his duty, that he had power to bind the company, and therefore that the evidence was admissible.

Note.—To be contrasted with this case is the earlier case of *Great Western Rly.* v. *Willis* (1865) 18 C.B. (N.S.) 748 (C.P.). There, in an action against a railway company for not delivering cattle promptly, the plaintiff gave evidence of a conversation a week after the transaction between himself and the company's night inspector, who had charge of the night cattle trains at a certain station, in the course of which the night inspector said the cattle had been forgotten. It was held that this statement was not an admission against the company, as the night inspector was a subordinate servant without authority to make such a statement, and also as the statement was made some time after the transaction.

Re Devala Provident Gold Mining Co. (1883) 22 Ch.D. 593 (Ch.D.). This was a summons by a shareholder for removal of his name from the share register, by reason of misrepresentation in the company's prospectus. The only evidence of the untruth of the representation was a statement made by the chairman in a speech to a meeting of the shareholders. It was alleged that the statement was material, that it was made by an agent of the company, and that the company itself had put the report in evidence as a true report of what the chairman said. It was held that the statement was not admissible against the company, on the ground that a statement in a report by an agent to his principal cannot be regarded as an admission by the principal so as to be admissible in favour of a third party against the principal. Fry J. said (pp. 595–596): "The only ground upon which, in my view, this statement could possibly be admitted would be that the chairman was the agent of the company, and that he was making the statement in the course of a transaction with a third party in which he was acting as the agent of the company, and that it was within the scope of his agency. If that were so, the statement would be admissible against the company. It appears to me, however, that it was not admissible, for it was made by the agent, not in a transaction between the company and a third party, but at a meeting of the company. It is the case of an agent making a report to his own principal, and in my view to when an agent is making a confidential report to his principal, the report is not admissible evidence in favour of a third party."

Note.—Justification for this limitation upon the reception of vicarious admissions is not clear. It would appear to derive from the notion that the admissibility of evidence of admissions depends not solely upon considerations of reliability, but also upon the logic of proceedings which are essentially adversarial (see the Introduction to this Chapter). Compare *The Solway* (1885) 10 P.D. 137. Note, too, that an agent's report to a principal could be rendered admissible under the Civil Evidence Act 1968, s.2.

R. v. **Evans** [1981] Crim.L.R. 699; [1981] C.L.Y. 425 (C.A.). Evidence was adduced at the trial for handling stolen goods that the managing clerk of the appellant's solicitors had approached the apellant's brother-in-law and stated that the appellant had asked him to ask a third party to say that the appellant had bought the relevant property from him (the third party). The Court of Appeal allowed the appellant's appeal against conviction, holding that the evidence ought not to have been admitted as it had not been shown that the managing clerk had the appellant's authority to act.

Note.—This decision is clearly consistent with the well established rule that the existence of agency must be established *aliunde* before admissions of an agent can be received against a principal. This can be implied from the surrounding circumstances (see, *e.g. R.* v. *Turner* (1975) 61 Cr.App.R. 67 (C.A.)), but was not so implied in *R.* v. *Evans*.

In an earlier Divisional Court case, *Edwards* v. *Brookes (Milk) Ltd.* [1963] 1 W.L.R. 795, it was held that an alleged agent's own statements and/or behaviour may in some circumstances constitute evidence sufficient to establish a prima facie case of his being an agent who might be impliedly authorised to make informal admissions. The court was at pains to point out that this did not involve contravention of the hearsay rule because the supposed agent's statements and/or behaviour could be regarded as objective facts. It might, however, be contended that, as the existence of the relationship was not itself a fact in issue or a relevant fact, but merely a "preliminary fact" (see Chapter 1, *supra*) bearing upon the admissibility of a particular piece of evidence, compliance with the hearsay rule would in principle not in any event be necessary. At the same time the case for Magistrates (and their Clerks) as a matter of practice observing the exclusionary rules of evidence when determining (or advising on the determination of) question of "preliminary fact" is quite strong. See, too, *G.(A.)* v. *G.(T.)* [1970] 2 Q.B. 643.

Williams v. **Innes** (1808) 1 Camp. 364 (K.B.). In an action against executors, who pleaded that they had fully administered the estate, the plaintiff, in order to prove assets, put in a letter from the defendants, telling her that if she wanted further information concerning the affairs of the deceased she should apply to a Mr. Ross, and she proposed to give in evidence what he said on the matter. The evidence was held admissible. Lord Ellenborough C.J. said (p. 365): "If a man refers another upon any particular business to a third person, he is bound by what this third person says or does concerning it, as much as if that had been said or done by himself."

Note.—This case is often quoted as an authority for the proposition that, if one party directs or requests another party to apply to any other person for information on a particular matter, such reference may constitute the other person an agent for that purpose; but the judgment is very short and general in its terms. It must be taken as applying only to cases of "particular business," not to every case of mere casual inquiry. In another case the same judge said: "Wherever a party refers to the evidence of another, he is bound by it—and this is constantly good evidence" (*Daniel* v. *Pitt* (1806) 1 Camp. 366). In a later criminal case, when a man referred a constable to his wife for information, a list of property, prepared by the wife and given to the police, was treated as an admission of possession by the husband (*R.* v. *Mallory* (1884) 13 Q.B.D. 33 (C.C.R.)).

BURR v. WARE RURAL DISTRICT COUNCIL

[1939] 2 All E.R. 688 (C.A.: 1939)

Admissions, made by a servant and relating to acts done by him in the course of his employment, but not themselves made in the course of that employment, are not admissible against the master.

An action was brought by the father of a motor cyclist killed in a collision between the motor cycle and a lorry driven by a servant of the defendant Council. The driver was the only person who could give evidence as to how the accident happened and he had made certain statements at the inquest on the motor cyclist. In the present proceedings the plaintiff further sought to administer an interrogatory to the Council asking that it should admit that their driver had made these statements. Hallett J. allowed the interrogatory, and the defendant Council appealed.

SIR WILFRID GREENE M.R.: This appeal must be allowed. The interrogatory which the plaintiff seeks to administer to the defendant corporation is one asking that the defendant corporation should admit that their lorry driver made certain statements at the inquest. It is not suggested that the lorry driver was the agent of the defendants to make admissions, and admissions by the lorry driver would not be evidence against the defendant in the absence of proof to that effect.

The judge thought that the case was really similar to that of *Sloan* v. *Hanson* ([1939] 1 All E.R. 333) decided in this court. In that case, this court confirmed an order of ASQUITH J., who had allowed an interrogatory asking whether or not the defendant had at an inquest made certain statements which were set out in conjunction with the interrogatory. In that case, the person whom it was sought to interrogate was the defendant himself, and the admission which the answer to that interrogatory would have elicited would have been an admission by the defendant himself. In the present case, however, the only result of the answer to the interrogatory would be, not an admission by the defendants as to the way in which their driver was driving, but an admission by the defendants that on a particular occasion their servant, not being an agent to make an admission, made a particular statement, which is a different thing altogether.

It is worth noticing that in *Griebart* v. *Morris* [1920] 1 K.B. 659 the interrogatories which were allowed were interrogatories relating, not to an admission by somebody in the employment of the defendant, but to the actual way in which the defendant's car was being driven, which is a different thing altogether.

In the present case, the authority of *Sloan* v. *Hanson* is, in my judgment, no authority to support the present order, which, in my opinion, cannot stand...

FINLAY L.JJ. and DU PARCQ agreed.

Note.—See, too, *Tustin* v. *Arnold* (1915) 84 L.J.K.B. 2214. But contrast *Beer* v. *W.H. Clench (1930), Ltd.* (1936) 52 T.L.R. 300 (D.C.), where the driver was discharging an employer's statutory duty to cause a record of hours of driving to be kept: the record kept by the driver was held to be admissible against the employer. The servant's statement might now be admissible against the master under the Civil Evidence Act 1968, s.2 (Part Two, *infra*).

Woolway v. **Rowe** (1834) 1 A. and E. 114 (K.B.). The statement of the plaintiff's father, the former owner of the plaintiff's land, that he had not the right claimed by the plaintiff in respect of it, was held addmissible; although the father was living and in court at the time. Lord Denman C.J. (delivering the judgment of the court) said (p. 118): "The first question raised in this case was, whether the declarations of a person formerly interested in the estate now the plaintiff's were admissible in evidence, when the party himself might have been called. We think they were receivable, on the ground of identity of interest. The fact of his being alive at the time of the trial, when perhaps his memory of facts was impaired, and when his interest was not the same, does not, in our opinion, affect the admissibility of those declarations which he formerly made on the subject of his own rights."

Note.—For a case where both parties derived title from the same predecessor, see *Falcon* v. *Famous Players Film Co.* [1926] 2 K.B. 474 (C.A.). Cases as to admissions by predecessors in title may be compared with cases as to declarations by deceased persons against proprietory interests (see *Peaceable d. Uncle* v. *Watson* (1811) 4 Taunt. 16 (C.P.), this Chapter: Section A, *supra*).

R. v. BLAKE AND TYE

6 Q.B. 126; **13 L.J.M.C. 131**; 8 Jur. 666; 115 E.R. 49 (Q.B.: 1844)

Acts and also statements by one of several conspirators are evidence against the other party or parties to the conspiracy, as if the acts or statements were done or made by him or them, so far as they were in the execution or furtherance of their common purpose, but not otherwise.

Blake was a "landing waiter" employed at the Custom House, and Tye was an agent for importers there. They were charged with conspiring to pass goods without paying full duty. Tye had made false entries in two books; in a day book the entries were necessary in order to carry out the fraud, in a cheque book the entry in a counterfoil was not thus necessary, but was for Tye's convenience only. The former were admissible against Blake, the latter was not.

LORD DENMAN C.J.: ... Upon the first point, the evidence was clearly receivable; it was an entry made in the course of the transaction, which could not have been proved by any other means. With regard to the other piece of evidence ... full effect might have been given to the conspiracy without it. ... It is a mere statement of what this party was doing. ... A mere statement made by one conspirator, or an act that he may choose to do, which is not necessary to carry the conspiracy to its end, is not evidence to affect another. ...

COLERIDE J.: ... Acts or declarations are not receivable unless they tend to the advancement of the common object. That assumes the object not to be then completed. If it has been accomplished, the act or statement is not receivable. This was a mere statement as to the share of the plunder. ...

PATTESON and WILLIAMS JJ. concurred.

Note.—The conduct of a managing director may be admissible on a charge against a limited company and others of conspiracy to defraud (R. v. I.C.R. Haullage, Ltd. [1944] K.B. 551 (C.C.A.), but compare R. v. McDonnell [1966] 1 Q.B. 233).

The operation of the principle laid down in R. v. Blake and Tye is not limited to prosecutions for conspiracy. Where the case for the prosecution is that in the commission of a crime a number of persons acted in concert and there is evidence of such concert, evidence of acts and words of one of the parties in furtherance of the common purpose may be given against the accused though he may not have been present then such acts were done or words spoken: see Tripodi v. R. (1961) 104 C.L.R. 1; [1961] A.L.R. 780 (High Court of Australia).

R. v. NORTON

[1910] 2 K.B. 496; 79 L.J.K.B. 756; 102 L.T. 926; 26 T.L.R. 550 (C.C.A.: 1910)

Admissions made by an accused person may be proved against him on a criminal charge. Such admissions may be made by his answer to, or words used in reply to, an accusation or statement made in his presence, or by his silence, conduct or demeanour when such statement is made, according to the circumstances.

On a charge of an offence against a girl under 13, it was proved that, on being asked by the prisoner who had done the act, she said "You." Being asked by another person, she said "Stevie Norton," and pointed to the prisoner. The prisoner said, "No, Madge, you are mistaken"; and then she said, "You have done it, Stephen Norton," and pointed to him again. According to one witness he then lifted his arms and said, "If I have done it I hope the Lord will strike me dead"; and according to another witness, "If you say so I might as well put my clothes on and go home." The prisoner was convicted. On appeal it was held that the evidence did not amount to an admission, and the conviction was quashed.

PICKFORD J. (delivering the judgment of the court, which included LORD ALVERSTONE C.J. and LORD COLERIDGE J.): ... As a general rule, statements as to the facts of a case under investigation are not evidence unless made by witnesses in the ordinary way, but to this rule there are exceptions. One is that statements made in the presence of a prisoner upon an occasion on which he might reasonably be expected to make some observation, explanation, or denial are admissible under certain circumstances. We think it is not strictly accurate, and may be misleading, to say that they are admissible in evidence against the prisoner, as such an expression may seem to imply that they are evidence of the facts stated in them and must be considered upon the footing of other evidence. Such statements are, however, never evidence of the facts stated in them; they are admissible only as introductory to, or explanatory of, the answer given to them by the person in whose presence they are made. Such answer may, of course, be given either by words or by conduct, e.g. by remaining silent on an occasion which demanded an answer.

If the answer given amounts to an admission of the statements or some part of them, they or that part become relevant as showing what facts are admitted; if the answer be not such an admission, the statements are irrelevant to the matter under consideration and should be disregarded. ...

... We think that the contents of such statements should not be given in evidence unless the judge is satisfied that there is evidence fit to be submitted to the jury that the prisoner by his answer to them, whether given by word or conduct, acknowledged the truth of the whole or part of them. If there be no such evidence, then the contents of the statement should be excluded; if there be such evidence, then they should be admitted, and the question whether the prisoner's answer, by words or conduct, did or did not in fact amount to an acknowledgment of them left to the jury.

In trials of prisoners on indictment, in which the most numerous and important of these cases arise, there is, as a rule, no difficulty in deciding whether there be such evidence or not, as the prisoner's answer appears upon the depositions, and the chance that the evidence with regard to it may be different on the trial is so small that it may be disregarded. When, however, the evidence of the prisoner's answer does not appear, there does not seem to be any practical difficulty in applying the rule above stated. The fact of a statement having been made in the prisoner's presence may be given in evidence, but not the contents, and the question asked, what the prisoner said or did on such a statement being made. If his answer, given either by words or conduct, be such as to be evidence from which an acknowledgement may be inferred, then the contents of the statement may be given and the question of admission or not in fact to the left to the jury; if it be not evidence from which such an acknowledgment may be inferred, then the contents of the statement should be excluded. To allow the contents of such statements to be given before it is ascertained that there is evidence of their being acknowledged to be true must be most prejudicial to the prisoner, as, whatever directions be given to the jury, it is almost impossible for them to dismiss such evidence entirely from their minds. It is perhaps too wide to say that in no case can the statements be given in evidence when they are denied by the prisoner, as it is possible that a denial may be given under such circumstances and in such a manner as to constitute evidence from which an acknowledgement may be inferred;

but, as above stated, we think they should be rejected unless there is some evidence of an acknowledgement of the truth. Where they are admitted we think the following is the proper direction to be given to the jury: That if they come to the conclusion that the prisoner had acknowledged the truth of the whole or any part of the facts stated they might take the statement, or so much of it as was acknowledged to be true (but no more), into consideration as evidence in the case generally, not because the statement standing alone afforded any evidence of the matter contained in it, but solely because of the prisoner's acknowledgement of its truth; but unless they found as a fact that there was such an acknowledgement they ought to disregard the statement altogether. . . .

Note.—That the accused, when cautioned and charged by the police (*R.* v. *Whitehead* [1929] 1 K.B. 99 (C.C.A.)), or at the hearing before the magistrates (*R.* v. *Naylor* [1933] 1 K.B. 685 (C.C.A.)), makes no denial does not amount to an admission (see also *R.* v. *Davis* (1959) 43 Cr.App.R 215 (C.C.A.); *R.* v. *Sullivan* (1966) 57 Cr.App.R. 102 (C.A.)). But although silence in such circumstances cannot amount to corroboration in a case where corroboration is required by law or practice (Chapter 10, *supra*), nevertheless the judge may in a proper case comment on the silence of the accused and on the fact that he has reserved his defence until the last possible moment, so depriving the police of any opportunity to verify it (*R.* v. *Littleboy* [1934] 2 K.B. 408 (C.C.A.)): but contrast *R.* v. *Gilbert* (1977) 66 Cr.App.R. 237 (C.A.)). The discretion should be exercised with restraint.

Notice of the defence of alibi is now necessary: Criminal Justice Act 1967, s.11 (Part Two, *infra*).

R. v. CHRISTIE

[1914] A.C. 545; 83 L.J.K.B. 1097; 111 L.T. 220; 30 T.L.R. 471; 24 Cox C.C. 249; 10 Cr.App.R. 141 (H.L.: 1914)

A statement or accusation made to or in the presence of an accused person may be evidence against him, although he actually denied or repudiated it at the time, if by his conduct or demeanour he may be held to have admitted it.

A statement made by a witness before the trial is not corroboration of the evidence he gives at the trial.

Christie was convicted of an indecent assault on a small boy, who gave his evidence without being sworn, under section 30 of the Children Act 1908 (now replaced). The boy described the assault and identified the prisoner, but he was not questioned as to a previous identification, nor was he cross-examined. The boy's mother then gave evidence that, shortly after the act alleged, she and the boy went towards the prisoner, and the boy said, "That is the man," describing the assault. Christie then said, "I am innocent." The mother was not cross-examined. A constable was then called as a witness, and confirmed the mother's story, saying that the boy went up to Christie, touched him and said, "That is the man," describing the assault, and that Christie said, "I am innocent." The constable was cross-examined, but his evidence on this point was not affected.

The Court of Criminal Appeal held that the boy's statement in Christie's presence was improperly admitted, as he had denied its truth, and they quashed the conviction. The House of Lords held (1) that the first part of the boy's statement, but not the second describing the assault, was admissible as part of the act of identification; (2) that the second part was admissible, as made in the presence of the accused and in view of his demeanour; but that, in general, where the evidence of a prisoner's assent to the truth of such statements is very slight, the judge should exclude them; (3) that the second part was not admissible either as part of the *res gestae*, or to corroborate the boy's testimony. The order quashing the conviction was affirmed on the ground of want of corroboration.

VISCOUNT HALDANE L.C.: My Lords, I have had the advantage of considering the opinions which three of your Lordships are about to express.... In the opinions about to be delivered by Lord Atkinson, Lord Moulton and Lord Reading the true view of the law appears to me to be expressed. The only point on which I desire to guard myself is the admissibility of the statement in question as evidence of identification. For the boy gave evidence at the trial, and if his evidence was required for the identification of the prisoner that evidence ought, in my opinion, to have been his direct evidence in the witness-box and not evidence of what he said elsewhere.... Subject to this observation I concur in the judgments about to be delivered.

LORD ATKINSON: ... The Attorney-General contended that the entire statement of the boy was admissible on each of four separate grounds:

(1) As part of the act of identification, or as explanatory of it.

(2) As a statement made in the presence of the prisoner in circumstances calling for some denial or explanation from him, the truth of which he admitted by his conduct and demeanour.

(3) As proof of the consistency of the boy's conduct before he was examined with his testimony at the trial.

(4) As part of the *res gestae*.

Your Lordships intimated during the course of the argument that you would not consider this third point. It is, therefore, unnecessary to allude to it further....

As to the first point, it cannot, I think, be open to doubt that if the boy had said nothing more, as he touched the sleeve of the coat of the accused, than "That is the man," the statement was so closely connected with the act which it accompanied, expressing, indeed, as it did, in words little if anything more than would have been implied by the gesture simpliciter, that it should have been admitted as part of the very act of identification itself. It is on the admissibility of the further statement made in answer to the question of the constable that the controversy arises. On the whole, I am of opinion, though not without some doubt, that this statement only amplifies what is implied by the words "That is the man," plus the act of touching him....

As to the second ground, the rule of law undoubtedly is that a statement made in the presence of an accused person, even upon an occasion which would be expected reasonably to call for some explanation or denial from him, is not evidence against him of the facts stated save so far as he accepts the statement, so as to make it, in effect, his own. If he accepts the statement in part only, then to that extent alone dogs it become his statement. He may accept the statement by word or conduct, action or demeanour, and it is the function of the jury which tries the case to determine whether his words, action, conduct, or demeanour at the time when a statement was made amounts to an acceptance of it in whole of in part. It by no means follows, I think, that a mere denial by the accused of the facts mentioned in the statement necessarily renders the statement inadmissible, because he may deny the statement in such a manner and under such circumstances as may lead a jury to disbelieve him, and constitute evidence from which an acknowledgement may be inferred by them.

Of course, if at the end of the case the presiding judge should be of opinion that no evidence has been given upon which the jury could reasonably find that the accused had accepted the statement so as to make it in whole or in part his own, the judge can instruct the jury to disregard the statement entirely. It is said that, despite this direction, grave injustice might be done to the accused, in as much as the jury, having once heard the statement, could not, or would not, rid their mind of it. It is, therefore, in the application of the rule that the difficulty arises. The question then is this: Is it to be taken as a rule of law that such a statement is not to be admitted in evidence until a foundation has been laid for its admission by proof of facts from which, in the opinion of the presiding judge, a jury might reasonably draw the inference that the accused had so accepted the statement as to make it in whole or in part his own, or is it to be laid down that the prosecutor is entitled to give the statement in evidence in the first instance, leaving it for the presiding judge, in case no such evidence as the above-mentioned should be ultimately produced, to tell the jury to disregard the statement altogether.

In my view the former is not a rule of law, but it is, I think, a rule which, in the interest of justice, it might be most prudent and proper to follow as a rule of practice....

The boy's statement was so separated by time and circumstances from the actual commission of the crime that it was not, I think, admissible as part of the *res gestae*....

Even, however, if the boy's statement was admissible in evidence, if properly dealt with, I think they verdict should be quashed. The deputy chairman never properly explained to the jury that it is what the accused accepts as his own of the statement made in his presence that is evidence against him, not the statement itself. Again, he treated the evidence of the mother of the boy and the constable, as to what the boy said and did on the occasion of the identification, as corroboration to his testimony at the trial, within the meaning of the 30th section of the Children Act of 1908. This is, of course, wholly erroneous. If the boy himself had been examined, either in chief or on cross-examination, and had detailed what took place at the identification, this portion of his evidence could not be treated as corroboration of the other portion proving the charge. He could not be his own corroborator. It can make no possible difference when others tell what he did and said on that occasion. Their evidence is no more "material corroborative evidence in support of his evidence at the trial implicating the accused" than his would be....

My Lords, I have been requested by my noble and learned friend LORD PARKER to express his concurrence in this judgment.

LORDS MOULTON and READING made speeches to the same effect; and LORD DUNEDIN concurred with the latter speech.

Note.—The requirement of corroboration of the evidence of an unsworn child is abolished by the Criminal Justice Act 1988, s.33(1) (Part Two, *infra*).

As to *res gestae*, see Chapter 15, *infra*.

HALL v. R.

[1971] 1 W.L.R. 298; [1971] 1 All E.R. 322; 55 Cr.App.R. 108 (P.C.: 1970)

A person is under no obligation to comment when informed that someone has accused him of an offence. Although there may be exceptional circumstances in which an inference may be drawn from a failure to give an explanation or make a disclaimer, silence alone on being so informed by a police officer cannot give rise to an inference that the person to whom the information is communicated accepts the truth of the accusation.

The appellant was charged jointly with two others, Thompson and Gordon, with unlawful possession of drugs. Premises, said to have been occupied by the three defendants, had been searched by the police, the appellant being absent at the time. Drugs were found in the rooms occupied by Thompson and Gordon. Thompson told the police that the bag containing the drugs found in his room had been brought there by the appellant. Shortly afterwards the appellant was brought to the premises by another police officer. He was told by the officer who had conducted the search that Thompson had said that the drugs belonged to him. He made no comment on this, but remained silent. All three defendants were then cautioned, and none of them said anything. All three were convicted. The appellant's appeal to the Court of Appeal of Jamaica was dismissed. He appealed to the Privy Council.

LORD DIPLOCK (delivering the judgment of the Board): The Court of Appeal had held...that the appellant's silence when told of the accusation made against him by Daphne Thompson amounted to an acknowledgement by him of the truth of the statement which Daphne Thompson had made....

In dealing with this question, the Court of Appeal cited the following paragraph from Archbold, *Criminal Pleading, Evidence & Practice* (37th ed., 1969), para. 1126: "A statement made in the presence of an accused person, accusing him of a crime, upon an occasion which may be expected reasonably to call for some explanation or denial from him, is not evidence against him of the facts stated, save in so far as he accepts the statement so as to make it in effect his own. If he accepts the statement in part only, then to that extent alone does it become his statement. He may accept the statement by word or conduct, action or demeanour, and it is the function of the jury which tries the case to determine whether his words, action, conduct or demeanour at the time when the statement was made amount to an acceptance of it in whole or in part." This statement, in their Lordships' view, states the law accurately. It is a citation from the speech of Lord Atkinson in *Rex* v. *Christie* [1914] A.C. 545, 555. But their Lordships do not consider that in the instant case the Court of Appeal applied it correctly. It is not suggested in the instant case that the appellant's acceptance of the suggestion of Daphne Thompson which was repeated to him by the police constable was shown by word or by any positive conduct, action or demeanour. All that is relied upon is his mere silence.

It is a clear and widely known principle of the common law in Jamaica, as in England, that a person is entitled to refrain from answering a question put to him for the purpose of discovering whether he has committed a criminal offence. *A fortiori* he is under no obligation to comment when he is informed that someone else has accused him of an offence. It may be that in very exceptional circumstances an inference may be drawn from a failure to give an explanation or a disclaimer, but in their Lordships' view silence alone on being informed by a police officer that someone else has made an accusation against him cannot give rise to an inference that the person to whom this information is communicated accepts the truth of the accusation. . . .

The caution merely serves to remind the accused of a right which he already possesses at common law. The fact that in a particular case he has not been reminded of it is no ground for inferring that his silence was not in exercise of that right, but was an acknowledgement of the truth of the accusation.

. . . Their Lordships have humbly advised Her Majesty that this appeal should be allowed and the appellant's conviction quashed.

Note.—In *R.* v. *Chandler* [1976] 1 W.L.R. 585 (C.A.) Lawton L.J. (delivering the judgment of the Court of Appeal) expressed "reservations" about the statement of the law contained in the paragraph commencing "It is a clear and widely known principle . . . " on the ground that it seems to conflict with *R.* v. *Christie* (*supra*) and with earlier authorities. His Lordship said (p. 589): "The law has long accepted that an accused person is not bound to incriminate himself; but it does not follow that a failure to answer an accusation or question when an answer could reasonably be expected may not provide some evidence in support of an accusation. Whether it does will depend upon the circumstances." His Lordship then cited with approval Lord Atkinson's words in *R.* v. *Christie* (*supra*) and commented (p. 590): "We are bound by *Rex* v. *Christie*, not by *Hall* v. *The Queen.*"

PARKES v. R.

[1976] 1 W.L.R. 1251; [1976] 3 All E.R. 380; 64 Cr.App.R. 25 (P.C.: 1976)

When a person is accused of a crime by a person speaking to him on even terms and it would be natural for him to reply, his silence in the face of the accusation together with his conduct may be taken into account by the jury when assessing the truth of the accusation.

The appellant was charged with the murder of a woman who had died from stab wounds. At the trial the dead woman's mother gave evidence that she had found her daughter injured and had gone to the appellant and said, "What she do you—why you stab her?" that she had repeated the question and that the appellant had made no answer and had tried to stab her when she threatened to hold him until the police came. He was convicted and his appeal to the Court of Appeal of Jamaica was dismissed. He appealed to the Privy Council.

LORD DIPLOCK (delivering the judgment of the Board): . . . On appeal to the Court of Appeal of Jamaica, the principal point argued on behalf of the defendant appears to have been that Smith C.J. was wrong in instructing the jury that the failure of the defendant to reply to the accusation twice made against him by Mrs. Graham that he had stabbed her daughter, coupled with his conduct immediately after that accusation had been made, were matters from which the jury could, if they thought fit, draw an inference that the defendant accepted the truth of the accusation. . . .

In support of the argument that the defendant's failure to answer Mrs. Graham's accusation that he had stabbed her daughter was not a matter from which the jury were entitled to draw any inference that the defendant accepted the truth of the accusation the defendant relied on the following passage in the judgment of this Board in *Hall* v. *The Queen* [1971] 1 W.L.R. 298, 301:

> "It is a clear and widely known principle of the common law in Jamaica, as in England, that a person is entitled to refrain from answering a question put to him for the purpose of discovering whether he has committed a criminal offence. *A fortiori* he is under an obligation to comment when he is informed that someone else has accused him of an offence. It may be that in very exceptional circumstances an inference may be drawn from a failure to give an explanation or a disclaimer, but in their Lordships' view silence alone on being informed by a police officer that someone else has made an accusation against him cannot give rise to an inference that the person to whom this information is communicated accepts the truth of the accusation."

As appears from this passage itself, it was concerned with a case where the person by whom the accusation was communicated to the accused was a police constable whom he knew was engaged in investigating a drug offence. There was no evidence of the defendant's demeanour or conduct when the accusation was made other than the mere fact that he failed to reply to the constable. The passage cited had been preceded by a quotation from a speech of Lord Atkinson in *Rex* v. *Christie* [1914] A.C. 545, 554, in which it was said that when a statement is made in the presence of an accused person:

> "He may accept the statement by word or conduct, action or demeanour, and it is the function of the jury which tries the case to determine whether his words, action, conduct or demeanour at the time when the statement was made amount to an acceptance of it in whole or in part."

In the instant case, there is no question of an accusation being made by or in the presence of a police officer or any other person in authority or charged with the investigation of the crime. It was a spontaneous charge made by a mother about an injury done to her daughter. In circumstances such as these, their Lordships agree with the Court of Appeal of Jamaica that the direction given by Cave J. in *Reg* v. *Mitchell* (1892) 17 Cox C.C. 503, 508 (to which their Lordships have supplied the emphasis) is applicable:

> "Now the whole admissibility of statements of this kind rests upon the consideration that if a charge is made against a person in that person's presence it is reasonable to expect that he or she will immediately deny it, and that the absence of such a denial is some evidence of an admission on the part of the person charged, and of the truth of the charge. *Undoubtedly, when persons are speaking on even terms,* and a charge is made, and the person charged says

nothing, and expresses no indignation, and does nothing to repel the charge, that is some evidence to show that he admits the charge to be true."

Here Mrs. Graham and the defendant were speaking on even terms. Furthermore, as the Chief Justice pointed out to the jury, the defendant's reaction to the twice-repeated accusation was not one of mere silence. He drew a knife and attempted to stab Mrs. Graham in order to escape when she threatened to detain him while the police were sent for. In their Lordships' view, the Chief Justice was perfectly entitled to instruct the jury that the defendant's reactions to the accusations including his silence were matters which they would take into account along with other evidence in deciding whether the defendant in fact committed the act with which he was charged. For these reasons their Lordships have humbly advised Her Majesty that the appeal be dismissed.

R. v. **Spinks** (1982) 74 Cr.App.R. 263 (C.A.). The appellant was convicted of doing, without lawful authority or reasonable excuse, an act—concealing a knife—with intent to impede the apprehension of a person named Fairey who had committed an arrestable offence, knowing him to be guilty of such an offence, contrary to section 4(1) of the Criminal Law Act 1967. The only evidence tendered at the trial showing that Fairey was guilty of an arrestable offence was his own out-of-court admission to the police made in the absence of the appellant. The Court of Appeal quashed the appellant's conviction, even though Fairey was in the event convicted of wounding with intent to do grievous bodily harm, having been charged on the same indictment as the appellant. Russell J., reading the judgment of the Court, said (p. 266): "The short point that is taken, therefore, is that the Crown had no admissible evidence as against the appellant to prove the first ingredient of the offence with which he was charged, namely, . . . that Fairey had committed the arrestable offence of wounding. The only evidence of that fact came from an out-of-court admission of a co-defendant which was not admissible against the appellant."

R. v. **Eden** [1970] 2 O.R. 161; [1970] 3 C.C.C. 280 (Court of Appeal for Ontario). The appellant had been convicted, along with two others, of taking a motor car without the owner's consent. After being stopped by the police the three defendants had been taken to a police car, and the questions had been addressed to them while they were sitting together on the rear seat. The answers were given by the other two defendants, the appellant remaining silent. The Ontario Court of Appeal held that evidence of what was said, although inculpating the appellant, ought not have been admitted in evidence against him and quashed his conviction. Gale C.J.O. (delivering the judgment of the court) said (O.R., p. 164): "When the appellant was seated in the back of the police cruiser alongside his two co-accused he was undoubtedly under arrest; notwithstanding the fact that the customary warning had not been given to him he was entirely within his rights in remaining silent and no imputation unfavourable to him should be placed upon his exercise of that right. To assume from his silence that he had conceded the accuracy of the statement would be in effect to place upon a prisoner under arrest the obligation to make exculpatory statements. For these reasons the fact that the appellant failed to contest the statement made in his presence was not evidence from which an inference of his guilt could be drawn."

Mahoney v. **Fielding** [1959] Qd. R. 749 (Full S.C. of Queensland). The accused was arrested on a charge of drunken driving. When he was put in the police car a third person shouted advice to him not to submit to any tests and to ring his own doctor. It was held that evidence of this had been wrongly admitted. Philip J. said (p. 484): "The evidence is quite inadmissible and very prejudicial. It was adduced for the improper purpose of planting in the magistrate's mind the idea that one of the appellant's companions thought that the appellant was so under the influence of alcohol as to need such a warning. One knows that it is widely held in police court circles that any statement made in the presence of a defendant is admissible. Of course, that is not the law."

E. STATUTORY EXCEPTIONS TO THE HEARSAY RULE

Note.—The selection of statutory enactments listed below is not exhaustive. Of general, as distinct from specific, importance are section 9 of the Criminal Justice Act 1967, sections 69–72 of the Police and Criminal Evidence Act 1984, and Part II of the Criminal Justice Act 1988. For all the listed provisions, except the Video Recording Act 1984, s.19, see Part Two, (*infra*).

Theft Act 1968, s.27(4).
Criminal Justice Act 1967, s.9.
Video Recording Act 1984, s.19.
Police and Criminal Evidence Act 1984, s.69–72.
Criminal Justice Act 1988, Part II.

Chapter 15

RES GESTAE

An item of evidence, otherwise inadmissible or of dubious admissibility, is sometimes received on the ostensible ground that it forms part of the *res gestae*.[1] Historically resort has been variously had to the notion of *res gestae* in order to facilitate the reception of similar fact evidence,[2] of opinion evidence and of hearsay evidence; but in relatively modern times its principal role has been the amelioration of the rigours of the hearsay rule. The recurrent, but far from consistent, theme of justification for the reception of such evidence has been its factual intimacy with other admissible evidence. More recently, and particularly since the Privy Council case of *Ratten* v. *R*.[3] focus has shifted to considerations bearing more directly on reliability. As a unitary doctrine *res gestae* defies even plausible logical analysis, but its influence upon the development of the law has on the whole been benign in that it has operated to soften the edges of over-rigid exclusionary rules.[4] In the sphere of hearsay it has provided an inclusionary cloak, under cover of which additional exceptions to the rule have crystallised; moreover, occasionally resort to it has served as a convenient pretext for the admission of evidence not falling within even a partially crystallised exception to the rule. Rational formulation of the underlying doctrine is made more difficult by the circumstance that in some instances the courts have made unnecessary use of *res gestae* terminology—unnecessary, either because the evidence has in reality been tendered as original rather than hearsay evidence, or because, although hearsay, it has fallen within an established exception to the hearsay rule. Conversely, in dealing with some situations apparently falling within a recognised category of *res gestae* the courts have not made use of the term.

Several attempts have been made by writers on the law of evidence to identify and classify the cases on or near the fringes of the hearsay rule (and the exceptions thereto) in which evidence has been received "as part of the *res gestae*." Many of these analyses appear to derive from that of Morgan whose pioneer article on the subject was published in 1922,[5] and all to some extent smack of *ex post facto* rationalisation. The

---

[1] Sometimes referred to as *res gestae*. The plural usage was emphatically rejected by Thayer.
[2] See Chapter 20, *infra*.
[3] [1972] A.C. 378 (P.C.) (*infra*).
[4] In 1953 its extension was recommended in the Report of the Evershed Committee on Supreme Court Practice and Procedure.
[5] Morgan, "A Suggested Classification of Utterances admissible as *Res Gestae*," 31 Yale Law Journal 299 (1922). See, too, Stone, "*Res Gestae Reagitatae*," 55 L.Q.R. 66 (1939).

late Sir Rupert Cross, perhaps somewhat conservatively, detailed four *res gestae* type exceptions to the hearsay rule.[6] These were: (1) statements made by a person contemporaneously with his performance of an act and explaining its significance; (2) spontaneous exclamations; (3) statements concerning the maker's contemporaneous state of mind or emotion; and (4) statements about the maker's contemporaneous physical sensation.

The boundaries of these four categories are in many respects ill-defined, and in some instances the categories seem to have been treated as over-lapping. However, some points appear to have become reasonably well settled: a contemporaneous explanatory statement to be admissible must have been made by the person doing the act which it explains and it must relate directly to that act; and a statement concerning the maker's contemporaneous state of mind or emotion is only received when that state of mind or emotion is *itself* in issue or relevant. At the same time there remain important uncertainties: the concept of spontaneity for the purposes of the reception of a "spontaneous" exclamation has been loosened in recent cases; it is far from clear whether mere intention qualifies as a state of mind for the purpose of the third category of *res gestae* exceptions; and the significance of contemporaneity in relation to admissibility as part of the *res gestae* has been greatly reduced.

Some of the materials set out in this Chapter illustrate cases in which otherwise inadmissible evidence has been received on the ground of its being so inextricably bound up with other evidence that the resultant amalgam should be regarded as evidence of a single, although sometimes continuing transaction. Other materials set out here relate to the above-mentioned four categories of hearsay evidence. Others illustrate the influence of the judgment of Lord Wilberforce in *Ratten* v. *R.* referred to above.

It is to be noted that, many of the cases illustrating the operation of the doctrine are civil cases, which pre-date the Civil Evidence Act 1968.[7] Since the coming into effect of that Act the doctrine of *res gestae* is, as such, no longer available to facilitate the admission of hearsay evidence in civil litigation.[8] But much evidence which would previously have been received as part of the *res gestae* is now admissible under the general provisions of that Act; and this admissibility is, of course, free of the restrictions surrounding the reception of *res gestae* evidence, although it is subject to the safeguards embodied in the Act. The otiose use of *res gestae* terminology in relation to original evidence is not affected by the Act; nor is any continued resort to the doctrine to explain the reception of opinion or similar fact evidence. Moreover, the scope of the doctrine of *res gestae* in criminal cases is, of course, in no way affected by the 1968 Act.

R. v. **Ellis** (1826) 6 B. &. C. 145 (K.B.). The prisoner was charged with stealing six shillings, marked money, from a till. Evidence was allowed of the taking not

---

[6] Cross, *Evidence* (5th ed., 1979), pp. 575–591.

[7] ss.1–10 (Part Two, *infra*).

[8] Except in Magistrates' Courts. See, too, the cryptic dictum of Lord Ackner in *R.* v. *Andrews* [1987] A.C. 281, 302 (H.L.), p. 366, *infra*.

only of that amount but also of other moneys taken during the day. Bayley J. said (pp. 147–148): "Generally speaking, it is not competent to a prosecutor to prove a man guilty of one felony, by proving him guilty of another unconnected felony; but where several felonies are connected together, and form part of one entire transaction, then the one is evidence to show the character of the other. Now all the evidence in this case tended to show that the prisoner was guilty of the felony charged in the indictment. It went to show the history of the till from the time when the marked money was put into it up to the time when it was found in the possession of the prisoner. I think, therefore, that the evidence was properly received."

Note.—Contrast *R.* v. *Birdseye* (1830) 4 C. & P. 386, where the alleged theft of a loaf half an hour after the alleged theft of some pork was held not to be part of the former act. See also *R.* v. *Rodley* [1913] 3 K.B. 468 (C.A.A.), where, on a charge of breaking and entering with intent to commit rape, evidence was held to have been wrongly admitted to the effect that on the same night about an hour later the prisoner had gone to a neighbouring farmhouse, climbed down the chimney into a woman's bedroom, and there had sexual connection with her with her consent.

O'Leary v. **R.** (1946) 73 C.L.R. 566 (H.C. (Aust.)). One, Ballard, an employee at a timber camp, and other fellow employees including the defendant, took part in a drunken orgy commencing on Saturday morning and continuing until late on Saturday evening. About midnight Ballard retired to his cubicle which was a short distance from that of the defendant; and in the early hours of the following morning he was found in a dying condition still in his cubicle. Examination showed that he had been struck on the head eight or nine times with a bottle and had then been soaked in kerosene and had his clothes set alight. Shortly after the discovery of Ballard the defendant was found to have a bottle in his possession, and a sweater belonging to him was picked up near Ballard's cubicle. At the defendant's trial for murder evidence was admitted that he had in the course of the orgy violently assaulted other employees; that some of these assaults were unprovoked and all took the form of sharp blows to the head; and that during the afternoon he had aimed a blow at Ballard. The defendant was convicted, and his appeal to the Full Supreme Court of South Australia was dismissed. The High Court of Australia refused his application for special leave to appeal, holding *inter alia* (McTiernan J. dissenting) that the evidence had been properly admitted. Rich J. said (p. 567): "I would...put the admissibility...on the ground that it forms part of the circumstances of crime, including the drunken condition of the prisoner, how he reached that condition, how long it continued and how, while in that condition, he was behaving. His violence, the fact that he exhibited this violence on slight or no provocation, and all the circumstances, form inseparable features of a transaction consisting of connected events." Dixon J. said (p. 577): "a connected series of events occurred which should be considered as one transaction." Williams J. said (p. 582): "It is evidence of certain significant incidents which took place in a series of connected occurrences which commenced with the drunken orgy on the sixth of July and concluded with Ballard's death in the early morning of the seventh...."

Note.—See, too *R.* v. *Wilkinson* [1934] 3 D.L.R. 50; 62 C.C.C. 63 (S.C. of Nova Scotia).

Howe v. **Malkin** (1878) 40 L.T. 196 (C.P.D.). An action for trespass involved an issue as to the position of a boundary. It was sought to prove a statement made by the plaintiff's father contemporaneously with the carrying out of work on the land by some builders. The evidence was rejected. Grove J. said

(p. 196): "It appears to me that the evidence was properly rejected; no act was shown to have been done by the plaintiff's father at the time of making the alleged statement, so that the declaration was by one person, and the accompanying act by another. That does not appear to me to come within the rule. The rule is that, though you cannot give in evidence a declaration *per se*, yet when there is an act accompanied by a statement which is so mixed up with it as to become part of the *res gestae*, evidence of such statement may be given. The statements here do not come fairly within that rule." Denman J. said (p. 197): "...in the present case the declarations sought to be given in evidence were not declarations accompanying an act, no evidence being tendered of any act whatever having been done by the declarant."

Note.—Contrast *R.* v. *Bliss* (1837) 7 Ad. & Ell. 550 (Q.B.) (Chapter 14, Section A, p. 324, *supra*).

Manchester Brewery Co. v. **Coombs** (1900), 82 L.T. 347 (Ch.D.). Under a contract between the plaintiff brewery company and the licensee of a public house the latter undertook to purchase all his beer from the former. The plaintiff company brought an action to restrain breach of this undertaking. The defendant licensee pleaded that the plaintiff was in breach of its obligation to supply good beer. At the trial the defendant licensee's counsel sought to ask him as a witness whether he had received complaints from customers about the quality of the beer. Farwell J. allowed the question and (presumably) the licensee's affirmative answer. Farwell J. said (p. 349): "...According to my recollection, this question has always been allowed in actions of this nature, and I think for this reason. Counsel can certainly ask as to facts—Did the customer order beer? Did he finish it? What did he do with it? If the matter is left there with the answer that he tasted and left it or threw it away, the judge cannot avoid drawing an inference, and the cross-examining counsel is driven to ask for some explanation. It is simpler, therefore, to allow the statement of the customer of the reason for his conduct to be given in chief...."

Note.—See, too, *R.* v. *Christie* [1914] A.C. 545 (H.L.) Chapter 14, Section D, *supra*.

Teper v. **R.** [1952] A.C. 480 (P.C.). The accused was convicted in British Guiana of setting fire to a shop belonging to his wife. To identify the accused as the person responsible for the fire, evidence was given by a police constable that he heard a woman shouting, "Your place burning and you going away from the fire," and that he then saw a car in which there was a man resembling the accused. This incident took place some distance from the burning shop, and nearly half-an-hour after the fire had started. The appeal was allowed, and the conviction quashed. Lord Normand (delivering the reasons of the Board) said (pp. 486 *et seq*.): "The rule against the admission of hearsay evidence is fundamental.... Nevertheless, the rule admits of certain carefully safeguarded and limited exceptions, one of which is that words may be proved when they form part of the *res gestae*.... It appears to rest ultimately on two propositions, that human utterance is both a fact and a means of communication, and that human action may be so interwoven with words that the significance of the action cannot be understood without the correlative words, and the dissociation of the words from the action would impede the discovery of truth. But the judicial applications of these two propositions, which do not always combine harmoniously, have never been precisely formulated in a general principle. Their Lordships will not attempt to arrive at a general formula, nor is it necessary to review all of the considerable number of cases cited in the argument. This, at least, may be said, that it is essential that the words sought to be proved by hearsay should be, if not absolutely contemporaneous with the action or event, at least so clearly associated with it, in time, place and circumstances, that they are part of the thing being done, and so an item or part of real evidence and not merely a reported statement: *R.* v. *Bedingfield* (1879) 14 Cox C.C. 341 (*supra*); *O'Hara* v. *Central S.M.T. Co.*, 1941 S.C. 363. . . . There was no other evidence of identification that was of any value, and the effect of this on the jury's mind would not improbably be to throw into relief the hearsay evidence and to give it prominence."

Note.—The reference to *R.* v. *Bedingfield* (*infra*) must now be re-assessed in the light of *R.* v. *Andrews* [1987] A.C. 281 (H.L.) (*infra*).

Any apparent holding that hearsay evidence of identification is never admissible cannot now be sustained in the light of subsequent cases such as *R.* v. *Turnbull* (1985) 80 Cr.App.R. 104 (C.A.) and *R.* v. *Andrews* [1987] A.C. 281 (H.L.) (*infra*). See too *R.* v. *Osbourne*; *R.* v. *Virtue* [1973] 1 Q.B. 678 (C.A.).

R. v. **Foster** (1834) 6 C. & P. 325 (Cen. Crim. Ct.). The accused was charged with manslaughter by driving over the deceased. A witness saw the vehicle drive by, but did not see the accident. He immediately afterwards went up to the injured man, who then made a statement as to the cause of the injury. The statement was admitted in evidence. Gurney B. said (p. 325): "What the deceased said at the instant, as to the cause of the accident, is clearly admissible." Park J. said (p. 325): "I am of opinion, that his evidence ought to be received. It is the best possible testimony that, under the circumstances, can be adduced to show what it was that had knocked the deceased down." Patterson J. concurred.

Note.—The general rule that the *res gestae* include oral statements has been traced back to *Thompson* v. *Trevanion* (1693) Skin. 402; when, in an action for assault on the plaintiff's wife, Holt C.J. allowed that what the wife said immediate upon the hurt received, and before she had time to devise or contrive anything for her own advantage, might be given in evidence.

Foster's case involved a somewhat liberal view of what is a contemporaneous statement. It is now acknowledged that the central focus is not on contemporaneity, which need only be "approximate": see *e.g. R.* v. *Andrews* [1987] A.C. 281 (H.L.) (*infra*).

R. v. **Bedingfield** (1879) 14 Cox C.C. 341 (Assizes). [This famous (and controversial) decision of Cockburn C.J. has recently been overruled: *R.* v. *Andrews* [1987] A.C. 281 (H.L.) (*infra*). A note of it is included here in the light of the many references to it to be found in the case-law.] At a murder trial it was proved that the deceased, with her throat cut, came suddenly out of a room, in which she had left the accused. Evidence was tendered to show that immediately after coming out of the room, and shortly before she died, she had made a remark implicating him. The actual words were not proved at the trial, but they were said to have been: "Oh dear, Aunt, see what Bedingfield has done to me." It was held that her statement was not admissible in evidence, either as a dying declaration, as it did not appear that she was in fear of death, or as *res gestae*, as it was made after the transaction was complete. Cockburn C.J. did indicate that the evidence would have been admissible on the latter ground had the utterance been at the time the act was actually being done, as for instance, if the deceased had been heard to say something such as "Don't Harry!"

Davies v. **Fortior Ltd.** [1952] 1 All E.R. 1359 (Q.B.D.). The plaintiff was the widow of a former employee of the defendant company and brought an action for negligence and breach of statutory duty under the Fatal Accidents

Act 1846 and under the Law Reform (Miscellaneous Provisions) Act 1934. The defendant company were engaged in chromium plating processes at their factory. The employee while working the processes concerned with the chromium plating of sheets of copper, fell from a platform into a bath of chromic acid. He died two days later. The defendant company denied that they had been guilty of negligence or of any breach of statutory duty, and said that the accident was occasioned solely by, or alternatively contributed to by, the negligence of the employee, who was a foreman, in failing to keep any or any proper look-out for his own safety. No one had witnessed the accident and there was no direct evidence to show how the employee fell into the bath. To support an inference that the employee had been guilty of some negligent conduct, *e.g.* sitting on the guard rail of the bath, the defendant company sought to give evidence that, within a period variously estimated by the witnesses at from a few seconds to two minutes after he had been assisted out of the bath, he had said several times "I shouldn't have done it." Donovan J. held that what the employee said immediately after the accident was admissible evidence as part of the *res gestae*. [The action was finally settled.]

Note.—See, too, *Cassels* v. *Toronto Transportation Commission* [1938] 1 D.L.R. 746 (Ont. C.A.); but contrast *R.* v. *Leland* [1951] O.R. 12; 98 C.C.C. 337 (Ont. C.A.).

RATTEN v. R.

[1972] A.C. 378; [1971] 3 All E.R. 801 (P.C.: 1971)

Evidence of a sobbing woman's statement, "Get me the police, please—," made by telephone is admissible as tending to show that the woman was alarmed, such evidence not being hearsay, or if containing an element of hearsay, being nevertheless safely admissible.

LORD WILBERFORCE (delivering the reasons of the Board, which included LORDS REID, HODSON, DIPLOCK and CROSS OF CHELSEA): The appellant was convicted...of the murder of his wife. His application to the Full Court of the Supreme Court of Victoria for leave to appeal was dismissed...By special leave he now appeals to the Board.

The death of the deceased took place in the kitchen of her house on May 7, 1970, as the result of a gunshot wound. The evidence established the times of certain events as follows:

(i) At 1.09 p.m., the appellant's father S. R. Ratten telephoned to the appellant from Melbourne; the call was a trunk call and so was timed and time recorded. It lasted 2.9 minutes. The conversation was perfectly normal: Mr. S. R. Ratten heard the voice of the deceased woman in the background apparently making comments of a normal character.

(ii) At about 1.15 p.m. a telephone call was made from the house and answered at the local exchange. The facts regarding this call are critical and will be examined later.

(iii) At about 1.20 p.m. a police officer, calling from the local police station, telephoned the appellant's house and spoke to the appellant. By this time the appellant's wife had been shot. Thus the shooting of the deceased, from which she died almost immediately, must have taken place between 1.12 p.m. and about 1.20 p.m.

The death of the deceased was caused by a wound from a shotgun held by the appellant. The appellant's account was that the discharge was accidental and occurred while he was cleaning his gun. . . .

It was relevant and important to inquire what was the action of the appellant immediately after the shooting. His evidence, which he first gave in a signed statement to the police on May 8, 1970, was that he immediately telephoned for an ambulance and that shortly afterwards the police telephoned him upon which he asked them to come immediately. He denied that any telephone call had been made by his wife, and also denied that he had telephoned for the police. It should be added that he gave evidence from the witness box at the trial, maintaining his account of events.

In these circumstances, and in order to rebut the appellant's account, the prosecution sought to introduce evidence from a telephonist at the local exchange as to the call made from the house at about 1.15 p.m.

The evidence as given by the telephonist. . . . was as follows:

"... I plugged into a number at Echuca, 1494 and I said—I opened the speak key and I said to the person 'Number please' and the reply I got was "Get me the police please.' I kept the speak key open as the person was hysterical.
  His Honour—You what?
  Witness—I kept the speak key open as the person was in an hysterical state [later, the witness added that the person sobbed] and I connected the call to Echuca 41 which is the police station. As I was connecting the call the person gave her address as 59, Mitchell Street."

The witness then said that the caller hung up but that she (the witness) after consulting her superior spoke to the police and told them that they were wanted at 59, Mitchell Street. It was in consequence of this that, as narrated above, the police telephoned to the house at about 1.20 p.m. and spoke to the accused. Echuca 1494 was the number of the appellant's house. . . .

Their Lordships must therefore proceed with the appeal on the basis that the jury was properly directed that, on the evidence, they might find that the telephone call at 1.15 p.m. or thereabouts was made by the deceased woman.

The next question related to the further facts sought to be proved concerning the telephone call. The objection taken against this evidence was that it was hearsay and that it did not come within any of the recognised exceptions to the rule against hearsay evidence.

In their Lordships' opinion the evidence was not hearsay evidence and was admissible as evidence of fact relevant to an issue.

The mere fact that evidence of a witness includes evidence as to words spoken by another person who is not called, is no objection to its admissibility. Words spoken are facts just as much as any other action by a human being. If the speaking of the words is a relevant fact, a witness may give evidence that they were spoken. A question of hearsay only arises when the words spoken are relied on "testimonially," *i.e.* as establishing some fact narrated by the words. . . .

The evidence relating to the act of telephoning by the deceased was, in their Lordship's view, factual and relevant. It can be analysed into the following elements.

(1) At about 1.15 p.m. the number Echuca 1494 rang. I plugged into that number.

(2) I opened the speak key and said "Number please."

(3) A female voice answered.

(4) The voice was hysterical and sobbed.

(5) The voice said "Get me the police please."

The factual items numbered (1)–(3) were relevant in order to show that contrary to the evidence of the appellant, a call was made, only some 3–5 minutes before the fatal shooting, by a woman. It not being suggested that there was anybody in the house other than the appellant, his wife and small children, this woman, the caller, could only have been the deceased. Items (4) and (5) were relevant as possibly showing (if the jury thought fit to draw the inference) that the deceased woman was at this time in a state of emotion or fear (*cf. Aveson* v. *Lord Kinnaird* (1805) 6 East 188, 193, *per* Lord Ellenborough C.J.). They were relevant and necessary, evidence in order to explain and complete the fact of the call being made. A telephone call is a composite act, made up of manual operations together with the utterance of words (*cf. McGregor* v. *Stokes* [1952] V.L.R. 347 and remarks of Salmond J. therein quoted). To confine the evidence to the first would be to deprive the act of most of its significance. The act had content when it was known that the call was made in a state of emotion. The knowledge that the caller desired the police to be called helped to indicate the nature of the emotion—anxiety or fear at an existing or impending emergency. It was a matter for the jury to decide what light (if any) this evidence, in the absence of any explanation from the appellant, who was in the house, threw upon what situation was occurring, or developing at the time.

If then, this evidence had been presented in this way, as evidence purely of relevant facts, its admissibility could hardly have been plausibly challenged. But the appellant submits that in fact this was not so. It is said that the evidence was tendered and admitted as evidence of an assertion by the deceased that she was being attacked by the accused, and that it was, so far, hearsay evidence, being put forward as evidence of the truth of facts asserted by his statement. It is claimed that the Chief Justice so presented the evidence to the jury and that, therefore, its admissibility, as hearsay, may be challenged.

Their Lordships, as already stated, do not consider that there is any hearsay element in the evidence, nor in their opinion was it so presented by the trial judge, but they think it right to deal with the appellant's submission on the assumption that there is: *i.e.* that the words said to have been used involve an assertion of the truth of some facts stated in them and that they may have been so understood by the jury. The Crown defended the admissibility of the words as part of the "res gestae" a contention which led to the citation of numerous authorities.

The expression "res gestae," like many Latin phrases, is often used to cover situations insufficiently analysed in clear English terms. In the context of the law of evidence it may be used in at least three different ways:

1. When a situation of fact (*e.g.* a killing) is being considered, the

question may arise when does the situation begin and when does it end. It may be arbitrary and artificial to confine the evidence to the firing of the gun or the insertion of the knife, without knowing in a broader sense, what was happening. Thus in *O'Leary* v. *The King* (1946) 73 C.L.R. 566 evidence was admitted of assaults, prior to killing, committed by the accused during what was said to be a continuous orgy. As Dixon J. said at p. 577:

> "Without evidence of what, during that time, was done by those men who took any significant part in the matter and especially evidence of the behaviour of the prisoner, the transaction of which the alleged murder formed an integral part could not be truly understood and, isolated from it, could only be presented as an unreal and not very intelligible event."

2. The evidence may be concerned with spoken words as such (apart from the truth of what they convey). The words are then themselves the *res gestae* or part of the *res gestae, i.e.* are the relevant facts or part of them.

3. A hearsay statement is made either by the victim of an attack or by a bystander—indicating directly or indirectly the identity of the attacker. The admissibility of the statement is then said to depend on whether it was made as part of the *res gestae*. A classical instance of this is the much debated case of *Reg.* v. *Bedingfield* (1879) 14 Cox C.C. 341, and there are other instances of its application in reported cases. These tend to apply different standards, and some of them carry less than conviction. The reason, why this is so, is that concentration tends to be focused upon the opaque or at least imprecise Latin phrase rather than upon the basic reason for excluding the type of evidence which this group of cases is concerned with. There is no doubt what this reason is: it is twofold. the first is that there may be uncertainty as to the exact words used because of their transmission through the evidence of another person than the speaker. The second is because of the risk of concoction of false evidence by persons who have been victims of assault or accident. The first matter goes to weight. The person testifying to the words used is liable to cross-examination: the accused person (as he could not at the time when earlier reported cases were decided) can give his own account if different. There is no such difference in kind or substance between evidence of what was said and evidence of what was done (for example between evidence of what the victim said as to an attack and evidence that he (or she) was seen in a terrified state or was heard to shriek) as to require a total rejection of one and admission of the other.

The possibility of concoction, or fabrication, where it exists, is on the other hand an entirely valid reason for exclusion, and is probably the real test which judges in fact apply. In their Lordships' opinion this should be recognised and applied directly as the relevant test: the test should be not the uncertain one whether the making of the statement was in some sense part of the event or transaction. This may often be difficult to establish: such external matters as the time which elapses between the events and the speaking of the words (or vice versa), and differences in location being relevant factors but not, taken by themselves, decisive criteria. As regards statements made after the event it must be for the judge, by preliminary ruling, to satisfy himself that the statement was so clearly made in circumstances of spontaneity or involvement in the event that the possibility of concoction can be disregarded. Conversely, if he considers that the statement was made by way of narrative of a detached prior event so that the speaker was so disengaged from it as to be able to construct or adapt his account, he should exclude it. And the same must in principle be true of statements made before the event. The test should be not the uncertain one, whether the making of the statement should be regarded as part of the event or transaction. This may often be difficult to show. But if the drama, leading up to the climax, has commenced and assumed such intensity and pressure that the utterance can safely be regarded as a true reflection of what was unrolling or actually happening, it ought to be received. The expression "res gestae" may conveniently sum up these criteria, but the reality of them must always be kept in mind: it is this that lies behind the best reasoned of the judges' rulings.

A few illustrations may be given. One of the earliest and as often happens also the clearest, is that of Holt C.J. at nisi prius in *Thompson* v. *Trevanion* (1693) Skin. 402. He allowed that "what the wife said immediate upon the hurt received, and before that she had time to device or contrive anything for her own advantage" might be given in evidence, a statement often quoted and approved. *Reg.* v. *Bedingfield*, 14 Cox C.C. 341 is more useful as a focus for discussion, than for the decision on the facts. . . .

In a lower key the evidence of the words of the careless pedestrian in *O'Hara* v. *Central S.M.T. Co. Ltd.*, 1941 S.C. 363 was admitted on the principle of spontaneity. The Lord President (Normand) said that there must be close association: the words should be at least de recenti and not after an interval which would allow time for reflection and concocting a story: see p. 381. Lord Fleming said, p. 386: "Obviously statements made after there has been time for deliberation are not likely to be entirely spontaneous, and may, indeed, be made for the express purpose of concealing the truth" and Lord Moncrieff refers to the "share in the event" which is taken by the person reported to have made the statement. He contrasts an exclamation "forced out of a witness by the emotion generated by an event" with a subsequent narrative (pp. 389–390). The Lord President reaffirmed the principle stated in this case in an appeal to this board in *Teper* v. *The Queen* [1952] A.C. 480, stressing the necessity for close association in time, place and circumstances between the statement and the crucial events.

In Australia, a leading authority is *Adelaide Chemical and Fertilizer Co. Ltd.* v. *Carlyle* (1940) 64 C.L.R. 514. . . . [There] Dixon J. with some caution reaches the conclusion that although English law, in the general view of lawyers, admits statements only as parts or details of a transaction not yet complete, while in America, greater recognition is given to the guarantee of truth provided by spontaneity and the lack of time to devise or contrive, yet English decisions do show some reliance on the greater trustworthiness of statements made at once without reflection.

In an earlier case in the High Court (*Brown* v. *The King* (1913) 17 C.L.R. 570) where evidence was excluded, Isaacs J. and Powers J. in their joint judgment put the exclusion on the ground that it was a mere narration respecting a concluded event, a narration not naturally or spontaneously emanating from or growing out of the main narration but arising as an independent and additional transaction (l.c. p. 597).

. . . .

These authorities show that there is ample support for the principle that hearsay evidence may be admitted if the statement providing it is made in such conditions (always being those of approximate but not exact contemporaneity) or involvement or pressure as to exclude the possibility of concoction or distortion to the advantage of the maker or the disadvantage of the accused.

Before applying it to the facts of the present case, there is one other matter to be considered, namely the nature of the proof required to establish the involvement of the speaker in the pressure of the drama, or the concatenation of events leading up to the crisis. On principle it would not appear right that the necessary association should be shown only by the statement itself, otherwise the statement would be lifting itself into the area of admissibility. There is little authority on this point.... Facts differ so greatly that it is impossible to lay down any precise general rule: it is difficult to imagine a case where there is no evidence at all of connection between statement and principal event other than the statement itself, but whether this is sufficiently shown must be a matter for the trial judge. Their Lordships would be disposed to agree that, amongst other things, he may take the statement itself into account.

In the present case, in their Lordships' judgment, there was ample evidence of the close and intimate connection between the statement ascribed to the deceased and the shooting which occurred very shortly afterwards. They were closely associated in place and in time. The way in which the statement came to be made (in a call for the police) and the tone of voice used, showed intrinsically that the statement was being forced from the deceased by an overwhelming pressure of contemporary event. It carried its own stamp of spontaneity and this was endorsed by the proved time sequence and the proved proximity of the deceased to the accused with his gun. Even on the assumption that there was an element of hearsay in the words used, they were safely admitted. The jury was, additionally, directed with great care as to the use to which they might be put. On all counts, therefore, their Lordships can find no error in law in the admission of the evidence. They should add that they see no reason why the judge should have excluded it as prejudicial in the exercise of discretion....

Their Lordships have previously announced that they must humbly advise Her Majesty that this appeal be dismissed.

Note.—That spontaneity does not now necessarily involve precise contemporaneity was illustrated in *R.* v. *Nye and Loan* (1977) 66 Cr.App.R. 252 (C.A.), where evidence of identification of an assailant by the victim of an attack, made by him a very short time after the attack but while he was still recovering from it, was received. Reference was also made to the possibility of error as distinct from concoction, in a case of spontaneity. After referring to *Ratten* v. *R.* Lawton L.J. said (pp. 256–257): "We have to apply the opinion of Lord Wilberforce. Was there spontaneity in this identification? It is difficult to imagine a more spantaneous identification. Mr. Lucas had been savagely attacked. He called for the help of the police and when police officers arrived, one of them asked what had happened. Mr. Lucas pointed out Loan to him and alleged that Loan was the man who had hit him. He did this in the presence of the crowd which had collected. Was there an opportunity for concoction? The interval of time was very short indeed. During part of that interval Mr. Lucas was sitting down in his car trying to overcome the effects of the blows which had been struck. Commonsense and experience of life tells us that in that interval he would not be thinking of concocting a case against anybody. He would have been trying to clear his head. So we can put out of mind altogether, in our judgment, any possibility of concoction. There is however the possibility of error, as Mr. Thom [counsel for the appellant] has pointed out to us and that, if we may put a gloss upon what Lord Wilberforce said, is an additional factor to be taken into consideration. Perhaps Lord Wilberforce envisaged error in the word 'concocted.' Was there in this case any real possibility of error?...There was no opportunity here for concoction and there was no chance of an error being made." For subsequent consideration of this additional factor see *R.* v. *Andrews* [1987] A.C. 281 (H.L.) (*infra*).

R. v. **Turnbull** (1985) 80 Cr.App.R. 104 (C.A.). A man who had been mortally wounded staggered into the bar of a public house. In response to questions put to him there, and shortly afterwards in an ambulance on the way to hospital, he was understood to say that "Ronnie Tommo" had done it. He died half an hour later in hospital. The appellant was subsequently charged with the man's murder. There was evidence that the appellant had been drinking with him shortly before the stabbing. At the trial the judge admitted evidence of the conversations which had taken place with witnesses in the public house and in the ambulance. The prosecution case was that the utterance of the words "Ronnie Tommo" by the deceased, who had a Scots accent and had consumed a great deal of alcohol, was an attempt at the name of the appellant who was also a Scotsman. The trial judge ruled that the evidence was admissible as part of the *res gestae*, it being evidence of something said at a time so closely linked with the event to which it referred that there was no possibility of concoction. The Court of Appeal held that the evidence had been rightly admitted on this ground. The court emphasised that it was as an exception to the hearsay rule that the evidence was admissible. In other respects heavy reliance was placed upon *Ratten* v. *R.* (*supra*). O'Connor L.J., giving the judgment of the court, cited extensively (pp. 108–109) from what Lord Wilberforce said there, including the words: "As regards statements made after the event, it must be for the judge, by preliminary ruling, to satisfy himself that the statement was so clearly made in circumstances of spontaneity or involvement in the event that the possibility of concoction can be disregarded." O'Connor L.J. concluded (p. 110): "In the present case the learned judge applied the right test and he ruled that there was here no such risk." The appeal was dismissed.

R. v. ANDREWS

[1987] A.C. 281; [1987] 1 All E.R. 513; 84 Cr.App.R. 382 (H.L.: 1987)

Hearsay evidence of a statement, in which a deceased victim identified his attacker, is admissible under the doctrine of res gestae as evidence of the truth of the facts stated, provided the statement was made in circumstances in which the possibility of concoction or distortion by the victim can be disregarded.
When such evidence is admitted, it is the duty of the judge to draw the attention of the jury to certain possible sources of unreliability.

Two men entered the flat of one, Morrow, and attacked him with knives. Shortly afterwards, badly wounded, he made his way to the flat below to obtain assistance. Within minutes of this two police officers arrived, and Morrow told them that a man named O'Neill and the defendant had attacked him. Two months later Morrow died as a result of his injuries. O'Neill and the defendant were jointly charged with aggravated burglary and murder. At the trial the Common Serjeant ruled in favour of admitting evidence of the deceased's statement to the police officers as evidence of the facts that he had asserted namely that he had said O'Neill and the defendant were his assailants. The defendant was convicted of aggravated burglary and manslaughter. His appeal against conviction to the Court of Appeal was dismissed. The court certified that the following point of law was involved in the decision: "where the victim of an attack tells a witness what has happened and does that in circumstances which satisfy the trial judge that there was no opportunity for concoction, is evidence of what the victim said admissible as to the truth of the facts stated as an exception to the hearsay rule?" The defendant's further appeal to the House of Lords was dismissed.

LORD ACKNER: ... Mr. Worsley [counsel for the prosecution] sought to have the statement of the deceased admitted as evidence of the truth of the facts that he had asserted, namely that he had been attacked by both O'Neill and the appellant.... Mr. Worsley based his submission that this hearsay evidence was admissible upon the so-called doctrine of "res gestae." He could not submit that the statement was a "dying declaration" since there was no evidence to suggest that at the time when the deceased made the statement (two months before his ultimate death) he was aware that he had been mortally injured. Mr. Worsley in support of his submission... relied essentially on a decision of the Privy Council, *Ratten* v. *The Queen* [1972] A.C. 378... which is the real issue in this appeal *viz.* that your Lordships should accept the analysis, reasoning and advice tendered by the Privy council as being good English law. [His Lordship then quoted very extensively from the judgment of Lord Wilberforce in *Ratten*'s case. He went on to point out that it had been approved in *R.* v. *Blastland* [1986] A.C. 41 at p. 58 (*infra*) and followed in *R.* v. *Nye and Loan* (1978) 66 Cr.App.R. 252 (See *Note* to *Ratten*'s case, *supra*) and in *R.* v. *Turnbull* (1984) 80 Cr.App.R. 104 (*supra*). He then dealt with the appellant's submission that the operation of the *res gestae* doctrine in England is limited to cases in which the statement was made contemporaneously with the act charged, and that in the light of the majority ruling in *Myers* v. *D.P.P.* [1965] A.C. 1001 (Chapter 13, *supra*) it cannot be extended.]... I do not accept that the principles identified by Lord Wilberforce involved any extension to the exception to the hearsay rule. Lord Wilberforce clarified the basis of the *res gestae* exception and isolated the matters of which the trial judge, by preliminary ruling, must satisfy himself before admitting the statement. I respectfully accept the accuracy and the value of this clarification. Thus it must, of course, follow that *Reg.* v. *Bedingfield*, 14 Cox C.C. 341 would not be so decided today. Indeed, there could, as Lord Wilberforce observed, hardly be a case where the words uttered carried more clearly the mark of spontaneity and intense involvement.

My Lords, may I therefore summarise the position which confronts the trial judge when faced in a criminal case with an application under the *res gestae* doctrine to admit evidence of statements, with a view to establishing the truth of some fact thus narrated, such evidence being truly categorised as "hearsay evidence?"

1. The primary question which the judge must ask himself is—can the possibility of concoction or distortion be disregarded.

2. To answer that question the judge must first consider the circumstances in which the particular statement was made, in order to satisfy himself that the event was so unusual or startling or dramatic as to dominate the thoughts of the victim, so that his utterance was an

instinctive reaction to that event, thus giving no real opportunity for reasoned reflection. In such a situation the judge would be entitled to conclude that the involvement or the pressure of the event would exclude the possibility of concoction or distortion, providing that the statement was made in conditions of approximate but not exact contemporaneity.

3. In order for the statement to be sufficiently "spontaneous" it must be so closely associated with the event which has excited the statement, that it can be fairly stated that the mind of the declarant was still dominated by the event. Thus the judge must be satisfied that the event, which provided the trigger mechanism for the statement, was still operative. The fact that the statement was made in answer to a question is but one factor to consider under this heading.

4. Quite apart from the time factor, there may be special features in the case, which relate to the possibility of concoction or distortion. In the instant appeal the defence relied upon evidence to support the contention that the deceased had a motive of his own to fabricate or concoct, namely, a malice which resided in him against O'Neill and the appellant because, so he believed, O'Neill had attacked and damaged his house and was accompanied by the appellant, who ran away on a previous occasion. The judge must be satisfied that the circumstances were such that having regard to the special feature of malice, there was no possibility of any concoction or distortion to the advantage of the maker or the disadvantage of the accused.

5. As to the possibility of error in the facts narrated in the statement, if only the ordinary fallibility of human recollection is relied upon, this goes to the weight to be attached to and not to the admissibility of the statement and is therefore a matter for the jury. However, here again there may be special features that may give rise to the possibility of error. In the instant case there was evidence that the deceased had drunk to excess, well over double the permitted limit for driving a motor car. Another example would be where the identification was made in circumstances of particular difficulty or where the declarant suffered from defective eyesight. In such circumstances the trial judge must consider whether he can exclude the possibility of error.

Croom-Johnson L.J., in giving the judgment of the Court of Appeal (Criminal Division) dismissing the appeal, stated, in my respectful view quite correctly, that the Common Serjeant had directed himself impeccably in his approach to the evidence that he heard. It is perhaps helpful to set out verbatim how the judge stated his conclusions:

> "I am satisfied that soon after receiving very serious stab wounds the deceased went downstairs for help unassisted and received some assistance. He was able to talk for a few minutes before he became unconscious. I am satisfied on the evidence—and not only the primary evidence but the inference of fact to which I am irresistibly driven—that the deceased only sustained the injuries a few minutes before the police arrived and subsequently, of course, the ambulance took him to hospital. Even if the period were longer than a few minutes, I am satisfied that there was no possibility in the circumstances of any concoction or fabrication of identification. I think that the injuries which the deceased sustained were of such a nature that it would drive out of his mind any possibility of him being activated by malice and I cannot

overlook as far as the identification was concerned, he was right over Mr. O'Neill who was a former co-defendant with the accused."

Where the trial judge has properly directed himself as to the correct approach to the evidence and there is material to entitle him to reach the conclusions which he did reach, then his decision is final, in the sense that it will not be interfered with on appeal. Of course, having ruled the statement admissible the judge must, as the Common Serjeant most certainly did, make it clear to the jury that it is for them to decide what was said and to be sure that the witnesses were not mistaken in what they believed had been said to them. Further, they must be satisfied that the declarant did not concoct or distort to his advantage or the disadvantage of the accused the statement relied upon and where there is material to raise the issue, that he was not activated by any malice or ill-will. Further where there are special features that bear on the possibility of mistake then the juries' attention must be invited to those matters.

My Lords, the doctrine of res gestae applied to civil as well as criminal proceedings. There is, however, special legislation as to the admissibility of hearsay evidence in civil proceedings. I wholly accept that the doctrine admits the hearsay statements, not only where the declarant is dead or otherwise not available but when he is called as a witness. Whatever may be the position in civil proceedings, I would, however, strongly deprecate any attempt in criminal prosecutions to use the doctrine as a device to avoid calling, when he is available, the maker of the statement. Thus to deprive the defence of the opportunity to cross-examine him, would not be consistent with the fundamental duty of the prosecution to place all the relevant material facts before the court, so as to ensure that justice is done.

My Lords, I would accordingly dismiss this appeal.

LORDS BRIDGE OF HARWICH, BRANDON OF OAKBROOK, GRIFFITHS and MACKAY OF CLASHFERN agreed.

Note.—The *obiter* reference in the last paragraph to the position in civil cases is not easily reconciled with the actual wording of section 1(1) of the Civil Evidence Act 1968 (Part Two, *infra*).

Tobi v. **Nicholas** (1988) 86 Cr.App.R. 323 (D.C.). The accused was charged with *inter alia* failing to stop after an automobile accident. The driver of a coach which had been damaged in the accident had told a police constable about 20 minutes later that a car driven by the accused had collided with his coach. At the trial the coach driver was not called as a witness, and the prosecution's application for an adjournment so that he might be called was refused. A Divisional Court held that, as the coach driver, although available, had not been called, the evidence of the police constable as to what he had said, particularly as to his identification of the accused, had been wrongly admitted. It was hearsay and not admissible as part of the *res gestae*. The principles laid down by Lord Ackner in *R.* v. *Andres* (*supra*) were applied, but the case was distinguished on its facts. Glidewell L.J. said (p. 334): "The event in this case was not so unusual or dramatic as in the ordinary way to dominate the thoughts of the victim. Of course anyone whose vehicle has been damaged is annoyed about it, but there is a world of difference between such an unfortunately commonplace situation and the thoughts of someone who has been assaulted and stabbed. Moreover in the circumstances of the present case, while no doubt Mr. Thomas [the coach driver] was still concerned about the damage to his coach, his accosting the defendant on the doorstep of his house in the presence of the police officer was some 20 minutes after the event in question, as he himself said. It cannot be said that the event was completely contemporaneous."

Note.—For a different point decided in the same case see the *Note* to the Road Traffic Offenders Act 1988, s.16 (Part Two, *infra*).

Thomas v. Connell (1838) 4 M. & W. 267 (Ex. Ch.). It was held on appeal that evidence of a bankrupt's statement that he knew he was insolvent was admissible to show his knowledge of that fact, but not to prove the fact itself, at the time when he made a payment alleged to be a fraudulent preference. Parke B. said (p. 269): "...if a fact be proved aliunde, it is clear that a particular person's knowledge of that fact may be proved by his declaration..."

R. v. Blastland [1986] A.C. 41 (H.L.). The appellant had been convicted of the buggery and murder of a 12 year old boy. His case was that he had attempted to bugger the boy but had desisted. He had then seen another man (Mark) nearby and had panicked and run home. He alleged that it was Mark who had committed the crimes, and he sought to call several witnesses who would give evidence that before the discovery of the boy's body Mark had told them that a boy had been murdered. The trial judge had excluded this evidence as hearsay. He had also rejected an application by the appellant to call Mark and treat him as a hostile witness. The purpose for which the appellant had sought to introduce the evidence was to show the truth of the implied assertion by Mark of his knowledge that a child had been murdered, and that he had this knowledge at a particular time,— namely a time when seemingly only the criminal (or someone who had witnessed the commission of the crime) could have possessed such knowledge. The fact of Mark's knowledge was not in the strict sense a fact in issue. It was, however, relevant to the defence put forward by the appellant. The appellant's appeal against conviction was dismissed by the Court of Appeal and by the House of Lords. The House of Lords unanimously held that the evidence of what Mark had allegedly said had been rightly excluded as hearsay. Lord Bridge of Harrow said (p. 62): "I do not think it would be appropriate to go further, by way of generalisation, than to say that the admissibility of a statement tendered in evidence as proof of the maker's knowledge or other state of mind must always depend on the degree of relevance of the state of mind sought to be proved to the issue in relation to which the evidence is tendered."

Note.—It is not altogether clear why the normal rules of relevance should not be applicable in this context. Nor is it clear why the disputed evidence was not sufficiently relevant to the defence raised by the appellant. It was, of course, not certain how Mark had come by the knowledge that a boy had been murdered, but as Lord Bridge had himself observed (p. 54), that this resulted from the fact that Mark was himself the culprit was one of the "two most obvious possibilities."

It is to be noted that, had the disputed evidence been admitted, it would have been open to the prosecution to call Mark to explain it or to rebut it.

R. v. Buckley (1873) 13 Cox C.C. 293 (Assizes). The accused was charged with the murder of a police officer. An issue was as to whether it was the accused who had committed the murder which had occurred on a certain night. Lush J. (after consulting his fellow Assize Judge, Mellor J., on the point) admitted evidence given by the deceased's superior officer of a statement made by the deceased to him the same morning to the effect that he had heard that the accused "was at his old game of thieving again" and that he "intended to watch his movements that night." The witness had then said, "I will send a man to assist you about nine o'clock"; and the deceased had replied "That will be too late, I will go about dusk, myself."

R. v. Wainwright (1875) 13 Cox C.C. 171 (Central Criminal Court). The accused was charged with murder. The prosecution sought to call a witness to testify that the girl, with whose murder he was charged, had told her on leaving her home that she was going to the accused's premises. Cockburn C.J. held this evidence to be inadmissible. He said (p. 172): "It was no part of the act of leaving, but only an incidental remark. It was only a statement of intention which might or might not have been carried out. She would have gone away under any circumstances."

R. v. Moghal (1977) 65 Cr.App.R. 56 (C.A.). The appellant had been convicted of murder. The victim had died in circumstances in which only the appellant or his mistress or both could have killed him. The mistress was tried first and was acquitted. At the subsequent trial of the appellant his defence was that his mistress alone had committed the murder. One of the grounds of his appeal against conviction was that the trial judge had wrongly excluded certain evidence including a tape recording by the mistress in which she had declared her intention to kill the victim. The prosecution had conceded that the mistress was the actual killer; but the Court of Appeal expressed the view that evidence of this declaration of intention to kill the deceased should have been admissible on the appellant's behalf, had the judge been asked to rule upon the matter. The court made no reference to *R. v. Thomson (infra)*.

R. v. Thomson [1912] 3 K.B. 19 (C.C.A.). The accused was charged with using an instrument for the purpose of procuring an abortion. The woman died subsequently from another cause. The defence was that the woman had operated on herself. To support this defence, it was proposed to ask a witness for the prosecution in cross-examination whether the woman had stated, some weeks before the operation, that she intended to operate on herself, and had said, a week after the operation, that she herself had done so. The judge held that this evidence was inadmissible; the accused was convicted; and the conviction was upheld on appeal. Lord Alverstone C.J. (delivering the judgment of the court) specifically rejected the submission that a distinction can be drawn between cases in which evidence of intention is tendered on behalf of the defence and those in which it is tendered on behalf of the prosecution.

LLOYD v. POWELL DUFFRYN STEAM COAL CO., LTD.

[1914] A.C. 733; 83 L.J.K.B. 1054; 111 L.T. 338; 30 T.L.R. 456 (H.L.: 1914)

Evidence of statements, acknowledging the paternity of a child and promising to marry the mother, was admissible as conduct relevant to paternity and dependency, and also as showing a state of mind.

In a claim for workmen's compensation under a statute now repealed, made on behalf of a posthumous illegitimate child as a dependant of its putative father, evidence of statements by the deceased workman, to the effect that he was the father of the child and that he intended to marry the mother before the child was born, was held admissible.

EARL LOREBURN: . . . Now the evidence thus rejected consisted of statements made by the deceased in which he acknowledged the paternity of the child and promised to marry the mother before the child should be born.... In considering whether the evidence was admissible or not the first question is, What were the issues? Paternity was one one issue. Whether the child was post-humous or illegitimate or both is immaterial. I think the evidence was properly allowed on the issue of paternity. If paternity has been established, the next issue is dependency....

The evidence in question went to show that if the father had not prematurely died this child would have been born legitimate, and its father would have been legally bound to maintain it, which is a strong fact to prove dependency. Accordingly the evidence was, in my opinion, admissible upon that ground also. Further it went to show that the child would need, and would have received, its father's support. On that ground too I think it was admissible....

LORD ATKINSON: ... [I]f a man, with full knowledge of the pregnancy of a woman with whom he has had sexual intercourse, becomes, during her pregnancy, engaged to be married to her, the fact of that contract having been entered into, though not carried out, is a most powerful piece of evidence on both the issues of fact, namely, the dependency and the paternity of the child, because by the marriage a relation would be created from which the presumption of the legitimacy of the child would arise, and by reason of that legitimacy the legal liability of the father to support and maintain the child would result. If the contract should be terminated the fact that it was made would be evidence of the second issue. I further think that the mere proposal of marriage made by a man under such circumstances, whether accepted or not, would be admissible evidence, certainly on the issue of paternity, although possibly not on that of dependency....

To treat the statements made by the deceased as statements made by a deceased person against his pecuniary interest, and therefore, though hearsay, proof of the facts stated, is wholly to mistake their true character and significance. The significance consists in the improbability that any man would make these statements, true or false, unless he believed himself to be the father of the child....

As I have already stated, I think the entering by these two people into an engagement to marry after the woman's condition had become known would, for the reasons I have mentioned, be admissible evidence on both issues....

LORD SHAW OF DUNFERMLINE: ... All the statements by the father, importing his knowledge of the condition of the mother, his intentions to set up a household, and the like, appear to me to be legitimate matter of proof on the point of paternity. In a question of status, I am of opinion that such statements, proved to have been made at the time and in the circumstances such as occurred in the present case, are part of the *res gestae* equally with actual contracts entered into by the deceased or conduct apart from words, both of which contracts and conduct could undoubtedly have been proved. I agree with the view that statements made at the time are, in this question of status, similarly admissible evidence....

LORD MOULTON: ... Now, it is well established in English jurisprudence, in accordance with the dictates of common sense, that the words and acts of a person are admissible as evidence of his state of mind. Indeed, they are the only possible evidence on such an issue. It was urged at the Bar that although the acts of the deceased might be put in evidence, his words might not. I fail to understand the distinction. Speaking is as much an act as doing.

It must be borne in mind that there is nothing in the admission of such evidence which clashes with the rooted objection in our jurisprudence to the admission of hearsay evidence. The testimony of the witnesses is to the act, *i.e.* to the deceased speaking these words, and it is the speaking of the words which is the matter that is put in evidence and which possesses evidential value. The evidence is, therefore, not in any respect open to the objection that it is secondary or hearsay evidence. The connection between the conversation and the information as to paternity is so close that it is probable that the evidence would be admissible under the head of *res gestae*, but its admissibility, on the grounds I have just mentioned, is so clear that is is not necessary to examine this further question. . . .

[The House unanimously allowed the appeal].

Note.—It is difficult to abstract a clear *ratio decidendi* from the judgments of the four Lords of Appeal who constituted the House of Lords in the *Lloyd* case. The admissibility of the evidence on the issue of dependency (*i.e.* as to whether, had he lived, the alleged father would in fact have maintained the child) can probably most easily be seen as resting on the exception to the hearsay rule covering declarations as to state of mind, provided this exception is taken to extend to cases of declaration (express or implied) of intention, and to cases in which the state of mind, although not in issue, is *per se* directly relevant to an issue. This was perhaps the approach taken by Lord Moulton. What is more difficult to explain is the reception of the evidence on the issue of paternity, unless it be regarded as evidence of declarations against interest. However, this latter justification for admissibility, although relied upon by the trial judge, was emphatically rejected in the Court of Appeal [1913] 2 K.B. 130, *sub nom. Ward* v. *H.S. Pitt & Co.*, and by a majority of the Law Lords.

The admissibility of the evidence would now depend upon the Civil Evidence Act 1968 (Part Two, *infra*).

Police v. **Machirus** [1977] 1 N.Z.L.R. 228 (New Zealand Court of Appeal). The accused was convicted of the offence of bookmaking. On arresting him at his flat the police had re-connected his telephone and had then received, within a short interval but after the accused had left, a number of incoming calls. The first caller attempted to place a bet. Evidence of the content of this call was admitted at the trial. The members of the New Zealand Court of Appeal were unanimous in holding that it was rightly admitted, but their reasons differed. Woodhouse J. did not treat the evidence as being hearsay (see Note to *R.* v. *Chapman* [1969] 2 Q.B. 436, Chapter 13, *supra*). On the other hand a majority (Richmond P. and Cooke J.) treated it as hearsay, but admissible hearsay. However, it is not altogether clear whether they regarded it as being admissible as an explanatory statement, or as a declaration as to state of mind—albeit of intention. Richmond P., having approved an earlier statement (*per* Salmond J. in *Davidson* v. *Quirke* [1923] N.Z.L.R. 552, 556) of "the principle that, notwithstanding the rule against hearsay, where the purpose or meaning of an act done is relevant, evidence of contemporaneous declaration accompanying and explaining the act is admissible in proof of such purpose or meaning," said (p. 290): "I think that the evidence was legally admissible to show that the purpose of the caller was to make a bet with someone called Peter, which happened to be the name by which the appellant was commonly known." But Cooke J. relied on the rule that (p. 294): "...a person's declaration of his contemporaneous state of mind—and a statement of his present intention must be within that category—is admissible evidence of the existence of that state of mind."

Aveson v. **Lord Kinnaird** (1805) 6 East 188 (K.B.). In an action upon a policy of insurance on the life of the plaintiff's wife, the question was whether the statement of the insured's good health, given at the time of effecting the policy, was false. The court allowed evidence to be given by a visitor to the effect that she had seen the deceased at the time, and had been told by her that she was in a bad state of health.

Note.—This case is one of the earliest accepted as authority for the proposition that evidence of a person's statement of contemporaneous physical sensation is admissible as part of the *res gestae*. For example, in *Gilbey* v. *Great Western Rail Co.* (1910) 102 L.T. 202 (C.A.) Cozens-Hardy M.R. entertained no doubt (p. 203) that: "Statements made by a workman to his wife of his sensations at the time, about the pains in his side or head, or what not—whether the statements were made by groans or by actions, or were verbal statements,—would be admissible to prove these sensations." There it was also held that the workman's assertion as to the cause of his condition was admissible.

The requirement of contemporaneity has given rise to some uncertainty and seems to have been a factor giving rise to the reluctance of the Court of Criminal Appeal to admit the evidence on this ground in *R.* v. *Black* (1922) 16 Cr.App.R. 118 (C.C.A.). In *Aveson* v. *Lord Kinnaird* itself the evidence was admitted to prove the existence of symptoms, not only at the time of the utterance, but also it seems 10 days previously. However, this could be explained on the basis that the prior existence of the symptoms was simply deducable from their presence at the time of the utterance.

In *Tickle* v. *Tickle* [1968] 1 W.L.R. 937 (D.C.) Sir Jocelyn Simon P., having cited *Aveson* v. *Kinnaird (Lord)*, said (p. 942): "If what a patient says about her state of health to a doctor is admissible as part of the *res gestae* notwithstanding the hearsay rule, it seems to me that what the doctor says to the patient is no less admissible when its adduction is required in order that justice should be done."

Chapter 16

HEARSAY EVIDENCE IN CIVIL CASES

BEFORE 1968 in addition to the many exceptions to the hearsay rule which had been developed at common law there had been several statutory inroads into the rule. The most important of these were the Evidence Act 1938,[1] which allowed for the reception in civil cases of certain written hearsay to prove facts of which direct oral evidence would have been admissible, and the Criminal Evidence Act 1965. This latter and the subsequently enacted Police and Criminal Evidence Act 1984, Part VII and Criminal Justice Act 1988, Part II,[2] have successively provided for the reception in criminal trials of an expanding range of documentary hearsay.

The approach to the hearsay problem taken in the Civil Evidence Act 1968[3] is, however, fundamentally different. Whereas the above-mentioned enactments simply created or create further exceptions to an exclusionary rule, the 1968 Act abrogates that rule itself in civil cases and substitutes for it an inclusionary pattern of rules providing for the admission of hearsay by virtue of Part I (ss.1 to 10) of the Act, any other statutory provision, or agreement between the parties, "but not otherwise."[4]

Section 2 of the Act renders admissible first-hand hearsay, whether oral, written or by conduct; but second-hand hearsay is excluded,[5] unless either it is written and comes within section 4 or section 5 of the Act, or it falls within one of the selected common law exceptions to the old hearsay rule which have been given statutory force by section 9. Section 4 provides for the admission of statements in documentary records, provided the records were compiled, pursuant to the discharge of a duty, from information supplied directly by a person having (or being reasonably supposed to have) personal knowledge of the facts, or indirectly from such a person via a person or persons each acting under a duty to pass on the information. Section 5 of the Act deals with the admissibility of statements produced by computers.

---

[1] The Evidence Act 1938 is still applicable in proceedings within the civil jurisdiction of magistrate's courts. See *R.* v. *Wood Green Crown Court, ex p. P.* (1982) 4 F.L.R. 206.
[2] See Part Two, *infra*.
[3] The provisions of this Act are set out in Part Two, *infra*: and the Rules of the Supreme Court (R.S.C., Ord. 38, rr. 20–34) which have been made pursuant to it, as extended by the Civil Evidence Act 1972, s.1(1) (Part Two, *infra*), are set out in Part Three, *infra*.
[4] s.1(1).
[5] See s.2(3).

The Act assumes a broad interpretation of the old hearsay rule in that its provisions extend to a witness's own prior statements. However, if the maker of the statement (in cases coming under section 2) or the original supplier of the information (in cases coming under section 4) has been, or is to be, called as a witness, the statement may only be received with leave of the court, and furthermore may usually not be given in evidence before the conclusion of the examination-in-chief of the maker or supplier.[6]

Some threads of continuity with pre-existing law are to be seen in sections 3 and 9 of the Act.

Section 3(1) provides that where a witness's prior inconsistent or contradictory statement is proved by virtue of sections 3, 4 or 5 of the Criminal Procedure Act 1865,[7] or his prior statement is proved to rebut the suggestion of fabrication,[8] evidence of the statement shall be admissible to prove the truth of any fact contained in it and of which direct oral evidence by the witness would be admissible. Section 3(2) expressly preserves the common law rules regulating the circumstances in which a document, used by a witness to refresh his memory, may be made evidence in proceedings[9]; but it provides that any statement contained in a document (or part of a document) made evidence in this way, which is the statement of the witness using the document to refresh his memory, shall be admissible as evidence of any fact so stated of which the witness's direct oral evidence would be admissible.

The general import of section 9 is to ensure that evidence, previously admissible by virtue of certain common law exceptions to the hearsay rule, shall continue to be admissible even though not made so by sections 2, 3, 4 or 5. This may be of particular importance in cases of second-hand oral hearsay. Subsections (1) and (2) of section 9 put on to a statutory basis the common law rule relating to the reception of evidence of informal admissions[10] and those relating to the reception of a wide range of public documents.[11] This statutory admissibility is not subject to any of the restrictions embodied in sections 2 to 7 of the Act; nor is it affected by the procedural safeguards laid down in the rules of court made pursuant to section 8 (*infra*).[12] Reliance may be placed upon subsections (1) and (2) even though the evidence would otherwise have been admissible under another provision of the Act. Subsections (3) and (4) of section 9 are concerned with the perpetuation of the common law rules rendering admissible (i) statements tending to establish a person's reputation for the purpose of showing his or her good or bad character,[13] and (ii) statements tending to establish reputation or family tradition for the purpose of proving or disproving pedigree, the existence of a marriage or the existence of any public or general right, or for the purpose of identifying any person or thing.[14] Evidence which was so admissible at common law is made admissible by virtue of these

---

[6] s.2(2) and s.4(2).
[7] Part Two, *infra*. See, too, Chap. 9, *supra*.
[8] See Chap. 9, *supra*.
[9] See Chap. 9, *supra*.
[10] s.9(1) and (2)(*a*).
[11] s.9(1) and (2)(*b*)–(*d*).
[12] s.9(5).
[13] s.9(3) and (4)(*a*).
[14] s.9(3) and (4)(*b*)–(*c*).

subsections—but only in so far as it is not capable of being rendered admissible under section 2 or 4.[15] When, despite this limitation upon the operation of the subsections, evidence is admissible by virtue of subsections (3) and (4), such admissibility is not subject to the restrictions in sections 2 to 7 or to the procedural safeguards laid down pursuant to section 8 (*infra*).[16] It is to be noted that subsection (3)(*b*) provides that evidence of reputation or family tradition received under Part I (ss.1 to 10) of the Act (whether under subsection (3)(*a*) or otherwise) shall be evidence of the actual matter reputed or handed down. Moreover, subsection (3) goes on to provide, without prejudice to this, that reputation for the purposes of Part I of the Act shall "be treated as fact and not as a statement or multiplicity of statements dealing with the matter reputed."

Section 6 contains provisions which are supplementary to sections 2, 3, 4 and 5; but subsection (3) would appear to be in large part otiose or inexplicable. That subsection is concerned with the weight, if any, to be attached to a statement admissible by virtue of section 2, 3, 4 or 5 and it ordains that in estimating such weight "regard shall be had to all the circumstances from which any inference can reasonably be drawn as to the accuracy or otherwise of the statement and, in particular—(*a*) in the case of a statement falling within section 2(1) or 3(1) or (2) of this Act, to the question whether or not the statement was made contemporaneously with the occurrence or existence of the fact stated, and to the question whether or not the maker of the statement had any incentive to conceal or misrepresent the facts; (*b*) . . . and (*c*) . . . [The subsection here makes corresponding provisions in regard to statements falling respectively within section 4(1) or 5(1)]." The reasons for, and the significance of, the singling out for particular mention of two factors (contemporaneity and the absence of any incentive to conceal or misrepresent) are not altogether clear. It is scarcely likely to have been the intention of Parliament that a significance, greater than that to which they are intrinsically entitled, should be accorded to these factors. And yet otherwise, specific reference to them would seem to be otiose.[17] Section 6(4) precludes the use of a statement admitted by virtue of section 2 or 3 as corroboration of evidence given by its maker; it similarly precludes the use of evidence admitted by virtue of section 4 as corroboration of evidence given by the original supplier of the information from which the record containing the statement was compiled.

Section 7 provides for the admissibility of evidence as to the credibility of the maker of a statement admitted under section 2 (and as to the credibility of the original supplier of information from which the record containing a statement admitted under section 4 was compiled), when the maker (or original supplier) is not called as a witness. The general principle permeating this section is that evidence affecting such person's credibility should be treated, so far as is practicable, in the same way as it would be treated had he been called as a witness. Evidence that the maker of the statement (or the original supplier) has made another inconsistent statement is treated along the same lines.

---

[15] s.9(3)(*a*).
[16] s.9(5).
[17] Perhaps the legislature intended the references to these factors to have no normative effect, but simply to serve as parenthetical reminders of their importance and to guard against their being overlooked.

However, it should be noted that rules of court may,[18] and do,[19] prevent a party from adducing, in relation to the maker (or original supplier) who is not called as a witness, evidence which could otherwise be adduced by him by virtue of section 7, unless such party has served a counter-notice requiring the maker (or original supplier) to be called as a witness.

A prime objective of the Civil Evidence Act is to replace inadmissibility by procedural safeguards as protection against hearsay evidence of suspect reliability. Section 8 of the Act, and the rules of court made pursuant to it,[20] play a central role in the achievement of this objective. The framework of these procedural safeguards is set out in section 8 itself. Under subsection (2)(a) rules of court "shall... require" a party wishing to put in a statement under section 2, 4 or 5 to notify every other party of his desire to do so and of such particulars as the rules may require. Similarly, rules of court "shall... enable"[21] a party receiving such a notice to serve a counter-notice if he requires any person, of whom particulars have been given, to be called as a witness. But a party will not be entitled to require such a person to be called if that person is "unavailable" within one of the categories set out in section 8(2)(b), viz., he is dead, beyond the seas, unfit to attend as a witness, cannot with reasonable diligence be identified or found, or cannot reasonably be expected to recall "matters relevant to the accuracy or otherwise of the statement."[22] However, under R.S.C., Ord. 38, r. 29, made pursuant to section 8(3), the court has an inclusionary discretion to admit a statement, although no notice of desire to tender it in evidence has been served, although a counter-notice requiring the maker of the statement (or original supplier of the information) to be called as a witness has not been complied with, and although none of the reasons for not calling him exists. At the same time section 8(3)(a) provides that, with one exception,[23] there can be no discretion to exclude a statement where there has been compliance with the notice procedures.

Section 10 is concerned with matters of interpretation relative to Part I of the Act and its application to arbitrations, etc. Mention may be made of the definition of "statement" contained in subsection (1), which is as follows: " 'statement' includes any representation of fact, whether made in words or otherwise." Consequent upon the Civil Evidence Act 1972, s.1,[24] the word "fact" must now be taken to include opinion.[25] The meaning of the word "statement" is of fundamental importance as it prescribes the whole ambit of the Part I of the Act. It is not conducive to clarity that resort has been made to an open-ended

---

[18] See. s.8(4).

[19] See R.S.C., Ord. 38, rr. 30 and 31 (Part Three, infra).

[20] See R.S.C., Ord. 38, rr. 21–29.

[21] s.8(2)(b).

[22] See R.S.C., Ord. 38, r. 25. Compare the corresponding provision in the Criminal Justice Act 1988, s. 23(2) (Part Two, infra). As to certification of unfitness, see s.8(5) of the 1968 Act.

[23] This exception relates to a case in which the statement in question was made by a person while giving evidence in former civil or criminal proceedings: s.8(3)(b) and R.S.C., Ord. 38, r. 28.

[24] Part Two, infra.

[25] For details of the effect of this upon evidence admitted by virtue of s.4 of the 1968 Act, see s.1(2) of the 1972 Act. (Part Two infra).

definition of this critical word by the use of the verb "includes."
Moreover, the choice of the noun "representation" is not entirely
happy. It does not seem apt to cover cases in which there is no intention
to communicate, such as that of an entry in a supposedly private diary,
or cases of implied assertions such as those hypothetically instanced by
Parke B. in the Court of Exchequer Chambers in *Wright* v. *Doe d.
Tatham*.[26] In order to bring such cases within the meaning of the word
"statement" (and thus within the scope of Part I of the Act) it may be
necessary to pray in aid the open-endedness of the definition. If the Act
were to be seen as not extending to, *e.g.* implied assertions, the
common law, with all its uncertainty in this area, would still be
applicable—and this is a prospect which few would contemplate with
equanimity.

Since the coming into force of the Civil Evidence Act 1968 there have
been relatively few reported cases dealing with its scope, interpretation
or operation. The materials set out in the present chapter illustrate
several somewhat miscellaneous aspects of the Act and the related Rules
of the Supreme Court, which have been considered by the courts.

RE KOSCOT INTERPLANETARY (U.K.) LTD.; RE KOSCOT A.G.

[1972] 3 All E.R. 829 (Ch.D.: 1972)

*For a statement to be admissible as evidence of a fact contained therein by
virtue of the Civil Evidence Act 1968, s.2(1), it must be established or
must appear that direct oral testimony by the maker of the statement
would be admissible as evidence of that fact.*

*A litigant who wishes to put in hearsay evidence by virtue of the Civil
Evidence Act 1968, s.4(1), must establish in some way that the
requirements of the subsection are satisfied. Accordingly, there must be
evidence as to the identity of the compiler of the record and that he was
acting under a duty when compiling it.*

*The exemption from giving notice conferred by R.S.C., Ord. 38, r. 21(4),
in relation to "evidence . . . to be given by affidavit" does not extend to
documents exhibited to an affidavit.*

MEGARRY J.: There are before me two petitions for winding up an
English and a Swiss company under the Companies Act 1967, s.35. The
petitions were filed by the Secretary of State for Trade and Industry,
and they state that it appears to him to be in the public interest that the
companies should be wound up. . . . A point of evidence has arisen
relating to an American company which, like the two companies in
question, has a name including the word "Koscot"; however, the two
companies in question before me are not subsidiaries of the American
company, but had, at least at the relevant time, shareholders who to a
substantial degree were common to the three companies.

The point that has arisen relates to some American material

---

[26] (1837) 7 Ad. & E11. 313 (Chap. 13, *supra*). Also, doubt might perhaps be entertained
as to the total appropriateness of describing some cases of negative hearsay as involving
representation, as, for instance, the case of a list of names of persons present tendered
to show the absence of a person whose name is not included.

concerning the American company and its methods of trading which, though not identical, had at the relevant time much in common with the methods of trading of the English company. This material consists, first, of a letter, document D41, sent to a member of the staff of the solicitor's office of the Department of Trade and Industry, and written by a Mr. O'Connell, an attorney in the Bureau of Consumer Protection in the Federal Trade Commission of Washington, in the District of Columbia. The letter makes a number of statements about the American company and proceedings against it in the American courts.

Secondly, there is a document, D70, some 16 pages long, setting out, State by State, a summary of proceedings against the American company and other companies that have been taken or are contemplated, and so on. Both the letter and the summary are included as exhibits to an affidavit of Mr. Gill, Deputy Inspector General of the Companies Inspection Branch of the Department of Trade and Industry, sworn very recently, on June 10, 1972. The letter forms a separate exhibit, whereas the summary is part of a report by the Council of Better Business Bureaus Inc., sent by Mr. O'Connell to Mr. Gill. The letter purports to be signed by Mr. O'Connell, whereas there is no signature anywhere on the report or on the summary. Indeed, there is nothing to indicate what human being or human beings prepared the report, save that an addendum to the report has typewritten words indicating that it is from a Mr. M. E. Brown, Director of the Trade Practices Division. The summary itself, however, remains wholly devoid of any authenticating name.

To the admission of this matter as evidence counsel for the respondents objected, on the ground that it constituted inadmissible hearsay; and counsel for the petitioner contended that the documents were admissible. . . .

The argument of counsel for the petitioner was based on two grounds. First, he said that quite apart from the Civil Evidence Act 1968 hearsay evidence was admissible on a petition such as this, whether that petition was unopposed, or, as here, opposed, and no matter how remote the hearsay was. . . . I can find nothing in the cases that supports any contention that in this type of case there is any open licence to admit hearsay evidence generally. . . . Accordingly, the contention of counsel for the petitioner on the first point fails.

Counsel for the petitioner's second head was based on the Civil Evidence Act 1968. For the letter from Mr. O'Connell, he relied on s.2(1). [His Lordship then read the subsection.] Counsel for the respondents' answer was simple and conclusive. If Mr. O'Connell were here and sought to repeat from the witness box the statements contained in his letter, most of it would in all probability be excluded as being hearsay; for he recounts matters about which it is at least improbable that he has any first-hand information. It certainly has not been established, nor does it appear, that he had first-hand knowledge of the facts that are stated in the letter. Accordingly, said counsel for the respondents, counsel for the petitioner had failed to satisfy the last 10 words of the subsection; he had not shown that the facts stated in the letter by Mr. O'Connell were facts "of which direct oral evidence by him would be admissible." This submission seems to me to be plainly right, and accordingly I hold that the letter is not made admissible by the subsection.

As regards the summary, counsel for the petitioner relied on section 4(1) of the 1968 Act. [His Lordship then read the subsection.] The Act does not define "record" but I very much doubt whether a compilation of the results of legal proceedings such as that now before me would normally fall within this description. If a member of the Bar, duly instructed by solicitors, goes to the library of his Inn, and from the law reports and newspapers there makes a summary of all the reported cases on a particular subject, or affecting a particular person or company, I do not think it can be said that this summary is a "record compiled by a person acting under a duty from information which was supplied by a person...who had, or may reasonably be supposed to have had, personal knowledge of the matters dealt with in that information" within the subsection. In any case, all that I have here is a document prepared by an unidentified person or persons from, it seems, information supplied by unidentified persons who may or may not have had any personal knowledge of the matters in question. When it is sought to put such a document in evidence, it may well be said that questions arise not merely on hearsay but also (if I may say) so on "whosay." I think that if a litigant wishes to put in hearsay evidence by virtue of section 4(1), he must establish in some way that the requirements of the subsection are satisfied. It will be observed that the phrase "may reasonably be supposed" governs only the requirement of personal knowledge, and that the other requirements are not softened in this way. Thus I do not see how a document can be shown to be, or to form part of, "a record compiled by a person acting under a duty" unless there is some evidence of who that person was, and that he was subject to such a duty. In saying that, I do not overlook section 6(2) of the Act, which was not debated before me.

Counsel for the petitioner also faced the difficulty that he had not satisfied the requirements of section 8 of the 1968 Act and R.S.C., Ord. 38, r. 21(1) by giving due notice of his intention to give in evidence the summary in dispute. He contended, however, that R.S.C., Ord. 38, r. 21(4), exempted him from this requirement. [His Lordship then read the sub-rule. See Part Three, *infra*.] However, the summary, of course, is not part of an affidavit, but is an exhibit to an affidavit, and in terms sub-rule (4) relates only to "any affidavit"....

It therefore seems to me that neither document is admissible in evidence for the purpose of establishing the truth of its contents. In saying that, I am not, of course, saying that the documents may not become admissible of some later stage in the proceedings if, for example, they are put to a witness in cross-examination, and he accepts them. It may also be that the documents might be admissible for some limited purpose other than establishing the truth of the statements contained in them. But for the purposes for which they were tendered, namely, of establishing such truth, I hold them inadmissible. I would only add that even if I am wrong on this, I should find it difficult to give any real weight to the summary, which might courteously be described as a masterpiece of distributive anonymity.

Ruling accordingly.

Taylor v. Taylor [1970] 1 W.L.R. 1148 (C.A.). A wife petitioned for divorce on the ground of her husband's adultery, alleging his incest with their 14-year-old daughter for which he had been convicted in 1962. The Court of Appeal held *inter alia* that, although hearsay, a transcript of the criminal proceedings was admissible in evidence both under section 2(1) and under section 4(1) of the 1968 Act together with R.S.C., Ord. 38, r. 28. Davies L.J. also said (p. 1154): "It may be, though I express no direct opinion on this, that the summing-up of the judge might not be covered by section 2(1) because that is dealing with a statement in evidence, and of course the judge cannot give evidence. But I think that the transcript of the summing-up would probably be admissible under section 4(1), since this is a record compiled by the shorthand writer in his capacity as such." [For another aspect of this decision see Chapter 19, *infra.*]

Knight v. **David** [1971] 1 W.L.R. 1671 (Ch.D.) The plaintiffs claimed title to certain land and wished to put in evidence a map made pursuant to the Tithe Act 1836. The defendants contended that the map would not be within section 4(1) of the Civil Evidence Act 1968 because (1) direct oral evidence of the title would not be admissible, and (2) there was nothing to show that the record compiled by the commissioners for the purposes of the 1836 Act was compiled from information supplied by persons having personal knowledge of the matter dealt with. Goulding J. rejected both contentions. Regarding the former his Lordship said (pp. 1675–1676): "The argument must fail if a living person could state in evidence that the machinery of the Act was carried out, and that a certain person was, and another was not, entered as proprietor of certain land. In my judgment such a statement would be admissible." Regarding counsel's second contention his Lordship said (p. 1676): "... having regard to the nature of the document and the lapse of time, it is right to infer that this condition [*i.e.* that the suppliers of the information 'had, or may reasonably be supposed to have had, personal knowledge of the matters dealt with'] is satisfied."

Note.—Goulding J. concluded (p. 1676): "Therefore, while I prefer to base my decision in common law, I should also be prepared to admit this evidence under section 4 of the Act of 1968." The reference to reliance upon the common law, seemingly as a declaration as to a public right (as to which see Chapter 14, Section A, *infra*), is puzzling. Admissibility under a common exception to the hearsay rule *as such* is no longer permissible (see the concluding three words of section 1(1) of the Act). Perhaps, however, a case could have been made for reception by virtue of section 9, which gives statutory effect to certain other previous common law heads of admissibility (see section 9(2)).

H. v. **Schering Chemicals Ltd.** [1983] 1 W.L.R. 143 (Q.B.D.). The plaintiffs claimed damages for personal injuries alleged to have been caused by the effect of a drug marketed and manufactured by the defendant pharmaceutical companies. They wished to introduce copies of certain specified documents which they claimed were records for the purposes of section 4 of the Civil Evidence Act 1968. The documents included summaries of the results of research, articles and letters published in medical journals concerning the drug. The plaintiffs wished to use the documents, not only in order to show the state of general medical knowledge of the drug, but also to show that the drug had in fact caused the injuries. Bingham J. held that the documents were not records and were therefore not admissible under section 4. His Lordship, having mentioned (p. 145) that the articles could be "referred to for the purpose of showing the state of general professional knowledge, which is of course relevant to the issue as to what the defendants knew or ought to have known at any given time." and that "the articles can be referred to by experts as part of the corpus of medical knowledge within the expertise of a medical expert," continued: "But the plaintiffs want to prove the facts and the results of the research summarised in the articles for the purpose of showing, on the strength of those facts and results, that the administering of the drug did cause the injuries complained of. ..." Holding that the documents were not records within the meaning of section 4, Bingham J. said (p. 146): "The intention of that section was, I believe, to admit in evidence records which a historian would regard as original or primary sources, that is, documents which either give effect to a transaction itself or which contain a contemporaneous register of information supplied by those with direct knowledge of the facts.... Judged by the same standard the documents in the present case, I think, are not records and are not primary or original sources. They are a digest or analysis of records which must exist or have existed, but they are not themselves those records. If the plaintiffs' submission were right it would, I think, mean that anyone who wrote a letter to 'The Times,' having done research and summarising that research in his letter, would find his letter admissible as evidence of the facts under section 4."

Note.—The somewhat restrictive approach taken by Bingham J. was adopted by Peter Gibson J. in *Savings Bank* v. *Gasco B.V.* [1984] 1 W.L.R. 271 (Ch.D.), where he held that a report on a company by Board of Trade inspectors, which included a compilation of information given to them by others and which expressed an opinion thereon, could not be considered as an original or primary source of information and was not therefore a "record" within the meaning of section 4.

See, too, *P.* v. *D.* [1985] C.L.Y. 1507.

RASOOL v. WEST MIDLANDS PASSENGER TRANSPORT EXECUTIVE

[1974] 3 All E.R. 638 (Q.B.D.: 1974)

The five factors, which (under the Civil Evidence Act 1968, s.8(2)(b) and R.S.C., Ord. 38, r. 25) excuse the calling of the maker of a statement as a witness, are to be treated disjunctively. Accordingly, if it is established on balance of probabilities that the maker of the statement is beyond the seas, it is not necessary to prove in addition that he cannot by reasonable diligence be found.
If the court is satisfied that as least one of the specified factors is established, it has no discretion to exclude the statement.

FINER J.: This is an appeal from the order of the district registrar... on the application of the defendants under R.S.C., Ord. 38, r. 27(1), whereby he determined that a Mrs. Celestine Collum could not be called as a witness at the hearing of the action on the ground that she had left her former known address and could not be found. The effect of the order will, it is contended, be to let in as evidence at the trial a written statement signed by Mrs. Collum and dated December 11, 1972, in which she gives her account as an eye-witness of an accident which happened on December 6, 1972, in which the plaintiff was knocked down by the defendants' omnibus in Birmingham and sustained, it would appear from the statement of claim, severe injuries which are the subject of his claim for compensation in the action....

The effect of the statement in dispute, taken at its face value, is highly prejudicial to the plaintiff....

In amending the law regarding the admissibility of hearsay evidence in civil proceedings, the Civil Evidence Act 1968, as appears from sections 1 and 8, left much of the detail to be worked out by rules of court which are now to be found in Part III of R.S.C., Ord. 38. Many of the questions which arise thus entail a reading of the 1968 Act and of the rules in close conjunction with each other. The scheme of things, so far as material in the present circumstances, may be summarised as follows.

[His Lordship then read section 2 of the Act, and referred to section 8 and to R.S.C., Ord. 38, rr. 21, 22(2) and (3), 25, 26(2) and 27(1)]. . . .

Now the short effect of all these complicated provisions seems to be as follows: that the system for adducing a written statement in evidence without calling the maker involved the service by the party wishing to take that course on the other parties of a notice in a prescribed form. A party receiving such a notice who objects to the proposal to put in the statement can, by an appropriate counter-notice, require the witness to be called, failing which the statement (subject to an overriding discretion which the court has to admit it under r. 29) will be excluded. This right of objection, however, is modified in the case where the stated reason for desiring to put the statement in evidence without calling the witness is one or other of the five reasons mentioned in section 8(2)(*b*) of the 1968 Act and rule 25. In such a case the objecting party must, despite the assertion in the notice that the witness cannot or should not be called because he is dead, or beyond the seas, or as the case may be, state in his counter-notice that the witness can or should be called. This raises the issues as to the truth or validity of the reason relied on, and that issue will be determined, as it is being now, under the procedure laid down by rule 27.

In the instant case, the defendants' notice to the plaintiff asserted that Mrs. Collum could not be called as a witness at the hearing because—

"She has left her former address number 325 Charles Road, Small Heath, Birmingham and cannot at present be found. It is understood that she is now beyond the seas and is probably resident in Jamaica."

Strictly speaking, this probably invokes only one of the five specified reasons, namely that despite the exercise of reasonable diligence it was not possible to find the witness. By common consent however, the notice at the hearing before myself was treated as invoking both that reason and the further reason that Mrs. Collum was beyond the seas.

The argument on appeal was primarily addressed to the sufficiency of the evidence adduced by the defendants to prove the reasons on which they rely. . . .

It seems to me that the standard of proof that the reason relied on is well founded must be the same as generally applies to other issues which arise in a civil proceeding, namely, proof on the balance of probabilities. . . . However, as I read section 8(2)(*b*) of the 1968 Act and the rules which reflect it, the five reasons that may be relied on for not calling a witness are disjunctive reasons. If the maker of the statement is beyond the seas it does not have to be proved also that he cannot by reasonable diligence be found. His whereabouts abroad may be precisely known, yet if it be established that he is indeed abroad that is in itself a sufficient reason for admitting the statement. It would follow that the application in this case (the terms of which were followed in the order) should not have been based on the ground that Mrs. Collum had left her former address, and could not be found. The real ground was that she was beyond the seas.

In finding, however, that the absence of the maker beyond the seas is a sufficient reason in itself for admitting the statement, even if no effort is made to trace the precise whereabouts of the proposed witness, or even if those whereabouts are known, I have deliberately elided the question whether the court nevertheless has any discretion to exclude it. At first sight it seems peculiar that there should be no such discretion.

Take the case of a witness who has been party to a conversation in which it is common ground that the plaintiff and defendant made a contract, but they dispute the terms they agreed. The witness lives at a known address in Paris, despite which the plaintiff seeks to adduce his evidence in the form of a statement, relying on the fact the witness is beyond the seas. Or in the present case, one may imagine that is was Mrs. Collum, a professed eye-witness to a serious accident whose statement may damn the plaintiff, who lived at a known address in Paris. Nevertheless, I find it a clear conclusion from the provisions of the statute and the rules which I have earlier mentioned that if the court is satisfied on any of the five specified reasons the statement becomes admissible, and there is no residuary discretion to exclude it by reference to other circumstances. The relevant provisions leave no room for such a discretion. The scheme of the law is that the counter-notice is ineffectual unless it raises an issue regarding the reason alleged in the notice which is ultimately determined in favour of the giver of the counter-notice. If the counter-notice is ineffectual, the notice takes effect. I consider that this would be the result even apart from section 8(3)(a), but that provision clinches the point by providing in terms that the rules cannot—with the exceptions provided for in section 8(3)(b), which has no application to the present case—confer on the court a discretion to exclude a statement where the requirements of the rules affecting its admissibility have been complied with.

The weight to be attached to the statement admitted in evidence remains a matter for the court. In the circumstances postulated in the examples I gave, where the whereabouts abroad of an important witness in a substantial case are known or can be easily ascertained, but the party relying on his evidence nevertheless adopts a method of adducing it which does not permit of cross-examination, no doubt the court would pay little attention to it. It may be that this is a risk which the defendants run if they make no efforts to find Mrs. Collum in Jamaica, so as to permit at least the possibility of evidence being taken on commission. But all that will be a matter for the trial judge.

I should add that in deciding as I have on the matter of discretion I have not overlooked section 18(5) of the 1968 Act which provides that nothing in the Act—

"shall prejudice ... any power of a court, in any legal proceedings, to exclude evidence (whether by preventing questions from being put or otherwise) at its discretion ... "

The exact meaning of this provision would be an interesting field for enquiry in appropriate circumstances, but it has no relevance that I can detect for the present case....

[His Lordship affirmed the order admitting the evidence, but on the ground that Mrs. Collum was "beyond the seas."]

Note.—In *Piermay Shipping Co.* v. *Chester* [1978] 1 W.L.R. 411 the Court of Appeal, approving *Rasool* v. *West Midlands Passenger Transport Executive* (*supra*), held that, on proof that the maker of a statement is abroad, it is unnecessary to show that any efforts have been made to secure his attendance as a witness, and that the court has no discretion to exclude evidence of his statement, provided there has been compliance with the other requirements of the Act and the relevant Rules of Court.

In *Rover International* v. *Cannon Films Ltd.* [1987] 1 W.L.R. 1597 (Ch.D.), a recent case concerned with the 1968 Act and in which the witness was resident in Guernsey, Harman J., having agreed that the Isle of Wight and the Scilly Islands although below the low-tide mark are not "beyond the seas," said (p. 1603): "In my view the purpose of the

Civil Evidence Act 1968, *i.e.* to get evidence in without the need for bringing persons to give the evidence here, can be considered in the light of the powers of the court to make people come and give evidence here. Where a subpoena will run, a witness can be compelled. A subpoena will not run in the Isle of Man or the Channel Islands and those islands are not parts of the United Kingdom in right of the Crown of England or the Crown of the Unions."

For the contrasting position in criminal cases see the Criminal Justice Act 1988, s.23(2) and *Note* thereon (Part Two, *infra*).

FORD v. LEWIS

[1971] 1 W.L.R. 623; [1971] 2 All E.R. 983 (C.A.: 1971)

For the discretion bestowed by R.S.C., Ord. 38, r. 29 (implementing the Civil Evidence Act 1968, s.8(3)(a)), to be properly exercised the court must be in possession of all relevant facts. Accordingly there can be no valid exercise of that discretion if there has, for any reason, been a deliberate withholding from the court of the reason for non-compliance with the notice procedure.

If that non-compliance resulted from a party's deliberate attempt to achieve tactical surprise a judge would (semble) not be acting judicially were he to exercise his discretion in favour of that party.

In 1960 the infant plaintiff, then aged five, and her parents were injured when a van driven by the defendant collided with them. The defendant denied negligence and alleged that the injuries suffered by the plaintiff were caused by the fact that her parents, who were in charge of her at the time, were in a state of intoxication. The action did not come on for hearing until 10 years later, and by that time the defendant had become a patient in a mental hospital, and it was agreed that he was unfit to be called as a witness. At the trial his counsel sought to put in evidence under the Civil Evidence Act 1968, s.2(1), a photostat copy of a written statement (proved to be in the defendant's handwriting) setting out his version of the accident, and also, under section 4(1) of the Act, hospital records stating that the plaintiff's father had been in an intoxicated state when admitted to hospital after the accident. No notice, as required by R.S.C., Ord. 38, rr. 21(1), 22 and 23, was served; and the reason for this omission was not disclosed to the trial judge. The judge, after offering the plaintiff's counsel an adjournment which was declined, admitted the documents in the exercise of his discretion under R.S.C., Ord. 38, r. 29(1). He accepted the statement attributed to the defendant and dismissed the action. The infant plaintiff appealed on the ground that the judge had wrongly exercised his discretion in permitting the admission of the defendant's statement and the hospital notes.

The Court of Appeal (EDMUND DAVIES and KARMINSKI L.JJ. (DAVIES L.J. dissenting)) allowed the appeal.

EDMUND DAVIES L.J.: ... [T]he point of substance involved in this appeal relates to the application of the Civil Evidence Act 1968 and R.S.C., Ord. 38 to the circumstances of this case....

... Rule 21 [of Order 38] ... makes it obligatory on the party desiring to adduce hearsay evidence by virtue of section 2 of the Act to serve notice on the other party of his intention to do so. If he does not, he will, subject to the court's discretion under rule 29, be precluded from giving the statement in evidence.... Rule 26 enables the party receiving such a notice to serve a counter-notice, requiring the other side to call as a witness at the trial any person to whom the original notice related. If that counter-notice is served, rule 27 provides the machinery whereby the necessity for the absent maker of the statement being actually called as a witness can be decided before the trial.

It is well known that the statutory provisions which led to the formulation of these rules were the subject-matter of considerable controversy.... A compromise was finally reached within the terms of section 8 of the Act of 1968 and its offspring R.S.C., Ord. 38. The object of the latter is expressed with admirable clarity in the notes thereto which appear in the *Supreme Court Practice* (1970), and I cannot do better than to quote them. I am quoting the thin supplement, para. 38.20.6:

> "The machinery of Part III of this Order is designed to achieve two main objectives, namely (*a*) that all questions concerning the giving of hearsay evidence at the trial should, so far as practicable, be dealt with and disposed of before the trial, so that the trial itself should proceed smoothly without unnecessary objections relating to such hearsay evidence, and (*b*) that in relation to any hearsay evidence which any party desires to adduce, there should be no surprises at the trial. In this latter respect, it is to be noted that the machinery of Part III of this Order makes a departure from the general rule of practice that a party is not required to disclose the evidence which he intends to adduce at the trial, for these rules do require such disclosure of the proposed hearsay evidence to be made. The principle is that if a party wishes to obtain the advantage of adducing secondary evidence at the trial, he should pay the price of disclosing such evidence before the trial, and affording the other party the opportunity to resist its admission in that form."

That being the object of Order 38, it is common ground that the defendant never did comply with it. For a substantial period his advisers had been in possession of a statement attributed to him which they had it in mind to place before the court of lieu of calling him as a witness. Despite their non-compliance, Veale J. allowed them to adduce it in evidence. It clearly played an effective part in leading him to dismiss the plaintiff's claim, for he made express reference to its contents in his judgment, saying: "It is not necessary for me to read it; it is only necessary for me to say that I think it rings true."

In proper circumstances, a trial judge is undoubtedly entitled to admit evidence of an out-of-court statement notwithstanding non-compliance with the initially mandatory requirements. Section 8(3)(*a*) of the Act of 1968 made express provision for this and was the foundation of rule 29 of Order 38. This provides that:

> "(1)... that court may, if it thinks it just to do so, allow a statement falling within section 2(1),... of the Act to be given in evidence... notwithstanding—(*a*) that the statement is one in relation to which rule 21(1) applies and that the party desiring to give the statement in evidence has failed to comply with that rule,..."

It was by virtue of this provision that Veale J. admitted the absentee defendant's out-of-court statement.

I think it is imperative to consider briefly the circumstances in which he was led to do so. He had himself addressed some sharp questions to the defence as to why they had not given the statutory notice, and he received no adequate answer—if, indeed, any real answer at all was forthcomming. But, his offer to adjourn the proceedings until the following assizes having been declined by plaintiff's counsel, the judge admitted the statement.

In these circumstances, it is urged on behalf of the defendant that this exercise of his discretion under rule 29 ought not now to be disturbed. For my part, I cannot accept this. Rule 29(1) empowers the court to admit such a statement as is here in question, notwithstanding failure to comply with the preceding rules, "if it thinks it just to do so." In order that the court may adjudicate upon the justice of relaxing the rules in favour of a defaulting party, it must surely be placed in possession of all the relevant facts. In the present case Veale J. was left ignorant of the vital fact that non-compliance by the defendant with the statutory requirement was due to no inability, inadvertence, or slackness on the part of his advisers, but resulted from a deliberate decision not to comply. This emerged from the completely candid statement of leading counsel for the defendant, who, in response to a direct inquiry from the Bench, took sole responsibility for the failure to give any notice of the kind required by rule 22. He was equally candid about his reason for advising this course of action, namely, that he suspected that, were the existence, nature and contents of the defendant's written statement made known to the plaintiff and her parents before the trial, if might have led to their evidence being in some way adjusted in order to meet and destroy it in advance. Put in plain words, this means that the tactics adopted were precisely those which the statutory provisions as to notice and counter-notice were designed to prevent, namely, the taking of a party by surprise by suddenly and without warning producing at the trial an out-of-court statement of someone not proposed to be called as a witness.

In these most unfortunate circumstances, it seems to me impossible that the defendant should be permitted to rely upon the judge's purported exercise of his discretion under rule 29. I hold that there can be no valid exercise of such discretion if there has (for any reason) been a deliberate withholding from the court of the reason for non-compliance. . . . A suitor who deliberately flouts the rules has no right to ask the court to exercise in his favour a discretionary indulgence created by those very same rules. Furthermore, a judge who, to his knowledge, finds himself confronted by such a situation would not, as I think, be acting judicially if he nevertheless exercised his discretion in favour of the recalcitrant suitor. The rules are there to be respected, and those who defy them should not be indulged or excused. Slackness is one thing; deliberate disobedience another. The former may be overlooked; the latter never, even though, as here, it derives from mistaken zeal on the client's behalf. To tolerate it would be dangerous to justice.

Nor do I think that the judge's offer of an adjournment cured the injustice done to the infant plaintiff, for I take the view that he would never have reached that stage had he known all the facts. . . .

A new trial was ordered.

Note.—See, too, *Rover International* v. *Cannon Films Ltd.* [1987] 1 W.L.R. 1597 (Ch.D.), where Harman J. said (p. 1600): "In my view, as a general proposition, the court should not exclude evidence unless it is satisfied that real prejudice has been caused or unless it is clear that a deliberate attempt has been made to take the other by surprise, a practice which it is the exact purpose of the rules to prevent." Compare, too, *Morris* v. *Stratford on Avon R.D.C.* (*infra*).

MORRIS v. STRATFORD ON AVON R.D.C.

[1973] 1 W.L.R. 1059; [1973] 3 All E.R. 263 (C.A.: 1973)

Non-compliance with the notice procedure prescribed by Rules of Court made pursuant to the Civil Evidence Act 1968, s.8, cannot lightly be overlooked; but it would be unfortunate if the matter were to be treated so that in every case those advising a party would feel it necessary to advise him to give advance notice if there was any possibility, however remote, that as a result of something that might happen thereafter an application might be made under the Act.

When an application to admit a statement under the Act is made (there having been a failure to comply with the notice requirements), if there is reason to suppose that otherwise injustice would be caused or that the other party would be materially prejudiced or embarrassed, the judge should either reject the statement or, in his discretion, admit it on terms.

The plaintiff, an employee of the defendants, was injured in the course of his employment. He issued a writ against the defendants claiming damaged for the alleged negligence of a fellow employee named Pattison. The defendants denied this negligence. At the trial, which took place some five years after the accident, the fellow employee's evidence as to what had happened was confused and inconsistent.

MEGAW L.J. (DAVIES L.J. and WALTON J. concurring):...At the end of the examination-in-chief of Mr. Pattison, counsel for the defendants asked the judge for leave to introduce in evidence a statement which Mr. Pattison had made some nine months after the accident. Apparently that statement was a proof of evidence which had been taken by a representative of the insurance company concerned. The application was made by counsel under the Civil Evidence Act 1968. Objection was taken by counsel for the plaintiff; but the judge, having heard certain submissions, exercised his discretion to admit the statement. In his judgment he refers to it and he quotes a part of it. For the plaintiff it is contended that the judge erred in admitting the statement.... But for myself,...I do not think that it can properly be said that the judge exercised his discretion wrongly.

Counsel for the plaintiff submits that the court, under the Civil Evidence Act 1968 and the Rules of Court made thereunder, has, in a case like this, not one but two discretions to exercise. The first discretion is that which is given to it by section 2 of the Act. That section, which provides for the admissibility of out-of-court statements as evidence of the facts stated, does say, in subsection (2)(*a*), that the statement "shall be given in evidence by virtue of this section on behalf of that party without the leave of the court": hence there is discretion coming in at *that* stage. Then in R.S.C., Ord. 38, r. 29, it is provided that "without prejudice to," *inter alia,* section 2(2)(*a*) of the Act, "the court may, if it thinks it just to do so, allow a statement falling within section 2(1)... of the Act to be given in evidence at the trial or hearing..."—and then (departing from the words of the rule), notwithstanding that the advance notices, which are required by the rules to be given where it is intended to seek to take advantage of the Act, have not been given.

I do not think it matters whether one regards these as being two separate discretions or as being one discretion with the matters which are relevant under Ord. 38, r. 29 being taken into account when the judge is dealing with the exercise of his discretion under section 2 of the Act or vice versa. There is no doubt that the judge has to consider all the relevant matters in exercising his discretion; and if the proper notices for which the Act and the rules provide have not been given, then the judge must consider that matter with case and must give the opposite party every opportunity to make submissions before he can properly decide whether or not the non-compliance with the rules is such that justice requires that the statement should be admitted.

Nothing that I say must be taken in any way as suggesting that non-compliance with the rules as to notices is a matter that can be lightly overlooked. On the other hand, there must be cases in which there is, sensibly and reasonably, no ground for supposing that a statement which is in existence is going to be used by a party. It would perhaps be unfortunate if the matter were to be so interpreted that, in every case, those who are advising a party felt it necessary to advise him that, if there is any possibility, however remote, that, as a result of something which may happen hereafter, an application might be sought to be made, then notice should be given in advance. But, quite clearly, if there is reason to suppose, on proper consideration of the evidence, that such an application may be made, then care must be taken that the proper notices should be given.

As I say, it is important that the notices should be given. We were told by counsel for the defendants, and I have no doubt whatever but that it is correct, that in the present case it had not crossed his mind that this statement would be one which there would be occasion to put in in evidence, and that it was only when the evidence of Mr. Pattison came to be taken that it occurred to him that it would be desirable that application should be made. In my judgment, no blame whatever attaches to counsel, for making the application at that state.

[His Lordship then distinguished *Ford* v. *Lewis* (*supra*).]

... [I]t is right that careful consideration should always be given, on an application of this sort, to matters such as those that were stressed before us by counsel for the plaintiff: for example, that the statement was taken as a proof of evidence and that it was not closely contemporary with the time of the accident but was taken some nine months later. Those are matters which of course go to weight; but they can be relevant on the question of a decision as to the exercise of discretion. Another matter which in my judgment must always be carefully watched, when an application of this sort is made under the Civil Evidence Act 1968 without proper notices having been given, is for the judge to make sure, so far as he can, that no injustice will be done to the other party by reason of the statement being allowed to be put in evidence. If there is ground to suppose that there will be any injustice caused, or that the other party will be materially prejudiced or embarrassed, then the judge should either refuse to allow the document to be admitted or, in his discretion, allow it on terms, such as an adjournment at the cost of the party seeking to put in the statement.

　...But, having regard to all the circumstances of which we have heard in this case, I am satisfied that there has been no such prejudice and that no injustice resulted. Accordingly, I take the view that Stirling J. was not wrong in the manner in which he exercised his discretion.

Chapter 17

CONFESSIONS AND IMPROPERLY OBTAINED EVIDENCE

EVIDENCE of a statement made by an accused person prior to his trial, if tendered as evidence of its truth, is very likely to be hearsay; but, to the extent that the statement was inculpatory, that is to say to the extent that it tends to show the accused's guilt, evidence of it will probably fall within the informal admission exception to the hearsay rule. Nevertheless, evidence of such a statement, if tendered by the prosecution in criminal proceedings, may be inadmissible unless certain additional requirements are satisfied. At common law this meant that it was incumbent upon the prosecution to establish that the inculpatory statement, or "confession," was not made as a result of an inducement held out by a person in authority and that it was not made as a result of oppression. An inducement could take the form of threat or of a promise. A person in authority was seen as being anyone whom it was reasonable to suppose that the accused, at the time he made the confession, had thought to be capable of influencing the outcome of the prosecution. What constituted oppression resisted precise definition and depended upon the circumstances, but its general nature was indicated by the Court of Appeal as being "something which tends to sap, and has sapped, that free will which must exist before a confession is voluntary."[1] It was, in fact, only relatively recently that oppression was clearly identified as a separate root of involuntariness. The classic statement of traditional common doctrine is that of Lord Sumner in *Ibrahim* v. *R.*[2]: "It has long been established as a positive rule of English law, that no statement by an accused is admissible in evidence against him unless it is shown by the prosecution to have been a voluntary statement, in the sense that it has not been obtained from him either by fear of prejudice or hope of advantage exercised or held out by a person in authority. The principle is as old as Lord Hale."[3] The

---

[1] *R.* v. *Prager* [1972] 1 W.L.R. 260, 266 (C.A.), where the Court of Appeal adopted this definition previously set out in a Note to *R.* v. *Priestley* (1965) 51 Cr.App.R. 1.
[2] [1914] A.C. 599, 610 (P.C.).
[3] As Cross points out (*Evidence*, (6th ed.), p. 534) the reference to Hale must be to later editions of his book. The first clear and authoritative statement of the rule was in *R.* v. *Warwickshall* (1783) Leach C.C. 263 (see *infra*). One of the last cases in which the scope and operation of the common law rule was reviewed was *D.P.P.* v. *Ping Lin* [1976] A.C. 574 (H.L.).

relationship between the inducement (or oppressive conduct) and the making of the confession had to be causal: a mere chronological sequence of events did not render the confession inadmissible. It is to be noted that the involuntariness of a confession only precluded reception of evidence of it if tendered by the prosecution: in other cases, for example one in which the evidence was tendered by a co-accused, involuntariness went only to its weight.

The formulation, and in significant measure the substance, of the pre-conditions of admissibility of evidence of a confession by an accused when tendered by the prosecution were changed by the Police and Criminal Evidence Act 1984, section 76. Oppression and the likelihood of unreliability have become the general controls upon admissibility. That the common law test of voluntariness has been discarded is clear. Oppression is now statutorily defined, but its relationship with the previously emerging common law test of oppression is less clear. Section 77 makes special provision for controlling confessions by mentally handicapped persons. For section 76 (and section 77), and some commentary thereon, see Part Two, *infra*. This Chapter sets out excerpts from cases on the interpretation of various aspects of the new statutory law. It contains, too, excerpts from several earlier cases which almost certainly survive, at least persuasively, as authorities.

If there is a dispute as to the existence or otherwise of a pre-condition of admissibility of evidence of a confession, that issue must be decided on the *voir dire* (colloquially described as a "trial within a trial") in the absence of the jury. This inquiry is not as to the truth of the confession, but as to the circumstances in which it was made. An accused who testifies on the *voir dire* should not be asked whether his confession was true. If, as a result of the *voir dire* the evidence of the confession is held to be inadmissible, no reference may be made to it when the trial on the merits is resumed. Moreover, the Crown may not call evidence, or cross-examine the accused, as to what was said on the *voir dire*. On the other hand, if the confession is found to be admissible, the accused may still contend that it was in fact made under pressure, or that it was in fact made in circumstances tending to make it unreliable, with a view to minimising the weight which the trier of fact will attach to it; but, although the trier of fact may in effect re-assess the questions of oppression and the circumstances in which the confession was made, they may only do so for the purpose of, and in the context of, deciding whether it was in fact true.[4] Here again the Crown cannot lead evidence of statements made by the accused on the *voir dire*; but, if the accused gives evidence himself and testifies as to the unreliability of the confession in a way inconsistent with what he said on the *voir dire*, he may be cross-examined on this.

There is the authority of the Supreme Court of Canada[5] to the effect that an involuntary statement which on its face is exculpatory (that is to say was, at the time it was made, apparently intended to exonerate) will also be excluded. This would appear to be correct in principle. If the statement was in fact really exculpatory it would seldom, if ever, be

---

[4] In some circumstances the judge is under a duty to direct the jury as to its possible unreliability: *R.* v. *McCarthy* (1980) 70 Cr.App.R. 270 (C.A.).

[5] *Piche* v. *R.* (1970) 11 D.L.R. (3d.) 709. However, the English Court of Appeal has recently expressed a contrary view by way of tentative *dictum* in *R.* v. *Sat-Bhambra* (1989) 88 Cr.App.R. 55, 61–62.

used by the prosecution. But, if the Crown wishes to use an *ex facie* exculpatory statement against the accused in order, for instance, to undermine a defence now raised and inconsistent with it, the circumstance that it was made under undue pressure might well tend to negative the significance of the fact that it was made at all.

It is well established[6] that, if the prosecution relies upon a confession, the whole statement becomes admissible, and the accused may rely upon such self-serving portions of it as there may be. A clear distinction is drawn in this regard between statements adduced by the Crown as part of its case against the accused and statements of an entirely self-serving nature adduced by the accused himself. Of course, it is quite possible that less weight will be attached to the exculpatory parts of the former than will be accorded to the inculpatory parts.

A confession, although made voluntarily may nevertheless be excluded by the trial judge in the exercise of his discretion. It now seems that there are probably three ways in which this may be done.

First, the judge may invoke his general discretion to exclude any evidence the likely prejudicial effect of which, in his view, so outweighs its true probative worth that its reception would be liable to deprive the accused of a fair trial.

Secondly, and more specifically, the judge has a discretion to exclude a confession or analogous evidence on the ground that it was improperly or unfairly obtained. In 1980 this specific discretion was exceptionally preserved in *R. v. Sang*.[7] There the House of Lords made it clear that an English trial judge has no discretion to refuse to admit otherwise admissible evidence simply on the ground that it was obtained by improper or unfair means "save with regard to admissions and confessions and generally with regard to evidence obtained from the accused after commission of the offence." It would seem that in practice much improperly or unfairly obtained evidence will fall into this latter category.[8] The discretion appears to have a certain mandatory aspect: if serious objection is taken to the means by which a confession was obtained, not only should the judge hold a *voir dire*, but also, should he find it to be admissible although perhaps obtained by questionable means, he must nevertheless then deliberately address himself to the exercise of this discretion.

These two common law discretions are impliedly, but clearly, preserved by section 82(3) of the 1984 Act (Part Two, *infra*).

Thirdly and somewhat confusingly, section 78(1) of that Act has conferred upon the court a further discretion to exclude. The relationship of this section with the doctrine laid down in *R. v. Sang* is not immediately obvious. (See the *Note* on *R. v. List* [1966] 1 W.L.R. 9, Chapter 1, Part A, *supra*).

Evidence of facts discovered in consequence of the accused having made an inadmissible confession is not itself inadmissible. This represents long-established doctrine,[9] and is specifically preserved by section 76(4)(*a*) of the 1984 Act. It is, however, to be noted that in a

---

[6] See, *e.g. R. v. Duncan* (1981) 73 Cr.App.R. 359 (C.A.) *infra*, recently approved by the House of Lords in *R. v. Sharp* [1988] 1 W.L.R. 7.

[7] [1980] A.C. 402, 437 (see, *infra*).

[8] In *R. v. Sang*, at least Lord Fraser, regarded it as covering not only cases in which the evidence or document is obtained from the accused personally but also cases in which it is obtained from premises occupied by him.

[9] *R. v. Warwickshall* (1783) 1 Leach. 263 (Old Bailey).

pre-Act case it was held that the contents of a documents produced in response to an inducement held out by a person in authority will not be received in evidence: in *R. v. Barker*,[10] although the document had come into existence before the inducement was held out, it was treated on the same footing as a confession made as a result of an inducement. Perhaps, therefore, a document would now similarly be excluded as a matter of law if produced in response to oppression or circumstances making for unreliability.[11]

The rationale of rules excluding confessions are complex and confused. Its diverse ingredients constitute a mixture rather than an amalgam. Considerations of reliability have undoubtedly played a large part in the development of the law. However, at common law an involuntary confession remained inadmissible even if palpably true. Moreover, under the Act a confession obtained by oppression will be excluded (s.76(2)(*b*)) regardless of its truth. Sometimes (but, perhaps significantly, not very often judicially) the confession rule is justified in terms of discouraging improper police methods. It is difficult to be confident about the practical efficacy as a deterrent of the rules relating to the inadmissibility of confessions: in any event it is possible to entertain doubts as to whether the law of evidence is an appropriate device for regulating the habits of law enforcement officers. Moreover, to exclude involuntary confessions with a view to inhibiting resort to undesirable practices, and yet to admit evidence of facts discovered as a result of a "lead" obtained in the course of such a confession, is cynically inconsistent. Nevertheless this factor has affected the evolution of the confession rule—most importantly perhaps in the common law limitation of operative inducements to those held out by persons in authority. Some apologists for the confession rule invoke the maxim that a person should not be put under pressure to incriminate himself. This irrational, but widely held, belief is a fundamental tenet of the "sporting theory" of justice[12]; but it is in itself an assertion rather than a reason. However, it too exerts a continuing influence in the development of this and related parts of the law, and a recent manifestation of this is perhaps to be seen in the nature and scope of the exception, emphasised in *R. v. Sang*,[13] to the doctrine (there re-affirmed) that there is no general discretion to exclude evidence on the ground that it was improperly or unfairly obtained.

R. v. Prager [1972] 1 W.L.R. 260 (C.A.). The defendant was convicted of espionage offences contrary to the Official Secrets Act 1911. A confession was admitted in evidence at his trial. This confession had been obtained after prolonged, but not uninterrupted, police questioning at a police station. It was not

---

[10] [1941] 2 K.B. 381 (C.C.A.).

[11] Probably no part of an inadmissible confession is rendered admissible by virtue of its accuracy being confirmed by a subsequent discovery. There is, however, authority which held that, on the contrary, so much (but only so much) of the confession as is confirmed by the subsequent discovery is rendered admissible. In *R. v. Garbett* (1847) 2 Car. & Kir. 474 (Ex.Ch.) it was even suggested that the whole confession might become admissible.

[12] In this particular sport the watchword "may the best man win" becomes "may the most successfully evasive man win."

[13] [1980] A.C. 402 (H.L.).

until after the questioning had continued for a total of more than five hours that any caution was administered. Thereafter the defendant made certain oral admissions. Later he was cautioned again, and he then made a written statement which, if true, constituted a complete admission of the two offences of which he was later convicted. The Court of Appeal refused his application for leave to appeal against conviction. In dealing with he issue of the voluntariness of the confession, Edmund Davies L.J., delivering the judgment of the court, accepted that a confession may be inadmissible, even in the absence of any threat or promise held out by a person in authority, if it was obtained by oppression. His Lordship said (p. 266): "The only reported judicial consideration of 'oppression' in the Judges's Rules of which we aware is that of Sachs J. in *R.* v. *Priestley* (1966) 52 Cr.App.R. 1, where he said: '. . . to my mind, this word, in the context of the principles under consideration imports something which tends to sap, and has sapped, that free will which must exist before a confession is voluntary. . . . Whether or not there is oppression in an individual case depends upon many elements. I am not going into all of them. They include such things as the length of time of any individual period of questioning, the length of time intervening between periods of questioning, whether the accused person had been given proper refreshment or not, and the characteristics of the person who makes the statement. What may be oppressive as regards a child, an invalid or an old man or somebody inexperienced in the ways of this world may turn out not to be oppressive when one finds that the accused person is of a tough character and an experienced man of the world.' In an address to the Bentham Club in 1978, Lord MacDermott described 'oppressive questioning' as 'questioning which by its nature, duration, or other attendant circumstances (including the fact of custody) excites hopes (such as the hope of release) or fears, or so affects the mind of the subject that his will crumbles and he speaks when otherwise he would have stayed silent.' We adopt these definitions or descriptions and apply them to the present case."

R. v. **Fulling** [1987] 1 Q.B. 427 (C.A.). The appellant had been convicted of obtaining property by deception. At the trial the prosecution had relied heavily upon evidence of her confession as corroboration of the evidence of an accomplice. On appeal the only issue was as to whether or not evidence of the confession had been rightly admitted. It had been represented to the trial judge that the confession was, or might have been, obtained by oppression within the meaning of section 76(2)(*a*) of the Police and Criminal Evidence Act 1984. The basis of this representation was that the police had told the appellant whilst in custody that her lover (who had also been arrested) had for the past three years been having an affair with another woman who was also in custody in connection with the same matter and who was being kept in a cell adjacent to that occupied by the appellant. Giving evidence on the *voir dire* the appellant said that these revelations so distressed her that she "just couldn't stand being in the cells any longer." Later in cross-examination she had said: "I agreed to a statement being taken, it was the only way I was going to be released from the cells"; but she conceded that she had not been offered bail in return for a statement. The police officers denied that they had made any such revelations as she had suggested. The trial judge held that, even on the assumption that the appellant's account was correct, oppression "cannot be made out on the evidence." He had taken the view that "the word oppression means something above and beyond that which is inherently oppressive in police custody and must import some impropriety, some oppression actively applied in an improper manner by the police" (quoted in the Court of Appeal at p. 430). Counsel for the appellant, having referred to several pre-Act decisions including *R.* v. *Priestley* and its citation in *R.* v. *Prager* (*supra*), submitted that on the strength of these the trial judge's ruling, particularly the words set out above, had been wrong. But Lord Lane C.J., delivering the judgment of the Court of Appeal, said (p. 431): "The point is one of statutory construction. The wording of the Act of 1984 does not follow the wording of earlier rules or decisions, nor is it expressed to be a consolidating Act, nor yet to be declaratory of the common law.... It is a codifying Act, and therefore the principles set out in *Bank of England* v. *Vagliano Brothers* [1891] A.C. 107, 144 apply. Lord Herschell, having pointed out that the Bills of Exchange Act 1882 which was under consideration was intended to be a codifying Act, said, at pp. 144–145: 'I think the proper course is in the first instance to examine the language of the statute and to ask what is its natural meaning, uninfluenced by any considerations derived from the previous state of the law, and not to start inquiring how the law previously stood, and then, assuming that it was probably intended to leave it unaltered, to see if the words of the enactment will bear an interpretation in conformity with this view. If a statute, intended to embody in a code a particular branch of the law, is to be treated in this fashion, it appears to me that its utility will be almost entirely destroyed, and the very object with which it was enacted will be frustrated. The purpose of such a statute surely was that on any point specifically dealt with by it, the law should be ascertained by interpreting the language used instead of, as before, by roaming over a vast number of authorities in order to discover what the law was, extracting it by a minute critical examination of the prior decisions, dependent upon a knowledge of the exact effect even of an obsolete proceeding such as a demurrer to evidence.'... Section 76(2) of the Act of 1984 distinguishes between two different ways in which a confession may be rendered inadmissible: (a) where it has been obtained by oppression; (b) where it has been made in consequence of anything said or done which was likely in the circumstances to render unreliable any confession which might be made by the defendant in consequence thereof. Paragraph (b) is wider than the old formulation, namely that the confession must be shown to be voluntary in the sense that it was not obtained by fear of prejudice or hope of advantage, excited or held out by a person in authority. It is wide enough to cover some of the circumstances which under the earlier rule were embraced by what seems to us to be the artificially wide definition of oppression approved in *Reg.* v. *Prager* [1972] 1 W.L.R. 260. This in turn leads us to believe that 'oppression' in section 76(2)(a) should be given its ordinary dictionary meaning. The *Oxford English Dictionary* as its third definition of the word runs as follows: 'Exercise of authority or power in a burdensome, harsh, or wrongful manner; unjust or cruel treatment of subjects, inferiors, etc.; the imposition of unreasonable or unjust burdens.' One of the quotations given under that paragraph runs as follows: 'There is not a word in our language which expresses more detestable wickedness than oppression.' We find it hard to envisage any circumstances in which such oppression would not entail some impropriety on the part of the interrogator. We do not think that the judge was wrong in using that test. What, however, is abundantly clear is that a confession may be invalidated under section 76(2)(b) where there is no suspicion of impropriety. No reliance was placed on the words of section 76(2)(b) either before the judge at the trial of before this court. Even if there had been such reliance, we do not consider that the policemen's remark was likely to make unreliable any confession of the appellant's own criminal activities, and she expressly exonerated—or tried to exonerate—her unfaithful lover. In those circumstances, in the judgment of the court, the judge was correct to reject the submission made to him under section 76 of the Act of 1984. The appeal is accordingly dismissed."

Note.—See too the open-ended definition of "oppression" in section 76(8) of the 1984 Act (Part II, *infra*).

Adjodha v. **The State** [1982] A.C. 204 (P.C.). The several appellants had all been convicted of murder. In the case of one the only prosecution evidence, and in the cases of the others the main prosecution evidence, was a signed confession statement; and the defence was that the appellants were not the authors of the confessions, three of them having been forced to sign and the fourth having been tricked into signing. At the trials no objection had been taken to the admissibility of the statements. The Court of Appeal of Trinidad and Tobago dismissed their appeals. But the Privy Council held that the appellants' allegations went to admissibility, and that they ought to have been investigated and ruled upon by the trial judge. Lord Bridge, giving the opinion of the Privy Council allowing the appeals, sought (p. 222) to distinguish the case in which an accused's contention is that the confession was never made at all: in such circumstances the issue would be for the jury. On the relative roles of judge and jury see Chapter 1, Section A, *supra*.

Note.—The Police and Criminal Evidence Act 1984, s.76(3), (Part II *infra*) provides that the "court may of its own motion" require the prosecution to demonstrate the admissibility of a confession. Presumably the finding in *Adjodha* v. *The State* that the judge will sometimes be under a *duty* to do so is not disturbed.

R. v. **Liverpool Juvenile Ct., ex p. R.** [1988] Q.B. 1 (D.C.). The defendant appeared before a juvenile court on a charge of burglary. It was clear that heavy reliance was to be placed upon evidence of a confession. The justices refused to hold a preliminary inquiry or *voir dire* and adjourned the trial to enable the defendant to seek judicial review of this refusal. His application for judicial review by way of an order of mandamus requiring the juvenile court to hold an inquiry into the admissibility of the confession was successful. Russell L.J., delivering the judgment of the Divisional Court, said (pp. 10–11): "To summarise the effect of this judgment I would, therefore, rule that: (1) The effect of section 76(2) of the Police and Criminal Evidence Act 1984 is that in summary proceedings justices must now hold a trial within a trial if it is represented to them by the defence that a confession was or may have been obtained by either of the improper processes appearing in sub-paragraphs (a) or (b) section 76(2). (2) In such a trial within a trial the defendant may give evidence confined to the question of admissibility and the justices will not be concerned with the truth or otherwise of the confession. (3) In consequence of paragraphs 1 and 2 above, the defendant is entitled to a ruling upon admissibility of a confession before, or at, the end of the prosecution case. (4) There remains a discretion open to the defendant as to the stage at which an attack is to be made upon an alleged confession. A trial within trial will only take place before the close of the prosecution case if it is represented to the court that the confession was, or may have been, obtained by one or other of the processes set out in sub-paragraphs (a) or (b) section 76(2). If no such representation is made the defendant is at liberty to raise admissibility or weight of the confession at any subsequent stage of the trial. For the avoidance of doubt, I consider that 'representation' is not the same as, nor does it include, cross-examination. Thus the court is not required to embark upon, nor is the defence bound to proceed upon, a *voire dire* merely because of a suggestion in cross-examination that the alleged confession was obtained improperly. (5) It should never be necessary to call the prosecution evidence relating to the obtaining of a confession twice."

Note.—In the context of "rule" (2) *Wong Kam-ming* v. *R.* [1980] A.C. 247 (P.C.) (*infra*) was expressly approved.

In elaboration of "rule" (4) Russell L.J. had earlier (p. 10) expressly accepted a submission of counsel that "should the defence not avail itself of the right to a trial within a trial by virtue of section 76(2) there remained an inherent jurisdiction in the court to exclude a confession at a later stage in the proceedings as well as by virtue of section 78 of the Act which specifically refers to 'the circumstances in which the evidence was obtained.' " The "inherent" jurisdiction is a common law power which has survived the Act.

Russell L.J. emphasised (p. 11) that these "rules" should not be taken as applicable in all *committal* proceedings. When at such proceedings justices refuse to undertake an enquiry pursuant to section 76(2) judicial review of their decision by way of certiorari may go to quash the proceedings. However, judicial review being a discretionary remedy, a Divisional Court should only in an exceptional case quash a conviction on that ground alone: *R.* v. *Oxford City Justices, ex p. Berry* [1988] 1 Q.B. 507 (D.C.).

WONG KAM-MING v. R.

[1980] A.C. 247; [1979] 1 All E.R. 939; 69 Cr.App.R. 47 (P.C.: 1978)

On a voir dire as to the admissibility of an accused's confession he should not be cross-examined by the prosecution as to its truth.

When a confession has been ruled inadmissible on a voir dire, the prosecution is not entitled at the trial of the general issue to adduce evidence as to what the accused said during the voir dire or to cross-examine him on the basis of what he said.

When a confession has been ruled admissible, and the accused subsequently testifies on the general issue as to the reliability of the confession and in doing so gives answers markedly different from his testimony on the voir dire, he may be cross-examined on the basis of those discrepancies.

The appellant was one of six men charged with murder and malicious wounding. The only evidence connecting him with the attack was his own signed statement to the police to the effect that he had been present at the scene and had "chopped" someone with a penknife. Defence counsel challenged the admissibility of this statement on the ground that it had not been made voluntarily. The judge held a *voir dire* in the absence of the jury. The appellant testified on the *voir dire* that he had made a statement but had not been cautioned, that police officers had offered him inducements to make it and that he had been forced to copy it out and sign it. Under cross-examination he admitted that he had been present and involved in the attack. The judge ruled the statement inadmissible. The trial then continued, and, in order to show that the appellant had been at the scene, prosecution counsel called two shorthand writers who had recorded the *voir dire* to testify that the defendant had admitted being present. This testimony was admitted over objection by the defence. The appellant gave evidence and was cross-examined as to discrepancies between his evidence and what he had said on the *voir dire*. The appellant was convicted of murder and malicious wounding. The Hong Kong Court of Appeal dismissed his appeal against conviction. His further appeal to the Privy Council was allowed, Lord Hailsham of St. Marylebone dissenting.

LORD EDMUND-DAVIES (delivering the judgment of the majority, which included LORDS DIPLOCK, SALMON and KEITH OF KINKEL of the Board): ... the conduct of the trial has been attacked in several respects, and these were conveniently summarised by the counsel for the defendant in framing the following questions. 1. During the cross-examination of a defendant in the *voir dire* as to the admissibility of his challenged statement, may questions be put as to its truth? 2. If "Yes," has the court a discretion to exclude such cross-examination, and (if so) was it properly exercised in the resent case? 3. Where, although the confession is held inadmissible, the answers to questions 1 and 2 are nevertheless in favour of the Crown, is the prosecution permitted, on resumption of the trial of the main issue, to adduce evidence of what the defendant said during the *voir dire*? 4. If "Yes," is there a discretion to exclude such evidence, and (if so) was it properly exercised here? 5. Even although it be held that the answer to question 3 is "No," may the defendant nevertheless be cross-examined upon what was said during the *voir dire*? Their Lordships proceed to consider these questions.

Questions 1 and 2: relevance of truth of extra-judicial statements

In *Rex* v. *Hammond* [1941] 3 All E.R. 318 prosecuting counsel was held entitled to ask the accused, when cross-examining him during the *voir dire*, whether a police statement which the accused alleged had been extorted by gross maltreatment was in fact true, and elicited the answer that it was. . . .

. . . .

Although much criticised, that decision has frequently been followed in England and Wales and in many other jurisdictions. . . .

. . . .

The sole object of the *voir dire* was to determine the voluntariness of the alleged confession in accordance with principles long established by such cases as *Ibrahim* v. *The King* [1914] A.C. 599. This was emphasised by this Board in *Chan Wei Keung* v. *The Queen* [1967] 2 A.C. 160, while the startling consequences of adopting the *Hammond* approach were well illustrated in the Canadian case of *Reg.* v. *Hnedish* (1958) 26 W.W.R. 685, 688, where Hall C.J. said: " . . . I do not see how under the guise of 'credibility' the court can transmute what is initially an inquiry as to the 'admissibility' of the confession into an inquisition of an accused. That would be repugnant to our accepted standards and principles of justice; it would invite and encourage brutality in the handling of persons suspected of having committed offences."

It is right to point out that counsel for the Crown did not seek to submit that the prosecution could in *every* case properly cross-examine the defendant during the *voir dire* regarding the truth of his challenged statement. . . . But he was unable to formulate an acceptable test of its propriety, and their Lordships have been driven to the conclusion that none exists. In other words, in their Lordships' view, *Rex* v. *Hammond* [1941] 3 All E.R. 318 was wrongly decided, and any decisions in Hong Kong which purported to follow it should be treated as overruled. The answer to question 1 is therefore "No," and it follows that question 2 does not fall to be considered.

Questions 3 and 4

Their Lordships turn to questions 3 and 4. As part of its case on the main issue, may the prosecution lead evidence regarding the testimony given by the defendant on the *voir dire*? . . .

. . . counsel for the Crown felt constrained to submit that, even were the trial judge to exclude a confession on the ground that torture had been used to extort it, any damaging statements made by the defendant on the *voir dire* could nevertheless properly be adduced as part of the prosecution's case. Boldness could go no further.

Fortunately for justice their Lordships have concluded that, where the confession has been excluded, the argument against ever admitting such evidence as part of the Crown case must prevail. But what if the confession is held *admissible*? In such circumstances, it is unlikely that the prosecution will need to do more than rely upon the confession itself. Nevertheless, in principle should they be prevented from proving in addition any admission made by the defendant on the *voir dire*? This question has exercised their Lordships a great deal, but even in the circumstances predicated it is preferable to maintain a clear distinction between the issue of voluntariness, which is alone relevant to the *voir dire*, and the issue of guilt falling to be decided in the main trial. To blur this distinction can lead, as has already been shown, to unfortunate consequences, and their Lordships have therefore concluded that the same exclusion evidence regarding the *voir dire* proceedings from the main trial must be observed, regardless of whether the challenged confession be excluded or admitted. It follows that question 3 must be answered in the negative, and question 4 accordingly does no arise.

Question 5

Question 5 remains for consideration by their Lordships. Notwithstanding the answer to question 3, in the event of the defendant giving evidence in the main trial, may he be cross-examined in respect of statements made by him during the *voir dire*? . . .

The problem is best approached in stages. . . .

In their Lordships' judgment, *Rex* v. *Treacy* [[1944] 2 All E.R. 229] was undoubtedly correct in prohibiting cross-examination as to the *contents* of confessions which the court has ruled inadmissible. But what if during the *voir dire* the accused has made self-incriminating statements not strictly related to the confession itself but which nevertheless have relevance to the issue of guilt or innocence of the charge preferred? May the accused be cross-examined so as to elicit those matters? In the light of their Lordships' earlier conclusion that the Crown may not adduce as part of its case evidence of what the accused said during a *voir dire* culminating in the exclusion of an impugned confession, can a different approach here be permitted from that condemned in *Rex* v. *Treacy*? Subject to what was said as to the court's discretion to exclude it in proper circumstances, counsel for the Crown submitted that it can be, citing in support section 13 of the Hong Kong Evidence Ordinance (c. 8), which was based on the familiar provision in section 4 of the Criminal Procedure Act 1865 of the United Kingdom, relating to the confrontation of a witness with his previous inconsistent statements. But these statutory provisions have no relevance if the earlier statements cannot be put in evidence. And, having already concluded that the *voir dire* statements of the defendant are not admissible during the presentation of the prosecution's case, their Lordships find it impossible in principle to distinguish between such cross-examination of the defendant on the basis of the *voir dire* as was permitted in the instant case . . . and that cross-examination based on the contents of an excluded confession which, it is common ground, was rightly condemned in *Rex* v. *Treacy* [1944] 2 All E.R. 229.

But what if the *voir dire* resulted in the impugned confession being *admitted*, and the defendant later elects to give evidence? If he then testifies to matters relating, for example, the the *reliability* of the confession (as opposed to its *voluntariness*, which *ex hypothesi*, is no longer in issue) and in so doing gives answers which are markedly different from his testimony given during the *voir dire* may he be cross-examined so as to establish that at the earlier stage of the trial he had told a different story? Great injustice could well result from the exclusion of such cross-examination, and their Lordships can see no justification in legal principle or on any other ground which renders it impermissible. As has already been observed, a defendant seeking to challenge the admissibility of a confession may for all practical purposes be *obliged* to testify in the *voir dire* if his challenge is to have any chance of succeeding, and his evidence is then (or certainly should be) restricted strictly to the issue of admissibility of the confession. But the situation is quite different where, the confession having been *admitted* despite his challenge, the defendant later elects to give evidence during the main trial and, in doing so, departs materially from the testimony he gave in the *voir dire*. Having so chosen to testify, why should the discrepancies not be elicited and demonstrated by cross-examination? In their Lordships' view, his earlier statements made in the *voir dire* provide as acceptable a basis for his cross-examination to that end as any other earlier statements made by him—including, of course, his confession which, though challenged, had been ruled admissible. Indeed, for such purpose and in such circumstances, his *voir dire* statements stand on no different basis than, for example, the sworn testimony given by a defendant in a previous trial where the jury had disagreed. No doubt the trial judge has a discretion and, indeed, a duty to ensure that the right of the prosecution to cross-examine or rebut is not used in a manner unfair or oppressive to the defendant and no doubt the judge is under an obligation to see to it that any statutory provisions bearing on the situation (such as those earlier referred to) are strictly complied with. But, subject thereto, their Lordships hold that cross-examination in the circumstances predicated which is directed to testing the credibility of the defendant by establishing the inconsistencies in his evidence is wholly permissible.

In the instant case, however, the challenged confession was excluded. It therefore follows that in the judgment of their Lordships no less than three substantial irregularities occurred in the trial: (1) in the *voir dire* the defendant was cross-examined with a view to establishing that his extra-judicial statement was true; (2) in the trial proper, the Crown was permitted to call as part of its case evidence regarding answers given by the defendant during the *voir dire*; and (3) the defendant was permitted to be cross-examined so as to demonstrate that what he had said in chief was inconsistent with his statement in the *voir dire*. As a result, evidence was wrongly placed before the jury.... But for that evidence, it is common ground that the submission of "no case" made by the defending counsel must have succeeded.

It follows that their Lordships will humbly advise Her Majesty that this appeal should be allowed and the conviction quashed.

LORD HAILSHAM OF ST. MARYLEBONE delivered a dissenting judgment.

Note.—For an example of particular permitted use of an inadmissible confession by a co-accused, see *Lui Mei Lin* v. *The Queen* [1989] A.C. 288 (P.C.), Chapter 23, *infra*.

R. v. **Brophy** [1982] A.C. 476 (H.L.). The defendant was tried in Northern Ireland for various allegations of murder and causing explosions and on a charge of being a member of the I.R.A. He challenged the admissibility of various confessions; and in his evidence-in-chief on the *voir dire* he admitted the I.R.A. charge. The trial judge excluded the confessions, but allowed evidence to be given of the defendant's admission during the *voir dire*. The defendant was acquitted on all counts except that dealing with membership of the I.R.A. His appeal against conviction on that count was allowed by the Court of Appeal in Northern Ireland. The Crown's appeal to the House of Lords was dismissed. The House, following *Wong Kam-ming* v. *R.* (*supra*), unanimously held that the defendant's evidence on the *voir dire* that he had been a member of the I.R.A. had been relevant to the issue there, and that it was therefore inadmissible at the substantive trial. Lord Fraser of Tullybelton said (p. 481): "Once it has been held that the material part of the respondent's evidence was relevant to the issue at the *voir dire*, a necessary consequence is, in my opinion, that it is not admissible in the substantive trial." Lord Fraser explained (p. 481) that where "evidence is given at the *voir dire* by an accused person in answer to questions by his counsel, and without objection by counsel for the Crown, his evidence ought in my opinion to be treated as relevant to the issue at the *voir dire*, unless it is clearly and obviously irrelevant." His Lordship emphasised, too, (p. 483) that: "The right of the accused to give evidence at the *voir dire* without affecting his right to remain silent at the substantive trial is in my opinion absolute and is not to made conditional on the exercise of a judicial discretion."

R. v. **Duncan** (1981) 73 Cr.App.R. 359 (C.A.). The appellant had made statements to a neighbour and to the police in the course of which he had in fact admitted having strangled a woman. He did not give evidence at his trial for murder. The trial judge ruled that, in so far as the appellant's statements were self-serving, they could not be admitted as evidence; and on this basis he withdrew the issue of provocation from the jury. The appellant was convicted of murder and appealed on the ground that the judge's ruling was wrong. The Court of Appeal (although dismissing the appeal on the basis that, even if the excluded evidence had been admitted, there would have been insufficient evidence of provocation for the issue to be put to the jury) held that in the case of a "mixed" statement, *i.e.* one which is partly inculpatory but partly exculpatory, if the inculpatory part is found to be admissible the exculpatory part is also admissible as evidence of its truth. Lord Cane C.J., delivering the judgment of the Court of Appeal, saw (p. 364) the earlier case of *R.* v. *McGregor* (1967) 51 Cr.App.R. 338 (C.A.), where Lord Parker C.J. had said (p. 378): "... if the prosecution are minded to put in an admission or a confession, they must put in the whole and not merely part of it," as "clear authority for the proposition that in the case of a 'mixed' statement both parts are evidence of the facts they state, though they are obviously not to be regarded as having equal weight." Lord Lane went on to approve the statement of James L.J. in *R.* v. *Donaldson and others* (1977) 64 Cr.App.R. 59 (C.A.) that "... there is a clear distinction to be made between statements of admission adduced by the Crown as part of the case against the defendant and statements entirely of a self-serving nature made and sought to be relied on by the defendant." His Lordship concluded (p. 365): "Where a 'mixed' statement is under consideration by the jury in a case where the defendant has not given evidence, it seems to us that the simplest, and, therefore, the method most likely to produce a just result, is for the jury to be told that the whole statement, both the incriminating parts and the excuses or explanations, must be considered by them in deciding where the truth lies. It is, to say the least, not helpful to try to explain to the jury that the exculpatory parts of the statement are something less than evidence of the facts they state. Equally, where appropriate, as it usually will be, the judge may, and should, point out that the incriminating parts are likely to be true (otherwise why say them?), whereas the excuses do not have the same weight. Nor is there any reason why, again where appropriate, the judge should not comment in relation to the exculpatory remarks upon the election of the accused not to give evidence."

Note.—R. v. *Duncan* has been followed in *R.* v. *Hamand* (1986) 82 Cr.App.R. 65 (C.A.) and was approved by the House of Lords in *R.* v. *Sharp* [1988] 1 W.L.R. 7; 86 Cr.App.R. 274, where Lord Mackay of Clashfern L.C. said (p. 9): "I particularly agree with the language used by Lord Lane C.J. in *Reg.* v. *Duncan* 73 Cr.App.R. 359 as a statement to be put before a jury in a case such as this." In *R.* v. *Sharp* the question certified for decision by the House was: "Where a statement made to a police officer out of court by a defendant contains both admissions and self-exculpatory parts do the exculpatory parts constitute evidence of the truth of the facts alleged therein?" The House unanimously answer this question in the affirmative, subject to the substitution of the words "a person" for the words "a police officer."

Mention may be made of a *per curiam* admonition in *R.* v. *McCarthy* (1980) 71 Cr.App.R. 142 (C.A.), decided a year before *R.* v. *Duncan*. There Lawton L.J., delivering the judgment of the Court of Appeal, said (p. 146): "If it is becoming a practice for counsel in criminal cases, where their clients have made exculpatory statements, not to call them in evidence, they should think very long and hard before they continue with that practice, because comment from the Bench is likely to lead the jury to think that there is something very odd about such tactics."

A statement prepared on legal advice containing an admission but substantially self-serving will be rightly excluded: *R.* v. *Newsome* (1980) 71 Cr.App.R. 325 (C.A.).

R. v. **Warwickshall** (1783) 1 Leach 263 (Old Bailey). The accused was charged, as an accessory after the fact, with having received stolen property knowing it to have been stolen. She made a full confession of guilt, and in consequence of this the property was found at her lodgings concealed in her bed. The accused's confession had, however, been obtained by promises of favour and was therefore held to be inadmissible. The court rejected the contention that, as the finding of the property in her house resulted from an inadmissible confession, evidence of that finding should also be inadmissible. Nares J. (and Eyre B.) said (p. 263): "A free and voluntary confession is deserving of the highest credit, because it is presumed to flow from the strongest sense of guilty, and therefore it is admitted as proof of the crime to which it refers; but a confession forced from the mind by the flattery of hope, or by the torture of fear, comes in so questionable a shape when it is to be considered as evidence of guilt, that no credit ought to be given to it; and therefore it is rejected. This principle respecting confessions has no application whatever as to the admission or rejection of facts, whether the knowledge of them be obtained in consequence of an extorted confession, or whether it arises from any other source; for a fact, if it exists at all, must exist invariably in the same manner, whether the confession from which it is derived be in other respects true or false. Facts thus obtained, however, must be fully and satisfactorily proved, without calling in the aid of any part of the confession from which they have been derived . . . "

Note.—The doctrine of *Warwickshall* is preserved in the Police and Criminal Evidence Act 1984, section 76(4)(*a*) (Part Two, *infra*).

In *R.* v. *Berriman* (1854) 6 Cox C.C. 388 (Surrey Assizes) the accused was indicted for concealing the birth of his child. Prosecuting counsel sought to ask a witness whether, in consequence of an answer improperly elicited from the accused by the magistrate at the preliminary examination, a search was made which resulted in the discovery of an infant's remains. Erle J. interjected (p. 389): "No: *Not in consequence of what she said.* You may ask him what search was made, and what things were found, but under the circumstances, I cannot allow that proceeding to be connected with the prisoner."

Pre-1984 Act authority was confused. In some cases it was held that evidence might be given connecting subsequent discovery with the inadmissible confession (*R.* v. *Gould* (1840) 9 C. and P. 364 (C.C.C.)); in others that part of the confession the truth of which was confirmed by the discovery was itself rendered admissible; and in at least one case that the whole confession was rendered admissible (*R.* v. *Garbett* 2 Car. & Kir. 474). For the present position (with which *R.* v. *Berriman* and *Chalmers* v. *H. M. Advocate (infra)* are consistent) see section 76(5) and (6) of the 1984 Act (Part Two, *infra*).

Chalmers v. **H.M. Advocate** 1954 S.C. (J.) 66; 1954 S.L.T. 177 (High Court of Justiciary). The accused was charged with murder. He had made a confession which was inadmissible and had then taken police officers to a cornfield where he had pointed out the purse of the murder victim. The full bench of the High Court of Justiciary held that evidence of the pointing out had been wrongly admitted and upheld Chalmers' appeal. The Lord Justice-General, Lord Cooper, said (S.L.T., at p. 183) "I take next the episode of the cornfield. This is related to the interrogation in two ways. In point of time the visit to the cornfield followed immediately after the further interrogation which followed the taking of the 'statement.' Moreover it is admitted that during the further interrogation the appellant was asked what happened to the purse, and that it was 'in consequence of' his answer to that question that he was taken to the cornfield 'to facilitate the search.' I therefore regard the visit to the cornfield under the surveillance of the police as part of the same transaction as the interrogation, and, if the interrogation and the 'statement' which emerged from it are inadmissible as 'unfair,' the same criticism must attach to the conducted visit to the cornfield. Next, I feel unable to accept the distinction drawn by the presiding Judge between statements and 'actings,' and I suspect that a fallacy lurks in the word 'actings.' The actings of an accused, if unattended by such circumstances as are here presented, are normally competent evidence against him. For instance, if the police had kept watch on the accused and had seen him go to the cornfield to retrieve the purse, such evidence would have been perfectly competent. Again, 'actings,' in the sense of the conduct, may be perfectly neutral as a communication of specific information; but 'actings,' in the sense of a gesture or sign, may be indistinguishable from a communication by word of mouth or by writing. The question here was—Where exactly is the purse? and this question might have been answered by an oral description of the place where it was, or by going to the place and silently pointing to that place. It seems to me to make no difference for present purposes which method of answering the question was adopted; from which it follows that, if, in the circumstances of this case, the 'statement' was inadmissible, the episode of the cornfield was equally inadmissible. The significance of the episode is plain, for it showed that the appellant knew where the purse was. If the police had simply produced, and proved the finding of, the purse, that evidence would have carried them little or no distance in this case towards implicating the appellant. It was essential that the appellant should be linked up with the purse, either by oral confession or by its equivalent—tacit admission of knowledge of its whereabouts obtained as a sequel to interrogation."

R. v. **Leatham** (1861) 8 Cox C.C. 498 (Queen's Bench). It was held that a document referred to by the defendant in an enquiry by Commissioners under the Corrupt Practices Act was admissible in evidence against him, even though the Act provided that the testimony before the Commissioners should not be admissible, Crompton J. interjected (p. 501): "Suppose by threats and promises a confession of murder is obtained, which would not be admissible, but you also obtain a clue to a place where a written confession may be found, or where the body of a person murdered is secreted; could not that latter evidence be made use of because the first clue to it came from the murderer? It matters not how you get it; if you steal it even, it would be admissible in evidence." In the course of his judgment he said (p. 503): "I do not at all see why we should suppose that the

Legislature, when they could so easily have said that no documents shall be used against him, as to which any clue has arisen on examination before the Commissioners, would not have said that. It would have been a most inconvenient thing if the Legislature had said so, because...you would have to enquire in every case, was this clue furnished by something the defendant said in his examination. He perhaps dropped some observation which led the Commissioners to institute another inquiry; and by sending officers to this place or that, something then comes out which is evidence against him; it would, in short, be the widest inquiry at *nisi prius* that could be conceived."

R. v. Barker [1941] 2 K.B. 381 (C.C.A.). The accused was convicted on an indictment charging him with conspiring with another to defraud the Inland Revenue. He was an accountant employed by that other to make tax returns. An Inland Revenue inspector had, at an interview with the accused, read a ministerial statement which had been published in *Hansard* to the effect that when a person voluntarily disclosed past tax frauds and was prepared to furnish full evidence, including books and documents, and to make a full and frank disclosure, criminal proceedings would not be instituted, but the Inland Revenue authorities could be satisfied with a pecuniary settlement. Thereupon the accused came forward and produced books and documents which disclosed tax irregularities. A prosecution was subsequently launched, and the trial judge admitted the books and documents produced in reliance upon this inducement. The accused's conviction was quashed by the Court of Criminal Appeal. Tucker J. (delivering the judgment of the court) said (p. 385): "...those documents stand on precisely the same footing as an oral or written confession which is brought into existence as the result of...a promise inducement or threat."

Note.—The actual decision, so far as it relates to income tax, is now negatived by the Taxes Management Act 1970, s.105 (Part Two, *infra*). Moreover, quite apart from this, it would appear to be inconsistent with the Police and Criminal Evidence Act 1984, s.76(4)(*a*) (Part Two, *infra*) unless the contents of the documents, although already in existence, are not to be regarded as "facts." Alternatively, the result could be supported on the basis of discretion; and that it might be so regarded has been hinted at by Lord Diplock in *R. v. Sang* [1980] A.C. 402, 435 (H.L.) *infra*.

R. v. Voisin [1918] 1 K.B. 531 (C.C.A.). The body of a woman was found in a parcel together with a piece of paper on which were written the words "Bladie Belgiam." The accused, while detained in custody for inquiries but who had not yet been charged, was asked by the police to write the words "Bloody Belgian." He expressed his willingness to do this and wrote "Bladie Belgiam." It was held that the writing had been properly admitted at the trial of the accused for murder. Lawrence J., giving the judgment of the court, said (p. 538): "The mere fact that the words were written at the request of police officers, or that he was detained in Bow Street, does not make the writing inadmissible in evidence. Those facts do not change the character of the writing, nor do they explain the resemblance between the handwriting and that upon the label, or account for the same misspellings occurring in both."

Note.—There was no question of an inadmissible confession, but it has been assumed that if the words had been written in such a confession, they ought still to have been admissible for the purpose of showing that the accused wrote (spoke or expressed himself) in a particular way: see, now, the Police and Criminal Evidence Act 1984, s.76(4)(*b*) (Part Two, *infra*).

Kuruma v. **R.** [1955] A.C. 197 (P.C.). The accused was charged with being in unlawful possession of two rounds of ammunition contrary to emergency regulations in Kenya. The ammunition was alleged to have been found in his pocket by two police officers, who (it was assumed), being of not sufficiently senior rank, had no power of search under the regulations. Evidence of the search was admitted, and the accused was convicted. The Court of Appeal for East Africa and the Judicial Committee of the Privy Council dismissed appeals against conviction. Lord Goddard C.J., on behalf of the Board, said (pp. 203–205): "In their Lordships' opinion the test to be applied in considering whether evidence is admissible is whether it is relevant to the matters in issue. If it is, it is admissible and the court is not concerned with how the evidence was obtained. While this proposition may not have been stated in so many words in any English case there are decisions which support it, and in their Lordships' opinion it is plainly right in principle.... No doubt in a criminal case the judge always has a discretion to disallow evidence if the strict rules of admissibility would operate unfairly against an accused. This was emphasised in the case before this Board of *Noor Mohamed* v. *R.* [1949] A.C. 182 at 191–192, and in the recent case in the House of Lords, *Harris* v. *Director of Public Prosecutions* [1952] A.C. 694. If, for instance, some admission of some piece of evidence, *e.g.* a document, had been obtained from a defendant by a trick, no doubt the judge might properly rule it out.... Their Lordships have no doubt that the evidence to which objection has been taken was properly admitted...."

Note.—It is to be observed that Lord Goddard appears to have intermingled considerations relating to impropriety or unfairness in the way in which evidence is obtained, with considerations relating to the unfairness of a trial which could result from the admission of evidence on the ground, for example, that its prejudicial effect would greatly outweigh its probative value (see, his Lordship's citation of two cases dealing with similar fact evidence).

R. v. SANG

[1980] A.C. 402; [1979] 2 All E.R. 1222; 69 Cr.App.R. 282 (H.L.: 1979)

The defence of entrapment being unknown to the substantive criminal law, the judge has no power to exclude otherwise admissible evidence of the commission of a crime on the ground that, if committed, it was at the instigation of an agent provocateur.

The judge in a criminal trial has a general discretion to refuse to admit evidence if in his opinion its probable prejudicial effect so outweighs its true probative worth as to make its reception unfair to the accused.

Save with regard to admissions and confessions and generally with regard to evidence obtained from the accused after commission of an offence, the judge has no discretion to refuse to admit relevant and otherwise admissible evidence solely on the ground that it was obtained by improper or unfair means.

LORD DIPLOCK: My Lords, the appellant was indicted...for conspiracy to utter counterfeit American bank notes. On his arraignment he pleaded not guilty to the charge and, in the absence of the jury, alleged, through his counsel, that he had been induced to commit the offence by an informer acting on the instructions of the police, and that, but for such persuasion, he would not have committed any crime of the kind with which he was charged. Faced, as he was, by recent decisions of the Criminal Division of the Court of Appeal that "entrapment" is no defence in English law (*Reg.* v. *McEvilly* (1973) 60 Cr.App.R. 150; *Reg.* v. *Mealey* (1974) 60 Cr.App.R. 59), counsel for the appellant sought to achieve by a different means the same effect as if it were. He submitted that if the judge were satisfied at a "trial within a trial" that the offence was instigated by an agent provocateur acting on the instructions of the police and, but for this, would not have been committed by the accused, the judge had a discretion to refuse to allow the prosecution to prove its case by evidence.

In support of this submission counsel was able to cite a number of dicta from impressive sources which, on the face of them, suggest that judges have a very wide discretion in criminal cases to exclude evidence tendered by the prosecution on the ground that it has been unfairly obtained. In addition there is one actual decision of the Court of Criminal Appeal in *Reg.* v. *Payne* [1963] 1 W.L.R. 637 where a conviction was quashed upon the ground that the judge ought to have exercised his discretion to exclude admissible evidence upon that ground—though this was not a case of entrapment....

In order to avoid what promised to be a lengthy "trial within a trial," which would be fruitless if Judge Buzzard [the trial judge] were to rule as a matter of law that he had no discretion to exclude relevant evidence tendered by the prosecution to prove the commission of the offence, even though it had been instigated by an agent provocateur and was one which the accused would never have committed but for such inducement, the judge first heard legal submissions on this question. He rules that even upon that assumption he had no discretion to exclude the prosecution's evidence. In consequence of this ruling the appellant withdrew his plea of not guilty and pleaded guilty....

The appeal to the Criminal Division of the Court of Appeal was dismissed.... But they certified as the point of law of general importance involved in their discretion a much wider question than is involved in the use of agents provocateurs. It is:

> "Does a trial judge have a discretion to refuse to allow evidence—being evidence other than evidence of admission—to be given in any circumstances in which such evidence is relevant and of more than minimal probative value."

. . . .

Before turning to that wider question however, I will deal with the narrower point of law upon which this appeal actually turns. I can do so briefly. The decisions in *Reg.* v. *McEvilly*, 60 Cr.App.R. 150 and *Reg.* v. *Mealey*, 60 Cr.App.R. 59 that there is no defence of "entrapment" known to English law are clearly right....

My Lords, this being the substantive law upon the matter, the suggestion that it can be evaded by the procedural device of preventing the prosecution from adducing evidence of the commission of the offence does not bear examination....

I understand your Lordships to be agreed that whatever be the ambit of the judicial discretion to exclude evidence it does not extend to excluding evidence of a crime because the crime was instigated by an agent provocateur....

I turn now to the wider question that has been certified. It does not purport to be concerned with self-incriminatory admissions made by the accused himself after commission of the crime though in dealing with the question I will find it necessary to say something about these. What the question is concerned with is the discretion of the trial judge to exclude all other kinds of evidence that are of more than minimal probative value.

Recognition that there may be circumstances in which a jury trial the judge has a discretion to prevent particular kinds of evidence that is admissible from being adduced before the jury, has grown up piecemeal. It appears first in cases arising under proviso (*f*) of section 1 of the Criminal Evidence Act 1898, which sets out the circumstances in which an accused may be cross-examined as to his previous convictions or bad character. . . .

Next the existence of a judicial discretion to exclude evidence of "similar facts," even where it was technically admissible, was recognised by Lord du Parcq, delivering the opinion of the Privy Council in *Noor Mohamed* v. *The King* [1949] A.C. 182, 192. . . .

[His Lordship then referred to Lord Moulton's speech in *R.* v. *Christie* [1914] A.C. 545, 559, which] was neither a "previous conviction" nor a "similar facts" case, but was one involving evidence of an accusation made in the presence of the accused by the child victim of an alleged indecent assault and the accused's failure to answer it, from which the prosecution sought to infer an admission by the accused that it was true. Lord Moulton's statement was not confined to evidence of inferential confessions but was general in its scope and has frequently been cited as applicable in cases of cross-examination as to bad character or previous convictions under the Criminal Evidence Act 1898 and "similar facts" cases. So I would hold that there has now developed a general rule of practice whereby in a trial by jury the judge has a discretion to exclude evidence which, though technically admissible, would probably have a prejudicial influence on the minds of the jury, which would be out of proportion to its true evidential value.

Ought your Lordships to go further and to hold that the discretion extends more widely than this, as the comparatively recent dicta to which I have already referred suggest? What has been regarded as the fountain head of all subsequent dicta on this topic is the statement by Lord Goddard delivering advice of the Privy Council in *Kuruma* v. *The Queen* [1955] A.C. 197. That was a case in which the evidence of unlawful possession of ammunition by the accused was obtained as a result of an illegal search of his person. The Board held that this evidence was admissible and had rightly been admitted; but Lord Goddard although he had earlier said at p. 203 that if evidence is admissible "the court is not concerned with how the evidence was obtained," nevertheless went on to say, at p. 204:

> "No doubt in a criminal case the judge always has a discretion to disallow evidence if the strict rules of admissibility would operate unfairly against an accused. This was emphasised in the case before this Board of *Noor Mohamed* v. *The King* [1949] A.C. 182, and in the recent case in the House of Lords, *Harris* v. *Director of Public Prosecutions* [1952] A.C. 694. *If, for instance, some admission of some piece of evidence, e.g. a document, had been obtained from a defendant by a trick, no doubt the judge might properly rule it out.*"

Up to the sentence that I have italicised there is nothing in this passage to suggest that when Lord Goddard spoke of admissible evidence operating "unfairly" against the accused he intended to refer to any wider aspects of unfairness than the probable prejudicial effect of the evidence upon the minds of the jury outweighing its true evidential value; though he no doubt also has in mind the discretion that had long been exercised in England under the Judges's Rules to refuse to admit confessions by the accused made after the crime even though strictly they may be admissible. The instance given in the passage I have italicised appears to me to deal with a case which falls within the latter category since the document "obtained from a defendant by a trick" is clearly analogous to a confession which the defendant has been unfairly induced to make, and had, indeed, been so treated in *Rex* v. *Barker* [1941] 2 K.B. 381 where an incriminating document obtained from the defendant by a promise of favours was held to be inadmissible.

It is interesting in this connection to observe that the only case that has been brought to your Lordships' attention in which an appellate court has actually excluded evidence on the ground that it had been unfairly obtained (*Reg.* v. *Payne* [1963] 1 W.L.R. 637) would appear to fall into this category. The defendant, charged with drunken driving, had been induced to submit himself to examination by a doctor to see if he was suffering from any illness or disability, upon the understanding that the doctor would not examine him for the purpose of seeing whether he were fit to drive. The doctor in fact gave evidence of the defendant's unfitness to drive based on his symptoms and behaviour in the course of that examination. The Court of Criminal Appeal quashed the conviction on the ground that the trial judge ought to have exercised his discretion to exclude the doctor's evidence. This again, as it seems to me, is analogous to unfairly inducing a defendant to confess to an offence, and the short judgment of the Court of Criminal Appeal is clearly based upon the maximum *nemo debet prodere se ipsum*.

. . . .

Nevertheless it has to be recognised that there is an unbroken series of dicta in judgments of appellate courts to the effect that there is a judicial discretion to exclude admissible evidence which has been "obtained" unfairly or by trickery or oppressively, although except in *Reg.* v. *Payne* [1963] 1 W.L.R. 637, there never has been a case in which those courts have come across conduct so unfair, so tricky or so oppressive as to justify them in holding that the discretion ought to have been exercised in favour of exclusion. In every one of the cases to which your Lordships have been referred where such dicta appear, the source from which the evidence sought to be excluded had been obtained has been the defendant himself or (in some of the search cases) premises occupied by him; and the dicta can be traced to a common ancestor in Lord Goddard's statement in *Kuruma* v. *The Queen* [1955] A.C. 197 which I have already cited. That statement was not, in my view, ever intended to acknowledge the existence of any wider discretion than to exclude (1) admissible evidence which would probably have a prejudicial influence upon the minds of the jury that would be out of proportion to its true evidential value; and (2) evidence tantamount to a self-incriminatory admission, which was obtained from the defendant, after the offence had been committed, by means which would justify a judge in excluding an actual confession which had the like self-incriminating effect. As a matter of language, although not as a matter of application, the subsequent dicta go much further than this; but in so far as they do so they have never yet been considered by this House.

My Lords, I propose to exclude, as the certified question does, detailed consideration of the role of the trial judge in relation to confessions and evidence obtained from the defendant after commission of the offence that is tantamount to a confession. . . .

Outside this limited field in which for historical reasons the function of the trial judge extended to imposing sanctions for improper conduct on the part of the prosecution before the commencement of the proceedings in inducing the accused by threats, favour or trickery to provide evidence against himself, your Lordships should, I think, make it clear that the function of the judge at a criminal trial as respects the admission of evidence is to ensure that the accused has a fair trial according to law. It is no part of a judge's function to exercise diciplinary powers over the police or prosecution as respects the way in which evidence to be used at the trial is obtained by them. If it was obtained illegally there will be a remedy in civil law; if it was obtained legally but in breach of the rules of conduct for the police, this is a matter for the appropriate disciplinary authority to deal with. What the judge at the trial is concerned with is not how the evidence sought to be adduced by the prosecution has been obtained, but with how it is used by the prosecution at the trial.

. . . However much the judge may dislike the way in which a particular piece of evidence was obtained before proceedings were commenced, if it is admissible evidence probative of the accused's guilt it is no part of his judicial function to exclude it for this reason. If your Lordships so hold you will be reverting to the law as it was laid down by Lord Moulton in *Rex* v. *Christie* [1914] A.C. 545, Lord du Parcq in *Noor Mohamed* v. *The King* [1949] A.C. 182 and Viscount Simon in *Harris* v. *Director of Public Prosecutions* [1952] A.C. 694 before the growth of what I believe to have been a misunderstanding of Lord Goddard's dictum in *Kuruma* v. *The Queen* [1955] A.C. 197.

I would accordingly answer the question certified in terms which have been suggested by my noble and learned friend, Viscount Dilhorne, in the course of our deliberations on this case. (1) A trial judge in a criminal trial has always a discretion to refuse to admit evidence if in his opinion its prejudicial effect outweighs its probative value. (2) Save with regard to admissions and confessions and generally with regard to evidence obtained from the accused after commission of the offence, he has no discretion to refuse to admit relevant admissible evidence on the ground that it was obtained by improper or unfair means. The court is not concerned with how it was obtained. It is no ground for the exercise of discretion to exclude that the evidence was obtained as the result of the activities of an agent provocateur. I would dismiss this appeal.

LORD FRASER OF TULLYBELTON: . . . The important question is whether the discretion (a) is limited to excluding evidence which is likely to have prejudicial value out of proportion to its evidential value or (b) extends to excluding other evidence which might operate unfairly against the accused and, if so, how far it extends. On the best consideration that I can give to the authorities, I have reached the opinion that the discretion is not limited to excluding evidence which is likely to have prejudicial effects out of proportion to its evidential value. . . .

I recognise that there does not appear to be any decision by an appellate court in England clearly based upon an exercise of the discretion except when the excluded evidence either (1) is more prejudicial than probative or (2) relates to an admission or confession. I do not regard the case of *Reg.* v. *Payne* [1963] 1 W.L.R. 637 as an authority in favour of such a discretion. The Court of Criminal Appeal held that evidence described by Lord Parker C.J. at p. 639 as "clearly admissible" ought to have been excluded and the conviction was quashed on that ground. The evidence in question was that of a doctor relating to a medical examination of an accused person who was charged with driving a motor car under the influence of drink. The accused had been induced by a trick to permit (and, I would suppose, co-operate in) a medical examination of himself and thus to provide material for incriminating evidence by the doctor who examined him and I regard the decision as being based, at least in part, on the maxim *nemo tenetur se ipsum accusare*. But notwithstanding the absence of direct decision on the point, the dicta are so numerous and so authoritative that I do not think that it would be right to disregard them, or to treat them as applicable only to cases where the prejudicial effect of the evidence would outweight its probative value. If they had been intended to have such a limited application, the references to the Scottish cases would be inexplicable. In any event, I would be against cutting down their application to that extent.

On the other hand, I doubt whether they were ever intended to apply to evidence obtained from sources other than the accused himself or from premises occupied by him. Indeed, it is not easy to see how evidence obtained from other sources, even if the means for obtaining it were improper, could lead to the accused being denied a fair trial. I accordingly agree with my noble and learned friends that the various statements with regard to the discretion to which I have referred should be treated as applying to evidence and documents obtained from an accused person or from premises occupied by him. That is enough to preserve the important principle that the judge has an overriding discretion to exclude evidence, the admission of which would prevent the accused from having a fair trial. That discretion will be preserved if the question in the appeal is answered in the way proposed in paragraph (2) at the end of the speech of my noble and learned friend, Lord Diplock, with which I agree.

. . . .

I have referred throughout to evidence being excluded by the judge from consideration by the jury, but it follows of course that the same evidence ought to be excluded by magistrates from their own consideration in cases where they are the judges both of law and of fact.

I would dismiss the appeal, and answer the question in the way proposed by my noble and learned friend, Lord Diplock.

LORD DILHORNE, LORD SALMON and LORD SCARMAN delivered concurring judgments.

Note.—Differing approaches have been taken in Common Law jurisdictions to the problem of the admissibility of illegally obtained evidence. In Canada the Supreme Court has consistently (although in recent cases by majority decisions) taken the view that a judge has no discretion to exclude evidence on the ground that it was illegally obtained. Even the judge's discretion to exclude evidence with a view to ensuring that the accused has a fair trial is narrower than it is in England. As Martland J. put it (D.L.R., pp. 689–690) in *R. v. Wray* [1971] S.C.R. 272; 11 D.L.R. (3d.) 673, "It is only the allowance of evidence gravely prejudicial to the accused, the admissibility of which is tenuous, and whose probative force in relation to the main issue before the Court is trifling, which can be said to operate unfairly." Earlier in his judgment his Lordship had stated the prevailing Canadian position when he said (pp. 685–686): "The exercise of a discretion of that kind is part of the function of the Court to ensure that the accused has a fair trial. But other than that, in my opinion, under our law, the function of the Court is to determine the issue before it, on the evidence admissible in law, and it does not extend to the exclusion of admissible evidence for any other reason." The position is, however, liable to be reviewed in the light of the recently enacted Canadian Charter of Rights and Freedoms. For a decision of the High Court of Australia demonstrating a less rigid and more sophisticated approach, see *Bunning v. Cross* (1978) 141 C.L.R. 54. There it was held that in Australia there exists a discretion to exclude evidence on the ground that it was improperly obtained. Its exercise depends, not simply upon consideration of fairness to the accused, but upon weighing against each other two competing requirements of public policy, thereby seeking to resolve the apparent conflict between the desirable goal of bringing to conviction the wrongdoer and the undesirable effect of curial approval, or even encouragement, being given to the unlawful or unfair conduct of those whose task it is to enforce the law. See, too, *Cleland* v. *R.* (1983) 57 A.L.J.R. 15 (H.C. Aust.). United States authorities are largely concerned with constitutional provisions and have an exclusionary tendency. Stress is laid upon the need to inhibit law enforcement officers from resorting to illegal or improper practices: see, *e.g., Mapp* v. *Ohio* 367 U.S. 643 (1961), rehear. den. 368 U.S. 871 (1961) (Supreme Court of the United States). However, the reach of *Mapp* v. *Ohio* has been limited in *United States* v. *Leon* 468 U.S. 897 (1984) and *Massachusetts* v. *Sheppard* 468 U.S. 981 (1984), evidence being held to be admissible if seized on the basis of reasonably held good faith. Recent Scots decisions perhaps go furthest in allowing considerable discretion to the trial judge. See the judgment of Lord Fraser of Tullybelton in *R.* v. *Sang* (*supra*).

Police and Criminal Evidence Act 1984, s.78 and s.82(3). (See Part Two, *infra*). To the (limited) extent that *R.* v. *Sang* permits exclusion its effect is preserved by section 82(3). To the extent that it does not do so its relationship with section 78 is not entirely clear. See the *Note* to *R.* v. *List* [1966] 1 W.L.R. 9 (Part One, Chapter 1, Section A, *supra*). But see, too *R.* v. *Mason* (*infra*).

The Scarman Amendment to the Police and Criminal Evidence Bill. This was considered at an early stage of the passage of the Bill through Parliament. What was intended as a slightly revised version of the Amendment as originally proposed by Lord Scarman is set out below. (Hansard H.L.Deb., Vol. 455, col. 427). The Amendment was eventually rejected but it provides a valuable study.

"(1) If it appears to the court in any proceedings that any evidence (other than a confession) proposed to be given by the prosecution may have been obtained improperly, the court shall not allow the evidence to be given unless—

    (a) the prosecution proves to the court beyond reasonable doubt that it was obtained lawfully and in accordance with a code of practice (where applicable) issued, approved and in force, under Part VI of this Act; or

    (b) the court is satisfied that anything improperly done in obtaining it was of no material significance in all the circumstances of the case and ought, therefore, to be disregarded; or

    (c) the court is satisfied that the probative value of the evidence, the gravity of the offence charged, and the circumstances in which the evidence was obtained are such that the public interest in the fair administration of the criminal law requires the evidence to be given, notwithstanding that it was obtained improperly.

(2) For the purposes of this section, evidence shall be treated as having been obtained improperly if it was obtained—

    (a) in breach of any provision of the Act or any other enactment or rule of law; or

    (b) in excess of any power conferred by or obtained under this Act or any other enactment; or

    (c) in breach of any provision of a code of practice issued, approved, and in force under Part VI of this Act; or

    (d) as a result of any material deception in obtaining or exercising any power under this Act or any other enactment."

R. v. O'Connor (1987) 85 Cr.App.R. 298 (C.A.). At the appellant's trial for conspiracy to obtain property by deception by taking part with a co-accused in a scheme to defraud an insurance company, evidence was admitted under the Police and Criminal Evidence Act 1984 s.74(1) of the co-accused's plea of guilty to the charge. As section 75 of the Act makes clear (see Part Two, *infra*), where evidence of conviction is admitted under section 74, it is not admitted simply as a plea, but with all the detail that was contained in the relevant count of the indictment. In these circumstances it was unrealistic to assume that, even though the judge had in effect invited the jury to disregard that evidence, it would in fact not be influenced by it when assessing the guilt of the appellant. The trial judge had therefore been in error in not having resort to the discretion given by section 78 of the 1984 Act so as to exclude the evidence.

Note.—Contrast *R. v. Robertson*; *R. v. Golder* [1987] 1 Q.B. 920 (C.A.), where the pleas and subsequent convictions of two co-accuseds did not on their face involve the appellant whose name did not appear in the relevant counts at all. The trial judge had, therefore, been right not to have resorted to section 78. Lord Lane C.J. did, however, state *per curiam* (p. 928): "Section 74 is a provision which should be sparingly used. There will be occasions where, although the evidence may be technically admissible, its effect is likely to be so slight that it will be wiser not to adduce it. This is particularly so when there is any danger of contravention of section 78."

Contrast, too, *R. v. Lunnon* (1989) 88 Cr.App.R. 71, where the Court of Appeal distinguished *R. v. O'Connor* on the grounds (1) that the plea of guilty was tendered only for the purpose of proving conspiracy and not for the purpose of implicating the defendant in it, and (2) that the summing-up to the jury had been entirely adequate in this regard. Moreover, in the circumstances the judge had rightly refused to exercise his discretion to exclude under section 78. See, too, *R. v. Bennett* [1988] Crim.L.R. 686; [1989] 6 C.L. 68 (C.A.).

In *R. v. Curry* [1988] Crim.L.R. 527; [1989] 3 C.L. 66 (C.A.) it was again emphasised that section 74 should be used sparingly, especially with regard to joint offences such as conspiracy or affray, and not where the evidence sought to be adduced under the section imported complicity of the person on trial.

R. v. Mason [1988] 1 W.L.R. 139 (C.A.). The appellant, whilst under arrest, was questioned by police officers about his involvement with arson caused by igniting inflammable liquid contained in bottles. The police officers had no evidence connecting him with the crime but told him, falsely, that his fingerprint had been found on a fragment of glass at the scene of the crime. Subsequently the police officers in a deliberate falsehood repeated this allegation to the appellant's solicitor. Thereupon, on advice, the appellant answered questions and confessed that he had handled the glass. The confession was admitted in evidence at the trial, over objection that it should be excluded in accordance with the Police and Criminal Evidence Act, s.78(1). The prosecution produced no further evidence; the accused did not testify and he was convicted. His appeal against conviction was resisted on the ground that section 78 ought not to apply to confessions because section 76 dealt with them specifically. However, the Court of Appeal, allowing the appeal, held that the word "evidence" in section 78(1) includes all evidence which could be introduced by the prosecution: accordingly a trial judge has a discretion under that section to exclude a confession in the interests of justice regardless of whether it falls to be considered under section 76(2). In the instant case the judge had erred in failing to take account of the vital fact that the police had practised deceit on the appellant's solicitor. In the course of delivering the judgment of the Court of Appeal, Watkin L.J. said (p. 144) of section 78 that it "in our opinion, does no more than to restate the power which judges had at common law before the Act of 1984 was passed."

Note.—*R. v. Mason* was distinguished in *Kinsella v. Marshall* [1988] 5 C.L. 61 (D.C.). There a plain clothes officer bought liquor sold in breach of licensing laws without revealing his identity as an officer, but evidence to this effect was admitted.

In *R.* v. *Samuel* [1988] Q.B. 615 the Court of Appeal held that improper prevention of an accused consulting a solicitor could impose a duty upon a trial judge to "address his mind" to the propriety of excluding evidence under section 78. *R.* v. *Samuel* was followed in *R.* v. *O'Leary* (1988) 87 Cr.App.R. 387 (C.A.), where it was held that the court should ask itself the question "Will its admission have such an effect on the fairness of the proceedings that I, the court, ought not to admit it?"

In *R.* v. *O'Loughlin and McLaughlin* (1987) 85 Cr.App.R. 157 (Cent. Cr.Ct.) it was indicated that depositions taken at committal proceedings by two women living abroad, who were said to be too frightened to give evidence in the light of threats that they had received, would be excluded under section 78. Contrast now the Criminal Justice Act 1988, s.23(3)(*b*) (Part Two, *infra*).

Morris v. **Beardmore** [1981] A.C. 446 (H.L.). The defendant was charged with failing to supply a specimen of breath contrary to the Road Traffic Act 1972, s.8(3), and also with failing to provide a specimen for a laboratory test contrary to section 9(3) of the Act. The police were trespassing on the defendant's property when they requested the specimen. The House of Lords held that the Justices had been right to dismiss the informations. The House held that in the absence of an express provision it is to be assumed that Parliament does not intend to authorise otherwise unlawful conduct. A constable must therefore be acting lawfully towards a person when he requires him to provide a specimen for a breath test under section 8(2). As at the time the constable was a trespasser in the defendant's house, the requirement to provide a specimen was not authorised by law. Reference was made by their Lordships to *R.* v. *Sang* (*supra*). Its irrelevance was explained (pp. 459–460) by Lord Edmund-Davies thus: "... I must certainly deal with the decision of this House in *Reg.* v. *Sang* [1980] A.C. 402, which it was suggested has some relevance, but which in my judgment has none. *Reg.* v. *Sang* was a case about what when I was young used to be called adjectival law, as contrasted with substantive law. Your Lordships were then considering whether evidence obtained in certain circumstances could be adduced in proof that the accused had committed the offence charged, whereas our present inquiry relates to the ingredients of the offence itself."

Note.—*Morris* v. *Beardmore* was followed in *Lambert* v. *Roberts* [1981] 2 All E.R. 15 (D.C.). It was, however, distinguished in *Fox* v. *Chief Constable of Gwent* [1985] 1 W.L.R. 1126 (H.L.) on the ground that, as a result of amendments to the Road Traffic Act 1972, lawful arrest was no longer an essential prerequisite of a breath test. But see, too, *Matto (Jit Singh)* v. *D.P.P.* [1987] R.T.R. 337; [1987] Crim.L.R. 641 (D.C.), where *Fox* v. *Chief Constable of Gwent* was itself distinguished but on a different ground. There a police officer had persisted with a request that the accused provide a breath sample although he was at the time on his own private property. It was held that, notwithstanding that subsequently there had been compliance with the Road Traffic Act 1972 when the test was carried out at the police station, evidence of what had happened following the accused's arrest should have been excluded in the light of what had occurred on the accused's property. The reference in section 78 of the 1984 Act to "the circumstances in which the evidence was obtained" was invoked.

OPINION EVIDENCE

A witness, it is traditionally asserted, must state the facts as he perceived them and not give his opinion about them. This reflects the fundamental doctrine of the common law that espouses trial by jury, judge or magistrate rather than trial by witness. It is for the trier of fact, not the witness, to draw inferences and, where necessary, to make value judgments. The application of this doctrine in simple cases presents little difficulty in practice. Whereas it is for a witness to depose that he saw the defendant's car mount the pavement, it is for the trier of fact to infer from this (taken perhaps with other facts) that it resulted from the defendant's act or from his having allowed his attention to wander, and to evaluate this inferred behaviour by reference to the law of negligence. However, the unqualified proposition that a witness must state facts not opinion is unacceptably simplistic. There are at least two major reasons for this.

First, a crude distinction between fact and opinion so patently does not stand up to even elementary philosophical analysis that it cannot form the basis of a strict legal rule. Virtually every statement made by a witness contains an element of inference. As Thayer pointed out nearly a century ago, "In a sense all testimony to matter of fact is opinion evidence; *i.e.* it is a conclusion formed from phenomena and mental impressions."[1] The inference which is involved in reaching the conclusion may be one which any rational person would draw, it may be subconscious, and it may be palpably correct; but it is still an inference. A witness when testifying can do no more than formulate in words his recollection of what he perceived with his senses,—what he saw, heard, smelled or felt, but testimony cannot aspire to direct and perfect reproduction of previously perceived date. An element of inference is inevitably involved in putting the witness's recollected version of his perception into words. Moreover, sometimes,—especially if the witness is to tell his story in his own way and/or in the way most helpful to the jury,—his testimony may well involve not only inference but also elements of value judgment: for example, he deposes that he tasted the beer, the quality of which is in dispute, and that it tasted "good." Statutory partial recognition of the inevitability of the presence of elements of opinion in testimony is reflected in the terminology of section 3(2) of the Civil Evidence Act 1972 (Part Two, *infra*) but this enactment is itself applicable only in civil cases.

---

[1] Thayer. *A Preliminary Treatise on Evidence at the Common Law* (1898), p. 524.

Secondly, there are some situations in which the drawing of a particular inference by a witness, although perhaps partially avoidable, is positively desirable in that it promotes the efficiency of the fact-finding process. There are many situations in which the witness is markedly better qualified to draw an inference than is the trier of fact. This may be because the drawing of the inference requires an expertise possessed by the witness but not possessed by the trier of fact: the case of the expert witness has long been openly recognised as constituting an exception to the opinion rule.[2] Or, it may be because the witness has had a specific experience which qualifies him, in a way in which the trier of fact can never become equally well qualified, to draw a certain inference. For example the witness, who was at the scene of the crime and saw its perpetrator, is by virtue of this experience better qualified than the trier of fact to identify the accused as that perpetrator; and this will usually remain so however fully and clearly the witness is able to describe the latter's individual features. Moreover, to allow the witness to draw rational inferences will often make for the saving of time and the avoidance of confusion. It is acknowledged, to some extent tacitly, that non-expert opinion evidence can be received in a wide range of situations, but, not surprisingly, the limits of this type of exception to the opinion rule are much less clearly defined than are the limits of the exception constituted by expert testimony.

Various additional justifications for the rule purporting to exclude opinion evidence have been adduced. Best wrote that "The rule is necessary to prevent the other rules of evidence being practically nullified,"[3] his point being that an opinion may have been formed on the basis of evidence, such as hearsay, which would itself be inadmissible. There is some force in this, but a witness can be cross-examined as to the grounds of his opinion, and, if these appear to be inadequate, the jury may be instructed to disregard the opinion.[4] The mere fact that a witness is relying upon inadmissible evidence will not automatically vitiate his opinion. Obviously much of an expert witness's expertise will have been acquired from hearsay sources; but if a witness's opinion is clearly based upon inadmissible evidence relating directly to the particular facts of the case, that opinion, especially if the witness is not an expert, is very likely to be unacceptable. It has also been said, and sometimes emphatically, that opinion evidence is inadmissible because it is irrelevant.[5] If this were the whole truth it would not be clear why a separate rule is required, for all irrelevant evidence is excluded. It cannot, however, be seriously contended that no opinion evidence has probative value. What would be more acceptable is a converse proposition, namely that when opinion evidence is overtly received this is partly justified by exceptional probative worth. Again, it has been objected that to the extent that a witness gives a mere opinion he cannot be prosecuted for perjury but this objection has not been influential at least in modern times.

---

[2] For the reception with leave of the court of expert reports (incorporating opinion) in criminal cases even if the maker of the report does not give oral evidence, see the Criminal Justice Act 1988, s.30 (Part Two, *infra*).

[3] Best, *Principles of the Law of Evidence* (12th ed., 1922).

[4] But here as elsewhere the efficacy of this sort of instruction may often be a matter for speculation.

[5] See, *e.g. Hollington* v. *Hewthorn* [1943] K.B. 587 (C.A.), *per* Goddard L.J. at p. 595.

It is the desirability of protecting the function of the trier of fact that forms the substantial bedrock of policy underpinning the rule which purports to exclude opinion evidence.[6] The formidable analytical and practical shortcomings of that rule, as historically and formally stated, ought not to be allowed to obscure the importance of this policy. Rather the nature of those shortcomings should be seen as simply indication the proper scope of the rule. The rule is directed against *de facto* usurpation by the witness of the role of the trier of fact. The trier of fact can always reject an opinion, but the danger to be guarded against is that a trier of fact may succumb to uncritical acceptance of a convincingly presented opinion. But at the same time the operation of the opinion rule must be circumscribed so as to prevent it becoming an instrument which actually inhibits the trier of fact in the efficient performance of its function. Thayer concluded that "there is ground for saying that, in the main, any rule excluding opinion evidence is limited to cases where, in the judgment of the court, it will not be helpful to the jury. Whether accepted in terms or not, this view largely governs the administration of the rule."[7] Prima facie and generally a witness's testimony should not be based upon inferences or contain value judgments. Departure from this doctrine is to be permitted only to the extent either that it is unavoidable or that it is positively helpful to the trier of fact. These "exceptional" situation are common and defy comprehensive classification, but they include cases in which a witness's expression of an opinion enables him to be more coherent and comprehensible, cases in which the inference involved is rational and commonplace, and cases in which for one reason or another the witness is markedly better qualified than is the trier of fact to draw the inference or to make the value judgment.

The risk of usurpation by the witness of the function of the trier of fact is often greatest if the witness expresses an opinion on the very question, or "ultimate issue," which the trier of fact has finally to decide. In such cases courts have in the past been especially wary about admitting opinion evidence. However, the Civil Evidence Act 1972, s.3 (Part Two, *infra*) provides that in civil cases expert evidence may be given even on an ultimate issue; and it also declares that non-expert opinion evidence may be given, seemingly even on an ultimate issue, if given "as a way of conveying relevant facts personally perceived" by the witness. Any discretion to exclude evidence is however expressly preserved.[8] In criminal cases expert opinion evidence is in practice often admitted although it concerns the ultimate issue, but the old common law rule will usually inhibit the reception of non-expert opinion in such circumstances.

Historically, the opinion rule has been classified as one of the four major exclusionary canons of the law of evidence,[9] but whereas the others,—the hearsay rule, the rule excluding similar fact evidence and that excluding some character evidence,—have been sources of masses of case law, the case law on the opinion rule is meagre. This is probably symptomatic of the true status of the rule. Although the regulation of a

---

[6] But for a somewhat differnt emphasis, see the judgment of Dixon J. in the Supreme Court of Canada in *Graat* v. *R.* (1983) 144 D.L.R. (3d.) 267.

[7] Thayer, *op. cit.* p. 525.

[8] s.5(3).

[9] See, *e.g.* Stephen, *A. Digest of the Law of Evidence* (1st ed., 1876, 12th (Revised) ed. 1948).

few specific problems, such as the reception of expert testimony, has
been subjected to fairly detailed formulation, the main body of the rule
is so flexible as to resist judicial analysis and in large measure to
preclude treatment at the appellate level. To quote Thayer again, the
rule as applied in practice "must allow a very great range of permissible
differences of judgment; and ... conclusions of that character ought not,
usually, to be regarded as subject to review by higher courts."[10]

There is also another and separate sense in which a witness is
required to confine his testimony to statements of fact: he must not
made assertions of legal doctrine. For him to do so would in effect to be
attempt to usurp the role, not of the jury, but of the judge. On the
other hand, an assertion that a legal criterion has or has not been
complied with, taking the form, *e.g.* that "X was negligent" or that "Y
is not insane within the *M'Naghten* Rules" *could* be no more than an
assertion of fact, but then only if it is clear that the assertion is as to
behaviour or condition and not as to the nature of a legal standard.[11]
But, of course, in such cases the assertion is likely to relate to the
ultimate issue of fact, and may be disallowed on that score. Also, it is to
be remembered that points of foreign law, although determined by the
judge,[12] are treated as questions of fact. Foreign law must therefore be
proved. This is usually done by expert testimony which often
incorporates expressions of opinion.

FRYER v. GATHERCOLE

4 Exch. 262; **14 Jur. 542;** 154 E.R. 1209 (Exchequer: 1849)

*On matters with respect to which it is practically impossible for any
witness to swear positively, an ordinary witness may give evidence of
his opinion; as on questions of identification, condition, comparison or
resemblance of persons or things.*

To prove the publication of a libellous pamphlet, a woman was called,
who deposed to having received from the defendant a copy of a
pamphlet, of which she read some portions. She lent it to several
persons in succession, who returned it to her, after which she wrote her
name on it; and, although there was no mark by which she could
identify it, she believed the copy produced to be the same but could not
swear that it was. It was held that this was proper evidence of
identification of the pamphlet.

POLLOCK C.B.: ... The question resolved itself into a question of
degree. The witness could say no more than this: "I believe the copy of
the pamphlet produced to be the same with that which I received from
the defendant, because when I lent that copy to other persons it was
returned to me, and I had no reason to believe it otherwise when I got

---

[10] Thayer, *op. cit.* p. 525.
[11] As a conflict between expert opinion is one of fact not law, it would be inappropriate
for the Court of Appeal to resolve it: see *dictum per curiam* in *Wilsher* v. *Essex Area
Health Authority* [1988] A.C. 1074, 1091 (H.L.).
[12] See Chapter 5, *supra.*

it back. I then for certainty put my name on it." If the name had been written in the first instance no doubt could have arisen.... As has been truly argued, there are many cases of identification where the law would be rendered ridiculous is positive certainly were required from witnesses.... The evidence in this case was therefore properly received; any objection to it goes merely to its value.

ALDERSON B.:... She lends it to A B, he has it in his possession out of her sight, he returns her a similar book on the same subject, and she believes it is the same copy. It is open to contend that A B may have substituted another copy, and that that returned is not the same which was lent. The jury may judge how far that is probable or reasonable.

PARKE B. (in course of argument):... In the identification of a person you compare in your mind the man you have seen with the man you see at the trial. The same rule belongs to every species of identification.

Note.—Evidence of opinion of the resemblance of pictures has been received in an action for infringement of copyright (*Lucas* v. *Williams & Sons* [1892] 2 Q.B. 113 (C.A.)). As to evidence of handwriting, see *R.* v. *Silverlock* [1894] 2 Q.B. 766 (C.C.R.) *infra*; as to evidence of opinion of the speed of motor vehicles, see the Road Traffic Regulation Act 1984, s.89 (Part Two, *infra*); and as to non-expert evidence of value, see *R.* v. *Beckett* (1913) 8 Cr. App. R. 204 (C.C.A.). Evidence of opinion by laymen has also been received in relation to age, health, intoxication, and the application of words. As to intoxication, see *R.* v. *Davies* (1962) 46 Cr. App. R. 292 (C.-M.A.C.) *infra*; *R.* v. *Neal* [1962] Crim. L.R. 698 (C.-M.A.C.). As to the application of words, see *Brunswick (Duke)* v. *Harmer* (1850) 3 Car. & Kir. 10; *R.* v. *Hendy* (1850) 4 Cox C.C. 243.

R. v. **Davies** [1962] 1 W.L.R. 1111 (C.-M.A.C.). The appellant was charged with having driven a vehicle on a road when unfit to drive through drink or drugs contrary to section 6 of the Road Traffic Act 1960. He appealed against conviction. Lord Parker C.J. (delivering the judgment of the Court) said (pp. 1112–1113): "The first point the [counsel for the appellant] took in this court was that certain evidence was wrongly admitted. The very first prosecution witness, the bombardier, found these vehicles in collision, and he gave evidence about a conversation which he had had with the appellant and how the appellant appeared to be behaving. He then said: 'I formed the impression that the accused was under the influence of drink and at that time he was in no condition to handle a motor-vehicle.' That is what he was allowed to say. The defence had strongly taken the stand that the witness should be allowed to speak only as to facts he had seen, because it was for the court to say what was the appellant's condition. Apparently the judge advocate advised the court that the witness could state the impression he formed as to the appellant's condition at the time he saw him if he was a witness who know what was entailed in the driving of a car. It is to be observed that the witness was allowed to speak about two matters which are quite distinct; one is what his impression was as to whether drink had been taken by the appellant, and the second was his opinion as to whether as the result of that drink he was fit or unfit to drive a car. The court has come clearly to the conclusion that a witness can quite properly give his general impression as to whether a driver had taken drink. He must describe of course the facts upon which he relies, but it seems to this court that he is perfectly entitled to give his impression as to whether drink had been taken or not. On the other hand, as regards the second matter, it cannot be said, as it seems to this court, that a witness, merely because he is a driver himself, is in the expert witness category so that it is proper to ask him his opinion as to fitness or unfitness to drive. That is the very matter which the court itself has to determine. Accordingly, in so far as this witness and two subsequent witnesses, . . . gave their opinion as to the appellant's ability or fitness to drive, the court was wrong in admitting that evidence." The appeal was however dismissed, there being ample other evidence to support the conviction.

R. v. **Chard** (1971) 56 Cr. App. R. 268 (C.A.). The applicant for leave to appeal had been convicted of murder. At the trial no question of insanity or of diminished responsibility had arisen, but the defence had sought to call a medical witness to give evidence concerning the applicant's intention to kill ro to do grevious bodily harm at the relevant time. The Court held that the judge had rightly refused to admit this evidence. Roskill L.J., delivering the judgment of the Court, said (pp. 270–271): " . . . one purpose of jury trials is to bring into the jury box a body of men and women who are able to judge ordinary day-to-day questions by their own standards, that is, the standards in the eyes of the law of theoretically ordinary reasonable men and women. That is something which they are well able by their ordinary experience to judge for themselves. Where the matters in issue go outside that experience and they are invited to deal with someone supposedly abnormal, for example, supposedly suffering from insanity or diminished responsibility, then plainly in such a case they are entitled to the benefit of expert evidence. But where, as in the present case, they are dealing with someone who by concession was on the medical evidence entirely normal, it seems to this Court abundantly plain on first principles of the admissibility of expert evidence, that it is not permissible to call a witness, whatever his personal experience, merely to tell the jury how he thinks an accused man's mind— assumedly a normal mind—operated at the time of the alleged crime with reference to the crucial question of what that man's intention was.

R. v. **Smith (Stanley)** [1979] 1 W.L.R. 1445 (C.A.). The applicant for leave to appeal had been convicted of murder. At the trial he had raised the defence of automatism while asleep. The Crown, contending that he had recently thought up the defence, obtained leave to cross examine him about interviews which he had with two psychiatrists while in custody and to call the psychiatrists to give their views on automatism. The Court of Appeal held that the judge had not erred in granting this leave, and, treating the application as an appeal, dismissed it. COunsel for the applicant argued that, as there was no question of insanity or diminished responsibility, automatism was a matter which could and should be decided by the jury in the light of their own experience and that they should not be assisted by expert evidence as to the accused's state of mind. Rejecting this argument, Geoffrey Lane L.J. (giving the judgment of the court) said (p. 1451): "This type of automatism—sleepwalking—call it what you like, is not something, we think, which is within the realm of the ordinary juryman's experience. It is something on which, speaking for ourselves as judges, we should like help were we to have to decide it and we see not why a jury should be deprived of that type of help."

Note.—In *R. v. Masih* [1986] C.L.Y. 579; [1986] Crim. L.R. 395, the Court of Appeal indicated that generally evidence that an accused had an I.Q. of 69 or less should be admitted on an issue of his capacity to understand.

R. v. **Stamford** [1972] 2 Q.B. 391 (C.A.). The defendant was charged with dispatching through the post packets containing indecent articles contrary to the Post Office Act 1953, s.11. The Court of Appeal held that whether a particular article was "indecent or obscene" for the purposes of the section was a matter for the jury and that the trial judge had been right to refuse to allow the defence to call evidence to explain the ordinary meaning of these words. Ashworth J., in the course of delivering the judgment of the court said (p. 399): "... In the speech of Lord Morris of Borth-y-Gest [in *Shaw* v. *D.P.P.* [1962] A.C. 220] the following appears, at p. 292: 'Even if accepted public standards may to some extent vary from generation to generation, current standards are in the keeping of juries, who can be trusted to maintain the corporate good sense of the community and to discern attacks upon values that must be preserved.' That says in a sentence all that need be said upon the task which is entrusted to juries and their competence to discharge their duty. They do not need assistance: they are themselves, so to speak, the custodians of the standards for the time being."

D.P.P. v. **Jordan** [1977] A.C. 699 (H.L.). A bookseller, charged with possessing obsence articles for publication for gain contrary to section 2(1) of the Obscene Publications Act 1959 as amended, raised the defence of "public good" pursuant to section 4(1) of that Act (Part Two, *infra*) and sought to call expert evidence to the effect that the material in question would be psychologically beneficial to persons with abnormal sexual tendencies in that it would relieve their sexual tensions and might divert them from anti-social activities. The accused contended that the evidence was admissible under section 4(2) (Part Two, *infra*) because the psychological health of the community was an object of general concern. The House of Lords held however, that the evidence had been rightly excluded. The House took the view that evidence tending to show that publication would benefit certain categories of persons, such as the sexually inadequate, the deviant and the perverted, was not evidence tending to show that publication would be "for the public good on the ground that it is in the interests ... of other objects of general concern" within the meaning of section 4(1).

R. v. TURNER

[1975] Q.B. 834; [1975] 1 All E.R. 70; 60 Cr. App. R. 80; [1975] Crim. L.R. 98
(C.A.: 1974)

Expert psychiatric testimony is, in the absence of mental illness, generally inadmissible either to show the accused's credibility as a witness or to show the likelihood of his having been provoked.
When psychiatric opinion evidence is admitted counsel should in examination-in-chief ask the witness to state the facts upon which his opinion is based, and these should be proved by admissible evidence.

LAWTON L.J. (delivering the judgment of court which included NIELD and CANTLEY JJ.): ... after a trial before Bridge J. the defendant was convicted of murder.... He has appealed against his conviction on the ground that the judge refused to admit evidence which a psychiatrist was prepared to give in support of his defence of provocation....
At about midnight on October 26/27, 1973, at Swindon while sitting in a motor car with a girl named Wendy Butterfield the defendant killed her by battering her about the head and face with a hammer. Fifteen blows were struck. Very shortly after striking these blows he went to a nearby farmhouse and told the occupants there he had killed his girl friend....
His defence was provocation. In the circumstances it could not have been any other. The basis for this defence was that he was deeply in love with the girl, whom he thought was pregnant by him. While he was in the motor car with her he said that she had told him with a grin that

while he had been in prison she had been sleeping with two other men, that she could make money in this way and that the child she was carrying was not his. He claimed that he had been very upset by what she had said. His hand had come across the hammer which was down by the side of the seat and he had hit her with it. He said: "It was never in my mind to do her any harm. I did not realise what I had in my hand. I knew it was heavy. . . . When I realised it was a hammer I stopped." If the jury rejected his evidence as to how the girl came to be killed (it was challenged by the prosecution) there was no foundation for the defence put forward. The defendant's credit as a witness was an important issue.

After the defendant had given evidence his counsel, Mr. Mildon, told Bridge J. he wanted to call a psychiatrist. He explained why. He said: "First of all, it may help the jury to accept as credible the defendant's account of what happened and, second, it may tell them why this man was provoked." The judge queried whether the evidence of a psychiatrist was admissible on these matters. There was some discussion, at the end of which the judge said that he wanted to see the evidence which the psychiatrist proposed to give. Mr. Mildon then handed to the judge a lengthy psychiatric report dated February 2, 1974, which had been prepared by a Dr. Smith. It was in a form with which judges have become familiar in recent years. At the beginning the doctor said that he had been asked to deal with various matters and in particular to assess the defendant's personality, his present mental state and to consider from the psychiatric point of view his emotional state and reaction at the time of the crime. Then followed a long account of the defendant's personality and medical history and his family background. Some of the information had come from medical records: most of it from the defendant himself but a little from his family and friends as is shown by the following passage: "From all accounts his personality has always been that of a placid, rather quiet and passive person who is quite sensitive to the feelings of other people. He was always regarded by his family and friends as an even-tempered person who is not in any way aggressive. . . . In general until the night of the crime he seems to have always displayed remarkably good impulse control.". . . The defendant himself had not put his character in issue. If the psychiatrist had given evidence in accordance with his report, the defendant would have been put before the jury by the psychiatrist as having a character and disposition which the prosecution considered in the light of his record he had not got. The opinion expressed at the end of this report was as follows: "At no time has this man appeared to show any evidence of mental illness as defined by the Mental Health Act 1959. His homicidal behaviour would appear to be understandable in terms of his relationship with Wendy Butterfield which, as I have endeavoured to outline above, was such as to make him particularly vulnerable to be overwhelmed by anger if she confirmed the accusation that had been made about her. If his statements are true that he was taken completely by surprise by her confession he would have appeared to have killed her in an explosive release of blind rage. His personality structure is consistent with someone who could behave in this way. There is no demonstrable clinical evidence to suggest that brain damage or organic disease of the brain diminished his sense of responsibility at the time he killed her, and since her death his behaviour would appear to have been consistent with someone suffering from profound grief. Although he would obviously benefit from psychotherapeutic counselling, in the absence of formal psychiatric illness there are no indications of recommending psychiatric treatment."

Mr. Calcutt [prosecution counsel] point out to the judge the difficulty presented by the references in the report to the defendant's alleged disposition and character. Thereupon the judge commented that the report contained "hearsay character evidence" which was inadmissible. He could have said that all the facts upon which the psychiatrist based his opinion were hearsay save for those which he observed for himself during his examination of the defendant such as his appearance of depression and his becoming emotional when discussing the deceased girl and his own family. It is not for this court to instruct psychiatrists how to draft their reports, but those who call psychiatrists as witnesses should remember that the facts upon which they base their opinions must be proved by admissible evidence. This elementary principle is frequently overlooked.

. . . . Before a court can assess the value of an opinion it must know the facts upon which it is based. If the expert has been misinformed about the facts or has taken irrelevant facts into consideration or has omitted to consider relevant ones, the opinion is likely to be valueless. In our judgment, counsel calling an expert should in examination in chief ask his witness to state the facts upon which his opinion is based. It is wrong to leave the other side to elicit the facts by cross-examination.

. . . . The evidence was tendered on the issues of provocation and credibility. The judge gave his ruling in relation to those issues. . . .

The first question on both these issues is whether the psychiatrist's opinion was relevant. A man's personality and mental make-up do have a bearing upon his conduct. A quick-tempered man will react more aggressively to an unpleasing situation than a placid one. Anyone having a florid imagination or a tendency to exaggerate is less likely to be a reliable witness than one who is precise and careful. These are matters of ordinary human experience. Opinions from knowledgeable persons about a man's personality and mental make-up play a part in many human judgments. In our judgment the psychiatrist's opinion was relevant. Relevance, however, does not result in evidence being admissible: it is a condition precedent to admissibility. Our law excludes evidence of many matters which in life outside the courts sensible people take into consideration when making decisions. Tow broad heads of exclusion are hearsay and opinion. As we have already pointed out, the psychiatrist's report contained a lot of hearsay which was inadmissible. A ruling on this ground, however, would merely have trimmed the psychiatrists's evidence: it would not have excluded it altogether. Was it inadmissible because of the rules relating to opinion evidence?

The foundation of these rules was laid by Lord Mansfield in *Folkes* v. *Chadd* (1782) 3 Doug. K.B. 157 and was well laid: the opinion of scientific men upon proven facts may be given by men of science within their own science. An expert's opinion is admissible to furnish the court with scientific information which is likely to be outside the experience and knowledge of a judge or jury. If on the proven facts a judge or jury can form their own conclusions without help, then the opinion of an expert is unnecessary. In such a case if it is given dressed up in scientific jargon it may make judgment more difficult. The fact that an expert witness has impressive scientific qualifications does not by that fact alone make his opinion on matters of human nature and behaviour within the limits of normality any more helpful than that of the jurors themselves; but there is a danger that they may think it does.

What, in plain English, was the psychiatrist in this case intending to say? First, that the defendant was not showing and never had shown any evidence of mental illness, as defined by the Mental Health Act 1959, and did not require any psychiatric treatment; secondly, that he had had a deep emotional relationship with the girl which was likely to have caused an explosive release of blind rage when she confessed her wantonness to him; thirdly, that after he had killed her he behaved like someone suffering from profound grief. The first part of his opinion was within his expert province and outside the experience of the jury but was of no relevance in the circumstances of this case. The second and third points dealt with matters which are well within ordinary human experience. We all know that both men and women who are deeply in love can, and sometime do, have outbursts of blind rage when discovering unexpected wantonness on the part of their loved ones; the wife taken in adultery is the classical example of the application of the defence of "provocation"; and when death or serious injury results, profound grief usually follows. Jurors do not need psychiatrists to tell them how ordinary folk who are not suffering from any mental illness are likely to react to the stresses and strains of life. It follows that the proposed evidence was not admissible to establish that the defendant was likely to have been provoked. The same reasoning applies to its suggested admissibility on the issue of credibility. The jury had to decide what reliance they could put upon the defendant's evidence. He had to be judged as someone who was not mentally disordered. This is what juries are empanelled to do. The law assumes they can perform their duties properly. The jury in this case did not need, and should not have been offered, the evidence of a psyciatrist to help them decide whether the defendant's evidence was truthful.

Mr. Mildon submitted that such help should not have been rejected by the judge because in *Lowery* v. *The Queen* [1974] A.C. 85 the Privy Council had approved of the admission of the evidence of a psychologist on the issue of credibility. We had to consider that case carefully before we could decide whether it had in any way put a new interpretation upon what have long been thought to be the rules relating to the calling of evidence on the issue of credibility, *viz.* that in general evidence can be called to impugn the credibility of witnesses but not led in chief to bolster it up. In *Lowery* v. *The Queen* evidence of a psychologist on behalf of one of two accused was admitted to establish that his version of the facts was more probable than that put forward by the other. In every case what is relevant and admissible depends on the issues raised in that case. In *Lowery* v. *The Queen* the issues were unusual; and the accused to whose disadvantage the psychologist's evidence went had in effect said before it was called that he was not the sort of man to have committed the offence. In giving the judgment of the Board, Lord Morris of Borth-y-Gest said, at p. 103: "The only question now arising is whether in the special circumstances above referred to it was open to King in defending himself to call Professor Cox to give the evidence that he gave. The evidence was relevant to and necessary for his case which involved negativing what Lowery had said and put forward; in their Lordships' view in agreement with that of the Court of Criminal Appeal the evidence was admissible." We adjudge *Lowery* v. *The Queen* [1974] A.C. 85 to have been decided on its special facts. We do not consider that it is an authority for the proposition that in all cases psychologists and psychiatrists can be called to prove the probability of the accused's veracity. If any such rule was applied in our courts, trial by psychiatrists would be likely to take the place of trial by jury and magistrates. We do not find that prospect attractive and the law does not at present provide for it.

In coming to the conclusion we have in this case we must not be taken to be discouraging the calling psychiatric evidence in cases where such evidence can be helpful within the present rules of evidence. These rules may be too restrictive of the admissibility of opinion evidence.... We have not overlooked what Lord Parker C.J. said in *Director of Public Prosecutions* v. *A. and B.C. Chewing Gum Ltd.* [1968] 1 Q.B. 159, 164 about the advance of science making more and more inroads into the old common law principle applicable to opinion evidence; but we are firmly of the opinion that psychiatry has not yet become a satisfactory substitute for the common sense of juries or magistrates on matters within their experience of life. The appeal is dismissed.

Note.—The decision in *R.* v. *Turner* must be taken to represent English law; but it is not altogether easy to reconcile with it the earlier Privy Council case of *Lowery* v. *R.* [1974] A.C. 85 referred to by Lawton L.J. (*supra*). If the evidence was admitted in *Lowery* simply on the issue of the comparative credibility of the two joint accuseds, the case can perhaps be plausibly distinguished from *Turner* on the ground that the appellant accused, to whose disadvantage the evidence admitted on behalf of his co-accused went, had already put his credibility in issue. If, however, as would seem to have been the case, the evidence in *Lowery* was in effect character evidence as to comparative likelihood of guilt, although its admissibility *qua* character evidence would again be permissible having regard to the fact that the appellant accused had already put his character in issue, the problem of it constituting opinion evidence remains. A mechanical and somewhat unattractive reconciliation of *Turner* and *Lowery* in this respect could be that, whereas expert evidence will not be received to show that a normal man is liable to lose control when a woman, towards whom he has a possessive attitude, admits infidelity, an expert witness may make a comparative assessment of the personal aggressiveness of two or more persons.

See, too, *R.* v. *MacKenney*; *R.* v. *Pinfold* (1983) 76 Cr. App. R. 271 (C.A.), Chapter 9, *supra.*

R. v. **Camplin** [1978] A.C. 705 (H.L.). The House of Lords laid down as a matter of substantive criminal law that, when determining an issue of provocation, a jury should take into account those factors, including the age and physical characteristics of the accused, which in their opinion would effect the gravity of taunts and insults addressed to the accused. It was, however, emphasised that the reasonableness of the accused's response remains an issue for the jury, and that evidence as to what would be reasonable in the particular circumstances is inadmissible. Lord Simon of Glaisdale said (p. 727): "It was suggested on behalf of the Director of Public Prosecutions that if .... it was open to the jury to consider such mental or physical characteristics of the defendant as might affect his self-control in the relevant situation, the jury might require evidence as to how a person of reasonable self-control would be likely to react in such circumstances—or at least that it would be open to either side to call such evidence. In other words, evidence would be required, or alternatively be admissible, to show, for example, how a pregnant woman or a 15 year old boy or a hunchback would, exercising reasonable self-control, react in the circumstances. I cannot agree. Evidence of the pregnancy or the age or the malformation would be admissible. But whether the defendant exercised reasonable self-control in the totality of the circumstances (which would include the pregnancy or the immaturity or the malformation) would be entirely a matter for consideration by the jury without further evidence. The jury would, as ever, use their collective common sense to determine whether the provocation was sufficient to make a person of reasonable self-control in the totality of the circumstances (including personal characteristics) act as the defendant did. I certainly do not think that that is beyond the capacity of a jury."

R. v. Lupien (1970) 9 D.L.R. (3d.) 1 (S.C. Can.). The respondent had been convicted on a charge of attempting to commit an act of gross indecency. He had been found by the police in an hotel bedroom with another man, who was a female impersonator. His main defence was that at all times, until just before the police entered the room, he thought that his companion was a woman, and it was sought to support his own evidence in this regard by the evidence of Dr. Newman, a highly qualified psychiatrist, who was present throughout the trial and who had interviewed the respondent and others and subjected the respondent to certain psychiatric tests for the purpose of determining what his normal state was in relation to sex. The trial judge had excluded this evidence. The Supreme Court of Canada, although divided as to the purpose for which this particular evidence was being tendered, were agreed that, although expert psychiatric testimony is not admissible to show the absence of the requisite intent on the part of an accused to commit the crime charged, it is admissible to show his lack of capacity to form that intent. Ritchie J., who would admit the evidence, said (pp. 9–10): "I agree . . . that if the evidence had been tendered for the purpose of showing that Lupien was a normal man, the conclusion as to how he would have acted under the circumstances would have been a question for the jury; but, with all respect, as I understand the record, the evidence was not tendered for this purpose at all but rather for the purpose of proving the doctor's opinion that this particular man had a certain type of defence mechanism that made him react violently against homosexual behaviour. . . . As I understand it, the evidence thus sought to be adduced was directed towards obtaining Dr. Newman's opinion to the effect that the respondent was so constituted as to be incapable of formulating the intention to commit a homosexual act. . . . "

DIRECTOR OF PUBLIC PROSECUTIONS v. A. AND B.C. CHEWING GUM LTD.

[1968] 1 Q.B. 159; [1967] 2 All E.R. 504 (Q.B.D.: 1967)

Expert testimony of a child psychiatrist is admissible to show the likely effect of allegedly obscene articles upon children.
In practice the common law principle excluding expert testimony on the ultimate issue is often disregarded in criminal cases.

The defendants were charged with contravening the Obscene Publications Act 1959, s.2(1), and the Obscene Publications Act 1964, s.1(1), by publishing for gain 43 obscene "bubble gum" battle cards. The cards were sold together with packets of bubble gum, and would be seen and read by children of five years and over, who would exchange them amongst themselves in order to obtain full sets. At the trial the prosecution sought to introduce evidence of experts in child psychiatry as to the likely effect of the cards on children.

The Justices refused to hear the witnesses and acquitted the defendants. The prosecutor appealed.

LORD PARKER C.J.: ...Now what was submitted to the justices and has been submitted to this court is that, as a general rule, a long-standing rule of common law, evidence is inadmissible if it is on the very issue the court has to determine. For my part, and I am only dealing with this case, I cannot think that the evidence tendered was on that very issue. There were two matters really for consideration. What sort of effect would these cards singly or together have upon children, and no doubt children of different ages; what would it lead them to do? Secondly, was what they were led to do a sign of corruption or depravity? As it seems to me, it would be perfectly proper to call a psychiatrist and to ask him in the first instance what his experience, if any, with children was, and to say what the effect on the minds of children of different groups would be if certain types of photographs or pictures were put before them, and indeed, having got his general evidence, to put one or more of the cards in question to him and say what would their effect be upon the child. For myself, I think it would be wrong to ask the direct question as to whether any particular cards tended to corrupt or deprave, because that final stage was a matter which was entirely for the justices. No doubt, however, in such a case the defence might well put it to the witness that a particular card or cards could not corrupt, and no doubt, whatever the strict position may be, that question coming from the defence would be allowed, if only to give the defence an opportunity of getting an answer "No" from the expert.

On that ground alone, as it seems to me, the evidence in the present case was admissible.

I myself would go a little further in that I cannot help feeling that with the advance of science more and more inroads have been made into the old common law principles. Those who practise in the criminal courts see every day cases of experts being called on the question of diminished responsibility, and although technically the final question "Do you think he was suffering from diminished responsibility?" is strictly inadmissible, it is allowed time and time again without any objection. No doubt when dealing with the effect of certain things on the mind science may still be less exact than evidence as to what effect some particular thing will have on the body, but that, as it seems to me, is purely a question of weight.

I said that I was confining my observations to this particular case, because I can quite see that when considering the effect of something on an adult an adult jury may be able to judge just as well as an adult witness called on the point. Indeed, there is nothing more than a jury or justices need to know. But certainly when you are dealing here with children of different age groups and children from five upwards, any jury and any justices need all the help they can get, information which they may not have, as to the effect on different children....

. . . .

I have come to a clear conclusion that the justices were wrong in this case and accordingly I would allow this appeal, and send the case back for rehearing by a different bench of magistrates.

WIDGERY and O'CONNOR JJ. agreed.

Note.—In *R.* v. *Anderson* [1972] 1 Q.B. 304 Lord Widgery C.J., delivering the judgment of the Court of Appeal, said (p. 313) of *D.P.P.* v. *A. and B.C. Chewing Gum Ltd.*: "That case in our judgment should be regarded as highly exceptional and confined to its own circumstances, namely, a case where the alleged obscene matter was directed at very young children, and was of itself of a somewhat unusual kind. In the ordinary run of the mill cases in the future the issue 'obscene or no' must be tried by the jury without the assistance of expert evidence on that issue, and we draw attention to the failure to observe that rule in this case in order that that failure may not occur again. We are not oblivious of the fact that some people, perhaps many people, will think a jury, unassisted by experts, a very unsatisfactory tribunal to decide such a matter. Those who feel like that must campaign elsewhere for a change of the law. We can only deal with the law as it stands, and that is how it stands on this point." In a later Court of Appeal case, *R. v. Stamford* [1972] 2 Q.B. 391 (C.A.) (*supra*), Ashworth J., delivering the judgment of the court, said (p. 397): "[it] was indeed a very special case involving young children, and the Divisional Court decided that in the circumstances evidence of psychiatrists expert in dealing with children could be admitted, but it is indeed a very special case not likely to be extended." Also, in *D.P.P.* v. *Jordan* [1977] A.C. 699 (H.L.) (*supra*) Lord Dilhorne expressed (p. 722) *obiter* some doubt as to the correctness of the decision on this point, observing that, "If an article is not manifestly obscene as tending to deprave and corrupt, it seems to me somewhat odd that a person should be liable to conviction for publishing obscene matter if the evidence of experts in psychiatry is required to establish its obscenity."

R. v. **Skirving**; **R.** v. **Grossman** [1985] Q.B. 819 (C.A.). The appellants, book distributors, had copies of a book, which was aimed at actual and potential abusers of cocaine and described in detail how to prepare the drug into "free base" for smoking as being the best method of ingestion for enabling the maximum effect to be obtained. They were convicted of having an obscene article for publication for gain contrary to the Obscene Publications Act 1959, s.2(1), as amended by the Obscene Publications Act 1964, s.1(1). Expert evidence had been admitted on behalf of the prosecution giving a scientific assessment of the characteristics of cocaine, the physical and metal effects on users or abusers and an explanation of the different effects of the various methods of ingesting the drug. The Court of Appeal held that this evidence had been rightly admitted, since it was not aimed at showing that the book had a tendency "to deprave and corrupt," but was tendered so as to equip the jury with information necessary for it to decide whether the book had that tendency. Lord Lane C.J. said (p. 827): "In our judgment the present case was one where without expert evidence the jury might very well have come to a conclusion unjust either to the defendants on the one side or to the prosecution on the other. The effects of cocaine and the effects of the various methods by which it is taken is not in the experience of the ordinary person; indeed it is true to say that the mystique which has tended to surround cocaine in the past is so at variance with the reality as it is now known that scientific evidence in this case was essential to ensure that justice was done between the prosecution on the one side and the defendants on the other. Without it the jury would have been in the dark. Without it the jury would have been guessing and no more. But once the jury were equipped with the information which had been given by the experts on one side or the other, and once they had heard the cross-examination they were in a position to come to a proper conclusion as to the effect of the drug."

Folkes v. **Chadd** (1782) 3 Doug. K.B. 157 (K.B.), A question having arisen as to whether a bank, erected for the purpose of preventing the sea overflowing certain meadows, contributed to the choking and decay of a harbour, the evidence of opinion of a celebrated engineer was allowed. Lord Mansfield C.J. (delivering the judgment of the court) said (p. 159): The question is, to what has this decay been owing.... That is matter of opinion; the whole case is a question of opinion, from facts agreed upon. Nobody can swear that it was the cause; nobody thought that it would produce this mischief when the bank was erected.... Mr. Smeaton is called.... It is objected that Mr. Smeaton is going to speak, not as to facts, but as to opinion. That opinion, however, is deduced from facts which are not disputed—the situation of banks, the course of tides and of winds, and the shifting of sands. His opinion deduced from all these facts, is, that, mathematically speaking, the bank may contribute to the mischief, but not sensibly. Mr. Smeaton understands the construction of harbours, the causes of their destruction, and how remedied. In matters of science no other witnesses can be called.... I cannot believe that where the question is, whether a defect arises from a natural or an artificial cause, the opinions of men of science are not to be received. Handwriting is proved every day by opinion; and for false evidence on such questions a man may be indicted for perjury....

Note.—The scope of evidence by experts in relation to patent cases has been described by the House of Lords as "the state of an art at a particular time and the meaning of any technical term used in connection therewith; whether any particular operation in connection with an art could be carried out and, generally, any explanation required as to facts of a scientific kind" (per Lord Tomlin in British Celanese Ltd. v. Courtaulds Ltd. (1935) 152 L.T. 537 at 543). Matters commonly made the subject of such evidence include causes of death, insanity, effects of poison, genuineness of works of art, value of articles, genuineness of handwriting, proper navigation of vessels, meaning of trade terms and foreign law.

In support of such evidence the witness may prove experiments, inspection and other acts upon which he bases his opinion, although they were made or done in the absence of the party (see R. v. Heseltine (1873) 12 Cox C.C. 404).

In a trial for murder it was held that a medical witness, who had not seen the body, might be asked whether, in his opinion, assuming the facts described by another witness who had seen the body to be true, the wounds could have been self-inflicted (R. v. Mason (1911) 7 Cr.App.R. 67 (C.C.A.)).

For various rules, which reduce controversy concerning matters of expertise and increase the usefulness of expert testimony, see R.S.C. Ord. 38, rr. 35–44 (Part Three, infra) made in accordance with the Civil Evidence Act 1972 s.2 (Part Two, infra). The general effect of these rules is that in civil cases parties wishing to call experts must apply to the court for leave to do so, and the court has power to order disclosure of an expert's report to the opposite party.

It is to be noted too that the Civil Evidence Act 1972, s.1 (Part Two, infra) enables hearsay evidence of opinion (including expert opinion) to be received in civil cases.

R. v. Oakley (1979) 70 Cr.App.R. 7; [1979] R.T.R. 417 (C.A.). The appellant had been convicted of causing death by dangerous driving contrary to the Road Traffic Act 1972, s.1(1). He had no recollection of the events, and there was no effective eye-witness. The prosecution called a police officer with 15 years' experience in the traffic division, who had attended a course on accident investigation, had passed the qualifying examination as an accident investigator and had attended more than 400 fatal road accidents. He gave evidence of his observations at the scene of the accident, produced a plan which he had prepared and gave expert evidence about his theories and conclusions. The accused appealed against conviction on the ground that the judge wrongly admitted that part of the police officer's testimony which related to his opinion as an expert. The appeal was dismissed, the Court of Appeal holding that a police officer may give opinion evidence as an expert to the extent that such evidence is within his expertise and is directed to the issues in the case. Whether a witness has kept within his expertise is a matter for the judge.

Note.—R. v. Oakley has been followed in R. v. Murphy [1980] 1 Q.B. 434 (C.A.), but is to be distinguished from the earlier case of Hinds v. London Transport Executive [1979] R.T.R. 103 (C.A.) where the Court of Appeal held that a consulting engineer's report, which ended with his opinion on the facts and his conclusions as to how a road accident occurred, should not be admitted. There Lord Denning M.R. said (p. 105): "Reading through the report, it is quite plain that it is merely giving arguments in favour of the plaintiff on the issues of negligence and causation and so forth. I cannot see that it contains any expert evidence at all. Some people try to call engineers in these cases but they are of no help to the court. They only give the arguments which counsel can give as well or better."

Foreign law, which in English courts is treated as a question of fact, is a subject upon which the opinion of experts is admissible, since competency to form an opinion thereon can only be acquired by study or experience. Although a question of fact, it is one which by statute is determinable by the judge and not the jury (Administration of Justice Act 1920, s.15; Supreme Court Act 1981, s.69(5); County Courts Act 1984, s.68 (all Part Two, *infra*).

Under the common law rule a person qualifies as an expert only if he has had practical experience in the country in question. This experience need not be as a qualified legal practitioner: for example a banker has been treated as an expert on foreign banking law (*de Beéche* v. *South American Stores, etc. Ltd.* [1935] A.C. 148 (H.L.); *Ajami* v. *Comptroller of Customs* [1954] 1 W.L.R. 1405 (P.C.)). Occasionally, however, expert testimony of a person without practical experience has been received (*Brailey* v. *Rhodesia Consolidated Ltd.* [1910] 2 Ch. 95); and in civil cases it is now provided by the Civil Evidence Act 1972, s.4(1) (Part Two, *infra*) that a person suitably qualified on account of his knowledge or experience may give evidence of foreign law. The section also re-affirms that the witness need not have acted, or be qualified to act, as a legal practitioner in the country in question.

R. v. **Silverlock** [1894] 2 Q.B. 766 (C.C.R.). In order to prove by comparison with admittedly genuine letters that an advertisement was in the handwriting of the accused, after objection the solicitor for the prosecution was allowed to be called as an expert. The solicitor testified that he had for the last ten years, and quite apart from his professional work, given considerable study and attention to handwriting and especially to old parish registers and wills; that he had on several occasions professionally compared handwriting, but had never before given evidence as to handwriting; also that he had formed an opinion that the defendant was guilty before he began to compare the handwriting. The prisoner was convicted, and the conviction was affirmed. Lord Russel of Killowen C.J. said (p. 771): "It is true that the witness who is called upon to give evidence founded on a comparison of handwriting must be *peritus*; he must be skilled in so doing; but we cannot say that he must have become *peritus*, but *peritus* in the way of his business, or in any definite way. The question is, is he *peritus*? Is he skilled? Has he an adequate knowledge? Looking at the matter practically, if a witness is not skilled the judge will tell the jury to disregard his evidence. There is no decision which requires that the evidence of a man who is skilled in comparing handwriting and has formed a reliable opinion from past experience, should be excluded because his experience has not been gained in the way of his business. It is, however, really unnecessary to consider this point; for it seems from the statement in the present case that the witness was not only *peritus*, but *peritus* in the way of business. When once it is determined that the evidence is admissible, the rest is merely a question of its value or weight, and this is entirely a question for the jury, who will attach more or less weight to it according as they believe the witness to be *peritus*.

Note.—The Criminal Procedure Act 1865, s.8 (Part Two, *infra*) contains statutory provision for the proof of handwriting by the comparison of the disputed writing with a specimen of genuine writing even by the evidence of non-experts or by the jury. But a comparison of documents by an ordinary witness is of little value, as indicated in the judgment above. In criminal cases tried with a jury there should be expert evidence with reference to a comparison of documents (*R.* v. *Harden* ([1963] 1 Q.B. 8 (C.C.A.)). See, too, *R.* v. *Smith* (1968) 52 Cr.App.R. 648 (C.A.)

An ordinary witness may prove handwriting with which he is familiar (*Doe* d. *Mudd* v.

Suckermore ((1837) 7 L.J.Q.B. 33, Chapter 24, *infra*) when a comparison of documents is not involved.

For a more recent case in which it has been emphasised that an expert can be qualified by skill and experience as an alternative to professional qualification, see *Longley (James) Ltd.* v. *South West Regional Health Authority* [1984] C.L.Y. 1519; (1983) 127 S.J. 597; 25 Build.L.R. 56.

R. v. **Holmes** [1953] 1 W.L.R. 686 (C.C.A.). The accused had been convicted of murder. He had unsuccessfully set up the defence of insanity. Both the doctor called for the prosecution and the doctor called for the defence had agreed that at the time of the trial, and probably earlier, he was suffering from a disease of the mind. At the trial the doctor called for the defence was asked in cross-examination whether in his opinion the conduct of the accused immediately after the murder would indicate that he knew (1) the nature of the act he was committing, or (2) that his act was contrary to law. The accused answered both questions in the affirmative. On his appeal against conviction it was held that this questioning had been proper. Lord Goddard C.J., giving the judgment of the Court, said (p. 688) that if such questioning were not permitted "it would put an insuperable difficulty in the way of the defence whenever they were trying to establish insanity."

Note.—On the admissibility of opinion evidence on the "ultimate issue" see too *R.* v. *Davies* [1962] 1 W.L.R. 1111 (C.-M.A.C.) (*supra*); *D.P.P.* v. *A. and B. C. Chewing Gum Ltd.* [1968] 1 Q.B. 159 (D.C.) (*supra*); the actual decision in *R.* v. *Smith (Stanley)* [1979] 1 W.L.R. 1445 (C.A.) (*supra*); *R.* v. *Lupien* [1970] S.C.R. 263 (S.C. Canada) (*supra*); the Civil Evidence Act 1972, s.3 (Part Two, *infra*).

For an interesting consideration of various matters relating to expert testimony, including the use of the hypothetical question technique for the avoidance of any altimate issue prohibition, see the judgment of the Ontario Court of Appeal in *R.* v. *Fisher* [1961] O.W.N. 94; 34 C.R. 320.

R. v. **Abadom** [1983] 1 W.L.R. 126 (C.A.). The accused had been convicted of a robbery which involved breaking a glass window pane. A principal scientific officer gave evidence at the trial that he had analysed fragments of glass from the broken window and fragments found in the appellant's shoes, and that he had found that they all had the same refractive index. He further testified that it was the practice of the Home Office Central Statistical Establishment to collate statistics of the refraction indices of broken glass which had been analysed in forensic laboratories, and that, having consulted those statistics, he had found that only 4 per cent. of the samples had the same refractive index as the fragments that he had analysed. He expressed the opinion that this was strong evidence that the fragments taken from the appellant's shoes had come from the broken window pane. The accused's appeal on the ground that the witness had been allowed to make use of inadmissible hearsay was dismissed. It was held that the witness could only give evidence of the refractive indices of the glass taken from the broken window and from the shoes that he himself had personally analysed, but once that basic fact had been established, he could not only draw on the work of others in forming the opinion, but it was an essential part of the function of an expert that he should take account of the work of others in his field of expertise. The witness had, therefore, properly drawn upon the statistical data compiled by the Home Office Central Research Establishment before forming his opinion.

Note.—See, too, *English Exporters (London) Ltd.* v. *Eldonwall Ltd.* [1973] Ch. 415 (Ch.D.); *City of St. John* v. *Irving Oil Ltd.* [1966] S.C.R. 581; 58 D.L.R. (2d.) 404 (S.C. Canada); *Ramsay* v. *Watson* (1961) 108 C.L.R. 642 (H.C. Australia).

R. v. **Bradshaw** (1986) 82 Cr.App.R. 79 (C.A.). The accused was convicted of murder. The only issue at the trial was diminished responsibility. He appealed against conviction on the ground that the judge had erred in ruling that the only appropriate course for the defence to take with a view to establishing this defence was to call the defendant himself to give evidence. The appeal on this ground was dismissed (see Chapter 8, *supra*), but the Court also considered a related matter, namely the extent to which this defence could be established by expert medical opinion involving reliance upon hearsay. Lord Lane C.J. said (p. 83): "Although as a concession to the defence doctors are sometimes allowed to base their opinions on what the defendant has told them (*i.e.* hearsay) without those matters being proved by admissible evidence, yet the strict (and correct) view is.... 'A doctor may not state what a patient told him about past symptoms as evidence of the existence of those symptoms because that would infringe the rule against hearsay, but he may give evidence of what the patient told him in order to explain the grounds on which he came to a conclusion with regard to the patient's condition.' Thus, if the doctor's opinion is based entirely on hearsay and is not supported by direct evidence, the judge will be justified in telling the jury that the defendant's case (if that is so) is based upon a flimsy or non-existent foundation and that they should reach their conclusion bearing that in mind."

Chapter 19

THE EVIDENTIAL SIGNIFICANCE OF EARLIER JUDICIAL FINDINGS: THE RETREAT FROM HOLLINGTON v. HEWTHORN

As was pointed out when considering the role of the doctrine of estoppel by record,[1] a judgment is conclusive as to the existence of the state of things which it brings about. But it does not follow this that the facts upon which the judgment was seemingly based cannot be disputed. Evidence that a person has been convicted of theft is conclusive as to the fact that he is a convicted person but not as to the fact that he stole. Similarly evidence that a person has been divorced, the judge having found adultery, is conclusive as to the termination of the marriage but not as to the fact of adultery. However, as has also been pointed out,[2] the parties to the earlier proceedings and those in privity with them will themselves often also be estopped from denying facts which formed the basis for the decision in those proceedings.

The present Chapter is concerned with a different matter; this is as to the extent (if at all) to which an earlier judgment is admissible in later proceedings as evidence of facts upon which it was seemingly founded even though the parties may not be the same. Common law doctrine on this matter was in 1943 revealed to the Court of Appeal in the heavily criticised case of *Hollington* v. *Hewthorn*.[3] The rule therein promulgated may be narrowly stated thus: evidence of a previous conviction is not admissible in subsequent civil proceedings to prove the facts upon which the conviction was based.[4] The Court's reasoning in *Hollington* v. *Hewthorn* was largely in terms of relevance, the view being taken that the previous conviction merely represented an opinion of the criminal court, and moreover an opinion based upon evidence unknown to the court trying the later civil action. Although there was surprisingly little authority on the point, it would seem that the philosophy of *Hollington* v. *Hewthorn* ought to be regarded as equally convincing or unconvincing when the subsequent proceedings are themselves also criminal. It would seem, too, that the same principle should also be applicable if the earlier finding was by a civil court, and *a fortiori* if it

---

[1] Chapter 6, *supra.*
[2] *Ibid.*
[3] [1943] K.B. 587.
[4] For the facts of *Hollington* v. *Hewthorn*, see *infra.*

was by a non-judicial tribunal. It was therefore surprising to find that the Court of Appeal had previously held in *Hill* v. *Clifford*,[5] a case seemingly not cited in *Hollington* v. *Hewthorn*, that a finding by the General Medical Council that a dentist had been guilty of professional misconduct was admissible as evidence of that misconduct in subsequent legal proceedings for the dissolution of the dentist's partnership. At the same time it would be contended that, even apart from the authority of *Hollington* v. *Hewthorn*, evidence of a previous acquittal, although of course admissible to show the fact of acquittal, should not be admissible to show innocence because, having regard to the rules relating to *quantum* of proof, the evidential significance of an acquittal is uncertain. Alternatively, it could, but for the analogy of *Hollington* v. *Hewthorn*, be argued that this consideration should go to weight and not admissibility.[6]

The rule in *Hollington* v. *Hewthorn* was itself abrogated by section 11 of the Civil Evidence Act 1968,[7] and the absence of any corresponding rule in relation to subsequent criminal proceedings has been established by section 74 of the Police and Criminal Evidence Act 1984.[8] Subsection 1 of each of these sections renders admissible what the rule had made inadmissible. Section 1(1) of the latter does not apply to convictions of the present accused. Otherwise, the rejection of the rule is in broad terms. No distinction is drawn between convictions following guilty pleas and those following not-guilty pleas, although their probative value may differ greatly. The latter represents a finding beyond reasonable doubt, whereas the former, particularly in the case of a trivial or technical offence, may indicate no more than the avoidance of trouble and expense.[9] Again no differentiation is made between convictions following trial by jury in a superior court and summary convictions. Moreover, the words of the subsections are mandatory: the evidence "shall be admissible."[10]

But each section does more than negative the rule in the sense of rendering admissible what under it was previously inadmissible; it shifts the legal burden of proof. Each provides by subsection 2 that a person proved to have been convicted of an offence "shall be taken to have committed that offence unless the contrary is provided."[11]

There has been some judicial disagreement as to whether the effect of section 1(2) of the 1968 Act is to do more than simply shift the legal

---

[5] [1907] 2 Ch. 236 (C.A.).

[6] In a pre-*Hollington* v. *Hewthorn* case, *Packer* v. *Clayton* (1932) 97 J.P. 14 (D.C.), Avory J. took the view that evidence of the respondent's acquittal of a sexual offence should have been admissible in subsequent affiliation proceedings.

[7] Part Two, *infra*.

[8] Part Two, *infra*.

[9] In civil cases the former plea of guilty might itself be admissible as an informal admission, but, of course, only subject to the safeguards governing the admissibility of such evidence. It is hard to see that the fact of conviction following such a plea has any appreciable *additional* probative worth.

[10] R.S.C., Ord. 18, r. 7A (Part Three, *infra*) requires a party to an action tried with pleadings to give particulars of the conviction and to indicate the issue to which he claims that it is relevant.

[11] Part Two, *infra*. It is to be observed that it is not enough to show that the conviction was unwarranted by the evidence adduced in the criminal case; it must be affirmatively shown that the crime was not in fact committed by the convicted person.

burden. As a matter of statutory interpretation it would seem unlikely; and Lord Denning M.R.'s contrary contention in *Stupple* v. *Royal Assurance Co.*[12] that the "conviction does not merely shift the burden of proof. It is a weighty piece of evidence in itself"[13] would be tantamount to the imposition upon the party asserting innocence a burden heavier than proof on balance of probabilities. This would constitute an unwarranted anomaly in a civil case.[14] One of the less unconvincing arguments in favour of the rule in *Hollington* v. *Hewthorn* was that to admit the evidence "for what it was worth" would be to involve the trier of fact in the impossible task of assessing the weight to be attached to a conviction based on evidence of which they had no knowledge. It would seem that the legislature has met this objection by specifying the effect of admission in terms, not of weight, but of the incidence of the legal burden of proof. An additional disadvantage of Lord Denning M.R.'s analysis is that it would resurrect the need to weigh the unknown.

Section 12 of the 1968 Act makes parallel statutory provision for the admissibility in subsequent civil proceedings of findings of adultery in prior matrimonial proceedings as evidence that the adultery was committed, and of findings of paternity in prior affiliation proceedings as evidence of actual paternity. As in the case of previous convictions the effect of admission is to shift the burden of proof.

Section 13 of the Civil Evidence Act 1968 deals with what the Law Reform Committee[15] and Parliament saw as a special case: the effect of a previous conviction in subsequent defamation proceedings. The Committee had taken the view that here the issue is not simply one of probative value and the efficiency of the fact-finding process in the later proceedings. A question of public policy arises: as a matter of substantive law no one ought to incur civil liability for having stated that another was in fact guilty of an offence of which he stood convicted. There must not be in effect a re-trial of a criminal case under the guise of a defamation action. Section 13 therefore provides that in defamation proceedings evidence of a previous conviction shall be conclusive evidence of guilt. This means that a defendant who has alleged that a plaintiff committed a crime has a complete defence in such proceedings if he can prove only that the plaintiff stands convicted of that crime. This position is not satisfactory. It is unjust that, even if the plaintiff can adduce overwhelming evidence of his innocence and even if that innocence was well-known to the defendant, he should be without redress unless he first successfully resorts to the often long, expensive, and difficult process of obtaining a pardon. Moreover, the danger against which section 13 was directed—the successful retrial of a criminal case under the guise of defamation proceedings—is in practice largely illusory, especially in the light of the shifting of the burden of proof effected by section 11. It will be rare for a plaintiff to be able to prove on balance of probabilities the contrary of what the Crown has already proved beyond reasonable doubt.[16] That is unless he did not in

---

[12] [1971] 1 Q.B. 50 (C.A.) *infra*.

[13] *Ibid.* p. 72 (C.A.).

[14] Contrast the clearly stated view of Buckley L.J., with which Winn L.J. seems to have agreed, and which is to be preferred.

[15] 15th Report (1967). Cmnd. 3391, paras. 26–33.

[16] But see *Hinds* v. *Sparks* [1964] Crim.L.R. 717 (*infra*), a case decided before the advantage of s.11 was available to the defendant.

fact commit the crime and his conviction was therefore wrong; and then that he had been wrongly convicted would be bad enough and it would add insult to injury to allow others to assert with impunity that he was rightly convicted.

It is interesting to contrast Parliament's rejection of the Law Reform Committee's concomitant recommendation that proof of an acquittal should be conclusive evidence of innocence in subsequent defamation proceedings. The fact of acquittal has limited probative significance, but it could be contended that as a matter of policy a person who has been acquitted ought to be immune from assertions that he was in fact guilty, even if the asserter can show on balance of probabilities that this is the case. This does smack of "re-trial" by journalist, and of "conviction" on something less than proof beyond reasonable doubt. But such seems to be the law[17] and it is not affected by the Act.

Section 1(3) of the Police and Criminal Evidence Act 1984 makes special provision for the case (excluded from the scope of subsections (1) and (2)), in which the previous conviction is of the accused himself. See the *General Note on section 74*, Part Two, *infra*.

It is to be noted that these statutory provisions do not ascribe evidentiary significance to earlier findings in civil courts (except in two cases[18]), to the findings of non-judicial tribunals[19] or to the findings of any foreign courts. Presumably the common law doctrine still obtains in these areas.

Hill v. **Clifford** [1907] 2 Ch. 236 (C.A.). Articles of partnership for practising as dentists between two persons named Clifford and the plaintiff provided that if a partner should be guilty of "professional misconduct" the other partner should be at liberty to determine the partnership. The General Medical Council, acting under the powers of the Dentists Act 1878, made an order directing the registrar to strike the Cliffords' names off the Register of Dentists on the ground that they had been guilty of conduct "which was infamous or disgraceful in a professional respect" within the terms of the Act. The plaintiff then gave notice determining the partnership. A question for determination by the Court of Appeal was the validity of this notice. A majority of the Court (Cozens-Hardy M.R. and Buckley L.J.) held that the order was admissible as prima facie evidence of the fact that the Cliffords had in fact been guilty of acts "infamous or disgraceful in a professional sense," and that, there being no rebutting evidence, that fact was proved.

Note.—See, too *Harvey* v. *R.* [1901] A.C. 601 (P.C.).

Hollington v. **Hewthorn** [1943] K.B. 587 (C.A). There was a collision between two cars on the highway in which the plaintiff's car was damaged. The two drivers were the only eye-witnesses. The driver of the defendant's car was convicted in a magistrates' court for the summary offence of careless driving. The plaintiff, who had not himself been involved in the accident, subsequently brought a civil action for negligence against the defendant and his convicted driver. But before the civil action came on for hearing the plaintiff's driver died. The plaintiff, deprived of his

---

[17] *Loughrans* v. *Odhams Press* [1963] C. L.Y. 2007; *The Times*, February 14, 1963 (*infra*).
[18] See the Civil Evidence Act 1968, s.12.
[19] See *Hill* v. *Clifford* (*infra*).

only witness, sought to put in evidence the conviction of the defendant driver to establish a prima facie case of negligence against him. The Court of Appeal held the conviction to be inadmissible in the civil action; and, the defendant calling no evidence, the plaintiff's action failed for want of any admissible evidence of the defendant driver's negligence.

Sutton v. **Sutton** [1970] 1 W.L.R. 183 (P.D.). After being divorced the parties had re-married each other in 1955, but in 1963 the husband left his wife, and a few months later the woman named joined him. The husband and the woman named petitioned for divorce on the ground of her adultery with, amongst others, the husband, and in 1966 in a defended suit Cairns J. found the adultery with the husband proved, expressly rejecting the contention that the woman named was only the husband's housekeeper. Subsequently the instant proceedings were brought by the wife who sought a divorce on the grounds of her husband's desertion and adultery with the woman named. Brandon J. held that the effect of the Civil Evidence Act 1968, s.12, was to place upon the respondent husband and the woman named the burden of disproving the adultery to which the finding of Cairns J. related. The learned judge said (p. 187): "As regards the standard of proof, it seems to me that in so far as there is a burden on the husband and Mrs. Gilchrist [the woman named] to disprove adultery, they have only to discharge that burden on a balance of probability. I think it would be wrong to construe section 12 as putting upon them a higher burden, for example, the burden of disproving adultery beyond reasonable doubt." Holding that they had not disproved adultery on balance of probability, he made a finding of adultery against them.

Taylor v. **Taylor** [1970] 1 W.L.R. 1148 (C.A.). A wife petitioned for divorce on the ground of her husband's adultery, alleging incest with their 14-year-old daughter for which he had been convicted in 1962. The husband denied adultery and cross-prayed for a divorce on the grounds of the wife's adultery. At the hearing the Commissioner found that the husband had been wrongly convicted of incest and dismissed the wife's petition. He granted the husband a decree nisi of divorce on the ground of the wife's adultery. The Court of Appeal held, however, that the Commissioner was wrong in holding that the husband had discharged the burden of proof under the Civil Evidence Act 1968, s.11, and that the wife was accordingly entitled to a finding that the husband had committed adultery. Davies L.J., delivering the leading judgment, said (p. 1152) of section 11: "That section obviously, on contradistinction to section 13 of the same Act, which deals with the effect of convictions when they fall to be considered in an action of defamation, means that the onus of proof of upsetting the previous conviction is on the person who seems to do so. It is probable, though I do not want to make any particular pronunciamento about it at the moment, that that is an onus of proof on balance of probabilities. But, having said that, it nevertheless is obvious that, when a man has been convicted by 12 of his fellow countrymen and countrywomen at a criminal trial, the verdict of the jury is a matter which is entitled to very great weight when the convicted person is seeking, in the words of the statute, to prove the contrary."

Note.—For another aspect of this case see pp. 378–379, *supra.*

STUPPLE v. ROYAL INSURANCE CO. LTD.

[1971] 1 Q.B. 50; [1970] 3 All E.R. 230; [1970] 2 Lloyd's Rep. 127 (C.A.: 1970)

The effect of the Civil Evidence Act 1968, section 11(2)(a) is to shift the legal burden of proof.

The plaintiff had been convicted of robbing a bank. The bank had been indemnified by the defendants. A sum of money found in the plaintiff's possession had been paid over to the defendants under the Police (Property) Act 1897. The plaintiff claimed this money, and the defendants counter-claimed for the balance of the indemnity. The plaintiff sought to show that he was not guilty of the robbery. The trial judge, Paull J., gave judgment for the defendants on the claim and the counterclaim, although he said that he would have taken a different view from that of the jury at the criminal trial had he been sitting as a juryman. The plaintiff's appeal to the Court of Appeal was dismissed.

LORD DENNING M.R.: . . . Mr Hawser, for Mr. Stupple, submitted that the only effect of the [Civil Evidence] Act was to shift the burden of proof. He said that, whereas previously the conviction was not admissible in evidence at all, now it was admissible in evidence, but the effect was simply to put on the man the burden of showing, on the balance of probabilities, that he was innocent. He claimed that Mr. Stupple had done so.

I do not accept Mr. Hawser's submission. I think that the conviction does not merely shift the burden of proof. It is a weighty piece of evidence of itself. . . .

. . . .

In my opinion, therefore, the weight to be given to a previous conviction is essentially for the judge at the civil trial. Just as he has to evaluate the oral evidence of a witness, so he should evaluate the probative force of a conviction.

. . . .

I regard the conviction of Stupple in these circumstances, after a four-and-a-half weeks trial, by a jury who were unanimous, as entitled to great weight in this civil action. . . .

WINN L.J.: . . . In my opinion the judge was right to hold that this enactment meant that, unless the defendant proved on a balance of probability, *viz.*, by a civil standard of proof, that he was innocent, he must be treated for all relevant purposes as having committed the offence of which he was convicted. I do not myself think that it was any requisite, or, indeed, any proper, part of the function of the judge to consider what view he himself might have taken of the case had he sat on it either as juryman or judge: nor was it on a correct view relevant to his decision whether there had been an unsuccessful application to the Court of Appeal for leave to appeal against the conviction. . . .

BUCKLEY L.J.: If, before 1968, A. sued B. for an act of B.'s of which B. had earlier been convicted in criminal proceedings, evidence of B.'s conviction was inadmissible in A.'s action. It merely demonstrated that another court had, on the material and arguments before it, concluded that B. was guilty of the act with which he was charged in the criminal proceedings. It did not prove any of the matters proved in the criminal proceedings, nor anything which A. would need to prove to make good his civil claim. Proof of B.'s conviction was accordingly irrelevant to A.'s action, and so was inadmissible: *Hollington* v. *F. Hewthorn & Co. Ltd.* [1943] 1 K.B. 587.

The Civil Evidence Act, 1968, has changed this. Section 11(1) makes proof of B.'s conviction admissible in evidence for the purpose of proving that B. did the act of which he has been convicted. If section 11(1) stood alone it would be clear that proof of the conviction would be some evidence of B.'s act: it would not be clear what weight it should be given. Under section 11(2)(a) however, if in A.'s action B. is proved to have been convicted he is to be taken to have committed the offence of which he was convicted unless the contrary is shown. The effect of proof of the conviction under this subsection is, as my Lord, the Master of the Rolls, has said, to shift the "legal" burden of proof in respect of B.'s act or alleged act from A., who would otherwise have to prove it to make good his claim, to B., who must disprove it to avoid the presumption of his having committed the offence prevailing. Once the conviction has been proved the task of the court, instead of being, as would otherwise be the case, to decide whether A. has successfully shown that on a balance of probability B. did the act, becomes to decide whether B. has successfully shown that, on a balance of probability, he did *not* do the act.

The judge in the present case rightly recognised that this was his function.

There remains, however, the problem of what weight, if any, should be accorded to the proved fact of conviction in deciding whether any other evidence adduced is sufficient to discharge the onus resting on B. In my judgment no weight is in this respect to be given to the mere fact of conviction.

If, as seems to be the case, I differ from Lord Denning M.R. in this respect, I do so with the greatest diffidence.

The effect of the bare proof of conviction is, I think, spent in bringing section 11(2)(a) into play. But very much weight may have to be given to such circumstances of the criminal proceedings as are brought out in the evidence in the civil action. Witnesses called in the civil proceedings may give different evidence from that which they gave in the criminal proceedings. Witnesses may be called in the civil proceedings who might have been but were not called in the criminal proceedings, or vice versa. The judge may feel that he should take account of the fact that the judge or jury in the criminal proceedings disbelieved a witness who is called in the civil proceedings or that the defendant pleaded guilty or not guilty, as the case may be. Many examples could be suggested of ways in which what occurred or did not occur in the criminal proceedings may have a bearing on the judge's decision in the civil proceedings: but the judge's duty in the civil proceedings is still to decide that case on the evidence adduced to him. He is not concerned with the evidence in the criminal proceedings except so far as it is reproduced in the evidence called before him, or is made evidence in the civil proceedings under the Civil Evidence Act, 1968, section 2, or is established before him in cross-examination. He is not concerned with the propriety of the conviction except so far as his view of the evidence before him may lead him incidentally to the conclusion that the conviction was justified or is open to criticism: but even if it does so, this must be a consequence of his decision and cannot be a reason for it. The propriety or otherwise of the conviction is irrelevant to the steps leading to his decision.

It was suggested in argument that so to view section 11 would result in the issues in the criminal proceedings being retried in the civil proceedings, and that this would be contrary to an intention on the part of the legislature to avoid this sort of duplication.

I do not myself think that this would be the result in most cases, and I do not discern any such general intention in the section. If the fact of conviction were meant to carry some weight in determining whether the convicted man has successfully discharged the onus under section 11(2)(a) of proving that he did not commit the offence, what weight should it carry? I cannot accept that this should depend on such considerations as, for instance, the status of the court which convicted, or whether the decision was unanimous or a majority verdict of a jury. I cannot discover any measure of the weight which the unexplored fact of conviction should carry. Although the section has made proof of conviction admissible and has given proof of conviction a particular statutory effect under section 11(2)(a), it remains, I think, as true today as before the Act that mere proof of conviction proves nothing relevant to the plaintiff's claim, and it clearly cannot be intended to shut out or, I think, to mitigate the effect of any evidence tending to show that the convicted person did not commit the offence. In my judgment, proof of conviction under this section gives rise to the statutory presumption laid down in section 11(2)(a), which, like any other presumption, will give way to evidence establishing the contrary on the balance of probability, without itself affording any evidential weight to be taken into account in determining whether that onus has been discharged.

With respect to the judge, I think that he was unnecessarily alarmed at the possibility of his reaching a different conclusion from the conclusion reached at the criminal trial, where both the burden of proof and the standard of proof differed from those in the action, and by the Court of Criminal Appeal. The conclusion which he did reach was one which, I think, was clearly open to him on the evidence before him, and I see no reason to disturb it.

Note.—For a more emphatic expression of Lord Denning M.R.'s somewhat idiosyncratic view as to the effect of section 11, see a later dictum in *McIlkenny* v. *Chief Constable* [1980] 1 Q.B. 283 (C.A.) (a case on estoppel which went to the House of Lords *sub nom. Hunter* v. *Chief Constable of the West Midlands Police* [1982] A.C. 529 (Chapter 6, *supra*)). Lord Denning said (p. 320) of the wording of section 11(2)(a): "How is a convicted man to prove 'the contrary?' That is, how is he to prove that he did not commit the offence? How is he to prove that he was innocent? Only, I suggest, by proving that the conviction was obtained by fraud or collusion, or by adducing fresh evidence. If the fresh evidence is inconclusive, he does not prove his innocence. It must be decisive, it must be conclusive, before he can be declared innocent."

Re Raphael [1973] 1 W.L.R. 998 (Ch.D.). The plaintiff applied to the court to pronounce against a purported will made by her deceased husband and alleged to be a forgery. The first named defendant, one of the two executors, had been convicted of forging the will. The certificate of conviction bore a notation showing that an appeal against the conviction was pending, but the grounds of appeal were not stated. Goulding J. held that, although the certificate was proof of a subsisting conviction for the purposes of the Civil Evidence Act 1968, s.11, proceedings would be adjourned until either the first defendant's appeal had been heard or the plaintiff was able to prove her case by other evidence. Goulding J. said (pp. 1001–1002): "Parliament cannot have intended that civil proceedings should be finally disposed of in reliance on a conviction subsequently liable to be quashed. The injustice of such a situation is especially apparent in relation to section 13 of the Act, whereunder proof of conviction is in actions for libel or slander not merely admissible, but conclusive, evidence of the offence. Why then does the statute not make special provision for the case? The answer, I think, may be twofold. First, it must be comparatively rare for a civil action to come to trial before criminal proceedings arising out of the same facts are disposed of, certainly in the class of personal injury cases which had notoriously drawn attention to the need for a change of law. Secondly, the legislature was well aware that civil courts have power to adjourn a trial when it is expedient in the interest of justice. It probably assumed that where possible injustice might otherwise result the hearing of the civil action would always be adjourned until after the determination of the criminal appeal."

Hinds v. **Sparks** [1964] Crim.L.R. 717; *The Times*, July 28 and 30, 1964. The plaintiff had been convicted of robbery and his conviction had been upheld by the Court of Criminal Appeal. Some years later he brought an action for libel against the defendant who had published a statement that he was guilty of the robbery of which he had been convicted. The defendant, upon whom, as the law as it then stood, the burden lay of proving that the plaintiff had in fact committed the robbery rested, failed to discharge it, and the plaintiff's action therefore succeeded. The defendant was in other words not able to show on balance probabilities what had already been proved beyond reasonable doubt.

Note.—This case would now be decided differently by virtue of the Civil Evidence Act 1968, s.13. Moreover, even without the absolute protection of that section, the defendant would now have had the advantage of s.11, which would have placed the burden of proof upon the plaintiff.

Loughrans v. **Odhams Press** [1963] C.L.Y. 2007 (Q.B.D.); *The Times*, February 14, 1963. The plaintiff had been acquitted of murder. Twenty years later he brought an action for libel against the defendants who had published a statement suggesting that he had in fact committed the murder of which he had been acquitted. The defendants successfully pleaded the defence of justification by proving on balance of probabilities that the plaintiff had been guilty.

Note.—There is no logical inconsistency in the defendant being able to prove to the civil standard what the prosecution had previously failed to prove to the higher criminal standard. But the position is open to criticism on policy grounds (see introduction to this chapter, *supra*).

Chapter 20

EVIDENCE OF DISPOSITION: SIMILAR FACTS

LEOPARDS may not change their spots, but there are acknowledged to be dangers in giving a dog a bad name. Many human beings are in many ways creatures of habit; but, if unduly heavy reliance is placed upon this generalisation by a trier of fact when determining whether a particular human being did in fact behave in a particular way on a particular occasion, serious injustice is liable to result. It is this consideration that constitutes the principal reason for the severe restrictions which the law places upon the reception of evidence of disposition.

The term "disposition" in this context denotes a tendency to behave— that is to say, to act, think or feel—in a certain way. Evidence of disposition may usefully be classified thus. (1) Evidence that a person has behaved on other occasions in the way in which he is alleged to have behaved on the instant occasion. Such evidence is traditionally designated "similar fact evidence," and selected materials relating to it are set out in the present Chapter. (2) Evidence of previous convictions, for which see Chapter 21. (3) Evidence of a person's general disposition (as distinct from specific examples of his actual behaviour) tendered to show that he did behave in the way in which he is said to have behaved, on the instant occasion. (4) Evidence that he has a reputation for that sort of behaviour. These two last-mentioned categories of evidence of disposition are usually subsumed under the heading of character evidence; materials relating to them are set out in Chapter 22. The reception or exclusion of evidence of the disposition of an accused person, when testifying as a witness in his own defence in criminal proceedings, poses special problems. The aim of provisos (e) and (f) to section 1 of the Criminal Evidence Act 1898 is to resolve those problems. Materials relating to these statutory provisions are set out in Chapter 23.

The problem with which the materials set out in the present Chapter are concerned—that of the admissibility of similar fact evidence—most frequently arises in criminal cases when such evidence is tendered on behalf of the prosecution. Very occasionally such evidence may be tendered by the defence or by a co-accused, and from time to time a question as to the admissibility of similar fact evidence may arise in civil litigation. A few cases concerned with some of these relatively infrequent situations are set out at the end of the Chapter, but the bulk of it is devoted to cases concerned with the admissibility of similar fact evidence tendered by the Crown in the criminal context.

Put in very broad terms this central problem is as to the admissibility of evidence showing or tending to show that on one or more other occasions the accused has behaved in a way similar to that in which the prosecution alleges that he behaved on the occasion to which the instant charge relates. The behaviour on the other occasion or occasions may or may not have led to a criminal conviction: but the disputed evidence is of the behaviour not of the conviction.[1] The other occasion or occasions are likely to be past but they may be more or less contemporaneous with, or even subsequent to, the occasion to which the charge relates. The Crown's objective in tendering the similar fact evidence is, of course, to make it more likely that the accused will be convicted on the present charge.

This is an area of the law of evidence in which over the decades an enormous bulk of authority has accumulated. In a collection of materials such as this book it would be impossible to do justice to this mass (or to do injustice to this morass) of case law. Ironically, despite the wealth[2] of authority, it is an area in which great uncertainty and confusion persists. In these circumstances resort has been had in this Chapter to an approach different from that adopted elsewhere and to a different arrangement of materials, the selection of which has inevitably been exceptionally arbitrary. The excerpts from cases concerned with similar fact evidence tendered by the prosecution in criminal cases are mostly set out in simple chronological sequence; although, in the *Notes* there are some backward and forward references. Excerpts from three civil cases are included at the end of the Chapter. The rest of this Introduction summarises the author's personal analysis of the present law and should be treated by the reader with an appropriate measure of reserve.[3] This analysis should be read in conjunction with the materials and the *Notes* thereon: for the avoidance of repetition there is considerable forward reference to them.

Although in the leading and perhaps watershed case of *Director of Public Prosecutions* v. *Boardman*[4] (*infra*) Lord Wilberforce, speaking of similar fact evidence, did say, "Questions of this kind arise in a number of different contexts and have, correspondingly, to be resolved in different ways"; his Lordship immediately went on to "think it desirable to confine ourselves to the present set of facts, and to situations of a similar character."[5] Historically the problem of the admissibility of similar fact evidence has been formulated in broad and general terms. This has reflected an assumption that it involves a single question inviting a single, if not necessarily simple, answer. This assumption may be a major cause both of the apparent intractability of the problem and of the actual uncertainty surrounding its resolution. The present thesis is that there are some four different types of case, or rather types of context, in which the problems can arise, and that each merits separate treatment. However, before attempting to identify these different manifestations, reference must be made to a threshold question—that of relevance. It is trite learning that irrelevant evidence of whatever sort cannot be received. Sometimes, however, courts have allowed them-

---

[1] For the position relating to evidence of previous convictions see Chap. 21, *infra*.
[2] The term is used loosely: it does not necessarily connote value.
[3] See, too, Carter, *Forbidden Reasoning Permissible: Similar Fact Evidence a Decade after Boardman*, (1985) 48 M.L.R. 29.
[4] [1975] A.C. 421 (H.L.).
[5] *Ibid*. pp. 442–443.

selves to become enmeshed in the intricacies of the similar fact rule prematurely and unnecessarily: these are cases in which, even if there were no similar fact rule, the disputed evidence would be rejected for lack of probative bearing upon a contested issue. A perfect illustration of this is provided by the facts of the Canadian case of *Leblanc* v. *R.*[6] (*infra*). There the only real dispute was as to whether the admitted behaviour of the accused amounted to culpable negligence. The disputed evidence was of his similar behaviour on other occasions. A majority of the Supreme Court held this evidence to be admissible within the framework of the similar fact rule. The perceptive minority, however, took the view that the evidence should have been rejected on the short ground that it had no probative bearing upon any issue that was in dispute. A slightly less obvious, but highly authoritative, example of the rejection of similar fact evidence on the same score is provided by the House of Lords case of *Harris* v. *Director of Public Prosecutions*[7] (*infra*). There the accused's conviction was quashed because the judge had failed to direct the jury to disregard evidence suggesting that the accused *might* have committed seven other offences (with which he was also charged but of which in the event he was acquitted) when considering his guilt of an eighth offence of which he was convicted, unless they believed that he had perpetrated the first seven offences. Absent such a finding, the similar "fact" evidence was in reality similar unproved allegation evidence: in the words of Viscount Simon, "the fact that someone perpetrated the earlier thefts when the accused may have been somewhere in the market does not provide material confirmation of his identity as the thief on the last occasion."[8]

Four differing, but sometimes overlapping, contexts in which the problem of the admissibility of relevant similar fact evidence may arise are as follows.

A. The classic similar fact situation. This is the situation in which the disputed evidence takes the form of what is often called propensity evidence. It is evidence indicating that the accused has on other occasions actually behaved in the way in which he is alleged to have behaved on the current occasion. It is evidence the adduction of which is likely to induce in the minds of the jury the belief that the accused has a propensity or tendency to behave in that way and for this reason is more likely to have behaved in that way on the instant occasion. This type of reasoning is prejudicial and unfair, because it does not make due allowance for the possibility of the accused having mended his ways temporarily or permanently. The term "prejudice" here denotes a specifically identifiable phenomenon, namely the discrepancy between true probative worth and the probative significance likely to be ascribed to evidence. What is important is not simply logical analysis: what is crucially involved is assessment of the way in which the mind of the jury is actually likely to operate at conscious and sub-conscious levels. It is against this, as Lord Hailsham has called it, "the forbidden type of

---

[6] (1976) 68 D.L.R. (2d) 243.

[7] [1952] A.C. 694.

[8] The case may be contrasted with *R.* v. *Mansfield* (1977) 65 Cr.App.R. 276 (C.A.), *infra*, but compared with *R.* v. *Tricoglus* (1977) 65 Cr.App.R. 16 (C.A.) referred to in the *Note* (*infra*) to *R.* v. *Mansfield*.

reasoning,"[9] that the first part of Lord Herschell's oft and over cited words in *Makin* v. *Attorney-General for New South Wales*[10] (*infra*) are directed. Lord Herschell said "It is undoubtedly not competent for the prosecution to adduce evidence tending to show that the accused has been guilty of criminal acts other than those covered by the indictment for the purpose of leading to the conclusion that the accused is a person likely from his criminal conduct or character to have committed the offence for which he is being tried."[11] A typical illustration of the rejection of such evidence is to be seen in *Noor Mohamed* v. *R.*,[12] (*infra*). Lord Herschell stated a general rule which is both well established and soundly based, but it does not and should not follow that it is to be indiscriminately applied in all cases. There can come a point where the true probative value of an item or pattern of similar fact evidence seems so great as adequately to underpin and justify the significance that a jury is likely to attach to it. Over the decades the judges have been curiously but consistently coy about stating this explicitly, although in *Boardman's* case there are dicta, particularly of Lord Wilberforce and Lord Cross in which the point is virtually conceded.[13] But traditionally the explanation of the admissibility of such evidence has almost invariably been in terms of the particular issue to which the evidence was relevant; for example it has been variously admitted to show *mens rea*, to prove identity, to show that the accused's purpose was not innocent, etc.[14] The inadequacy of this sort of purported justification for admissibility is that it disregards the basic point that propensity evidence is objectionable not for what it proves but for the way in which it proves it. Decisions such as those in *R.* v. *Ball*,[15] *Thompson* v. *R.*,[16] *R.* v. *Armstrong*[17] and *R.* v. *Straffen*[18] (all *infra*) are not convincingly explicable except on the basis that similar fact evidence is sometimes admissible even though, whatever its purported justification, it is virtually certain that the jury will use it in the way which Lord Herschell forbade. Nor is this unreasonable: if real probative worth completely underwrites any reasonably likely prejudice, why exclude? Rationally the true test for the admissibility of propensity-type similar fact evidence should depend upon its true probative worth. The matter then becomes one of degree, but the test should remain a very stern one. The courts should be constantly mindful of the force of the words of Kennedy J. in *R.* v. *Bond*[19]: "Nothing can so certainly be counted upon to make a prejudice against an accused upon his trial as the disclosure to the jury of other misconduct of a kind similar to that which is the subject of the indictment, and, indeed, when the crime

---

[9] *Boardman* v. *Director of Public Prosecutions* [1975] A.C. 421, 453.
[10] [1894] A.C. 57 (P.C.).
[11] *Ibid.* p. 65.
[12] [1949] A.C. 182 (P.C.).
[13] See, too, Scarman L.J. delivering the judgment of the Court of Appeal in *R.* v. *Scarrott* [1978] Q.B. 1016 (*infra*).
[14] At other times similar fact evidence has been admitted on a different type of pretext, namely in order to "show system." But a system is little more than a specific, consistently practised and well-organised propensity.
[15] [1911] A.C. 47 (H.L.).
[16] [1918] A.C. 221 (H.L.).
[17] [1922] 2 K.B. 555 (C.A.).
[18] [1952] 2 Q.B. 911 (P.C.).
[19] [1906] 2 K.B. 389, 395–396 (C.C.R.), *infra*.

alleged is one of a revolting character, such as the charge against Bond
in the present case, and the hearer is a person who has not been trained
to think judicially, the prejudice must sometimes be almost insurmount-
able." In assessing true probative worth the nature of the issue upon
which it bears will, of course, often be a factor to take into account, but
not itself the sole criterion. So, too, the degree of similarity, the
importance of which is heavily emphasised in the *Boardman* case,
should be seen as a factor affecting, rather than a criterion determining,
probative work. There are many other factors which may fall to be
considered as well. How firmly established are the similar facts? How
well do they establish the propensity? How often have they occurred?
How regularly? How recently? Are they acts intrinsically likely to be
repeated? Is the propensity continuing or intermittent? etc., etc.

   B. Similar fact evidence can be admitted if it has substantial probative
value in a way which does not depend upon the forbidden type of
reasoning. It is with this that the latter part of Lord Herschell's famous
dictum in *Makin* v. *Attorney-General for New South Wales* was (albeit
perhaps infelicitously formulated) probably largely concerned. Distinguishing the exclusion of "evidence tending to show that the accused has
been guilty of criminal acts other than those covered by the indictment,
for the purpose of leading to the conclusion that the accused is a person
likely from his criminal conduct or character to have committed the
offence for which he is being tried," the Lord Chancellor continued:
"On the other hand, the mere fact that the evidence adduced tends to
show the commission of other crimes does not render it inadmissible if it
be relevant to an issue before the jury, and it may be so relevant if it
bears upon the question whether the acts alleged to constitute the crime
charged in the indictment were designed or accidental, or to rebut a
defence which would otherwise be open to the accused." The words "if
it be relevant to an issue before the jury," if left unqualified, would in
effect deprive the exclusionary rule of substance, for no evidence is
admissible unless it is relevant to an issue before the trier of fact. It is,
however, not unreasonable to suppose that these words were intended
to refer only to evidence the relevance of which does not necessarily
involve what has now been dubbed the "forbidden type of reasoning"
and which for convenience can be referred to simply as the forbidden
reasoning.
   Simple illustrations of admissibility of evidence of this sort are
provided by cases of what may be termed specific or particular
relevance. Suppose, for example, that an accused is charged with theft,
it being part of the prosecution case that he knew the key to a
combination lock. Evidence of the fact that he had previously stolen the
victim's diary containing a record of that key would be admissible, not
to show that the accused was in the habit of stealing, but to show that
he knew the key. Suppose again that an accused is charged with stealing
one part of a ten-pound note that has been torn in half. Evidence that
he had previously stolen the other part of the note would surely be
admissible to show that he had a particular interest in acquiring the first
part, and not to show that he had a predilection for the acquisition of
mutilated bank notes. The Canadian case of *R.* v. *Ducsharm*[20] (*infra*)
provides a further illustration of this type of admissibility. Again, similar

---

[20] [1956] 1 D.L.R. 732 (Ont. C.A.), *infra*.

fact evidence may be admissible on grounds reminiscent of the *res gestae* justification for the reception of hearsay evidence: the similar fact evidence is admitted on the ground that it forms an essential "part of the story." The term *"res gestae"* may, or may not, be used. Examples are provided by *R. v. Salisbury*[21] (*infra*) and the Australian case of *O'Leary v. R.*[22]

In many of the cases in this somewhat miscellaneous category the disputed evidence may in addition have some relevance in a way involving resort to the forbidden reasoning, but the consequential dangers are seen as being offset by the need to admit the evidence on other grounds. It is, however, important that the jury be directed in the clearest terms with regard to the specific and limited way in which the evidence may be used.

C. Important examples of the reception of evidence that has substantial relevance in a way not involving resort to the forbidden reasoning are to be found in situations in which the disputed evidence does not establish that the accused has behaved in a similar way on any other particular occasion, but rather indicates the repetition of a pattern of similar events which is unlikely to have resulted from coincidence. It is with this type of situation that Lord Herschell's concluding words seem to have been concerned: his Lordship said " . . . it may be so relevant if it bears upon the question whether the acts alleged to constitute the crime charged in the indictment were *designed or accidental, or to rebut a defence which would otherwise be open to the accused.*"[23] This type of situation was exemplified by the facts of *Makin's* case itself, by those of *R. v. Smith*[24] (*infra*) and by those of the civil case of *Mood Music Publishing Company v. de Wolfe*[25] (*infra*). The essence of the situation is that a defence or explanation has been, or is clearly going to be, put forward, which when viewed in isolation appears distinctly plausible, but which, if seen in the chronological context of similar patterns of events, becomes markedly implausible. When so viewed the defence or explanation ceases to be in any real sense "open" to the accused.

The value of this type of evidence does not depend upon any assumption that a defendant has not mended his ways: it rests upon the much more sure ground of the laws of chance. Assuming that the coincidence which the admission of the evidence would throw up is sufficiently marked, the matter becomes one not of admissibility but of weight. If this is substantial the evidence may safely be received—and this even though the jury may in fact, perhaps in a confused and partial way, use it as if it were propensity evidence. As Lord Herschell indicated, the "mere fact" that it tends to show the commission of other crimes does not render the evidence inadmissible.

D. Another type of so-called similar fact case is that in which the disputed evidence is of similar, but as yet unproved, allegations. It is a

---

[21] (1831) 5 C. & P. 155.
[22] (1946) 73 C.L.R. 566. See p. 354, *supra*.
[23] [1894] A.C. 57, at p. 65 (P.C.). Italics supplied.
[24] (1915) 11 Cr.App.R. 229 (C.C.A.).
[25] [1976] 1 Ch. 119 (C.A.). See, too, the succinct formulation by Neill L.J. in *Thorpe v. Chief Constable, Manchester* [1989] 1 W.L.R. 665, 674 (C.A.), p. 480, *infra*.

situation which is often presented when an application is being made on behalf of an accused, who is being charged on several counts, for separate trials in respect of counts involving separate but similar allegations. Whether such an application is to be granted is basically within the judge's discretion. In principle, however, it would seem that a judge ought not to refuse the application unless *inter alia* he is satisfied that the evidence in respect of each such count would be admissible on the others. This was emphasised by Lord Wilberforce and Lord Cross in the *Boardman* case (*infra*): but see, now, the later Court of Appeal case *R.* v. *Glinchey*,[26] (*infra*). Looked at from the viewpoint of "the prohibited reasoning" the reception in these circumstances of this type of similar allegation evidence is liable to be exceptionally dangerous. It seldom has great true probative value and it is almost always prejudicial. Moreover looked at from this standpoint there is a further difficulty: the similar facts from which the propensity is to be inferred are themselves being established in part by reliance upon the facts to be implied from the propensity. There is thus an element of circular reasoning. Accordingly, any assumption, made for the purpose of dealing with an application for separate trials, that the evidence would be admissible, must depend upon quite different considerations. These considerations concern not the supposed propensities of the accused, but the reliability of prosecution witnesses. If different and independent witnesses are going to make similar allegations about the behaviour of the accused on different occasions, and if the defence must be that they are all lying or mistaken, the similar allegation evidence can be received in order to demonstrate the suggestion of improbable coincidence implicit in such a defence. It is objectively highly improbable that different and independent witnesses should all be lying or mistaken and should all be telling remarkably similar lies or making remarkably similar mistakes and all about the same man. The similar allegation evidence would then be available to indicate something, not about the accused's propensities, but rather about the credibility of the prosecution witnesses. The value of the evidence, and thus the likelihood of its admissibility, should be assessed within this framework. This sort of situation is somewhat specialised and obviously will not arise in all applications for separate trials, but it is illustrated by the case of *R.* v. *Sims*[27] (*infra*), as subsequently explained and expurgated.

Finally it may be mentioned that there are a few statutes which render similar fact evidence admissible in certain specific circumstances and for particular purposes. The most important of these enactments is the Theft Act 1968, s.27(3)(*a*).[28] This provides that where a person is proceeded against only for handling stolen goods and evidence has been given of the other ingredients of the offence "evidence that he has had in his possession, or has undertaken or assisted in the retention, removal, disposal or realisation of, stolen goods from any theft taking place not earlier than 12 months before the offence charged" shall be

---

[26] (1983) 78 Cr.App.R. 282.

[27] [1946] K.B. 531 (C.A.). See, too, *R.* v. *Scarrott* [1978] Q.B. 1016 (C.A.) (*infra*).

[28] Part Two, *infra* s.27(3)(*b*) deals correspondingly with evidence of previous convictions (Chap. 21, *infra*). See, too, the presumption that arises from the accused's possession of the property mentioned in the indictment shortly after the theft; Chapter 4, *supra*. See, too, the Official Secrets Act 1911, s.1(2), Part Two, *infra*.

admissible, but only for the purpose of proving that he knew or believed the goods to be stolen goods.

R. v. **Salisbury** (1831) 5 C. & P. 155. A postman was indicted for the larceny of a letter containing banknotes belonging to one, Cox. The prosecution case was that these notes had been inserted in another letter from which the original contents had previously been taken and they were traced to the possession of the accused. It was held that evidence of the interception of this other letter was admissible as going to proof of an essential link in the chain of events leading up to establishing the larceny of Cox's notes.

Note.—See, too, *e.g.* the following: (1) *R.* v. *Cobden* (1862) 3 F. & F. 833, where the accused jointly with others was charged with burglary, and evidence of other thefts on the night in question was held to be admissible because "the events of that night relating to those burglaries are so intermixed that it is impossible to separate them" (*per* Bramwell B.); (2) *O'Leary* v. *R.* (1946) 73 C.L.R. 566 (H.C. Australia), Chapter 15 *infra*; (3) *R.* v. *Ducsharm* [1956] 1 D.L.R. 732 (Ontario C.A.) *infra*; (4) *R.* v. *Asif* (1986) 82 Cr.App.R. 123 (C.A.), where it was held that, on a proper construction of the Finance Act 1972, s.38, a number of different similar offences can be indicted as one composite offence.

MAKIN v. ATTORNEY-GENERAL FOR NEW SOUTH WALES

[1894] A.C. 57; 63 L.J.P.C. 41; 69 L.T. 778; 6 R. 373 (P.C.: 1893)

Evidence of similar behaviour by an accused person on other occasions is generally inadmissible for the purpose of showing that he is therefore a person more likely to have committed the offence with which he is being charged. Such evidence may, however, be admissible if it is relevant in some other way.

The prisoners were charged with the murder of an infant child, which they had received from its mother for adoption on payment of a sum insufficient for its support. The child's body had been found buried in the garden of a house occupied by them. Evidence was held admissible that other children had been received by the prisoners on like terms, and that other children's bodies had been found buried in a similar manner in the gardens of other houses occupied by the prisoners. The ground upon which the Privy Council found this evidence to have been properly admitted seems to have been that the Crown, in the context of discharging its obligation to prove that the Makins had deliberately killed the child with whose murder they were charged, was entitled to rely upon evidence which served to negative the possibility that its death resulted from accident or natural causes.

LORD HERSCHELL L.C. (delivering the advice of the Board, which included LORDS WATSON, HALSBURY, ASHBOURNE, MACNAGHTEN, MORRIS and SHAND: ... The question which their Lordships had to determine was the admissibility of the evidence relating to the finding of other bodies, and to the fact that other children had been entrusted to the appellants.

In their Lordship's opinion the principles which must govern the decision of the case are clear, though the application of them is by no means free from difficulty. It is undoubtedly not competent for the prosecution to adduce evidence tending to show that the accused has been guilty of criminal acts other than those covered by the indictment, for the purpose of leading to the conclusion that the accused is a person likely from his criminal conduct or character to have committed the offence for which he is being tried. On the other hand, the mere fact that the evidence adduced tends to show the commission of other crimes does not render it inadmissible if it be relevant to an issue before the jury, and it may be so relevant if it bears upon the question whether the acts alleged to constitute the crime charged in the indictment were designed or accidental, or to rebut a defence which would otherwise be open to the accused. . . .

The leading authority relied on by the Crown was the case of *R.* v. *Geering* (1849) 18 L.J.M.C. 215, where on the trial of a prisoner for the murder of her husband by administering arsenic evidence was tendered, with the view of showing that two sons of the prisoner who had formed part of the same family, and for whom as well as for her husband the prisoner had cooked their food, had died of poison, the symptoms in all these cases being the same. The evidence was admitted by Pollock C.B., who tried the case; he held that it was admissible inasmuch as its tendency was to prove that the death of the husband was occasioned by arsenic, and was relevant to the question whether such taking was accidental or not. . . .

Under these circumstances [of the present case] their Lordships cannot see that it was irrelevant to the issue to be tried by the jury that several other infants had been received from their mothers on like representations, and upon payment of a sum inadequate for the support of the child for more than a very limited period, or that the bodies of infants had been found buried in a similar manner in the gardens of several houses occupied by the prisoners. . . .

R. v. **Bond** [1906] 2 K.B. 389 (C.C.R.). The accused, a medical practitioner, was convicted of unlawfully using instruments upon a woman named Jones with the intent to procure an abortion. The trial judge admitted the evidence of another woman, Taylor, to the effect that the accused had performed a similar operation on her with similar intent some nine months previously. In the course of her examination-in-chief Taylor further testified that the accused had subsequently told her that he had "put dozens of girls right." Both women had at the material times been living at the accused's house and were pregnant by him. The defence was that instruments had been used on Jones in the course of a lawful medical examination. The only real issue before the jury was as to intent. The Court for Crown Cases Reserved held by a majority of five to two that Taylor's evidence had been rightly admitted. Most of the majority judgments and the dissenting judgment of Lord Alverstone C.J. (with whom Ridley J. agreed) proceed on the assumption that for an item of similar fact evidence to be admissible it must be seen to fit into one of the several categories of relevance which constitute exceptions to Lord Herschell's first and exclusionary proposition. There is, however, an apparent lack of unanimity amongst the judges as to the particular category into which the disputed evidence in the instant case fell. It is variously regarded by some of them as "negativing accident or mistake," as "negativing innocence of intent" and as "proof of system." Some of the judges treat certain categories of relevance as overlapping, and A. T. Lawrence J. concluded (p. 425) that Taylor's evidence was trebly admissible—it showed that Jones's illness was the result "of design and not of accident," it showed "scheme or system" and it "tended to rebut the defence [the accused] set up of an innocent operation." The majority of their Lordships were also divided as to whether Taylor's evidence of her own experience with the accused would have been admissible had she not also testified as to what the accused had said to her about his having "put dozens of girls right."

Note.—Although it is likely that the evidence admitted in *R.* v. *Bond* (and perhaps even the evidence of Taylor's own experience standing by itself) would be admitted were the case to be decided today, the framework of reasoning within which the judgments were set has now been finally dismantled by the House of Lords in *Director of Public Prosecutions* v. *Boardman* [1975] A.C. 421 (*infra*). The notion that Lord Herschell's second and inclusionary proposition represents a miscellany of exceptions to his first proposition has been discarded. As Lord Hailsham put it (p. 452) in the *Boardman* case, the second proposition "is not an exception grafted on to the first. It is an independent proposition introduced by the words: 'On the other hand' and the two propositions together cover the entire field. If one applies the other does not." Whilst respectfully agreeing with this contemporary analysis of the relationship between Lord Herschell's two propositions, it is submitted that it has also to be acknowledged that evidence falling within the first (and therefore falling outside the second) proposition will sometimes be admitted if its true probative worth appears to be very great.

R. v. **Ball** [1911] A.C. 47 (H.L.). Two accused, brother and sister, were convicted of incest. The Court of Criminal Appeal had quashed the convictions on the ground that certain similar fact evidence had been wrongly admitted: it had not been properly admissible in the first instance and nothing had occurred in the conduct of the defence to render it admissible as evidence in rebuttal. The House of Lords reversed the order of the Court of Criminal Appeal. Lord Loreburn L.C. said (p. 71): " ... Certain evidence, which was obviously admissible, was given to establish that at all events there was ample opportunity for this offence, and that there were circumstances which, to say the least, were very suggestive of incest. Also these two persons lived together and occupied the same bedroom and the same bed. Further evidence was then tendered to show that these persons had previously carnally known each other and had a child in 1908. The object was to establish that they had a guilty passion towards each other, and that therefore the proper inference from their occupying the same bedroom and the same bed was an inference of guilt, or—which is the same thing in another way—that the defence of innocent living together as brother and sister ought to fail.... I consider that this evidence was clearly admissible on the issue that this crime was committed—not to prove the mens rea, as Darling J. considered, but to establish the guilty relations between the parties and the existence of a sexual passion between them as elements in proving that they had illicit connection in fact on or between the dates charged. Their passion for each other was as much evidence as was their presence together in bed of the fact that they had guilty relations with each other. My Lords, I agree that Courts ought to be very careful to preserve the time-honoured law of England, that you cannot convict a man of one crime by proving that he had committed some other crime; that, and all other safeguards of our criminal law, will be jealously guarded; but here I think the evidence went directly to prove the actual crime for which these parties were indicted."

Note.—Darling J., delivering the judgment of the Court of Criminal Appeal, had said ([1911] A.C. 47, 57): "If on the facts of this case an act of intercourse was proved, no question could arise as to the mens rea with which the act was done, for the statute forbids the act as in itself criminal. If without the admission of the disputed evidence the fact of the two accused persons occupying the same bed on the date or dates charged was insufficient proof that intercourse took place between them on that date or those dates, then the fact that intercourse took place between them on former occasions could only be tendered to show that they were persons likely to have intercourse on the particular dates—a ground on which evidence is not receivable. It would be tendering evidence of the former commission of similar acts, not to show the mens rea with which the act was committed, but to show the commission of the act itself. We are of opinion that such evidence is not receivable."

The Irish Court of Criminal Appeal in *The People (Attorney-General)* v. *Dempsey* [1961] I.R. 288, applying the principle of *R.* v. *Ball*, held admissible evidence of intercourse between a boy and a girl on several other occasions in order to show the nature of their relationship and thus to rebut the defence of its innocence. The accused was charged with having unlawful carnal knowledge of her on two particular occasions. However, in *R.* v. *Barry* (1986) 83 Cr.App.R. 7 in the English Court of Appeal, *R.* v. *Ball* was referred to (p. 10) as a "dubious authority." But contrast *R.* v. *Williams* (1987) 84 Cr.App.R. 299 (C.A.) (*infra*).

R. v. **Smith** (1915) 11 Cr.App.R. 229 (C.C.A.). The appellant was charged with the murder of a woman with whom he had recently gone through a bigamous marriage ceremony. She had been found dead in her bath. The accused, who stood to benefit financially from her death, had sought to show that it resulted from an epileptic fit. At the trial evidence was given that two other women had died on subsequent dates, that the appellant had gone through a form of marriage with each of these women, and that both had died in their baths in circumstances very similar to those surrounding the death of the victim in the instant case. In each case the accused again stood to benefit financially by the woman's death. The Court of Criminal Appeal held that this evidence had been rightly admitted. Counsel *arguendo* quoted the words of the trial judge to the jury: "And then comes in the purpose, and the only purpose, for which you are allowed to consider the evidence as to the other deaths. If you find an accident which benefits a person and you find that the person has been sufficiently fortunate to have that accident happen to him a number of times, benefiting him each time, you draw a very strong, frequently irresistible inference, that the occurrence of so many accidents benefiting him is such a coincidence that it cannot have happened unless it was design." Lord Reading C.J. then interjected (p. 233): "I think that puts it very accurately, and states exactly why the evidence is admissible."

THOMPSON v. R.

[1918] A.C. 221; 87 L.J.K.B. 478; 118 L.T. 418; 34 T.L.R. 204; 26 Cox 189 (H.L.: 1918)

Similar fact evidence may be admissible as tending to identify the accused as the perpetrator of the crime charged by showing that both possess certain markedly similar characteristic propensities.

The appellant was charged with having on March 16, 1917, committed acts of gross indecency with boys, contrary to the Criminal Law Amendment Act 1885, s.11. It was not disputed that the offences had been committed. The appellant's defence was that he was not the man and he adduced evidence of an alibi. It was proved that the man who committed the offence had made an appointment to meet the boys three days later at the time and place where the offence was committed, and that the appellant met the boys at the appointed time and place and gave them money. The prosecution tendered evidence that on this latter occasion, when the appellant was arrested, powder puffs were found in his possession and that a number of indecent photographs of boys were later found in his rooms. This evidence was admitted by the trial judge over defence objection, and the appellant was convicted. He appealed against conviction on the ground that this evidence had been improperly admitted. His appeal was dismissed by the Court of Criminal Appeal, as was his further appeal to the House of Lords.

LORD FINLAY L.C.: ... The whole question is as to the identity of the person who came to the spot on the 19th with the person who committed the acts on the 16th. What was done on the 16th shows that the person who did it was a person with abnormal propensities of this kind. The possession of the articles tends to show that the person who came on the 19th, the prisoner, had abnormal propensities of the same kind. The criminal of the 16th and the prisoner had this feature in common, and it appears to me that the evidence which is objected to afforded some evidence tending to show the probability of the truth of the boys' story as to identity.

In my opinion Lawrence J. was right in admitting the evidence, and this appeal should be dismissed.

LORD PARKER OF WADDINGTON: My Lords, I also have come to the conclusion, though with some hesitation, that the evidence in question was admissible. I think, however, that it was admissible on one ground only. The real issue was the identity of the accused with the man who committed the crime of March 16. If the abnormal propensity of the criminal of March 16, manifested by the nature of the crime and the appointment for its repetition, can be regarded as one of the indicia by which his identity can be established, the evidence is admissible as showing that the accused had the same abnormal propensity. For the reasons about to be explained by my noble and learned friend Lord Sumner, I have come to the conclusion that it may be so regarded. But it would, in my opinion, be wrong to treat your Lordships' decision in the present case as laying down any principle capable of general application.

LORD SUMNER: ... No one doubts that it does not tend to prove a man guilty of a particular crime to show that he is the kind of man who would commit a crime, or that he is generally disposed to crime and even to a particular crime; but, sometimes for one reason sometimes for another, evidence is admissible, notwithstanding that its general character is to show that the accused had in him the makings of a criminal, for example, in proving guilty knowledge, or intent, or system, or in rebutting an appearance of innocence which, unexplained, the facts might wear. In cases of coining, uttering, procuring abortion, demanding by menaces, false pretences, and sundry species of frauds such evidence is constantly and properly admitted. Before an issue can be said to be raised, which would permit the introduction of such evidence so obviously prejudicial to the accused, it must have been raised in substance if not in so many words, and the issue so raised must be one to which the prejudicial evidence is relevant. The mere theory that a plea of not guilty puts everything material in issue is not enough for this purpose. The prosecution cannot credit the accused with fancy defences in order to rebut them at the outset with some damning piece of prejudice.... In the present case, even before the justices, it became clear that the accused made one case, and one case only, and so it has been throughout. He said that he was not the man. . . .

As was admitted, there was a stronger case for the admissibility of the powder puffs than of the photographs. I think the powder puffs were clearly admissible. The criminal made an appointment with the boys for the following Monday, and to the place of that appointment at the appointed time there came the appellant, equipped with articles recognised by the court as "used for the carrying out of their design" by persons of the class to which the criminal belonged. They are direct evidence that the appellant was keeping the criminal's appointment and was the same man. . . .

The photographs thus become the turning point of the case. The principles on which the admissibility of evidence of identification rest are in no need of restatement. . . . All lawyers recognise, as part of their professional premisses, that there is all the difference in the world between evidence proving that the accused is a bad man and evidence proving that he is *the* man. . . . There must be something to connect the circumstance tendered in evidence, not only with the accused, but with his participation in the crime. It is this something which is expressed in the judgment under appeal in the words "ordinary men do not keep indecent photographs of naked boys in their possession. Men who commit the offences charged do. . . . The man who did the acts on March 16 was a man who would be likely to have such photographs in his possession. The man arrested on the 19th in fact had such photographs in his possession at his rooms.". . . As applied to the facts of the case I think the meaning of the above passage may be restated more fully as follows: The actual criminal made an appointment to meet the same boys at the same time and place three days later and presumably for the same purpose. This tends to show that his act was not an isolated act, but was an incident in the habitual gratification of a particular propensity. The appellant, as his possession of the photographs tends to show, is a person with the same propensity. Indeed, he went to the place of the appointment with some of the outfit, and he had the rest of it at home. The evidence tends to attach to the accused a peculiarity which, though not purely physical, I think may be recognised as properly bearing that name. Experience tends to show that these offences against nature connote an inversion of normal characteristics which, while demanding punishment as offending against social morality, also partake of the nature of an abnormal physical property. A thief, a cheat, a coiner, or housebreaker is only a particular specimen of the genus rogue, and, though no doubt each tends to keep to his own line of business, they all alike possess the by no means extraordinary mental characteristic that they propose somehow to get their living dishonestly. So common a characteristic is not a recognisable mark of the individual. Persons, however, who commit the offences now under consideration seek the habitual gratification of a particular perverted lust, which not only takes them out of the class of ordinary men gone wrong, but stamps them with the hall-mark of a specialised and extraordinary class as much as if they carried on their bodies some physical peculiarity. So expanded and understood, I accept the passage which I have quoted above, and think that the photographs, found as they were and after a short interval of time, tend to show that the accused has this recognisable propensity, which it was shown was also the propensity of the criminal of March 16. It was accordingly admissible evidence of his identity with that criminal. . . .

Lords Dunedin, Atkinson and Parmoor gave concurring judgments.

Note.—For an extension of the "hallmark" principle for the purpose of establishing identity, see *R.* v. *Davis; R.* v. *Murphy* (1971) 56 Cr.App.R. 249 (C.A.).

R. v. **Armstrong** [1922] 2 K.B. 555 (C.C.A.). The accused, a solicitor, was charged with murdering his wife by poisoning her with arsenic. His defence was that she had committed suicide. On arrest he was found to be in possession of a considerable amount of arsenic, but he said that he bought it and kept it for the purpose of killing weeds in his garden. It was proved that he had purchased it a short time before his wife's death. The trial judge admitted evidence suggesting that he had attempted to poison a fellow solicitor with arsenic some eight months after his wife's death. He was convicted of the murder of his wife. The Court of Criminal Appeal held that there was ample evidence to support this verdict without reference to the similar fact evidence, but that this latter had been rightly admitted. Admissibility was said to be justifiable on the ground that it suggested that the appellant was lying when he said that he had purchased the arsenic for an innocent purpose.

Note.—As no defence of accident was raised the decision is perplexing. The jury must surely have treated the evidence as simply tending to establish a propensity in the accused to commit the type of offence with which he was being charged. Although it has never been overruled, the case has probably outlived its usefulness as an authority. Contrast *Noor Mohamed* v. *R.* [1949] A.C. 182 (P.C.) (*infra*).

R. v. SIMS

[1946] K.B. 531; [1946] 1 All E.R. 697; 31 Cr.App.R. 158 (C.C.A.: 1946)

When several strikingly similar allegations are made (in each case by a different person) of the misbehaviour of the accused on different occasions, evidence of each such allegation may be admissible as tending to negative the possibility of the other such allegations being false.

The accused was tried on an indictment containing 10 counts. Counts 1 and 2 contained charges of sodomy and gross indecency respectively with a man, A.M.; counts 3 and 4 contained similar charges in respect of another man, C.M.; counts 5 and 6 contained similar charges in respect of another man, H.S.; count 7 contained a charge of gross indecency with another man, E.G.W.; and counts 8, 9 and 10 contained charges of gross indecency with three boys. At the trial the accused made an application that the counts be tried separately in respect of each separate man or boy. The judge refused the application so far as the four men were concerned and the accused was thereupon tried on the first seven counts. He was found guilty on counts 1, 3 and 5, but acquitted on counts 2, 4, 6 and 7. He appealed against conviction.

Lord Goddard C.J. (reading the judgment, which he stated had been largely prepared by Denning J., of the court which included

OLIVER, CROOM-JOHNSON, DENNING and LUNSKEY JJ.): The important point involved in this appeal is whether the judge ought to have ordered separate trials in respect of each man involved.... We do not think that the mere fact that evidence is admissible on one count and inadmissible on another is by itself a ground for separate trials: because often the matter can be made clear in the summing up without prejudice to the accused. In such a case as the present, however, it is asking too much to expect any jury when considering one charge to disregard the evidence on the others, and if such evidence is inadmissible, the prejudice created by it would be improper and would be too great for any direction to overcome....

The question, therefore, is whether the evidence was admissible ... we are of opinion that on the trial of one of the counts in this case, the evidence on the others would be admissible. The evidence of each man was that the accused invited him into the house and there committed the acts charged. The acts they describe bear a striking similarity. That is a special feature sufficient in itself to justify the admissibility of the evidence; but we think it should be put on a broader basis. Sodomy is a crime in a special category.... On this account, in regard to this crime we think that the repetition of the acts is itself a specific feature connecting the accused with the crime and that evidence of this kind is admissible to show the nature of the act done by the accused. The probative force of all the acts together is much greater than one alone; for, whereas the jury might think one man might be telling an untruth, three or four are hardly likely to tell the same untruth unless they were conspiring together. If there is nothing to suggest a conspiracy their evidence would seem to be overwhelming. Whilst it would no doubt be in the interests of the prisoner that each case should be considered separately without the evidence on the others, we think that the interests of justice require that on each case the evidence on the others should be considered, and that, even apart from the defence raised by him, the evidence would be admissible.

In this case the matter can be put in another and very simple way. The visits of the men to the prisoner's house were either for a guilty or an innocent purpose: that they all speak to the commission of the same class of acts upon them tends to show that in each case the visits were to the former and not the latter purpose. The same considerations would apply to a case where a man is charged with a series of indecent offences against children, whether boys or girls: that they all complain of the same sort of conduct shows that the interest the prisoner was taking in them was not of a paternal or friendly nature but for the purpose of satisfying lust.

If we are right in thinking that the evidence was admissible, it is plain that the accused would not be prejudiced or embarrassed by reason of all the counts being tried together, and there was no reason for the judge to direct the jury that, in considering whether a particular charge was proved, they were to shut out other charges from their minds....

... we are of opinion that this appeal should be dismissed.

Note.—The notion that, homosexual offences being in a special category, the repetition of the acts in such cases is itself a special feature connecting the accused with the crime and thus warranting the admissibility of similar fact evidence, has now been decisively rejected by the House of Lords in *Director of Public Prosecutions* v. *Boardman* [1975] A.C. 421 (*infra*). There are also other features of the judgment in *R.* v. *Sims* which no longer represent the law,—in particular the suggestion that prima facie any similar fact evidence is admissible if it is "logically probative": see *Noor Mohamed* v. *R.* [1949] A.C. 182 (*infra*). For an analysis of the modern significance of the *Sims* case see especially the judgment of Lord Hailsham in *Director of Public Prosecutions* v. *Boardman*. It is submitted that *R.* v. *Sims*, as expurgated, now stands for the proposition in the headnote set out above. On this assumption the actual decision in *R.* v. *Chandor* [1958] 1 Q.B. 545, where on facts generally similar to those in *R.* v. *Sims* the Court of Criminal Appeal held that the evidence was wrongly admitted, must be distinguished on the ground that there the accusations of the three boys involved were not so strikingly similar as to make it a sufficiently remarkable coincidence if they were untrue. The report of *R.* v. *Chandor* does not detail the degree of similarity that was established, but counsel for the appellant is recorded (p. 547) as contending that "there was no striking similarity between the alleged offences," and this seemingly was not contradicted.

The principle stated in the headnote seems to have been followed in *R.* v. *Barrington* [1981] 1 W.L.R. 419 (C.A.), although *R.* v. *Sims* was not cited.

NOOR MOHAMED v. R.

[1949] A.C. 182; [1949] 1 All E.R. 365; 65 T.L.R. 124 (P.C.: 1948)

The general rule is that similar fact evidence, which, if believed, would be impressive only because it would tend to show the accused to be a person likely from his criminal conduct or character to have committed the offence for which he is being tried, and which would otherwise be of no real substance, is not admissible.

The appellant had been convicted of murdering a woman names Ayesha with whom he had been living. The appellant had cyanide lawfully in his possession for the purposes of his business as a goldsmith. There was no doubt that Ayesha had died as a result of cyanide poisoning, but there was no evidence that the poison had been administered to her by the accused. He was on bad terms with her, and there was some suggestion that she had committed suicide. The trial judge admitted evidence from which it might have been inferred that the accused had some two or three years previously caused the death of his wife, Gooriah, with whom he had also been on bad terms, by persuading her to take cyanide as a cure for toothache. The Privy Council held that this evidence had been wrongly admitted and quashed the appellant's conviction.

LORD DU PARQ (delivering the reasons of the Board, which included LORDS UTHWATT and OAKSEY, SIR MADHAVAN IVAIR and SIR JOHN BEAUMONT): . . . Their Lordships have considered with care the question whether the evidence now in question can be said to be relevant to any issue in the case. They have asked themselves, adopting the language of Lord Sumner in *Thompson's* case ([1918] A.C. 221, 236), "What exactly does this purport to prove?" At the trial the learned counsel for the Crown, when submitting that the evidence should be admitted, referred to the possible defences of accident and suicide. In his address to the jury he said, according to the note, that the evidence was led "to meet the defence of suicide," and pointed out that the circumstances surrounding the deaths of the two women "followed a similar pattern." At their Lordships' bar it was submitted that this similarity of circumstances would lead to the inference that the appellant administered poison to Ayesha with felonious intent.

There can be little doubt that the manner of Ayesha's death, even without the evidence as to the death of Gooriah, would arouse suspicion against the appellant in the mind of a reasonable man. The facts proved as to the death of Gooriah would certainly tend to deepen that suspicion, and might well tilt the balance against the accused in the estimation of a jury. It by no means follows that this evidence ought to be admitted. If an examination of it shows that it is impressive just because it appears to demonstrate, in the words of Lord Herschell in *Makin's* case ([1894] A.C. 57, 65) "that the accused is a person likely from his criminal conduct or character to have committed the offence for which he is being tried," and if it is otherwise of no real substance, then it was certainly wrongly admitted. After fully considering all the facts which, if accepted, it revealed, their Lordships are not satisfied that its admission can be justified on any of the grounds which have been suggested or on any other ground. Assuming that it is consistent with the evidence relating to the death of Ayesha that she took her own life, or that she took poison accidentally (one of which assumptions must be made for the purpose of the Crown's argument at the trial) there is nothing in the circumstances of Gooriah's death to negative these possible views. Even if the appellant deliberately caused Gooriah to take poison (an assumption not lightly to be made, since he was never charged with having murdered her) it does not follow that Ayesha may not have committed suicide. As to the argument from similarity of circumstances, it seems on analysis to amount to no more than this, that if the appellant murdered one woman because he was jealous of her, it is probable that he murdered another for the same reason. If the appellant were proved to have administered poison to Ayesha in circumstances consistent with accident, then proof that he had previously administered poison to Gooriah in similar circumstances might well have been admissible. There was, however, no direct evidence in either case that the appellant had administered the poison. It is true that in the case of Gooriah there was evidence from which it might be inferred that he persuaded her to take the poison by a trick, but this evidence cannot properly be used to found an inference that a similar trick was used to deceive Ayesha, and so to fill a gap in the available evidence.... The effect of the admission of the impugned evidence may well have been that the jury came to the conclusion that the appellant was guilty of the murder of Gooriah, with which he had never been charged, and having thus adjudged him a murderer, were satisfied with something short of conclusive proof that he had murdered Ayesha. In these circumstances the verdict cannot stand....

Note.—Lord du Parq also adverted (p. 191) to the judge's discretion to exclude prejudicial but legally admissible similar fact evidence. See, too, *Harris* v. *Director of Public Prosecutions* [1952] A.C. 694 (H.L.) (*infra*). However, the practical importance of this may be reassessed in the light of the implications of the decision in *Director of Public Prosecutions* v. *Boardman* [1975] A.C. 421 (*infra*): to the extent that (but only to the extent that) similar fact evidence is now admissible by virtue of its high probative value as compared with its probable prejudicial effect, it is *ex hypothesi* unlikely to be excluded in the exercise of such a discretion.

Lord du Parq also criticised (pp. 194 *et seq.*) the approach, canvassed in *R.* v. *Sims* [1946] K.B. 531 (C.A.) (*supra*), that all similar fact evidence is prima facie admissible if it is logically probative. That approach probably never did, and certainly does not now, represent the law. See, too, *R.* v. *Hall* [1952] 1 K.B. 302 (C.C.A.).

The actual decision in *Noor* *Mohamed* v. *R.* may be contrasted with that in *R.* v. *Armstrong*, [1922] 2 K.B. 555 (C.C.A.) (*supra*).

HARRIS v. DIRECTOR OF PUBLIC PROSECUTIONS

[1952] A.C. 694; [1952] 1 T.L.R. 1075; [1952] 1 All E.R. 1044; 36 Cr.App.R. 39
(H.L.: 1952)

*To be admissible, evidence of similar facts must be relevant to an issue
before the jury.*

A police constable was indicted on eight counts, each of which alleged
a separate breaking into the same office in a market and larceny there.
All the counts were tried together. The evidence showed that on each
occasion the thief had entered the building by the same method, and
had stolen part only of the money which he could have taken. On the
last occasion the accused was found by detectives near the building very
soon after the ringing of an alarm bell, which might have warned the
thief to hide the stolen money where it was discovered. The accused was
acquitted on the first seven counts, but was convicted on the eighth
count. His appeal was dismissed by the Court of Criminal Appeal, but
was allowed by the House of Lords.

VISCOUNT SIMON: . . . In my opinion, the principle laid down by Lord
Herschell L.C. in *Makin's* case ([1894] A.C. 57 at 65) remains the
proper principle to apply. . . .
The substance of the matter appears to me to be that the prosecution
may adduce all proper evidence which tends to prove the charge. I do
not understand Lord Herschell's words to mean that the prosecution
must withhold such evidence until after the accused has set up a specific
defence which calls for rebuttal. Where, for instance, *mens rea* is an
essential element in guilt, and the facts of the occurrence which is the
subject of the charge, standing by themselves, would be consistent with
mere accident, there would be nothing wrong in the prosecution seeking
to establish the true situation by offering, as part of its case in the first
instance, evidence of similar action by the accused at another time
which would go to show that he intended to do what he did on the
occasion charged and was thus acting criminally. . . . What Lord Sumner
meant when he denied the right of the prosecution to "credit the
accused with fancy defences" (in *Thompson* v. *R.* [1918] A.C. 221 at
232) was that evidence of similar facts involving the accused ought not
to be dragged in to his prejudice without reasonable cause.
. . . .
A criminal trial in this country is conducted for the purpose of
deciding whether the prosecution has proved that the accused is guilty of
the particular crime charged, and evidence of "similar facts" should be
excluded unless such evidence has a really material bearing on the issues
to be decided. . . .
Applying the above general propositions to the case before us, it
appears to me that the only difficulty arises from the form of the
summing-up. The judge, having decided that the eight counts should be
tried together, did not warn the jury that the evidence called in support
of the earlier counts did not in itself provide confirmation of the last

charge. Yet, if the eighth count had been the only charge to be tried, it is difficult to see how the fact that there had been similar thefts of the same pattern before would confirm the allegation that the appellant was the thief on July 22. The eighth count raised two issues: (1) Was the money stolen on July 22? (2) Is it proved that it was the appellant who stole it? Previous events could not confirm (1), which indeed was proved beyond dispute. As for (2), the accused denied that he was the thief and the fact that someone perpetrated the earlier thefts when the accused may have been somewhere in the market does not provide material confirmation of his identity as the thief on the last occasion. The case against him on July 22 depended on the facts of that date. Yet the jury may well have been swayed, however logically, in reaching its verdict on the eighth count by the earlier evidence. It should have been warned of this danger. . . .

LORDS PORTER, MORTON and TUCKER concurred. LORD OAKSEY dissented.

Note.—Lord Simon also referred to the role of judicial discretion; but, in the light of subsequently introduced flexibility in the law (see *infra*), the importance of this in the present context is now greatly reduced.

Le Blanc v. **R.** (1976) 68 D.L.R. (3d.) 243; [1977] 1 S.C.R. 339 (S.C. Can.). The accused was charged with causing death by criminal negligence. He was a bush pilot who was due to pick up the deceased and his companion. As he approached the pick-up point and in order to frighten the men on the ground as a joke he tried to make a "pass" (*i.e.* fly very low) over them. He miscalculated, flew too low and hit and killed the deceased. The weather was ideal, and the mechanical efficiency of the plane was established. The accused testified and admitted that he was making a "pass" and offered no further explanation or excuse. The judge allowed the Crown to prove as part of its case that on three earlier occasions he accused had made similar passes, although then without mishap. The judge instructed the jury that this similar fact evidence was led to counter possible defences (which had not been raised) of mechanical misfunction or accident from causes beyond the pilot's control. He further charged them that such evidence confirmed the testimony of a passenger in the accused's plane (which had not been contradicted) that the accused intended to frighten the persons on the ground by making a "pass." The accused was convicted, and his appeal to the Court of Appeal for Quebec was dismissed. In dismissing his further appeal the Supreme Court of Canada divided by six to three. The majority, taking the view that the requisite *mens rea* involved "advertent" negligence, held that the similar fact evidence was admissible as tending to show this. A powerfully constituted minority (Laskin C.J., Dickson J. and Beetz J.) pointed out that the accused's intention to make a "pass" was not in issue and that no question of subjective intent arose. The sole issue was as to whether his admitted behaviour constituted criminal negligence. His behaviour on other occasions was not relevant to this issue.

R. v. STRAFFEN

[1952] 2 Q.B. 911; [1952] 2 T.L.R. 589; [1952] 2 All E.R. 657; 36 Cr.App.R. 132
(C.C.A.: 1952)

Similarities between the circumstances of the accused's behaviour on previous occasions and the circumstances of the criminal's behaviour on the instant occasion may be so striking as to render evidence of the former admissible for the purpose of identifying the accused as the criminal.

In 1951 the appellant was charged with the murder, by manual strangulation, of two little girls at Bath on July 15 and August 8 respectively. He was found unfit to plead by reason of insanity and was committed to Broadmoor Institution. On April 29, 1952, he escaped from Broadmoor and was at large from 2.40 p.m. until 6.40 p.m. of that day, when he was arrested and returned to Broadmoor. At about 6 a.m. on the following morning the body of Linda Bowyer, the subject of the present murder charge, was found. She had died from manual strangulation some 12 to 15 hours before. About two-and-a-half hours after the discovery of the dead body of the child, two detective officers visited the appellant at Broadmoor. He denied that he had murdered the child, though he admitted that he had been in the neighbourhood of the place where her body was found and that he had seen her. There were also other passers-by who might have committed the crime. At the appellant's trial for the murder of Linda Bowyer Cassels J. admitted evidence of the oral statements made by the appellant to the police officers and also the evidence of the doctor who was called as a witness in connection with the murders at Bath and of a pathologist who was tendered as a witness in the present case and who had studied the depositions, the photographs and the post-mortem reports in the Bath cases. The evidence was tendered to prove the similarities between the circumstances of the three cases and the method employed by the murderer in each. The accused was convicted and appealed against conviction.

SLADE J. (giving the judgment of the court which included DEVLIN and GORMAN JJ.): ... Cassels J., ... admitted evidence in regard to the murders alleged to have been committed by the appellant at Bath on the ground that it was material to establish the identity of the murderer of Linda Bowyer, and the question is: Was that evidence properly admitted? The general rule, of course, is to exclude evidence which tends to show that the accused has been guilty of criminal acts other than those covered by the indictment, and it is an irrefragable rule that evidence of such offences shall not be admitted for the purpose of proving that the accused is a person of criminal disposition, or even that he has a propensity for committing the particular type of crime with which he is being charged. But, apart from statute, there are certain recognised exceptions to the general rule under which evidence is admissible of other crimes committed by the accused, in spite of the fact that it tends to prove that he is of a criminal disposition, because it tends to prove that he committed the particular crime with which he is charged. I take the law on this point from the well-known case of *Makin v. Attorney-General of New South Wales* [1894] A.C. 57, 64.... Lord Herschell there said: "It is undoubtedly not competent for the prosecution to adduce evidence tending to show that the accused has been guilty of criminal acts other than those covered by the indictment for the purpose of leading to the conclusion that the accused is a person likely, from his criminal conduct or character, to have committed the offence for which he is being tried. On the other hand, the mere fact that the evidence adduced tends to show the commission of other crimes does not render it inadmissible if it be relevant to an issue before the jury, and it may be so relevant if it bears upon the question whether the acts charged in the indictment were designed or accidental, or to rebut a defence which would otherwise be open to the accused."

Here the evidence was admitted by Cassels J. on the latter ground, namely, that it tended to rebut a defence which was otherwise open to the accused, that is, that he was not the person who committed the murder.

In the recent case of *Harris* v. *Director of Public Prosecutions* [1952] A.C. 694, in the House of Lords, Lord Simon said: "In my opinion the principle laid down by Lord Herschell in *Makin's* case remains the proper principle to apply, and I see no reason for modifying it."...Further on Lord Simon said: "The substance of the matter appears to me to be that the prosecution may adduce all proper evidence which tends to prove the charge"; and after dealing with *Thompson* v. *The King* [1918] A.C. 221 he said: "It is the fact that he (Thompson) was involved in other occurrences which may negative the inference of accident or establish his mens rea by showing 'system.' Or, again, the other occurrences may sometimes assist to prove his identity, as, for instance, in *Perkins* v. *Jeffery* [1915] 2 K.B. 702. But evidence of other occurrences which merely tend to deepen suspicion does not go to prove guilt."

That being the law, the question is whether, in this case, the evidence does or does not fall within the category of admissibility as being relevant to prove the crime charged by showing that it was the accused who committed it. The grounds on which the admissibility of the evidence was urged by the Solicitor-General in the court below was the similarity of the circumstances surrounding the murders in the case of the two Bath murders on the one hand and [this] murder on the other. He stated the similarities to be, first, that each of the victims was a young girl; secondly, that each was killed by manual strangulation; thirdly, that in none of the cases was there any attempt at sexual interference or any apparent motive for the crime; fourthly, that in no case was there any evidence of a struggle; and fifthly, that in none of the three cases was any attempt made to conceal the body, though that could easily have been done.

Those similarities were fortified by the evidence of the doctor who examined the bodies of the two girls murdered at Bath and by the pathologist called in the case of Linda Bowyer, who had studied the depositions, the photographs and the post-mortem reports in the two cases at Bath. The evidence with regard to the Bath murders was tendered and admitted for the purpose of showing that the same person killed all three little girls; that is to say, that the person who strangled Brenda Goddard and Cicily Batstone, in the circumstances described, also manually strangled Linda Bowyer in similar circumstances as regards the method of death, the precision of the strangulation, and the other similar circumstances to which I have referred. In the opinion of the court that evidence was rightly admitted, not for the purpose of showing, to use Mr. Elam's [defence counsel's] words, that the appellant was "a professional strangler," but to show that he strangled Linda Bowyer; in other words, for the purpose of identifying the murderer of Linda Bowyer as being the same individual as the person who had murdered the other two girls in precisely the same way.

I can see no distinction in principle between the present case and

Thompson v. *The King*, to which we were referred, and, indeed, I think one cannot distinguish abnormal propensities from identification. Abnormal propensity is a means of identification. In *Thompson's* case evidence was admitted to prove his identity which showed that he was a person who suffered from the abnormal propensity of homosexuality. It is an abnormal propensity to strangle young girls and to do so without any apparent motive, without any attempt at sexual interference, and to leave their dead bodies where they can be seen and where, presumably, their deaths would be detected. In the judgment of the court, that evidence was admissible because it tended to identify the person who murdered Linda Bowyer with the person who confessed in his statements to having murdered the other two girls a year before, in exactly similar circumstances.

Mr. Elam asked: "How far does the admissibility of such evidence go? Would it extend to the case of a burglar, housebreaker, thief, and so on?" Speaking for myself, I think that if the question of identity arose in a case of housebreaking and it were possible to adduce evidence that there was some hallmark or other peculiarity in relation to earlier housebreakings which were also apparent in the case of the housebreaking charged, so as to stamp the accused man, not only with the housebreaking charged but with the earlier housebreakings, and there was a confession or other evidence that he had committed the earlier housebreakings, that would fall within the same principle of admissibility, not to prove his propensity for housebreaking, but to prove that he was the person who had committed the housebreaking charged.

I should repeat, perhaps, as I stated at the beginning of this judgment, that the sole ground of his appeal is the admissibility of the evidence as a matter of law. It is unnecessary, therefore, to consider whether, when evidence is admissible, its prejudicial effect is so disproportionate to its probative value that the judge, in the exercise of his discretion, ought not to have allowed its admission. That point does not arise in this appeal since Mr. Elam very properly said that if the evidence was admissible, he conceded that the discretion of the judge at the trial was judicially exercised. In the circumstances this appeal is dismissed.

Note.—Perkins v. *Jeffery* [1915] 2 K.B. 702 (D.C.) was a case of indecent exposure, where evidence of similar facts was allowed, partly to establish the identity of the accused.

R. v. **Ducsharm** [1956] 1 D.L.R. 732; [1955] O.R. 824; 113 C.C.C. 1 (Ont. C.A.). The defendant appealed from a murder conviction on the ground *inter alia* that evidence had been wrongly admitted of his having at various times broken into premises near the scene of the crime. It was held by a unanimous Ontario Court of Appeal that this evidence was only admissible to the extent that the timing of a break-in indicated that he was in the vicinity of the murder about the time that it was committed. Pickup C.J.O. said (p. 735): "The weight of this evidence was for the jury but, being admitted merely as a circumstance tending to show the presence of the accused in the vicinity of the crime, the jury should have been instructed that it was admitted for that purpose only and that they must not consider it for any purpose other than as assisting them to determine whether or not the accused was in the vicinity of the crime when it was committed."

Note.—See, too, *R.* v. *Mackie* (1973) 57 Cr.App.R. 463 (C.A.). There the appellant was convicted of the manslaughter of a child aged three to whom he stood *in loco parentis*. The child had fallen downstairs and been killed when running away from the appellant. The prosecution case was that the appellant had disciplined the boy excessively in the past and this explained why the boy should be frightened and be running away from the appellant in fear of being ill-treated again. The Court of Appeal held that the evidence of injuries previously sustained by the boy at the hands of the appellant was rightly admitted. Such evidence had some propensity-type relevance, but it was admitted on the specific issue of the boy's state of mind, proof of this being an essential part of the prosecution case. In terms of prejudicial effect, this should perhaps be seen as borderline.

But see, to, *R.* v. *O'Neale* [1988] R.T.R. 124 (C.A.). There it was held that, on a charge of causing death by reckless driving, evidence of the fact that the accused was in breach of the law relating to holders of provisional licences was inadmissible *per se*. It would be admissible only if it could be specifically shown to be causally connected with the ensuing accident, *i.e.*, if it could be shown that the absence of a qualified supervising driver had contributed to the manner of the accused's driving. The Court of Appeal allowed the appeal on the ground that the trial judge had not given an adequate instruction to the jury on this "vital distinction." Purchas LJ. said (p. 128): "They may have thought that the appellant's driving without 'L' plates and without a qualified driver was evidence from which they could come to the conclusion that he was the sort of person who ignored obvious risks and safety precautions and that this would be relevant to establish that the driving was reckless upon the occasion in question. ... [T]he judge should have directed the jury that they must be satisfied that there was a causal connection between the appellant's failure to comply with the requirements for holders of provisional licences and the driving in question."

DIRECTOR OF PUBLIC PROSECUTIONS v. BOARDMAN

[1975] A.C. 421; *sub nom. Boardman* v. *D.P.P.* [1974] 3 All E.R. 887; 60 Cr.App. 165 (H.L.: 1974)

Similar fact evidence is admissible if its true probative worth is so great as to offset any likely prejudicial effect, or if it has a real relevance which is independent of a tendency to show that the accused is the sort of person who would be likely to have committed the offence with which he is charged. Any admission of similar fact evidence is exceptional, and that the evidence is "strikingly" similar is an important factor to be taken into account.

There is no special rule applicable to heterosexual or to homosexual offences.

No distinction is to be drawn between cases in which the defence is "innocent association" and those of complete denial.

The appellant, the headmaster of a boarding school for boys in Cambridge, was charged with, *inter alia*, buggery with S, a pupil aged 16, and with inciting H, a pupil aged 17, to commit buggery with him. There was no application for separate trials. The judge ruled and directed the jury that the evidence of S on the count concerning him was admissible as corroborative evidence in relation to the count concerning H, and vice versa. The appellant was convicted on both counts. His appeal against conviction of these two counts on the ground, *inter alia*, that the judge's ruling as to the admissibility of the boys' evidence had been wrong was dismissed by the Court of Appeal. He further appealed to the House of Lords. Their Lordships were unanimous in dismissing this appeal, although a majority of them regarded it as a borderline case.

LORD WILBERFORCE: My Lords, the question for decision in this appeal is whether, on a charge against the appellant of buggery with one boy, evidence was admissible that the appellant had incited another boy to buggery, and vice versa. The judge ruled that, in the particular circumstances of this case, the evidence was admissible. We have to decide whether this ruling was correct; for reasons which others of your Lordships have given, we cannot answer the question certified in the terms in which it is stated. Whether in the field of sexual conduct or otherwise, there is no general or automatic answer to be given to the question whether evidence of facts similar to those the subject of a particular charge ought to be admitted. In each case it is necessary to estimate (i) whether, and if so how strongly, the evidence as to other facts tends to support, *i.e.* to make more credible, the evidence given as to the fact in question, (ii) whether such evidence, if given, is likely to be prejudicial to the accused. Both these elements involve questions of degree.

It falls to the judge, in the first place by way of preliminary ruling, and indeed on an application for separate trials if such is made (see the opinion of my noble and learned friend Lord Cross of Chelsea), to estimate the respective and relative weight of these two factors and only to allow the evidence to be put before the jury if he is satisfied that the answer to the first question is clearly positive, and, on the assumption, which is likely, that the second question must be similarly answered, that on a combination of the two the interests of justice clearly require that the evidence be admitted.

Questions of this kind arise in a number of different contexts and have, correspondingly, to be resolved in different ways. I think that it is desirable to confine ourselves to the present set of facts, and to situations of a similar character. In my understanding we are not here concerned with cases of "system" or "underlying unity" (*cf. Moorov v. H.M. Advocate*, 1930 J.C. 68), words whose vagueness is liable to result in their misapplication, nor with a case involving proof of identity, or an alibi, nor, even, is this a case where evidence is adduced to rebut a particular defence. It is sometimes said that evidence of "similar facts" may be called to rebut a defence of innocent association, a proposition which I regard with suspicion since it seems a specious manner of outflanking the exclusionary rule. But we need not consider the validity or scope of this proposition. The Court of Appeal dealt with the case on the basis, submitted by the appellant's counsel, that no defence of innocent association was set up; in my opinion we should take the same course.

This is simply a case where evidence of facts similar in character to those forming the subject of the charge is sought to be given in support of the evidence on that charge. Though the case was one in which separate charges relating to different complainants were tried jointly, the principle must be the same as would arise if there were only one charge relating to one complainant. If the appellant were being tried on a charge relating to S, could the prosecution call H as a witness to give evidence about facts relating to H? The judge should apply just as strict a rule in the one case as in the other. If, as I believe, the general rule is that such evidence cannot be allowed, it requires exceptional circumstances to justify the admission. This

House should not, in my opinion, encourage erosion of the general rule.

We can dispose at once of the suggestion that there is a special rule or principle applicable to sexual, or to homosexual, offences.... Evidence that an offence of a sexual character was committed by A against B cannot be supported by evidence that an offence of a sexual character was committed by A against C, or against C, D and E.

The question certified suggests that the contrary may be true if the offences take a "particular form." I do not know what this means: all sexual activity has some form or other and the varieties are not unlimited: how particular must it be for a special rule to apply? The general salutary rule of exclusion must not be eroded through so vague an epithet. The danger of it being so is indeed well shown in the present case for the judge excluded the (similar fact) evidence of one boy because it showed "normal" homosexual acts while admitting the (similar fact) evidence of another boy because the homosexual acts assumed a different, and, in his view, "abnormal," pattern. Distinctions such as this, rightly called fine distinctions by the judge, lend an unattractive unreality to the law.

If the evidence was to be received, then it must be on some general principle not confined to sexual offences. There are obvious difficulties in the way of formulating any such rule in such a manner as, on the one hand, to enable clear guidance to be given to juries, and, on the other hand, to avoid undue rigidity.

The prevailing formulation is to be found in the judgment of the Court of Criminal Appeal in *Rex* v. *Sims* [1946] K.B. 531 where it was said, at pp. 539–540:

> "The evidence of each man was that the accused invited him into the house and there committed the acts charged. The acts they describe bear a striking similarity. That is a special feature sufficient in itself to justify the admissibility of the evidence;... The probative force of all the acts together is much greater than one alone; for, whereas the jury might think that one man might be telling an untruth, three or four are hardly likely to tell the same untruth unless they were conspiring together. If there is nothing to suggest a conspiracy their evidence would seem to be overwhelming."

Sims has not received universal approbation or uniform commentary, but I think that it must be taken that this passage has received at least the general approval of this House in *Reg.* v. *Kilbourne* [1973] A.C. 529. For my part, since the statement is evidently related to the facts of that particular case, I should deprecate its literal use in other cases. It is certainly neither clear nor comprehensive. A suitable adaptation, and, if necessary, expansion, should be allowed to judges in order to suit the facts involved. The basic principle must be that the admission of similar fact evidence (of the kind now in question) is exceptional and requires a strong degree of probative force. This probative force is derived, if at all, from the circumstance that the facts testified to by the several witnesses bear to each other such a striking similarity that they must, when judged by experience and common sense, either all be true, or have arisen from a cause common to the witnesses or from pure coincidence. The jury may, therefore, properly be asked to judge whether the right conclusion is that all are true, so that each story is supported by the other(s).

I use the words "a cause common to the witnesses" to include not only (as in *Rex* v. *Sims* [1946] K.B. 531) the possibility that the witnesses may have invented a story in concert but also the possibility that a similar story may have arisen by a process of infection from media of publicity or simply from fashion. In the sexual field, and in others, this may be a real possibility: something much more than mere similarity and absence of proved conspiracy is needed if this evidence is to be allowed. This is well illustrated by *Reg.* v. *Kilbourne* [1973] A.C. 529 where the judge excluded "intra group" evidence because of the possibility, *as it appeared to him*, of collaboration between boys who knew each other well. This is, in my respectful opinion, the right course rather than to admit the evidence unless a case of collaboration or concoction is made out.

If this test is to be applied fairly, much depends in the first place upon the experience and common sense of the judge. As was said by Lord Simon of Glaisdale in *Reg.* v. *Kilbourne*, at p. 756, in judging whether one fact is probative of another, experience plays as large a place as logic. And in matters of experience it is for the judge to keep close to current mores. What is striking in one age is normal in another: the perversions of yesterday may be the routine or the fashion of tomorrow. The ultimate test has to be applied by the jury using similar qualities of experience and common sense after a fair presentation of the dangers either way of admission or of rejection. Finally, whether the judge has properly used and stated the ingredients of experience and common sense may be reviewed by the Court of Appeal.

The present case is, to my mind, right on the border-line. There were only two relevant witnesses, S and H. The striking similarity as presented to the jury was and was only the active character of the sexual performance to which the accused was said to have invited the complainants. In relation to the incident which was the subject of the second charge, the language used by the boy was not specific: the "similarity" was derived from an earlier incident in connection with which the boy used a verb connoting an active role. I agree with, I think, all your Lordships in thinking that all of this, relating not very specifically to the one striking element, common to two boys only, is, if sufficient, only just sufficient. Perhaps other similarities could have been found in the accused's approaches to the boys (I do not myself find them particularly striking), but the judge did not rest upon them or direct the jury as to their "similarity." I do not think that these ought now to be relied upon. The dilution of the "striking" fact by more prosaic details might have weakened the impact upon the jury rather than strengthened it. The judge dealt properly and fairly with the possibility of a conspiracy between the boys.

These matters lie largely within the field of the judge's discretion, and of the jury's task; the Court of Appeal has reviewed the whole matter in a careful judgment. I do not think that there is anything which justifies the interference of this House. But I confess to some fear that the case, if regarded as an example, may be setting the standard of "striking similarity" too low.

. . . .

I would dismiss the appeal.

LORD HAILSHAM OF ST. MARYLEBONE: . . . I do not know that the matter can be better stated than it was by Lord Herschell L.C. in *Makin* v. *Attorney-General for New South Wales* [1894] A.C. 57, 65, . . . It is perhaps helpful to remind oneself that what is *not* to be admitted is a chain of reasoning and not necessarily a state of facts. If the inadmissible chain of reasoning is the *only* purpose for which the evidence is adduced as a matter of law, the evidence itself is not admissible. If there is some other relevant, probative purpose than for the forbidden type of reasoning, the evidence is admitted, but should be made subject to a warning from the judge that the jury must eschew the forbidden reasoning. The judge has also a discretion, not as a matter of law but as a matter of good practice, to exclude evidence whose prejudicial effect, though the evidence be technically admissible on the decided cases, may be so great in the particular circumstances as to outweigh its probative value to the extent that a verdict of guilty might be considered unsafe or unsatisfactory if ensuing (*cf. per* Lord Simon in *Harris* v. *Director of Public Prosecutions* [1952] A.C. 694, 707). In all these cases it is for the judge to ensure as a matter of law in the first place, and as a matter of discretion where the matter is free, that a properly instructed jury, applying their minds to the facts, can come to the conclusion that they are satisfied so that they are sure that to treat the matter as pure coincidence by reason of the "nexus," "pattern," "system," "striking resemblances" or whatever phrase is used is "an affront to common sense" [*Reg.* v. *Kilbourne* [1973] A.C. 729, *per* Lord Simon of Glaisdale, at p. 759]. In this the ordinary rules of logic and common sense prevail, whether the case is one of burglary and the burglar has left some "signature" as the mark of his presence, or false pretences and the pretences alleged have too many common characteristics to have happened coincidentally, or whether the dispute is one of identity and the accused in a series of offences has some notable physical features or behavioural or psychological characteristics or, as in some cases, is in possession of incriminating articles, like a jemmy, a set of skeleton keys or, in abortion cases, the apparatus of the abortionist. Attempts to codify the rules of common sense are to be resisted. The first rule in *Makin* [1894] A.C. 57, 65 is designed to exclude a particular kind of inference being drawn which might upset the presumption of innocence by introducing more heat than light. When that is the only purpose for which the evidence is being tendered, it should be excluded altogether, as in *Reg.* v. *Horwood* [1970] 1 Q.B. 133. Where the purpose is an inference of another kind, subject to the judge's overriding discretion to exclude, the evidence is admissible, if in fact the evidence be logically probative. Even then it is for the jury to assess its weight, which may be greater or less according as to how far it accords with other evidence, and according as to how far that other evidence may be conclusive.

There are two further points of a general character that I would add. The "striking resemblances" or "unusual features," or whatever phrase is considered appropriate, to ignore which would affront common sense, may either be in the objective facts, as for instance in *Rex* v. *Smith, Notable British Trials Series*, or *Reg.* v. *Straffen* [1952] 2 Q.B. 911, or may constitute a striking similarity in the accounts by witnesses of disputed transactions. For instance, whilst it would certainly not be enough to identify the culprit in a series of burglaries that he climbed in through a ground floor window, the fact that he left the same humorous limerick on the walls of the sitting room, or an esoteric symbol written in lipstick on the mirror, might well be enough. In a sex case, to adopt an example given in argument in the Court of Appeal, whilst a repeated homosexual act by itself might be quite insufficient to admit the evidence as confirmatory of identity or design, the fact that it was alleged to have been performed wearing the ceremonial head-dress of a Red Indian chief or other eccentric garb might well in appropriate circumstances suffice. . . .

LORD CROSS OF CHELSEA: My Lords, on the hearing of a criminal charge the prosecution is not as a general rule allowed to adduce evidence that the accused has done acts other than those with which he is charged in order to show that he is the sort of person who would be likely to have committed the offence in question. As my noble and learned friend, Lord Simon of Glaisdale, pointed out in the recent case of *Reg.* v. *Kilbourne* [1973] A.C. 729, 757, the reason for this general rule is not that the law regards such evidence as inherently irrelevant but that it is believed that if it were generally admitted jurors would in many cases think that it was more relevant than it was, so that, as it is put, its prejudicial effect would outweigh its probative value. Circumstances, however, may arise in which such evidence is so very relevant that to exclude it would be an affront to common sense. Take, for example, *Reg.* v. *Straffen* [1952] 2 Q.B. 911. There a young girl was found strangled. It was a most unusual murder for there had been no attempt to assault her sexually or to conceal the body though this might easily have been done. The accused, who had just escaped from Broadmoor and was in the neighbourhood at the time of the crime, had previously committed two murders of young girls, each of which had the same peculiar features. It would, indeed, have been a most extraordinary coincidence if this third murder had been committed by someone else and though an ultra-cautious jury might still have acquitted him it would have been absurd for the law to have prevented the evidence of the other murders being put before them although it was simply evidence to show that Straffen was a man likely to commit a murder of that particular kind. As Viscount Simon said in *Harris* v. *Director of Public Prosecutions* [1952] A.C. 694, 705, it is not possible to compile an exhaustive list of the sort of cases in which "similar fact" evidence— to use a compendious phrase—is admissible. The question must always be whether the similar fact evidence taken together with the other evidence would do no more than raise or strengthen a suspicion that the accused committed the offence with which he is charged or would point so strongly to his guilt that only an ultra-cautious jury, if they accepted it as true, would acquit in face of it. In the end—although the admissibility of such evidence is a question of law, not of discretion—the question as I see it must be one of degree. . . .

The setting in which the question arises in this case is familiar enough. When A is charged with an offence against B in what circumstances (if any) can the prosecution strengthen B's evidence by calling C and D to say that A committed similar offences against them? This problem was considered by a full Court of Appeal in *Rex* v. *Sims* [1946] K.B. 531. The facts there were that the defendant was charged on different counts with homosexual offences of a similar character involving four different men. Each said that the defendant had invited him to his house and then had homosexual relations with him. The defendant admitted that each of the men had in fact visited him at his invitation on the occasions in question, but he denied that he had been guilty of any improper conduct with any of them. The court gave three separate reasons for saying that on each count the evidence of the other men as to what the defendant had done to them was admissible to support the evidence of the man with whom the offence to which the count related was alleged to have been committed. The first reason was expressed in the following terms, at pp. 539–540.

> "The evidence of each man was that the accused invited him into the house and there committed the acts charged. The acts they describe bear a striking similarity. . . . The probative force of all the acts together is much greater than one alone; for, whereas the jury might think one man might be telling an untruth, three or four are hardly likely to tell the same untruth unless they are conspiring. If there is nothing to suggest a conspiracy their evidence would seem to be overwhelming."

The second reason was that homosexual offences formed a special class in respect of which "similar fact" evidence was more readily admissible than in other cases. The third reason was that "similar fact" evidence was always admissible to rebut a defence of "innocent association." . . . The attitude of the ordinary man to homosexuality has changed very much even since *Rex* v. *Sims* was decided and what was said on that subject in 1917 by Lord Sumner in *Thompson* v. *The King* [1918] A.C. 221, 235—from which the view that homosexual offences form a class apart appears to stem—sounds nowadays like a voice from another world. Speaking for myself I have also great difficulty in accepting the third reason. If I am charged with a sexual offence why should it make any difference to the admissibility or non-admissibility of similar fact evidence whether my case is that the meeting at which the offence is said to have been committed never took place or that I committed no offence in the course of it? In each case I am saying that my accuser is lying. . . .

If the decision in *Rex* v. *Sims* [1946] K.B. 531 is to be justified it must, as I see it, be for the first reason. One must, however, bear in mind that such a case as *Rex* v. *Sims* or this case differs materially from such cases as *Reg.* v. *Straffen* [1952] 2 Q.B. 911 or *Rex* v. *Smith* (the "brides in the bath" case), 11 Cr.App.R. 229. In those cases there was no direct evidence that the accused had committed the offence with which he was charged but equally there was no question of any witness for the prosecution telling lies. . . . In such cases as *Rex* v. *Sims* [1946] K.B. 531 or this case on the other hand there is, it is true, some direct evidence that the offence was committed by the accused but he says that that evidence is false and the similar fact evidence—which he says is also false—is sought to be let in in order to strengthen the case for saying that his denials are untrue. In such circumstances the first question which arises is obviously whether his accusers may not have put their heads together to concoct false evidence and if there is any real chance of this having occurred the similar fact evidence must be excluded. In *Reg.* v. *Kilbourne* [1973] A.C. 729 it was only allowed to be given by boys of a different group from the boy an alleged offence against whom was being considered. But even if collaboration is out of the way it remains possible that the charge made by the complainant is false and that it is simply a coincidence that others should be making or should have made independently allegations of a similar character against the accused. The likelihood of such a coincidence obviously becomes less and less the more people there are who make the similar allegations and the more striking are the similarities in the various stories. In the end, as I have said, it is a question of degree.

Before I come to the particular facts of this case there is one other matter to which I wish to refer. When in a case of this sort the prosecution wishes to adduce "similar fact" evidence which the defence says is inadmissible, the question whether it is admissible ought, if possible, to be decided in the absence of the jury at the outset of the trial and if it is decided that the evidence is inadmissible and the accused is being charged in the same indictment with offences against the other men the charges relating to the different persons ought to be tried separately. If they are tried together the judge will, of course, have to tell the jury that in considering whether the accused is guilty of the offence alleged against him by A they must put out of mind the fact— which they know—that B and C are making similar allegations against him. But, as the Court of Criminal Appeal said in *Rex* v. *Sims* [1946] K.B. 531, 536, it is asking too much of any jury to tell them to perform mental gymnastics of this sort. If the charges are tried together it is inevitable that the jurors will be influenced, consciously or unconsciously, by the fact that the accused is being charged not with a single offence against one person but with three separate offences against three persons. It is said, I know, that to order separate trials in all these cases would be highly inconvenient. If and so far as this is true it is a reason for doubting the wisdom of the general rule excluding similar fact evidence. But so long as there is that general rule the courts ought to strive to give effect to it loyally and not, while paying lip service to it, in effect let in the inadmissible evidence by trying all the charges together.

. . . .

The appellant who was in his 40s was charged with having committed homosexual offences with three pupils at his school: buggery with S, aged 16, incitement to buggery with H, aged 17, and incitement to buggery with A, aged 18. All three charges were tried together. In his summing up the judge told the jury—rightly as it is agreed—that there was no evidence to suggest that the three boys were in league with one another and that the case for the defence was that each had independently for reasons of his own made up a false story. He then directed them that in considering whether they thought that S was telling the truth they could take into account the evidence given by H and vice versa, but that they must not treat the evidence of either S or H as supporting that given by A or that given by A as supporting that given by either S or H. The jury convicted the appellant on all three counts but his conviction on count 3 was quashed by the Court of Appeal for reasons to which it is unnecessary to refer here and counsel for the Director of Public Prosecutions did not argue that the judge was wrong to draw the distinction which he did between counts 1 and 2 and count 3 with regard to the admission of similar fact evidence. We must therefore treat this case, as the Court of Appeal treated it, as though A were out of the picture and there were simply two charges concerning S and H. In *Reg.* v. *Kilbourne* [1973] A.C. 729 my noble and learned friend, Lord Reid, expressed the view, at pp. 750–751, that in a case of this sort "similar fact" evidence could only be admitted if it showed that the accused was pursuing what could be "loosely called a system" and that two instances would not be enough to constitute a system." I naturally hesitate to differ from my noble and learned friend but I am not myself prepared to draw a line of this sort. On the other hand, I think that when you have so few as two instances you need to proceed with great caution. It is by no means unheard of for a boy to accuse a schoolmaster falsely of having made homosexual advances to him. If two boys make accusations of that sort at about the same time independently of one another then no doubt the ordinary man would tend to think that there was "probably something in it." But it is just this instinctive reaction of the ordinary man which the general rule is intended to counter and I think that one needs to find very striking peculiarities common to the two stories to justify the admission of one to support the other. The feature in the two stories upon which attention was concentrated in the courts below is that both youths said that the appellant suggested not that he should bugger them but that they should bugger him. This was said to be an "unusual" suggestion. If I thought that the outcome of this appeal depended on whether such a suggestion was in fact "unusual" I would be in favour of allowing it. It is no doubt unusual for a middle-aged man to yield to the urge to commit buggery or to try to commit buggery with youths or young men but whether it is unusual for such a middle-aged man to wish to play the passive rather than the active role I have no idea whatever and I am not prepared, in the absence of any evidence on the point, to make any assumption one way or the other. As I see it, however, the point is not whether what the appellant is said to have suggested would be, as coming from a middle-aged active homosexual, in itself particularly unusual but whether it would be unlikely that two youths who were saying untruly that the appellant had made homosexual advances to them would have put such a suggestion into his mouth. In one passage in his summing up the judge touched on this aspect of the matter and said that the jury might think it more likely that if their stories were untrue S and H would have said that the appellant wished to bugger or did bugger them than that he wished them to bugger or induced them to bugger him. There is, I think, force in that observation, but I do not think that this similarity standing alone would be sufficient to warrant the admission of the evidence. My noble and learned friends, Lord Morris of Borth-y-Gest, Lord Hailsham of St. Marylebone and Lord Salmon, point, however, to other features common to the two stories which, it may be said, two liars concocting false stories independently of one another would have been unlikely to hit upon and, although I must say that I regard this as very much a border-line case, I am not prepared to dissent from their view that the "similar fact" evidence was admissible here and that the appeal should be dismissed.

LORD SALMON: . . . My Lords, whether or not evidence is relevant and admissible against an accused is solely a question of law. The test must be: is the evidence capable of tending to persuade a reasonable jury of the accused's guilt on some ground other than his bad character and disposition to commit the sort of crime with which he is charged? In the case of an alleged homosexual offence, just as in the case of an alleged burglary, evidence which proves merely that the accused has committed crimes in the past and is therefore disposed to commit the crime charged is clearly inadmissible. It has, however, never been doubted that if the crime charged is committed in a uniquely or strikingly similar manner to other crimes committed by the accused the manner in which the other crimes were committed may be evidence upon which a jury could reasonably conclude that the accused was guilty of the crime charged. The similarity would have to be so unique or striking that common sense makes it inexplicable on the basis of coincidence. I would stress that the question as to whether the evidence is capable of being so regarded by a reasonable jury is a question of law. There is no easy way out by leaving it to the jury to see how they decide it. If a trial judge wrongly lets in the evidence and the jury convict, then, subject to the proviso [to section 2(1) of the Criminal Appeal Act 1968], the conviction must be quashed. . . .

If a trial judge rightly rules that the evidence is relevant and admissible, he still, of course, has a discretion to exclude it on the ground that its probative value is minimal and altogether outweighed by its likely prejudicial effect. Once, however, he lets in evidence which is in law admissible, it is only in a very clear case that an appellate tribunal would interfere with the exercise of his discretion. . . .

LORD MORRIS OF BORTH-Y-GEST delivered a concurring judgment.

Note.—For post-*Boardman* cases, see *R.* v. *Rance and Heron* (1975) 62 Cr.App.R. 462 (C.A.), *infra*; *R.* v. *Mustafa* (1976) 65 Cr.App.R. 26 (C.A.); *R.* v. *Scarrott* [1978] Q.B. 1016 (C.A.), *infra*.; and *R.* v. *Mansfield* (1977) 65 Cr.App.R. 276 (C.A.), *infra*; *R.* v. *Tricoglus* (1976) 65 Cr.App.R. 16 (C.A.); *R.* v. *Johannsen* (1976) 65 Cr.App.R. 101 (C.A.); *R.* v. *Novac* (1976) 65 Cr.App.R. 107 (C.A.); *R.* v. *Inder* (1977) 67 Cr.App.R. 143 (C.A.), Chapter 23, *infra*; *R.* v. *Clarke* (1978) 67 Cr.App.R. 398 (C.A.); *R.* v. *Seaman* (1978) 67 Cr.App.R. 234 (C.A.); *R.* v. *Barringon* [1981] 1 W.L.R. 419 (C.A.); *R.* v. *Blackstock* (1979) 70 Cr.App.R. 34 (C.A.); *R.* v. *McGlinchey* (1984) 78 Cr.App.R. 282 (C.A.), *infra*; *R.* v. *Asif* (1985) 82 Cr.App.R. 123 (C.A.); *R.* v. *Butler* (1987) 84 Cr.App.R. 12 (C.A.), *infra*; *R.* v. *Williams* (1987) 84 Cr.App.R. 299 (C.A.), *infra*; *R.* v. *Lunt* (1987) 85 Cr.App.R. 241 (C.A.), *infra*. See, too, a secondary *ratio* (or dicta) in *R.* v. *Anderson* [1988] Q.B. 678 (C.A.) (Chapter 23, *infra*).

See, too, *R.* v. *Lewis* (1983) 76 Cr.App.R. 33 (C.A.), a case in which the general principles laid down in *R.* v. *Boardman* appear to have been avoided or flouted (and for a critical commentary, see (1985) 48 Mod.L.R. 29, esp., pp. 37–42).

R. v. **Rance and Herron** (1975) 62 Cr.App.R. 118 (C.A.). The applicant, Rance, who was the managing director of a building company, was charged with corruptly procuring a payment to Herron, and Herron was charged with receiving it. The payment was made on a certificate signed by Rance falsely naming Herron as a sub-contractor. Rance's defence was that he must have been tricked into signing the document not knowing what it was and that it was for this reason alone that he would seem to have been implicated in what was undoubtedly a transaction of bribery. Evidence was admitted of two other payments made in strikingly similar circumstances to two persons named respectively McKenna and Bowes. In each case corrupt payments were made on certificates signed by Rance and containing false statements as to work done by the recipient of the money. Rance's application for leave to appeal against conviction was refused. Lord Widgery C.J. said (p. 121): "The gist of what is being said both by Lord Cross and by Lord Salmon [in *D.P.P.* v. *Boardman* (*supra*)] is that evidence is admissible as similar fact evidence if, but only if, it goes beyond showing a tendency to commit crimes of this kind and is positively probative in regard to the crime now charged. That, we think, is the test which we have to apply on the question of the correctness or otherwise of the admission of the similar fact evidence in this case. We think quite clearly that the evidence of the other transactions—Bowes and McKenna—did, if accepted by the jury, go beyond merely showing that Rance was a person who was not above passing a bribe. The essence of each of these three cases is that a bribe was paid out to a councillor in respect of a contract in which Rance's company was interested, and in every case (each of the three—the instant one and the other two) there is the bogus document of some kind with Rance's signature on it which is the basis upon which the bribe was to be covered up. We have no doubt in saying that in those circumstances the similar fact evidence of Bowes's case and McKenna's case did go beyond merely showing a tendency on the part of Rance to commit the offence. Therefore it passed the test in *D.P.P.* v. *Boardman* (*supra*) and so far was correctly admitted." The court then went on to reject the submission that evidence of similar facts must necessarily be excluded if the correctness of the evidence as to the occurrence of those facts is itself challenged. Lord Widgery C.J. said (p. 122): "The question of whether the evidence relating to the similar facts is accepted or not is a question for the jury,... If the judge is satisfied that the evidence, if accepted by the jury, goes beyond evidence of mere disposition, he should let the evidence in and then leave it to the jury to make what they think of it,... " Regarding the need to warn the jury as to the use to which admitted similar fact evidence can properly be put Lord Widgery said (p. 122): "For our part we think that in this type of case it is a very suitable and proper thing that the judge should consider whether to give a warning of that kind, but we decline to say as a matter of principle that it must always be done and at pains of the conviction being set aside if not. If, as in the present case, the whole approach to the admission of similar facts has been for the purpose of showing something other than disposition, we do not regard it as necessarily fatal that the judge has not in terms spelt out to the jury that they must not allow the evidence to be used for what Lord Hailsham calls "the forbidden purpose." In this case we are satisfied, looking at the summing-up as a whole, that it is not."

Note.—The consideration given by the court to the relative roles of judge and jury appears to contain some conflation which could be misleading.

The admissibility of evidence is, as Lord Salmon reaffirmed in *D.P.P.* v. *Boardman*, "Solely a question of law." The determination of preliminary issues of fact for the purpose of ruling upon admissibility is accordingly a matter for the judge. To the extent that the admissibility of an item of similar fact evidence depends upon its having great probative worth one of the factors which a judge may have to take into account is his assessment of the accuracy of the evidence that similar facts occurred. Of course, if the evidence is admitted, it will then be for the jury to decide how much weight to attach to it, and in this context the jury must themselves consider the accuracy of the evidence of the similar facts.

At the same time, if admissibility is being considered on the basis that the similar fact evidence would serve to rebut the defence of accident or otherwise highlight an improbable coincidence, the judge will first decide whether a reasonable jury could believe that the similar facts occurred, and, if so, he will then make his determination of admissibility on the hypothesis that the jury will in fact believe this.

In an appropriate case the jury should be carefully instructed to disregard the similar fact evidence unless they do believe it.

See, generally, *R.* v. *Scarrott* [1978] Q.B. 1016 (C.A.) (*infra*).

R. v. **Mansfield** (1977) 65 Cr.App.R. 276 (C.A.). [This case is also reported: [1978] 1 W.L.R. 1002 and [1978] 1 All E.R. 134. There is some variation between the reports, and in the Weekly Law Reports the point relating to the admissibility of similar fact evidence is referred to only briefly.] The accused had been convicted of starting three fires. At his trial he had submitted that there should be separate trials in respect of each of these fires because the alleged similarities between them were not sufficiently striking to justify admission of the evidence relating to all of them in respect of each one of them. The judge refused to sever the indictment, and the trial proceeded. In the course of his summing-up the judge instructed the jury to ask themselves whether they felt sure that the three fires had all been started by the same person. If (and seemingly only if) they did so feel, they could then take account of the evidence relating to the first two fires when considering the accused's guilt in respect of the third fire. The Court of Appeal, dismissing Mansfield's appeal against conviction, held that there was a sufficient degree of similarity between the three fires to justify admission of the evidence in respect of all of them in considering each count. Accordingly, the judge had not acted improperly in refusing to sever the indictment, and no misdirection was involved in the judge's charge to the jury as to the way in which they should treat the similar fact evidence. The Court of Appeal took the view that the decision of the House of Lords in *Harris* v. *Director of Public Prosecutions* [1952] A.C. 694 (*supra*) could be distinguished on the ground that in that case there was virtually no evidence connecting the accused and the first seven of the eight thefts, whereas in the instant case there was "overwhelming evidence that in relation to the first two fires the appellant was not only in the vicinity but he had ample opportunity of starting those fires and in relation to each of them he behaved afterwards in a manner which aroused suspicion."

Note.—This case could perhaps generate some unease. Not only is it variously reported, but the judgment of the Court of Appeal is scarcely pellucid. Also, not only had there been an earlier trial at which the jury had failed to agree, but at this second trial the judge had exhorted the jury to reach a unanimous verdict in order to avoid the "great public inconvenience and expense" which would be involved in a third trial,—a procedure of which the Court of Appeal disapproved after "anxious consideration," although holding the judge had not in any way tried to pressurise the jury.

The similarity of the circumstances surrounding the three fires could suggest that they were all started by the same person, but it could not in itself suggest that the accused was that person. The Court of Appeal, however, seems to have taken the view that, once it was accepted that the fires were all started by one person, then any evidence suggesting that the accused started any one fire would automatically suggest that he started the other fires as well. The formal logic of this is impeccable; —but logic sometimes makes little allowance for the way in which the minds of members of juries are likely to work in fact, and sometimes to work to the prejudice of the accused.

Contrast *R.* v. *Tricoglus* (1977) 65 Cr.App.R. 16 (C.A.) where the striking similarity between two rapes strongly suggested that both were perpetrated by the same man but provided little indication that that man was the accused, and the conviction was quashed.

R. v. SCARROTT

[1978] Q.B. 1016; [1978] 1 All E.R. 672; 65 Cr.App.R. 125; [1977] Crim.L.R. 745
(C.A.: 1977)

For similar fact evidence to be admissible as being "strikingly similar" it must have "positive probative value." This is not to be inferred from the mere similarity of commonplace facts.
There are procedural guidelines to assist trial judges in ruling on similar fact evidence.

The defendant was tried on an indictment containing 13 counts, charging him with buggery, attempted buggery, assault with intent to commit buggery and indecent assault involving eight boys over a period of four-and-a-half years. His counsel's application to sever the indictment asking for separate trials in respect of each boy was refused. During the course of the trial the judge ruled that the evidence given by each boy relating to the count, or counts, concerning him had a striking similarity to the evidence given by the other boys and was therefore admissible on the other counts. The defendant was convicted on one count of buggery, one count of attempted buggery and eight counts of indecent assault on seven boys. His appeal against conviction was dismissed. The judgment of the Court of Appeal, given by Scarman L.J., is especially valuable for the procedural guidelines which are laid down for trial judges when ruling on similar fact evidence.

SCARMAN L.J. (delivering the judgment of the court, which included ROSKILL L.J. and WIEN J.): ... Positive probative value is what the law requires, if similar fact evidence is to be admissible. Such probative value is not provided by the mere repetition of similar facts; there has to be some feature or features in the evidence sought to be adduced which provides a link—an underlying link as it has been called in some of the cases. The existence of such a link is not to be inferred from mere similarity of facts which are themselves so commonplace that they can provide no sure ground for saying that they point to the commission by the accused of the offence under consideration.

Lord Cross of Chelsea put the matter, as we think, in its correct perspective at the end of the day when, in the course of his speech in *Reg.* v. *Boardman* [1975] A.C. 421, 459, he said: "The likelihood of such a coincidence obviously becomes less and less the more people there are who make the similar allegations and the more striking are the similarities in various stories. In the end, as I have said, it is a question of degree." ... ultimately the task of judgment is to assess the evidence, and, in this class of case, the degree of similarity. That must be a matter for judgment upon the particular circumstances of each case.

We therefore have to consider in this appeal whether the evidence sought to be adduced by the Crown does reveal similarities which may be described as striking, or, as we prefer to put it, which may be described as giving to the evidence positive probative value. ...

.... If the judge was right to have ruled this evidence as admissible, he was certainly also correct in the way in which he left it to the jury. As Lord Salmon said in the passage already quoted, admissibility is a question of law for the judge and, therefore, at the stage when he is making his ruling he has to make up his mind whether the evidence possesses features of striking similarity or not. He cannot leave it to the jury. But, having made up his mind to admit the evidence, the judge is certainly right to do what Judge Vowden did in this case and tell the jury that when they come to consider whether the evidence is worthy of acceptance and whether the evidence is to be treated as corroboration, then it is a matter for them, at that stage, to consider whether the similarities are sufficiently striking for them to accept the evidence as corroboration just as it is a matter for them to decide at that stage whether the evidence that they have under consideration is credible or not. This is so, even though it is a question of law for the judge on his ruling to make up his mind as to whether there are similarities sufficiently striking to allow the evidence to go before the jury. The jury still have, as ever in our criminal trials, the last word when they come to consider whether they will accept the evidence and what effect they will give it.

....

We have come to the conclusion that the evidence does possess that positive, probative value, does possess striking similarities. It is necessary to repeat the features which are strikingly similar: the ages of the boys, the way in which their resistance was worn down, the location of the offences and the offences themselves. Taken together, these similarities are inexplicable on the basis of coincidence. We have come to the conclusion, therefore, that the judge was right to admit this evidence and that he was right to submit it to the jury in the way that he did. ...

We think, however, that, in this very difficult class of case where trial judges do face a very complex problem in both the conduct of the trial

and in summing up, we should attempt to give some practical guidance
to judges at certain stages of the trial. What we now say is not to be
considered as any advance or development of the law; it is merely an
attempt upon the basis of *Reg.* v. *Kilbourne* [1973] A.C. 729 and *Reg.* v.
Boardman [1975] A.C. 421 to give some guidance which may be helpful
to judges who have this very difficult task to discharge.

The help that we can give deals really with a number of phases of the
trial process. The first phase is before arrangement when a defendant
submits that the indictment should be severed. Of course the question as
to whether a judge should allow an indictment to contain a number of
counts initially has to be dealt with under the discretion given to a judge
by the Indictment Rules 1971, and in particular rule 9, which only
repeats the law as it has been ever since 1915: "Charges for any offences
may be joined in the same indictment if those charges are founded on
the same facts, or form or are a part of a series of offences of the same
or a similar character." It is not very difficult for a judge to reach a
conclusion under that rule, but, having come to the conclusion, as Judge
Vowden plainly did in this case, that the offences were of a similar
character and a series, he then has to consider how to deal with the
application to sever. It appears to us that when such an application at
this stage is made a judge must, as Lawton L.J. said in *Reg.* v.
Johannsen [now reported (1977) 65 Cr.App.R. 101] act not on some
judicial speculation as to what may happen in the trial but on such
factual material as is then available to him, *i.e.* the depositions or the
statements, according to the nature of the committal proceedings. He
must ask himself at that stage, whether in his judgment it would be
open to a jury, properly directed and warned, to treat the evidence
available upon a study of the depositions or statements as strikingly
similar to the evidence to be adduced in respect of the various counts
and he must, we think, be able even at that stage to take the matter a
little further; he must be able to say that if this evidence is believed, it
could be accepted as admissible similar fact evidence or, as in the
circumstances of this class of case, as evidence capable of corroborating
the direct evidence. Of course he will also at this stage, as at all stages
of a criminal trial when a ruling is required of him, consider whether the
evidence appears to be, upon the information then available, independent or untainted evidence and whether there is a real chance that there
is falsity or conspiracy to give false evidence and he must also consider
at this, as at every stage when a ruling is sought, the balance, upon the
information then available to him, between the possible prejudicial
effect of the evidence and its probative value. If the judge takes all
those well-known matters into account, and reaches his decision upon
the basis of the factual information which is available to him, it does not
seem to us possible to fault the exercise of his discretion whichever way
it goes. It is important to appreciate that at this stage, the pre-
arraignment stage, the ultimate decision of the judge is an exercise of
judicial discretion. So long as he does not err in law, takes into account
all relevant matters and excludes consideration of irrelevant matters, his
discretion will stand. Of course at this stage the judge is taking no final
decision as to the admissibility of evidence. If he decides to allow the
multi-count indictment to proceed, it will still be for his ruling as to
whether the evidence, for instance, on counts 1 to 7 will be admitted as
similar fact evidence to assist in the proof of the offence charged in
count 8 and so on throughout the indictment. It does not follow that
because a multi-count indictment has been allowed to proceed that

therefore the evidence given will be evidence on all the counts contained in the indictment. Similarly, if he decides at this stage to sever and if the trial proceeds upon the basis of only, let us say, one count, it will be open to the prosecution, at the appropriate moment, to adduce evidence relating to the other (and now put aside) counts as similar fact evidence of that count and it will then be for the judge to rule, in accordance with the laws of evidence, whether the evidence is admissible or not.

The next phase of the trial process, on which we think, in the light of the authorities, we can give some practical guidance, is when the judge's ruling is sought as to the admissibility of the similar fact evidence. His task, though a difficult exercise of judgment, can be stated in simple terms. He first has to reach a view upon what he then knows of the facts of the case and of the nature of the evidence to be adduced as to whether the evidence possesses the features of striking similarity or probative value which have been canvassed earlier in this judgment. If he reaches the view that it does, he then has to consider whether the evidence is such that it ought to be put to the jury. He may be impressed with the very real possibility that the evidence is tainted by conspiracy or ganging up, the group objection, or he may, because of the group objection or for some other reason, take the view that, though strikingly similar and therefore, prima facie, admissible, the evidence is so prejudicial that its prejudicial effect outweighs its probative value. If he admits the evidence, he will in his summing up have to make sure that the jury is left with the task of deciding whether to accept the evidence and whether to treat the evidence as in fact corroboration or not. Here Judge Vowden, as I have already mentioned, very correctly did that, notwithstanding he had already made his ruling as to striking similarities.

R. v. **McGlinchey** (1984) 78 Cr.App.R. 283 (C.A.). The defendant was charged on an indictment containing, *inter alia*, three counts—count 3 with handling photographic equipment, count 4 with burglary occurring 10 days later, and count 5 with handling four days later still a stolen credit card which was one of the articles stolen in the count 4 burglary. The trial judge rejected a submission that counts 4 and 5 should be severed from count 3. The defendant was convicted on counts 3 and 5, but acquitted on count 4. The Court of Appeal held that the judge had properly exercised his discretion. The court took the opportunity to restate the principles which apply to the exercise of judicial discretion relating to severance of counts in an indictment. In the course of this French J., delivering the judgment of the court said (pp. 385–385): "(2) Rule 9 [of the Indictment Rules 1971] does not mean that joinder of offences can only be sanctioned if they arise out of the same facts or are part of a system of conduct. (3) A sufficient nexus must exist between the offences. (4) A sufficient nexus will exist if evidence of one offence would be admissible on the trial of another, but the rule is not confined to such cases. (5) All that is necessary to satisfy the rule is that the offences should exhibit such similar features that they can conveniently be tried together in the general interests of justice, including those of the defendants, the Crown, the witnesses and the public. (6) The manifest intention of the 1915 [Indictments] Act is that charges which either are founded on the same facts or relate to a series of offences of the same or similar character, properly can, and normally should, be joined in one indictment and a joint trial of the charges will normally follow, although the judge has a discretionary power to direct separate trials under section 5(3) of the 1915 Act. (7) The judge has no duty to direct separate trials under section 5(3) unless in his opinion there is some special feature of the case which would make a joint trial of several counts prejudicial or embarrassing to the accused and separate trials are required in the interests of justice...." French J. referred to "dicta" of Lords Wilberforce and Cross in the *Boardman* case but regarded it as "inconceivable" that their Lordships had intended to cast doubt on the general validity of the earlier decision of the House in *Ludlow* v. *Metropolitan Police Commissioner* [1971] A.C. 29, from which (together with *R.* v. *Kray* [1970] 1 Q.B. 125) the principles now restated were derived.

Note.—Included amongst the "dicta" referred to by French J. was that of Lord Cross ([1975] A.C. 421, 459) that, "If the charges are tried together it is inevitable that the jurors will be influenced, consciously or unconsciously, by the fact that the accused is being charged not with a single offence against one person but with three separate offences against three persons. It is said, I know, that to order separate trials in all these cases would be highly inconvenient. If and so far as this is true it is a reason for doubting the wisdom of the general rule excluding similar fact evidence. But so long as there is that general rule the courts ought to strive to give effect to it loyally and not, while paying lip service to it, in effect let in inadmissible evidence by trying all the charges together." This would appear to be an unequivocal and clear statement. In *R.* v. *McGlinchey* the Court of Appeal sought to confine its scope to circumstances such as those in *Boardman* itself. Such a limitation would appear to be devoid of policy justification; moreover it is to be remembered that it was heavily emphasised in *R.* v. *Boardman* that there is no special rule governing the direct admissibility of similar fact evidence in sexual and homosexual cases.

R. v. **Butler** (1987) 84 Cr.App.R. 12 (C.A.). The appellant was charged with rape and indecent assault on two young women. Forensic evidence supported their stories. Both had been picked up at bus stops, asked to perform similar sex acts, and then raped. At the trial the judge admitted evidence from a former girl friend of the appellant concerning a sexual relationship she had had with him before her marriage. They had at times indulged in sexual activity in his car in a way identical with what had taken place on the nights when the two victims were indecently assaulted and raped. She also identified the scenes of the rapes as being places where she had been with the appellant for sexual purposes. She had been a consenting party. The Court of Appeal held that this evidence had been properly admitted. The trial judge had identified eight particular features which the prosecution had submitted showed a "striking similarity." Sir Ralph Kilner Brown, giving the judgment of the Court of Appeal, said (p. 17): "The judge took the view, with which we concur, that these were not only strikingly similar but in their weight were very substantial indeed."

R. v. **Williams** (1987) 84 Cr.App.R. 299 (C.A.). The appellant was charged with making a threat to kill contrary to the Offences against the Person Act 1861, s.16. The trial judge admitted evidence that the appellant had previously assaulted the same intended victim. The Court of Appeal held that this evidence had been rightly admitted. Hodgson J., reading the judgment of the court, referred to the "somewhat unusual mental element required for the commission of this offence" and said (p. 300): "The prosecution therefore had to establish both that the appellant made the threats to Mrs. Edwards and that he intended that she should fear they would be carried out." The evidence had been admitted as tending to show that the appellant intended his threats to be taken seriously.

Note.—It is not altogether clear why the disputed evidence would tend to show the appellant's intention that the victim should fear, although it might well tend to show that she would in fact fear. Moreover and more importantly, it might be taken to indicate the appellant's ill-will towards the victim. It is to be noted in this latter connection that the court seems to have disassociated itself from what had been said in *R.* v. *Berry* (1986) 83

Cr.App.R. 7 (C.A.) casting doubt on *R.* v. *Ball* [1911] A.C. 47 (H.L.) (*supra*). Viewed in this way, the actual effect of the evidence in *R.* v. *Williams* involved the assumption that the appellant's ill-will was continuing, just as the effect of the disputed evidence in *R.* v. *Ball* involved the assumption that the couple's "guilty passion" was continuing. What is relied upon is the existence of a propensity—albeit a mental or emotional propensity. Such reliance by the jury might, given the weight of the evidence, be very reasonable.

R. v. **Lunt** (1987) 85 Cr.App.R. 241 (C.A.). The appellant and co-defendants were charged with offences involving the use of a stolen cheque-book and card. Evidence was admitted of a statement made by one of the co-defendants dealing, not only with the occasions when one forged cheque was so used to obtain goods, but also with numerous other occasions when 24 forged cheques from the stolen cheque book were similarly used to obtain goods and services. The Court of Appeal held that the evidence had been rightly admitted as being "positively probative" to rebut the appellant's defence of "innocent association." It was also reaffirmed that similar fact evidence is not automatically to be excluded on the ground that it is provided by an accomplice. All that is then required is the usual "mandatory warning" with regard to the evidence of an accomplice, and this warning had been given in the instant case.

HOLLINGHAM v. HEAD

4 C.B.(N.S.) 388; **27** **L.J.C.P. 241;** 4 Jur.(N.S.) 379; 6 W.R. 442; 140 E.R. 1135
(Common Pleas: 1858)

In civil cases the fact that a person has done a thing on other occasions is not usually admissible to show that he did it on the occasion in question, unless at least it clearly renders this reasonably likely.

The question being whether the plaintiff had sold guano to the defendant on certain special terms, the fact that he had sold guano to other persons on such terms was inadmissible as evidence.

WILLES J.: ... The question is, whether in an action for goods sold and delivered, it is competent for the defendant to show, by way of defence, that the plaintiff has entered into contracts with other persons in a particular form, for the purpose of inducing the jury to come to the conclusion that the contract sued upon was in that particular form, and so to defeat the action; and I am of opinion that it is not competent for the defendant to do so. ...

It may be often difficult to decide upon the admissibility of evidence, where it is offered for the purpose of establishing probability, but to be admissible it must at least afford a reasonable inference as to the principal matter in dispute. ... It appears to me that the evidence, which was proposed to be given in this case, would not have shown that it was probable that the plaintiff had made the contract, which the defendant contended he had made; for I do not see how the fact that a man has once or more in his life acted in a particular way makes it probable that he so acted on a given occasion. The admission of such evidence would be fraught with the greatest inconvenience. Where, indeed, the question is one of guilty knowledge or intent, as in the case of uttering forged documents or base coin, such evidence is admissible as tending to establish a necessary ingredient of the crime. But if the evidence were admissible in this case, it would be difficult to say that in any case, where the question was whether or not goods had been sold upon credit, the defendant might not call evidence to prove that other persons had received credit from the plaintiff; or in an action for an assault, that the plaintiff might not prove that the defendant had assaulted other persons generally, or persons of a particular class.

To obviate the prejudice, the injustice, and the waste of time to which the admission of such evidence would lead, and bearing in mind the extent to which it might be carried, and that litigants are mortal, it is necessary not only to adhere to the rule but to lay it down strictly. I think, therefore, the fact that the plaintiff had entered into contracts of a particular kind with other persons on other occasions could not properly be admitted in evidence, where no custom of trade to make such contracts, and no connection between such and the one in question, was shown to exist. . . .

BYLES and WILLIAMS JJ. delivered concurring judgments.

Note.—In other civil cases, however, evidence of similar facts has sometimes been regarded as relevant to the case of either party, and thus admissible. In *Hales* v. *Kerr* [1908] 2 K.B. 601 (D.C.), an action for negligence in shaving the plaintiff with a dirty razor and thereby infecting him with ringworm, evidence was admissible that other persons shaved in the defendant's shop had been similarly infected. See, too, *Sattin* v. *National Union Bank* (1978) 122 S.J. 367 (C.A.). In *Joy* v. *Phillips, Mills & Co. Ltd.* [1916] 1 K.B. 849 (C.A.), on a claim for workman's compensation by the father of a stable boy, who was kicked by a horse and found dying with a halter in his hand, evidence was admitted that the boy had previously teased horses with a halter. Again, the practice of a deceased workman and others, in not using a safety belt, has been treated as the appropriate basis of an inference that the deceased would not have worn one if it had been available (see *McWilliams* v. *Sir William Arrol & Co. Ltd.* [1962] 1 W.L.R. 295 (H.L.)).

As to identifying the principle of an agent, see *Woodward* v. *Buchanan* (1870) L.R. 5 Q.B. 285; *Blake* v. *Albion Life Assurance Society* (1878) 4 C.P.D. 94 (D.C.).

Evidence of previous familiarity between persons accused of adultery has been received.

As to rebutting a defence of apology by evidence of other libels, see *Barrett* v. *Long* (1851) 3 H.L.Cas. 395.

See, too, *R.* v. *Riley* (1887) 18 Q.B.D. 481 (p. 182, *supra*) concerning evidence of similar conduct on other occasions between the prosecutrix and the accused in cases of rape, etc.

MOOD MUSIC PUBLISHING CO. LTD. v. DE WOLFE PUBLISHING LTD.

[1976] 1 Ch. 119; [1976] 1 All E.R. 463 (C.A.: 1975)

Similar fact evidence may be admissible to rebut an allegation of coincidence.
Similar fact evidence is more readily admissible in civil cases generally than it is in criminal cases.

The plaintiffs and the defendants were both music publishers. The plaintiffs brought an action for infringement of copyright. The defendants admitted the similarity of a musical work produced by themselves to a work in which the plaintiffs owned the copyright, but they alleged that this similarity resulted from sheer coincidence. To rebut this the plaintiffs were allowed by the trial judge to adduce evidence of other works produced by the defendants bearing marked similarity to works in which other persons owned the copyright. The defendants appealed against the judge's ruling, contending that evidence of similar facts should not be introduced in a civil action for breach of copyright when there was no allegation of fraud or dishonesty and when they had not had proper notice.

LORD DENNING M.R.:...The admissibility of evidence as to "similar facts" has been much considered in the criminal law.... The criminal courts have been very careful not to admit such evidence unless its probative value is so strong that it should be received in the interests of justice: and its admission will not operate unfairly to the accused. In civil cases the courts have followed a similar line but have not been so chary of admitting it. In civil cases the courts will admit evidence of similar facts if it is logically probative, that is, if it is logically relevant in determining the matter which is in issue: provided that it is not oppressive or unfair to the other side: and also that the other side has fair notice of it and is able to deal with it. Instances are *Brown* v. *Eastern & Midlands Railway Co.* (1889) 22 Q.B.D. 391; *Moore* v. *Ransome's Dock Committee* (1898) 14 T.L.R. 539 and *Hales* v. *Kerr* [1908] 2 K.B. 601.

The matter in issue in the present case is whether the resemblances which "Girl in the Dark" bear to "Sogno Nostalgico" are mere coincidences or are due to copying. Upon that issue it is very relevant to know that there are these other cases of musical works which were undoubtedly the subject of copyright, but that the defendants have nevertheless produced musical works bearing close resemblance to them. Whereas it might be due to mere coincidence in one case, it is very unlikely that they would be coincidences in four cases. It is rather like *Rex* v. *Sims* [1946] K.B. 531, 540, where it was said: "The probative force of all the acts together is much greater than one alone." So the probative force of four resemblances together is much better than one alone....

It seems to me the judge was right.... I would dismiss the appeal.

ORR and BROWNE L.JJ. agreed.

Note.—In *Thorpe* v. *Chief Constable of Greater Manchester Police* [1989] 1 W.L.R. 665 (C.A.), an action brought against the police claiming damages for assault, unlawful arrest, false imprisonment and malicious prosecution, it was held that courts will not order discovery of certificates of previous convictions (or adjudications of guilt in police disciplinary proceedings) except in rare cases in which these might be necessary to prove admissible similar facts. Neill L.J., having referred to *Mood Music Publishing Co. Ltd.* v. *De Wolfe Ltd.* (*supra*) as the "leading modern authority on 'similar fact' evidence in civil proceedings," said (p. 674): "Evidence of 'similar facts' is relevant both in criminal and in civil cases to rebut defences such as accident or coincidence or sometimes to prove a system of conduct. Such evidence is not admissible, however, merely to show that the party concerned has a disposition to commit the conduct alleged." In *Thorpe* discovery was refused because there was no reason to suppose that any defence of accident or coincidence was likely to be raised, and there was no basis for any suggestion that the evidence could prove "system."

The phrase "a system of conduct" could in some circumstances be unduly restrictive, and "positive probative value" (see *R.* v. *Scarrott* [1978] Q.B. 1016 (C.A.) *supra*) is perhaps to be preferred.

The importance of Neill L.J.'s formulation lies in the re-affirmation of the distinction between admissibility on this basis (however stated) and admissibility for the purpose of rebutting a defence such as accident or coincidence.

Chapter 21

EVIDENCE OF DISPOSITION: PREVIOUS CONVICTIONS

A party's conviction on a particular occasion may always be proved when the fact of that conviction is in issue. Thus in a civil action for libel, in which the defendant seeks to justify his allegation that the plaintiff is a convicted criminal, proof of the plaintiff's conviction will be admissible. Thus, too, in criminal proceedings, if the accused enters a plea of *autrefois convict*, evidence will be admissible to prove his prior conviction of the offence with which he is then charged; and some statutes prescribe the fact of previous conviction as an ingredient of a crime.[1]

Evidence of a party's previous conviction which is merely relevant to an issue may now be admitted as tending the show the truth of the facts upon which the conviction was based[2]; but, of course, it will not be so admissible unless evidence of those facts would itself be admissible. Whether this latter will be the case will usually be controlled by the similar fact rule[3] and/or the rules relating to character evidence generally.[4] To this general pattern of the law there are, however, some very exceptional cases of statutory admissibility of convictions for specified limited purposes. The most important of these is to be found in section 27(3)(*b*) of the Theft Act 1968.[5] It provides that where a person is proceeded against only for handling stolen goods and evidence has been given of the other ingredients of the offence, "evidence that he has within the five years preceding the date of the offence charged been convicted of theft or handling stolen goods" will be admissible, but only for the purpose of proving that he knew or believed the goods to be stolen goods. The accused must be given seven days' written notice of the prosecution's intention to prove the prior conviction. Also, in defamation proceedings evidence of the plaintiff's previous convictions for offences bearing upon the alleged defamation may be given in mitigation of damages.[6]

---

[1] See, *e.g.* The Firearms Act 1968, s.21.
[2] See the Civil Evidence Act 1968, ss.11–13; and the Police and Criminal Evidence Act 1984, s.74 (both Part Two, *infra*).
[3] Chapter 20, *supra*.
[4] Chapter 22, *infra*.
[5] Part Two, *infra*. Section 27(3)(*a*) deals correspondingly with similar fact evidence (Chap. 20, *supra*).
[6] *Goody* v. *Odhams Press* [1967] 1 Q.B. 333 (C.A.). See, too, the Official Secrets Act 1911, s.1(2), Part Two, *infra*.

In civil cases a party who himself gives evidence may be cross-examined about his previous convictions, not only when they are in issue, but also with a view to shaking his credibility as a witness. If he then denies that he has been convicted, the fact may be proved under the Criminal Procedure Act 1865, s.6.[7] If the accused testifies in a criminal case he may only be cross-examined as to his previous convictions, even for the sole purpose of shaking his credibility, to the extent that this permitted under proviso (f) to section 1 of the Criminal Evidence Act 1898.[8]

In a criminal case after conviction proof of previous criminal convictions may be given in order to help the court on the question of sentence. Formal proof is not required, unless the previous conviction is denied by the accused, and the judge may then call for strict proof.[9]

Two overriding limitations upon the admissibility of evidence of previous convictions are created by the provisions of the Children and Young Persons Act 1963[10] and the Rehabilitation of Offenders Act 1974.[11] The former provides by section 16(2) that, in criminal proceedings against a person of 25 years or more, evidence of his conviction for an offence while under the age of 14 "shall be disregarded for the purposes of any evidence relating to his previous convictions": nor may he be cross-examined about them. The general effect of the Rehabilitation of Offenders Act 1974 is that, once a conviction has become "spent," no evidence is admissible in most civil proceedings to show that the person thus "rehabilitated" was charged with, committed or was convicted of, the offence to which the conviction related, unless this is permitted by the judge on the ground that justice cannot otherwise be done. Convictions leading to a life sentence or a fixed term of more than 30 months' imprisonment cannot become "spent." Otherwise a conviction becomes "spent" after the expiration of a period of time the duration of which varies according to the length of the sentence. A further conviction during the running of a rehabilitation period may delay rehabilitation or preclude it altogether. The Act does not apply in criminal proceedings, but a Practice Direction made in 1975[12] provides that reference should not be made to a spent conviction even in such proceedings unless it cannot reasonably be avoided, and then only with the authority of the judge which should not be given unless the interests of justice so require.

Evidence of an acquittal of a party may be received if the fact of acquittal is actually in issue, as for example in an action for malicious prosecution. Otherwise, evidence of an acquittal, which of course itself shows no more than that commission has not been proved beyond reasonable doubt, is generally excluded. However, there can be exceptional circumstances in which evidence of an acquittal, although not itself in issue will be admitted—for instance if a previous acquittal is

---

[7] Part Two, *infra*.

[8] Part Two, *infra*. Materials illustrating the operation of this proviso are set out in Chap. 23, *infra*.

[9] *R. v. Nicholson* [1962] Crim.L.R. 624 (C.C.A.).

[10] Part Two, *infra*.

[11] Part Two, *infra*. The provisions of the Act, which is no masterpiece of drafting, are detailed and complex.

[12] See *Note* to the Act, Part Two, *infra*.

relevant so as to qualify the significance of evidence of previous convictions which has been admitted.[13]

If evidence of a previous acquittal is given accidentally the judge has a discretion as to whether or not to discharge the jury, and his direction that they should disregard the reference to the acquittal may be sufficient: *R.* v. *Palmer* [1983] C.L.Y. 632; [1983] Crim.L.R. 252 (C.A.).

---

[13] *R.* v. *Doosti* (1986) 82 Cr.App.R. 181 (C.A.); see, too, *R.* v. *Hay* (1983) 77 Cr.App. 70 (C.A.).

Chapter 22

EVIDENCE OF DISPOSITION: CHARACTER

THE term "character" is used in the law of evidence to denote sometimes a person's actual disposition, sometimes his reputed disposition or reputation, and sometimes both his actual disposition and his reputation. Evidence of a party's character is generally inadmissible on the grounds that it is often irrelevant or of dubious relevance, its admission would frequently be prejudicial, and to permit its reception could facilitate resort to unfair tactical surprise and/or give rise to prolonged diversionary consideration of side issues.

In civil cases evidence of the defendant's character will not be admissible for the purpose of showing that he behaved in the way alleged by the plaintiff, even though it might in fact have a tendency to do so. Evidence of the plaintiff's character, although also generally inadmissible, will be admissible if it is in issue or if it is directly relevant to a question of liability or of damages. For example, in an action for defamation the plaintiff's character will be directly in issue if justification is pleaded. His character will also be relevant to the amount of damages which, if he is successful, he will be entitled to recover. The traditional rule that the character of the parties to a civil action is usually regarded as irrelevant generally applies to both plaintiff and defendant. However, not only is it established that the rule does not cover cases in which the plaintiff's character is in issue or directly relevant to a question of liability or damages, but it must also be recognised that at the present day, when the role of the exclusionary rules of evidence is being increasingly curtailed in civil cases, evidence bearing upon the character of a party is frequently introduced without exception being taken. When the character of a non-party is in issue or is relevant in civil litigation, evidence of it is admissible.

If a party to civil proceedings himself gives evidence he becomes liable to cross-examination as to his credibility *qua* witness. In this regard and for this purpose his position is no more protected than is that of a non-party witness, as to which see Chapter 9.[1] In a jury trial the judge has the unenviable task of explaining to the jury the need to separate the issue of a party-witness's credibility from issues of liability and damages.

In criminal cases the prosecution may not, subject to minor statutory exceptions, lead evidence of the accused's bad character or seek to elicit

---

[1] See too R. v. *Knightsbridge Cr.Ct., ex p. Goonatilleke* [1986] 1 Q.B. 1 (D.C.).

it by cross-examination unless the accused "puts his character in issue."
If the accused does this by calling witnesses to testify as to his good
character and/or by cross-examining prosecution witnesses with a view to
establishing it, the prosecution may give evidence of his bad character in
rebuttal, but in this context character, whether good or bad, is (anyhow
theoretically) given the special meaning of reputation. By way of
contrast, in cases of statutory admissibility[2] of evidence of the accused's
character as part of the prosecution case it seems clear that evidence of
actual disposition may also be received. Evidence of the character of the
prosecutor or of that of a non-party in criminal proceedings is admissible
to the extent that it is in issue or relevant, but there are special
limitations upon the reception and effect of evidence of the complainant's character in prosecutions or rape and kindred offences.[3]

SCOTT v. SAMPSON

8 Q.B.D. 491; **51 L.J.Q.B. 380;** 46 L.T. 412; 30 W.R. 541 (Q.B.: 1882)

*In actions for defamation, when justification has been pleaded as a
defence, evidence of the plaintiff's reputation is relevant to damages and
admissible. But evidence cannot be given of rumours or suspicions to
the same effect as the matter complained of, or of particular acts of
misconduct by the plaintiff.*

This was an action for libel. The plaintiff, a journalist, alleged that
the defendant had published words to the effect that he had obtained
money under a threat of publishing facts injurious to a lady, and
systematically abused his position as a dramatic critic and journalist for
the purpose of extorting money. The judge at the trial refused to receive
evidence of the plaintiff's character, of specific acts of misconduct, and
also of rumours prior to the alleged libel to the same effect as the
matters complained of. On an application for a new trial it was held that
the evidence of reputation was admissible, but the other evidence was
not admissible, though a new trial was refused on other grounds.

CAVE J.: . . . [In a libel action the plaintiff] complains of an injury to
his reputation, and seeks to recover damages for that injury, and it
seems most material that the jury who have to award those damages
should know, if the fact is so, that he is a man of no reputation. . . . To
enable the jury to estimate the probable quantum of injury sustained, a
knowledge of the party's previous character is not only material, but
seems to be absolutely essential. . . ."
As to the second head of evidence, or evidence of rumours and
suspicions to the same effect as the defamatory matter complained of, it
would seem that upon principle such evidence is not admissible, as only
indirectly tending to affect the plaintiff's reputation. If these rumours
and suspicions have, in fact, affected the plaintiff's reputation, that may

---

[2] *e.g.* Under the Official Secrets Act 1911, s.1(2), Part Two, *infra.* See too the Criminal
Evidence Act 1898, s.1(f), Part Two, *infra,* and *R.* v. *Dunkley* [1927] 1 K.B. 323
(C.C.A.).
[3] See the Sexual Offences (Amendment) Act 1976, s.2, Part Two, *infra.*

be proved by general evidence of reputation. If they have not affected it, they are not relevant to the issue.... Unlike evidence of general reputation, it is particularly difficult for the plaintiff to meet and rebut such evidence; for all that those who know him best can say is that they have not heard anything of these rumours. Moreover, it may be that it is the defendant who himself has started them....

As to the third head, or evidence of facts and circumstances tending to show the disposition of the plaintiff, both principle and authority seem equally against its admission. At the most it tends to prove not that the plaintiff has not, but that he ought not to have, a good reputation, and to admit evidence of this kind is, in effect, to throw upon the plaintiff the difficulty of showing a uniform propriety of conduct during his whole life. It would give rise to interminable issues which would have but a very remote bearing on the question in dispute, which is to what extent the reputation which he actually possesses has been damaged by the defamatory matter complained of....

Note.—*Scott* v. *Sampson* has been approved by the House of Lords in *Plato Films Ltd.* v. *Speidel* [1961] A.C. 1090; although doubts were expressed there, particularly by Lord Radcliffe, about the difficulty and rationality of drawing a clear distinction between reputation and specific acts. Moreover, the evidence of reputation must relate to the aspect of the plaintiff's life to which the defamation relates.

Evidence of the plaintiff's previous convictions for relevant offences may be proved in mitigation of damages: *Goody* v. *Odhams Press Ltd.* [1967] 1 Q.B. 333, 340 (C.A.). See, too, the Civil Evidence Act 1968, s.13 (Part Two, *infra*).

On the issue of the truth of the allegedly defamatory statement (as distinct from that of damages) the admissibility of evidence of rumours or suspicions, or of specific acts, will depend upon the pleadings: *Maisel* v. *Financial Times Ltd.* (1915) 84 L.J.K.B. 2145 (C.A.).

For the position of the plaintiff who is cross-examined as to credit, see *Hobbs* v. *Tinling & Co. Ltd.* [1929] 2 K.B. 1 (C.A.), *infra*.

HOBBS v. TINLING & CO. LTD.

[1929] 2 K.B. 1; 98 L.J.K.B. 421; 141 L.T. 121; 45 T.L.R. 328; (C.A.: 1929)

In actions for defamation, when justification has not been pleaded as a defence, cross-examination as to the plaintiff's character is permissible as cross-examination to credit.

In an action for libel the defendants did not plead justification, but gave notice under the relevant rule (see now R.S.C., Ord. 82, r. 7) of their intention to give in evidence certain matters in mitigation of damages. The plaintiff at the trial gave evidence of good character, and was thereupon cross-examined as to specific incidents neither mentioned in the libel nor in the particulars given. It was held that the cross-examination was admissible as to credit, but that, the incidents alleged being denied by the plaintiff, no evidence was admissible in rebuttal, and that the jury should have been directed (1) that his denials, even if unbelieved, afforded no evidence that the incidents had taken place, and (2) that the cross-examination was not admissible to mitigate damages.

SCRUTTON L.J.:...The civil wrong of defamation by a published written or printed statement, commonly known as libel, is committed by any one who publishes such a statement expressed in such a way that it would be understood by reasonable people to injure appreciably the reputation of another amongst reasonable people acquainted with him. A plaintiff may recover general damages for such a statement without proving his actual reputation or any actual damage.... It follows that a defendant may reduce the damages for libel by proving that the plaintiff had already a bad reputation....

Questions have, of course, arisen as to the circumstances under which evidence can be given to mitigate damages, and the judgment of Cave J., concurred in by Matthew J., in *Scott* v. *Sampson* [*supra*], which carefully considered the authorities has, I think, been accepted as an accurate statement of the law. The defendant may mitigate damages by giving evidence to prove that the plaintiff is a man of bad general reputation, and the plaintiff may rebut it by "coming prepared with friends who have known him to prove that his reputation has been good." On the other hand, the defendant may not give evidence of rumours at the time of publication to the same effect as the libel, nor may the defendant give evidence of specific facts and circumstances to show the disposition of the plaintiff, as distinct from general evidence that he has that reputation. If those specific facts are to the same effect as the libel, which he has not justified, he cannot justify under the plea of mitigation of damages. If those facts are different from the libel they do not prove actual reputation, which can be proved under the first head, but that he ought not to have such a reputation....

In my opinion, just as you cannot prove specific instances of misconduct, as distinguished from general reputation, whether involved in the libel or not, in order to mitigate damages, so also you cannot achieve that purpose by cross-examination as to such specific instances.

There is, however, another purpose for which cross-examination as to specific instances not involved in the libel can be used. When a witness has given evidence material to the issues in that case you can cross-examine him on matters not directly material to the case in order to ask the jury to infer from his answers that he is not worthy of belief, not a credible person, and therefore that they should not accept his answers on questions material to the case as true. This is cross-examination as to his credibility, commonly called cross-examination to credit. But as it is on matters not directly material to the case, the party cross-examining is not allowed to call evidence in chief to contradict his answers. To permit this would involve the court in an interminable series of controversies not directly material to the case on alleged facts of which the witness had no notice when he came into court, and which he or the party calling him might not be prepared without notice to meet. This rule, which has been established by cases in which the party cross-examining has desired to call rebutting evidence in chief, has been expressed in various ways.... But this does not go to the extent contended for by the appellant's counsel that the jury must believe the answers given by the witness. No case has been found where such a contention has been put forward, and if the jury, hearing the answers given by the witness, do not believe him they are entitled to do so, and to use the view thus obtained as to his credibility in rejecting answers given by him on matters material to the case. But rejecting his denials, does not prove the fact he denies, of which there is, and can be, no other evidence. It only destroys his credibility in respect of other evidence....

The Lord Chief Justice gave a wrong direction when he ruled that specific acts of misconduct, not the subject of the libel, might be given in evidence, by questions in cross-examination in mitigation of damages.

GREER L.J.: . . . It seems to be convenient at this stage to state certain rules of law that have been established by the decisions. (1) It is not permissible for a plaintiff to give evidence of particular facts in support of his claim to have a good character, nor is it open to a defendant to give evidence, or to cross-examine as to particular instances with the object of diminishing the damages . . . (2) On the other hand, if a plaintiff in chief gives evidence of any fact, and the defendant disputes that fact, the defendant is entitled to cross-examine to credit, and in particular to cross-examine about details of misconduct, but it has been laid down in a number of cases that the defendant is bound to be content with the plaintiff's answers. He cannot contradict them, but must be content to let them go to the jury as the only evidence on the matters involved in the cross-examination. . . .

SANKEY L.J. delivered a judgment to the same effect.

R. v. Clarke (1817) 2 Stark. 241 (Nisi Prius). Upon an indictment for assault with intent to commit rape, it was proposed, on the part of the defendant, to call witnesses to impugn the character of the prosecutrix, both generally and particularly. Holroyd J. said (p. 244): "It is clear that no evidence can be received of particular facts, and such evidence could not have been received, although the prosecutrix had been cross-examined as to those facts, because her answers upon those facts must have been taken as conclusive. With respect to such facts the case is clear. Then, with respect to general evidence; such evidence, it has been held, is admissible in all cases where character is in issue, and therefore the only question is, whether the character of the prosecutrix is involved in the present issue. In the case of an indictment for a rape, evidence that a woman had a bad character previous to the supposed commission of the offence is admissible; but the defendant cannot go into evidence of particular facts. This is the law upon an indictment for rape, and I am of opinion that the same principles apply to the case of an indictment for an assault with intent to commit rape."

Note.—At common law the complainant in this type of case may be cross-examined about the intercourse with the accused on other occasions and with other men. In the latter (*R. v. Holmes* (1871) L.R. 1 C.C.R. 334), but not in the former (*R. v. Riley* (1887) 18 Q.B.D. 481), event, her answers must be treated as final. The accused may, however, adduce evidence tending to show the complainant's bad reputation for chastity, as in *R. v. Clarke*; and she may be contradicted by other evidence if she denies that she is a prostitute or a woman who has demanded money after sexual intercourse, see *R. v. Bashir*; *R. v. Manzur* [1969] 1 W.L.R. 1303 and *R. v. Krausz* (1973) 57 Cr.App.R. 466 (C.A.).

The common law has been modified by statute so far as evidence of the complainant's sexual intercourse with other men is concerned. See the Sexual Offences (Amendment) Act 1976, s.2, and *Note* thereon, (Part Two, *infra*).

R. v. Cox (1987) 84 Cr.App.R. 132 (C.A.). The accused was charged with rape. His defence was that the complainant had consented. He alleged that she had subsequently accused him of rape because she feared that her boyfriend might leave her if he thought that she had consented to sexual intercourse with the accused. The accused sought leave to cross-examine her about an earlier occasion in which she had had intercourse with another man in similar circumstances and had afterwards falsely accused him of rape. The Court of Appeal held that the judge, in refusing leave, had wrongly exercised his discretion under the Sexual Offences (Amendment) Act 1976, s.2 (Part Two, *infra*).

R. v. ROWTON

34 L.J.M.C. 57; 11 L.T. 745; 13 W.R. 436; 11 Jur.(N.S.) 325; 10 Cox C.C. 25; Le. & Ca. 520; 169 E.R. 1497 (C.C.R.: 1865)

An accused person in a criminal trial can adduce evidence of his good character. The prosecution may rebut such evidence by evidence of his bad character, although they cannot give evidence of his bad character as part of their original case.
Evidence of character must not be evidence of particular facts, but must be evidence of general reputation only, having reference to the nature of the charge.

On a trial for indecent assault, where the defendant had called evidence of his good character, a witness called by the prosecution to rebut such evidence was asked, "What is the defendant's general character for decency and morality of conduct?" The witness said, "I know nothing of the neighbourhood's opinion, because I was only a boy at school when I knew him; but my own opinion, and the opinion of my brothers, who were also pupils of his, is that his character is that of a man capable of the grossest indecency and the most flagrant immorality." It was held by a majority of the judges that this answer was not admissible in evidence.

COCKBURN C.J.:...Two questions present themselves, the first, whether, when evidence in favour of the character of the prisoner has been given on his behalf, evidence of his bad character can be adduced upon the part of the prosecution to rebut the evidence so given. I am clearly of opinion that such evidence may properly be received....

Assuming, then, that evidence was properly received to rebut the prior evidence of good character, adduced by the prisoner, the question still presents itself of whether the answer which was given to the question, which is perfectly legitimate in its character, was an answer which it was proper to leave to the jury? Now, in determining this, it becomes necessary in the first instance, to consider what is the meaning of evidence of character. It is laid down in the books that a prisoner is entitled to give evidence as to his general character. What does that mean? Does it mean evidence as to his reputation amongst those to whom his conduct and position are known, or does it mean evidence of disposition? I think it means evidence of reputation only.... No one ever heard of a question put deliberately to a witness called on behalf of a prisoner as to the prisoner's disposition of mind; the way, and the only way the law allows of your getting at the disposition and tendency of his mind, is by evidence as to his general character found upon the knowledge of those who know anything about him and his general conduct. Now, that is the sense in which I find the word "character" used and applied in all the books of the text-writers of authority upon the subject of evidence....

No one pretends that, according to the present practice, examination can be made as to a specific fact, though every one would agree that evidence of one fact of honesty or dishonesty, as the case might be, would weigh infinitely more than the opinions of a man's friends or neighbours as to his general character. The truth is, this part of our law is an anomaly. Although, logically speaking, it is quite clear that an antecedent bad character would form quite as reasonable a ground for the presumption and probability of guilt, as previous good character lays the foundation for the presumption of innocence, yet the prosecution cannot go into evidence as to the prisoner's bad character. The allowing evidence of a prisoner's good character to be given has grown from a desire to administer the law with mercy, as far as possible. . . .

When we come to consider the question of what, in the strict interpretation of the law, is the limit of such evidence, I must say that, in my judgment, it must be restrained to this: the evidence must be of the man's general reputation, and not the individual opinion of the witness. . . . The witness who acknowledged that he knew nothing of the general character, and had no opportunity of knowing it in the sense of reputation, would not be allowed to give an opinion as to a man's character in the more limited sense of his disposition.

If that be the true doctrine on the subject of the admissibility of evidence to character in favour of the prisoner, the next question that presents itself is, within what limits must the evidence be confined which is adduced in rebutting evidence to meet the evidence which the prisoner has brought forward? I think that that evidence must be of the same character and kept within the same limits; that while the prisoner can give evidence of general good character, so the evidence called to rebut it must be evidence of the same general description, showing that the evidence which has been given to establish a good reputation on the one hand is not true, because the man's general reputation was bad.

Now, then, what is the answer in the present case? The witness, it seems, disclaims all knowledge as to the general reputation of the accused; what he says is this: "I know nothing of the neighbourhood's opinion." I take the witness in this expression to mean to say, "I know nothing of the opinion of those with whom the man has in the ordinary occupations of life been brought immediately into contact. I knew him, and so did two brothers of mind when we were at school, and in my opinion his disposition" (for in that sense the word "character" is used by the witness)—"in my opinion his disposition is such that he is capable of committing the class of offences with which he is charged." I am strongly of opinion that that answer was not admissible in evidence. . . . I take my stand on this: I find it uniformly laid down in the books of authority that the evidence to character must be evidence to general character in the sense of reputation. . . .

POLLOCK C.B., WILLIAMS, BLACKBURN, BYLES, KEATING, MELLOR and SHEE JJ. and MARTIN, CHANNELL and PIGGOTT BB. concurred; ERLE C.J. and WILLES J. dissented.

Note.—This case was decided before an accused person could give evidence on his own behalf. Though the decision is still good law, and also applies when the accused himself gives evidence of his own good character, in such circumstances the accused is liable to be cross-examined as to character. There are special rules on this subject, which are dealt with separately in Chapter 23, and in such cases character sometimes seems to have a wider meaning than reputation. But criminal cases still occur in which the accused does not give evidence, when the general position is as illustrated by *R.* v. *Butterwasser* [1948] 1 K.B. 4 (C.C.A.), *infra.*

R. v. **Redgrave** (1982) 74 Cr.App.R. 10 (C.A.). The accused was charged with importuning for immoral purposes contrary to the Sexual Offences Act 1956, s.32. He sought to tender detailed evidence of his heterosexual relationships with girls in order to rebut inferences that, on the occasion to which the charge related, he had been making homosexual approaches to plain-clothed police officers. The Court of Appeal held that the trial judge had been right to exclude the evidence tendered by the accused. The accused could not rely upon evidence of particular facts in order to show that he had no actual disposition to behave in the way which the prosecution alleged. Lawton L.J., delivering the judgment of the Court said (pp. 14–15): " . . . although disposition to commit the kind of offence charged was relevant, the law is as decided in *Rowtin*, *viz.*, that the defendant could do no more than say, or call witnesses to prove, that he was not by general repute the kind of young man who would have behaved in the kind of way that the Crown alleged." His Lordship did, however, go on to say (p. 15): "It has long been the practice of judges to allow some relaxation of the law of evidence on behalf of defendants. Had this young man been a married man, or alternatively had he confined his relationship to one girl, it might not have been all that objectionable for him to have given evidence in general terms that his relationship with his wife or the girl was satisfactory. That would have been an indulgence on the part of the court."

R. v. **Winfield** [1939] 4 All E.R. 164; 27 Cr.App.R. 139 (C.C.A.). The appellant was convicted of indecent assault upon a woman. At his trial he had called a witness and asked her questions designed to establish his good character with regard to sexual morality. The prosecution had then been allowed to cross-examine the witness on the appellant's previous convictions of offences involving dishonesty. The Court of Criminal Appeal held this to have been proper. Humphreys J. said (Cr.App.R., p. 141): " . . . there is no such thing known to our procedure as putting half a prisoner's character in issue and leaving out the other half. A prisoner, who has a bad character for dishonesty, is not entitled to say that he has never acted indecently towards women and claim that he has not put the rest of his character in issue." (The accused's conviction was quashed on other grounds).

Note.—This decision has been criticised. It runs counter to views expressed as long ago as 1851 by Baron Alderson in *R.* v. *Shrimpton* (1851) 2 Den. 319, 322, and to the dictates of common-sense. As the learned editor of the last edition of Cockle's Statutes and Cases wrote (Nokes, *Introduction to Evidence* (4th ed., 1967), p. 140), "If a man is charged with forgery, cross-examination as to his conviction for cruelty to animals can have no purpose but prejudice." By the same token there would seem to be no reason to suppose *a priori* that, for example, a rapist is likely to be dishonest. *Winfield's* case has been approved by the House of Lords in *Stirland* v. *D.P.P.* [1944] A.C. 315 (Chapter 23, *infra*), but their Lordships were there primarily concerned with a different matter, namely the interpretation of the Criminal Evidence Act 1898.

R. v. BUTTERWASSER

[1948] 1 K.B. 4; 63 T.L.R. 463; 32 Cr.App.R. 81; [1947] 2 All E.R. 415
(C.C.A.: 1947)

Evidence of the bad character or conviction of an accused person is not generally admissible if he does not testify or put his character in issue.

The accused was charged with wounding with intent to do grievous bodily harm. The prosecutor and his wife gave evidence that the accused slashed the prosecutor's face with a razor, and they were cross-examined as to their bad record. A police officer gave evidence of the accused's bad character and read out a record of his previous convictions. The accused did not give evidence. The accused was found guilty of the charge, but his conviction was quashed on appeal.

LORD GODDARD C.J. (giving the judgment of the court, which included HILBERY and LYNSKEY JJ.): We have to consider whether what was done in this case was in accordance with law. When it became clear that the appellant's counsel, after having attacked the witnesses for the prosecution, was not going to call the appellant, the prosecution sought and were allowed to give evidence-in-chief of the prisoner's bad character. A police officer was called, who testified to the prisoner's previous convictions and general character. In the opinion of the court, that was a course which cannot possibly be allowed as the law is at present.... It is, of course, permissible, where a prisoner takes advantage of the [Criminal Evidence] Act 1898 [see Chapter 23, *infra*] which made prisoners competent witnesses on their trial in all cases, and goes into the witness box and attacks the witnesses for the prosecution, to cross-examine him with regard to convictions and matters of character; and no doubt if a conviction is put to him and he denies it, the provisions of Denman's Act [*i.e.* The Criminal Procedure Act 1865, s.6, Part Two, *infra*] would apply and the conviction could be proved against him. But it is admitted that there is no authority, and I do not see on what principle it could be said, that if a man does not go into the box and put his own character in issue, he can have evidence given against him of previous bad character when all that he has done is to attack the witnesses for the prosecution. The reason is that by attacking the witnesses for the prosecution and suggesting they are unreliable, he is not putting his character in issue; he is putting their character in issue. And the reason why, if he gives evidence, he can be cross-examined if he has attacked the witness for the prosecution is that the statute says he can. It seems to the court, therefore, that it is impossible to say that because the prisoner in this case attacked the witnesses for the prosecution but did not himself give evidence, evidence of his bad character was admissible....

Note.—*R.* v. *Butterwasser* was followed in *R.* v. *de Vere* [1982] 1 Q.B. 75 (C.A.), where it was also indicated that an averment of good character, even if not evidence in the strict sense, may sometimes have the effect if putting the accused's character in issue.

R. v. **Bellis** [1966] 1 W.L.R. 234 (C.C.A.). The defendant was convicted of knowingly having explosives in his possession or control. He appealed against conviction on the ground *inter alia* that the Deputy Chairman had misdirected the jury as to the way in which they should treat evidence of his good character. The Court of Criminal Appeal dismissed the appeal. Widgery J., delivering the judgment of the court, said (pp. 235–236): "Criticism is made of the direction of the Deputy Chairman when he dealt with the fact that the defendant was of previous good character. Having told the jury that mere possession of a good character was not, as it were, a ticket to an acquittal, he went on to say: 'But it is something which you must take into account in his favour really on the basis that a person of good character is less likely to commit this type of offence than a man of bad character.' The criticism levelled at that direction is that in the submission of Mr. Gower [defence counsel] the proper direction to the jury in regard to the defendant's good character is that possession of a good character makes his testimony more worthy of belief than that of a man of bad character. The complaint is that the observation should have been directed to the credibility of the defendant rather than to suggest that possession of a good character made it less likely that he would commit this type of offence. Although there is, as Mr. Parker [prosecuting counsel] says, no formal or standard direction in these terms, this court does take the view that possession of a good character is a matter which primarily goes to credibility, but it is to be observed in this case that the direction actually employed by the Deputy Chairman is certainly not less favourable to this defendant, because logically if he directed them that the defendant was more credible by reason of his good character, it would have followed from that that he was less likely to have committed the offence. There is in our view nothing in this point which would in any way cause us to interfere with the verdict of the jury."

Note.—See, too, *R.* v. *Richardson*; *R.* v. *Longman* [1966] 1 Q.B. 299 (C.A.), and *R.* v. *Falconer-Atlee* (1974) 58 Cr.App.R. 348 (C.A.). The notion that evidence of character is irrelevant to the issue of guilt and can therefore bear only on credibility dies hard. But it is a notion that is not easy to accept. If an accused testifies, evidence of his character may often bear upon his credibility *qua* witness, although whether it will be admissible will depend upon the Criminal Evidence Act 1898, s.1, proviso (*f*). But, if relevance reflects probative significance in the light of logic and human experience, evidence of character may well in addition be relevant to the issue of guilt. Moreover, evidence of character may be received in cases in which the accused does not testify; in such cases *ex hypothesi* no issue of his credibility can arise. Notwithstanding recent intimations to the contrary, it is respectfully submitted that Patteson J. with characteristic perspicacity indicated the true position as long ago as 1837 when, in *R.* v. *Stannard* (1837) 7 C. & P. 673, he said: "I cannot in principle make any distinction between evidence of facts and evidence of character; the latter is equally laid before the jury as the former, as being relevant to the question of guilty or not guilty; the object of laying it before the jury is to induce them to believe, from the improbability that a person of good character should have conducted himself as alleged, that there is some mistake or misrepresentation in the evidence on the part of the prosecution, and it is strictly evidence in the case." See *R.* v. *Bryant and Oxley* (1977) 67 Cr.App.R. 157 (C.A.), where it was held that it would be a misdirection for the judge to convey to the jury that evidence of good character is only relevant and admissible when the defendant testifies.

Chapter 23

EVIDENCE OF DISPOSITION: CRIMINAL EVIDENCE ACT 1898

A primary effect of the Criminal Evidence Act 1898[1] was to confer upon an accused person the right to give evidence in his own defence.[2] Parliament was then faced with two inter-acting questions, namely, as to the extent to which an accused when testifying should be allowed to claim the privilege against self-incrimination available to the ordinary witness, and as to the extent to which he should be able to retain whilst under cross-examination the sort of protection against disclosure of evidence of disposition which he would enjoy if he did not himself testify. Provisos (e) and (f) to section 1 of the 1898 Act represent Parliament's attempt to accommodate these problems.

Proviso (e) lays down in broad terms that the accused when testifying in pursuance of the Act "may be asked any question in cross-examination notwithstanding that it would tend to criminate him as to the offence charged." The accused is thus deprived of the privilege against self-incrimination in so far as, but of course only so far as, the offence charged is concerned, and to that extent he is placed in a less protected position than that of an ordinary witness. If proviso (e) stood alone the position would be both clear and unsatisfactory. But it does not stand alone for proviso (f) contains a protective prohibition. This is to the effect that an accused when testifying shall not be asked, or, if asked, required to answer "any question tending to show that he has committed or been convicted of or been charged with any offence other than that wherewith he is then charged, or is of bad character," except in four (although listed under only three sub-clauses) situations. Viewed in isolation the protective prohibition of proviso (f) places the accused in a more protected position than that of the ordinary witness in that the latter may be asked many of the prohibited questions with a view to shaking his credibility.

Proviso (e) has inclusionary effect, whereas the effect of proviso (f) is exclusionary. At one time it was contended that the apparent inconsistency thus presented is to be resolved by confining the prohibitive effect of proviso (f) to questioning as to credit as distinct

---

[1] Part Two, *infra*.
[2] See Chap. 8, *supra*.

from guilt or alternatively to guilt as distinct from credit. These motions lingered on as late as 1962 in dissenting opinions in *Jones* v. *Director of Public Prosecutions*,[3] but were decisively rejected by the majority of the House of Lords in that case and can now be disregarded. The apparent generality of proviso (*e*) must now be seen as qualified by the prohibition contained in proviso (*f*): "any question" in the former proviso must be construed as meaning any question not prohibited by the latter. At the same time, of course, in the four exceptional situations in which the operation of proviso (*f*) is curtailed, the generality of proviso (*e*) is *pro tanto* restored.

Several points concerning the interpretation and scope of the proviso (*f*) prohibition are to be noted. It only restricts cross-examination and does not prevent questions being put or answered during examination-in-chief on the infrequent occasions on which an accused wishes to testify as to matters dealt with in the proviso. More importantly and more surprisingly it has been held by a majority of the House of Lords in the *Jones* case[4] that the words "tending to show" mean "making known to the jury": thus, if earlier in the trial the jury has become aware of the accused's dubious past, the proviso does not apply. The word "charged" in proviso (*f*) means "charged in court."[5] At the same time it is to be remembered that questioning as to informal "charges" or accusations will often (although not always)[6] be excluded on the score of irrelevance, and also that in any event the judge has an overriding discretion to exclude prejudicial evidence of marginal probative worth.

The four exceptional situations in which the prohibitive effect of proviso (*f*) is curtailed are as follows.

1. The first is the case where, as proviso (*f*)(i) lays down, proof that the accused has committed or been convicted of another offence "is admissible evidence to show that he is guilty of the offence wherewith he is then charged." Admissible evidence in this sub-clause means evidence which would be admissible even if the accused had not testified. In such circumstances there is no reason to restrict cross-examination of the accused himself concerning the similar facts or previous convictions.[7]

2. The second exceptional situation is, as laid down in the first part of proviso (*f*)(ii), that in which the accused has "personally or by his advocate asked questions of the witnesses for the prosecution with a view to establishing his own good character, or has given evidence of his good character." The general effect of this exception is to permit questioning of the accused as to his bad character when other evidence

[3] [1962] A.C. 635 (H.L.), *infra*.
[4] *Jones* v. *Director of Public Prosecutions* (footnote 3, *supra*): it has been followed in *R.* v. *Anderson* [1988] Q.B. 678 (C.A.) (*infra*).
[5] *Stirland* v. *Director of Public Prosecutions* [1944] A.C. 315 (H.L.).
[6] See *Maxwell* v. *Director of Public Prosecutions* [1935] A.C. 309 (H.L.), *infra*, and *R.* v. *Waldman* (1934) 24 Cr.App.R. 204 (C.C.A.).
[7] It could be contended that, on a strictly logical interpretation of the whole proviso, once an exception is made operative the whole of the prohibition is negatived. On this view the effect of cross-examination as to similar facts or previous convictions becoming permissible by virtue of proviso (*f*)(i) would be to allow as well questioning as to bad character and (so far as the prohibition is concerned) earlier charges. Although the structure and wording of the proviso is not very felicitous, the logic of this contention is not entirely convincing and in policy terms it is not easily supportable. There is, however, implicit support for it in several of the cases.

of his bad character would be admissible, he having put his character in issue.[8]

It may be generalised that the underlying purpose of proviso (f)(i) and of the first part of proviso (f)(ii) seems to be to carry, into the new statutory situation, created by the accused himself being under cross-examination, the general law relating, respectively, to the admissibility of evidence of similar facts and previous convictions, and to the admissibility of character evidence. It should follow from this that answers to the permitted questioning may be used to establish the guilt of the accused in addition to any bearing which they have upon his credit *qua* witness. This is the case so far as answers to questions allowed by virtue of proviso (f)(i) are concerned, but the authorities are inconclusive as to the use that may be made of answers elicited in response to cross-examination permitted by virtue of the first limb of proviso (f)(ii).

3. Thirdly, the accused is to be seen, at least as a matter of law, as having "thrown away his shield" when, in the words of the latter part of proviso (f)(ii), "the nature or conduct of the defence is such as to involve imputations upon the character of the prosecutor or the witness for the prosecution." There is no totally satisfying explanation for this exception. First, it is to be noted that here, unlike in the first two cases in which cross-examination is allowed, the permission does not reflect the legal position if the accused does not give evidence, for the casting of imputations does not then render admissible otherwise inadmissible evidence of disposition.[9] Secondly, it is to be observed that the permission extends to cases in which the imputations are not cast by the accused personally: the suggestion that the sub-clause reflects a "tit-for-tat" policy, even if this were otherwise acceptable, is not adequate as an explanation in so far as it is an argument which relates only to the accused's credibility as a witness. Thirdly, the sub-clause is not designed to inhibit simply the casting of gratuitous, unnecessary or irrelevant imputations: it can and sometimes does inhibit the putting forward of a perfectly proper defence by an accused person with a bad record. Fourthly, the truth of the imputation is seemingly immaterial. Not surprisingly in these circumstances English judges have, now for some 90 years, sought to mitigate the rigours of Parliament's mandate. Their endeavours have taken several forms of which four may be mentioned. First and especially during the decades immediately following the passage of the Act, there was a marked although varying tendency to construe the word "imputation" restrictively—sometimes very restrictively. Secondly, and especially since the House of Lords case of *Selvey* v. *Director of Public Prosecutions*,[10] a very heavy discretionary gloss been placed upon the words of the statute. Although it is said that as a matter of law the words must be given "their ordinary natural meaning,"[11] a judge may in his discretion curtail cross-examination to the extent that in his view the answers elicited by it would be liable to be unfairly prejudicial to the accused. The significance of the matter

---

[8] A comment similar to that made in the preceding footnote may be made in relation to the effect of this sub-clause becoming operative.

[9] This was confirmed as regards character evidence in *R.* v. *Butterwasser* [1948] 1 K.B. 4 (C.C.A.), Chap. 22, *supra*. Followed in *R.* v. *de Vere* [1982] 2 Q.B. 75 (C.A.).

[10] [1970] A.C. 304 (H.L.), *infra*.

[11] *Ibid. per* Lord Dilhorne, p. 339.

being treated as one of discretion rather than of law is twofold. Even though cross-examination has become legally permissible Crown counsel seeking to take advantage of this must first seek leave to do so. Again, an appellate court will be exceptionally reluctant to interfere with the judge's ruling. The third way in which the judges at one time sought to contain the significance of the sub-clause was by endeavouring to ensure that the answers obtained in response to the permitted cross-examination are used only for the purpose of discrediting the accused *qua* witness and not for the purpose of establishing his guilt.[12] However, the position has become uncertain.[13] In any event the success of such endeavours can in practice only be partial. Fourthly, it is the usual practice, especially in cases in which the accused is not represented by counsel, for the judge to warn the accused of the risk he is running if the nature or conducting of his defence seems to be leading to the casting of imputations.

When cross-examination is permitted by virtue of this exception to the proviso (*f*) prohibition, it is, of course, in the great majority of cases conducted only by the prosecution counsel. There is, however, some authority for the view that counsel for a co-accused may at the judge's discretion also cross-examine the accused if his evidence was prejudicial to the co-accused.

4. It is by the fourth exception to the prohibition, namely that embodied in proviso (*f*)(iii), that protection is principally accorded to a co-accused. This sub-clause, as amended by the Criminal Evidence Act 1979,[14] allows cross-examination when the accused has 'given evidence against any other person charged in the same proceedings.'' It would obviously be unfair to a co-accused to prevent him from probing the credibility of a person who from his point of view is *de facto* a prosecution witness.[15] When proviso (*f*)(iii) comes into operation the co-accused may cross-examine as of right but, his cross-examination must be directed to the credit of the first accused not to his guilt. There is authority for suggesting that prosecution counsel may also be allowed to cross-examine one of two accused under proviso (*f*)(iii); but this will only be allowed in exceptional cases, and then only with the leave of the judge. There has been some case-law concerned with what is meant by evidence "against" a co-accused. The principle seems to be that, whatever the accused's intention may have been, if the likely overall effect of his evidence would be to increase the chance of the co-accused being convicted, the sub-clause will become operative.

---

[12] *R. v. Richardson* [1969] 1 Q.B. 299 (C.A.); *R. v. Inder* (1977) 67 Cr.App.R. 143 (C.A.), *infra*.
[13] *R. v. Burke* (1986) 82 Cr.App.R. 156 (C.A.); *R. v. Powell* [1985] 1 W.L.R. 1365 (C.A.), *infra*.
[14] Part Two, *infra*.
[15] A co-accused may, of course, cross-examine an accused who testifies even though the accused's evidence does not impeach him: *R. v. Hilton* [1972] 1 Q.B. 421 (C.A.) (see Chap. 9, Section B, *supra*). But the co-accused can only invoke proviso (*f*)(iii) so as to allow his cross-examination to extend to questions within the proviso (*f*) prohibition if the accused has given evidence "against" him.

JONES v. DIRECTOR OF PUBLIC PROSECUTIONS

[1962] A.C. 635; [1962] 2 W.L.R. 575; [1962] 1 All E.R. 569; 46 Cr.App.R. 129
(H.L.: 1962)

*Under the Criminal Evidence Act 1898, section 1(e) and (f), questions in
cross-examination of the accused are (the exceptional cases apart)
inadmissible if they tend to show that he has committed or been
convicted of or charged with another offence, or is of bad character.
But such questioning which does not reveal to the jury anything which
has not previously been disclosed are outside this prohibition.*

General Note.—This interpretation of the words "tending to show" in the prohibition
represents the view of the majority (Viscount Simonds, Lord Reid and Lord Morris of
Borth-y-Gest). Lord Denning and Lord Devlin expressly rejected this view, but would
dismiss the appeal on the different and broader ground that the disputed cross-
examination was relevant to the accused's liability as distinct from simply his credibility.
The majority, although agreeing that it was so relevant, would have found that this was
not sufficient to render it admissible under the Act. None of their Lordships would have
held that the case fell within the first (or any) exception to the prohibition.

The accused was charged with the murder of a young girl. He had
previously been convicted of the rape of another young girl, after giving
a false explanation of his movements at the relevant time. At the trial
for murder, both in cross-examination of a prosecution witness and in
evidence by the accused, reference was made to his having previously
been in trouble with the police. The accused gave a similar explanation
of his movements in relation to the murder, and was cross-examined as
to the similarity of the two explanations. He was convicted, and his
appeals to the Court of Criminal Appeal and the House of Lords were
dismissed.

VISCOUNT SIMONDS: My Lords, the questions raised in this appeal are
important. . . . Both of them arise upon the simple issue whether certain
questions put to the appellant in cross-examination upon his trial for
murder . . . were barred by the Criminal Evidence Act, 1898. . . . The
first and more important of them is whether, even if the questions that
were asked tended to show that the appellant had committed or been
convicted of or charged with any other offence than that wherewith he
was then charged (see section 1(f) of the Act), yet they were admissible
on the ground that they were relevant to an issue in the case that they
tended to criminate him as to the offence charged. . . . The second
question is whether these questions did in fact tend to show that he had
committed or been convicted of or charged with some other offence.
The answer to this question depends partly on the meaning of the words
"tend to show" and partly on a consideration of all the circumstances of
the case. Reason and authority demand that the questions that are
challenged cannot be considered in isolation.

My Lords, in my opinion, the answer to the first question depends
first and last upon the construction of section 1 of the Act, and
particularly of provisos (e) and (f). . . . It appears to me that no
language could be plainer than that by which the Act, for the first time
making an accused person a competent witness on his trial, provides first
what questions he may be asked and then what questions he may not be
asked. I do not understand upon what canon of construction it can be

said that the second proviso is in some way subordinate to the first. On the contrary, as if to make it clear that the first proviso is not generally paramount, there are particular qualifications introduced to the second proviso. . . .

. . . .

I turn to the second question. Here it is common ground that the challenged questions must be regarded not in isolation but in relation to the evidence that had already been given: see *R.* v. *Ellis* [1910] 2 K.B. 746 (C.C.A.). So regarded they do not appear to me to tend to show to the jury anything that had not been shown before. . . . As to the meaning of the words "tend to show" I see no difficulty. It is not the intention of the question that matters but the effect of the question and, presumably, the possible answer. Nor is the word "show" in its context ambiguous. Primarily it may mean a visual demonstration but in relation to the giving of oral evidence it can only mean "make known." The issue, then, is whether the challenged questions made known anything to the jury which they did not know before. Learned counsel for the defence had, for reasons which were, no doubt, adequate and probably imperative, made it known to the jury that the appellant had previously been in trouble with the police. In doing so he took a calculated risk. I think that it would be too strict a view to hold that the challenged questions tended to make known to the jury that the appellant had committed or been convicted of or charged with any other offence than that of the murder for which he was standing his trial. They had been told that he had been in trouble with the police: what the trouble was they were not told. He was asked whether on some occasion he had answered certain questions in a certain way. He was not asked what the occasion was. Vagueness was matched with vagueness. The jury could not be expected to know what your Lordships now are told that his trouble with the police referred to one incident and his answers to questions to another. This was the view taken by the experienced judges of the Court of Criminal Appeal and I agree with them. . . .

LORD REID: . . . The accused had been convicted in March 1961 of the rape of another young girl in September 1960; For what seem good reasons this conviction was not proved in the murder trial. In the course of that trial the accused put forward an alibi which corresponded with his second alibi in the murder trial. In each case he narrated a long conversation with his wife on the day after the night of the alibi, and the two conversations corresponded almost word for word. Obviously it was highly relevant to put this before the jury in the murder trial to show that the alibi put forward in evidence in the murder trial could not be credible. It is the cross-examination for this purpose which is said to be prohibited by the Act of 1898. . . .

It is well established that the 1898 Act has no application to evidence given by any person other than the accused: where it was competent before that Act for a witness to prove or refer to a previous conviction of the accused, that is still competent. What the Act does is to alter the old rules as regards the accused. It might merely have provided that the accused should be a competent witness; then the ordinary rules would have applied to him. But it goes on to afford to him protection which the ordinary rules would not give him: it expressly prohibits certain kinds of question being put to him. That must mean questions which would be competent and relevant under the ordinary rules, because there was no need to prohibit any question which would in any event have been excluded by the ordinary rules. So what must now be considered is what kinds of question, which would have been competent and relevant under the ordinary rules of evidence, does the Act prohibit....

....

The questions prohibited are those which "tend to show" certain things. Does this mean tend to prove or tend to suggest?... In my judgment, "tends to show" means tends to suggest to the jury. But the crucial point in the present case is whether the questions are to be considered in isolation or whether they are to be considered in light of all that had gone before them at the trial. If the questions or line of questioning has to be considered in isolation I think that the questions with which this appeal is concerned would tend to show at least that the accused had previously been charged with an offence. The jury would be likely to jump to that conclusion, if this was the first they had heard of this matter. But I do not think that the questions ought to be considered in isolation. If the test is the effect the questions would be likely o have on the minds of the jury that necessarily implies that one must have regard to what the jury had already heard. If the jury already knew that the accused had been charged with an offence, a question inferring that he had been charged would add nothing and it would be absurd to prohibit it. If the obvious purpose of this provision is to protect the accused from possible prejudice, as I think it is, then "show" must mean "reveal," because it is only a revelation of something new which could cause such prejudice.

.... I am of opinion that this appeal should be dismissed on the ground that these questions were not prohibited because they did not "tend to show" any of the matters specified in proviso (f).

But, in case it should be thought that some of the views which I have expressed are not in accord with what was said by Lord Simon in *Stirland* v. *Director of Public Prosecutions* (above, p. 281), I must say something about that case. That was a case where the accused had put his character in issue and the questions which it was held ought not to have been put to him in cross-examination dealt with an occasion when a former employer had questioned him about a suspected forgery. But the case did not turn on proviso (f) because the second exception in the proviso was satisfied by the accused having given evidence of his good character and therefore the proviso was excluded.

Lord Simon did, however, state six rules which should govern cross-examination to credit of an accused person. First he set out proviso (f). Then comes the rule which gives rise to the difficulty: "2. He may, however, be cross-examined as to any of the evidence he has given in chief, including statements concerning his good record, with a view to testing his veracity or accuracy or to showing that he is not to be believed on his oath." Applied to a case where the accused has put his character in issue I think that is correct, because then proviso (f) does not apply. But I do not think that Lord Simon can have meant it to apply in its general form to a case where proviso (f) does operate because earlier in his speech he said: "This House has laid it down in *Maxwell* v. *Director of Public Prosecutions* (above, p. 276) that, while paragraph (f) of this section absolutely prohibits any question of the kind there indicated being put to the accused in the witness box unless one or other of the conditions (i), (ii) or (iii) is satisfied, it does not follow that such questions are in all circumstances justified whenever one or other of the conditions is fulfilled." Thus he recognised the absolute character of the prohibition except where one or other of the conditions is satisfied, so he cannot have intended to say that there is another case, not covered by the conditions, where the proviso also does not apply, namely, where questions are put with a view to testing the veracity of the accused's evidence in chief. But if he did mean that it was certainly *obiter* and I would not agree with it. It would in effect be legislating by adding a fourth condition to proviso (*f*). The Attorney-General refused to take this point and I think he was perfectly right.

It is said that the views which I have expressed involve overruling two decisions of the Court of Criminal Appeal, *Rex* v. *Chitson* ([1909] 2 K.B. 945) and *Rex* v. *Kennaway* ([1917] 1 K.B. 25). I do not think so. I think the decisions were right but the reasons given for them were not. In the former case the accused was charged with having had carnal knowledge of a girl aged 14. Giving evidence, she said that the accused told her that he had previously done the same thing to another girl, who, she said, was under 16. No objection was taken to this evidence, I assume rightly. So before the accused gave evidence the jury already knew that he was alleged to have committed another offence. If the views which I have already expressed are right, cross-examining the accused about this matter disclosed nothing new to them and therefore did not offend against the prohibition in proviso (*f*). But the judgment of the court was not based on that ground: it was said that although the questions tended to prove that the accused was of bad character they also tend to show that he was guilty of the offence with which he was charged. For the reasons which I have given I do not think that that is sufficient to avoid the prohibition in proviso (*f*).

Rex v. *Kennaway* was a prosecution for forgery. Accomplices giving evidence for the prosecution described the fraudulent scheme of which the forgery was a part and related a conversation with the accused in which he stated to them that some years earlier he had forged another will in pursuance of a similar scheme. Then in cross-examination the accused was asked a number of questions about this other forgery. Those questions were held to have been properly put to him. Here, again, these questions disclosed nothing new to the jury and I can see no valid objection to them. But again that was not the ground of the court's decision. Their ground of decision was similar to that in *Chitson's* case, and I need not repeat what I have said about that case. . . .

LORD DENNING (dissenting on the construction of the words "tending to show"): My Lords, much of the discussion before your Lordships was directed to the effect of section 1(*f*) of the Criminal Evidence Act, 1898: and, if that were the sole paragraph for consideration, I should have thought that counsel for the Crown ought not to have asked the questions he did. . . . But I do not think it rests on section 1(*f*). In my judgment, the questions were admissible under section 1(*e*), which says that a person charged "may be asked any question in cross-examination notwithstanding that it would tend to criminate him as to the offence charged." As to this subsection, Viscount Sankey L.C., speaking for all in this House in *Maxwell's* case, said that under section 1(*e*) "a witness may be cross-examined in respect of the offence charged, and cannot refuse to answer questions directly relevant to the offence on the ground that they tend to incriminate him: thus if he denies the offence, he may be cross-examined to refute the denial." I would add that, if he gives an explanation in an attempt to exculpate himself, he may be cross-examined to refuse his explanation. And nonetheless so because it tends incidentally to show that he had previously been charged with another offence....

The situation is precisely covered by the second proposition in *Stirland's* case where Viscount Simon L.C., in this House, with the assent of all present, said that, notwithstanding the prohibition in section 1(*f*), the accused man, "may, however, be cross-examined as to any of the evidence he has given in-chief, including statements concerning his good record," and including, I would add, any explanation offered by him, "with a view to testing is veracity or accuracy or to showing that he is not to be believed on his oath."

It is noteworthy that everyone at the trial of Jones acted on this view of the law. No one suggested that the questions were absolutely prohibited. All that was suggested was that it was a matter of discretion. And that is, I think, the true position. The judge was entitled in his discretion to exclude them if he thought that they were so prejudicial as to outweigh their probative value. It was his discretion, not that of the prosecution. He did not exclude them but permitted them to be asked. They were, therefore, properly put.

In conclusion I would say that I view with concern the suggestion that the reasoning in *Rex* v. *Chitson* and *Rex* v. *Kennaway* was wrong and that what Viscount Simon L.C. said in *Stirland's* case is no longer a safe guide. Those cases have governed the practice in our criminal courts for years: and the result has been wholly beneficial. It is not, in my opinion, right to resort now to a literal reading of the Act so as to displace them....

I would dismiss the appeal.

LORD MORRIS OF BORTH-Y-GEST:...It is submitted on behalf of the appellant that the cross-examination came within the prohibition of "any question tending to show that he has committed or been convicted of or been charged with any offence other than that wherewith he is then charged, or is of bad character," and that none of the permitting provisions contained in (*f*) were applicable. It therefore becomes necessary to consider whether the cross-examination tended to show that the appellant had (a) committed or (b) been convicted of or (c) been charged with some other offence. This cannot be decided by taking any questions in isolation: they must be examined in their context and, as was said in *R.* v. *Ellis* [1910] 2 K.B. 746 at 757 (C.C.A.): "Each question must be judged by the light of others asked before and after." Nor is the matter to be decided by determining what was the object with which the questions were put. It is the result of putting the questions that must be regarded and not the purpose which inspired them. Furthermore, if the questions tend to show the commission of or a conviction for or a charge of another offence or tend to show bad character, then they must not be put unless the permitting provisions apply even though they would be admissible on other grounds....

There is a contrast between proviso (*e*) and proviso (*f*). Proviso (*e*) shows that an accused person who avails himself of his opportunity to give evidence "may be asked" questions in cross-examination although they would tend "to criminate him as to the offence charged." That denotes questions on matters directly relevant to the charge. Then proviso (*f*) gives the accused person a "shield." He "shall not be asked" certain questions unless certain conditions apply. Proviso (*e*) permits questions to be asked: the corollary is that they must be answered.

Proviso (f) does not say that certain questions may be asked; it says that certain questions may not be asked. This means that even if the questions are relevant and have to do with the issue before the court they cannot be asked unless covered by the permitting provisions of proviso (f). "The substantive part of that proviso is negative in form and as such is universal an is absolute unless the exceptions come into play."

In *Stirland* v. *Director of Public Prosecutions* it was held that the word "charged" in proviso (f) means "accused before a court." In his speech in that case Viscount Simon referred to *Maxwell's* case as follows: "This House has laid it down in *Maxwell* v. *Director of Public Prosecutions* that, while paragraph (f) of this section absolutely prohibits any question of the kind there indicated being put to the accused in the witness box unless one or other of the conditions (i), (ii) or (iii) is satisfied, it does not follow that such questions are in all circumstances justified whenever one or other of the conditions is fulfilled." Later in his speech Viscount Simon formulated certain propositions. The first two were as follows: "1. The accused in the witness box may not be asked any question 'tending to show that he has committed or been convicted of or been charged with any offence other than that wherewith he is then charged, or is of bad character, unless' one or other of the three conditions set out in para. (f) of section 1 of the Act of 1898 is fulfilled. 2. He may, however, be cross-examined as to any of the evidence he has given in-chief, including statements concerning his good record, with a view to testing his veracity or accuracy or to showing that he is not to be believed on his oath."

The second proposition could not be read as modifying anything that was said in *Maxwell's* case or as suggesting that the prohibition in proviso (f) is other than "absolute" unless any one of the three conditions is fulfilled. Viscount Simon pointed out in his speech how undesirable it would be if the rules governing cross-examination to credit of an accused person in the witness box should be complicated by refined distinctions involving a close study and comparison of decided cases. My Lords, it seems to me that the clearest guidance as to provisos (e) and (f) was given in *Maxwell's* case. . . .

Having regard to what has been laid down in *Maxwell's* case and in *Stirland's* case, I do not find it necessary to embark upon "a close study and comparison" of earlier cases such as *Rex* v. *Chitson* and *Rex* v. *Kennaway*. If the results reached in those cases can be supported it must not be on any line of reasoning that runs counter to what has been laid down in *Maxwell's* case and in *Stirland's* case.

It was submitted on behalf of the appellant that in cases in which proof of the commission of or the conviction of an offence other than that charged would, within the first permitting provision of proviso (f), be "admissible evidence" to show that the accused is guilty of the offence wherewith he is then charged, questions could only be put to the accused if as part of the case for the prosecution substantive evidence in regard to such other offence had already been given. I cannot agree. The admission of the accused when asked questions in cross-examination would be proof and there is no essential requirement that proof should be given in any other way or at any earlier stage. In practice I do not think that such a situation would be likely to arise. If the prosecution consider that proof of the commission of or the conviction of some other offence would be "admissible evidence" to show guilt in regard to the offence charged (*e.g.* within the principles laid down in the case of *Makin* v. *Att.-Gen. for New South Wales* [1894] A.C. 57, then such proof from the points of view of effectiveness and convenience would be given, if allowed as admissible, as part of the case for the prosecution. I agree with the Court of Criminal Appeal that in general it would be undesirable if the matter was first raised in cross-examination.

I pass now to a consideration of the questions which were put in cross-examination. Were they questions "tending to show that" the appellant had "committed or been convicted of or been charged with" any offence other than that charged? . . .

My Lords, it seems to me that, on the assumption that the jury could reasonably interpret the question in cross-examination as involving that there had been some prior charge against the appellant or that he was of bad character, the jury would only link the matters with what he had himself brought out, *i.e.* that he had been in trouble with the police.

. . . I consider, in agreement with the Court of Criminal Appeal, that in the proviso the words "tending to show" have the meaning of tending to reveal or tending to disclose. . . .

For reasons and purposes which the defence found to be entirely necessary for their case the defence decided to lift the "shield" which the appellant otherwise have possessed. . . .

LORD DEVLIN (dissenting on the construction of the words "tending to show"): My Lords, I would dismiss this appeal on the short ground that the questions objected to were relevant to an issue in the case upon which the appellant had testified in chief. It is not disputed that the issue to which the questions related was a relevant one. It concerned the identification of the appellant as being at the material time at the scene of the crime. . . .

[LORD DEVLIN dissented too on some other points, holding the test for admissibility to be relevance, not revelation.]

Note.—The majority view was followed in *R.* v. *Anderson* [1988] Q.B. 678 (C.A.) (*infra*) and must, of course, be taken to represent English law. It would appear, too, to represent Scots law: see *Dodds* v. *H.M. Advocate* [1987] S.C.C.R. 768 (H.C. Just.) dealing with the Criminal Procedure (Scotland) Act 1975, s. 141 (*f*), which is the equivalent of section 1(*f*) of the 1898 English Act.

So far as the interpretation of the words "tending to show" is concerned it can only be observed, first that in this type of context elsewhere in the law of evidence the word "show" is usually treated as synonymous with the word "prove"; secondly, that, as a matter of linguistic usage, revelation implies something more or less instantaneous, and a tendency to reveal is thus unusual; and thirdly (and most importantly) that the interpretation of the majority may operate harshly upon the accused, for in the words of Lord Denning (p. 667): "It is one thing to confess to having been in trouble before. It is quite another thing to have it emphasised against you with devastating detail."

More welcome is the majority view that, but for the fact that the accused had already referred to his previous trouble, the appeal would have been allowed. This finally disposes of the notion that the prohibition of section 1, proviso (*f*), applies only to cross-examination as to credit. It must now be seen as applying as well to cross-examination as to guilt and thus as constituting an exception to the generality of section 1, proviso (*e*). This had previously been implicit in several decisions (*e.g. R.* v. *Cokar* [1960] 2 Q.B. 207 (C.C.A.), *infra*). Some other earlier decisions (or the reasons given for them) must now, however, be reappraised in this regard: see, *e.g. R.* v. *Chitson* immediately *infra*.

R. v. **Chitson** [1909] 2 K.B. 945 (C.C.A.). The accused was charged with having had carnal knowledge of a girl aged fourteen. The girl gave evidence that on the day after the connection had taken place the accused had told her that he had previously done the same thing with another girl, who was alleged by the prosecution to have been under age at the time. The judge allowed the accused to be asked in cross-examination whether he had made the statement attributed to him by the prosecutrix and whether it was true. His appeal against conviction was dismissed.

Note.—The cross-examination of the accused as to whether he had had immoral relations with the second girl was held to be relevant to his guilt and would now therefore, having regard to the majority view in the *Jones* case, not be permissible but for the fact that the prosecutrix had already made known to the jury that the accused was alleged to be a man of bad character.

R. v. Anderson [1988] Q.B. 678 (C.A.). The appellant and co-defendants were tried on a count of conspiracy to cause explosions likely to endanger life or cause serious injury to property. She denied that she had taken part in the conspiracy as charged and, without the prosecution being forewarned, explained evidence against her by claiming that she had been concerned in attempting to smuggle members of the I.R.A., who had escaped from prison in Ireland, through Scotland to Denmark. The trial judge allowed the prosecution to question her in order to establish that she had been "wanted by the police prior to her arrest," the purpose of this being to show that it was unlikely that such a person would in fact have been selected to help escaped prisoners or that such a person would herself have been willing to undertake a task involving a double risk of identification. On the question being put, the appellant admitted that she had been a "wanted" person. She was convicted of the conspiracy as charged.

The Court of Appeal held that the questioning did not involve a contravention of the proviso (*f*) to section 1 of the Criminal Evidence Act 1898, and that the trial judge had not erred in refusing to exercise his discretion nevertheless to disallow the questioning. The Court, following the majority view in *Jones* v. *Director of Public Prosecutions* [*supra*], held that proviso (*f*) did not protect the appellant because, as she had by her own evidence stated that she had committed other offences, the questions did not tend to show, in the sense of revealing for the first time, her involvement. The Court did, however, proffer an additional reason for dismissing the appeal, namely that the evidence would in any event have been admissible as similar fact evidence to rebut the particular defence that had been raised.

Note.—For comment upon the Court's reliance upon the majority decision in *Jones* v. *Director of Public Prosecutions* see *Note* to that case, *supra*. With regard to the court's additional line of reasoning it is surprising that no actual mention was made of the first exception to the prohibition contained in proviso (*f*). Proviso (*f*)(i) specifically excludes operation of the prohibition where proof that the accused "has committed or been convicted of such offence is admissible evidence to show that he is guilty of the offence charged." The phrase "is admissible evidence" must surely mean would be admissible even if the accused had not testified. (See the Introduction to this Chapter; and see observations of Lord Parker C.J. in *R.* v. *Cokar* [1960] 2 Q.B. 207 (C.C.A.).

R. v. Weekes (1983) 77 Cr.App.R. 207 (C.A.). The accused was before the Crown Court on two indictments. Having pleaded guilty to three counts, a fresh indictment containing ten counts, but excluding the three matters to which he had pleaded guilty, was prepared. The trial judge allowed the prosecution, as a matter of discretion and regardless of the 1898, s.1(*f*), to cross-examine the accused about the three matters. The Court of Appeal, quashing the conviction, held that the judge had erred in law. Bristow J. said (p. 209): "He [the trial judge] expressly admitted the questioning not upon the basis of the Act. In the judgment of this Court, he was wrong to do so. However tiresome it might be, the only power which he had to allow the questioning of the appellant on those lines was if the situation fell within section 1(f). . . . " (His Lordship added that the evidence might have been admissible under section 1(f)(ii) if the judge had found on the facts that the nature or conduct of the defence was such as to involve imputations upon the character of the prosecutor of witnesses for the prosecution).

R. v. de Vere [1982] 1 Q.B. 75 (C.A.). The accused was charged with obtaining property and services by deception. He did not give evidence but (as was then permissible) made an unsworn statement from the dock in which he attacked prosecution witnesses. The trial judge then allowed the prosecution to adduce evidence under section 1(f)(ii) of the 1898 Act to the effect that the accused was not a man of substance and indeed had previous convictions for fraud. The Court of Appeal held that section 1 (including proviso (f)(ii)) is only applicable when the accused gives evidence, and that the trial judge had, therefore, been wrong to invoke it. (The Court also held that the accused had put his character in issue, not by attacking the character of prosecution witnesses but by setting himself up as a man of substance, and that the evidence in rebuttable was therefore admissible at common law: see Chapter 22, *supra*).

MAXWELL v. DIRECTOR OF PUBLIC PROSECUTIONS

[1935] A.C. 309; 103 L.J.K.B. 501; 151 L.T. 477; 50 T.L.R. 499; 24 Cr.App.R. 152; 30 Cox C.C. 160; 32 L.G.R. 335 (H.L.: 1934)

Under the Criminal Evidence Act 1898, section 1(f)(ii), cross-examination by the prosecution as to a prisoner's character is allowed when he puts his character in issue. This cross-examination, however, is subject to the common law rule as to relevance. The fact that a person has on a previous occasion been charged with an offence and acquitted is not usually relevant either to his guilt or to impeach his credibility as a witness.

The prisoner was charged with the manslaughter of a woman by performing an illegal operation on her. Having given evidence of his own good character, he was cross-examined as to a previous case where a patient of his had died in suspicious circumstances, in which he had been prosecuted and acquitted. It was held that the questions were not admissible; and the appeal from conviction was allowed.

VISCOUNT SANKEY L.C.: The question is whether it was permissible in the particular facts of the case, under the Criminal Evidence Act 1898, s.1, proviso (f), for the prosecution to ask the prisoner whether on a previous occasion he had been charged with a similar offence, the charge having been tried and having resulted in an acquittal. . . . It must first of all be stated that it has been admitted throughout that the prisoner in saying that he had lived a good, clean, moral life had put his character in issue, and had in the words of proviso (f)(ii) "given evidence of his good character." The first question here is, What consequences follow from that?

This involves the proper construction of section 1(f) of that Act. . . . When Parliament by the Act of 1898 effected a change in the general law and made the prisoner in every case a competent witness, it was in an evident difficulty, and it pursued the familiar English system of a compromise. It was clear that if you allowed a prisoner to go into the witness-box, it was impossible to allow him to be treated as an ordinary witness. Had that been permitted, a prisoner who went into the box to give evidence on oath could have been asked about any previous conviction, with the result that an old offender would seldom, if ever, have been acquitted. This would have offended against one of the most deeply rooted and jealously guarded principles of our criminal law....

Some middle way, therefore, had to be discovered, and the result was that a certain amount of protection was accorded to a prisoner who gave evidence on his own behalf. As it has been expressed, he was presented with a shield and it was provided that he was not to be asked, and that, if he was asked, he should not be required to answer, any question tending to show that he had committed or been convicted or or been charged with any offence other than that wherewith he was then charged, or was of bad character. Apart, however, from this protection, he was placed in the position of an ordinary witness in an ordinary civil case. The laws of evidence were not otherwise altered by the Criminal Evidence Act 1898, and the prisoner who was a witness in his own case could not be asked questions which were irrelevant or had nothing to do with the issue which the court was endeavouring to decide. As has already been pointed out, the prisoner in the present case threw away his shield and, therefore, the learned counsel for the prosecution was entitled to ask him, and he could be required to answer, any question tending to show that he had committed or been convicted of or been charged with an offence, but subject to the consideration that the question asked him must be one which was relevant and admissible in the case of an ordinary witness. The Act does not in terms say that in any case a prisoner may be asked or required to answer questions falling within proviso (f), or impose any such affirmative or absolute burden upon him. I think this conclusion is confirmed by a study of the words of the statute. In section 1, proviso (e), it has been enacted that a witness may be cross-examined in respect of the offence charged, and cannot refuse to answer questions directly relevant to the offence on the ground that they tend to incriminate him: thus if he denies the offence, he may be cross-examined to refute the denial. These are matters directly relevant to the charge on which he is being tried. Proviso (f), however, is dealing with matters outside and not directly relevant to the particular offence charged; such matters, to be admissible at all, must in general fall under two main classes: one is the class of evidence which goes to show not that the prisoner did the acts charged, but that, if he did these acts, he did them as part of a system or intentionally, so as to refute a defence that if he did them he did them innocently or inadvertently, as, for instance, in *Makin* v. *Att.-Gen. for New South Wales* ([1894] A.C. 57) where the charge was one of murder; another illustration of such cases is *R.* v. *Bond* [1906] 2 K.B. 389. This rule applies to cases where guilty knowledge or design or intention is of the essence of the offence.

The other main class is where it is sought to show that the prisoner is not a person to be believed on his oath, which is generally attempted by what is called cross-examination to credit. Closely allied with this latter type of question is the rule that, if the prisoner by himself or his witnesses seek to give evidence of his own good character, for the purpose of showing that it is unlikely that he committed the offence charged, he raises by way of defence an issue as to his good character, so that he may fairly be cross-examined on that issue, just as any witness called by him to prove his good character may be cross-examined to show the contrary. All these matters are dealt with in proviso (*f*). The substantive part of that proviso is negative in form and as such is universal and is absolute unless the exceptions come into play. Then come the three exceptions: but it does not follow that when the absolute prohibition is superseded by a permission, that the permission is as absolute as the prohibition. When it is sought to justify a question it must not only be brought within terms of the permission, but also must be capable of justification according to the general rules of evidence and in particular must satisfy the test of relevance. Exception (i) deals with the former of the two main classes of evidence referred to above, that is, evidence falling within the rule that where issues of intention or design are involved in the charge or defence, the prisoner may be asked questions relevant to these matters, even though he has himself raised no questions of his good character. Exceptions (ii) and (iii) come into play where the prisoner by himself or his witnesses has put his character in issue, or has attacked the character of others. Dealing with exceptions (i) and (ii), it is clear that the test of relevance is wider in (ii) than in (i); in the latter, proof that the prisoner has committed or been convicted of some other offence can only be admitted if it goes to show that he was guilty of the offence charged. In the former (exception (ii)), the questions permissible must be relevant to the issue of his own good character and if not so relevant cannot be admissible. But it seems clear that the mere fact of a charge cannot in general be evidence of bad character or be regarded otherwise than as a misfortune. It seemed to be contended on behalf of the respondent that a charge was *per se* such evidence that the man charged, even though acquitted, must thereafter remain under a cloud, however innocent. I find it impossible to accept any such view. The mere fact that a man has been charged with an offence is no proof that he committed the offence. Such a fact is, therefore, irrelevant; it neither goes to show that the prisoner did the acts for which he is actually being tried nor does it go to his credibility as a witness. Such questions must, therefore, be excluded on the principle which is fundamental in the law of evidence as conceived in this country, especially in criminal cases, because if allowed, they are likely to lead the minds of the jury astray into false issues; not merely do they tend to introduce suspicion as if it were evidence, but they tend to distract the jury from the true issue—namely, whether the prisoner in fact committed the offence on which he is actually standing his trial. It is of the utmost importance for a fair trial that the evidence should be prima facie limited to matters relating to the transaction which forms the subject of the indictment and that any departure from these matters should be strictly confined.

It does not result from this conclusion that the word "charged" in proviso (*f*) is otiose: it is clearly not so as regards the prohibition; and when the exceptions come into play there may still be cases in which a prisoner may be asked about a charge as a step in cross-examination leading to a question whether he was convicted on the charge, or in order to elicit some evidence as to statements made or evidence given by the prisoner in the course of the trial on a charge which failed, which tend to throw doubt on the evidence which he is actually giving, though cases of this last class must be rare and the cross-examination permissible only with great safeguards.

Again, a man charged with an offence against the person may perhaps be asked whether he had uttered threats against the person attacked because he was angry with him for bringing a charge which turned out to be unfounded. Other probabilities may be imagined. Thus, if a prisoner has been acquitted on a plea of *autrefois convict* such an acquittal might be relevant to his credit, though it would seem that what was in truth relevant to his credit was the previous conviction and not the fact that he was erroneously again charged with the same offence; again, it may be, though it is perhaps a remote supposition, that an acquittal of a prisoner charged with rape on the plea of consent may possibly be relevant to a prisoner's credit.

But these instances all involve the crucial test of relevance. And in general no question whether a prisoner has been convicted or charged or acquitted should be asked or, if asked, allowed by the judge, who has a discretion under proviso (*f*), unless it helps to elucidate the particular issue which the jury is investigating, or goes to credibility, that is, tends to show that he is not to be believed on oath; indeed, the question whether a man has been convicted, charged or acquitted ought not to be admitted, even if it goes to credibility, if there is any risk of the jury being misled into thinking that it goes not to credibility but to the probability of his having committed the offence of which he is charged. I think that it is impossible in the present case to say that the fact that the prisoner had been acquitted on a previous charge of murder or manslaughter was relevant, or that it tended in the present case to destroy his credibility as a witness.

LORDS BLANESBURGH, ATKIN, THANKERTON and WRIGHT concurred.

Note.—*Maxwell* v. *Director of Public Prosecutions* was followed in *R.* v. *Cokar* [1960] 2 Q.B. 207 (C.C.A.). There, at his trial for burglary, the accused gave evidence that he had entered a dwelling house only for warmth and sleep, having been found asleep in a chair before a fire. It was held that he should not have been cross-examined as to a previous acquittal in similar circumstances with a view to showing his knowledge of the defence of innocent purpose, and his conviction was accordingly quashed. (It is to be noted that by clear implication this decision was a precursor of the view of the scope of the proviso (*f*) prohibition adopted by the majority in *Jones* v. *Director of Public Prosecutions* [1962] A.C. 635, *supra*. On the minority view in the *Jones* case, as the questioning in *R.* v. *Cokar* went to guilt, it would have been outside the prohibition and there would accordingly have been no need to involve exception (*f*)(i)).

The *Maxwell* principle applied to an abandoned charge (*R.* v. *Wadey* (1935) 25 Cr.App.R. 104 (C.C.A.): *R.* v. *Nicoloudis* (1954) 38 Cr.App.R. 118 (C.C.A.)). In *R.* v. *Waldman* (1934) 24 Cr.App.R. 204 (C.C.A.), however, the prisoner on a charge of receiving put his character in issue and was thereupon cross-examined on two previous cases, one of which resulted in a conviction and the other an acquittal; and the Court of Criminal Appeal held that this circumstance made the case distinguishable from *Maxwell's* case, upholding the conviction.

STIRLAND v. DIRECTOR OF PUBLIC PROSECUTIONS

[1944] A.C. 315; 113 L.J.K.B. 394; 171 L.T. 78; 60 T.L.R. 461; [1944] 2 All E.R. 13; 30 Cr.App.R. 40; 42 L.G.R. 263 (H.L.: 1944)

Under the Criminal Evidence Act 1898, section 1(f)(ii), cross-examination by the prosecution as to a prisoner's antecedents is allowed when he puts his character in issue. Such antecedents may include previous

*charges when the accused has expressly sworn to the contrary. The
words "been charged with any offence" mean "brought before a
criminal court," and do not extend to accusations which have not led
to a criminal prosecution. A denial by the accused that he has ever
been "charged" before will usually be construed in the same way.*

The prisoner was accused of forgery, and gave evidence of his own
good character, including his good record with a previous employer. He
also called a witness to say he had never been "charged" before. He
was then cross-examined as to whether that employer had suspected and
questioned him about a suggested forgery. It was held that the question
was improper and should have been disallowed, but that no miscarriage
of justice had occurred.

VISCOUNT SIMON L.C.: . . . When the appellant denied that he had
ever been 'charged" he may fairly be understood to use the word in the
sense it bears in the statute, and to mean that he had never previously
been brought before a criminal court. Questions as to whether his
former employer had suspected him of forgery were not therefore any
challenge to the veracity of what he had said. . . .
It is most undesirable that the rules which should govern cross-
examination to credit of an accused person in the witness-box should be
complicated by refined distinctions. . . . The following propositions seem
to cover the ground. (I am omitting the rule which admits evidence
tending to prove other offences where this evidence is relevant . . . as
helping to negative accident or establish system, intent, or the like.)
(1) The accused in the witness-box may not be asked any question
"tending to show that he had committed or been convicted of or been
charged with any offence other than that wherewith he is then charged
or is of bad character" unless one or other of the three conditions laid
down in section 1(f) of the Act of 1898 is fulfilled.
(2) He may, however, be cross-examined as to any of the evidence he
has given in chief, including statements as to his own good record, with
a view to testing his veracity or accuracy or to showing he is not to be
believed on his oath.
(3) An accused who puts his character in issue must be regarded as
putting the whole of his past record in issue. He cannot assert his good
character in certain respects without exposing himself to inquiry as to
the rest of his record so far as this tends to disprove a claim for good
character.
(4) An accused is not to be regarded as depriving himself of the
protection of the section because the proper conduct of his defence
necessitates the making of injurious reflections on the prosecutor or his
witnesses.
(5) It is no disproof of good character that a man has been suspected
or accused of a previous crime. Such questions as "Were you
suspected?" or "Were you accused?" are inadmissible because they are
irrelevant to the issue of character and can only be asked if the accused
has sworn expressly to the contrary.
(6) The fact that a question put to the accused is irrelevant is in itself
no reason for quashing a conviction, though it should have been
disallowed by the judge. . . .

LORDS RUSSELL OF KILLOWEN, THANKERTON, WRIGHT and PONTER
concurred.

Note.—As to rule (2)—see the criticism in *Jones* v. *D.P.P.* [1962] A.C. 635 (H.L.), *supra.* As to rule (3)—this apparently recognises the practice approved in *R.* v. *Winfield* (1939) 27 Cr.App.R. 139 (C.C.A.), Chapter 22, *supra.* As to rule (4)—see below.

R. v. **Ellis** [1910] 2 K.B. 746 (C.C.A.). The accused, an antique dealer, was charged with obtaining cheques from a customer named Dickens by false pretences. He had agreed to sell at cost plus 10 per cent. profit. The prosecution alleged that he had represented the cost to be higher than it really was. In the course of his examination-in-chief the accused answered questions about his conduct towards the customer with a view to negativing any intent to defraud. The Court of Criminal Appeal held that he ought not to have been asked questions under section 1(*f*)(ii) because evidence had not been given with a view to establishing good character. Bray J., delivering the judgment of the court, said (pp. 762–763):" Mr.Bodkin [prosecution counsel] suggested that [defence counsel] had in his opening speech to the jury endeavoured to establish the appellant's general good character. We do not think that this was so, but if it were so, that is not within the statute; he must have asked questions of the witnesses for the prosecution, or he must have given evidence with a view to establishing the appellant's good character. It was said that in the examination-in-chief of the appellant Mr. Elliott had asked questions relating to his purchase of this business, to his general relations with Mr. Dickins, and to other transactions under the cost plus 10 per cent. agreement. In our opinion it would not be correct to say that the appellant had given evidence of his own good character. It may or may not have been relevant to go into other sales on the cost price plus 10 per cent. basis. Mr. Bodkin thought it was not and objected, and Mr. Elliott did not further pursue that line of examination, but its object was not to set up the appellant's good character, it was to negative fraud. In our opinion, if we were to give the slightest colour to the idea that a general examination as to the surrounding circumstances was such evidence of good character as to entitle the prosecution to prove or to cross-examine as to other offences or convictions, we should deprive the prisoner of the protection which the statute has given him. Sub-clause (ii) of section 1, clause (*f*), of the Criminal Evidence Act 1898, was not intended to apply to a case like this. It was intended to apply to cases where witnesses to character were called, or where evidence of the good character of the prisoner was sought to be elicited from the witnesses for the prosecution. In civil actions evidence of good character is not, as a rule, admissible. It is admissible in criminal cases, and it is to this class of evidence that the statute refers, not to mere assertions of innocence or repudiation of guilt on the part of the prisoner, nor to reasons given by him for such assertion or repudiation."

Note.—See, too, *R.* v. *Lee* [1976] 1 W.L.R. 71 (C.A.) and *Malindi* v. *R.* [1967] A.C. 439 (P.C.).

R. v. COOK

[1959] 2 Q.B. 340; [1959] 2 All E.R. 97; 43 Cr.App.R. 138; (C.C.A.: 1959)

Although the Criminal Evidence Act 1898, section 1(f)(ii), makes admissible cross-examination of the accused as to his previous convictions when he has made imputations on the prosecution, the judge in his discretion should protect the accused from too severe an application of the statutory provision.

On a charge of false pretences and receiving stolen cheque forms, the accused in cross-examination of a police officer and in evidence asserted that incriminating statements made by him to the police were procured by a threat to charge the accused's wife, which allegation was denied. The chairman of quarter sessions allowed the accused to be cross-examined by the prosecution as to his previous convictions, and he was found guilty. The Court of Criminal Appeal held that the defence was so conducted as to involve an imputation on a prosecution witness; that it was not clear that the chairman had exercised his discretion in permitting cross-examination as to the accused's record; that the appellate court should exercise a discretion; that the questions as to the accused's record should not have been put, but that there had been no miscarriage of justice, and the appeal failed.

DEVLIN J. (reading the judgment of the court, which included LORD PARKER C.J., DONOVAN, MCNAIR and HINCHCLIFFE JJ.): . . . Counsel- . . . put to the appellant, and the appellant agreed, that he had a long record of crime behind him; details of various convictions for offences of dishonesty were then put. In the circumstances of this case and under the provisions of section 1(*f*)(ii) of the Criminal Evidence Act 1898, those questions were permissible only if the nature or conduct of the defence was such as to involve imputations on the character of Detective-Constable Thomas.

It is clear from the subsection as a whole that it does not intend that the introduction of a prisoner's previous convictions should be other than exceptional. The difficulty about its phraseology is that unless it is given some restricted meaning, a prisoner's bad character, if he had one, would emerge almost as a matter of course. Counsel for the defence could not submit that a witness for the prosecution was untruthful without making an imputation upon his character; a prisoner charged with assault could not assert that the prosecutor struck first without imputing to him a similar crime. The authorities show that this court has endeavoured to surmount this difficulty in two ways. First, it has in a number of cases construed the words of the subsection as benevolently as possible in favour of the accused. Secondly, it has laid it down that, in cases which fall within the subsection, the trial judge must not allow as a matter of course questions designed to show bad character; he must weigh the prejudicial effect of such questions against the damage done by the attack on the prosecution's witnesses, and must generally exercise his discretion so as to secure a trial that is fair both to the prosecution and to the defence.

The judgments in many of the earlier cases are based upon a limited construction of the statute. Thus, in *R. v. Rouse* [1904] 1 K.B. 184 (C.C.R.) it was held that a statement by the prisoner in cross-examination that the prosecutor was a liar must be regarded only as an emphatic denial of the truth of the charge against him and did not enable the prosecution to put his character in issue. Cases of rape have given rise to a peculiar difficulty; the prisoner cannot assert that the connection was with the consent of the prosecutrix without making imputations against her chastity. There was for a long time a difference of opinion about the effect of this; it was not definitely settled in favour of the defence until *R. v. Turner* [1944] K.B. 463 (C.C.A.), a case which was shortly after approved by the House of Lords in *Stirland* v. *Director of Public Prosecutions* [1944] A.C. 315. At the same time this court has refused as a general rule to read words into the section that are not there. This was plainly laid down by a full court in *R.* v. *Hudson* [1912] 2 K.B. 464 at 470 (C.C.A.) in the following terms: "We think that the words of the section, 'unless...the nature or conduct of the defence is such as to involve imputations,' etc., must receive their ordinary and natural interpretation, and that it is not legitimate to qualify them by adding or inserting the words 'unnecessarily' or 'unjustifiably' or 'for purposes other than that of developing the defence,' or other similar words...."

The alternative approach to the problem has been by the application of the general rule that the trial judge must always exercise his discretion so as to prevent the introduction of material whose prejudicial effect would outweigh its evidential value....

In our opinion the difficulties created by this subsection are as a general rule best dealt with in accordance with the principle in *R.* v. *Hudson* (above) as applied in *R.* v. *Jenkins* (1945) 31 Cr.App.R. 1. The attempt to give the words a limited construction has led to decisions which it is difficult to reconcile; now that it is clearly established that the trial judge has a discretion and that he must exercise it so as to secure that the defence is not unfairly prejudiced, there is nothing to be gained by seeking to strain the words of the subsection in favour of the defence. We think, therefore, that the words should be given their natural and ordinary meaning and that the trial judge should, in his discretion, do what is necessary in the circumstances to protect the prisoner from an application of the subsection that would be too severe. It may be that, as indicated in *O'Hara* v. *H.M. Advocate*, 1948 J.C. 90, cases of rape should be regarded as *sui generis*; certainly the peculiar questions to which they give rise have been settled by *R.* v. *Turner* (above) and that case has determined how the discretion should be exercised. No equally clear guidance can be given in cases where the subject-matter is not so specialised. In particular, no firm rule has been, or can be, laid down to govern the sort of circumstances we have to consider here where the defence involves a suggestion of impropriety against the police officer. The cases on this subject-matter—in particular *R.* v. *Preston* [1909] 1 K.B. 568 (C.C.A.), *R.* v. *Jones* (1923) 39 T.L.R. 457 (C.C.A.), and *R.* v. *Clark* [1955] 2 Q.B. 469 (C.C.A.)—indicate the factors to be borne in mind and the sort of question that a judge should ask himself. Is a deliberate attack being made upon the conduct of the police officer calculated to discredit him wholly as a witness? If there is, a judge might well feel that he must withdraw the protection which he would desire to extend as far as possible to an accused who was endeavouring only to develop a line of defence. If there is a real issue about the conduct of an important witness which the jury will inevitably have to settle in order to arrive at their verdict, then, as Singleton J. put it in *R.* v. *Jenkins* (above) and Lord Goddard C.J. repeated in *R.* v. *Clark* (above), the jury is entitled to know the credit of the man on whose word the witness's character is being impugned.

We now apply these principles to the circumstances of this case. In our judgment, when the prosecution's evidence of an admission made to a police officer is met by saying that it was extorted by means of a threat that otherwise the prisoner's wife would be charged, the defence is so conducted as to involve an imputation on the character of the police officer. The issue, therefore, becomes one of discretion. It is well settled that this court will not interfere with the exercise of a discretion by the judge below unless he has erred in principle or there is no material on which he could properly have arrived at his decision. But in this case we are not satisfied that the learned chairman really exercised his discretion at all. He allowed the questions to be put because he thought that counsel was strictly entitled to do so, although he, he chairman, queried whether it was necessary. Accordingly, it falls to us to exercise our own discretion in the matter.

[Counsel] did not dispute that the conduct imputed to the police officer was grossly improper, but he submitted that it was not like a charge of fabrication or concoction which goes to the root of a witness's integrity and which, if accepted, destroys the whole of his evidence on every point in the case. He submitted also that the attack was not pointedly directed against the witness under cross-examination, but was made against the police generally. The charge was not elaborated or pressed; it was repeated several times, but that was probably because the prisoner is a man who often repeats himself. Finally, (counsel) made the substantial point that no warning was given to the accused before his convictions were put to him. In cases of this sort where there is no hard and fast rule, some warning to the defence that it is going too far is of great importance; and it has always been the practice for prosecuting counsel to indicate in advance that he is going to claim his rights under the subsection, or for the judge to give the defence a caution. This is especially needful when the prisoner, as here, was not represented, though it is fair to say that he professed familiarity with the law and rejected the legal aid that had been assigned to him. We have come to the conclusion that the questions ought not to have been put....

SELVEY v. DIRECTOR OF PUBLIC PROSECUTIONS

[1970] A.C. 304; 52 Cr.App.R. 443; [1968] 2 All E.R. 497 (H.L.: 1968)

Except in cases of rape (either because these are sui generis, or because the issue of non-consent is raised by the prosecution), an accused person loses the protection of the Criminal Evidence Act 1898, section 1(f), if the nature or conduct of his defence involves imputations on the prosecutor or a prosecution witness, even though the imputations are a necessary part of his defence.

When as a matter of law the protection is thus lost, a judge nevertheless has a discretion to admit or exclude the previous record or character of an accused person and to allow or disallow cross-examination on it. There is no general rule that this discretion should be exercised in favour of the accused, even though the imputations do form a necessary part of the defence.

The appellant was charged with committing buggery with the complainant, who was cross-examined by defence counsel on the basis that he carried indecent photographs with him, that he had already committed buggery that same afternoon with another person, and that having been refused £1 when he offered himself to the appellant, he had blamed the appellant for his condition (to which a doctor testified). On the view that the appellant's defence involved an attack on the complainant's character, the judge gave the prosecution leave to put to the appellant his previous sexual convictions (which were disclosed as indecent assaults on young boys, and persistently importuning male persons). The appellant was convicted. His appeal was dismissed by the Court of Appeal which, however, gave leave to appeal to the House of Lords, certifying that two points of law of general public importance were involved: (i) If the making of the imputation is necessary for the proper development of the defence, is the cross-examination permitted by section 1(*f*)(ii) of the Act of 1898? (ii) Is there a general rule as to the exercise of the judge's discretion as stated in *R.* v. *Flynn* [1963] 1 Q.B. 729? The House of Lords dismissed the appeal.

VISCOUNT DILHORNE: ... The cases to which I have referred, some of which it is not possible to reconcile, in my opinion finally establish the following propositions:

(1) The words of the statute must be given their ordinary natural meaning (*Hudson* [1912] 2 K.B. 464; *Jenkins*, 31 Cr.App.R. 1; *Cook* [1959] 1 Q.B. 340).

(2) The section permits cross-examination of the accused as to character both when imputations on the character of the prosecutor and his witness are cast to show their unreliability as witnesses independently of the evidence given by them and also when the casting of such imputations is necessary to enable the accused to establish his defence (*Hudson*; *Jenkins*; *Cook*).

(3) In rape cases the accused can allege consent without placing himself in peril of such cross-examination (*Sheean*, 21 Cox C.C. 561; *Turner* [1944] K.B. 463). This may be because such cases are *sui generis* (*per* Devlin J. in *Rex* v. *Cook* [1959] 2 Q.B. 340, 347), or on the ground that the issue is one raised by the prosecution.

(4) If what is said amounts in reality to no more than a denial of the charge expressed, it may be, in emphatic language, it should not be regarded as coming within the section (*Rouse* [1904] 1 K.B. 184; *Rex* v. *Grout* (1909) 3 Cr.App.R. 64; *Rex* v. *Jones*, 17 Cr.App.R. 117; *Clark* [1955] 2 Q.B. 469).

Applying these propositions to this case, it is in my opinion clear beyond all doubt that the cross-examination of the accused was permissible under the statute.

I now turn to the question whether a judge has discretion to refuse to permit such cross-examination of the accused when it is permissible under the section. Mr. Caulfield [counsel for the respondent] submitted that there was no such discretion and contended that a judge at a criminal trial had no power to exclude evidence which was admissible....

.... [But] it has been said in many cases that a judge has such a discretion. In *Rex* v. *Christie* [1914] A.C. 545 where the question was as to the admissibility of a statement made in the presence and hearing of the accused, Lord Moulton said, at p. 559: ...

"The law is so much on its guard against the accused being prejudiced by evidence which, though admissible, would probably have a prejudicial influence on the minds of the jury which would be out of proportion to its true evidential value, that there has grown up a practice of a very salutary nature, under which the judge intimates to the counsel for the prosecution that he should not press for the admission of evidence which would be open to this objection, and such an intimation from the tribunal trying the case is usually sufficient to prevent the evidence being pressed in all cases where the scruples of the tribunal in this respect are reasonable. Under the influence of this practice, which is based on an anxiety to secure for everyone a fair trial, there has grown up a custom of not admitting certain kinds of evidence which is so constantly followed that it almost amounts to a rule of procedure."

In *Watson*, 8 Cr.App.R. 249, 254, the first case when the exercise of discretion in relation to cases coming within the section was mentioned, Pickford J. said:

"It has been pointed out that to apply the rule" [in *Hudson* [1912] 2 K.B. 464] "strictly is to put a hardship on a prisoner with a bad character. That may be so, but it does not follow that a judge necessarily allows the prisoner to be cross-examined to character; he has a discretion not to allow it, and the prisoner has that protection."

In *Maxwell* [1935] A.C. 309 and in *Stirland* [1944] A.C. 315 it was said in this House that a judge has that discretion. In *Jenkins*, 31 Cr.App.R. 1, 15, Singleton J. said:

"If and when such a situation arises" (the question whether the accused should be cross-examined as to character) "it is open to counsel to apply to the presiding judge that he may be allowed to take the course indicated.... Such an application will not always be granted, for the judge has a discretion in the matter. He may feel that even though the position is established in law, still the putting of such questions as to the character of the accused person may be fraught with results which immeasurably outweigh the result of questions put by the defence and which make a fair trial of the accused person almost impossible. On the other hand, in the ordinary and normal case he may feel that if the credit of the prosecutor or his witnesses has been attacked, it is only fair that the jury should have before them material on which they can form their judgment whether the accused person is any more worthy to be believed than those he has attacked. It is obviously unfair that the jury should be left in the dark about the accused person's character if the conduct of his defence has attacked the character of the prosecutor or the witnesses for the prosecution within the meaning of the section. The essential thing is a fair trial and that the legislature sought to ensure by section 1, subsection (*f*)."

Similar views were expressed in *Noor Mohamed* v. *The King* [1949] A.C. 182 by Lord du Parcq, in *Harris* v. *Director of Public Prosecutions* [1952] A.C. 694, in *Cook* [1959] 2 Q.B. 340, in *Jones* v. *Director of Public Prosecutions* [1962] A.C. 635, and in other cases.

In the light of what was said in all these cases by judges of great eminence, one is tempted to say, as Lord Hewart said in *Dunkley* [1927] 1 K.B. 323 that it is far too late in the day even to consider the argument that a judge has no such discretion. Let it suffice for me to say that in my opinion the existence of such a discretion is now clearly established.

Mr. Caulfield posed the question, on what principles, should such a discretion be exercised. In *Reg.* v. *Flynn* [1963] 1 Q.B. 729, 737 the court said:

"... where ... the very nature of the defence necessarily involves an imputation, against a prosecution witness or witnesses, the discretion should, in the opinion of this court, be as a general rule exercised in favour of the accused, that is to say, evidence as to his bad character or criminal record should be excluded. If it were otherwise, it comes to this, that the Act of 1898, the very Act which gave the charter, so to speak, to an accused person to give evidence on oath in the witness box, would be a mere trap because he would be unable to put forward any defence, no matter how true, which involved an imputation on the character of the prosecutor or any of his witnesses, without running the risk, if he had the misfortune to have a record, of his previous convictions being brought up in court while being tried on a wholly different matter."

No authority is given for this supposed general rule. In my opinion, the court was wrong in thinking that there was any such rule. If there was any such general rule, it would amount under the guise of the exercise of discretion, to the insertion of a proviso to the statute of the very kind that was said in *Hudson* [1912] 2 K.B. 464 not to be legitimate.

I do not think it possible to improve upon the guidance given by Singleton J. in the passage quoted above from *Jenkins*, 31 Cr.App.R. 1, 15, by Lord du Parcq in *Noor Mohamed* [1949] A.C. 182 or by Devlin J., in *Cook* [1959] 2 Q.B. 340 as to the matters which should be borne in mind in relation to the exercise of the discretion. It is now so well established that on a charge of rape the allegation that the women consented, although involving an imputation on her character, should not expose an accused to cross-examination as to character, that it is possible to say, if the refusal to allow it is a matter of discretion, that there is a general rule that the discretion should be so exercised. Apart from this, there is not, I think, any general rule as to the exercise of discretion. It must depend on the circumstances of each case and the overriding duty of the judge to ensure that a trial is fair.

It is desirable that a warning should be given when it becomes apparent that the defence is taking a course which may expose the accused to such cross-examination. That was not given in this case but the failure to give such a warning would not, in my opinion, justify in this case the allowing of the appeal.

In my opinion the cross-examination of the accused was permissible under the section and it cannot be said the judge exercised his discretion wrongly in allowing it to take place. . . .

LORD GUEST: . . . If I had thought that there was no discretion in English law for a judge to disallow admissible evidence, as counsel for the Crown argued, I should have striven hard and long to give a benevolent construction to section 1(f)(ii), which would exclude such cases as *Rouse* [1904] 1 K.B. 184, "liar," *Rex* v. *Rappolt*, 6 Cr.App.R. 156, "horrible liar," *Rex* v. *Jones*, 17 Cr.App.R. 117, "fabricated evidence," *Rex* v. *Turner* [1944] K.B. 463, rape and other sexual offences, *Reg.* v. *Brown* (1960) 44 Cr.App.R. 181, "self defence." I cannot believe that Parliament can have intended that in such cases an accused could only put forward such a defence at peril of having his character put before the jury. This would be to defeat the benevolent purposes of the 1898 Act which was for the first time to allow the accused to give evidence on his own behalf in all criminal cases. This would deprive the accused of the advantage of the Act. But I am not persuaded by the Crown's argument and I am satisfied upon a review of all the authorities that in English law such a discretion does exist. . . .

I find it unnecessary to say much more on the principles upon which discretion should be exercised. The guiding star should be fairness to the accused. This idea is best expressed by Devlin J. in *Reg.* v. *Cook* [1959] 2 Q.B. 340. In following this star the fact that the imputation was a necessary part of the accused's defence is a consideration which will no doubt be taken into account by the trial judge. If, however, the accused or his counsel goes beyond developing his defence in order to blacken the character of a prosecution witness, this no doubt will be another factor to be taken into account. If it is suggested that the exercise of this discretion may be whimsical and depend on the individual idiosyncrasies of the judge, this is inevitable where it is a question of discretion; but I am satisfied that this is a lesser risk than attempting to shackle the judge's power within a straitjacket. . . .

LORD HODSON and LORD PEARCE (with whom LORD WILBERFORCE agreed) delivered concurring judgments.

Note.—Implicit in Lord Dilhorne's first proposition is confirmation of rejection of any suggestion that an accused will not expose himself to cross-examination concerning his record if he casts an imputation which is essential for the proper conduct of his defence. This notion which found favour in some of the early cases was first decisively rejected by the full Court of Criminal Appeal in *R.* v. *Hudson* [1912] 2 K.B. 464. There the accused was charged with larceny and his defence was that the crime had been committed not by him but by a prosecution witness. The putting of this defence was held to involve an imputation for the purposes of the proviso. See, too, in addition to the other cases cited by Lord Dilhorne *R.* v. *Sargvon* (1967) 51 Cr.App.R. 394 (C.A.) and *R.* v. *Bishop* [1975] Q.B. 274 (C.A.), *infra*. In *R.* v. *Turner*, one of the rape cases referred to by Lord Dilhorne under this third proposition, the Court of Criminal Appeal held that the accused's allegations, not only that the prosecutrix had consented to intercourse, but also that she had been guilty of acts of gross indecency as a preliminary, did not as a matter of law constitute an imputation for the purposes of proviso (*f*)(ii).

R. v. **Bishop** [1975] 1 Q.B. 274 (C.A.). The accused was charged with theft from a bedroom. In evidence he explained the presence of his fingerprints in the room by saying that he had a homosexual relationship with the occupier and had often been there by invitation. The occupier, who was called as a prosecution witness, denied this. The Court of Appeal held that Bishop's allegation constituted an imputation and that therefore the prosecution had properly been allowed to cross-examine him as to his criminal record. Homosexual acts committed in private between consenting adults being no longer criminal, the allegation was not of unlawful conduct, but this did not prevent it from constituting or involving an imputation. The court took the view that this imputation could reflect upon the witness's reliability both generally and in the witness box. The court also affirmed that an accused may lose the protection of the proviso (*f*) prohibition even though he does not intend to discredit the prosecution witness: the criterion being purely objective, what is important is not the accused's motive but the likely actual effect of the "nature or conduct of the defence."

Note.—This decision may be regarded as being indicative of a return to a stricter interpretation of proviso (*f*)(ii) so far as the purely legal position is concerned, this being co-relative to the placing by the House of Lords in *Selvey's* case (*supra*) of its *imprimatur* upon the existence of a discretion. At all events *R.* v. *Bishop* is not easy to reconcile with some earlier cases, such as *R.* v. *Westfall* (1912) 7 Cr.App.R. 176, where an allegation by an accused charged with robbery that the prosecutor was a habitual drunkard was held not to constitute an imputation.

R. v. Tanner (1977) 66 Cr.App.R. 56 (C.A.). The appellant had been indicted on two counts of theft. Police officers testified at the trial that when he was being questioned about the two thefts he had made admissions about the transactions on which the charges were based. The appellant denied those admissions and other parts of the interviews with the police officers. Defence counsel did not cross-examine the officers but merely suggested that they were wrong in saying that the appellant had admitted the offences. However, later in the trial the appellant during his cross-examination said in answer to a question by the trial judge that the police evidence on the matter was a complete invention. The judge then allowed the prosecution to cross-examine the appellant about his previous convictions. The appellant's appeal against conviction was dismissed. The Court of Appeal held that a distinction (although sometimes a "very narrow" one) must be drawn between a case in which the defendant merely denies, even emphatically denies, the truth of the evidence of a prosecution witness, and a case where, as here, he makes specific allegations of serious improprieties against a witness. Approving dicta of two Lord Chief Justices, that of Lord Hewart in *R. v. Jones* (1924) 17 Cr.App.R. 117 (C.C.A.) and that of Lord Goddard in *R. v. Clark* [1955] 2 Q.B. 469, Browne L.J. (giving the judgment of the Court) indicated that even the statement, "the police constable is a liar," would not constitute an imputation, but a suggestion that the police officers had conspired to fabricate evidence and to defeat the ends of justice would do so. The court further found that there was no reason to suppose that in the instant case the trial judge had wrongly exercised his discretion in allowing the cross-examination which had been rendered legally admissible by "the nature or conduct of the defence."

Note.—To be contrasted with *R. v. Tanner* is *R. v. Nelson* (1978) 68 Cr.App.R. 12 (C.A.), where counsel for the appellant had put it to a police officer in cross-examination that the accused had not made the admissions which he was alleged to have made when being interrogated, that the whole alleged conversation had never taken place, and by implication that the police officers's note-book had been fabricated: the Court of Appeal nevertheless held that cross-examination of the accused had been improperly allowed. In the later case of *R. v. Britzman* [1983] 1 W.L.R. 350 (C.A.) Lawton L.J., giving the judgment of the Court, preferred the decision in *R. v. Tanner* to that in *R. v. Nelson*. Subsequently in *R. v. St. Louis and Case* (1984) 79 Cr.App.R. 53 (C.A.) a distinction was drawn (p. 60) "between accusations going essentially to the credit of a police officer and suggestions made in cross-examination that are essential to a plea of 'not guilty' albeit made with emphasis." *R. v. Britzman* was approved, but distinguished on the ground that there "the only inference to be drawn from the flat denial that the alleged conversation had taken place—a matter about which there could be no room for mistake, misunderstanding or confusion—was an imputation of conspiracy to commit perjury; it did not go to the central part of the defence." (It is to be noted the central focus in *R. v. St. Louis and Case* would appear to have been as to the propriety of resort to the proviso to section 2(1) of the Criminal Appeal Act 1968).

R. v. Inder (1977) 67 Cr.App.R. 143 (C.A.). The appellant was charged with one offence of buggery and with seven of indecent assault relating to six boys. He had a bad record for this type of offence. During the evidence of one boy the appellant alleged that the evidence against him had been faked and that the boy had been blackmailing him. The trial judge then ruled that this constituted an imputation upon the boy's character and he accordingly allowed the appellant's bad record to be let in. The appellant was convicted on the buggery count and on four of the indecent assault counts. The Court of Appeal allowed his appeal and quashed the conviction. The court held that cross-examination of the appellant as to his record had been properly permitted; but, as this cross-examination was permissible only by virtue of proviso (f)(ii) to section 1, the accused having cast imputations upon the police, the judge ought to have warned the jury that the evidence elicited by it could only go to the appellant's credit as a witness and not to his guilt as an accused person. The judge had failed to do this adequately. The court held that evidence of earlier offences was not admissible as similar fact evidence because the similarities were not sufficiently striking but merely represented "the stock in trade of the seducer of small boys and were not unique but appear in the vast majority of cases that come before the courts."

Note.—Had the evidence of earlier offences been admissible as similar fact evidence (as to which see Chapter 23, supra), cross-examination of the accused would then also have been permissible under the proviso (f)(i), and in this event the appellant's answers would have been additionally available on the issue of his guilt.

R. v. Powell [1985] 1 W.L.R. 1364 (C.A.). The accused was charged with knowingly living off immoral earnings. His defence was that the prosecution evidence was a complete fabrication; he also gave evidence of his own good character. The prosecution was allowed to prove three earlier convictions for allowing his premises to be used for the purposes of prostitution. The jury were warned that the evidence of these convictions went only to credibility. The Court of Appeal held that the fact that the convictions were for offences not involving dishonesty, and the fact that they were for offences closely resembling the offences charged, were both matters for the judge to take into consideration when exercising his discretion, but neither was a bar to allowing cross-examination. The Court held that there were no grounds for interfering with the judge's exercise of his discretion, either on the basis that the accused had given evidence of his own good character or on the basis of his attack on the police witnesses.

Note.—The Court of Appeal declined to follow its earlier decision in R. v. Watts (1983) 77 Cr.App.R. 126, where in similar circumstances it had quashed a conviction on the ground that "it would have been extremely difficult if not impossible" for the jury to use the similar fact evidence on the issue of the credibility of the police witnesses but at the same time ignore it on the issue of the accused's guilt.

It is in fact not easy to see that evidence of previous convictions or activity not involving dishonesty will often have much relevance on the issue, of credibility. Moreover, the decision in R. v. Powell clearly means that similar fact evidence, of a type that is usually excluded, may be admissible, albeit technically on the issue of credibility, if the accused testifies (but not otherwise) and "the nature or conduct of the defence is such as to involve imputations on the character of the prosecutor or the witnesses for the prosecution." It is a position that is difficult to justify either in logic or in policy.

R. v. Owen (1986) 83 Cr.App.R. 100 (C.A.). The appellant was charged with the theft of a purse. Police officers who arrested him said that they had seem him reach inside his jacket pocket and drop the purse. When interviewed, the appellant said the officers had lied. Evidence of the interview was given at the trial. Leave was granted to cross-examine as to previous offences of dishonesty without revealing that they were similar to the offence charged. It was held that, despite the restraint exercised by the appellant's counsel, it was a necessary implication in the questions addressed to the officers that they had concocted their evidence. Neill L.J., giving the judgment of the Court, listed (pp. 104–105) seven points which it is necessary to bear in mind in this context. (1) The judge has two separate tasks to perform: first a determination as to whether as a matter of law an imputation has been cast; secondly, if it has, whether as a matter of discretion cross-examination should not be allowed. (2) ". . . in many cases imputations on the character of the witnesses for the prosecution may be made even though no explicit allegation of fabrication is made and even though counsel for the accused has conducted his cross-examination with delicacy and restraint." (3) In exercising his discretion a judge "must weigh the prejudicial effect of the questions to be directed to the accused against the damage done by the attack on the prosecution's witness, and must generally exercise his discretion so as to secure a trial that is fair to the prosecution and the defence." (4) Sometimes to allow questioning might "make a fair trial of the accused almost impossible." (5) "In the normal and ordinary case, however, the trial judge may feel that if the credit of the prosecution or his witnesses has been attacked, it is only fair that the jury should have before them material on which they can form their judgment whether the accused person is any more worthy to be believed than those he has attacked." (6) "The fact that the accused's convictions are not for offences of dishonesty, but may be for offences bearing a close resemblance to the offences charged, are matters for the judge to take into consideration when exercising his discretion, but they certainly do not oblige the judge to disallow the proposed cross-examination: see *Powell*" (*infra*). (7) The appellate court will not interfere with the exercise of the judge's discretion merely because it would itself have exercised the discretion differently, but only if the judge "erred in principle or there was no material on which he could properly arrive at his decision."

Note.—See, too, the earlier case of *R.* v. *Burke* (1986) 82 Cr.App.R. 156 (C.A.) from which some of these propositions derive.

MURDOCH v. TAYLOR

[1965] A.C. 574; [1965] 1 All E.R. 406; 49 Cr.App.R. 119 (H.L.: 1965)

Under the Criminal Evidence Act 1898, section 1(f)(iii), evidence is "given... against" a co-accused (whether in examination-in-chief or under cross-examination), if it supports the prosecution case in a material respect or undermines the defence of the co-accused; the test is an objective not a subjective one. When section 1(f)(iii) is applicable the judge has no discretion to disallow cross-examination of an accused by a co-accused, but he has a discretion to disallow such cross-examination by the prosecution.

The appellant, Murdoch, was charged jointly with one Lynch with knowingly receiving stolen property. Under cross-examination the appellant said that the stolen property had nothing to do with him, and gave answers to the effect that the box containing the property had been in the control and possession of Lynch. Counsel for Lynch was permitted to cross-examine the appellant as to his previous convictions. Both accused were found guilty. An appeal by Murdoch to the Court of Criminal Appeal on the ground that he had not given evidence "against" his co-accused was dismissed, as was his appeal to the House of Lords.

Lords Evershed and Morris of Borth-y-Gest concurred with Lord Donovan. Lord Reid concurred with Lord Donovan on the issue of discretion, but was doubtful of the majority's interpretation of "against." Lord Pearce concurred with Lord Donovan, but dissented from the view that no discretion existed in the case of cross-examination by a co-accused.

Lord Donovan: ... It is now contended on behalf of Murdoch, first, that he had given no evidence against Lynch within the meaning of proviso (*f*)(iii). That expression in this context connotes, it is said, only evidence given in examination-in-chief and not evidence given in cross-examination. Alternatively, it refers only to evidence given with a hostile intent against a co-accused so that the test to be applied is subjective and not objective. In the further alternative, it is argued that, whatever be the true meaning of the expression, a trial judge has in all cases a discretion whether or not to allow questions to be put pursuant to proviso (*f*)(iii) just as he has in relation to proviso (*f*)(ii) of the section. . . .

. . . . The effect upon the jury is the same whether the evidence be given in examination-in-chief or in cross-examination; and the desirability of the co-accused being able to meet it by cross-examination as to credit is of the same importance, however the evidence is given. I feel no difficulty in holding that the first of the appellant's contentions must be rejected.

The like considerations also lead me to reject the argument that proviso (*f*)(iii) refers only to evidence given by one accused against the other with hostile intent. Again, it is the effect of the evidence upon the minds of the jury which matters, not the state of mind of the person who gives it. . . . In my opinion, the test to be applied in order to determine whether one accused has given evidence against his co-accused is objective and not subjective.

What kind of evidence is contemplated by proviso (*f*)(iii), that is, what *is* "evidence against" a co-accused is perhaps the most difficult part of the case. At one end of the scale is evidence which does no more than contradict something which a co-accused has said without further advancing the prosecution's case in any significant degree. I agree with the view expressed by Winn J. in giving judgment in *Stannard* [[1965] 2 Q.B. 1] that this is not the kind of evidence contemplated by proviso (*f*)(iii). At the other end of the scale is evidence which, if the jury believes it, would establish the co-accused's guilt, for example, in a case of theft: "I saw him steal the purse" or in a case of assault "I saw him strike the blow." It is this kind of evidence which alone, so the appellant contends, will satisfy the words "has given evidence against." Again, I regret I cannot share that view. There may well be evidence which regarded in isolation would be quite innocuous from the co-accused's point of view and, so regarded, could not be regarded as evidence "against" him. For example, what would be proved if one co-accused said of his co-accused: "He told me he knew of an easy job and persuaded me to help him?" If such evidence is kept unrelated to anything else it proves nothing criminal. But juries hear the whole of the evidence and they will consider particular parts of it, not in isolation but in conjunction with all the other evidence, and part of that other evidence may establish that "job" meant a housebreaking job. Then the item of evidence I have taken as an example obviously becomes evidence "against" the accused. If, therefore, the effect of the evidence upon the minds of the jury is to be taken as the test, it cannot be right to regard it in isolation in order to decide whether it is evidence against the co-accused. If Parliament had meant by proviso (*f*)(iii) to refer to evidence which was by itself conclusive against the co-accused it would have been easy to say so.

The test prescribed by the Court of Criminal Appeal in *Stannard* (above) was whether the evidence in question tended to support the prosecution's case in a material respect or to undermine the defence. I have no substantial quarrel with this definition. I would, however, observe that some danger may lurk in the use of the expression "tended to." There will probably be occasions when it could be said that evidence given by one accused "tended to" support the prosecution's case simply because it differed from the evidence of his co-accused; and the addition of the words "in a material respect" might not wholly remove the danger. The difficulty is not really one of conception but of expression. I myself would omit the words "tended to" and simply say that "evidence against" means evidence which supports the prosecution's case in a material respect or which undermines the defence of the co-accused. . . .

On the question of discretion, I agree with the Court of Criminal Appeal that a trial judge has no discretion whether to allow an accused person to be cross-examined as to his past criminal offences once he has given evidence against his co-accused. Proviso (f)(iii) in terms confers no such discretion and, in my opinion, none can be implied. It is true that in relation to proviso (f)(ii) such a discretion does exist; that is to say, in the cases where the accused has attempted to establish his own good character or where the nature and conduct of the defence is such as to involve imputations on the character of the prosecutor or of a witness for the prosecution.

But in these cases it will normally, if not invariably, be the prosecution which will want to bring out the accused's bad character—not some co-accused; and in such cases it seems to me quite proper that the court should retain some control of the matter. For its duty is to secure a fair trial and the prejudicial value of evidence establishing the accused's bad character may at times wholly outweigh the value of such evidence as tending to show that he was guilty of the crime alleged.

These considerations lead me to the view that if, in any given case (which I think would be rare), the prosecution sought to avail itself of the provisions of proviso (f)(iii) then here, again, the court should keep control of the matter in the like way. Otherwise, if two accused gave evidence one against the other, but neither wished to cross-examine as to character, the prosecution could step in as of right and reveal the criminal records of both, if both possessed them. I cannot think that Parliament in the Act of 1898 ever intended such an unfair procedure. So far as concerns the prosecution, therefore, the matter should be one for the exercise of the judge's discretion, as it is in the case of proviso (f)(ii). But when it is the co-accused who seeks to exercise the right conferred by proviso (f)(iii) different considerations come into play. He seeks to defend himself; to say to the jury that the man who is giving evidence against him is unworthy of belief; and to support that assertion by proof of bad character. The right to do this cannot, in my opinion, be fettered in any way. . . .

Note.—In *Matusevich* v. *R.* (1977) 51 A.L.J.R. 657 a majority of the High Court of Australia, construing a proviso generally similar to proviso (f)(iii), doubted whether the prosecution can ever take advantage of it.

R. v. **Varley** (1982) 75 Cr.App.R. 241 (C.A.). The appellant and his co-accused, Dibble, were charged jointly with robbery. At the trial Dibble contended that he took part in the joint venture under duress from the appellant. The appellant denied that he had taken part in the robbery or that he had forced Dibble to commit it. Dibble's counsel was granted leave to cross-examine the appellant about his previous convictions on the basis that the appellant had given evidence against Dibble. The Court of Appeal held this to be proper because the appellant's evidence, not only contradicted Dibble's evidence, but also suggested that he had participated in the robbery on his own and had not acted under duress. Kilner Brown J., giving the judgment of the Court, referred to Lord Donovan's definition in *Murdoch* v. *Taylor* that " 'evidence against' means evidence which supports the prosecution's case in a material respect or which undermines the defence of the co-accused" (*supra*), and continued (p. 246): "There are three reported cases in the Court of Appeal (Criminal Division) in which this interpretation has been considered and to which we were referred. They are *Davis (Alan)* (1974) 60 Cr.App.R. 157; [1975] 1 W.L.R. 345; *Bruce and Others* (1975) 61 Cr.App.R. 123; [1975] 1 W.L.R. 1252 and *Hatton* (1977) 64 Cr.App.R. 88. Now putting all the reported cases together, are there established principles which might serve as guidance to trial judges when called upon to give rulings in this very difficult area of the law? We venture to think that they are these and, if they are borne in mind, it may not be necessary to investigate all the relevant authorities. (1) If it is established that a person jointly charged has given evidence against the co-defendant that defendant has a right to cross-examine the other as to previous convictions and the trial judge has no discretion to refuse the application. (2) Such evidence may be given either in chief or during cross-examination. (3) It has to be objectively decided whether the evidence either supports the prosecution case in a material respect or undermines the defence of the co-accused. A hostile intent is irrelevant. (4) If consideration has to be given to the undermining of the other's defence care must be taken to see that the evidence clearly undermines the defence. Inconvenience to or inconsistency with the other's defence is not of itself sufficient. (5) Mere denial of participation in a joint venture is not of itself sufficient to rank as evidence against the co-defendant. For the proviso to section 1(*f*)(iii) to apply, such denial must lead to the conclusion that if the witness did not participate then it must have been the other who did. (6) Where the one defendant asserts or in due course would assert one view of the joint venture which is directly contradicted by the other such contradiction may be evidence against the co-defendant."

Note.—In *R.* v. *Bruce and others* it was said: "The fact that Bruce's evidence undermined [the co-accused's] defence by supplying with him another does not make it evidence against him. If and only if such evidence undermines a co-accused's defence so as to make his acquittal less likely, is it given against him.... Bruce's evidence did not undermine [the co-accused's] defence. He should not have been asked questions about his previous convictions." (*per* Stephenson L.J., giving the judgment of the Court of Appeal [1975] 1 W.L.R. 1252, 1259). This decision was distinguished in *R.* v. *Hatton* (1976) 64 Cr.App.R. 88 (C.A.). Hatton's evidence had supported a material part of the prosecution case against the co-accused thereby making his conviction more likely. The sixth proposition listed *supra* in *R.* v. *Varley* will not always lie easily with what was said in *R.* v. *Bruce* or with the distinction drawn in *R.* v. *Hatton*, in that the proposition appears to indicate that mere contradiction can sometimes constitute evidence against a co-accused.

In *R.* v. *Davis (Alan)* [1975] 1 W.L.R. 345 Davis and a co-accused were jointly charged with theft. The circumstances were such that the theft must have perpetrated either by the accused or by the co-accused or by both. Although Davis tried to avoid saying that the co-accused had committed the theft, his own denial that he had himself done so, was treated as tantamount to giving evidence against the co-accused.

In elaboration of the second proposition listed *supra* in *R.* v. *Varley*, it is to be noted that proviso (*f*)(iii) may operate even though the evidence given by the accused against his co-accused is itself simply in rebuttal of evidence already given against him by the co-accused.

Lui Mei Lin v. **The Queen** [1989] A.C. 228 (P.C.). The appellant and two co-accuseds had been jointly tried for forgery. The trial judge ruled that a statement made to the police by one of the co-defendants implicating the appellant was inadmissible as a confession. The co-defendant gave evidence at the trial which incriminated the appellant, but which differed in certain material respects from his inadmissible statement to the police. The Privy Council held that the trial judge was wrong in not allowing the appellant's counsel to cross-examine the co-defendant on his previous inconsistent statement. Accordingly the appellant's conviction was quashed. Although the co-defendant's statement could not be adduced in evidence against him or relied upon in support of the prosecution's case, since the co-defendant had given evidence incriminating the appellant, she was entitled to cross-examine him on it (*qua* prior inconsistent statement) in order to shake his credibility. Lord Roskill said (p. 298): "... the right to cross-examine is, as Lord Donovan stated in *Murdoch* v. *Taylor* [1965] A.C. 754, 593, unfettered, the only limit being relevancy." His Lordship emphasised (p. 298) that "... the trial judge should warn the jury that they must not use the statement in any way as evidence in support of the prosecution's case and that its only relevance is to test the credibility of the evidence which the maker of the statement has given against his co-accused."

Note.—This appeal was from the Court of Appeal of Hong Kong. In the course of delivery the opinion of the Privy Council Lord Roskill said (p. 297): "Counsel for the Crown invited their Lordships to distinguish *Murdoch* v. *Taylor* [1965] A.C. 574 on the ground that the rights there in question were under a statute and that what was there allowed to be put in cross-examination were the previous convictions of the co-accused. Their Lordships agree that this is so but find no sufficient ground of distinction in that fact."

Chapter 24

DOCUMENTARY EVIDENCE

THIS Chapter deals mainly with private documents. The materials which are set out are concerned with four different, but related, topics. Those in the first Section are concerned with ways in which the contents of a document are proved; those in the second Section with the way in which the fact of a document's proper execution is proved; those in the third Section with the extent to which other (or extrinsic) evidence is admissible to prove the terms of a transaction which is wholly or partially embodied in a document or the meaning of words used in it; and those in the last Section with the use of extrinsic evidence as an aid to interpretation.

An old-established dogma of the law of evidence is that a party seeking to rely upon the contents of a document must adduce primary evidence of them. This is sometimes seen as the only significant survival of the so-called Best Evidence Rule, although, as Sir Rupert Cross pointed out,[1] it in fact pre-dates that Rule by several centuries. The perfect and most common item of primary evidence is the original of the document in question. There may be more than one original, as when a document is produced in duplicate. So, too, in some circumstances a signed copy may qualify as an original, but an unsigned carbon copy of a letter or one produced on a duplicating machine does not. In the case of a telegram the original of the written message sent is that accepted or recorded at the telegraph office, but the original of the message received is the written message reaching the recipient. Apart from the original document there are two other recognised categories of primary evidence. An informal admission by a party to litigation constitutes primary evidence against him of the contents of a document. Secondly, in the case of many private documents which have to be officially filed, a copy issued on filing by the relevant office will be treated as an original.

The general rule that the contents of a document must be proved by primary evidence has its limitations and is, moreover, subject to a multiplicity of exceptions. The rule itself is only applicable when direct reliance is being placed upon the content of the document. Nor does it apply when the reference to the content of the document is solely for the purpose of identifying it. And, of course, a case in which the only issue is as to the physical existence of the document is outside the scope of the rule, and is, indeed, outside the scope of documentary, as distinct from real, evidence.[2]

---

[1] Cross, *Evidence* (6th ed., 1985), p. 601.
[2] See Chapter 25, *infra*.

The exceptional cases in which secondary evidence is admissible to prove the contents of a document include the following:

(1) Cases in which the original can be shown to have been destroyed or cannot be found after due search: *Brewster* v. *Sewell, infra.*

(2) Cases in which, although the original is still in existence, its production is physically or legally impossible: inscriptions on monuments exemplify the former, and certain documents in public custody the latter, type of situation: *Mortimer* v. *M'Callan, infra.*

(3) Cases in which the document comes within a wide range of public documents.[3]

(4) Cases in which the original is in the possession of a stranger to the litigation who lawfully refuses to produce it by, for example, either claiming a privilege or invoking the doctrine of State or diplomatic immunity: *R.* v. *Nowaz, infra.*

(5) Cases in which the original is in the possession of another party to the litigation who refuses to produce it after a notice to produce has been served on him. A notice to produce advises the party upon whom it is served to produce specified documents at the trial. It does not compel production, but its service followed by non-compliance permits the reception of secondary evidence. Service of notice to produce is thus to be distinguished from service of a *subpoena duces tecum* which compels production and can be resorted to, when a party is not in a position to adduce secondary evidence, or when an aspect of the original itself, *e.g.* handwriting, is in issue or relevant. Express notice to produce is dispensed with when the document sought itself impliedly constitutes such a notice.

(6) Civil cases in which evidence of the contents of a document is admissible as hearsay under the Civil Evidence Act 1968, ss.2, 4 or 5.[4] Criminal cases in which the secondary evidence takes the form of a copy by virtue of the wide provisions of s.27 of the Criminal Justice Act 1988.[5]

(7) Cases falling under the Bankers' Books Act 1879.[6] This provides for the admission, subject to certain conditions and safeguards, of copies of an entry in a banker's book as prima facie evidence of the entry and of the matters, transactions and accounts therein recorded.

(8) Cases falling under the Solicitors Act 1974, s.18. This provides that a list purporting to be published by authority of the Law Society shall be evidence that persons named in it hold practising certificates "until the contrary is proved."[7]

Traditional learning as to what constitutes secondary evidence, when it is admissible to prove the contents of a document, is epitomised in the aphorism of Chief Baron Abinger that "there are no degrees of secondary evidence."[8] Generally, therefore, there is no differentiation (as regards admissibility as distinct from weight) between various types of copy, or probably even copies of copies, provided, of course, that in this latter case a witness testifies that the copy is a true copy of the first copy and that it was a true copy of the original. So, too, oral evidence

---

[3] See *Mortimer* v. *M'Callan* (1840) 6 M. & W. 58 and *Note* thereto (*infra*).
[4] Civil Evidence Act 1968, s.6(1) (Part Two, *infra*).
[5] Part Two, *infra*.
[6] Part Two, *infra*.
[7] Part Two, *infra*.
[8] *Doe d. Gilbert* v. *Ross* (1840) 7 M. & W. 102.

can be received without accounting for the absence of any copies which may be in existence. But to the generalisation that there are no degrees of secondary evidence there are exceptions, for example it has long been established that the contents of a will admitted to probate cannot be proved by oral testimony if either the original or the probate is still in existence; and in the case of a wide variety of public documents oral evidence of contents will not be admissible if a copy is available. See, too, in criminal cases the wide exception now created by section 27 of the Criminal Justice Act 1988 (Part Two, *infra*).

It is usually not sufficient merely to produce even an original document. Generally there is the further requirement that the document produced be proved to have been signed or otherwise executed by the person whose document it purports to be, unless either (1) such due execution is admitted; or (2) it is a public document covered by a statute which not only enables the document's contents to be proved by means of copies but also dispenses with proof of execution; or (3) it, being not less than 20^9 years old and coming from proper custody, is within the scope of the presumption of formal validity.

Proof of execution usually involves proof of handwriting. This may take various forms: the direct testimony or an admissible hearsay statement of the alleged signatory, the testimony of someone (whether an attesting witness or not) who saw the document executed, other admissible hearsay to this effect, or the opinion of a person well acquainted with the writing of the alleged signatory. Handwriting may also be proved under the Criminal Procedure Act 1865, s.8,[10] by comparison of the writing which is before the court with a document which has been proved to have been signed or written by the alleged signatory of that document. The comparison may be by an expert, a non-expert or the court itself; but conclusions based on comparison by non-experts or by the court are treated, especially in criminal cases, with very great reserve.

In addition to signature proper execution sometimes involves attestation. Historically in such cases one of the subscribing witnesses had to be called as a witness unless they were all unavailable, but the application of this strict rule is now limited to testamentary documents by the Evidence Act 1938, s.3.[11]

Some documents require stamping.[12] In civil proceedings objection for failure to stamp must be taken by the court and cannot be waived by the parties, but, if the original of a document either cannot be found or is not produced after due notice, it will be presumed to have been stamped. In criminal proceedings unstamped documents are admissible.

In addition to the important presumption of due execution attaching to a document not less than 20 years old produced from proper custody referred to above, there are several other presumptions which facilitate proof of execution and related matters. A document is presumed to have been executed on the date it bears. Alterations in a deed are presumed to have been made prior to execution, although alterations in a will are presumed to have been made after execution. Also, although

---

[9] At common law the period was 30 years, but 20 years was substituted for both civil and criminal cases by the Evidence Act 1938, s.4 (Part Two, *infra*).

[10] Part Two, *infra*.

[11] Part Two, *infra*.

[12] See the Stamp Act 1891 (Part Two, *infra*).

there is probably no presumption that a deed, whether or not less than 20 years old, has been sealed, circumstantial evidence may perhaps establish a prima facie case of this.

It is said that a document is not only exclusive, but is also conclusive, as to its terms. Whereas the former characteristic is reflected in the rule that usually it is by primary evidence alone that the contents of a document can be proved, the latter, *i.e.* the document's conclusiveness, is epitomised in what is often, although not entirely felicitously, identified as the Parol Evidence Rule. The essence of this rule is that in the words of Sir Rupert Cross, "Extrinsic evidence is generally inadmissible when it would, if accepted, have the effect of adding to, varying or contradicting the terms of a judicial record, a transaction required by law to be in writing, or a document constituting a valid and effective contract or other transaction."[13] Extrinsic evidence mostly takes the form of oral evidence,—hence the use of the term parol evidence, but it may consist of other documents or occasionally of real evidence.[14] The materials included in the first part of the third Section of this Chapter illustrate the limits of, and the exceptions to, the so-called Parol Evidence Rule. In other words they are concerned with the admissibility of extrinsic evidence about the matter to which a document relates.

The position in this regard of transactions required by law to be in writing is clear. If a transaction is a legal nullity to the extent that it is not in writing, although extrinsic evidence may be received in order to show its true meaning, such evidence is not admissible for the purpose of adding to, contradicting or varying that meaning.

It is in the other cases, especially those involving contractual transactions, that the presumed intention of the parties appears to have the dominant role to play.[15] Extrinsic evidence may be admissible to show a consensual collateral transaction inducing the execution of the document. Again, the position may be seen to depend upon whether the parties intended their transaction to be completely or only partially embodied in the document. Sometimes the intrinsic validity of the transaction embodied in the document may be in dispute. Or the true nature of the transaction may be in doubt. A convenient solvent of many problems such as these is to be found in the presumed intention of the parties. In some instances, however, intention is somewhat constructive, as when a party is allowed to incorprate a trade usage or custom provided only that this is not actually inconsistent with the express terms of the document embodying the transaction. Also, it would seem that, subject to the terms of the statute under which it is kept, the contents of a public register are not necessarily conclusive in the face of extrinsic evidence.

The group of materials set out in the fourth Section of this Chapter concern the extent to which parol evidence is admissible to assist in the interpretation of a document when its meaning is obscure. This question is sometimes confused with that of the admissibility of extrinsic evidence

---

[13] Cross, *Evidence* (6th ed., 1985) pp. 615–616.

[14] See Chapter 25, *infra.*

[15] Indeed the Law Commission, doubting the independent existence of the Parol Evidence Rule, has concluded that evidence previously subsumed under it "will only be excluded when its reception would be inconsistent with the intention of the parties." Law Commission No. 154, p. 27 (1986) Cmnd. 9700.

which would have the effect of adding to, varying or contradicting the terms of a document; but in fact the questions are separate. Rules of interpretation or construction indicate permitted techniques for the discovery of the meaning of a document, whereas the purpose of the so-called Parol Evidence Rule itself is to control deviation from that meaning.

A. PROOF OF THE CONTENTS OF A DOCUMENT

MACDONNELL v. EVANS

21 L.J.C.P. 141; 18 L.T. 241; 16 Jur. 103; **11 C.B. 930;** 138 E.R. 742 (Common Pleas: 1852)

A party tendering a private document should give the best evidence. Generally, the best evidence is the original document which is primary evidence of its contents.

In an action on a bill of exchange, a witness called by the plaintiff was asked in cross-examination by the defendant's counsel who produced a letter purporting to have been written by the witness: "Did you not write that letter in answer to a letter charging you with forgery?" Counsel for the plaintiff objected to the question of the ground that it was an attempt to get in evidence the contents of the other letter without producing the document itself. It was held that the objection was valid.

JERVIS C.J.: ... [The] rule is, that the best evidence in the possession or power of the party must be produced. What the best evidence is must depend upon circumstances. Generally speaking, the original document is the best evidence; but circumstances may arise in which secondary evidence of the contents may be given. In the present case, those circumstances do not exist.... It was sought to give secondary evidence of the contents of a letter, without in any way accounting for its absence, or showing any attempt to obtain it. It is enough for us to decide upon the application of the general rule. The best evidence of the contents of the document was not tendered....

MAULE J.: ... It is a general rule ... that, if you want to get at the contents of a written document, the proper way is, to produce it, if you can. That is a rule in which the common sense of mankind concurs. If the paper is in the possession of the party who seeks to have the jury infer something from its contents, he should let them see it. That is the general and ordinary rule; the contents can only be proved by the writing itself. If the document does not exist, or the party seeking to show its contents cannot get at it, he is at liberty to give secondary evidence, because in that case no better is to be had.... Here the very form of the question, "Did you not write that letter in answer to a letter containing so and so?" assumes that there is another letter in existence, the production of which would be the best proof of its contents. There was nothing to show why that letter was not forthcoming. Our decision does not, and need not, go further than that. . . .

CRESSWELL and WILLIAMS JJ. concurred.

Note.—Duplicate originals, or copies executed by all parties to a transaction, are primary evidence against all such parties. Counterparts, or copies executed by different parties, are primary evidence only against the party executing the counterpart.

R. v. Holy Trinity Hull (Inhabitants) (1827) 7 B. & C. 611 (K.B.). Parol evidence was admitted to prove the fact of a tenancy, although it had been created by a written document. A legal relationship had been created by a written document, but the mere fact of the relationship was proved by other evidence without production of the document. Bailey J. said (p. 614): "The general rule is that the contents of a written document cannot be proved without producing it. But, although there may be a written instrument between a landlord and tenant, defining the terms of the tenancy, the fact of the tenancy may be proved by parol without proving the terms of it. It was unnecessary in this case to prove by the written instrument either the fact of tenancy or the value of the premises." Littledale J. added (p. 614): "Payment of rent as rent is evidence of tenancy, and may be proved without producing the written instrument."

Note.—Where it was necessary to prove the amount of the rent (*Augustien* v. *Challis* (1847) 1 Exch. 279) or the length of the tenancy (*Twyman* v. *Knowles* (1853) 13 C.B. 222), as distinct from its mere existence, it was held that the lease must be produced. The critical question is as to whether reliance is necessarily being placed upon the contents of the document. In *R. v. Holy Trinity, Hull (Inhabitants)* this was not the case: contrast the position in *R. v. Elworthy* (1867) L.R. 1 C.C.R. 103 (C.C.C.R.) (*infra*).

Slatterie v. Pooley (1840) 10 L.J. Ex. 8 (Exch.). See Chapter 14, p. 334, *supra.*

Brewster v. Sewell (1820) 3 B. and Ald. 296 (K.B.). In 1813 a fire occurred at the plaintiff's premises, and the insurance company paid the claim. A fresh policy was afterwards taken out by the plaintiff. In 1819 the plaintiff had occasion to give evidence concerning the earlier policy, but he could not produce the original. He produced evidence to the effect that search had been made in every place in which the document, if still in existence, would be likely to be found, but it could not be found; and that he had treated it as a worthless document after the new policy had been issued, and did not remember what had become of it. It was held that sufficient search for such an apparently useless document had been made to allow secondary evidence to be given. Abbott C.J. said (pp. 298–299): "All evidence is to be considered with regard to the matter with respect to which it is produced. Now it appears to be a very different thing, whether the subject of inquiry be a useless paper, which may reasonably be supposed to be lost, or whether it be an important document which the party might have an interest in keeping, and for the non-production of which no satisfactory reason is assigned. This is the case of a policy of insurance by which a company undertook to indemnify the plaintiff against losses by fire. A fire took place, and a loss was paid. That having taken place, the original policy became mere waste paper. There was no reason to suppose that the policy could, at any future time be called for, to answer any reasonable purpose whatever. . . . This being a case, therefore, where the loss or destruction of the paper may almost be presumed, very slight evidence of its loss or destruction is sufficient. . . . "

Note.—In *Kajala* v. *Noble* (1982) 75 Cr.App.R. 149 (D.C.) it was held that the best evidence rule is limited to written documents in the strict sense of the term, and has no relevance to tapes or films.

Mortimer v. **M'Callan** (1840) 6 M. and W. 58 (Ex.). In order to prove acceptance of certain stock by the defendant, evidence was adduced that a person unknown to the clerk in the Bank of England came there with one Taylor, and made an entry of his acceptance of the stock. A witness was then called who proved that he had inspected the Bank books, and that the signature to the acceptance of the stock was in the defendant's handwriting. It was held that this evidence was admissible to prove the acceptance of the stock by the defendant, and that it was not necessary that the Bank books themselves should be produced, on the ground of public convenience. Lord Abinger C.B. said (pp. 67–69): "It has been established by a series of decisions, the first of them I think by Lord Mansfield, that the books of the Bank of England being of great concernment to the whole of the national creditors, the removal of them would be so inconvenient, that copies of them might be received in evidence. It was founded upon the principle, that the public inconvenience, from the removal of documents of that sort, would justify the introduction of secondary evidence. That principle has been adopted in a variety of cases, and has never been questioned since.... I think it was competent evidence, for the purpose of proving the identity of the party who accepted this stock, to show that an entry in the books of the Bank of England was the handwriting of that party. The principle of law is, that where you cannot get the best possible evidence, you must take the next best; and where the law was laid down that you cannot remove the document in which the writing is made, you are to be entitled to the next best evidence of it, by proving whose writing it was...." Alderson B. said (p. 72): "The Bank books are not capable of being produced without so much public inconvenience, that the courts have directed them to remain in the Bank, and copies of them to be received in evidence for the purpose for which the books are receivable. Then, if they are not removable on the ground of public inconvenience, that is upon the same footing in point of principle as in the case of that which is not removable by the physical nature of the thing itself. Inscriptions upon tombstones or on a wall are proved every day in this way for that reason. The necessity of the case in the one instance and in the other case the general inconvenience which would follow from the books being removed, supplies the reason of the rule...."

Note.—The position of public documentation *vis-à-vis* the hearsay rule has been stated in Chapters 13 and 15, *supra*. It is another aspect of their admissibility, the matter of proof of their contents by secondary evidence, that is here in question. General provisions for the proof of public documents are made by the Evidence Acts 1845, s.1, and 1851, s.14 (both Part Two, *infra*). In addition there are numerous other statutory provisions on the proof of public documents of various kinds.

There are four chief methods of proof by public documents, *i.e.* by—

(1) Examined Copies. Copies proved by oral evidence to have been examined with, and to correspond with, the originals. The witness may either have examined the original himself with the copy, or have examined the copy while another person, not called as a witness, read from the original. All public documents may be proved in this manner, but certified or office copies are generally used when available.

(2) Certified Copies. Copies signed and certified as correct by officials having custody of the originals. They are allowed as evidence by various statutes, and are used chiefly to prove entries in registers, proceedings of corporations and companies, and by-laws.

(3) Office Copies. Copies made by officials having custody of judicial documents, and sealed with the seal of the court. They are the usual method of proving judicial documents, such as judgments, orders and affidavits.

(4) Government Printer's Copies. Copies supplied by the Government Printer, Queen's Printer, or under the authority of the Stationery Office. They are the usual and proper method of proving proclamations, orders and regulations.

It will be observed that, in the above case, the books of the Bank of England were treated as public documents. But the books of other banks were not so treated as public. See the Bankers' Books Evidence Act 1879 (Part Two, *infra*).

R. v. Nowaz [1976] 1 W.L.R. 830 (C.A.). The accused was convicted of making a false declaration contrary to the Perjury Act 1911, s.5(*a*), in that he gave a false name in his application for registration as a citizen of the United Kingdom and Colonies. At his trial a police officer gave oral evidence relating to a photograph, which was produced, and to the contents of a passport application, which had been submitted to a Pakistani consulate. The consul, who had shown the document and given one photograph to the police officer, claimed diplomatic immunity from attending the trial or producing the documents. The Court of Appeal held that the secondary evidence had been rightly admitted.

Note.—An earlier case, illustrating the rule that secondary evidence of a document is admissible when the original is in the hands of a non-party who cannot be compelled to produce it on the ground of privilege and who refuses to do so, is *Mills* v. *Oddy* (1834) 6 C. and P. 728 (Nisi Prius). There the privilege relied upon was in respect of title deeds (for which see Chapter 11, Section C, *supra*). The same principle applies to a document in the possession of a person outside the jurisdiction, who similarly cannot be compelled to produce the document: *Kilgour* v. *Owen* (1889) 88 Law Times (journal) p. 7.

DWYER v. COLLINS

21 L.J.Ex. 225; 19 L.T. 186; 16 Jur. 569; 7 Exch. 639; 155 E.R. 1104 (Exchequer: 1852)

Secondary evidence of a document is admissible when the original is in the possession of the opposite party, who refuses to produce it after a proper notice to produce has been served on him.
When the document is in court at the time of the trial, a notice to produce it immediately is sufficient to render secondary evidence of its contents admissible if it is not produced.

In an action on a bill of exchange, the plaintiff's attorney, who was called by the defendant as a witness, admitted that he had the bill in court but he declined to produce it. Secondary evidence of its contents was allowed.

PARKE B. (delivering the judgment of the court, which included POLLOCK C.B., PLATT and MARTIN BB.): . . . The next question is, whether the bill being admitted to be in court, parol evidence was admissible on its non-production by the attorney on demand, or whether previous notice to produce was necessary. On principle the answer must depend on this: why the notice to produce is required. If it be to give to the opponent notice that such a document would be used by the party to the cause, so that the opponent may be enabled to prepare evidence to explain or confirm it, then, no doubt, a notice at the trial, although the document be in court, is too late; but if it be merely to enable the party to have the document in court, to produce it if he likes, and if he does not, to enable his opponent to give parol evidence—if it be merely to exclude the argument that the opponent has not taken all reasonable means to procure the original, which he must do before he can be permitted to make use of secondary evidence, then the demand of production at the trial is sufficient. . . .

We think the plaintiff's alleged principle is not the true one on which the notice to produce is required, but that it is merely to give sufficient opportunity to the opposite party to produce it if he pleases, and thereby to secure the best evidence of its contents, and the request to produce it immediately is quite sufficient for that purpose if the document be in court. . . .

Note.—As to cases where notice to produce is implied by the service of a list of documents, see R.S.C., Ord. 27, r. 4(3) (Part Three, *infra*).

In *Wharam* v. *Routledge* (1805) 5 Esp. 235 (Nisi Prius) it was held that an opponent who produces a document, when called for on notice to produce, may then insist that it be put in evidence by the party calling for it, if the latter uses it or inspects it. It is not clear that this will apply to cases coming within Ord. 27, r. 4(3).

An opponent who refuses to produce a document, and so allows secondary evidence of its contents to be given by the other party, cannot afterwards use the original as evidence, except by consent: *Doe d. Thompson* v. *Hodgson* (1840) 12 A. & E. 135 (Q.B.).

R. v. **Elworthy** (1867) L.R. 1 C.C.R. 103 (C.C.C.R.). A solicitor was indicted for perjury, in having sworn there was no draft of a certain statutory declaration. No notice to produce this draft had been given to the accused, in whose possession it was. The materiality of the draft turned, not upon its mere existence, but upon its contents and the fact of certain alterations having been made in it. It was held, therefore, that, as the Crown could not produce the original, they should have given notice to the accused to produce it; and that secondary evidence of its contents was not admissible, as the nature of the proceedings was not such as to excuse notice to produce.

Note.—In some circumstances notice to produce is excused, so that secondary evidence of a document, the original being in the possession of an opponent, may be given without previous notice to produce. These circumstances include cases where the document is itself the subject-matter of the litigation, or is itself a notice to the opponent; and it has been seen that a notice in court may be sufficient (*Dwyer* v. *Collins* (1852) 7 Ex. 639, *supra*).

R. v. **Collins** (1960) 44 Cr.App.R. 170 (C.C.A.). The accused was convicted of obtaining money by false pretences. The prosecution evidence admitted at the trial included a copy of a carbon-copy letter written to the accused by his bank manager, but it was not proved that this copy was in the same terms as the original letter. There was also oral evidence by a person who had read the original letter before handing it to the accused. The Court of Criminal Appeal held that, as the accused had been called upon to produce the original letter but had failed to do so, secondary evidence of its contents was admissible. It further held, however, that, although the oral testimony constituted secondary evidence, the copy of the carbon-copy letter did not. Had it been proved that it was in the same terms as the original it seems that it would have qualified as secondary evidence.

Note.—See now the Criminal Justice Act 1988, s.27 (Part Two, *infra*).

R. v. LLANFAETHLY (INHABITANTS)

23 L.J.M.C. 33; 2 W.R. 61; 17 Jur. 1123; 2 E. & B. 940; 2 C.L.R. 230; 118 E.R. 1018 (Q.B.: 1853)

Secondary evidence of a document is not admissible if a stranger or third person wrongfully refuses to produce the original, after being served with a subpoena to do so; such a person may be compelled to produce the original.

A *subpoena* had been served on a witness to produce a rate-book, supposed to be in his possession. He did not attend, and the rate-book was not produced. It was held that parol evidence of rating was not admissible, the witness having improperly neglected to produce the book.

LORD CAMPBELL C.J.: ... It has been held that if, under a *subpoena duces tecum*, the witness appears and stands on his privilege and refuses to produce the document, and the judge admits the objection, secondary evidence is then admissible. But here no privilege existed, and the witness would have been bound to produce the rate-book, and would have been punishable for contempt if he had refused to do so. ...

ERLE J.: The appellants had the duty cast upon them of establishing the contents of the rate-book, and they must therefore either produce it or account satisfactorily for its absence. They have not done either of these things by serving the party who is supposed to have the rate-book, but who, in fact, had it not, with a *subpoena* to produce it. I am further of opinion that, even if they had served the party in whose possession it really was, to produce the book, and that party had disobeyed the *subpoena*, secondary evidence of its contents would not have been admissible. ...

Note.—A party should do all that he legally may to compel production of a document by a stranger before he can put in secondary evidence against an opponent. Otherwise secondary evidence of an unreliable character might be tendered against a party by collusion between his opponent and the stranger. If production can be compelled by *subpoena*, this must be attempted.

B. PROOF OF THE EXECUTION OF A DOCUMENT

Introductory Note.—The general rule is that a document will not be admitted into evidence except on proof of execution. However, in the case of many public documents, proof is excused by statute. Execution of a private document may be admitted, or it may in appropriate cases be presumed. Moreover proof is not necessary when the document is produced by an opponent who himself claims some interest under it. Otherwise due execution must be proved: this may involve proof of handwriting and in a few (but important) cases proof of attestation. In addition certain documents must be stamped for the purposes of stamp duty.

With regard to the requirement of attestation, a distinction must now be drawn between testamentary documents and other documents. In a case of the former (except where probate is sought in common form) in order to prove due execution one of the attesting witnesses must be called, unless none is available. If the witness denies execution (or refuses to give evidence) other evidence then becomes admissible. If no attesting witness is available, secondary evidence of attestation by proof of handwriting of one of the attesting witnesses is normally required. Only if this is clearly not available will other evidence of due execution (such as that of a non-attesting witness to the execution) be admissible. The relatively few kinds of documents, other than testamentary documents, which require attestation need not be proved by the evidence of an attesting witness. Proof may be by evidence of the handwriting of an attesting witness, or failing this, by other evidence. See the Evidence Act 1938, s.3 (Part Three, *infra*).

DOE d. MUDD v. SUCKERMORE

7 L.J.Q.B. 33; 5 A. & E. 703; 2 N. & P. 16; W.W. & D. 405; 111 E.R. 1331
(Q.B.: 1837)

Handwriting may be proved not only by the alleged signatory or a person who saw a particular document signed, but also by any person acquainted with the handwriting of the person said to have signed the document; for example, by having seen him write at any time, or having received documents purporting to be in his handwriting, or having observed or dealt with documents purporting to be in his handwriting in the ordinary course of business.

In an action of ejectment the signature of an attesting witness to a will was in dispute. He was called as a witness in the case and swore to his signature. He also admitted that two other signatures on other documents were his. An inspector of the Bank of England was called to prove that the signature to the will was not genuine. He stated that it was his duty at the Bank to compare signatures on powers of attorney and other documents, that he had never seen the attesting witness write, and that his only knowledge of his handwriting had been derived from comparison of the signatures produced in the case. There was a division of judicial opinion as to whether the inspector's evidence was admissible, which does not affect the observations extracted below.

COLERIDGE J.: ... The rule was as to the proof of handwriting, where the witness has not seen the party write the document in question, may be stated generally thus: either the witness has seen the party write on some other occasion, or he has corresponded with him, and transactions have taken place between them, upon the faith that letters purporting to have been written or signed by him have been so written or signed. On either supposition, the witness is supposed to have received into his mind an impression, not so much of the manner in which the writer has formed the letters in the particular instances, as of the general character of his handwriting; and he is called on to speak as to the writing in question, by reference to the standard so formed in his mind. It is obvious that the weight of this evidence may vary in every conceivable degree; but the principle appears to be sound....

LORD DENMAN C.J.: ... He did not see him sign it; nor has he ever seen him write; but this is professedly immaterial, if he has had other adequate means of obtaining a knowledge of his hand.... The clerk who constantly read the letters, the broker who was ever consulted upon them, is as competent to judge whether another signature is that of the writer of the letters, as the merchant to whom they were addressed. The servant who has habitually carried letters addressed by me to others has an opportunity of obtaining a knowledge of my writing though he never saw me write, or received a letter from me....

WILLIAMS and PATTESON JJ. delivered judgments to the same effect on this aspect of the case.

Note.—Handwriting or a signature may also be proved by comparison of the document in question with another document proved or admitted to have been written by the person in question. See the Criminal Procedure Act 1865, ss.7 and 8 (Part Two, *infra*), which applies in civil as well as criminal cases.

MEATH (BISHOP) v. WINCHESTER (MARQUIS)

3 Bing.N.C. 183; 4 Cl. & F. 445; 10 Bli.(N.S.) 330; 3 Scott 561; 6 E.R. 125
(H.L.: 1836)

Ancient documents prove themselves; that is, they are presumed to have been duly executed. This rule, however, applies only to those coming from proper custody; that is, from any custody consistent with their genuineness and legitimate origin, in which they might reasonably be expected to be found.

Documents which had belonged to a deceased bishop by virtue of his office, and which were found among his private papers in possession of his family, were held to be produced from proper custody, although the most proper custody would have been in the hands of his successor, the bishop for the time being.

This case was brought to the House of Lords from the Exchequer Chamber in Ireland by writ of error. Their Lordships put certain questions to the judges, whose opinion was delivered by Tindal C.J.

TINDAL C.J.: . . . These documents were found in a place in which, and under the care of persons with whom, papers of Bishop Dopping might naturally and reasonably be expected to be found; and that is precisely the custody which gives authenticity to documents found within it; for it is not necessary that they should be found in the best and most proper place of deposit. If documents continue in such custody there never would be any question as to their authenticity; but it is when documents are found in other than their proper place of deposit that the investigation commences, whether it was reasonable and natural under the circumstances in the particular case, to expect that they should have been in the place where they are actually found; for it is obvious that whilst there can be only one place of deposit strictly and absolutely proper, there may be various and many that are reasonable an probable, though differing in degree; some being more so, some less; and in those cases the proposition to be determined is, whether the actual custody is so reasonably and probably to be accounted for that it impresses the mind with the conviction that the instrument found in such custody must be genuine. . . .

Note.—An ancient document is one which is not less than 20 years old: Evidence Act 1938, s.4 (Part Two, *infra*). Previously the period was 30 years. It has been held that the following documents were produced from proper custody—expired leases produced by either lessor or lessee, a will produced by a tenant for life claiming under it, a settlement produced by an equitable tenant for life claiming under it, and Bibles produced by members of the family to which entries in them related.

In practice due execution is often admitted or presumed. Due execution may be formally admitted in civil proceedings and under the Criminal Justice Act 1967, section 10

(Part Two, *infra*). A party upon whom a list of documents is served by way of discovery may be deemed to have admitted that an original document was written, signed or executed as it purports to have been, unless its authenticity has been denied in his pleadings or by notice: see R.S.C., Ord. 27, r. 4, (Part Three, *infra*). The authenticity of a document may also be deemed to have been admitted by a party who, served with a notice to admit authenticity, has failed to serve a notice of non-admission in reply. Proof of due execution is also unnecessary when the document in question is in the possession of an opponent, but he refuses to comply with a notice to produce it.

Anderson v. **Weston** (1840) 6 Bing.N.C. 296 (C.P.). In an action on a bill of exchange, the date of the drawing and indorsement of the bill was material, but no evidence was given other than the date on the bill. Tindal C.J. left it to the jury to find the date of the indorsement, and a verdict was found in favour of the plaintiff. On motion to enter a nonsuit the verdict was upheld. Bonsanquet J. said (pp. 300–301): "Now when a deed is produced, and the execution of that deed is proved by the subscribing witness, or by accounting for the absence of the subscribing witness by death or otherwise, and proving the signature, and that deed bears a date, as far as my experience goes, that date has uniformly been taken to be prima facie evidence that the deed was executed at the time when it purports to bear date. It is the practice in cross-examination to inquire whether the deed was executed when it bears date, but I certainly never heard it contended that it was part of the proof of the person producing the instrument, not only to give evidence of the execution of the instrument, but in the first instance, and before any evidence is offered to render doubtful the time of making the instrument, that it was executed at the time it bears date. This is the case not merely with respect to instruments binding on the person of the party in the cause, but also with respect to his title where a deed of conveyance comes from third parties."

Note.—As Bonsanquet J. went on to indicate the presumption will often be important in demonstrating that the document is in fact 30 (now 20) years old.

Alterations in a deed are rebuttably presumed to have been made before execution: *Doe d. Tatum* v. *Catomore* (1851) 16 Q.B. 745 (C.B.). Alterations to a will are presumed to have been made after the execution. To presume that an alteration in a deed was made after execution would invalidate the whole deed, whereas a similar presumption does not invalidate a testamentary instrument. However, the Wills Act 1837, s.21, provides that no alteration in a will shall be effective unless executed as a will.

There is some authority which suggests that a deed, even less than 20 years old, will be presumed to have been duly sealed: see *R.* v. *Sandilands* (1871) L.R. 6 C.P. 411 (C.P.); *National Provincial Bank of England* v. *Jackson* (1886) 33 Ch.D. 1, 11 and 14; and *Re Balkis Consolidated Co. Ltd.* (1888) 58 L.T. 300. But any inference of sealing must then depend upon particular circumstances.

C. EXTRINSIC EVIDENCE AFFECTING THE CONTENTS OF A DOCUMENT

ALLEN v. PINK

4 M. & W. 140; 1 H. & H. 207; 7 L.J.Ex. 206; 150 E.R. 1376 (Exchequer: 1838)

Parol evidence of an oral transaction is not excluded by the fact that a writing was made concerning or relating to it, unless the writing was in

*fact the transaction itself, and not merely a memorandum of, or a
portion of, the transaction.*

The plaintiff bought of the defendant a horse, and received from him
the following memorandum: "Bought of G. Pink a horse for the sum of
£7 2s. 6d. G. Pink." The horse having proved vicious, the plaintiff sued
for the return of the price, and adduced evidence of an oral warranty of
the horse. It was held that such evidence was admissible, as the
agreement itself had not been reduced into writing, the memorandum
only referring to a portion of it.

LORD ABINGER C.B.: . . . The general principle is quite true, that if
there has been a parol agreement, which is afterwards reduced by the
parties into writing, that writing alone must be looked to to ascertain
the terms of the contract; but the principle does not apply here; there
was no evidence of any agreement by the plaintiff that the whole
contract should be reduced into writing by the defendant; the contract is
first concluded by parol, and afterwards the paper is drawn up, which
appears to have been meant merely as a memorandum of the
transaction, or an informal receipt for the money, not as containing the
terms of the contract itself. . . .

BOLLAND and ALDERSON BB. concurred.

Note.—This type of case should not be regarded as an exception to the rule prohibiting
parol evidence in variation or contradiction of a written document, but rather as falling
outside the scope of that rule. The rule is concerned with written transactions, not
transactions which are merely evidenced by writing. The question whether the parties
intended a writing to record a transaction may sometimes be answered by perusal of the
document itself; as when it is signed over a stamp (see *Hutton* v. *Watling* [1948] Ch. 398
(C.A.)).
   When the law requires a note or memorandum in writing, parol evidence may
nevertheless be admissible (1) to connect two documents, so as to form a complete
memorandum (see *Long* v. *Millar* (1879) 4 C.P.D. 450 (C.A.); compare *Timmins* v.
Moreland Street Property Co. Ltd. [1958] Ch. 110 (C.A.)); (2) to show that the
memorandum is incomplete (see *Beckett* v. *Nurse* [1948] 1 K.B. 535 (C.A.)); or (3) to
prove the terms of the contract, when part performance takes the place of a statutory
memorandum on a claim to the equitable remedy of specific performance (see *Chapronière*
v. *Lambert* [1917] 2 Ch. 356 (C.A.)).

Meres v. **Ansell** (1771) 3 Wils. K.B. 275. An agreement in writing had been
made between the parties for the exchange of land, no mention being made
therein as to a particular piece of land in dispute. The defendant called evidence
to show that at the same time it was verbally agreed that the land in dispute was
to be included in the agreement. On this evidence a verdict was found for the
defendant. The court granted a new trial on the ground that such evidence was
inadmissible.

Henderson v. **Arthur** [1907] 1 K.B. 10 (C.A.). A lease provided for the
payment of rent in advance. The lessee was not allowed to adduce evidence of a
prior parol undertaking to accept rent in arrears.

Note.—*Meres* v. *Ansell* and *Henderson* v. *Arthur* are classic illustrations of the operation
of the parol evidence rule. Most judicial formulations of the rule relate to its application in
cases of contract. For example, in *Bank of Australasia* v. *Palmer* [1897] A.C. 540 (P.C.)

Lord Morris said (at p. 545): "Parol testimony cannot be received to contradict, vary, add to or subtract from the terms of a written contract or the terms in which the parties have deliberately agreed to record any part of this contract."

ANGELL v. DUKE

L.R. 10 Q.B. 174; 44 L.J.Q.B. 78; **32 L.T. 320;** 39 J.P. 677; 23 W.R. 548 (Q.B.: 1875)

Parol evidence is not admissible to prove oral terms which are inconsistent with written terms, if the whole contract between the parties is contained in a document.

The defendant let to the plaintiff, by written agreement, a house and the furniture therein. The plaintiff offered evidence of an oral agreement, to the effect that the defendant would send in additional furniture. It was held that such evidence was inadmissible, as being inconsistent with the written agreement.

COCKBURN C.J.: ... To allow the plaintiff to recover in this action would be to allow a parol agreement to conflict with a written agreement afterwards entered into. I agree with the cases which have been cited to this extent, that they may be instances of collateral parol agreements which would be admissible, but this is not the case here; something passes between the parties during the course of the negotiations, but afterwards the plaintiff enters into a written agreement to take the house and the furniture in the house, which is specified. Having once executed that, without making the terms of the alleged parol agreement a part of it, he cannot afterwards set up the parol agreement.

BLACKBURN, MELLOR and FIELD JJ. concurred.

Note.—In *Humble* v. *Hunter* (1848) 12 Q.B. 310, a third party set up the case that the plaintiff had acted as his agent and claimed the right as undisclosed principal of coming in to claim the benefit of his agent's contract. It was held that he was precluded by a rule of evidence; namely, there being a written contract in which the alleged "agent" was described as "owner," so that evidence was not admissible to contradict the word "owner" by showing that it really meant "agent." This case was distinguished in *Fred. Drughorn Ltd.* v. *Rederiaktiebolaget Trans-Atlantic* [1919] A.C. 203 (H.L.), where the word was "charterer"; and there are other cases where the court was allowed oral evidence to show the capacity of signatories to a document.

DOBELL v. STEVENS

3 L.J.(o.s.) K.B. 89; **3 B. & C. 623;** 5 Dow. & Ry. K.B. 490; 107 E.R. 864 (K.B.: 1825)

Parol evidence is admissible to show that a writing is not a valid transaction. Such evidence may therefore be given to prove fraud, or other matter affecting the validity of a document.

The plaintiff sued the defendant for damages for fraudulently misrepresenting the takings of a public-house, sold to the plaintiff by the defendant. A written contract for the sale and an assignment of the lease of the premises were afterwards executed; but neither of these documents mentioned the alleged oral representation. Parol evidence of the representation was allowed to go to the jury, who found a verdict thereon for the plaintiff. On a motion for a new trial, the defendant urged that parol evidence was inadmissible, as "the contract having been reduced into writing the parties must be bound by that, and cannot add to it by evidence of previous conversations." It was held that the evidence was rightly admitted.

ABBOTT C.J.: Whether any fraud or deceit had or had not been practised in this case was peculiarly a question for the jury; nor has any complaint been made against the mode in which that question was presented to their consideration. If, then, this motion be sustainable at all, it must be sustainable on the ground that evidence of a fraudulent or deceitful representation could not be received, in as much as it was not noticed in the written agreement, or in the conveyance which was afterwards executed by the parties.... Here the plaintiff did rely on the assertion of the defendant, and that was his inducement to make the purchase. The representation was not of any matter of quality pertaining to the thing sold, and therefore likely to be mentioned in the conveyance, but was altogether collateral to it ... and the jury having found that that which was untruly represented was fraudulently and deceitfully represented, I think that we ought not to grant a rule for a new trial.

BAYLEY, HOLROYD and LITTLEDALE JJ. concurred.

Note.—The principle of this case may be taken as applicable to any matter affecting the validity of the document or transaction. "When the parties have recorded their contract in writing, the rule that they are not at liberty to alter or vary it, comes into effect. That which they put down is final as to what they mean; it is the binding record of the agreement. But they are always at liberty to show whether it is the binding record of the agreement. Suppose that the signature were made in the course of a dramatic representation, or suppose a printed form of agreement were used, and the witness, by mistake, signed his name in the space meant for the principal, and vice versa, would not the parties be at liberty to show the real state of the case?" (*Per* Bramwell B. in *Wake* v. *Harrop* (1861) 7 Jur. 710). Yet mistake in a notice required by statute may not be within this exception (see *Sidney Bolsom Investment Trust Ltd.* v. *E Karmios & Co. (London) Ltd.* [1956] 1 Q.B. 529 (C.A.)). However, the exception has been applied to different forms of mistake; also to illegality, want of consideration and other invalidating factors.

Extrinsic evidence may also be admissible to show the real nature of a transaction when this is relevant or in issue. In *Re Duke of Marlborough, Davis* v. *Whitehead* [1894] 2 Ch. 133 it was received to show that an apparent sale was really a mortgage. In *Inland Revenue Commissioners* v. *Church Commissioners for England* [1977] A.C. 329 (H.L.) the particular importance in revenue cases of admissibility to show the true nature of a transaction was emphasised.

PYM v. CAMPBELL

25 L.J.Q.B. 277; 27 L.T. 122; 4 W.R. 528; 2 Jur.(N.S.) 641; 6 E. & B. 370; 119 E.R. 903 (Q.B.: 1856)

Parol evidence is admissible to prove a condition precedent, to the effect that a document, apparently a complete and operative transaction on its face, was in fact conditional upon the happening of a certain event which has not occurred.

The defendants , agreed in writing to buy from the plaintiff an invention. Evidence was tendered by the defendants to the effect that they declined to purchase unless one Abernethy, an engineer, approved of the machine; that, as Abernethy was absent, and one of the defendants could not conveniently return to sign the document after seeing him, it was expressly agreed orally that the written document was signed conditionally upon Abernethy's approval being obtained; and that Abernethy had disapproved of the machine. It was held that such evidence was admissible to show that the written document was not operative.

ERLE J.: . . . There was a paper signed by the parties, and there would be a very strong presumption that it contained all the terms agreed upon, and if the jury had found that it was signed *animo contrahendi*, I am clearly of opinion that no evidence to vary it would be admissible. But the matter goes a step farther here, for the jury have found that the parties, when they signed the paper, expressly said, "We do not agree to the terms contained in it; we are prevented by the absence of a person whose judgment we desire to have from making up our minds definitely, and therefore, although we put our names to the paper we do so without making an agreement." I grant that there may be danger in admitting such evidence, and that a jury ought to look very scrupulously at such a case; but if it is a true case, all that can be said about the danger of admitting parol evidence tells equally against the party seeking to set up as an agreement a document which was never intended so to operate. The distinction is, that the evidence is admitted not to vary or alter an actual agreement, but to show that the paper was not at the time an agreement.

CROMPTON J. and LORD CAMPBELL C.J. delivered judgments to the same effect.

Note.—In *Davis* v. *Jones* (1856) 17 C.B. 625 it was held that parol evidence was admissible to show that a written contract, which was updated, was not intended to operate from its delivery, but from a future uncertain period.

DE LASSALLE v. GUILDFORD

[1901] 2 K.B. 215; 70 L.J.K.B. 533; 84 L.T. 549; 17 T.L.R. 384; 49 W.R. 467
(C.A.: 1901)

Parol evidence is admissible to prove matters collateral to a written transaction in the case of a warranty given by one of the parties to the other at the time of entering into the written transaction, provided the warranty is not inconsistent with the writing.

The plaintiff, being the tenant of the defendant, sued for breach of warranty as to the condition of the drains of the demised premises. It appeared that the plaintiff raised the question of the drains before he finally took a lease of the house, and he refused to hand over the

counterpart lease and complete the transaction until the defendant
assured him that the drains were in good order. The lease itself
contained no reference to the drains. The drains afterwards appeared to
be out of order, and in consequence the plaintiff and his family suffered
in health, and he was put to expense. The jury found that there was a
representation that the drains were in good order, but no fraud or
breach of covenant, and assessed damages. The judge gave judgment for
the defendant on the ground that, if there were a warranty, it was not
collateral to the lease. On appeal it was held that there was a collateral
warranty and the plaintiff was entitled to judgment.

A. L. SMITH M.R. (delivering the judgment of the court, which
included COLLINS and ROMER L.JJ.): . . . To create a warranty no special
form of words is necessary. It must be a collateral undertaking forming
part of the contract by agreement of the parties express or implied, and
must be given during the course of the dealing which leads to the
bargain, and should then enter into the bargain as part of it. It was laid
down by Buller J. as long ago as 1789 in *Pasley* v. *Freeman*, 3 T.R. 51:
"It was rightly held by Holt C.J." in *Crosse* v. *Gardner* (1688) Carth.
90, and *Medina* v. *Stoughton* (1699) Salk. 210, "and has been uniformly
adopted ever since, that an affirmation at the time of sale is a warranty
provided it appear on evidence to have been so intended." . . .
    What is it the defendant asserts? I paraphrase the evidence: "You
need have no certificate of a sanitary inspector—it is quite unnecessary;
the drains are in perfect condition. I give you my word on the subject.
Will that satisfy you? If so, hand me over the counterpart." What more
deliberate and emphatic assertion of a fact could well be made during
the course of the dealing which led up to the counterpart lease being
handed over to the defendant? . . .
    The next question is, Was the warranty collateral to the lease so that
it might be given in evidence and given effect to? It appears to me in
this case clear that the lease did not cover the whole ground, and that it
did not contain the whole of the contract between the parties. The lease
is entirely silent about the drains, though there is a covenant that the
lessee during the term should do the inside repairs, and the lessor the
outside repairs, which would, I suppose, include the drains which
happened to be inside or outside the house. There is nothing in the
lease as to the then condition of the drains—*i.e.* at the time of the
taking of the lease, which was the vital point in hand. Then why is not
the warranty collateral to anything which is to be found in the lease?
The present contract or warranty by the defendant was entirely
independent of what was to happen during the tenancy. It was what
induced the tenancy, and it in no way affected the terms of the tenancy
during the three years, which was all the lease dealt with. The warranty
in no way contradicts the lease, and without the warranty the lease
never would have been executed. Three cases were cited in which parol
collateral agreements outside leases had been allowed in evidence and
given effect to by the court, namely: *Morgan* v. *Griffith* [*Note, infra*],
Erskine v. *Adeane* [*Note, infra*], and *Angell* v. *Duke* [*supra*]. The first
two cases related to parol agreements collateral to leases as to keeping
down rabbits, and the last case to a parol collateral agreement to do
repairs and to send in additional furniture. . . . In the rabbit cases the
agreements were held collateral to the leases, and did not contradict the
terms of the leases. It was argued by the learned counsel for the
defendant that the collateral agreements in the rabbit cases were

agreements that something should be done after the lease was taken, and that in the present case the agreement or warranty is that the drains were then in good order. This is true; but if in the rabbit cases the agreements were collateral and outside the leases, the leases not containing the whole terms and the collateral agreements not contradicting the leases, I cannot see why the warranty in this case is not collateral also.... In my opinion, even if the jury had not found a warranty, the true inference is that there was a warranty given in this case collateral to the lease, and therefore the judgment entered for the defendant must be set aside, and judgment entered for the plaintiff....

Note.—In *Morgan* v. *Griffith* (1871) L.R. 6 Ex. 70 the plaintiff took a lease of land from the defendant, reserving to the latter the sporting rights. Evidence was admitted of a collateral verbal agreement by which the defendant promised to destroy the rabbits if the plaintiff would sign the lease, although the lease was silent on the point. *Erskine* v. *Adeane* (1873) 8 Ch.App. 756 is a similar case.

GOSS v. NUGENT

2 L.J.K.B. 127; **5 B. & Ad. 58;** 2 Nev. & M.K.B. 28; 110 E.R. 713 (K.B.: 1833)

Parol evidence is admissible to prove a subsequent oral agreement modifying the terms of a written document, unless writing is required by law to render the transaction in question enforceable.

The plaintiff agreed to sell fourteen lots of freehold land to the defendant, by a written agreement, undertaking to make a good title to each lot. He offered evidence of a subsequent oral agreement discharging him from the duty of making a good title to one of the lots. It was held that such evidence would have been admissible but for the Statute of Frauds, which required writing in the case of agreements relating to land.

DENMAN C.J. (delivering the judgment of the court, which included TAUNTON, LITTLEDALE, PARKE and PATTESON JJ.): By the general rules of the common law, if there be a contract which has been reduced into writing, verbal evidence is not allowed to be given of what passed between the parties, either before the written instrument was made, or during the time that it was in a state of preparation, so as to add to or subtract from, or in any manner to vary or qualify the written contract; but after the agreement has been reduced into writing, it is competent to the parties, at any time before breach of it, by a new contract not in writing, either altogether to waive, dissolve, or annul the former agreement, or in any manner to add to, or subtract from, or vary or qualify the terms of it, and thus to make a new contract; which is to be proved, partly by the written agreement, and partly by the subsequent verbal terms engrafted upon what will be thus left of the written agreement.

And if the present contract was not subject to the control of any Act of Parliament, we think that it would have been competent for the parties, by word of mouth, to dispense with requiring a good title to be made to the lot in question, and that the action might be maintained.

But the Statute of Frauds has made certain regulations as to contracts for the sale of lands....

We think the object of the Statute of Frauds was to exclude all oral evidence as to contracts for the sale of lands, and that any contract which is sought to be enforced must be proved by writing only. . . .

Note.—The provisions of the Statute of Frauds which relate to contracts for the sale of land have been repealed and re-enacted by the Law of Property Act 1925, s.40. The principle of the above case remains unaffected. Extrinsic evidence is also admissible for the purpose of construing (as distinct from altering or supplementing) a contract to which the statute applies: *Perrylease Ltd.* v. *Imecar A.G.* [1988] 1 W.L.R. 463 (Q.B.D).

Although parol evidence cannot be given to modify or vary a contract required by statute to be evidenced by writing, parol evidence of an agreement to rescind such a contract is admissible. Rescission may be proved by giving evidence of a new agreement which, though unenforceable itself as not being in writing, may yet serve to rescind an enforceable contract.

Wigglesworth v. **Dallison** (1779) 1 Doug. K.B. 201 (K.B.). In a case of an agricultural lease, evidence was allowed of a custom whereby, contrary to the general law, the tenant, on leaving at the end of his term, was allowed to take away his "way-going crop, that is to say, all the corn growing upon the said lands which hath before the expiration of such term been sown by such tenant upon any part of such lands"; although the lease was in writing and no mention was therein made of such custom. Lord Mansfield C.J. said (p. 207): "The custom does not alter or contradict the agreement in the lease; it only superadds a right which is consequential to the taking, as a heriot may be due by custom, although not mentioned in the grant or lease."

Note.—This case illustrates a blatant if unimportant exception to the general rule, namely that evidence is admissible of any local custom of general application in order that it may bind the parties to the written transaction, unless it is inconsistent with the writing. See, too, *Re Sutro & Co. Heilbut, Symons & Co.* [1917] 2 K.B. 348 (C.A.); but contrast the approach in *Brown* v. *Byrne* (1854) 3 E. & B. 703 (Q.B.) (*infra*).

Kemp v. **Elisha** [1918] 1 K.B. 228 (C.A.). The plaintiff, a member of the public, was injured by the alleged negligence of the driver of a taxicab. He brought an action against the defendant, whose name was entered in the register of licences of hackney carriages kept at Scotland Yard as being the proprietor of the cab in his capacity as managing director of a limited company. At the trial the plaintiff put in a certified copy of the entry in the register for the purpose of proving that the defendant, being registered as the proprietor of the cab, was liable for the acts of the driver. The defendant tendered evidence to show that he was in fact neither owner nor part-owner of the cab and was accordingly not liable. The trial judge rejected this evidence on the ground that the register was conclusive; but the Court of Appeal held that the register was not conclusive and that therefore the evidence had been wrongly rejected. The Court treated the matter as one of statutory interpretation, but the principle seems to have been accepted that, subject to the terms of the particular statute under which a public register is set up, extrinsic evidence is admissible to disprove its accuracy.

Note.—See, too, *The Recepta* (1889) 14 P.D. 131 in which oral evidence was received to show the gross tonnage of a vessel was different from that recorded in the register of shipping.

D. EXTRINSIC EVIDENCE AND INTERPRETATION

Introductory Note.—Problems concerning the extent to which extrinsic evidence may be used as an aid to interpretation have mostly arisen in relation to wills. Much of the earlier case law concerning wills must now, in cases in which the testator died after December 31, 1982, be read in conjunction with section 21 of the Administration of Justice Act 1982 (Part Two, *infra*). The provisions of section 22 of the Act may also be relevant. This latter section extends the equitable doctrine of ratification to wills, and thus allows words to be added to (as well as ommitted from) the probate.

COLPOYS v. COLPOYS

Jac. 451; 37 E.R. 921 (Ch.: 1822)

Parol evidence is admissible to explain patent ambiguities; but probably only when they cannot be otherwise explained by construction of the context.

Evidence of the nature and amount of a testator's property was held admissible to explain the meaning of certain bequests ambiguous in themselves.

PLUMER M.R.: . . . The admission of extrinsic circumstances to govern the construction of a written instrument, is in all cases an exception to the general rule of law, which excludes everything *dehors* the instrument. It is only from necessity, and then with great jealousy and caution, that courts, either of law or equity, will suffer this rule to be departed from. It must be the case of an ambiguity, which cannot otherwise be removed, and which may by these means be clearly and satisfactorily explained. This is always permitted in the case of a latent ambiguity, which not appearing on the face of the instrument, but arising entirely from extrinsic circumstances, may always be removed by a reference to extrinsic circumstances.

In the case of a patent ambiguity, that is one appearing on the face of the instrument, as a general rule a reference to matter *dehors* the instrument is forbidden. It must, if possible, be removed by construction, and not by averment. But in many cases this is impracticable; where the terms used are wholly indefinite and equivocal, and carry on the face of them no certain or explicit meaning, and the instrument furnishes no materials by which the ambiguity thus arising can be removed: if in such cases the court were to reject the only mode by which the meaning could be ascertained, *viz.*, the resort to extrinsic circumstances, the instrument must become inoperative and void. As a minor evil, therefore, common sense, and the law of England (which are seldom at variance), warrant the departure from the general rule, and call in the light of extrinsic evidence. The books are full of instances sanctioned by the highest authorities both in law and equity. When the person or thing is designated on the face of the instrument, by terms imperfect and equivocal, admitting either of no meaning at all by themselves, or of a variety of different meanings, referring tacitly or expressly for the ascertainment and completion of the meaning to extrinsic circumstances, it has never been considered an objection to the reception of the evidence of these circumstances, that the ambiguity was patent, manifested on the face of the instrument. When a legacy is given to a man by his surname, and the Christian name is not mentioned; is not that a patent ambiguity? Yet, it is decided, that evidence is admissible (*Price* v. *Page* (1799) 4 Ves. Jr. 680). So where there is a gift of the testator's stock, that is ambiguous, it has different meanings when used by a farmer and a merchant. . . .

Note.—Extrinsic evidence is, however, not admissible to fill in a total blank: *Bayliss* v. *Attorney-General* (1741) 2 Atk. 239 (Ch.); *Hunt* v. *Hort* (1791) 3 Br.C.C. 311.

Doe d. Gord v. Needs 1836 2 M. & W. 129 (Exch.). A will made various bequests to "George Gord the son of John Gord" and others to "George Gord the son of George Gord," but in one passage the testator wrote "George Gord son of Gord" (presumably by inadvertence, there being, as the court pointed out, no blank in front of "Gord"). There appeared by extrinsic evidence to be two persons answering such description, and further evidence was allowed of the circumstances of the testator's statements of intention to show which of the two persons he meant, notwithstanding the fact that there were two such persons was also apparent on the face of the will itself. Parke B. said (pp. 140–141): " . . . The evidence of the declarations of the testator was not the effect of varying the instrument in any way whatever; it only enables the court to reject one of the subjects, or objects, to which the description in the will applies; and to determine which of the two the devisor understood to be signified by the description which he used in the will. . . . "

Note.—At common law extrinsic evidence of the testator's intention had to be circumstantial, except in cases of equivocation, that is to say cases in which the words of the will apply equally to two or more persons or objects. To solve such an equivocation direct evidence of the testator's intention was exceptionally admissible: *Doe d. Gords* v. *Needs* provides an illustration of this. Now in the case of a will taking effect after December 31, 1982 the area in which direct evidence of intention is admissible has been expanded from merely solving equivocations to resolving other types of ambiguity. It is, however, to be remembered that the evidence, whether circumstantial or direct, may only be used to assist in interpretation of the words used. See *Re Williams (dec'd)* [1985] 1 W.L.R. 905 (Ch.D.), referred to in *Note* on the Administration of Justice Act 1982, s.21 (Part Two, *infra*).

In cases of contract, if the agreement (when viewed objectively) is ambiguous, extrinsic circumstantial evidence and occasionally direct evidence, is allowed to show intention. However, evidence of statements made by parties during negotiations is not necessarily admissible: *Prenn* v. *Simmonds* [1971] 1 W.L.R. 1381 (H.L.). So, too, opinions written by counsel in relation to, and shortly before, drafting trust deeds have been held to be admissible to show what was intended by the words used in the deed: *Rabin* v. *Gerson Berger Association Ltd.* [1986] 1 W.L.R. 526 (C.A.).

Smith v. Wilson (1832) 1 L.J.K.B. 194 (K.B.). In a lease it was provided that at the end of the term the tenant should leave not less than 10,000 rabbits on the premises, to be taken and paid for by the landlord, at the rate of £60 "per thousand." It was held that evidence was admissible to show that the custom of that part of the country, in counting rabbits, was to allow six score (*i.e.* 120) to the 100. Lord Tenterden C.J. said (p. 195): "I think that where in a deed, or in a declaration, or other pleading, a term is used, to which an Act of Parliament has given a definite meaning, the use of the term will be governed by the meaning given by the Act of Parliament. There is no Act of Parliament which provides that a hundred rabbits shall consist of five score to the hundred. Then we must suppose that the parties to his deed used the word "thousand" with reference to the subject-matter, according to the meaning which it received in that part of the country. I cannot say, then, that evidence to show what was the acception of the term "thousand," with reference to this subject-matter ought not to have been received at all."

Note.—As a foreign language might be translated by verbal evidence, so might local, technical, obsolete, trade, or family language be translated. "There is no doubt that not only where the language of the instrument is such as the court does not understand, it is competent to receive evidence of the proper meaning of that language, as when it is written in a foreign tongue; but it is also competent, where technical words or peculiar terms, or indeed any expressions are used, which at the time the instrument was written had acquired an appropriate meaning, either generally or by local usage, or amongst particular classes" (*Shore* v. *Wilson* (1842) 9 Cl. & F. 355, 525 at 555).

In *de Beéche* v. *South American Stores, etc., Ltd.* [1935] A.C. 148 at 158 (H.L.), where evidence was admitted that the expression "payable in Chile in first-class bills on London" had a special mercantile meaning in Chile, Lord Sankey L.C. stated three conditions precedent to the admissibility of such evidence: "(1) the evidence must not conflict with a statutory definition; (2) the evidence must be of a usage common the place in question; and (3) the evidence must expound and not contradict the terms of the contract."

See also *Morrell* v. *Frith* (1838) 3 M. & W. 402 (Chapter 1, Section C, *supra*); *Wigglesworth* v. *Dallison* (1779) 1 Doug. K.B. 201 (*supra*); *Brown* v. *Byrne* (1854) 3 E. & B. 703 (*infra*); *Kell* v. *Charmer* (1856) 23 Beav. 195 (*infra*).

Brown v. **Byrne** (1854) 23 L.J.Q.B. 313 (Q.B.). A bill of lading specified a certain amount as payable for freight. Parol evidence was offered of a custom whereby three months' credit or discount was allowed for freight. The evidence was held admissible. Coleridge J. said (p. 316): "Mercantile contracts are very commonly framed in a language peculiar to merchants; the intention of the parties, though perfectly well known to themselves, would often be defeated if this language were strictly construed according to its ordinary import in the world at large: evidence, therefore, of mercantile custom and usage is admitted in order to expound it and arrive at its true meaning. Again, in all contracts, as to the subject-matter of which known usages prevail, parties are found to proceed with the tacit assumption of these usages; they commonly reduce into writing the special particulars of their agreement but omit to specify these known usages, which are included, however, as of course, by mutual understanding: evidence therefore of such incidents is receivable. The contract in truth is partly express and in writing, partly implied or understood and unwritten. But, in these cases, a restriction is established on the soundest principle, that the evidence received must not be of a particular which is repugnant to, or inconsistent with, the written contract. Merely that it varies the apparent contract is not enough to exclude the evidence; for it is impossible to add any material incident to the written terms of a contract without altering its effect, more or less. Neither, in the construction of a contract among merchants, tradesmen, or others, will the evidence be excluded because the words are in their ordinary meaning unambiguous; for the principle of admission is, that words perfectly unambiguous in their ordinary meaning are used by the contractors in a different sense from that. What words more plain than "a thousand," "a week," "a day?" Yet the cases are familiar in which "a thousand" has been held to mean twelve hundred, "a week" a week only during the theatrical season, "a day" a working day. In such cases the evidence neither adds to, nor qualifies, nor contradicts the written contract; it only ascertains it, by expounding the language. Here the contract is, to pay freight on delivery at a certain rate per pound: is it inconsistent with this to allege that, by the custom, the shipowner, on payment, is bound to allow three months' discount? We think not...*Webb* v. *Plummer* (1819) 2 B. & Ald. 746 and *Hutton* v. *Warren* (1836) 1 M. & W. 466 are cases which illustrate this principle. In the first of these, by the custom of the country the outgoing tenant was bound to do certain acts, and entitled to receive certain compensation; but the lease which formed the written contract bound him to do the same acts in substance and specially provided for his payment as to some of them, omitting the others; and the court held that the expression as to some excluded the implication as to the remainder, and that the language of the lease was equivalent to a stipulation that the lessor should pay for the things mentioned and no more. The custom therefore would have been repugnant to the contract. But in the latter case, in which the former was expressly recognised, the court held that a specific provision, as to a matter *dehors* the custom, left the custom untouched and in full force. This latter case appears to us like the present: the contract settles the right of freight; whether or not discount is to be allowed on the payment, it leaves open; and to that the usage applies...."

Note.—In this case the importation of the custom is by interpretation of the words used. Contrast, *e.g. Wigglesworth* v. *Dallison* (1779) 1 Doug. K.B. 201 (*supra*) where evidence of a custom seems to have been admitted as an explicit exception to the parol evidence rule.

Kell v. **Charmer** (1856) 23 Beav. 195 (Ch.). A testator gave legacies by his will as follows: "I give and bequeath to my son William the sum of i. x. x.; to my son Robert Charles the sum of o. x. x." Evidence was given by the shopman of the testator to the effect that the testator had carried on the business of a jeweller, in the course of which he had used certain private marks or symbols to denote prices or sums of money, and that, according to such marks or symbols as used by him, i. x. x. meant £100 and o. x. x. meant £200. Romilly M.R. held that this evidence was admissible to determine the amount of the legacies.

Higgins v. **Dawson** [1902] A.C. 1 (H.L.). A testator, after directing payment of his debts, funeral and testamentary expenses, and bequeathing a number of pecuniary legacies, gave "all the residue and remainder of the sum of £9,187 lent on mortgage to A, and £4,000 lent on mortgage to B, after payment of my debts, funeral and testamentary expenses," to certain persons, there being no general residuary gift. The question being whether the pecuniary legacies were to be paid out of the two mortgages, or only out of the general personal estate excluding the mortgages, it was held that the latter construction was correct; and that, the words in inverted commas being unambiguous, evidence of the circumstance surrounding the testator at the date of the execution of the will (*viz.*, that if the legacies were to be paid out of the then general personal estate, without resorting to the mortgages, the legacies could not be paid in full) was not admissible to explain the words "residue and remainder" in the will.

Note.—If the testator had died after December 31, 1982, evidence (other than direct evidence of the testator's intention) would have been admissible in an attempt to show ambiguity. In the event of this ambiguity being shown, evidence, including direct evidence of the testator's intention, would have been admissible to resolve that ambiguity (Administration of Justice Act, 1982, s.21, Part Two, *infra*).

Chapter 25

REAL EVIDENCE

THE term "real evidence" is used rather loosely. Sometimes and most narrowly it denotes a material object that has allegedly played some role in the sequence of events giving rise to the trial and which is physically produced in court for inspection—the knife that bears stains of blood, or the suit that does not fit the customer for whom the tailor contracted to make it. Although real evidence in this sense usually takes the form of an inanimate object, it may be an animal or even a human being— the dog that is vicious or the person who has been injured.[1] Real evidence is, however, often given an extended meaning so as to cover what is occasionally alternatively referred to as "demonstrative evidence." Such evidence consists of material that illustrates or explains relevant matters. This may be constituted by, for example, a photograph or a film of actual events, or tape recordings of actual conversations. Or, again, it may consist of a reconstruction of events, a demonstration, a diagram, or a scale model.

The term "real evidence" has also been seen as being apt when a site or an object is inspected out of court, often at the *locus in quo*. This procedure, to which resort is liable to be had, either because a physical object is immovable or is too large to be produced in court, or because a site cannot be adequately described testimonially, is usually referred to as a "view." There is some doubt as to whether a view can by itself constitute evidence. In *Goold* v. *Evans & Co.*[2] (*infra*), although Denning L.J. expressed the opinion that it can,[3] Hodson L.J. thought that it cannot.[4] However, what is inspected may not be just a static situation but may include activity. If a person were to demonstrate in court his inability, as a result of an accident, to raise his arm, this in itself would be admissible as real evidence; and the position would probably be no different if the demonstration were to take place out of

---

[1] However, although the demeanour of a witness generally simply bears upon the weight to be attached to testimonial evidence, it has been pointed out that "When the court acts on the remarks or behaviour of a witness as constituting a contempt, it may be said to accept real evidence because it is not asked to do more than act on its powers of perception in determining the existence of a fact in issue—the contemptuous conduct." (Cross: *Evidence*, 6th ed., (1985) p. 41).

[2] [1951] 2 T.L.R. 1189 (C.A.).

[3] *Ibid.* p. 1191. See, too, dicta of the Privy Council in *Karamat* v. *The Queen* [1956] A.C. 256 and *Tameshwar* v. *The Queen* [1957] A.C. 476 suggesting that for some purposes at least a view should be treated as evidence.

[4] *Ibid.* pp. 1191–1192.

court, for example in the hospital to which the person was confined. But in cases in which alleged earlier activities are simulated or re-enacted, either in court or out of court, the position is more complex. It would seem that in principle such demonstration should be equated with testimonial evidence and that the demonstrator should be sworn and made liable to cross-examination. Perhaps Hodson L.J. was pointing the way in *Goold* v. *Evans & Co.* (*infra*), but authority is scanty.

The common law adopts a slightly ambivalent attitude towards the reception of some kinds of real evidence. One consideration is that cross-examination is the life-blood of the adversary system, and a physical object is immune from the probing question. Of course, it is true that it is relatively infrequently that a piece of real evidence is tendered in isolation: it is usually accompanied by testimony of a witness to explain it—for example to prove where it was found, its condition, the use to which it was put, or to identify it; and this oral testimony can itself be tested by cross-examination. In some areas of the subject contemporary doubt and uncertainty results from recent technological advances. In much recent case law principle is not always easy to discern, and rules have not yet been fully developed.

Moreover and more generally, the diverse nature of the types of evidence to be accommodated under the omnibus heading of real and/or demonstrative evidence makes the formulation of defensible rules of general applicability difficult.

A document may constitute real evidence. Whether it does so will depend upon the purpose for which the document is tendered. If it is produced *qua* chattel and without regard to the message which it contains, for instance simply in order to show that it exists, the quality of the paper of which it is made or the fact that it is torn, it is treated as real not documentary evidence. If, on the other hand, it is produced *qua* statement, it is documentary evidence and a hearsay problem may arise. Whether such problem does arise will in its turn depend upon whether the statement is tendered as evidence of its truth, or is circumstantially relevant, *e.g.* it is tendered to show that, true or false, it was made. It is to be remembered that a document the *content* of which is circumstantially relevant is nevertheless documentary rather than real evidence.[5] Similar principles apply to tape-recordings and other mechanically, photographically or electronically produced statements. Thus, if a tape-recording is played over in court simply to show that the words used were uttered with a particular accent, the tape will usually be regarded as a piece of real evidence, but if it is played in order to show that particular words were uttered it will constitute documentary evidence.[6]

Whereas generally the original of a private document must be produced in order to prove its contents unless its absence can be explained, other evidence relating to a physical object may be given without producing, or accounting for, the absence of the object itself.

---

[5] But see *R.* v. *Rice* [1963] 1 Q.B. 857 (C.A.), Chapter 13, *supra.* For situations in which a computer print-out is tendered as documentary evidence, see the Civil Evidence Act 1968, s.5 and the Police and Criminal Evidence Act 1984, s.69 (both Part Two, *infra*).

[6] It is to be noted that the court must be satisfied that the tape is original and has not been altered. A transcript of a tape is also admissible if the court is satisfied as to its accuracy. See *R.* v. *Stevenson* [1971] 1 W.L.R. 1 (Assizes) and *R.* v. *Robson* [1972] 1 W.L.R. 651 (Cent. C.C.).

However, failure to produce an easily portable object may, not only go to the weight of that other evidence, but may also give rise to a presumption.[7] Although vestigial remains of the Best Evidence Rule are still to be found in the law regulating the admissibility of documentary evidence, that "Rule" has no role to perform in the corresponding parts of the law concerning the admissibility of real evidence.

Line v. **Taylor** (1862) 3 F. and F. 731 (Assizes). In an action for knowingly keeping a fierce and mischievous dog, which bit and wounded the plaintiff, the defendant's counsel proposed that the dog should be brought into court, in charge of his keeper, to be inspected by the jury. Despite objection by counsel for the plaintiff, the dog was accordingly brought in, led by his keeper, with a chain. The jury had him brought up to them, and at their desire the keeper let go of him. They examined him, and appeared to be of opinion that, from the expression of his eyes and other indications, he was not of a vicious disposition. Erle C.J. told the jury that they might judge partly from their knowledge of dogs and partly from their own observance of the animal in question.

Note.—It will be observed that the jury were also invited to use their own previously acquired general knowledge of dogs, thus importing into the case of notion sometimes confused with judicial (and jury) notice. See Chapter 7, *supra*.

In actions in the High Court, there is a restriction upon the use of models and plans in particular circumstances (R.S.C., Ord. 38, r. 5; Part Three, *infra*). As to the custody of things exhibited in the High Court, see Order 35, r. 12.

Goold v. **Evans and Co.** [1951] 2 T.L.R. 1189 (C.A.). A trial judge, in the course of hearing an action for damages for injury to a workman allegedly caused by his employers' negligence, viewed the premises and saw an operation which purported to be similar to that in which the workman had been engaged at the time of the accident. Owing to a mistake the workman was not informed of the date of the view and did not attend it. The judge found for the defendants, but the Court of Appeal held that there must be a new trial before another judge. Whether a view is regarded as technical evidence or not, both parties must be given the opportunity to be present at it. Denning L.J. (p. 1191) said "... I think that a view is part of the evidence, just as much as an exhibit. It is real evidence." His Lordship distinguished the situation in which the judge goes by himself and informally to see a site. Hodson L.J., however, said (p. 1191) that counsel had "... I think, rightly contended that a view is not in itself evidence. A view does not do away with the necessity of evidence. What I think happened in this case was something more than a view, because the view took place and an operation was performed, purporting to be the same operation as that which had been carried out when the plaintiff was injured. Whether words were spoken or not, or whether there was merely a silent representation of the operation, it seems to me that evidence was at that time being given."

Note.—The right of the judge to inspect a place or thing, *e.g.* under R.S.C., Ord. 35, r. 8(1) (Part Three, *infra*), is to be distinguished from a view, whether or not the latter is for all purposes to be regarded as evidence. It is not improper, although often undesirable, for a judge to inspect, as distinct from holding a view, without the parties' consent and in

---

[7] In the famous case of *Armory* v. *Delamirie* (1721) 1 Str. 505 (K.B.) the Chief Justice Pratt instructed the jury that, on the defendant's failure to produce the purloined jewel, they should presume its maximum value.

their absence: *Salsbury* v. *Woodland* [1970] 1 Q.B. 324 (C.A.); *Parry* v. *Boyle* (1986) 83 Cr.App.R. 310 (D.C.).

BUCKINGHAM v. DAILY NEWS LTD.

[1956] 2 Q.B. 534; [1956] 2 All E.R. 904 (C.A.: 1956)

A view may include a demonstration and constitute real evidence.

The plaintiff, who was employed by the defendants, was injured when cleaning a machine. In this action for damages for negligence the judge inspected the machine and watched a demonstration by the plaintiff as to how the machine was cleaned. The judge did not accept the plaintiff's oral evidence, and gave judgments for the defendants. The Court of Appeal was unanimous in dismissing the plaintiff's appeal.

BIRKETT L.J.: . . . When the case started, the judge, having been invited, with the consent of counsel upon both sides, as I think very wisely and very properly, to go to Bouverie Street to see the machine, decided to go. He went accompanied by the counsel on both sides and by the plaintiff, and they saw the machine on which the plaintiff had been working with the very blades. [Counsel] says that, with the machines running, there was a great deal of noise going on; and no doubt it was difficult to hear what was said. It was said . . . that the plaintiff showed the judge at Bouverie Street on this machine exactly what he was doing with the tucking blades on the day on which the accident took place.

. . . [T]he substantial submission that [counsel] makes is that what the judge did in this case was something forbidden by law, according to the authorities; namely, that he cast to the winds the evidence that was given for the plaintiff in this case and substituted for that evidence the impression which he had gained when he made the view at Bouverie Street. . . .

He cited in support of that submission *London General Omnibus Co. Ltd.* v. *Lavell* [1901] 1 Ch. 135 (C.A.). . . .

That was the main case upon which [counsel] relied, and he said that the doctrine that is laid down there is that a judge has no right to substitute his own opinion for the evidence; and that, he said, is what in this case this judge had done.

. . . In a case which I tried it was alleged that an accident had been caused by a defective stairway. The parties said: We would like you to see it; you can form your own view by seeing the stairway. I went to see the stairway. I had in mind what was said upon the one side and the other, and could make up my own mind whether, in my view, every relevant fact being before me, it was a reasonable thing to say it was a dangerous stairway, or a dangerous floor, a too-highly polished floor, and matters of that kind. As a judge of first instance, I visited factories, workshops, shops, cinemas—all for the purpose of seeing for myself the nature of the place where the accident occurred—the very material upon which the accident was itself founded.

Then, in addition to that, there are the exhibits that are brought into court. I have seen the model of the side of a house, with all the elaborate modern scaffolding, in order to save me and the parties making a journey to where the house was, the parties having agreed that that model was a faithful representation of the scaffolding and the house. I have seen models of aeroplanes in which it was alleged that accidents had occurred, such models being brought into court by the wish of the parties, so that I could see for myself and form my own opinion.

My own view in that respect is supported by what was said by Denning L.J. in *Goold* v. *Evans & Co.* [1951] 2 T.L.R. 1189 (C.A.)....

Denning L.J. said: "It is a fundamental principle of our law that a judge must act on the evidence before him and not on outside information; and, further, the evidence on which he acts must be given in the presence of both parties, or, at any rate, each party must be given an opportunity of being present. Speaking for myself, I think that a view is part of the evidence, just as much as an exhibit. It is real evidence. The tribunal sees the real thing instead of having a drawing or a photograph of it. But, even if a view is not evidence, the same principles apply."

I would very respectfully adopt that language, and say that when a judge goes to see machinery, and sees it in operation when the parties are present and everything is done regularly and in order, it is just the same as though the machinery were brought into court and the demonstration made in the well of the court, so that the judge or judges may see it....

...It is not a proper description of what occurred to say that the judge cast to the winds the evidence that was given, and substituted therefor his own opinion. What the judge manifestly was doing in this judgment was to say: I have in mind the evidence given by the plaintiff; I have taken each witness in turn and stated the substance of what they have said; but I also must bear in mind that I was invited to see the particular operation going on and I did see it. I express my view with regard to it. My own view is contrary to the view of the witnesses which has been given before me, and to that extent, impliedly and implicitly, I reject that evidence.

  . . . .

PARKER L.J.:...It is just as much a part of the evidence as if the machine had been brought into the well of the court and the plaintiff had there demonstrated what took place....

DENNING L.J.:...It follows from our decision today that the observations of Lord Alverstone C.J. in the *London General Omnibus* case [1901] 1 Ch. 135 (C.A.) unduly restrict the function of a view. Everyday practice in these courts shows that, where the matter for decision is one of ordinary common sense, the judge of fact is entitled to form his own judgment on the real evidence of a view, just as much as on the oral evidence of witnesses.

  . . . .

Note.—It may be noted that there was other real evidence in this case, as the swab (like a household dish-cloth) used for cleaning the machine was produced in the Court of Appeal.

Demonstrations of where witnesses were at the relevant time are also permissible on trials for crime. Then usually the judge, counsel, the jury, witnesses and the accused should all attend; see *Tameshwar* v. *R.* [1957] A.C. 476 (P.C.) as interpreted in *R.* v. *Hunter* [1985] 1 W.L.R. 614 (C.A.) *infra*.

An inspection should not be made (at least in criminal trials) after the end of the summing-up. See *R.* v. *Nixon* [1968] 1 W.L.R. 577 (C.A.); *Parry* v. *Boyle* (1986) 83 Cr.App.R. 310 (D.C.).

As to an ordinary view in a criminal case, see *R.* v. *Martin* (1872) L.R. 1 C.C.R. 378. As to views in civil cases see the Common Law Procedure Act 1852 s.114; R.S.C., Ord. 29, r. 2(1); Ord. 35, r. 8, (Part Three *infra*). See, too, C.C.R., Ord. 13, r. 11, Ord. 23, r. 14.

Li Shu-Ling v. **The Queen** [1989] A.C. 270 (P.C.). After confessing to murder, the appellant was invited by the police to reconstruct the crime on video. He was reminded that he was still under caution and was told that he need not reconstruct the crime if he did not want to. He agreed to do so. The Privy Council, affirming the decision of the Court of Appeal of Hong Kong, held that the video was admissible evidence of the appellant's confession. It was emphasised that such a video recording should be shown to an accused as soon as practicable after its completion, and that he should be given an opportunity to make, and have recorded, any comments he wished to make about it.

R. v. **Hunter** [1985] 1 W.L.R. 613 (C.A.). The accused was charged with importing cannabis through Newport docks. The judge decided that the jury should see the docks. They did so accompanied by counsel, the clerk and some witnesses. The judge did not go himself. Nor was the shorthand writer sent. At the view the jury asked some question of the witnesses and they were answered through the clerk. The Court of Appeal, allowing the defendant's appeal against conviction, held that the judge should have been present in order to control what had occurred. There had been a fundamental illegality, and the conviction was quashed. Boreham J., giving the judgment of the Court of Appeal, said (p. 617): "The judge should be present at every stage of the trial. A view is a stage of the trial. Whether or not a witness is present, in our view the judge should always be present."

R. v. **Senat; R.** v. **Sin** (1968) 52 Cr.App.R. 282 (C.A.). Tape-recordings of incriminating telephone conversations tapped on behalf of a party to divorce proceedings held to have been rightly admitted at a criminal trial. No question of their exclusion, on the grounds of their having been illegally obtained or of their amounting to a confession, arose because the tapping had not been the work of the police. There was no suggestion that they had been tampered with in any way or had been mistranscribed, or that voices had been wrongly identified. Counsel's contention, that, even if they were legally admissible, the trial judge ought in his discretion to have excluded them on the ground that it was difficult for the accused to criticise them after a lapse of two years, was also rejected by the Court of Appeal. Although a trial judge has a general discretion in a criminal case to exclude admissible evidence if its admission would be likely to make the trial unfair, there was no reason to suppose that this discretion had been wrongly exercised.

Note.—See, too, *R.* v. *Maqsud Ali* [1966] 1 Q.B. 688 (C.C.A.).

The Statue of Liberty [1968] 1 W.L.R. 739 (P.D.). In an action arising out of a collision between two ships in the river Thames the plaintiffs were allowed to adduce in evidence film recorded by radar apparatus on shore. Sir Jocelyn Simon P. said (p. 740): "If tape-recordings are admissible, it seems that a photograph of radar reception is equally admissible—or indeed, any other type of photograph. It would be an absurd distinction that a photograph should be admissible if the camera were operated manually by a photographer, but not if it were operated by a trip or clock mechanism. Similarly, if evidence of weather conditions were relevant, the law would affront common sense if it were to say that those could be proved by a person who looked at a barometer from time to time, but not by producing a barograph record. So, too, with other types of denial recordings. Again, cards from clocking-in-and-out machines are frequently admitted in accident cases. The law is now bound to take cognizance of the fact that mechanical means replace human effort."

R. v. Dodson; R. v. Williams [1984] 1 W.L.R. 971 (C.A.). The two accused had been convicted of attempted robbery of building society premises. The trial judge had allowed in evidence photographs of the raiders taken by automatic security cameras. The Court of Appeal held that this evidence had as a matter of law, been rightly admitted both on the issue of commission of the crime and on the issue of the identity of the criminals. It was, of course, for the jury to assess the weight of the evidence. Watkins L.J., giving the judgment of the Court of Appeal, said (p. 979): "They are called upon to do no more than the average person in domestic, social and other situations does from time to time, namely to say whether he is sure that a person shown in a photograph is the person he is then looking at or whom he has seen recently. It is, however, imperative that a jury is warned by a judge in summing up of the perils of the deciding whether by this means alone or with some form of supporting evidence a defendant has committed the crime alleged. . . . In the present case we do not doubt that the jury was made well aware of the need to exercise particular caution in this respect."

Note.—See, too, *R.* v. *Cook* [1987] Q.B. 417 (C.A.), where a "photofit" was likened to a photograph. This presents basic difficulties as to the nature of hearsay: see Chapter 13, *supra.*

R. v. Wood (1982) 76 Cr.App.R. 23 (C.A.). The accused was convicted of handling stolen processed metals. The prosecution had relied upon records in the prosecutor's possession of the chemical composition of the consignment from which the metal had allegedly been stolen. Their records were copies of figures from computer print-outs supplied by chemists. The computer had been programmed to make calculations from ratios fed into it to produce metal percentages. Similar tests were carried out using the computer on the metal handled by the defendant in order to show that it was of the same composition. The Court of Appeal, dismissing the accused's appeal against conviction, found that the computer was being used simply as a calculator. The print-outs were not hearsay but pieces of real evidence, proof of which depended upon the testimony of the chemist, and the relevance of which depended on his testimony, the testimony of the programmer and other expert evidence. Lord Lane L.C.J. delivering the judgment of the court, said (pp. 26–27): "The computer in the present case was being used as a calculator. Its programming and its use were covered by oral evidence. . . . The computer was rightly described as a tool. It did not contribute its own knowledge. It merely did a sophisticated calculation which could have been done manually by the chemist and was in fact done by chemists using the computer programmed by Mr. Kellie whom the Crown called as a witness."

Note.—See, too, *Castle* v. *Cross* [1984] 1 W.L.R. 1372 (D.C.), where it was held that readings from an Intoximeter 300 (for analysing specimens of breath) were no different from readings from other recording and measuring machines. The fact that it was a sophisticated machine and produced a computer print-out of its analysis did not alter the fact that it had been used simply as a tool in the hands of a skilled operator. The print-out was admissible in evidence, and the operator should have been allowed to give evidence of his observations and, if necessary, to interpret them. See, too, *Sophocleus* v. *Ringer* [1987]

86 Cr.App.R. 227 (D.C.), where it was held that the Police and Criminal Evidence Act, s.69, (Part Two, *infra*) was not apt in such circumstances.

R. v. HUNT

3 B. & Ald. 444, 566; 106 E.R. 725, 768 (K.B.: 1820)

The existence of characteristics of physical objects may be proved by oral evidence. An original writing must be produced, or its absence accounted for, only when it is tendered as documentary evidence.

On a charge of conspiracy, seditious meeting and riot, it appeared in evidence that there were various flags and banners, bearing inscriptions and devices of a seditious and inflammatory tendency, and that they were seized by the police officers on dispersion of the mob. On parol evidence of such inscriptions and devices being tendered, it was objected that the flags or banners ought to have been produced, or that notice should have been given to produce the originals. This objection was overruled, and the parol evidence was held admissible.

ABBOTT C.J.: ... With respect to the last point, the reception of the evidence as to the inscriptions on the flags or banners, I think it was not necessary either to produce the flags or to give notice to the defendants to produce them. The cases requiring the production of a writing itself will be found to apply to writings of a very different character. There is no authority to show that in a criminal case ensigns, banners, or other things exhibited to public view, and of which the effect depends upon such public exhibition, must be produced or accounted for on the part either of the prosecutor or of the defendants. And in many instances the proof of such matters from eye-witnesses, speaking to what they saw on the occasion, has been received, and its competency was never, to my knowledge, called in question until the present time. Inscriptions used on such occasions are the public expression of the sentiments of those who bear and adopt them, and have rather the character of speeches than of writings. If we were to hold that words inscribed on a banner so exhibited could not be proved without the production of the banner, I know not upon what reason a witness should be allowed to mention the colour of the banner or even to say that he saw a banner displayed, for the banner itself may be said to be the best possible evidence of its existence and its colour. And if such parol proof may be received generally, the proof at this trial was properly received: notwithstanding the allegation that the things themselves, or some of them, were in the hands of a constable then at York; for, in the first place, this fact did not appear (if indeed it appeared at any time distinctly) until after the evidence was received; and, in the second place, if it had appeared distinctly at the time when the parol evidence was offered, still that particular fact would not affect the competency of the other proof, such other proof being competent upon general principles. Its proper effect would only be to furnish matter of observation to the jury on the part of the defendants, that the prosecutor chose to offer only the fallible testimony of witnesses where he had it in his power to produce the infallible testimony of the thing themselves. ...

BAYLEY, HOLROYD and BEST JJ. concurred.

Note.—The evidence would appear to have been documentary rather than real in that the contents of the statements were relevant, and the actual decision has been the subject of some criticism, but it has been followed in relation to oral evidence of things generally. See, *e.g. R.* v. *Francis, infra.* See also *Redford* v. *Birley* (1822) 3 Stark. 76 at 96, 113; *R.* v. *Fursey* (1836) 6 C. & P. 81. Perhaps the judgment may be explained on the ground that the inscriptions were simply marks of identity. See *Martin* v. *White* [1910] 1 K.B. 665 (D.C.).

R. v. FRANCIS

L.R. 2 C.C.R. 128; **43 L.J.M.C. 97;** 30 L.T. 503; 22 W.R. 663; 12 Cox C.C. 612
(C.C.R.: 1874)

Non-production of a physical object, which might be produced for inspection by the court, does not render oral evidence respecting it inadmissible.

The prisoner was indicted for false pretences, by having falsely represented a ring to be a diamond ring. In order to prove his guilty knowledge, evidence was admitted of attempts on other occasions to obtain money on a false ring. It was held that oral evidence of the nature of the latter ring was admissible although it was not produced in court.

LORD COLERIDGE C.J. (delivering the judgment of the court, which included BLACKBURN and LUSH JJ., PIGOTT and CLEASBY BB.): ... It was objected that the evidence of what took place at Leicester was not properly received, because the cluster ring which he there attempted to pass was not produced in court, and that the evidence of two witnesses who saw it, and swore to its being false, was not admissible. No doubt if there was not admissible evidence that this ring was false it ought not to have been left to the jury; but though the non-production of the article may afford ground for observation more or less weighty, according to circumstances, it only goes to the weight, not to the admissibility, of the evidence, and no question as to the weight of this evidence is now before us. Where the question is as to the effect of a written instrument, the instrument itself is primary evidence of its contents, and until it is produced, or the non-production is excused, no secondary evidence can be received. But there is no case whatever deciding that, when the issue as to the state of a chattel, *e.g.* the soundness of a horse, or the equality of the bulk of the goods to the sample, the production of the chattel is primary evidence, and that no other evidence can be given till the chattel is produced in court for the inspection of the jury. The law of evidence is the same in criminal and civil suits.

Note.—This case is also an illustration of the admissibility of evidence of similar facts: see Chapter 20, *supra.*

In *Hocking* v. *Ahlquist Bros. Ltd.* [1944] K.B. 120 (K.B.D.) the defendants were accused of infringing statutory regulations which, during scarcity of materials in war-time, imposed restrictions on the method of making garments. The offending garments were not produced at the trial, and it was argued on behalf of the accused that evidence could therefore not be given by witnesses who had inspected them. The court, on a case stated, decided that this argument was erroneous. Viscount Caldecote C.J. said (pp. 122–124): "[I]n my judgment, it is much too late, even if it was ever possible, to suppose that evidence of the nature of chattels cannot be given by witnesses who have seen them and speak to their condition. To suppose that all the articles about which issues are raised in a great variety of cases ought to be produced in court would lead to consequences which would show how impossible the suggested rule would be in practice...."

The rule also applies where a person accused of murder has destroyed or concealed the body of his victim (see *R.* v. *Onufrejczyk* [1955] 1 Q.B. 388 (C.C.A.)).

EVIDENCE ON APPEAL

AFTER a civil case has been tried with a jury the party against whom judgment has been given may apply to the Court of Appeal for an order for a new trial and, if his application is successful, the verdict of the jury will be set aside. Where the appeal is on a point of law, two types of question relating to evidence may arise, namely (1) as to whether the judge wrongly admitted or rejected evidence, or (2) as to whether there was no evidence which could properly have been left to the jury in favour of the proponent of the issue in question (*i.e.* as to whether the judge had erred in finding that the evidential burden on that issue had been discharged), or, alternatively, as to whether an issue was wrongly withdrawn from the jury (*i.e.* as to whether the judge had erred in finding that the evidential burden had not been discharged).[1] A new trial may also be ordered on the ground that the jury's verdict was against the weight of the evidence. But this is a rare occurrence: it will reflect an indisputable and gross failure of the jury to recognise that a legal burden of proof was, or was not, discharged. For a new trial to be ordered on this ground there must be such a preponderance of evidence "as to make it unreasonable, and almost perverse, that the jury when instructed and assisted properly by the judge should return such a verdict."[2]

When, as is usual, a civil case has been heard before a judge sitting alone an appeal will take the form of a re-hearing which usually leads to judgment for one of the parties rather than an order for a new trial. Appeals on matters of law may be on the ground that evidence was wrongly admitted or rejected. Although the Court of Appeal has power to reverse the trial judge on a question of fact, it will only do so if, either the finding is of a fact which was wrongly inferred from admitted or indisputable primary facts, or (very occasionally) if the judge was palpably wrong in his assessment of testimony or other primary evidence.

Notwithstanding that in other respects the appeal is a re-hearing,[3] the appellate court does not receive oral evidence save in exceptional circumstances, but relies upon a transcript or the shorthand note of

---

[1] In a case in which there was no evidence which could properly have been left to the jury, the Court of Appeal will enter judgment for the opponent rather than order a retrial.

[2] *Per* Lord Selborne in *Metropolitan Rail Co.* v. *Wright* (1886) 11 App.Cas. 152, 153 (H.L.).

[3] R.S.C., Ord. 59, r. 3(1).

evidence in the court below. However, in all civil cases the Court of Appeal does have the power to consider fresh evidence. But the special grounds upon which this power can be exercised are very limited unless the new evidence relates to events occurring subsequent to the judgment under appeal.[4]

The Criminal Appeal Act 1968, s.1(1),[5] provides that a person convicted of an offence on indictment may appeal to the Court of Appeal against his conviction. Under section 2(1)(a) of the Act one of the bases upon which the Court of Appeal should allow an appeal is that the Court thinks that the conviction should be set aside on the ground that under all the circumstances of the case it is unsafe or unsatisfactory. The other grounds are error of law[6] (including the wrong reception or rejection of evidence and that an issue was wrongly left to, or withdrawn from, the jury) and "material irregularity in the course of the trial."[7] It is to be remembered, however, that the duty of the Court of Appeal to allow an appeal against conviction, on whatever ground, is qualified by the important and overriding proviso to section 2 of the 1968 Act which enables the Court to dismiss an appeal "if they consider that no miscarriage of justice has actually occurred."[8]

In a criminal case the Court of Appeal can hear fresh evidence under the conditions and circumstances set out in the Criminal Appeal Act 1968, s.23.[9] Having done so, it can order a retrial if it "appears to the Court that the interests of justice so require" and subject to the limitations set out in section 7 of the 1968 Act as amended.[10]

The materials set out in this chapter, illustrate the attitude of appellate courts to (1) the evidence adduced in the lower court, and (2) the admission of fresh evidence on appeal.

S.S. HONTESTROOM v. S.S. SAGAPORACK

[1927] A.C. 37; 95 L.J.P. 153; 136 L.T. 33; 42 T.L.R. 741; 17 Asp. 123 (H.L.: 1926)

An appellate court, not having seen the witnesses, is in a position of disadvantage as compared with the trial judge, and ought not to reverse the findings which are based on his estimate of the witnesses, unless it can be shown that he has manifestly taken an erroneous view.

These were actions arising out of two collisions in the Thames.

LORD SUMNER: ... If you begin by scrutinising the Hontestroom's story on the shorthand note ... and if it then impresses you unfavourably, if thereafter you follow her up to her starboarding ... with growing

---

[4] R.S.C., Ord. 59, r. 10(2) (Part Three, *infra*).
[5] Part Two, *infra*.
[6] s.2(1)(b).
[7] s.2(1)(c).
[8] For the power in civil cases see R.S.C., Ord. 59, r. 11(2) (Part Three, *infra*).
[9] Part Two, *infra*.
[10] Part Two, *infra*. The Court of Appeal should make its own assessment of the new evidence rather than conjecture as to the effect it might have had on the jury: *R.* v. *Byrne* (1988) 88 Cr.App.R. 33 (C.A.).

doubt, and if you finally come upon a manoeuvre of the Sagaporack, which is requisite to save the Hontestroom from blame but is not to be found in her preliminary act, I can well understand that you would cry: "What need have we of further testimony? Let there be judgment for the defendant." But suppose the sequence is otherwise, as at the trial it was. Watching the witnesses in the box and not merely perusing the shorthand notes, listening to what they say without any previous preparation of an adverse kind...a judge in the Admiralty Court watches the case as it is built up by the witnesses themselves. He reads their faces, not the shorthand note....

Not to have seen the witnesses puts appellate judges in a permanent position of disadvantage as against the trial judge, and unless it can be shown that he has failed to use or has palpably misused his advantage, the higher court ought not to take the responsibility of reversing conclusions so arrived at, merely on the result of their own comparisons and criticisms of the witnesses and of their own view of the probabilities of the case. The course of the trial and the whole substance of the judgment must be looked at, and the matter does not depend on the question whether a witness has been cross-examined to credit or has been pronounced by the judge in terms to be unworthy of it. If his estimate of the man forms any substantial part of his reasons for his judgment the trial judge's conclusions of fact should, as I understand the decisions, be left alone....

VISCOUNT DUNEDIN and LORD CARSON agreed.

LORDS PHILLIMORE and BLANESBURGH dissented.

Note.—The statement of the law in the text has been approved (see *Powell* v. *Streatham Manor Nursing Home* [1935] A.C. 243 (H.L.); *Thomas* v. *Thomas* [1947] A.C. 484 (H.L.)). But when a finding of fact by the trial court is really an inference from other facts specifically found, the appellate court may be equally competent to draw the appropriate inference: see *Benmax* v. *Austin Motor Co. Ltd., infra.*

BENMAX v. AUSTIN MOTOR CO. LTD.

[1955] A.C. 370; [1955] 1 All E.R. 326 (H.L.: 1955)

There is a distinction between on one hand a finding of a specific primary fact and on the other hand a finding of fact which is really an inference drawn from a primary fact or primary facts. In the latter case an appellate tribunal will more readily form an independent opinion that it will in the former case, because whereas the former involves evaluation of the evidence of witnesses, often being founded on their credibility or demeanour, the latter usually does not.

This was an appeal from an order of the Court of Appeal reversing the judgment of the trial judge, Lloyd-Jacobs J., in an action in which the appellant, as plaintiff, had sought an injunction to restrain the respondents, as defendants, from infringing letters patent granted to him. By their defence the respondents *inter alia* alleged that the letters patent were invalid on the ground that the invention claimed therein was either not new, or was obvious and did not involve any inventive step.

VISCOUNT SIMONDS: . . . Counsel for the appellant urged in the forefront of his argument that the existence of an inventive step was a question of fact which had been decided by the trial judge, Lloyd-Jacob J., in favour of the appellant, and therefore that the Court of Appeal should not have reversed his decision except for certain reasons which clearly were not present in this case. I think it convenient therefore to state my view on this question, though I am aware that it does not entirely agree with observations made in this House by noble Lords for whose opinion I have the highest regard. Fifty years ago, in *Montgomerie & Co. Ltd.* v. *Wallace-James* [1904] A.C. 73, 75, Lord Halsbury L.C. said: "But where no question" arises as to truthfulness, and where the question is as to the proper inferences to be drawn from truthful evidence, then the original tribunal is in no better position to decide than the judges of an Appellate Court." And in *Mersey Docks and Harbour Board* v. *Procter* [1923] A.C. 253, 258–259, Lord Cave L.C. said: "The procedure on an appeal from a judge sitting without a jury is not governed by the rules applicable to a motion for a new trial after a verdict of a jury. In such a case it is the duty of the Court of Appeal to make up its own mind, not disregarding the judgment appealed from and giving special weight to that judgment in cases where the credibility of witnesses comes into question, but with full liberty to draw its own inference from the facts proved or admitted, and to decide accordingly." It appears to me that these statements are consonant with the Rules of the Supreme Court [now R.S.C., Ord. 59, r. 3(1) which prescribes that an appeal to the Court of Appeal shall be by way of re-hearing, and Ord. 59, r. 10(3), which provides that the "Court of Appeal shall have power to draw inferences of fact and to give any judgment and make any order which ought to have been given or made. . . ."] This does not mean that an appellate court should lightly differ from the finding of a trial judge on a question of fact, and I would say that it would be difficult for it to do so where the finding turned solely on the credibility of a witness. But I cannot help thinking that some confusion may have arisen from failure to distinguish between the finding of a specific fact and a finding of fact which is really an inference from facts specifically found, or, as it has sometimes been said, between the perception and evaluation of facts. An example of this distinction may be seen in any case in which a plaintiff alleges negligence on the part of the defendant. Here it must first be determined what the defendant in fact did and, secondly, whether what he did amounted in the circumstances (which must also so far as relevant be found as specific facts) to negligence. A jury finds that the defendant has been negligent, and that is an end of the matter unless its verdict can be upset according to well established rules. A judge sitting without a jury would fall short of his duty if he did not first find the facts and then draw from them the inference of fact whether or not the defendant had been negligent. This is a simple illustration of a process in which it may often be difficult to say what is simple fact and what is inference from fact, or, to repeat what I have said, what is perception, what evaluation. Nor is it of any importance to do so except to explain why, as I think, different views have been expressed as to the duty of an appellate tribunal in relation to a finding by a trial judge. For I have found, on the one hand, universal reluctance to reject a finding of specific fact, particularly where the finding could be founded on the credibility or bearing of a witness, and, on the other hand, no less a willingness to form an independent opinion about the proper inference of fact, subject only to the weight which should, as a matter of course, be given to the opinion of the learned judge. For I have found, on the one hand, universal reluctance to reject a finding of specific fact, particularly where the finding could be founded on the credibility or bearing of a witness, and, on the other hand, no less a willingness to form an independent opinion about the proper inference of fact, subject only to the weight which should, as a matter of course, be given to the opinion of the learned judge. But the statement of the proper function of the appellate court will be influenced by the extent to which the mind of the speaker is directed to the one or the other of the two aspects of the problem.

In a case like that under appeal where, so far as I can see, there can be no dispute about any relevant specific fact, much less any dispute arising out of the credibility of witnesses, but the sole question is whether the proper inference from those facts is that the patent in suit disclosed an inventive step, I do not hesitate to say that an appellate court should form an independent opinion, though it will naturally attach importance to the judgments of the trial judge. . . .

I would dismiss this appeal.

LORDS MORTON OF HENRYTON (with whose judgment LORD TUCKER agreed), REID and LORD SOMERVELL OF HARROW delivered concurring judgments.

Note.—The principle enunciated in *Benmax* v. *Austin Motor Co. Ltd.* seems to have been applied in *Whitehouse* v. *Jordan* [1981] 1 W.L.R. 246 (H.L.).

Joyce v. **Yeomans** [1981] 1 W.L.R. 549 (C.A.). The defendant's liability for negligent driving was admitted. At the trial, on quantum of damages only, there was a difference of opinion, between a medical expert who gave evidence for the defendant and two experts called by the plaintiff, as to the cause of some of the plaintiff's injuries. The trial judge preferred the evidence of the defendant's witness. The plaintiff appealed on the ground *inter alia* that the judge had erred in this. The Court of Appeal dismissed the appeal. Brandon L.J. said (p. 556): "I do not think that the authorities on the right of an appellate court to interfere with the findings of fact of a trial judge based on witnesses of simple fact are entirely applicable to cases where the finding is based on expert evidence, but I certainly would not go to the other extreme and say that the trial judge has no advantage over an appellate court because the witnesses are expert. I think he has certain advantages—not perhaps so great as those applicable where witnesses are witnesses of fact, but nevertheless significant advantages which an appellate court ought not to ignore."

Note.—See, too, *Wilsher* v. *Essex Area Health Authority* [1988] A.C. 1074 (H.L.) (for facts, see Chapter 4, Section B, *supra*). There Lord Bridge of Harwich said *obiter* (p. 1091): "Where expert witnesses are radically at issue about complex technical questions within their own field and are examined and cross-examined at length about their conflicting theories, I believe that the judge's advantage in seeing them and leaving them is scarcely less important than when he has to resolve some conflict of primary fact between lay witnesses in purely mundane matters."

BRADDOCK v. TILLOTSON'S NEWSPAPERS LTD.

[1950] 1 K.B. 47; [1949] 2 All E.R. 306; 65 T.L.R. 553 (C.A.: 1949)

Leave to call fresh evidence on appeal in relation to an issue will be granted only when the evidence could not reasonably have been discovered before the trial, and would probably have led to a different result. When the fresh evidence relates to the credit of a witness, its effect must be more certain.

The plaintiff in an action for libel applied to the Court of Appeal to have one of the defendants' witnesses recalled for cross-examination to credit. The application was refused.

TUCKER L.J.: . . . It has been the invariable practice of the Court of Appeal in this country to confine the admission of fresh evidence, in circumstances such as this, to evidence which could not reasonably have been discovered before the trial, and to evidence which, if believed, either would be conclusive or, as has been said by some judges, to evidence which would lead to the reasonable probability that the verdict would have been different. But the practice has hitherto been confined to evidence relating to an issue in the case, or at any rate to an issue which could and might yet be raised if there were a new trial in the action. No case has been cited in which this court has ever admitted or has ever been asked to admit evidence going to credit only. . . .

There has been some variation in the language used by judges as to the quality of new evidence required by the court, before it shall be admitted, namely, whether it must be such as is presumably to be believed, and if believed would be conclusive; or that it is sufficient if there is a reasonable possibility that, if brought before the jury, a different verdict would have been given.

These varying expressions have, so far as the decision of the courts in this country are concerned, always been directed to evidence directly relevant to the main issue in the action, or to some issue which could, or would, have been raised at the trial if the evidence has been discovered. It is not necessary in this case to express any opinion as to which is the better view with regard to the quality of the evidence in such a case. If, however, this court is to depart from its invariable practice of confining such evidence to the relevant issues and is to admit fresh evidence directed solely to credit, I am of opinion that such a course would, if ever only be justified where the evidence is of such a nature and the circumstances of the case are such that no reasonable jury could be expected to act upon the evidence of the witness whose character had been called in question. It would, in my view, be wrong for this court to admit fresh evidence directed solely to credit, merely because there is a possibility, or merely a reasonable probability, that such evidence would result in a different verdict. There are two conflicting principles operating in these matters; one is that everything should be done in order to ascertain the truth; the other is that there should be some finality in litigation, and, so far as possible, a reasonable limitation of costs. It is in order to achieve the latter result that it is necessary for the court to impose some limit to the reopening of decided issues, even at the risk that injustice may result, or it may appear that there is a possibility of injustice resulting. . . .

COHEN L.J.: . . . I think that if this court is to extend the ambit of cases in which it allows further evidence to be adduced on appeal to include the cases where the further evidence is directed only to the credit of a witness called at the trial, it can, if it be right at all, only be right to do so in a case where the court is satisfied that the additional evidence *must* have led a reasonable jury to a different conclusion from that actually arrived at in the case. . . .

SINGLETON L.J. delivered a concurring judgment.

Note.—There are numerous reported cases on this subject, some of which show that a further condition of allowing fresh evidence is that it must be credible, and that it may relate to the credit of a witness (see, for example, *Ladd* v. *Marshall* [1954] 1 W.L.R. 1489 (C.A.); *Roe* v. *Robert McGregor & Sons* [1968] 1 W.L.R. 925 (C.A.)), or to misleading the court (*Meek* v. *Fleming* [1961] 2 Q.B. 366 (C.A.)).

As to the evidence being credible, and such as might have caused a reasonable doubt in the minds of the jury, in criminal cases, see also *R.* v. *Parks* [1961] 1 W.L.R. 1484 (C.C.A.). See, too, *R.* v. *Pedrini* [1964] Crim.L.R. 719 (C.C.A.), where one of the prosecution witnesses was alleged to be insane; and *R.* v. *Flower* [1966] 1 Q.B. 146 (C.C.A.).

Fresh evidence is admissible on an appeal against sentence where the purpose of the evidence is to show that a special verdict taken from a jury is unsafe or unsatisfactory, and that the special verdict formed the basis of the sentence: *R.* v. *Frankum* (1983) 5 Cr.App.R. (S) 259 (C.A.).

Fresh evidence is even admissible in exceptional cases in which an appeal is being heard against a conviction following a plea of guilty: *R.* v. *Foster* [1985] Q.B. 115 (C.A.).

Transcontainer Express v. **Custodian Security** [1988] 1 Lloyd's Rep. 128; [1988] 1 F.T.L.R. 54 (C.A.). The plaintiffs, carriers, had to compensate the owners of goods which had been stolen in transit. They sought to recover these and other expenses from the defendant who had provided a 24 hour security service in the area where the goods were at the time of the theft. The claim was in tort, and the plaintiff alleging that the defendant was a sub-bailee for reward. The judge concluded that the defendant had not taken reasonable care, but dismissed the plaintiff's claim on the ground that the defendant's duty to take care extended only to those with a possessory or proprietary interest in the goods, which the plaintiff did not have. On appeal the plaintiff sought to argue that at the time of theft he had an immediate right to possession of the goods. The Court of Appeal held that it could only agree to such a new point being raised if it were satisfied that no new evidence could have been adduced on the point. On the facts it was perfectly possible that the defendant would have wanted to call evidence of contractual and other arrangements between the plaintiff and the owner of the goods. So the new point could not be taken on appeal.

Part Two

STATUTES ON EVIDENCE

WITNESSES ACT 1806

46 Geo. 3, c. 37

Be it therefore declared... that a witness cannot be law refuse to answer a question relevant to the matter in issue, the answering of which has no tendency to accuse himself, or to expose him to penalty or forfeiture of any nature whatsoever, by reason only or on the sole ground that the answering of such question may establish, or tend to establish that he owes a debt, or is otherwise subject to a civil suit, either at the instance of his Majesty, or of any other person or persons.

Note.—See, too, the Civil Evidence Act 1968, s.14(1) and s.16(1) (*infra*).

EVIDENCE ACT 1845

8 & 9 Vict. c. 113

1. ... Whenever by any Act now in force or hereafter to be in force any certificate, official or public document or proceeding of any corporation or joint stock or other company, or any certified copy of any document, bye-law, entry in any register or other book, or of any other proceeding shall be receivable in evidence of any particular in any court of justice, or before any legal tribunal, or either House of Parliament, or any committee of either House, or in any judicial proceeding, the same shall respectively be admitted in evidence, provided they respectively purport to be sealed or impressed with a stamp, or sealed and signed, or signed alone, as required, or impressed with a stamp and signed, as directed by the respective Acts made or to be hereafter made, without any proof of the seal or stamp, where a seal or stamp is necessary, or of the signature or of the official character of the person appearing to have signed the same, and without any further proof thereof, in every case in which the original record could have been received in evidence.

Note.—See *Mortimer* v. *M'Callan* (1840) 6 M. & W. 58 (Part One, Chapter 24, *supra*) and the Evidence Act 1851, s.14 (*infra*).

2. All courts, judges, justices, masters in chancery, masters of courts, commissioners judicially acting, and other judicial officers, shall henceforth take judicial notice of the signature of any of the equity or common law judges of the superior courts at Westminster, provided such signature be attached or appended to any decree, order, certificate, or other judicial or official document.

3. All copies of private and local and personal Acts of Parliament not public Acts, if purporting to be printed by the Queen's printers, and all copies of the journals of either House of Parliament, and of royal proclamations, purporting to be printed by the printers to the crown or by the printers to either House of Parliament, or by any or either of them, shall be admitted as evidence thereof by all courts, judges, justices, and others, without any proof being given that such copies were so printed.

Note.—For minor repeals see the Statute Law Revision Act 1891. See also the Documentary Evidence Act 1868 (*infra*). By the Documentary Evidence Act 1882 a Stationery Office copy is made the equivalent of a Queen's Printer's copy. As to judicial notice, see Part One, Chapter 7, *supra*. As to proof of public documents, see Part One, Chapter 24, *supra*.

EVIDENCE ACT 1851

14 & 15 VICT. C. 99

2. On the trial of any issue joined, or of any matter or question, or on any inquiry arising in any suit, action, or other proceeding in any court of justice, or before any person having by law, or by consent of parties, authority to hear, receive, and examine evidence, the parties thereto, and the persons in whose behalf any such suit, action or other proceeding may be brought or defended, shall, except as hereinafter excepted, be competent and compellable to give evidence, either *viva voce* or by deposition, according to the practice of the court, on behalf of either or any of the parties to the said suit, action, or other proceeding.

3. But nothing herein contained shall render any person who in any criminal proceeding is charged with the commission of any indictable offence, or any offence punishable on summary conviction, competent or compellable to give evidence for or against himself or herself, or shall render any person compellable to answer any question tending to criminate himself or herself, or shall in any criminal proceeding render any husband competent or compellable to give evidence for or against his wife, or any wife competent or compellable to give evidence for or against her husband.

Note.—As to the evidence of accused persons and their spouses, see the Criminal Evidence Act 1898 and the Police and Criminal Evidence Act 1984 (both *infra*), and Part One, Chapter 23 (*supra*).

7. All proclamations, treaties, and other acts of state of any foreign state or of any British colony, and all judgments, decrees, orders, and other judicial proceedings of any court of justice in any foreign state or in any British Colony, and any affidavits, pleadings, and other legal documents filed or deposited in any such court, may be proved in any court of justice, or before any person having by law or by consent of parties authority to hear, receive, and examine evidence, either by examined copies or by copies authenticated as hereinafter mentioned; that is to say, if the document sought to be proved be a proclamation, treaty, or other act of state, the authenticated copy to be admissible in evidence must purport to be sealed with the seal of the foreign state or British colony to which the original document belongs; and if the document sought to be proved be a judgment, decree, order, or other judicial proceeding of any foreign or colonial court, or an affidavit, pleading, or other legal document filed or deposited in any such court, the authenticated copy to be admissible in evidence must purport either to be sealed with the seal of the foreign or colonial court having no seal to be signed by the judge, or, if there be more than one judge, by any one of the judges of the said court; and such judge shall attach to his signature a statement in writing on the said copy that the court whereof he is a judge has no seal; but if any of the aforesaid authenticated copies shall purport to be sealed or signed as hereinbefore respectively directed, the same shall respectively be admitted in evidence in every case in which the original document could have been received in evidence without any proof of the seal where a seal is necessary, or of the signature, or of the truth of the statement attached thereto, where such signature and statement are necessary or of the judicial character of the person appearing to have made such signature and statement.

14. Whenever any book or other document is of such a public nature as to be admissible in evidence on its mere production from the proper custody, and no statute exists which renders its contents provable by means of a copy, any copy thereof or extra therefrom shall be admissible in evidence in any court of justice, or before any person now or hereafter having by law or by consent of parties authority to hear, receive, and examine evidence, provided it be proved to be an examined copy or extract, or provided it purport to be signed and certified as a true copy or extract by the officer to whose custody the original is intrusted, and which officer is hereby required to furnish such certified copy or extract to any person applying at a reasonable time for the same, upon payment of a reasonable sum for the same, not exceeding fourpence for every folio of ninety words.

Note.—See *Mortimer* v. *M'Callan* (1840) 6 M. & W. 58 (Part One, Chapter 24, *supra*).

EVIDENCE AMENDMENT ACT 1853

16 & 17 Vict c. 83

1. On the trial of any issue joined, or of any matter or question, or on any inquiry arising in any suit, action, or other proceeding in any court of justice, or before any person having by law or by consent of parties authority to hear, receive, and examine evidence, the husbands and wives of the parties thereto, and of the persons in whose behalf any such suit, action, or other proceeding may be brought or instituted, or opposed or defended, shall, except as hereinafter excepted, by competent and compellable to give evidence either *viva voce* or by deposition according to the practice of the court, on behalf of either or any of the parties to the said suit, action, or other proceeding.

Note.—As to criminal proceedings see the Criminal Evidence Act 1898 and the Police and Criminal Evidence Act 1984 (both *infra*).

BRITISH LAW ASCERTAINMENT ACT 1859

22 & 23 Vict c. 63

1. If in any action depending in any court within Her Majesty's dominions it shall be the opinion of such court that it is necessary or expedient for the proper disposal of such action to ascertain the law applicable to the facts of the case as administered in any other part of Her Majesty's dominions on any point on which the law of such other part of Her Majesty's dominions is different from that in which the court is situate, it shall be competent to the court in which such action may depend to direct a case to be prepared setting forth the facts, as these may be ascertained by verdict of a jury or other mode competent, or may be agreed upon by the parties, or settled by such person or persons as may have been appointed by the court for that purpose in the event of the parties not agreeing; and upon such case being approved of by such court or a judge thereof, they shall settle the questions of law arising out of the same on which they desire to have the opinion of another court, and shall pronounce an order remitting the same, together with the case, to the court in such other part of Her Majesty's dominions, being one of the superior courts thereof, whose opinion is desired upon the law administered by them as applicable to the facts set forth in such case, and desiring them to pronounce their opinion on the questions submitted to them in the terms of the Act; and it shall be competent to any of the parties to the action to present a petition to the court whose opinion is to be obtained, praying such last-mentioned court to hear parties or their counsel, and to pronounce their opinion thereon in terms of this Act, or to pronounce their opinion without hearing parties or counsel; and the court to which such petition shall be presented shall, if they think fit, appoint an early day for hearing parties or their counsel on such case, and shall thereafter pronounce their opinion upon the questions of law as administered by them which are submitted to them by the court; and in order to their pronouncing such opinion they shall be entitled to take such further procedure thereupon as to them shall seem proper.

2. Upon such opinion being pronounced, a copy thereof, certified by an officer of such court, shall be given to each of the parties to the action by whom the same shall be required, and shall be deemed and held to contain a correct record of such opinion.

Note.—Compare Art. 177 of the Treaty of Rome.

CRIMINAL PROCEDURE ACT 1865

28 & 29 Vict c. 18

1. The provisions of section two of this Act shall apply to every trial . . . ; and . . . the provisions of sections from three to eight, inclusive, of this Act shall apply to all courts of judicature, as well criminal as all others, and to all persons having, by law or by consent of parties, authority to hear, receive, and examine evidence.

3. A party producing a witness shall not be allowed to impeach his credit by general evidence of bad character, but he may, in case the witness shall, in the opinion of the judge, prove adverse, contradict him by other evidence, or, by leave of the judge, prove that he has made at other times a statement inconsistent with his present testimony; but before such last-mentioned proof can be given the circumstances of the supposed statement, sufficient to designate the particular occasion, must be mentioned to the witness, and he must be asked whether or not he has made such statement.

Note.—See the Civil Evidence Act 1968, s.3(1) (*infra*), and Part One, Chapter 9 (*supra*). There is a judicial discretion independent of section 3 to allow cross-examination of a party's own hostile witness: *R.* v. *Thompson* (1976) 64 Cr.App.R. 86 (C.A.) (Part One, Chapter 9, *infra*).

4. If a witness, upon cross-examination as to a former statement made by him relative to the subject matter of the indictment or proceeding, and inconsistent with his present testimony, does not distinctly admit that he has made such statement, proof may be given that he did in fact make it; but before such proof can be given the circumstances of the supposed statement, sufficient to designate the particular occasion, must be mentioned to the witness, and he must be asked whether or not he has made such statement.

Note.—See the Civil Evidence Act 1968, s.3(1) (*infra*). Section 4 does not apply to cross-examination of a party's own hostile witness: *R.* v. *Booth* (1982) 74 Cr.App.R. 123 (C.A.).

5. A witness may be cross-examined as to previous statements made by him in writing or reduced into writing relative to the subject matter of the indictment or proceeding, without such writing being shown to him; but if it is intended to contradict such witness by the writing, his attention must, before such contradictory proof can be given, be called to those parts of the writing which are to be used for the purpose of so contradicting him: provided always, that it shall be competent for the judge, at any time during the trial, to require the production of the writing for his inspection, and he may thereupon make such use of it for the purposes of the trial as he may think fit.

Note.—See the Civil Evidence Act 1968, s.3(1) (*infra*). The proviso with regard to the judge making such use of the writing as he thinks fit does not extend to directing the jury to treat it as evidence of the truth of the facts stated: *R.* v. *Birch* (1924) 18 Cr.App.R. 26 (C.C.A.). Nor can the cross-examiner make it evidence by asking the witness to read it out: *R.* v. *Gillespie and Simpson* (1967) 51 Cr.App.R. 12 (C.A.).

6. A witness may be questioned as to whether he has been convicted of any felony or misdemeanour, and upon being so questioned, if he either denies or does not admit the fact, or refuses to answer, it shall be lawful for the cross-examining party to prove such conviction. . . .

Note.—As to proof of previous convictions, see the Police and Criminal Evidence Act 1984, s.73 (*infra*). In civil actions a witness may usually not be asked about his "spent" convictions: Rehabilitation of Offenders Act 1974 (*infra*).

7. It shall not be necessary to prove by the attesting witness any instrument to the validity of which attestation is not requisite, and such instrument may be proved as if there had been no attesting witness thereto.

Note.—Compare the Merchant Shipping Act 1894, s.694 (*infra*) and the Evidence Act 1938, s.3 (*infra*).

8. Comparison of a disputed writing with any writing proved to the satisfaction of the judge to be genuine shall be permitted to be made by witnesses; and such writings, and the evidence of witnesses respecting the same, may be submitted to the court and jury as evidence of the genuineness or otherwise of the writing in dispute.

Note.—For the meaning of "satisfaction of the judge," see *R.* v. *Ewing* [1983] Q.B. 1039 (C.A.) (Part One, Chapter 3, *supra*). Although the Act does not require the evidence of expert witnesses, in a number of criminal cases this has been thought desirable (see *R.* v. *Rickard* (1918) 13 Cr.App.R. 140; *R.* v. *Day* (1940) 27 Cr.App.R. 168 (C.C.A.)) or necessary (see *R.* v. *Tilley* [1961] 1 W.L.R. 1309 (C.C.A.); *R.* v. *Harden* [1963] 1 Q.B. 8 (C.C.A.). For a special mode of proof of some documents, see Magistrates' Courts Rules 1981, as amended, Rule 67 (Part Three, *infra*).

CRIMINAL LAW AMENDMENT ACT 1867

30 & 31 Vict. c. 35

6. An officer to whom a statement taken under section 105 of the Magistrates' Courts Act 1980, is sent in pursuance of rules made under section 144 of that Act shall preserve the same, and file it of record; and if afterwards, upon the trial of any offender or offence to which the same may relate, the person who made the same statement shall be proved to be dead, or if it shall be proved that there is no reasonable probability that such person will ever be able to travel or to give evidence, it shall be lawful to read such statement in evidence, either for or against the accused, without further proof thereof, if the same purports to be signed by the justice by or before whom it purports to be taken, and provided it be proved to the satisfaction of the court that reasonable notice of the intention to take such statement has been served upon the person (whether prosecutor or accused) against whom it is proposed to be read in evidence, and that such person, or his counsel or attorney, had or might have had, if he had chosen to be present, full opportunity of cross-examining the deceased person who made the same.

Note.—For the Magistrates' Courts Act 1980, s.105, see *infra*.

For other situations in which a deposition may be read at a criminal trial see, *e.g.* Criminal Justice Act 1925, s.13(3); Children and Young Persons Act 1933, s.43; Magistrates' Courts Act 1980, s.102(7) (all *infra*): also Children and Young Persons Act 1963, s.27.

DOCUMENTARY EVIDENCE ACT 1868

31 & 32 Vict. c. 37

2. Prima facie evidence of any proclamation, order, or regulation issued before or after the passing of this Act by Her Majesty, or by the Privy Council, also of any proclamation, order, or regulation issued before or after the passing of this Act by or under the authority of any such department of the Government or officer as is mentioned in the first column of the schedule hereto, may be given in all courts of justice, and in all legal proceedings whatsoever, in all or any of the modes hereinafter mentioned; that is to say:

(1) By the production of a copy of the Gazette purporting to contain such proclamation, order or regulation.

(2) By the production of a copy of such proclamation, order, or regulation, purporting to be printed by the Government printer, or, where the question arises in a court in any British colony or possession, of a copy purporting to be printed under the authority of the legislature of such British colony or possession.

(3) By the production, in the case of any proclamation, order, or regulation issued by Her Majesty or by the Privy Council, of a copy or extract purporting to be certified to be true by the clerk

of the Privy Council, or by any one of the lords or others of the Privy Council, and, in the case of any proclamation, order, or regulation issued by or under the authority of any of the said departments or officers, by the production of a copy or extract purporting to be certified to be true by the person or persons specified in the second column of the said schedule in connection with such department or officer.

Any copy or extract made in pursuance of this Act may be in print or in writing, or partly in print and partly in writing.

No proof shall be required of the handwriting or official position of any person certifying, in pursuance of this Act, to the truth of any copy of an extract from any proclamation, order, or regulation.

Note.—The schedule referred to above originally comprised the principal departments of State as they then existed. Later legislation has frequently added new bodies.

See too the Documentary Evidence Act 1882. For proof of local authority by-laws see Local Government Act 1972, s.210. Dominion and Colonial regulations are proved by an appropriate Government Printer's copy: Evidence (Colonial Statutes) Act 1907.

PREVENTION OF CRIMES ACT 1871

24 & 35 Vict. c. 112

A previous conviction in any one part of the United Kingdom may be proved against a prisoner in any other part of the United Kingdom.

Note.—Regarding summary convictions see the Magistrates' Courts Act 1980, s.104.

BANKERS' BOOKS EVIDENCE ACT 1879

42 & 43 Vict. c. 11

3. Subject to the provisions of this Act, a copy of any entry in a banker's book shall in all legal proceedings be received as prima facie evidence of such entry, and of the matters, transactions, and accounts therein recorded.

Note.—An arbitration is a legal proceeding within this Act (see s.10). See too the Solicitors Act 1974, s.86.

4. A copy of an entry in a banker's book shall not be received in evidence under this Act unless it be first proved that the book was at the time of the making of the entry one of the ordinary books of the bank, and that the entry was made in the usual and ordinary court of business, and that the book is in the custody or control of the bank.

Such proof may be given by a partner or officer of the bank, and may be given orally or by an affidavit sworn before any commissioner or person authorised to take affidavits.

5. A copy of an entry in a banker's book shall not be received in evidence under this Act unless it be further proved that the copy has been examined with the original entry and is correct.

Such proof shall be given by some person who has examined the copy with the original entry, and may be given either orally or by an affidavit sworn before any commissioner or person authorised to take affidavits.

6. A banker or officer of a bank shall not, in any legal proceeding to which the bank is not a party, be compellable to produce any banker's book the contents of which can be proved under this Act, or to appear as a witness to prove the matters, transactions, and accounts therein recorded, unless by order of a judge made for special cause.

7. On the application of any party to a legal proceeding a court or judge may order that such party be at liberty to inspect and take copies of any entries in a banker's book for any of the purposes of such proceedings. An order under this section may be made either with or without summoning the bank or any other party, and shall be served on the bank three clear days before the same is to be obeyed, unless the court or judge otherwise directs.

Note.—A magistrate before whom criminal proceedings are pending is a court within this section (*R.* v. *Kinghorn* [1908] 2 K.B. 949).

An order made under this section should be limited in point of time: *R.* v. *Marlborough Street Stipendiary Magistrate* (1980) 70 Cr.App.R. 291 (D.C.). The power to make an order must not be exercised for the purpose of "fishing" in order to see whether there is a case: the court should proceed with caution and should be satisfied that there is other evidence to support the charge: *R.* v. *Nottingham Justices, ex p. Lynn* (1984) 79 Cr.App.R. 238 (D.C.).

The fact that the holder of an account is not a compellable witness may justify the making of an order permitting inspection of the account: *R.* v. *Andover Justices, ex p. Rhodes* [1980] Crim.L.R. 644 (D.C.). It is desirable that notice be given to a person affected by an order.

In *R.* v. *Grossman* (1981) 73 Cr.App.R. 302 the Court of Appeal emphasised that it is only in exceptional circumstances that an order can be made for the inspection of the account of a bank's customer who is not a party to the proceedings. Only if the public interest in helping the prosecution outweighs the private interest of confidentiality should inspection be ordered. *R.* v. *Grossman* was followed in *Mackinnon* v. *Donaldson, Lufkin and Jenrette Corporation* [1986] Ch. 482 (Ch.D.), where Hoffman J. held that in particular a non-party foreign bank, which would owe a duty of confidence to its customers regulated by the law of the country where the customer's account was kept, should only in extremely exceptional circumstances be required to produce documents outside the jurisdiction concerning business transacted outside the jurisdiction.

9. (1). In this Act the expressions "bank" and "banker" mean—

(a) an institution authorised under the Banking Act 1987 or a municipal bank within the meaning of that Act; [as revised by Banking Act 1987, Sched. 6, 1(1)]

(b) ....

(c) the National Savings Bank; and

(d) the Post Office, in the exercise of its powers to provide banking services.

(2) Expressions in this Act relating to "bankers' books" include ledgers, day books, cash books, account books and other records used in the ordinary business of the bank, whether those records are in written form or are kept in microfilms, magnetic tape or any other form of mechanical or electronic data retrieval mechanism.

Note.—The words "other records" are to be construed *ejusdem generis* and accordingly do not include cheques and credit slips: *Williams* v. *Williams* [1988] Q.B. 161 (C.A.).

BILLS OF EXCHANGE ACT 1882

45 & 46 Vict. c. 61

30.—(1) Every party whose signature appears on a bill is prima facie deemed to have become a party thereto for value.

(2) Every holder of a bill is prima facie deemed to be a holder in due course; but if in an action on a bill it is admitted or proved that the acceptance, issue, or subsequent negotiation of the bill is affected with fraud, duress, or force and fear, or illegality, the burden of proof is shifted, unless and until the holder proves that, subsequent to the alleged fraud or illegality, value has in good faith been given for the bill.

Note.—Compare the Prevention of Corruption Act 1916, s.2 (*infra*).

For a discussion of the incidence and shifting of the burden of proof, see Part One, Chapter 2 and Chapter 3, Section B (*supra*).

PARTNERSHIP ACT 1890

53 & 54 Vict. c. 39

2. In determining whether a partnership does or does not exist, regard shall be had to the following rules:

(1)...

(2)...

(3) The receipt by a person of a share of the profits of a business is prima facie evidence that he is a partner in the business but the receipt of such a share, or of a payment contingent on or varying with the profits of a business, does not of itself make him a partner in the business; and in particular—[then follow five examples of events which as a matter of substantive law do not make a person "a partner in the business or liable as such"].

15. An admission or representation made by any partner concerning the partnership affairs, and in the ordinary course of its business, is evidence against the firm.

Note.—As to admissions by agents, see Part One, Chapter 14, Section D (*supra*).

STAMP ACT 1891

54 & 55 Vict. c. 39

12.—(5) Every instrument stamped with the particular stamp denoting either that it is not chargeable with any duty, or is duly stamped, shall be admissible in evidence, and available for all purposes notwithstanding any objection relating to duty.

14.—(1) Upon the production of an instrument chargeable with any duty as evidence in any court of civil judicature in any part of the United Kingdom, or before any arbitrator or referee, notice shall be taken by the judge, arbitrator or referee of any omission or insufficiency of the stamp thereon, and if the instrument is one which may legally be stamped after the execution thereof, it may, on payment to the officer of the court whose duty it is to read the instrument, or to the arbitrator or referee, of the amount of unpaid duty, and the penalty payable on stamping the same, and of a further sum of one pound, be receivable in evidence, saving all just exceptions on other grounds.

(4) Save as aforesaid, an instrument executed in any part of the United Kingdom, or relating, wheresoever executed, to any property situate, or to any matter or thing done or to be done, in any part of the United Kingdom, shall not, except in criminal proceedings, be given in evidence, or be available for any purpose whatever, unless it is duly stamped in accordance with the law in force at the time when it was first executed.

Note.—As to the effect on the right to a new trial of any ruling on stamps, see R.S.C., Ord. 59, r. 11(5). See, too, *Maugham* v. *Hubbard* (1828) 8 B. & C. 14, in which it was held that an unstamped document, which would ordinarily require stamping, although inadmissible as evidence, may be used for the purpose of refreshing a witness's memory. This seems still to be the position despite the stricter working of the 1891 Act, which replaced earlier Acts: *Birchall* v. *Bullough* [1896] 1 Q.B. 325 (D.C.). But another view was expressed in *Fengl* v. *Fengl* [1914] P. 274 (D.C.).

MERCHANT SHIPPING ACT 1894

57 & 58 VICT. c. 60

691.—(1) Whenever in the course of any legal proceeding instituted in any part of Her Majesty's dominions before any judge or magistrate, or before any person authorised by law or by consent of parties to receive evidence, the testimony of any witness is required in relation to the subject-matter of that proceeding, then upon due proof, if the proceeding is instituted in the United Kingdom, that the witness cannot be found in that kingdom, or if in any British possession, that he cannot be found in that possession, any deposition that the witness may have previously made on oath in relation to the same subject-matter before any justice or magistrate in Her Majesty's dominions, or any British consular officer elsewhere, shall be admissible in evidence, provided that:

(*a*) if the deposition was made in the United Kingdom, it shall not be admissible in any proceeding instituted in the United Kingdom; and

(*b*) if the deposition was made in any British possession, it shall not be admissible in any proceeding instituted in that British possession; and

(*c*) if the proceeding is criminal it shall not be admissible, unless it was made in the presence of the person accused.

(2) A deposition so made shall be authenticated by the signature of the judge, magistrate, or consular officer before whom it is made; and the judge, magistrate, or consular officer shall certify if the fact is so, that the accused was present at the taking thereof.

(3) It shall not be necessary in any case to prove the signature or official character of the person appearing to have signed any such deposition, and in any criminal proceeding a certificate under this section shall, unless the contrary is proved, be sufficient evidence of the accused having been present in manner thereby certified.

(4) Nothing herein contained shall affect any case in which depositions taken in any proceeding are rendered admissible in evidence by any Act of Parliament, or by any Act or ordinance of the legislature of any colony, so far as regards that colony, or interfere with the power of any

colonial legislature to make those depositions admissible in evidence, or interfere with the practice of any court in which depositions not authenticated as hereinbefore mentioned are admissible.

694. Where any document is required by this Act to be executed in the presence of, or to be attested by any witness or witnesses, that document may be proved by the evidence of any person who is able to bear witness to the requisite facts without calling the attesting witness or the attesting witnesses or any of them.

Note.—See, too, the Evidence Act 1938, s.3 (*infra*); and compare the Criminal Procedure Act 1865, s.7 (*supra*), which deals with a situation in which attestation is not in any event required.

CRIMINAL EVIDENCE ACT 1898

61 & 62 Vict. c. 36

1. Every person charged with an offence shall be a competent witness for the defence at every stage of the proceedings, whether the person so charged is charged solely or jointly with any other person. Provided as follows:

(*a*) A person so charged shall not be called as a witness in pursuance of this Act except upon his own application;

(*b*) The failure of any person charged with an offence to give evidence shall not be made the subject of any comment by the prosecution;

[(*c*) and (*d*) repealed].

(*e*) a person charged and being a witness in pursuance of this Act may be asked any question in cross-examination notwithstanding that it would tend to criminate him as to the offence charged;

(*f*) A person charged and called as a witness in pursuance of this Act shall not be asked, and if asked shall not be required to answer, any question tending to show that he has committed or been convicted of or been charged with any offence other than that wherewith he is then charged, or is of bad character, unless.—

    (*i*) the proof that he has committed or been convicted of such other offence is admissible evidence to show that he is guilty of the offence wherewith he is then charged; or

    (*ii*) he has personally or by his advocate asked questions of the witnesses for the prosecution with a view to establish his own good character, or has given evidence of his good character, or the nature of conduct of the defence is such as to involve imputations on the character of the prosecutor or the witnesses for the prosecution; or

    (*iii*) he has given evidence against any other person charged in the same proceedings:

(*g*) Every person called as a witness in pursuance of this Act shall, unless otherwise ordered by the court, give his evidence from the witness box or other place from which the other witnesses give their evidence:

[(*h*) repealed].

Note.—The word "offence" includes the plural thereby giving a defendant the choice of giving evidence in relation to each or all of the offences charged, but he does not have the right to have an indictment severed where offences are properly joined simply because he wishes to give evidence on particular counts only: *R.* v. *Phillips* (1988) 86 Cr.App.R. 18 (C.A.).

As to proviso *(b)*, the right of comment by the judge is unaffected, but should be exercised fairly. See Part One, Chapter 8 *(supra)*.

As to the competence and compellability of the spouse of the accused, see the Police and Criminal Evidence Act 1984, s.80 *(infra)*.

As to relation between provisos *(e)* and *(f)*, see *Jones* v. *D.P.P.* [1962] A.C. 635 (H.L.) (Part One, Chapter 23, *supra*).

For commentary, cases and annotations on provisos *(e)* and *(f)*, see Part One, Chapter 23 *(supra)*.

Proviso *(f)* must be read subject to the Children and Young Persons Act 1963, s.16(2) *(infra)*. In proviso *(f)* (iii) the words "in the same proceedings" were substituted for the words "with the same offence" by the Criminal Evidence Act 1979, s.1.

2. Where the only witness to the facts of the case called by the defence is the person charged, he shall be called as a witness immediately after the close of the evidence for the prosecution.

Note.—As to the time for taking the evidence of the accused when there are one or more other defence witnesses to the facts of the case, see the Police and Criminal Evidence Act 1984, s.79 *(infra)*.

PERJURY ACT 1911

1 & 2 GEO. 5, c. 6

13. A person shall not be liable to be convicted of any offence against this Act, or of any offence declared by any other Act to be perjury or subornation of perjury, or to be punishable as perjury or subornation of perjury solely upon the evidence of one witness as to the falsity of any statement alleged to be false.

Note.—When the prosecution seeks to show that a particular statement was untrue, the trial judge must bring section 13 to the attention of the jury: *R.* v. *Rider* (1986) 83 Cr.App.R. 207 (C.A.). Corroboration is not required of the fact that the accused knew that he was making an untrue statement: *R.* v. *O'Connor* [1980] Crim.L.R. 43 (C.A.). As to corroboration generally, see Part One, Chapter 10, *(supra)*.

14. On a prosecution—
  (*a*) for perjury alleged to have been committed on the trial of an indictment for misdemeanour; or
  (*b*) for procuring or suborning the commission of perjury on any such trial,
the fact of the former trial shall be sufficiently proved by the production of a certificate containing the substance and effect (omitting the formal parts) of the indictment and trial purporting to be signed by the clerk of the court, or other person having the custody of the records of the court where the indictment was tried, or by the deputy of that clerk or other person, without proof of the signature or official character of the clerk or person appearing to have signed the certificate.

OFFICIAL SECRETS ACT 1911

1 & 2 GEO. 5, c. 28

1.—(1) If any person for any purpose prejudicial to the safety or interests of the State—[indulges in various forms of espionage] he shall be guilty of felony.

(2) On a prosecution under this section, it shall not be necessary to show that the accused person was guilty of any particular act tending to show a purpose prejudicial to the safety or interests of the State, and, notwithstanding that no such act is proved against him, he may be convicted if, from the circumstances of the case, or his conduct, or his known character as proved, it appears that his purpose was a purpose prejudicial to the safety or interests of the State; and if any sketch, plan, model, article, note, document, or information relating to or used in any prohibited place within the meaning of this Act, or anything in such a place, or any secret official code word or pass word is made, obtained, collected, recorded, published or communicated by any person other than a person acting under lawful authority, it shall be deemed to have been made, obtained, collected, recorded, published or communicated for a purpose prejudicial to the safety or interests of the State unless the contrary is proved.

Note.—For an extension of the Act see too the European Communities Act 1972, s.11(2).

PREVENTION OF CORRUPTION ACT 1916

6 & 7 GEO, 5, C. 64

2. Where in any proceedings against a person for an offence under the Prevention of Corruption Act, 1906, or the Public Bodies Corrupt Practices Act, 1889, it is proved that any money, gift, or other consideration has been paid or given to or received by a person in the employment of His Majesty or any Government Department or a public body by or from a person, or agent of a person, holding or seeking to obtain a contract from His Majesty or any Government Department or public body, the money, gift, or consideration shall be deemed to have been paid or given and received corruptly as such inducement or reward as is mentioned in such Act unless the contrary is proved.

Note.—For the interaction of presumptions and burdens generally, and for comments by the Court of Appeal in *R.* v. *Braithwaite* [1983] 1 W.L.R. 385 on the effect of section 2, see Part One, Chapter 4, Section B (*supra*). Compare the Bills of Exchange Act 1882, s.30(2) (*supra*).

ADMINISTRATION OF JUSTICE ACT 1920

10 & 11 GEO. 5, C. 81

15. Where for the purpose of disposing of any action or other matter which is being tried by a judge with a jury in any court in England or Wales it is necessary to ascertain the law of any other country which is applicable to the facts of the case, any question as to the effect of the evidence given with respect to that law shall, instead of being submitted to the jury, be decided by the judge alone.

Note.—This section no longer applies to the High Court; but a similar provision is to be found in the Supreme Court Act 1981, s.69(5) (*infra*). For County Courts, see the County Courts Act 1984, s.68 (*infra*). The section has been held to extend to criminal proceedings: *R.* v. *Hammer* [1923] 2 K.B. 786 (C.C.A.).

LAW OF PROPERTY ACT 1925

15 & 16 Geo. 5, c. 20

184. In all cases where, after the commencement of this Act, two or more persons have died in circumstances rendering it uncertain which of them survived the other or others, such deaths shall (subject to any order of the court), for all purposes affecting the title to property, be presumed to have occurred in order of seniority, and accordingly the younger shall be deemed to have survived the elder.

Note.— In *Hickman* v. *Peacey* [1945] A.C. 304 a majority of the House of Lords held that this section applies even in a case in which the deaths are likely to have been simultaneous, because it is uncertain which, if either, survived.

See too the Family Law Reform Act 1987, ss.18 and 21. The former section provides that for the purposes of Part IV of the Administration of Estates Act 1925 (which deals with succession on intestacy) "a person whose father and mother were not married to each other at the time of his birth shall be presumed not to have been survived by his father, or by any person related to him only through his father, unless the contrary is proved." Section 21 lays down that, for the purposes of obtaining a grant of probate or administration, there is a rebuttable presumption that the deceased left no surviving relatives who are illegitimate or whose relationship is traced through illegitimacy. These sections have only prospective effect.

CRIMINAL JUSTICE ACT 1925

15 & 16 Geo. 5, c. 86

12.—(4) Any statement made by the accused in proceedings before examining justices in answer to the charge and taken down in accordance with rules made under section 144 of the Magistrates' Courts Act 1980 may, whether signed by the accused or not, be given in evidence on his trial without further proof:

Provided that, if the said rules require the statement to be signed by any of the examining justices, and it is proved that any signature to the statement purporting to be that of an examining justice is not his signature, the statement shall not be admissible by virtue of this section.

(6) Nothing in this section or the said rules shall prevent the prosecutor in any case from giving in evidence at the trial any admission or confession or other statement of the accused made at any time which is by law admissible as evidence against the accused.

*Note.—*Compare the Criminal Law Amendment Act 1867, s.6 (*supra*). The rules referred to are the Magistrates' Courts Rules 1981 (Part Three, *infra*).

13.—(3) Where any person has been committed for trial for any offence, the deposition of any person taken before the examining justices may, if the conditions hereinafter set out are satisfied, without further proof be read as evidence on the trial of that person, whether for that offence or for any other offence arising out of the same transaction, or set of circumstances, as that offence.

The conditions hereinbefore referred to are the following:

(*a*) The deposition must be the deposition either of a witness in respect of whom a conditional witness order, or an order treated as a conditional witness order, has been made under section 1 of the Criminal Procedure (Attendance of

Witnesses) Act 1965, or of a witness who is proved at the trial by the oath of a credible witness to be dead or insane, or so ill as not to be able to travel, or to be kept out of the way by means of the procurement of the accused or on his behalf:

(b) It must be proved at the trial, either by a certificate purporting to be signed by the justice before whom the deposition purports to have been taken or by the clerk to the examining justices, or by the oath of a credible witness, that the deposition was taken in the presence of the accused and that the accused or his counsel or solicitor had full opportunity of cross-examining the witness:

(c) The deposition must purport to be signed by the justice before whom it purports to have been taken:

Provided that the provisions of this subsection shall not have effect in any case in which it is proved—

(i) That the deposition, or, where the proof required by paragraph (b) of this subsection is given by means of a certificate, that the certificate, was not in fact signed by the justice by whom it purports to have been signed; or

(ii) Where the deposition is the deposition of a witness in respect of whom such an order as aforesaid has been made that the witness has been duly notified that he is required to attend the trial.

Note.—For the Criminal Procedure (Attendance of Witnesses) Act 1965, see *infra*. See also the Magistrates' Courts Act 1980, s.102(7), (*infra*).

The admission of a deposition is always subject to the discretion of the trial judge: *R.* v. *Blithing* (1983) 77 Cr.App.R. 86 (C.A.).

EVIDENCE (FOREIGN, DOMINION AND COLONIAL DOCUMENTS) ACT 1933

23 & 24 Geo. 5, c. 4

1.—(2) An Order in Council made under section 5 of the Oaths and Evidence (Overseas Authorities and Countries) Act 1963 may provide that in all parts of the United Kingdom—

(a) a register of the country to which the Order relates, being such a register as is specified in the Order, shall be deemed to be a public register kept under the authority of the law of that country and recognised by the courts thereof as an authentic record, and to be a document of such a public nature as to be admissible as evidence of the matters regularly recorded therein;

(b) such matters as may be specified in the Order shall, if recorded in such a register, be deemed, until the contrary is proved, to be regularly recorded therein;

(c) subject to any condition specified in the Order and to any requirements of rules of court a document purporting to be issued in the country to which the Order relates as an official copy of an entry in such a register as is so specified, and purporting to be authenticated as such in the manner specified in the Order as appropriate in the case of such a register, shall, without evidence as to the custody of the register or of inability to produce it and without any further or other proof,

be received as evidence that the register contains such an
entry;
   (d) subject as aforesaid a certificate purporting to be given in the
       country to which the Order relates as an official certificate of
       any such class as is specified in the Order, and purporting to
       be siged by the officer, and to be authenticated in the
       manner, specified in the Order as appropriate in the case of a
       certificate of that class, shall be received as evidence of the
       facts stated in the certificate;
   (e) no official document issued in the country to which the Order
       relates as proof of any matters for the proof of which
       provision is made by the Order shall, if otherwise admissible
       in evidence, be inadmissible by reason only that it is not
       authenticated by the process known as legislation.
   (3) Official books of record preserved in a central registry and
containing entries copied from original registers may, if those entries
were copied by officials in the course of their duty themselves be treated
for the purposes of this section as registers.
   (4) In this section the expression "country" means a Dominion, the
Isle of Man, any of the Channel Islands, a British colony or
protectorate, a foreign country, a colony or protectorate of a foreign
country, or any mandated territory:
   Provided that where a part of a country is under both a local and a
central legislature, an Order under this section may be made as well
with respect to that part, as with respect to all the parts under that
central legislature.

   Note.—The powers were first exercised in respect of various registers and certificates of
Belgium (1933), France (1937), Australia (1938) and New Zealand (1959). Thereafter
Orders under this Act, or this Act as modified by the Oaths and Evidence (Overseas
Authorities and Countries) Act 1963, s.5, have been made in respect of numerous
Commonwealth countries.
   For alternative means of proving the celebration of a marriage outside England and
Wales and its validity under the *lex loci celebrationis* in matrimonial proceedings, see the
Matrimonial Causes Rules 1977 (as amended), Rule 40.

CHILDREN AND YOUNG PERSONS ACT 1933

23 & 24 GEO. 5, c. 12

   4.—(2) If a person having the custody, charge, or care of a child or
young person is charged with an offence under this section, and it is
proved that the child or young person was in any street, premises, or
place for any such purpose as aforesaid, and that the person charged
allowed the child or young person to be in the street, premises, or
place, he shall be presumed to have allowed him to be in the street,
premises or place for that purpose unless the contrary is proved.
   (3) If any person while singing, playing, performing or offering
anything for sale in a street or public place has with him a child who has
been lent or hired out to him, the child shall, for the purposes of this
section, be deemed to be in that street or place for the purpose of
inducing the giving of alms.

   Note.—This section relates to the use of children, etc., for begging. Whereas subs. (2)
creates a rebuttable (but compelling) presumption, subs. (3) would appear to create an
irrebuttable presumption. See Part One, Chapter 4 (*supra*).

38.—(1) Where, in any proceedings against any person for any offence, any child of tender years called as a witness does not in the opinion of the court understand the nature of an oath, his evidence may be received, though not given upon oath, if, in the opinion of the court, he is possessed of sufficient intelligence to justify the reception of the evidence, and understands the duty of speaking the truth; and his evidence, though not given on oath, but otherwise taken and reduced into writing in accordance with the provisions of section 17 of the Indictable Offences Act 1848, or of this Part of this Act, shall be deemed to be a deposition within the meaning of that section and that Part respectively.

(2) If any child whose evidence is received as aforesaid wilfully gives false evidence in such circumstances that he would, if the the evidence had been given an oath, have been guilty of perjury, he shall be liable on summary conviction to be dealt with as if he had been summarily convicted of a indictable offence punishable in the case of an adult with imprisonment.

Note.—Section 17 of the Indictable Offences Act 1848 has been repealed: see now the Magistrates' Courts Rules 1981.

The meaning of "child of tender years" was considered in *R.* v. *Lal Khan* (1981) 73 Cr.App.R. 190 (C.A.) It was said there that, although the meaning may well depend upon the type of child, "under the age of 14" may be a good general working rule.

A proviso to subsection (1) that an accused could not be convicted on the uncorroborated evidence of an unsworn child was abolished by the Criminal Justice Act 1988, s.34(1).

42.—(1) Where a justice of the peace is satisfied by the evidence of a duly qualified medical practitioner that the attendance before a court of any child or young person in respect of whom any of the offences mentioned in the First Schedule to this Act is alleged to have been committed would involve serious danger to his life or health, the justice may take in writing the deposition of the child or young person on oath, and shall thereupon subscribe the deposition and add thereto a statement of his reason for taking it and of the day when and place where it was taken, and of the names of the persons (if any) present at the taking thereof.

43. Where, in any proceedings in respect of any of the offences mentioned in the First Schedule to this Act, the court is satisfied by the evidence of a duly qualified medical practitioner that the attendance before the court of any child or young person in respect of whom the offence is alleged to have been committed would involve serious danger to his life or health, any deposition of the child or young person taken under the Indictable Offences Act 1848, or this Part of this Act, shall be admissible in evidence either for or against the accused person without further proof thereof if it purports to be signed by the justice by or before whom it purports to be taken:

Provided that the deposition shall not be admissible in evidence against the accused person unless it is proved that reasonable notice of the intention to take the deposition has been served upon him and that he or his counsel or solicitor had, or might have had if he had chosen to be present, an opportunity of cross-examining the child or young person making the deposition.

Note.—Contrast the Magistrates' Courts Act 1980 (*infra*). As to the Indictable Offences Act 1848 see *Note* to section 38 (*supra*).

50. It shall be conclusively presumed that no child under the age of ten years can be guilty of any offence.

Note.—This is a rule of substantive law expressed as a presumption; and in appropriate cases it might operate as a defence to a charge under section 38(2) (*supra*).

99.—(1) Where a person, whether charged with an offence or not, is brought before any court otherwise than for the purpose of giving evidence, and it appears to the court that he is a child or young person, the court shall make due inquiry as to the age of that person, and for that purpose shall take such evidence as may be forthcomming at the hearing of the case, but an order or judgment of the court shall not be invalidated by any subsequent proof that the age of that person has not been correctly stated to the court, and the age presumed or declared by the court to be the age of the person so brought before it shall, for the purposes of this Act, be deemed to be the true age of that person, and, where it appears to the court that the person so brought before it has attained the age of seventeen years, that person shall for the purposes of this Act be deemed not to be a child or young person.

Note.—By the Children and Young Persons Act 1969, s.70(3), the reference in section 99(1) of the 1933 Act to "this Act" is to be construed as including reference to the 1969 Act.

(2) Where in any charge or indictment for any offence under this Act or any of the offences mentioned in the First Schedule to this Act, except as provided in that Schedule, it is alleged that the person by or in respect of whom the offence was committed was a child or young person or was under or had attained any specified age, and he appears to the court to have been at the date of the commission of the alleged offence a child or young person, or to have been under or to have attained the specified age, as the case may be, he shall for the purposes of this Act be presumed at that date to have been a child or young person or to have been under or to have attained that age, as the case may be, unless the contrary is proved.

Note.—Similar provisions as to presuming the age of a person will be found in the Criminal Justice Act 1948, s.80(3) and the Sexual Offences Act 1956, s.28(5). Compare the Police and Criminal Evidence Act 1984, s.80(6), (*infra*).

FIRST SCHEDULE

Note.—This Schedule, which has been amended by the Sexual Offences Act 1956, includes the murder or manslaughter of a child or young person; infanticide; various offences under the Offences against the Person Act 1861, the Act of 1933, the Sexual Offences Act 1956, and the Protection of Children Act 1978, s.1(*a*); and any other offence involving bodily injury to a child or young person. See also the Indecency with Children Act 1960, s.1(3); the Suicide Act 1961, Sched. I.

EVIDENCE ACT 1938

1 & 2 Geo. 6, c. 28

Note.—Sections 1, 2 and part of 6 of this Act were repealed by the Civil Evidence Act 1968 (*infra*), but the Act is still generally applicable in proceedings within the civil jurisdiction of magistrates' courts. See Part One, Chapter 16 (*supra*).

3. Subject as hereinafter provided, in any proceedings, whether civil or criminal, an instrument to the validity of which attestation is requisite may, instead of being proved by an attesting witness, be proved in the manner in which it might be proved if no attesting witness were alive:

Provided that nothing in this section shall apply to the proof of wills or other testamentary documents.

Note.—Compare the Criminal Procedure Act 1865, s.7 (*supra*). See, too, Part One, Chapter 24, Section B (*supra*); and see the Merchant Shipping Act 1894, s.694 (*supra*).

4. In any proceedings, whether civil or criminal, there shall, in the case of a document proved, or purporting, to be not less than twenty years old, be made any presumption which immediately before the commencement of this Act would have been made in the case of a document of like character proved, or purporting, to be not less than thirty years old.

WELSH COURTS ACT 1942

5 & 6 GEO. 6, c. 40

2. The Lord Chancellor may make rules prescribing a translation in the Welsh language of any form for the time being prescribed by law as the form of any oath or affirmation to be administered and taken or made by any person in any court, and an oath of affirmation administered and taken or made in any court in Wales in the translation prescribed by such rules shall, without interpretation, be of the like effect as if it had been administered and taken or made in the English language.

Note.—The relevant rules are the Welsh Courts (Oaths and Interpreters) Rules 1943–1972, as amended. See too the Welsh Language Act 1967, and the Oaths Act 1978 (*infra*).

CROWN PROCEEDINGS ACT 1947

10 & 11 GEO. 6, c. 44

28.—(1) Subject to and in accordance with rules of court and county court rules:—

    (*a*) in any civil proceedings in the High Court or a county court to which the Crown is a party, the Crown may be required by the court to make discovery of documents and produce documents for inspection; and

    (*b*) in any such proceedings as aforesaid, the Crown may be required by the court to answer interrogatories:

Provided that this section shall be without prejudice to any rule of law which authorises or requires the withholding of any document or the refusal to answer any question on the ground that the disclosure of the document or the answering of the question would in injurious to the public interest.

Any order of the court made under the powers conferred by paragraph (*b*) of this subsection shall direct by what officer of the Crown the interrogatories are to be answered.

(2) Without prejudice to the proviso to the preceding subsection, any rules made for the purposes of this section shall be such as to secure

that the existence of a document will not be disclosed if, in the opinion of a Minister of the Crown, it would be injurious to the public interest to disclose the existence thereof.

Note.—For public interest immunity, see Part One, Chapter 12 (*supra*).

CRIMINAL JUSTICE ACT 1948

11 & 12 Geo 6, c. 58

39.—(1) A previous conviction may be proved against any person in any criminal proceedings by the production of such evidence of the conviction as is mentioned in this section, and by showing that his finger-prints and those of the person convicted are the finger-prints of the same person.

(2) A certificate purporting to be signed by or on behalf of the Commissioner of Police of the Metropolis, containing particulars relating to a conviction extracted from the criminal records kept by him, and certifying that the copies of the finger-prints exhibited to the certificate are copies of the finger-prints appearing from the said records to have been taken . . . from the person convicted on the occasion of the conviction, shall be evidence of the conviction and evidence that the copies of the finger-prints exhibited to the certificate are copies of the finger-prints of the person convicted.

(3) A certificate purporting to be signed by or on behalf of the governor of a prison or remand centre in which any person has been detained in connection with any criminal proceedings, certifying that the finger-prints exhibited thereto were taken from him while he was so detained, shall be evidence in those proceedings that the finger-prints exhibited to the certificate are the finger-prints of that person.

(4) A certificate, purporting to be signed by or on behalf of the Commissioner of Police of the Metropolis, and certifying that the finger-prints, copies of which are certified as aforesaid by or on behalf of the Commissioner to be copies of the finger-prints of a person previously convicted and the finger-prints certified by or on behalf of the governor as aforesaid, or otherwise shown, to be the finger-prints of the person against whom the previous conviction is sought to be proved are the finger-prints of the same person shall be evidence of the matter so certified.

(5) The method of proving a previous conviction authorised by this section shall be in addition to any other method of proving the conviction.

Note.—References to finger-prints include references to palm-prints (Criminal Justice Act 1967, s.33).

For another method of proving previous convictions, see the Police and Criminal Evidence Act 1984, s.73 (*infra*).

41.—(1) In any criminal proceedings, a certificate purporting to be signed by a constable, or by a person having the prescribed qualifications, and certifying that a plan or drawing exhibited thereto is a plan or drawing made by him of the place or object specified in the certificate, and that the plan or drawing is correctly drawn to a scale so specified, shall be evidence of the relative position of the things shown on the plan or drawing.

MAINTENANCE ORDERS ACT 1950

14 Geo. 6, c. 37

22.—(2) For the purposes of subsection (1) of the section, a court in any part of the United Kingdom may take notice of the law in force in any other part of the United Kingdom.

Note.—Subsection (1) deals with the variation of maintenance orders registered in courts of summary jurisdiction.

As the law in other parts of the United Kingdom is mainly foreign law, the provision above constitutes an exception of the general rule as to proof of foreign law. On judicial notice generally, see Part One, Chapter 7, (*supra*).

SEXUAL OFFENCES ACT 1956

4 & 5 Eliz. 2, c. 69

2.—(1) It is an offence for a person to procure a woman, by threats or intimidation, to have unlawful sexual intercourse in any part of the world.

(2) A person shall not be convicted of an offence under this section on the evidence of one witness only, unless the witness is corroborated in some material particular by evidence implicating the accused.

Note.—There is a similar provision on corroboration in section 3 (procurement of a woman by false pretences), 4 (administering drugs to obtain or facilitate intercourse), 22 (causing the prostitution of a woman) and 23 (procuration of a girl under 21 years of age).

47. Where in any of the foregoing sections the description of an offence is expressed to be subject to exceptions mentioned in the section, proof of the exception is to lie on the person relying on it.

Note.—See also the Magistrates' Courts Act 1980, s.101 (*infra*).

HOMICIDE ACT 1957

5 & 6 Eliz 2, c. 11

2.—(1) Where a person kills or is a party to the killing of another, he shall not be convicted of murder if he was suffering from such abnormality of mind (whether arising from a condition of arrested or retarded development of mind or any inherent causes or induced by disease or injury) as substantially impaired his mental responsibility for his acts and omissions in doing or being a party to the killing.

(2) On a charge of murder, it shall be for the defence to prove that the person charged is by virtue of this section not liable to be convicted of murder.

Note.—In *R.* v. *Dix* (1982) 74 Cr.App.R. 306 (C.A.) Shaw L.J. said (p.311) that "while the sub-section does not in terms require that medical evidence be adduced in support of a defence of diminished responsibility, it makes it a practical necessity if that defence is to begin to run at all."

As to the rebuttal of a plea of diminished responsibility see now the Criminal Procedure (Insanity) Act 1964, s.6 (*infra*).

As to the distinction regarding burden of proof between insanity and diminished responsibility, see *R.* v. *Burns* (1973) 58 Cr.App.R. 364 (C.A.) (Part One, Chapter 2, *supra*).

As to comment by the judge on the failure of the accused to give evidence on an issue of diminished responsibility, see *R.* v. *Bathurst* [1968] 2 Q.B. 99 (C.A.) (Part One, Chapter 8, *supra*).

4.—(1) It shall be manslaughter, and shall not be murder, for a person acting in pursuance of a suicide pact between him and another to kill the other or be a party to the other being killed by a third person.

(2) Where it is shown that a person charged with the murder of another killed the other or was a party to his being killed, it shall be for the defence to prove that the person charged was acting in pursuance of a suicide pact between him and the other.

OBSCENE PUBLICATIONS ACT 1959

7 & 8 ELIZ. 2, c. 66

4.—(1) Subject to subsection (1A) of this section a person shall not be convicted of an offence against section two of this Act, and an order for forfeiture shall not be made under the foregoing section, if it is proved that publication of the article in question is justified as being for the public good on the ground that it is in the interests of science, literature, art or learning, or of other objects of general concern.

(1A) Subsection (1) of this section shall not apply where the article in question is a moving picture film or soundtrack, but—

> (*a*) a person shall not be convicted of an offence against section 2 of this Act in relation to any such film or soundtrack, and
>
> (*b*) an order for forfeiture of any such film or soundtrack shall not be made under section 3 of this Act.

if it is proved that publication of the film or soundtrack is justified as being for the public good on the ground that it is in the interests of drama, opera, ballet or any other art, or of literature or learning.

(2) It is hereby declared that the opinion of experts as to the literary, artistic, scientific or other merits of an article may be admitted in any proceedings under this Act either to establish or to negative the said ground.

(3) In this section "moving picture soundtrack" means any sound record designed for playing with a moving picture film, whether incorporated with the film or not.

Note.—Section 2 makes the publication of an obscene article a statutory offence, in substitution of the common law on this subject; and the possession of an obscene article for publication for gain in an offence under the Obscene Publications Act 1964.

Subsections (1A) and (3) were introduced by the Criminal Law Act 1977, s.53(6) and (7).

For the interpretation of section 4 see *D.P.P.* v. *Jordan* [1977] A.C. 699 (H.L.) (Part One, Chapter 18, *supra*). Section 4(2) is without prejudice to the possibility of reception at common law of opinion evidence in relation to other issues: *D.P.P.* v. *A. and B.C. Chewing Gum Ltd.* [1968] 1 Q.B. 159 (D.C.).

CHILDREN AND YOUNG PERSONS ACT 1963

1963, c. 37

16.—(2) In any proceedings for an offence committed or alleged to have been committed by a person of or over the age of 21, any offence of which he was found guilty while under the age of 14 shall be disregarded for the purposes of any evidence relating to his previous convictions; and he shall not be asked, and if asked shall not be required to answer, any question relating to such an offence, notwithstanding that the question would otherwise be admissible under section 1 of the Criminal Evidence Act 1898.

Note.—For the Criminal Evidence Act 1898, see, *supra.*

26. In any proceedings, other than proceedings for an offence, before a juvenile court, and on any appeal from a decision of a juvenile court in any such proceedings, any document purporting to be a certificate of a fully registered medical practitioner as to any person's physical or mental condition shall be admissible as evidence of that condition.

LICENSING ACT 1964

1964, c. 26

196.—(1) Evidence that a transaction in the nature of a sale of intoxicating liquor took place shall, in any proceedings relating to an offence under this Act, be evidence of the sale of the liquor without proof that money passed.

(2) Evidence that consumption of intoxicating liquor was about to take place shall in any proceedings be evidence of the consumption of intoxicating liquor without proof of actual consumption.

(3) Evidence that any person, other than the occupier of licensed premises or a servant employed in licensed premises, or, as the case may be, other than the occupier of a licensed canteen or a servant employed in such a canteen consumed or intended to consume intoxicating liquor in the premises or, as the case may be, canteen, shall be evidence that the liquor was sold by or on behalf of the holder of the justices' licence occasional licence or canteen licence, as the case may be, to that person.

Note.—The words "be evidence" in subsection (3) mean shall be prima facie and rebuttable evidence: see *Harbottle* v. *Gill* (1877) 4 I.J.P. 742. Presumably the phrase has a similar meaning in subsections (1) and (2).

DIPLOMATIC PRIVILEGES ACT 1964

1964, c. 81

4. If in any proceedings any question arises whether or not any person is entitled to any privilege or immunity under this Act a certificate issued by or under the authority of the Secretary of State stating any fact relating to that question shall be conclusive evidence of that fact.

Note.—The Consular Relations Act 1968, s.11, and the International Organisations Act 1968, s.8, are similarly worded. See, too, the State Immunity Act 1978, s.21 (*infra*). See also Part One, Chapter 5 (*supra*).

CRIMINAL PROCEDURE (INSANITY) ACT 1964

1964, c. 84

6. Where on a trial for murder the accused contends—
  (*a*) that at the time of the alleged offence he was insane so as not to be responsible according to law for his actions; or
  (*b*) that at that time he was suffering from such abnormality of mind as is specified in subsection (1) of section 2 of the Homicide Act 1957 (diminished responsibility),
the court shall allow the prosecution to adduce or elicit evidence tending to prove the other of those contentions, and may give directions as to the stage of the proceedings at which the prosecution may adduce such evidence.

CRIMINAL PROCEDURE (ATTENDANCE OF WITNESSES) ACT 1965

1965, c. 69

1.—(1) A magistrates' court acting as examining justices shall in respect of each witness examined by the court, other than the accused and any witness of his merely to his character, make an order (in this Act referred to as a witness order) requiring him to attend and give evidence before the Crown Court.

(2) Where it appears to the court, after taking into account any representation made by the accused or the prosecutor, that the attendance at the trial of any witness is unnecessary on the ground that this evidence is unlikely to be required or is unlikely to be disputed, then—
  (*a*) any witness order to be made by the court in his case shall be a conditional order requiring him to attend the trial if notice in that behalf is given to him and not otherwise; and
  (*b*) if a witness order other than a conditional order has previously been made by the court in his case, the court shall direct that that order be treated as a conditional order.

(3) A magistrates' court on committing any person for trial shall inform him of his right to require the attendance at the trial of any witness in respect of whom a conditional witness order, or an order treated as a conditional witness order, has been made, and of the steps he must take for the purpose of enforcing the attendance.

Note.—For the scope of the inherent power of the judge to prevent a defendant from calling a witness who is not necessary to the defence, see *R.* v. *Morley* [1988] Q.B. 601 (C.A.).

Section 2 deals with the power to issue (for the purpose of criminal proceedings before the Crown Court) a witness summons requiring attendance. Section 3 provides for punishment for disobedience to a witness order or witness summons. Section 4 allows a High Court judge to issue a warrant for the arrest of a witness.

CRIMINAL JUSTICE ACT 1967

1967, c. 80

8.—A court or jury, in determining whether a person has committed an offence—

(a) shall not be bound in law to infer that he intended or foresaw a result of his action by reason only of its being a natural and probable consequence of those actions; but

(b) shall decide whether he did intend to foresee that result by reference to all the evidence, drawing such inferences from the evidence as appear proper in the circumstances.

9.—(1) In any criminal proceedings, other than committal proceedings, a written statement by any person shall, if such of the conditions mentioned in the next following subsection as are applicable are satisfied, be admissible as evidence to the like extent as oral evidence to the like effect by that person.

(2) The said conditions are—

(a) the statement purports to be signed by the person who made it;

(b) the statement contains a declaration by that person to the effect that it is true to the best of his knowledge and belief and that he made the statement knowing that, if it were tendered in evidence, he would be liable to prosecution if he wilfully stated in it anything which he knew to be false or did not believe to be true;

(c) before the hearing at which the statement is tendered in evidence, a copy of the statement is served, by or on behalf of the party proposing to tender it, on each of the other parties to the proceedings; and

(d) none of the other parties or their solicitors, within seven days from the service of the copy of the statement, serves a notice on the party so proposing objecting to the statements being tendered in evidence under this section:

Provided that the conditions mentioned in paragraphs (c) and (d) of this subsection shall not apply if the parties agree before or during the hearing the statement shall be so tendered.

Note.—For the position of an objecting party who has not complied with s.9(2)(d), see *Lister* v. *Quaife* [1983] 1 W.L.R. 48 (D.C.). See too comments of Stephen Brown J. at p. 55 on the desirability of calling oral evidence upon issues central to a contested case.

(3) The following provisions shall also have effect in relation to any written statement tendered in evidence under this section, that is to say—

(a) if the statement is made by a person under the age of 21, it shall give his age;

(b) if it is made by a person who cannot read it, it shall be read to him before he signs it and shall be accompanied by a declaration by the person who so read the statement to the effect that it was so read; and

(c) if it refers to any other document as an exhibit, the copy served on any other party to the proceedings under paragraph (c) of the last foregoing subsection shall be accompanied by a copy of that document or by such information as may be necessary in order to enable the party on whom it is served to inspect that document or a copy thereof.

(3A) In the case of a statement which indicates in pursuance of subsection (3)(a) of this section that the person making it has not attained the age of 14, subsection (2)(b) of this section have effect as if for the words from "made" onwards there were substituted the words "understands the importance of telling the truth in it."

(4) Notwithstanding that a written statement made by any person may be admissible as evidence by virtue of this section—

    (*a*) the party by whom or on whose behalf a copy of the statement was served may call that person to give evidence; and

    (*b*) the court may, of his own motion or on the application of any party to the proceedings, require that person to attend before the court and give evidence.

Note.—The section also contains further elaborate consequential provisions. Moreover, and for practical purposes most importantly, it must be read in the light of the *Practice Direction (Crimes: Evidence by Written Statements)* [1986] 1 W.L.R. 805. This deals with the preparation and editing of written statements tendered under section 9 (as well as with those tendered under the Magistrates' Courts Act 1980, s.102).

Section 9 applies to written statements made in Scotland and Northern Ireland: Criminal Justice Act 1972, s.46(1).

10.—(1) Subject to the provisions of this section, any fact of which oral evidence may be given in any criminal proceedings may be admitted for the purpose of those proceedings by or on behalf of the prosecutor or defendant, and the admission by any party of any such fact under this section shall as against that party be conclusive evidence in those proceedings of the fact admitted.

(2) An admission under this section—

    (*a*) may be made before or at the proceedings;

    (*b*) if made otherwise than in court, shall be in writing;

    (*c*) if made in writing by an individual, shall purport to be signed by the person making it and, if so made by a body corporate, shall purport to be signed by a director or manager, or the secretary or clerk, or some other similar officer of the body corporate;

    (*d*) if made on behalf of a defendant who is an individual, shall be made by his counsel or solicitor;

    (*e*) if made at any stage before the trial by a defendant who is an individual, must be approved by his counsel or solicitor (whether at the time it was made or subsequently) before or at the proceedings in question.

(3) An admission under this section for the purpose of proceedings relating to any matter shall be treated as an admission for the purpose of any subsequent criminal proceedings relating to that matter (including any appeal or retrial).

(4) An admission under this section may with the leave of the court be withdrawn in the proceedings for the purpose of which it is made or any subsequent criminal proceedings relating to the same matter.

Note.—As to formal admissions in Magistrates' Courts, see to the Magistrates' Courts Rules 1981, r. 71 (Part Three, *infra*).

11.—(1) On a trial on indictment the defendant shall not without the leave of the court adduce evidence in support of an alibi unless, before the end of the prescribed period, he gives notice of particulars of the alibi.

(4) Any evidence tendered to disprove an alibi may, subject to any directions by the court as to the time it is to be given, be given before or after evidence is given in support of the alibi.

Note.—This section also contains consequential provisions. The prescribed period is seven days from the end of the proceedings before the examining magistrates.

If prosecuting counsel wishes to put in a defendant's alibi notice as part of the Crown case, he should first give most careful consideration to what he is doing and should be prepared later to justify what he has done: *R.* v. *Watts* (1980) 71 Cr.App.R. 136 (C.A.).

For other aspects of the scope and operation of the section, see *R.* v. *Lewis* [1969] 2 Q.B. 1 (C.A.); *R.* v. *Sullivan* [1971] 1 Q.B. 253 (C.A.); and *R.* v. *Cooper* (1969) 79 Cr.App.R. 229 (C.A.).

89.—(1) If any person in a written statement tendered in evidence in criminal proceedings by virtue of section 9 of this Act, or in proceedings before a court-martial by virtue of the said section 9 as extended by section 12, *supra*, above or by section 99A of the Army Act 1955 or section 99A of the Air Force Act 1955, wilfully makes a statement material in those proceedings which he knows to be false or does not believe to be true, he shall be liable on conviction on indictment to imprisonment for a term not exceeding two years or a fine or both.

(2) The Perjury Act 1911 shall have effect as if this section were contained in that Act.

Note.—The section applies to written statements made in Scotland and Northern Ireland: Criminal Justice Act 1972, s.46(1). For the Perjury Act 1911 see *supra*.

CRIMINAL APPEAL ACT 1968

1968, c. 19

1.—(1) Subject to subsection (3) below a person convicted of an offence on indictment may appeal to the Court of Appeal against his conviction.

(2) The appeal may be—
  (*a*) on any ground which involves a question of law alone; and
  (*b*) with the leave of the Court of Appeal, on any ground which involves a question of fact alone, or a question of mixed law and fact, or on any other ground which appears to the Court of Appeal to be a sufficient ground of appeal;
but if the judge of the court of trial grants a certificate that the case is fit for appeal on a ground which involves a question of fact, or a question of mixed law and fact, an appeal lies under this section without the leave of the Court of Appeal.

(3) Where a person is convicted before the Crown Court of a scheduled offence it shall not be open to him to appeal to the Court of Appeal against conviction on the ground that the decision of the court which convicted him for trial as to the value involved was mistaken.

(4) In subsection (3) above "scheduled offence" and "the value involved" have the same meaning as they have in section 22 of the Magistrates' Courts Act 1980 (certain offences against the property to be tried summarily if value of property or damage is small).

Note.—This Act repeals the Criminal Appeal Act 1907, and some sections of the Criminal Appeal Acts of 1964 and 1966.

2.—(1) Except as provided by this Act, the Court of Appeal shall allow an appeal against conviction if they think—

(a) that the conviction should be set aside on the ground that under all the circumstances of the case it is unsafe or unsatisfactory; or

(b) that the judgment of the court of trial should be set aside on the ground of a wrong decision of any question of law; or

(c) that there was a material irregularity in the course of the trial, and in any other case shall dismiss the appeal:

Provided that the Court may, notwithstanding that they are of opinion that the point raised in the appeal might be decided in favour of the appellant, dismiss the appeal if they consider that no miscarriage of justice has actually occurred.

Note.—In subsection (1)(a) the word "conviction" was substituted for the words "verdict of the jury" by the Criminal Law Act 1977, s.44. This enables a person who has pleaded guilty to appeal against conviction. But the fact that a person has been found fit to plead and has pleaded guilty without equivocation after receiving expert advice may be relevant to the applicability of section 2(1)(a): *R.* v. *Lee* [1984] 1 W.L.R. 578 (C.A.); *R.* v. *Foster* [1985] 1 Q.B. 115 (C.A.)

(2) In the case of an appeal against conviction the Court shall, if they allow the appeal, quash the conviction.

(3) An order of the Court of Appeal quashing a conviction shall, except when under section 7 below the appellant is ordered to be retried, operate as a direction to the court of trial to enter, instead of the record of conviction, a judgment and verdict of acquittal.

7.—(1) Where the Court of Appeal allow an appeal against conviction and it appears to the Court that the interests of justice so require, they may order the appellant to be retried.

Note.—The limitation of this power to cases, in which the appeal is allowed only by reason of evidence received or available under section 23 (*infra*), was removed by the Criminal Jurisdiction Act 1988, s.43.

(2) A person shall not under this section be ordered to be retried for any offence other than—

(a) the offence of which he was convicted at the original trial and in respect of which his appeal is allowed as mentioned in subsection (1) above;

(b) an offence of which he could have been convicted at the original trial on an indictment for the first-mentioned offence; or

(c) an offence charged in an alternative count of the indictment in respect of which the jury were discharged from giving a verdict in consequence of convicting him of the first-mentioned offence.

23.—(1) For the purposes of this Part of this Act the Court of Appeal may, if they think it necessary or expedient in the interests of justice—

(a) order the production of any document, exhibit or other thing connected with the proceedings, the production of which appears to them necessary for the determination of the case;

(b) order any witness who would have been a compellable witness in the proceedings from which the appeal lies to attend for examination and be examined before the Court, whether or not he was called in those proceedings; and

(c) subject to subsection (3) below, receive the evidence, if tendered, of any witness.

(2) Without prejudice to subsection (1) above, where evidence is tendered to the Court of Appeal thereunder the Court shall, unless they are satisfied that the evidence, if received, would not afford any ground for allowing the appeal, exercise their power of receiving it if—

(a) it appears to them that the evidence is likely to be credible and would have been admissible in the proceedings from which the appeal lies on an issue which is the subject of the appeal; and

(b) they are satisfied that it was not adduced in those proceedings but there is a reasonable explanation for the failure to adduce it.

Note.—When the Court of Appeal hears fresh evidence the test (as to whether the appeal should be allowed) is whether the court has a reasonable doubt, not whether the jury might have reached a different conclusion if it heard the evidence: *R.* v. *Byrne* (1989) 88 Cr.App.R. 33 (C.A.).

Subsection (2) is mandatory and is important, when the evidence relates to an issue being raised for the first time in the Court of Appeal (see *R.* v. *Melville* [1976] 1 W.L.R. 181, 185 (C.A.)), and in cases where there is no reasonable explanation for failure to adduce the evidence at the trial (see, *e.g. R.* v. *Merry* (1970) 54 Cr.App.R. 274 (C.A.) and *R.* v. *Frankum* (1983) 5 Cr.App.R. (S); [1984] Crim.L.R. 434 (C.A.)).

For a case in which the accused had pleaded guilty, see *R.* v. *Lee* [1984] 1 W.L.R. 578; (1983) 79 Cr.App.R. 108 (C.A.). For a case in which he had been granted a free pardon, see *R.* v. *Foster* [1985] Q.B. 115 (C.A.).

(3) Subsection (1)(c) above applies to any witness (including the appellant) who is competent but not compellable, and applies also to the appellant's husband or wife where the appellant makes an application for that purpose and the evidence of the husband or wife could not have been given in the proceedings from which the appeal lies except on such an application.

(4) For purposes of this Part of this Act, the Court of Appeal may, if they think it necessary or expedient in the interests of justice, order the examination of any witness whose attendance might be required under subsection (1)(b) above to be conducted, in manner provided by rules of court, before any judge or officer of the Court or other person appointed by the Court for the purpose, and allow the admission of any depositions so taken as evidence before the Court.

THEFT ACT 1968

1968, c. 60

27.—(3) Where a person is being proceeded against for handling stolen goods (but not for any offence other than handling stolen goods), then at any stage of the proceedings, if evidence has been given of his having or arranging to have in his possession the goods the subject of the charge, or of his undertaking or assisting in, or arranging to undertake or assist in, their retention, removal, disposal or realisation, the following evidence shall be admissible for the purpose of proving that he knew or believed the goods to be stolen goods—

(a) evidence that he has had in his possession, or has undertaken or assisted in the retention, removal, disposal or realisation of, stolen goods from any theft taking place not earlier than twelve months before the offence charged; and

(b) (provided that seven days' notice in writing has been given to him of the intention to prove the conviction) evidence that he has within the five years preceding the date of the offence charged been convicted of theft or for handling stolen goods.

(4) In any proceedings for theft of any thing in the course of transmission (whether by post or otherwise), or for handling stolen goods from such a theft, a statutory declaration made by any person that he despatched or received or failed to receive any goods or postal packet, or that any goods or postal packet when despatched or received by him were in a particular state or condition, shall be admissible as evidence of the facts stated in the declaration, subject to the following conditions:—

(a) a statutory declaration shall only be admissible where and to the extent to which oral evidence to the like effect would have been admissible in the proceedings; and

(b) a statutory declaration shall only be admissible if at least seven days before the hearing or trial a copy of it has been given to the person charged, and he has not, at least three days before the hearing or trial or within such further time as the court may in special circumstances allow, given the prosecutor written notice requiring the attendance at the hearing or trial of the person making the declaration.

(5) This section is to be construed in accordance with section 24 of this Act; and in subsection (3)(b) above the reference to handling stolen goods shall include any corresponding offence committed before the commencement of this Act.

Note.—By section 22 a person handles stolen goods if (otherwise than in the course of stealing) knowingly or believing them to be stolen goods he dishonestly receives the goods, or dishonestly undertakes or assists in their retention, removal, disposal or realisation by or for the benefit of another person, or if he arranges to do so. Section 24 deals with the scope of offences relating to stolen goods.

Note that evidence admissible by virtue of section 27(3) may be used only on the issue of knowledge. A judge's failure to make this clear to the jury may constitute a misdirection. Moreover, the judge has an overriding discretion to exclude the evidence if it may be unduly prejudicial. See *R. v. Wilkins* (1975) 60 Cr.App.R. 300 (C.A.); see, too, *R. v. Perry* [1984] Crim.L.R. 680 (C.A.). Evidence that may be given under the subsection is limited to the fact that on the previous occasion the accused had been found in possession of stolen goods, etc., (or had been convicted of theft or of handling stolen goods). It does not extend, *e.g.* to evidence as to the circumstances, etc., of the finding or conviction: *R. v. Wood* [1987] 1 W.L.R. 779 (C.A.). See, too, *R. v. Fowler* (1988) 86 Cr.App.R. 219 (C.A.).

Section 27(3) has been described as "an object of practically unique curiosity, eccentric in conception, irresolute in its development, erratic of application, its adverse influence only contained by bold judicial contrivance" (Munday: [1988] Crim.L.R. 345, 354).

30.—(1) This Act shall apply in relation to the parties to a marriage, and to property belonging to the wife or husband whether or not by reason of an interest derived from the marriage, as it would apply if they were not married and any such interest subsisted independently of the marriage.

(2) Subject to subsection (4) below, a person shall have the same right to bring proceedings against that person's wife or husband for any

CIVIL EVIDENCE ACT 1968   599

offence (whether under this Act or otherwise) as if they were not
married, and a person bringing any such proceedings shall be competent
to give evidence for the prosecution at every stage of the proceedings.

Note.—Compare the Criminal Evidence Act 1898, s.1 (*supra*). Section 30(4) requires
that in certain circumstances the proceedings be instituted by or with the consent of the
Director of Public Prosecutions.

31.—(1) A person shall not be excused, by reason that to do so may
incriminate that person or the wife or husband of that person of an
offence under this Act—
  (*a*) from answering any question put to that person in proceedings
       for the recovery or administration of any property, for the
       execution of any trust or for an account of any property or
       dealings with property; or
  (*b*) from complying with any order made in any such proceedings;
but no statement or admission made by a person in answering a
question put or complying with an order made as aforesaid shall, in
proceedings or an offence under this Act, be admissible in evidence
against that person or (unless they married after the making of the
statement or admission) against the wife or husband of that person.

Note.—This subsection is made applicable to the Theft Act 1978 by section 5(2) of the
Act. See, too, the Supreme Court Act, 1981, s.72 (*infra*) and the Criminal Damage Act
1971, s.9 (*infra*) for similar provisions.
The scope of section 31 was considered in *Khan* v. *Khan* [1982] 2 All E.R. 60 (C.A.).

CIVIL EVIDENCE ACT 1968

1968, c. 64

Note.—Part I (ss.1–10) of this Act is based upon recommendations in the Thirteenth
Report of the Law Reform Committee (Cmnd. 2964). Sections 11, 12 and 13 give effect
with some modifications to the recommendations in the Committee's Fifteenth Report
(Cmnd. 3391), and subsequent sections embody various recommendations in the
Committee's Sixteenth Report (Cmnd. 3742). Part I and section 20(2) do not appear to
apply in bankruptcy proceedings. Moreover, although they now do apply in County Courts
and in the Mayor's and City of London Court (S.I. 1969 No. 1104; S.I. 1970 No. 18), they
do not yet apply in other inferior courts. In Magistrates' Courts, therefore, the
admissibility of hearsay evidence even in civil proceedings is governed by the common law
as modified by especially the Evidence Act 1938. The application of the 1968 Act has been
extended to proceedings before the Disciplinary Tribunal, which was established by the
Solicitors Act 1974, s.46, by the Solicitors (Disciplinary Proceedings) Rules 1975 (S.I. 1975
No. 727), r. 41.

Part I

Hearsay Evidence

Note.—For the extension of the application of this Part of the Act (except section 5) to
statements of opinion see the Civil Evidence Act 1972, s.1 (*infra*).
For a general survey of sections 1–10 of the 1968 Act itself, see Part One, Chapter 16
(*supra*).

1.—(1) In any civil proceedings a statement other than one made by a
person while giving oral evidence in those proceedings shall be

admissible as evidence of any fact stated therein to the extent that it is so admissible by virtue of any provision of this Part of this Act or by virtue of any other statutory provision or by agreement of the parties, but not otherwise.

(2) In this section "statutory provision" means any provision contained in, or in an instrument made under, this or any other Act, including any Act passed after this Act.

2.—(1) In any civil proceedings a statement made, whether orally or in a document or otherwise, by any person, whether called as a witness in those proceedings or not, shall, subject to this section and to rules of court, be admissible as evidence of any fact stated therein of which direct oral evidence by him would be admissible.

Note.—For the requirement that the maker of the statement have direct first-hand knowledge of the facts stated therein, see *Re Koscot Interplanetary (U.K.)*; *Re Koscot A.G.* [1972] 3 All E.R. 829 (Part One, Chapter 16, *supra*).

(2) Where in any civil proceedings a party desiring to give a statement in evidence by virtue of this section has called or intends to call as a witness in the proceedings the person by whom the statement was made, the statement—

(*a*) shall not be given in evidence by virtue of this section on behalf of the party without the leave of the court; and

(*b*) without prejudice to paragraph (*a*) above, shall not be given in evidence by virtue of this section on behalf of that party before the conclusion of the examination-in-chief of the person by whom it was made, except—

(*i*) where before that person is called the court allows evidence of the making of the statement to be given on behalf of that party by some other person; or

(*ii*) in so far as the court allows the person by whom the statement was made to narrate it in the course of his examination-in-chief on the ground that to prevent him from doing so would adversely affect the intelligibility of his evidence.

Note.—For a relaxation of the requirements of section 2(2) in relation to experts' reports see the Civil Evidence Act 1972, s.2 (*infra*).

As to section 2(2)(*a*), see *Morris* v. *Stratford on Avon R.D.C.* [1973] 1 W.L.R. 1059 (Part One, Chapter 16, *supra*).

(3) Where in any civil proceedings a statement which was made otherwise than in a document is admissible by virtue of this section, no evidence other than direct oral evidence by the person who made the statement or any person who heard or otherwise perceived it being made shall be admissible for the purpose of proving it:

Provided that if the statement in question was made by a person while giving oral evidence in some other legal proceedings (whether civil or criminal), it may be proved in any manner authorised by the court.

Note.—On the proviso to section 2(3) see *Tremelbye (Selangor) Ltd.* v. *Stekel* [1971] 1 W.L.R. 226 (Ch.D.). For an extension of section 2 to statements by deceased persons, see the Inheritance (Provision for Family and Dependants) Act 1975, s.21 (*infra*).

3.—(1) Where in any civil proceedings—
(*a*) a previous inconsistent or contradictory statement made by a person called as a witness in those proceedings is proved by virtue of section 3, 4 or 5 of the Criminal Procedure Act 1865; or
(*b*) a previous statement made by a person called as aforesaid is proved for the purpose of rebutting a suggestion that his evidence has been fabricated.

that statement shall by virtue of this subsection be admissible as evidence of any fact stated therein of which direct oral evidence by him would be admissible.

Note.—On the admissibility of a witness's prior consistent and inconsistent statements see Part One, Chapter 9 (*supra*).

(2) Nothing in this Act shall affect any of the rules of law relating to the circumstances in which, where a person called as a witness in any civil proceedings is cross-examined on a document used by him to refresh his memory, that document may be made evidence in those proceedings; and where a document or any part of a document is received in evidence in any such proceedings by virtue of any such rule of law, any statement made in that document or part by the person using the document to refresh his memory shall by virtue of this subsection be admissible as evidence of any fact stated therein of which direct oral evidence by him would be admissible.

Note.—On the use of a document to refresh a witness's memory see Part One, Chapter 9 (*supra*).

4.—(1) Without prejudice to section 5 of this Act, in any civil proceedings a statement contained in a document shall, subject to this section and to rules of court, be admissible as evidence of any fact stated therein of which direct oral evidence would be admissible, if the document is, or forms part of, a record compiled by a person acting under a duty from information which was supplied by a person (whether acting under a duty or not) who had, or may reasonably be supposed to have had, personal knowledge of the matters dealt with in that information and which, if not supplied by that person to the compiler of the record directly, was supplied by him to the compiler of the record indirectly through one or more intermediaries each acting under a duty.

Note.—For a case in which personal knowledge had to be presumed see *Knight* v. *David* [1971] 1 W.L.R. 1671, but contrast *Re Koscot Interplanetary (U.K.); Re Koscot A.G.* [1972] 3 All E.R. 829, both Part One, Chapter 16 (*supra*).
For the meaning of "record" see *H.* v. *Schering Chemicals* [1983] 1 W.L.R. 143 (Q.B.D.) (Part One, Chapter 16, *supra*).

(2) Where in any civil proceedings a party desiring to give a statement in evidence by virtue of this section has called or intends to call as a witness in the proceedings the person who originally supplied the information from which the record containing the statement was compiled, the statement—
(*a*) shall not be given in evidence by virtue of this section on behalf of that party without the leave of the court; and
(*b*) without prejudice to paragraph (*a*) above, shall not without the leave of the court be given in evidence by virtue of this

section on behalf of that party before the conclusion of the examination-in-chief of the person who originally supplied the said information.

(3) Any reference in this section to a person acting under a duty includes a reference to a person acting in the course of any trade, business, profession or other occupation in which he is engaged or employed or for the purposes of any paid or unpaid office held by him.

5.—(1) In any civil proceedings a statement contained in a document produced by a computer shall, subject to rules of court, be admissible as evidence of any fact stated therein of which direct oral evidence would be admissible, if it is shown that the conditions mentioned in subsection (2) below are satisfied in relation to the statement and computer in question.

(2) The said conditions are—

(a) that the document containing the statement was produced by the computer during a period over which the computer was used regularly to store or process information for the purposes of any activities regularly carried on over that period, whether for profit or not, by any body, whether corporate or not, or by any individual;

(b) that over that period there was regularly supplied to the computer in the ordinary course of those activities information of the kind contained in the statement or of the kind from which the information so contained is derived;

(c) that throughout the material part of that period the computer was operating properly or, if not, that any respect in which it was not operating properly or was out of operation during that part of that period was not such as to affect the production of the document or the accuracy of its contents; and

(d) that the information contained in the statement reproduces or is derived from information supplied to the computer in the ordinary course of those activities.

(3) Where over a period the function of storing or processing information for the purposes of any activities regularly carried on over that period as mentioned in subsection (2)(a) above was regularly performed by computers, whether—

(a) by a combination of computers operating over that period; or

(b) by different computers operating in succession over that period; or

(c) by different combinations of computers operating in succession over that period; or

(d) in any other manner involving the successive operation over that period, in whatever order, of one or more computers and one or more combinations of computers.

all the computers used for that purpose during that period shall be treated for the purposes of this Part of this Act as constituting a single computer; and references in this Part of this Act to a computer shall be construed accordingly.

(4) In any civil proceedings where it is desired to give a statement in evidence by virtue of this section, a certificate doing any of the following things, that is to say—

(a) identifying the document containing the statement and describing the manner in which it was produced;

(b) giving such particulars of any device involved in the production of that document as may be appropriate for the purpose of showing that the document was produced by a computer;

(c) dealing with any of the matters to which the conditions mentioned in subsection (2) above relate.

and purporting to be signed by a person occupying a responsible position in relation to the operation of the relevant device or the management of the relevant activities (whichever is appropriate) shall be evidence of any matter stated in the certificate; and for the purposes of this subsection it shall be sufficient for a matter to be stated to the best of the knowledge and belief of the person stating it.

(5) For the purposes of this Part of this Act—

(a) information shall be taken to be supplied to a computer if it is supplied thereto in any appropriate form and whether it is so supplied directly or (with or without human intervention) by means of any appropriate equipment;

(b) where, in the course of activities carried on by any individual or body, information is supplied with a view to its being stored or processed for the purposes of those activities by a computer operated otherwise than in the course of those activities, that information, if duly supplied to that computer, shall be taken to be supplied to it in the course of those activities;

(c) a document shall be taken to have been produced by a computer whether it was produced by it directly or (with or without human intervention) by means of any appropriate equipment.

(6) Subject to subsection (3) above, in this Part of this Act "computer" means any device for storing and processing information, and any reference to information being derived from other information is a reference to its being derived therefrom by calculation, comparison or any other process.

6.—(1) Where in civil proceedings a statement contained in a document is proposed to be given in evidence by virtue of section 2, 4 or 5 of this Act it may, subject to any rules of court, be proved by the production of that document or (whether or not that document is still in existence) by the production of a copy of that document, or of the material part thereof, authenticated in such manner as the court may approve.

(2) For the purpose of deciding whether or not a statement is admissible in evidence by virtue of section 2, 4 or 5 of this Act, the court may draw any reasonable inference from the circumstances in which the statement was made or otherwise came into being or from any other circumstances, including, in the case of a statement contained in a document, the form and contents of that document.

(3) In estimating the weight, if any, to be attached to a statement admissible in evidence by virtue of sections 2, 3, 4, or 5 of this Act regard shall be had to all the circumstances from which any inference can reasonably be drawn as to the accuracy or otherwise of the statement and, in particular—

(a) in the case of a statement falling within sections 2(1) or 3(1) or (2) of this Act, to the question whether or not the statement was made contemporaneously with the occurrence or existence of the facts stated, and to the question whether or not the maker of the statement had any incentive to conceal or misrepresent the facts;

(*b*) in the case of a statement falling within section 4(1) of this Act, to the question whether or not the person who originally supplied the information from which the record containing the statement was compiled did so contemporaneously with the occurrence or existence of the facts dealt with in that information, and to the question whether or not that person, or any person concerned with compiling or keeping the record containing the statement, had any incentive to conceal or misrepresent the facts; and

(*c*) in the case of a statement falling within section 5(1) of this Act, to question whether or not the information which the information contained in the statement reproduces or is derived from was supplied to the relevant computer, or recorded for the purpose of being supplied thereto, contemporaneously with the occurrence or existence of the facts dealt with in that information, and to the question whether or not any person concerned with the supply of information to that computer or with the operation of that computer or any equipment by means of which the document containing the statement was produced by it, had any incentive to conceal or misrepresent the facts.

(4) For the purpose of any enactment or rule of law or practice requiring evidence to be corroborated or regulating the manner in which uncorroborated evidence is to be treated—

(*a*) a statement which is admissible in evidence by virtue of section 2 or 3 of this Act shall not be capable of corroborating evidence given by the maker of the statement; and

(*b*) a statement which is admissible in evidence by virtue of section 4 of this Act shall not be capable of corroborating evidence given by the person who originally supplied the information from which the record containing the statement was compiled.

(5) If any person in a certificate tendered in evidence in civil proceedings by virtue of section 5(4) of this Act wilfully makes a statement material in those proceedings which he knows to be false or does not believe to be true, he shall be liable on conviction on indictment to imprisonment for a term not exceeding two years or a fine or both.

7.—(1) Subject to rules of court, where in any civil proceedings a statement made by a person who is not called as a witness in those proceedings is given in evidence by virtue of section 2 of this Act—

(*a*) any evidence which, if that person had been so called would be admissible for the purpose of destroying or supporting his credibility as a witness shall be admissible for that purpose in those proceedings; and

(*b*) evidence tending to prove that, whether before or after he made that statement, that person made (whether orally or in a document or otherwise) another statement inconsistent therewith shall be admissible for the purpose of showing that that person has contradicted himself:

Provided that nothing in this subsection shall enable evidence to be given of any matter of which, if the person in question had been called as a witness and had denied that matter in cross-examination, evidence could not have been adduced by the cross-examining party.

(2) Subsection (1) above shall apply in relation to a statement given in evidence by virtue of section 4 of this Act as it applies in relation to a statement given in evidence by virtue of section 2 of this Act, except that references to the person who made the statement and to his making the statement shall be construed respectively as references to the person who originally supplied the information from which the record containing the statement was compiled and to his supplying that information.

(3) Section 3(1) of this Act shall apply to any statement proved by virtue of subsection (1)(*b*) above as it applies to a previous inconsistent or contradictory statement made by a person called as a witness which is proved as mentioned in paragraph (*a*) of the said section 3(1).

8.—(1) Provision shall be made by rules of court as to the procedure which, subject to any exceptions provided for in the rules, must be followed and the other conditions which, subject as aforesaid, must be fulfilled before a statement can be given in evidence in civil proceedings by virtue of section 2, 4, or 5 of this Act.

Note.—For the relevant Rules see R.S.C., Ord. 38, rr. 20–34 (Part Three, *infra*).

(2) Rules of court made in pursuance of subsection (1) above shall in particular, subject to such exceptions (if any) as may be provided for in the rules—

(*a*) require a party to any civil proceedings who desires to give in evidence any such statement as is mentioned in that subsection to give to every other party to the proceedings such notice of his desire to do so and such particulars of or relating to the statement as may be specified in the rules, including particulars of such one or more of the persons connected with the making or recording of the statement or, in the case of a statement falling within section 5(1) of this Act, such one or more of the persons concerned as mentioned in section 6(3)(*c*) of this Act as the rules may in any case require; and

(*b*) enable any party who receives such notice as aforesaid by counter-notice to require any person of whom particulars were given with the notice to be called as a witness in the proceedings unless that person is dead, or beyond the seas, or unfit by reason of his bodily or mental condition to attend as a witness, or cannot with reasonable diligence be identified or found, or cannot reasonably be expected (having regard to the time which has elapsed since he was connected or concerned as aforesaid and to all the circumstances) to have any recollection of matters relevant to the accuracy or otherwise of the statement.

Note.—See *Rasool* v. *West Midlands Passenger Transport Executive* [1974] 3 All E.R. 638 and *Piermay Shipping Co.* v. *Chester* [1978] 1 W.L.R. 411 (C.A.) (both Part One, Chapter 16, *supra*).

(3) Rules of court made in pursuance of subsection (1) above—

(*a*) may confer on the court in any civil proceedings a discretion to allow a statement falling within sections 2(1), 4(1) or 5(1) of this Act to be given in evidence notwithstanding that any requirement of the rules affecting the admissibility of that statement has not been complied with, but except in pursuance of paragraph (*b*) below shall not confer on the court a discretion to exclude such a statement where the requirements of the rules affecting its admissibility have been complied with;

(*b*) may confer on the court power, where a party to any civil proceedings has given notice that he desires to give in evidence—

(*i*) a statement falling within section 2(1) of this Act which was made by a person, whether orally or in a document, in the course of giving evidence in some other legal proceedings (whether civil or criminal); or

(*ii*) a statement falling within section 4(1) of this Act which is contained in a record of any direct oral evidence given in some other legal proceedings (whether civil or criminal).

to give directions on the application of any party to the proceedings as to whether, and if so on what conditions, the party desiring to give the statement in evidence will be permitted to do so and (where applicable) as to the manner in which that statement and any other evidence given in those other proceedings is to be proved; and

(*c*) may make different provisions for different circumstances, and in particular may make different provisions with respect to statements falling within sections 2(1), 4(1) and 5(1) of this Act respectively;

and any discretion conferred on the court by rules of court made as aforesaid may be either a general discretion or a discretion exercisable only in such circumstances as may be specified in the rules.

Note.—For the manner of exercise of the discretion conferred by s.8(3)(*a*) see *Ford* v. *Lewis* [1971] 1 W.L.R. 623 (C.A.) and *Morris* v. *Stratford U.D.C.* [1973] 1 W.L.R. 1059 (C.A.) (both Part One, Chapter 16, *supra*).

(4) Rules of court may make provision for preventing a party to any civil proceedings (subject to any exceptions provided for in the rules) from adducing in relation to a person who is not called as a witness in those proceedings any evidence which could otherwise be adduced by him by virtue of section 7 of this Act unless that party has in pursuance of the rules given in respect of that person such a counter-notice as is mentioned in subsection (2)(*b*) above.

(5) In deciding for the purposes of any rules of court made in pursuance of this section whether or not a person is fit to attend as a witness, a court may act on a certificate purporting to be a certificate of a fully registered medical practitioner.

(6) Nothing of the foregoing provisions of this section shall prejudice the generality of section 75 of the County Courts Act 1984, section 144 of the Magistrates' Courts Act 1980 or any other enactment conferring power to make rules of court; and nothing in section 75(2) of the County Courts Act 1984 or any other enactment restricting the matters with respect to which rules of court may be made shall prejudice the making of rules of court with respect to any matter mentioned in the foregoing provisions of this section or the operation of any rules of court made with respect to any such matter.

Note.—For modification of some of the requirements of section 8 in relation to reports of experts see the Civil Evidence Act 1972, s.2 (*infra*).

9.—(1) In any civil proceedings a statement which, if this Part of this Act had not been passed, would by virtue of any rule of law mentioned in subsection (2) below have been admissible as evidence of any fact stated therein shall be admissible as evidence of that fact by virtue of this subsection.

(2) The rules of law referred to in subsection (1) above are the following, that is to say any rule of law—

(a) whereby in any civil proceedings an admission adverse to a party to the proceedings, whether made by that party or by another person, may be given in evidence against that party for the purpose of proving any fact stated in the admission;

(b) whereby in any civil proceedings published works dealing with matters of a public nature (for example, histories, scientific works, dictionaries and maps) are admissible as evidence of facts of a public nature stated therein;

(c) whereby in any civil proceedings public documents (for example, public registers, and returns made under public authority with respect to matters of public interest) are admissible as evidence of facts stated therein; or

(d) whereby in any civil proceedings records (for example, the records of certain courts, treaties, Crown grants, pardons and commissions) are admissible as evidence of facts stated therein.

In this subsection "admission" includes any representation of fact, whether made in words or otherwise.

(3) In any civil proceedings a statement which tends to establish reputation or family tradition with respect to any matter and which, if this Act had not been passed, would have been admissible in evidence by virtue of any rule of law mentioned in subsection (4) below—

(a) shall be admissible in evidence by virtue of this paragraph in so far as it is not capable of being rendered admissible under sections 2 or 4 of this Act; and

(b) if given in evidence under this Part of this Act (whether by virtue of paragraph (a) above or otherwise) shall by virtue of this paragraph be admissible as evidence of the matter reputed or handed down;

and, without prejudice to paragraph (b) above, reputation shall for the purposes of this Part of this Act be treated as a fact and not as a statement or multiplicity of statements dealing with the matter reputed.

(4) The rules of law referred to in subsection (3) above are the following, that is to say any rule of law—

(a) whereby in any civil proceedings evidence of a person's reputation is admissible for the purpose of establishing his good or bad character;

(b) whereby in any civil proceedings involving a question of pedigree or in which the existence of a marriage is in issue evidence of reputation or family tradition is admissible for the purpose of proving or disproving pedigree or the existence of the marriage, as the case may be; or

(c) whereby in any civil proceedings evidence of reputation or family tradition is admissible for the purpose of proving or disproving the existence of any public or general right or of identifying any person or thing.

(5) It is hereby declared that in so far as any statement is admissible in any civil proceedings by virtue of subsection (1) or (3)(*a*) above, it may be given in evidence in those proceedings notwithstanding anything in sections 2 to 7 of this Act or in any rules of court made in pursuance of section 8 of this Act.

(6) The words in which any rule of law mentioned in subsection (2) or (4) above is there described are intended only to identify the rule in question and shall not be construed as altering that rule in any way.

10.—(1) In this Part of this Act—

"computer" has the meaning assigned by section 5 of this Act;

"document" includes, in addition to a document in writing—

(*a*) any map, plan, graph or drawing;

(*b*) any photograph;

(*c*) any disc, tape, sound track or other device in which sounds or other data (not being visual images) are embodied so as to be capable (with or without the aid of some other equipment) of being reproduced therefrom; and

(*d*) any film, negative, tape or other device in which one or more visual images are embodied so as to be capable (as aforesaid) of being reproduced therefrom;

"film" includes a microfilm;

"statement" includes any representation of fact, whether made in words or otherwise.

(2) In this Part of this Act any reference to a copy of a document includes—

(*a*) in the case of a document falling within paragraph (*c*) but not (*d*) of the definition of "document" in the foregoing subsection, a transcript of the sounds or other data embodied therein;

(*b*) in the case of a document falling within paragraph (*d*) but not (*c*) of that definition, a reproduction or still reproduction of the image or images embodied therein, whether enlarged or not;

(*c*) in the case of a document falling within both those paragraphs, such a transcript together with such a still reproduction; and

(*d*) in the case of a document not falling within the said paragraph (*d*) of which a visual image is embodied in a document falling within that paragraph, a reproduction of that image, whether enlarged or not.

and any reference to a copy of the material part of a document shall be construed accordingly.

(3) For the purposes of the application of this Part of this Act in relation to any such civil proceedings as are mentioned in section 18(1)(*a*) and (*b*) of this Act, other than civil proceedings on a reference or arbitration under section 64 of the County Courts Act 1984, any rules of court made for the purposes of this Act under section 99 of the Supreme Court of Judicature (Consolidation) Act 1925 shall (except in so far as their operation is excluded by agreement) apply, subject to such modifications as may be appropriate, in like manner as they apply in relation to civil proceedings in the High Court:

(3A) For the purposes of the application of this part of this Act in relation to proceedings on an arbitration under section 64 of the County Courts Act 1984 any rules made for the purposes of this Act under section 75 of that Act shall (except in so far as their operation is precluded by agreement) apply, subject to such modifications as may be appropriate, in like manner as they apply in relation to proceedings in the County Court.

Note.—The Supreme Court of Judicature (Consolidation) Act 1925, s.99, was repealed by the Supreme Court Act 1981. See now ss.84 and 85 of that Act.

(4) If any question arises as to what are, for the purposes of any such civil proceedings as are mentioned in section 18(1)(*a*) or (*b*) of this Act, the appropriate modifications of any such rule of court as is mentioned in sub-section (3) above, that question shall, in default of agreement, be determined by the tribunal or the arbitrator or umpire, as the case may be.

PART II

MISCELLANEOUS AND GENERAL

Note.—On sections 11–13 of the Act see Part One, Chapter 19, *supra*. Note, too, that the provisions of these sections with regard to previous convictions must be read subject to the Rehabilitation of Offenders Act 1974 (Part Two, *infra*).

On various points dealt with in sections 14–16 see Part One, Chapter 11, *supra*.

11.—(1) In any civil proceedings the fact that a person has been convicted of an offence by or before any court in the United Kingdom or by a court-martial there or elsewhere shall (subject to subsection (3) below) be admissible in evidence for the purpose of proving, where to do so is relevant to any issue in those proceedings, that he committed that offence, whether he was so convicted upon plea of guilty or otherwise and whether or not he is a party to the civil proceedings; but no conviction other than a subsisting one shall be admissible in evidence by virtue of this section.

Note.—See R.S.C., Ord. 18, r. 7A (Part Three, *infra*). For meaning of "subsisting" see *In re Raphael, dec'd.* [1973] 1 W.L.R. 998 (Part One, Chapter 19, *supra*). In *Union Carbide Corporation* v. *Naturin* [1987] F.S.R. 538 the Court of Appeal held that the section did not apply to convictions in a French court.

For the position in criminal proceedings see the Police and Criminal Evidence Act 1984, ss.73–75 (*infra*).

(2) In any civil proceedings in which by virtue of this section a person is proved to have been convicted of an offence by or before any court in the United Kingdom or by a court-martial there or elsewhere—

(*a*) he shall be taken to have committed that offence unless the contrary is proved; and

(*b*) without prejudice to the reception of any other admissible evidence for the purpose of identifying the facts on which the conviction was based, the contents of any document which is admissible as evidence of the conviction, and the contents of the information, complaint, indictment or charge-sheet on which the person in question was convicted, shall be admissible in evidence for that purpose.

Note.—For significance of section 11(2)(*a*) see *Stupple* v. *Royal Insurance Co. Ltd.* [1971] 1 Q.B. 50 (C.A.) (Part One, Chapter 19, *supra*). See, too, dicta of Lord Diplock on sections 11 and 13 in *Hunter* v. *Chief Constable of West Midlands Police* [1982] A.C. 529 (H.L.) at pp. 543–544.

(3) Nothing in this section shall prejudice the operation of section 13 of this Act or any other enactment whereby a conviction or a finding of fact in any criminal proceedings is for the purposes of any other proceedings made conclusive evidence of any fact.

(4) Where in any civil proceedings the contents of any document are admissible in evidence by virtue of subsection (2) above, a copy of that document, or of the material part thereof, purporting to be certified or otherwise authenticated by or on behalf of the court or authority having custody of that document shall be admissible in evidence and shall be taken to be a true copy of that document or part unless the contrary is shown.

(5) Nothing in any of the following enactments, that is to say—
  (*a*) section 13 of the Powers of Criminal Courts Act 1973 (under which a conviction leading to probation or discharge is to be disregarded except as therein mentioned);
  (*b*) section 9 of the Criminal Justice (Scotland) Act 1949 (which makes similar provision in respect of convictions on indictment in Scotland); and
  (*c*) section 8 of the Probation Act (Northern Ireland) 1950 (which corresponds to the said section 12) or any corresponding enactment of the Parliament of Northern Ireland for the time being in force,
shall affect the operation of this section; and for the purposes of this section any order made by a court of summary jurisdiction in Scotland under section 1 or section 2 of the said Act of 1949 shall be treated as a conviction.

(6) In this section "court-martial" means a court-martial constituted under the Army Act 1955, the Air Force Act 1955 or the Naval Discipline Act 1957 or a disciplinary court constituted under section 50 of the said Act of 1957, and in relation to a court-martial "conviction," as regards a court-martial constituted under either of the said Acts of 1955, means a finding of guilty which is, or falls to be treated as, a finding of the court duly confirmed and, as regards a court-martial or disciplinary court constituted under the said Act of 1957, means a finding of guilty which is, or falls to be treated as, the finding of the court, and "convicted" shall be construed accordingly.

12.—(1) In any civil proceedings—
  (*a*) the fact that a person has been found guilty of adultery in any matrimonial proceedings; and
  (*b*) the fact that a person has been found to be the father of a child in relevant proceedings before any court in England and Wales or has been adjudged to be the father of a child in affiliation proceedings before any court in the United Kingdom,
shall (subject to subsection (3) below) be admissible in evidence for the purpose of proving, where to do so is relevant to any issue in those civil proceedings, that he committed the adultery to which the finding relates or, as the case may be, is (or was) the father of that child, whether or not he offered any defence to the allegation of adultery or paternity and whether or not he is a party to the civil proceedings; but no finding or

adjudication other than a subsisting one shall be admissible in evidence by virtue of this section.

(2) In any civil proceedings in which by virtue of this section a person is proved to have been found guilty of adultery as mentioned in subsection (1)(*a*) above or to have been found or adjudged to be the father of a child as mentioned in subsection (1)(*b*) above—

(*a*) he shall be taken to have committed the adultery to which the finding relates or, as the case may be, to be (or have been) the father of that child, unless the contrary is proved; and

(*b*) without prejudice to the reception of any other admissible evidence for the purpose of identifying the facts on which the finding or adjudication was based, the contents of any document which was before the court, or which contains any pronouncement of the court, in the other proceedings in question shall be admissible in evidence for that purpose.

(3) Nothing in this section shall prejudice the operation of any enactment whereby a finding of fact in any matrimonial or affiliation proceedings is for the purposes of any other proceedings made conclusive evidence of any fact.

(4) Subsection (4) of section 11 of this Act shall apply for the purposes of this section as if the reference to subsection (2) were a reference to subsection (2) of this section.

(5) In this section—

"matrimonial proceedings" means any matrimonial cause in the High Court or a county court in England and Wales or in the High Court in Northern Ireland, any consistorial action in Scotland, or any appeal arising out of any such cause or action;

"relevant proceedings" means [any proceedings brought by public bodies].

"affiliation proceedings" means, in relation to Scotland, any action of affiliation and aliment;

and in this subsection "consistorial action" does not include an action of aliment only between husband and wife raised in the Court of Session or an action of interim aliment raised in the sheriff court.

Note.—Section 12 was amended by the Family Law Reform Act 1987, s.29.

13.—(1) In an action for libel or slander in which the question whether a person did or did not commit a criminal offence is relevant to an issue arising in the action, proof that, at the time when that issue falls to be determined, that person stands convicted of that offence shall be conclusive evidence that he committed that offence; and his conviction thereof shall be admissible in evidence accordingly.

(2) In any such action as aforesaid in which by virtue of this section a person is proved to have been convicted of an offence, the contents of any document which is admissible as evidence of the conviction, and the contents of the information, complaint, indictment or charge-sheet on which that person was convicted, shall, without prejudice to the reception of any other admissible evidence for the purpose of identifying the facts on which the conviction was based, be admissible in evidence for the purpose of identifying those facts.

(3) For the purposes of this section a person shall be taken to stand convicted of an offence if but only if there subsists against him a conviction of that offence by or before a court in the United Kingdom or by a court-martial there or elsewhere.

(4) Subsections (4) to (6) of section 11 of this Act shall apply for the purposes of this section as they apply for the purposes of that section, but as if in the said subsection (4) the reference to subsection (2) were a reference to subsection (2) of this section.

Note.—An effect of this section is to reverse decisions such as that in *Hinds* v. *Sparks* [1964] Crim.L.R. 717 (Part One, Chapter 19, *supra*), but decisions such as that in *Loughrans* v. *Odham's Press* [1963] C.L.Y. 2007 (Part One, Chapter 19, *supra*) are unaffected. Contrast the recommendation of the Law Reform Committee (15th Report (1967) Cmnd. 3391), para. 41(9): "... in defamation actions, where the statement complained of alleges that the plaintiff had been guilty of a criminal offence, proof that he has been convicted of that offence and that the conviction has not been set aside should be conclusive evidence of his guilt, and proof that he was acquitted of that offence should be conclusive evidence of his innocence."

14.—(1) The right of a person in any legal proceedings other than criminal proceedings to refuse to answer any question or produce any document or thing if to do so would tend to expose that person to proceedings for an offence or for the recovery of a penalty—

  (*a*) shall apply only as regards criminal offences under the law of any part of the United Kingdom and penalties provided for by such law; and

  (*b*) shall include a like right to refuse to answer any question or produce any document or thing if to do so would tend to expose the husband or wife of that person to proceedings for any such criminal offence or for the recovery of any such penalty.

Note.—A penalty in this section includes, not only a penalty imposed as a result of proceedings, but also a penalty imposed by administrative action and recoverable by proceedings. See *In re Westinghouse Uranium Contract* [1978] A.C. 547 (H.L.). Proceedings for committal for contempt of court are not "criminal" proceedings nor are they covered by the word "penalty": *Garvin* v. *Domus Publishing Ltd.* [1989] Ch. 335 (Ch.D.).

In *Arab Monetary Fund* v. *Hashim* [1989] 1 W.L.R. 565 (Ch.D.) it was indicated that, although the Act makes it clear that in civil cases there is no privilege against self-incrimination in relation to possible criminal offences under non-U.K. law, the possibility of such self-incrimination is a factor which could be taken into account in the exercise of a court's discretionary power to grant an interlocutory injunction under the Supreme Court Act 1981, s. 37.

The common law position (which still obtains in criminal law proceedings) relating to questions the answer to which would tend to incriminate a spouse is not clear.

(2) In so far as any existing enactment conferring (in whatever words) powers of inspection or investigation confers on a person (in whatever words) any right otherwise than in criminal proceedings to refuse to answer any question or give any evidence tending to incriminate that person, subsection (1) above shall apply to that right as it applies to the right described in that subsection; and every such existing enactment shall be construed accordingly.

(3) In so far as any existing enactment provides (in whatever words) that in any proceedings other than criminal proceedings a person shall not be excused from answering any question or giving any evidence on the ground that to do so may incriminate that person, that enactment shall be construed as providing also that in such proceedings a person shall not be excused from answering any question or giving any

evidence on the ground that to do so may incriminate the husband or wife of that person.

(4) Where any existing enactment (however worded) that—
    (*a*) confers powers of inspection or investigation; or
    (*b*) provides as mentioned in subsection (3) above,
further provides (in whatever words) that any answer or evidence given by a person shall not be admissible in evidence against that person in any proceedings or class of proceedings (however described, and whether criminal or not), that enactment shall be construed as providing also that any answer or evidence given by that person shall not be admissible in evidence against the husband or wife of that person in the proceedings or class of proceedings in question.

(5) In this section "existing enactment" means any enactment passed before this Act; and the references to giving evidence are references to giving evidence in any manner, whether by furnishing information, making discovery, producing documents or otherwise.

15. [This section was repealed by the Patents Act 1977, s.132(7), Sched. 6. See now the Copyright, Designs and Patents Act 1988, s.280 (*infra*)].

16.—(1) The following rules of law are hereby abrogated except in relation to criminal proceedings, that is to say—
    (*a*) the rule whereby, in any legal proceedings, a person cannot be compelled to answer any question or produce any document or thing if to do so would tend to expose him to a forfeiture; and
    (*b*) the rule whereby, in any legal proceedings, a person other than a party to the proceedings cannot be compelled to produce any deed or other document relating to his title to any land.

(2) The rule of law whereby, in any civil proceedings, a party to the proceedings cannot be compelled to produce any document relating solely to his own case and in no way tending to impeach that case or support the case of any opposing party is hereby abrogated.

(3) and (4) [These subsections respectively abrogate in civil cases the privileges relating to marital communications and to marital intercourse. For corresponding abrogation in criminal cases see the Police and Criminal Evidence Act 1984, s.80(9) and Sched. 7].

(5) A witness in any proceedings instituted in consequence of adultery, whether a party to the proceedings or not, shall not be excused from answering any question by reason that it tends to show that he or she has been guilty of adultery.

17.—(1) In relation to England and Wales—
    (*a*) section 1(3) of the Tribunals of Inquiry (Evidence) Act 1921 (under which a witness before a tribunal to which that Act has been applied is entitled to the same privileges as if he were a witness before the High Court) shall have effect as if after the word "witness," in the second place where it occurs, there were inserted the words "in civil proceedings"; and
    (*b*) section 8(5) of the Parliamentary Commissioner Act 1967 (which provides that, subject as there mentioned, no person shall be compelled for the purposes of an investigation under that Act to give any evidence or produce any document which he could not be compelled to give or produce in proceedings before the High Court) shall have effect as if before the word "proceedings" there were inserted the word "civil";

and, so far as it applies to England and Wales, any other existing enactment, however framed or worded, which in relation to any tribunal, investigation or inquiry (however described) confers on persons required to answer questions or give evidence any privilege described by reference to the privileges of witnesses in proceedings before any court shall, unless the contrary intention appears, be construed as referring to the privileges of witnesses in civil proceedings before that court.

Note.—Section 17(2) was repealed by the Evidence (Proceedings in Other Jurisdictions) Act 1977, s.8(2), Sched. 2.

(3) Without prejudice to the generality of subsections (2) to (4) of section 14 of this Act, the enactments mentioned in the Schedule to this Act shall have effect subject to the amendments provided for by that Schedule (being verbal amendments to bring those enactments into conformity with the provisions of that section).

(4) Subsection (5) of section 14 of this Act shall apply for the purposes of this section as it applies for the purposes of that section.

18.—(1) In this Act "civil proceedings" includes, in addition to civil proceedings in any of the ordinary courts of law—

(*a*) civil proceedings before any other tribunal, being proceedings in relation to which the strict rules of evidence apply; and

(*b*) an arbitration or reference, whether under an enactment or not, but does not include civil proceedings in relation to which the strict rules of evidence do not apply.

Note.—The enforcement of an interlocutory order made in civil proceedings to protect one of the parties to the action is properly classified as a civil proceeding within section 18(1)(*a*) even if the remedy sought is punitive and the burden of proof is that applicable in criminal proceedings: *Savings and Investment Bank Ltd.* v. *Gasco Investments (Netherlands) B.V. (No. 2)* [1988] Ch. 422 (C.A.).

Contrary to earlier assumptions it has now been made clear that courts hearing custody or access applications are not conducting "civil proceedings in relation to which the strict rules of evidence do not apply" within section 18(1)(*b*): *Re H; Re K* (1989) 139 New L.J. 864 (C.A.).

(2) In this Act—

"court" does not include a court-martial, and, in relation to an arbitration or reference, means the arbitrator or umpire and, in relation to proceedings before a tribunal (not being one of the ordinary courts of law), means the tribunal;

"legal proceedings" includes an arbitration or reference, whether under an enactment or not;

and for the avoidance of doubt it is hereby declared that in this Act, and in any amendment made by this Act in any other enactment, references to a person's husband or wife do not include references to a person who is no longer married to that person.

(3) Any reference in this Act to any other enactment is a reference thereto as amended, and includes a reference thereto as applied, by or under any other enactment.

(4) Nothing in this Act shall prejudice the operation of any enactment which provides (in whatever words) that any answer or evidence given by a person in specified circumstances shall not be admissible in evidence against him or some other person in any proceedings or class of proceedings (however described).

In this subsection the reference to giving evidence is a reference to giving evidence in any manner, whether by furnishing information, making discovery, producing documents or otherwise.

(5) Nothing in this Act shall prejudice—

(*a*) any power of a court, in any legal proceedings, to exclude evidence (whether by preventing questions from being put or otherwise) at its discretion; or

(*b*) the operation of any agreement (whenever made) between the parties to any legal proceedings as to the evidence which is to be admissible (whether generally or for any particular purpose) in those proceedings.

(6) It is hereby declared that where, by reason of any defect of speech or hearing from which he is suffering, a person called as a witness in any legal proceedings gives his evidence in writing or by signs, that evidence is to be treated for the purposes of this Act as being given orally.

FAMILY LAW REFORM ACT 1969

1969, c. 46

20.—(1) In any civil proceedings in which the parentage of any person falls to be determined, the court may, either of its own motion or on an application by any party to the proceedings, give a direction—

(a) for the use of scientific tests to ascertain whether such tests show that a party to the proceedings is or is not the father or mother of that person; and

(b) for the taking, within a period specified in the direction, of bodily samples from all or any of the following, namely, that person, any party who is alleged to be the father or mother of that person and any other party to the proceedings;

and the court may at any time revoke or vary a direction previously given by it under this subsection.

(2) The person responsible for carrying out scientific tests in pursuance of a direction under subsection (1) above shall make to the court a report in which he shall state—

(a) the results of the tests;

(b) whether any party to whom the report relates is or is not excluded by the results from being the father or mother of the person whose parentage is to be determined; and

(c) in relation to any party who is not so excluded, the value, if any, of the results in determining whether that party is the father or mother of that person;

and the report shall be received by the court as evidence in the proceedings of the matters stated in it.

(2A) Where the proceedings in which the parentage of any person falls to be determined are proceedings on an application under section 56 of the Family Law Act 1986, any reference in subsection (1) or (2) of this section to any party to the proceedings shall include a reference to any person named in the application.

(3) A report under subsection (2) of this section shall be in the form prescribed by regulations made under section 22 of this Act.

(4) Where a report has been made to a court under subsection (2) of this section, any party may, with the leave of the court, or shall, if the court so directs, obtain from the person who made the report a written

statement explaining or amplifying any statement made in the report, and that statement shall be deemed for the purposes of this section (except subsection (3) thereof) to form part of the report made to the court.

(5) Where a direction is given under this section in any proceedings, a party to the proceedings, unless the court otherwise directs, shall not be entitled to call as a witness the person responsible for carrying out the tests taken for the purpose of giving effect to the direction, or any person by whom any thing necessary for the purpose of enabling those tests to be carried out was done, unless within 14 days after receiving a copy of the report he serves notice on the other parties to the proceedings, or on such of them as the court may direct, of his intention to call that person; and where any such person is called as a witness the party who called him shall be entitled to cross-examine him.

(6) Where a direction is given under this section the party on whose application the direction is given shall pay the cost of taking and testing bodily samples for the purpose of giving effect to the direction (including any expenses reasonably incurred by any person in taking any steps required of him for the purpose), and of making a report to the court under this section, but the amount paid shall be treated as costs incurred by him in the proceedings.

Note.—The section does not apply to proceedings under the Maintenance Orders (Reciprocal Enforcement) Act 1972: see section 44(1) of that Act.

Subsections (1), (2) and (2A) were substituted for the original subsections (1) and (2) by the Family Law Reform Act 1987, s.23(1). Tests may now be used to determine parentage, including maternity, and are not, as under the previous provision, limited to paternity.

26. Any presumption of law as to the legitimacy or illegitimacy of any person may in any civil proceedings be rebutted by evidence which shows that it is more probable than not that that person is illegitimate or legitimate, as the case may be, and it shall not be necessary to prove that fact beyond reasonable doubt in order to rebut the presumption.

Note.—The position in criminal cases is not changed by the section; but it is unlikely that the common law presumption rebuttable only by proof beyond reasonable doubt would be allowed to operate against an accused in, *e.g.* a prosecution for incest.

For the limited effect of the section upon the standard of proof required in certain civil cases see *Serio* v. *Serio* (1983) 13 Fam. Law 255 (C.A.) (Part One, Chapter 3, *supra*).

See, too, Part One, Chapter 4, (*supra*) on presumptions generally.

TAXES MANAGEMENT ACT 1970

1970, c. 9

105.—(1) Statements made or documents produced by or on behalf of a person shall not be inadmissible in any such proceedings as are mentioned in subsection (2) below by reason only that it has been drawn to his attention that—

(a) in relation to tax, the Board may accept pecuniary settlements instead of instituting proceedings, and

(b) though no undertaking can be given as to whether or not the Board will accept such a settlement in the case of any particular person, it is the practice of the Board to be influenced by the fact that a person has made a full confession

of fraud or default to which he has been a party and has given
full facilities for investigation.
and that he was or may have been induced thereby to make statements
or produce the documents.

(2) The proceedings mentioned in subsection (1) above are—

    (*a*) any criminal proceedings against the person in question for
any form of fraud or wilful default in connection with or in
relation to tax, and

    (*b*) any proceedings against him for the recovery of any sum due
from him, whether by way of tax or penalty, in connection
with or in relation to tax.

Note.—This section has the effect of reversing the decision in *R.* v. *Barker* [1941] 2 K.B.
381 (C.A.) (Part One, Chapter 17, *supra*).

VEHICLES (EXCISE) ACT 1971

1971, c. 10

33. If in any proceedings under sections 8, 16(7) or 26(2) of this Act
any question arises—

    (*a*) as to the number of mechanically propelled vehicles used, or

    (*b*) as to the character, weight, horse-power or cylinder capacity
of any mechanically propelled vehicle, or

    (*c*) as to the number of persons for which a mechanically
propelled vehicle has seating capacity, or

    (*d*) as to the purpose for which any mechanically propelled
vehicle has been used,

the burden of proof in respect of the matter in question shall lie on the
defendant.

Note.—Section 8 of this Act is concerned with using and keeping vehicles without a
licence; section 16(7) with the misuse of trade licences; and section 26(2) with the giving of
false information.

For the Civil Evidence Act 1968, see *supra*.

CRIMINAL DAMAGE ACT 1971

1971, c. 48

9. A person shall not be excused, by reason that to do so may
incriminate that person or the wife or husband of that person of an
offence under this Act—

    (*a*) from answering any question put to that person in proceedings
for the recovery or administration of any property, for the
execution of any trust or for an account of any property or
dealings with property: or

    (*b*) from complying with any order made in any such proceedings;

but no statement or admission made by a person in answering a
question put or complying with an order made as aforesaid shall, in
proceedings for an offence under this Act, be admissible in evidence
against that person or (unless they married after the making of the
statement or admission) against the wife or husband of that person.

Note.—This is the counterpart of the Theft Act 1968, s.31(1). See *supra*.

MAINTENANCE ORDERS (RECIPROCAL ENFORCEMENT) ACT 1972

1972, c. 18

Note.—This Act makes provision relating to the admissibility of evidence given in a reciprocating country (s.13); the obtaining of evidence needed for certain proceedings in a reciprocating country (s.14); the admissibility of evidence given in a convention country (s.36); the obtaining of evidence for the purpose of proceedings in a United Kingdom court (s.37); and the taking of evidence at the request of a court in a convention country (s.38). See, too, section 44(1) (the non-applicability of the Family Law Reform Act 1969, s.20, *supra*) and section 44(2) as amended (the non-applicability of the Evidence (Proceedings in Other Jurisdictions) Act 1975, *supra*). The convention referred to is the United Nations Convention on the Recovery Abroad of Maintenance 1956.

CIVIL EVIDENCE ACT 1972

1972, c. 30

Note.—For comment on some of the provisions of the Act, see Part One, Chapter 18 (*supra*).

1.—(1) Subject to the provisions of this section, Part I (hearsay evidence) of the Civil Evidence Act 1968, except section 5 (statements produced by computers), shall apply in relation to statements of opinion as it applies in relation to statements of fact, subject to the necessary modifications and in particular the modification that any reference to a fact stated in a statement shall be construed as a reference to a matter dealt with herein.

(2) Section 4 (admissibility of certain records) of the Civil Evidence Act 1968, as applied by subsection (1) above, shall not render admissible in any civil proceedings a statement of opinion contained in a record unless that statement would be admissible in those proceedings if made in the course of giving oral evidence by the person who originally supplied the information from which the record was compiled; but where a statement of opinion contained in a record deals with a matter on which the person who originally supplied the information from which the record was compiled is (or would if living be) qualified to give oral expert evidence, the said section 4, as applied by subsection (1) above, shall have effect in relation to that statement as if so much of subsection (1) of that section as requires personal knowledge on the part of that person were omitted.

2.—(1) If and so far as rules of court so provide, subsection (2) of section 2 of the Civil Evidence Act 1968 (which imposes restrictions on the giving of a statement in evidence by virtue of that section on behalf of a party who has called or intends to call as a witness the maker of the statement) shall not apply to statements (whether of fact or opinion) contained in expert records.

(2) In so far as they relate to statements (whether of fact or opinion) contained in expert reports, rules of court made in pursuance of subsection (1) of section 8 of Civil Evidence Act 1968 as to the procedure to be followed and the other conditions to be fulfilled before a statement can be given in evidence in civil proceedings by virtue of section 2 of that Act (admissibility of out-of-court statements) shall not be subject to the requirements of subsection (2) of the said section 8 (which specifies certain matters of procedure for which provision must

CIVIL EVIDENCE ACT 1972

ordinarily be made by rules of court made in pursuance of the said subsection (1)).

(3) Notwithstanding any enactment or rule of law by virtue of which documents prepared for the purpose of pending or contemplated civil proceedings or in connection with the obtaining or giving of legal advice are in certain circumstances privileged from disclosure, provision may be made by rules of court—

(a) for enabling the court in any civil proceedings to direct, with respect to medical matters or matters of any other class which may be specified in the direction, that the parties or some of them shall each by such date as may be so specified (or such later date as may be permitted or agreed in accordance with the rules) disclose to the other or others in the form of one or more expert reports the expert evidence on matters of that class which he proposes to adduce as part of his case at the trial; and

(b) for prohibiting a party who fails to comply with a direction given in any such proceedings under rules of court made by virtue of paragraph (a) above from adducing in evidence by virtue of section 2 of the Civil Evidence Act 1968 (admissibility of out-of-court statements), except with the leave of the court, any statement (whether of fact or opinion) contained in any expert report whatsoever in so far as that statement deals with matters of any class specified in the direction.

(4) Provision may be made by rules of court as to the conditions subject to which oral expert evidence may be given in civil proceedings.

(5) Without prejudice to the generality of subsection (4) above, rules of court made in pursuance of that subsection may make provision for prohibiting a party who fails to comply with a direction given as mentioned in subsection (3)(b) above from adducing, except with the leave of the court, any oral expert evidence whatsoever with respect to matters of any class specified in the direction.

(6) Any rules of court made in pursuance of this section may make different provision for different classes of cases, for expert reports dealing with matters of different classes, and for other different circumstances.

(7) References in this section to an expert report are references to a written report by a person dealing wholly or mainly with matters on which he is (or would if living be) qualified to give expert evidence.

(8) Nothing in the foregoing provisions of this section shall prejudice the generality of section 75 of the County Courts Act 1984, section 144 of the Magistrates' Courts Act 1980 or any other enactment conferring power to make rules of court; and nothing in section 75(2) of the County Courts Act 1984 or any other enactment restricting the matters with respect to which rules of court may be made shall prejudice the making of rules of court in pursuance of this section or the operation of any rules of court so made.

Note.—See R.S.C., Ord. 38, rr. 35–44 (Part Three, *infra*).

3.—(1) Subject to any rules of court made in pursuance of Part I of the Civil Evidence Act 1968 or this Act, where a person is called as a witness in any civil proceedings, his opinion on any relevant matter on which he is qualified to give expert evidence shall be admissible in evidence.

(2) It is hereby declared that where a person is called as a witness in any civil proceedings, a statement of opinion by him on any relevant matter on which he is not qualified to give expert evidence, if made as a way of conveying relevant facts personally perceived by him, is admissible as evidence of what he perceived.

(3) In this section "relevant matter" includes an issue in the proceedings in question.

4.—(1) It is hereby declared that in civil proceedings a person who is suitably qualified to do so on account of his knowledge or experience is competent to give expert evidence as to the law of any country or territory outside the United Kingdom, or of any part of the United Kingdom other than England and Wales, irrespective of whether he has acted or is entitled to act as a legal practitioner there.

Note.—At common law a person did not qualify as an expert on foreign law unless he had had practical experience (although not necessarily as a lawyer) in the country in question. Knowledge derived solely from study did not suffice: *Bristow* v. *Sequeville* (1850) 19 L.J. Ex. 289. This rule would presumably still apply in the rare event of a point of foreign law falling to be determined in a criminal case.

(2) Where any question as to the law of any country or territory outside the United Kingdom, or of any part of the United Kingdom other than England and Wales, with respect to any matter has been determined (whether before or after the passing of this Act) in any such proceedings as are mentioned in subsection (4) below, then in any civil proceedings (not being proceedings before a court which can take judicial notice of the law of that country, territory or part with respect to that matter)—

    (*a*) any finding made or decision given on that question in the first-mentioned proceedings shall, if reported or recorded in citable form, be admissible in evidence for the purpose of proving the law of that country, territory or part with respect to that matter; and

    (*b*) if that finding or decision, as so reported or recorded, is adduced for that purpose, the law of that country, territory or part with respect to that matter shall be taken to be in accordance with that finding or decision unless the contrary is proved:

Provided that paragraph (*b*) above shall not apply in the case of a finding or decision which conflicts with another finding or decision in the same question adduced by virtue of this subsection in the same proceedings.

(3) Except with the leave of the court, a party to any civil proceedings shall not be permitted to adduce any such finding or decision as is mentioned in subsection (2) above by virtue of that subsection unless he has in accordance with rules of court given to every other party to the proceedings notice that he intends to do so.

(4) The proceedings referred to in subsection (2) above are the following, whether civil or criminal, namely—

    (*a*) proceedings at first instance in any of the following courts, namely the High Court, the Crown Court, a court of quarter sessions, the Court of Chancery of the County Palatine of

Lancaster and the Court of Chancery of the County Palatine of Durham;

(b) appeals arising out of any such proceedings as are mentioned in paragraph (a) above;

(c) proceedings before the Judicial Committee of the Privy Council on appeal (whether to Her Majesty in Council or to the Judicial Committee as such) from any decision of any court outside the United Kingdom.

(5) For the purposes of this section a finding or decision on any such question as is mentioned in subsection (2) above shall be taken to be reported or recorded in citable form if, but only if, it is reported or recorded in writing in a report, transcript or other document which, if that question had been a question as to the law of England and Wales, could be cited as an authority in legal proceedings in England and Wales.

Note.—Common law doctrine was that an earlier finding by an English court of a point of foreign law, being a finding of fact, did not constitute a precedent.

5.—(1) In this Act "civil proceedings" and "court" have the meanings assigned by section 18(1) and (2) of the Civil Evidence Act 1968.

(2) Subsections (3) and (4) of section 10 of the Civil Evidence Act 1968 shall apply for the purposes of the application of sections 2 and 4 of this Act in relation to any such civil proceedings as are mentioned in section 18(1)(a) and (b) of that Act (that is to say civil proceedings before a tribunal other than one of the ordinary courts of law, being proceedings in relation to which the strict rules of evidence apply, and an arbitration or reference, whether under an enactment or not) as they apply for the purposes of the application of Part I of that Act in relation to any such civil proceedings.

(3) Nothing in this Act shall prejudice—

(a) any power of a court, in any civil proceedings, to exclude evidence (whether by preventing questions from being put or otherwise) at its discretion; or

(b) the operation of any agreement (whenever made) between the parties to any civil proceedings as to the evidence which is to be admissible (whether generally or for any particular purpose) in those proceedings.

EUROPEAN COMMUNITIES ACT 1972

1972, c. 68

3.—(1) For the purposes of all legal proceedings any question as to the meaning or effect of any of the Treaties, or as to the validity, meaning or effect of any Community instrument, shall be treated as a question of law (and, if not referred to the European Court, be for determination as such in accordance with the principles laid down by and any relevant decision of the European Court or any court attached thereto).

(2) Judicial notice shall be taken of the Treaties, of the Official Journal of the Communities and of any decision of, or expression of opinion by, the European Court or any court attached thereto on any such question as aforesaid; and the Official Journal shall be admissible

as evidence of any instrument or other act thereby communicated of any of the Communities or of any Community institution.

(3) Evidence of any instrument issued by a Community institution, including any judgment or order of the European Court or any court attached thereto, or of any document in the custody of a Community institution, or any entry in or extract from such a document, may be given in any legal proceedings by production of a copy certified as a true copy by an official of that institution; and any document purporting to be such a copy shall be received in evidence without proof of the official position or handwriting of the person signing the certificate.

(4) Evidence of any Community instrument may also be given in any legal proceedings—

    (a) by production of a copy purporting to be printed by the Queen's Printer;

    (b) where the instrument is in the custody of a government department (including a department of the Government of Northern Ireland), by production of a copy certified on behalf of the department to be a true copy by an officer of the department generally or specially authorised so to do;

and any document purporting to be such a copy as is mentioned in paragraph (b) above of an instrument in the custody of a department shall be received in evidence without proof of the official position or handwriting of the person signing the certificate, or of his authority to do so, or of the document being in the custody of the department.

Note.—Section 3(1) was considered in *R.* v. *Goldstein* [1983] 1 W.L.R. 151 (H.L.). On judicial notice, see Part One, Chapter 7 (*supra*).

MATRIMONIAL CAUSES ACT 1973

1973, c. 18

19.—(1) Any married person who alleges that reasonable grounds exist for supposing that the other party to the marriage is dead may present a petition to the court to have it presumed that the other party is dead and to have the marriage dissolved, and the court may, if satisfied that such reasonable grounds exist, grant a decree of presumption of death and dissolution of the marriage.

(3) In any proceedings under this section the fact that for a period of seven years or more the other party to the marriage has been continually absent from the petitioner and the petitioner has no reason to believe that the other party has been living within that time shall be evidence that the other party is dead until the contrary is proved.

48.—(1) The evidence of a husband or wife shall be admissible in any proceedings to prove that marital intercourse did or did not take place between them during any period.

(2) In any proceedings for nullity of marriage, evidence on the question of sexual capacity shall be heard in camera unless in any case the judge is satisfied that in the interests of justice any such evidence ought to be heard in open court.

SOLICITORS ACT 1974

1974, c. 47

18.—(1) Any list purporting to be published by authority of the Society and to contain the names of solicitors who have obtained practising certificates for the current year before 2nd January in that year shall, until the contrary is proved, be evidence that the persons so named as solicitors holding practising certificates for the current year are solicitors holding such certificates.

(2) The absence from any such list of the name of any person shall, until the contrary is proved, be evidence that that person is not qualified to practise as a solicitor under a certificate for the current year, but in the case of any such person an extract from the roll certified as correct by the Society shall be evidence of the facts appearing in the extract.

REHABILITATION OF OFFENDERS ACT 1974

1974, c. 53

4.—(1) Subject to sections 7 and 8 below, a person who has become a rehabilitated person for the purposes of this Act in respect of a conviction shall be treated for all purposes in law as a person who has not committed or been charged with or prosecuted for or convicted of or sentenced for the offence or offences which were the subject of that conviction; and, notwithstanding the provisions of any other enactment or rule of law to the contrary, but subject as aforesaid—

(*a*) no evidence shall be admissible in any proceedings before a judicial authority exercising its jurisdiction or functions in Great Britain to prove that any such person has committed or been charged with or prosecuted for or convicted of or sentenced for any offence which was the subject of a spent conviction; and

(*b*) a person shall not, in any such proceedings, be asked, and, if asked, shall not be required to answer, any question relating to his past which cannot be answered without acknowledging or referring to a spent conviction or spent convictions or any circumstances ancillary thereto.

Note.—Section 7 (part of which is set out below) deals with limitations upon rehabilitation under the Act. Section 8 deals with its impact in defamation proceedings. Certain additional exceptions to the applicability of section 4(1) are to be found in the Rehabilitation of Offences Act 1974 (Exceptions) Order 1975, (S.I. 1975 No. 1023), Sched. 3; (Exceptions) (Amendment) Order 1986 (S.I. 1986 No. 1249); and (Exceptions) (Amendment) Order 1986 (S.I. 1986 No. 2268).

(5) For the purposes of this section and section 7 below any of the following are circumstances ancillary to a conviction, that is to say—

(*a*) the offence or offences which were the subject of that conviction;

(*b*) the conduct constituting that offence or those offences; and

(*c*) any process or proceedings preliminary to that conviction, any sentence imposed in respect of that conviction, any proceedings (whether by way of appeal or otherwise) for reviewing that conviction or any such sentence, and anything done in pursuance of or undergone in compliance with any such sentence.

(6) For the purposes of this section and section 7 below "proceedings before a judicial authority" includes, in addition to proceedings before any of the ordinary courts of law, proceedings before any tribunal, body or person having power—

(a) by virtue of any enactment, law, custom or practice;

(b) under the rules governing any association, institution, profession, occupation or employment; or

(c) under any provision of an agreement providing for arbitration with respect to questions arising thereunder;

to determine any question affecting the rights, privileges, obligations or liabilities of any person, or to receive evidence affecting the determination of any such question.

5.(1)— The sentences excluded from rehabilitation under this Act are—

(a) a sentence of imprisonment for life;

(b) a sentence of imprisonment, youth custody or corrective training for a term exceeding 30 months;

(c) a sentence of preventive detention;

(d) a sentence of detention during Her Majesty's pleasure or for life, or under section 205(2) or (3) of the Criminal Procedure (Scotland) Act 1975, or for a term exceeding 30 months, passed under section 53 of the Children and Young Persons Act 1933 (young offenders convicted of grave crimes) or under section 206 of the said Act of 1975 (detention of children convicted on indictment) or a corresponding court-martial punishment; and

(e) a sentence of custody for life;

and any other sentence is a sentence subject to rehabilitation under this Act.

Note.—The rest of section 5 deals with the length of rehabilitation periods for particular sentences.

7.—(2) Nothing in section 4(1) above shall affect the determination of any issue, or prevent the admission or requirement of any evidence, relating to a person's previous convictions or to circumstances ancillary thereto—

(a) in any criminal proceedings before a court in Great Britain (including any appeal or reference in a criminal matter);

(b) in any service disciplinary proceedings or in any proceedings on appeal from any service disciplinary proceedings;

(c) in any proceedings relating to adoption or to the guardianship, wardship, marriage, custody, care or control of, or access to, any minor, or to the provision by any person of accommodation, care or schooling for minors;

(d) in any care proceedings under section 1 of the Children and Young Persons Act 1969 or on appeal from any such proceedings, or in any proceedings relating to the variation or discharge of a care order or supervision order under that Act;

(e) in any proceedings before a children's hearing under the Social Work (Scotland) Act 1968 or on appeal for any such hearing;

(f) in any proceedings in which he is a party or a witness, provided that, on the occasion when the issue or the admission or requirement of the evidence falls to be determined, he consents to the determination of the issue or, as the case may be, the admission or requirement of the evidence notwithstanding the provisions of section 4(1).

In the application of this subsection to Scotland, "minor" means a child under the age of 18, including a pupil child.

(3) If at any stage in any proceedings before a judicial authority in Great Britain (not being proceedings to which, by virtue of any of paragraphs (a) to (e) of subsection (2) above or of any order for the time being in force under subsection (6) below, section 4(1) above has no application, or proceedings to which section 8 below applies) the authority is satisfied, in the light of any considerations which appear to it to be relevant (including any evidence which has been or may thereafter be put before it), that justice cannot be done in the case except by admitting or requiring evidence relating to a person's spent convictions or to circumstances ancillary thereto, that authority may admit or, as the case may be, require the evidence in question notwithstanding the provisions of subsection (1) of section 4 above, and may determine any issue to which the evidence relates in disregard, so far as necessary, of those provisions.

(4) The Secretary of State may by order exclude the application of section 4(1) above in relation to any proceedings specified in the order (other than proceedings to which section 8 below applies) to such extent and for such purposes as may be so specified.

(5) No order made by a court with respect to any person otherwise than on a conviction shall be included in any list or statement of that person's previous convictions given or made to any court which is considering how to deal with him in respect of any offence.

Note.—The Act does not apply to evidence given in criminal proceedings, but see Lord Widgery C.J.'s Practice Direction [1975] 1 W.L.R. 1065 (D.C.): "When the Bill was before the House of Commons...the hope was expressed that the Lord Chief Justice would issue a Practice Direction for the guidance of the Crown Court with a view to reducing disclosure of spent conviction to a minimum. . . . It is not possible to give general directions...but it is recommended that both court and counsel should give effect to the general intention of Parliament by never referring to a spent conviction when such reference can be reasonably avoided. . . . "

Counsel should seek leave before disclosing a spent conviction in criminal proceedings; but his failure to do so is not necessarily a ground for appeal: *R.* v. *Sullivan* [1982] Crim.L.R. 175 (C.A.). For examples of circumstances in which leave to appeal should be given, see *R.* v. *Nye* (1982) 75 Cr.App.R. 247 (C.A.) at p. 250. For a criminal case in which evidence of the complainant's spent conviction was held to have been wrongly excluded, see *R.* v. *Paraskeva* (1982) 76 Cr.App.R. 162 (C.A.).

For the limited scope of the Act in proceedings arising pursuant to the Banking Act 1987, see section 97 of that Act.

INHERITANCE (PROVISION FOR FAMILY AND DEPENDANTS) ACT 1975

1975, c. 63

21. In any proceedings under this Act a statement made by the deceased, whether orally or in a document or otherwise, shall be admissible under section 2 of the Civil Evidence Act 1968 as evidence of any fact stated therein in like manner as if the statement were a statement falling within section 2(1) of that Act; and any reference in that Act to a statement admissible, or given or proposed to be given, in evidence under section 2 thereof or to the admissibility or the giving in evidence of a statement by virtue of that section or to any statement falling within section 2(1) of that Act shall be construed accordingly.

Note.—For the position in criminal cases see Part One, Chapter 14, Section A (supra).

LOCAL LAND CHARGES ACT 1975

1975, c. 76

12. An office copy of an entry in any local land charges register shall be admissible in evidence in all proceedings and between all parties to the same extent as the original would be admissible.

SEXUAL OFFENCES AMENDMENT ACT 1976

1976, c. 82

2.—(1) If at a trial any person is for the time being charged with a rape offence to which he pleads not guilty, then, except with the leave of the judge, no evidence and no question in cross-examination shall be adduced or asked at the trial, by or on behalf of any defendant at the trial, about any sexual experience of a complainant with a person other than that defendant.

(2) The judge shall not give leave in pursuance of the preceding subsection for any evidence or question except on an application made to him in the absence of the jury by or on behalf of a defendant; and on such an application the judge shall give leave if and only if he is satisfied that it would be unfair to that defendant to refuse to allow the evidence to be adduced or the question to be asked.

(3) In subsection (1) of this section 'complainant' means a woman upon whom, in a charge for a rape offence to which the trial in question relates, it is alleged that rape was committed, attempted or proposed.

(4) Nothing in this section authorises evidence to be adduced or a question to be asked which cannot be adduced or asked apart from this section.

Note.—"A rape offence" is defined in section 7(2) (as amended by the Criminal Justice Act 1988, s.150(6)) as "rape, attempted rape, aiding, abetting, counselling and procuring rape or attempted rape, incitement to rape, conspiracy to rape and burglary with intent to rape."

The Act only restricts the admission of evidence and cross-examination of the victim of a rape offence, so defined, whereas there are several sexual offences against females which are outside this definition and in which the victim's sexual experience may be, or may be thought to be, relevant. It is not clear whether the restriction extends to evidence or cross-examination which merely *implies* sexual activity: see *R.* v. *Hinds and Butler* [1979] Crim.L.R. 111 (Crown Ct.). It was assumed in *R.* v. *Viola* [1982] 1 W.L.R. 1138 (C.A.) that "sexual experience" includes sexual activity falling short of intercourse.

Evidence and cross-examination relevant to an issue such as consent are likely to be admitted, whereas evidence and cross-examination going to credit—at least when the implication is that the victim should not be believed simply because she engages in extra-marital sexual activity—are likely to be excluded: *R.* v. *Viola, ibid.* However, in *R.* v. *Viola* it was held *per curiam* (p. 1142) that, once the judge concludes that he is satisfied that exclusion of the evidence and/or questioning would be unfair to the defendant, he has no discretion and the evidence has to be admitted and/or the questioning allowed. See *R.* v. *Cox* (1987) 84 Cr.App.R. 132 (C.A.) (Part One, Chapter 22, *supra*). See, also, *R.* v. *Mills* (1979) 68 Cr.App.R. 327 (C.A.), *R.* v. *Fenlon*; *R.* v. *Neal* (1980) 71 Cr.App.R. 307 (C.A.); and *R.* v. *Barton* 85 Cr.App.R. 5 (C.A.).

3. Where a magistrates' court inquires into a rape offence as examining justices, then, except with the consent of the court, evidence shall not be adduced and a question shall not be asked at the inquiry which, if the inquiry were a trial at which a person is charged as mentioned in subsection (1) of the preceding section and each of the accused at the inquiry were charged at the trial with the offences of which he is accused at the inquiry, could not be adduced or asked without leave in pursuance of that section.

(2) On an application for consent in pursuance of the preceding subsection for any evidence or question the court shall—

(*a*) refuse the consent unless the court is satisfied that leave in respect of the evidence or question would be likely to be given at a relevant trial; and

(*b*) give the consent if the court is so satisfied.

(3) Where a person charged with a rape offence is tried for that offence either by court-martial or summarily before a magistrates' court in pursuance of section 24(1) of the Magistrates' Courts Act 1980 (which provides for the summary trial in certain cases of persons under the age of 17 who are charged with indictable offences) the preceding section shall have effect in relation to the trial as if—

(*a*) the words "in the absence of the jury" in subsection (2) were omitted; and

(*b*) for any reference to the judge there were substituted—

(*i*) in the case of a trial by court-martial for which a judge advocate is appointed, a reference to the judge advocate, and

(*ii*) in any other case, a reference to the court.

PATENTS ACT 1977

1977, c. 37

100.—(1) If the invention for which a patent is granted is a process for obtaining a new product, the same product produced by a person other than the proprietor of the patent or a licensee of his shall, unless the contrary is proved, be taken in any proceedings to have been obtained by that process.

(2) In considering whether a party has discharged the burden imposed upon him by this section, the court shall not require him to disclose any manufacturing or commercial secrets if it appears to the court that it would be unreasonable to do so.

Note.—See, too, the Copyright, Designs and Patents Act 1988, section 280 (*infra*).

OATHS ACT 1978

1978, c. 19

Note.—This Act consolidates the Oaths Act 1838 and the Oaths Acts 1888 to 1977. Sections 1 to 3 deal with the administration of oaths. Section 1(3) allows for the administration of an oath "in any lawful manner" to a person who is neither a Christian nor a Jew.

4.—(1) In any case in which an oath may lawfully be and has been administered to any person, if it has been administered in a form and manner other than that prescribed by law, he is bound by it if it has been administered in such form and with such ceremonies as he may have declared to be binding.

(2) Where an oath has been duly administered and taken, the fact that the person to whom it was administered had, at the time of taking it, no religious belief, shall not for any purpose affect the validity of the oath.

5.—(1) Any person who objects to being sworn shall be permitted to make his solemn affirmation instead of taking an oath.

(2) Subsection (1) above shall apply in relation to a person to whom it is not reasonably practicable without inconvenience or delay to administer an oath in the manner appropriate to his religious belief as it applies in relation to a person objecting to be sworn.

(3) A person who may be permitted under subsection (2) above to make his solemn affirmation may also be required to do so.

(4) A solemn affirmation shall be of the same force and effect as an oath.

Note.—Section 6 sets out the form of an affirmation. See too the Welsh Courts Act 1942 (*supra*).

A competent witness who does not object to being sworn should give evidence on oath irrespective of his or her belief in the divine sanction of an oath: *R.* v. *Bellamy* (1985) 82 Cr.App.R. 22 (C.A.).

As to the position of child witnesses, see Part One, Chapter 8 (*supra*) and the Children and Young Persons Act 1963, s.28.

The Oaths and Evidence (Overseas Authorities and Countries) Act 1963 authorises the administration of oaths and the performance of notarial acts by representatives of, and other persons empowered by the authorities of, countries overseas for the taking of evidence for foreign civil proceedings.

INTERPRETATION ACT 1978

1978, c. 30

3. Every Act is a public Act to be judicially noticed as such, unless the contrary is expressly provided by the Act.

Note.—This section derives from the Interpretation Act 1889, s.9. It applies to Acts passed after 1978 and to existing Acts passed after 1850: s.22(1) and Sched. 2, para. 2. Judicial Notice is taken at common law of public Acts passed before 1851, but a private Act passed before that date must be pleaded and proved unless it provides to the contrary. On judicial notice generally, see Part One, Chapter 7 (*supra*).

Dominion and Colonial statutes and ordinances are proved by a Government Printers' copy: Evidence (Colonial Statutes) Act 1907.

STATE IMMUNITY ACT 1978

1978, c. 33

21. A certificate by or on behalf of the Secretary of State shall be conclusive evidence on any question—

(a) whether any country is a State for the purposes of Part I of this Act, whether any territory is a constituent territory of a federal State for those purposes or as to the person or persons to be regarded for those purposes as the head or government of a State;

(b) whether a State is a party to the Brussels Convention mentioned in Part I of this Act.

(c) whether a State is a party to the European Convention on State Immunity, whether it has made a declaration under Article 24 of that Convention or as to the territories in respect of which the United Kingdom or any other State is a party;

(d) whether, and if so when, a document has been served or received as mentioned in section 12(1) or (5) above.

Note.—This Act codifies the law on state immunity to be applied in the United Kingdom. The Brussels Convention is the International Convention for the Unification of Certain Rules relating to the Immunity of State-owned Vessels 1926 (Cmd. 5672) and the Protocol to it (Cmd. 5081). Article 24 of the European Convention on State Immunity 1972 (Cmnd. 5081) permits a state by making an appropriate declaration to grant immunity on a more restricted basis than would otherwise stem from ratification. Section 12 deals with service of process against a state and with judgments in default of a state's appearance.

See too the Diplomatic Privileges Act 1964, s.4 (*supra*), the Consular Relations Act 1968, s.11, and the International Organisation Act 1968, s.8.

PROTECTION OF CHILDREN ACT 1978

1978, c. 37

2.—(3) In proceedings under this Act a person is to be taken as having been a child at any material time if it appears from the evidence as a whole that he was then under the age of 16.

Note.—Compare the Police and Criminal Evidence Act 1984, s.80(6) (*infra*) and the Magistrates' Courts Act 1980, s.150(4) (*infra*).

MAGISTRATES' COURTS ACT 1980

1980, c. 43

98. Subject to the provisions of any enactment or rule of law authorising the reception of unsworn evidence, evidence given before a magistrates' court shall be given on oath.

101. Where the defendant to an information or complaint relies for his defence on any exception, exemption, proviso, excuse or qualification, whether or not it accompanies the description of the offence or matter of complaint in the enactment creating the offence or on which the complaint is founded, the burden of proving the exception, exemption, proviso, excuse or qualification shall be on him; and this notwithstanding that the information or complaint contains an allegation negativing the exception, exemption, proviso, excuse or qualification.

Note.—It is accepted that the words "the burden of proof" impose a legal burden: see, *e.g. R.* v. *Hunt* [1987] A.C. 352 (H.L.) (Part One, Chapter 2, *supra*) (*per* Lord Ackner at p. 385).

102.—(1) In committal proceedings a written statement by any person shall, if the conditions mentioned in subsection (2) below are satisfied, be admissible as evidence to the like extent as oral evidence to the like effect by that person.

(2) The said conditions are—

    (a) the statement purports to be signed by the person who made it;

    (b) the statement contains a declaration by that person to the effect that it is true to the best of his knowledge and belief and that he made the statement knowing that, if it were tendered in evidence, he would be liable to prosecution if he wilfully stated in it anything which he knew to be false or did not believe to be true;

    (c) before the statement is tendered in evidence, a copy of the statement is given, by or on behalf of the party proposing to tender it, to each of the other parties to the proceedings; and

    (d) none of the other parties, before the statement is tendered in evidence at the committal proceedings, objects to the statement being so tendered under this section.

(3) The following provisions shall also have effect in relation to any written statement tendered in evidence under this section, that is to say—

    (a) if the statement is made by a person under 21 years old, it shall give his age;

    (b) if it is made by a person who cannot reread it, it shall be read to him before he signs it and shall be accompanied by a declaration by the person who so read the statement to the effect that it was so read; and

    (c) if it refers to any other document as an exhibit, the copy given to any other party to the proceedings under subsection (2)(c) above shall be accompanied by a copy of that document or by such information as may be necessary in order to enable the party to whom it is given to inspect that document or a copy thereof.

(4) Notwithstanding that a written statement made by any person may be admissible in committal proceedings by virtue of this section, the court before which the proceedings are held may, of its own motion or on the application of any party to the proceedings, require that person to attend before the court and give evidence.

(5) So much of any statement as is admitted in evidence by virtue of this section shall, unless the court commits the accused for trial by virtue of section 6(2) above or the court otherwise directs, be read aloud at the hearing, and where the court so directs an account shall be given orally of so much of any statement as is not read aloud.

(6) Any document or object referred to as an exhibit and identified in a written statement tendered in evidence under this section shall be treated as if it had been produced as an exhibit and identified in court by the maker of the statement.

(7) Subsection (3) of section 13 of the Criminal Justices Act 1925 (reading of deposition as evidence at the trial) shall apply to any written statement tendered in evidence in committal proceedings under this section as it applies to a deposition taken in such proceedings, but in its application to any such statement that subsection shall have effect as if paragraph (b) thereof were omitted.

(8) In section 2(2) of the Administration of Justice (Miscellaneous

Provisions) Act 1933, procedure for preferring bills of indictment) the reference in proviso (i) to facts disclosed in any deposition taken before a justice in the presence of the accused shall be construed as including a reference to facts disclosed in any such written statement as aforesaid, and section 40 of the Criminal Justice Act 1988 (power to join in indictment count for common assault, etc.) shall be given a corresponding construction.

(9) Section 28 above shall not apply to any such statement as aforesaid.

(10) A person whose written statement is tendered in evidence in committal proceedings under this section shall be treated for the purposes of section 1 of the Criminal Procedure (Attendance of Witnesses) Act 1965 (witness orders) as a witness who has been examined by the court.

Note.—Section 102 must be read in the light of the *Practice Direction (Crime: Evidence by Written Statements)* [1986] 1 W.L.R. 805, which deals with the preparation and editing of written statements tendered under this section (in addition to those tendered under the Criminal Justice Act 1967, s.9 (*infra*)).

103.—(1) In any proceedings before a magistrates' court inquiring into an offence to which this section applies as examining justices—

(a) a child shall not be called as a witness for the prosecution; but

(b) any statement made by or taken from a child shall be admissible in evidence of any matter of which his oral testimony would be admissible,

except in a case where the application of this subsection is excluded under subsection (3) below.

(2) This section applies—

(a) to an offence which involves an assault, or injury or a threat of injury to, a person;

(b) to an offence under section 1 of the Children and Young Persons Act 1933 (cruelty to persons under 16);

(c) to an offence under the Sexual Offences Act 1956, the Indecency with Children Act 1960, the Sexual Offences Act 1967, section 54 of the Criminal Law Act 1977 or the Protection of Children Act 1978; and

(d) to an offence which consists of attempting or conspiring to commit, or of aiding, abetting, counselling, procuring or inciting the commission of, an offence falling within paragraph (a), (b) or (c) above.

(3) The application of subsection (1) above is excluded—

(a) where at or before the time when the statement is tendered in evidence the defence objects to its admission; or

(b) where the prosecution requires the attendance of the child for the purpose of establishing the identity of any person; or

(c) where the court is satisfied that it has not been possible to obtain from the child a statement that may be given in evidence under this section; or

(d) where the inquiry into the offence takes place after the court has discontinued to try it summarily and the child has given evidence in the summary trial.

(4) Section 28 above shall not apply to any statement admitted in pursuance of subsection (1) above.

(5) In this section "child" means a person under the age of 14.

Note.—This section was substituted for the original section by the Criminal Justice Act 1988, s.33. The change which it has introduced is to extend to cases involving allegations of assault or cruelty the previous rule forbidding (subject to exceptions re-enacted in subsection (3)) the calling of children to give evidence at committal hearings. The practical importance of the rule is often limited by subsection 3(*a*) and (*b*). It is to be noted that the child may, or may not, be the alleged victim.

105.—(1) Where a person appears to a justice of the peace to be able and willing to give material information relating to an indictable offence or to any person accused of an indictable offence, and—

    (*a*) the justice is satisfied, on a representation made by a duly qualified medical practitioner, that the person able and willing to make the statement is dangerously ill and unlikely to recover; and

    (*b*) it is not practicable for examining justices to take the evidence of the sick person in accordance with the provisions of this Act and the rules,

the justice may take in writing the deposition of the sick person on oath.

(2) A deposition taken under this section may be given in evidence before examining justices inquiring into an information against the offender or in respect of the offence to which the deposition relates, but subject to the same conditions as apply, under section 6 of the Criminal Law Amendment Act 1867, to its being given in evidence upon the trial of the offender or offence.

150.—(4) Where the age of any person at any time is material for the purposes of any provision of this Act regulating the powers of a magistrates' court, his age at the material time shall be deemed to be or to have been that which appears to the court after considering any available evidence to be or to have been his age at that time.

HIGHWAYS ACT 1980

1980, c. 66

32. A court or other tribunal, before determining whether a way has or has not been dedicated as a highway, or the date on which such dedication, if any, took place, shall take into consideration any map, plan or history of the locality or other relevant document which is tendered in evidence, and shall give such weight thereto as the court or tribunal considers justified by the circumstances, including the antiquity of the tendered document, the status of the person by whom and the purpose for which it was made or compiled, and the custody in which it has been kept and from which it is produced.

Note.—This provision re-enacts the Highways Act 1959, s.35, which was a partial re-enactment of the Rights of Way Act 1932, s.3.

ANIMAL HEALTH ACT 1981

1981, c. 22

79.—(2) Where the owner or person in charge of an animal is charged with an offence against this Act relative to disease or to any illness of the animal, he shall be presumed to have known of the existence of the disease or illness unless and until he shows to the court's satisfaction that—

    (a) he had not knowledge of the existence of that disease or illness, and

    (b) he could not with reasonable diligence have obtained that knowledge.

(3) Where a person—

    (a) is charged with an offence against this Act in not having duly cleansed or disinfected any place, vessel, aircraft, vehicle or thing belonging to him or under his charge, and

    (b) a presumption against him on the part of the prosecution is raised,

it shall lie on him to prove the due cleansing and disinfection mentioned in paragraph (a).

(4) Every offence against this Act shall be deemed to have been committed, and every cause of complaint or matter for summary proceeding under this Act or an order of the Minister or regulation of a local authority shall be deemed to have arisen, either in any place—

    (a) where it actually was committed or arose; or

    (b) where the person charged or complained of or proceeded against happens to be at the time of the institution or commencement of the charge, complaint or proceeding.

Note.—These subsections illustrate some distinctions, verbal and/or real, relating to burdens and presumptions (see Part One, Chapter 4, Section B, *supra*). Whereas subsection (2), although couched in terms of a presumption, indicates the incidence of the legal burden of proof on the issue of knowledge, subsection (4) lays down what is sometimes described as an irrebuttable or conclusive presumption of law. The significance of subsection (3)(b) is, however, not altogether clear. Either it means that what the subsection in effect does is simply to propound a presumption of fact. Or, alternatively, it may denote a compelling presumption of law,—the adduction by the prosecution of some affirmative evidence of the non-existence of the presumed fact (due cleansing and disinfection) being one of the basic facts, *i.e.* one of the facts to be established before the presumption is operative.

CRIMINAL ATTEMPTS ACT 1981

1981, c. 47

2.—(1) Any provision to which this section applies shall have effect with respect to an offence under section 1 above of attempting to commit an offence as it has effect with respect to the offence attempted.

(2) This section applies to provisions of any of the following descriptions made by or under any enactment (whenever passed)—

    . . . .

    (g) provisions whereby a person may not be convicted or committed for trial on the uncorroborated evidence of one witness (including any provision requiring the evidence of not less than two credible witnesses);

Note.—This Act abolished the common law offence of attempt and replaced it with a statutory offence. Section 2 is designed to ensure that any statutory rule, such as is mentioned in subsection (2) as applicable to a particular substantive offence, shall be equally applicable to an attempt to commit that offence. As regards subsection (2)(g) there are two types of rules about corroboration—one simply requiring it, and the other requiring that the jury be warned of the risks of convicting on uncorroborated evidence (see Part One, Chapter 10, *supra*). Only the former rules are "made by or under any enactment," *e.g.* the Perjury Act 1911, s.13, the Sexual Offences Act 1956, s.2(2) (both *supra*) and the Road Traffic Regulation Act 1984, s.89(2) (*infra*). It is, however, not unreasonable to suppose that as a matter of common law a mandatory warning rule (such as that relating to the evidence of an accomplice) will be equally applicable in a prosecution for an attempt under this Act.

4.—(3) Where, in proceedings against a person for an offence under section 1 above, there is evidence sufficient in law to support a finding that he did an act falling within subsection (1) of that section, the question whether or not his act fell within that subsection is a question of fact.

Note.—Section 1(1) outlines the ingredients of the newly created statutory offence of attempting to commit an offence.

Section 4(4) is similar to section 4(3), except that it deals with proceedings against a person for an attempt under some other special statutory provision. These two subsections apparently represent a somewhat convoluted, and probably largely unnecessary, codification of the respective functions of judge and jury as had been laid down by a majority of the House of Lords in *D.P.P.* v. *Stonehouse* [1978] A.C. 55 (Part One, Chapter 1, Section D, *supra*).

CONTEMPT OF COURT ACT 1981

1981, c. 49

10. No court may require a person to disclose, nor is any person guilty of contempt of court for refusing to disclose, the source of information contained in a publication for which he is responsible, unless it be established to the satisfaction of the court that disclosure is necessary in the interests of justice or national security or for the prevention of disorder or crime.

Note.—See Part One, Chapter 11, Section C, *supra*.

SUPREME COURT ACT 1981

1981, c. 54

69.—(5) Where for the purpose of disposing of any action or other matter which is being tried in the High Court by a judge with a jury it is necessary to ascertain the law of any other country which is applicable to the facts of the case, any question as to the effect of the evidence given with respect to that law shall, instead of being submitted to the jury, be decided by the judge alone.

Note.—Judicial notice is not taken of foreign law. The content of foreign law is proved as a fact—usually by expert testimony. Although an issue of fact, it is determined by the judge.

72.—(1) In any proceedings to which this subsection applies a person shall not be excused, by reason that to do so would tend to expose that person, or his or her spouse, to proceedings for a related offence or for the recovery of a related penalty—

    (*a*) from answering any question put to that person in the first-mentioned proceedings; or

(b) from complying with any order made in those proceedings.

(2) Subsection (1) applies to the following civil proceedings in the High Court, namely—

(a) proceedings for infringement of rights pertaining to any intellectual property or for passing off;

(b) proceedings brought to obtain disclosure of information relating to any infringement of such rights or to any passing off; and

(c) proceedings brought to prevent any apprehended infringement of such rights or any apprehended passing off.

(3) Subject to subsection (4), no statement or admission made by a person—

(a) in answering a question put to him in any proceedings to which subsection (1) applies; or

(b) in complying with any order made in any such proceedings, shall, in proceedings for any related offence or for the recovery of any related penalty, be admissible in evidence against that person or (unless they married after the making of the statement or admission) against the spouse of that person.

(4) Nothing in subsection (3) shall render any statement or admission made by a person as there mentioned inadmissible in evidence against that person in proceedings for perjury or contempt of court.

(5) In this section—

"intellectual property" means any patent, trade mark, copyright, registered design, technical or commercial information or other intellectual property;

"related offence," in relation to any proceedings to which subsection (1) applies, means—

(a) in the case of proceedings within subsection (2)(a) or (b)—

(i) any offence committed by or in the course of the infringement or passing off to which those proceedings relate; or

(ii) any offence not within sub-paragraph (i) committed in connection with that infringement or passing off, being an offence involving fraud or dishonesty;

(b) in the case of proceedings within subsection (2)(c), any offence revealed by the facts on which the plaintiff relies in those proceedings;

"related penalty," in relation to any proceedings to which subsection (1) applies means—

(a) in the case of proceedings within subsection (2)(a) or (b), any penalty incurred in respect of anything done or omitted in connection with the infringement or passing off to which those proceedings relate;

(b) in the case of proceedings within subsection (2)(c), any penalty incurred in respect of any act or omission revealed by the facts on which the plaintiff relies in those proceedings.

(6) Any reference in this section to civil proceedings in the High Court of any description includes a reference to proceedings on appeal arising out of civil proceedings in the High Court of that description.

Note.—Section 54(6) of the Cable and Broadcasting Act 1984 extends the scope of this section to certain High Court proceedings brought by virtue of that section of that Act.

As to the meaning of the words "any offence" in the definition of "related offence" in section 72(5)(b), see *Universal City Studios* v. *Hubbard* [1984] Ch. 225 (C.A.).

132. Every document purporting to be sealed or stamped with the seal or stamp of the Supreme Court or of any office of the Supreme Court shall be received in evidence in all parts of the United Kingdom without further proof.

Note.—See, too, R.S.C, Ord. 38, r. 10(2).

CIVIL JURISDICTION AND JUDGMENTS ACT 1982

1982, c. 27

11.—(1) For the purposes of the 1968 Convention—
  (a) a document, duly authenticated, which purports to be a copy of a judgment given by a court of a Contracting State other than the United Kingdom shall without further proof be deemed to be a true copy, unless the contrary is shown; and
  (b) the original or a copy of any such document as is mentioned in Articles 46(2) or 47 (supporting documents to be produced by a party seeking recognition or enforcement of a judgment) shall be evidence, and in Scotland sufficient evidence, of any matter to which it relates.

(2) A document purporting to be a copy of a judgment given by any such court as is mentioned in subsection (1)(a) is duly authenticated for the purpose of this section if it purports—
  (a) to bear the seal of that court; or
  (b) to be certified by any person in his capacity as a judge or officer of that court to be a true copy of a judgment given by that court.

(3) Nothing in this section shall prejudice the admission in evidence of any document which is admissible apart from this section.

Note.—The primary purpose of this Act is to give effect to the Brussels Convention of 1968 on jurisdiction and the enforcement of judgments in civil and commercial matters. Members of the EEC are (or will become) "Contracting States." Section 11 of the Act makes provision relating to the proof in the United Kingdom of the judgments of the courts of other Contracting States.

CRIMINAL JUSTICE ACT 1982

1982, c. 48

72.—(1) Subject to subsections (2) and (3) below, in any criminal proceedings the accused shall not be entitled to make a statement without being sworn, and accordingly, if he gives evidence, he shall do so on oath and be liable to cross-examination; but this section shall not affect the right of the accused, if not represented by counsel or a solicitor, to address the court or jury otherwise than on oath on any matter on which, if he were so represented, counsel or a solicitor could address the court or jury on his behalf.

(2) Nothing in subsection (1) above shall prevent the accused making a statement without being sworn—
  (a) if it is one which he is required by law to make personally; or

(b) if he makes it by way of mitigation before the court passes sentence upon him.

Note.—This section abolished the common law right of an accused person to make an unsworn statement from the dock without being subject to cross-examination.

ADMINISTRATION OF JUSTICE ACT 1982

1982, c. 53

21.—(1) This section applies to a will—

(a) in so far as any part of it is meaningless:

(b) in so far as the language used in any part of it is ambiguous on the face of it;

(c) in so far as evidence, other than evidence of the testator's intention, shows that the language used in any part of it is ambiguous in the light of surrounding circumstances.

(2) In so far as this section applies to a will extrinsic evidence, including evidence of the testator's intention, may be admitted to assist in its interpretation.

Note.—See *Re Williams (dec'd)* [1985] 1 W.L.R. 905 (Ch.D), where it was said that the purpose of admitting extrinsic evidence is to assist in the construction of the will, and not to facilitate its rewriting.

REPRESENTATION OF THE PEOPLE ACT 1983

1983, c. 2

141.—(1) A person called as a witness respecting an election before any election court shall not be excused from answering any question relating to any offence at or connected with the election—

(a) on the ground that the answer to it may incriminate or tend to incriminate—

(i) that person or that person's husband or wife, or

(ii) in Scotland, that person; or

(b) on the ground of privilege.

(2) An answer by a person to a question put by or before any election court shall not, except in the case of any criminal proceeding for perjury in respect of the evidence, be in any proceeding, civil or criminal, admissible in evidence against—

(a) that person or that person's husband or wife; or

(b) in Scotland, that person.

ROAD TRAFFIC REGULATION ACT 1984

1984, c. 27

89.—(1) A person who drives a motor vehicle on a road at a speed exceeding a limit imposed by or under any enactment to which this section applies shall be guilty of an offence.

(2) A person prosecuted for such an offence shall not be liable to be convicted solely on the evidence of one witness to the effect that, in the opinion of the witness, the person prosecuted was driving the vehicle at a speed exceeding a specified limit.

(4) If a person who employs other person to drive motor vehicles on roads publishes or issues any time-table or schedule, or gives any directions, under which any journey, or any stage or part of any journey, is to be completed within some specified time, and it is not practicable in the circumstances of the case for that journey (or that stage or part of it) to be completed in the specified time without the commission of such an offence as is mentioned in subsection (1) above, the publication or issue of the time-table or schedule, or the giving of the directions, may be produced as prima facie evidence that the employer procured or (as the case may be) incited the persons employed by him to drive the vehicles to commit such an offence.

Note.—For the interpretation of s.89(2) see *Nicholas* v. *Penny* [1950] 2 K.B. 466 (D.C.) and *Note* thereon (Part One, Chapter 10, Section A, *supra*).

Subsection (4) appears to create a permissive rebuttable presumption. See Part One, Chapter 4, (*supra*).

COUNTY COURTS ACT 1984

1984 c. 28

56. The High Court shall have the same power to issue a commission, request or order to examine witnesses abroad for the purpose of proceedings in a county court as it has for the purpose of an action or matter in the High Court.

68. Where, for the purpose of disposing of any proceedings which are being tried in a county court by the judge with a jury, it is necessary to ascertain the law of any other country which is applicable to the facts of the case, any question as to the effect of the evidence given with respect to that law shall, instead of being submitted to the jury, be decided by the judge alone.

Note.—See *Note* to section 69(5) of the Supreme Court Act 1981 (*supra*).

DATA PROTECTION ACT 1984

1984, c. 35

31.—(2) Personal data are exempt from the subject access provisions if the data consist of information in respect of which a claim to legal professional privilege (or, in Scotland, to confidentiality as between client and professional legal advisor) could be maintained in legal proceedings.

Note.—A "Data subject" is an individual who is the subject of personal data. His or her general right of access to personal data is set out in section 21.

For legal professional privilege generally, see Part One, Chapter 11, Section B (*supra*).

POLICE AND CRIMINAL EVIDENCE ACT 1984

1984, c. 60

Part II

Powers of Entry Search and Seizure

10.—(1) Subject to subsection (2) below, in this Act "items subject to legal privilege" means—

(a) communications between a professional legal adviser and his client or any person representing his client made in connection with the giving of legal advice to the client;

(b) communications between a professional legal adviser and his client or any person representing his client or between such an adviser or his client or any such representative and any other person made in connection with or in contemplation of legal proceedings and for the purposes of such proceedings; and

(c) items enclosed with or referred to in such communications and made—

(i) in connection with the giving of legal advice; or

(ii) in connection with or in contemplation of legal proceedings and for the purposes of such proceedings,

when they are in the possession of a person who is entitled to possession of them.

(2) Items held with the intention of further a criminal purpose are not items subject to legal privilege.

Note.—The Act does not allow search warrants to be issued to the police for items subject to legal proceedings (s.8(1)(*d*) and s.9(2)), or allow such items to be sought after arrest (s.18), or allow their seizure (s.19(6)).

For the interpretation of section 10 see *R. v. Central Criminal Court, ex p. Francis and Francis* [1989] A.C. 346 (H.L.), (Chapter 11, Section B, *supra*).

Part V

Questioning and Treatment of Persons by Police

62.—(1) An intimate sample may be taken from a person in police detention only—

(a) if a police officer of at least the rank of superintendent authorises it to be taken; and

(b) if the appropriate consent is given.

(2)–(9). . . .

(10) Where the appropriate consent to the taking of an intimate sample from a person was refused without good cause, in any proceedings against that person for an offence—

    (a) the court, in determining—
        (i) whether to commit that person for trial; or
        (ii) whether there is a case to answer; and
    (b) the court or jury, in determining whether that person is guilty of the offence charged,

may draw such inferences from the refusal as appear proper; and the refusal may, on the basis of such inferences, be treated as, or as capable of amounting to, corroboration of any evidence against the person in relation to which the refusal is material.

Note.—"Intimate sample" means a sample of blood, semen or any other tissue fluid, urine, saliva or pubic hair, or a swab taken from a person's body orifice (s.65). Whether a refusal of consent was made with "good cause" is a question of fact. Under comparable road traffic legislation it is for the accused to provide some evidence of a reasonable excuse and for the prosecution then to negative the defence to the satisfaction of the jury or magistrates (see, *e.g. R.* v. *Clarke* [1969] 1 W.L.R. 1109 (C.A.)). For sufficiency of evidence generally, see Part One, Chapter 1, Section B (*supra*).

For corroboration generally, see Part One, Chapter 10 (*supra*).

PART VI

CODES OF PRACTICE—GENERAL

66. The Secretary of State shall issue codes of practice in connection with—
    (a) the exercise by police officers of statutory powers—
        (i) to search a person without first arresting him; or
        (ii) to search a vehicle without making an arrest;
    (b) the detention, treatment, questioning and identification of persons by police officers;
    (c) searches of premises by police officers; and
    (d) the seizure of property found by police officers on persons or premises.

Note.—Four Codes of Practice have been issued:

A. Code of Practice for the Exercise by Police Officers of Statutory Powers of Stop and Search.

B. Code of Practice for the Searching of Premises by Police Officers and the Seizure of Property found by Police Officers on Persons or Premises.

C. Code of Practice For the Detention, Treatment and Questioning of Persons by Police Officers.

D. Code of Practice for the Identification of Persons by Police Officers.

These Codes came into force (subject to various transitional arrangements) on January 1, 1986. They superseded previous provisions (including the Judges' Rules) and introduce much wholly new material. A failure on the part of a law enforcement officer to comply with a Code may trigger off the exclusionary discretion embodied in section 78 (*infra*): see, *e.g. R.* v. *Foster* [1987] Crim.L.R. 821; although such failure "shall not of itself render him liable to any criminal or civil proceedings" (section 67(10)). In *R.* v. *Delaney* [1988] C.L.Y. 545 (C.A.) it was re-affirmed that a failure to observe the Code does not automatically lead to the rejection of evidence.

PART VII

DOCUMENTARY EVIDENCE IN CRIMINAL PROCEEDINGS

68. [This section has been repealed by the Criminal Justice Act 1988, Sched. 16. See now Part II of that Act (*infra*).]

69.—(1) In any proceedings, a statement in a document produced by a computer shall not be admissible as evidence of any fact stated therein unless it is shown—

(*a*) that there are no reasonable grounds for believing that the statement is inaccurate because of improper use of the computer;

(*b*) that at all material times the computer was operating properly, or if not, that any respect in which it was not operating properly or was out of operation was not such as to affect the production of the document or the accuracy of its contents; and

(*c*) that any relevant conditions specified in rules of court under subsection (2) below are satisfied.

(2) Provision may be made by rules of court requiring that in any proceedings where it is desired to give a statement in evidence by virtue of this section such information concerning the statement as may be required by the rules shall be provided in such form and at such time as may be so required.

General Notes on section 69—

(i) The section is to be read with Parts II and III of Schedule 3 of the Act (see s.70, *infra*).

(ii) Compliance with the conditions set out in subsection (1) may be established by a certificate "(*a*) identifying the document containing the statement and describing the manner in which it was produced; (*b*) giving such particulars of any device involved in the production of that document as may be appropriate for the purpose of showing that the document was produced by a computer; (*c*) dealing with any of the matters mentioned in subsection (1) of section 69 . . . and (*d*) purporting to be signed by a person occupying a responsible position in relation to the operation of the computer" (Sched. 3, para. 8). Notwithstanding that such a certificate is to be treated as "evidence of anything stated in it" (Sched. 3, para. 8) a court may require oral evidence to be given of anything of which evidence could be given by means of the certificate (Sched. 3, para. 9). It is sufficient for a matter to be stated to the best of the knowledge and belief of the signatory (Sched. 3, para. 8). But a person who in a certificate makes a statement which he knows to be false or does not believe to be true commits a criminal offence (Sched. 3, para. 10).

(iii) "Proceedings" means criminal proceedings, and for the scope of this and for the meaning of "statement" see s.72(1) *infra*. "Computer" is not defined: compare the Civil Evidence Act 1968, s.5(6) (*supra*).

(iv) Hearsay statements produced by computer must draw their admissibility from some source other than section 69—usually this source (which was formerly section 68) will now be the Criminal Justice Act 1988, ss.23 and 24 (*infra*). Section 69 lays down *additional* conditions which are to be satisfied for computer-produced hearsay to be admitted: sections 23 and 24 of the 1988 Act are "subject to section 69" of the 1984 Act: see *R. v. Minors* [1989] 1 W.L.R. 441 (C.A.).

(v) The better view probably is that real, as distinct from documentary, evidence is unaffected by section 69. An example of this would be the case in which the computer is operating simply as a mechanical device: see *R. v. Wood* (1982) 76 Cr.App.R. 23 (C.A.); *Castle v. Cross* [1984] 1 W.L.R. 1372 (D.C.), and *Sophocleus v. Ringer* [1988] R.T.R. 52 (D.C.). On real evidence generally see Part I, Chapter 25, (*supra*).

(vi) In estimating the weight, if any, to be attached to a statement by a computer "regard shall be had to all the circumstances from which any inference can reasonably be drawn as to the accuracy or otherwise of the statement and, in particular—(*a*) to the question whether or not the information which the information contained in the statement reproduces or is derived from was supplied to the relevant computer, or recorded for the purpose of being supplied to it, contemporaneously with the occurrence or existence of the facts dealt with in that information; and (*b*) to the question whether or not any person concerned with the supply of information to that computer, or with the operation of that computer or any equipment by means of which the document containing the statement was produced by it, had any incentive to conceal or misrepresent the facts" (Sched. 3, para. 11).

(vii) In considering the admissibility of a statement the court may draw any reasonable inference from the circumstances in which it was made or otherwise came into being, or from any other circumstances, including the form and contents of the document in which it is contained (Sched. 3, para. 14).

(viii) Section 72(2) preserves all existing common law and statutory discretions to exclude evidence otherwise admissible under the section. See, too, section 78.

70.—(1) Part I of Schedule 3 to this Act shall have effect for the purpose of supplementing section 68 above.

(2) Part II of that Schedule shall have effect for the purpose of supplementing section 69 above.

(3) Part III of that Schedule shall have effect for the purpose of supplementing both sections.

71. In any proceedings the contents of a document may (whether or not the document is still in existence) be proved by the production of an enlargement of a microfilm copy of that document or of the material part of it, authenticated in such manner as the court may approve.

Note.—This section modifies the common law rule that secondary evidence is normally only admissible if the original is unavailable (see Part One, Chapter 24, *supra*). For the meaning of "copy," see section 72 (*infra*).

72.—(1) In this Part of this Act—

"copy" and "statement" have the same meanings as in Part I of the Civil Evidence Act 1968; and

"proceedings" means criminal proceedings, including—

> (*a*) proceedings in the United Kingdom or elsewhere before a court-martial constituted under the Army Act 1955 or the Air Force Act 1955;
>
> (*b*) proceedings in the United Kingdom or elsewhere before the Courts-Martial Appeal Court—
>
>> (*i*) on an appeal from a court-martial so constituted or from a court-martial constituted under the Naval Discipline Act 1957; or
>>
>> (*ii*) on a reference under section 34 of the Courts-Martial (Appeals) Act 1968; and
>
> (*c*) proceedings before a Standing Civilian Court.

(2) Nothing in this Part of this Act shall prejudice any power of a court to exclude evidence (whether by preventing questions from being put or otherwise) at its discretion.

Note.—In connection with subsection (2) see, too, section 78; and in connection with both provisions see the *Note* on *R.* v. *List* [1966] 1 W.L.R. 9 (Part One, Chapter 1, Section A, *supra*).

PART VIII

EVIDENCE IN CRIMINAL PROCEEDINGS—GENERAL

Convictions and acquittals

73.—(1) Where in any proceedings the fact that a person has in the United Kingdom been convicted or acquitted of an offence otherwise than by a Service court is admissible in evidence, it may be proved by producing a certificate of conviction or, as the case may be, of acquittal relating to that offence, and proving that the person named in the certificate as having been convicted or acquitted of the offence is the person whose conviction or acquittal of the offence is to be proved.

(2) For the purposes of this section a certificate of conviction or of acquittal—

> (*a*) shall, as regards a conviction or acquittal on indictment, consist of a certificate, signed by the clerk of the court where the conviction or acquittal took place, giving the substance and effect (omitting the formal parts) of the indictment and of the conviction or acquittal; and
>
> (*b*) shall, as regards a conviction or acquittal on a summary trial, consist of a copy of the conviction or of the dismissal of the information, signed by the clerk of the court where the conviction or acquittal took place or by the clerk of the court, if any, to which a memorandum of the conviction or acquittal was sent;

and a document purporting to be a duly signed certificate of conviction or acquittal under this section shall be taken to be such a certificate unless the contrary is proved.

(3) References in this section to the clerk of a court include references to his deputy and to any other person having the custody of the court record.

(4) The method of proving a conviction or acquittal authorised by this section shall be in addition to and not to the exclusion of any other authorised manner of proving a conviction or acquittal.

General Notes on Section 73—
(i) The only purpose of this section is to revise the rules governing the method of proving a conviction or acquittal which is admissible in evidence. It does not affect that admissibility itself.

(ii) The section supersedes section 13 of the Evidence Act 1851, part of section 6 of the Criminal Evidence Act 1865, and section 18 of the Prevention of Crimes Act 1871.

(iii) Other accepted methods of proving a conviction, such as evidence by a person present in court and finger-print evidence (see the Criminal Justice Act 1948, s.39, *supra*), are preserved.

74.—(1) In any proceedings the fact that a person other than the accused has been convicted of an offence by or before any court in the United Kingdom or by a Service court outside the United Kingdom shall be admissible in evidence for the purpose of proving, where to do so is relevant to any issue in those proceedings, that that person committed that offence, whether or not any other evidence of his having committed that offence is given.

Note.—A "Service court" is a court martial or standing civilian court (see s.82).

(2) In any proceedings in which by virtue of this section a person other than the accused is proved to have been convicted of an offence by or before any court in the United Kingdom or by a Service court outside the United Kingdom, he shall be taken to have committed that offence unless the contrary is proved.

(3) In any proceedings where evidence is admissible of the fact that the accused has committed an offence, in so far as that evidence is relevant to any matter in issue in the proceedings for a reason other than a tendency to show in the accused a disposition to commit the kind of offence with which he is charged, if the accused is proved to have been convicted of the offence—

(*a*) by or before any court in the United Kingdom; or

(*b*) by a Service court outside the United Kingdom,

he shall be taken to have committed that offence unless the contrary is proved.

(4) Nothing in this section shall prejudice—

(*a*) the admissibility in evidence of any conviction which would be admissible apart from this section; or

(*b*) the operation of any enactment whereby a conviction or a finding of fact in any proceedings is for the purposes of any other proceedings made conclusive evidence of any fact.

Note.—In connection with section 4(*a*) see, *e.g.* the Criminal Procedure Act 1865, s.6 (*supra*). As regards section 4(*b*) it would appear that there is in fact no existing provision of a Public General Act which renders a conviction conclusive evidence of a fact.

General Notes on Section 74—
(i) At common law evidence that a person had been convicted of an offence was not admissible in subsequent proceedings for the purpose of proving his actual commission of that offence or the facts upon which the conviction had been based. This rule was abrogated in relation to subsequent civil proceedings by section 11 of the Civil Evidence Act 1968 (*supra*). Section 74 deals with the position in relation to subsequent criminal proceedings. See, generally, Part One, Chapter 19 (*supra*).
(ii) Subsections (1) and (2) provide for the admission, in subsequent criminal proceedings, of evidence of the previous conviction of *a person other than the accused* in order to prove that person's commission of the offence. The effect of reception of the evidence is to shift this legal burden of proof on the issue of commission. (See, too, the Civil Evidence Act 1968, s.11, *supra*). The standard of proof required to discharge this burden is presumably, the balance of probabilities when it rests upon the defence, but beyond reasonable doubt when it rests upon the prosecution.
(iii) The term "issue" in subsection (1) applies not only to facts in issue in the strict sense but also to relevant facts: *R.* v. *Robertson*; *R.* v. *Golder* [1987] 1 Q.B. 920 (C.A.).
(iv) Subsection (3) makes similar, but qualified, provision with regard to evidence of a previous conviction of *the accused.*
(v) A previous conviction of an accused is admissible to prove his actual commission of the offence only if his commission of it, either is (exceptionally) admissible at common law, or is admissible by virtue of some specific statutory provision (*e.g.* the Theft Act 1968, s.27(3), *supra*). Section 74(3), unlike section 74(1), does not therefore widen admissibility of evidence of the fact of commission.
(vi) If evidence that the accused has committed a similar crime to that charged is relevant solely on a "propensity" basis but is nevertheless (exceptionally) admissible at common law, commission of the earlier offence cannot be proved by virtue of section 74(3). In such a case the common law survives, and commission must be proved by means other than by proof of conviction. It is, however, submitted that the qualified wording of section 74(3) does not inhibit proof of commission by way of proof of conviction if the similar fact evidence is relevant and admissible on a "non-propensity" basis. For a discussion of the distinction between "propensity" evidence and similar fact evidence relevant in other ways, see Part One, Chapter 20 (*supra*).

(vii) For the need to use sections 74 and 75 "sparingly," and its relationship with s.78, see *per curiam* statement in *R.* v. *Robertson*; *R.* v. *Golder* [1987] 1 Q.B. 920 (C.A.) (Part One, Chapter 17, *Note* on *R.* v. *O'Connor* (1987) 85 Cr.App.R. 298 (C.A.)).

75.—(1) Where evidence that a person has been convicted of an offence is admissible by virtue of section 74 above, then without prejudice to the reception of any other admissible evidence for the purpose of identifying the facts on which the conviction was based—

(a) the contents of any document which is admissible as evidence of the conviction; and

(b) the contents of the information, complaint, indictment or charge-sheet on which the person in question was convicted,

shall be admissible in evidence for that purpose.

(2) Where in any proceedings the contents of any document are admissible in evidence by virtue of subsection (1) above, a copy of that document, or of the material part of it, purporting to be certified or otherwise authenticated by or on behalf of the court or authority having custody of that document shall be admissible in evidence and shall be taken to be a true copy of that document or part unless the contrary is shown.

(3) Nothing in any of the following—

(a) section 13 of the Powers of Criminal Courts Act 1973 (under which a conviction leading to probation or discharge is to be disregarded except as mentioned in that section);

(b) section 392 of the Criminal Procedure (Scotland) Act 1975 (which makes similar provision in respect of convictions on indictment in Scotland); and

(c) section 8 of the Probation Act (Northern Ireland) 1950 (which corresponds to section 13 of the Powers of Criminal Courts Act 1973) or any legislation which is in force in Northern Ireland for the time being and corresponds to that section,

shall affect the operation of section 74 above; and for the purposes of that section any order made by a court of summary jurisdiction in Scotland under section 182 or section 183 of the said Act of 1975 shall be treated as a conviction.

(4) Nothing in section 74 above shall be construed as rendering admissible in any proceedings evidence of any conviction other than a subsisting one.

Note.—A "subsisting" conviction is one which has not been quashed on appeal or been the subject of a Royal Pardon. It may seemingly, however, be "spent," the Rehabilitation of Offenders Act 1974 (*supra*) does not apply to evidence tendered in criminal proceedings.

Confessions

General Note on sections 76 and 77.—Section 76 changes, drastically in form and significantly in substance, the common law relating to the admissibility of evidence, tendered by the prosecution in criminal proceedings, of a confession by an accused person. The test of voluntariness (see Part One, Chapter 17, *supra*) is replaced by a rule of admissibility subject to two, sometimes overlapping, rules of exclusion (subsection (2)(*a*) and (2)(*b*)).

Section 77 lays down additional requirements in the case of a confession made, in the absence of an independent adult, by a mentally-handicapped accused.

On the law governing confessions and related matters generally, see Part One, Chapter 17, (*supra*).

76.—(1) In any proceedings a confession made by an accused person may be given in evidence against him in so far as it is relevant to any matter in issue in the proceedings and is not excluded by the court in pursuance of this section.

Note.—But section 82(3) preserves any power of the court to exclude a confession in its discretion. For the meaning of "confession" see s.82(1).

(2) If, in any proceedings where the prosecution proposes to give in evidence a confession made by an accused person, it is represented to the court that the confession was or may have been obtained—

    (*a*) by oppression of the person who made it; or

    (*b*) in consequence of anything said or done which was likely, in the circumstances existing at the time, to render unreliable any confession which might be made by him in consequence thereof,

the court shall not allow the confession to be given in evidence against him except in so far as the prosecution proves to the court beyond reasonable doubt that the confession (notwithstanding that it may be true) was not obtained as aforesaid.

Note.—Presumably, despite the wording, it is still possible to challenge a confession which the prosecution does not "propose" to give in evidence but has already done so. On the other hand the case of evidence given on behalf of a co-accused is not covered.

"Oppression" is partially defined in s.76(8). *cf.* Code of Practice for the Detention, Treatment and Questioning of Persons by Police Officers, para. 11.1: "No police officer may try to obtain answers to questions or to elicit a statement by the use of oppression..."

"[A]nything said or done" is not limited to conduct directed at the accused or to conduct emanating from his interrogators. But, if it does emanate from a person in authority, it may be more likely to have influenced the accused. The phrase does extend to conduct of the accused: *R.* v. *Goldenberg* (1989) 88 Cr.App.R. 285 (C.A.). The conduct must have *caused* the likelihood of unreliability; but, for a pre-Act case in which several different factors had, or may have had, a causative effect in the context of voluntariness see *R.* v. *Rennie* [1982] 1 W.L.R. 64 (C.A.). There Lord Lane C.J. said (p. 70): "The answer will not be found from any refined analysis of the concept of causation ... Although the question is for the judge, he should approach it much as would a jury, were it for them." These words have been cited with approval in a post-Act case, *R.* v. *Phillips* (1988) 86 Cr.App.R. 18 (C.A.).

It is not clear whether the court can exclude a confession made in consequence of something "said or done" if it was sanctioned by the provisions of the Act or by the *Codes of Practice* (see s.66).

The test under section 2(*b*) is put in terms, not of the actual unreliability of the confession in question, but of the likelihood of "any" confession being unreliable. "Any" presumably does not mean "every" but rather "at least one." Common sense requires that the actual confession be excluded if the thing "said or done" was likely to render *it* unreliable, although any confession might not have been so rendered.

It is important to assess reliability in the context of the particular accused, regard being had to factors such as age, experience, mental ability, etc.

The necessary proof by the prosecution "to the court beyond reasonable doubt" will normally be on the *voir dire* (or at a "trial within the trial") conducted by the judge in the absence of the jury. For details see Part One, Chapter 17 (*supra*). When a judge, who has ruled a confession admissible in evidence, changes his mind in the light of further evidence before the jury, he is not bound to discharge the jury but may conclude that the matter is capable of remedy by an appropriate direction. The force of section 76 is apparently seen as being spent, and the judge's power would seemingly, therefore, derive from section 82(3) (*infra*): see *R.* v. *Sat-Bhambra* (1988) 88 Cr.App.R. 55 (C.A.).

Given the wording of the subsections (1) and (2) it might be (unattractively) argued that an admission made by an accused during the *voir dire* would itself be admissible as a confession since it would almost certainly satisfy the conditions laid down in subsection (2) and would, therefore, at least as a matter of law, be admissible under subsection (1). This result may well not have been intended, and it would cast doubt upon the authority of *Wong Kam-ming* v. *R.* [1980] A.C. 247 (Part One, Chapter 17, *supra*) in which the Privy Council put the law on a rational basis and which was followed by the House of Lords in *R.* v. *Brophy* [1982] A.C. 476. Moreover, *Wong Kam-ming* v. *R.* has been applied in at least one post-Act case: *R.* v. *Liverpool Juvenile Court, ex p. R.* [1988] Q.B. 1 (D.C.) (Part One, Chapter 17, *supra*).

(3) In any proceedings where the prosecution proposes to give in evidence a confession made by an accused person, the court may of its own motion require the prosecution, as a condition of allowing it to do so, to prove that the confession was not obtained as mentioned in subsection (2) above.

Note.—This may have particular importance in Magistrates' Courts where an accused is less likely to be represented.

(4) The fact that a confession is wholly or partly excluded in pursuance of this section shall not affect the admissibility in evidence—
  (a) of any facts discovered as a result of the confession; or
  (b) where the confession is relevant as showing that the accused speaks, writes or expresses himself in a particular way, of so much of the confession as is necessary to show that he does so.
(5) Evidence that a fact to which this subsection applies was discovered as a result of a statement made by an accused person shall not be admissible unless evidence of how it was discovered is given by him or on his behalf.
(6) Subsection (5) above applies—
  (a) to any fact discovered as a result of a confession which is wholly excluded in pursuance of this section; and
  (b) to any fact discovered as a result of a confession which is partly so excluded, if the fact is discovered as a result of the excluded part of the confession.

Note.—See Part One, Chapter 17 (*supra*). Whereas subsection (4) restates existing law, subsections (5) and (6) qualify the substance of subsection (4)(a). The effect of subsection (5) can be illustrated thus: if an accused under physical pressure tells the police where stolen goods are hidden, the goods can be produced and evidence can be given of any fingerprints on them. But evidence cannot be given, except by the accused or someone on his behalf, as to how the police came to look for them in the place where they were found.

(7) Nothing in Part VII of this Act shall prejudice the admissibility of a confession made by an accused person.
(8) In this section "oppression" includes torture, inhuman or degrading treatment, and the use or threat or violence (whether or not amounting to torture).

Note.—This "definition" of "oppression" does not purport to be exhaustive. Much of the pre-Act case law on the subject is seemingly now of limited importance: *R.* v. *Fulling* [1987] 1 Q.B. 426 (C.A.), (Part One, Chapter 17, *supra*); and see *e.g. R.* v. *Davison* [1988] Crim.L.R. 442; [1989] 4 C.L. 70 (Cent.C.C.); and more generally see Chapter 17.

77.—(1) Without prejudice to the general duty of the court at a trial on indictment to direct the jury on any matter on which it appears to the court appropriate to do so, where at such a trial—

  (*a*) the case against the accused depends wholly or substantially on a confession by him; and

  (*b*) the court is satisfied—

     (*i*) that he is mentally handicapped; and

     (*ii*) that the confession was not made in the presence of an independent person,

the court shall warn the jury that there is special need for caution before convicting the accused in reliance on the confession, and shall explain that the need arises because of the circumstances mentioned in paragraphs (*a*) and (*b*) above.

(2) In any case where at the summary trial of a person for an offence it appears to the court that a warning under subsection (1) above would be required if the trial were on indictment, the court shall treat the case as one in which there is a special need for caution before convicting the accused on his confession.

Note.—This section only operates in a case in which the confession is not inadmissible. Presumably it is for the defence to satisfy the court on the balance of probabilities that the facts giving rise to the warning requirement do exist.

The concept of corroboration (as to which, see Part One, Chapter 10, *supra*) is avoided. However, the desirability of corroboration is mentioned in the Code of Practice for the Detention etc., para. 13B.

There is no statement of the consequences of the failure to warn. As the rule is mandatory, presumably such failure would constitute a misdirection.

(3) In this section—

"independent person" does not include a police officer or a person employed for, or engaged on, police purposes;

"mentally handicapped," in relation to a person, means that he is in a state of arrested or incomplete development of mind which includes significant impairment of intelligence and social functioning; and

"police purposes" has the meaning assigned to it by section 64 of the Police Act 1964.

Note.—Nor is a Customs and Excise officer or any person acting under the authority of the Commissioners of Customs and Excise an "independent person": S.I. 1985 No. 1800 Art. 10.

The (presumably exhaustive) definition of mentally handicapped does not seem to cover cases of temporary impairment (such as that resulting from concussion), cases of acquired mental illness, or cases of pure senility.

Miscellaneous

78.—(1) In any proceedings the court may refuse to allow evidence on which the prosecution proposes to rely to be given if it appears to the court that, having regard to all the circumstances, including the circumstances in which the evidence was obtained, the admission of the evidence would have such an adverse effect on the fairness of the proceedings that the court ought not to admit it.

(2) Nothing in this section shall prejudice any rule of law requiring a court to exclude evidence.

Note.—See, too, sections 72(2) and 82(3). For the impact of all these provisions on common law discretions see the *Note* to *R.* v. *List* [1966] 1 W.L.R. 9 (Part One, Chapter 1, Section A, *supra*).

For illustrations of the way in which section 78 is operating see Part One, Chapter 17, esp. pp. 410–412, *supra*.

The right of a detained person to have access to legal advise is set out in section 58 of the Act. It would appear that failure to comply with its provisions will often lead to successful invocation of section 78: see, *e.g. R.* v. *Smith* [1987] Crim.L.R. 579; [1987] C.L.Y. 565; *R.* v. *Deacon* [1987] Crim.L.R. 404; [1987] C.L.Y. 611; but contrast *R.* v. *Walters* [1987] Crim.L.R. 577.

Cases in which it would be appropriate for a judge to hold a "trial within a trial" in order to decide whether to exclude evidence under the section will be rare: *R.* v. *Beveridge* (1987) 85 Cr.App.R. 225 (C.A.).

79. If at the trial of any person for an offence—

 (*a*) the defence intends to call two or more witnesses to the facts of the case; and

 (*b*) those witnesses include the accused,

the accused shall be called before the other witness or witnesses unless the court in its discretion otherwise directs.

Note.—This section clarifies a common law rule and puts it on a statutory footing. A character witness is presumably not a witness "to the facts of the case." The discretion of the court to allow another defence witness to testify before the accused is no longer confined to the formal or uncontroversial witness—although this will still be the most common case. The purpose of the rule is to prevent the accused from tailoring his evidence so as to fit that of other defence witnesses. There is no danger of the converse because other witnesses must remain out of court until after an accused's testimony has been given.

80.—(1) In any proceedings the wife or husband of the accused shall be competent to give evidence—

 (*a*) subject to subsection (4) below, for the prosecution; and

 (*b*) on behalf of the accused or any person jointly charged with the accused.

(2) In any proceedings the wife or husband of the accused shall, subject to subsection (4) below, be compellable to give evidence on behalf of the accused.

(3) In any proceedings the wife or husband of the accused shall, subject to subsection (4) below, be compellable to give evidence for the prosecution or on behalf of any person jointly charged with the accused if and only if—

 (*a*) the offence charged involves an assault on, or injury or a threat of injury to, the wife or husband of the accused or a person who was at the material time under the age of sixteen; or

 (*b*) the offence charged is a sexual offence alleged to have been committed in respect of a person who was at the material time under that age; or

 (*c*) the offence charged consists of attempting or conspiring to commit, or of aiding, abetting, counselling, procuring or inciting the commission of, an offence falling within paragraph (*a*) or (*b*) above.

(4) Where a husband and wife are jointly charged with an offence neither spouse shall at the trial be competent or compellable by virtue of subsection (1)(*a*), (2) or (3) above to give evidence in respect of that offence unless that spouse is not, or is no longer, liable to be convicted

of that offence at the trial as a result of pleading guilty or for any other reason.

Note.—This section effects major changes in the law relating to the testimonial competence and compellability of the spouse of the accused. The Criminal Evidence Act 1898, s.1, had made a spouse a competent witness for the accused and (but in most cases only with the accused's consent) for a co-accused. For certain specified offences the spouse also became a competent witness for the prosecution. In none of these situations was the spouse compellable. By virtue of section 80 a spouse now becomes a compellable witness for the accused; and a competent witness for the prosecution, and for a co-accused without the accused's consent in all cases except where the spouses are jointly on trial (see subsection (4)). Moreover, the spouse now becomes a compellable witness for the prosecution (and for a co-accused if not jointly on trial with the accused) in the cases specified in subsection (3). The effect of subsection (3)(a) is to reverse the majority decision of the House of Lords in *Hoskyn* v. *Metropolitan Police Commissioner* [1979] A.C. 274.

It is not clear whether "offence charged" in subsection (3)(a) refers to the nature or definition of the offence, or to the alleged facts of a particular case: would it cover a case of careless driving causing injury?

(5) In any proceedings a person who has been but is no longer married to the accused shall be competent and compellable to give evidence as if that person and the accused had never been married.

Note.—This subsection has the effect of reversing *R*. v. *Algar* [1954] 1 Q.B. 279 (C.C.A.). Judicially separated persons are still spouses, but cohabitees are not (see, however, the presumption of the validity of marriage, Part One, Chapter 4, *supra*).

(6) Where in any proceedings the age of any person at any time is material for the purposes of subsection (3) above, his age at the material time shall for the purposes of that provision be deemed to be or to have been that which appears to the court to be or to have been his age at that time.

(7) In subsection (3)(b) above "sexual offence" means an offence under the Sexual Offences Act 1956, the Indecency with Children Act 1960, the Sexual Offences Act 1967, section 54 of the Criminal Law Act 1977 or the Protection of Children Act 1978.

(8) The failure of the wife or husband of the accused to give evidence shall not be made the subject of any comment by the prosecution.

Note.—Subsection (8) preserves section 1, prov. (b) of the Criminal Evidence Act 1898. Comment by the judge is not prohibited, but for common law limitations upon this see Part One, Chapter 8 (*supra*).

(9) Section 1(d) of the Criminal Evidence Act 1898 (communications between husband and wife) and section 43(1) of the Matrimonial Causes Act 1965 (evidence as to marital intercourse) shall cease to have effect.

Note.—This subsection abolishes two old statutory privileges already abolished in civil cases (Civil Evidence Act 1968, s.16(3) and (4), *supra*). One related to communications between spouses made during their marriage; the other related to evidence that marital intercourse did or did not take place during any period.

81.—(1) Crown Court Rules may make provision for—
    (a) requiring any party to proceedings before the court to disclose to the other party or parties any expert evidence which he proposes to adduce in the proceedings; and

    (b) prohibiting a party who fails to comply in respect of any evidence with any requirement imposed by virtue of paragraph (a) above from adducing that evidence without the leave of the court.

(2) Crown Court Rules made by virtue of this section may specify the kinds of expert evidence to which they apply and may exempt facts or matters of any description specified in the rules.

Note.—See the Crown Court (Advance Notice of Expert Evidence) Rules 1987, S.I. No. 716 (L.2). Non-compliance with Rules renders the expert evidence inadmissible except with leave of the court. Contrast the Criminal Justice Act 1967, s.11(1) (*supra*), under which there is a requirement that notice be given of an alibi.

PART VII—SUPPLEMENTARY

82.—(1) In this Part of this Act—

"confession," includes any statement wholly or partly adverse to the person who made it, whether made to a person in authority or not and whether made in words or otherwise;

Note.—A nod or a wink would be an example of a confession made "otherwise" than in words.

There is a provisional *dictum* of the Court of Appeal in *R.* v. *Sat-Bhambra* (1989) 88 Cr.App.R. 55, 61–2, to the effect that a statement, on its face wholly exculpatory but being relied upon by the prosecution to prove guilt, is not covered by the definition. In other words the requirement of "adversity" cannot be satisfied by the way in which the prosecution is in fact seeking to use the confession, *e.g.* to show inconsistency with a different explanation being given by the accused. However, contrast *Piché* v. *R.* (1970) 11 D.L.R. (3d.) 700 (S.C.Can.).

"court-martial" means a court-martial constituted under the Army Act 1955, the Air Force Act 1955 or the Naval Discipline Act 1957 or a disciplinary court constituted under section 50 of the said Act of 1957;

"proceedings" means criminal proceedings, including—

    (a) proceedings in the United Kingdom or elsewhere before a court-martial so constituted or from a court-martial constituted under the Army Act 1955 or the Air Force Act 1955;

    (b) proceedings in the United Kingdom or elsewhere before the Courts-Martial Appeal Court—

        (i) on an appeal from a court-martial constituted under the Naval Discipline Act 1957; or

        (ii) on a reference under section 34 of the Courts-Martial (Appeals) Act 1968; and

    (c) proceedings before a Standing Civilian Court; and

"Service court" means a court-martial or a Standing Civilian Court.

(2) In this Part of this Act references to conviction before a Service court are references:—

    (a) as regards a court-martial constituted under the Army Act 1955 or the Air Force Act 1955, to a finding of guilty which is, or falls to be treated as, a finding of the court duly confirmed;

    (b) as regards—

      (*i*) a court-martial; or
     (*ii*) a disciplinary court,
constituted under the Naval Discipline Act 1957, to a finding
of guilty which is, or falls to be treated as, the finding of the
court;
and "convicted" shall be construed accordingly.

(3) Nothing in this Part of this Act shall prejudice any power of a
court to exclude evidence (whether by preventing questions from being
put or otherwise) at its discretion.

Note.—In connection with subsection (3) see, too, section 78; and in connection with
both provisions, see the *Note* on *R.* v. *List* [1966] 1 W.L.R. 9 (Part One, Chapter 1,
Section A, *supra*) and *R.* v. *Sang* [1980] A.C. 402 (H.L.) (Part One, Chapter 17, *supra*).

COMPANIES ACT 1985

1985, c. 6

452.—(1) Nothing in sections 431 to 446 requires the disclosure to the
Secretary of State or to an inspector appointed by him—
    (*a*)   by any person of information which he would in an action in
          the High Court or the Court of Sessions be entitled to refuse
          to disclose on grounds of legal professional privilege except, if
          he is a lawyer, the name and address of his client,
    (*b*)   by a company's bankers (as such) of information as to the
          affairs of any of their customers other than the company.

(2) Nothing in sections 447 to 451 compels the production by any
person of a document which he would in an action in the High Court or
the Court of Session be entitled to refuse to produce on grounds of legal
professional privilege, or authorises the taking of possession of any such
document which is in the person's possession.

Note.—The sections referred to deal with the investigation of companies and their
affairs, and the requisition of documents. The privilege is, of course, that of the client;
and if he waives it the inspectors will be able to obtain documents from his lawyers. See
Part One, Chapter 11, Section B (*supra*).

732.—(3) Where proceedings are instituted under the Companies Acts
against any person by the Director of Public Prosecutions or by or on
behalf of the Secretary of State or the Lord Advocate, nothing in those
Acts is to be taken to require any person to disclose any information
which he is entitled to refuse to disclose on grounds of legal professional
privilege.

Note.—This reiterates that legal professional privilege is unaffected in proceedings for
non-disclosure brought by one of the Public Authorities.

ADMINISTRATION OF JUSTICE ACT 1985

1985, c. 61

33.—(1) Any communication made—
    (*a*) to or by a licensed conveyancer in the course of his acting as
         such for a client; or

(b) to or by a recognised body in the course of its acting as such
      for a client,
shall in any legal proceedings be privileged from disclosure in like
manner as if the licensed conveyancer or body had at all material times
been acting as the client's solicitor.

Note.—Contrast the Copyright, Designs and Patents Act 1988, s.280 and *Note* thereon
(*infra*). On privilege generally, see Part One, Chapter 11 (*supra*).

INSOLVENCY ACT 1986

1986, c. 45

433. In any proceedings (whether or not under this Act)—
  (a) a statement of affairs prepared for the purposes of any
        provision of this Act which is derived from the Insolvency Act
        1985, and
  (b) any other statement made in pursuance of a requirement
        imposed by or under any such provision or by or under rules
        made under this Act,
may be used in evidence against any person making or concurring in
making the statement.

Note.—This Act deals with the insolvency of individuals and of corporations.
The making of a "statement of affairs" may take place for various purposes: see sections
22, 47, 66, 131 and 288.

CRIMINAL JUSTICE ACT 1987

1987, c. 38

2.—(9) A person shall not under this section be required to disclose
any information or produce any document which he would be entitled to
refuse to disclose or produce on grounds of legal professional privilege
in proceedings in the High Court, except that a lawyer may be required
to furnish the name and address of his client.

Note.—Section 1 established a Serious Fraud Office under a Director answerable to the
Attorney-General. Section 2 deals with the Office's investigatory powers.

CRIMINAL JUSTICE ACT 1988

1988, c. 33

PART I

EXTRADITION

13.—(1) For the purposes of this Part of this Act foreign documents
may be authenticated by the oath of a witness, but shall in any case be
deemed duly authenticated—

(*a*) if they purport to be signed or certified by a judge, magistrate or officer of the foreign state where they were issued; and

(*b*) if they purport to be certified by the Minister of Justice, or some other Minister of State, of the foreign state.

(2) Judicial notice shall be taken of such certification as is mentioned in subsection (1)(*b*) above and documents authenticated by such certification shall be received in evidence without further proof.

Note.—It is to be noted that, although the section makes foreign documents receivable (if properly signed and certified), it does not *itself* effect admissibility. Thus if, for example, the document contains hearsay, that part of it could be inadmissible in the extradition proceedings unless otherwise admissible.

Judicial notice taken under subsection (2) is only of the fact of certification.

For judicial notice generally see Part One, Chapter 7 (*supra*).

PART II

DOCUMENTARY EVIDENCE IN CRIMINAL PROCEEDINGS

Note.—This Part of the Act provides for the admissibility in criminal proceedings of a wide range of documentary hearsay. In doing so it replaces, and greatly extends the scope of, section 68 of the Police and Criminal Evidence Act 1984. Most importantly, whereas that section dealt only with records of a business type compiled by persons acting under a duty, section 23 of this Act extends admissibility in certain circumstances to first-hand hearsay contained in a personal document. Although it deals only with documentary hearsay, it is to be noted that "document" is given a very wide meaning (see the Civil Evidence Act 1968, s.10, incorporated here by Sched. 2, para. 5) so as to include film, tape recordings and computer discs. For a critical commentary on this Part of the Act, see *Birch*, [1989] Crim.L.R., pp. 15–31.

23.—(1) Subject—

(*a*) to subsection (4) below;

(*b*) to paragraph 1A of Schedule 2 to the Criminal Appeal Act 1968 (evidence given orally at original trial to be given orally at retrial); and

(*c*) to section 69 of the Police and Criminal Evidence Act 1984 (evidence from computer records),

a statement made by a person in a document shall be admissible in criminal proceedings as evidence of any fact of which direct oral evidence by him would be admissible if—

(*i*) the requirements of one of the paragraphs of subsection (2) below are satisfied; or

(*ii*) the requirements of subsection (3) below are satisfied.

(2) The requirements mentioned in subsection (1)(i) above are—

(*a*) that the person who made the statement is dead or by reason of his bodily or mental condition unfit to attend as a witness;

(*b*) that—

(*i*) the person who made the statement is outside the United Kingdom; and

(*ii*) it is not reasonably practicable to secure his attendance; or

(*c*) that all reasonable steps have been taken to find the person who made the statement, but that he cannot be found.

(3) The requirements mentioned in subsection (1)(ii) above are—
(*a*) that the statement was made to a police officer or some other person charged with the duty of investigating offences or charging offenders; and
(*b*) that the person who made it does not give oral evidence through fear or because he is kept out of the way.

(4) Subsection (1) above does not render admissible a confession made by an accused person that would not be admissible under section 76 of the Police and Criminal Evidence Act 1984.

Note.—"statement made by a person" presumably includes, for example, a statement dictated by that person to a typist. It is to be noted that a statement made by a person *to* a police officer (subsection (3)) is seen as being made *by* that person in a document.

"fact" presumably does not cover opinion. (Contrast the position in civil cases by virtue of the Civil Evidence Act 1972, s.1(1) (*supra*)).

"direct oral evidence" means, *e.g.*, evidence not itself containing a hearsay ingredient.

"would be admissible" must clearly be construed as including "would have been admissible" in order to cover the case in which the maker has died.

Subsection (2)(*b*) requires that the declarant be abroad *and* that it is not reasonably practicable to secure his attendance (contrast the Civil Evidence Act 1968, s.8(2)(*b*) and *Rasool* v. *West Midlands Passenger Transport Executive* [1974] 3 All E.R. 638 (Part I, Chapter 16, *supra*)). The phrase "outside the United Kingdom" is to be contrasted with the archaic imprecise phrase "beyond the seas" used in the Civil Evidence Act 1968, s.8(2)(*b*) (*supra*). Seemingly now, however, absence in Northern Ireland will not qualify, but absence in the Isle of Man or the Channel Islands will.

In considering whether "all reasonable steps" have been taken for the purpose of subsection 2(*c*) account may presumably be taken of the nature of the resources available to the party tendering the evidence. Resources available to the police will often be greater than those available to the accused.

See, too, *R.* v. *Bray* (1989) 88 Cr.App.R. 354 (C.A.).

Unqualified reference to "fear" in subsection 3(*b*) is difficult to justify. Fairness to the accused will often require that the subsection should not be operative in the absence of evidence that the fear has been induced by him, or at least by someone acting for him.

24.—(1) Subject—
(*a*) to subsections (3) and (4) below;
(*b*) to paragraph 1A of Schedule 2 to the Criminal Appeal Act 1968; and
(*c*) to section 69 of the Police and Criminal Evidence Act 1984, a statement in a document shall be admissible in criminal proceedings as evidence of any fact of which direct oral evidence would be admissible, if the following conditions are satisfied—
(*i*) the document was created or received by a person in the course of a trade, business, profession or other occupation, or as the holder of a paid or unpaid office; and
(*ii*) the information contained in the document was supplied by a person (whether or not the maker of the statement) who had, or may reasonably be supposed to have had, personal knowledge of the matters dealt with.

(2) Subsection (1) above applies whether the information contained in the document was supplied directly or indirectly but, if it was supplied indirectly, only if each person through whom it was supplied received it—
(*a*) in the course of a trade, business, profession or other occupation; or
(*b*) as the holder of a paid or unpaid office.

(3) Subsection (1) above does not render admissible a confession made by an accused person that would not be admissible under section 76 of the Police and Criminal Evidence Act 1984.

(4) A statement prepared otherwise than in accordance with section 29 below or an order under paragraph 6 of Schedule 13 to this Act or under section 30 or 31 below for the purposes—

    (*a*) of pending or contemplated criminal proceedings; or

    (*b*) of a criminal investigation,

shall not be admissible by virtue of subsection (1) above unless—

    (*i*) the requirements of one of the paragraphs of subsection (2) of section 23 above are satisfied; or

    (*ii*) the requirements of subsection (3) of that section are satisfied; or

    (*iii*) the person who made the statement cannot reasonably be expected (having regard to the time which has elapsed since he made the statement and to all the circumstances) to have any recollection of the matters dealt with in the statement.

Note.—This section is characterised by a multiplicity of terminology. Not only is a differentiation made between a "document," a "statement in a document" and "information contained in the document," but also the persons involved, in addition to the "maker of the statement," may include the creator of the document, the recipient of the document, the direct supplier of information, and indirect suppliers of information. Moreover sometimes (but not always) some (but not all) of these rôles may be performed by the same person.

The position would seem to be that, for a statement in a document to be admissible in evidence under the section, two distinct conditions must be cumulatively satisfied. The first of these conditions is relatively clear, whereas the second is perhaps less clear.

First, the document must in effect be a business, etc., document (subsection 1(*c*)(i)). If not created by a person in the course of business, etc., it must have been received by a person in such circumstances. It is to be noted that, in contrast with the corresponding provision (section 4) of the Civil Evidence Act 1968 (and with the now repealed section 68 of the Police and Criminal Evidence Act 1984), the document need not form part of a record.

However, subsection (1)(*c*)(ii), embodying the second condition, is open to two possible interpretations. It might be seen as referring to the nature of the document and to the general nature of the information contained in it. Alternatively it might be seen as referring more specifically to any information contained in the actual statement for which reception in evidence is being sought. If this latter, and in some ways preferable, interpretation is accepted, it must be conceded that the phrase "information contained in the document" would more aptly have read "information contained in the statement."

On either interpretation, the information must have been supplied by a person "who had, or may reasonably be supposed to have had, personal knowledge of the matters dealt with." That person may be the maker of the statement himself; or he may be someone else who has supplied the information directly to the maker; or he may be someone who has supplied it to the maker through an intermediary (or a succession of intermediaries). However, in this last mentioned case it must be further shown that each intermediary received the information in the course of business, etc. To this extent provision is made for the admission of multiple hearsay. Under this section (except where subsection (4) is applicable) it is no longer necessary that a reason be given for the non-availability of the witness (contrast the Civil Evidence Act 1968, s.8).

In a criminal trial it is likely (and certainly desirable if the evidence is tendered by the prosecution) that "personal knowledge" will be less readily assumed than it is in a civil case under the Civil Evidence Act 1968 (as to which see *Knight* v. *David* [1971] 1 W.L.R. 1571 (Ch.D.) (Part One, Chapter 16, *supra*)). But the words, "or may reasonably be supposed to have had," would presumably cover facts like those in *Myers* v. *D.P.P.* [1965] A.C. 1001 (H.L.) (Part One, Chapter 13, *supra*).

It is to be noted that subsection (4) lays down a further pre-condition for the reception under this section of statements prepared for the purposes of "pending or contemplated criminal proceedings" or of "a criminal investigation" (*e.g.* a deposition, or a witness's proof of evidence). Moreover, further restrictions are imposed upon the admissibility of such evidence, either under this section or under section 23, by section 26. In all such cases leave of the court is required, and leave shall not be given "unless it is of the opinion that the statement ought to be admitted in the interests of justice," and the court is required in this context to have regard to factors specified in section 26(*b*)(i), (ii) and (iii). To use proofs of evidence could easily constitute a device to avoid cross-examination.

The inclusion here of subsection 4(*b*)(iii), as contrasted with the absence of any corresponding provision in section 23, is presumably on the ground that it is appropriate for business documents, because, for example, it would be unreasonable to expect a bank clerk to remember the details of a transaction which passed through his hands, whereas in the case of personal documents, such as letters or diaries, one might expect the person concerned to recall the incident recorded. It is to be remembered, too, that, if he gives oral evidence, he will in any event often be permitted to refresh his memory from the written record.

For sections 29, 30 and 31, see *infra*; Schedule 13 deals with evidence before Courts-Martial, etc.

25.—(1) If, having regard to all the circumstances—
    (*a*) the Crown Court—
        (*i*) on a trial on indictment;
        (*ii*) on an appeal from a magistrates' court; or
        (*iii*) on the hearing of an application under section 6 of the Criminal Justice Act 1987 (applications for dismissal of charges of fraud transferred from magistrates' court to Crown Court); or
    (*b*) the criminal division of the Court of Appeal; or
    (*c*) a magistrates' court on a trial of an information,
is of the opinion that in the interests of justice a statement which is admissible by virtue of section 23 or 24 above nevertheless ought not to be admitted, it may direct that the statement shall not be admitted.

(2) Without prejudice to the generality of subsection (1) above, it shall be the duty of the court to have regard—
    (*a*) to the nature and source of the document containing the statement and to whether or not, having regard to its nature and source and to any other circumstances that appear to the court to be relevant, it is likely that the document is authentic;
    (*b*) to the extent to which the statement appears to supply evidence which would otherwise not be readily available;
    (*c*) to the relevance of the evidence that it appears to supply to any issue which is likely to have to be determined in the proceedings; and
    (*d*) to any risk, having regard in particular to whether it is likely to be possible to controvert the statement if the person making it does not attend to give oral evidence in the proceedings, that its admission or exclusion will result in unfairness to the accused or, if there is more than one, to any of them.

Note.—This section embodies an exclusionary discretion: the onus is upon the party seeking to exclude to show that it is not in the interests of justice that the document be admitted. Section 28(1)(*b*) makes it clear that the statutory discretion embodied in this section is cumulative to the general common law discretion of the judge in a criminal trial to exclude evidence if its likely prejudicial effect so outweighs its probative value that its reception might result in an unjust conviction (see *R.* v. *List* [1966] 1 W.L.R. 9 (Part I, Chapter 1, Section A, *supra*)). However, given the width of the statutory discretion it is perhaps unlikely that resort will often have to be made to the common law in the context of evidence otherwise admissible by virtue of sections 23 or 24.

To be contrasted with the exclusionary nature of the discretion deriving from section 25, is the inclusionary discretion embodied in section 26 and to be operative in the case of documents prepared for the proceedings.

Subsection (2) contains a list of factors which the court must consider when exercising its discretion to exclude a statement in the interests of justice. This list is not comprehensive. Para. (d) would seem to indicate a wide basis for excluding statements, in that "controversion" by cross-examination is obviously always prevented when reliance is simply on documentary evidence.

26. Where a statement which is admissible in criminal proceedings by virtue of section 23 or 24 above appears to the court to have been prepared, otherwise than in accordance with section 29 below or an order under paragraph 6 of Schedule 13 to this Act or under section 30 or 31 below, for the purposes—

    (*a*) of pending or contemplated criminal proceedings; or

    (*b*) of a criminal investigation,

the statement shall not be given in evidence in any criminal proceedings without the leave of the court, and the court shall not give leave unless it is of the opinion that the statement ought to be admitted in the interests of justice; and in considering whether its admission would be in the interests of justice, it shall be the duty of the court to have regard—

    (*i*) to the contents of the statement;

    (*ii*) to any risk, having regard in particular to whether it is likely to be possible to controvert the statement if the person making it does not attend to give oral evidence in the proceedings, that its admission or exclusion will result in unfairness to the accused or, if there is more than one, to any of them; and

    (*iii*) to any other circumstances that appear to the court to be relevant.

Note.—The section imposes more exacting requirements for admissibility of statements in documents that appear to have been prepared for purposes of criminal proceedings or investigations. First, leave must be obtained before such documents are admissible. The burden is thus placed upon the party seeking to admit. Secondly, the factors (*b*)(i)–(iii) to which the court must have regard when considering whether the statement ought to be admitted in the interests of justice in this specific context differ from those which the court must consider in exercising its exclusionary discretion under section 25. The significance of this difference and, indeed, the general relationship between the two sections is not obvious.

Documentary evidence admitted under the Criminal Justice Act 1967, s.9, (*supra*) or under the Magistrates' Courts Act 1980, s.102, (*supra*) is unaffected by section 26, because this section applies only to documents admissible by virtue of sections 23 or 24.

27. Where a statement contained in a document is admissible as evidence in criminal proceedings, it may be proved—

    (*a*) by the production of that document; or

    (*b*) (whether or not that document is still in existence) by the production of a copy of that document, or of the material part of it,

authenticated in such manner as the court may approve; and it is immaterial for the purposes of this subsection how many removes there are between a copy and the original.

Note.—On its face the scope of this section is wide (especially in the light of the definition of "document" imported from the Civil Evidence Act 1968, s.10(1). Moreover, it is not limited to documents admitted by virtue of this Act. Note, too, the removal of the restriction to "first-hand" copies.

For definitions of "copy", "document" and "statement" see Sched. 2, para. 5 to this Act (*infra*) and the Civil Evidence Act 1968, s.10 (*supra*). For proof of the contents of a document by microfilm copy see the Police and Criminal Evidence Act 1984, s.71 (*supra*).

28.—(1) Nothing in this Part of this Act shall prejudice—
    (*a*) the admissibility of a statement not made by a person while giving oral evidence in court which is admissible otherwise than by virtue of this Part of this Act; or
    (*b*) any power of a court to exclude at its discretion a statement admissible by virtue of this Part of this Act.

(2) Schedule 2 to this Act shall have effect for the purpose of supplementing this Part of this Act.

Note.—The reference to the "power of a court to exclude at its discretion" includes the general common law power to exclude to the advantage of an accused (see *Note* to *R*. v. *List* [1966] 1 W.L.R. 9, Part One, Chapter 1, Section A, *supra*) and the power embodied in the Police and Criminal Evidence Act, s.78 (*supra*). For Schedule 2, see *infra*.

PART III

OTHER PROVISIONS ABOUT EVIDENCE IN CRIMINAL PROCEEDINGS

29.—(1) Where on an application made in accordance with the following provisions of this section it appears to a justice of the peace or judge that criminal proceedings—
    (*a*) have been instituted; or
    (*b*) are likely to be instituted if evidence is obtained for the purpose,
he may order that a letter of request shall be issued to a court or tribunal or appropriate authority specified in the order and exercising jurisdiction in a place outside the United Kingdom, requesting it to assist in obtaining for the purposes of the proceedings evidence specified in the letter.

(2) In subsection (1) above "appropriate authority" means any central authority designated by a state to receive requests for assistance in legal matters.

(3) An application for an order under this section may be made by a prosecuting authority.

(4) If proceedings have already been instituted, a person charged with an offence in the proceedings may make such an application.

(5) Without prejudice to the generality of any enactment conferring power to make them—
    (*a*) Crown Court Rules;
    (*b*) Criminal Appeal Rules; and
    (*c*) rules under section 144 of the Magistrates' Courts Act 1980,
may make such provision as appears to the authority making any of them to be necessary or expedient for the purposes of this section and in particular for the appointment of a person before whom evidence may be taken in pursuance of a letter of request.

(6) In exercising the discretion conferred by section 25 above in relation to a statement contained in evidence taken in pursuance of a letter of request, the court shall have regard—

    (*a*) to whether it was possible to challenge the statement by questioning the person who made it; and

    (*b*) to whether the local law allowed the parties to the criminal proceedings to be legally represented when the evidence was being taken.

Note.—This section outlines a procedure whereby requests may be made to foreign courts for assistance in obtaining evidence abroad.

30.—(1) An expert report shall be admissible as evidence in criminal proceedings, whether or not the person making it attends to give oral evidence in those proceedings.

(2) If it is proposed that the person making the report shall not give oral evidence, the report shall only be admissible with the leave of the court.

(3) For the purpose of determining whether to give leave the court shall have regard—

    (*a*) to the contents of the report;

    (*b*) to the reasons why it is proposed that the person making the report shall not give oral evidence;

    (*c*) to any risk, having regard in particular to whether it is likely to be possible to controvert statements in the report if the person making it does not attend to give oral evidence in the proceedings, that its admission or exclusion will result in unfairness to the accused or, if there is more than one, to any of them; and

    (*d*) to any other circumstances that appear to the court to be relevant.

(4) An expert report, when admitted, shall be evidence of any fact or opinion of which the person making it could have given oral evidence.

(5) In this section "expert report" means a written report by a person dealing wholly or mainly with matters on which he is (or would if living be) qualified to give expert evidence.

Note.—This section allows expert evidence sometimes to be given in purely documentary form. The effect of subsection (1) is to create an exception to the hearsay rule.

Admission of an expert report under the section requires the leave of the court. If leave is granted questions of weight will be determined in accordance with Sched. 2, para. 3 (*infra*).

The section should be read with the Police and Criminal Evidence Act 1984, s.81 (*supra*), and Crown Court Rules made pursuant to it.

31. For the purpose of helping members of juries to understand complicated issues of fact or technical terms Crown Court Rules may make provision—

    (*a*) as to the furnishing of evidence in any form, notwithstanding the existence of admissible material from which the evidence to be given in that form would be derived; and

    (*b*) as to the furnishing of glossaries for such purposes as may be specified

in any case where the court gives leave for, or requires, evidence or a glossary to be so furnished.

Note.—This section stems from a recommendation of the *Roskill Committee* and *A Report of Four Research Studies carried out for the Roskill Committee* (H.M.S.O. 1986). It is primarily designed to allow the evidence to be made more simple for juries in complex fraud cases. Para. (a) of the subsection is concerned with the presentation of evidence itself. Para. (b) is concerned with additional material for the interpretation of the evidence. Note that section 26 does not apply to this material.

32.—(1) A person other than the accused may give evidence through a live television link on a trial on indictment or an appeal to the criminal division of the Court of Appeal or the hearing of a reference under section 17 of the Criminal Appeal Act 1968 if—

    (*a*) the witness is outside the United Kingdom; or

    (*b*) the witness is under the age of 14 and the offence charged is one to which subsection (2) below applies,

but evidence may not be so given without the leave of the court.

(2) This subsection applies—

    (*a*) to an offence which involves an assault on, or injury or a threat of injury to, a person;

    (*b*) to an offence under section 1 of the Children and Young Persons Act 1933 (cruelty to persons under 16);

    (*c*) to an offence under the Sexual Offences Act 1956, the Indecency with Children Act 1960, the Sexual Offences Act 1967, section 54 of the Criminal Law Act 1977 or the Protection of Children Act 1978; and

    (*d*) to an offence which consists of attempting or conspiring to commit, or of aiding, abetting, counselling, procuring or inciting the commission of, an offence falling within paragraph (*a*), (*b*) or (*c*) above.

(3) A statement made on oath by a witness outside the United Kingdom and given in evidence through a link by virtue of this section shall be treated for the purposes of section 1 of the Perjury Act 1911 as having been made in the proceedings in which it is given in evidence.

(4) Without prejudice to the generality of any enactment conferring power to make rules to which this subsection applies, such rules may make such provision as appears to the authority making them to be necessary or expedient for the purposes of this section.

(5) The rules to which subsection (4) above applies are—

    (*a*) Crown Court Rules; and

    (*b*) Criminal Appeal Rules.

Note.—The section creates a discretion to admit evidence by live television link in a limited range of circumstances. Evidence allowed by virtue of the section is in most respects given in the usual way and subject to the usual constraints, except that the witness is not in the court room.

Much evidence of this type would also qualify as documentary evidence under section 23. However, as it will usually have been prepared for the investigation of the offence, it will not be admissible under that section unless the court has been satisfied that this would be in the interests of justice.

33. [Provision is made for the substitution of a new section 103 of the Magistrates' Courts Act 1980 (*supra*).]

34.—(1) The proviso to subsection (1) of section 38 of the Children and Young Persons Act 1933 (under which, where the unsworn evidence of a child of tender years admitted by virtue of that section is given on behalf of the prosecution, the accused is not liable to be convicted unless that evidence is corroborated by some other material evidence in support thereof implicating him) shall cease to have effect.

(2) Any requirement whereby at a trial on indictment it is obligatory for the court to give the jury a warning about convicting the accused on the uncorroborated evidence of a child is abrogated in relation to cases where such a warning is required by reason only that the evidence is the evidence of a child.

(3) Unsworn evidence admitted by virtue of section 38 of the Children and Young Persons Act 1933 may corroborate evidence (sworn or unsworn) given by any other person.

Note.—It is to be observed that subsection (2) applies only to trials on indictment. Perhaps a Magistrates' Clerk ought to warn Magistrates. Moreover, it is arguable that a warning is still required even at a trial on indictment if the child is giving unsworn evidence on the ground that it is then not required "by reason *only* that the evidence is the evidence of a child" but also by reason of the fact that the evidence is unsworn. There is certainly room for the view that, if the only prosecution evidence is that of a child whom the judge has found unfit to be sworn, the attention of the jury should be drawn to any risks involved in convicting.

In any event the section does not remove the requirement that the judge give a corroboration warning if this is necessary because, for example, he or she is an accomplice. Nor does it affect the position in cases in which corroboration is required as a matter of law (see, *e.g.*, the Sexual Offences Act 1956, s.2 and *Note* thereon (*supra*)).

For corroboration generally see Part One, Chapter 10 (*supra*).

Schedule 2

Documentary Evidence—Supplementary

1. Where a statement is admitted as evidence in criminal proceedings by virtue of Part II of this Act—

   (*a*) any evidence which, if the person making the statement had been called as a witness, would have been admissible as relevant to his credibility as a witness shall be admissible for that purpose in those proceedings;

   (*b*) evidence may, with the leave of the court, be given of any matter which, if that person had been called as a witness, could have been put to him in cross-examination as relevant to his credibility as a witness but of which evidence could not have been adduced by the cross-examining party; and

   (*c*) evidence tending to prove that that person, whether before or after making the statement, made (whether orally or not) some other statement which is inconsistent with it shall be admissible for the purpose of showing that he has contradicted himself.

2. A statement which is given in evidence by virtue of Part II of this Act shall not be capable of corroborating evidence given by the person making it.

3. In estimating the weight, if any, to be attached to such a statement regard shall be had to all the circumstances from which any inference can reasonably be drawn as to its accuracy or otherwise.

4. Without prejudice to the generality of any enactment conferring power to make them—

   (*a*) Crown Court Rules;

(b) Criminal Appeal Rules; and
(c) rules under section 144 of the Magistrates' Courts Act 1980,
may make such provision as appears to the authority making any of
them to be necessary or expedient for the purposes of Part II of this
Act.
5. Expressions used in Part II of this Act and in Part I of the Civil
Evidence Act 1968 are to be construed in Part II of this Act in
accordance with section 10 of that Act.
6. In Part II of this Act "confession" has the meaning assigned to it
by section 82 of the Police and Criminal Evidence Act 1984.

Note.—Paragraph 1 deals with attacking and supporting the credibility of the person
making the statement. In so far as paras. 1(b) and 1(c) both admit prior inconsistent
statements going to credit, they overlap. It is to be noted that para. 1(b), if strictly
construed, would appear to permit a party, against whom a document is tendered, to call
evidence discrediting the maker of the statement even though an answer in actual cross-
examination would have been final.
It is to be noted that in para. 3, dealing with the estimation of weight, the curious
singling-out of two factors (that of contemporaneity and that of incentive to conceal or
misrepresent) for particular attention, which is contained in the corresponding provision
(section 6(3)) of the Civil Evidence Act 1968 (see Part I, Chapter 16, *supra*), is omitted
here.
Paragraph 5 provides that an expression used, both in Part II of this Act and in Part I
of the Civil Evidence Act 1968, is to be construed in the present context in accordance
with section 10 of the 1968 Act. For comment on, in particular, the definition of
"statement," see the Introduction to Chapter 16, *supra*.

COPYRIGHT, DESIGNS AND PATENTS ACT 1988

1988, c. 48

280.—(1) This section applies to communications as to any matter
relating to the protection of any invention, design, technical information, trade mark or service mark, or as to any matter involving passing
off.
(2) Any such communication—
    (a) between a person and his patent agent, or
    (b) for the purpose of obtaining, or in response to a request for,
        information which a person is seeking for the purpose of
        instructing his patent agent,
is privileged from disclosure in legal proceedings in England, Wales or
Northern Ireland in the same way as a communication between a
person and his solicitor or, as the case may be, a communication for
the purpose of obtaining, or in response to a request for, information
which a person seeks for the purpose of instructing his solicitor.
(3) In subsection (2) "patent agent" means—
    (a) a registered patent agent or a person who is on the
        European list,
    (b) a partnership entitled to describe itself as a firm of patent
        agents or as a firm carrying on the business of a European
        patent attorney, or
    (c) a body corporate entitled to describe itself as a patent agent
        or as a company carrying on the business of a European
        patent attorney.
(4) It is hereby declared that in Scotland the rules of law which
confer privilege from disclosure in legal proceedings in respect of

communications extend to such communications as are mentioned in this section.

Note.—This section replaces the Patents Act 1977, s.104, which had in its turn replaced the Civil Evidence Act 1968, s.15. Section 104 is broader in scope than the earlier legislation in several ways,—most importantly the privilege is now no longer confined to advice in connection with actual or contemplated proceedings, and moreover it is now available in criminal as well as civil proceedings.

Section 284 of the Act confers a new privilege respecting communications with registered trade mark agents. The form of words used in this section mirrors that used in section 280.

For the position of licensed conveyancers see the Administration of Justice Act 1985, s.33 (*infra*).

ROAD TRAFFIC OFFENDERS ACT 1988

1988, c. 53

11.—(1) In any proceedings in England and Wales for an offence to which this section applies, a certificate in the prescribed form, purporting to be signed by a constable and certifying that a person specified in the certificate stated to the constable—

(*a*) that a particular motor vehicle was being driven or used by, or belonged to, that person on a particular occasion, or

(*b*) that a particular motor vehicle on a particular occasion was used by, or belonged to, a firm and that he was, at the time of the statement, a partner in that firm, or

(*c*) that a particular motor vehicle on a particular occasion was used by, or belonged to, a corporation and that he was, at the time of the statement, a director, officer or employee of that corporation,

shall be admissible as evidence for the purpose of determining by whom the vehicle was being driven or used, or to whom it belonged, as the case may be, on that occasion.

(2) Nothing in subsection (1) above makes a certificate admissible as evidence in proceedings for an offence except in a case where and to the like extent to which oral evidence to the like effect would have been admissible in those proceedings.

(3) Nothing in subsection (1) above makes a certificate admissible as evidence in proceedings for an offence—

(*a*) unless a copy of it has, not less than seven days before the hearing or trial, been served in the prescribed manner on the person charged with the offence, or

(*b*) if that person, not later than three days before the hearing or trial or within such further time as the court may in special circumstances allow, serves a notice in the prescribed form and manner on the prosecutor requiring attendance at the trial of the person who signed the certificate.

(4) In this section "prescribed" means prescribed by rules made by the Secretary of State by statutory instrument.

(5) Schedule 1 to this Act shows the offences to which this section applies.

Note.—This section replaces the Road Traffic Regulation Act 1984, s.113. Section 112 of that Act imposes a duty to provide information as to the identity of the driver of a vehicle. This may involve a driver in incriminating himself in breach of the general privilege against incrimination.

Schedule 1 to the 1988 Act lists a very wide range of traffic offences to which section 11 applies.

12.—(1) Where on the summary trial in England and Wales of an information for an offence to which this subsection applies—
- (a) it is proved to the satisfaction of the court, on oath or in a manner prescribed by rules made under section 144 of the Magistrates' Courts Act 1980, that a requirement under section 172(2) of the Road Traffic Act 1988 to give information as to the identity of the driver of a particular vehicle on the particular occasion to which the information relates has been served on the accused by post, and
- (b) a statement in writing is produced to the court purporting to be signed by the accused that the accused was the driver of that vehicle on that occasion,

the court may accept that statement as evidence that the accused was the driver of that vehicle on that occasion.

(2) Schedule 1 to this Act shows the offences to which subsection (1) above applies.

(3) Where on the summary trial in England and Wales of an information for an offence to which section 112 of the Road Traffic Regulation Act 1984 applies—
- (a) it is proved to the satisfaction of the court, on oath or in manner prescribed by rules made under section 144 of the Magistrates' Courts Act 1980, that a requirement under section 112(2) of the Road Traffic Regulation Act 1984 to give information as to the identity of the driver of a particular vehicle on the particular occasion to which the information relates has been served on the accused by post, and
- (b) a statement in writing is produced to the court purporting to be signed by the accused that the accused was the driver of that vehicle on that occasion,

the court may accept that statement as evidence that the accused was the driver of that vehicle of that occasion.

Note.—Subsection (1) of this section replaces the Road Traffic Regulation Act 1984, s.114.

Regarding Schedule 1 of the Act and the Road Traffic Regulation Act 1984, s.112, see *Note* to section 11, (*supra*).

The phrase in section 12(1) and (3) that "the court may accept that statement as evidence" presumably not only denotes admissibility but also creates a permissive presumption of law, *i.e.* it enables (but does not require) the court to find on the basis of the statement alone that the accused was the driver on the occasion in question.

As to the nature of permissive presumptions of law see Part One, Chapter 4, *supra*.

15.—(1) This section and section 16 of this Act apply in respect of proceedings for an offence under section 4 or 5 of the Road Traffic Act 1988 (motor vehicles: drink and drugs); and expressions used in this section and section 16 of this Act have the same meaning as in sections 4 to 10 of that Act.

(2) Evidence of the proportion of alcohol or any drug in a specimen of breath, blood or urine provided by the accused shall, in all cases, be taken into account and, subject to subsection (3) below, it shall be assumed that the proportion of alcohol in the accused's breath, blood or

urine at the time of the alleged offence was not less than in the specimen.

(3) If the proceedings are for an offence under section 5 of that Act or, where the accused is alleged to have been unfit through drink, for an offence under section 4 of that Act, that assumption shall not be made if the accused proves—

(a) that he consumed alcohol after he had ceased to drive, attempt to drive or be in charge of a motor vehicle on a road or other public place and before he provided the specimen, and

(b) that had he not done so the proportion of alcohol in his breath, blood or urine would not have exceeded the prescribed limit and, if the proceedings are for an offence under section 4 of that Act, would not have been such as to impair his ability to drive properly.

(4) A specimen of blood shall be disregarded unless it was taken from the accused with his consent by a medical practitioner.

(5) Where, at the time a specimen of blood or urine was provided by the accused, he asked to be provided with such a specimen, evidence of the proportion of alcohol or any drug found in the specimen is not admissible on behalf of the prosecution unless—

(a) the specimen in which the alcohol or drug was found is one of two parts into which the specimen provided by the accused was divided at the time it was provided, and

(b) the other part was supplied by the accused.

Note.—This section is a partial replacement of the Road Traffic Act 1972, s.10.

Section 15(3) does not confine challenge to any particular type of evidence. The defendant may adduce evidence of the amount of alcohol that he had in fact consumed: see *Cracknell* v. *Willis* (1988) 86 Cr.App.R. 196; [1988] R.T.R. 1 (H.L.)—although itself a case concerned with the previous Road Traffic Act 1972, s.10.

16.—(1) Evidence of the proportion of alcohol or a drug in a specimen of breath, blood or urine may, subject to subsections (3) and (4) below and to section 15(5) of this Act, be given by the production of a document or documents purporting to be whichever of the following is appropriate, that is to say—

(a) a statement automatically produced by the device by which the proportion of alcohol in a specimen of breath was measured and a certificate signed by a constable (which may but need not be contained in the same document as the statement) that the statement relates to a specimen provided by the accused at the date and time shown in the statement, and

(b) a certificate signed by an authorised analyst as to the proportion of alcohol or any drug found in a specimen of blood or urine identified in the certificate.

(2) Subject to subsections (3) and (4) below, evidence that a specimen of blood was taken from the accused with his consent by a medical practitioner may be given by the production of a document purporting to certify that fact and to be signed by a medical practitioner.

(3) Subject to subsection (4) below—

(a) a document purporting to be such a statement or such a certificate (or both such a statement and such a certificate) as is mentioned in subsection (1)(a) above is admissible in evidence on behalf of the prosecution in pursuance of this section only if a copy of it either has been handed to the accused when the document was produced or has been served on him not later than seven days before the hearing, and

(b) any other document is so admissible only if a copy of it has been served on the accused not later than seven days before the hearing.

(4) A document purporting to be a certificate (or so much of a document as purports to be a certificate) is not so admissible if the accused, not later than three days before the hearing or within such further time as the court may in special circumstances allow, has served notice on the prosecutor requiring the attendance at the hearing of the person by whom the document purports to be signed.

(5) In Scotland—

(a) a document produced in evidence on behalf of the prosecution in pursuance of subsection (1) or (2) above and, where the person by whom the document was signed is called as a witness, the evidence of that person, shall be sufficient evidence of the facts stated in the document, and

(b) a written execution purporting to be signed by the person who handed to or served on the accused or the prosecutor a copy of the document or of the notice in terms of subsection (3) or (4) above, together with, where appropriate, a post office receipt for the registered or recorded delivery letter shall be sufficient evidence of the handing or service of such a copy or notice.

(6) A copy of a certificate required by this section to be served on the accused or a notice required by this section to be served on the prosecutor may be served personally or sent by registered post or recorded delivery service.

(7) . . . .

Note.—This section is a partial replacement of the Road Traffic Act 1972, s.10.

Under section 16(3) a doctor's certificate is not admissible unless a copy has been served on the defendant at least seven days prior to the hearing, even if counsel for the defendant purports to waive any objection to the admissibility of the certificate: see *Tobi* v. *Nicholas* (1988) 86 Cr.App.R. 323 (D.C.), although it too is a case based upon the previous Road Traffic Act 1972, s.10.

20. On the prosecution of a person for any speeding offence, evidence of the measurement of any speed by a device designed or adapted for measuring by radar the speed of motor vehicles shall not be admissible unless the device is of a type approved by the Secretary of State.

Note.—This section re-enacts the Road Traffic Regulation Act 1984, s.90.

Part Three

RULES ON EVIDENCE

THE RULES OF THE SUPREME COURT 1965, AS AMENDED[1]

ORDER 18

PLEADINGS

Facts, not evidence, to be pleaded

7.—(1) Subject to the provisions of this rule, and rules 7A, 10, 11 and 12, every pleading must contain, and contain only, a statement in a summary form of the material facts on which the party pleading relies for his claim or defence, as the case may be, but not the evidence by which those facts are to be proved, and the statement must be as brief as the nature of the case admits.

Note.—Rules 10, 11 and 12 relate respectively to departure, points of law, and particulars.

(2) Without prejudice to paragraph (1), the effect of any document or the purport of any conversation referred to in the pleading must, if material, be briefly stated, and the precise words of the document or conversation shall not be stated, except in so far as those words are themselves material.

(3) A party need not plead any fact if it is presumed by law to be true or the burden of disproving it lies on the other party, unless the other party has specifically denied it in his pleading.

(4) A statement that a thing has been done or that an event has occurred, being a thing or event the doing or occurrence of which, as the case may be, constitutes a condition precedent necessary for the case of a party is to be implied in his pleading.

Conviction, etc., to be adduced in evidence: matters to be pleaded

7A.—(1) If in any action which is to be tried with pleadings any party intends, in reliance on section 11 of the Civil Evidence Act 1968 (convictions as evidence in civil proceedings) to adduce evidence that a person was convicted of an offence by or before a court in the United Kingdom or by a court-martial there or elsewhere, he must include in his pleading a statement of his intention with particulars of—

(*a*) the conviction and the date thereof,
(*b*) the court or court-martial which made the conviction, and
(*c*) the issue in the proceedings to which the conviction is relevant.

---

[1] Amendments up to and including those contained in Supplement No. 53 (July 1988) are incorporated.

(2) If in any action which is to be tried with pleadings any party intends, in reliance on section 12 of the said Act of 1968 (findings of adultery and paternity as evidence in civil proceedings) to adduce evidence that a person was found guilty of adultery in matrimonial proceedings or was adjudged to be the father of a child in affiliation proceedings before a court in the United Kingdom, he must include in his pleading a statement of his intention with particulars of—

    (*a*) the finding of adjudication and the date thereof,

    (*b*) the court which made the finding or adjudication and the proceedings in which it was made, and

    (*c*) the issue in the proceedings to which the finding or adjudication is relevant.

(3) Where a party's pleading includes such a statement as is mentioned in paragraph (1) or (2), then if the opposite party—

    (*a*) denies the conviction, finding of adultery or adjudication of paternity to which the statement relates, or

    (*b*) alleges that the conviction, finding or adjudication was erroneous or

    (*c*) denies that the conviction, finding or adjudication is relevant to any issue in the proceedings,

he must make the denial or allegation in his pleading.

ORDER 24

DISCOVERY AND INSPECTION OF DOCUMENTS

Mutual discovery of documents

1.—(1) After the close of pleadings in an action begun by writ there shall, subject to and in accordance with the provisions of this Order, be discovery by the parties to the action of the documents which are or have been in their possession, custody or power relating to matters in question in the action.

(2) Nothing in this Order shall be taken as preventing the parties of an action agreeing to dispense with or limit the discovery of documents which they would otherwise be required to make to each other.

Inspection of documents referred to in pleadings and affidavits

10.—(1) Any party to a cause or matter shall be entitled at any time to serve a notice on any other party in whose pleadings or affidavits reference is made to any document requiring him to produce that document for the inspection of the party giving the notice and to permit him to take copies thereof.

Document disclosure of which would be injurious to public interest: saving

15. The foregoing provisions of this Order shall be without prejudice to any rule of law which authorises or requires the withholding of any document on the ground that the disclosure of it would be injurious to the public interest.

ORDER 26

INTERROGATORIES

Use of answers to interrogatories at trial

7. A party may put in evidence at the trial of a cause or matter, or of any issue therein, some only of the answers to interrogatories, or part only of such an answer, without putting in evidence the other answers or, as the case may be, the whole of that answer, but the Court may look at the whole of the answers and if of opinion that any other answer or other part of an answer is so connected with an answer or part thereof used in evidence that the one ought not to be so used without the other, the court may direct that that other answer or part shall be put in evidence.

ORDER 27

ADMISSIONS

Admission of case of other party

1. Without prejudice to Order 18, rule 13, a party to cause or matter may give notice, by his pleading or otherwise in writing, that he admits the truth of the whole or any part of the case of any other party.

Note.—Ord. 18, r. 13, relates to admissions and denials in pleadings.

Notice to admit facts

2.—(1) A party to a cause or matter may not later than 21 days after the cause or matter is set down for trial serve on any other party a notice requiring him to admit, for the purpose of that cause or matter only, such facts, or such part of his case, as may be specified in the notice.

(2) An admission made in compliance with a notice under this rule shall not be used against the party by whom it was made in any cause or matter other than the cause or matter for the purpose of which it was made or in favour of any person other than the person by whom the notice was given, and the Court may at any time allow a party to amend or withdraw an admission so made by him on such terms as may be just.

Admission and production of documents specified in list of documents

4.—(1) Subject to paragraph (2) and without prejudice to the right of a party to object to the admission in evidence of any document, a party on whom a list of documents is served in pursuance of any provision of Order 24 shall, unless the Court otherwise orders, be deemed to admit—

(*a*) that any document described in the list as an original document is such a document and was printed, written, signed or executed as it purports respectively to have been, and

(*b*) that any document described therein as a copy is a true copy.

This paragraph does not apply to a document the authenticity of which the party has denied in his pleading.

(2) If before the expiration of 21 days after inspection of the documents specified in a list of documents or after the time limited for inspection of those documents expires, whichever is the later, the party on whom the list is served serves on the party whose list it is a notice stating, in relation to any document specified therein, that he does not admit the authenticity of that document and requires it to be proved at the trial, he shall not be deemed to make any admission in relation to that document under paragraph (1).

(3) A party to a cause or matter by whom a list of documents is served on any other party in pursuance of any provision of Order 24 shall be deemed to have been served by that other party with a notice requiring him to produce at the trial of the cause or matter such of the documents specified in the list as are in his possession, custody or power.

(4) The foregoing provisions of this rule apply in relation to an affidavit made in compliance with an order under Order 24, rule 7, as they apply in relation to a list of documents served in pursuance of any provision of that Order.

Note.—For Ord. 24, see *supra.*

Notices to admit or produce documents

5.—(1) Except where rule 4(1) applies, a party to a cause or matter may within 21 days after the cause or matter is set down for trial serve on any other party a notice requiring him to admit the authenticity of the documents specified in the notice.

(2) If a party on whom a notice under paragraph (1) is served desires to challenge the authenticity of any document therein specified he must, within 21 days after service of the notice, serve on the party by whom it was given a notice stating that he does not admit the authenticity of the document and requires it to be proved at the trial.

(3) A party who fails to give a notice of non-admission in accordance with paragraph (2) in relation to any document shall be deemed to have admitted the authenticity of that document unless the Court otherwise orders.

(4) Except where rule 4(3) applies, a party to a cause or matter may serve on any other party a notice requiring him to produce the documents specified in the notice at the trial of the cause or matter.

ORDER 35

Proceedings at Trial

Order of speeches

7.—(1) The judge before whom an action is tried (whether with or without a jury) may give directions as to the party to begin and the order of speeches at the trial, and, subject to any such directions, the party to begin and the order of speeches shall be that provided by this rule.

(2) Subject to paragraph (6), the plaintiff shall begin by opening his case.

(3) If the defendant elects not to adduce evidence, then, whether or not the defendant has in the course of cross-examination of a witness for

the plaintiff or otherwise put in a document, the plaintiff may, after the evidence on his behalf has been given, make a second speech closing his case and the defendant shall then state his case.

(4) If the defendant elects to adduce evidence, he may, after any evidence on behalf of the plaintiff has been given, open his case and, after the evidence on his behalf has been given, make a second speech closing his case, and at the close of the defendant's case the plaintiff may make a speech in reply.

(5) Where there are two or more defendants who appear separately or are separately represented, then—

(a) if none of them elects to adduce evidence, each of them shall state his case in the order in which his name appears on the record;

(b) if each of them elects to adduce evidence, each of them may open his case and the evidence on behalf of each of them shall be given in the order aforesaid and the speech of each of them closing his case shall be made in that order after the evidence on behalf of all the defendants has been given;

(c) if some of them elect to adduce evidence and some do not, those who do not shall state their cases in the order aforesaid after the speech of the plaintiff in reply to the other defendants.

(6) Where the burden of proof of all the issues in the action lies on the defendant or, where there are two or more defendants and they appear separately or are separately represented, on one of the defendants, the defendant or that defendant, as the case may be, shall be entitled to begin, and in that case paragraphs (2), (3) and (4) shall have effect in relation to, and as between, him and the plaintiff as if for references to the plaintiff and the defendant there were substituted references to the defendant and the plaintiff respectively.

(7) Where, as between the plaintiff and any defendant, the party who would, but for this paragraph, be entitled to make the final speech raises any fresh point of law in that speech or cities in that speech any authority not previously cited, the opposite party may make a further speech in reply, but only in relation to that point of law or that authority, as the case may be.

Inspection by judge or jury

8.—(1) The judge by whom any cause or matter is tried may inspect any place or thing with respect to which any question arises in the cause or matter.

(2) Where a cause or matter is tried with a jury and the judge inspects any place or thing under paragraph (1), he may authorise the jury to inspect it also.

ORDER 38

EVIDENCE

I. GENERAL RULES

1. Subject to the provisions of these rules and of the Civil Evidence Act 1968 and the Civil Evidence Act 1972 and any other enactment relating to evidence, and fact required to be proved at the trial of any action begun by writ by the evidence of witnesses shall be proved by the examination of the witnesses orally and in open court.

Evidence by affidavit

2.—(1) The Court may, at or before the trial of an action begun by writ, order that the affidavit of any witness may be read at the trial if in the circumstances of the case it thinks it reasonable so to order.

(2) An order under paragraph (1) may be made on such terms as to the filing and giving of copies of the affidavits and as to the production of the deponents for the cross-examination as the Court thinks fit but, subject to any such terms and to any subsequent order of the Court, the deponents shall not be subject to cross-examination and need not attend the trial for the purpose.

(3) In any cause or matter begun by originating summons, originating motion or petition, and on any application made by summons or motion, evidence may be given by affidavit unless in the case of any such cause, matter or application any provision of these rules otherwise provides or the Court otherwise directs, but the Court may, on the application of any party, order the attendance for cross-examination of the person making any such affidavit, and where, after such an order has been made, the person in question does not attend, his affidavit shall not be used as evidence without the leave of the Court.

Exchange of witness's statements

2A.—(1) This rule applies to any cause or matter which is proceeding in the Chancery Division, the Commercial Court, the Admiralty Court or as official referees' business, and in this rule "the Court" includes an official referee.

(2) At any stage in any cause or matter to which this rule applies, the Court may, if it thinks fit for the purpose of disposing fairly and expeditiously of the cause or matter and saving costs, direct any party to serve on the other parties, on such terms as the Court shall think just, written statements of the oral evidence which the party intends to lead on any issues of fact to be decided at the trial.

(3) Directions given under paragraph (2) may—
  (a) make different provision with regard to different issues of fact or different witnesses;
  (b) require any written statement served to be signed by the intended witness;
  (c) require that statements be filed with the Court.

(4) Subject to paragraph (6), where the party serving a statement under paragraph (2) does not call the witness to whose evidence it relates no other party may put the statement in evidence at the trial.

(5) Subject to paragraph (6) and unless the Court otherwise orders, where the party serving the statement does call such a witness at the trial—
  (a) that party may not without the consent of the other parties or the leave of the Court lead evidence from that witness the substance of which is not included in the statement served, except in relation to new matters which have arisen in the course of the trial;

(b) the Court may, on such terms as it thinks fit, direct that the statement served, or part of it, shall stand as the evidence in chief of the witness or part of such evidence;

(c) whether or not the statement or any part of it is referred to during the evidence in chief of the witness, any party may put the statement or any part of it in cross-examination of that witness.

(6) Where any statement served is one to which the Civil Evidence Acts 1968 and 1972 apply, paragraphs (4) and (5) shall take effect subject to the provisions of those Acts and of Parts III and IV of this Order. The service of a statement pursuant to a direction given under paragraph (2) shall not, unless expressly so stated by the party serving the same, be treated as a notice under the said Acts.

(7) Where a party fails to comply with a direction given under paragraph (2) he shall not be entitled to adduce evidence to which such direction related without the leave of the Court.

(8) Nothing in this rule shall deprive any part of his right to treat any communication as privileged or make admissible evidence otherwise inadmissible.

Note.—See *Comfort Hotels Ltd.* v. *Wembley Stadium Ltd.* [1978] 1 W.L.R. 872 (Ch.D.)

Evidence of particular facts

3.—(1) Without prejudice to rule 2, the Court may, at or before the trial of any action, order that evidence of any particular fact shall be given at the trial in such manner as may be specified by the order.

(2) The power conferred by paragraph (1) extends in particular to ordering that evidence of any particular fact may be given at the trial—

(a) by statement on oath of information or belief, or

(b) by the production of documents or entries in books, or

(c) by copies of documents or entries in books, or

(d) in the case of a fact which is or was a matter of common knowledge either generally or in a particular district, by the production of a specified newspaper which contains a statement of that fact.

Limitation of expert evidence

4. The Court may, at or before the trial of any action, order that the number of medical or other expert witnesses who may be called at the trial shall be limited as specified by the order.

Limitation of plans, etc., in evidence

5. Unless, at or before the trial, the Court for special reasons otherwise orders, no plan, photograph or model shall be receivable in evidence at the trial of an action unless at least 10 days before the commencement of the trial the parties, other than the party producing it, have been given an opportunity to inspect it and to agree to the admission thereof without further proof.

Note.—For consideration of the exercise of the discretion to order for "special reasons," see *McGuinness* v. *Kellogg Co. of G.B. Ltd.* [1988] 1 W.L.R. 913 (C.A.).

Revocation or variation of orders under rules 2 to 5

6. Any order under rules 2 to 5 (including an order made on appeal) may, on sufficient cause being shown, be revoked or varied by a subsequent order of the Court made at or before the trial.

Evidence of finding on foreign law

7.—(1) A party to any cause or matter who intends to adduce in evidence a finding or decision on a question of foreign law by virtue of section 4(2) of the Civil Evidence Act 1972 shall—

> (*a*) in the case of an action to which Order 25, rule 1, applies, within 14 days after the pleadings in the action are deemed to be closed, and
>
> (*b*) in the case of any other cause or matter, within 21 days after the date on which an appointment for the first hearing of the cause or matter is obtained,

or, in either case, within such other period as the Court may specify, serve notice of his intention on every other party to the proceedings.

(2) The notice shall specify the question on which the finding or decision was given or made and specify the document in which it is reported or recorded in citable form.

(3) In any cause or matter in which evidence may be given by affidavit, an affidavit specifying the matters contained in paragraph (2) shall constitute notice under paragraph (1) if served within the period mentioned in that paragraph.

Depositions: when receivable in evidence at trial

9.—(1) No deposition taken in any cause or matter shall be received in evidence at the trial of the cause or matter unless—

> (*a*) the deposition taken in pursuance of an order under Order 39, rule 1, and
>
> (*b*) either the party against whom the evidence is offered consents or it is proved to the satisfaction of the Court that the deponent is dead, or beyond the jurisdiction of the Court or unable from sickness or other infirmity to attend the trial.

(2) A party intending to use any deposition in evidence at the trial of a cause or matter must, a reasonable time before the trial, give notice of his intention to do so to the other party.

(3) A deposition purporting to be signed by the person before whom it was taken shall be receivable in evidence without proof of the signature being the signature of that person.

Note.—Ord. 39, rr. 1 (*infra*) and 2 provide for the examination of witnesses before examiners at home and abroad.

Court documents admissible or receivable in evidence

10.—(1) Office copies of writs, records, pleadings and documents filed in the High Court shall be admissible in evidence in any cause or matter and between all parties to the same extent as the original would be admissible.

(2) Without prejudice to the provisions of any enactment, every document purporting to be sealed with the seal of any office or department of the Supreme Court shall be received in evidence without further proof, and any document purporting to be so sealed and to be a

copy of a document filed in, or issued out of, that office or department shall be deemed to be an office copy of that document without further proof unless the contrary is shown.

Evidence at trial may be used in subsequent proceedings

12. Any evidence taken at the trial of any cause or matter may be used in any subsequent proceedings in that cause or matter.

Order to produce document at proceeding other than trial

13.—(1) At any stage in a cause or matter the Court may order any person to attend any proceeding in the cause or matter and produce any document, to be specified or described in the order, the production of which appears to the Court to be necessary for the purpose of that proceeding.

(2) No person shall be compelled by an order under paragraph (1) to produce any document at a proceeding in a cause or matter which he could not be compelled to produce at the trial of that cause or matter.

III. HEARSAY EVIDENCE

Interpretation and application

20.—(1) In this Part of this Order "the Act" means the Civil Evidence Act 1968 and any expressions used in this Part of this Order and in Part I of the Act have the same meanings in this Part of this Order as they have in the said Part I.

(2) This Part of this Order shall apply in relation to the trial or hearing of an issue or question arising in a cause or matter, and to a reference, inquiry and assessment of damages, as it applies in relation to the trial or hearing of a cause or matter.

Notice of intention to give certain statements in evidence

21.—(1) Subject to the provisions of this rule, a party to a cause or matter who desires to give in evidence at the trial or hearing of the cause or matter any statement which is admissible in evidence by virtue of section 2, 4 or 5 of the Act must—

    (*a*) in the case of a cause or matter which is required to be set down for trial or hearing or adjourned into court, within 21 days after it is set down or so adjourned, or within such other period as the Court may specify, and

    (*b*) in the case of any other cause or matter, within 21 days after the date on which an appointment for the first hearing of the cause or matter is obtained, or within such other period as the Court may specify,

serve on every other party to the cause or matter notice of his desire to do so, and the notice must comply with the provisions of rule 22, 23 or 24, as the circumstances of the case require.

(2) Paragraph (1) shall not apply in relation to any statement which is admissible as evidence of any fact stated therein by virtue not only of the said section 2, 4 or 5 but by virtue also of any other statutory provision within the meaning of section 1 of the Act.

(3) Paragraph (1) shall not apply in relation to any statement which any part to a probate action desires to give in evidence at the trial of

that action and which is alleged to have been made by the deceased person whose estate is the subject of the action.

(4) Where by virtue of any provision of these rules or of any order or direction of the Court the evidence in any proceedings is to be given by affidavit then, without prejudice to paragraph (2), paragraph (1) shall not apply in relation to any statement which any party to the proceedings desires to have included in any affidavit to be used on his behalf in the proceedings, but nothing in this paragraph shall affect the operation of Order 41, rule 5, or the powers of the Court under Order 38, rule 3.

Note.—See *Re Koscot Interplanetary (U.K.) Ltd.*; *Re Koscot A.G.* [1972] 3 All E.R. 829, Part One, Chapter 16, *supra*.

(5) Order 65, rule 9, shall not apply to a notice under this rule but the Court may direct that the notice need not be served on any party who at the time when service is to be effected is in default as to acknowledgment of service or who has no address for service.

Statement admissible by virtue of section 2 of the Act: contents of notice

22.—(1) If the statement is admissible by virtue of section 2 of the Act and was made otherwise than in a document, the notice must contain particulars of—

    (*a*) the time, place and circumstances at or in which the statement was made;

    (*b*) the person by whom, and the person to whom, the statement was made; and

    (*c*) the substance of the statement or, if material, the words used.

(2) If the statement is admissible by virtue of the said section 2 and was made in a document, a copy or transcript of the document, or of the relevant part thereof, must be annexed to the notice and the notice must contain such (if any) of the particulars mentioned in paragraph (1)(*a*) and (*b*) as are not apparent on the face of the document or part.

(3) If the party giving the notice alleges that any person, particulars of whom are contained in the notice, cannot or should not be called as a witness at the trial or hearing for any of the reasons specified in rule 25, the notice must contain a statement to that effect specifying the reason relied on.

Statement admissible by virtue of section 4 of the Act: contents of notice

23.—(1) If the statement is admissible by virtue of section 4 of the Act, the notice must have annexed to it a copy or transcript of the document containing the statement, or of the relevant part thereof, and must contain—

    (*a*) particulars of—

        (*i*) the person by whom the record containing the statement was compiled;

        (*ii*) the person who originally supplied the information from which the record was compiled; and

        (*iii*) any other person through whom that information was supplied to the compiler of that record;

    and, in the case of any such person as is referred to in (i) or (iii) above, a description of the duty under which that person was acting when compiling that record or supplying information from which that record was compiled, as the case may be;

(b) if not apparent on the face of the document annexed to the notice, a description of the nature of the record which, or part of which, contains the statement; and

(c) particulars of the time, place and circumstances at or in which that record or part was complied.

(2) If the party giving the notice alleges that any person, particulars of whom are contained in the notice, cannot or should not be called as a witness at the trial or hearing for any of the reasons specified in rule 25, the notice must contain a statement to that effect specifying the reason relied on.

Statement admissible by virtue of section 5 of the Act: contents of notice

24.—(1) If the statement is contained in a document produced by a computer and is admissible by virtue of section 5 of the Act, the notice must have annexed to it a copy or transcript of the document containing the statement, or of the relevant part thereof, and must contain particulars of—

(a) a person who occupied a responsible position in relation to the management of the relevant activities for the purposes of which the computer was used regularly during the material period to store or process information;

(b) a person who at the material time occupied such a position in relation to the supply of information to the computer, being information which is reproduced in the statement or information from which the information contained in the statement is derived;

(c) a person who occupied such a position in relation to the operation of the computer during the material period;

and where there are two or more persons who fall within any of the foregoing subparagraphs and some only of those persons are at the date of service of the notice capable of being called as witnesses at the trial or hearing, the person particulars of whom are to be contained in the notice must be such one of those persons as is at that date so capable.

(2) The notice must also state whether the computer was operating properly throughout the material period and, if not, whether any respect in which it was not operating properly or was out of operation during any part of that period was such as to affect the production of the document in which the statement is contained or the accuracy of its contents.

(3) If the party giving the notice alleges that any person, particulars of whom are contained in the notice, cannot or should not be called as a witness at the trial or hearing for any of the reasons specified in rule 25, the notice must contain a statement to that effect specifying the reason relied on.

Reasons for not calling a person as a witness

25. The reasons referred to in rules 22(3), 23(2) and 24(3) are that the person in question is dead, or beyond the seas, or unfit by reason of his bodily or mental condition to attend as a witness or that despite the exercise of reasonable diligence it has not been possible to identify or find him or that he cannot reasonably be expected to have any recollection of matters relevant to the accuracy or otherwise of the statement to which the notice relates.

Note.—See *Rasool* v. *West Midlands Passenger Transport Executive* [1974] 3 All E.R. 638 (Q.B.D.) and *Piermay Shipping Co.* v. *Chester* [1978] 1 W.L.R. 411 (C.A.), both in Part One, Chapter 16, *supra.*

Counter-notice requiring person to be called as a witness

26.—(1) Subject to paragraphs (2) and (3), any party to a cause or matter on whom a notice under rule 21 is served may within 21 days after service of the notice on him serve on the party who gave the notice a counter-notice requiring that party to call as a witness at the trial or hearing of the cause or matter any person (naming him) particulars of whom are contained in the notice.

(2) Where any notice under rule 21 contains a statement that any person particulars of whom are contained in the notice cannot or should not be called as a witness for the reason specified therein, a party shall not be entitled to serve a counter-notice under this rule requiring that person to be called as a witness at the trial or hearing of the cause or matter unless he contends that that person can or, as the case may be, should be called, and in that case he must include in his counter-notice a statement to that effect.

(3) Where a statement to which a notice under rule 21 relates is one to which rule 28 applies, no party on whom the notice is served shall be entitled to serve a counter-notice under this rule in relation to that statement, but the foregoing provision is without prejudice to the right of any party to apply to the Court under rule 28 for directions with respect to the admissibility of that statement.

(4) If any party to a cause or matter by whom a notice under rule 21 is served fails to comply with a counter-notice duly served on him under this rule, then, unless any of the reasons specified in rule 25 applies in relation to the person named in the counter-notice, and without prejudice to the powers of the Court under rule 29, the statement to which the notice under rule 21 relates shall not be admissible at the trial or hearing of the cause or matter as evidence of any fact stated therein by virtue of section 2, 4 or 5 of the Act, as the case may be.

Determination of question whether person can or should be called as a witness

27.—(1) Where in any cause or matter a question arises whether any of the reasons specified in rule 25 applies in relation to a person particulars of whom are contained in a notice under rule 21, the Court may, on the application of any party to the cause or matter, determine that question before the trial or hearing of the cause or matter or give directions for it to be determined before the trial or hearing and for the manner in which it is to be so determined.

(2) Unless the Court otherwise directs, the summons by which an application under paragraph (1) is made must be served by the party making the application on every other party to the cause or matter.

(3) Where any such question as is referred to in paragraph (1) has been determined under or by virtue of that paragraph, no application to have it determined afresh at the trial or hearing of the cause or matter may be made unless the evidence which it is sought to adduce

in support of the application could not with reasonable diligence have been adduced at the hearing which resulted in the determination.

Directions with respect to statement made in previous proceedings

28. Where a party to a cause or matter has given notice in accordance with rule 21 that he desires to give in evidence at the trial or hearing of the cause or matter—

(*a*) a statement falling within section 2(1) of the Act which was made by a person, whether orally or in a document, in the course of giving evidence in some other legal proceedings (whether civil or criminal), or

(*b*) a statement falling within section 4(1) of the Act which is contained in a record of direct oral evidence given in some other legal proceedings (whether civil or criminal),

any party to the cause or matter may apply to the Court for directions under this rule, and the Court hearing such an application may give directions as to whether, and if so on what conditions, the party desiring to give the statement in evidence will be permitted to do so and (where applicable) as to the manner in which that statement and any other evidence given in those other proceedings is to be proved.

Note.—Conditions imposed by the court when permitting under this rule reception of a statement made in previous proceedings may include the condition that any opposing party be permitted to cross-examine on it: see *Tremelbye (Selangor) Ltd.* v. *Stekel* [1971] 1 W.L.R. 226, (Ch.D.).

Power of Court to allow statements to be given in evidence

29.—(1) Without prejudice to section 2(2)(*a*) and 4(2)(*a*) of the Act and rule 28, the Court may, if it thinks it just to do so, allow a statement falling within section 2(1), 4(1) or 5(1) of the Act to be given in evidence at the trial or hearing of a cause or matter notwithstanding—

(*a*) that the statement is one in relation to which rule 21(1) applies and that the party desiring to give the statement in evidence has failed to comply with that rule, or

(*b*) that that party has failed to comply with any requirement of a counter-notice relating to that statement which was served on him in accordance with rule 26.

(2) Without prejudice to the generality of paragraph (1), the Court may exercise its power under that paragraph to allow a statement to be given in evidence at the trial or hearing of a cause or matter if a refusal to exercise that power might oblige the party desiring to give the statement in evidence to call as a witness at the trial or hearing an opposite party or a person who is or was at the material time the servant or agent of an opposite party.

Restriction on adducing evidence as to credibility of maker, etc., of certain statements

30. Where—

(*a*) a notice given under rule 21 in a cause or matter related to a statement which is admissible by virtue of section 2 or 4 of the Act, and

(*b*) the person who made the statement, or, as the case may be, the person who originally supplied the information from which the record containing the statement was compiled, is not called as a witness at the trial or hearing of the cause or matter, and

(c) none of the reasons mentioned in rule 25 applies so as to prevent the party who gave the notice from calling that person as a witness,

no other party to the cause or matter shall be entitled, except with the leave of the Court, to adduce in relation to that person any evidence which could otherwise be adduced by him by virtue of section 7 of the Act unless he gave a counter-notice under rule 26 in respect of that person or applied under rule 28 for a direction that that person be called as a witness at the trial or hearing of the cause or matter.

Notice required of intention to give evidence of certain inconsistent statements

31.—(1) Where a person, particulars of whom were contained in a notice given under rule 21 in a cause or matter, is not to be called as a witness at the trial or hearing of the cause or matter, any party to the cause or matter who is entitled and intends to adduce in relation to that person any evidence which is admissible for the purpose mentioned in section 7(1)(b) of the Act must, not more than 21 days after service of that notice on him, serve on the party who gave that notice, notice of his intention to do so.

(2) Rule 22(1) and (2) shall apply to a notice under this rule as if the notice were a notice under rule 21 and the statement to which the notice relates were a statement admissible by virtue of section 2 of the Act.

(3) The Court may, if it thinks it just to do so, allow a party to give in evidence at the trial or hearing of a cause or matter any evidence which is admissible for the purpose mentioned in the said section 7(1)(b) notwithstanding that that party has failed to comply with the provisions of paragraph (1).

Costs

32. If—

(a) a party to a cause or matter serves a counter-notice under rule 26 in respect of any person who is called as a witness at the trial of the cause or matter in compliance with a requirement of the counter-notice, and

(b) it appears to the Court that it was unreasonable to require that person to be called as a witness,

then, without prejudice to Order 62 and, in particular, to rule 10(1) thereof, the Court may direct that any costs to that party in respect of the preparation and service of the counter-notice shall not be allowed to him and that any costs occasioned by the counter-notice to any other party shall be paid by him to that other party.

Certain powers exercisable in chambers

33. The jurisdiction of the court under sections 2(2)(a), 2(3), 4(2)(a) and 6(1) of the Act may be exercised in chambers.

Statements of opinion

34. Where a party to a cause or matter desires to give in evidence by virtue of Part 1 of the Act, as extended by section 1(1) of the Civil Evidence Act 1972, a statement of opinion other than a statement to which Part IV of this Order applies, the provisions of rules 20 to 23 and 25 to 33 shall apply with such modifications as the Court may direct or the circumstances of the case may require.

IV. Expert Evidence

Interpretation

35. In this Part of this Order a reference to a summons for directions includes a reference to any summons or application to which, under any of these Rules, Order 25, rules 2 to 7, apply and expressions used in this Part of this Order which are used in the Civil Evidence Act 1972 have the same meanings in this Part of this Order as in that Act.

Note.—Expert evidence in this Order includes the evidence of "in house" experts and the parties themselves: *Shell Pensions Trust* v. *Pell Frischmann and Partners (A Firm)* [1986] 2 All E.R. 911 (His Honour Judge Newey Q.C.).

Restrictions on adducing expert evidence

36.—(1) Except with the leave of the Court or where all parties agree, no expert evidence may be adduced at the trial or hearing of any cause or matter unless the party seeking to adduce the evidence
> (*a*) has applied to the Court to determine whether a direction should be given under rule 37 or 41 (whichever is appropriate) and has complied with any direction given on the application, or
> (*b*) has complied with automatic directions taking effect under Order 25, rule 8(1)(*b*).

(2) Nothing in paragraph (1) shall apply to evidence which is permitted to be given by affidavit or shall affect the enforcement under any other provision of these rules (except Order 45, rule 5) of a direction given under this Part of this Order.

Note.—For rules 37 and 41 see *infra*. Order 45, rule 5 deals with the enforcement of judgments to do or abstain from doing any act.

Direction that expert report be disclosed

37. Where in any cause or matter an application is made under rule 36(1) in respect of oral expert evidence, then, unless the Court considers that there are special reasons for not doing so, it shall direct that the substance of the evidence be disclosed in the form of a written report or reports to such other parties and within such period as the Court may specify.

Meeting of experts

38. In any cause or matter the Court may, if it thinks fit, direct that there be a meeting "without prejudice" of such experts within such period before or after the disclosure of their reports as the Court may specify, for the purpose of identifying those parts of their evidence which are in issue. Where such a meeting takes place the experts may prepare a joint statement indicating those parts of their evidence on which they are, and those on which they are not, in agreement.

[Rule **44** is revoked.]

Disclosure of part of expert evidence

39. Where the Court considers that any circumstances rendering it undesirable to give a direction under rule 37 relate to part only of the evidence sought to be adduced, the Court may, if it thinks fits, direct disclosure of the remainder.

Expert evidence contained in statement

41. Where an application is made under rule 36 in respect of expert evidence contained in a statement and the applicant alleges that the maker of the statement cannot or should not be called as a witness, the Court may direct that the provisions of rules 20 to 23 and 25 to 33 shall apply with such modifications as the Court thinks fit.

Note.—For rules 20 to 23 and 25 to 33 see *supra*.

Putting in evidence expert report disclosed by another party

42. A party to any cause or matter may put in evidence any expert report disclosed to him by any other party in accordance with this Part of this Order.

Time for putting expert report in evidence

43. Where a party to any cause or matter calls as a witness the maker of a report which has been disclosed in accordance with a direction given under rule 37, the report may be put in evidence at the commencement of its maker's examination in chief or at such other time as the Court may direct.

Revocation and variation of directions

44. Any direction given under this Part of this Order may on sufficient cause being shown by revoked or varied by a subsequent direction given at or before the trial of the cause or matter.

ORDER 39

EVIDENCE BY DEPOSITION: EXAMINERS OF THE COURT

Power to order depositions to be taken

1.—(1) The Court may, in any cause or matter where it appears necessary for the purposes of justice, make an order (in Form No. 32 in Appendix A) for the examination on oath before a judge, an officer or examiner of the Court or some other person, at any place, of any person.

(2) An order under paragraph (1) may be made on such terms (including, in particular, terms as to the giving of discovery before the examination takes place) as the Court thinks fit, and may contain an order for the production of any document which appears to the court to be necessary for the purposes of the examination.

Conduct of examination

8.—(1) Subject to any directions contained in the order for examination—

(a) any person ordered to be examined before the examiner may be cross-examined and re-examined, and

(b) the examination, cross-examination and re-examination of persons before the examiner shall be conducted in like manner as at the trial of a cause or matter.

(2) The examiner may put any question to any person examined before him as to the meaning of any answer made by that person or as to any matter arising in the course of the examination.

(3) The examiner may, if necessary, adjourn the examination from time to time.

Objection to questions

10.—(1) If any person being examined before the examiner objects to answer any question put to him, or if objection is taken to any such question, that question, the ground for the objection and the answer to any such question to which objection is taken must be set out in the deposition of that person or in a statement annexed thereto.

(2) The validity of the ground for objecting to answer any such question or for objection to any such question shall be decided by the Court and not by the examiner, but the examiner must state to the parties his opinion thereon, and the statement of his opinion must be set out in the deposition or in a statement annexed thereto.

(3) If the Court decides against the person taking the objection it may order him to pay the costs occasioned by his objection.

Taking of depositions

11.—(1) The deposition of any person examined before the examiner must be taken down by the examiner or a shorthand writer or some other person in the presence of the examiner but, subject to paragraph (2) and rule 10(1), the deposition need not set out every question and answer so long as it contains as nearly as may be the statement of the person examined.

(2) The examiner may direct the exact words of any particular question and the answer thereto to be set out in the deposition if that question and answer appear to him to have special importance.

(3) The deposition of any person shall be read to him, and he shall be asked to sign it, in the presence of such of the parties as may attend, but the parties may agree in writing to dispense with the foregoing provision.

If a person refuses to sign a deposition when asked under this paragraph to do so, the examiner must sign the deposition.

ORDER 40

COURT EXPERT

Appointment of expert to report on certain questions

1.—(1) If any cause or matter which is to be tried without a jury and in which any question for an expert witness arises the Court may at any time, on the application of any party, appoint an independent expert or, if more than one such question arises, two or more such experts, to inquire and report upon any question of fact or opinion not involving questions of law or of construction.

An expert appointed under this paragraph is referred to in this Order as a "court expert."

(2) Any court expert in a cause or matter shall, if possible, be a person agreed between the parties and, failing agreement, shall be nominated by the Court.

(3) The question to be submitted to the court expert and the instructions (if any) given to him shall, failing agreement between the parties, be settled by the Court.

(4) In this rule "expert", in relation to any question arising in a cause or matter, means any person who has such knowledge or experience of or in connection with that question that his opinion on it would be admissible in evidence.

Report of court expert

2.—(1) The Court expert must send his report to the Court, together with such number of copies thereof as the Court may direct, and the proper officer must send copies of the report to the parties or their solicitors.

(2) The Court may direct the court expert to make a further or supplemental report.

(3) Any part of a court expert's report which is not accepted by all the parties to the cause or matter in which it is made shall be treated as information furnished to the Court and be given such weight as the Court thinks fit.

Experiments and tests

3. If the court expert is of opinion that an experiment or test of any kind (other than one of a trifling character) is necessary to enable him to make a satisfactory report he shall inform the parties or their solicitors and shall, if possible, make an arrangement with them as to the expenses involved, the persons to attend and other relevant matters; and if the parties are unable to agree on any of those matters it shall be settled by the Court.

Cross-examination of court expert

4. Any party may, within 14 days after receiving a copy of the court expert's report, apply to the Court for leave to cross-examine the expert on his report, and on that application the Court shall make an order for the cross-examination of the expert by all the parties either—

(a) at the trial, or

(b) before an examiner at such time and place as may be specified in the order.

Calling of expert witnesses

6. Where a court expert is appointed in a cause or matter, any party may, on giving to the other parties a reasonable time before the trial notice of his intention to do so, call one expert witness to give evidence on the question reported on by the court expert but no party may call more than one such witness without the leave of the Court, and the Court shall not grant leave unless it considers the circumstances of the case to be exceptional.

ORDER 41

AFFIDAVITS

Contents of affidavit

5.—(1) Subject to Order 14, rules 2(2) and 4(2), to Order 86, rule 2(1), to paragraph (2) of this rule and to any order made under Order 38, rule 3, an affidavit may contain only such facts as the deponent is able of his own knowledge to prove.

(2) An affidavit sworn for the purpose of being used in interlocutory proceedings may contain statements of information or belief with the sources and grounds thereof.

Note.—Ord. 14, which relates to summary judgments, by r. 2(2) and r. 4(2) permits an affidavit to contain statements of information or belief with the sources and grounds thereof. As to Ord. 38, r. 3, see *supra.* Ord. 86 relates to applications for summary judgment in actions for specific performance of certain agreements concerning property, for their rescission, or for forfeiture or return of any deposit made under them; and r. 2(1) permits an affidavit to contain a statement of the facts on which the cause of action is based, and the deponent's belief that there is no defence to the action.

ORDER 55

APPEALS TO HIGH COURT FROM COURT, TRIBUNAL OR PERSON: GENERAL

Powers of court hearing appeal

7.—(1) In addition to the power conferred by rule 6(3), the Court hearing an appeal to which this Order applies shall have the powers conferred by the following provisions of this rule.

(2) The Court shall have power to receive further evidence on questions of fact, and the evidence may be given in such manner as the Court may direct either by oral examination in court, by affidavit, by deposition taken before an examiner or in some other manner.

(3) The Court shall have power to draw any inferences of fact which might have been drawn in the proceedings out of which the appeal arose.

(4) It shall be the duty of the appellant to apply to the judge or other person presiding at the proceedings in which the decision appealed against was given for a signed copy of any note made by him of the proceedings and to furnish that copy for the use of the Court; and in default of production of such a note, or, if such note is incomplete, in addition to such note, the Court may hear and determine the appeal on any other evidence or statement of what occurred in those proceedings as appears to the Court to be sufficient.

Except where the Court otherwise directs, an affidavit or note by a person present at the proceedings shall not be used in evidence under this paragraph unless it was previously submitted to the person presiding at the proceedings for his comments.

(7) The Court shall not be bound to allow the appeal on the ground merely of misdirection, or of the improper admission or rejection of evidence, unless in the opinion of the Court substantial wrong or miscarriage has been thereby occasioned.

Note.—Rule 6(3) gives the court power to amend the notice of motion, or to make any other order to ensure the determination on the merits of the question in controversy.

ORDER 59

APPEALS TO THE COURT OF APPEAL

General powers of the Court

10.—(1) In relation to an appeal the Court of Appeal shall have all the powers and duties as to amendment and otherwise of the High Court including, without prejudice to the generality of the foregoing words, the powers of the Court under Order 36 to refer any question or issue of fact for trial before, or inquiry and report by, an official referee.

In relation to a reference made to an official referee, any thing required or authorised under Order 36, rule 9, to be done by, to or before the Court shall be done by, to or before the Court of Appeal.

(2) The Court of Appeal shall have power to receive further evidence on questions of fact, either by oral examination in court, by affidavit, or by deposition taken before an examiner, but, in the case of an appeal from a judgment after trial or hearing of any cause or matter on the merits, no such further evidence (other than evidence as to matters which have occurred after the date of the trial or hearing) shall be admitted except on special grounds.

Note.—See Part One, Chapter 26, *supra.* Seemingly (but suprisingly) rule 10(2) applies even in the case of an appeal against a summary judgment: *Langdale* v. *Darby* [1982] 1 W.L.R. 1123 (H.L.).

(3) The Court of Appeal shall have power to draw inferences of fact and to give any judgment and make any order which ought to have been given or made, and to make such further or other order as the case may require.

Powers of the Court as to new trials

11.—(1) On the hearing of any appeal the Court of Appeal may, if it thinks fit, make any such order as could be made in pursuance of an application for a new trial or to set aside a verdict, finding or judgment of the court below.

(2) The Court of Appeal shall not be bound to order a new trial on the ground of misdirection, or of the improper admission or rejection of evidence, or because the verdict of the jury was not taken upon a question which the judge at the trial was not asked to leave to them, unless in the opinion of the Court of Appeal some substantial wrong or miscarriage has been thereby occasioned.

Note.—See Part One, Chapter 26, *supra.*

Evidence on appeal

12. Where any question of fact is involved in an appeal, the evidence taken in the court below bearing on the question shall, subject to any direction of the Court of Appeal or a single judge or the registrar, be brought before that Court as follows:—

(*a*) in the case of evidence taken by affidavit, by the production of a true copy of such affidavit;

(*b*) in the case of evidence given orally, by a copy of so much of the transcript of the official shorthand note as is relevant or by a copy of the judge's note, where he has intimated that in the event of an appeal his note will be sufficient, or by such other means as the Court of Appeal or a single judge or the registrar may direct.

Note.—See Part One, Chapter 26, *supra*.

ORDER 82

DEFAMATION ACTIONS

Interrogatories not allowed in certain cases

6. In an action for libel or slander where the defendant pleads that the words or matters complained of are fair comment on a matter of public interest or were published on a privileged occasion, no interrogatories as to the defendant's sources of information or grounds of belief shall be allowed.

THE COUNTY COURT RULES 1981, AS AMENDED

ORDER 14

DISCOVERY AND INTERROGATORIES

Order for production to court

7. At any stage of the proceedings in an action or matter the court may, subject to rule 8, order any party to produce to the court any document in his possession, custody or power relating to any matter in question in the proceedings and the court may deal with the document when produced in such manner as it thinks fit.

Discovery etc. to be ordered only if necessary

8.—(1) On the hearing of an application under rule 1, 2 or 5, the court, if satisfied that the discovery, disclosure or production sought is not necessary, or not necessary at that stage of the action or matter, may dismiss or adjourn the application and shall in any case refuse to make an order if and so far as it is of opinion that discovery, disclosure or production, as the case may be, is not necessary either for disposing fairly of the action or matter or for saving costs.

Use of documents

8A. Any undertaking, whether express or implied, not to use a document for any purpose other than those of the proceedings in which it is disclosed shall cease to apply to such a document after it has been read to or by the court, or referred to, in open court, unless the court for special reasons has otherwise ordered on the application of a party or the person to whom the document belongs.

Saving for public interest

9. The foregoing provisions of this Order shall be without prejudice to any rule of law which authorises or requires the withholding of any document on the ground that the disclosure of it would be injurious to the public interest.

Note.—Rule 1 of this Order deals with discovery of documents, rule 2 with disclosure of particular documents, and rule 5 with orders for production for inspection.
For public interest immunity, see Part I, Chapter 11, *supra*.

ORDER 20

EVIDENCE

PART I—ADMISSIONS

Admission of other party's case.

1. A party to an action or matter may give notice, by his pleading or otherwise in writing, that he admits the truth of the whole or any part of the case of any other party, and no costs incurred after the receipt of the notice in respect of the proof of any matters which the admission renders it unnecessary to prove shall be allowed.

Note.—Compare R.S.C., Ord. 27, r. 1, *supra.*

Notice to admit facts

2.—(1) A party to an action or matter may, not later than 14 days before the trial or hearing, serve on any other party a notice requiring him to admit, for the purpose of that action or matter only, such facts, or such part of his case, as may be specified in the notice.

(2) If the party served with a notice to admit facts under paragraph (1) does not deliver a written admission of the facts within 7 days after service of the notice on him, the costs of proving the facts shall be paid by him unless the court otherwise orders.

(3) An admission made in compliance with a notice under paragraph (1) shall not be used against the party by whom it was made in any action or matter other than the one for the purpose of which it was made or in favour of any person other than the one by whom the notice was given and the court may at any time allow a party to amend or withdraw an admission so made by him on such terms as may be just.

Notice to admit or produce documents

3.—(1) Without prejudice to rule 11 and any presumption of law as to the authenticity of a document, a party to an action or matter who desires to adduce any document in evidence may, not later than 14 days before the trial or hearing, serve on any other party a notice requiring him to admit the authenticity of the document.

(2) If the party served with a notice under paragraph (1) desires to challenge the authenticity of the document, he must, within 7 days after service of the notice, serve on the party by whom it was given a notice that he does not admit the authenticity of the document and requires it to be proved at the trial, and in that case the costs of proving the document shall be paid by him unless the court otherwise orders.

(3) A party who fails to give notice of non-admission under paragraph (2) shall be deemed to have admitted the authenticity of the document unless the court otherwise orders.

(4) A party to an action or matter may serve on any other party a notice requiring him to produce the document specified in the notice at the trial or hearing of the action or matter.

PART II—EVIDENCE GENERALLY

Evidence generally to be given orally and in open court

4. Subject to any provision made by or under any Act or rule and to any rule of law, any fact required to be proved at the hearing of an action or matter by the evidence of witnesses shall be proved by the examination of the witnesses orally and in open court.

Evidence in chambers

5. In any proceedings in chambers evidence may be given by affidavit unless by any provision of these rules it is otherwise provided or the court otherwise directs, but the court may, on the application of any party, order the attendance for cross-examination of the person making any such affidavit, and where, after such an order has been made, the person in question does not attend, his affidavit shall not be used in evidence without the leave of the court.

Evidence by affidavit on order

6.—(1) In any case to which rule 5 does not apply the court may, at or before the hearing of an action or matter, order that the affidavit of any witness may be read at the hearing if in the circumstances of the case it thinks it reasonable to do so.

(2) An order under paragraph (1) may be made on such terms as to the filing and giving of copies of the affidavit and as to the production of the deponent for cross-examination as the court thinks fit but, subject to such terms and to any subsequent order of the court, the deponent shall not be subject to cross-examination and need not attend the hearing for the purpose.

Use of affidavit on notice

7.—(1) Where a party desires to use at the hearing of an action or matter an affidavit which is not rendered admissible by rule 5 and in respect of which no order has been made under rule 6, he may, not less than 14 days before the hearing, give notice of his desire, accompanied by a copy of the affidavit, to the party against whom it is to be used, and unless that party, within 7 days after receipt of the notice, gives notice to the other party that he objects to the use of the affidavit, he shall be taken to have consented to its use and accordingly the affidavits may be used at the hearing.

(2) Where—
    (*a*) the defendant in a fixed date action has not delivered a defence within the time limited by Order 9, rule 2, or
    (*b*) the defendant in a default or fixed date action does not appear on a pre-trial review of the action.

evidence by affidavit shall be admissible in support of the plaintiff's claim without notice being given under paragraph (1), unless the court otherwise orders.

Evidence of particular facts

8. The court may, at or before the trial or hearing of any action or matter and on or before any application in the course of proceedings or any pre-trial review, order that evidence of any particular fact shall be given at the hearing of the action or matter or, as the case may be, on the application or pre-trial review in such manner as may be specified in the order, and in particular—

    (a) by the production of documents or entries in books, or
    (b) by copies of documents or entries in books, or
    (c) in the case of a fact which is or was a matter of common knowledge either generally or in a particular district, by the production of a specified newspaper which contains a statement of that fact.

Savings and revocation or variation of orders

9.—(1) Nothing in rules 5 to 8 or in any order made thereunder shall affect the weight, if any, to be attached to a statement admissible in evidence under any of those rules or under any such order, or the power of the court, when the statement is tendered in evidence, to refuse to admit it if in the interest of justice the court thinks fit to do so.

   . . . .

Form and contents of affidavit

10.—(1) Subject to the following paragraphs of this rule, the provisions of the R.S.C. with respect to—

    (a) the form and contents of an affidavit;
    (b) the making of an affidavit by two or more deponents or by a blind or illiterate deponent;
    (c) the use of any affidavit which contains an interlineation, erasure or other alteration or is otherwise defective;
    (d) the striking out of any matter which is scandalous, irrelevant or otherwise oppressive;
    (e) the insufficiency of an affidavit sworn before any agent, partner or clerk of a party's solicitor; and
    (f) the making and marking of exhibits to an affidavit.

shall apply in relation to an affidavit for use in a county court as they apply in relation to an affidavit for use in the High Court.

   . . . .

(4) Unless the court otherwise orders, an affidavit may be used notwithstanding that it contains statements of information or belief.

(5) Every affidavit shall state which of the facts deposed to are within the deponent's knowledge and which are based on information or belief and shall give, in the former case, his means of knowledge and, in the latter case, the sources and grounds of the information or belief.

Documents produced from proper custody

11.—(1) Where a document which would, if duly proved, be admissible in evidence is produced to the court from proper custody, it shall be admitted without further proof if—

    (a) in the opinion of the court it appears genuine; and
    (b) no objection is taken to its admission.

(2) If objection is taken to the admission of any document so produced, the court may adjourn the hearing of the action or matter for proof of the document and, if it is proved, the party objecting shall pay the costs occasioned by the objection unless the court otherwise orders.

PART III—SUMMONING AND EXAMINATION OF WITNESSES

Evidence by deposition

13.—(1) The court may, in any action or matter where it appears necessary for the purposes of justice, make an order in the appropriate form for the examination on oath of any person (in this rule called "the witness") at any place in England and Wales.

(2) The examination may be ordered to take place before any of the following persons (in this rule called "the examiner"), that is to say—
  (*a*) any officer of the court making the order, or
  (*b*) any officer of the court for the district in which the witness resides or carries on business, or
  (*c*) such other person as the court may appoint.

(3) The order shall specify the day and place fixed for the examination and shall be served on the witness personally a reasonable time before the day so fixed and at the same time there shall be paid or tendered to the witness the sums prescribed by rule 12(7).

A copy of the order shall also be sent to every party to the action or matter.

. . .

(5) Subject to the following paragraphs of this rule, the provisions of the R.S.C. with respect to—
  (*a*) the documents to be furnished to the examiner,
  (*b*) the conduct of the examination,
  (*c*) the making of objections to questions put to the witness,
  (*d*) the taking and signing of the deposition,
  (*e*) the making of a special report by the examiner, and
  (*f*) the reception of the deposition in evidence at the hearing of the action or matter,
shall apply in relation to the examination of a witness pursuant to an order under paragraph (1) as they apply in relation to the examination of a witness pursuant to an order made in a cause or matter in the High Court.

PART IV—HEARSAY EVIDENCE

Note.—Rule 14 and rules 15–24 correspond with R.S.C., Ord. 38, rr. 20–32.

Order 20, r. 14(3) of C.C.R. 1981 excludes the application of the rules in Part IV to an arbitration under the County Courts Act 1984, s.64.

Evidence of findings on foreign law

25.—(1) Subject to the provisions of this rule, a party who intends to adduce in evidence a finding or decision on a question of foreign law by virtue of section 4(2) of the Civil Evidence Act 1972 shall, not less than 14 days before the day fixed for the trial or hearing or within such other period as the court may specify, serve notice of his intention on every other party to the proceedings.

(2) The notice shall specify the question on which the finding or decision was given or made and specify the document in which it is reported or recorded in citable form.

(3) In any action or matter in which evidence may be given by affidavit, an affidavit specifying the matter contained in paragraph (2) shall constitute notice under paragraph (1) if served within the period mentioned in that paragraph.

(4) Unless in any particular case the court otherwise directs, paragraph (1) shall not apply to an action or matter in which no defence or answer has been filed.

Statements of opinion

26. Where a party to an action or matter desires to give in evidence by virtue of Part I of the Act of 1968 as extended by section 1(1) of the Civil Evidence Act 1972, a statement of opinion other than a statement to which Part III of this Order applies, the provisions of rules 14 to 24 of this Order (except so much of rule 16 as applies R.S.C. Order 38, rule 24) shall apply with such modifications as the court may direct or the circumstances of the case may require.

PART V—EXPERT EVIDENCE

Restrictions on adducing expert evidence

27.—(1) Except with the leave of the court or where all parties agree, no expert evidence may be adduced at the trial or hearing of an action or matter, unless the party seeking to adduce the evidence has applied to the court to determine whether a direction should be given under rule 37, 38 or 41 (whichever is appropriate) of R.S.C. Order 38, as applied by rule 28 of this Order, and has complied with any direction given on the application.

(2) Nothing in paragraph (1) shall apply to expert evidence which is permitted to be given by affidavit or which is to be adduced in an action or matter in which no defence or answer has been filed or in proceedings referred to arbitration under section 64 of the Act.

(3) Nothing in paragraph (1) shall affect the enforcement under any other provision of these rules (except Order 29, rule 1) of a direction given under this Part of this Order.

Application of R.S.C.

28. R.S.C. Order 38, rules 37 to 44 shall apply in relation to an application under rule 27 of this Order as they apply in relation to an application under rule 36(1) of the said Order 38.

ORDER 21

Inspection by judge or jury

6.—(1) The judge by whom any action or matter is heard may inspect any place or thing with respect to which any question arises in the proceedings.

(2) Where an action or matter is tried with a jury and the judge inspects any place or thing under paragraph (1), he may authorise the jury to inspect it also.

MAGISTRATES' COURTS RULES 1981, AS AMENDED

Taking depositions of witnesses and statement of accused

7.—(1) This rule does not apply to committal proceedings where under section 6(2) of the Act of 1980 a magistrates' court commits a person for trial without consideration of the evidence.

(2) A magistrates' court inquiring into an offence as examining justices shall cause the evidence of each witness, including the evidence of the accused, but not including any witness of his merely to his character, to be put into writing; and as soon as may be after the examination of such a witness shall cause his deposition to be read to him in the presence and hearing of the accused, and shall require the witness to sign the deposition:

Provided that where the evidence has been given in the absence of the accused under section 4(4) of the Act of 1980 this shall be recorded on the deposition of the witness and the deposition need not be read in the presence and hearing of the accused.

(3) The depositions shall be authenticated by a certificate signed by one of the examining justices.

(4) Where the accused is not represented by counsel or a solicitor before a statement made in writing by or taken in writing from a child is received in evidence under subsection (1) of section 103 of the Act of 1980 the court shall cause the effect of that subsection to be explained to the accused in ordinary language and, if the defence does not object to the application of that subsection, shall inform him that he may ask questions about the circumstances in which the statement was made or taken.

(5) Any such statement as aforesaid which is received in evidence shall be made an exhibit.

(6) After the evidence for the prosecution (including any statements tendered under section 102 of the Act of 1980, has been given and after hearing any submission, if any is made, the court shall, unless it then decides not to commit for trial, cause the charge to be written down, if this has not already been done, and, if the accused is not represented by counsel or a solicitor, shall read the charge to him and explain it in ordinary language.

(9) The court shall then say to the accused—

"I must warn you that if this court should commit you for trial you may not be permitted at that trial to give evidence of an alibi or to call witnesses in support of an alibi unless you have earlier given particulars of the alibi and of the witnesses. You may give those particulars now to this court or to the solicitor for the prosecution not later than 7 days from the end of these committal proceedings,"

698

or words to that effect and, if it appears to the court that the accused may not understand the meaning of the term "alibi," the court shall explain it to him:

Provided that the court shall not be required to give this warning in any case where it appears to the court that, having regard to the nature of the offence with which the accused is charged, it is unnecessary to do so.

(10) After complying with the requirements of this rule relating to the statement of the accused, and whether or not he has made a statement in answer to the charge, the court shall give him an opportunity to give evidence himself and to call witnesses.

(11) Where the accused is represented by counsel or a solicitor, his counsel or solicitor shall be heard on his behalf, either before or after the evidence for the defence is taken, at his discretion, and may, if the accused gives evidence himself and calls witnesses, be heard on his behalf with the leave of the court both before and after the evidence is taken:

Provided that, where the court gives leave to counsel or the solicitor for the accused to be heard after, as well as before, the evidence is taken, counsel or the solicitor for the prosecution shall be entitled to be heard immediately before counsel or the solicitor for the accused is heard for the second time.

. . . .

Order of evidence and speeches: information

13.—(1) On the summary trial of an information, where the accused does not plead guilty, the prosecutor shall call the evidence for the prosecution, and before doing so may address the court.

(2) At the conclusion of the evidence for the prosecution, the accused may address the court, whether or not he afterwards calls evidence.

(3) At the conclusion of the evidence, if any, for the defence, the prosecutor may call evidence to rebut that evidence.

(4) At the conclusion of the evidence for the defence and the evidence, if any, in rebuttal, the accused may address the court if he has not already done so.

(5) Either party may, with the leave of the court, address the court a second time, but where the court grants leave to one party it shall not refuse leave to the other.

(6) Where both parties address the court twice the prosecutor shall address the court for the second time before the accused does so.

Note.—This rule does not prevent justices, in their discretion, from permitting the clerk to examine witnesses on behalf of an unrepresented party who is not competent or desirous of doing so: *Simms* v. *Moore* [1970] 2 Q.B. 327 (D.C.).

Order of evidence and speeches: complaint

14.—(1) On the hearing of a complaint, except where the court determines under section 53(3) of the Act of 1980 to make the order with the consent of the defendant without hearing evidence, the complainant shall call his evidence, and before doing so may address the court.

(2) At the conclusion of the evidence for the complainant the defendant may address the court, whether or not he afterwards calls evidence.

(3) At the conclusion of the evidence, if any, for the defence, the complainant may call evidence to rebut that evidence.

(4) At the conclusion of the evidence for the defence and the evidence, if any, in rebuttal, the defendant may address the court if he has not already done so.

(5) Either party may, with the leave of the court, address the court a second time, but where the court grants leave to one party it shall not refuse leave to the other.

(6) Where the defendant obtains leave to address the court for a second time his second address shall be made before the second address, if any, of the complainant.

Deposition of person dangerously ill

33.—(1) Where a justice of the peace takes the deposition of a person under section 105 of the Act of 1980 and the deposition relates to an offence with which a person has been charged, the justice shall give the person, whether prosecutor or accused, against whom it is proposed to use it reasonable notice of the intention to take the deposition, and shall give that person or his counsel or solicitor full opportunity of cross-examining the deponent.

(2) The justice shall sign the deposition and add to it a statement of his reason for taking it, the day when, and the place where it was taken and the names of any persons present when it was taken.

(3) The justice shall send the deposition, with the statement, to the clerk to the justices for the petty sessions area for which the justice acts and the clerk shall—

> (*a*) if the deposition relates to an offence for which a person has been committed for trial, send the deposition and statement to the appropriate officer of the Crown Court;
>
> (*b*) if the deposition relates to proceedings which are pending before a magistrates' court acting for another area, send the deposition and statement to the clerk of that court.

Proof of service, handwriting, etc.

67.—(1) The service on any person of a summons, process, notice or document required or authorised to be served in any proceedings before a magistrates' court, and the handwriting or seal of a justice of the peace or other person on any warrant, summons, notice, process or documents issued or made in any such proceedings, may be proved in any legal proceedings by a document purporting to be a solemn declaration in the prescribed form made before a justice of the peace, commissioner for oaths, clerk of a magistrates' court or registrar of a county court or a sheriff or sheriff clerk (in Scotland) or a clerk of petty sessions (in Northern Ireland).

(2) The service of any process or other document required or authorised to be served, the proper addressing, pre-paying and posting or registration for the purposes of service of a letter containing such a document, and the place, date and time of posting or registration of any such letter, may be proved in any proceedings before a magistrates' court by a document purporting to be a certificate signed by the person by whom the service was effected or the letter posted or registered.

(3) References in paragraph (2) to the service of any process shall, in their application to a witness summons, be construed as including

references to the payment or tender to the witness of his costs and expenses.

Proof of proceedings

68. The register of a magistrates' court, or any document purporting to be an extract from the register and to be certified by the clerk as a true extract, shall be admissible in any legal proceedings as evidence of the proceedings of the court entered in the register.

EVIDENCE—CRIMINAL PROCEEDINGS

Written statements in committal proceedings or summary trial

70.—(1) Written statements to be tendered in evidence under section 102 of the Act of 1980 or section 9 of the Criminal Justice Act 1967 shall be in the prescribed form.

(2) When a copy of such a statement is given to or served on any party to the proceedings a copy of the statement and of any exhibit which accompanied it shall be given to the clerk of the magistrates' court as soon as practicable thereafter, and where a copy of any such statement is given or served by or on behalf of the prosecutor, the accused shall be given notice by or on behalf of the prosecutor of his right to object to the statement being tendered in evidence.

(3) Where before a magistrates' court enquiring into an offence as examining justices the accused objects to a written statement being tendered in evidence and he has been given a copy of the statement but has not given notice of his intention to object to the statement being tendered in evidence, the court shall if necessary, adjourn to enable the witness to be called.

(4) Where a written statement to be tendered in evidence under the said section 102 or 9 refers to any document or object as an exhibit, that document or object shall wherever possible be identified by means of a label or other mark of identification signed by the maker of the statement, and before a magistrates' court treats any document ör object referred to as an exhibit in such a written statement as an exhibit produced and identified in court by the maker of the statement, the court shall be satisfied that the document or object is sufficiently described in the statement for it to be identified.

(5) If it appears to a magistrates' court that any part of a written statement is inadmissible there shall be written against that part—

(a) in the case of a written statement tendered in evidence under the said section 102 the words "Treated as inadmissible" together with the signature and name of the examining justice or, where there is more than one examining justice, the signature and name of one of the examining justices by whom the statement is so treated;

(b) in the case of a written statement tendered in evidence under the said section 9 the words "Ruled inadmissible" together with the signature and name of the justice or, where there is more than one justice, the signature and name of one of the justices who ruled the statement to be inadmissible.

(6) Where a written statement is tendered in evidence under the said section 102 or 9 before a magistrates' court the name and address of

the maker of the statement shall be read aloud unless the court otherwise directs.

(7) Where under subsection (5) of the said section 102 or subsection (6) of the said section 9 in any proceedings before a magistrates' court any part of a written statement has to be read aloud, or an account has to be given orally of so much of any written statement as is not read aloud, the statement shall be read or the account given by or on behalf of the party which has tendered the statement in evidence.

(8) Written statements tendered in evidence under the said section 102 before a magistrates' court acting as examining justices shall be authenticated by a certificate signed by one of the examining justices.

. . . .

Proof by formal admission

71.—Where under section 10 of the Criminal Justice Act 1967 a fact is admitted orally in court by or on behalf of the prosecutor or defendant for the purposes of the summary trial of an offence or proceedings before a magistrates' court acting as examining justices the court shall cause the admission to be written down and signed by or on behalf of the party making the admission.

INDEX